Commentary
on the
OLD TESTAMENT

Commentary on the OLD TESTAMENT

IN TEN VOLUMES

by

C. F. KEIL and F. DELITZSCH

Translated from the German by James Martin

VOLUME V

Psalms

by F. DELITZSCH

Three Volumes in One

WILLIAM B. EERDMANS PUBLISHING COMPANY
Grand Rapids, Michigan

COMMENTARY ON THE OLD TESTAMENT
by C. F. Keil and F. Delitzsch
Translated from the German

Volumes translated by James Martin
THE PENTATEUCH
JOSHUA, JUDGES, RUTH
THE BOOKS OF SAMUEL
THE BOOKS OF THE KINGS
THE PROPHECIES OF ISAIAH
THE PROPHECIES OF EZEKIEL
THE TWELVE MINOR PROPHETS

Volumes translated by Andrew Harper
THE BOOKS OF THE CHRONICLES

Volumes translated by Sophia Taylor
THE BOOKS OF EZRA, NEHEMIAH, ESTHER

Volumes translated by Francis Bolton
THE BOOK OF JOB
THE PSALMS

Volumes translated by M. G. Easton
PROVERBS OF SOLOMON
THE SONG OF SONG AND ECCLESIASTES
THE BOOK OF DANIEL

Volumes translated by David Patrick
THE PROPHECIES OF JEREMIAH, VOL. I

Volumes translated by James Kennedy
THE PROPHECIES OF JEREMIAH, VOL. II

ISBN 0-8028-8039-8

Reprinted, June 1984

PREFACE

SEVEN whole years have passed since the publication of
my *Commentar über den Psalter* (2 vols. 1859–60), and
during this period large and important contributions have been
made towards the exposition of the Psalms. Of Hupfeld's
Commentary the last two volumes (vol. iii., 1860; vol. iv., 1862)
have appeared since the completion of my own. Hitzig's
(1835–36) has appeared in a new form (2 vols., 1863–65),
enriched by the fruit of nearly thirty years' progressive study.
And the Commentary of Ewald has taken the field for the
third time (1866), with proud words scorning down all fellow-
workers, in order that all honour may be given to itself alone.
In addition to these, Böttcher's *Neue Kritische Aehrenlese*,
issued by Mühlau after the author's death, has furnished valuable contributions towards the exposition of the Psalms (Abth.
2, 1864); Von Ortenberg in the department of textual criticism (*Zur Textkritik der Psalmen*, 1861), and Kurtz in that of
theology (*Zur Theologie der Psalmen*, in the *Dorpater Zeitschrift*,
1864–65), have promoted the interpretation of the Psalms; and
side by side with these, Böhl's *Zwölf Messianische Psalmen*
("Twelve Messianic Psalms," 1862) and Kamphausen's exposition of the Psalms in Bunsen's *Bibelwerk* (1863) also claim
attention.

I had therefore no lack of external inducements for the
revision of my own Commentary; but I was also not unconscious of its defects. Despite all this, Hupfeld's inconsiderate
and condemnatory judgment caused me pain. In an essay

on the faithful representation of the text of the Old Testament
according to the Masora (*Lutherische Zeitschrift*, 1863) I incidentally gave expression to this feeling. On the 20th of
October 1863 Hupfeld wrote to me, "I have only just seen
your complaint of my judgment at the close of my work on
the Psalms. The complaint is so gentle in its tone, it partakes
so little of the bitterness of my verdict, and at the same time
strikes chords that are not yet deadened within me, and which
have not yet forgotten how to bring back the echo of happier
times of common research and to revive the feeling of gratitude
for faithful companionship, that it has touched my heart and
conscience." He closes his letter with the hope that he may
one day have an opportunity of expressing publicly how that
harsh and untempered judgment is now repugnant to his own
feelings. Up to the present time I have made no use whatever of this letter. I regarded it as a private matter between
ourselves. Since, however, Riehm has transferred that judgment unaltered to the second edition of the first volume of the
Commentary of Hupfeld, I owe it not to myself alone, but also
to him who is since deceased, to explain that this has not been
done in accordance with his wish.

Hitzig's new Commentary has been of the greatest service
to me in the revision and re-working of my own. In it I found
mine uniformly taken into account from beginning to end,
either with or without direct mention, and subjected to severe
but kindly-disposed criticism; and here and there not without
a ready recognition of the scientific advance which could not
but be observed in it. In comparison with such an unmerciful
judgment as that which Hupfeld pronounced upon me, and
which he would a few years later with very similar language pronounced upon him, I here met with reasonable criticism of the
matter, and, notwithstanding the full consciousness of the
thoroughly original inquirer, an appreciation of the toil bestowed by others upon their work.

I am the more encouraged to hope that all those who do not

hold scientific love of truth and progress to be the exclusive privilege of their own tendencies, will find in this new thoroughly revised edition of my Commentary much that is instructive, and much that is more correctly apprehended. The fact that I have still further pressed the Oriental learning of Fleischer and Wetzstein into the service of Biblical science will not be unwelcome to my readers. But that I have also laid Jewish investigators under contribution is due to my desire to see the partition wall between Synagogue and Church broken down. The exposition of Scripture has not only to serve the Church of the present, but also to help in building up the Church of the future. In this spirit I commend the present work to the grace and blessing of the God of the history of redemption.

DELITZSCH.

ERLANGEN, 7*th July* 1867.

NOTE ON יהוה.

Jahve is (1) the traditional pronunciation, and (2) the pronunciation to be presupposed in accordance with the laws of formation and of vowel sounds. It is the traditional, for Theodoret and Epiphanius transcribe Ἰαβέ. The mode of pronunciation Ἀϊά (not Ἰαβά), on the contrary, is the reproduction of the form of the name יה, and the mode of pronunciation Ἰαῶ of the form of the name יהו, which although occurring only in the Old Testament in composition, had once, according to traces that can be relied on, an independent existence. Also the testimonies of the Talmud and post-talmudical writings require the final sound to be הָ, and the corresponding name by which God calls Himself, אֶהְיֶה, is authentic security for this ending. When it is further considered that יַהְוְ (whence יְהוּ) according to analogous contractions has grown out of יַהְוֶה, and not out of יְהֹוָה, and that the Hebrew language exhibits no proof of any transition from הָ to הַ which would not at the same time be a transition from the masculine to the feminine, it must be conceded that the pronunciation *Jahve* is to be regarded as the original pronunciation. The mode of pronunciation *Jehova* has only come up within the last three hundred years; our own "*Jahavā*" [in the first edition] was an innovation. We now acknowledge the patristic 'Ιαβέ, and hope to have another opportunity of substantiating in detail what is maintained in this prefatory note.

NOTE BY THE TRANSLATOR.

Any justification of the retention of the exact orthography of the author, explained above, ought to be needless. The *J* has been retained, inasmuch as this representative of the Hebrew *Jod* or *Yod* is become thoroughly naturalized in our Scripture names although wrongly pronounced (compare as an exception to this the *y* sound of the *j* in the word "Hallelujah," which may perhaps be accounted for by the Greek form of the word adopted in our version of the New Testament). Although the quiescent final *h* (*He*) has been, with Dr. Delitzsch, omitted here, it is still retained in other Scripture names in accordance with the customary orthography.

The Hebrew numbering of the verses is followed in the text of each Psalm, and in the references generally. In a few instances only, where the difference between the Hebrew and the English divisions might prove perplexing to the English reader, both are given; *e.g.* Lev. vi. 5 [12], Joel iv. [iii.] 3. To the student Baer's critical text of the Psalter (*Liber Psalmorum Hebraicus. Textum masorethicum accuratius quam adhuc factum est expressit, brevem de accentibus metricis institutionem præmisit, notas criticas adjecit S. Baer. Præfatus est Fr. Delitzsch.* 1861. Lipsiæ, Dörffling et Franke. Cr. 8vo, pp. xiv. 134), often referred to by Dr. Delitzsch, will be found to be a useful companion to this Commentary, and more particularly as illustrating the pointings and accentuation adopted or mentioned in the notes.

It is almost superfluous to say that it has been altogether impracticable to follow Dr. Delitzsch in his acrostic reproduction of the Alphabetical Psalms.

F. B.

Elland, 31*st January* 1871.

TABLE OF CONTENTS

INTRODUCTION TO THE PSALTER.

EXPOSITION OF THE PSALTER.

FIRST BOOK OF THE PSALTER, PS. I.–XLI.

INTRODUCTION

TO THE PSALTER.

Πάντα ὥσπερ ἐν μεγάλῳ τινὶ καὶ κοινῷ ταμιείῳ τῇ βίβλῳ τῶν ψαλμῶν τεθησαύρισται.

Basil.

I. POSITION OF THE PSALTER AMONG THE HAGIOGRAPHA, AND MORE ESPECIALLY AMONG THE POETICAL BOOKS.

The Psalter is everywhere regarded as an essential part of the *Kethubîm* or *Hagiographa*; but its position among these varies. It seems to follow from Luke xxiv. 44 that it opened the Kethubim in the earliest period of the Christian era.* The order of the books in the Hebrew MSS. of the German class, upon which our printed editions in general use are based, is actually this: Psalms, Proverbs, Job, and the five Megilloth. But the Masora and the MSS. of the Spanish class begin the Kethubim with the Chronicles which they awkwardly separate from Ezra and Nehemiah, and then range the Psalms, Job, Proverbs and the five Megilloth next.** And according to the Talmud (*Baba Bathra* 14 *b*)

---

* Also from 2 Macc. ii. 13, where τὰ τοῦ Δαυίδ appears to be the designation of the כתובים according to their beginning; and from Philo, *De vita contempl.* (*Opp.* II. 475 *ed. Mangey*), where he makes the following distinction νόμους καὶ λόγια θεσπισθέντα διὰ προφητῶν καὶ ὕμνους καὶ τὰ ἄλλα οἷς ἐπιστήμη καὶ εὐσέβεια συναύξονται καὶ τελειοῦνται.

** In all the Masoretic lists the twenty four bcoks are arranged in the following order: 1) בראשׁית; 2) שׁמות אלה וְ; 3) וַיקרא; 4) וידבר (also במדבר); 5) אלה הדברים; 6) יהושׁע; 7) שׁופטים; 8) שׁמואל; 9) מלכים; 10) ישׁעיה; 11) ירמיה; 12) יחזקאל; 13) תרי עשׂר; 14) דברי הימים; 15) תהלות; 16) איוב; 17) משׁלי; 18) רות; 19) שׁיר השׁירים; 20) קהלת; 21) קינות (איכה); 22) אחשׁורושׁ (מגלה); 23) דניאל; 24) עזרא. The Masoretic abbreviation for the three pre‑eminently poetical books is accordingly, not א״מת but (in agreement with their Talmudic order) ה״אם (as also in Chajug'), *vid.* Elia Levita, *Masoreth ha-Masoreth* p. 19. 73 (*ed. Ven.* 1538) [ed. Ginsburg, 1867, p. 120, 248].

the following is the right order: Ruth, Psalms, Job, Proverbs; the Book of Ruth precedes the Psalter as its prologue, for Ruth is the ancestor of him to whom the sacred lyric owes its richest and most flourishing era. It is undoubtedly the most natural order that the Psalter should open the division of the Kethubim, and for this reason: that, according to the stock which forms the basis of it, it represents the time of David, and then afterwards in like manner the Proverbs and Job represent the Chokma-literature of the age of Solomon. But it is at once evident that it could have no other place but among the Kethubim.

The codex of the giving of the Law, which is the foundation of the old covenant and of the nationality of Israel, as also of all its subsequent literature, occupies the first place in the canon. Under the collective title of נביאים, a series of historical writings of a prophetic character, which trace the history of Israel from the occupation of Canaan to the first gleam of light in the gloomy retributive condition of the Babylonish Exile (*Prophetæ priores*) is first attached to these five books of the Thôra; and then a series of strictly prophetical writings by the prophets themselves which extend to the time of Darius Nothus, and indeed to the time of Nehemiah's second sojourn in Jerusalem under this Persian king (*Prophetæ posteriores*). Regarded chronologically, the first series would better correspond to the second if the historical books of the Persian period (Chronicles with Ezra, Nehemiah, and Esther) were joined to it; but for a very good reason this has not been done. The Israelitish literature has marked out two sharply defined and distinct methods of writing history, viz. the annalistic and the prophetic. The so-called Elohistic and so-called Jehovistic form of historical writing in the Pentateuch might serve as general types of these. The historical books of the Persian period are, however, of the annalistic, not of the prophetic character (although the Chronicles have taken up and incorporated many remnants of the prophetic form of historical writing, and the Books of the Kings, *vice versâ*, many remnants of the annalistic): they could not therefore stand among the *Prophetæ priores*. But with the Book of Ruth it is different. This short book is so like the end of the Book of the Judges (ch. xvii—xxi), that it might very well stand between Judges and Samuel; and it did originally stand after the Book of the Judges, just as the Lamentations of Jeremiah stood after his prophecies. It is only on liturgical grounds that they have both been placed with the so-called Megilloth (Canticles, Ruth, Lamentations, Ecclesiastes, and Esther, as they are arranged in our ordinary copies according to the calendar of the festivals). All the remaining books could manifestly only be classed under the third division of the canon, which (as could hardly have been otherwise in connection with תורה and נביאים) has been entitled, in the most general way, כתובים,—a title which, as the grandson of Ben-Sira renders it in his prologue [to Ecclesiasticus], means simply τὰ ἄλλα πάτρια βιβλία, or τὰ λοιπὰ τῶν βιβλίων, and nothing more. For if it were intended to mean writings, written ברוח הקדש, — as the third degree of inspiration which is combined with the greatest spontaneity of spirit, is styled according to the synagogue notion of inspiration, — then the words ברוח הקדש would and ought to stand with it.

II. NAMES OF THE PSALTER.

At the close of the seventy-second Psalm (ver. 20) we find the subscription: "*Are ended the prayers of David, the Son of Jesse.*" The whole of the preceding Psalms are here comprehended under the name תְּפִלּוֹת. This strikes one as strange, because with the exception of Ps. xvii (and further on Ps. lxxxvi, xc, cii, cxlii) they are all inscribed otherwise; and because in part, as *e. g.* Ps. i and ii, they contain no supplicatory address to God and have therefore not the form of prayers. Nevertheless the collective name *Tephilloth* is suitable to all Psalms. The essence of prayer is a direct and undiverted looking towards God, and the absorption of the mind in the thought of Him. Of this nature of prayer all Psalms partake; even the didactic and laudatory, though containing no supplicatory address, — like Hannah's song of praise which is introduced with ותתפלל (1 Sam. ii. 1). The title inscribed on the Psalter is תְּהִלִּים (סֵפֶר) for which תִּלִּים (apocopated תִּלִּי) is also commonly used, as Hippolytus (*ed.*

de Lagarde p. 188) testifies: ‘Εβραῖοι περιέγραψαν τὴν βίβλον Σέφρα Θελείμ.* This name may also seem strange, for the Psalms for the most part are hardly hymns in the proper sense: the majority are elegiac or didactic; and only a solitary one, Ps. cxlv, is directly inscribed תהלה. But even this collective name of the Psalms is admissible, for they all partake of the nature of the hymn, to wit the purpose of the hymn, the glorifying of God. The narrative Psalms praise the *magnalia Dei,* the plaintive likewise praise Him, since they are directed to Him as the only helper, and close with grateful confidence that He will hear and answer. The verb הלֵּל includes both the *Magnificat* and the *De profundis.*

The language of the Masora gives the preference to the feminine form of the name, instead of תהלים, and throughout calls the Psalter ספר תהלות (*e. g.* on 2 Sam. xxii. 5).** In the Syriac it is styled *kᵉtobo dᵉmazmûre,* in the Koran *zabûr* (not as Golius and Freytag point it, *zubûr*), which in the usage of the Arabic language signifies nothing more than "writing" (synon. *kitâb: vid.* on iii. 1), but is perhaps a corruption of *mizmor* from which a plural *mezâmîr* is formed, by a change of vowels, in Jewish-Oriental MSS. In the Old Testament writings a plural of *mizamor* does not occur. Also in the post-biblical usage *mizmorîm* or *mizmoroth* is found only in solitary instances as the name for the Psalms. In Hellenistic Greek the corresponding word ψαλμοί (from ψάλλειν = זמֵּר) is the more common; the Psalm collection is called βίβλος ψαλμῶν (Lk. xx. 42, Acts i. 20) or ψαλτήριον, the name of the instrument (*psantērîn* in the Book of Daniel)*** being

---

* In Eusebius, vi. 25: Σέφηρ Θιλλήν; Jerome (in the Preface to his translation of the Psalms *juxta Hebraicam veritatem*) points it still differently: *SEPHAR THALLIM quod interpretatur volumen hymnorum.* Accordingly at the end of the *Psalterium ex Hebræo, Cod.* 19 in the Convent Library of St. Gall we find the subscription: *Sephar Tallim Quod interpretatur volumen Ymnorum explicit.*

** It is an erroneous opinion of Buxtorf in his *Tiberias* and also of Jewish Masoretes, that the Masora calls the Psalter הליֵלא (*hallêla*). It is only the so-called *Hallel,* Ps. cxiii—cxix, that bears this name, for in the Masora on 2 Sam. xxii. 5, Ps. cxvi. 3 *a* is called הברו דהלילא (the similar passage in the Hallel) in relation to xviii. 5 *a.*

*** Νάβλα — say Eusebius and others of the Greek Fathers — παρ’ ‘Εβραίοις λέγεται τὸ ψαλτήριον, ὃ δὴ μόνον τῶν μουσικῶν ὀργάνων ὀρθότατον

transferred metaphorically to the songs that are sung with its accompaniment. Psalms are songs for the lyre, and therefore lyric poems in the strictest sense.

III. THE HISTORY OF PSALM COMPOSITION.

Before we can seek to obtain a clear idea of the origin of the Psalm-collection we must take a general survey of the course of the development of psalm writing. The lyric is the earliest kind of poetry in general, and the Hebrew poetry, the oldest example of the poetry of antiquity that has come down to us, is therefore essentially lyric. Neither the Epos nor the Drama, but only the *Mashal,* has branched off from it and attained an independent form. Even prophecy, which is distinguished from psalmody by a higher impulse which the mind of the writer receives from the power of the divine mind, shares with the latter the common designation of נִבָּא (1 Chron. xxv. 1 — 3), and the psalm-singer, מְשׁרֵר, is also as such called חֹזֶה (1 Chron. xxv. 5; 2 Chron. xxix. 30, xxxv. 15, cf. 1 Chron. xv. 19 and freq.); for just as the sacred lyric often rises to the height of prophetic vision, so the prophetic epic of the future, because it is not entirely freed from the sub-

---

καὶ μὴ συνεργούμενον εἰς ἦχον ἐκ τῶν κατωτάτω μερῶν, ἀλλ᾽ ἄνωθεν ἔχων τὸν ὑπηχοῦντα χαλκόν. Augustine describes this instrument still more clearly *in Ps.* xlii and elsewhere: *Psalterium istud organum dicitur quod de superiore parte habet testudinem, illud scilicet tympanum et concavum lignum cui chordæ innitentes resonant, cithara vero id ipsum lignum cavum et sonorum ex inferiore parte habet.* In the cithern the strings pass over the sound-board, in the harp and lyre the vibrating body runs round the strings which are left free (without a bridge) and is either curved or angular as in the case of the harp, or encompasses the strings as in the lyre. Harps with an upper sounding body (whether of metal or wood, viz. *lignum concavum* i. e. with a hollow and hence sonorous wood, which protects the strings like a *testudo* and serves as a *tympanum*) are found both on Egyptian and on Assyrian monuments. By the *psalterium* described by Augustine, Cassiodorus and Isidorus understand the *trigonum,* which is in the form of an inverted sharp-cornered triangle; but it cannot be this that is intended because the horizontal strings of this instrument are surrounded by a three-sided sounding body, so that it must be a triangular lyre. Moreover there is also a trigon belonging to the Macedonian era which is formed like a harp (*vid.* Weiss' *Kostümkunde,* Fig. 347) and this further tends to support our view.

jectivity of the prophet, frequently passes into the strain of the psalm.

The time of Moses was the period of Israel's birth as a nation and also of its national lyric. The Israelites brought instruments with them out of Egypt and these were the accompaniments of their first song (Ex. xv.) — the oldest hymn, which re-echoes through all hymns of the following ages and also through the Psalter (comp. ver. 2 with Ps. cxviii. 14; ver. 3 with Ps. xxiv. 8; ver. 4, xiv. 27 with Ps. cxxxvi. 15; ver. 8 with Ps. lxxviii. 13; ver. 11 with Ps. lxxvii. 14, lxxxvi. 8, lxxxix. 7 sq.; ver. 13, 17 with Ps. lxxviii. 54, and other parallels of a similar kind). If we add to these, Ps. xc and Deut. xxxii, we then have the prototypes of all Psalms, the hymnic, elegiac, and prophetico-didactic. All three classes of songs are still wanting in the strophic symmetry which characterises the later art. But even Deborah's song of victory, arranged in hexastichs, — a song of triumph composed eight centuries before Pindar and far outstripping him, — exhibits to us the strophic art approximating to its perfect development. It has been thought strange that the very beginnings of the poesy of Israel are so perfect, but the history of Israel, and also the history of its literature, comes under a different law from that of a constant development from a lower to a higher grade. The redemptive period of Moses, unique in its way, influences as a creative beginning, every future development. There is a constant progression, but of such a kind as only to develope that which had begun in the Mosaic age with all the primal force and fulness of a divine creation. We see, however, how closely the stages of this progress are linked together, from the fact that Hannah the singer of the Old Testament *Magnificat,* was the mother of him who anointed, as King, the sweet singer of Israel, on whose tongue was the word of the Lord.

In David the sacred lyric attained its full maturity. Many things combined to make the time of David its golden age. Samuel had laid the foundation of this both by his energetic reforms in general, and by founding the schools of the prophets in particular, in which under his guidance (1 Sam. xix. 19 sq.), in conjunction with the awakening and fostering of the prophetic gift, music and song were taught. Through these *cœnobia*, whence sprang a spiritual awakening hitherto unknown in Israel, David also passed. Here his poetic talent, if not awakened, was however cultivated. He was a musician and poet born. Even as a Bethlehemite shepherd he played upon the harp, and with his natural gift he combined a heart deeply imbued with religious feeling. But the Psalter contains as few traces of David's Psalms before his anointing (*vid.* on Ps. viii, cxliv.) as the New Testament does of the writings of the Apostles before the time of Pentecost. It was only from the time when the Spirit of Jahve came upon him at his anointing as king of Israel, and raised him to the dignity of his calling in connection with the covenant of redemption, that he sang Psalms, which have become an integral part of the canon. They are the fruit not only of his high gifts and the inspiration of the Spirit of God (2 Sam. xxiii. 2), but also of his own experience and of the experience of his people interwoven with his own. David's path from his anointing onwards, lay through affliction to glory. Song however, as a Hìndu proverb says, is the offspring of suffering, the *çloka* springs from the *çoka*. His life was marked by vicissitudes which at one time prompted him to elegiac strains, at another to praise and thanksgiving; at the same time he was the founder of the kingship of promise, a prophecy of the future Christ, and his life, thus typically moulded, could not express itself otherwise than in typical or even consciously prophetic language. Raised to the throne, he did not forget the harp which had been his companion and solace when he fled before Saul, but rewarded it with all honour. He appointed 4000 Levites, the fourth division of the whole Levitical order, as singers and musicians in connection with the service in the tabernacle on Zion and partly in Gibeon, the place of the Mosaic tabernacle. These he divided into 24 classes under the Precentors, Asaph, Heman, and Ethan=Jeduthun (1 Chron. xxv. comp. xv. 17 sqq.), and multiplied the instruments, particularly the stringed instruments, by his own invention (1 Chron. xxiii. 5, Neh. xii. 36 *). In David's time there were three places of sacrifice:

---

* I tended, says David in the Greek Psalter, at the close of Ps. cl., my father's sheep, my hands made pipes (ὄργανον = עוגב) and my fingers put together (or: tuned) harps (ψαλτήριον = נבל) cf. *Numeri Rabba* c. xv (f. 264 *a*) and the Targum on Am. vi. 5.

on Zion beside the ark (2 Sam. vi. 17 sq.), in Gibeon beside the Mosaic tabernacle (1 Chron. xvi. 39 sq.) and later, on the threshing-floor of Ornan, afterwards the Temple-hill (1 Chron. xxi. 28—30). Thus others also were stimulated in many ways to consecrate their offerings to the God of Israel. Beside the 73 Psalms bearing the inscription לדוד, — Psalms the direct Davidic authorship of which is attested, at least in the case of some fifty, by their creative originality, their impassioned and predominantly plaintive strain, their graceful flow and movement, their ancient but clear language, which becomes harsh and obscure only when describing the dissolute conduct of the ungodly, — the collection contains the following which are named after cotemporary singers appointed by David: 12 לאסף (Ps. l. lxxiii—lxxxiii) of which the contents and spirit are chiefly prophetic, and 12 by the Levite family of singers, the בני־קרה (Ps. xlii—xlix, lxxxiv, lxxxv, lxxxvii, lxxxviii, including Ps. xliii), bearing a predominantly regal and priestly impress. Both the Psalms of the Ezrahites, Ps. lxxxviii by Heman and lxxxix by Ethan, belong to the time of Solomon whose name, with the exception of Ps. lxxii, is borne only by Ps. cxxvii. Under Solomon psalm-poesy began to decline; all the existing productions of the mind of that age bear the mark of thoughtful contemplation rather than of direct conception, for restless eagerness had yielded to enjoyable contentment, national concentration to cosmopolitan expansion. It was the age of the Chokma, which brought the apophthegm to its artistic perfection, and also produced a species of drama. Solomon himself is the perfecter of the *Mashal,* that form of poetic composition belonging strictly to the Chokma. Certainly according to 1 Kings v. 12 [Hebr.; iv. 32, Engl.] he was also the author of 1005 songs, but in the canon we only find two Psalms by him and the dramatic Song of Songs. This may perhaps be explained by the fact that he spake of trees from the cedar to the hyssop, that his poems, mostly of a worldly character, pertained rather to the realm of nature than to the kingdom of grace.

Only twice after this did psalm-poesy rise to any height and then only for a short period: viz. under Jehoshaphat and under Hezekiah. Under both these kings the glorious services of the Temple rose from the desecration and decay into

which they had fallen to the full splendour of their ancient
glory. Moreover there were two great and marvellous deliverances which aroused the spirit of poesy during the reigns of
these kings: under Jehoshaphat, the overthrow of the neighbouring nations when they had banded together for the ex-
stirpation of Judah, predicted by Jahaziel, the Asaphite; under Hezekiah the overthrow of Sennacherib's host foretold by
Isaiah. These kings also rendered great service to the cause
of social progress. Jehoshaphat by an institution designed
to raise the educational status of the people, which reminds
one of the Carlovingian *missi* (2 Chron. xvii. 7—9); Hezekiah,
whom one may regard as the Pisistratus of Israelitish literature, by the establishment of a commission charged with collecting the relics of the early literature (Prov. xxv. 1); he
also revived the ancient sacred music and restored the Psalms
of David and Asaph to their liturgical use (2 Chron. xxix.
25 sqq). And he was himself a poet, as his מכתב (מכתם?)
(Isa. xxxviii) shews, though certainly a reproductive rather
than a creative poet. Both from the time of Jehoshaphat
and from the time of Hezekiah we possess in the Psalter not
a few Psalms, chiefly Asaphic and Korahitic, which, although
bearing no historical heading, unmistakeably confront us with
the peculiar circumstances of those times.* With the exception of these two periods of revival the latter part of the regal period produced scarcely any psalm writers, but is all the
more rich in prophets. When the lyric became mute, prophecy
raised its trumpet voice in order to revive the religious life of
the nation, which previously had expressed itself in psalms. In
the writings of the prophets, which represent the λεῖμμα χάριτος
in Israel, we do indeed find even psalms, as Jon. ch. ii, Isa. xii,
Hab. iii, but these are more imitations of the ancient congregational hymns than original compositions. It was not until
after the Exile that a time of new creations set in.

As the Reformation gave birth to the German church-
hymn, and the Thirty years' war, without which perhaps
there might have been no Paul Gerhardt, called it into life
afresh, so the Davidic age gave birth to psalm-poesy and the

---

* With regard to the time of Jehoshaphat even Nic. Nonne has acknowledged this in his *Diss. de Tzippor et Deror* (Bremen 1741, 4to.) which
has reference to Ps. lxxxiv. 4.

tion as we now have it was made: whereas Hitzig going somewhat deeper ascribes Ps. i. ii. cl. with others, and the arrangement of the whole, to Hyrcanus' son, Alexander Jannæus.

On the other hand both the existence and possibility of Maccabean psalms is disputed not only by Hengstenberg, Hävernick, and Keil but also by Gesenius, Hassler, Ewald, Thenius, Böttcher, and Dillmann. For our own part we admit the possibility. It has been said that the ardent enthusiasm of the Maccabean period was more human than divine, more nationally patriotic than theocratically national in its character, but the Book of Daniel exhibits to us, in a prophetic representation of that period, a holy people of the Most High contending with the god-opposing power in the world, and claims for this contest the highest significance in relation to the history of redemption. The history of the canon, also, does not exclude the possibility of there being Maccabean psalms. For although the chronicler by 1 Chron. xvi. 36 brings us to the safe conclusion that in his day the Psalter (comp. τὰ τοῦ Δαυίδ, 2 Macc. ii. 13*) was already a whole divided into five books (*vid.* on Ps. xcvi. cv. cvi): it might nevertheless, after having been completely arranged still remain open for later insertions (just as the ספר הישר cited in the Book of Joshua and 2 Sam. i., was an anthology which had grown together in the course of time). When Judas Maccabæus, by gathering together the national literature, followed in the footsteps of Nehemiah (2 Macc. ii. 14: ὡσαύτως δὲ καὶ Ἰούδας τὰ διεσκορπισμένα διὰ τὸν πόλεμον τὸν γεγονότα ἡμῖν ἐπισυνήγαγε πάντα, καὶ ἔστι παρ᾽ ἡμῖν), we might perhaps suppose that the Psalter was at that time enriched by some additions. And when Jewish tradition assigns to the so-called Great Synagogue (כנסת הגדולה) a share in the compilation of the canon, this is not unfavourable to the supposition of Maccabean psalms, since this συναγωγὴ μεγάλη was still in existence under the domination of the Seleucidæ (1 Macc. xiv. 28).

It is utterly at variance with historical fact to maintain that the Maccabean period was altogether incapable of producing psalms worthy of incorporation in the canon. Al-

---

* In the early phraseology of the Eastern and Western churches the Psalter is simply called *David*, *e. g.* in Chrysostom: ἐκμαθόντες ὅλον τὸν Δαβίδ, and at the close of the Æthiopic Psalter: "David is ended".

though the Maccabean period had no prophets, it is nevertheless to be supposed that many possessed the gift of poesy,
and that the Spirit of faith, which is essentially one and the
same with the Spirit of prophecy, might sanctify this gift
and cause it to bear fruit. An actual proof of this is furnished
by the so-called Psalter of Solomon (Ψαλτήριον Σαλομῶντος
in distinction from the canonical Psalter of David)* consisting
of 18 psalms, which certainly come far behind the originality
and artistic beauty of the canonical Psalms; but they shew
at the same time, that the feelings of believers, even throughout the whole time of the Maccabees, found utterance in expressive spiritual songs. Maccabean psalms are therefore not
an absolute impossibility — no doubt they were many; and
that some of them were incorporated in the Psalter, cannot
be denied *à priori*. But still the history of the canon does
not favour this supposition. And the circumstance of the
LXX version of the Psalms (according to which citations are
made even in the first Book of the Maccabees) inscribing several Psalms Ἀγγαίου καὶ Ζαχαρίου, while however it does not
assign the date of the later period to any, is against it. And
if Maccabean psalms be supposed to exist in the Psalter they
can at any rate only be few, because they must have been inserted in a collection which was already arranged. And since
the Maccabean movement, though beginning with lofty aspira-
tions, gravitated, in its onward course, towards things carnal,
we can no longer expect to find psalms relating to it, or
at least none belonging to the period after Judas Maccabæus;
and from all that we know of the character and disposition
of Alexander Jannæus it is morally impossible that this des-
pot should be the author of the first and second Psalms and
should have closed the collection.

IV. ORIGIN OF THE COLLECTION.

The Psalter, as we now have it, consists of five books.**
Τοῦτό σε μὴ παρέλθοι, ὦ φιλόλογε — says Hippolytus, whose

---

* First made known by De la Cerda in his *Adversaria sacra* (1626)
and afterwards incorporated by Fabricius in his *Codex Pseudepigraphus
V. T.* pp. 914 sqq. (1713).

** The Karaite Jerocham (about 950 A. D.) says מגלות (rolls) instead
of ספרים.

words are afterwards quoted by Epiphanius — ὅτι καὶ τὸ ψαλτήριον εἰς πέντε διεῖλον βιβλία οἱ Ἑβραῖοι, ὥστε εἶναι καὶ αὐτὸ ἄλλον πεντάτευχον. This accords with the Midrash on Ps. i. 1: Moses gave the Israelites the five books of the Thôra and corresponding to these (כנגדם) David gave them the book of Psalms which consists of five books (ספר תהלים שיש בו חמשה ספרים). The division of the Psalter into five parts makes it the copy and echo of the Thôra, which it also resembles in this particular: that as in the Thôra Elohistic and Jehovistic sections alternate, so here a group of Elohistic Psalms (xlii—lxxxiv) is surrounded on both sides by groups of Jehovistic (i—xli, lxxxv—cl). The five books are as follow: — i—xli, xlii—lxxii, lxxiii—lxxxix, xc—cvi, cvii—cl.* Each of the first four books closes with a doxology, which one might erroneously regard as a part of the preceding Psalm (xli. 14, lxxii. 18 sq., lxxxix. 53, cvi. 48), and the place of the fifth doxology is occupied by Ps. cl. as a full toned finale to the whole (like the relation of Ps. cxxxiv to the so-called Songs of degrees). These doxologies very much resemble the language of the liturgical *Beracha* of the second Temple. The אָמֵן וְאָמֵן coupled with וֹ (cf. on the contrary Num. v. 22 and also Neh. viii. 6) is exclusively peculiar to them in Old Testament writings. Even in the time of the writer of the Chronicles the Psalter was a whole divided into five parts, which were indicated by these landmarks. We infer this from 1 Chron. xvi. 36. The chronicler in the free manner which characterises Thucydides or Livy in reporting a speech, there reproduces David's festal hymn that resounded in Israel after the bringing home of the ark; and he does it in such a way that after he has once fallen into the track of Ps. cvi., he also puts into the mouth of David the *beracha* which follows that Ps. From this we see that the Psalter was already divided into books at that period; the closing doxologies had already become thoroughly grafted upon the body of the Psalms after which they stand. The chronicler however wrote under the pontificate of Johanan, the son of Eliashib, the predecessor of Jaddua, towards the end of the Persian supremacy, but a considerable time before the commencement of the Grecian.

---

* The Karaite Jefeth ben Eli calls them ספר אשרי‎, כאיל ס׳ &c.

Next to this application of the *beracha* of the Fourth book by the chronicler, Ps. lxxii. 20 is a significant mark for determining the history of the origin of the Psalter. The words: *"are ended the prayers of David the son of Jesse"*, are without doubt the subscription to the oldest psalm-collection, which preceded the present psalm-pentateuch. The collector certainly has removed this subscription from its original place close after lxxii. 17, by the interpolation of the *beracha* lxxii. 18 sq., but left it, at the same time, untouched. The collectors and those who worked up the older documents within the range of the Biblical literature appear to have been extremely conscientious in this respect and they thereby make it easier for us to gain an insight into the origin of their works, — as, *e. g.* the composer of the Books of Samuel gives intact the list of officers from a later document 2 Sam. viii. 16—18 (which closed with that, so far as we at present have it in its incorporated state), as well as the list from an older document (2 Sam. xx. 23—26); or, as not merely the author of the Book of Kings in the middle of the Exile, but also the chronicler towards the end of the Persian period, have transferred unaltered, to their pages, the statement that the staves of the ark are to be found in the rings of the ark "to this day", which has its origin in some annalistic document (1 Kings viii. 8, 2 Chron. v. 9). But unfortunately that subscription, which has been so faithfully preserved, furnishes us less help than we could wish. We only gather from it that the present collection was preceded by a primary collection of very much more limited compass which formed its basis and that this closed with the Salomonic Ps. lxxii; for the collector would surely not have placed the subscription, referring only to the prayers of David, after this Psalm if he had not found it there already. And from this point it becomes natural to suppose that Solomon himself, prompted perhaps by the liturgical requirements of the new Temple, compiled this primary collection, and by the addition of Ps. lxxii may have caused it to be understood that he was the originator of the collection.

But to the question whether the primary collection also contained only Davidic songs properly so called or whether the subscribed designation תהלות דוד is only intended *a potiori,* the answer is entirely wanting. If we adopt the latter supposition, one is at a loss to understand for what reason only Ps. l. of the Psalms of Asaph was inserted in it. For this psalm is really one of the old Asaphic psalms and might therefore have been an integral part of the primary collection. On the other hand it is altogether impossible for all the Korahitic psalms xlii — xlix to have belonged to it, for some of them, and most undoubtedly xlvii and xlviii were composed in the time of Jehoshaphat, the most remarkable event of which, as the chronicler narrates, was foretold by an Asaphite and celebrated by Korahitic singers. It is therefore, apart from other psalms which bring us down to the Assyrian period (as lxvi, lxvii) and the time of Jeremiah (as lxxi) and bear in themselves traces of the time of the Exile (as lxix, 35 sqq.), absolutely impossible that the primary collection should have consisted of Ps. ii — lxxii, or rather (since Ps. ii appears as though it ought to be assigned to the later time of the kings, perhaps the time of Isaiah) of Ps. iii — lxxii. And if we leave the later insertions out of consideration, there is no arrangement left for the Psalms of David and his cotemporaries, which should in any way bear the impress of the Davidic and Salomonic mind. Even the old Jewish teachers were struck by this, and in the Midrash on Ps. iii we are told, that when Joshua ben Levi was endeavouring to put the Ps. in order, a voice from heaven cried out to him: arouse not the slumberer (אל־תפיחי את־הישן) i. e. do not disturb David in his grave! Why Ps. iii follows directly upon Ps. ii, or as it is expressed in the Midrash פרשת אבשלום follows פרשת גוג ומגוג, may certainly be more satisfactorily explained than is done there: but to speak generally the mode of the arrangement of the first two books of the Psalms is of a similar nature to that of the last three, viz., that which in my *Symbolæ ad Psalmos illustrandos isagogicæ* (1846) is shewn to run through the entire Psalter, more according to external than internal points of contact.*

---

* The right view has been long since perceived by Eusebius, who in his exposition of Ps. lxiii (LXX. lxii), among other things expresses himself thus: ἐγὼ δὲ ἡγοῦμαι τῆς τῶν ἐγγεγραμμένων διανοίας ἕνεκεν ἐφεξῆς ἀλλήλων τοὺς ψαλμοὺς κεῖσθαι κατὰ τὸ πλεῖστον, οὕτως ἐν πολλοῖς ἐπιτηρήσας καὶ εὑρών, διὸ καὶ συνῆφθαι αὐτοὺς ὡσανεὶ συγγένειαν ἔχοντας καὶ ἀκολουθίαν πρὸς ἀλλήλους· ἔνθεν μὴ κατὰ τοὺς χρόνους ἐμφέρεσθαι, ἀλλὰ κατὰ τὴν τῆς διανοίας ἀκολουθίαν (in Montfaucon's *Collectio Nova,* t. i. p. 300). This ἀκολουθία διανοίας is however not always central and deep. The attempts of Luther (Walch, iv. col. 646 sqq.) and especially of So-

On the other side it cannot be denied that the ground-work of the collection that formed the basis of the present Psalter must lie within the limits of Ps. iii—lxxii, for nowhere else do old Davidic psalms stand so closely and numerously together as here. The Third book (Ps. lxxiii—lxxxix) exhibits a marked difference in this respect. We may therefore suppose that the chief bulk of the oldest hymn book of the Israelitish church is contained in Ps. iii—lxxii. But we must at the same time admit, that its contents have been dispersed and newly arranged in later redactions and more especially in the last of all; and yet, amidst these changes the connection of the subscription, lxxii. 20, with the psalm of Solomon was preserved. The two groups iii—lxxii, lxxiii—lxxxix, although not preserved in the original arrangement, and augmented by several kinds of interpolations, at least represent the first two stages of the growth of the Psalter. The primary collection may be Salomonic. The after portion of the second group was, at the earliest, added in the time of Jehoshaphat, at which time probably the book of the Proverbs of Solomon was also compiled. But with a greater probability of being in the right we incline to assign them to the time of Hezekiah, not merely because some of the psalms among them seem as though they ought to be referred to the overthrow of Assyria under Hezekiah rather than to the overthrow of the allied neighbouring nations under Jehoshaphat, but chiefly because just in the same manner "the men of Hezekiah" appended an after gleaning to the older Salomonic book of Proverbs (Prov. xxv. 1), and because of Hezekiah it is recorded, that he brought the Psalms of David and of Asaph (the bulk of which are contained in the Third book of the Psalms) into use again (2 Chron. xxix. 30). In the time of Ezra and Nehemiah the collection was next extended by the songs composed during and (which are still more numerous) after the Exile. But a gleaning of old songs also had been reserved for this time. A psalm of Moses was placed first, in order to give a pleasing relief to the beginning of the new psalter by this glance back into the earliest time. And to the 56 Davidic psalms of the first three books, there are

____

lomon Gesner, to prove a link of internal progress in the Psalter are not convincing.

Exile brought back to life again that which had become dead. The divine chastisement did not fail to produce the effect designed. Even though it should not admit of proof, that many of the Psalms have had portions added to them, from which it would be manifest how constantly they were then used as forms of supplication, still it is placed beyond all doubt, that the Psalter contains many psalms belonging to the time of the Exile, as *e. g.* Ps. cii. Still far more new psalms were composed after the Return. When those who returned from exile, among whom were many Asaphites, * again felt themselves to be a nation, and after the restoration of the Temple to be also a church, the harps which in Babylon hung upon the willows, were tuned afresh and a rich new flow of song was the fruit of this re-awakened first love. But this did not continue long. A sanctity founded on good works and the service of the letter took the place of that outward, coarse idolatry from which the people, now returned to their fatherland, had been weaned while undergoing punishment in the land of the stranger. Nevertheless in the era of the Seleucidæ the oppressed and injured national feeling revived under the Maccabees in its old life and vigour. Prophecy had then long been dumb, a fact lamented in many passages in the 1st Book of the Maccabees. It cannot be maintained that psalm-poesy flourished again at that time. Hitzig has recently endeavoured to bring forward positive proof, that it is Maccabean psalms, which form the proper groundwork of the Psalter. He regards the Maccabean prince Alexander Jannæus as the writer of Ps. i and ii, refers Ps. xliv. to 1 Macc. v. 56—62, and maintains both in his *Commentary* of 1835—36 and in the later edition of 1863 — 65 that from Ps. lxxiii onwards there is not a single pre-Maccabean psalm in the collection and that, from that point, the Psalter mirrors the prominent events of the time of the Maccabees in chronological order. Hitzig has been followed by von Lengerke and Olshausen. They both mark the reign of John Hyrcanus (B. C. 135 — 107) as the time when the latest psalms were composed and when the collec-

---

* In Barhebræus on Job and in his *Chronikon* several traditions are referred to "Asaph the Hebrew priest, the brother of Ezra the writer of the Scriptures."

seventeen more added here in the last two. They are certainly not all directly Davidic, but partly the result of the writer throwing himself into David's temper of mind and circumstances. One chief store of such older psalms were perhaps the historical works of an annalistic or even prophetic character, rescued from the age before the Exile. It is from such sources that the historical notes prefixed to the Davidic hymns (and also to one in the Fifth book: Ps. cxlii) come. On the whole there is unmistakeably an advance from the earliest to the latest; and we may say, with Ewald, that in Ps. i—xli the real bulk of the Davidic and, in general, of the older songs is contained, in Ps. xlii—lxxxix predominantly songs of the middle period, in Ps. xc — cl the large mass of later and very late songs. But moreover it is with the Psalm-collection as with the collection of the prophecies of Isaiah, Jeremiah, and Ezekiel: the chronological order and the arrangement according to the matter are at variance; and in many places the former is intentionally and significantly disregarded in favour of the latter. We have often already referred to one chief point of view of this arrangement according to matter, viz., the imitation of the Thôra; it was perhaps this which led to the opening of the Fourth book, which corresponds to the Book of Numbers, with a psalm of Moses of this character.

V. ARRANGEMENT AND INSCRIPTIONS.

Among the Fathers, Gregory of Nyssa has attempted to shew that the Psalter in its five books leads upward as by five steps to moral perfection, ἀεὶ πρὸς τὸ ὑψηλότερον τὴν ψυχὴν ὑπερτιθείς, ὡς ἂν ἐπὶ τὸ ἀκρότατον ἐφίκηται τῶν ἀγαθῶν;* and down to the most recent times attempts have been made to trace in the five books a gradation of principal thoughts, which influence and run through the whole collection.** We fear that in this direction, investigation has set before itself an unattainable end. Nevertheless, as we shall see, the collection bears the impress of one ordering mind. For its opening is

---

* *Opp. ed. Paris*, (1638) t. i. p. 288.
** Thus especially Stähelin, *Zur Einleitung in die Psalmen*, 1859, 4to.

formed by a didactic-prophetic couplet of psalms (Ps. i. ii), introductory to the whole Psalter and therefore in the earliest times regarded as one psalm, which opens and closes with אשרי; and its close is formed by four psalms (Ps. cxlvi —cxlix) which begin and end with הללו־יה. We do not include Ps. cl. for this psalm takes the place of the *beracha* of the Fifth book, exactly as the recurring verse Isa. xlviii. 22 is repeated in lvii. 21 with fuller emphasis, but is omitted at the close of the third part of this address of Isaiah to the exiles, its place being occupied by a terrifying description of the hopeless end of the wicked. The opening of the Psalter celebrates the blessedness of those who walk according to the will of God in redemption, which has been revealed in the law and in history; the close of the Psalter calls upon all creatures to praise this God of redemption, as it were on the ground of the completion of this great work. Bede has already called attention to the fact that the Psalter from Ps. cxlvi ends in a complete strain of praise; the end of the Psalter soars upward to a happy climax. The assumption that there was an evident predilection for attempting to make the number 150 complete, as Ewald supposes, cannot be established; the reckoning 147 (according to a Haggadah book mentioned in *Jer. Sabbath* xvi, parallel with the years of Jacob's life), and the reckoning 149, which frequently occurs both in Karaitic and Rabbinic MSS., have also been adopted; the numbering of the whole and of particular psalms varies.*

There are in the Psalter 73 psalms bearing the inscription לדוד, viz. (reckoning exactly) 37 in book i; 18 in book ii; 1 in book iii; 2 in book iv; 15 in book v. The redaction has designed the pleasing effect of closing the collection with an imposing group of Davidic psalms, just as it begins with the bulk of the Davidic psalms. And the Hallelujahs which begin with Ps. cxlvi (after the 15 Davidic psalms) are the preludes of the closing doxology.

---

* The LXX, like our Hebrew text, reckons 150 psalms, but with variations in separate instances, by making ix and x, and cxiv and cxv into one, and in place of these, dividing cxvi and cxlvii each into two. The combination of ix and x, of cxiv and cxv into one has also been adopted by others; cxxxiv and cxxxv, but especially i and ii, appear here and there as one psalm. Kimchi reckons 149 by making Ps. cxiv and cxv into one. The ancient Syriac version combines Ps. cxiv and cxv as one, but reckons 150 by dividing Ps. cxlvii.

The Korahitic and Asaphic psalms are found exclusively in the Second and Third books. There are 12 Asaphic psalms: l. lxxiii—lxxxiii, and also 12 Korahitic: xlii. xliii. xliv—xlix. lxxxiv. lxxxv. lxxxvii. lxxxviii, assuming that Ps. xliii is to be regarded as an independent twin psalm to xlii and that Ps. lxxxviii is to be reckoned among the Korahitic psalms. In both of these divisions we find psalms belonging to the time of the Exile and to the time after the Exile (lxxiv. lxxix. lxxxv). The fact of their being found exclusively in the Second and Third books cannot therefore be explained on purely chronological grounds. Korahitic psalms, followed by an Asaphic, open the Second book; Asaphic psalms, followed by four Korahitic, open the Third book.

The way in which Davidic psalms are interspersed clearly sets before us the principle by which the arrangement according to the matter, which the collector has chosen, is governed. It is the principle of homogeneousness, which is the old Semitic mode of arranging things: for in the alphabet, the hand and the hollow of the hand, water and fish, the eye and the mouth, the back and front of the head have been placed together. In like manner also the psalms follow one another according to their relationship as manifested by prominent external and internal marks. The Asaphic psalm, Ps. l, is followed by the Davidic psalm, li., because they both similarly disparage the material animal sacrifice, as compared with that which is personal and spiritual. And the Davidic psalm lxxxvi is inserted between the Korahitic psalms lxxxv and lxxxvii, because it is related both to Ps. lxxxv. 8 by the prayer: *"Shew me Thy way, O Jahve"* and *"give Thy conquering strength unto Thy servant"*, and to Ps. lxxxvii by the prospect of the conversion of the heathen to the God of Israel. This phenomenon, that psalms with similar prominent thoughts, or even with only markedly similar passages, especially at the beginning and the end, are thus strung together, may be observed throughout the whole collection. Thus *e. g.* Ps. lvi with the inscription, *"after* (the melody): *the mute dove among strangers"*, is placed after Ps. lv on account of the occurrence of the words: *"Oh that I had wings like a dove!"* &c., in that psalm; thus Ps. xxxiv and xxxv stand together as being the only psalms in which "the Angel of Jahve" occurs; and just so Ps. ix and x which coincide in the expression עתות בצרה.

Closely connected with this principle of arrangement is the circumstance that the Elohimic psalms (*i. e.,* those which, according to a peculiar style of composition as I have shewn in my *Symbolæ,* not from the caprice of an editor, * almost exclusively call God אלהים, and beside this make use of such compound names of God as יהוה אלהים צבאות, יהוה צבאות and the like) are placed together without any intermixture of Jehovic psalms. In Ps. i—xli the divine name יהוה predominates; it occurs 272 times and אלהים only 15 times, and for the most part under circumstances where יהוה was not admissible. With Ps. xlii the Elohimic style begins; the last psalm of this kind is the Korahitic psalm lxxxiv, which for this very reason is placed after the Elohimic psalms of Asaph. In the Ps. lxxxv — cl יהוה again becomes prominent, with such exclusiveness, that in the psalms of the Fourth and Fifth books יהוה occurs 339 times (not 239 as in *Symbolæ* p. 5), and אלהים of the true God only once (cxliv. 9). Among the psalms of David 18 are Elohimic, among the Korahitic 9, and the Asaphic are all Elohimic. Including one psalm of Solomon and four anonymous psalms, there are 44 in all (reckoning Ps. xlii and xliii as two). They form the middle portion of the Psalter, and have on their right 41 and on their left 65 Jahve-psalms.

Community in species of composition also belongs to the manifold grounds on which the order according to the subject-matter is determined. Thus the מַשְׂכִּיל (xlii—xliii. xliv. xlv. lii—lv) and מִכְתָּם (lvi—lx) stand together among the Elohim-psalms. In like manner we have in the last two books the שִׁיר הַמַּצֲלוֹת (cxx—cxxxiv) and, divided into groups, those beginning with הוֹדוּ (cv—cvii) and those beginning and ending with הַלְלוּיָהּ (cxi—cxvii, cxlvi—cl) — whence it follows that these titles to the psalms are older than the final redaction of the collection.

It could not possibly be otherwise than that the inscriptions of the psalms, after the harmless position which the mono-

---

* This is Ewald's view (which is also supported by Riehm in *Stud. u. Krit.* 1857 S. 168). A closer insight into the characteristic peculiarity of the Elohim-psalms, which is manifest in other respects also, proves it to be superficial and erroneous.

graphs of Sonntag (1687), Celsius (1718), Irhof (1728) take with regard to them, should at length become a subject for criticism; but the custom which has gained ground since the last decade of the past century of rejecting what has been historically handed down, has at present grown into a despicable habit of forming a decision too hastily, which in any other department of literature where the judgment is not so prejudiced by the drift of the enquiry, would be regarded as folly. Instances like Hab. iii. 1 and 2 Sam. i. 18, comp. Ps. lx. 1, shew that David and other psalm-writers might have appended their names to their psalms and the definition of their purport. And the great antiquity of these and similar inscriptions also follows from the fact that the LXX found them already in existence and did not understand them; that they also cannot be explained from the Books of the Chronicles (including the Book of Ezra, which belongs to these) in which much is said about music, and appear in these books, like much besides, as an old treasure of the language revived, so that the key to the understanding of them must have been lost very early, as also appears from the fact that in the last two books of the Psalter they are of more rare, and in the first three of more frequent occurrence.

VI. THE STROPHE-SYSTEM OF THE PSALMS.

The early Hebrew poetry has neither rhyme nor metre, both of which (first rhyme and then afterwards metre) were first adopted by Jewish poesy in the seventh century after Christ. True, attempts at rhyme are not wanting in the poetry and prophecy of the Old Testament, especially in the *tephilla* style, Ps. cvi. 4—7 cf. Jer. iii. 21—25, where the earnestness of the prayer naturally causes the heaping up of similar flexional endings; but this assonance, in the transition state towards rhyme proper, had not yet assumed such an established form as is found in Syriac.* It is also just as difficult to point out verses of four lines only, which have a uniform or mixed metre running through them. Notwithstanding, Augustine, *Ep.* cxiii *ad Memorium,* is perfectly warranted in saying of the Psalms: *certis eos constare numeris*

---

* *Vid.* Zingerle in the *Deutsch. Morgenländ. Zeitschrift.* X. 110 ff.

credo illis qui eam linguam probe callent, and it is not a mere
fancy when Philo, Josephus, Eusebius, Jerome and others have
detected in the Old Testament songs, and especially in the
Psalms, something resembling the Greek and Latin metres.
For the Hebrew poetry indeed had a certain syllabic measure, since, — apart from the audible *Shebâ* and the *Chateph,*
both of which represent the primitive shortenings, — all syllables with a full vowel are intermediate, and in ascending become long, in descending short, or in other words, in one
position are strongly accented, in another more or less slurred over. Hence the most manifold rhythms arise, *e. g.* the
anapæstic *wenashlîcha miménnu abothêmo* (ii. 3) or the dactylic
áz jedabbér elêmo beappó (ii. 5). The poetic discourse is freer
in its movement than the Syriac poetry with its constant ascending (‿ ‿́) or descending spondees (‿́ ‿); it represents
all kinds of syllabic movements and thus obtains the appearance of a lively mixture of the Greek and Latin metres. But
it is only an appearance — for the forms of verse, which con-
form to the laws of quantity, are altogether foreign to early
Hebrew poetry, as also to the oldest poetry; and these rhythms
which vary according to the emotions are not metres, for, as
Augustine says in his work *De Musica, "Omne metrum rhythmus,
non omnis rhythmus etiam metrum est."* Yet there is not a single
instance of a definite rhythm running through the whole in a
shorter or longer poem, but the rhythms always vary according to the thoughts and feelings; as *e. g.* the evening song
Ps. iv towards the end rises to the anapæstic measure: *ki-
attá Jahawé lebadád,* in order then quietly to subside in the
iambic: *labétach tôshibéni.** With this alternation of rise and

---

* Bellermann's *Versuch über die Metrik der Hebräer* (1813) is comparatively the best on this subject even down to the present time; for
Saalschütz (*Von der Form der hebr. Poesie,* 1825, and elsewhere) proceeds
on the erroneous assumption that the present system of accentuation
does not indicate the actual strong toned syllable of the words — by
following the pronunciation of the German and Polish Jews he perceives,
almost throughout, a spondæo-dactylic rhythm (*e. g.* Judg. xiv. 18 *lúle
charáshtem beegláthi*). But the traditional accentuation is proved to be
a faithful continuation of the ancient proper pronunciation of the Hebrew; the trochaic pronunciation is more Syrian, and the tendency to
draw the accent from the final syllable to the penult, regardless of the
conditions originally governing it, is a phenomenon which belongs only

fall, long and short syllables, harmonizing in lively passages with the subject, there is combined, in Hebrew poetry, an expressiveness of accent which is hardly to be found anywhere else to such an extent. Thus *e. g.* Ps. ii. 5*a* sounds like pealing thunder, and 5*b* corresponds to it as the flashing lightning. And there are a number of dull toned Psalms as xvii. xlix. lviii. lix. lxxiii, in which the description drags heavily on and is hard to be understood, and in which more particularly the suffixes in *mo* are heaped up, because the indignant mood of the writer impresses itself upon the style and makes itself heard in the very sound of the words. The *non plus ultra* of such poetry, whose very tones heighten the expression, is the cycle of the prophecies of Jeremiah chap. xxiv—xxvii.

Under the point of view of rhythm the so-called *parallelismus membrorum* has also been rightly placed: that fundamental law of the higher, especially poetic, style for which this appropriate name has been coined, not very long since.* The relation of the two parallel members does not really differ from that of the two halves on either side of the principal cæsura of the hexameter and pentameter; and this is particularly manifest in the double long line of the cæsural schema (more correctly: the diæretic schema) *e. g.* Ps. xlviii. 6, 7: *They beheld, straightway they marvelled, | bewildered they took to flight. Trembling took hold upon them there | anguish, as a woman in travail.* Here the one thought is expanded in the same verse in two parallel members. But from the fact of the rhythmical organization being carried out without reference to the logical requirements of the sentence, as in the same psalm vers. 4, 8: *Elohim in her palaces | was known as a refuge. With an east wind Thou breakest | the ships of Tarshish,* we

---

to the later period of the language (*vid.* Hupfeld in the *Deutsch. Morgenl. Zeitschr.* vi. 187).

  * Abenezra calls it כָּפוּל *duplicatum,* and Kimchi כֶּפֶל עִנְיָן בְּמִלּוֹת שׁוֹנוֹת, *duplicatio sententiæ verbis variatis;* both regard it as an elegant form of expression (דרך צחות). Even the punctuation does not proceed from a real understanding of the rhythmical relation of the members of the verse to one another, and when it divides every verse that is marked off by *Silluk* wherever it is possible into two parts, it must not be inferred that this rhythmical relation is actually always one consisting of two members merely, although (as Hupfeld has shewn in his admirable treatise on the twofold law of the rhythm and accent, in the *D. M. Z.* 1852), wherever it exists it always consists of at least two members.

see that the rhythm is not called into existence as a necessity of such expansion of the thought, but *vice versâ* this mode of expanding the thought results from the requirements of the rhythm. Here is neither synonymous or identical (tautological), nor antithetical, nor synthetical parallelism, but merely that which De Wette calls rhythmical, merely the rhythmical rise and fall, the diastole and systole, which poetry is otherwise (without binding itself) wont to accomplish by two different kinds of ascending and descending logical organization. The ascending and descending rhythm does not usually exist within the compass of one line, but it is distributed over two lines which bear the relation to one another of rhythmical antecedent and consequent, of προῳδός and ἐπῳδός. This distich is the simplest ground-form of the strophe, which is visible in the earliest song, handed down to us, Gen. iv. 23 sq. The whole Ps. cxix is composed in such distichs, which is the usual form of the apophthegm; the acrostic letter stands there at the head of each distich, just as at the head of each line in the likewise distichic pair, Ps. cxi, cxii. The tristich is an outgrowth from the distich, the ascending rhythm being prolonged through two lines and the fall commencing only in the third, *e. g.* xxv. 7 (the ח of this alphabetical Psalm):

Have not the sins of my youth and my transgressions in remembrance,
According to Thy mercy remember Thou me
For Thy goodness' sake, O Jahve!

This at least is the natural origin of the tristich, which moreover in connection with a most varied logical organization still has the inalienable peculiarity, that the full fall is reserved until the third line, *e. g.* in the first two strophes of the Lamentations of Jeremiah, where each line is a long line in two parts consisting of rise and fall, the principal fall, however, after the cæsura of the third long line, closes the strophe:

Ah! how doth the city sit solitary, otherwise full of people!
She is become as a widow, the great one among nations,
The princess among provinces, she is become tributary.

By night she weepeth sore and her tears are upon her cheeks;
There is not one to comfort her of all her lovers,
All her friends have betrayed her, they are become her enemies.

If we now further enquire, whether Hebrew poesy goes beyond these simplest beginnings of the strophe-formation and even

extends the network of the rhythmical period, by combining
the two and three line strophe with ascending and descending
rhythm into greater strophic wholes rounded off into themselves, the alphabetical Psalm xxxvii furnishes us with a
safe answer to the question, for this is almost entirely tetrastichic, *e. g.*

> About evil-doers fret not thyself,
> About the workers of iniquity be thou not envious.
> For as grass they shall soon be cut down,
> And as the green herb they shall wither,

but it admits of the compass of the strophe increasing even
to the pentastich, (ver. 25, 26) since the unmistakeable landmarks of the order, the letters, allow a freer movement:

> Now I, who once was young, am become old,
> Yet have I not seen the righteous forsaken
> And his seed begging bread.
> He ever giveth and lendeth
> And his seed is blessed.

From this point the sure guidance of the alphabetical
Psalms* fails us in investigating the Hebrew strophe-system.
But in our further confirmatory investigations we will take
with us from these Psalms, the important conclusion that the
verse bounded by *Sôph pasûk,* the placing of which harmonizes
with the accentuation first mentioned in the post-Talmudic
tractate *Sofrim,* ** is by no means (as, since Köster, 1831, it
has been almost universally supposed) the original form of
the strophe but that strophes are a whole consisting of an
equal or symmetrical number of stichs.*** Hupfeld (*Ps.* iv.

---

* Even the older critics now and then supposed that we were to
make these Ps. the starting point of our enquiries. For instance, Serpilius says: "It may perhaps strike some one whether an opinion as to
some of the modes of the Davidic species of verse and poetry might
not be formed from his, so-to-speak, alphabetical psalms."

** Even if, and this is what Hupfeld and Riehm (*Luth. Zeitschr.* 1866,
S. 300) advance, the Old Testament books were divided into verses,
פסוקים, even before the time of the Masoretes, still the division into
verses, as we now have it and especially that of the three poetical books,
is Masoretic.

*** It was these stichs, of which the Talmud (*B. Kiddushin* 30 *a*) counts
eight more in the Psalter than in the Thôra, viz. 5896, which were originally called פסוקים. Also in Augustine we find *versus* thus used like
στίχος. With him the words *Populus ejus et oves pascuæ ejus* are one
versus. There is no Hebrew MS. which could have formed the basis of

450) has objected against this, that "this is diametrically opposed to the nature of rhythm = parallelism, which cannot stand on one leg, but needs two, that the distich is therefore the rhythmical unit."

But does it therefore follow, that a strophe is to be measured according to the number of distichs? The distich is itself only the smallest strophe, viz. one consisting of two lines. And it is even forbidden to measure a greater strophe by the number of distichs, because the rhythmical unit, of which the distich is the ground-form, can just as well be tristichic, and consequently these so-called rhythmical units form neither according to time nor space parts of equal value. But this applies still less to the Masoretic verses. True, we have shewn in our larger Commentary on the Psalms, ii. 522 sq., in agreement with Hupfeld, and in opposition to Ewald, that the accentuation proceeds upon the law of dichotomy. But the Masoretic division of the verses is not only obliged sometimes to give up the law of dichotomy, because the verse (as *e. g.* xviii. 2, xxv. 1, xcii. 9,) does not admit of being properly divided into two parts ; and it subjects not only verses of three members (as *e. g.* i. 1, ii. 2) in which the third member is embellishingly or synthetically related to the other two — both are phenomena which in themselves furnish proof in favour of the relative independence of the lines of the verse — but also verses of four members where the sense requires it (as i. 3, xviii. 16) and where it does not require it (as xxii. 15, xl. 6), to the law of dichotomy. And these Masoretic verses of such various compass

the arrangement of the Psalms in stichs; those which we possess only break the Masoretic verse, (if the space of the line admits of it) for ease of writing into the two halves, without even regarding the general injunction in c. xiv of the tractate *Sofrim* and that of Ben-Bileam in his *Horajoth ha-Kore*, that the breaks are to be regulated by the beginnings of the verses and the two great pausal accents. Nowhere in the MSS., which divide and break up the words most capriciously, is there to be seen any trace of the recognition of those old פסוקים being preserved. These were not merely lines determined by the space, as were chiefly also the στίχοι or ἔπη according to the number of which, the compass of Greek works was recorded, but lines determined by the sense, κῶλα (Suidas: κῶλον ὁ ἀπηρτισμένην ἔννοιαν ἔχων στίχος), as Jerome wrote his Latin translation of the Old Testament after the model of the Greek and Roman orators (*e. g.* the MSS. of Demosthenes), *per cola et commata* i. e. in lines breaking off according to the sense.

are to be the constituent parts according to which strophes
of a like cipher shall be measured! A strophe only becomes
a strophe by virtue of its symmetrical relation to others, to
the ear it must have the same time, to the eye the same form
and it must consequently represent the same number of lines
(clauses). The fact of these clauses, according to the special
characteristic of Hebrew poetry, moving on with that rising
and falling movement which we call parallelism until they
come to the close of the strophe where it gently falls to rest, is a
thing *sui generis,* and, within the province of the strophe, somewhat of a substitute for metre; but the strophe itself is a section which comes to thorough repose by this species of rhythmical movement. So far, then, from placing the rhythm on
one leg only, we give it its two: but measure the strophe
not by the two feet of the Masoretic verses or even couplets
of verses, but by the equal, or symmetrically alternating number of the members present, which consist mostly of two feet,
often enough however of three, and sometimes even of four feet.

Whether and how a psalm is laid out in strophes, is shewn
by seeing first of all what its pauses are, where the flow of
thoughts and feelings falls in order to rise anew, and then
by trying whether these pauses have a like or symmetrically
correspondent number of stichs *(e. g.* 6. 6. 6. 6 or 6. 7. 6. 7)
or, if their compass is too great for them to be at once regarded as one strophe, whether they cannot be divided into
smaller wholes of an equal or symmetrical number of stichs.
For the peculiarity of the Hebrew strophe does not consist
in a run of definite metres closely united to form one harmonious whole (for instance, like the Sapphic strophe, which
the four membered verses, Isa. xvi. 9, 10, with their short
closing lines corresponding to the Adonic verse, strikingly
resemble), but in a closed train of thought which is unrolled
after the distichic and tristichic ground-form of the rhythmical period. The strophe-schemata, which are thus evolved,
are very diverse. We find not only that all the strophes of
a poem are of the same compass *(e. g.* 4. 4. 4. 4), but also
that the poem is made up of symmetrical relations formed
of strophes of different compass. The condition laid down
by some, * that only a poem that consists of strophes of equal

---

* For instance Meier in his *Geschichte der poetischen Nationallitera-*

length can be regarded as strophic, is refuted not only by the Syriac* but also by the post-biblical Jewish poetry. ** We find the following variations: strophes of the same compass followed by those of different compass (*e. g.* 4. 4. 6. 6); as in the chiasmus, the outer and inner strophes of the same compass (*e. g.* 4. 6. 6. 4); the first and third, the second and fourth corresponding to one another (*e. g.* 4. 6. 4. 6); the mingling of the strophes repeated antistrophically, *i. e.* in the inverted order (*e. g.* 4. 6. 7. 7. 6. 4); strophes of equal compass surrounding one of much greater compass (*e. g.* 4. 4. 10. 4. 4.), what Köster calls the pyramidal schema; strophes of equal compass followed by a short closing stanza (*e. g.* 3. 3. 2); a longer strophe forming the base of the whole (*e. g.* 5. 3. 3. 7), and these are far from being all the different figures, which the Old Testament songs and more especially the Psalms present to us, when we arrange their contents in stichs.

With regard to the compass of the strophe, we may expect to find it consisting of as many as twelve lines according to the Syrian and the synagogue poetry. The line usually consists of three words, or at least only of three larger words; in this respect the Hebrew exhibits a capacity for short but emphatic expressions, which are inadmissible in German [or English]. This measure is often most uniformly preserved throughout a considerable length, not only in the Psalms but also in the Book of Job. For there is far more reason for saying that the strophe lies at the basis of the arrangement of the Book of Job, than for G. Hermann's observation of strophic arrangement in the Bucolic writers and Köchly's in the older portions of Homer.

VII. TEMPLE MUSIC AND PSALMODY.

The Thôra contains no directions respecting the use of song and music in divine worship except the commands con-

---

tur der Hebräer, S. 67, who maintains that strophes of unequal length are opposed to the simplest laws of the lyric song and melody. But the demands which melody imposes on the formation of the verse and the strophe were not so stringent among the ancients as now, and moreover — is not the sonnet a lyric poem?

* *vid.* Zingerle in the *D. M. Z.* x. 123, 124.

** *vid.* Zunz, *Synagogale Poesie des Mittelalters*, S. 92—94.

cerning the ritualistic use of silver trumpets to be blown by the priests (Numb. ch. x). David is really the creator of liturgical music, and to his arrangements, as we see from the Chronicles, every thing was afterwards referred, and in times when it had fallen into disuse, restored. So long as David lived, the superintendence of the liturgical music was in his hands (1 Chron. xxv. 2). The instrument by means of which the three choir-masters (Heman, Asaph, and Ethan-Jeduthun) directed the choir was the cymbals (מְצִלְתַּיִם or צֶלְצְלִים*) which served instead of wands for beating time; the harps (נְבָלִים) represented the soprano, and the bass (the male voice in opposition to the female) was represented by the citherns an octave lower (1 Chron. xv. 17—21), which, to infer from the word לְנַצֵּחַ used there, were used at the practice of the pieces by the מְנַצֵּחַ appointed. In a Psalm where סֶלָה is appended (vid. on Ps. iii), the stringed instruments (which הִגָּיוֹן סֶלָה ix. 17 definitely expresses), and the instruments generally, are to join in** in such a way as to give intensity to that which is being sung. To these instruments, besides those mentioned in Ps. cl, 2 Sam. vi. 5, belonged also the flute, the liturgical use of which (vid. on v. 1) in the time of the first as of the second Temple is undoubted: it formed the peculiar musical accompaniment of the *hallel* (vid. Ps. cxiii) and of the nightly torch-light festival on the semi-festival days of the Feast of Tabernacles (*Succa* 15 a). The trumpets (הַצֹּצְרוֹת) were blown exclusively by the priests to whom no part was assigned in the singing (as probably also the horn שׁוֹפָר lxxxi. 4, xcviii. 6, cl. 3), and according to 2 Chron. v. 12 sq. (where the number of the two Mosaic trumpets appears to be raised to 120) took their turn *unisono* with the singing and the music of the Levites. At the dedication of Solomon's Temple the Levites sing and play and the priests sound trumpets נֶגְדָּם, 2 Chron. vii. 6, and at

---

* Talmudic צֶלְצַל. The usual Levitic orchestra of the temple of Herod consisted of 2 Nabla players, 9 Cithern players and one who struck the *Zelazal*, viz. Ben-Arza (*Erachin* 10 a, &c.; *Tamid* vii. 3), who also had the oversight of the *duchan* (*Tosiphta* to *Shekalim* ii).

** Comp. Mattheson's "*Erläutertes Selah*" 1745: Selah is a word marking a prelude, interlude, or after-piece with instruments, a sign indicating the places where the instruments play alone, in short a so-called *ritornello*.

the inauguration of the purified Temple under Hezekiah the music of the Levites and priests sound in concert until all the burnt offerings are laid upon the altar fire, and then (probably as the wine is being poured on) began (without any further thought of the priests) the song of the Levites, 2 Chron. xxix. 26—30. In the second Temple it was otherwise: the sounding of the trumpets by the priests and the Levitical song with its accompanying music alternated, they were not simultaneous. The congregation did not usually sing with the choir, but only uttered their Amen; nevertheless they joined in the *Hallel* and in some psalms after the first clause with its repetition, after the second with hallelujah (Maimonides, *Hilchoth Megilla*, 3). 1 Chron. xvi. 36 points to a similar arrangement in the time of the first Temple. Just so does Jer. xxxiii. 11 in reference to the *"Give thanks unto the Lord, for He is good"*. Antiphonal singing on the part of the congregation is also to be inferred from Ezra iii. 10 sq. The Psalter itself is moreover acquainted with an allotment of the עלמות, comp. מְשֹׁרְרוֹת Ezra ii. 65 (whose treble was represented by the Levite boys in the second Temple, *vid.* on xlvi 1) in choral worship and speaks of a praising of God "in full choirs", xxvi. 12, lxviii. 27. And responsive singing is of ancient date in Israel: even Miriam with the women answered the men (לָהֶם Ex. xv. 21) in alternating song, and Nehemiah (ch. xii. 27 sqq.) at the dedication of the city walls placed the Levites in two great companies which are there called תודות, in the midst of the procession moving towards the Temple. In the time of the second Temple each day of the week had its psalm. The psalm for Sunday was xxiv, for Monday xlviii, Tuesday lxxxii, Wednesday xciv, Thursday lxxxi, Friday xciii, the Sabbath xcii. This arrangement is at least as old as the time of the Ptolemies and the Seleucidæ, for the statements of the Talmud are supported by the inscriptions of Ps. xxiv, xlviii, xciv, xciii in the LXX, and as respects the connection of the daily psalms with the drink-offering, by Sir. l. 14—16. The psalms for the days of the week were sung, to wit, at the time of the drink-offering (נֶסֶךְ) which was joined with the morning *Tamîd*[*]: two priests, who stood on

---

[*] According to the maxim אין אומר שירה אלא על היין, "no one singeth except over the wine."

the right and left of the player upon the cymbal *(Zelazal)* by whom the signal was given, sounded the trumpets at the nine pauses (פרקים), into which it was divided when sung by the Levites, and the people bowed down and worshipped.* The Levites standing upon the *suggestus* (דּוּכָן), — *i. e.* upon a broad staircase consisting of a few steps, which led up from the court of the laity to that of the priests, — who were both singers and musicians, and consequently played only on stringed instruments and instruments of percussion, not wind-instruments, were at least twelve in number, with 9 citherns, 2 harps, and one cymbal: on certain days the flute was added to this number.** The usual *suggestus* on the steps at the side of the altar was changed for another only in a few cases; for it is noticed as something special that the singers had a different position at the festival of water-drawing during the Feast of Tabernacles (*vid.* introduction to Ps. cxx — cxxxiv), and that the flute-players who accompanied the *Hallel* stood before the altar, לפני המזבח (*Erachin* 10 *a*). The treble was taken

---

* *B. Rosh ha-Shana*, 31 *a*. *Tamîd* vii. 3, comp. the introduction to Ps. xxiv. xcii and xciv.

** According to *B. Erachin* 10 *a* the following were the customary accompaniments of the daily service: 1) 21 trumpet blasts, to as many as 48; 2) 2 nablas, to 6 at most; 2 flutes (חלילין), to 12 at most. Blowing the flute is called striking the flute, הִכָּה הֶחָלִיל. On 12 days of the year the flute was played before the altar: on the 14th of Nisan at the slaying of the Passover (at which the *Hallel* was sung), on the 14th of Ijar at the slaying of the little Passover, on the 1st and 7th days of the Passover and on the eight days of the Feast of Tabernacles. The mouth-piece (אַבּוּב according to the explanation of Maimonides) was not of metal but a reed (comp. Arab. *anbûb*, the blade of the reed), because it sounds more melodious. And it was never more than one flute (אבוב יחידי, playing a solo), which continued at the end of a strain and closed it, because this produces the finest close (חלּוּק). On the 12 days mentioned, the *Hallel* was sung with flute accompaniment. On other days, the Psalm appointed for the day was accompanied by nablas, cymbals and citherns. This passage of the treatise *Erachin* also tells who were the flute-players. On the flute-playing at the festival of water-drawing, *vid.* my *Geschichte der jüdischen Poesie* S. 195. In the Temple of Herod, according to *Erachin* 10 *b*, there was also an organ. This was however not a water-organ (הדרולים, *hydraulis*), but a wind-organ (מַגְרֵפָה) with a hundred different tones (מיני זמר), whose thunder-like sound, according to Jerome (*Opp. ed. Mart.* v. 191), was heard *ab Jerusalem usque ad montem Oliveti et amplius*, vid. Saalschütz, *Archäol* i. 281—284.

by the Levite youths, who stood below the *suggestus* at
the feet of the Levites (*vid.* on Ps. xlvi). The daily שִׁיר הַקָּרְבָּן
(*i. e.* the week‑day psalm which concluded the morning sa‑
crifice) was sung in nine (or perhaps more correctly 3*) pau‑
ses, and the pauses were indicated by the trumpet-blasts of
the priests (*vid.* on Ps. xxxviii. lxxxi. 4). Beside the seven
Psalms which were sung week by week, there were others ap‑
pointed for the services of the festivals and intervening days
(*vid.* on Ps. lxxxi), and in *Biccurim* 3, 4 we read that when
a procession bearing the firstfruits accompanied by flute
playing had reached the hill on which the Temple stood and
the firstfruits had been brought up in baskets, at the entrance
of the offerers into the *Azara,* Ps. xxx was struck up by the
Levites. This singing was distinct from the mode of deliver‑
ing the *Tefilla* (*vid.* on Ps. xliv *ad fin.*) and the benediction of
the priests (*vid.* on Ps. lxvii), both of which were unaccom‑
panied by music. Distinct also, as it seems, from the mode
of delivering the *Hallel,* which was more as a recitative, than
sung (*Pesachim* 64 *a,* קָרְאוּ אֶת הַהֲלֵּל). It was probably similar
to the Arabic, which delights in shrieking, long-winded, tril‑
ling, and especially also nasal tones. For it is related of one
of the chief singers that in order to multiply the tones, he
placed his thumb in his mouth and his fore finger בֵּין הַנִּימִין
(between the hairs, *i. e.* according to Rashi: on the furrow
of the upper lip against the partition of the nostrils), and thus
(by forming mouth and nose into a trumpet) produced sounds,
before the volume of which the priests started back in aston‑
ishment.** This mode of psalm-singing in the Temple of He‑
rod was no longer the original mode, and if the present ac‑
centuation of the Psalms represents the fixed form of the
Temple song, it nevertheless does not convey to us any im‑

------

* This is the view of Maimonides, who distributes the 9 trumpet-
blasts by which the morning sacrifice, according to *Succa* 53 *b*, was ac‑
companied, over the 3 pauses of the song. The hymn *Haazinu,* Deut. xxxii,
which is called שִׁירַת הַלְוִים *par excellence*, was sung at the Sabbath
Musaph - sacrifice — each Sabbath a division of the hymn, which was
divided into six parts — so that it began anew on every seventh Sabbath,
vid. J. Megilla, sect. iii, *ad fin.*

** *vid. B. Joma* 38 *b* and *J. Shekalim* ɤ. 3, comp. *Canticum Rabba* on
Canticles iii. 6.

pression of that before the Exile. It does, however, neither the one nor the other.

The accents are only musical, and indirectly interpunctional, signs for the chanting pronunciation of the synagogue. And moreover we no longer possess the key to the accents of the three metrical (*i. e.* consisting of symmetrical stichs and strophes) books as musical signs. For the so-called Sarka-tables (which give the value of the accents as notes, beginning with *Zarka,* זרקא), *e. g.* at the end of the second edition of Nägelsbach's *Gramm.,* relate only to the reading of the penta-teuchal and prophetic pericope, — consequently to the system of prose accents. In the German synagogue there is no tradition concerning the value of the so-called metrical accents as notes, for the Psalms were not recited according to the accents; but for all the Psalms, there are only two different modes, at least in the German ritual, *viz.* 1) the customary one according to which verse after verse is recited by the leader and the congregation, as *e. g.* Ps. xcv — xcix. xxix. every Friday evening; and 2) that peculiar to Ps. cxix in which the first seven verses of the eight are recited alternately by the leader and the congregation, but the eighth as a concluding verse is always closed by the congregation with a cadence. This psalmody does not always follow the accents. We can only by supposition approximately determine how the Psalms were to be recited according to them. For we still possess at least a few statements of Ben-Asher, Shemtob and Moses Provenzalo (in his grammatical didactic poem בְּשֵׁם קַדְמוֹן) concerning the intonation of single metrical accents. *Pazer* and *Shalshéleth* have a like intonation, which rises with a trill; though *Shalshéleth* is more prolonged, about a third longer than that of the prose books. *Legarme* (in form *Mahpach* or *Azla* followed by *Psik*) has a clear high pitch, before *Zinnor,* however, a deeper and more broken tone; *Rebia magnum* a soft tone tending to repose. By *Silluk* the tone first rises and then diminishes. The tone of *Mercha* is according to its name *andante* and sinking into the depths; the tone of *Tarcha* corresponds to *adagio.* Further hints cannot be traced: though we may infer with respect to *Ole we-jored (Mercha mahpa-chatum)* and *Athnach,* that their intonation ought to form a cadence, as that *Rebia parvum* and *Zinnor (Zarka)* had an intonation hurrying on to the following distinctive accent. Further, if we place *Dechi (Tiphcha initiale)* and *Rebia gereshatum* beside the remaining six *servi* among the notes, we may indeed produce a sarka-table of the metrical accentuation, although we cannot guarantee its exact agreement with the original manner of singing.

Following Gerbert *(De musica sacra)* and Martini *(Storia della musica),* the view is at present very general that in the eight Gregorian tones together with the extra tone *(tonus peregrinus),** used only for Ps. cxiii (= cxiv—cxv in the Hebrew numeration), we have a remnant of the ancient Temple song; and this in itself is by no means improbable in connection with the Jewish nationality of the primitive church and its gradual severance at the first from the Temple and synagogue. In the convents of Bethlehem, which St. Paula founded, psalms were sung at six hours of prayer from early morn till midnight, and she herself was so well versed in Hebrew, *ut Psalmos hebraice caneret et sermonem absque ulla Latinæ linguæ proprietate personaret (Ep.* 108 *ad Eustoch.* c. 26). This points to a connection between the church and synagogue psalm-melodies in the *mos orientalium partium,* the oriental psalmody, which was introduced by Ambrose into the Milanese church. Nevertheless, at the same time the Jewish element has undergone scarcely any change; it has been developed under the influence of the Greek style, but is, notwithstanding, still recognizable.** Pethachja of Ratisbon, the Jewish traveller in the 12th century, when in Bagdad, the ancient seat of the Geonim (נאונים), heard the Psalms sung in a manner altogether peculiar;*** and Benjamin of Tudela, in the same century, became acquainted in Bagdad with a skilful singer of the Psalms used in divine worship. Saadia on Ps. vi. 1,

---

* *vid.* Friedr. Hommel's *Psalter nach der deutschen Uebersetzung* D. *M. Luthers für den Gesang eingerichtet,* 1859. The Psalms are there arranged in stichs, rightly assuming it to be the original mode and the most appropriate, that antiphonal song ought to alternate not according to the verses, as at the present day in the Romish and English church, but according to the two members of the verse.

** *vid.* Saalschütz, *Geschichte und Würdigung der Musik bei den Hebräern,* 1829, S. 121, and Otto Strauss, *Geschichtliche Betrachtung über den Psalter als Gesang- und Gebetbuch,* 1859.

*** *vid. Literaturblatt des Orients,* 4th year, col. 541.

infers from עַל־הַשְּׁמִינִית that there were eight different melodies (الكان). And eight נְגִינֹת are also mentioned elsewhere;* perhaps not without reference to those eight church-tones, which are also found among the Armenians.** Moreover the two modes of using the accents in chanting, which are attested in the ancient service-books,*** may perhaps be not altogether unconnected with the distinction between the festival and the simpler ferial manner in the Gregorian style of church-music.

VIII. TRANSLATIONS OF THE PSALMS.

The earliest translation of the Psalms is the Greek Alexandrine version. When the grandson of the son of Sirach came to Egypt in the year 132 B. C., not only the Law and the Prophets, but also the Hagiographa were already translated into the Greek; of course therefore also the Psalms, by which the Hagiographa are directly named in Luke xxiv. 44. The story of the LXX (LXXII) translators, in its original form, refers only to the Thôra; the translations of the other books are later and by different authors. All these translators used a text consisting only of consonants, and these moreover were here and there more or less indistinct; this text had numerous glosses, and was certainly not yet, as later, settled on the Masoretic basis. This they translated literally, in ignorance of the higher exegetical and artistic functions of the translator, and frequently the translation itself is obscure. From Philo, Josephus and the New Testament we see that we possess the text of this translation substantially in its original form, so that criticism, which since the middle of the last century has acquired many hitherto unknown helps,† more especially also in the province of the Psalms, will not need to reverse its judgment of the character of the

---

* Steinschneider, *Jewish Literature* p. 336 sq.

** Petermann, *Ueber die Musik der Armenier* in the *Deutsche Morgenl. Zeischrift* v. 368 f.

*** Zunz, *Synagogale Poesie*, S. 115.

† To this period belong 1) the *Psalterium Veronense* published by Blanchini 1740, the Greek text in Roman characters with the Italic at the side belonging to the 5th or 6th century (*vid.* Tischendorf's edition of the LXX, 1856, *Prolegg.* p. lviii sq.); 2) the *Psalterium Turicense pur-*

work. Nevertheless, this translation, as being the oldest key to the understanding of the language of the Old Testament writings, as being the oldest mirror of the Old Testament text, which is not to be exempted from modest critical investigation, and as an important check upon the interpretation of Scripture handed down in the Talmud, in the Midrash, and in that portion of the national literature in general, not originating in Egypt, — is invaluable.

In one other respect this version claims a still greater significance. Next to the Book of Isaiah, no book is so frequently cited in the New Testament as the Psalter. The Epistle to the Hebrews has grown up entirely from the roots of the language of the Old Testament psalms. The Apocalypse, the only book which does not admit of being referred back to any earlier formula as its basis, is nevertheless not without references to the Psalter: Ps. ii in particular has a significant part in the moulding of the apocalyptic conceptions and language. These New Testament citations, with few exceptions (as John xiii. 18), are based upon the LXX, even where this translation (as. *e. g.,* Ps. xix. 5, li. 6, cxvi. 10), only in a general way, correctly reproduces the original text. The explanation of this New Testament use of the LXX is to be found in the high esteem in which this translation was held among the Jewish people: it was accounted, not only by the Hellenistic, but also by the Palestinian Jews, as a providential and almost miraculous production; and this esteem was justified by the fact, that, although altogether of unequal birth with the canonical writ-

---

pureum described by Breitinger 1748, Greek Text likewise of the 5th or 6th century (*vid. ibid.* p. lix sq.); 3) *Palmorum Fragmenta papyracea Londinensia* (in the British Museum), Ps. x. 2—xviii. 6, xx. 14—xxxiv. 6, of the 4th century, given in Tischendorf's *Monumenta Sacra Inedita. Nova Collectio* t. i; 4) *Fragmenta Psalmorum Tischendorfiana* Ps. cxli (ii). 7—8, cxlii (iii). 1—3, cxliv (v). 7—13, of the 5th or 4th century in the *Monumenta* t. ii. There still remain unused to the present time 1) the *Psalterium Græco-Latinum* of the library at St. Gall, *Cod.* 17 in 4to, Greek text in uncial characters with the Latin at the side; 2) *Psalterium Gallico-Romano-Hebraico-Græcum* of the year 909, *Cod.* 230 in the public library at Bamberg (*vid.* a description of this MS. by Schönfelder in the *Serapeum*, 1865, No. 21) written by Solomon, abbot of St. Gall and bishop of Constance (d. 920), and brought to Bamberg by the emperor Henry II (d. 1024), who had received it as a gift when in St. Gall; as regards the criticism of the text of the LXX it is of like importance with the *Veronense* which it resembles.

ings, it nevertheless occupies a position in the history of divine revelation which forms a distinct epoch. For it was the first opportunity afforded to the gentile world of becoming acquainted with the Old Testament revelation, and thus the first introduction of Japheth into the tents of Shem. At the same time therewith, a distinct breaking down of the barriers of the Old Testament particularism was effected. The Alexandrine translation was, therefore, an event which prepared the way for that Christianity, in which the appointment of the religion of Israel to be the religion of the world is perfected. This version, at the outset, created for Christianity the language which it was to use; for the New Testament Scriptures are written in the popular Greek dialect (κοινή) with an Alexandrine colouring. And in a general way we may say that Alexandrinism moulded the forms beforehand, which Christianity was afterwards to fill up with the substance of the gospel. As the way of Jesus Christ lay by Egypt (Matth. ii. 15), so the way of Christianity also lay by Egypt, and Alexandria in particular.

Equally worthy of respect on account of its antiquity and independence, though not of the same importance as the LXX from a religio-historical point of view, is the Targum or Chaldee version of the Psalms: a version which only in a few passages assumes the form of a paraphrase with reference to Midrash interpretations. The date of its composition is uncertain. But as there was a written Targum to the Book of Job* even during the time of the Temple, there was also a Targum of the Psalms, though bearing in itself traces of manifold revisions, which probably had its origin during the duration of the Temple. In distinction from the Targums of Onkelos to the Pentateuch and of Jonathan to the minor Prophets the Targum of the Psalms belongs to the so-called Jerusalem group,** for the Aramaic idiom in which it is written, — while, as the Jerusalem Talmud shews, it is always distinguished in no small degree from the Palestinian popular dialect as being the language of the literature — abounds in the same manner as the former in Greek words

---

* *vid. Tosefta* to *Sabb.* xvi, *Jer. Sabb.* xiv, §. 1, *Bab. Sabb.* 115 *a*, *Sofrim* v, 15.

** *vid.* Geiger, *Urschrift und Uebersetzungen der Bibel, S.* 166 f.

(as אַנְגְּלִין ἄγγελοι, אַבְסַדְרִין ἐξέδραι, קִירִים κύριος), and like it also closely approximates, in sound and formation, to the Syriac. From this translation which excels the LXX in grammatical accuracy and has at its basis a more settled and stricter text, we learn the meaning of the Psalms as understood in the synagogue, as the interpretation became fixed, under the influence of early tradition, in the first centuries of the Christian era. The text of the Targum itself is at the present day in a very neglected condition. The most correct texts are to be found in Buxtorf and Norzi's Bibles. Critical observations on the Targums of the Hagiographa are given in the treatise עיטה אור by Benzion Berkowitz (Wilna, 1843).

The third most important translation of the Psalms is the *Peshîto*, the old version of the Syrian church, which was made not later than in the second century. Its author translated from the original text, which he had without the vowel points, and perhaps also in a rather incorrect form: as is seen from such errors as xvii. 15 (אמונתך instead of תמונתך), lxxxiii. 12 (שדמו ואבדמי *dele eos et perde eos* instead of שיתמו נדיבמו), cxxxix. 16 (גמלי *retributionem meam* instead of גלמי). In other errors he is influenced by the LXX, as lvi. 9 (בנגדך LXX ἐνώπιόν σου instead of בנאדך), he follows this version in such departures from the better text sometimes not without additional reason, as xc. 5 (*generationes eorum annus erunt,* i. e. זרעותיו שנה יהיו, LXX τὰ ἐξουδενώματα αὐτῶν ἔτη ἔσονται), cx. 3 (*populus tuus gloriosus,* i. e. עמך נְדִבֹת in the sense of נדיבה, Job xxx. 15, nobility, rank, LXX μετὰ σοῦ ἡ ἀρχή). The fact that he had the LXX before him beside the original text is manifest, and cannot be done away by the supposition that the text of the Peshîto has been greatly distorted out of the later Hexaplarian translation; although even this is probable, for the LXX won such universal respect in the church that the Syrians were almost ashamed of their ancient version, which disagreed with it in many points, and it was this very circumstance which gave rise in the year 617 A. D. to the preparation of a new Syriac translation from the Hexaplarian LXX-text. It is not however merely between the Peshîto and the LXX, but also between the Peshîto and the Targum, that a not accidental mutual relation exists, which becomes at once apparent in Ps. i (*e. g.* in the translation of לצים by

ממיקני and of תורת by נמוסא) and hardly admits of explanation by the use of the Christian Peshîto on the part of the Jewish Targumist.* It may be more readily supposed that the old Syriac translator of the Psalms, of whom we are now speaking, was a Jewish Christian and did not despise the welcome assistance of the Targum, which was already at hand, in whatever form it might be. It is evident that he was a Christian from passages like xix. 5, cx. 3, also from lxviii. 19 comp. with Ephes. iv. 8, Jer. xxxi. 31 comp. with Hebr. viii. 8; and his knowledge of the Hebrew language, with which, as was then generally the case, the knowledge of Greek was united, shews that he was a Jewish Christian. Moreover the translation has its peculiar Targum characteristics: tropical expressions are rendered literally, and by a remarkable process of reasoning interrogative clauses are turned into express declarations: lxxxviii. 11—13 is an instance of this with a bold inversion of the true meaning to its opposite. In general the author shuns no violence in order to give a pleasing sense to a difficult passage e. g. xii. 6 b, lx. 6. The musical and historical inscriptions, and consequently also the סלה (including הגיון סלה ix. 17) he leaves untranslated, and the division of verses he adopts is not the later Masoretic. All these peculiarities make the *Peshîto* all the more interesting as a memorial in exegetico-historical and critical enquiry: and yet, since Dathe's edition, 1768, who took the text of Erpenius as his ground-work and added valuable notes,** scarcely anything has been done in this direction.

In the second century new Greek translations were also made. The high veneration which the LXX had hitherto enjoyed was completely reversed when the rupture between the synagogue and the church took place, so that the day when this translation was completed was no longer compared to the day of the giving of the Law, but to the day of

----

* Although more recently we are told, Hai Gaon (in Babylonia) when he came upon a difficult passage in his Academical lectures on the Psalms enquired of the patriarch of the Eastern church how he interpreted it, *vid.* Steinschneider, *Jewish Literature*, p. 125 sq.

** The fragments of the translation of the Ps., which are cited under the name ὁ Σύρος, Dathe has also there collected in his preface.

the golden calf. Nor was it possible that it should be otherwise than that its defects should become more and more perceptible. Even the New Testament writers found it requiring correction here and there, or altogether unfit for use, for the Palestinian text of the Old Testament which had been handed down, was not merely as regards the consonants but also as to pronunciation substantially the same as that which has been fixed by the Masoretes since the sixth century. Consequently Aquila of Pontus (a proselyte from heathenism to Judaism) in the first half of the 2nd century, made a Greek translation of the Old Testament, which imitated the original text word for word even at the risk of un-Greek expressions, and in the choice of the Greek words used is determined by the etymology of the Hebrew words. Not to lose any of the weighty words he translates the first sentence of the Thôra thus: Ἐν κεφαλαίῳ ἔκτισεν ὁ Θεὸς σὺν (את) τὸν οὐρανὸν καὶ σὺν (את) τὴν γῆν. In the fragments of the translation of the Psalms, one of which has been preserved in the Talmudic literature (*vid.* on Ps. xlviii. 15), we do not meet with such instances of violence in favour of literalness, although also even there he forces the Greek into the form of the Hebrew, and always renders the words according to their primary meaning (*e. g.* דביר χρηματιστήριον, מגלה εἴλημα, פתח ἄνοιγμα, רהב ὅρμημα, אמן πεπιστευμένως), sometimes unhappily and misled by the usage the language had acquired in his time. In some passages he reads the text differently from our present pointing (*e. g.* x. 4 ὅταν ὑψωθῇ), but he moreover follows the tradition (*e. g.* סלה ἀεί, שׁדי ἱκανός, מבתם τοῦ ταπεινόφρονος καὶ ἁπλοῦ = מך ותם) and also does not despise whatever the LXX may offer that is of any worth (*e. g.* במנים ἐν χορδαῖς), as his translation throughout, although an independent one, relies more or less upon the pioneering work of its predecessor, the LXX. His talent as a translator is unmistakeable. He has perfect command of the Hebrew, and handles the treasures of the Greek with a master-hand. For instance, in the causative forms he is never in difficulty for a corresponding Greek word (הפיל πτωματίζειν, הריץ δρομοῦν, השׂכיל ἐπιστημοῦν and the like). The fact that he translated for the synagogue in opposition to the church is betrayed by passages like ii. 12, xxii. 17, cx. 3 and perhaps also lxxxiv. 10, comp. Dan. ix. 26, where he prefers ἠλειμμένου to Χριστοῦ: nevertheless one must not in this respect charge him with evil intentions throughout. Even Jerome, on calmer reflection, moderated his indignation against Aquila's translation to a less harsh judgment: *ut amicæ menti fatear, quæ ad nostram fidem pertineant roborandam plura reperio*, and praised it even at the expense of the translations of Theodotion and Symmachus: *Isti Semichristiani Judaice transtulerunt, et Judæus Aquila interpretatus est ut Christianus.*

The translation of Theodotion is not an original work. It is based upon the LXX and brings this version, which was still the most widely used, into closer relation to the original text, by making use of Aquila's translation. The fragments that are preserved to us of passages independently translated contain nothing pre-eminently characteristic. Symmachus also takes the LXX as his basis, but in re-moulding it according to the original text he acts far more decidedly and independently than Theodotion, and distinguishes himself from Aquila by endeavouring to unite literalness with clearness and verbal accuracy: his translation of the Psalms has even a poetic inspiration about it. Both Aquila and Symmachus issued their translations twice, so that some passages are extant translated in a twofold form (*vid.* cx. 3).

Beside the LXX. Aq. Symm. and Theod. there are also a fifth, sixth and seventh Greek translation of the Psalms. The fifth is said to have been found in Jericho under the emperor Caracalla, the sixth in Nicopolis under the emperor Alexander Severus. The former, in its remains, shews a knowledge of the language and tradition, the latter is sometimes (xxxvii. 35, Hab. iii. 13) paraphrastic. A seventh is also mentioned besides, it is most like Theodotion. In the Hexapla of Origen, which properly contains only six columns (the Hebrew text, the Hebr. text in Greek characters, Aq., Symm., LXX, Theod.), in the Ps. and elsewhere a *Quinta* (E), *Sexta* (ς), and *Septima* (Z) are added to these six columns: thus the Hexapla (apart from the Seventh) became an Octapla. Of the remains of these old versions as compiled by Origen, after the labours of his predecessors Nobilius and Drusius, the most complete collection is that of Bernard de Montfaucon in his *Hexaplorum Origenis quæ supersunt* (2 vols. *folio,* Paris 1713); the rich gleanings since handed down from many different quarters* are unfortunately still scattered and uncollated.

Euthymius Zigadenus mentions beside the LXX, Aq., Symm., Theod., V., and VI., as a Seventh version that of Lucian which attempts to restore the original Septuagint-text by a comparison with the original text. Lucian died as a martyr 311 A. D. in Nicomedia, whither he had been dragged from Antioch. The autograph of this translation was found in Nicomedia, hidden in a small rough-plastered tower.** We are as little able to form a conception of this Septuagint-recension of Lucian as of that of the cotemporary Egyptian bishop Hesychius, since not a single specimen of either is extant. It would be interesting to know the difference of treatment of the two critics from that of Origen, who corrected the text of the κοινή after the Hebrew original by means of Theodotion's, *obelis jugulans quæ abundare videbantur, et quæ deerant sub asteriscis interserens,* which produced a confusion that might easily have been foreseen.

From the old Latin translation, the so-called *Itala,* made from the LXX, we possess the Psalter complete: Blanchini has published this translation of the Psalms (1740) from the Veronese Psalter, and Sabbatier in the second volume of his *Latinæ Versiones Antiquæ* (1751) from the Psalter of the monastery of St. Germain. The text in Faber Stapulensis' *Quincuplex Psalterium* (1509) is compiled from Augustine; for Augustine, like Hilary, Ambrose, Prosper, and Cassiodorus, expounds the Psalms according to the old Latin text. Jerome first of all carefully revised this in Rome, and thus originated the *Psalterium Romanum,* which has been the longest retained

---

* Thus *e. g.* Montfaucon was only able to make use of the Psalter-MS. *Cod. Vat.* 754 for 16 Psalms; Adler has compared it to the end and found in it valuable Hexapla fragments (*vid. Repert. für Bibl. u. Morgenl. Lit.* xiv. S. 183 f.). The Psalm-commentary of Barhebræus and the *Psalterium Mediolanense* have also been begun to be worked with this object; but as yet, not the Syriac Psalter of the Medici library mentioned by Montfaucon, *Bibliotheca Bibliothecarum* i. 240 and supposed to be based upon the *Quinta.*

** Comp. the Athanasian synopsis in Montfaucon, *Hexapla* t. 1 p. 59 and the contribution from a Syriac MS. in the *Repertorium für Bibl. u. Morgenl. Lit. ib.* (1784) S. 48 f.

by the church of Milan and the Basilica of the Vatican. He
then in Bethlehem prepared a second more carefully revised
edition, according to the Hexaplarian Septuagint-text* with
daggers (as a sign of additions in the LXX contrary to the
original) and asterisks (a sign of additions in the LXX from
Theodotion in accordance with the original), and this second
edition which was first adopted by the Gallican churches
obtained the name of the *Psalterium Gallicanum.* It is not
essentially different from the Psalter of the Vulgate, and
appeared, with its critical signs, from a MS. of Bruno, bishop
of Würzburg (died 1045), for the first time in the year 1494
(then edited by Cochleus, 1533): both Psalters, the Romish
and the Gallican, are placed opposite one another in Faber's
Quincuplex Psalterium, in t. x. p. 1 of the *Opp. Hieronymi, ed.
Vallarsi* and elsewhere.

The Latin Psalters, springing from the common or from
the Hexaplarian Septuagint-text, as also the Hexapla-Syriac
and the remaining Oriental versions based upon the LXX and
the Peshîto, have only an indirectly exegetico-historical value.
On the contrary Jerome's translation of the Psalter, *juxta
Hebraicam veritatem,* is the first scientific work of translation,
and, like the whole of his independent translation of the
Old Testament from the original text, a bold act by which
he has rendered an invaluable service to the church, without
allowing himself to be deterred by the cry raised against such
innovations. This independent translation of Jerome has
become the Vulgate of the church: but in a text in many
ways estranged from its original form, with the simple exception of the Psalter. For the new translation of this book
was opposed by the inflexible liturgical use it had attained;
the texts of the *Psalterium Romanum* and *Gallicanum* maintained their ground and became (with the omission of the
critical signs) an essential portion of the Vulgate. On this
account it is the more to be desired that Jerome's Latin Psalter

---

* *Illud breviter admoneo* — says Jerome, Ep. cvi. *ad Sunniam et Frete-
lam* — *ut sciatis, aliam esse editionem, quam Origenes et Cæsareensis Eusebius omnesque Græciæ tractatores* Κοινήν, *id est, Communem appellant atque
Vulgatam et a plerisque nunc* Λουκιανός *dicitur; aliam Septuaginta Inter-
pretum, quæ in* Ἑξαπλοῖς *codicibus reperitur et a nobis in Latinum sermonem fideliter versa est et Hierosolymæ atque in Orientis ecclesiis decantatur.*

ex Hebræo (*Opp. ed. Vallarsi* t. ix. p. iii) were made more generally known and accessible by a critical edition published separately. It is not necessary to search far for critical helps for such an undertaking. There is an excellent MS., *Cod.* 19, in the library of St. Gall, presented by the abbot Hartmot (died 895).

Origen and Jerome learnt the language of the Old Testament from Jewish teachers. All the advantages of Origen's philological learning are lost to us, excepting a few insignificant remains, with his Hexapla: this gigantic bible which would be the oldest direct monument of the Old Testament text if it were but extant. Whereas in Jerome's Old Testament translated from the original text (*canon Hebraicæ veritatis*) we have the maturest fruit of the philological attainments of this indefatigable, steady investigator inspired with a zeal for knowledge. It is a work of the greatest critical and historical value in reference to language and exegesis. The translation of the Psalter is dedicated to Sophronius who had promised to translate it into Greek: this Greek translation is not preserved to us.

Jerome's translation of the Psalter has not its equal either in the synagogue or the church until the time of Saadia Gaon of Fajum, the Arabian translator of the Psalms. Two MSS. of his translation of the Psalms are to be found at Oxford; but the most important, which also contains his annotations complete, is in Munich. Schnurrer (1791) contributed Ps. xvi, xl and cx to Eichhorn's *Biblioth. der Bibl. Lit.* iii, from *Cod. Pocock.* 281, then Haneberg (1840) Ps. lxviii and several others from the Munich Cod.; the most extensive excerpts from *Cod. Pocock.* 281 and *Cod. Huntingt.* 416 (with various readings from *Cod. Mon.* appended) are given by Ewald in the first vol. of his *Beiträge zur ältesten Ausleg. u. Spracherklärung des A. T.* 1844. The gain which can be drawn from Saadia for the interpretation of the Psalms, according to the requirements of the present day, is very limited; but he promises a more interesting and rich advantage to philology and the history of exegesis. Saadia stands in the midst of the still ever mysterious process of development out of which the finally established and pointed text of the Old Testament came forth. He has written a treatise on the punctuation

(ניקוד) to which Rashi refers in Ps. xlv. 10, but in his treatment of the Old Testament text shews himself to be unfettered by its established punctuation. His translation is the first scientific work on the Psalms in the synagogue. The translation of Jerome is five hundred years older, but only the translation of Luther has been able to stand side by side with it and that because he was the first to go back to the fountain head of the original text.

The task, which is assigned to the translator of the sacred Scriptures, was recognised by Luther as by no one before him, and he has discharged it as no one up to the present day since his time has done. What Cicero said of his translation of the two controversial speeches of Demosthenes and Æschines holds good also of Luther: *Non converti ut interpres, sed ut orator, sententiis iisdem et earum formis tanquam figuris, verbis ad nostram consuetudinem aptis: in quibus non verbum pro verbo necesse habui reddere, sed genus omnium verborum vimque servavi; non enim ea me adnumerare lectori putavi oportere, sed tanquam adpendere* — he has lived in thought and feeling in the original text in order not to reproduce it literally with a slavish adherence to its form, but to re-mould it into good and yet spiritually renewed German and at the same time to preserve its spirit free and true to its deepest meaning. This is especially the case with his translation of the Psalms, in which even Moses Mendelssohn has thought it to his advantage to follow him. To deny that here and there it is capable of improvement by a more correct understanding of the sense and in general by greater faithfulness to the original (without departing from the spirit of the German language), would indicate an ungrateful indifference to the advance which has been made in biblical interpretation — an advance not merely promised, but which we see actually achieved.

IX. HISTORY OF THE EXPOSITION OF THE PSALMS.

If we now take a glance over the history of the exposition of the Psalms, we shall see from it how late it was before the proper function of scientific exposition was recognised. We begin with the apostolic exposition. The Old Testament according to its very nature tends towards and centres in

Christ.   Therefore the innermost truth of the Old Testament has been revealed in the revelation of Jesus Christ.   But not all at once: His passion, resurrection, and ascension are three steps of this progressive opening up of the Old Testament, and of the Psalms in particular.   Our Lord himself, both before and after His resurrection, unfolded the meaning of the Psalms from His own life and its vicissitudes; He shewed how what was written in the Law of Moses, in the Prophets and in the Psalms was fulfilled in Him; He revealed to His disciples the meaning τοῦ συνιέναι τὰς γραφάς Luke xxiv. 44 sq. Jesus Christ's exposition of the Psalms is the beginning and the goal of Christian Psalm-interpretation.   This began, as that of the Christian church, and in fact first of all that of the Apostles, at Pentecost when the Spirit, whose instrument David acknowledges himself to have been (2 Sam. xxiii. 2), descended upon the Apostles as the Spirit of Jesus, the ful-filler and fulfilment of prophecy.   This Spirit of the glorified Jesus completed what, in His humiliation and after His resur-rection, he had begun: He opened up to the disciples the meaning of the Psalms.   How strongly they were drawn to the Psalms is seen from the fact that they are quoted about seventy times in the New Testament, which, next to Isaiah, is more frequently than any other Old Testament book.   From these interpretations of the Psalms the church will have to draw to the end of time.   For only the end will be like the begin-ning and even surpass it.   But we must not seek in the New Testament Scriptures what they are not designed to furnish, viz., an answer to questions belonging to the lower grades of knowledge, to grammar, to cotemporary history and to criticism. The highest and final questions of the spiritual meaning of Scripture find their answer here; the grammatico-historico-critical under-structure, — as it were, the candlestick of the new light, — it was left for succeeding ages to produce.

The post-apostolic, patristic exposition was not ca-pable of this.   The interpreters of the early church with the exception of Origen and Jerome possessed no knowledge of the Hebrew tongue, and even these two not sufficient to be able to rise to freedom from a dependence upon the LXX which only led them into frequent error.   Of Origen's Commentary and Homilies on the Ps. we possess only fragments translated

by Rufinus, and his ὑπόμνημα εἰς τοὺς ψαλμούς (edited complete
by Kleopas, 1855, from a MS. in the monastery of Mar-Saba).
Jerome, *contra Rufinum* i. § 19, indeed mentions *Commentarioli*
on the Ps. by himself, but the *Breviarium in Psalterium* (in t.
vii. p. ii of his *Opp. ed. Vallarsi*) bearing his name is allowed
not to be genuine, and is worthless as regards the history of
the text and the language. The almost complete Commentary
(on Ps. i—cxix according to the Hebrew reckoning) of Eusebius, made known by Montfaucon (*Collectio nova Patrum et
Scriptorum Græc.* t. i) is unsuspected. Eusebius, though living
in Palestine and having a valuable library at command,
is nevertheless so ignorant of the Hebrew, that he considers
it is possible Μαριαμ (מרחם) in Ps. cx may refer to Mary.
But by contributions from the Hexapla he has preserved
many acceptable treasures of historical value in connection
v ith the translation, but of little worth in other respects,
for the interpretation is superficial, and capriciously allegorical
and forced. Athanasius in his short explanation of the Psalms
(in t. i p. ii of the Benedictine edition) is entirely dependent
on Philo for the meaning of the Hebrew names and words.
His book: πρὸς Μαρκελλῖνον εἰς τὴν ἑρμηνείαν τῶν ψαλμῶν (in
the same vol. of the Benedictine edition) is a very beautiful
essay. It treats of the riches contained in the Psalms, classi-
fies them according to their different points of view, and gives
directions how to use them profitably in the manifold circumstances and moods of the outward and inner life. Johann
Reuchlin has translated this little book of Athanasius into
Latin, and Jörg Spalatin from the Latin of Reuchlin into
German (1516. 4to.). Of a similar kind are the two books of
Gregory of Nyssa εἰς τὴν ἐπιγραφὴν τῶν ψαλμῶν (*Opp. ed.
Paris,* t. i), which treat of the arrangement and inscriptions;
but in respect of the latter he is so led astray by the LXX,
that he sets down the want of titles of 12 Ps. (this is the
number according to Gregory), which have titles in the LXX,
to Jewish ἀπιστία and κακία. Nevertheless there are several
valuable observations in this introduction of the great Nyssene.
About cotemporaneously with Athanasius, Hilarius Picta-
viensis, in the Western church, wrote his allegorizing (after
Origen's example) *Tractatus in librum Psalmorum* with an
extensive prologue, which strongly reminds one of Hippolytus'

We still have his exposition of Ps. i. ii. **ix.** xiii. xiv. li. lii. liii—lxix. xci. cxviii—cl (according to the numbering of the LXX); according to Jerome (*Ep. ad Augustin.* cxii*) it is transferred from Origen and Eusebius. It is throughout ingenious and pithy, but more useful to the dogmatic theologian than to the exegete (t. xxvii. xxviii of the *Collectio Patrum* by Caillau and Guillon).** Somewhat later, but yet within the last twenty years of the fourth century (about 386 — 397), come Ambrose's *Enarrationes in Ps.* i. xxxv—xl. xliii. xlv. xlvii. xlviii. lxi. cxviii (in t. ii of the Benedictine edition). The exposition of Ps. i is likewise an introduction to the whole Psalter, taken partly from Basil. He and Ambrose have pronounced the highest eulogiums on the Psalter. The latter says: *Psalmus enim benedictio populi est, Dei laus, plebis laudatio, plausus omnium, sermo universorum, vox Ecclesiæ, fidei canora confessio, auctoritatis plena devotio, libertatis lætitia, clamor jucunditatis, lætitiæ resultatio. Ab iracundia mitigat, a sollicitudine abdicat, a mærore allevat. Nocturna arma, diurna magisteria; scutum in timore, festum in sanctitate, imago tranquillitatis, pignus pacis atque concordiæ, citharæ modo ex diversis et disparibus vocibus unam exprimens cantilenam. Diei ortus psalmum resultat, psalmum resonat occasus.* After such and similar prefatory language we are led to expect from the exposition great fervour and depth of perception: and such are really its characteristics, but not to so large an extent as might have been the case had Ambrose — whose style of writing is as musical as that of Hilary is stiff and angular — worked

------

* The following Greek expositors of the Psalms are mentioned there: 1) Origen, 2) Eusebius of Cæsarea, 3) Theodore of Heraclea (the *Anonymus* in Corderius' *Catena*), 4) Asterius of Scythopolis, 5) Apollinaris (Apolinarios) of Laodicea, 6) Didymus of Alexandria. Then the following Latin expositors: 1) Hilary of Poictiers, who translated or rather remodelled Origen's Homilies on the Psalms (Jerome himself says of him, *Ep.* lvii *ad Pammach.* : *captivos sensus in suam linguam victoris jure transposuit*), 2) Eusebius of Vercelli, translator of the commentary of Eusebius of Cæsarea, and 3) Ambrose, who was partly dependent upon Origen. Of Apollinaris the elder, we have a Μετάφρασις τοῦ ψαλτῆρος διὰ στίχων ἡρωϊκῶν preserved to us. He has also translated the Pentateuch and other Old Testament books into heroic verse.

** *vid.* the characteristics of this commentary in Reinkens, *Hilarius von Poitiers* (1864) S. 291—308.

out these expositions, which were partly delivered as sermons, partly dictated, with his own hand.

The most comprehensive work of the early church on the Psalms was that of Chrysostom, which was probably written while at Antioch. We possess only the exposition of 58 Ps. or (including Ps. iii and xli, which in their present form do not belong to this work) 60 Ps. (in t. v of Montfaucon's edition). Photius and Suidas place this commentary on the Psalms in the highest rank among the works of Chrysostom. It is composed in the form of sermons, the style is brilliant, and the contents more ethical than dogmatic. Sometimes the Hebrew text according to the Hexapla is quoted, and the Greek versions which depart from the original are frequently compared, but, unfortunately, generally without any name. There is hardly any trace in it of the renowned philologico-historical tendency of the school of Antioch. Theodoret (in t. ii p. ii of the Halle edition) was the first to set before himself the middle course between an extravagant allegorising and an unspiritual adherence to the literal historical sense (by which he doubtless has reference to Theodore of Mopsuestia), and thus to a certain extent he makes a beginning in distinguishing between the province of exegesis and practical application. But this scientific commencement, with even more of the grammatico-historical tendency, is still defective and wanting in independence. For example, the question whether all the Psalms are by David or not, is briefly decided in the affirmative, with κρατείτω τῶν πλειόνων ἡ ψῆφος.* The designed, minute comparison of the Greek translators is most thankworthy; in other respects, this expositor, like the Syrians generally, is wanting in the mystic depth which might compensate for the want of scientific insight. All this may be also said of Euthymius Zigadenus (Zigabenus): his commentary on the

---

* In the Talmud R. Meir, *Pesachim* 117 *a*, adopts the view that David is the author of all the Ps.: כל תשבחות שבספר תהלים כולן דוד אמרן, while in *Bathra* 14 *b* ten authors are supposed: דוד כתב ספר תהלים על ידי עשׂרה זקנים, *vid.* on this, Midrash to Cant. iv. 4 and Eccl. vii. 19. In the former passage לתלפיות is explained as an emblematic name of the Psalter: ספר שאמרוהו לו פיות הרבה, the book of David, to which the mouths of many have contributed. And there are two modern commentaries, viz. by Klauss, 1832, and Randegger, 1841, which are written with the design of proving all the Psalms to be Davidic.

Psalms (in Greek in t. iv of the Venetian edition of the *Opp. Theophylacti*), written at the desire of the emperor Alexius Comnenus, is nothing but a skilful compilation, in the preparation of which he made good use of the Psalm-catena, likewise a compilation, of the somewhat earlier Νικήτας Σερρῶν*, which is to be found on Mount Athos and is still unprinted.

The Western counterpart to Chrysostom's commentary are Augustine's *Enarrationes in Psalmos* (in t. iv of the Benedictine edition). The psalm-singing in the Milanese church had contributed greatly to Augustine's conversion. But his love to his Lord was fired still more by the reading of the Psalms when he was preparing himself in solitude for his baptism. His commentary consists of sermons which he wrote down in part himself and in part dictated. Only the thirty-two *sermones* on Ps. cxviii (cxix), which he ventured upon last of all, were not actually delivered. He does not adopt the text of Jerome as his basis, but makes use of the older Latin version, the original text of which he sought to establish, and here and there to correct, by the LXX; whereas Arnobius, the Semi-Pelagian, in his paraphrastic Africano-Latin commentary on the Psalms (first edition by Erasmus, *Basileæ, Froben.* 1522, who, as also Trithemius, erroneously regarded the author as one and the same with the Apologist) no longer uses the so-called Itala, but takes Jerome's translation as his basis. The work of Augustine far surpassing that of Chrysostom in richness and depth of thought, has become, in the Western church, the chief mine of all later exposition of the Psalms. Cassiodorus in his *Expositiones in omnes Psalmos* (in t. ii of the Bened. ed.) draws largely from Augustine, though not devoid of independence.

What the Greek church has done for the exposition of the Psalms has been garnered up many times since Photius in so-called Σειραί, *Catenæ*. That of Nicetas archbishop of Serra in Macedonia (about 1070), is still unprinted. One, extending only to Ps. l, appeared at Venice 1569, and a complete one, edited by Corderius, at Antwerp 1643 (3 vols., from

---

* This information is found in the modern Greek edition of Euthemius' Commentary on the Ps. by Nicodemos the Agiorite (2 vols. Constantinople 1819—21), which also contains extracts from this catena of Nicetas Serronius.

Vienna and Munich MSS.). Folckmann (1601) made extracts from the Catena of Nicetas Heracleota, and Aloysius Lippomanus began a Catena from Greek and Latin writers on the largest scale (one folio vol. on Ps. i—x, *Romæ* 1585). The defects to be found in the ancient exposition of the Psalms are in general the same in the Greek and in the Western expositors. To their want of acquaintance with the text of the original was added their unmethodical, irregular mode of procedure, their arbitrary straining of the prophetic character of the Psalms (as *e. g.* Tertullian, *De spectaculis,* takes the whole of Ps. i as a prophecy concerning Joseph of Arimathea), their unhistorical perception, before which all differences between the two Testaments vanish, and their misleading predilection for the allegorical method. In all this, the meaning of the Psalms, as understood by the apostles, remains unused; they appropriate it without rightly apprehending it, and do not place the Psalms in the light of the New Testament fulfilment of them, but at once turn them into New Testament language and thoughts. But the church has never found such rapturous delight in the Psalms, which it was never weary of singing day and night, never used them with richer results even to martyrdom, than at that period. Instead of profane popular songs, as one passed through the country one might hear psalms resounding over the fields and vineyards. *Quocunque te verteris,* writes Jerome to the widow of Marcellus from the Holy Land, *arator stivam tenens Alleluja decantat, sudans messor psalmis se avocat et curva attondens vitem falce vinitor aliquid Davidicum canit. Hæc sunt in hac provincia carmina, hæ (ut vulgo dicitur) amatoriæ cantiones, hic pastorum sibilus, hæc arma culturæ.* The delights of country life he commends to Marcella in the following among other words: *Vere ager floribus pingitur et inter querulas aves Psalmi dulcius cantabuntur.* In Sidonius Apollinaris we find even psalm-singing in the mouth of the men who tow the boats, and the poet takes from this a beautiful admonition for Christians in their voyage and journey through this life:

> *Curvorum hinc chorus helciariorum*
> *Responsantibus Alleluja ripis*
> *Ad Christum levat amicum celeusma.*
> *Sic, sic psallite, nauta et viator!*

And how many martyrs have endured every form of martyrdom with psalms upon their lips! That which the church in those days failed to furnish in writing towards the exposition of the Psalms, it more than compensated for by preserving the vitality of the Psalms with its blood. Practice made far more rapid progress than theory.* These patristic works are patterns for every age of the true fervour which should characterise the expositor of the Psalms.

The mediæval church exposition did not make any essential advance upon the patristic. After Cassiodorus, came Haymo (d. 853) and Remigius of Auxerre (d. about 900), still less independent compilers; the commentary of the former, edited by Erasmus, appeared *Trib.* 1531, of the latter, first *Colon.* 1536, and then in the *Bibl. maxima Lugdunensis*. That of Petrus Lombardus (d. about 1160) is a catena taken directly from earlier expositors from Jerome to Alcuin. Of a more independent character are the commentaries of Thomas Aquinas, who however only completed 51 Ps., and Alexander of Hales, if the Commentary which appeared under his name (*Venet.* 1496) is not rather to be attributed to cardinal Hugo. Besides these, Bonaventura (d. 1274) and Albertus Magnus (d. 1280) stand out prominently in the Middle Ages as expositors of the Psalms; and on the border of the Middle Ages Michael Ayguanus (about 1400) whose commentary has been frequently reprinted since its first appearance, *Mediol.* 1510. If you know one of these expositors, you know them all. The most that they have to offer us is an echo of the earlier writers. By their dependence on the letter of the Vulgate, and consequently indirectly of the LXX, they only too frequently light upon a false track and miss the meaning. The *literalis sensus* is completely buried in *mysticæ intelligentiæ*. Without observing the distinction between the two economies, the conversion of the Psalms into New Testament language and

---

* *vid.* besides the essay by Otto Strauss, already mentioned: Armknecht, *Die heilige Psalmodie oder der psalmodirende König David und die singende Urkirche*, 1855; and W. von Gülick, *Das Psalterium nach seinem Hauptinhalte in seiner wissenschaftlichen und praktischen Bedeutung* (a Catholic prize essay) 1858; partly also Rudelbach's *Hymnologische Studien* in the *Luther. Zeitschrift* 1855, 4, 1856, 2. and especiallyno penitential psalm-singing Zöckler's *Geschichte der Askese* (1863) S. 256—264.

thought, regardless of the intermediate steps of development,
is here continued. Thus, for example, Albertus Magnus in his
commentary (*Opp.* t. vii), on the principle: *Constat, quod totus
liber iste de Christo,* at once expounds *Beatus vir* (Ps. i. 1),
and the whole Ps., *de Christo et ejus corpore ecclesia.* But as
we find in the Fathers occasional instances of deep insight
into the meaning of passages, and occasional flashes of thought
of lasting value, so even here the reading, especially of the
mystics, will repay one. — The greatest authority in psalm-
exposition for the Middle Ages was Augustine. From Augustine, and perhaps we may add from Cassiodorus, Notker
Labeo (d. 1022), the monk of St. Gall, drew the short annotations which, verse by verse, accompany his German translation of the Psalms (vol. ii of H. Hattemer's *Denkmahle des
Mittelalters*). In like manner the Latin Psalter-catena of bishop Bruno of Würzburg (d. 1045), mentioned above, is compiled from Augustine and Cassiodorus, but also from Jerome,
Bede and Gregory. And the Syriac annotations to the Psalms
of Gregory Barhebræus (d. 1286), — of which Tullberg and
Koraen, Upsala 1842, and Schröter, Breslau 1857, have published specimens, — are merely of importance in connection
with the history of exposition, and are moreover in no way
distinguished from the mediæval method.

The mediæval synagogue exposition is wanting in the
recognition of Christ, and consequently in the fundamental
condition required for a spiritual understanding of the Psalms.
But as we are indebted to the Jews for the transmission
of the codex of the Old Testament, we also owe the transmission of the knowledge of Hebrew to them. So far the
Jewish interpreters give us what the Christian interpreters
of the same period were not able to tender. The interpretations of passages from the Psalms scattered up and down
in the Talmud are mostly unsound, arbitrary, and strange.
And the Midrash on the Ps., bearing the title שׁוֹחר טוֹב (*vid.*
Zunz, *Vorträge*, §. 266 ff.), and the Midrash-catenæ entitled
ילקוּט, of which at present only ילקוט שמעוני (by Simeon Kara
ha-Darshan) is known, and ילקוט מכירי (by Machir b. Abba-
Mari), contain far more that is limitlessly digressive than
what is to the point and usable. This class of psalm-exposition was always employed for the thoroughly practical end

of stimulating and edifying discourse. It is only since about
900 A. D., when indirectly under Syro-Arabian influence, the
study of grammar began to be cultivated among the Jews,
that the exposition and the application of Scripture began
to be disentangled. At the head of this new era of Jewish
exegesis stands Saadia Gaon (d. 941—2), from whose Arabic
translation and annotations of the Ps. Haneberg (1840) and
Ewald (1844) have published extracts. The Karaites, Salmon
b. Jerocham and Jefeth, both of whom have also expounded
the Psalms, are warm opponents of Saadia; but Jefeth whose
commentary on the Psalms* has been in part made known by
Bargès (since 1846), nevertheless already recognises the influence of grammar, which Saadia raised to the dignity of a
science, but which Salmon utterly discards. The next great
expositor of the Psalms is Rashi (*i. e.* Rabbi Salomo Isaaki)
of Troyes (d. 1105), who has interpreted the whole of the
Old Testament (except the Chronicles) and the whole of the
Talmud;** and he has not only treasured up with pithy brevity the traditional interpretations scattered about in the
Talmud and Midrash, but also (especially in the Psalms) made
use of every existing grammatico-lexical help. Aben-Ezra
of Toledo (d. 1167) and David Kimchi of Narbonne (d. about
1250) are less dependent upon tradition, which for the most
part expended itself upon strange interpretations. The former is the more independent and genial, but seldom happy
in his characteristic fancies; the latter is less original, but
gifted with a keener appreciation of that which is simple and
natural, and of all the Jewish expositors he is the pre-
eminently . grammatico - historical interpreter. Gecatilia's
(Mose ha-Cohen Chiquitilla) commentary on the Psalms written in Arabic is only known to us from quotations, principally in Aben-Ezra. In later commentaries, as those of Mose
Alshêch (Venice 1601) and Joel Shoëb (Salonica 1569), the
simplicity and elegance of the older expositors degenerates
into the most repulsive scholasticism. The commentary of

---

* It is to be found in MS. partly in Paris, partly in St. Peters-
burg: the former having been brought thither from Egypt by Munk in
1841 and the latter by Tischendorf in 1853.

** But on some parts of the Talmud, *e. g.* the tractate *Maccoth*, we
have not any commentary by Rashi.

Obadia Sforno (d. at Bologna 1550), Reuchlin's teacher, is too much given to philosophising, but is at least withal clear and brief. Their knowledge of the Hebrew gives all these expositors a marked advantage over their Christian cotemporaries, but the veil of Moses over their eyes is thicker in proportion to their conscious opposition to Christianity. Nevertheless the church has not left these preparatory works unused. The Jewish Christians, Nicolaus de Lyra (d. about 1340), the author of the *Postillæ perpetuæ*, and Archbishop Paul de Santa Maria of Burgos (d. 1435), the author of the *Additiones ad Lyram*, took the lead in this respect. Independently, like the last mentioned writers, Augustinus Justinianus of Genoa, in his *Octaplus Psalterii* (Genoa, 1516, folio), drew chiefly from the Midrash and Sohar. The preference however was generally given to the use of Aben-Ezra and Kimchi; *e. g.* Bucer, who acknowledges his obligation to these, says: *neque enim candidi ingenii est dissimulare, per quos profeceris.* Justinianus, Pagninus, and Felix were the three highest authorities on the original text at the commencement of the Reformation. The first two had gained their knowledge of the original from Jewish sources and Felix Pratensis, whose *Psalterium ex hebreo diligentissime ad verbum fere translatum*, 1522, appeared under Leo X., was a proselyte.

We have now reached the threshold of the Reformation exposition. Psalmody in the reigning church had sunk to a lifeless form of service. The exposition of the Psalms lost itself in the dependency of compilation and the chaos of the schools. *Et ipsa quamvis frigida tractatione Psalmorum* — says Luther in his preface to Bugenhagen's Latin Psalter — *aliquis tamen odor vitae oblatus est plerisque bonæ mentis hominibus, et utcunque ex verbis illis etiam non intellectis semper aliquid consolationis et aurulæ senserunt e Psalmis pii, veluti ex roseto leniter spirantis.* Now, however, when a new light dawned upon the church through the Reformation — the light of a grammatical and deeply spiritual understanding of Scripture, represented in Germany by Reuchlin and in France by Vatablus — then the rose-garden of the Psalter began to breathe forth its perfumes as with the renewed freshness of a May day; and born again from the Psalter, German hymns resounded from the shores of the Baltic to the foot of the Alps with all the fervour of a newly quickened first-love. "It is marvellous"—says the Spanish Carmelite Thomas à Jesu,— "how greatly the hymns of Luther helped forward the Lutheran cause. Not only the churches and schools echo with them, but even the private houses, the workshops, the markets, streets, and fields." For converted into imperishable hymns (by Luther, Albinus, Franck, Gerhardt, Jonas, Musculus, Poliander, Ringwaldt, and many more) the ancient Psalms were transferred anew into the psalmody of the German as of the Scandinavian* Lutheran church. In the French church Clément Marot translated into verse 30 Ps., then 19 more (1541—43) and Theodore Beza added the rest (1562).** Calvin introduced the Psalms in Marot's version as early as 1542 into the service of the Geneva church, and the Psalms have since continued to be the favorite hymns of the Reformed church. Goudimel, the martyr of St. Bartholemew's night and teacher of Palestrina, composed the melodies and chorales. The English Established church adopted the Psalms direct as they are, as a portion of its liturgy, the Congregational church followed the example of the sister-churches of the Continent. And how industriously the Psalter was moulded into Greek verse, as by Olympia Morata (d. 1555)*** and under the influence of Melanthon† into Latin! The paraphrases of Helius Eoban Hesse (of whom Martin Herz, 1860, has given a biographical sketch)††, Joh. Major, Jacob Micyllus (whose life Classen has written, 1859), Joh. Stigel (whose memory has been revived by Paulus Cassel 1860), Gre. Bersmann (d. 1611), and also that begun by Geo. Buchanan during his sojourn in a Portuguese monastery, are not only learned performances, but productions of an inward

---

* The Swedish hymns taken from the Psalms have been recently remodelled for congregational use and augmented by Runeberg (Oerebro 1858).

** *vid.* Félix Bovet, Les Psaumes de Marot et de Bèze, in the Lausanne magazine, *Le Chrétien Evangélique*, 1866, No. 4.

*** *vid.* examples in Bonnet's life of Olympia Morata. Germ. transl. by Merschmann 1860 S. 131—135.

† *vid.* Wilhelm Thilo, *Melanchthon im Dienste an heil. Schrift* (Berlin, 1859), S. 28.

†† His Psalms (to which Veit Dietrich wrote notes) passed through forty editions in seventy years.

spiritual need; although one must assent to the judgment expressed by Harless, that the best attempts of this kind only satisfy one in proportion as we are able first of all to banish the remembrance of the original from our mind.

But since the time of the Reformation the exegetical functions of psalm-exposition have been more clearly apprehended and more happily discharged than ever before. In Luther, who opened his academical lectures in 1514 with the Ps. (in Latin in Luther's own hand writing in Wolfenbüttel) and began to publish a part of them in 1519 under the title *Operationes in duas Psalmorum decades,* the depth of experience of the Fathers is united to the Pauline recognition (which he gave back to the church) of the doctrine of free grace. It is true, he is not entirely free from the allegorising which he rejected *in thesi,* and, in general, from a departure *a sensu literæ,* and there is also still wanting in Luther the historical insight into the distinctive character of the two Testaments; but with respect to experimental, mystical, and withal sound, understanding he is incomparable. His interpretations of the Psalms, especially of the penitential Ps. and of Ps. xc, excel every thing hitherto produced, and are still a perpetual mine of wealth. Bugenhagen's exposition of the Psalms (Basel 1524, 4to. and freq.) continued the interrupted work of Luther, who in a brief but forcible preface says in its praise, that it is the first worthy of the name of an exposition. Penetration and delicacy of judgment distinguish the interpretation of the five books of the Psalms by Aretius Felinus *i. e.* Martin Bucer (1529, 4to. and freq.). The *Autophyes* (= *a se et per se Existens*), by which throughout he translates יהוה, gives it a remarkable appearance. But about the same time, as an exegete, Calvin came forward at the side of the German reformer. His commentary (first published at Geneva 1564) combines with great psychological penetration more discernment of the types and greater freedom of historical perception, but is not without many errors arising from this freedom. Calvin's strict historical method of interpretation becomes a caricature in Esrom Rüdinger, the schoolmaster of the Moravian brethren, who died at Altorf in 1591 without being able, as he had intended, to issue his commentary, which appeared in 1580 — 81, in a new and revised form. His is an original work which, after trying many conjectures, at last assigns even the first Psalm to the era of the Seleucidæ.

Within the range of the p o s t - R e f o r m a t i o n exposition the first that meets us is Reinhard Bakius, the persevering and talented pastor of Magdeburg and Grimma during the Thirty-years' war, whose *Comm. exegetico-practicus* on the Ps. (in the first edition by his son 1664) is a work of extensive reading and good sense, in many respects a welcome supplement to Luther, crammed full of all kinds of notable things about the Psalms, under which, however, the thread of simple exposition is lost. Martin Geier keeps the work of the exposition most distinctly before him, adhering more closely to it and restraining himself from digression. His lectures on the Psalms delivered at Leipzig extended over a period of eighteen years. Deep piety and extensive learning adorn his commentary (1668), but the free spirit of the men of the Reformation is no longer here. Geier is not capable of turning from dogmatics, and throwing himself into the exegesis: a traditional standard of exegesis had become fixed, to overstep which was accounted as heterodox. In the Reformed church Cocceius stands prominently forward (d. 1669). He was an original and gifted man, but starting from false principles of hermeneutics, too fond of an eschatological literalness of interpretation.

Not only the two Protestant churches, but also the Romish church took part in the advancing work of psalm-exposition. Its most prominent expositors from 1550—1650 are Genebrardus, Agellius, and De Muis, all of whom possessing a knowledge of the Semitic languages, go back to the original, and Bellarmin, who brings to the work not merely uncommon natural talents, but, within the limits of papistical restraint, a deep spiritual penetration. Later on psalm-exposition in the Romish church degenerated into scholasticism. This is at its height in Le Blanc's *Psalmorum Davidicorum Analysis* and in Joh. Lorinus' *Commentaria in Psalmos* (6 folio vols. 1665 — 1676). In the protestant churches, however, a lamentable decline from the spirit of the men of the Reformation in like manner manifested itself. The *Adnotationes uberiores in Hagiographa* (t. i. 1745, 4to: Ps. and Prov.) of Joh. Heinrich Michaelis are a mass of raw materials:

the glossarial annotations groan beneath the burden of numberless unsifted examples and parallel passages. What had been done during the past sixteen hundred years remains almost entirely unnoticed; Luther is not explored, even Calvin within the pale of his own church no longer exerts any influence over the exposition of Scripture. After 1750, the exposition of Scripture lost that spiritual and ecclesiastical character which had gained strength in the seventeenth century, but had also gradually become torpid; whereas in the Romish church, as the Psalm-expositions of De Sacy, Berthier and La Harpe shew, it never sank so low as to deny the existence of revealed religion. That love for the Ps., which produced the evangelical hymn-psalter of that truly Christian poet and minister Christoph Karl Ludwig von Pfeil (1747),* prefaced by Bengel, degenerated to a merely literary, or at most poetical, interest, — exegesis became carnal and unspiritual. The remnant of what was spiritual in this age of decline, is represented by Burk in his *Gnomon* to the Ps. (1760) which follows the model of Bengel, and by Chr. A. Crusius in the second part of his *Hypomnemata ad Theologiam Propheticam* (1761), a work which follows the track newly opened up by Bengel, and is rich in germs of progressive knowledge (*vid.* my *Biblisch-prophetische Theologie*, 1845). We may see the character of the theology of that age from Joh. Dav. Michaelis' translation of the Old Testament, with notes for the unlearned (1771), and his writings on separate Psalms. From a linguistic and historical point of view we may find something of value here; but besides, only wordy, discursive, tasteless trifling and spiritual deadness. It has been the honour of Herder that he has freed psalm-exposition from this want of taste, and the merit of Hengstenberg (first of all in his Lectures), that he has brought it back out of this want of spirituality to the believing consciousness of the church.

The transition to modern exposition is marked by Rosenmüller's *Scholia* to the Ps. (first published in 1798—1804), a compilation written in pure clear language with exegetical tact and with a thankworthy use of older expositors who had become unknown, as Rüdinger, Bucer, and

---

* *vid.* his Life by Heinr. Merz (1863), S. 111—117.

Agellius, and also of Jewish writers. De Wette's commentary on the Psalms (first published in 1811, 5 th edition by Gustav Baur, 1856) was far more independent and forms an epoch in exegesis. De Wette is precise and clear, and also not without a perception of the beautiful; but his position in relation to the Scripture writers is too much like that of a reviewer, his research too sceptical, and his estimate of the Ps. does not sufficiently recognise their place in the history of redemption. He regards them as national hymns, partly in the most ordinary patriotic sense, and when his theological perception fails him, he helps himself out with sarcasm against the theocratic element, which he carries to the extreme of disgust. Nevertheless, De Wette's commentary opens up a new epoch so far as it has first of all set in order the hitherto existing chaos of psalm-exposition, and introduced into it taste and grammatical accuracy, after the example of Herder and under the influence of Gesenius. He is far more independent than Rosenmüller, who though not wanting in taste and tact, is only a compiler. In investigating the historical circumstances which gave rise to the composition of the different psalms, De Wette is more negative than assumptive. Hitzig in his historical and critical commentary (1835. 36), which has appeared recently in a revised form (Bd. 1, 1863, Bd. 2. Abth. 1, 1864, Abth. 2, 1865), has sought to supplement positively the negative criticism of De Wette, by ascribing to David fourteen Ps. of the seventy three that bear the inscription לדוד, assigning all the Ps. from the lxxiii onwards, together with i. ii. lx (these three, as also cxlii—cxliv, cl, by Alexander Jannæus) to the Maccabean period (*e. g.* cxxxviii —cxli to Alexander's father, John Hyrcanus), and also inferring the authors (Zechariah, 2 Chron. xxvi. 5; Isaiah, Jeremiah) or at least the date of composition of all the rest.

Von Lengerke, in his commentary compiled half from Hengstenberg, half from Hitzig (1847), has attached himself to this so-called positive criticism, which always arrives at positive results and regards Maccabean psalms as the primary stock of the Psalter. Von Lengerke maintains that not a single Ps. can with certainty be ascribed to David. Olshausen (in his *Comment.* 1853), who only leaves a few Ps., as ii. xx. xxi, to the time of the kings prior to the Exile, and with a propensity, which he is not able to resist, brings down all the others to the time of the Maccabees, even to the beginning of the reign of John Hyrcanus, also belongs to the positive school. Whereas Hupfeld in his commentary, 1855—1862 (4 vols.), considers it unworthy of earnest investigation, to lower one's self to such "childish trifling with hypotheses" and remains true to De Wette's negative criticism: but he seeks to carry it out in a different way. He also maintains that none of the Ps. admit of being with certainty ascribed to David; and proceeds on the assumption, that although only a part of the inscriptions are false, for that very reason none of them can be used by us.

We stand neither on the side of this scepticism, which everywhere negatives tradition, nor on the side of that self-confidence, which mostly negatives it and places in opposition to it its own positive counter-assumptions; but we do not on this account fail to recognise the great merit which Olshausen, Hupfeld and Hitzig have acquired by their expositions of the Psalms. In Olshausen we prize his prominent talent for critical conjectures; in Hupfeld grammatical thoroughness, and solid study so far as it is carried; in Hitzig the stimulating originality everywhere manifest, his happy perspicacity in tracing out the connection of the thoughts, and the marvellous amount of reading which is displayed in support of the usage of language and of that which is admissible according to syntax. The commentary of Ewald (*Poetische Bücher*, 1839, 40. 2nd edition 1866), apart from the introductory portion, according to its plan only fragmentarily meets the requirements of exposition, but in the argument which precedes each Ps. gives evidence of a special gift for perceiving the emotions and throbbings of the heart and entering into the changes of feeling.

None of these expositors are in truly spiritual *rapport* with the spirit of the psalmists. The much abused commentary of Hengstenberg 1842—1847 (4 vols. 2nd edition 1849—1852) consequently opened a new track, in as much as it primarily set the exposition of the Psalms in its right relation to the church once more, and was not confined to the historico-grammatical function of exposition. The kindred spirited works of Umbreit (*Christliche Erbauung aus dem Psalter* 1835) and Stier (*Siebenzig Psalmen* 1834. 36), which extend only to a selection from the Psalms, may be regarded as its forerunners, and the commentary of Tholuck (1847) who excludes verbal criticism and seeks to present the results of exegetical progress in a practical form for the use of the people, as its counterpart.   For the sake of completeness we may also mention the commentary of Köster (1837) which has become of importance for its appreciation of the artistic form of the Psalms, especially the strophe-system, and Vaihinger's (1845). Out of Germany, no work on the Psalms has appeared which could be placed side by side with those of Hengstenberg, Hupfeld and Hitzig. And yet the inexhaustible task demands the combined work of many hands. Would that the examples set by Björk, by Perret-Gentil, Armand de Mestral and J. F. Thrupp, of noble rivalry with German scholarship might find many imitators in the countries of the Scandinavian, Latin, and English tongues! Would that the zealous industry of Bade and Reinke, the noble endeavours of Schegg and König, might set an example to many in the Romish church! Would that also the Greek church on the basis of the criticism of the LXX defended by Pharmakides against Oikonomos, far surpassing the works on the Ps. of Nicodimos and Anthimos, which are drawn from the Fathers, might continue in that rival connection with German scholarship of which the Prolegomena to the Psalm-commentary of the Jerusalem patriarch Anthimos, by Dionysios Kleopas (Jerusalem 1855. 4to.) give evidence! *Non plus ultra* is the watchword of the church with regard to the word of God, and *plus ultra* is its watchword with regard to the understanding of that word.   Common work upon the Scriptures is the finest union of the severed churches and the surest harbinger of their future unity. The exposition of Scripture will rear the Church of the Future.

X. THEOLOGICAL PRELIMINARY CONSIDERATIONS.

The expositor of the Psalms can place himself on the standpoint of the poet, or the standpoint of the Old Testament church, or the standpoint of the church of the present dispensation — a primary condition of exegetical progress is the keeping of these three standpoints distinct, and, in accordance therewith, the distinguishing between the two

Testaments, and in general, between the different steps in the development of the revelation, and in the perception of the plan, of redemption. For as redemption itself has a progressive history, so has the revelation and growing perception of it a progressive history also, which extends from paradise, through time, on into eternity. Redemption realizes itself in a system of facts, in which the divine purpose of love for the deliverance of sinful humanity unfolds itself, and the revelation of salvation is given in advance of this gradually developing course of events in order to guarantee its divine authorship and as a means by which it may be rightly understood. In the Psalms we have five centuries and more of this progressive realizing, disclosing, and perception of salvation laid open before us. If we add to this the fact that one psalm is by Moses, and that the retrospective portions of the historical psalms refer back even to the patriarchal age, then, from the call of Abraham down to the restoration of Israel's position among the nations after the Exile, there is scarcely a single event of importance in sacred history which does not find some expression in the Psalter. And it is not merely facts external to it, which echo therein in lyric strains, but, because David, — next to Abraham undoubtedly the most significant character of sacred history in the Old Testament, — is its chief composer, it is itself a direct integral part of the history of redemption. And it is also a source of information for the history of the revelation of redemption, in as much as it flowed not from the Spirit of faith merely, but mainly also from the Spirit of prophecy: but, pre-eminently, it is the most important memorial of the progressive recognition of the plan of salvation, since it shews how, between the giving of the Law from Sinai and the proclamation of the Gospel from Sion, the final, great salvation was heralded in the consciousness and life of the Jewish church.

We will consider 1) the relation of the Psalms to the prophecy of the future Christ. When man whom God had created, had corrupted himself by sin, God did not leave him to that doom of wrath which he had chosen for himself, but visited him on the evening of that most unfortunate of all days, in order to make that doom the disciplinary medium of His love. This visitation of Jahve Elohim was

the first step in the history of redemption towards the goal
of the incarnation, and the so-called protevangelium was the
first laying of the foundation of His verbal revelation of law
and gospel — a revelation in accordance with the plan of
salvation, and preparing the way towards this goal of the
incarnation and the recovery of man. The way of this salvation, which opens up its own historical course, and at the
same time announces itself in a form adapted to the human
consciousness, runs all through Israel, and the Psalms shew
us how this seed-corn of words and acts of divine love has
expanded with a vital energy in the believing hearts of Israel.
They bear the impress of the period, during which the preparation of the way of salvation was centred in Israel and
the hope of redemption was a national hope. For after mankind was separated into different nations, salvation was confined within the limits of a chosen nation, that it might
mature there, and then bursting its bounds become the property of the human race. At that period the promise of the
future Mediator was in its third stage. The hope of over-
coming the tendency in mankind to be led astray into evil
was attached to the seed of the woman, and the hope of a
blessing for all peoples, to the seed of Abraham: but, at this
period, when David became the creator of psalm-poesy for
the sanctuary service, the promise had assumed a Messianic
character and pointed the hope of the believing ones towards
the king of Israel, and in fact to David and his seed: the
salvation and glory of Israel first, and indirectly of the nations,
was looked for from the mediatorship of Jahve's Anointed.

The fact that among all the Davidic psalms there is only
a single one, viz. Ps. cx, in which David (as in his last words
2 Sam. xxiii. 1—7) looks forth into the future of his seed
and has the Messiah definitely before his mind, can only be
explained by the consideration, that he was hitherto himself
the object of Messianic hope, and that this hope was first
gradually (especially in consequence of his deep fall) separated from himself individually, and transferred to the future.
Therefore when Solomon came to the throne the Messianic
desires and hopes of Israel were directed towards him, as
Ps. lxxii shews; they belonged only to the one final Christ
of God, but they clung for a long time enquiringly and with

a perfect right (on the ground of 2 Sam. vii) to the direct son of David. Also in Ps. xlv it is a son of David, cotemporary with the Korahite singer, to whom the Messianic promise is applied as a marriage benediction, wishing that the promise may be realized in him.

But it soon became evident that He, in whom the full realization of the idea of the Messiah is to be found, had not yet appeared either in the person of this king or of Solomon. And when in the later time of the kings the Davidic line became more and more inconsistent with its vocation in the sacred history, then the hope of the Messiah was completely weaned of its expectation of immediate fulfilment, and the present became merely the dark ground from which the image of the Messiah, as purely future, stood forth in relief. The בֶּן־דָּוִד, in whom the prophecy of the later time of the kings centres, and whom also Ps. ii sets forth before the kings of the earth that they may render homage to Him, is an eschatological character (although the אחרית was looked for as dawning close upon the border of the present). In the mouth of the congregation Ps. xlv and cxxxii, since their contents referred to the future, have become too prophetically and eschatologically Messianic. But it is remarkable that the number of these psalms which are not merely typically Messianic is so small, and that the church of the period after the Exile has not enriched the Psalter with a single psalm that is Messianic in the stricter sense. In the later portion of the Psalter, in distinction from the strictly Messianic psalms, the theocratic psalms are more numerously represented, *i. e.* those psalms which do not speak of the kingdom of Jahve's Anointed which shall conquer and bless the world, not of the Christocracy, in which the theocracy reaches the pinnacle of its representation, but of the theocracy as such, which is complete inwardly and outwardly in its own representation of itself, — not of the advent of a human king, but of Jahve Himself, with the kingdom of God manifest in all its glory. For the announcement of salvation in the Old Testament runs on in two parallel lines: the one has as its termination the Anointed of Jahve, who rules all nations out of Zion, the other, the LORD Himself sitting above the Cherubim, to whom all the earth does homage. These two lines do not meet in the Old Testament; it is only the fulfilment that makes it plain, that the advent of the Anointed one and the advent of Jahve is one and the same. And of these two lines the divine is the one that preponderates in the Psalter; the hope of Israel, especially after the kingship had ceased in Israel, is directed generally beyond the human mediation directly towards Jahve, the Author of salvation. The fundamental article of the Old Testament faith runs ישׁועתה ליהוה (Ps. iii. 9, Jon. ii. 10). The Messiah is not yet recognised as a God-man. Consequently the Psalms contain neither prayer to Him, nor prayer in His name. But prayer to Jahve and for Jahve's sake is essentially the same. For Jesus is in Jahve. Jahve is the Saviour. And the Saviour when he shall appear, is nothing but the visible manifestation of the ישׁועה of this God (Isa. xlix. 6).

In considering the goal of the Old Testament history in its relation to the God-man, we distinguish five classes of psalms which are directed towards this goal. After 2 Sam. vii the Messianic promise is no longer in a general way connected with the tribe of Judah, but with David; and is referred not merely to the endless duration of his kingdom, but also to one scion of his house, in whom that to which God has appointed the seed of David in its relation to Israel first, and from Israel to all the other nations, shall be fully realised, and without whom the kingdom of David is like a headless trunk. Psalms in which the poet, looking beyond his own age, comforts himself with the vision of this king in whom the promise is finally fulfilled, we call eschatological psalms, and in fact directly eschatologically Messianic psalms. These connect themselves not merely with the already existing prophetic utterances, but carry them even further, and are only distinguished from prophecy proper by their lyric form; for prophecy is a discourse and the psalms are spiritual songs.

The Messianic character of the Psalms is, however, not confined to prophecy proper, the subject of which is that which is future. Just as nature exhibits a series of stages of life in which the lower order of existence points to the next order above it and indirectly to the highest, so that, for instance, in the globular form of a drop we read the intimation of the struggle after organism, as it were, in the simplest barest outline: so also the progress of history is typical, and not only as a whole, but also most surprisingly in single traits, the life of David is a *vaticinium reale* of the life of Him, whom prophecy calls directly עבדי דוד Ezek. xxxiv. 23 sq. xxxvii. 24 sq. and דוד מלכם Hos. iii. 5, Jer. xxx. 9, as the David who is, as it were, raised from the dead in a glorified form. Those psalms in which David himself (or even a poet throwing himself into David's position and mood) gives expression in lyric verse to prominent typical events and features of his life, we call typically Messianic psalms. This class, however, is not confined to those, of which David is directly or indirectly the subject, for the course of suffering of all the Old Testament saints, and especially of the prophets in their calling (*vid.* on xxxiv. 20 sq. and Ps. lxix), was to a certain extent a τύπος τοῦ μέλλοντος. All these psalms, not less than those of the first class, may be quoted in the New Testament with the words ἵνα πληρωθῇ, with this difference only, that in the former it is the prophetic word, in the latter the prophetic history, that is fulfilled. The older theologians, especially the Lutheran, contended against the supposition of such typological citations of the Old Testament in the New: they were destitute of that perception of the organic element in history granted to our age, and consequently were lacking in the true counterpoise to their rigid notions of inspiration.

But there is also a class of Psalms which we call typico-prophetically Messianic, viz. those in which David, describing his outward and inward experiences, — experiences even in themselves typical, — is carried beyond the limits of his individuality and present condition, and utters concerning himself that which, transcending human experience, is intended to become historically true only in Christ. Such psalms are typical, in as much as their contents is grounded in the individual, but typical, history of David; they are, however, at the same time prophetic, in as much as they express present individual experience in laments, hopes, and descriptions which point far forward beyond the present and are only fully realised in Christ. The psychological possibility of such psalms has been called in question; but they would only be psychologically impossible, if one were obliged to suppose that David's self-consciousness must under such circumstances pass over into that of his antitype; but it is in reality quite otherwise. As the poet in order to describe his experiences in verse, idealises them, *i. e.* seizes the idea of them at the very root, and, stripping off all that is adventitious and insignificant, rises into the region of the ideal: so David also in these psalms idealises his experiences, which even in itself results in the reduction of them to all that is essential to their continuance as types. This he does, however, not from his own poetic impulse, but under the inspiration of the Spirit of God; and a still further result which follows from this is, that the description of his typical fortunes and their corresponding states of feeling is moulded into the prophetic description of the fortunes and feelings of his antitype.

Beside these three classes of Messianic psalms one may regard psalms like xlv and lxxii as a fourth class of indirectly eschatologically Messianic psalms. They are those in which, according to the time of their composition, Messianic hopes are referred to a cotemporary king, but without having been fulfilled in him; so that, in the mouth of the church, still expecting their final accomplishment, these psalms have become eschatological hymns and their exposition as such, by the side of their chronological interpretation, is fully warranted.

A fifth class is formed by the eschatologically Jehovic psalms, which are taken up with describing the advent of Jahve and the consummation of His kingdom, which is all through brought about by judgment (*vid.* Ps. xciii). The number of these psalms in the Psalter greatly preponderates. They contain the other premiss to the divine-human end of the history of salvation. There are sudden flashes of light thrown upon this end in the prophets. But it remains reserved to the history itself to draw the inference of the *unio personalis* from these human and divine premises. The Redeemer, in whom the Old Testament faith reposed, is Jahve. The centre of the hope lay in the divine not in the human king. That the Redeemer, when He should appear, would be God and man in one person was alien to the mind of the Old Testament church. And the perception of the fact that He would be sacrifice and priest in one person, only penetrates in single rays into the Old Testament darkness, the cynosure of which is יהוה, and יהוה only.

Coming now to consider 2) the relation of the Psalms to the legal sacrifice, we shall find this also different from what we might expect from the stand-point of fulfilment. Passages certainly are not wanting where the outward legal sacrifice is acknowledged as an act of worship on the part of the individual and of the congregation (lxvi. 15, li. 21); but those occur more frequently, in which in comparison with the λογικὴ λατρεία it is so lightly esteemed, that without respect to its divine institution it appears as something not at all desired by God, as a shell to be cast away, and as a form to be broken in pieces (xl. 7 sq. l. li. 18 sq.). But it is not this that surprises us. It is just in this respect that the psalms contribute their share towards the progress of sacred history. It is that process of spiritualisation which begins even in Deuteronomy, and which is continued by reason of the memorable words of Samuel, 1 Sam. xv. 22 sq. It is the spirit of the New Testament, growing more and more in strength, which here and in other parts of the Psalter shakes the legal barriers and casts off the στοιχεῖα τοῦ κόσμου as a butterfly does its chrysalis shell. But what is substituted for the sacrifice thus criticised and rejected? Contrition, prayer, thankgiving, yielding one's self to God in the doing of His will, as Prov. xxi. 3 to do justly, Hos. vi. 6 kindness, Mic. vi. 6—8 acting justly, love, and humility, Jer. vii. 21—23 obedience. This it is that surprises one. The disparaged sacrifice is regarded only as a symbol not as a type; it is only considered in its ethical character, not in its relation to the history of redemption. Its nature is unfolded only so far as it is a gift to God (קרבן), not so far as the offering is appointed for atonement (כפרה); in one word: the mystery of the blood remains undisclosed. Where the New Testament mind is obliged to think of the sprinkling with the blood of Jesus Christ, it is, in Ps. li. 9, the sprinkling of the legal ritual of purification and atonement that is mentioned, and that manifestly figuratively but yet without the significance of the figure. Whence is it? — Because the sacrifice with blood, as such, in the Old Testament remains a question to which Isaiah, in ch. liii, gives almost the only distinct answer in accordance with its historical fulfilment; for passages like Dan. ix. 24 sqq. Zech. xii. 10, xiii. 7 are themselves questionable and enigmatical. The prophetic representation of the passion and sacrifice of Christ is only given in direct prophetic language thus late on, and it is only the evangelic history of the fulfilment that shews, how exactly the Spirit which spoke by David has moulded that which he says concerning himself, the type, into correspondence with the antitype. The confidence of faith under the Old Testament, as it finds expression in the Psalms, rested upon Jahve even in reference to the atonement, as in reference to redemption in general. As He is the Saviour, so is He also the one who makes the atonement (מכפר), from whom expiation is earnestly sought and hoped for (lxxix. 9, lxv. 4, lxxviii. 38, lxxxv. 3 and other passages). It is Jahve who at the end of His course of the redemptive history is the God-man, and the blood given by Him as the medium of atonement (Lev. xvii. 11) is, in the antitype, His own blood.

Advancing from this point, we come to examine 3) t h e relation of the Psalms to the New Testament righteousness of faith and to the New Testament morality which flows from the primary command of infinite love. Both with respect to the atonement and to redemption the Psalms undergo a complete metamorphosis in the consciousness of the praying New Testament church— a metamorphosis, rendered possible by the unveiling and particularising of salvation that has since taken place, and to which they can without any reserve be accommodated. There are only two points in which the prayers of the Psalms appear to be difficult of amalgamation with the Christian consciousness. These are the moral self-confidence bordering on self-righteousness, which is frequently maintained before God in the Psalms, and the warmth of feeling against enemies and persecutors which finds vent in fearful cursings. The self-righteousness here is a mere appearance; for the righteousness to which the psalmists appeal is not the merit of works, not a sum of good works, which are reckoned up before God as claiming a reward, but a godly direction of the will and a godly form of life, which has its root in the surrender of

one's whole self to God and regards itself as the operation
and work of justifying, sanctifying, preserving and ruling
grace (lxxiii. 25 sq. xxv. 5—7, xix. 14 and other passages).
There is not wanting an acknowledgement of the innate sinfulness of our nature (li. 7), of the man's exposure to punishment before God apart from His grace (cxliii. 2), of the many,
and for the most part unperceived, sins of the converted (xix.
13), of the forgiveness of sins as a fundamental condition
to the attainment of happiness (xxxii. 1 sq.), of the necessity
of a new divinely-created heart (li. 12), in short, of the way
of salvation which consists of penitential contrition, pardon,
and newness of life.

On the other hand it is not less true, that in the light
of the vicarious atonement and of the Spirit of regeneration
it becomes possible to form a far more penetrating and subtle
moral judgment of one's self; it is not less true, that the tribulation, which the New Testament believer experiences, though
it does not produce such a strong and overwhelming sense
of divine wrath as that which is often expressed in the psalms,
nevertheless sinks deeper into his inmost nature in the
presence of the cross on Golgotha and of the heaven that
is opened up to him, in as much as it appears to him to
be sent by a love that chastens, proves, and prepares him
for the future; and it is not less true, that after the righteousness of God — which takes over our unrighteousness
and is accounted even in the Old Testament as a gift of
grace — lies before us for believing appropriation as a
righteousness redemptively wrought out by the active and
passive obedience of Jesus, the distinctive as well as the
reciprocally conditioned character of righteousness of faith
and of righteousness of life is become a more clearly perceived fact of the inner life, and one which exercises a more
powerful influence over the conduct of that life.* Nevertheless even such personal testimonies, as Ps. xvii. 1—5, do not

---

* cf. Kurtz, *Zur Theologie der Psalmen*, III: *The self-righteousness of
the psalmists*, in the *Dorpater Zeitschrift* 1865 S. 352—358: "The Old
Testament righteousness of faith, represented by the *evangelium visibile*
of the sacrificial worship, had not as yet the fundamental and primary,
helpful position assigned to it, especially by Paul, in the New Testament,

resist conversion into New Testament forms of thought and experience, for they do not hinder the mind from thinking specially, at the same time, of righteousness of faith, of God's acts which are performed through the medium of sacraments, and of that life resulting from the new birth, which maintains itself victorious in the old man; moreover the Christian ought to be himself earnestly warned by them to examine himself whether his faith is really manifest as an energising power of a new life; and the difference between the two Testaments loses its harshness even here, in the presence of the great verities which condemn all moral infirmity, viz. that the church of Christ is a community of the holy, that the blood of Jesus Christ cleanseth us from all sin, and that whosoever is born of God doth not commit sin.

But as to the so-called imprecatory psalms,* in the position occupied by the Christian and by the church towards the enemies of Christ, the desire for their removal is certainly outweighed by the desire for their conversion: but assuming, that they will not be converted and will not anticipate their punishment by penitence, the transition from a feeling of love to that of wrath is warranted in the New Testament (*e. g.* Gal. v. 12), and assuming their absolute Satanic hardness of heart the Christian even may not shrink from praying for their final overthrow. For the kingdom of God comes not only by the way of mercy but also of judgment; and the coming of the kingdom of God is the goal of the Old as well as of the New Testament saint (*vid.* ix. 21, lix. 14 and other passages), and every wish that judgment may descend upon those who oppose the coming of the kingdom of God is cherished even in the Psalms on the assumption of their lasting impenitence (*vid.* vii. 13 sq. cix. 17). Where, however, as in Ps. lxix and cix, the imprecations go into particulars and extend to the descendents of the unfortunate one

---

but only a more secondary position; justification is conceived not as a condition of the sanctification which is to be striven after, but as a supplementing of that which is wanting in the sanctification thus defectively striven after.

* cf. Kurtz, *ibid.* IV: *The imprecatory Psalms, ibid.* S. 359—372 and our discussions in the introductions to Ps. xxxv and cix, which belong to this class.

and even on to eternity, the only justification of them is this, that they flow from the prophetic spirit, and for the Christian they admit of no other adoption, except as, reiterating them, he gives the glory to the justice of God, and commends himself the more earnestly to His favour.

Also 4) the relation of the Psalms to the Last Things is such, that in order to be used as prayers expressive of the New Testament faith they require deepening and adjusting. For what Julius Africanus says of the Old Testament: οὐδέπω δέδοτο ἐλπὶς ἀναστάσεως σαφής, holds good at least of the time before Isaiah. For Isaiah is the first to foretell, in one of his latest apocalyptic cycles (ch. xxiv—xxvii), the first resurrection, *i. e.* the re-quickening of the martyr-church that has succumbed to death (ch. xxvi. 19), just as with an extended vision he foretells the termination of death itself (ch. xxv. 8); and the Book of Daniel — that Old Testament apocalypse, sealed until the time of its fulfilment — first foretells the general resurrection, *i. e.* the awakening of some to life and others to judgment (ch. xii. 2). Between these two prophecies comes Ezekiel's vision of Israel's return from the Exile under the figure of a creative quickening of a vast field of corpses (ch. xxxvii) — a figure which at least assumes that what is represented is not impossible to the wonder-working power of God, which is true to His promises. But also in the latest psalms the perception of salvation nowhere appears to have made such advance, that these words of prophecy foretelling the resurrection should have been converted into a dogmatic element of the church's belief. The hope, that the bones committed, like seed, to the ground would spring forth again, finds expression first only in a bold, but differently expressed figure (cxli. 7); the hopeless darkness of Sheôl (vi. 6, xxx. 10, lxxxviii. 11—13) remained unillumined, and where deliverance from death and Hades is spoken of, what is meant is the preservation of the living, either experienced (*e. g.* lxxxvi. 13) or hoped for (*e. g.* cxviii. 17) from falling a prey to death and Hades, and we find in connection with it other passages which express the impossibility of escaping this universal final destiny (lxxxix. 49). The hope of eternal life after death is nowhere definitely expressed, as even in the Book of Job the longing for it is never able to expand into a hope, because no light of promise shines into that night, which reigns over Job's mind, — a night, which the conflict of temptation through which he is passing makes darker than it is in itself. The pearl which appears above the waves of temptation is only too quickly swallowed up again by them.

Also in the Psalms we find passages in which the hope of not falling a prey to death is expressed so broadly, that the thought of the final destiny of all men being inevitable is completely swallowed up by the living one's confidence of living in the strength of God (lvi. 14 and esp. xvi. 9—11); passages in which the covenant relation with Jahve is contrasted with this present life and its possession, in such a manner that the opposite of a life extending beyond the present time is implied (xvii. 14 sq., lxiii. 4); passages in which the end of the ungodly is compared with the end of the righteous as death and life, defeat and triumph (xlix. 15), so that the inference forces itself upon one, that the former die although they seem to live for ever, and the latter live for ever although they die at once; and passages in which the psalmist, though only by way of allusion, looks forward to a being borne away to God, like Enoch and Elijah (xlix. 16, lxxiii. 24). Nowhere, however, is there any general creed to be found, but we see how the belief in a future life struggles to be free, at first only, as an individual conclusion of the believing mind from premises which experience has established. And far from the grave being penetrated by a glimpse of heaven, it has, on the contrary, to the ecstasy of the life derived from God, as it were altogether vanished; for life in opposition to death only appears as the lengthening of the line of the present *ad infinitum.* Hence it is that we no more find in the Psalms than in the Book of Job a perfectly satisfactory theodicy with reference to that distribution of human fortunes in this world, which is incompatible with God's justice. — Ps. vii. xlix. lxxiii. certainly border on the right solution of the mystery, but it stops short at mere hint and presage, so that the utterances that touch upon it admit of different interpretation.*

---

* *vid.* Kurtz, *ibid.* II: *The doctrine of retribution in the Psalms*, *ibid.* S. 316—352.

But on the other hand, death and life in the mind of the psalmists are such deep-rooted notions (*i. e.* taken hold of at the very roots, which are grounded in the principles of divine wrath and divine love), that it is easy for the New Testament faith, to which they have become clear even to their back ground of hell and heaven, to adjust and deepen the meaning of all utterances in the Psalms that refer to them. It is by no means contrary to the meaning of the psalmist when, as in passages like Ps. vi. 6, Gehenna is substituted for Hades to adapt it to the New Testament saint; for since the descent of Jesus Christ into Hades there is no longer any *limbus patrum,* the way of all who die in the Lord is not earthwards but upwards, Hades exists only as the vestibule of hell. The psalmists indeed dread it, but only as the realm of wrath or of seclusion from God's love, which is the true life of man. Nor is it contrary to the idea of the poets to think of the future vision of God's face in all its glory in Ps. xvii. 15 and of the resurrection morn in Ps. xlix. 15; for the hopes expressed there, though to the Old Testament consciousness they referred to this side the grave, are future according to their New Testament fulfilment, which is the only truly satisfying one. There is, as Oetinger says, no essential New Testament truth not contained in the Psalms either νοΐ (according to its unfolded meaning), or at least πνεύματι. The Old Testament barrier encompasses the germinating New Testament life, which at a future time shall burst it. The eschatology of the Old Testament leaves a dark background, which, as is designed, is divided by the New Testament revelation into light and darkness, and is to be illumined into a wide perspective extending into the eternity beyond time. Everywhere, where it begins to dawn in this eschatological darkness of the Old Testament, it is the first morning rays of the New Testament sun-rise which is already announcing itself. The Christian also here cannot refrain from leaping the barrier of the psalmists, and understanding the Psalms according to the mind of the Spirit whose purpose in the midst of the development of salvation and of the perception of it, is directed towards its goal and consummation. Thus understood the Psalms are the hymns of the New Testament Israel as of the Old. The church by using the language of the Psalms in supplication celebrates the unity of the two Testaments, and scholarship in expounding them honours their distinctiveness. Both are in the right; the former in regarding the Psalms in the light of the one great salvation, the latter in carefully distinguishing the eras in the history, and the steps in the perception, of this salvation.

EXPOSITION

OF THE PSALTER

*Cum consummaverit homo, tunc incipiet, et cum quieverit,
aporiabitur (novis aporiis urgebitur).*

Sir. xviii. 6 (applied by Augustine to the
expositor of the Psalter).

FIRST BOOK OF THE PSALTER

Ps. I.—XLI.

PSALM I.

THE RADICALLY DISTINCT LOT OF THE PIOUS AND THE UNGODLY.

1 BLESSED is the man who walketh not in the counsel of
  the ungodly,
And standeth not in the way of sinners,
And sitteth not in the company of scorners,
2 But his delight is in the Law of Jahve
And in His Law doth he meditate day and night —
3 And he is like a tree planted by the water-courses,
Which bringeth forth its fruit in its season,
And its leaf withereth not,
And whatsoever he doeth, he carrieth through.

4 Not thus are the ungodly,
But they are like the chaff which the wind driveth away.
5 Therefore the ungodly cannot stand in the judgment,
Nor sinners in the congregation of the righteous;
6 For Jahve knoweth the way of the righteous,
But the way of the ungodly perisheth.

The collection of the Psalms and that of the prophecies
of Isaiah resemble one another in the fact, that the one begins
with a discourse that bears no superscription, and the other

with a Psalm of the same character; and these form the prologues to the two collections. From Acts xiii. 33, where the words: *Thou art My Son* . . . are quoted as being found ἐν τῷ πρώτῳ ψαλμῷ, we see that in early times Ps. i. was regarded as the prologue to the collection. The reading ἐν τῷ ψαλμῷ τῷ δευτέρῳ, rejected by Griesbach, is an old correction. But this way of numbering the Psalms is based upon tradition. A scholium from Origen and Eusebius says of Ps. i. and ii.: ἐν τῷ Ἑβραϊκῷ συνημμένοι, and just so Apollinaris:

Ἐπιγραφῆς ὁ ψαλμὸς εὑρέθη δίχα,
Ἡνωμένος δὲ τοῖς παρ᾽ Ἑβραίοις στίχοις.

For it is an old Jewish way of looking at it, as Albertus Magnus observes: *Psalmus primus incipit a beatitudine et terminatur a beatitudine, i. e.* it begins with אשרי i. 1 and ends with אשרי ii. 12, so that consequently Ps. i. and ii., as is said in *B. Berachoth* 9 *b* (cf. *Jer. Taanith* ii. 2), form one Psalm (חדא פרשה). As regards the subject-matter this is certainly not so. It is true Ps. i. and ii. coincide in some respects (in the former יהגה, in the latter יהגו; in the former ודרך · · תאבד, in the latter ותאבדו דרך; in the former אשרי at the beginning, in the latter, at the end), but these coincidences of phraseology are not sufficient to justify the conclusion of unity of authorship (Hitz.), much less that the two Psalms are so intimately connected as to form one whole. These two anonymous hymns are only so far related, as that the one is adapted to form the *procemium* of the Psalter from its ethical, the other from its prophetic character. The question, however, arises whether this was in the mind of the collector. Perhaps Ps. ii. is only attached to Ps. i. on account of those coincidences; Ps. i. being the proper prologue of the Psalter in its pentateuchal arrangement after the pattern of the Tôra. For the Psalter is the Yea and Amen in the form of hymns to the word of God given in the Tôra. Therefore it begins with a Psalm which contrasts the lot of him who loves the Tôra with the lot of the ungodly, — an echo of that exhortation, Josh. i. 8, in which, after the death of Moses, Jahve charges his successor Joshua to do all that is written in the book of the Tôra. As the New Testament sermon on the Mount, as a sermon on the spiritualized Law,

begins with μακάριοι, so the Old Testament Psalter, directed
entirely to the application of the Law to the inner life, begins
with אַשְׁרֵי. The First book of the Psalms begins with two
אַשְׁרֵי i. 1, ii. 12, and closes with two אַשְׁרֵי xl. 5, xli. 2. A
number of Psalms begin with אַשְׁרֵי, Ps. xxxii. xli. cxii.
cxix. cxxviii.; but we must not therefore suppose the existence
of a special kind of *ashrê*-psalms; for, *e. g.*, Ps. xxxii. is a
מַשְׂכִּיל, Ps. cxii. a *Hallelujah*, Ps. cxxviii. a שִׁיר הַמַּעֲלוֹת.

As regards the time of the composition of the Psalm,
we do not wish to lay any stress on the fact that 2 Chron.
xxii. 5 sounds like an allusion to it. But 1st, it is earlier than
the time of Jeremiah; for Jeremiah was acquainted with it.
The words of curse and blessing, Jer. xvii. 5—8, are like an
expository and embellished paraphrase of it. It is customary
with Jeremiah to reproduce the prophecies of his predecessors, and more especially the words of the Psalms, in the
flow of his discourse and to transform their style to his
own. In the present instance the following circumstance
also favours the priority of the Psalm: Jeremiah refers the
curse corresponding to the blessing to Jehoiakim and thus
applies the Psalm to the history of his own times. It is 2ndly,
not earlier than the time of Solomon. For לֵצִים occurring
only here in the whole Psalter, a word which came into use,
for the unbelievers, in the time of the Chokma (*vid.* the
definition of the word, Prov. xxi. 24), points us to the time
of Solomon and onwards. But since it contains no indications of cotemporary history whatever, we give up the attempt
to define more minutely the date of its composition, and say
with St. Columba (against the reference of the Psalm to Joash
the *protegé* of Jehoiada, which some incline to): *Non audiendi
sunt hi, qui ad excludendam Psalmorum veram expositionem
falsas similitudines ab historia petitas conantur inducere.**

Vers. 1—3. The exclamatory אַשְׁרֵי, as also xxxii. 2, xl.
5, Prov. viii. 34, has *Gaja* (*Metheg*) by the *Aleph*, and in some

---

* *vid.* Zeuss, *Grammatica Celtica* (1853) ii. 1065. The Commentary
of Columba on the Psalms, with Irish explanations, and coming from
the monastery of Bobbio, is among the treasures of the Ambrosiana.

Codd. even a second by שְׁ, because it is intended to be read
ashᵉrê as an exception, on account of the significance of the
word (Baer, in *Comm.* ii. 495). It is the construct of the *pluralet.* אֲשָׁרִים (from אָשַׁר, cogn. כָּשַׁר, יָשַׁר, to be straight, right,
well-ordered), and always in the form אַשְׁרֵי, even before the
light suffixes (Olsh. § 135, *c*), as an exclamation: O the
blessedness of so and so. The man who is characterised
as blessed is first described according to the things he does
not do, then (which is the chief thought of the whole Ps.)
according to what he actually does: he is not a companion
of the unrighteous, but he abides by the revealed word of
God. רְשָׁעִים are the godless, whose moral condition is lax,
devoid of stay, and as it were gone beyond the reasonable
bounds of a true unity (wanting in stability of character),
so that they are like a tossed and stormy sea, Isa. lvii. 20
sq.;* חַטָּאִים (from the *sing.* חַטָּא, instead of which חֹטֵא is
usually found) sinners, ἁμαρτωλοί, who pass their lives in
sin, especially coarse and manifest sin; לֵצִים (from לוּץ, as מֵת
from מוּת) scoffers, who make that which is divine, holy, and
true a subject of frivolous jesting. The three appellations
form a climax: *impii corde, peccatores opere, illusores ore*, in
accordance with which עֵצָה (from יָעַץ, *figere, statuere*), resolution, bias of the will, and thus way of thinking, is used in
reference to the first, as in Job xxi. 16, xxii. 18; in reference

---

* Nevertheless we have not to compare רָעַשׁ, רָגַשׁ, for רָשַׁע, but the
Arabic in the two roots رسع and رسغ shews for רשע the primary
notion to be slack, loose, in opposition to صلق צרק to be hard, firm,
tight; as رمح صلق i. e. according to the Kamus صلب متين
مستو a hard, firm and straight spear. We too transfer the idea of being
lax and loose to the province of ethics: the difference is only one of
degree. The same two primary notions are also opposed to one another
in speaking of the intellect: حكم wise, prop. thick, firm, stout, solid,
and سخف foolish, simple, prop. thin, loose, without stay, like a bad
piece of weaving, *vid.* Fleischer's translation of Samachschari's *Golden
Necklace* pp. 26 and 27 Anm. 76. Thus רָשָׁע means the loose man and
indeed as a moral-religious notion loose from God, godless [comp. *Bibl.
Psychol.* p. 189. transl.].

to the second, דֶּרֶךְ mode of conduct, action, life; in reference to the third, מוֹשָׁב which like the Arabic *meǵlis* signifies both seat (Job xxix. 7) and assembling (cvii. 32), be it official or social (cf. xxvi. 4 sq., Jer. xv. 17). On הָלַךְ בְּ, in an ethical sense, cf. Mic. vi. 16, Jer. vii. 24. Therefore: Blessed is he who does not walk in the state of mind which the ungodly cherish, much less that he should associate with the vicious life of sinners, or even delight in the company of those who scoff at religion. The description now continues with כִּי אִם (*imo si*, Ges. § 155, 2, *i*): but (if) his delight is, = (substantival instead of the verbal clause:) he delights (חֵפֶץ cf. خفض *f. i.* with the primary notion of firmly adhering, *vid.* on Job xl. 17) in תּוֹרַת ה׳, the teaching of Jahve, which is become Israel's νόμος, rule of life; in this he meditates profoundly by day and night (two *acc.* with the old accusative terminations *am* and *ah*). The *perff.* in ver. 1 describe what he all along has never done, the *fut.* יֶהְגֶּה, what he is always striving to do; הָגָה of a deep (cf. هَج *depressum esse*), dull sound, as if vibrating between within and without, here signifies the quiet soliloquy (cf. هاجس *mussitando secum loqui*) of one who is searching and thinking.

With וְהָיָה,* in ver. 3, the development of the אשׁרי now begins; it is the *præt. consec.*: he becomes in consequence of this, he is thereby, like a tree planted beside the water-courses, which yields its fruit at the proper season and its leaf does not fall off. In distinction from נָטוּעַ, according to *Jalkut* § 614, שָׁתוּל means firmly planted, so that no winds that may rage around it are able to remove it from its place (אין מזיזין אתו ממקומו). In פַּלְגֵי מַיִם, both מַיִם and the plur. serve to give intensity to the figure; פֶּלֶג (Arab. *falǵ*, from פלג to divide, Job xxxviii. 25) means the brook meandering

---

* By the *Shebà* stands *Metheg* (*Gaja*), as it does wherever a word, with *Shebà* in the first syllable, has *Olewejored*, *Rebia magnum*, or *Dechî* without a conjunctive preceding, in case at least one vowel and no *Metheg* — except perhaps that standing before *Shebà compos.* — lies between the *Shebà* and the tone, *e. g.* נִנְתָּקָה (with *Dechî*) ii. 3, וְאֶעֱנֵהוּ xci. 15 and the like. The intonation of the accent is said in these instances to begin, by anticipation, with the fugitive *ĕ*.

and cleaving its course for itself through the soil and stones;
the *plur.* denotes either one brook regarded from its abundance of water, or even several which from different directions supply the tree with nourishing and refreshing moisture. In the relative clause the whole emphasis does not
rest on בְּעִתּוֹ (Calvin: *impii, licet præcoces fructus ostentent,
nihil tamen producunt nisi abortivum*), but פִּרְיוֹ is the first,
בְּעִתּוֹ the second tone-word: the fruit which one expects from
it, it yields (equivalent to יַעֲשֶׂה it produces, elsewhere), and
that at its appointed, proper time (= בְּעִדָּתוֹ, for עֵת is = עֶדֶת
or עֶדֶת, like לֶדֶת, רֶדֶת, from וָעַד), without ever disappointing
that hope in the course of the recurring seasons. The clause
וְעָלֵהוּ לֹא יִבּוֹל is the other half of the relative clause: and
its foliage does not fall off or wither (נָבֵל like the synon.
ذَبُل, from the root בל).

The green foliage is an emblem of faith, which converts
the water of life of the divine word into sap and strength,
and the fruit, an emblem of works, which gradually ripen
and scatter their blessings around; a tree that has lost
its leaves, does not bring its fruit to maturity. It is only
with וְכֹל, where the language becomes unemblematic, that
the man who loves the Law of God again becomes the direct
subject. The accentuation treats this member of the verse as
the third member of the relative clause; one may, however,
say of a thriving plant צָלֵחַ, but not הִצְלִיחַ. This *Hiph.* (from
צלח, صلح, to divide, press forward, press through, *vid.* xlv.
5) signifies both causative: to cause anything to go through,
or prosper (Gen. xxxiv. 23), and transitive: to carry through,
and intransitive: to succeed, prosper (Judg. xviii. 5). With
the first meaning, Jahve would be the subject; with the
third, the project of the righteous; with the middle one, the
righteous man himself. This last is the most natural: everything he takes in hand he brings to a successful issue (an
expression like 2 Chron. vii. 11, xxxi. 21, Dan. viii. 24). What
a richly flowing brook is to the tree that is planted on its
bank, such is the word of God to him who devotes himself to
it: it makes him, according to his position and calling, ever
fruitful in good and well-timed deeds and keeps him fresh

in his inner and outward life, and whatsoever such an one
undertakes, he brings to a successful issue, for the might of
the word and of the blessing of God is in his actions.

Vers. 4—6. The ungodly (הרשעים, with the demonstrative art.) are the opposite of a tree planted by the water-
courses: they are כמץ, like chaff (from מוץ to press out),
which the wind drives away, *viz.* from the loftily situated
threshing-floor (Isa. xvii. 13), *i. e.* without root below, without
fruit above, devoid of all the vigour and freshness of life,
lying loose upon the threshing-floor and a prey of the slightest breeze, — thus utterly worthless and unstable. With
עַל־כֵּן an inference is drawn from this moral characteristic of
the ungodly: just on account of their inner worthlessness and
instability they do not stand בַּמִּשְׁפָּט. This is the word for
the judgment of just recompense to which God brings
each individual man and all without exception with all their
works (Eccl. xii. 14), — His righteous government, which
takes cognisance of the whole life of each individual and
the history of nations and recompenses according to desert.
In this judgment the ungodly cannot stand (קוּם to continue
to stand, like עָמַד cxxx. 3 to keep one's self erect), nor
sinners בַּעֲדַת צַדִּיקִים. The congregation (עֵדָה = *ĭdah*, from
יָעַד, וָעַד) of the righteous is the congregation of Jahve
(עֲדַת ה'), which, according to its nature which is ordained
and inwrought by God, is a congregation of the righteous,
to which consequently the unrighteous belong only outwardly and visibly: οὐ γὰρ πάντες οἱ ἐξ Ἰσραὴλ, οὗτοι Ἰσραήλ,
Rom. ix. 6. God's judgment, when and wheresoever he may
hold it, shall trace back this appearance to its nothingness.
When the time of the divine decision shall come, which also
separates outwardly that which is now inwardly separate, viz.
righteous and unrighteous, wheat and chaff, then shall the
unrighteous be driven away like chaff before the storm, and
their temporary prosperity, which had no divine roots, come
to a fearful end. For Jahve knoweth the way of the righteous, יוֹדֵעַ as in xxxvii. 18, Mat. vii. 23, 2 Tim. ii. 19, and
frequently. What is intended is, as the schoolmen say, a *nosse
con affectu et effectu*, a knowledge which is in living, intimate
relationship to its subject and at the same time is inclined

to it and bound to it by love. The way, *i. e.* the life's course,
of the righteous has God as its goal; God knows this way,
which on this very account also unfailingly reaches its goal.
On the contrary, the way of the ungodly תאֹבֵד, perishes,
because left to itself, — goes down to אֲבַדּוֹן, loses itself,
without reaching the goal set before it, in darkest night. The
way of the righteous only is דֶּרֶךְ עוֹלָם, cxxxix. 24, a way
that ends in eternal life. Ps. cxii. which begins with אַשְׁרֵי
ends with the same fearful תֹּאבֵד.

PSALM II.

THE KINGDOM OF GOD AND OF HIS CHRIST, TO WHICH EVERYTHING MUST BOW.

1 WHY do the people rage,
   And the nations imagine a vain thing?!
2 The kings of the earth rise in rebellion,
   And the rulers take counsel together —
   Against Jahve and against His Anointed.
3 "Up! let us burst their bands asunder,
   And cast away their cords from us!"

4 He who is enthroned in the heavens laughs,
   The Lord hath them in derision.
5 Then shall He speak to them in His wrath,
   And thunder them down in His hot displeasure:
6 "— And yet have I set My King
   Upon Zion, My holy hill."

(The Divine King:)

7 "I will speak concerning a decree!
   Jahve saith unto me: Thou art My Son,
   This day have I begotten Thee.
8 Demand of Me, and I will give Thee the nations for
      Thine inheritance,
   And the ends of the earth for Thy possession.
9 Thou shalt break them with an iron sceptre,
   Like a potter's vessel shalt Thou dash them in pieces."

10 And now, O ye kings, be wise,
    Be admonished, ye judges of the earth!
11 Serve Jahve with fear,
    And rejoice with trembling.
12 Kiss the Son, lest He be angry and ye perish,
    For His wrath may kindle suddenly —
    Blessed are all they who hide in Him!

The didactic Ps. i. which began with אשרי, is now followed by a prophetic Psalm, which closes with אשרי. It coincides also in other respects with Ps. i., but still more with Psalms of the earlier time of the kings (lix. 9, lxxxiii. 3—9) and with Isaiah's prophetic style. The rising of the confederate nations and their rulers against Jahve and His Anointed will be dashed to pieces against the imperturbable all-conquering power of dominion, which Jahve has entrusted to His King set upon Zion, His Son. This is the fundamental thought, which is worked out with the vivid directness of dramatic representation. The words of the singer and seer begin and end the Psalm. The rebels, Jahve, and His Anointed come forward, and speak for themselves; but the framework is formed by the composer's discourse, which, like the chorus of the Greek drama, expresses the reflexions and feelings which are produced on the spectators and hearers. The poem before us is not purely lyric. The personality of the poet is kept in the back-ground. The Lord's Anointed who speaks in the middle of the Psalm is not the anonymous poet himself. It may, however, be a king of the time, who is here regarded in the light of the Messianic promise, or that King of the future, in whom at a future period the mission of the Davidic kingship in the world shall be fulfilled: at all events this Lord's Anointed comes forward with the divine power and glory, with which the Messiah appears in the prophets.

The Psalm is anonymous. For this very reason we may not assign it to David (Hofm.) nor to Solomon (Ew.); for nothing is to be inferred from Acts iv. 25, since in the New Testament "hymn of David" and "psalm" are co-ordinate ideas, and it is always far more hazardous to ascribe an anonymous Psalm to David or Solomon, than to deny to one inscribed לְדָוִד or לִשְׁלֹמֹה direct authorship from David or Solomon. But the subject of the Psalm is neither David (Kurtz) nor Solomon (Bleek). It might be David, for in his reign there is at least one coalition of the peoples like that from which our Psalm takes its rise, *vid.* 2 Sam. x. 6: on the contrary it cannot be Solomon, because in his reign, though troubled towards its close (1 Kings xi. 14 sqq.), no such event occurs, but would then have to be inferred to have happened from this Psalm. We might rather guess at Uzziah (Meier) or Hezekiah (Maurer), both of whom inherited the kingdom in a weakened condition and found the neighbouring peoples alienated from the house of David. The situation might correspond to these times, for the rebellious peoples, which are brought before us, have been hitherto subject to Jahve and His Anointed. But all historical indications which might support the one supposition or the other are wanting. If the God-anointed one, who speaks in ver. 7, were the psalmist himself, we should at least know the Psalm was composed by a king filled with a lofty Messianic consciousness. But the dramatic movement of the Psalm up to the וְעַתָּה (ver. 10) which follows, is opposed to such an identification of the God-anointed one with the poet. But that Alexander Jannæus (Hitz.), that blood-thirsty ruler, so justly hated by his people, who inaugurated his reign by fratricide, may be both at the same time, is a supposition which turns the moral and covenant character of the Psalm into detestable falsehood. The Old Testament knows no kingship to which is promised the dominion of the world and to which sonship is ascribed (2 Sam. vii. 14, Ps. lxxxix. 28), but the Davidic. The events of his own time, which influenced the mind of the poet, are no longer clear to us. But from these he is carried away into those tumults of the peoples which shall end in all kingdoms becoming the kingdom of God and of His Christ (Apoc. xi. 15, xii. 10).

In the New Testament this Psalm is cited more frequently than any other. According to Acts iv. 25—28, vers. 1 and 2 have been fulfilled in the confederate hostility of Israel and the Gentiles against Jesus the holy servant of God and

against His confessors.　In the Epistle to the Hebrews, Ps. cx.
and ii. stand side by side, the former as a witness of the eternal
priesthood of Jesus after the order of Melchisedek, the latter
as a witness of His sonship, which is superior to that of the
angels. Paul teaches us in Acts xiii. 33, comp. Rom. i. 4,
how the "to-day" is to be understood. The "to-day" according to its proper fulfilment, is the day of Jesus' resurrection.
Born from the dead to the life at the right hand of God,
He entered on this day, which the church therefore calls *dies
regalis*, upon His eternal kingship.

The New Testament echo of this Psalm however goes still
deeper and further. The two names of the future One in
use in the time of Jesus, ὁ Χριστός and ὁ υἱὸς τοῦ θεοῦ, John
i. 50, Mat. xxvi. 63 (in the mouth of Nathanael and of the
High Priest) refer back to this Ps. and Dan. ix. 25, just as
ὁ υἱὸς τοῦ ἀνθρώπου incontrovertibly refers to Ps. viii. 5 and
Dan. vii. 13. The view maintained by De Wette and Hupfeld,
that the Psalm is not applicable to the Christian conceptions
of the Messiah, seems almost as though these were to be
gauged according to the authoritative utterances of the pro-
fessorial chair and not according to the language of the
Apostles. Even in the Apocalypse, ch. xix. 15, xii. 5, Jesus
appears exactly as this Psalm represents Him, as ποιμαίνων
τὰ ἔθνη ἐν ῥάβδῳ σιδηρᾷ. The office of the Messiah is not only
that of Saviour but also of Judge. Redemption is the beginning and the judgment the end of His work. It is to this
end that the Psalm refers. The Lord himself frequently refers in the Gospels to the fact of His bearing side by side
with the sceptre of peace and the shepherd's staff, the sceptre
of iron also, Mat. xxiv. 50 sq., xxi. 44, Luke xix. 27. The
day of His coming is indeed a day of judgment — the great
day of the ὀργὴ τοῦ ἀγνίου, Apoc. vi. 17, before which the
ultra-spiritual Messianic creations of enlightened exegetes
will melt away, just as the carnal Messianic hopes of the
Jews did before His first coming.

Vers. 1—3. The Psalm begins with a seven line strophe,
ruled by an interrogative Wherefore. The mischievous under-

taking condemns itself. It it groundless and fruitless. This certainty is expressed, with a tinge of involuntary astonishment, in the question. לָמָּה followed by a *præt.* enquires the ground of such lawlessness: wherefore have the peoples banded together so tumultuously (Aquila: ἐθορυβήθησαν)? and followed by a *fut.*, the aim of this ineffectual action: wherefore do they imagine emptiness? רִיק might be adverbial and equivalent to לָרִיק, but it is here, as in iv. 3, a governed accusative; for הָגָה which signifies in itself only quiet inward musing and yearning, expressing itself by a dull muttering (here: something deceitful, as in xxxviii. 13), requires an object. By this רִיק the involuntary astonishment of the question justifies itself: to what purpose is this empty affair, *i. e.* devoid of reason and continuance? For the psalmist, himself a subject and member of the divine kingdom, is too well acquainted with Jahve and His Anointed not to recognise beforehand the unwarrantableness and impotency of such rebellion. That these two things are kept in view, is implied by ver. 2, which further depicts the position of affairs without being subordinated to the למה. The *fut.* describes what is going on at the present time: they set themselves in position, they take up a defiant position (הִתְיַצֵּב as in 1 Sam. xvii. 16), after which we again (comp. the reverse order in lxxxiii. 6) have a transition to the *perf.* which is the more uncoloured expression of the actual: נוֹסַד (with יַחַד as the exponent of reciprocity) prop. to press close and firm upon one another, then (like سَاوَرَ, which, according to the correct observation of the Turkish Kamus, in its signification *clam cum aliquo locutus est*, starts from the very same primary meaning of pressing close to any object): to deliberate confidentially together (as xxxi. 14 and נוֹעַץ lxxi. 10). The subjects מַלְכֵי־אֶרֶץ and רוֹזְנִים (according to the Arabic *razuna*, to be weighty: the grave, dignitaries, σεμνοί, *augusti*) are only in accordance with the poetic style without the article. It is a general rising of the people of the earth against Jahve and His מָשִׁיחַ, Χριστός, the king anointed by Him by means of the holy oil and most intimately allied to Him. The psalmist hears (ver. 3) the decision of the deliberating

princes. The pathetic suff. *êmō* instead of *êhém* refers back
to Jahve and His Anointed. The cohortatives express the
mutual kindling of feeling; the sound and rhythm of the exclamation correspond to the dull murmur of hatred and
threatening defiance: the rhythm is iambic, and then anapæstic. First they determine to break asunder the fetters
(מֹאסְרוֹת = מוֹסְרוֹת) to which the אֶת, which is significant in
the poetical style, points, then to cast away the cords from
them (מִמֶּנּוּ *a nobis*, this is the Palestinian mode of writing,
whereas the Babylonians said and wrote מִמֶּנּוּ *a nobis* in distinction from מִמֶּנּוּ *ab eo*, B. *Sota* 35 *a*) partly with the vexation
of captives, partly with the triumph of freedmen. They are,
therefore, at present subjects of Jahve and His Anointed,
and not merely because the whole world is Jahve's, but
because He has helped His Anointed to obtain dominion
over them. It is a battle for freedom, upon which they are
entering, but a freedom that is opposed to God.

Vers. 4—6. Above the scene of this wild tumult of battle
and imperious arrogance the psalmist in this six line strophe
beholds Jahve, and in spirit hears His voice of thunder against
the rebels. In contrast to earthly rulers and events Jahve
is called יוֹשֵׁב בַּשָּׁמַיִם : He is enthroned above them in unapproachable majesty and ever-abiding glory; He is called
אֲדֹנָי as He who controls whatever takes place below with absolute power according to the plan His wisdom has devised,
which brooks no hindrance in execution. The *futt.* describe
not what He will do, but what He does continually (cf. Isa.
xviii. 4 sq.). לָמוֹ also belongs, according to lix. 9, xxxvii.
13, to יִשְׂחָק (שׂחק׳ which is more usual in the post-pentateu-
chal language = צחק). He laughs at the defiant ones, for between them and Him there is an infinite distance; He derides
them by allowing the boundless stupidity of the infinitely little
one to come to a climax and then He thrusts him down to the
earth undeceived. This climax, the extreme limit of the
divine forbearance, is determined by the אָז, as in Deut. xxix.
19, cf. שָׁם xiv. 5, xxxvi. 13, which is a "then" referring to the
future and pointing towards the crisis which then supervenes.
Then He begins at once to utter the actual language of His
wrath to his foes and confounds them in the heat of His

anger, disconcerts them utterly, both outwardly and in spirit.
בָּהַל, بهل, cogn. בָּלָה, means orginally to let loose, let go,
then in Hebrew sometimes, externally, to overthrow, sometimes, of the mind, to confound and disconcert.

Ver. 5 *a* is like a peal of thunder (cf. Isa. x. 33); בַּחֲרוֹנוֹ,
5 *b*, like the lightning's destructive flash. And as the first
strophe closed with the words of the rebels, so this second
closes with Jahve's own words. With וַאֲנִי begins an adverbial
clause like Gen. xv. 2, xviii. 13, Ps. l. 17. The suppressed
principal clause (cf. Isa. iii. 14; Ew. § 341, *c*) is easily supplied: ye are revolting, whilst notwithstanding I . . . With
וַאֲנִי He opposes His irresistible will to their vain untertaking.
It has been shewn by Böttcher, that we must not translate
"I have anointed" (Targ., Symm.). נָסַךְ, نسك, certainly means
to pour out, but not to pour upon, and the meaning of pouring wide and firm (of casting metal, libation, anointing)
then, as in הִצִּיק, הִצִּיג, goes over into the meaning of setting
firmly in any place (*fundere* into *fundare, constituere,* as
LXX., Syr., Jer., and Luther translate), so that consequently
נָסִיךְ the word for prince cannot be compared with מָשִׁיחַ,
but with נָצִיב.* The Targum rightly inserts וּמְנִיתֵיהּ (*et præ-
feci eum*) after רַבִּיתִי (*unxi*), for the place of the anointing is
not עַל־צִיּוֹן. History makes no mention of a king of Israel
being anointed on Zion. Zion is mentioned as the royal seat
of the Anointed One; there He is installed, that He may
reign there, and rule from thence, cx. 2. It is the hill of the
city of David (2 Sam. v. 7, 9, 1 Kings viii. 1) including Moriah, that is intended. That hill of holiness, *i. e.* holy hill,
which is the resting-place of the divine presence and therefore excels all the heights of the earth, is assigned to Him
as the seat of His throne.

---

* Even the Jalkut on the Psalms, § 620, wavers in the explanation
of נסכתי between אמשחתיה I have anointed him, (after Dan. x. 3),
אתיכתיה I have cast him (after Exod. xxxii. 4 and freq.), and גדלתיו I have
made him great (after Mic. v. 4). Aquila, by rendering it καὶ ἐδιασάμην
(from διάζεσθαι = ὑφαίνειν), adds a fourth possible rendering. A fifth is נָסַךְ
to purify, consecrate (Hitz.), which does not exist, for the Arabic *nasaka*
obtains this meaning from the primary signification of cleansing by flooding with water (*e. g.* washing away the briny elements of a field). Also
in Prov. viii. 23 נִסַּכְתִּי means I am cast = placed.

Vers. 7—9. The Anointed One himself now speaks and expresses what he is, and is able to do, by virtue of the divine decree. No transitional word or formula of introduction denotes this sudden transition from the speech of Jahve to that of His Christ. The psalmist is the seer: his Psalm is the mirrored picture of what he saw and the echo of what he heard. As Jahve in opposition to the rebels acknowledges the king upon Zion, so the king on Zion appeals to Him in opposition to the rebels. The name of God, יְהֹוָה, has *Rebia magnum* and, on account of the compass of the full intonation of this accent, a *Gaja* by the *Shebâ* (comp. אֱלֹהָי xxv. 2, אֱלֹהִים lxviii. 8, אֲדֹנָי xc. 1).* The construction of סָפֵר with אֶל (as lxix. 27, comp. אָמַר Gen. xx. 2, Jer. xxvii. 19, דִּבֶּר 2 Chron. xxxii. 19, הוֹדִיעַ Isa. xxxviii. 19): to narrate or make an announcement with respect to… is minute, and therefore solemn. Self-confident and fearless, he can and will oppose to those, who now renounce their allegiance to him, a חֹק, *i. e.* an authentic, inviolable appointment, which can neither be changed nor shaken. All the ancient versions, with the exception of the Syriac, read חֹק־יְהוָֹה together. The line of the strophe becomes thereby more symmetrical, but the expression loses in force. אֶל־חֹק rightly has *Olewejored*. It is the amplificative use of the noun when it is not more precisely determined, known in Arabic grammar: such a decree! majestic as to its author and its matter. Jahve has declared to Him: בְּנִי אַתָּה,** and that on the definite day

____

* We may observe here, in general, that this *Gaja* (*Metheg*) which draws the *Shebâ* into the intonation is placed even beside words with the lesser distinctives *Zinnor* and *Rebia parvum* only by the Masorete *Ben-Naphtali*, not by *Ben-Asher* (both about 950 A. D.). This is a point which has not been observed throughout even in Baer's edition of the Psalter so that consequently *e. g.* in v. 11 it is to be written אֱלֹהִים; in vi. 2 on the other hand (with *Dechi*) יְהוָֹה, not יְהֹוָה.

** Even in pause here אַתָּה remains without a lengthened *ā* (*Psalter* ii. 468), but the word is become *Milel,* while out of pause, according to Ben-Asher, it is *Milra*; but even out of pause (as in lxxxix. 10, 12, xc. 2) it is accented on the *penult.* by Ben-Naphtali. The *Athnach* of the books תאם (Ps., Job, Prov.), corresponding to the *Zakeph* of the 21 other books, has only a half pausal power, and as a rule none at all where it follows *Olewejored*, cf. ix. 7, xiv. 4, xxv. 7, xxvii. 4, xxxi. 14, xxxv. 15, &c. (Baer, *Thorath Emeth* p. 37).

on which He has begotten or born him into this relationship
of son. The verb יָלַד (with the changeable vowel *i**) unites in
itself, like| γεννᾶν, the ideas of begetting and bearing (LXX.
γεγέννηκα, Aq. ἔτεκον); what is intended is an operation of
divine power exalted above both, and indeed, since it refers to
a setting up (נסך) in the kingship, the begetting into a royal
existence, which takes place in and by the act of anointing
(משׁח). Whether it be David, or a son of David, or the
other David, that is intended, in any case 2 Sam. vii. is to be
accounted as the first and oldest proclamation of this decree;
for there David, with reference to his own anointing, and
at the same time with the promise of everlasting dominion,
receives the witness of the eternal sonship to which Jahve has
appointed the seed of David in relation to Himself as Father,
so that David and his seed can say to Jahve: אָבִי אַתָּה, Thou
art my Father, lxxxix. 27, as Jahve can to him: בְּנִי אַתָּה, Thou
art My son. From this sonship of the Anointed one to Jahve,
the Creator and Possessor of the world, flows His claim to
and expectation of the dominion of the world. The cohortative, natural after challenges, follows upon שְׁאַל, Ges.
§ 128, 1. Jahve has appointed the dominion of the world
to His Son: on His part therefore it needs only the desire for
it, to appropriate to Himself that which is allotted to Him.
He needs only to be willing, and that He is willing is shewn
by His appealing to the authority delegated to Him by Jahve
against the rebels. This authority has a supplement in ver.
9, which is most terrible for the rebellious ones. The *suff.*
refer to the גּוֹיִם, the ἔθνη, sunk in heathenism. For these his
sceptre of dominion (cx. 2) becomes a rod of iron, which will
shatter them into a thousand pieces like a brittle image of
clay (Jer. xix. 11). With נִפֵּץ alternates רָעַע (= רָעַץ *frangere*),
fut. תָּרֹעַ; whereas the LXX. (Syr., Jer.), which renders ποι-
μανεῖς αὐτοὺς ἐν ῥάβδῳ (as 1 Cor. iv. 21) σιδηρᾷ, points it
תִּרְעֵם from רָעָה. The staff of iron, according to the Hebrew
text the instrument of punitive power, becomes thus with

---

* The changeable *i* goes back either to a primary form שָׁאַל, יָרַשׁ, יָלַד;
or it originates directly from *Pathach*; forms like יְרֻשּׁה and שְׁאֵלָה favour
the former, *ē* in a closed syllable generally going over into *Segol* favours
the latter.

reference to שֵׁבֶט as the shepherd's staff xxiii. 4, Mic. vii. 14, an instrument of despotism.

Vers. 10—12. The poet closes with a practical application to the great of the earth of that which he has seen and heard. With וְעַתָּה, καὶ νῦν (1 John ii. 28), *itaque*, appropriate conclusions are drawn from some general moral matter of fact (*e. g.* Prov. v. 7) or some fact connected with the history of redemption (*e. g.* Isa. xxviii. 22). The exhortation is not addressed to those whom he has seen in a state of rebellion, but to kings in general with reference to what he has prophetically seen and heard. שֹׁפְטֵי אָרֶץ are not those who judge the earth, but the judges, *i. e.* rulers (Amos ii. 3, cf. i. 8), belonging to the earth, throughout its length or breadth. The *Hiph.* הִשְׂכִּיל signifies to shew intelligence or discernment; the *Niph.* נוֹסַר as a so-called *Niph. tolerativum*, to let one's self be chastened or instructed, like נוֹעָץ Prov. xiii. 10, to allow one's self to be advised, נִדְרַשׁ Ezek. xiv. 3, to allow one's self to be sought, נִמְצָא to allow one's self to be found, 1 Chron. xxviii. 9, and frequently. This general call to reflection is followed, in ver. 11, by a special exhortation in reference to Jahve, and in ver. 12, in reference to the Son. עִבְדוּ and גִּילוּ answer to each other: the latter is not according to Hos. x. 5 in the sense of חָילוּ xcvi. 9, but, — since "to shake with trembling" (Hitz.) is a tautology, and as an imperative גִּילוּ everywhere else signifies: rejoice, — according to c. 2, in the sense of rapturous manifestation of joy at the happiness and honour of being permitted to be servants of such a God. The LXX. correctly renders it: ἀγαλλιᾶσθε αὐτῷ ἐν τρόμῳ. Their rejoicing, in order that it may not run to the excess of security and haughtiness, is to be blended with trembling (בְּ as Zeph. iii. 17), viz. with the trembling of reverence and self-control, for God is a consuming fire, Hebr. xii. 28.

The second exhortation, which now follows, having reference to their relationship to the Anointed One, has been missed by all the ancient versions except the Syriac, as though its clearness had blinded the translators, since they render בַר, either בֹּר purity, chastity, discipline (LXX., Targ., Ital., Vulg.), or בַּר pure, unmixed (Aq., Symm., Jer.:

adorate pure). Thus also Hupfeld renders it "yield sincerely", whereas it is rendered by Ewald "receive wholesome warning", and by Hitzig "submit to duty" (בַּר like the Arabic *birr* = בֹּר); Olshausen even thinks, there may be some mistake in בר, and Diestel decides for בּו instead of בר. But the context and the usage of the language require *osculamini filium*. The *Piel* נָשַׁק means to kiss, and never anything else; and while בֹּר in Hebrew means purity and nothing more, and בַּר as an adverb, *pure,* cannot be supported, nothing is more natural here, after Jahve has acknowledged His Anointed One as His Son, than that בַּר (Prov. xxxi. 2, even בְּנִי = בְּרִי) — which has nothing strange about it when found in solemn discourse, and here helps one over the dissonance of בֶּן פֶּן — should, in a like absolute manner to חֹק, denote the unique son, and in fact the Son of God.* The exhortation to submit to Jahve is followed, as Aben-Ezra has observed, by the exhortation to do homage to Jahve's Son. To kiss is equivalent to to do homage. Samuel kisses Saul (1 Sam. x. 1), saying that thereby he does homage to him.**

The subject to what follows is now, however, not the Son, but Jahve. It is certainly at least quite as natural to the New Testament consciousness to refer "lest He be angry" to the Son (*vid.* Apoc. vi. 16 sq.), and since the warning against putting trust (חֲסוֹת) in princes, cxviii. 9, cxlvi. 3, cannot be applied to the Christ of God, the reference of בּו to Him (Hengst.) cannot be regarded as impossible. But since חָסָה בְּ is the usual word for taking confiding refuge in Jahve, and

---

* Apart from the fact of בר not having the article, its indefiniteness comes under the point of view of that which, because it combines with it the idea of the majestic, great, and terrible, is called by the Arabian grammarians لتعظيم التنكير or۱ لتكثير or لتهويل; by the boundlessness which lies in it it challenges the imagination to magnify the notion which it thus expresses. An Arabic expositor would here (as in ver. 7 above) render it "Kiss a son and such a son!" (*vid. Ibn Hishâm* in De Sacy's *Anthol. Grammat.* p. ٨٥, where it is to be translated *hic est vir, qualis vir!*). Examples which support this doctrine are בְּיָד Isa. xxviii. 2 by a hand, viz. God's almighty hand which is the hand of hands, and Isa. xxxi. 8 מִפְּנֵי־חֶרֶב before a sword, viz. the divine sword which brooks no opposing weapon.

** On this *vid.* Scacchi *Myrothecium*, t. iii. (1637) c. 35.

the future day of wrath is always referred to in the Old Testament (*e. g.* cx. 5) as the day of the wrath of God, we refer the *ne irascatur* to Him whose son the Anointed One is; therefore it is to be rendered: lest Jahve be angry and ye perish דֶּרֶךְ. This דֶּרֶךְ is the *accus.* of more exact definition. If the way of any one perish, i. 6, he himself is lost with regard to the way, since this leads him into the abyss. It is questionable whether כִּמְעַט means "for a little" in the sense of *brevi* or *facile.* The *usus loquendi* and position of the words favour the latter (Hupf.). Everywhere else כִּמְעַט means by itself (without such additions as in Ezr. ix. 8, Isa. xxvi. 20, Ezek. xvi. 47) "for a little, nearly, easily." At least this meaning is secured to it when it occurs after hypothetical antecedent clauses as in lxxxi. 15, 2 Sam. xix. 37, Job xxxii. 22. Therefore it is to be rendered: for His wrath might kindle easily, or might kindle suddenly. The poet warns the rulers in their own highest interest not to challenge the wrathful zeal of Jahve for His Christ, which according to ver. 5 is inevitable. Well is it with all those who have nothing to fear from this outburst of wrath, because they hide themselves in Jahve as their refuge. The construct state חוֹסֵי connects בּוֹ, without a genitive relation, with itself as forming together one notion, Ges. § 116, 1. חסה the usual word for fleeing confidingly to Jahve, means according to its radical notion not so much *refugere, confugere,* as *se abdere, condere,* and is therefore never combined with אֶל, but always with בְּ. *

---

* On old names of towns, which show this ancient חסה. Wetzstein's remark on Job xxiv. 8 [ii. p. 22 n. 2]. The Arabic still has حسى in the reference of the primary meaning to water which, sucked in and hidden, flows under the sand and only comes to sight on digging. The rocky bottom on which it collects beneath the surface of the sand and by which it is prevented from oozing away or drying up is called حَسَى ḥasâ or حِسَى ḥisâ a hiding-place or place of protection, and a fountain dug there is called عين الحسى.

PSALM III.

MORNING HYMN OF ONE IN DISTRESS, BUT CONFIDENT IN GOD.

2 JAHVE, how many are my oppressors!
   Many rise up against me,
3 Many say of my soul:
   "There is no help for him in God". (*Sela*)

4 But Thou, O Jahve, art a shield for me,
   My glory and the lifter up of my head.
5 I cried unto Jahve with my voice
   And He answered me from His holy hill. (*Sela*)

6 I laid me down, and slept;
   I awaked, for Jahve sustaineth me.
7 I will not be afraid of ten thousands of the people
   Who have set themselves against me round about.

8 Arise, O Jahve, help me, O my God!
   For Thou smitest all mine enemies on the cheek,
   Thou breakest the teeth of the ungodly.
9 To Jahve belongeth salvation —
   Upon Thy people be Thy blessing! (*Sela*)

The two Psalms forming the prologue, which treat of cognate themes, the one ethical, from the standpoint of the הכמה, and the other related to the history of redemption from the standpoint of the נבואה, are now followed by a morning prayer; for morning and evening prayers are surely the first that one expects to find in a prayer- and hymnbook. The morning hymn, Ps. iii., which has the mention of the "holy hill" in common with Ps. ii., naturally precedes the evening hymn Ps. iv.; for that Ps. iii. is an evening hymn as some are of opinion, rests on grammatical misconception.

With Ps. iii., begin, as already stated, the hymns arranged for music. By מִזְמוֹר לְדָוִד, *a Psalm of David*, the hymn which follows is marked as one designed for musical accompaniment. Since מזמור occurs exclusively in the inscriptions of the Psalms, it is no doubt a technical expression coined by David. זָמַר (root זם) is an onomatopoetic word, which in *Kal* signifies to cut off, and in fact to prune or lop (the vine) (cf. Arabic زبر to write, from the buzzing noise of the style or reed on the writing material). The signification of singing and playing proper to the *Piel* are not connected with the signification "to nip". For neithertherhythmical division (Schultens) nor the articulated speaking (Hitz.) furnish a probable explanation, since the cæsura and syllable are not natural but artificial notions, nor also the nipping of the strings (Böttch., Ges.), for which the language has coined the word נִגֵּן (of like root with נָגַע). Moreover, the earliest passages in which זִמְרָה and זִמֵּר occur (Gen. xliii. 11, Exod. xv. 2, Judges v. 3), speak rather of song than music and both words frequently denote song in distinction from music, *e. g.* xcviii. 5, lxxxi. 3, cf. Cant. ii. 12. Also, if זִמֵּר originally means, like ψάλλειν, *carpere (pulsare) fides,* such names of instruments as Arab. *zemr* the hautboy and *zummâra* the pipe would not be formed. But זִמֵּר means, as Hupfeld has shewn, as indirect an onomatope as *canere,* "to make music" in the widest sense; the more accurate usage of the language, however, distinguishes זִמֵּר and שִׁיר as to play and to sing. With בְּ of the instrument זִמֵּר denotes song with musical accompaniment (like the Æthiopic זמר *instrumento canere*) and זִמְרָה (Aram. זְמַר) is sometimes, as in Amos v. 23, absolutely: music. Accordingly מִזְמוֹר signifies technically the music and שִׁיר the words. And therefore we translate the former by "Psalm", for ὁ ψαλμός ἐστιν — says Gregory of Nyssa — ἡ διὰ τοῦ ὀργάνου τοῦ μουσικοῦ μελωδία, ᾠδὴ δὲ ἡ διὰ στόματος γενομένου τοῦ μέλους μετὰ ῥημάτων ἐκφώνησις.

That Ps. iii. is a hymn arranged for music is also manifest from the סֶלָה which occurs here 3 times. It is found in the Psalter, as Bruno has correctly calculated, 71 times (17 times in the 1st book, 30 in the 2nd, 20 in the 3rd, 4 in the 4th) and, with the exception of the anonymous Ps. lxvi. lxvii., always in those that are inscribed by the name of David and of the psalmists famed from the time of David. That it is a marginal note referring to the Davidic Temple-music is clearly seen from the fact, that all the Psalms with סלה have the לַמְנַצֵּחַ which relates to the musical execution, with the exception of eight (xxxii. xlviii. l. lxxxii. lxxxiii. lxxxvii. lxxxix. cxliii.) which, however, from the designation מִזְמוֹר

are at least manifestly designed for music. The Tephilla of
Habbakuk, ch. iii., the only portion of Scripture in which
סלה occurs out of the Psalter, as an exception has the למנצח
at the end. Including the three סלה of this tephilla, the
word does not occur less than 74 times in the Old Testament.

Now as to the meaning of this musical *nota bene*, 1st,
every explanation as an abbreviation, — the best of which is
סב לְמַעְלָה הַשָּׁר = (turn thyself towards above *i. e.* towards
the front, O Singer! therefore: *da capo*), — is to be rejected,
because such abbreviations fail of any further support in the
Old Testament. Also 2ndly, the derivation from סָלָה = שָׁלָה
silere, according to which it denotes a pause, or orders the
singers to be silent while the music strikes up, is inadmissible, because סלה in this sense is neither Hebrew nor Aramaic and moreover in Hebrew itself the interchange of שׁ
with ס (שִׂרְיוֹן, סִרְיוֹן) is extremely rare. There is but one verbal stem with which סָלָה can be combined, viz. סָלַל or סָלָה
(סְלָא). The primary notion of this verbal stem is that of
lifting up, from which, with reference to the derivatives סֻלָּם
a ladder and מְסִלָּה in the signification an ascent, or steps,
2 Chron. ix. 11, comes the general meaning for סֶלָה, of a
musical rise. When the tradition of the Mishna explains the
word as a synonym of נֶצַח and the Targum, the Quinta, and
the Sexta (and although variously Aquila and sometimes
the Syriac version) render it in accordance therewith "for
ever (always)", — in favour of which Jerome also at last
decides, *Ep. ad Marcellam "quid sit Sela"*), — the original musical signification is converted into a corresponding logical
or lexical one. But it is apparent from the διάψαλμα of the
LXX. (adopted by Symm., Theod., and the Syr.), that the
musical meaning amounts to a strengthening of some kind
or other; for διάψαλμα signifies, according to its formation
(— μα = — μενον), not the pause as Gregory of Nyssa defines it:
ἡ μεταξὺ τῆς ψαλμῳδίας γενομένη κατὰ τὸ ἀθρόον ἐπηρέμησις
πρὸς ὑποδοχὴν τοῦ θεόθεν ἐπικρινομένου νοήματος, but either the
interlude, especially of the stringed instruments, (like διαύ-
λιον (διαύλειον), according to Hesychius the interlude of the
flutes between the choruses), or an intensified playing (as
διαψάλλειν τριγώνοις is found in a fragment of the comedian

Eupolis in Athenæus of the strong play of triangular harps).*
According to the pointing of the word as we now have it, it
ought apparently to be regarded as a noun סַל with the *ah* of
direction (synonymous with נֵוָה, up! Job xxii. 29); for the omission of the *Dagesh* beside the *ah* of direction is not without
example (cf. 1 Kings ii. 40 גָּתָה which is the proper reading,
instead of גַּתָּה, and referred to by Ewald) and the —, with
Dag. forte implicitum, is usual before liquids instead of —, as
פַּדֶּנָה Gen. xxviii. 2, הָרָה Gen. xiv. 10 instead of *paddannah,*
harrah, as also כַּרְמֶלָה 1 Sam. xxv. 5 instead of כַּרְמְלָה. But
the present pointing of this word, which is uniformly included
in the accentuation of the Masoretic verse, is scarcely the
genuine pointing: it looks like an imitation of נֵצַח. The word
may originally have been pronounced סַלָּה (*elevatio* after the
form דָּלָה, בַּתָּה). The combination הִגָּיוֹן סלה ix. 17, in which
הגיון refers to the playing of the stringed instruments (xcii. 4)
leads one to infer that סלה is a note which refers not to the
singing but to the instrumental accompaniment. But to
understand by this a heaping up of weighty expressive accords and powerful harmonies in general, would be to confound ancient with modern music. What is meant is the
joining in of the orchestra, or a reinforcement of the instruments, or even a transition from *piano* to *forte.*

Three times in this Psalm we meet with this Hebrew *forte.*
In sixteen Psalms (vii. xx. xxi. xliv. xlvii. xlviii. l. liv. lx.
lxi. lxxv. lxxxi. lxxxii. lxxxiii. lxxxv. cxliii.) we find it only
once; in fifteen Psalms (iv. ix. xxiv. xxxix. xlix. lii. lv. lvii.
lix. lxii. lxvii. lxxvi. lxxxiv. lxxxvii. lxxxviii.), twice; in but
seven Psalms (iii. xxxii. xlvi. lxvi. lxviii. lxxvii. cxl. and also
Hab. iii.), three times; and only in one (lxxxix.), four times.
It never stands at the beginning of a Psalm, for the ancient
music was not as yet so fully developed, that סלה should
absolutely correspond to the *ritornello.* Moreover, it does
not always stand at the close of a strophe so as to be the
sign of a regular interlude, but it is always placed where
the instruments are to join in simultaneously and take up

---

* On the explanations of διάψαλμα in the Fathers and the old lexicographers. *vid.* Suicer's *Thes. Eccl.* and Augusti's *Christl. Archäologie,*
Th. ii.

the melody — a thing which frequently happens in the midst
of the strophe. In the Psalm before us it stands at the close
of the 1st, 2nd, and 4th strophes. The reason of its omission
after the third is evident.

Not a few of the Psalms bear the date of the time of
the persecution under Saul, but only this and probably
Ps. lxiii. have that of Absolom. The Psalter however contains other Psalms which reflect this second time of persecution. It is therefore all the more easy to accept as tradition the inscription: *when he fled before Absolom, his son.* And
what is there in the contents of the Psalm against this statement? All the leading features of the Psalm accord with it,
viz. the mockery of one who is rejected of God 2 Sam. xvi.
7 sq., the danger by night 2 Sam. xvii. 1, the multitudes of
the people 2 Sam. xv. 13, xvii. 11, and the high position of
honour held by the psalmist. Hitzig prefers to refer this
and the following Psalm to the surprize by the Amalekites
during David's settlement in Ziklag. But since at that time
Zion and Jerusalem were not free some different interpretation of ver. 5 *b* becomes necessary. And the fact that the
Psalm does not contain any reference to Absolom does not
militate against the inscription. It is explained by the tone
of 2 Sam. xix. 1 [xviii. 33 Engl.]. And if Psalms belonging
to the time of Absolom's rebellion required any such reference
to make them known, then we should have none at all

Vers. 2—3. The first strophe contains the lament concerning the existing distress. From its combination with the
exclamative מָה, רַבּוּ is accented on the *ultima* (and also in
civ. 24); the accentuation of the *perf.* of verbs עע very frequently (even without the *Waw consec.*) follows the example
of the strong verb, Ges. § 67 rem. 12. A declaration then
takes the place of the summons and the רַבִּים implied in the
predicate רַבּוּ now becomes the subject of participial predicates, which more minutely describe the continuing condition
of affairs. The לְ of לְנַפְשִׁי signifies "in the direction of", followed by an address in xi. 1 (= "to"), or, as here and frequently (*e. g.* Gen. xxi. 7) followed by narration (= "of",

concerning). לְנַפְשִׁי instead of לִי implies that the words of the adversaries pronounce a judgment upon his inmost life, or upon his personal relationship to God. יְשׁוּעָתָה is an intensive form for יְשׁוּעָה, whether it be with a double feminine termination (Ges., Ew., Olsh.), or, with an original (accusative) *ah* of the direction: we regard this latter view, with Hupfeld, as more in accordance with the usage and analogy of the language (comp. xliv. 27 with lxxx. 3, and לַיְלָה prop. νύχτα, then as common Greek ἡ νύχτα, νύχθα). God is the ground of help; to have no more help in Him is equivalent to being rooted out of favour with God. Open enemies as well as disconcerted friends look upon him as one henceforth cast away. David had plunged himself into the deepest abyss of wretchedness by his adultery with Bathsheba, at the beginning of the very year in which, by the renewal of the Syro-Ammonitish war, he had reached the pinnacle of worldly power. The rebellion of Absolom belonged to the series of dire calamities which began to come upon him from that time. Plausible reasons were not wanting for such words as these which give up his cause as lost.

Vers. 4—5. But cleansed by penitence he stands in a totally different relationship to God and God to him from that which men suppose. Every hour he has reason to fear some overwhelming attack but Jahve is the shield which covers him behind and before (בְּעַד *constr.* of בַּעַד = بَعْدَ prop. *pone, post*). His kingdom is taken from him, but Jahve is his glory. With covered head and dejected countenance he ascended the Mount of Olives (2 Sam. xv. 30), but Jahve is the "lifter up of his head", inasmuch as He comforts and helps him. The primary passage of this believing utterance "God is a shield" is Gen. xv. 1 (cf. Deut. xxxiii. 29). Very far from praying in vain, he is assured, that when he prays his prayer will be heard and answered. The rendering "I cried and He answered me" is erroneous here where אֶקְרָא does not stand in an historical connection. The future of sequence does not require it, as is evident from lv. 17 sq. (comp. on cxx. 1); it is only an expression of confidence in the answer on God's part, which will follow his prayer. In constructions like קוֹלִי אֶקְרָא, Hitzig and Hupfeld regard קוֹלִי as the narrower subject-notion beside the more general one (as xliv. 3, lxix. 11, lxxxiii. 19): my voice — I cried; but the position of the words is not favourable to this in the passage before us and in xvii. 10, xxvii. 7, lvii. 5, lxvi. 17, cxlii. 2, Isa. xxvi. 9, though it may be in lxix. 11, cviii. 2. According to Ew. § 281, *c*, קוֹלִי is an accusative of more precise definition, as without doubt in Isa. x. 30 cf. Ps. lx. 7, xvii. 13 sq.; the cry is thereby described as a loud cry.* To this cry, as וַיַּעֲנֵנִי as being a pure mood of sequence implies, succeeds the answer, or, which better corresponds to the original meaning of עָנָה (comp. عَنَّ to meet, stand opposite) reply;** and it it comes from the place whither it was directed: מֵהַר קָדְשׁוֹ. He had removed the ark from Kirjath Jearim to Zion. He had not taken it with him when he left Jerusalem and fled before Absolom, 2 Sam. xv. 25. He was therefore separated by a hostile power from the resting-place of the divine presence. But his prayer urged its way on to the cherubim-throne; and to the answer of Him who is enthroned there, there is no separating barrier of space or created things.

Vers. 6—7. That this God will protect him, His protection during the past night is now a pledge to him in the early morning. It is a violation of the rules of grammar to translate וָאִישָׁנָה: I shall go to sleep, or: I am going to sleep. The 1 *pers. fut. consec.* which is indicated by the וָ, is fond of taking an *ah* of direction, which gives subjective intensity to the idea of sequence: "and thus I then fell asleep", cf. vii. 5, cxix. 55, and frequently, Gen. xxxii. 6, and more especially

* Böttcher, *Collectanea* pp. 166 sq., also adopts the view, that נַפְשִׁי, פִּי, קוֹלִי are each *appositum vicarium subjecti* and therefore *nomin.* in such passages. But 1) the fact that אֶת never stands beside them is explained by the consideration that it is not suited to an adverbial collateral definition. And 2) that elsewhere the same notions appear as direct subjects, just as 3) that elsewhere they alternate with the verbal subject-notion in the parallel member of the verse (cxxx. 5, Prov. viii. 4) — these last two admit of no inference. The controverted question of the syntax is, moreover, an old one and has been treated of at length by Kimchi in his *Book of Roots s. r.* אוה.

** *vid.* Redslob in his treatise: *Die Integrität der Stelle Hos.* vii. 4—10 *in Frage gestellt* S. 7.

so in the later style, Ezra ix. 3, Neh. xiii. 21, *vid.* Ges. § 49, 2, Böttcher,. *Neue Aehrenlese,* No. 412. It is a retrospective glance at the past night. Awaking in health and safety, he feels grateful to Him to whom he owes it: יהוה יְסָמְכֵנִי. It is the result of the fact that Jahve supports him, and that God's hand is his pillow.* Because this loving, almighty hand is beneath his head (Cant. ii. 6) he is inaccessible and there-fore also devoid of fear. שִׁית (שׁוּת) carries its object in itself: to take up one's position, as in Isa. xxii. 7, synon. חָנָה xxviii. 3 and שִׂים 1 Kings xx. 12, cf. ἐπιτιθέναι τινί. David does not put a merely possible case. All Israel, that is to say ten thousands, myriads, were gone over to Absolom. Here, at the close of the third strophe, סלה is wanting because the לֹא אִירָא (I will not fear) is not uttered in a tone of triumph, but is only a quiet, meek expression of believing confidence. If the instruments struck up boldly and suddenly here, then a cry for help, urged forth by the difficulties that still continually sur-rounded him, would not be able to follow.

Vers. 8—9. The bold קוּמָה is taken from the mouth of Moses, Num. x. 35. God is said to arise when He takes a decisive part in what takes place in this world. Instead of *ḳûmah* it is accented *ḳumáh* as *Milra,* in order (since the reading קומה אדני is assumed) that the final *āh* may be sharply cut off from the guttural initial of the next word, and thus render a clear, exact pronunciation of the latter possible (Hitz., Ew. § 228, *b*).** Beside יהוה we have אֱלֹהַי, with the

____

* Referred to the other David, ver. 6 has become an Easter-morning call, *vid.* Val. Herberger's *Paradies-Blümlein aus dem Lustgarten der Psalmen* (Neue Ausg. 1857) S. 25.

** This is the traditional reason of the accentuation *shubáh*, *ḳumáh*, *shitháh* before יהוה: it is intended to prevent the one or other of the two gutturals being swallowed up (שלא יבולעו) by too rapid speaking. Hence it is that the same thing takes place even when another word, not the name of God, follows, if it begins with א or the like, and is closely con-nected with it by meaning and accentuation: *e. g.* Judges iv. 18 סוּרָה twice *Milra* before א; Ps. lvii. 9 עוּרָה, *Milra* before ה; לָמָה, *Milra* before ה, Exod. v. 22; נָחָת Is. xi. 2, and הֵבֵאת Gen. xxvi. 10, *Milra* before ע; and the following fact favours it, viz. that for a similar reason *Pasek* is placed were two ' would come together, *e. g.* Gen. xxi. 14 *Adonaj jir'eh* with the stroke of separation between the two words, cf. Ex. xv. 18, Prov. viii. 21. The fact that in Jer. xl. 5, וְשֻׁבָה remains *Milel,* is accounted

suff. of appropriating faith. The cry for help is then substantiated by כִּי and the retrospective *perf.* They are not
such *perff* of prophetically certain hope as in vi. 9, vii. 7,
ix. 5 sq., for the logical connection requires an appeal to
previous experience in the present passage: they express facts
of experience, which are taken from many single events (hence
כֹל) down to the present time. The verb הִכָּה is construed
with a double accusative, as *e. g.*, *Iliad* xvi. 597 τὸν μὲν ἄρα
Γλαῦχος στῆθος μέσον οὔτασε δουρί. The idea of contempt (Job
xvi. 10) is combined with that of rendering harmless in this
"smiting upon the cheek". What is meant is a striking in of
the jaw-bone and therewith a breaking of the teeth in pieces
(שִׁבַּר). David means, an ignominious end has always come
upon the ungodly who rose up against him and against God's
order in general, as their punishment. The enemies are conceived of as monsters given to biting, and the picture of their
fate is fashioned according to this conception. Jahve has the
power and the will to defend His Anointed against their hostility: לַה׳ הַיְשׁוּעָה *penes Jovam est salus.* יְשׁוּעָה (from יָשַׁע, وَسِعَ,
amplum esse) signifies breadth as applied to perfect freedom
of motion, removal of all straitness and oppression, prosperity without exposure to danger and unbeclouded. In the לְ
of possession lies the idea of the exclusiveness of the possession and of perfect freedom of disposal. At Jahve's free
disposal stands הַיְשׁוּעָה, salvation, in all its fulness (just so
in Jon. ii. 10, Apoc. vii. 10). In connection therewith David
first of all thinks of his own need of deliverance. But as a
true king he cannot before God think of himself, without
connecting himself with his people. Therefore he closes
with the intercessory inference: עַל־עַמְּךָ בִרְכָתֶךָ Upon Thy
people be Thy blessing! We may supply תְּהִי or תָּבֹא. Instead
of cursing his faithless people he implores a blessing upon

for by its being separated from the following אֶל־גְּדַלְיָה by *Pazer*; a real
exception, however (*Michlol* 112 *b*), — and not as Norzi from misapprehension observes, a controverted one, — is שְׁבָה, *Milel* before הָעִיר 2 Sam.
xv. 27, but it is by no means sufficient to oppose the purely orthophonic
(not rhythmical) ground of this *ultima*-accentuation. Even the semi-gut-
tural ר sometimes has a like influence over the tone: *ribáh ribî* xliii. 1,
cxix. 154.

those who have been piteously led astray and deceived. This
"upon Thy people be Thy blessing!" has its counterpart in
the "Father forgive them" of the other David, whom His
people crucified. The one concluding word of the Psalm
— observes Ewald — casts a bright light into the very
depths of his noble soul.

PSALM IV.
EVENING HYMN OF ONE WHO IS UNMOVED BEFORE BACK-BITERS AND MEN OF LITTLE FAITH.

2 WHEN I call answer me, O God of my righteousness,
Who hast made space for me in straitness;
Be merciful unto me and hear my prayer!

3 Ye sons of men, how long shall my honour become shame,
Since ye love appearance, ye seek after leasing?! (*Sela*)
4 Know then, that Jahve hath marked out the godly man
for Himself;
Jahve heareth when I call to Him.

5 Be ye angry, yet sin ye not! —
Commune with your own heart upon your bed and be
still! (*Sela.*)
6 Offer the sacrifices of righteousness,
And put your trust in Jahve!

7 Many say: "How can we experience good!?"
O lift up the light of Thy countenance upon us, Jahve!
8 Thou hast put gladness into my heart,
More than in the time when their corn and wine abound.

9 In peace will I lay me down and forthwith sleep,
For Thou, O Jahve, in seclusion
Makest me to dwell securely.

The Davidic morning hymn is now followed by a Davidic
evening hymn. It is evident that they belong together from
the mutual relation of iv. 7 with iii. 3, and iii. 6 with iv. 9.
They are the only two Psalms in which the direct words of
others are taken up into a prayer with the formula "many
say", רבים אמרים. The history and chronological position of
the one is explained from the inscription of the other. From

the *quousque* iv. 3, and the words of the feeble-faiths iv. 7, it follows that Ps. iv. is the later of the two.

It is at the head of this Psalm that we are first met by לַמְנַצֵּחַ (or לַמְנַצֵּחַ with *Gaja*, Hab. iii. 19), which still calls for investigation. It is found fifty five times in the Psalter, not 54 as is usually reckoned: viz. 19 times in book i., 25 times in book ii., 8 times in book iii., 3 times in book v. Only two of the Psalms, at the head of which it is found, are anonymous: viz. lxvi., lxvii. All the others bear the names of David and of the psalmists celebrated from David's time, viz. 39 of David, 9 of the Korahites, 5 of Asaph. No fewer than 30 of these Psalms are Elohimic. למנצח is always the first word of the inscription; only in Ps. lxxxviii., which is easily liable to be overlooked in reckoning, is it otherwise, because there two different inscriptions are put together.

The meaning of the verb נִצַּח is evident from the Chronicles and the Book of Ezra, which belongs to them. The predilection of the chronicler for the history of religious worship and antiquarian lore is also of use in reference to this word. He uses it in the history of the time of David, of Solomon, of Josiah, of Zerubbabel and Joshua, and always in connection with the accounts of the Temple-service and the building of single parts of the Temple. To discharge the official duties of the Temple-service is called נַצֵּחַ עַל־מְלֶאבֶת בֵּית־יְהֹוָה 1 Chron. xxiii. 4 (comp. 28—32), and the expression is used in Ezra iii. 8 sq. of the oversight of the work and workmen for the building of the Temple. The same 3300 (3600) overseers, who are called הָרֹדִים בָּעָם הָעֹשִׂים בַּמְּלָאכָה in 1 Kings v. 30 are described by the chronicler (2 Chron. ii. 1) as מְנַצְּחִים עֲלֵיהֶם. In connection with the repair of the Temple under Josiah we read that Levites were appointed לְנַצֵּחַ (2 Chron. xxxiv. 12), namely לְכֹל עֹשֵׂה מְלָאכָה (ver. 13), instead of which we find it said in ii. 17 לְהַעֲבִיד, to keep the people at their work. The primary notion of נצח is that of shining, and in fact of the purest and most dazzling brightness; this then passes over to the notion of shining over or outshining, and in fact both of uninterrupted continuance and of excellence and superiority (*vid. Ithpa.* Dan. vi. 4, and cf. 1 Chron. xxiii. 4 with ix. 13; 1 Cor. xv. 54 with Isa. xxv. 8).

Thus, therefore, מְנַצֵּחַ is one who shews eminent ability in any departement, and then it gains the general signification of master, director, chief overseer. At the head of the Psalms it is commonly understood of the director of the Temple-music. מְנַצֵּחַ *est dux cantus* — Luther says in one place — *quem nos dicimus den Kapellenmeister* [the band-master], *qui orditur et gubernat cantum,* ἔξαρχος *(Opp. lat.* xvii. 134 *ed. Erl.).* But 1st, even the Psalms of Asaph have this למנצה at the beginning, and he was himself a director of the Temple-music, and in fact the chief-director (חָרֹאשׁ) 1 Chron. xvi. 5, or at any rate he was one of the three (Heman, Asaph, Ethan), to whom the 24 classes of the 4000 Levite singers under the Davidico-Salomonic sanctuary were subordinate; 2ndly, the passage of the chronicler (1 Chron. xv. 17—21) which is most prominent in reference to this question, does not accord with this explanation. According to this passage the three directors of the Temple-music managed the cymbals לְהַשְׁמִיעַ, to sound aloud; eight other musicians of high rank the nablas and six others the citherns לְנַצֵּחַ. This expression cannot mean "to direct", for the direction belonged to the three, and the cymbals were also better adapted to it than the citherns. It means "to take the lead in the playing": the cymbals directed and the citherns, better adapted to take the lead in the playing, were related to them, somewhat as the violins to the clarinets now-a-days. Hence מְנַצֵּחַ is not the director of the Temple-music but in general the master of song, and למנצה addresses the Psalm to him whose duty it is to arrange it and to train the Levite choristers; it therefore defines the Psalm as belonging to the songs of the Temple worship that require musical accompaniment. The translation of the Targum (Luther) also corresponds to this general sense of the expression: לְשַׁבְּחָא "to be sung liturgically", and the LXX.: εἰς τὸ τέλος, if this signifies "to the execution" and does not on the contrary ascribe an eschatological meaning to the Psalm.*

---

* Thus *e. g.* Eusebius: εἰς τὸ τέλος ὡς ἂν μακροῖς ὕστερον χρόνοις ἐπὶ συντελείᾳ τοῦ αἰῶνος μελλόντων πληροῦσθαι, and Theodoret: σημαίνει τὸ εἰς τὸ τέλος ὅτι μακροῖς ὕστερον χρόνοις πληρωθήσεται τὰ προφητευόμενα, with which accords *Pesachim* 117 *a* נגון לעתיד לבא ניצוח, *i. e.*

The בִּנְגִינוֹת which is added is not governed by it. This can be seen at once from Hab. iii. 19: to the chief singer, with an accompaniment of my stringed instruments (*vid.* my *Commentary*), which Hitzig renders: to the chief singer of my musical pieces; but נַצֵּחַ בְּ is not a phrase that can be supported, and נְגִינָה does not mean a piece of music. The *Piel,* נִגֵּן, complete with בְּיַד, signifies to touch the strings (cogn. נגע), to play a stringed instrument. Whence comes נְגִינוֹת (lxxvii. 7, Isa. xxxviii. 20) which is almost always used as a *pluralet.*: the play of the stringed instruments, and the superscribed בִּנְגִינוֹת Ps. iv. vi. liv. lv. lxvii. lxxvi.: with an accompaniment of the stringed instruments; and בְ is used as in xlix. 5, Isa. xxx. 29, 32. The hymn is to be sung in company with, probably with the sole accompaniment of, the stringed instruments. The fact of the inscribed words למנצח בנגינות preceding מזמור לדוד probably arises from the fact of their being written originally at the top over the chief title which gave the generic name of the hymn and the author.

Ver. 2. Jahve is אֱלֹהֵי צֶדֶק, the possessor of righteousness, the author of righteousness, and the vindicator of misjudged and persecuted righteousness. This God of righteousness David believingly calls his God (cf. xxiv. 5, lix. 11); for the righteousness he possesses, he possesses in Him, and the righteousness he looks for, he looks for in Him. That this is not in vain, his previous experience assures him: Thou hast made a breadth (space) for me when in a strait. In connection with this confirmatory relation of בַּצָּר הִרְחַבְתָּ לִּי it is more probable that we have before us an attributive clause (Hitz.), than that we have an independent one, and at any rate it is a retrospective clause. הרחבת is not precative (Böttch.), for the *perf.* of certainty with a precative colouring is confined

Psalms with למנצח and בנגינות refer to the last days. Gregory of Nyssa combines the different translations by rendering: εἰς τέλος, ὅπερ ἐστὶν ἡ νίκη. Ewald's view, that τέλος in this formula means consecration, celebration, worship, is improbable; in this signification it is not a Septuagint word.

to such exclamatory utterances as Job xxi. 16 (which see).
He bases his prayer on two things, viz. on his fellowship
with God, the righteous God, and on His justifying grace
which he has already experienced. He has been many times
in a strait already, and God has made a broad place for him.
The idea of the expansion of the breathing (of the stream
of air) and of space is attached to the ח ך of רחב, root רח
(*Deutsch. Morgenl. Zeitschr*. xii. 657). What is meant is the
expansion of the straitened heart, xxv. 17. Isa. lx. 5, and
the widening of a straitened position, xviii. 20, cxviii. 5. On
the *Dag.* in לִי *vid.* on lxxxiv. 4.

Vers. 3—4. Righteous in his relation to God he turns
rebukingly towards those who contemn him whose honour is
God's honour, viz. to the partisans of Absolom. In contrast
with בְּנֵי אָדָם, men who are lost in the multitude, בְּנֵי אִישׁ
d notes such as stand prominently forward out of the multitude; passages like xlix. 3, lxii. 10, Prov. viii. 4, Isa. ii. 9,
v. 15, shew this distinction. In this and the preceding Psalm
David makes as little mention of his degenerate son as he
does of the deluded king in the Psalms belonging to the
period of his persecution by Saul. The address is directed
to the aristocratic party, whose tool Absolom has become.
To these he says: till when (עַד־מֶה beside the non-guttural
which follows with *Segol,* without any manifest reason, as in
x. 13, Isa. i. 5, Jer. xvi. 10), *i. e.* how long shall my honour
become a mockery, namely to you and by you, just as we can
also say in Latin *quousque tandem dignitas mea ludibrio?* The
two following members are circumstantial clauses subordinate to the principal clause with עַד־מֶה (similar to Isa. i.
5 *a*; Ew. § 341, *b*). The energetic *fut.* with *Nun parag.* does
not usually stand at the head of independent clauses; it is
therefore to be rendered: since ye love רִיק, that which is
empty — the proper name for their high rank is hollow
appearance — how long will ye pursue after כָּזָב, falsehood?
— they seek to find out every possible lying pretext, in
order to trail the honour of the legitimate king in the
dust. The assertion that the personal honour of David,
not his kingly dignity, is meant by כְּבוֹדִי, separates what
is inseparable. They are eager to injure his official at the

same time as his personal reputation. Therefore David appeals in opposition to them (ver. 4) not only to the divine
choice, but also to his personal relationship to God, on which
that choice is based. The ו of וּדְעוּ is, as in 2 Kings iv. 41,
the ו of sequence: so know then. The *Hiph.* הִפְלָה (from
פָּלָה = פָּלָא, cogn. פָּלַל, prop. to divide) to make a separation, make a distinction Exod. ix. 4, xi. 7, then to distinguish in an extraordinary and remarkable way Exod. viii.
18, and to shew Ps. xvii. 7, cf. xxxi. 22, so that consequently what is meant is not the mere selection (בָּחַר), but
the remarkable selection to a remarkable position of honour
(LXX., Vulg. *mirificavit,* Windberg   translation of the Psalms
gewunderlichet). לוֹ belongs to the verb, as in cxxxv. 4, and
the principal accent lies on חָסִיד: he whom Jahve Himself, not
men, has thus remarkably distinguished is a חָסִיד, a pious
man, *i. e.* either, like the Syriac רְחִימָא = חֲסִידָא: God's favourite, or, according to the biblical usage of the language (cf. xii
2 with Isa. lvii. 1), in an active signification like פָּרִיץ פָּלִיט,
and the like: a lover of God, from חָסַד (root חם حس *strin-*
gere, whence *ḥassa* to curry, *maḥassa* a curry-comb) prop.
to feel one's self drawn, *i. e.* strongly affected (comp. *ḥiss* a
mental impression), in Hebrew, of a strong ardent affection.
As a חסיד he does not call upon God in vain, but finds a
ready hearing. Their undertaking consequently runs counter
to the miraculously evidenced will of God and must fail by
reason of the loving relationship in which the dethroned
and debased one stands to God.

Vers. 5—6. The address is continued: they are to repent
and cleave to Jahve instead of allowing themselves to be carried away by arrogance and discontent. The LXX. has rendered it correctly: ὀργίζεσθε καὶ μὴ ἁμαρτάνετε (cf. Ephes.
iv. 26): if ye will be angry beware of sinning, viz. back-
biting and rebellion (cf. the similar paratactic combinations xxviii. 1, Josh. vi. 18, Isa. xii. 1). In connection with
the rendering *contremiscite* we feel to miss any expression
of that before which they are to tremble (viz. the sure
punishment which God decrees). He warns his adversaries
against blind passion, and counsels them to quiet converse
with their own hearts, and solitary meditation, in order that

they may not imperil their own salvation. To commune with
one's own heart, without the addition of the object, is equivalent to to think alone by one's self, and the bed or resting-
place, without requiring to be understood literally, points to a
condition of mind that is favourable to quiet contemplation.
The heart is the seat of the conscience, and the Spirit of God
(as Hamann, *Werke* i. 98, observes on this subject) disguises
itself as our own voice that we may see His exhortation, His
counsel, and His wisdom well up out of our own stony heart.
The second *imper.* continues the first: and cease, prop. be
still (דֹמּוּ from the sound of the closed mouth checking the
discourse), *i. e.* come to your right mind by self-examination,
cease your tumult — a warning coming with the semblance
of command by reason of the consciousness of innocence on
his part; and this impression has to be rendered here by the
striking in of the music. The dehortation passes over into
exhortation in ver. 6. Of course the sacrifices were continued
in the sanctuary while David, with his faithful followers,
was a fugitive from Jerusalem. Referring to this, David
cries out to the Absolomites: offer זִבְחֵי־צֶדֶק. Here at least
these are not offerings consisting of actions which are in accordance with the will of God, instead of slaughtered animals,
but sacrifices offered with a right mind, conformed to the will
of God, instead of the hypocritical mind with which they consecrate their evil doings and think to flatter God. In li. 21,
Deut. xxxiii. 19 also, "the sacrifices of righteousness" are real
sacrifices, not merely symbols of moral acts. Not less full of
meaning is the exhortation וּבִטְחוּ אֶל־ה׳. The verb בָּטַח is
construed with אֶל as in xxxi. 7, lvi. 4, lxxxvi. 2, combining
with the notion of trusting that of drawing near to, hanging
on, attaching one's self to any one. The Arabic word بَطَح,

expandere, has preserved the primary notion of the word, a
notion which, as in the synon. بَسَط, when referred to the
effect which is produced on the heart, countenance and whole
nature of the man by a joyous cheerful state of mind, passes
over to the notion of this state of mind itself, so that בָּטַח
(like the Arab. *inbasaṭa* to be cheerful, fearless, bold, *lit.*
expanded (cf. רָהַב Isa. lx. 5) = unstraitened) consequently

signifies to be courageous, confident. They are to renounce
the self-trust which blinds them in their opposition to the
king who is deprived of all human assistance. If they will
trustingly submit themselves to God, then at the same time
the murmuring and rancorous discontent, from which the
rebellion has sprung, will be stilled. Thus far the address to
the rebellious magnates goes.

Vers. 7—8. Looking into his own small camp David is
conscious of a disheartened feeling which is gaining power
over him. The words: who will make us see, *i. e.* (as in xxxiv.
13) experience any good? can be taken as expressive of a
wish according to 2 Sam. xxiii. 15, Isa. xlii. 23; but the situation gives it the character of a despondent question arising
from a disheartened view of the future. The gloom has now,
lasted so long with David's companions in tribulation that
their faith is turned to fear, their hope to despair. David
therefore prays as he looks upon them: Oh lift upon us
(נְסָה־עָלֵינוּ)* the light of Thy countenance. The form of the
petition reminds one of the priestly benediction in Num. vi.
There it is: יָאֵר ה׳ פָּנָיו in the second portion, in the third יִשָּׂא
ה׳ פָּנָיו, here these two wishes are blended into one prayer;
and moreover in נְסָה there is an allusion to נֵם a banner, for
the *imper.* of נָשָׂא, the regular form of which is שָׂא, will also
admit of the form נְשָׂא (x. 12), but the mode of writing נְסָה
(without example elsewhere, for נִסָּה Job iv. 2 signifies "to be
attempted") is only explained by the mingling of the verbs

נָשָׂא and נָסַם, نصّ, *extollere* (lx. 6); ה׳ נִסִּי (cf. lx. 6) is, moreover, a primeval word of the Tôra (Ex. xvii. 15). If we may
suppose that this mingling is not merely a mingling of forms
in writing, but also a mingling of the ideas in those forms,
then we have three thoughts in this prayer which are brought
before the eye and ear in the briefest possible expression:

---

* The *Metheg* which stands in the second syllable before the tone
stands by the *Shebâ*, in the metrical books, if this syllable is the first
in a word marked with a greater distinctive without any conjunctive preceding it, and beginning with *Shebâ*; it is, therefore, not נְסָה־עָלֵינוּ but
נְסָה־עָלֵינוּ, cf. li. 2 בְּבוֹא־, lxix. 28 תִּנָּה־, lxxxi. 3 שְׂאוּ־, cxvi. 17 לְךָ־,
cxix. 175 תְּחִי־. The reason and object are the same as stated in note
p. 84 *supra*.

may Jahve cause His face to shine upon them; may He lift
upon them the light of His countenance so that they may
have it above them like the sun in the sky, and may that
light be a banner promising them the victory, around which
they shall rally.

David, however, despite the hopelessness of the present,
is even now at peace in His God. The joy which Jahve has
put into his heart in the midst of outward trial and adversity
is מֵעֵת דְּגָנָם וְתִירוֹשָׁם רָבּוּ. The expression is as concise as possible: (1) *gaudium præ* equivalent to *gaudium magnum præ* =
majus quam; then (2) מֵעֵת after the analogy of the *comparatio
decurtata* (*e. g.* xviii. 34 my feet are like hinds, *i. e.* like the
feet of hinds) is equivalent to מִשְׂמְחַת עֵת; (3) אֲשֶׁר is omitted
after עֵת according to Ges. § 123, 3, for עֵת is the construct
state, and what follows is the second member of the genitival
relation, dependent upon it (cf. xc. 15, Isa. xxix. 1); the
plurality of things: corn and new wine, inasmuch as it is
the stores of both that are specially meant, is exceptionally
joined with the *plur.* instead of the *sing.*, and the chief word
rābbu stands at the end by way of emphasis. The *suff.* does
not refer to the people of the land in general (as in lxv.
10), but, in accordance with the contrast, to the Absolomites,
to those of the nation who have fallen away from David.
When David came to Mahanaim, while the rebels were encamped in Gilead, the country round about him was hostile,
so that he had to receive provisions by stealth, 2 Sam. xvii.
26—29. Perhaps it was at the time of the feast of tabernacles. The harvest and the vintage were over. A rich
harvest of corn and new wine was garnered. The followers
of Absolom had, in these rich stores which were at their
disposal, a powerful reserve upon which to fall back. David
and his host were like a band of beggars or marauders.
But the king brought down from the sceptre to the beggar's
staff is nevertheless happier than they, the rebels against
him. What he possesses in his heart is a richer treasure
than all that they have in their barns and cellars.

Ver. 9. Thus then he lies down to sleep, cheerfully and
peacefully. The hymn closes as it began with a three line
verse. יַחְדָּו (*lit.* in its unions = collectively, Olshausen, § 135, *c*,

like כֻּלוֹ altogether, בְּעִתּוֹ at the right time) is by no means unemphatic; nor is it so in xix. 10 where it means "all together, without exception". With synonymous verbs it denotes the combination of that which they imply, as Isa. xlii. 14. It is similar in cxli. 10 where it expresses the coincidence of the fall of his enemies and the escape of the persecuted one. So here: he wishes to go to sleep and also at once he falls asleep (וְאִישָׁן in a likewise cohortative sense = וְאִישָׁנָה). His God makes him to dwell in seclusion free of care. לְבָדָד is a first definition of condition, and לָבֶטַח a second. The former is not, after Deut. xxxii. 12, equivalent to לְבַדְּךָ, an addition which would be without any implied antithesis and consequently meaningless. One must therefore, as is indeed required by the situation, understand לְבָדָד according to Num. xxiii. 9, Mic. vii, 14, Deut. xxxiii. 28, Jer. xlix. 31. He needs no guards for he is guarded round about by Jahve and kept in safety. The seclusion, בָּדָד, in which he is, is security, בֶּטַח, because Jahve is near him. Under what a many phases and how sweetly the nature of faith is expressed in this and the foregoing Psalm: his righteousness, exaltation, joy, peace, contentment in God! And how delicately conceived is the rhythm! In the last line the evening hymn itself sinks to rest. The iambics with which it closes are like the last strains of a lullaby which die away softly and as though falling asleep themselves. Dante is right when he says in his *Convito,* that the sweetness of the music and harmony of the Hebrew Psalter is lost in the Greek and Latin translations.

PSALM V.

MORNING PRAYER BEFORE GOING TO THE HOUSE OF GOD.

2 GIVE ear to my words, O Jahve,
　　Consider my meditation!
3 Hearken unto my loud cry, my King and my God,
　　For unto Thee do I pray.
4 Jahve, in the morning shalt Thou hear my voice
　　In the morning will I prepare an offering for Thee and
　　　　look forth.

5 For Thou art not a God that hath pleasure in wickedness,
  An evil man cannot dwell with Thee.
6 Boasters cannot stand in Thy sight,
  Thou hatest all workers of iniquity;
7 Thou destroyest them that speak lies,
  The man of blood-guiltiness and malice Jahve abhorreth.

8 Yet I, through Thy rich grace, may enter Thy house,
  I may worship towards Thy holy Temple in Thy fear.
9 Jahve, lead me by Thy righteousness, because of them
        that lie in wait for me,
  Make Thy way even before my face —
10 For in his mouth is nothing certain,
                their inward part is an abyss,
  An open sepulchre is their throat,
                with a smooth tongue.

11 Punish them, Elohim, let them fall from their counsels,
   In the multitude of their transgressions cast them away,
                who defy Thee;
12 That all they who trust in Thee may rejoice,
                may ever shout for joy;
   And defend Thou them that they may exult in Thee,
                who love Thy name.
13 For Thou, even Thou, dost bless the righteous —
   Jahve! with favour dost Thou compass him as with
       a shield.

The evening prayer is now followed by a second morning prayer, which like the former draws to a close with כִּי־אַתָּה (iv. 9, v. 13). The situation is different from that in Ps. iii. In that Psalm David is fleeing, here he is in Jerusalem and anticipates going up to the Temple service. If this Psalm also belongs to the time of the rebellion of Absolom, it must have been written when the fire which afterwards broke forth was already smouldering in secret.

The inscription אֶל־הַנְּחִילוֹת is certainly not a motto indicative of its contents (LXX., Vulg., Luther, Hengstenberg). As such it would stand after מִזְמוֹר. Whatever is connected with לַמְנַצֵּחַ, always has reference to the music. If נחילות

came from נָחַל it might according to the biblical use of this verb signify "inheritances", or according to its use in the Talmud "swarms", and in fact swarms of bees (نَحْل); and נְחִילוֹת ought then to be the beginning of a popular melody to which the Psalm is adapted. Hai Gaon understands it to denote a melody resembling the hum of bees; Reggio a song that sings of bees. Or is נְחִילוֹת equivalent to נְחָלוֹת *(excavatæ)* and this a special name for the flutes (הַחֲלִילִים)? The use of the flute in the service of the sanctuary is attested by Isa. xxx. 29, cf. 1 Sam. x. 5, 1 Kings i. 40.* The *præp.* אֶל was, then, more appropriate than עַל; because, as Redslob has observed, the singer cannot play the flute at the same time, but can only sing to the playing of another.

The Psalm consists of four six line strophes. The lines of the strophes here and there approximate to the cæsura-schema. They consist of a rising and a sudden lowering. The German language, which uses so many more words, is not adapted to this cæsura-schema [and the same may be said of the English].

Vers. 2—4. *The introit:* Prayer to be heard. The thoughts are simple but the language is carefully chosen. אֲמָרִים is the *plur.* of אֹמֶר (אֵמֶר), one of the words peculiar to the poetic prophetical style. The denominative הַאֲזִין (like *audire* = *aus*, οὖς, *dare*) belongs more to poetry than prose. הָגִיג (like אָבִיב) or הֶגִיג (like מְחִיר) occurs only in two Psalms לְדָוִד, viz. here and xxxix. 4. It is derived from הָגָה = הָגַג (*vid.* i. 2) and signifies that which is spoken meditatively, here praying in rapt devotion. Beginning thus the prayer gradually rises to a *vox clamoris.* שַׁוְעִי from שָׁוַע, to be distinguished from שַׁוְּעִי (*inf. Pi.*) xxviii. 2, xxxi. 23, is one word with the Aram. צְוַח, Æthiop. צוע (to call). On הַקְשִׁיב used of intent listening, *vid.* x. 17. The invocation מַלְכִּי וֵאלֹהָי, when it is a king who utters it, is all the more significant. David, and in general the theocratic king, is only the representative of the Invisible One, whom he with all Israel adores

---

* On the use of the flute in the second Temple, *vid.* Introduction p. 33.

as his King. Prayer to Him is his first work as he begins the day. In the morning, בֹּקֶר (as in lv. 18 for בַּבֹּקֶר, lxxxviii. 14), shalt Thou hear my cry, is equivalent to my cry which goes forth with the early morn. Hupfeld considers the mention of the morning as only a "poetical expression" and when getting rid of the meaning *prima luce,* he also gets rid of the beautiful and obvious reference to the daily sacrifice. The verb עָרַךְ is the word used of laying the wood in order for the sacrifice, Lev. i. 7, and the pieces of the sacrifice, Lev. i. 8, 12, vi. 5, of putting the sacred lamps in order, Ex. xxvii. 21, Lev. xxiv. 3 sq., and of setting the shew-bread in order, Ex. xl. 23, Lev. xxiv. 8. The laying of the wood in order for the morning offering of a lamb (Lev. vi. 5 [12], cf. Num. xxviii. 4) was one of the first duties of the priest, as soon as the day began to dawn; the lamb was slain before sun-rise and when the sun appeared above the horizon laid piece by piece upon the altar. The morning prayer is compared to this morning sacrifice. This is in its way also a sacrifice. The object which David has in his mind in connection with אֶעֱרָךְ is תְּפִלָּתִי. As the priests, with the early morning, lay the wood and pieces of the sacrifices of the *Tamîd* upon the altar, so he brings his prayer before God as a spiritual sacrifice and looks out for an answer (צָפָה *speculari* as in Hab. ii. 1), perhaps as the priest looks out for fire from heaven to consume the sacrifice, or looks to the smoke to see that it rises up straight towards heaven.

Vers. 5—7: The basing of the prayer on God's holiness. The verbal adjective חָפֵץ (coming from the primitive signification of adhering firmly which is still preserved in خفض *fut.* i.) is in the *sing.* always (xxxiv. 13, xxxv. 27) joined with the accusative. רָע is conceived as a person, for although גּוּר may have a material object, it cannot well have a material subject. יְגֻרְךָ is used for brevity of expression instead of יָגוּר עִמָּךְ (Ges. § 121, 4). The verb גּוּר (to turn in, to take up one's abode with or near any one) frequently has an accusative object, cxx. 5, Judges v. 17, and Isa. xxxiii. 14 according to which the light of the divine holiness is to sinners a consuming fire, which they cannot endure. Now there follow specific designations of the wicked. הוֹלֲלִים *part. Kal*

= *hôlᵃlîm*, or even *Poal* = *hôlᵃlîm* (= מְהוֹלֲלִים),* are the foolish, and more especially foolish boasters; the primary notion of the verb is not that of being hollow, but that of sounding, then of loud boisterous, non-sensical behaviour. Of such it is said, that they are not able to maintain their position when they become manifest before the eye of God (לְנֶגֶד as in ci. 7 manifest before any one, from נָגַד to come forward, be visible far off, be distinctly visible). פֹּעֲלֵי אָוֶן are those who work (οἱ ἐργαζόμενοι Mat. vii. 23) iniquity; אָוֶן breath (ἄνεμος) is sometimes trouble, in connection with which one pants, sometimes wickedness, in which there is not even a trace of any thing noble, true, or pure. Such men Jahve hates; for if He did not hate evil (xi. 5), His love would not be a holy love. In דִּבְרֵי, דִּבְרֵי כָזָב is the usual form in combination when the *plur.* is used, instead of מְדַבְּרֵי. It is the same in lviii. 4. The style of expression is also Davidic in other respects, viz. אִישׁ דָּמִים וּמִרְמָה as in lv. 24, and אָבַד as in ix. 6, cf. xxi. 11. תִּעֵב (in Amos, ch. vi. 8 תֵּאֵב) appears to be a secondary formation from עוּב, like תָּאַב to desire, from אָבָה, and therefore to be of a cognate root with the Aram. עַיֵּב to despise, treat with indignity, and the Arabic ʿaib a stain (cf. on Lam. ii. 1). The fact that, as Hengstenberg has observed, wickedness and the wicked are described in a sevenfold manner is perhaps merely accidental.

Vers. 8—10. Since the Psalm is a morning hymn, the *futt.* in ver. 8 state what he, on the contrary, may and will do (lxvi. 13). By the greatness and fulness of divine favour (lxix. 14) he has access (εἴσοδον, for בוֹא means, according to its root, "to enter") to the sanctuary, and he will accordingly repair thither to-day. It is the tabernacle on Zion in which was the ark of the covenant that is meant here. That

---

* On the rule, according to which here, as in שׁוֹרְרָי ver. 9 and the like, a simple *Shebâ mobile* goes over into *Chateph pathach* with *Gaja* preceding it, *vid.* the observations on giving a faithful representation of the O. T. text according to the Masora in the *Luther. Zeitschr.* 1863. S. 411. The Babylonian Ben-Naphtali (about 940) prefers the simple *Shebâ* in such cases, as also in others; Ben-Âsher of the school of Tiberias, whom the Masora follows, and whom consequently our Masoretic text ought to follow, prefers the *Chateph, vid. Psalter* ii. 460—467.

daily liturgical service was celebrated there must be assumed, since the ark of the covenant is the sign and pledge of Jahve's presence; and it is, moreover, attested by 1 Chron. xvi. 37 sq. It is also to be supposed that sacrifice was offered daily before the tabernacle. For it is not to be inferred from 1 Chron. xvi, 39 sqq. that sacrifice was only offered regularly on the *Bama* (high place) in Gibeon before the Mosaic tabernacle.* It is true sacrifice was offered in Gibeon, where the old tabernacle and the old altars (or at least the altar of burnt-offering) were, and also that after the removal of the ark to Zion both David (1 Chron. xxi. 29 sq.) and Solomon (1 Kings iii. 4, 2 Chron. i. 2—6) worshipped and sacrificed in Gibeon. But it is self-evident sacrifices might have been offered where the ark was, and that even with greater right than in Gibeon; and since both David, upon its arrival (2 Sam. vi. 17 sq.), and Solomon after his accession (1 Kings iii. 15), offered sacrifices through the priests who were placed there, it is probable, — and by a comparison of the Davidic Psalms not to be doubted,—that there was a daily service, in conjunction with sacrifices, before the ark on Zion.

But, moreover, is it really the אֹהֶל on Zion which is meant here in ver. 8 by the house of God? It is still maintained by renowned critics that the tabernacle pitched by David over the sacred ark is never called בית ה׳ or היכל or משכן ה׳ or מקדש or קדש. But why could it not have all these names? We will not appeal to the fact that the house of God at Shilo (1 Sam. i. 9, iii. 3) is called בית and היכל ה׳, since it may be objected that it was really more of a temple than a tabernacle,** although in the same book, ch. ii. 22 it is called אֹהֶל מוֹעֵד, and in connection with the other appellations the poetic colouring of the historical style of 1 Sam.

---

* Thus, in particular, Stähelin, *Zur Kritik der Psalmen* in the *Deutsch. Morgenl. Zeitschr.* vi (1852) S. 108 and *Zur Einleitung in die Psalmen.* An academical programme, 1859. 4to.

** *vid.* C. H. Graf, *Commentatio de templo Silonensi ad illustrandum locum Jud.* xviii. 30, 31. (1855, 4to.), in which he seeks to prove that the sanctuary in Shilo was a temple to Jahve that lasted until the dissolution of the kingdom of Israel.

i.—iii. is to be taken into consideration. Moreover, we put aside passages like Ex. xxiii. 19, xxxiv. 26, since it may be said that the future Temple was present to the mind of the Lawgiver. But in Josh. vi. 24, 2 Sam. xii. 20, the sanctuary is called בֵּית ה׳ without being conceived of as a temple. Why then cannot the tabernacle, which David pitched for the ark of the covenant when removed to Zion (2 Sam. vi. 17), be called בֵּית ה׳? It is only when אֹהֶל and בַּיִת are placed in opposition to one another that the latter has the notion of a dwelling built of more solid materials; but in itself *beit* (*bêt*) in Semitic is the generic term for housing of every kind whether it be made of wool, felt, and hair-cloth, or of earth, stone, and wood; consequently it is just as much a tent as a house (in the stricter sense of the word), whether the latter be a hut built of wood and clay or a palace.* If a dwelling-house is frequently called אֹהֶל, then a tent that any one dwells in may the more naturally be called his בַּיִת. And this we find is actually the case with the dwellings of the patriarchs, which, although they were not generally solid houses (Gen. xxxiii. 17), are called בַּיִת (Gen. xxvii. 15). Moreover, הֵיכָל (from יָכַל = כּוּל to hold, *capacem esse*), although it signifies a palace does not necessarily signify one of stone, for the heavens are also called Jahve's הֵיכָל, *e. g.* xviii. 7, and not necessarily one of gigantic proportions, for even the Holy of holies of Solomon's Temple, and this *par excellence*, is called הֵיכָל, and once, 1 Kings vi. 3, הֵיכַל הַבַּיִת. Of the spaciousness and general character of the Davidic tabernacle we know indeed nothing: it certainly had its splendour, and was not so much a substitute for the original tabernacle, which according

---

* The Turkish Kamus says: "بيت is a house (Turk. *ew*) in the signification of *châne* (Persic the same), whether it be made of hair, therefore a tent, or built of stone and tiles". And further on: "*Beit* originally signified a place specially designed for persons to retire to at night [from بَات he has passed the night, if it does not perhaps come from the בוא, Arab. بَى, which stands next to it in this passage, *vid. Job* ii. 125]; but later on the meaning was extended and the special reference to the night time was lost." Even at the present day the Beduin does not call his tent *ahl*, but always *bêt* and in fact *bêt sha'r* (בֵּית שֵׂעָר), the modern expression for the older *bêt wabar* (hair-house).

to the testimony of the chronicler remained in Gibeon, as a substitute for the Temple that was still to be built. But, however insignificant it may have been, Jahve had His throne there, and it was therefore the הֵיכַל of a great king, just as the wall-less place in the open field where God manifested Himself with His angels to the homeless Jacob was בֵּית אֱלֹהִים (Gen. xxviii. 17).

Into this tabernacle of God, *i. e.* into its front court, will David enter (בּוֹא with *acc.* as in lxvi. 13) this morning, there will he prostrate himself in worship, προσκυνεῖν (הִשְׁתַּחֲוָה reflexive of the *Pilel* שָׁחֲוָה, Ges. § 75, rem. 18), towards (אֶל as in xxviii. 2, 1 Kings viii. 29, 35, cf. לְ xcix. 5, 9) Jahve's הֵיכַל קֹדֶשׁ, *i. e.* the דְּבִיר, the Holy of holies xxviii. 2, and that "in Thy fear", *i. e.* in reverence before Thee (*genit. objectivus*). The going into the Temple which David purposes, leads his thoughts on to his way through life, and the special δέησις, which only begins here, moulds itself accordingly: he prays for God's gracious guidance as in xxvii. 11, lxxxvi. 11, and frequently. The direction of God, by which he wishes to be guided he calls צְדָקָה. Such is the general expression for the determination of conduct by an ethical rule. The rule, acting in accordance with which, God is called *par excellence* צַדִּיק, is the order of salvation which opens up the way of mercy to sinners. When God forgives those who walk in this way their sins, and stands near to bless and protect them, He shews Himself not less צַדִּיק (just), than when He destroys those who despise Him, in the heat of His rejected love. By this righteousness, which accords with the counsel and order of mercy, David prays to be led לְמַעַן שׁוֹרְרָי, in order that the malicious desire of those who lie in wait for him may not be fulfilled, but put to shame, and that the honour of God may not be sullied by him. שׁוֹרֵר is equivalent to מְשׁוֹרֵר (Aquila ἐφοδεύων, Jerome *insidiator*) from the *Pilel* שׁוֹרֵר to fix one's eyes sharply upon, especially of hostile observation. David further prays that God will make his way (*i. e.* the way in which a man must walk according to God's will) even and straight before him, the praying one, in order that he may walk therein without going astray and unimpeded. The adj. יָשָׁר signifies both the straightness of a line and the evenness of a surface. The fut. of the *Hiph.* הִישִׁיר is יִישִׁיר in Prov. iv. 25, and accordingly the *Keri* substitutes for the *imper.* הוֹשֵׁר the corresponding form הַיְשַׁר, just as in Isa. xlv. 2 it removes the *Hiphil* form אוֹשֵׁר (cf. Gen. viii. 17 הוֹצֵא *Keri* הַיְצֵא), without any grammatical, but certainly not without some traditional ground.

כִּי in ver. 10 is closely connected with לְמַעַן שׁוֹרְרָי: on account of my way-layers, for the following are their characteristics. אֵין is separated by בְּפִיהוּ (=בְּפִיו lxii. 5) from נְכוֹנָה the word it governs; this was the more easily possible as the usage of the language almost entirely lost sight of the fact that אֵין is the construct of אַיִן, Ges. § 152, 1. In his mouth is nothing that should stand firm, keep its ground, remain the same (cf. Job xlii. 7 sq.). The singular suffix of בְּפִיהוּ has a distributive meaning: *in ore uniuscujusque eorum.* Hence the *sing.* at once passes over into the *plur.*: קִרְבָּם הַוּוֹת their inward part, *i. e.* that towards which it goes forth and in which it has its rise (*vid.* xlix. 12) is הַוּוֹת corruption, from

הָוָה which comes from הָיָה = هَوَى to yawn, gape, χαίνειν, *hiare,* a yawning abyss and a gaping vacuum, and then, inasmuch as, starting from the primary idea of an empty space, the verbal significations *libere ferri* (especially from below upwards) and more particularly *animo ad* or *in aliquid ferri* are developed, it obtains the pathological sense of strong desire, passion, just as it does also the intellectual sense of a loose way of thinking proceding from a self-willed tendency (*vid.* Fleischer on Job xxxvii. 6). In Hebrew the prevalent meaning of the word is corruption, lvii. 2, which is a metaphor for the abyss, *barathrum,* (so far, but only so far Schultens on Prov. x. 3 is right), and proceeding from this meaning it denotes both that which is physically corruptible (Job. vi. 30) and, as in the present passage and frequently, that which is corruptible from an ethical point of view. The meaning strong desire, in which הַוָּה looks as though it only differed from אַוָּה in one letter, occurs only in lii. 9, Prov. x. 3, Mic. vii. 3. The substance of their inward part is that which is corruptible in every way, and their throat, as the organ of speech, as in cxv. 7, cxlix. 6, cf. lxix. 4, is (perhaps a figure connected with the primary meaning of הַוּוֹת) a grave, which yawns like the jaws, which open and snatch and swallow down whatever comes in their way. To this "they make smooth their tongue" is added as a circumstantial clause. Their throat is thus formed and adapted, while they make smooth their tongue (cf. Prov. ii. 16), in order to conceal their real design beneath flattering language. From this meaning, הֶחֱלִיק directly signifies to flatter in xxxvi. 3, Prov. xxix. 5. The last two lines of the strophe are formed according to the cæsura schema. This schema is also continued in the concluding strophe.

Vers. 11—13. The verb אָשֵׁם or אָשַׁם unites in itself the three closely allied meanings of becoming guilty (*e. g.* Lev. v. 19), of a feeling of guilt (Lev. v. 4 sq.), and of expiation (Ps. xxxiv. 22 sq.); just as the verbal adj. אָשֵׁם also signifies both liable to punishment and expiating, and the substantive אָשָׁם both the guilt to be expiated and the expiation. The *Hiph.* הֶאֱשִׁים signifies to cause any one to render the expiation due to his fault, to make him do penance. As an exception God is here, in the midst of the Jehovic Psalms, called אֱלֹהִים, perhaps not altogether unintentionally as being God the Judge. The מִן of מִמֹּעֲצוֹתֵיהֶם (with *Gaja* by the מִן and a transition of the counter-tone *Metheg* into *Galgal*, as in Hos. xi. 6 into *Meajla, vid. Psalter* ii. 526) is certainly that of the cause in Hos. xi. 6, but here it is to be explained with Olsh. and Hitz. according to Sir. xiv. 2, Judith xi. 6 (cf. Hos. x. 6): may they fall from their own counsels, *i. e.* founder in the execution of them. Therefore מִן in the sense of "down from, away", a sense which the parallel הַדִּיחֵמוֹ, thrust them away (cf. דֹּחוּ from דָּחָה xxxvi. 13), presupposes. The בְּ of בְּרֹב is to be understood according to John viii. 21, 24 "ye shall die ἐν ταῖς ἁμαρτίαις ὑμῶν". The multitude of their transgressions shall remain unforgiven and in this state God is to cast them into hades. The ground of this terrible prayer is set forth by כִּי מָרוּ בָךְ. The tone of מָרוּ for a well-known reason (cf. *e. g.,* xxxvii. 40, lxiv. 11, lxxii. 17) has retreated to the *penult.* מָרָה, root מר, prop. to be or hold one's self stiff towards any one, compare

تَمَارَ ,مَارَ, to press and stiffen against one another in wrestling, تَمَارِي ,مَارِي, to struggle against anything, whether with outward or mental and moral opposition. Their obstinacy is not obstinacy against a man, but against God Himself; their sin is, therefore, Satanic and on that account unpardonable. All the prayers of this character are based upon the assumption expressed in vii. 13, that those against whom they are directed do not wish for mercy. Accordingly their removal is prayed for. Their removal will make the *ecclesia pressa* free and therefore joyous. From this point of view the prayer in ver. 12 is inspired by the prospect of the result of their removal. The *futt.* do not express a wish, but a consequence. The division of the verse is, however, incorrect. The rise of the first half of the verse closes with בָךְ (the pausal form by *Pazer*), its fall is לְעוֹלָם יְרַנֵּנוּ; then the rise begins anew in the second half, extending to בָךְ which ought likewise to be pointed בָךְ, and אֹהֲבֵי שְׁמֶךָ is its fall. וְתָסֵךְ עֲלֵימוֹ (from הֵסֵךְ *Hiph.* of סָכַךְ xci. 4) is awkward in this sequence of thoughts. Hupfeld and Hitzig render it: "they shall rejoice for ever whom Thou defendest"; but then it ought not only to be pointed יְרַנְּנוּ, but the וְ must also be removed, and yet there is nothing to characterise תסך עלימו as being virtually a subject. On the other hand it does not harmonise with the other consecutive futures. It must therefore, like יִפָּלוּ, be the optative: "And do Thou defend them, then shall those who love Thy name rejoice in Thee". And then upon this this joy of those who love the name of Jahve (*i. e.* God in His revelation of Himself in redemption) lxix. 37, cxix. 132, is based by כִּי־אַתָּה from a fact of universal experience which is the sum of all His historical self-attestations. עֲלֵימוֹ is used instead of עֲלֵיהֶם as a graver form of expression, just like הַדִּיחֵמוֹ for הַדִּיחֵם as an indignant one. The form וְיַעְלְצוּ (Ges. § 63, 3) is chosen instead of the יַעֲלְצוּ found in xxv. 2, lxviii. 4, in order to assist the rhythm. The *futt.* are continuative. תַּעְטְרֶנּוּ, *cinges eum,* is not a contracted *Hiph.* according to 1 Sam. xvii. 25, but *Kal* as in 1 Sam. xxiii. 26; here it is used like the *Piel* in viii. 6 with a double accusative. The צִנָּה (from צָנַן صان *med. Waw,* Æthiop. צון to hedge round, guard) is a shield of a largest dimensions; larger than מָגֵן 1 Kings x. 16 sq. (cf. 1 Sam. xvii. 7, where Goliath has his צִנָּה borne by a shield-bearer). כַּצִּנָּה "like a shield" is equivalent to: as with a shield (Ges. § 118, 3, rem.). The name of God, יהוה, is correctly drawn to the second member of the verse by the accentuation, in order to balance it with the first; and for this reason the first clause does not begin with כי־אתה יהוה here as it does elsewhere (iv. 9, xii. 8). רָצוֹן delight, goodwill, is also a synonym for the divine blessing in Deut. xxxiii. 23.

PSALM VI.
A CRY FOR MERCY UNDER JUDGMENT.

2 JAHVE, not in Thy wrath rebuke me,
  And not in Thy hot displeasure chasten me!
3 Be gracious unto me, for I am fading away;
  Oh heal me, Jahve, for my bones are affrighted,
4 And my soul is affrighted exceedingly —
  And Thou, O Jahve, how long?!

5 Return, Jahve, rescue my soul,
  Save me for Thy mercy's sake.
6 For in death there is no remembrance of Thee,
  In Sheôl who can give Thee thanks?
7 I am exhausted with my groaning,
  Every night make I my bed to swim —
  With my tears I flood my couch.
8 Sunken is mine eye with grief,
  It is grown old because of all mine oppressors.

9 Depart from me all ye who deal wickedly!
  For Jahve hath heard my loud weeping,
10 Jahve hath heard my supplication:
  Jahve will accept my prayer.
11 All mine enemies shall be ashamed and affrighted
        exceedingly,
  They shall turn away ashamed suddenly.

The morning prayer, Ps. v., is followed by a *"Psalm of David"*, which, even if not composed in the morning, looks

back upon a sleepless, tearful night. It consists of three
strophes. In the middle one, which is a third longer than
the other two, the poet, by means of a calmer outpouring
of his heart, struggles on from the cry of distress in the first
strophe to the believing confidence of the last. The hostility
of men seems to him as a punishment of divine wrath, and
consequently (but this is not so clearly expressed as in
Ps. xxxviii., which is its counterpart) as the result of his sin;
and this persecution, which to him has God's wrath behind
it and sin as the sting of its bitterness, makes him sorrowful and sick even unto death. Because the Psalm contains
no confession of sin, one might be inclined to think that the
church has wrongly reckoned it as the first of the seven
(probably selected with reference to the seven days of the
week) *Psalmi pœnitentiales* (vi. xxxii. xxxviii. li. cii. cxxx.
cxliii.). A. H. Francke in his *Introductio in Psalterium* says,
it is rather *Psalmus precatorius hominis gravissimi tentati a
pœnitente probe distinguendi.* But this is a mistake. The man
who is tempted is distinguished from a penitent man by this,
that the feeling of wrath is with the one perfectly groundless and with the other well-grounded. Job was one who
was tempted thus. Our psalmist, however, is a penitent, who
accordingly seeks that the punitive chastisement of God, as
the just God, may for him be changed into the loving chastisement of God, as the merciful One.

We recognise here the language of penitently believing
prayer, which has been coined by David. Compare ver. 2
with xxxviii. 2; 3 with xli. 5; 5 with cix. 26; 6 with xxx. 10;
7 with lxix. 4; 8 with xxxi. 10; 11 with xxxv. 4. 26. The
language of Heman's Psalm is perceptibly different, comp.
ver. 6 with lxxxvii. 11—13; 8 with lxxxviii. 10. And the
corresponding strains in Jeremiah (comp. ver. 2, xxxviii. 2
with Jer. x. 24; 3 and 5 with Jer. xvii. 14; 7 with Jer. xlv.
3) are echoes, which to us prove that the Psalm belongs to
an earlier age, not that it was composed by the prophet
(Hitzig). It is at once probable, from the almost anthological relationship in which Jeremiah stands to the earlier
literature, that in the present instance also he is the repro-
ducer. And this idea is confirmed by the fact that in ch. x. 25,

after language resembling the Psalm before us, he continues in words taken from Ps. lxxix. 6 sq. When Hitzig maintains that David could no more have composed this disconcertedly despondent Psalm than Isaiah could the words in Isa. xxi. 3, 4, we refer, in answer to him, to Isa. xxii. 4 and to the many attestations that David did weep, 2 Sam. i. 12, iii. 32, xii. 21, xv. 30, xix. 1.

The accompanying musical direction runs: *To the Precentor, with accompaniment of stringed instruments, upon the Octave.* The LXX. translates ὑπὲρ τῆς ὀγδόης, and the Fathers associate with it the thought of the octave of eternal happiness, ἡ ὀγδόη ἐκείνη, as Gregory of Nyssa says, ἥτίς ἐστιν ὁ ἐφεξῆς αἰών. But there is no doubt whatever that עַל־הַשְּׁמִינִית has reference to music. It is also found by Ps. xii., and besides in 1 Chron. xv. 21. From this latter passage it is at least clear that it is not the name of an instrument. An instrument with eight strings could not have been called an *octave* instead of an *octachord.* In that passage they played upon nablas עַל־עֲלָמוֹת, and with citherns עַל־הַשְּׁמִינִית. If עֲלָמוֹת denotes maidens = maidens' voices *i. e. soprano,* then, as it seems, הַשְּׁמִינִית is a designation of the bass, and עַל־הֹשׁמינית equivalent to *all' ottava bassa.* The fact that Ps. xlvi., which is accompanied by the direction עַל־עֲלָמוֹת, is a joyous song, whereas Ps. vi. is a plaintive one and Ps. xii. not less gloomy and sad, accords with this. These two were to be played in the lower octave, that one in the higher.

Vers. 2—4. There is a chastisement which proceeds from God's love to the man as being pardoned and which is designed to purify or to prove him, and a chastisement which proceeds from God's wrath against the man as striving obstinately against, or as fallen away from, favour, and which satisfies divine justice. Ps. xciv. 12, cxviii. 17, Prov. iii. 11 sq. speak of this loving chastisement. The man who should decline it, would act against his own salvation. Accordingly David, like Jeremiah (ch. x. 24), does not pray for the removal of the chastisement but of the chastisement *in wrath,* or what is the same thing, of the judgment proceeding from wrath [*Zorngericht*]. בְּאַפְּךָ and בַּחֲמָתְךָ stand in the middle, between אַל and the verbs, for the sake of emphasis. Hengstenberg indeed finds a different antithesis here. He says: "The contrast is not that of chastisement in love with chastisement in wrath, but that of loving rescue in contrast with chastisement, which always proceeds from the principle of wrath". If what is here meant is, that always when God chastens a man his wrath is the true and proper motive, it is an error, for the refutation of which one whole book of the Bible, viz. the Book of Job, has been written. For there the friends think that God is angry with Job; but we know from the prologue that, so far from being angry with him, he on the contrary glories in him. Here, in this Psalm, assuming David to be its author, and his adultery the occasion of it, it is certainly quite otherwise. The chastisement under which David is brought low, has God's wrath as its motive: it is punitive chastisement and remains such, so long as David remains fallen from favour. But if in sincere penitence he again struggles through to favour, then the punitive becomes a loving chastisement: God's relationship to him becomes an essentially different relationship. The evil, which is the result of his sin and as such indeed originates in the principle of wrath, becomes the means of discipline and purifying which love employs, and this it is that he here implores for himself. And thus Dante Alighieri* correctly and beautifully paraphrases the verse:

> *Signor, non mi riprender con furore,*
> *E non voler correggermi con ira,*
> *Ma con dolcezza e con perfetto amore.*

In חָנֵּנִי David prays God to let him experience His loving-kindness and tender mercy in place of the punishment He has a right to inflict; for anguish of soul has already reduced him to the extreme even of bodily sickness: he is withered up and weary. אֻמְלָל has *Pathach*, and consequently seems to be the 3 *pers. Pul.* as in Joel i. 10, Nah. i. 4; but this

---

* Provided he is the author of *I sètte Salmi Penitenziali trasportati alla volgar poesia*, *vid.* Dante Alighieri's Lyric poems, translated and annotated by Kannegiesser and Witte (1842) i. 203 sq., ii. 208 sq.

cannot be according to the rules of grammar. It is an adjective, like רַעֲנָן, שַׁאֲנָן, with the passive pointing. The formation אמלל (from אמל أَمَلَ with the primary meaning to stretch out lengthwise) is analogous to the IX. and XI. forms of the Arabic verb which serve especially to express colours and defects (Caspari § 59). The two words אֻמְלַל אָנִי have the double accent *Mercha-Mahpach* together, and according to the exact mode of writing (*vid.* Baer in my *Psalter* ii. 492) the *Mahpach*, (the sign resembling *Mahpach* or rather *Jethib*), ought to stand between the two words, since it at the same time represents the *Makkeph*. The principal tone of the united pair, therefore, lies on *āni*; and accordingly the adj. אֻמְלָל is shortened to אֻמְלַל (cf. מָרְמָם, הֲפַכְפַּךְ, אֲדַמְדָּם, and the like)—a contraction which proves that אמלל is not treated as *part. Pul.* (= מְאָמְלָל), for its characteristic *ā* is unchangeable. The prayer for healing is based upon the plea that his bones (Job iv. 14, Isa. xxxviii. 13) are affrighted. We have no German word exactly corresponding to this נִבְהַל which (from the radical notion "to let go", cogn. בָּלַה) expresses a condition of outward overthrow and inward consternation, and is therefore the effect of fright which disconcerts one and of excitement that deprives one of self-control.* His soul is still more shaken than his body. The affliction is therefore not a merely bodily ailment in which only a timorous man loses heart. God's love is hidden from him. God's wrath seems as though it would wear him completely away. It is an affliction beyond all other afflictions. Hence he enquires: And Thou, O Jahve, how long?! Instead of אתה it is written את, which the *Keri* says is to be read אַתָּה, while in three passages (Num. xi. 15, Deut. v. 24, Ezek. xxviii. 14) אַתְּ is admitted as *masc.*

Vers. 5—8. God has turned away from him, hence the prayer שׁוּבָה, viz. אֵלָי. The tone of שׁוּבָה is on the *ult.*, because it is assumed to be read שׁוּבָה אֲדֹנָי. The *ultima* accentuation is intended to secure its distinct pronunciation to the final syllable of שׁובה, which is liable to be drowned and

---

* We have translated Dr. Delitzsch's word *erschreckt* literally—the *vexed* of the Authorized Version seems hardly equal to the meaning.

escape notice in connection with the coming together of the
two aspirates (*vid.* on iii. 8). May God turn to him again,
rescue (חַלֵּץ from חלץ, which is transitive in Hebr. and Aram.,
to free, *expedire, exuere,* Arab. خَلَصَ to be pure, prop. to
be loose, free) his soul, in which his affliction has taken
deep root, from this affliction, and extend to him salvation
on the ground of His mercy towards sinners. He founds
this cry for help upon his yearning to be able still longer
to praise God, — a happy employ, the possibility of which
would be cut off from him if he should die. זָכַר, as frequently
הִזְכִּיר, is used of remembering one with reverence and honour;
הוֹדָה (from וָדָה) has the *dat. honoris* after it. שְׁאוֹל, ver. 6*b*,
ᾅδης (Apoc. xx. 13), alternates with מָוֶת. Such is the name
of the underground abode of the dead, the gate of which is
the grave, the yawning abyss, into which everything mortal
descends (from שָׁאַל = שׁוּל سال, to be loose, relaxed, to hang
down, sink down: a sinking in, that which is sunken in*,
a depth). The writers of the Psalms all (which is no small
objection against Maccabean Psalms) know only of one
single gathering-place of the dead in the depth of the earth,
where they indeed live, but it is only a *quasi* life, because
they are secluded from the light of this world and, what is
the most lamentable, from the light of God's presence.
Hence the Christian can only join in the prayer of ver. 6 of
this Psalm and similar passages (xxx. 10, lxxxviii. 11—13,
cxv. 17, Isa. xxxviii. 18 sq.) so far as he transfers the notion
of hades to that of gehenna.** In hell there is really no
remembrance and no praising of God. David's fear of death
as something in itself unhappy, is also, according to its

-----

* The form corresponds to the Arabic form فِعَال, which, though
originally a verbal abstract, has carried over the passive meaning into
the province of the concrete, *e. g. kitâb = maktûb* and *ilâh,* אֱלֹהַּ =
ma'lûh = ma'bûd (the feared, revered One).

** An adumbration of this relationship of Christianity to the religion
of the Old Testament is the relationship of Islam to the religion of the
Arab wandering tribes, which is called the "religion of Abraham" (*Din
Ibrâhîm),* and knows no life after death; while Islam has taken from
the later Judaism and from Christianity the hope of a resurrection and
heavenly blessedness.

ultimate ground, nothing but the fear of an unhappy death. In these "pains of hell" he is wearied with (בְ as in lxix. 4) groaning, and bedews his couch every night with a river of tears. Just as the *Hiph.* הִשְׂחָה signifies to cause to swim from שָׂחָה to swim, so the *Hiph.* הִמְסָה signifies to dissolve, cause to melt, from מָסָה (cogn. מָסַס) to melt. דִּמְעָה, in Arabic a *nom. unit.* a tear, is in Hebrew a flood of tears.

In ver. 8 עֵינִי does not signify my "appearance" (Num. xi. 7), but, as becomes clear from xxxi. 10, lxxxviii. 10, Job xvii. 7, "my eye"; the eye reflects the whole state of a man's health. The verb עָשַׁשׁ appears to be a denominative from עָשׁ: to be moth-eaten.* The signification *senescere* for the verb עָתֵק is more certain. The closing words בְּכָל־צוֹרְרָי (cf. Num. x. 9 הַצַּר הַצֹּרֵר the oppressing oppressor, from the root צר صر to press, squeeze, and especially to bind together, *constringere, coartare***), in which the writer indicates, partially at least, the cause of his grief (כַּעַם, in Job xviii. 7 כַּעַשׁ), are as it were the socket into which the following strophe is inserted.

Vers. 9—11. Even before his plaintive prayer is ended the divine light and comfort come quickly into his heart, as Frisch says in his *"Neuklingende Harfe Davids"*. His enemies mock him as one forsaken of God, but even in the face of his enemies he becomes conscious that this is not his condition. Thrice in vers. 9, 10 his confidence that God will answer him flashes forth: He hears his loud sobbing, the voice of his weeping that rises towards heaven, He hears his supplication, and He graciously accepts his prayer. The twofold שָׁמַע expresses the fact and יִקַּח its consequence. That which he seems to have to suffer, shall in reality be the lot of his enemies, viz. the end of those who are rejected of God:

---

* Reuchlin in his grammatical analysis of the seven Penitential Psalms, which he published in 1512 after his *Ll. III de Rudimentis Hebraicis* (1506), explains it thus: עָשְׁשָׁה *Verminavit. Sic a vermibus dictum qui turbant res claras puras et nitidas*, and in the *Rudim.* p. 412: *Turbatus est a furore oculus meus, corrosus et obfuscatus, quasi vitro laternæ obductus.*

** In Arabic צִיר *ḍir* is the word for a step-mother as the oppressor of the step-children; and צָרְר *ḍirr*, a concubine as the oppressor of her rival.

they shall be put to shame. The בּוֹשׁ, Syr. ܒܗܶܬ, Chald. בְּהִת, בְּהֵת, which we meet with here for the first time, is not connected with the Arab. بهت but (since the Old Arabic as a rule has ث as a mediating vowel between שׁ and ܙ, ת) with باث which signifies "to turn up and scatter about things that lie together (either beside or upon each other)" *eruere et diruere, disturbare,*—a root which also appears in the reduplicated form بثّ: to root up and disperse, whence بَثّ sorrow and anxiety, according to which therefore בּוֹשׁ (= בּוֹשׁ as بَاتَ = بَوَتَ) prop. signifies *disturbare*, to be perplexed, lose one's self-control, and denotes shame according to a similar, but somewhat differently applied conception to *confundi*, συγχεῖσθαι, συγχύνεσθαι. וְיִבָּהֲלוּ points back to vers. 2, 3: the lot at which the malicious have rejoiced, shall come upon themselves. As is implied in יָשֻׁבוּ יֵבֹשׁוּ, a higher power turns back the assailants filled with shame (ix. 4, xxxv. 4).

What an impressive finish we have here in these three *Milels, jashûbu jebôshu râga‘,* in relation to the tripping measure of the preceding words addressed to his enemies! And, if not intentional, .yet how remarkable is the coincidence, that shame follows the involuntary reverse of the foes, and that יבשׁו in its letters and sound is the reverse of וישבו! What music there is in the Psalter! If composers could but understand it!!

PSALM VII.

APPEAL TO THE JUDGE OF THE WHOLE EARTH AGAINST SLANDER AND REQUITING GOOD WITH EVIL.

2 JAHVE, my God, in Thee do I hide myself;
  Save me from all my persecutors, and deliver me!
3 Lest he tear my soul like a lion,
  Rending it in pieces while there is none to deliver.

4 Jahve, my God, if I have done this,
  If iniquity cling to my hands,
5 If I have rewarded evil to him that was at peace with me
  And plundered mine enemy without cause:

6 Then let the enemy persecute my soul and take [it],
   And tread down my life to the earth,
   And lay my dignity in the dust. *(Sela.)*

7 Arise, Jahve, in Thine anger,
   Lift up Thyself against the rage of mine oppressors,
   And awake for me, Thou hast indeed arranged justice!
8 And let the host of the nations stand round about Thee
   And over it do Thou return again on high!
9 Jahve shall judge the peoples —
   Jahve, judge me according to my righteousness and my
        innocence in me!

10 Oh let the wickedness of the wicked come to an end,
           establish the righteous,
   Thou art He who trieth the hearts and reins, a just God.
11 My shield is borne by Elohim,
   The Saviour of the upright in heart.

12 Elohim is a righteous Judge
   And a God threatening day by day.
13 If a man will not repent, He whetteth His sword,
   He hath bent His bow and made it ready,
14 And against him He directeth the weapon of death,
   His arrows He maketh burning arrows.

15 Behold, he travaileth with evil: he conceiveth trouble
        and bringeth forth falsehood.
16 He hath digged a pit and hollowed it out,
   And falleth into the hollow that he is making.
17 His trouble cometh back upon his own head,
   And his violent dealing cometh down upon his own pate.
18 I will give thanks to Jahve according to His righteousness,
   And will sing praise to the name of Jahve, the Most High.

In the second part of Ps. vi. David meets his enemies
with strong self-confidence in God. Ps. vii., which even
Hitzig ascribes to David, continues this theme and exhibits
to us, in a prominent example taken from the time of persecution under Saul, his purity of conscience and joyousness
of faith. One need only read 1 Sam. xxiv.—xxvi. to see how
this Psalm abounds in unmistakeable references to this por-

tion of David's life. The superscribed statement of the events that gave rise to its composition point to this. Such statements are found exclusively only by the Davidic Psalms.* The inscription runs: *Shiggajon of David, which he sang to Jahve on account of the sayings of Cush a Benjamite.* עַל־דִּבְרֵי is intentionally chosen instead of עַל which has other functions in these superscriptions. Although דְּבַר and דִּבְרֵי can mean a thing, business, affairs (Ex. xxii. 8, 1 Sam. x. 2, and freq.) and עַל־דִּבְרֵי "in reference to" (Deut. iv. 21, Jer. vii. 22) or "on occasion of" (Jer. xiv. 1), still we must here keep to the most natural signification: "on account of the words (speeches)". *Cûsh* (LXX. falsely Χουσί = כּוּשִׁי; Luther, likewise under misapprehension, "the Moor") must have been one of the many servants of Saul, his kinsman, one of the talebearers like Doeg and the Ziphites, who shamefully slandered David before Saul, and roused him against David. The epithet בֶּן־יְמִינִי (as in 1 Sam. ix. 1, 21, cf. אִישׁ־יְמִינִי 2 Sam. xx. 1) describes him as "a Benjamite" and does not assume any knowledge of him, as would be the case if it were הַבִּנְיָמִינִי, or rather (in accordance with biblical usage) בֶּן־הַיְמִינִי. And this accords with the actual fact, for there is no mention of him elsewhere in Scripture history. The statement על־דברי וגו' is hardly from David's hand, but written by some one else, whether from tradition or from the דברי הימים of David, where this Psalm may have been interwoven with the history of its occasion. Whereas there is nothing against our regarding שִׁגָּיוֹן לְדָוִד, or at least שׁגיון, as a note appended by David himself.

Since שִׁגָּיוֹן (after the form חִזָּיוֹן a vision) belongs to the same class as superscribed appellations like מִזְמוֹר and מַשְׂכִּיל, and the *Tephilla* of Habakkuk, ch. iii. 1 (*vid.* my *Commentary*), has the addition שׁגיון, עַל־שִׁגְיֹנוֹת must be the name of a kind of lyric composition, and in fact a kind described according to the rhythm of its language or melody. Now since שָׁגָה means to go astray, wander, reel, and is cognate with שָׁגַע (whence comes שִׁגָּעוֹן madness, a word formed in the same manner)

שִׁגָּיוֹן may mean in the language of prosody a reeling poem, *i. e.* one composed in a most excited movement and with a rapid change of the strongest emotions, therefore a dithyrambic poem, and שִׁגְּיֹנוֹת dithyrambic rhythms, variously and violently mixed together. Thus Ewald and Rödiger understand it, and thus even Tarnov, Geier, and other old expositors who translate it *cantio erratica*. What we therefore look for is that this Psalm shall consist, as Ainsworth expresses it (1627), "of sundry variable and wandering verses", that it shall wander through the most diverse rhythms as in a state of intoxication — an expectation which is in fact realized. The musical accompaniment also had its part in the general effect produced. Moreover, the contents of the Psalm corresponds to this poetic musical style. It is the most solemn pathos of exalted self-consciousness which is expressed in it. And in common with Hab. iii. it gives expression to the joy which arises from zealous anger against the enemies of God and from the contemplation of their speedy overthrow. Painful unrest, defiant self-confidence, triumphant ecstacy, calm trust, prophetic certainty — all these states of mind find expression in the irregular arrangement of the strophes of this Davidic dithyramb, the ancient customary Psalm for the feast of Purim (*Sofrim* xviii. § 2).

Vers. 2—3. With this word of faith, love, and hope בְּךָ חָסִיתִי (as in cxli. 8), this holy *captatio benevolentiæ*, David also begins in xi. 1, xvi. 1, xxxi. 2, cf. lxxi. 1. The *perf.* is inchoative: in Thee have I taken my refuge, equivalent to: in Thee do I trust. The transition from the multitude of his persecutors to the *sing.* in ver. 3 is explained most naturally, as one looks at the inscription, thus: that of the many the one who is just at the time the worst of all comes prominently before his mind. The verb טָרַף from the primary signification *carpere* (which corresponds still more exactly to חרף) means both to tear off and to tear in pieces (whence טְרֵפָה that which is torn in pieces); and פָּרַק from its primary signification *frangere* means both to break loose and to break in pieces, therefore to liberate, *e. g.* in cxxxvi. 24. and to break in small pieces, 1 Kings xix. 11. The persecutors are conceived of as wild animals, as lions which rend their prey and craunch its bones. Thus blood-thirsty are they for his soul, *i. e.* his life. After the painful unrest of this first strophe, the second begins the tone of defiant self-consciousness.

Vers. 4—6. According to the inscription זאת points to the substance of those slanderous sayings of the Benjamite. With אִם־יֶשׁ־עָוֶל בְּכַפָּי one may compare David's words to Saul אֵין בְּיָדִי רָעָה 1 Sam. xxiv. 12, xxvi. 18; and from this comparison one will at once see in a small compass the difference between poetical and prose expression. שֹׁלְמִי (Targ. לְבַעֵל שְׁלָמִי) is the name he gives (with reference to Saul) to him who stands on a peaceful, friendly footing with him, cf. the adject. שָׁלֵם, lv. 21, and אִישׁ שָׁלוֹם, xli. 10. The verb גָּמַל, cogn. גָּמַר, signifies originally to finish, complete, (root גם, כם, cf. כִּימָה to be or to make full, to gather into a heap). One says גָּמַל טוֹב and גָּמַל רַע, and also without a material object גָּמַל עָלַי or גְּמָלָנִי *benefecit* or *malefecit mihi*. But we join גָמַלְתִּי with רָע according to the Targum and contrary to the accentuation, and not with שֹׁלְמִי (Olsh., Böttch., Hitz.), although שָׁלֵם beside מְשַׁלֵּם, as *e. g.* דֹּבֵר beside מְדַבֵּר might mean "requiting". The poet would then have written: אִם שִׁלַּמְתִּי גֹמְלִי רָע *i. e.* if I have retaliated upon him that hath done evil to me. In ver. 5 we do not render it according the meaning of חָלַץ which is usual elsewhere: but rather I rescued . . . (Louis de Dieu, Ewald § 345, *a*, and Hupfeld). Why cannot חָלַץ in accordance with its primary signification *expedire, exuere* (according to which even the signification of rescuing, taken exactly, does not proceed from the idea of drawing out, but of making loose, *exuere vinclis*) signify here *exuere = spoliare*, as it does in Aramaic? And how extremely appropriate it is as an allusion to the incident in the cave, when David did not rescue Saul, but, without indeed designing to take חֲלִיצָה, *exuviæ,* cut off the hem of his garment! As Hengstenberg observes, "He affirms his innocence in the most general terms, thereby shewing that his conduct towards Saul was not anything exceptional, but sprang from his whole disposition and mode of action". On the 1 *pers. fut. conv.* with *ah, vid.* on iii. 6. רֵיקָם belongs to צוֹרְרִי, like xxv. 3, lxix. 5.

In the apodosis, ver. 6, the *fut. Kal* of רָדַף is made
into three syllables, in a way altogether without example,
since, by first making the *Shebâ* audible, from יִרְדֹּף it is become
יְרַדֹּף (like יְצַחַק Gen. xxi. 6, תְּהַלֵּךְ Ps. lxxiii. 9, Ex. ix. 23,
שָׁמְעָה xxxix. 13), and this is then sharpened by an euphonic
*Dag. forte.** Other ways of explaining it, as that by Chajug
יִתְרֹדֵף =, or by Kimchi as a mixed form from *Kal* and *Piel,***
have been already refuted by Baer, *Thorath Emeth,* p. 33.
This dactylic jussive form of *Kal* is followed by the regular
jussives of *Hiph.* יַשֵּׂג and יִשְׁכֵּן. The rhythm is similar so that
in the primary passage Ex. xv. 9, which also finds its echo
in Ps. xviii. 38, — viz. iambic with anapæsts inspersed. By
its parallelism with נַפְשִׁי and חַיַּי, כְּבוֹדִי acquires the signification "my soul", as Saadia, Gecatilia and Aben-Ezra have
rendered it — a signification which is secured to it by xvi. 9,
xxx. 13, lvii. 9, cviii. 2, Gen. xlix. 6. Man's soul is his *doxa*,
and this it is as being the copy of the divine *doxa* (*Bibl.
Psychol.* S. 98, [tr.p. 119], and frequently). Moreover, "let
him lay in the dust" is at least quite as favourable to this sense
of כבודי as to the sense of personal and official dignity (iii.
4, iv. 3). To lay down in the dust is equivalent to: to lay in
the dust of death, xxii. 16. שֹׁכְנֵי עָפָר, Isa. xxvi. 19, are the
dead. According to the biblical conception the soul is capable of being killed (Num. xxxv. 11), and mortal (Num.
xxiii. 10). It binds spirit and body together and this bond
is cut asunder by death. David will submit willingly to
death in case he has ever acted dishonourably.

Here the music is to strike up, in order to give intensity
to the expression of this courageous confession. In the next
strophe his affirmation of innocence rises to a challenging
appeal to the judgment-seat of God and a prophetic certainty
that that judgment is near at hand.

---

* The *Dag.* is of the same kind as the *Dag.* in גְּמַלִּים among nouns;
Arabic popular dialect *farassi* (my horse), *vid.* Wetzstein's *Inschriften*
S. 366.

** Pinsker's view, that the pointing יְרַדֹּף is designed to leave the
reader at liberty to choose between the reading יִרְדֹּף and יְרַדֵּף, cannot
be supported. There are no safe examples for the supposition that the
variations of tradition found expression in this way.

Vers. 7—9. In the consciousness of his own innocence
he calls upon Jahve to sit in judgment and to do justice to
His own. His vision widens and extends from the enemies
immediately around to the whole world in its hostility towards Jahve and His anointed one. In the very same way
special judgments and the judgment of the world are portrayed side by side, as it were on one canvas, in the prophets.
The truth of this combination lies in the fact of the final
judgment being only the finale of that judgment which is in
constant execution in the world itself. The language here
takes the highest and most majestic flight conceivable. By
קוּמָה (*Milra*, as in iii. 8), which is one of David's words of
prayer that he has taken from the lips of Moses (ix. 20, x. 12),
he calls upon Jahve to interpose. The parallel is הִנָּשֵׂא lift
Thyself up, shew Thyself in Thy majesty, xciv. 2, Isa. xxxiii.
10. The anger, in which He is to arise, is the principle of His
judicial righteousness. With this His anger He is to gird Himself (lxxvi. 11) against the ragings of the oppressors of God's
anointed one, *i. e.* taking vengeance on their many and manifold manifestations of hostility. עַבְרוֹת is a shorter form of the
construct (instead of עֶבְרוֹת Job xl. 11, cf. xxi. 31) of עֶבְרָה
which describes the anger as running over, breaking forth
from within and passing over into words and deeds (cf. Arab.

فشّ used of water: it overflows the dam, of wrath: it breaks
forth). It is contrary to the usage of the language to make
מִשְׁפָּט the object to עוּרָה in opposition to the accents, and it
is unnatural to regard it as the accus. of direction = לְמִשְׁפָּט
(xxxv. 23), as Hitzig does. The accents rightly unite עוּרָה
אֵלָי: awake (stir thyself) for me *i. e.* to help me (אֵלַי like
לְקִלְאָתִי, lix. 5). The view, that צִוִּיתָ is then precative and
equivalent to צַוֵּה: command judgment, is one that cannot be
established according to syntax either here, or in lxxi. 3. It
ought at least to have been וְצִוִּיתָ with *Waw consec.* On the
other hand the relative rendering: Thou who hast ordered
judgment (Maurer, Hengst.), is admissible, but unnecessary.
We take it by itself in a confirmatory sense, not as a circumstantial clause: having commanded judgment (Ewald),
but as a co-ordinate clause: Thou hast indeed enjoined the
maintaining of right (Hupfeld).

The psalmist now, so to speak, arranges the judgment scene: the assembly of the nations is to form a circle round about Jahve, in the midst of which He will sit in judgment, and after the judgment He is to soar away (Gen. xvii. 22) aloft over it and return to the heights of heaven like a victor after the battle (see lxviii. 19). Although it strikes one as strange that the termination of the judgment itself is not definitely expressed, yet the rendering of Hupfeld and others: sit Thou again upon Thy heavenly judgment-seat to judge, is to be rejected on account of the שׁוּבָה (cf. on the other hand xxi. 14) which is not suited to it; שׁוּב לַמָּרוֹם can only mean Jahve's return to His rest after the execution of judgment. That which vers. 7 and 8 in the boldness of faith desire, the beginning of ver. 9 expresses as a prophetic hope, from which proceeds the prayer, that the Judge of the earth may also do justice to him (שָׁפְטֵנִי *vindica me,* as in xxvi. 1, xxxv. 24) according to his righteousness and the purity of which he is conscious, as dwelling in him. עָלַי is to be closely connected with תֻּמִּי, just as one says נַפְשִׁי עָלַי (*Psychol.* S. 152 [tr. p. 180]). That which the individual as ego, distinguishes from itself as being in it, as subject, it denotes by עָלַי. In explaining it elliptically: "come upon me" (Ew., Olsh., Hupf.) this psychologically intelligible usage of the language is not recognised. On תֹּם *vid.* on xxv. 21, xxvi. 1.

Vers. 10—11. In this strophe we hear the calm language of courageous trust, to which the rising and calmly subsiding cæsural schema is particularly adapted. He is now concerned about the cessation of evil: Oh let it come to an end (גְּמָר intransitive as in xii. 2, lxxvii. 9)... His prayer is therefore not directed against the individuals as such but against the wickedness that is in them. This Psalm is the key to all Psalms which contain prayers against one's enemies. Just in the same manner וּתְכוֹנֵן is intended to express a wish; it is one of the comparatively rare voluntatives of the 2 *pers.* (Ew. § 229): and mayst Thou be pleased to establish.... To the termination of evil which is desired corresponds, in a positive form of expression, the desired security and establishment of the righteous, whom it had injured and whose continuance was endangered by it. וּבֹחֵן is the beginning of a circumstantial clause, introduced by וֹ, but without the personal pronoun, which is not unfrequently omitted both in the leading participial clause, as in Isa. xxix. 8 (which see), and in the minor participial clause as here (cf. lv. 20): *cum sis* = *quoniam es*. The reins are the seat of the emotions, just as the heart is the seat of the thoughts and feelings. Reins and heart lie naked before God — a description of the only καρδιογνώστης, which is repeated in Jer. xi. 20, xx. 12, Apoc. ii. 23. In the thesis the adjective is used with אֱלֹהִים in the *sing.* as in lxxviii. 56, cf. lviii. 12. God is the righteous God, and by his knowledge of the inmost part He is fully capable of always shewing Himself both righteous in anger and righteous in mercy according to the requirements and necessity of the case. Therefore David can courageously add מָגִנִּי עַל־אֱלֹהִים, my shield doth God carry; לְ (lxxxix. 19) would signify: He has it, it (my shield) belongs to Him, עַל (1 Chron. xviii. 7) signifies: He bears it, or if one takes shield in the sense of protection: He has taken my protection upon Himself, has undertaken it (as in lxii. 8, cf. Judges xix. 20), as He is in general the Saviour of all who are devoted to Him with an upright heart, *i. e.* a heart sincere, guileless (cf. xxxii. with ver. 2). צַדִּים is intentionally repeated at the end of the first two lines — the favourite palindrome, found more especially in Isa. xl.—lxvi. And to the mixed character of this Psalm belongs the fact of its being both Elohimic and Jehovic. From the calm language of heartfelt trust in God the next strophe passes over into the language of earnest warning, which is again more excited and somewhat after the style of didactic poetry.

Vers. 12—14. If God will in the end let His wrath break forth, He will not do it without having previously given threatenings thereof every day, viz. to the ungodly, cf. Isa. lxvi. 14, Mal. i. 4. He makes these feel His זַעַם beforehand in order to strike a wholesome terror into them. The subject of the conditional clause אִם־לֹא יָשׁוּב is any ungodly person whatever; and the subject of the principal clause, as its continuation in ver. 14 shews, is God. If a man (any one) does not repent, then Jahve will whet His sword (cf. Deut. xxxii. 41). This sense of the words accords with the connection; whereas with the rendering: "forsooth He (Elohim) will again whet His sword" (Böttch., Ew., Hupf.) יָשׁוּב, which would moreover stand close by יִלְטוֹשׁ (cf. *e. g.* Gen. xxx. 31), is meaningless; and the אִם־לֹא of asseveration is devoid of purpose. Judgment is being gradually prepared, as the *fut.* implies; but, as the *perff.* imply, it is also on the other hand like a bow that is already strung against the sinner with the arrow pointed towards him, so that it can be executed at any moment. כּוֹנֵן of the making ready, and הֵכִין of the aiming, are used alternately. לוֹ, referring to the sinner, stands first by way of emphasis as in Gen. xlix. 10, 1 Sam. ii. 3, and is equivalent to אֵלָיו, Ezek. iv. 3. "Burning" arrows are fire-arrows (דֹּלְקִים, זִיקוֹת, *malleoli*); and God's fire-arrows are the lightnings sent forth by Him, xviii. 15, Zech. ix. 14. The *fut.* יִפְעָל denotes the simultaneous charging of the arrows aimed at the sinner, with the fire of His wrath. The case illustrated by Cush is generalised: by the sword and arrow the manifold energy of the divine anger is symbolised, and it is only the divine forbearance that prevents it from immediately breaking forth. The conception is not coarsely material, but the vividness of the idea of itself suggests the form of its embodiment.

Vers. 15—18. This closing strophe foretells to the enemy of God, as if dictated by the judge, what awaits him; and concludes with a prospect of thanksgiving and praise. Man brings forth what he has conceived, he reaps what he has sown. Starting from this primary passage, we find the punishment which sin brings with it frequently represented under these figures of הָרָה and יָלַד (הוֹלִיד, חִבֵּל, חִיל), זָרַע and קָצַר, and first of all in Job xv. 35. The act, guilt, and punishment of sin appear in general as notions that run into one another. David sees in the sin of his enemies their self-destruction. It is singular, that travail is first spoken of, and then only afterwards pregnancy. For חִבֵּל signifies, as in Cant. viii. 5, ὠδίνειν, not: to conceive (Hitz.). The Arab. *ḥabila* (synonym of *ḥamala*) is not to conceive in distinction from being pregnant, but it is both: to be and to become pregnant. The accentuation indicates the correct relationship of the three members of the sentence. First of all comes

the general statement: Behold he shall travail with, *i. e.*
bring forth with writhing as in the pains of labour, אָוֶן, evil,
as the result which proceeds from his wickedness. Then, by
this thought being divided into its two factors (Hupf.) it goes
on to say: that is, he shall conceive *(concipere)* עָמָל, and
bear שֶׁקֶר. The former signifies trouble, *molestia*, just as
πονηρία signifies that which makes πόνον; the latter falsehood,
viz. self-deception, delusion, vanity, inasmuch as the burden
prepared for others, returns as a heavy and oppressive
burden upon the sinner himself, as is said in ver. 17; cf. Isa.
lix. 4, where אָוֶן instead of שֶׁקֶר denotes the accursed wages
of sin which consist in the unmasking of its nothingness,
and in the undeceiving of its self-delusion. He diggeth a
pit for himself, is another turn of the same thought, lvii, 7,
Eccl. x. 8. Ver. 16*a* mentions the digging, and 16*b* the subsequent falling into the pit; the aorist וַיִּפֹּל is, for instance,
like ver. 13*b*, xvi. 9, xxix. 10. The attributive יִפְעָל is virtually a genitive to שַׁחַת, and is rightly taken by Ges. § 123,
3, *a* as present: in the midst of the execution of the work
of destruction prepared for others it becomes his own. The
trouble, עָמָל, prepared for others returns upon his own head
(בְּרֹאשׁוֹ, clinging to it, just as עַל־רֹאשׁוֹ signifies descending
and resting upon it), and the violence, חָמָם, done to others,
being turned back by the Judge who dwells above (Mic. i.
12), descends upon his own pate (קָדְקֳדוֹ with ŏ by *q*, as *e. g.* in
Gen. ii. 23). Thus is the righteousness of God revealed in
wrath upon the oppressor and in mercy upon him who is
innocently oppressed. Then will the rescued one, then will
David, give thanks unto Jahve, as is due to Him after the
revelation of His righteousness, and will sing of the name of
Jahve the Most High (עֶלְיוֹן as an appended name of God is
always used without the *art., e. g.,* lvii. 3). In the revelation
of Himself He has made Himself a name. He has, however,
revealed Himself as the almighty Judge and Deliverer, as
the God of salvation, who rules over everything that takes
place here below. It is this name, which He has made by
His acts, that David will then echo back to Him in his song
of thanksgiving.

PSALM VIII.

THE PRAISE OF THE CREATOR'S GLORY SUNG BY THE STARRY HEAVENS TO PUNY MAN,

2 JAHVE, our Lord,
  How excellent is Thy name in all the earth,
  Who hast covered the heavens with Thy glory!
3 Out of the mouth of children and sucklings hast Thou
      founded a power,
  Because of Thine adversaries,
  To still the enemy and the revengeful.

4 When I see Thy heavens, the work of Thy fingers,
  The moon and the stars which Thou hast ordained:
5 What is mortal man, that Thou art mindful of him,
  And the son of man that Thou carest for him!
6 And hast made him a little less than divine,
  And crowned him with glory and honour.

7 Thou madest him to have dominion over the works of
      Thy hands,
  Thou hast put all things under his feet:
8 Sheep and oxen all together,
  And also the beasts of the field,
9 The fowls of heaven and the fishes of the sea,
  Whatsoever passeth through the paths of the sea.

10 Jahve, our Lord,
  How excellent is Thy name in all the earth!

Ps. vii. closed with a similar prospect of his enemies being undeceived by the execution of the divine judgments to Ps. vi. The former is the pendant or companion to the latter, and enters into detail, illustrating it by examples. Now if at the same time we call to mind the fact, that Ps. vi., if it be not a morning hymn, at any rate looks back upon sleepless nights of weeping, then the idea of the arrangement becomes at once clear, when we find a hymn of the night following Ps. vi. with its pendant, Ps. vii. David composes even at night; Jahve's song, as a Korahite psalmist says of himself in xlii. 9, was his companionship even in the loneliness of the night. The omission of any reference to the sun in ver. 4 shews that Ps. viii. is a hymn of this kind composed in the night, or at least one in which the writer transfers himself in thought to the night season. The poet has the starry heavens before him, he begins with the glorious revelation of Jahve's power on earth and in the heavens, and then pauses at man, comparatively puny man, to whom Jahve condescends in love and whom He has made lord over His creation. This Psalm, like Ps. civ. and others, is a lyric echo of the Mosaic account of the creation. Ewald calls it a flash of lightning cast into the darkness of the creation.

Even Hitzig acknowledges David's authorship here; whereas Hupfeld is silent, and Olshausen says that nothing can be said about it. The idea, that David composed it when a shepherd boy on the plains of Judah, is rightly rejected again by Hitzig after he has been at the pains to support it. (This thought is pleasingly worked out by Nachtigal, *Psalmen gesungen vor David's Thronbesteigung*, 1797, after the opinion of E. G. von Bengel, *cum magna veri specie*.) For, just as the Gospels do not contain any discourses of our Lord belonging to the time prior to His baptism, and just as the New Testament canon does not contain any writings of the Apostles from the time prior to Pentecost, so the Old Testament canon contains no Psalms of David belonging to the time prior to his anointing. It is only from that time, when he is the anointed one of the God of Jacob, that he becomes the sweet singer of Israel, on whose tongue is the word of Jahve, 2 Sam. xxiii. 1 sq.

The inscription runs: *To the Precentor, on the Gittith, a Psalm of David.* The Targum translates it *super cithara, quam David de Gath attulit.* According to which it is a Philistine cithern, just as there was (according to Athenæus and Pollux) a peculiar Phœnician and Carian flute played at the festivals of Adonis, called γίγγρας, and also an Egyptian flute and a Doric lyre. All the Psalms bearing the inscription עַל־הַגִּתִּית (viii. lxxxi. lxxxiv.) are of a laudatory character. The gittith was, therefore, an instrument giving forth a joyous sound, or (what better accords with its occurring exclusively in the inscriptions of the Psalms), a joyous melody, perhaps a march of the Gittite guard, 2 Sam. xv. 18 (Hitzig).

Kurtz makes this Psalm into four tetrastichic strophes, by taking ver. 2 *a b* and ver. 10 by themselves as the opening and close of the hymn, and putting ver. 2 *c* (Thou whose majesty . . .) to the first strophe. But אֲשֶׁר is not rightly adapted to begin a strophe; the poet, we think, would in this case have written אתה אשר תנה הודו.

Vers. 2—3. Here, for the first time, the subject speaking in the Psalm is not one individual, but a number of persons; and who should they be but the church of Jahve, which (as in Neh. x. 30) can call Jahve its Lord (אֲדֹנֵינוּ, like אֲדֹנָי, from אֲדֹנִים *plur. excellentiæ*, Ges. § 108, 2); but knowing also at the same time that what it has become by grace it is called to be for the good of the whole earth? The שֵׁם of God is the impress (cognate Arabic *wasm,* a sign, Greek σῆμα) of His nature, which we see in His works of creation and His acts of salvation, a nature which can only be known from this visible and comprehensible representation *(nomen = gnomen).** This name of God is certainly not yet so known and praised everywhere, as the church to which it has been made known by a positive revelation can know and praise it; but, nevertheless, it, viz. the divine name uttered in creation and its works, by which God has made Himself known and capable of being recognised and named, is אַדִּיר *amplum et gloriosum*, everywhere through out the earth, even if it were entirely without any echo. The clause with אֲשֶׁר must not be rendered: Who, do Thou be pleased to put Thy glory upon the heavens (Gesenius even: *quam tuam magnificentiam pone in cælis*), for such a use of the *imperat.* after אשר is unheard of; and, moreover, although it is true a thought admissible in its connection with the redemptive history (lvii. 6, 12) is thus obtained, it is here, however, one that runs counter to the fundamental tone, and to the circumstances, of the Psalm. For the primary thought of the Psalm is this, that

* cf. Oehler's art. *Name* in Herzog's *Real-Encyklopädie.*

the God, whose glory the heavens reflect, has also glorified
Himself in the earth and in man; and the situation of the
poet is this, that he has the moon and stars before his eyes:
how then could he wish that heaven to be made glorious
whose glory is shining into his eyes! It is just as impracticable to take תֵּנָה as a contraction of נְתָנָה, like תַּתָּה 2 Sam.
xxii. 41, = נָתַתָּה, as Ammonius and others, and last of all
Böhl, have done, or with Thenius (*Stud. u. Krit.* 1860 S. 712 f.)
to read it so at once. For even if the thought: "which (the
earth) gives (announces) Thy glory all over the heavens"
is not contrary to the connection, and if נָתַן עֹז, lxviii. 34,
and נָתַן כָּבוֹד, Jer. xiii. 16, can be compared with this נָתַן
הוֹד, still the phrase נָתַן הוֹד עַל means nothing but to lay
majesty on any one, to clothe him with it, Num. xxvii. 20,
1 Chron. xxix. 25, Dan. xi. 21, cf. Ps. xxi. 6; and this is
just the thought one looks for, viz., that the name of the
God, who has put His glory upon the heavens (cxlviii. 13)
is also glorious here below. We must, therefore, take תְּנָה,
although it is always the form of the *imper.* elsewhere, as
infin., just as רְדָה occurs once in Gen. xlvi. 3 as *infin.* (like
the Arab. *rĭda* a giving to drink, *lĭda* a bringing forth —
forms to which לְדָה and the like in Hebrew certainly more
exactly correspond). תְּנָה הוֹדְךָ signifies the setting of Thy
glory (prop. τὸ τιθέναι τὴν δόξαν σου) just like דֵּעָה אֶת־ה' the
the knowledge of Jahve, and Obad. ver. 5, שִׂים קִנֶּךָ, probably
the setting of thy nest, Ges. § 133. 1. It may be interpreted:
O Thou whose laying of Thy glory is upon the heavens, *i. e.*
Thou who hast chosen this as the place on which Thou hast
laid Thy glory (Hengst.). In accordance with this Jerome
translates it: *qui posuisti gloriam tuam super cœlos.* Thus
also the Syriac version with the Targum: *dᵉjabt* (ריהבת)
shubhoch ʿal shᵉmajo, and Symmachus: ὃς ἔταξας τὸν ἔπαινόν
σου ὑπεράνω τῶν οὐρανῶν. This use of the *nomen verbale* and
the genitival relation of אֲשֶׁר to תְּנָה הוֹדְךָ, which is taken
as one notion, is still remarkable. Hitzig considers that
no reasonable man would think and write thus; but thereby
at the same time utterly condemns his own conjecture תֵּן
הַהוֹדְךָ (whose extending of glory over the heavens). This,
moreover, goes beyond the limits of the language, which is

only acquainted with תֵּן as the name of an animal. All difficulty would vanish if one might, with Hupfeld, read נָתַתָּה.
But תנה has not the slightest appearance of being a corruption of נתתה. It might be more readily supposed that
תְּנָה is an erroneous pointing for תָּנָה (to stretch or extend,
cf. Hos. viii. 10 to stretch forth, distribute): Thou whose
glory stretches over the heavens, — an interpretation which
is more probable than that it is, with Paulus and Kurtz,
to be read תֻּנָּה: Thou whose glory is praised (*pass.* of the
תִּנָּה in Judges v. 11, xi. 40, which belongs to the dialect of
Northern Palestine), instead of which one would more readily expect יְתֻנֶּה. The verbal notion, which is tacitly implied
in cxiii. 4, cxlviii. 13, would then be expressed here. But perhaps the author wrote תְּנָה הוֹדְךָ instead of נָתַתָּ הוֹדְךָ, because
he wishes to describe the setting out of the heavens with
divine splendour* as being constantly repeated and not as
done once for all.

There now follows, in ver. 3, the confirmation of ver.
2 *a*: also all over the earth, despite its distance from the
heavens above, Jahve's name is glorious; for even children,
yea even sucklings glorify him there, and in fact not mutely
and passively by their mere existence, but with their mouth.
עוֹלֵל (= מְעוֹלֵל) or עוֹלָל is a child that is more mature and capable of spontaneous action, from עוֹלֵל (*Poel* of עָלַל *ludere*),**
according to 1 Sam. xxii. 19, xv. 3, distinct from יוֹנֵק, *i. e.*
a suckling, not, however, *infans,* but, — since the Hebrew

---

* In the first Sidonian inscription אַדִּיר occurs as a by-name of the
heavens (שמם אדרם).

** According to this derivation עוֹלֵל (cf. Beduin עאלול, '*âlûl* a young
ox) is related to תְּעָלוּל; whereas עוּל as a synonym of יונק signifies one
who is supported, sustained. For the radical signification of עוּל according to the Arabic عَال *fut. o.* is "to weigh heavy, to be heavy, to lie
upon; to have anything incumbent upon one's self, to carry, support, preserve",
whence '*ajjil* the maintained child of the house, and '*ajjila* (Damascene
'*êla*) he who is dependent upon one for support and the family depending upon the paterfamilias for sustenance. Neither عَال *fut. o.*, nor
غَال *fut. i.* usually applied to a pregnant woman who still suckles, has
the direct signification to suckle. Moreover, the demon *Ghul* does not
receive its name from swallowing up or sucking out (Ges.), but from
destroying (غَال *fut. o.*)

women were accustomed to suckle their children for a long
period, — a little child which is able to lisp and speak (*vid.*
2 Macc. vii. 27). Out of the mouth of beings such as these
Jahve has founded for Himself עֹז. The LXX. translates it
the utterance of praise, αἶνον; and עֹז certainly sometimes has
the meaning of power ascribed to God in praise, and so a laudatory acknowledgment of His might; but this is only when
connected with verbs of giving, xxix. 1, lxviii. 35, xcvi. 7.
In itself, when standing alone, it cannot mean this. It is in
this passage: might, or victorious power, which God creates
for Himself out of the mouths of children that confess Him.
This offensive and defensive power, as Luther has observed
on this passage, is conceived of as a strong building, עֹז as
מָעֹוז (Jer. xvi. 19) *i. e.* a fortress, refuge, bulwark, fortifica-
tion, for the foundation of which He has taken the mouth,
i. e. the stammering of children; and this He has done because
of His enemies, to restrain (הִשְׁבִּית to cause any one to sit
or lie down, rest, to put him to silence, *e. g.* Isa. xvi. 10,
Ezek. vii. 24) such as are enraged against Him and His, and
are inspired with a thirst for vengeance which expresses
itself in curses (the same combination is found in xliv. 17).
Those meant, are the fierce and calumniating opponents of
revelation. Jahve has placed the mouth of children in opposition to these, as a strong defensive controversive power.
He has chosen that which is foolish and weak in the eyes
of the world to put to shame the wise and that which is
strong (1 Cor. i. 27). It is by obscure and naturally feeble
instruments that He makes His name glorious here below,
and overcomes whatsoever is opposed to this glorifying.

Vers. 4—6. Stier wrongly translates: For I shall behold.
The principal thought towards which the rest tends is ver. 5
(parallel are vers. 2 *a*, 3), and consequently ver. 4 is the protasis
(par., ver. 2 *b*), and כִּי accordingly is = *quum, quando,* in the
sense of *quoties.* As often as he gazes at the heavens which
bear upon themselves the name of God in characters of light
(wherefore he says שָׁמֶיךָ), the heavens with their boundless
spaces (an idea which lies in the *plur.* שָׁמַיִם) extending
beyond the reach of mortal eye, the moon (יָרֵחַ, dialectic
ורח, perhaps, as Maurer derives it, from יָרֵחַ = יָרַק *subflavum*

esse), and beyond this the innumerable stars which are lost
in infinite space (כּוֹכָבִים = כַּבְכָּבִים prop. round, ball-shaped,
spherical bodies) to which Jahve appointed their fixed place
on the vault of heaven which He has formed with all the
skill of His creative wisdom (כּוּנֵן to place and set up, in the
sense of existence and duration): so often does the thought
"what is mortal man....?" increase in power and intensity.
The most natural thought would be: frail, puny man is as
nothing before all this; but this thought is passed over
in order to celebrate, with grateful emotion and astonished
adoration, the divine love which appears in all the more
glorious light, — a love which condescends to poor man,
the dust of earth. Even if אֱנוֹשׁ does not come from אָנַשׁ
to be fragile, nevertheless, according to the usage of the
language, it describes man from the side of his impotence,
frailty, and mortality (*vid.* ciii. 15, Isa. li. 12, and on Gen.
iv. 26). בֶּן־אָדָם, also, is not without a similar collateral
reference. With retrospective reference to עוֹלְלִים וְיֹנְקִים, בֶּן־אָדָם
is equivalent to יְלוּד־אִשָּׁה in Job xiv. 1: man, who is not,
like the stars, God's directly creative work, but comes into
being through human agency, born of woman. From both
designations it follows that it is the existing generation of
man that is spoken of. Man, as we see him in ourselves and
others, this weak and dependent being is, nevertheless, not
forgotten by God, God remembers him and looks about
after him (פָּקַד of observing attentively, especially visitation,
and with the *accus.* it is generally used of lovingly provident
visitation, *e. g.* Jer. xv. 15). He does not leave him to himself, but enters into personal intercourse with him, he is
the special and favoured object whither His eye turns (cf.
cxliv. 3, and the parody of the tempted one in Job vii.
17 sq.)

It is not until ver. 6 that the writer glances back at creation. וַתְּחַסְּרֵהוּ (differing from the *fut. consec.* Job vii. 18)
describes that which happened formerly. חִסַּר מִן signifies
to cause to be short of, wanting in something, to deprive
any one of something (cf. Eccl. iv. 8). מִן is here neither
comparative *(paullo inferiorem eum fecisti Deo)*, nor negative
(paullum derogasti ei, ne esset Deus), but partitive *(paullum*

derogasti ei divinæ naturæ); and, without אֱלֹהִים being on that account an abstract plural, *paullum Deorum,* = *Dei (vid. Genesis* S. 66 sq.), is equivalent to *paullum numinis Deorum.* According to Gen. i. 27 man is created בְּצֶלֶם אֱלֹהִים, he is a being in the image of God, and, therefore, nearly a divine being. But when God says: "let us make man in our image after our likeness", He there connects Himself with the angels. The translation of the LXX. ἠλάττωσας αὐτὸν βραχύ τι παρ᾽ ἀγγέλους, with which the Targum and the prevailing Jewish interpretations also harmonize, is, therefore, not unwarranted. Because in the biblical mode of conception the angels are so closely connected with God as the nearest creaturely effulgence of His nature, it is really possible that in מֵאֱלֹהִים David may have thought of God including the angels. Since man is in the image of God, he is at the same time in the likeness of an angel, and since he is only a little less than divine, he is also only a little less than angelic. The position, somewhat exalted above the angels, which he occupies by being the bond between all created things, in so far as mind and matter are united in him, is here left out of consideration. The writer has only this one thing in his mind, that man is inferior to God, who is רוּחַ, and to the angels who are רוּחוֹת (Isa. xxxi. 3, Heb. i. 14) in this respect, that he is a material being, and on this very account a finite and mortal being; as Theodoret well and briefly observes: τῷ θνητῷ τῶν ἀγγέλων ἠλάττωται. This is the מְעַט in which whatever is wanting to him to make him a divine being is concentrated. But it is nothing more than מְעַט. The assertion in ver. 6 *a* refers to the fact of the nature of man being in the image of God, and especially to the spirit breathed into him from God; ver. 6 *b*, to his godlike position as ruler in accordance with this his participation in the divine nature: *honore ac decore coronasti eum.* כָּבוֹד is the manifestation of glory described from the side of its weightiness and fulness; הוֹד (cf. הֵד, הֵידָד) from the side of its far resounding announcement of itself (*vid.* on Job xxxix. 20); הָדָר from the side of its brilliancy, majesty, and beauty. הוֹד וְהָדָר, xcvi. 6, or also הֲדַר כְּבוֹד הוֹד ה', cxlv. 5, is the appellation of the divine *doxa*, with the image of which man is adorned as with a regal crown. The preceding *fut. consec.* also stamps תְּעַטְּרֵהוּ and תַּמְשִׁילֵהוּ as historical retrospects. The next strophe unfolds the regal glory of man: he is the lord of all things, the lord of all earthly creatures.

Vers. 7—9. Man is a king, and not a king without territory; the world around, with the works of creative wisdom which fill it, is his kingdom. The words "put under his feet" sound like a paraphrase of the רְדָה in Gen. i. 26, 28. כֹּל is unlimited, as in Job xiii. 1, xlii. 2, Isa. xliv. 24. But the expansion of the expression in vers. 8, 9 extends only to the earth, and is limited even there to the different classes of creatures in the regions of land, air, and water. The poet is enthusiastic in his survey of this province of man's dominion. And his lofty poetic language corresponds to this enthusiasm. The enumeration begins with the domestic animals and passes on from these to the wild beasts — together the creatures that dwell on *terra firma.* צֹנֶה (צְנָא Num. xxxii. 24) from צֹנֶה (צְנָא), ضنى (ضنأ), as also ضان *fut. o., proliferum esse* is, in poetry, equivalent to צֹאן, which is otherwise the usual name for small cattle. אֲלָפִים (in Aramaic, as the name of the letter shews, a prose word) is in Hebrew poetically equivalent to בָּקָר; the oxen which willingly accommodate themselves to the service of man, especially of the husbandman, are so called from אָלַף to yield to. Wild animals, which in prose are called חַיַּת הָאָרֶץ, (הַשָּׂדֶה) here bear the poetical name בַּהֲמוֹת שָׂדָי, as in Joel ii. 22, cf. i. 20, 1 Sam. xvii. 44. שָׂדָי (in pause שָׂדָי) is the primitive form of שָׂדֶה, which is not declined, and has thereby obtained a collective signification. From the land animals the description passes on to the fowls of the air and the fishes of the water. צִפּוֹר is the softer word, instead of עוֹף; and שָׁמַיִם is used without the *art.* according to poetical usage, whereas הַיָּם without the *art.* would have sounded too scanty and not sufficiently measured. In connection with יַמִּים the article may be again omitted, just as with שָׁמָיִם. עֹבֵר is a collective participle. If the following were intended: he (or: since he), viz. man, passes through the paths of the sea

(Böttcher, Cassel, and even Aben-Ezra and Kimchi), then
it would not have been expressed in such a monostich, and
in a form so liable to lead one astray. The words may be
a comprehensive designation of that portion of the animal
kingdom which is found in the sea; and this also intended
to include all from the smallest worm to the gigantic leviathan: ὁππόσα ποντοπόρους παρεπιστείβουσι κελεύθους (Apollinaris). If man thus rules over every living thing that is round
about him from the nearest to the most remote, even that
which is apparently the most untameable: then it is clear
that every lifeless created thing in his vicinity must serve
him as its king. The poet regards man in the light of the
purpose for which he was created.

Ver. 10. He has now demonstrated what he expressed
in ver. 2, that the name of Jahve whose glory is reflected
by the heavens, is also glorious on earth. Thus, then, he
can as a conclusion repeat the thought with which he began,
in a wider and more comprehensive meaning, and weave
his Psalm together, as it were, into a wreath.

It is just this Psalm, of which one would have least
expected it, that is frequently quoted in the New Testament
and applied to the Messiah. Indeed Jesus' designation of
Himself by ὁ υἱὸς τοῦ ἀνθρώπου, however far it may refer
back to the Old Testament Scriptures, leans no less upon
this Psalm than upon Dan. vii. 13. The use the writer of
the Epistle to the Hebrews (ch. ii. 6 — 8) makes of vers.
5—7 of this Psalm shews us how the New Testament application to the Messiah is effected. The psalmist regards
man as one who glorifies God and as a prince created of God.
The deformation of this position by sin he leaves unheeded.
But both sides of the mode of regarding it are warranted.
On the one hand, we see that which man has become by
creation still in operation even in his present state; on the
other hand, we see it distorted and stunted. If we compare
what the Psalm says with this shady side of the reality,
from which side it is incongruous with the end of man's
creation, then the song which treats of the man of the present becomes a prophecy of the man of the future. The

Psalm undergoes this metamorphosis in the New Testament consciousness, which looks more to the loss than to that which remains of the original. In fact, the centre of the New Testament consciousness is Jesus the Restorer of that which is lost. The dominion of the world lost to fallen man, and only retained by him in a ruined condition, is allotted to mankind, when redeemed by Him, in fuller and more perfect reality. This dominion is not yet in the actual possession of mankind, but in the person of Jesus it now sits enthroned at the right hand of God. In Him the idea of humanity is transcendently realised, *i. e.* according to a very much higher standard than that laid down when the world was founded. He has entered into the state — only a little (βραχύ τι) beneath the angels — of created humanity for a little while (βραχύ τι), in order to raise redeemed humanity above the angels. Everything (כֹּל) is really put under Him with just as little limitation as is expressed in this Psalm: not merely the animal kindom, not merely the world itself, but the universe with all the ruling powers in it, whether they be in subjection or in hostility to God, yea even the power of death (1 Cor. xv. 27, cf. Ephes. i. 22). Moreover, by redemption, more than heretofore, the confession which comes from the mouth of little children is become a bulwark founded of God, in order that against it the resistance of the opponents of revelation may be broken. We have an example of this in Mat. xxi. 16, where our Lord points the pharisees and scribes, who are enraged at the Hosanna of the children, to Ps. viii. 3. Redemption demands of man, before everything else, that he should become as a little child, and reveals its mysteries to infants, which are hidden from the wise and intelligent. Thus, therefore, it is μικροὶ καὶ νήπιοι, whose tongue is loosed by the Spirit of God, who are to put to shame the unbelieving; and all that this Psalm says of the man of the present becomes in the light of the New Testament in its relation to the history of redemption, a prophecy of the Son of man κατ᾽ ἐξοχήν, and of the new humanity.

PSALM IX.

ПYMN TO THE RIGHTEOUS JUDGE AFTER A DEFEAT OF HOSTILE PEOPLES.

2 א I WILL give thanks to Jahve with my whole heart,
   א I will recount all Thy marvellous works —
3 א I will be glad and rejoice in Thee,
   א I will sing praise to Thy name, O Most High!

4 ב When mine enemies turned back,
   When they fell and perished before Thine angry face.
5   For Thou hast maintained my right and my cause,
   Thou hast sat down on the throne, a righteous Judge.

6 ג Thou didst rebuke peoples, Thou didst destroy the
      wicked,
   Their name didst Thou blot out for ever and ever.
7 ה The enemy are perished, perpetual ruins;
   And cities hast Thou rooted out, effaced is their very
      memory.

8 ו But Jahve sits enthroned for ever,
   He hath set His throne for judgment.
9   And He shall judge the earth in righteousness,
   He shall minister judgment to the nations in up-
      rightness.

10 ו So will Jahve be a stronghold to the oppressed,
    A stronghold in times of trouble;
11   Thus shall they trust in Thee who know Thy name,
    Because Thou hast not forsaken them who ask after
       Thee, Jahve!

12 ז Sing praises to Jahve, who dwelleth in Zion,
    Declare among the peoples His deeds;
13   That the Avenger of blood hath remembered them,
    He hath not forgotten the cry of the sufferer.

14 ח "Have mercy upon me, O Jahve; behold mine affliction
      from them that hate me,
    "My lifter-up from the gates of death,

15 "That I may tell all Thy praise,
 "That in the gates of the daughter of Zion I may rejoice in Thy salvation!"

16 ט The peoples have sunk down in the pit they have
   made,
  In the net, that they hid, were their own feet taken.
17 Jahve hath made Himself known: He hath executed
   judgment,
  Snaring the wicked in the work of his own hands.
        (*Stringed Instruments*, *Sela*.)

18 י Yea back to Hades must the wicked return,
  All the heathen, that forget God.
19 For the poor shall not always be forgotten,
  The hope of the afflicted is (not) perished for ever.

20 ק Arise, Jahve, let not mortal man be defiant,
  Let the heathen be judged in Thy sight!
21 Put them in fear, O Jahve,
  Let the heathen know they are mortals! (*Sela*).

Just as Ps. vii. is placed after Ps. vi. as exemplifying
it, so Ps. ix. follows Ps. viii. as an illustration of the glorifying of the divine name on earth. And what a beautiful
idea it is that Ps. viii., the Psalm which celebrates Jahve's
name as being glorious in the earth, is introduced between
a Psalm that closes with the words "I will sing of the name
of Jahve, the Most High" (vii. 18) and one which begins: "I
will sing of Thy name, O Most High!" (ix. 3).

The LXX. translates the inscription עַל־מוּת לַבֵּן by ὑπὲρ
τῶν κρυφίων τοῦ υἱοῦ (Vulg. *pro occultis filii*) as though it were
עַל־עֲלָמוֹת. Luther's rendering is still bolder: of beautiful
(perhaps properly: lily-white) youth. Both renderings are
opposed to the text, in which עַל occurs only once. The
Targum understands בֵּן of the duellist Goliath (= אִישׁ הַבֵּנַיִם);
and some of the Rabbis regard לַבֵּן even as a transposition
of נָבָל: on the death of Nabal. Hengstenberg has revived
this view, regarding נָבָל as a collective designation of all
Nabal-like fools. All these and other curious conceits arise
from the erroneous idea that these words are an inscription

referring to the contents of the Psalm. But, on the contrary,
they indicate the tune or melody, and that by means of the
familiar words of the song, — perhaps some popular song, —
with which this air had become most intimately associated.
At the end of Ps. xlviii. this indication of the air is simply
expressed by עַל־מוּת. The view of the Jewish expositors, who
refer לַבֵּן to the musician בֵּן mentioned in 1 Chron. xv. 18,
has, therefore, some probability in its favour. But this name
excites critical suspicion. Why may not a well-known song
have begun מוּת לַבֵּן "dying (is) to the son" . . ., or (if one is
inclined to depart from the pointing, although there is
nothing to render this suspicious) מָוֶת לִבֵּן "Death makes
white"?

Even Hitzig does not allow himself to be misled as to
the ancient Davidic origin of Ps. ix. and x. by the fact of
their having an alphabetical arrangement. These two Psalms
have the honour of being ranked among the thirteen Psalms
which are acknowledged by him to be genuine Davidic Psalms.
Thus, therefore, the alphabetical arrangement found in
other Psalms cannot, in itself, bring us down to "the times
of poetic trifling and degenerated taste." Nor can the freedom, with which the alphabetical arrangement is handled
in Ps. ix. and x. be regarded as an indication of an
earlier antiquity than these times. For the Old Testament
poets, even in other instances, do not allow themselves to
be fettered by forms of this character (*vid.* on Ps. cxlv.,
cf. on xlii. 2); and the fact, that in Ps. ix. x. the alphabetical
arrangement is not fully carried out, is accounted for otherwise than by the license in which David, in distinction from
later poets, indulged. In reality this pair of Psalms shews,
that even David was given to acrostic composition. And
why should he not be? Even among the Romans, Ennius
(Cicero, *De Divin.* ii. 54 § 111), who belongs not to the
leaden, but to the iron age, out of which the golden age first
developed itself, composed in acrostics. And our oldest
Germanic epics are clothed in the garb of alliteration,
which Vilmar calls the most characteristic and most elevated
style that the poetic spirit of our nation has created. Moreover, the alphabetical form is adapted to the common people,

as is evident from Augustine's *Retract.* i. 20. It is not a paltry substitute for the departed poetic spirit, not merely an accessory to please the eye, an outward embellishment — it is in itself indicative of mental power. The didactic poet regards the array of the linguistic elements as the steps by which he leads his pupils up into the sanctuary of wisdom, or as the many-celled casket in which he stores the pearls of the teachings of his wisdom. The lyric writer regards it as the keys on which he strikes every note, in order to give the fullest expression to his feelings. Even the prophet does not disdain to allow the order of the letters to exert an influence over the course of his thoughts, as we see from Nah. i. 3—7.* Therefore, when among the nine** alphabetical Psalms (ix. x. xxv. xxxiv. xxxvii. cxi. cxii. cxix. cxlv.) four bear the inscription לדוד (ix. xxv. xxxiv. cxlv.), we shall not at once regard them as non-Davidic just because they indicate an alphabetical plan which is more or less fully carried out.

This is not the place to speak of the relation of the anonymous Ps. x. to Ps. ix., since Ps. ix. is not in any way wanting in internal roundness and finish. It is thoroughly hymnic. The idea that ver. 14 passes from thanksgiving into supplication rests on a misinterpretation, as we shall presently see. This Psalm is a thoroughly national song of thanksgiving for victory by David, belonging to the time when Jahve was already enthroned on Zion, and therefore, to the time after the ark was brought home. Was it composed after the triumphant termination of the Syro-Ammonitish war? — The judgment of extermination already executed, ix. 8 sq., harmonises with what is recorded in 2 Sam. xii. 31; and the גוים, who are actually living within the borders of Israel, appear to be Philistines according to the annalistic passage about the Philistine feuds, 2 Sam. xxi. 15 sqq., cf. viii. 1 in connection with 1 Sam. xiii. 6.

---

* This observation is due to Pastor Frohnmeyer of Würtemberg.

** The *Psalterium Brunonis* (ed. by Cochleus, 1533) overlooks Ps. ix. x., reckoning only seven alphabetical Psalms.

Vers. 2—3. In this first strophe of the Psalm, which is laid out in tetrastichs, — the normative strophe, — the alphabetical form is carried out in the fullest possible way: we have four lines, each of which begins with א. It is the prelude of the song. The poet rouses himself up to a joyful utterance of Jahve's praise. With his whole heart (cxxxviii. 1), *i. e.* all his powers of mind and soul as centred in his heart taking part in the act, will he thankfully and intelligently confess God, and declare His wondrous acts which exceed human desire and comprehension (xxvi. 7); he will rejoice and be glad in Jahve, as the ground of his rejoicing and as the sphere of his joy; and with voice and with harp he will sing of the name of the Most High. עֶלְיוֹן is not an attributive of the name of God (Hitz.: Thine exalted name), but, as it is everywhere from Gen. xiv. 18—22 onward (*e. g.* xcvii. 9), an attributive name of God. As an attributive to שְׁמָךְ one would expect to find הָעֶלְיוֹן.

Vers. 4—5. The call upon himself to thanksgiving sounds forth, and the ב-strophe continues it by expressing the ground of it. The preposition בְּ in this instance expresses both the time and the reason together (as in lxxvi. 10, 2 Chron. xxviii. 6); in Latin it is *recedentibus hostibus meis retro.* אָחוֹר serves to strengthen the notion of being driven back, as in lvi. 10, cf. xliv. 11; and just as, in Latin, verbs compounded of *re* are strengthened by *retro.* In ver. 4*b* finite verbs take the place of the infinitive construct; here we have *futt.* with a present signification, just as in 2 Chron. xvi. 7 we find a *præt.* intended as perfect. For the rendering which Hitzig adopts: When mine enemies retreat backwards, they stumble ... is opposed both by the absence of any syntactic indication in ver. 4*b* of an apodosis (cf. xxvii. 2); and also by the fact that יִכָּשְׁלוּ is well adapted to be a continuation of the description of שׁוּב אָחוֹר (cf. John xviii. 6), but is tame as a principal clause to the definitive clause בשוב אויבי אחור. Moreover, אָחוֹר does not signify backwards (which would rather be אֲחֹרַנִּית [Gen. ix. 23, 1 Sam. iv. 18]), but back, or into the rear. The מִן of מִפָּנֶיךָ is the מִן of the cause, whence the action proceeds. What is intended is God's angry countenance, the look of which sets his enemies on fire as if they were fuel (xxi. 10), in antithesis to God's countenance as beaming with the light of His love. Now, while this is taking place, and because of its taking place, will he sing praise to God. From ver. 2 we see that the Psalm is composed directly after the victory and while the destructive consequences of it to the vanquished are still in operation. David sees in it all an act of Jahve's judicial power. To execute any one's right, מִשְׁפָּט (Mic. vii. 9), to bring to an issue any one's suit or lawful demand, דִּין (cxl. 13), is equivalent to: to assist him and his good cause in securing their right. The phrases are also used in a judicial sense without the suffix. The genitive object after these principal words never denotes the person against whom, but the person on whose behalf, the third party steps forward with his judicial authority. Jahve has seated Himself upon His judgment-seat as a judge of righteousness (as in Jer. xi. 20), *i. e.* as a judge whose judicial mode of procedure is righteousness, justice,* and has decided in his favour. In יָשַׁב לְ (as in cxxxii. 11), which is distinguished in this respect from יָשַׁב עַל (xlvii. 9), the idea of motion, *considĕre*, comes prominently forward.

Vers. 6—7. The strophe with ג, which is perhaps intended to represent ד and ה as well, continues the confirmation of the cause for thanksgiving laid down in ver. 4. He does not celebrate the judicial act of God on his behalf, which he has just experienced, alone, but in connection with, and, as it were, as the sum of many others which have preceded it. If this is the case, then in ver. 6 beside the Ammonites one may at the same time (with Hengstenb.) think of the Amalekites (1 Sam. viii. 12), who had been threatened since the time of Moses with a "blotting out of their remembrance" (Ex. xvii. 14, Deut. xxv. 19, cf. Num. xxiv. 20). The divine threatening is the word of omnipotence which detroys in distinction from the word of omnipotence that

---

* Also Prov. viii. 16 is probably to be read כָּל־שֹׁפְטֵי צֶדֶק, with Norzi, according to the Targum, Syriac version, and old Codices; at any rate this is an old various reading, and one in accordance with the sense, side by side with כָּל־שֹׁפְטֵי אָרֶץ.

creates. רָשָׁע in close connection with גּוֹיִם is individualising, cf. ver. 18 with vers. 16, 17. וָעֶד is a sharpened pausal form for וָעַד, the *Pathach* going into a *Segol* (פתח קטן); perhaps it is in order to avoid the threefold *a*-sound in לעולם ועד (Nägelsbach § 8 *extr.*). In ver. 7 הָאוֹיֵב (with *Azla legarme*) appears to be a vocative. In that case נָתַשְׁתָּ ought also to be addressed to the enemy. But if it be interpreted: "Thou hast destroyed thine own cities, their memorial is perished", destroyed, viz. at the challenge of Israel, then the thought is forced; and if we render it: "the cities, which thou hast destroyed, perished is the remembrance of them", *i. e.* one no longer thinks of thine acts of conquest, then we have a thought that is in itself awkward and one that finds no support in any of the numerous parallels which speak of a blotting out and leaving no trace behind. But, moreover, in both these interpretations the fact that זִכְרָם is strengthened by הֵמָּה is lost sight of, and the twofold masculine זִכְרָם הֵמָּה is referred to עָרִים (which is carelessly done by most expositors), whereas עִיר, with but few exceptions, is feminine; consequently זכרם המה, so far as this is not absolutely impossible, must be referred to the enemies themselves (cf. xxxiv. 17, cix. 15). האויב might more readily be *nom. absol.*: "the enemy — it is at end for ever with his destructions", but הָרְבָּה never has an active but always only a neuter signification; or: "the enemy — ruins are finished for ever", but the signification to be destroyed is more natural for תָּמַם than to be completed, when it is used of *ruinæ*. Moreover, in connection with both these renderings the retrospective pronoun (חָרְבוֹתָיו) is wanting, and this is also the case with the reading חֲרָבוֹת (LXX., Vulg., Syr.), which leaves it uncertain whose swords are meant. But why may we not rather connect האויב at once with תַּמּוּ as subject? In other instances תַּמּוּ is also joined to a singular collective subject, *e. g.* Isa. xvi. 4; here it precedes, like הָאֹרֵב in Judg. xx. 37. חֳרָבוֹת לָנֶצַח is a nominative of the product, corresponding to the factitive object with verbs of making: the enemies are destroyed as ruins for ever, *i. e.* so that they are become ruins; or, more in accordance with the accentuation: the enemy, destroyed as ruins are they for ever. With respect to what follows the accentuation also contains hints worthy of our attention. It does not take נָתַשְׁתָּ (with the regular *Pathach* by *Athnach* after *Olewejored, vid.* on ii. 7) as a relative clause, and consequently does not require זכרם המה to be referred back to ערים.

We interpret the passage thus: and cities (viz. such as were hostile) thou hast destroyed (נָתַשׁ *evellere, exstirpare*), perished is their (the enemies') memorial. Thus it also now becomes intelligible, why זִכְרָם, according to the rule Ges. § 121, 3, is so remarkably strengthened by the addition of הֵמָּה (cf. Num. xiv. 32, 1 Sam. xx. 42, Prov. xxii. 19, xxiii. 15, Ezek. xxxiv. 11). Hupfeld, whose interpretation is exactly the same as ours, thinks it might perhaps be the enemies themselves and the cities set over against one another. But the contrast follows in ver. 8: their, even their memorial is perished, while on the contrary Jahve endures for ever and is enthroned as judge. This contrast also retrospectively gives support to the explanation, that זכרם refers not to the cities, but to האויב as a collective. With this interpretation of ver. 7 we have no occasion to read זִכְרָם מֵהֵמָּה (Targ.), nor זֵכֶר מֵהֵמָּה (Paul., Hitz.). The latter is strongly commended by Job xi. 20, cf. Jer. x. 2; but still it is not quite admissible, since זֵכֶר here is not subjective (their own remembrance) but objective (remembrance of them). But may not עָרִים perhaps here, as in cxxxix. 20, mean zealots = adversaries (from עִיר *fervere, zelare*)? We reply in the negative, because the Psalm bears neither an Aramaising nor a North Palestinian impress. Even in connection with this meaning, the harshness of the ערים without any suffix would still remain. But, that the cities that are, as it were, plucked up by the root are cities of the enemy, is evident from the context.

Vers. 8—9. Without a trace even of the remembrance of them the enemies are destroyed, while on the other hand Jahve endureth for ever. This strophe is the continuation of the preceding with the most intimate connnection of contrast (just as the ב-strophe expresses the ground for what is said in the preceding strophe). The verb יֵשֵׁב has not the general signification "to remain" here (like עָמַד to endure), but just the same meaning as in xxix. 10. Everything that is opposed to Him comes to a terrible end, whereas He sits,

or (which the *fut.* implies) abides, enthroned for ever, and
that as Judge: He hath prepared His throne for the purpose
of judgment. This same God, who has just given proof that
He lives and reigns, will by and bye judge the nations still
more comprehensively, strictly, and impartially. תֵּבֵל, a
word exclusively poetic and always without the article,
signifies first (in distinction from אֶרֶץ the body of the earth
and אֲדָמָה the covering or soil of the earth) the fertile (from
יָבַל) surface of the globe, the οἰκουμένη. It is the last Judgment, of which all preceding judgments are harbingers and
pledges, that is intended. In later Psalms this Davidic utterance concerning the future is repeated.

Vers. 10—11. Thus judging the nations Jahve shews
Himself to be, as a second ו-strophe says, the refuge and
help of His own. The voluntative with *Waw* of sequence
expresses that which the poet desires for his own sake and
for the sake of the result mentioned in ver. 11. מִשְׂגָּב, a high,
steep place, where one is removed from danger, is a figure
familiar to David from the experiences of his time of persecution. דַּךְ (in pause דָּךְ) is properly one who is crushed
(from דָּכָה = דָּכָא, דָּכַךְ to crush, break in pieces, דָּקַק to pulverize), therefore one who is overwhelmed to the extreme,
even to being completely crushed. The parallel is לְעִתּוֹת בַּצָּרָה
with the datival לְ (as probably also in x. 1). עִתּוֹת from עֵת
(time, and then both continuance, lxxxi. 16, and condition)
signifies the public relations of the time, or even the vicissitudes of private life, xxxi. 16; and בַּצָּרָה is not הַצָּרָה with
בְּ (Böttch.), which gives an expression that is meaninglessly
minute ("for times in the need"), but one word, formed from
בָּצַר (to cut off, Arab. to see, prop. to discern keenly), just
like בַּקָּשָׁה from בָּקַשׁ, prop. a cutting off, or being cut off,
i. e. either restraint, especially motionlessness (= בַּצֹּרֶת, Jer.
xvii. 8, *plur.* בַּצָּרוֹת Jer. xiv. 1), or distress, in which the
prospect of deliverance is cut off. Since God is a final refuge
for such circumstances of hopelessness in life, *i. e.* for those
who are in such circumstances, the confidence of His people
is strengthened, refreshed, and quickened. They who know
His name, to them He has now revealed its character fully,
and that by His acts; and they who inquire after Him, or

trouble and concern themselves about Him (this is what דָרַשׁ signifies in distinction from בִּקֵּשׁ), have now experienced that He also does not forget them, but makes Himself known to them in the fulness of His power and mercy.

Vers. 12—13. Thus then the ז-strophe summons to the praise of this God who has done, and will still do, such things. The summons contains a moral claim, and therefore applies to all, and to each one individually. Jahve, who is to be praised everywhere and by every one, is called יֹשֵׁב צִיּוֹן, which does not mean: He who sits enthroned in Zion, but He who inhabiteth Zion, Ges. § 138, 1. Such is the name by which He is called since the time when IIis earthly throne, the ark, was fixed on the castle hill of Jerusalem, lxxvi. 3. It is the epithet applied to Him during the period of the typical kingship of promise. That Jahve's salvation shall be proclaimed from Zion to all the world, even outside Israel, for their salvation, is, as we see here and elsewhere, an idea which throbs with life even in the Davidic Psalms; later prophecy beholds its realisation in its wider connections with the history of the future. That which shall be proclaimed to the nations is called עֲלִילוֹתָיו, a designation which the *magnalia Dei* have obtained in the Psalms and the prophets since the time of Hannah's song, 1 Sam. ii. 3 (from עָלַל, root על, to come over or upon anything, to influence a person or a thing, as it were, from above, to subject them to one's energy, to act upon them).

With כִּי, *quod*, in ver. 13, the subject of the proclamation of salvation is unfolded as to its substance. The *prætt.* state that which is really past; for that which God has done is the assumption that forms the basis of the discourse in praise of God on account of His mighty acts. They consist in avenging and rescuing His persecuted church, — persecuted even to martyrdom. The אוֹתָם, standing by way of emphasis before its verb, refers to those who are mentioned afterwards (cf. ver. 21): the *Chethîb* calls them עֲנִיִּים, the *Kerî* עֲנָוִים. Both words alternate elsewhere also, the *Kerî* at one time placing the latter, at another the former, in the place of the one that stands in the text. They are both referable to עָנָה to bend (to bring low, Isa. xxv. 5). The neuter signification

of the verb עָנָה = עָנוּ, عَنَا *fut. o.*, underlies the noun עֱנוּ (cf.
שְׁלִי), for which in Num. xii. 3 there is a *Kerî* עָנָיו with an
incorrect *Jod* (like שָׁלֵיו Job xxi. 23). This is manifest from
the substantive עֲנָוָה, which does not signify affliction, but
passiveness, *i. e.* humility and gentleness; and the noun עָנִי
is passive, and therefore does not, like עָנָו, signify one who
is lowly-minded, in a state of עֲנָוָה, but one who is bowed
down by afflictions, עָנִי. But because the twin virtues denoted
by עֲנָוָה are acquired in the school of affliction, there comes
to be connected with עָנִי — but only secondarily — the
notion of that moral and spiritual condition which is aimed
at by dispensations of affliction, and is joined with a suffering life, rather than with one of worldly happiness and prosperity, — a condition which, as Num. xii. 3 shews, is properly described by עָנָו (ταπεινός and πραΰς). It shall be
proclaimed beyond Israel, even among the nations, that the
Avenger of blood, דֹּרֵשׁ דָּמִים, thinks of them (His דֹּרְשִׁים), and
has been as earnest in His concern for them as they in theirs
for Him. דָּמִים always signifies human blood that is shed
by violence and unnaturally; the *plur.* is the plural of the
product discussed by Dietrich, *Abhandl.* S. 40. דָּרַשׁ to demand back from any one that which he has destroyed, and
therefore to demand a reckoning, indemnification, satisfaction for it, Gen. ix. 5, then absolutely to punish, 2 Chron.
xxiv. 22.

Vers. 14—15. To take this strophe as a prayer of David
at the present time, is to destroy the unity and hymnic
character of the Psalm, since that which is here put in the
form of prayer appears in what has preceded and in what
follows as something he has experienced. The strophe
represents to us how the עֲנָיִים (עֲנָוִים) cried to Jahve before
the deliverance now experienced. Instead of the form חָנֵּנִי
used everywhere else the resolved, and as it were tremulous,
form חָנְנֵנִי is designedly chosen. According to a better attested
reading it is חָנְנֵנִי (*Pathach* with *Gaja* in the first syllable),
which is regarded by Chajug̃ and others as the *imper. Piel*,
but more correctly (Ewald § 251, *c*) as the *imper. Kal* from
the intransitive imperative form חֲנַן. מְרוֹמְמִי is the vocative,
cf. xvii. 7. The gates of death, *i. e.* the gates of the realm

of the dead (שְׁאוֹל, Isa. xxxviii. 10), are in the deep; he who
is in peril of death is said to have sunk down to them; he
who is snatched from peril of death is lifted up, so that they
do not swallow him up and close behind him. The church,
already very near to the gates of death, cried to the God
who can snatch from death. Its final purpose in connection
with such deliverance is that it may glorify God. The form
תְּהִלָּתֶיךָ is *sing.* with a plural suffix just like שִׂנְאָתֶיךָ Ezek.
xxxv. 11, אַשְׁמָתֵינוּ Ezra ix. 15. The punctuists maintained (as
עֲצָתֶיךָ in Isa. xlvii. 13 shews) the possibility of a plural inflexion of a collective singular. In antithesis to the gates
of death, which are represented as beneath the ground, we
have the gates of the daughter of Zion standing on high.
צִיּוֹן is *gen. appositionis* (Ges. § 116, 5). The daughter of Zion
(Zion itself) is the church in its childlike, bride-like, and
conjugal relation to Jahve. In the gates of the daughter of
Zion is equivalent to: before all God's people, cxvi. 14. For
the gates are the places of public resort and business. At
this period the Old Testament mind knew nothing of the
songs of praise of the redeemed in heaven. On the other
side of the grave is the silence of death. If the church desires
to praise God, it must continue in life and not die.

Vers. 16—17. And, as this פ-strophe says, the church
is able to praise God; for it is rescued from death, and those
who desired that death might overtake it, have fallen a prey
to death themselves. Having interpreted the ה-strophe as
the representation of the earlier צַעֲקַת עֲנִיִּים we have no need
to supply *dicendo* or *dicturus*, as Seb. Schmidt does, before
this strophe, but it continues the *prætt.* preceding the ה-
strophe, which celebrate that which has just been experienced.
The verb טָבַע (root טב, whence also טָבַל) signifies originally
to press upon anything with anything flat, to be pressed
into, then, as here and in lxix. 3, 15, to sink in. זוּ טָמָנוּ
(pausal form in connection with *Mugrash*) in the parallel
member of the verse corresponds to the attributive עָשׂוּ (cf.
יִפְעָל, vii. 16). The union of the epicene זוּ with רֶשֶׁת by
Makkeph proceeds from the view, that זוּ is demonstrative as
in xii. 8: the net there (which they have hidden). The punctuation, it is true, recognises a relative זוּ, xvii. 9, lxviii. 29,

but it mostly takes it as demonstrative, inasmuch as it connects it closely with the preceding noun, either by *Makkeph* (xxxii. 8, lxii. 12, cxlii. 4, cxliii. 8) or by marking the noun with a conjunctive accent (x. 2, xxxi. 5, cxxxii. 12). The verb לָכַד (Arabic to hang on, adhere to, IV. to hold fast to) has the signification of seizing and catching in Hebrew.

In ver. 17 Ben Naphtali points נוֹדָע with *ā*: Jahve is known (*part. Niph.*); Ben Asher נוֹדַע, Jahve has made Himself known (3 *pers. præt. Niph.* in a reflexive signification, as in Ezek. xxxviii. 23). The readings of Ben Asher have become the *textus receptus.* That by which Jahve has made Himself known is stated immediately: He has executed judgment or right, by ensnaring the evil-doer (רָשָׁע, as in ver. 6) in his own craftily planned work designed for the destruction of Israel. Thus Gussetius has already interpreted it. נוֹקֵשׁ is *part. Kal* from נָקַשׁ. If it were *part. Niph.* from יָקַשׁ the *ē*, which occurs elsewhere only in a few עָע verbs, as נָמֵם *liquefactus*, would be without an example. But it is not to be translated, with Ges. and Hengst.: "the wicked is snared in the work of his own hands", in which case it would have to be pointed נוֹקַשׁ (3 *præt. Niph.*), as in the old versions. Jahve is the subject, and the suffix refers to the evil-doer. The thought is the same as in Job xxxiv. 11, Isa. i. 31. This figure of the net, רֶשֶׁת (from יָרַשׁ *capere*), is peculiar to the Psalms that are inscribed לדוד. The music, and in fact, as the combination הגיון סלה indicates, the playing of the stringed instruments (xcii. 4), increases here; or the music is increased after a solo of the stringed instruments. The song here soars aloft to the climax of triumph.

Vers. 18—19. Just as in vers. 8 sqq. the prospect of a final universal judgment was opened up by Jahve's act of judgment experienced in the present, so here the grateful restrospect of what has just happened passes over into a confident contemplation of the future, which is thereby guaranteed. The LXX. translates יָשׁוּבוּ by ἀποστραφήτωσαν, Jer. *convertantur*, a meaning which it may have (cf. *e. g.* 2 Chron. xviii. 25); but why should it not be ἀναστραφήτωσαν, or rather: ἀναστραφήσονται, since ver. 19 shews that ver. 18 is not a wish but a prospect of that which is sure to come to pass? To be resolved into dust again, to sink away into nothing (*re-dactio in pulverem, in nihilum*) is man's return to his original condition, — man who was formed from the dust, who was called into being out of nothing. To die is to return to the dust, civ. 29, cf. Gen. iii. 19, and here it is called the return to Sheôl, as in Job xxx. 23 to death, and in xc. 3 to atoms, inasmuch as the state of shadowy existence in Hades, the condition of worn out life, the state of decay is to a certain extent the renewal (*Repristination*) of that which man was before he came into being. As to outward form לִשְׁאוֹלָה may be compared with לִישֻׁעָתֶךָ in lxxx. 3; the ל in both instances is that of the direction or aim, and might very well come before שְׁאוֹלָה, because this form of the word may signify both ἐν ᾅδου and εἰς ᾅδου (cf. מִבָּבֶלָה Jer. xxvii. 16). R. Abba ben Zabda, in *Genesis Rabba* cap. 50, explains the double sign of the direction as giving intensity to it: *in imum ambitum orci.* The heathen receive the epithet of שְׁכֵחֵי אֱלֹהִים (which is more neuter than שֹׁכְחֵי, l. 22); for God has not left them without a witness of Himself, that they could not know of Him, their alienation from God is a forgetfulness of Him, the guilt of which they have incurred themselves, and from which they are to turn to God (Isa. xix. 22). But because they do not do this, and even rise up in hostility against the nation and the God of the revelation that unfolds the plan of redemption, they will be obliged to return to the earth, and in fact to Hades, in order that the persecuted church may obtain its longed for peace and its promised dominion. Jahve will at last acknowledge this *ecclesia pressa*; and although its hope seems likely to perish, inasmuch as it remains again and again unfulfilled, nevertheless it will not always continue thus. The strongly accented לֹא rules both members of ver. 19, as in xxxv. 19, xxxviii. 2, and also frequently elsewhere (Ewald § 351, *a*). אֶבְיוֹן, from אָבָה to wish, is one eager to obtain anything = a needy person. The Arabic

أَبَى, which means the very opposite, and according to which it would mean "one who restrains himself", viz. because he is obliged to, must be left out of consideration.

Vers. 20—21. By reason of the act of judgment already

witnessed the prayer now becomes all the more confident in respect of the state of things which is still continually threatened. From י the poet takes a leap to ק which, however, seems to be a substitute for the כ which one would expect to find, since the following Psalm begins with ל. David's קוּמָה (iii. 8, vii. 7) is taken from the lips of Moses, Num. x. 35. "Jahve arises, comes, appears" are kindred expressions in the Old Testament, all of which point to a final personal appearing of God to take part in human history from which He has now, as it were, retired into a state of repose becoming invisible to human eyes. Hupfeld and others wrongly translate "let not man become strong". The verb עָזַז does not only mean to be or become strong, but also to feel strong, powerful, possessed of power, and to act accordingly, therefore: to defy, lii. 9, like עַז defiant, impudent (post-biblical עַזּוּת shamelessness). אֱנוֹשׁ, as in 2 Chron. xiv. 10, is man, impotent in comparison with God, and frail in himself. The enemies of the church of God are not unfrequently designated by this name, which indicates the impotence of their pretended power (Isa. li. 7, 12). David prays that God may repress the arrogance of these defiant ones, by arising and manifesting Himself in all the greatness of His omnipotence, after His forbearance with them so long has seemed to them to be the result of impotence. He is to arise as the Judge of the world, judging the heathen, while they are compelled to appear before Him, and, as it were, defile before Him (עַל־פְּנֵי), He is to lay מוֹרָה on them. If "razor" be the meaning it is equivocally expressed; and if, according to Isa. vii. 20, we associate with it the idea of an ignominious rasure, or of throat-cutting, it is a figure unworthy of the passage. The signification master (LXX., Syr., Vulg., and Luther) rests upon the reading מוֹרֶה, which we do not with Thenius and others prefer to the traditional reading (even Jerome translates: *pone, Domine, terrorem eis*); for מוֹרָה, which according to the Masora is instead of מוֹרָא (like מִבְלָה Hab. iii. 17 for מִבְלָא), is perfectly appropriate. Hitzig objects that fear is not a thing which one lays upon any one; but מוֹרָא means not merely fear, but an object, or as Hitzig himself explains it in Mal. ii. 5 a "lever", of fear. It is not meant

that God is to cause them to be overcome with terror (עַל),
nor that He is to put terror into them (בְּ), but that He is to
make them (לְ in no way differing from xxi. 4, cxl. 6, Job
xiv. 13) an object of terror, from which to their dismay, as
the wish is further expressed in ver. 21*b*, they shall come to
know (Hos. ix. 7) that they are mortal men. As in x. 12,
xlix. 12, l. 21, lxiv. 6, Gen. xii. 13, Job xxxv. 14, Amos v.
12, Hos. vii. 2, יֵדְעוּ is followed by an only half indirect
speech, without כִּי or אֲשֶׁר. סֶלָה has *Dag. forte conj.* according to the rule of the אתי מרחיק (concerning which *vid.* on lii.
5), because it is erroneously regarded as an essential part
of the text.

PSALM X.

PLAINTIVE AND SUPPLICATORY PRAYER UNDER THE PRESSURE OF HEATHENISH FOES AT HOME AND ABROAD.

1 לְ WHY, Jahve, standest Thou afar off,
    Why hidest Thou Thyself in times of trouble!?
2   Through the pride of the evil-doer the afflicted burneth
        with fear,
    They are taken in the plots which they have devised.

3   For the evil-doer boasteth of his soul's desire,
    And the covetous renounceth [and] despiseth Jahve.
4   The evil-doer in his scornfulness — : "With nothing
        will He punish!
    There is no God!" is the sum of his thoughts.

5   Sure are his ways at all times;
    Far above are Thy judgments, out of his sight;
    All his adversaries, he puffeth at them.

6   He saith in his heart: with nothing shall I be moved,
    From one generation to another I am he to whom no
        misfortune comes.
7   Of cursing is his mouth full, and of deceit and oppres-
        sion,
    Under his tongue is trouble and evil.

8   He sitteth in the lurking-places of the villages,
In the secret corners doth he slay the innocent;
His eyes, they lie in wait for the weak.

9   He lieth in wait in the secret corner as a lion in his
        lair,
He lieth in wait to carry off the afflicted,
He carrieth off the afflicted, drawing him away in
        his net.

10   He croucheth, he cowereth and there fall into his claws
        — the weak.

11   He saith in his heart: "God hath forgotten,
He hath hidden His face, He hath never seen."

12 ק Arise, Jahve; O God lift up Thine hand,
Forget not the sufferer!

13   Wherefore should the evil-doer blaspheme the Deity,
Saying in his heart: Thou dost not punish?!

14 ר Thou dost indeed see it; for Thou beholdest trouble
        and grief,   to lay it in Thy hand;
The weak committeth himself to Thee,
Thou art the helper of the orphan.

15 שׁ Break Thou the arm of the evil-doer;
And the wicked man — punish his evil-doing, that it
        may vanish before Thee!

16   Jahve is King for ever and ever,
The heathen are perished out of His land.

17 ת The desire of the sufferers hast Thou heard, Jahve,
Thou didst establish their heart, didst cause Thine ear
        to hear,

18   To obtain justice for the orphan and the oppressed,
That man of the earth may no more terrrify.

This Psalm and Ps. xxxiii. are the only ones that are anonymous in the First book of the Psalms. But Ps. x. has something peculiar about it. The LXX. gives it with Ps. ix. as one Psalm, and not without a certain amount of warrant for so doing. Both are laid out in tetrastichs; only in the middle portion of Ps. x. some three line strophes are mixed with the four line. And assuming that the ק-strophe, with which Ps. ix. closes, stands in the place of a כ-strophe which one would look for after the י-strophe, then Ps. x., beginning with ל, continues the order of the letters. At any rate it begins in the middle of the alphabet, whereas Ps. ix. begins at the beginning. It is true the ל-strophe is then followed by strophes without the letters that come next in order; but their number exactly corresponds to the letters between ל and ק, ר, שׁ, ת with which the last four strophes of the Psalm begin, viz. six, corresponding to the letters מ, נ, ס, ע, פ, צ, which are not introduced acrostically. In addition to this it is to be remarked that Ps. ix. and x. are most intimately related to one another by the occurrence of rare expressions, as לְעִתּוֹת בַּצָּרָה and דַּךְ; by the use of words in the same sense, as אֱנוֹשׁ and גּוֹיִם; by striking thoughts, as "Jahve doth not forget" and "Arise"; and by similarities of style, as the use of the *oratio directa* instead of *obliqua*, ix. 21, x. 13. And yet it is impossible that the two Psalms should be only one. Notwithstanding all their community of character they are also radically different. Ps. ix. is a thanksgiving Psalm, Ps. x. is a supplicatory Psalm. In the latter the personality of the psalmist, which is prominent in the former, keeps entirely in the background. The enemies whose defeat Ps. ix. celebrates with thanksgiving and towards whose final removal it looks forward are גּוֹיִם, therefore foreign foes; whereas in Ps. x. apostates and persecutors of his own nation stand in the foreground, and the גוים are only mentioned in the last two strophes. In their form also the two Psalms differ insofar as Ps. x. has no musical mark defining its use, and the tetrastich strophe structure of Ps. ix., as we have already observed, it not carried out with the same consistency in Ps. x. And is anything really wanting to the perfect unity of Ps. ix.? If it is connected with Ps. x. and they are read together *uno tenore*, then the latter becomes a tail-piece which disfigures the whole. There are only two things possible: Ps. x. is a pendant to Ps. ix. composed either by David himself, or by some other poet, and

closely allied to it by its continuance of the alphabetical
order. But the possibility of the latter becomes very slight
when we consider that Ps. x. is not inferior to Ps. ix. in the
antiquity of the language and the characteristic nature of
the thoughts. Accordingly the mutual coincidences point to
the same author, and the two Psalms must be regarded as
"two co-ordinate halves of one whole, which make a higher
unity" (Hitz.). That hard, dull, and tersely laconic language
of deep-seated indignation at moral abominations for which
the language has, as it were, no one word, we detect also
elsewhere in some Psalms of David and of his time, those
Psalms, which we are accustomed to designate as Psalms
written in the indignant style (*in grollendem Stil*).

Vers. 1—2. The Psalm opens with the plaintive inquiry,
why Jahve tarries in the deliverance of His oppressed people.
It is not a complaining murmuring at the delay that is expressed by the question, but an ardent desire that God may
not delay to act as it becomes His nature and His promise.
לָמָה, which belongs to both members of the sentence, has
the accent on the *ultima*, as *e. g.* before עֲזַבְתָּנִי in xxii. 2, and
before הֲרֵעֹתָה in Ex. v. 22, in order that neither of the two
gutturals, pointed with *a*, should be lost to the ear in rapid
speaking (*vid.* on iii. 8, and Luzzatto on Isa. xi. 2, נָחָה עָלָיו).*
For according to the primitive pronunciation (even before
the Masoretic) it is to be read: *lamáh Adonaj*; so that consequently ה and א are coincident. The poet asks why in the
present hopeless condition of affairs (on בַּצָּרָה *vid.* on ix. 10)
Jahve stands in the distance (בְּרָחוֹק, only here, instead of
מֵרָחוֹק), as an idle spectator, and why does He cover (תַּעְלִים

---

* According to the Masora לָמָה without *Dag.* is always *Milra* with
the single exception of Job vii. 20, and לָמָה with *Dag.* is *Milel*; but,
when the following closely connected word begins with one of the letters
אהע it becomes *Milra*, with five exceptions, viz. xlix. 6, 1 Sam. xxviii.
15, 2 Sam, xiv. 31 (three instances in which the guttural of the second
word has the vowel *i*), and 2 Sam. ii. 22, and Jer. xv. 18. In the Babylonian system of pointing, למה is always written without *Dag.* and with
the accent on the penultimate, *vid.* Pinsker, *Einleitung in das Babylonisch-
hebräische Punktationssystem*, S. 182—184.

with orthophonic *Dagesh*, in order that it may not be pronounced תַּעְלִים), viz. His eyes, so as not to see the desperate
condition of His people, or also His ears (Lam. iii. 56) so
as not to hear their supplication. For by the insolent treatment of the ungodly the poor burns with fear (Ges., Stier,
Hupf.), not vexation (Hengst.). The assault is a πύρωσις,
1 Pet. iv, 12. The verb דָּלַק which calls to mind דַּלֶּקֶת, πυρε-
τός, is perhaps chosen with reference to the heat of feeling
under oppression, which is the result of the persecution, of the
דְּלֹק אַחֲרָיו (בּוֹ) of the ungodly. There is no harshness in the
transition from the singular to the plural, because עָנִי and
רָשָׁע are individualising designations of two different classes
of men. The subject to יִתְּפְשׂוּ is the עֲנִיִּים, and the subject
to חָשָׁבוּ is the רְשָׁעִים. The futures describe what usually
takes place. Those who, apart from this, are afflicted are
held ensnared in the crafty and malicious devices which the
ungodly have contrived and plotted against them, without
being able to disentangle themselves. The punctuation,
which places *Tarcha* by זוּ, mistakes the relative and interprets it: "in the plots there, which they have devised".

Vers. 3—4. The prominent features of the situation are
supported by a detailed description. The *prætt.* express
those features of their character that have become a matter
of actual experience. הִלֵּל, to praise aloud, generally with the
accus., is here used with עַל of the thing which calls forth
praise. Far from hiding the shameful desire or passion
(cxii. 10) of his soul, he makes it an object and ground of
high and sounding praise, imagining himself to be above
all restraint human or divine. Hupfeld translates wrongly:
"and he blesses the plunderer, he blasphemes Jahve". But
the רָשָׁע who persecutes the godly, is himself a בֹּצֵעַ, a cove-
tous or rapacious person; for such is the designation (elsewhere with בֶּצַע Prov. i. 19, or בֶּצַע רָע Hab. ii. 9) not merely
of one who "cuts off" (بضع), *i. e.* obtains unjust gain, by
trading, but also by plunder, πλεονέκτης. The verb בֵּרֵך (here
in connection with *Mugrash,* as in Num. xxiii. 20 with *Tiphcha*
בֵּרֵך) never directly signifies *maledicere* in biblical Hebrew as
it does in the later Talmudic (whence בִּרְכַּת הַשֵּׁם blasphemy,
B. Sanhedrin 56 *a*, and frequently), but to take leave of any
one with a benediction, and then to bid farewell, to dismiss,

to decline and abandon generally, Job i. 5, and frequently
(cf. the word *remercier, abdanken;* and the phrase "*das Zeit-
liche segnen*" = to depart this life). The declaration without
a conjunction is climactic, like Isa. i. 4, Amos iv. 5, Jer.
xv. 7. נִאֵץ, properly to prick, sting, is used of utter rejection by word and deed.* In ver. 4, "the evil-doer according to his haughtiness" (cf. Prov. xvi. 18) is *nom. absol.,*
and בַּל־יִדְרֹשׁ אֵין אֱלֹהִים (contrary to the accentuation) is virtually the predicate to בָּל־מְזִמּוֹתָיו. This word, which denotes
the intrigues of the ungodly, in ver. 2, has in this verse, the
general meaning: thoughts (from זמם, زمّ, to join, combine),
but not without being easily associated with the secondary
idea of that which is subtly devised. The whole texture of
his thoughts is, *i. e.* proceeds from and tends towards the
thought, that he (viz. Jahve, whom he does not like to name)
will punish with nothing (בַּל the strongest form of subjective
negation), that in fact there is no God at all. This second
follows from the first; for to deny the existence of a living,
acting, all-punishing (in one word: a personal) God, is
equivalent to denying the existence of any real and true
God whatever (Ewald).

Ver. 5. This strophe, consisting of only three lines,
describes his happiness which he allows nothing to disturb.
The signification: to be lasting (prop. stiff, strong) is secured to the verb חִיל (whence חַיִל) by Job xx. 21. He takes
whatever ways he choses, they always lead to the desired
end; he stands fast, he neither stumbles nor goes astray,
cf. Jer. xii. 1. The *Chethîb* דרכו (דְּרָכָו) has no other meaning
than that given to it by the *Kerî* (cf. xxiv. 6, lviii. 8). Whatever might cast a cloud over his happiness does not trouble
him: neither the judgments of God, which are removed high
as the heavens out of his sight, and consequently do not
disturb his conscience (cf. xxviii. 5, Isa. v. 12; and the opposite, xviii. 23), nor his adversaries whom he bloweth upon
contemptuously. מָרוֹם is the predicate: *altissime remota.*
And הֵפִיחַ בְּ, to breathe upon, does not in any case signify:

---

* *Pasek* stands between נִאֵץ and יְהוָה, because to blaspheme God
is a terrible thought and not to be spoken of without hesitancy, cf.
the *Pasek* in lxxiv. 18, lxxxix. 52, Isa. xxxvii. 24 (2 Kings xix. 23).

actually to blow away or down (to express which נָשַׁב or נָשַׁף would be used), but either to "snub", or, what is more appropriate to ver. 5 *b*, to blow upon them disdainfully, to puff at them, like הִפִּיחַ in Mal. i. 13, and *flare rosas* (to despise the roses) in Prudentius. The meaning is not that he drives his enemies away without much difficulty, but that by his proud and haughty bearing he gives them to understand how little they interfere with him.

Vers. 6 — 7. Then in his boundless carnal security he gives free course to his wicked tongue. That which the believer can say by reason of his fellowship with God, בַּל־אֶמּוֹט (xxx. 7, xvi. 8), is said by him in godless self-confidence. He looks upon himself in age after age, *i. e.* in the endless future, as אֲשֶׁר לֹא בְרָע, *i. e.* as one who (אֲשֶׁר as in Isa. viii. 20) will never be in evil case (בְרָע as in Ex. v. 19, 2 Sam. xvi. 8). It might perhaps also be interpreted according to Zech. viii. 20, 23 (*vid.* Köhler, *in loc.*): in all time to come (it will come to pass) that I am not in misfortune. But then the personal pronoun (אֲנִי or הוּא) ought not be omitted; whereas with our interpretation it is supplied from אֶמּוֹט, and there is no need to supply anything if the clause is taken as an apposition: in all time to come he who ... In connection with such unbounded self-confidence his mouth is full of אָלָה, cursing, *execratio* (not perjury, *perjurium*, a meaning the word never has), מִרְמוֹת, deceit and craft of every kind, and תֹּךְ, oppression, violence. And that which he has under his tongue, and consequently always in readiness for being put forth (cxl. 4, cf. lxvi. 17), is trouble for others, and in itself matured wickedness. Paul has made use of this ver. 7 in his contemplative description of the corruptness of mankind, Rom. iii. 14.

Ver. 8. The ungodly is described as a lier in wait; and one is reminded by it of such a state of anarchy, as that described in Hos. vi. 9 for instance. The picture fixes upon one simple feature in which the meanness of the ungodly culminates; and it is possible that it is intended to be taken as emblematical rather than literally. חָצֵר (from חָצַר to surround, cf. حظر ,حصر, and especially حضر) is a farm premises walled in (Arab. *ḥaḏar, ḥaḏâr, ḥaḏâra*), then losing the special characteristic of being walled round it

comes to mean generally a settled abode (with a house of
clay or stone) in opposition to a roaming life in tents (cf.
Lev. xxv. 31, Gen. xxv. 16). In such a place where men are
more sure of falling into his hands than in the open plain,
he lies in wait (יֵשֵׁב, like لَهُ قَعَدَ *subsedit* = *insidiatus est ei*),
murders unobserved him who had never provoked his ven-
geance, and his eyes לְהֶלְכָה יִצְפֹּנוּ. צָפָה to spie, xxxvii. 32,
might have been used instead of צָפַן; but צָפַן also obtains the
meaning, to lie in ambush (lvi. 7, Prov. i. 11, 18) from the
primary notion of restraining one's self (ضفن *fut. i.* in Beduin Arabic: to keep still, to be immoveably lost in thought,
vid. on Job xxiv. 1), which takes a transitive turn in צָפַן
"to conceal". חֶלְכָה, the dative of the object, is pointed just
as though it came from חַיִל: Thy host, *i. e.* Thy church, O
Jahve. The pausal form accordingly is חֶלְכָה with *Segol*, in
ver. 14, not with *Tsere* as in incorrect editions. And the
appeal against this interpretation, which is found in the
plur. חלכאים ver. 10, is set aside by the fact that this plural
is taken as a double word: host (חֵל = חֵיל = חַיִל as in Obad.
ver. 20) of the troubled ones (בָּאִים, not as Ben-Labrat supposes, for נִבְאִים, but from כָּאָה weary, and mellow and de-
cayed), as the *Kerî* (which is followed by the Syriac version)
and the Masora direct, and accordingly it is pointed חֵלְכָּאִים
with *Tsere*. The punctuation therefore sets aside a word
which was unintelligible to it, and cannot be binding on us.
There is a verb הָלַךְ, which, it is true, does not occur in the
Old Testament, but in the Arabic, from the root حلك *firmus
fuit, firmum fecit* (whence also حلك intrans. to be firm,
fermé, i. e. closed), it gains the signification in reference to
colour: to be dark (cognate with חָכַל, whence חַכְלִילִי) and is
also transferred to the gloom and blackness of misfortune.*
From this an abstract is formed חֶלֶךְ or חֹלֶךְ (like חֹפֶשׁ):

---

* Cf. Samachschari's *Golden Necklaces*, Proverb 67, which Fleischer
translates: "Which is blacker: the plumage of the raven, which is black
as coal, or thy life, O stranger among strangers?" The word "blacker"
is here expressed by أَحْلَكُ, just as the verb حلك with its infinitives حَلَكَ or حُلْكَة and its derivatives is applied to sorrow and
misery.

blackness, misfortune, or also of a defective development
of the senses: imbecility; and from this an adjective חֶלְכָּה
‌= חֶלְכַי, or also (cf. חָפְשִׁי, עָלְפֶּה Ezek. xxxi. 15 = one in a
condition of languishing, עָלַף) חָלְכָּה = חֶלְכַי, *plur.* חֶלְכָּאִים,
after the form הוֹדָאִים, from הוֹדִי, Ew. § 189,*g.*

Ver. 9. The picture of the רָשָׁע, who is become as it
were a beast of prey, is now worked out further. The *lustrum*
of the lion is called סֹךְ Jer. xxv. 38, or סֻכָּה Job xxxviii. 40:
a thicket, from סָכַךְ, which means both to interweave and
to plait over = to cover (without any connection with שׁוֹךְ
a thorn, Arab. *shôk*, a thistle). The figure of the lion is
reversed in the second line, the עָנִי himself being compared
to the beast of prey and the רָשָׁע to a hunter who drives
him into the pit-fall and when he has fallen in hastens to
drag him away (מֶשַׁךְ, as in xxviii. 3, Job xxiv. 22) in, or by
means of (Hos. xi. 4, Job xl. 25), his net, in which he has
become entangled.

Vers. 10—11. The comparison to the lion is still in force
here and the description recurs to its commencement in the
second strophe, by tracing back the persecution of the ungodly to its final cause. Instead of the *Chethib* ודכה (וְדָכָה
perf. consec.), the *Kerî* reads יִדְכֶּה more in accordance with
the Hebrew use of the tenses. Job xxxviii. 40 is the rule
for the interpretation. The two futures depict the settled
and familiar lying in wait of the plunderer. True, the *Kal*
דָּכָה in the signification "to crouch down" finds no support
elsewhere; but the Arab. *dakka* to make even (cf. رصﺪ *firmiter inhæsit loco*, of the crouching down of beasts of prey,
of hunters, and of foes) and the Arab. *daǵǵa,* compared by
Hitzig, to move stealthily along, to creep, and *duǵjeh* a
hunter's hiding-place exhibit synonymous significations. The
ταπεινώσει αὐτόν of the LXX. is not far out of the way. And
one can still discern in it the assumption that the text is
to be read וְדָכֶה יִשַׁח: and crushed he sinks (Aquila: ὁ δὲ
λασθεὶς καμφθήσεται); but even דָּכָה is not found elsewhere,
and if the poet meant that, why could he not have written
נִדְכָּה? (cf. moreover Judges v. 27). If דָּכָה is taken in the
sense of a position in which one is the least likely to be
seen, then the first two verbs refer to the sculker, but the
third according to the usual *schema* (as *e. g.* cxxiv. 5) is the

predicate to חֶלְכָּאִים (חֵלְכָאִים) going before it. Crouching down as low as possible he lies on the watch, and the feeble and defenceless fall into his strong ones, עֲצוּמָיו, *i. e.* claws. Thus the ungodly slays the righteous, thinking within himself: God has forgotten, He has hidden His face, *i. e.* He does not concern Himself about these poor creatures and does not wish to know anything about them (the denial of the truth expressed in ix. 13, 19.); He has in fact never been one who sees, and never will be. These two thoughts are blended; בַּל with the *perf.* as in xxi. 3, and the addition of לָנֶצַח (cf. xciv. 7) denies the possibility of God seeing now any more than formerly, as being an absolute absurdity. The thought of a personal God would disturb the ungodly in his doings, he therefore prefers to deny His existence, and thinks: there is only fate and fate is blind, only an absolute and it has no eyes, only a notion and that cannot interfere in the affairs of men.

Vers. 12—13. The six strophes, in which the consecutive letters from מ to צ are wanting, are completed, and now the acrostic strophes begin again with ק. In contrast to those who have no God, or only a lifeless idol, the psalmist calls upon his God, the living God, to destroy the appearance that He is not an omniscient Being, by arising to action. We have more than one name of God used here; אֵל is a vocative just as in xvi. 1, lxxxiii, 2, cxxxix. 17, 23. He is to lift up His hand in order to help and to punish (נָשָׂא יָד, whence comes the *imperat.* נְשָׂא = שָׂא, cf. נָסָה iv. 7, like שְׁלַח יָד cxxxviii. 7 and נָטָה יָד Ex. vii. 5 elsewhere). Forget not is equivalent to: fulfil the לֹא שָׁכַח of ix. 13, put to shame the שָׁכַח אֵל of the ungodly, ver. 11! Our translation follows the *Kerî* עֲנָוִים. That which is complained of in vers. 3, 4 is put in the form of a question to God in ver. 13: wherefore (עַל־מֶה, instead of which we find עַל־מָה in Num. xxii. 32, Jer. ix. 11, because the following words begin with letters of a different class) does it come to pass, *i. e.* is it permitted to come to pass? On the *perf.* in this interrogative clause *vid.* xi. 3. מַדּוּעַ inquires the cause, לָמָה the aim, and עַל־מֶה the motive, or in general the reason: on what ground, since God's holiness can suffer no injury to His honour?

On לֹא תִדְרשׁ with כִּי, the *oratio directa* instead of *obliqua*, *vid.* on ix. 21.

Ver. 14. Now comes the confirmation of his cry to God: It is with Him entirely different from what the ungodly imagine. They think that He will not punish; but He does see (cf. 2 Chron. xxiv. 22), and the psalmist knows and confesses it: רָאִתָה (defective = רָאִיתָה xxxv. 22), Thou hast seen and dost see what is done to Thine own, what is done to the innocent. This he supports by a conclusion *a genere ad speciem* thus: the trouble which is prepared for others, and the sorrow (כַּעַס, as in Eccl. vii. 3) which they cause them, does not escape the all-seeing eye of God, He notes it all, to give it into (lay it in) His hand. "To give anything into any one's hand" is equivalent to, into his power (1 Kings xx. 28, and frequently), or into any one's care (Gen. xxxii. 17, and frequently); but here God gives (lays) the things which are not to be administered, but requited, into His own hand. The expression is meant to be understood according to lvi. 9, cf. Isa. xlix. 16: He is observant of the afflictions of His saints, laying them up in His hand and preserving them there in order, in His own time, to restore them to His saints in joy, and to their enemies in punishment. Thus, therefore, the feeble and helpless (read חֵלְכָה or חֵלְכֶה; according to the Masoretic text חֵלְכָה Thy host, not חֵלְכָה, which is contrary to the character of the form, as pausal form for חֶלְכָה) can leave to Him, viz. all his burden (יְהָבוֹ, lv. 23), everything that vexes and disquiets him. Jahve has been and will be the Helper of the fatherless. יָתוֹם stands prominent by way of emphasis, like אוֹתָם ix. 13, and Bakius rightly remarks *in voce pupilli synecdoche est, complectens omnes illos, qui humanis præsidiis destituuntur.*

Vers. 15—16. The desire for Jahve's interposition now rises again with fresh earnestness. It is a mistake to regard דָּרַשׁ and מָצָא as correlative notions. In the phrase to seek and not find, when used of that which has totally disappeared, we never have דָּרַשׁ, but always בִּקֵּשׁ, xxxvii. 36, Isa. xli. 12, Jer. l. 20, and frequently. The verb דָּרַשׁ signifies here exactly the same as in vers. 4, 13, and ix. 13: "and the wicked (*nom. absol.* as in ver. 4) — mayst Thou punish his

wickedness, mayst Thou find nothing more of it". It is not
without a meaning that, instead of the form of expression
usual elsewhere (xxxvii. 36, Job xx. 8), the address to Jahve
is retained: that which is no longer visible to the eye of
God, not merely of man, has absolutely vanished out of
existence. This absolute conquest of evil is to be as surely
looked for, as that Jahve's universal kingship, which has
been an element of the creed of God's people ever since the
call and redemption of Israel (Ex. xv. 18), cannot remain
without being perfectly and visibly realised. His absolute
and eternal kingship must at length be realised, even in all
the universality and endless duration foretold in Zech. xiv.
9, Dan. vii. 14, Apoc. xi. 15. Losing himself in the contemplation of this kingship, and beholding the kingdom of God,
the kingdom of good, as realised, the psalmist's vision
stretches beyond the foes of the church at home to its foes
in general; and, inasmuch as the heathen in Israel and the
heathen world outside of Israel are blended together into
one to his mind, he comprehends them all in the collective
name of גוֹיִם, and sees the land of Jahve (Lev. xxv. 23),
the holy land, purified of all oppressors hostile to the church
and its God. It is the same that is foretold by Isaiah (lii. 1),
Nahum (ii. 1), and in other passages, which, by the anticipation of faith, here stands before the mind of the supplaint
as an accomplished fact — viz. the consummation of the
judgment, which has been celebrated in the hymnic half
(Ps. ix.) of this double Psalm as a judgment already executed
in part.

Vers. 17—18. Still standing on this eminence from which
he seems to behold the end, the poet basks in the realisation of that which has been obtained in answer to prayer.
The ardent longing of the meek and lowly sufferers for the
arising, the *parusia* of Jahve (Isa. xxvi. 8), has now been
heard by Him, and that under circumstances which find expression in the following *futt.*, which have a past signification: God has given and preserved to their hearts the right
disposition towards Himself (הֵכִין, as in lxxviii. 8, Job xi,
13, Sir. ii. 17 ἑτοιμάζειν καρδίας, post-biblical כֵּוֵּן* and to be

____

* *B. Berachoth* 31*a*: the man who prays must direct his heart
steadfastly towards God (יְכַוֵּן לִבּוֹ לַשָּׁמַיִם).

understood according to 1 Sam. vii. 3, 2 Chron. xx. 33, cf.
לֵב נָכוֹן li. 12, lxxviii. 37; it is equivalent to "the single eye"
in the language of the New Testament), just as, on the other
hand, He has set His ear in the attitude of close attention
to their prayer, and even to their most secret sighings (הִקְשִׁיב
with אֹזֶן, as in Prov. ii. 2; to stiffen the ear, from קָשַׁב, قَسَبَ,
root קשׁ to be hard, rigid, firm, from which we also have
קָשֶׁה, قَسَا, קָשׁוּחַ, قَسَم, قَسَن, cf. on Isa. xxi. 7). It was a mutual relation, the design of which was finally and speedily
to obtain justice for the fatherless and oppressed, yea crushed,
few, in order that mortal man of the earth may no longer
(בַּל, as in Isa. xiv. 21, and in post-biblical Hebrew בַּל and
לְבַל instead of פֶּן) terrify. From the parallel conclusion, ix.
20, 21, it is to be inferred that אֱנוֹשׁ does not refer to the
oppressed but to the oppressor, and is therefore intended
as the subject; and then the phrase מִן־הָאָרֶץ also belongs to
it, as in xvii. 14, people of the world, lxxx. 14 boar of the
woods, whereas in Prov. xxx. 14 מֵאֶרֶץ belongs to the verb
(to devour from off the earth). It is only in this combination
that אֱנוֹשׁ מִן־הָאָרֶץ forms with לַעֲרֹץ a significant paronoma-
sia, by contrasting the conduct of the tyrant with his true
nature: a mortal of the earth, *i. e.* a being who, far removed
from any possibility of vying with the God who is in heaven,
has the earth as his birth-place. It is not מִן־הָאֲדָמָה, for the
earth is not referred to as the material out of which man
is formed, but as his ancestral house, his home, his bound,
just as in the expression of John ὁ ὢν ἐκ τῆς γῆς, iii. 31
(Lat. *ut non amplius terreat homo terrenus*). A similar play
of words was attempted before in ix. 20 אַל־יָעֹז אֱנוֹשׁ. The
Hebrew verb עָרַץ signifies both to give way to fear, Deut.
vii. 21, and to put in fear, Isa. ii. 19, 21, xlvii. 12. It does
mean "to defy, rebel against", although it might have this
meaning according to the Arabic عرض (to come in the way,
withstand, according to which Wetzstein explains עָרוּץ Job
xxx. 6, like عِرْض, "a valley that runs slantwise across a
district, a gorge that blocks up the traveller's way".*). It
is related to عرض to vibrate, tremble (*e. g.* of lightning).

---

* *Zeitschrift für Allgem. Erdkunde* xviii (1865) 1, S. 30.

PSALM XI.

REFUSAL TO FLEE WHEN IN A PERILOUS SITUATION.

1 IN Jahve put I my trust — how say ye to my soul:
"Flee to your mountain [as] a bird!

2 "For, lo, the wicked have bent the bow,
"They have made ready their arrow upon the string,
"To shoot the upright in heart in the dark.

3 "When the pillars are pulled down,
"The righteous — what will he do?!"

4 Jahve in His holy temple,
Jahve, who hath His throne in heaven —
His eyes behold, His eyelids try the children of men.

5 Jahve, He trieth the righteous,
And the wicked and him that loveth violence His soul
hateth.

6 Upon the wicked He shall rain snares;
Fire, brimstone, and burning wind is the portion of
their cup.

7 For Jahve is righteous, loving righteousness:
The upright shall behold His countenance.

Ps. xi., which likewise confidently sets the all-seeing eye
of Jahve before the ungodly who carry out their murderous
designs under cover of the darkness, is placed after Ps. x.
The life of David (to whom even Hitzig and Ewald ascribe
this Psalm) is threatened, the pillars of the state are shaken,
they counsel the king to flee to the mountains. These are
indications of the time when the rebellion of Absolom was
secretly preparing, but still clearly discernible. Although
hurrying on with a swift measure and clear in the principal thoughts, still this Psalm is not free from difficult points,
just as it is with all the Psalms which contain similar dark
passages from the internal condition of Israel. The gloomy
condition of the nation seems to be reflected in the very
language. The strophic plan is not easily discernible; nevertheless we cannot go far wrong in dividing the Psalm into
two seven line strophes with a two line *epiphonema*.

Vers. 1—3. David rejects the advice of his friends to
save his life by flight. Hidden in Jahve (xvi. 1, xxxvi. 8)
he needs no other refuge. However well-meant and well-
grounded the advice, he considers it too full of fear and is
himself too confident in God, to follow it. David also introduces his friends as speaking in other passages in the Psalms
belonging to the period of the Absolom persecution, iii. 3,
iv. 7. Their want of courage, which he afterwards had to
reprove and endeavour to restore, shewed itself even before
the storm had burst, as we see here. With the words "how
can you say" he rejects their proposal as unreasonable, and
turns it as a reproach against them. If the *Chethîb*, נוּדִי, is
adopted, then those who are well-disposed, say to David,
including with him his nearest subjects who are faithful to
him: retreat to your mountain, (ye) birds (צִפּוֹר collective
as in viii. 9, cxlviii. 10); or, since this address sounds too
derisive to be appropriate to the lips of those who are supposed to be speaking here: like birds (*comparatio decurtata*
as in xxii. 14, lviii. 9, Job xxiv. 5, Isa. xxi. 8). הָרְכֶם which
seems more natural in connection with the vocative rendering of צִפּוֹר (cf. Isa. xviii. 6 with Ezek. xxxix. 4) may also
be explained, with the comparative rendering, without any
need for the conjecture הר כמו צפור (cf. Deut. xxxiii. 19), as a
retrospective glance at the time of the persecution under Saul:
to the mountains, which formerly so effectually protected
you (cf. 1 Sam. xxvi. 20, xxiii. 14). But the *Kerî*, which is
followed by the ancient versions, exchanges נוּדוּ for נוּדִי, cf.
שְׁחִי Isa. li. 23. Even reading it thus we should not take
צִפּוֹר, which certainly is epicœne, as vocative: flee to your
mountain, O bird (Hitz.); and for this reason, that this form
of address is not appropriate to the idea of those who pro-
fer their counsel. But we should take it as an equation
instead of a comparison: fly to your mountain (which gave
you shelter formerly), a bird, *i. e.* after the manner of a bird
that flies away to its mountain home when it is chased in
the plain. But this *Kerî* appears to be a needless correction,
which removes the difficulty of נוּדוּ coming after לְנַפְשִׁי, by
putting another in the place of this *synallage numeri.**

---

* According to the above rendering: "Flee ye to your mountain,

In ver. 2 the faint-hearted ones give as the ground of their advice, the fearful peril which threatens from the side of crafty and malicious foes. As הִנֵּה implies, this danger is imminent. The perfect overrides the future: they are not only already in the act of bending the bow, they have made ready their arrow, *i. e.* their deadly weapon, upon the string (יֶתֶר = מֵיתָר, xxi. 13, Arab. *watar,* from יָתַר, *watara,* to stretch tight, extend, so that the thing is continued in one straight line) and even taken aim, in order to discharge it (יָרָה with לְ of the aim, as in lxiv. 5, with *acc.* of the object) in the dark (*i. e.* secretly, like an assassin) at the upright (those who by their character are opposed to them). In ver. 3 the faint-hearted still further support their advice from the present total subversion of justice. הַשָּׁתוֹת are either the highest ranks, who support the edifice of the state, according to Isa. xix. 10, or, according to lxxxii. 5, Ezek. xxx. 4, the foundations of the state, upon whom the existence and well-being of the land depends. We prefer the latter, since the king and those who are loyal to him, who are associated in thought with צַדִּיק, are compared to the שָׁתוֹת. The construction of the clause beginning with כִּי is like Job xxxviii. 41. The *fut.* has a present signification. The *perf.* in the principal clause, as it frequently does elsewhere (*e. g.* xxxix. 8, lx. 11, Gen. xxi. 7, Num. xxiii. 10, Job xii. 9, 2 Kings xx. 9) in interrogative sentences, corresponds to the Latin conjunctive (here *quid fecerit*), and is to be expressed in English by the auxiliary verbs: when the bases of the state are shattered, what can the righteous do? he can do nothing. And all counter-effort is so useless that it is well to be as far from danger as possible.

Vers. 4—6. The words of David's counsellors who fear for him are now ended. And David justifies his confidence in God with which he began his song. Jahve sits enthroned

---

a bird" it would require to be accented נוּדוּ הַרְכֶם צִפּוֹן (as a transformation from נוּדוּ הַרְכֶם צִפּוֹר, *vid.* Baer's *Accentssystem* XVIII. 2). The interpunction as we have it, נוּדוּ הַרְכֶם צִפּוֹר, harmonises with the interpretation of Varenius as of Löb Spira (*Pentateuch-Comm.* 1815): *Fugite (o socii Davidis), mons vester (h. e. præsidium vestrum,* Ps. xxx. 8, *cui innitimini) est avis errans.*

above all that takes place on earth that disheartens those of little faith. At an infinite distance above the earth, and also above Jerusalem, now in rebellion, is a הֵיכַל קֹדֶשׁ, xviii. 7, xxix. 9, and in this holy temple is Jahve, the Holy One. Above the earth are the heavens, and in heaven is the throne of Jahve, the King of kings. And this temple, this palace in the heavens, is the place whence issues the final decision of all earthly matters, Hab. ii. 20, Mic. i. 2. For His throne above is also the super-terrestrial judgment-seat, ix. 8, ciii. 19. Jahve who sits thereon is the all-seeing and omniscient One. חָזָה prop. to split, cf. *cernere,* is used here according to its radical meaning, of a sharp piercing glance. בָּחַן prop. to try metals by fire, of a fixed and penetrating look that sees into a thing to the foundation of its inmost nature. The mention of the eyelids is intentional. When we observe a thing closely or ponder over it, we draw the eyelids together, in order that our vision may be more concentrated and direct, and become, as it were, one ray piercing through the object. Thus are men open to the all-seeing eyes, the all-searching looks of Jahve: the just and the unjust alike. He tries the righteous, *i. e.* He knows that in the depth of his soul there is an upright nature that will abide all testing (xvii. 3, Job xxiii. 10), so that He lovingly protects him, just as the righteous lovingly depends upon Him. And His soul hates (*i. e.* He hates him with all the energy of His perfectly and essentially holy nature) the evil-doer and him that delights in the violence of the strong towards the weak. And the more intense this hatred, the more fearful will be the judgments in which it bursts forth.

Ver. 7, which assumes a declaration of something that is near at hand, is opposed to our rendering the voluntative form of the *fut.,* יַמְטֵר, as expressive of a wish. The shorter form of the future is frequently indicative in the sense of the future, *e. g.* lxxii. 13, or of the present, *e. g.* lviii. 5, or of the past, xviii. 12. Thus it here affirms a fact of the future which follows as a necessity from vers. 4, 5. Assuming that פֶּחִים might be equivalent to פֶּחָמִים, even then the Hebrew פֶּחָם, according to the general usage of the language, in distinction from גַּחֶלֶת, does not denote burning, but black coals. It ought therefore to have been פֶּחֲמֵי אֵשׁ. Hitzig reads פֶּחָים from פִּיחַ ashes; but a rain of ashes is no medium of punishment. Böttcher translates it "lumps" according to Ex. xxxix. 3, Num. xvii. 3; but in these passages the word means thin plates. We adhere to the signification snares, Job xxii. 10, cf. xxi. 17, Prov. xxii. 5; and following the accentuation, we understand it to be a means of punishment by itself. First of all descends a whole discharge of missiles which render all attempt at flight impossible, viz. lightnings; for the lightning striking out its course and travelling from one point in the distance, bending itself like a serpent, may really be compared to a snare, or noose, thrown down from above. In addition to fire and brimstone (Gen. xix. 24) we have also רוּחַ זִלְעָפוֹת. The LXX. renders it πνεῦμα καταιγίδος, and the Targum וַעֲפָא עָלְעוּלָא, *procella turbinea*. The root is not לעף, which cannot be sustained as a cognate form of לאב, להב to burn, but זעף, which (as Sam. v. 10 shews) exactly corresponds to the Latin *æstuare* which combines in itself the characteristics of heat and violent motion, therefore perhaps: a wind of flames, *i. e.* the deadly simoom, which, according to the present division of the verse is represented in connection with אֵשׁ וְגָפְרִית, as the breath of the divine wrath pouring itself forth like a stream of brimstone, Isa. xxx. 33. It thus also becomes clear how this can be called the portion of their cup, *i. e.* what is adjudged to them as the contents of their cup which they must drain off. מְנָת (only found in the Davidic Psalms, with the exception of 2 Chron. xxxi. 4) is both *absolutivus* and *constructivus* according to Olshausen (§§ 108, *c*, 165, *i*), and is derived from *manajath,* or *manawath,* with the original feminine termination *ath,* the final weak radical being blended with it. According to Hupfeld it is *constr.*, springing from מְנָיַת, like קְצָת (in Dan. and Neh.) from קַצְוַת. But probably it is best to regard it as = מְנָוֹת or מְנָיַת, like גְּלוֹת = גָּלֹות.

Ver. 7. Thus then Jahve is in covenant with David. Even though he cannot defend himself against his enemies, still, when Jahve gives free course to His hatred in judgment, they will then have to do with the powers of wrath and death, which they will not be able to escape. When the closing distich bases this different relation of God towards the righteous and the unrighteous and this judgment of the

latter on the righteousness of God, we at once perceive what
a totally different and blessed end awaits the righteous. As
Jahve Himself is righteous, so also on His part (1 Sam. xii.
7, Mic. vi. 5, and frequently) and on the part of man (Isa.
xxxiii. 15) He loves צְדָקוֹת, the works of righteousness. The
object of אָהֵב (= אֹהֵב) stands at the head of the sentence,
as in xcix. 4, cf. x. 14. In ver. 7*b* יָשָׁר designates the upright
as a class, hence it is the more natural for the predicate to
follow in the *plur.* (cf. ix. 7, Job viii. 19) than to precede
as elsewhere (Prov. xxviii. 1, Isa. xvi. 4). The rendering:
"His countenance looks upon the upright man" (Hengst. and
others) is not a probable one, just because one expects to
find something respecting the end of the upright in contrast
to that of the ungodly. This rendering is also contrary
to the general usage of the language, according to which
פנים is always used only as that which is to be seen, not as
that which itself sees. It ought to have been עֵינֵימוֹ, xxxiii.
18, xxxiv. 16, Job xxxvi. 7. It must therefore be translated
according to xvii. 15, cxl. 13: the upright (*quisquis probus
est*) shall behold His countenance. The pathetic form פָּנִימוֹ
instead of פָּנָיו was specially admissible here, where God is
spoken of (as in Deut. xxxiii. 2, cf. Isa. xliv. 15). It ought
not to be denied any longer that *mo* is sometimes (*e. g.* Job
xx. 23, cf. xxii. 2, xxvii. 23) a dignified singular suffix. To
behold the face of God is in itself impossible to mortals
without dying. But when God reveals Himself in love, then
He makes His countenance bearable to the creature. And
to enjoy this vision of God softened by love is the highest
honour God in His mercy can confer on a man; it is the
blessedness itself that is reserved for the upright, cxl. 14.
It is not possible to say that what is intended is a future
vision of God; but it is just as little possible to say that
it is exclusively a vision in this world. To the Old Testament conception the future עוֹלָם is certainly lost in the night
of Sheôl. But faith broke through this night, and consoled
itself with a future beholding of God, Job xix. 26. The redemption of the New Testament has realised this aspiration
of faith, since the Redeemer has broken through the night
of the realm of the dead, has borne on high with Him the

Old Testament saints, and translated them into the sphere
of the divine love revealed in heaven.

PSALM XII.

LAMENT AND CONSOLATION IN THE MIDST OF PREVAILING FALSEHOOD.

2 HELP, Jahve, for the godly man ceaseth,
   For the faithful have vanished- from among the children
      of men!
3 They speak falsehood one with another,
   Flattering lips with a double heart, they speak.

4 May Jahve root out all flattering lips,
   The tongue that speaketh great swelling words,
5 Which say: to our tongue we impart strength,
   Our lips are with us, who is lord over us?!

6 "Because of the desolation of the afflicted, the sighing
      of the poor,
   "Will I now arise — saith Jahve —
   "In safety will I set him who languisheth for it." —
7 The words of Jahve are pure words,
   Silver melted down in the furnace, to the earth,
   Purified seven times.

8 Thou, O Jahve, wilt defend them,
   Thou wilt preserve him from this generation for ever;
9 The wicked strut about on every side,
   When vileness among the children of men is exalted.

Ps. xi. is appropriately followed by Ps. xii., which is of
a kindred character: a prayer for the deliverance of the poor
and miserable in a time of universal moral corruption, and
more particularly of prevailing faithlessness and boasting.
The inscription: *To the Precentor, on the Octave, a Psalm of
David* points us to the time when the Temple music was being
established, *i. e.* the time of David—incomparably the best
age in the history of Israel, and yet, viewed in the light of the

spirit of holiness, an age so radically corrupt. The true people
of Jahve were even then, as ever, a church of confessors and
martyrs, and the sighing for the coming of Jahve was then
not less deep than the cry "Come, Lord Jesus!" at the present
time.

This Ps. xii. together with Ps. ii. is a second example of
the way in which the psalmist, when under great excitement
of spirit, passes over into the tone of one who directly hears
God's words, and therefore into the tone of an inspired
prophet. Just as lyric poetry in general, as being a direct
and solemn expression of strong inward feeling, is the
earliest form of poetry: so psalm-poetry contains in itself
not only the *mashal,* the epos, and the drama in their preformative stages, but prophecy also, as we have it in the
prophetic writings of its most flourishing period, has, as it
were, sprung from the bosom of psalm-poetry. It is throughout a blending of prophetical epic and subjective lyric elements, and is in many respects the echo of earlier psalms,
and even in some instances (as *e.g.* Isa. xii., Hab. iii.) transforms itself into the strain of a psalm. Hence Asaph is called
הַחֹזֶה in 2 Chron. xxix. 30, not from the special character
of his Psalms, but from his being a psalmist in general; for
Jeduthun has the same name given to him in 2 Chron. xxxv.
15, and נִבָּא in 1 Chron. xxv. 2 sq. (cf. προφητεύειν, Luke i.
67) is used directly as an epithet for psalm-singing with
accompaniment — a clear proof that in prophecy the co-
operation of a human element is no less to be acknowledged,
than the influence of a divine element in psalm-poesy.

The direct words of Jahve, and the psalmist's Amen to
them, form the middle portion of this Psalm — a six line
strophe, which is surrounded by four line strophes.

Vers. 2 — 3. The sigh of supplication, הוֹשִׁיעָה, has its
object within itself: work deliverance, give help; and the
motive is expressed by the complaint which follows. The
verb גָּמַר to complete, means here, as in vii. 10, to have an
end; and the ἀπ. λεγ. פָּסַם is equivalent to אָפֵס in lxxvii. 9,
to come to the extremity, to cease. It is at once clear from
the predicate being placed first in the *plur.,* that אֱמוּנִים in
this passage is not an *abstractum,* as *e. g.* in Prov. xiii. 17.;
moreover the parallelism is against it, just as in xxxi. 24.

חָסִיד is the pious man, as one who practises חֶסֶד towards God and man. אֵמוּן, primary form אָמוּן (plur. אֱמוּנִים; whereas from אָמוּן we should expect אֱמוּנִים), — used as an adjective (cf. on the contrary Deut. xxxii. 20) here just as in xxxi. 24, 2 Sam. xx. 19, — is the reliable, faithful, conscientious man, literally one who is firm, *i. e.* whose word and meaning is firm, so that one can rely upon it and be certain in relation to it.* We find similar complaints of the universal prevalence of wickedness in Mic. vii. 2, Isa. lvii. 1, Jer. vii. 28, and elsewhere. They contain their own limitation. For although those who complain thus without pharisaic self-righteousness would convict themselves of being affected by the prevailing corruption, they are still, in their penitence, in their sufferings for righteousness' sake, and in their cry for help, a standing proof that humanity has not yet, without exception, become a *massa perdita*. That which the writer especially laments, is the prevailing untruthfulness. Men speak שָׁוְא (= שָׁוְא from שׁוא), desolation and emptiness under a disguise that conceals its true nature, falsehood (xli. 7), and hypocrisy (Job xxxv. 13), ἕκαστος πρὸς τὸν πλησίον αὐτοῦ (LXX., cf. Ephes. iv. 25, where the greatness of the sin finds ιts confirmation according to the teaching of the New Testament: ὅτι ἐσμὲν ἀλλήλων μέλη). They speak lips of smoothnesses (חֲלָקוֹת, plural from חֲלָקָה, *lævitates*, or from חָלָק, *lævia*), *i. e.* the smoothest, most deceitful language (accusative of the object as in Isa. xix. 18) with a double heart, inasmuch, namely, as the meaning they deceitfully express to others, and even to themselves, differs from the purpose they actually cherish, or even (cf. 1 Chron. xii. 33 בלא לב ולב, and James i. 8 δίψυχος, wavering) inasmuch as the purpose they now so flatteringly put forth quickly changes to the very opposite.

Vers. 4—5. In this instance the voluntative has its own proper signification: may He root out (cf. cix. 15, and the oppositive xi. 6). Flattering lips and a vaunting tongue are

---

*The Aryan root *man* to remain, abide (Neo-Persic *mânden*), also takes a similar course, signifying usually "to continue in any course, wait, hope." So the old Persic *man*, Zend *upaman*, cf. μένειν with its derivatives which are applied in several ways in the New Testament to characterise πίστις.

one, insofar as the braggart becomes a flatterer when it serves his own selfish interest. אֲשֶׁר refers to lips and tongue, which are put for their possessors. The *Hiph.* הִגְבִּיר may mean either to impart strength, or to give proof of strength. The combination with לְ, not בְּ, favours the former: we will give emphasis to our tongue (this is their self-confident declaration). Hupfeld renders it, contrary to the meaning of the *Hiph.*: over our tongue we have power, and Ewald and Olshausen, on the ground of an erroneous interpretation of Dan. ix. 27, render: we make or have a firm covenant with our tongue. They describe their lips as being their confederates (אֵת as in 2 Kings ix. 32), and by the expression "who is lord over us" they declare themselves to be absolutely free, and exalted above all authority. If any authority were to assert itself over them, their mouth would put it down and their tongue would thrash it into submission. But Jahve, whom this making of themselves into gods challenges, will not always suffer His own people to be thus enslaved.

Vers. 6—7. In ver. 6 the psalmist hears Jahve Himself speak; and in ver. 7 he adds his Amen. The two מִן in ver. 6 denote the motive, עַתָּה the decisive turning-point from forebearance to the execution of judgment, and יֹאמַר the divine determination, which has just now made itself audible; cf. Isaiah's echo of it, Isa. xxxiii. 10. Jahve has hitherto looked on with seeming inactivity and indifference, now He will arise and place in יֵשַׁע, *i. e* a condition of safety (cf. שִׁית בַּחַיִּים, lxvi. 9), him who languishes for deliverance. It is not to be explained: him whom he, *i. e.* the boaster, blows upon, which would be expressed by יָפִיחַ בּוֹ, cf. x, 5; but, with Ewald, Hengstenberg, Olshausen, and Böttcher, according to Hab. ii. 3, where הֵפִיחַ לְ occurs in the sense of panting after an object: him who longs for it. יָפִיחַ is, however, not a participial adjective = יָפֵחַ, but the *fut.*, and יָפִיחַ לוֹ is therefore a relative clause occupying the place of the object, just as we find the same thing occurring in Job xxiv. 19, Isa. xli. 2, 25, and frequently. Hupfeld's rendering: "in order that he may gain breath (*respiret*)" leaves אָשִׁית without an object, and accords more with Aramaic and Arabic than with

Hebrew usage, which would express this idea by יָנוּחַ לוֹ or
יִרְוַח לוֹ.

In ver. 7 the announcement of Jahve is followed by
its echo in the heart of the seer: the words (אֲמָרוֹת instead
of אִמְרוֹת by changing the *Shebâ* which closes the syllable
into an audible one, as *e.g.* in אַשְׁרֵי) of Jahve are pure words,
i. e. intended, and to be fulfilled, absolutely as they run
without any admixture whatever of untruthfulness. The
poetical אִמְרָה (after the form זִמְרָה) serves pre-eminently as
the designation of the divine power-words of promise. The
figure, which is indicated in other instances, when God's
word is said to be צְרוּפָה (xviii. 31, cxix. 140, Prov. xxx. 5),
is here worked out: silver melted and thus purified בַּעֲלִיל
לָאָרֶץ. עֲלִיל signifies either a smelting-pot from עָלַל, غَلّ,
immittere, whence also עָל (Hitz.); or, what is more probable
since the language has the epithets כּוּר and מַצְרֵף for this: a
workshop, from עָלַל, عَلّ, *operari* (prop. to set about a thing),
first that which is wrought at (after the form שְׁבִיל, פְּסִיל, מְעִיל),
then the place where the work is carried on. From this also
comes the Talm. בַּעֲלִיל = בְּגָלוּי *manifeste*, occurring in the
Mishna *Rosh ha-Shana* i. 5 and elsewhere, and which in its
first meaning corresponds to the French *en effet*.* According to this, the ל in לָאָרֶץ is not the ל of property: in a fining-
pot built into the earth, for which לארץ without anything
further would be an inadequate and colourless expression.
But in accordance with the usual meaning of לארץ as a
collateral definition it is: smelted (purified) down to the
earth. As Olshausen observes on this subject, "Silver that
is purified in the furnace and flows down to the ground can
be seen in every smelting hut; the pure liquid silver flows
down out of the smelting furnace, in which the ore is piled
up." For it cannot be ל of reference: "purified with respect
to the earth", since ארץ does not denote the earth as a material and cannot therefore mean an earthy element. We
ought then to read לָאָבֶץ, which would not mean "to a white
brilliancy", *i. e.* to a pure bright mass (Böttch.), but "with

------

* On this word with reference to this passage of the Psalm *vid.*
Steinschneider's *Hebr. Bibliographie* 1861, S. 83.

respect to the *stannum,* lead" (*vid.* on Isa. i. 25). The verb
זָקַק to strain, filter, cause to ooze through, corresponds to
the German *seihen, seigen,* old High German *sîhan,* Greek
σακκεῖν (σακκίζειν), to clean by passing through a cloth as a
strainer, שֵׂק. God's word is solid silver smelted and leaving
all impurity behind, and, as it were, having passed seven
times through the smelting furnace, *i. e.* the purest silver,
entirely purged from dross. Silver is the emblem of everything precious and pure (*vid.* Bähr, *Symbol.* i, 284); and
seven is the number indicating the completion of any process (*Bibl. Psychol.* S. 57., transl. p. 71).

Vers. 8 — 9. The supplicatory complaint contained in
the first strophe has passed into an ardent wish in the second; and now in the fourth there arises a consolatory hope
based upon the divine utterance which was heard in the
third strophe. The suffix *ēm* in ver. 8*a* refers to the miserable and poor; the suffix *ennu* in ver. 8*b* (him, not: us,
which would be pointed תִּצְּרֵנוּ, and more especially since it
is not preceded by תִּשְׁמְרֵנוּ) refers back to the man who
yearns for deliverance mentioned in the divine utterance,
ver. 6. The "preserving for ever" is so constant, that neither
now nor at any future time will they succumb to this generation. The oppression shall not become a thorough depression, the trial shall not exceed their power of endurance.
What follows in ver. 9 is a more minute description of this
depraved generation. הַדּוֹר is the generation whole and entire
bearing one general character and doing homage to the one
spirit of the age (cf. *e. g.* Prov. xxx. 11 — 14, where the
characteristics of a corrupt age are portrayed). זוּ (always
without the article, Ew. § 293,*a*) points to the present and
the character it has assumed, which is again described here
finally in a few outlines of a more general kind than in
vers. 3—5. The wicked march about on every side (הִתְהַלֵּךְ
used of going about unopposed with an arrogant and vaunting mien), when (while) vileness among (לְ) the children
of men rises to eminence (רוּם as in Prov. xi. 11, cf. מְשֹׁל
Prov. xxix. 2), so that they come to be under its dominion. Vileness is called זֻלּוּת from זָלַל (cogn. דָּלַל) to be
supple and lax, narrow, low, weak and worthless. The form
is passive just as is the Talm. זִילוּת (from זִיל = זְלִיל), and it

is the epithet applied to that which is depreciated, despised,
and to be despised; here it is the opposite of the disposition
and conduct of the noble man, נָדִיב, Isa. xxxii. 8, — a base-
ness which is utterly devoid not only of all nobler principles and motives, but also of all nobler feelings and impulses. The כְּ of כְּרֻם is not the expression of simultaneousness (as *e. g.* in Prov. x. 25): immediately it is exalted —
for then ver. 9 would give expression to a general observation, instead of being descriptive — but כְּרֻם is equivalent
to בְּרֻם, only it is intentionally used instead of the latter,
to express a coincidence that is based upon an intimate relation of cause and effect, and is not merely accidental.
The wicked are puffed up on all sides, and encompass the
better disposed on every side as their enemies. Such is the
state of things, and it cannot be otherwise at a time when
men allow meanness to gain the ascendency among and over
them, as is the case at the present moment. Thus even at
last the depressing view of the present prevails in the amidst
of the confession of a more consolatory hope. The present
is gloomy. But in the central hexastich the future is lighted
up as a consolation against this gloominess. The Psalm is
a ring and this central oracle is its jewel.

P S A L M XIII.

SUPPLIANT CRY OF ONE WHO IS UTTERLY UNDONE.

2 HOW long, Jahve, wilt Thou forget me,
   How long wilt Thou veil Thy face from me?!
3 How long shall I cherish cares in my soul,
   Sorrow in my heart by day?!
   How long shall mine enemy be exalted over me?!

4 Look, answer me, Jahve, my God,
   Lighten mine eyes, that I fall not asleep in death,
5 That mine enemy may not say: "I have prevailed against
       him",
   That mine oppressors may not rejoice, when I stumble.

6 And as for me, in Thy mercy do I trust,
My heart shall rejoice at Thy salvation;
I will sing of Jahve, because He hath dealt bountifully
with me.

The יָרוּם of the personal cry with which David opens Ps. xiii. harmonizes with כְּרֻם of the general lament which he introduces into Ps. xii.; and for this reason the collector has coupled these two Psalms together. Hitzig assigns Ps. xiii. to the time when Saul posted watchers to hunt David from place to place, and when, having been long and unceasingly persecuted, David dared to cherish a hope of escaping death only by indefatigable vigilance and endurance. Perhaps this view is correct. The Psalm consists of three strophes, or if it be preferred, three groups of decreasing magnitude. A long deep sigh is followed, as from a relieved breast, by an already much more gentle and half calm prayer; and this again by the believing joy which anticipates the certainty of being answered. This song as it were casts up constantly lessening waves, until it becomes still as the sea when smooth as a mirror, and the only motion discernible at last is that of the joyous ripple of calm repose.

Vers. 2—3. The complicated question: till when, how long . . . for ever (as in lxxiv. 10, lxxix. 5, lxxxix. 47), is the expression of a complicated condition of soul, in which, as Luther briefly and forcibly describes it, amidst the feeling of anguish under divine wrath "hope itself despairs and despair nevertheless begins to hope". The self-contradiction of the question is to be explained by the conflict which is going on within between the flesh and the spirit. The dejected heart thinks: God has forgotten me for ever. But the spirit, which thrusts away this thought, changes it into a question which sets upon it the mark of a mere appearance not a reality: how long shall it seem as though Thou forgettest me for ever? It is in the nature of the divine wrath, that the feeling of it is always accompanied by an impression that it will last for ever; and consequently it becomes a foretaste of hell itself. But faith holds fast the love that is behind the wrath; it sees in the display of anger only a self-masking of the loving countenance of the God of love, and longs for the time when this loving countenance shall be again unveiled to it. Thrice does David send forth this cry of faith out of the inmost depths of his spirit. To place or set up contrivances, plans, or proposals in his soul, viz. as to the means by which he may be able to escape from this painful condition, is equivalent to, to make the soul the place of such thoughts, or the place where such thoughts are fabricated (cf. Prov. xxvi. 24). One such עֵצָה chases the other in his soul, because he recognises the vanity of one after another as soon us they spring up. With respect to the יוֹמָם which follows, we must think of these cares as taking possession of his soul in the night time; for the night leaves a man alone with his affliction and makes it doubly felt by him. It cannot be proved from Ezek. xxx. 16 (cf. Zeph. ii. 4 בַּצָּהֳרָיִם), that יוֹמָם like יוֹם (Jer. vii. 25, short for יוֹם יוֹם) may mean "daily" (Ew. § 313, a). יומם does not mean this here, but is the antithesis to לַיְלָה which is to be supplied in thought in ver. 3 a. By night he proposes plan after plan, each one as worthless as the other; and by day, or all the day through, when he sees his distress with open eyes, sorrow (יָגוֹן) is in his heart, as it were, as the feeling the night leaves behind it and as the direct reflex of his helpless and hopeless condition. He is persecuted, and his foe is in the ascendant. רוּם is both to be exalted and to rise, raise one's self, *i. e.* to rise to position and arrogantly to assume dignity to one's self (*sich brüsten*). The strophe closes with ʿad-āna which is used for the fourth time.

Vers. 4—5. In contrast to God's seeming to have forgotten him and to wish neither to see nor know anything of his need, he prays: הַבִּיטָה (cf. Isa. lxiii. 15). In contrast to his being in perplexity what course to take and unable to help himself, he prays: עֲנֵנִי, answer me, who cry for help, viz. by the fulfilment of my prayer as a real, actual answer. In contrast to the triumphing of his foe: הָאִירָה עֵינַי, in order that the triumph of his enemy may not be made complete by his dying. To lighten the eyes that are dimmed with sorrow and ready to break, is equivalent to, to impart new life (Ezra ix. 8), which is reflected in the fresh clear brightness of the eye (1 Sam. xiv. 27, 29). The lightening light, to which הָאִיר points, is the light of love beaming from the divine countenance, xxxi. 17. Light, love, and life are closely allied notions in the Scriptures. He, upon whom God looks down in love, continues in life, new powers of life are imparted to him, it is not his lot to sleep the death, *i. e.* the sleep of death, Jer. li. 39, 57, cf. Ps. lxxvi. 6. הַמָּוֶת is the accusative of effect or sequence: to sleep so that the sleep becomes death (LXX. εἰς θάνατον), Ew. § 281, *e.* Such is the light of life for which he prays, in order that his foe may not be able at last to say יְכָלְתִּיו (with accusative object, as in Jer. xxxviii. 5) = יְכֹלְתִּי לוֹ, cxxix. 2, Gen. xxxii. 26, I am able for him, a match for him, I am superior to him, have gained the mastery over him. כִּי, on account of the future which follows, had better be taken as temporal (*quum*) than as expressing the reason (*quod*), cf. בְּמוֹט רַגְלִי, xxxviii. 17.

Ver. 6. Three lines of joyous anticipation now follow the five of lament and four of prayer. By וַאֲנִי he sets himself in opposition to his foes. The latter desire his death, but he trusts in the mercy of God, who will turn and terminate his affliction. בָּטַח בְּ denotes faith as clinging fast to God, just as חָסָה בְ denotes it as confidence which hides itself in Him. The voluntative יָגֵל pre-supposes the sure realisation of the hope. The perfect in ver. 6*c* is to be properly understood thus: the celebration follows the fact that inspires him to song. גָּמַל עַל to do good to any one, as in cxvi. 7, cxix. 17, cf. the radically cognate נָמַר (על) lvii. 3. With the two iambics *gamál'aláj* the song sinks to rest. In the storm-tossed soul of the suppliant all has now become calm. Though it rage without as much now as ever — peace reigns in the depth of his heart.

PSALM XIV.

THE PREVAILING CORRUPTION AND THE REDEMPTION DESIRED

1 THE fool hath said in his heart: "There is no God";
  Corrupt, abominable are their doings,
  There is none that doeth good.

2 Jahve looketh down from heaven upon the children of
          men
  To see if there be any that have understanding,
  If any that seek after God.

3 They are all fallen away, altogether they are corrupt,
  There is none that doeth good,
  Not even one.

4 "Are they so utterly devoid of understanding, all the
          workers of iniquity,
  Who eating up my people, eat up bread,
  They call not on Jahve?"

5 Then were they in great fear,
  For God is in the righteous generation.

6 Would ye bring to shame the counsel of the afflicted,
  For Jahve is indeed his refuge!

7 Oh that the salvation of Israel were come out of Zion!
  When Jahve turneth the captivity of His people,
  Jacob shall rejoice, Israel shall be glad.

Just as the general lamentation of Ps. xii. assumes a
personal character in Ps. xiii., so in Ps. xiv. it becomes
again general; and the personal desire יָגֵל לִבִּי, xiii. 6, so full
of hope, corresponds to יָגֵל יַעֲקֹב, which is extended to the
whole people of God in xiv. 7. Moreover, Ps. xiv., as being
a gloomy picture of the times in which the dawn of the divine day is discernible in the background, is more closely
allied to Ps. xii. than to Ps. xiii., although this latter is
not inserted between them without some recognised reason.
In the reprobation of the moral and religious character of
the men of the age, which Ps. xiv. has in common with Ps.
xii., we at once have a confirmation of the לְדָוִד. But xiv. 7
does not necessitate our coming down to the time of the
Exile.

In Ps. liii. we find this Psalm which is Jehovic, occurring again as Elohimic. The position of Ps. xiv. in the
primary collection favours the presumption, that it is the
earlier and more original composition. And since this
presumption will bear the test of a critical comparison of

the two Psalms, we may leave the treatment of Ps. liii. to
its proper place, without bringing it forward here. It is not
as though Ps. xiv. were intact. It is marked out as seven
three-line verses, but vers. 5 and 6, which ought to be the
fifth and sixth three lines, are only two; and the original
form appears to be destroyed by some deficiency. The difficulty is got over in Ps. liii., by making the two two-line
verses into one three-line verse, so that it consists only of
six three-line verses. And in that Psalm the announcement
of judgment is applied to foreign enemies, a circumstance
which has influenced some critics and led them astray in the
interpretation of Ps. xiv.

Ver. 1. The perfect אָמַר, as in i. 1, x. 3, is the so-called
abstract present (Ges. § 126, 3), expressing a fact of universal experience, inferred from a number of single instances. The Old Testament language is unusually rich in epithets
for the unwise. The simple, פֶּתִי, and the silly, כְּסִיל, for the
lowest branches of this scale; the fool, אֱוִיל, and the madman, הוֹלֵל, the uppermost. In the middle comes the notion
of the simpleton or maniac, נָבָל, — a word from the verbal
stem נָבֵל which, according as that which forms the centre
of the group of consonants lies either in נב (*Genesis* S. 636),
or in בל (comp. אבל, אול, אמל, קמל), signifies either to be
extended, to relax, to become frail, to wither, or to be prominent, *eminere*, Arab. *nabula;* so that consequently נָבָל
means the relaxed, powerless, expressed in New Testament
language: πνεῦμα οὐκ ἔχοντα. Thus Isaiah (ch. xxxii. 6) describes the נָבָל: "a simpleton speaks simpleness and his heart
does godless things, to practice tricks and to say foolish
things against Jahve, to leave the soul of the hungry empty,
and to refuse drink to the thirsty." Accordingly נָבָל is the
synonym of לֵץ the scoffer (*vid.* the definition in Prov. xxi. 24).
A free spirit of this class is reckoned according to the
Scriptures among the empty, hollow, and devoid of mind.
The thought, אֵין אֱלֹהִים, which is the root of the thought
and action of such a man, is the climax of imbecility. It is
not merely practical atheism, that is intended by this maxim
of the נָבָל. The heart according to Scripture language is not
only the seat of volition, but also of thought. The נָבָל is

not content with acting as though there were no God, but directly denies that there is a God, *i.e.* a personal God. The psalmist makes this prominent as the very extreme and depth of human depravity, that there can be among men those who deny the existence of a God. The subject of what follows are, then, not these atheists but men in general, among whom such characters are to be found: they make the mode of action, (their) doings, corrupt, they make it abominable. עֲלִילָה, a poetical brevity of expression for עֲלִילוֹתָם, belongs to both verbs, which have *Tarcha* and *Mercha* (the two usual conjunctives of *Mugrash*) in correct texts; and is in fact not used as an adverbial accusative (Hengstenberg and others), but as an object, since הִשְׁחִית is just the word that is generally used in this combination with עֲלִילָה Zeph. iii. 7 or, what is the same thing, דֶּרֶךְ Gen. vi. 12; and הִתְעִיב (cf. 1 Kings xxi. 26) is only added to give a superlative intensity to the expression. The negative: "there is none that doeth good" is just as unrestricted as in xii. 2. But further on the psalmist distinguishes between a דּוֹר צַדִּיק, which experiences this corruption in the form of persecution, and the corrupt mass of mankind. He means what he says of mankind as κόσμος, in which, at first the few rescued by grace from the mass of corruption are lost sight of by him, just as in the words of God, Gen. vi. 5, 12. Since it is only grace that frees any from the general corruption, it may also be said, that men are described just as they are by nature; although, be it admitted, it is not hereditary sin but actual sin, which springs up from it, and grows apace if grace do not interpose, that is here spoken of.

Ver. 2. The second tristich appeals to the infallible decision of God Himself. The verb הִשְׁקִיף means to look forth, by bending one's self forward. It is the proper word for looking out of a window, 2 Kings ix. 30 (cf. *Niph.* Judges v. 28, and frequently), and for God's looking down from heaven upon the earth, cii. 20, and frequently; and it is cognate and synonymous with הִשְׁגִּיחַ, xxxiii. 13, 14; cf., moreover, Cant. ii. 9. The *perf.* is used in the sense of the perfect only insofar as the divine survey is antecedent to its result as given in ver. 3. Just as הִשְׁחִיתוּ reminds one of the history of the Flood, so does לִרְאוֹת of the history of the building of the tower of Babel, Gen. xi. 5, cf. xviii. 21. God's judgment rests upon a knowledge of the matter of fact, which is represented in such passages after the manner of men. God's all-seeing, all-piercing eyes scrutinise the whole human race. Is there one who shews discernment in thought and act, one to whom fellowship with God is the highest good, and consequently that after which he strives? — this is God's question, and He delights in such persons, and certainly none such would escape His longing search. On אֶת־אֱלֹהִים, τὸν Θεόν, *vid.*, Ges. § 117. 2.

Ver. 3. The third tristich bewails the condition in which He finds humanity. The universality of corruption is expressed in as strong terms as possible. הַכֹּל they all (*lit.* the totality); יַחְדָּו with one another (*lit.* in its or their unions, *i. e.*, *universi*); אֵין גַּם־אֶחָד not a single one who might form an exception. סָר (probably not 3 *præt.* but *partic.*, which passes at once into the finite verb) signifies to depart, viz. from the ways of God, therefore to fall away (ἀποστάτης). נֶאֱלָח, as in Job xv. 16, denotes the moral corruptness as a becoming sour, putrefaction, and suppuration. Instead of אֵין גַּם־אֶחָד, the LXX. translates οὐκ ἔστιν ἕως ἑνός (as though it were עַד־אֶחָד, which is the more familiar form of expression). Paul quotes the first three verses of this Psalm (Rom. iii. 10—12) in order to shew how the assertion, that Jews and heathen all are included under sin, is in accordance with the teaching of Scripture. What the psalmist says, applies primarily to Israel, his immediate neighbours, but at the same time to the heathen, as is self-evident. What is lamented is neither the pseudo-Israelitish corruption in particular, nor that of the heathen, but the universal corruption of man which prevails not less in Israel than in the heathen world. The citations of the apostle which follow his quotation of the Psalm, from τάφος ἀνεῳγμένος to ἀπέναντι τῶν ὀφθαλμῶν αὐτῶν were early incorporated in the Psalm in the Κοινή of the LXX. They appear as an integral part of it in the *Cod. Alex.*, in the Greco-Latin *Psalterium Veronense*, and in the Syriac *Psalterium Mediolanense*. They are also found in Apollinaris' paraphrase of the Psalms as a later interpolation; the *Cod. Vat.* has them in the margin; and the words σύντριμμα καὶ ταλαιπωρία ἐν ταῖς ὁδοῖς αὐτῶν have found admittance in the translation, which is more Rabbinical than Old Hebrew, מַזָּל רַע וּפְגַע רַע בְּדַרְכֵיהֶם even in a Hebrew codex (Kennicott 649). Origen rightly excluded this apostolic Mosaic work of Old Testament testimonies from his text of the Psalm; and the true representation of the matter is to be found in Jerome, in the preface to the xvi. book of his commentary on Isaiah.*

Ver. 4. Thus utterly cheerless is the issue of the divine scrutiny. It ought at least to have been different in Israel, the nation of the positive revelation. But even there wickedness prevails and makes God's purpose of mercy of none effect. The divine outburst of indignation which the psalmist hears here, is applicable to the sinners in Israel. Also in Isa. iii. 13 — 15 the Judge of the world addresses Himself to the heads of Israel in particular. This one feature of the Psalm before us is raised to the consistency of a special prophetic picture in the Psalm of Asaph, lxxxii. That which is here clothed in the form of a question, הֲלֹא יָדְעוּ, is reversed into an assertion in ver. 5 of that Psalm. It is not to be translated: will they not have to feel (which ought to be יֵדְעוּ); but also not as Hupfeld renders it: have they not experienced. "Not to know" is intended to be used as absolutely in the signification *non sapere,* and consequently *insipientem esse,* as it is in lxxxii. 5, lxxiii. 22, xcii. 7, Isa. xliv. 18, cf. 9, xlv. 20, and frequently. The perfect is to be judged after the analogy of *novisse* (Ges. § 126, 3), therefore it is to be rendered: have they attained to no knowledge, are they devoid of all knowledge, and therefore like the brutes, yea, according to Isa. i. 2, 3 even worse than the brutes, all the workers of iniquity? The two clauses which follow are, logically at least, attributive clauses. The subordination of אָכְלוּ לֶחֶם to the participle as a circumstantial clause in the sense of כֶּאֱכָל לֶחֶם is syntactically inadmissible; neither can אכלו לחם, with Hupfeld, be understood of a brutish and secure passing away of life; for, as Olshausen, rightly observes אָכַל לֶחֶם does not signify to feast and carouse, but simply to eat, take a meal. Hengstenberg correctly translates it

---

* Cf. Plüschke's Monograph on the Milanese *Psalterium Syriacum,* 1835, p. 28—39.

„who eating my people, eat bread", *i. e.* who think that they
are not doing anything more sinful, — indeed rather what
is justifiable, irreproachable and lawful to them, — than
when they are eating bread; cf. the further carrying out of
this thought in Mic. iii. 1—3 (especially ver. 3 *extr.:* "just
as in the pot and as flesh within the caldron."). Instead of
ה' לֹא קָרָאוּ Jeremiah says in ch. x. 21 (cf., however, x. 25):
וְאֶת־ה' לֹא דָרָשׁוּ. The meaning is like that in Hos. vii. 7. They
do not pray as it becomes man who is endowed with mind,
therefore they are like cattle, and act like beasts of prey.

Ver. 5. When Jahve thus bursts forth in scorn His
word, which never fails in its working, smites down these
brutish men, who are without knowledge and conscience.
The local demonstrative שָׁם is used as temporal in this
passage just as in lxvi, 6, Hos. ii. 17, Zeph. i. 14, Job xxiii.
7, xxxv. 12, and is joined with the perfect of certainty, as
in xxxvi. 13, where it has not so much a temporal as a local
sense. It does not mean "there = at a future time", as pointing into the indefinite future, but "there = then", when God
shall thus speak to them in His anger. Intensity is here
given to the verb פָּחַד by the addition of a substantival object
of the same root, just as is frequently the case in the more
elevated style, *e. g.* Hab. iii. 9; and as is done in other cases
by the addition of the adverbial infinitive. Then, when God's
long-suffering changes into wrath, terror at His judgment
seizes them and they tremble through and through. This
judgment of wrath, however, is on the other hand a revelation of love. Jahve avenges and thus delivers those whom
He calls עַמִּי (My people); and who are here called דּוֹר צַדִּיק,
the generation of the righteous, in opposition to the corrupted humanity of the time (xii. 8), as being conformed to
the will of God and held together by a superior spirit to
the prevailing spirit of the age. They are so called inasmuch as דּוֹר passes over from the signification *generatio* to
that of *genus hominum* here and also elsewhere, when it is
not merely a temporal, but a moral notion; cf. xxiv. 6,
lxxiii. 15, cxii. 2, where it uniformly denotes the whole of
the children of God who are in bondage in the world and
longing for deliverance, not Israel collectively in antithesis
to the Scythians and the heathen in general (Hitzig).

Ver. 6. The psalmist himself meets the oppressed full of joyous confidence, by reason of the self-manifestation of God in judgment, of which he is now become so confident and which so fills him with comfort. Instead of the sixth tristich, which we expected, we have another distich. The *Hiph.* הֵבִישׁ with a personal object signifies: to put any one to shame, *i. e.* to bring it about that any one must be ashamed, *e. g.* xliv. 8 (cf. liii. 6, where the accusative of the person has to be supplied), or absolutely: to act shamefully, as in the phrase used in Proverbs, בֵּן מֵבִישׁ (a prodigal son). It appears only here with a neuter accusative of the object, not in the signification to defame (Hitz.), — a meaning it never has (not even in Prov. xiii. 5, where it is blended with הִבְאִישׁ to make stinking, *i. e.* a reproach, Gen. xxxiv. 30), — but to confound, put to shame = to frustrate (Hupf.), which is at once the most natural meaning in connection with עֵצַת. But it is not to be rendered: ye put to shame, because ..., for to what purpose is this statement with this inapplicable reason in support of it? The *fut.* תָּבִישׁוּ is used with a like shade of meaning as in Lev. xix. 17, and the imperative elsewhere; and כִּי gives the reason for the tacitly implied clause, or if a line is really lost from the strophe, the lost clause (cf. Isa. viii. 9 sq.): ye will not accomplish it. עֵצָה is whatsoever the pious man, who as such suffers reproach, plans to do for the glory of his God, or even in accordance with the will of his God. All this the children of the world, who are in possession of worldly power, seek to frustrate; but viewed in the light of the final decision their attempt is futile: Jahve is his refuge, or, literally the place whither he flees to hide himself and finds a hiding or concealment (צֵל, טָלַל, סֵתֶר, سِتْر, Arabic also نَزَى). מַחְסֵהוּ has an orthophonic *Dag.*, which obviates the necessity for the reading מַחְסֵהוּ (cf. תַּעְלִים x. 1, טַעְמוּ xxxiv. 1, לֶאְסֹר cv. 22, and similar instances).

Ver. 7. This tristich sounds like a liturgical addition belonging to the time of the Exile, unless one is disposed to assign the whole Psalm to this period on account of it. For elsewhere in a similar connection, as *e. g.* in Ps. cxxvi., שׁוּב שְׁבוּת means to turn the captivity, or to bring back the captives. שׁוּב has here, — as in cxxvi. 4, Nah. ii. 3 (followed by אֵת), cf. Ezek xlvii. 7, the *Kal* being preferred to the *Hiph.* הֵשִׁיב (Jer. xxxii. 44, xxxiii. 11) in favour of the alliteration with שְׁבוּת (from שָׁבָה to make any one a prisoner of war), — a transitive signification, which Hengstenberg (who interprets it: to turn back, to turn to the captivity, of God's merciful visitation), vainly hesitates to admit. But Isa. lxvi. 6, for instance, shews that the exiles also never looked for redemption anywhere but from Zion. Not as though they had thought, that Jahve still dwelt among the ruins of His habitation, which indeed on the contrary was become a ruin because He had forsaken it (as we read in Ezekiel); but the moment of His return to His people is also the moment when He entered again upon the occupation of His sanctuary, and His sanctuary, again appropriated by Jahve even before it was actually reared, is the spot whence issues the kindling of the divine judgment on the enemies of Israel, as well as the spot whence issues the brightness of the reverse side of this judgment, viz. the final deliverance, hence even during the Exile, Jerusalem is the point (the *kibla*) whither the eye of the praying captive was directed, Dan. vi. 11. There would therefore be nothing strange if a psalm-writer belonging to the Exile should express his longing for deliverance in these words: who gives = oh that one would give = oh that the salvation of Israel were come out of Zion! But since שׁוּב שְׁבוּת also signifies metaphorically to turn misfortune, as in Job xlii. 10, Ezek. xvi. 53 (perhaps also in Ps. lxxxv. 2, cf. ver. 5), inasmuch as the idea of שְׁבוּת has been generalised exactly like the German "*Elend*", exile (Old High German *elilenti* = sojourn in another country, banishment, homelessness), therefore the inscribed לדוד cannot be called in question from this quarter. Even Hitzig renders: "if Jahve would but turn the misfortune of His people", regarding this Psalm as composed by Jeremiah during the time the Scythians were in the land. If this rendering is possible, and that it is is undeniable, then we retain the inscription לדוד. And we do so the more readily, as Jeremiah's supposed authorship rests upon a non-recognition of his reproductive character, and the history of the prophet's times makes no allusion to any incursion by the Scythians.

The condition of the true people of God in the time of Absolom was really a שְׁבוּת in more than a figurative sense. But we require no such comparison with cotemporary history, since in these closing words we have only the gathering up into a brief form of the view which prevails in other parts of the Psalm, viz. that the "righteous generation" in the midst of the world, and even of the so-called Israel, finds itself in a state of oppression, imprisonment, and bondage. If God will turn this condition of His people, who are His people indeed and of a truth, then shall Jacob rejoice and Israel be glad. It is the grateful duty of the redeemed to rejoice. — And how could they do otherwise!

PSALM XV.

THE CONDITIONS OF ACCESS TO GOD.

1 JAHVE, who may sojourn in Thy tabernacle,
Who may dwell on Thy holy mountain?

2 He that walketh uprightly, and worketh righteousness,
And speaketh truth in his heart.

3 That taketh not slander upon his tongue,
Nor doeth evil to his companion,
Nor bringeth a reproach upon his neighbour;

4 That is displeasing in his own eyes, to be despised,
But those who fear Jahve he honoureth;
He sweareth to [his own] hurt — he changeth not.

5 He putteth not out his money to usury,
And taketh not a bribe against the innocent —
He that doeth these things shall never be moved.

The preceeding Psalm distinguished דּוֹר צַדִּיק, a righteous generation, from the mass of the universal corruption, and closed with a longing for the salvation out of Zion. Ps. xv. answers the question: who belongs to this דּוֹר צַדִּיק. and whom shall the future salvation avail? Ps. xxiv., composed in connection with the removal of the Ark to Zion, is very similar. The state of mind expressed in this Psalm exactly corresponds to the unhypocritical piety and genuine lowliness which were manifest in David in their most beauteous light on that occasion; cf. ver. 4*b* with 2 Sam. vi. 19; ver. 4*a* with 2 Sam. vi. 21 sq. The fact, however, that Zion (Moriah) is called simply הַר הַקֹּדֶשׁ in ver. 1, rather favours the time of the Absolomic exile, when David was cut off from the sanctuary of his God, whilst it was in the possession of men the very opposite of those described in this Psalm (*vid.* iv. 6). Nothing can be maintained with any certainty except that the Psalm assumes the elevation of Zion to the special designation of "the holy mountain" and the removal of the Ark to the אֹהֶל erected there (2 Sam. vi. 17). Isa. xxxiii. 13—16 is a fine variation of this Psalm.

Vers. 1—2. That which is expanded in the tristichic portion of the Psalm, is all contained in this distichic portion *in nuce*. The address to God is not merely a favourite form (Hupfeld), but the question is really, as its words imply, directed to God. The answer, however, is not therefore to be taken as a direct answer from God, as it might be in a prophetical connection: the psalmist addresses himself to God in prayer, he as it were reads the heart of God, and answers to himself the question just asked, in accordance with the mind of God. גּוּר and שָׁכֵן which are usually distinguished from each other like παροικεῖν and κατοικεῖν in Hellenistic Greek, are alike in meaning in this instance. It is not a merely temporary גּוּר (lxi. 5), but for ever, that is intended. The only difference between the two interchangeable notions is this, the one denotes the finding of an abiding place of rest starting from the idea of a wandering life, the other the possession of an abiding place of rest starting from the idea of settled family life.* The holy

---

* In the Arabic جام اللّه is "one under the protection of God, dwelling as it were in the fortress of God." *vid.* Fleischer's Samachschari, S. 1, Anm. 1.

tabernacle and the holy mountain are here thought of in their spiritual character as the places of the divine presence and of the church of God assembled round the symbol of it; and accordingly the sojourning and dwelling there is not to be understood literally, but in a spiritual sense. This spiritual depth of view, first of all with local limitations, is also to be found in xxvii. 4, 5, lxi. 5. This is present even where the idea of earnestness and regularity in attending the sanctuary rises in intensity to that of constantly dwelling therein, lxv. 5, lxxxiv. 4—5; while elsewhere, as in xxiv. 3, the outward materiality of the Old Testament is not exceeded. Thus we see the idea of the sanctuary at one time contracting itself within the Old Testament limits, and at another expanding more in accordance with the spirit of the New Testament; since in this matter, as in the matter of sacrifice, the spirit of the New Testament already shews signs of life, and works powerfully through its cosmical veil, without that veil being as yet rent. The answer to the question, so like the spirit of the New Testament in its intention, is also itself no less New Testament in its character: Not every one who saith Lord, Lord, but they who do the will of God, shall enjoy the rights of friendship with Him. But His will concerns the very substance of the Law, viz. our duties towards all men, and the inward state of the heart towards God.

In the expression הוֹלֵךְ תָּמִים (here and in Prov. xxviii. 18), תמים is either a closer definition of the subject: one walking as an upright man, like הוֹלֵךְ רָכִיל one going about as a slanderer, cf. הַיָּשָׁר הוֹלֵךְ Mic. ii. 7 "the upright as one walking"; or it is an accusative of the object, as in הוֹלֵךְ צְדָקוֹת Isa. xxxiii. 15: one who walks uprightness, *i. e.* one who makes uprightness his way, his mode of action; since תמים may mean *integrum = integritas,* and this is strongly favoured by הֹלְכִים בְּתָמִים, which is used interchangeably with it in Ps. lxxxiv. 12 (those who walk in uprightness). Instead of עָשָׂה צְדָקָה we have the poetical form of expression פֹּעַל צֶדֶק. The characterising of the outward walk and action is followed in ver. 2*b* by the characterising of the inward nature: speaking truth in his heart, not: with his heart (not merely

with his mouth); for in the phrase בְּ אָמַר בְּלֵב‎, בְּ‎ is always the
Beth of the place, not of the instrument — the meaning
therefore is: it is not falsehood and deceit that he thinks
and plans inwardly, but truth (Hitz.). We have three characteristics here: a spotless walk, conduct ordered according
to God's will, and a truth-loving mode of thought.

Vers. 3 — 5. The distich which contains the question
and that containing the general answer are now followed
by three tristichs, which work the answer out in detail.
The description is continued in independent clauses, which,
however, have logically the value of relative clauses. The
perff. have the signification of abstract presents, for they
are the expression of tried qualities, of the habitual mode
of action, of that which the man, who is the subject of the
question, never did and what consequently it is not his
wont to do. רָגַל‎ means to go about, whether in order to
spie out (which is it usual meaning), or to gossip and slander
(here, and the *Piel* in 2 Sam. xix. 28; cf. רָכִיל, רָכַל‎). Instead
בִּלְשֹׁנוֹ‎ we have עַל־לְשֹׁנוֹ‎ (with *Dag.* in the second ל‎, in order
that it may be read with emphasis and not slurred over*),
because a word lies upon the tongue ere it is uttered, the
speaker brings it up as it were from within on to his tongue
or lips, xvi. 4, l. 16, Ezek. xxxvi. 3. The assonance of
לְרֵעֵהוּ רָעָה‎ is well conceived. To do evil to him who is bound
to us by the ties of kindred and friendship, is a sin which
will bring its own punishment. קָרוֹב‎ is also the parallel
word to רֵעַ‎ in Exod. xxxii. 27. Both are here intended to
refer not merely to persons of the same nation; for whatever
is sinful in itself and under any circumstances whatever, is
also sinful in relation to every man according to the morality of the Old Testament. The assertion of Hupfeld and
others that נָשָׂא‎ in conjunction with חֶרְפָּה‎ means *efferre* =
effari, is opposed by its combination with עַל‎ and its use
elsewhere in the phrase נשׂא חרפה‎ "to bear reproach" (lxix. 8).
It means (since נשׂא‎ is just as much *tollere* as *ferre*) to bring
reproach on any one, or load any one with reproach. Re-

---

* *vid.* the rule for this orthophonic *Dag.* in the *Luther. Zeitschrift,*
1863, S. 413.

proach is a burden which is more easily put on than cast off; *audacter calumniare, semper aliquid hæret.*

In ver. 4a the interpretation "he is little in his own eyes, despised," of which Hupfeld, rejecting it, says that Hitzig has picked it up out of the dust, is to be retained. Even the Targ., Saad., Aben-Ezra, Kimchi, Urbino (in his Grammar, אהל מועד) take נבזה בעיניו together, even though explaining it differently, and it is accordingly accented by Baer נִבְזֶה בְּעֵינָיו וְנִמְאָס (*Mahpach, Asla Legarme, Rebia magnum*).* God exalts him who is קָטָן בְּעֵינָיו, 1 Sam. xv. 17. David, when he brought up the ark of his God, could not sufficiently degrade himself (נָקֵל), and appeared שָׁפָל בְּעֵינָיו, 2 Sam. vi. 22. This lowliness, which David also confesses in Ps. cxxxi., is noted here and throughout the whole of the Old Testament, *e. g.,* Isa. lvii. 15, as a condition of being well-pleasing before God; just as it is in reality the chief of all virtues. On the other hand, it is mostly translated either, according to the usual accentuation, with which the *Beth* of בעיניו is dageshed: the reprobate is despised in his eyes (Rashi, Hupf.), or in accordance with the above accentuation: despised in his eyes is the reprobate (Maurer, Hengst., Olsh., Luzzatto); but this would say but little, and be badly expressed. For the placing together of two participles without an article, and moreover of similar meaning, with the design of the one being taken as subject and the other as predicate, is to be repudiated simply on the ground of style; and the difference among expositors shews how equivocal the expression is.

On the other hand, when we translate it: "despicable is he in his own eyes, worthy to be despised" (Ges. § 134, 1), we can appeal to xiv. 1, where הִשְׁחִיתוּ is intensified just in the same way by הִתְעִיבוּ, as נִבְזֶה is here by נִמְאָס; cf. also Gen. xxx. 31, Job xxxi. 23, Isa. xliii. 4. The antithesis of

---

* The usual accentuation נבזה | בְּעֵינָיו נמאם forcibly separates בעיניו from נבזה to which according to its position it belongs. And Heidenheim's accentuation נבזה בעיניו נמאם is to be rejected on accentuological grounds, because of two like distinctives the second has always a less distinctive value than the first. We are consequently only left to the one given above. The MSS. vary.

ver. 4*b* to ver. 4*a* is also thus fully met: he himself seems
to himself unworthy of any respect, whereas he constantly
shews respect to others; and the standard by which he
judges is the fear of God. His own fear of Jahve is manifest
from the self-denying strictness with which he performs
his vows. This sense of נִשְׁבַּע לְהָרַע is entirely misapprehended
when it is rendered: he swears to his neighbour (רֵעַ = רַע),
which ought to be לְרֵעֵהוּ, or: he swears to the wicked (and
keeps to what he has thus solemnly promised), which ought
to be לָרָע; for to what purpose would be the omission of
the elision of the article, which is extremely rarely (xxxvi. 6)
not attended to in the classic style of the period before the
Exile?   The words have reference to Lev. v. 4: if any one
swear, thoughtlessly pronouncing לְהָרַע אוֹ לְהֵיטִיב, to do evil
or to do good, etc. The subject spoken of is oaths which are
forgotten, and the forgetting of which must be atoned for
by an *asham,* whether the nature of the oath be something
unpleasant and injurious, or agreeable and profitable, to
the person making the vow. The retrospective reference of
להרע to the subject is self-evident; for to injure another is
indeed a sin, the vowing and performance of which, not its
omission, would require to be expiated.   On לְהָרַע = לְהָרֵעַ
vid. Ges. § 67, rem. 6.   The hypothetical antecedent (cf.
e. g., 2 Kings v. 13) is followed by וְלֹא יָמִר as an apodosis.
The verb הֵמִיר is native to the law of vows, which, if any
one has vowed an animal in sacrifice, forbids both changing it for its money value (הֶחֱלִיף) and exchanging it for
another, be it טוֹב בְּרָע אוֹ־רַע בְּטוֹב, Lev. xxvii. 10, 33.   The
psalmist of course does not use these words in the technical
sense in which they are used in the Law. Swearing includes
making a vow, and לֹא יָמִר disavows not merely any exchanging of that which was solemnly promised, but also
any alteration of that which was sworn: he does not misuse
the name of God in anywise, לַשָּׁוְא.

   In ver. 5*a* the psalmist also has a passage of the Tôra
before his mind, viz. Lev. xxv. 37, cf. Exod. xxii. 24, Deut.
xxiii. 20, Ezek. xviii. 8.   נָתַן בְּנֶשֶׁךְ signifies to give a thing
away in order to take usury (נֶשֶׁךְ from נָשַׁךְ to bite, δάκνειν)
for it. The receiver or demander of interest is מַשִּׁיךְ, the

one who pays interest נָשׁוּךְ, the interest itself נֶשֶׁךְ. The trait
of character described in ver. 5*b* also recalls the language
of the Mosaic law: שֹׁחַד לֹא לָקַח, the prohibition Exod.
xxiii. 8, Deut. xvi. 19; and עַל־נָקִי, the curse Deut. xxvii. 25:
on account of the innocent, *i. e.* against him, to condemn
him.　Whether it be as a loan or as a gift, he gives without
conditions, and if he attain the dignity of a judge he is proof
against bribery, especially with reference to the destruction
of the innocent.　And now instead of closing in conformity
with the description of character already given: such a man
shall dwell, etc., the concluding sentence takes a different
form, moulded in accordance with the spiritual meaning of
the opening question: he who doeth these things shall never
be moved (יִמּוֹט *fut. Niph.*), he stands fast, being upheld by
Jahve, hidden in His fellowship; nothing from without, no
misfortune, can cause his overthrow.

PSALM XVI.

REFUGE IN GOD, THE HIGHEST GOOD, IN THE PRESENCE
OF DISTRESS AND OF DEATH.

1 PRESERVE me, O God, for in Thee do I hide myself
2 I say unto Jahve: "Thou art my Lord,
　Besides Thee I have no good",
　3 And to the saints who are in the earth:
　"These are the excellent, in whom is all my delight".

4 Their sorrows shall be multiplied who have bartered
　　　　for an idol —
　I will not pour out their drink-offerings of blood,
　Nor take their names upon my lips.
5 Jahve is the portion of my land and of my cup,
　Thou makest my lot illustrious.

6 The lines have fallen unto me in pleasant places,
　Yea, the heritage appears fair to me.
　7 I will bless Jahve, who hath given me counsel;
　In the night-seasons also my reins instruct me.

8 I have set Jahve always before me,
   For He is at my right hand — therefore I shall not
   be moved.

 9 Therefore my heart is glad, and my glory exulteth,
   My flesh also shall dwell free of care.
10 For Thou wilt not abandon my soul to Hades,
   Nor give up Thy Holy One to see the pit;
11 Thou wilt make me know the path of life —
   Fulness of joy is in Thy countenance,
   Pleasures are in Thy right hand for evermore.

The preceding Psalm closed with the words לֹא יִמּוֹט; this word of promise is repeated in xvi. 8 as an utterance of faith in the mouth of David. We are here confronted by a pattern of the unchangeable believing confidence of a friend of God; for the writer of Ps. xvi. is in danger of death, as is to be inferred from the prayer expressed in ver. 1 and the expectation in ver. 10. But there is no trace of anything like bitter complaint, gloomy conflict, or hard struggle: the cry for help is immediately swallowed up by an overpowering and blessed consciousness and a bright hope. There reigns in the whole Psalm, a settled calm, an inward joy, and a joyous confidence, which is certain that everything that it can desire for the present and for the future it possesses in its God.

The Psalm is inscribed לְדָוִד; and Hitzig also confesses that "David may be inferred from its language". Whatever can mark a Psalm as Davidic we find combined in this Psalm: thoughts crowding together in compressed language, which becomes in ver. 4 bold even to harshness, but then becomes clear and moves more rapidly; an antiquated, peculiar, and highly poetic impress (אֲדֹנָי, *my Lord*, מְנָת, נַחֲלָת, תּוֹמִיךְ, שֶׁפֶר); and a well-devised grouping of the strophes. In addition to all these, there are manifold points of contact with indisputably genuine Davidic Psalms (comp. *e. g.*, ver. 5 with xi. 6; ver. 10 with iv. 4; ver. 11 with xvii. 15), and with indisputably ancient portions of the Pentateuch (Exod. xxiii. 13, xix. 6, Gen. xlix. 6). Scarcely any other Psalm shews so clearly as this, what deep roots psalm-poetry has struck into the Tôra, both as it regards the matter and the language. Concerning the circumstances of its composition, *vid.* on Ps. xxx.

The superscription מִכְתָּם לְדָוִד, Ps. xvi. has in common with Ps. lvi.—lx. After the analogy of the other superscriptions, it must have a technical meaning. This at once militates against Hitzig's explanation, that it is a poem hitherto unknown, an ἀνέκδοτον, according to the Arabic *mâktum*, hidden, secret, just as also against the meaning κειμήλιον, which says nothing further to help us. The LXX. translates it στηλογραφία (εἰς στηλογραφίαν), instead of which the Old Latin version has *tituli inscriptio* (Hesychius τίτλος· πτυχίον ἐπίγραμμα ἔχον). That this translation accords with the tradition is shewn by that of the Targum גְּלִיפָא תְרִיצָא *sculptura recta* (not *erecta* as Hupfeld renders it). Both versions give the verb the meaning כָּתַם *insculpere*, which is supported both by a comparison with כָּתַב, cogn. חָצַב, עָצַב, and by חָתַם *imprimere* (*sigillum*). Moreover, the sin of Israel is called נִכְתָּם in Jer. ii. 22 (cf. xvii. 1) as being a deeply impressed spot, not to be wiped out. If we now look more closely into the *Michtam* Psalms as a whole, we find they have two prevailing features in common. Sometimes significant and remarkable words are introduced by וַיֹּאמַר, אָמַרְתִּי, דִּבֶּר, xvi. 2, lviii. 12, lx. 8, cf. Isa. xxxviii. 10, 11 (in Hezekiah's psalm, which is inscribed מִכְתָּם = מִכְתָּב as it is perhaps to be read); sometimes words of this character are repeated after the manner of a refrain, as in Ps. lvi.: *I will not fear, what can man do to me!* in Ps. lvii.: *Be Thou exalted, Elohim, above the heavens, Thy glory above all the earth!* and in Ps. lix.: *For Elohim is my high tower, my merciful God.* Hezekiah's psalm unites this characteristic with the other. Accordingly מכתם, like ἐπίγραμμα,* appears to mean first of all an inscription and then to be equivalent to an inscription-poem or epigram, a poem containing pithy sayings; since in the Psalms of this order some expressive sentence, after the style of an inscription or a motto on a

---

* In modern Jewish poetry מכתם is actually the name for the epigram.

monument, is brought prominently forward, by being either specially introduced or repeated as a refrain.

The strophe-schema is 5. 5. 6. 7. The last strophe, which has grown to seven lines, is an expression of joyous hopes in the face of death, which extend onward even into eternity.

Vers. 1—3.   The Psalm begins with a prayer that is based upon faith, the special meaning of which becomes clear from ver. 10: May God preserve him (which He is able to do as being אֵל, the Almighty, able to do all things), who has no other refuge in which he has hidden and will hide but Him. This short introit is excepted from the parallelism; so far therefore it is monostichic, — a sigh expressing everything in few words. And the emphatic pronunciation שָׁמְרֵנִי *shām^ereni* harmonises with it; for it is to be read thus, just as in lxxxvi. 2, cxix. 167 *shām^erah* (cf. on Isa. xxxviii. 14 עָשְׁקָה), according to the express testimony of the Masora.*

The text of the next two verses (so it appears) needs to be improved in two respects. The reading אָמַרְתְּ as addressed to the soul (Targ.), cf. Lam. iii. 24 sq., is opposed by the absence of any mention of the thing addressed. It rests upon a misconception of the defective form of writing, אָמַרְתִּ (Ges. § 44, rem. 4).   Hitzig and Ewald (§ 190, *d*) suppose that in such cases a rejection of the final vowel, which really occurs in the language of the people, after the manner of the Aramaic (אֲמֶרֶת or אִמְרֵת), lies at the bottom of the form. And it does really seem as though the frequent occurrence of this defective form (ידעת = ידעתי cxl. 13, Job xlii. 2, בניתי = בנית 1 Kings viii. 48, עשית = עשיתי Ezek. xvi. 59, cf. 2 Kings xviii. 20, אמרת now pointed אָמַרְתְּ, with Isa. xxxvi. 5) has its occasion at least in some such cutting away of the *i*, peculiar to the language of the common people; although,

---

* The Masora observes ב' גרשין בספרא, *i. e.* twice in the Psalter שמרה is in the imperative, the ŏ being displaced by *Gaja (Metheg)* and changed into *ā*, *vid.* Baer, *Torath Emeth* p. 22 sq. In spite of this the grammarians are not agreed as to the pronunciation of the imperative and infinitive forms when so pointed. Luzzatto, like Lonzano, reads it *shŏm^ereni.*

if David wrote it so, אָמַרְתְּ is not intended to be read otherwise than it is in xxxi. 15, cxl. 7.*

First of all David gives expression to his confession of
Jahve, to whom he submits himself unconditionally, and
whom he sets above everything else without exception.
Since the suffix of אֲדֹנָי (properly *domini mei* = *domine mi*,
Gen. xviii. 3, cf. xix. 2), which has become mostly lost sight
of in the usage of the language, now and then retains its
original meaning, as it does indisputably in xxxv. 23, it is
certainly to be rendered also here: "Thou art my Lord" and
not "Thou art the Lord". The emphasis lies expressly on
the "my". It is the unreserved and joyous feeling of dependence (more that of the little child, than of the servant),
which is expressed in this first confession. For, as the second
clause of the confession says: Jahve, who is his Lord, is also
his benefactor, yea even his highest good. The preposition
עַל frequently introduces that which extends beyond something else, Gen. xlviii. 22 (cf. lxxxix. 8, xcv. 3), and to this
passage may be added Gen. xxxi. 50, xxxii. 12, Exod.
xxxv. 22, Num. xxxi. 8, Deut. xix. 9, xxii. 6, the one thing
being above, or co-ordinate with, the other. So also here:
"my good, *i. e.* whatever makes me truly happy, is not above
Thee", *i. e.* in addition to Thee, beside Thee; according to
the sense it is equivalent to out of Thee or without Thee
(as the Targ., Symm., and Jerome render it), Thou alone,
without exception, art my good. In connection with this
rendering of the עַל, the בַּל (poetic, and contracted from
בְּלִי), which is unknown to the literature before David's
time, presents no difficulty. As in Prov. xxiii. 7 it is short
for בַּל־תִּהְיֶה. Hengstenberg remarks, "Just as *Thou art the
Lord!* is the response of the soul to the words *I am the Lord
thy God* (Exod. xx. 2), so *Thou only art my salvation!* is the
response to *Thou shalt have no other gods beside Me*
(עַל־פָּנַי)". The psalmist knows no fountain of true hap-

---

* Pinsker's view (*Einleit.* S. 100—102), who considers פָּעַלְתָּ to
have sprung from פָּעֲלָה as the primary form of the 1. *pers. sing*, from
which then came פָּעַלְתִּי and later still פָּעַלְתִּי, is untenable according
to the history of the language.

piness but Jahve, in Him he possesses all, his treasure is in Heaven.

Such is his confession to Jahve. But he also has those on earth to whom he makes confession. Transposing the ו we read:

$$\text{וְלִקְדוֹשִׁים אֲשֶׁר בָּאָרֶץ}$$
$$\text{הֵמָּה אַדִּירֵי כָּל־חֶפְצִי־בָם:}$$

While Diestel's alteration: "to the saints, who are in his land, he makes himself glorious, and all his delight is in them," is altogether strange to this verse: the above transfer of the *Waw** suffices to remove its difficulties, and that in a way quite in accordance with the connection. Now it is clear, that לקדושים, as has been supposed by some, is the dative governed by אָמַרְתִּי, the influence of which is thus carried forward; it is clear what is meant by the addition אשר בארץ, which distinguishes the object of his affection here below from the One above, who is incomparably the highest; it is clear, as to what הֵמָּה defines, whereas otherwise this purely descriptive relative clause אֲשֶׁר בָּאָרֶץ הֵמָּה (which von Ortenberg transposes into אֲשֶׁר אַרְצָה בָהֵמָּה) appears to be useless and surprises one both on account of its redundancy (since המה is superfluous, cf. *e. g.* 2 Sam. vii. 9, ii. 18) and on account of its arrangement of the words (an arrangement, which is usual in connection with a negative construction, Deut. xx. 15, 2 Chron. viii. 7, cf. Gen. ix. 3, Ezek. xii. 10); it is clear, in what sense אדירי alternates with קדושים, since it is not those who are accounted by the world as אדירים on account of their worldly power and possessions (cxxxvi. 18, 2 Chron. xxiii. 20), but the holy, prized by him as being also glorious, partakers of higher glory and worthy of higher honour; and moreover, this corrected arrangement of the verse harmonises with the *Michtam* character of the Psalm. The thought thus obtained, is the thought one expected (love to God and love to His saints), and the one which one is also obliged to wring from the text as we have it, either by translating with De Welte, Maurer, Dietrich and others:

---

* Approved by Kamphausen and by the critic in the *Liter. Blatt* of the *Allgem. Kirchen-Zeitung* 1864 S. 107.

"the saints who are in the land, they are the excellent in
whom I have all my delight", — a *Waw apodoseos*, with
which one could only be satisfied if it were וְהֵמָּ֫ר (cf. 2 Sam.
xv. 34) — or: "the saints who are in the land and the
glorious — all my delight is in them". By both these interpretations, לְ would be the exponent of the *nom. absol.* which
is elsewhere detached and placed at the beginning of a sentence, and this לְ of reference (Ew. § 310, *a*) is really common to every style (Num. xviii. 8, Isa. xxxii. 1, Eccl. ix. 4);
whereas the לְ understood of the fellowship in which he
stands when thus making confession to Jahve: associating
myself with the saints (Hengst.), with (von Lengerke), among
the saints (Hupf., Thenius), would be a preposition most
liable to be misapprehended, and makes ver. 3 a cumber-
some appendage of ver. 2.   But if לְ be taken as the *Lamed*
of reference then the elliptical construct וְאַדִּירֵי, to which
הָאָרֶץ ought to be supplied, remains a stumbling-block not
to be easily set aside. For such an isolation of the connecting form from its genitive cannot be shown to be syntactically possible in Hebrew (*vid.* on 2 Kings ix. 17, Thenius,
and Keil); nor are we compelled to suppose in this instance
what cannot be proved elsewhere, since כָּל־חֶפְצִי־בָם is,
without any harshness, subordinate to ואדירי as a genitival
notion (Ges. § 116, 3).   And still in connection with the
reading ואדירי, both the formation of the sentence which,
beginning with לְ, leads one to expect an apodosis, and the
relation of ver. 3 to ver. 2, according to which the central
point of the declaration must lie just within כל־חפצי־בם,
are opposed to this rendering of the words ואדירי כל־
חפצי־בם.

Thus, therefore, we come back to the above easy improvement of the text.   קְדוֹשִׁים are those in whom the will
of Jahve concerning Israel, that it should be a holy nation
(Exod. xix. 6, Deut. vii. 6), has been fulfilled, viz. the living
members of the *ecclesia sanctorum* in this world (for there
is also one in the other world, lxxxix. 6).   Glory, δόξα, is
the outward manifestation of holiness.   It is ordained of
God for the sanctified (cf. Rom. viii. 30), whose moral nobility is now for the present veiled under the menial form

of the עָנִי; and in the eyes of David they already possess it. His spiritual vision pierces through the outward form of the servant. His verdict is like the verdict of God, who is his all in all. The saints, and they only, are the excellent to him. His whole delight is centred in them, all his respect and affection is given to them. The congregation of the saints is his *Chephzibah,* Isa. lxii. 4 (cf. 2 Kings xxi. 1).

Vers. 4—5. As he loves the saints so, on the other hand, he abhors the apostates and their idols. אַחֵר מָהָרוּ is to be construed as an appositional relative clause to the preceding: *multi sunt cruciatus* (cf. xxxii. 10) *eorum, eorum scil. qui alium permutant.* The expression would flow on more smoothly if it were יַרְבּוּ: they multiply, or increase their pains, who ..., so that אַחֵר מהרו would be the subject, for instance like ה' אֲהֵבוֹ (he whom Jahve loves), Isa. xlviii. 14. This ver. 4 forms a perfect antithesis to ver. 3. In David's eyes the saints are already the glorified, in whom his delight centres; while, as he knows, a future full of anguish is in store for the idolatrous, and their worship, yea, their very names are an abomination to him. The suffixes of נִסְכֵּיהֶם and שְׁמוֹתָם might be referred to the idols according to Exod. xxiii. 13, Hos. ii. 19, if אַחֵר be taken collectively as equivalent to אַחֵרִם, as in Job viii. 19. But it is more natural to assign the same reference to them as to the suffix of עַצְּבוֹתָם, which does not signify "their idols" (for idols are עֲצַבִּים), but their torments, pains (from עַצֶּבֶת derived from עָצֵב), cxlvii. 3, Job ix. 28. The thought is similar to 1 Tim. vi. 10, ἑαυτοὺς περιέπειραν ὀδύναις ποικίλαις. אַחֵר is a general designation of the broadest kind for everything that is not God, but which man makes his idol beside God and in opposition to God (cf. Isa. xlii. 8, xlviii. 11). מָהָרוּ cannot mean *festinant,* for in this signification it is only found in *Piel* מִהֵר, and that once with a local, but not a personal, accusative of the direction, Nah. ii. 6. It is therefore to be rendered (and the *perf.* is also better adapted to this meaning): they have taken in exchange that which is not God (מָהַר like הֵמִיר, cvi. 20, Jer. ii. 11). Perhaps (cf. the phrase זָנָה אַחֲרֵי) the secondary meaning of wooing and fondling is connected with it; for מָהַר is the proper word for acquiring

a wife by paying down the price asked by her father, Exod.
xxii. 15. With such persons, who may seem to be אַדִּירִים
in the eyes of the world, but for whom a future full of anguish is in store, David has nothing whatever to do: he will
not pour out drink-offerings as they pour them out. נִסְכֵּיהֶם
has the *Dag. lene*, as it always has. They are not called מִדָּם
as actually consisting of blood, or of wine actually mingled
with blood; but consisting as it were of blood, because they
are offered with blood-stained hands and blood-guilty con-
sciences. מִן is the *min* of derivation; in this instance (as in
Amos iv. 5, cf. Hos. vi. 8) of the material, and is used in
other instances also for similar virtually adjectival expressions, x. 18, xvii. 14, lxxx. 14.

In ver. 4 *c* the expression of his abhorrence attains its
climax: even their names, *i. e.* the names of their false gods,
which they call out, he shuns taking upon his lips, just as
is actually forbidden in the Tôra, Exod. xxiii. 13 (cf. *Const.
Apost.* V. 10 εἴδωλον μνημονεύειν ὀνόματα δαιμονικά). He takes
the side of Jahve. Whatever he may wish for, he possesses
in Him; and whatever he has in Him, is always secured to
him by Him. חֶלְקִי does not here mean food (Böttch.), for in this
sense חֵלֶק (Lev. vi. 10) and מָנָה (1 Sam. i. 4) are identical;
and parallel passages like cxlii. 6 shew what חלקי means when
applied to Jahve. According to xi. 6, כּוֹסִי is also a genitive
just like חלקי; מְנָת חֵלֶק is the share of landed property assigned to any one; מְנָת כּוֹם the share of the cup according
to paternal apportionment. The tribe of Levi received no
territory in the distribution of the country, from which
they might have maintained themselves; Jahve was to be
their חֵלֶק, Num. xviii. 20, and the gifts consecrated to Jahve
were to be their food, Deut. x. 9, xviii. 1 sq. But nevertheless all Israel is βασίλειον ἱεράτευμα, Exod. xix. 6, towards
which even קְדוֹשִׁים and אדרים in ver. 3 pointed; so that,
therefore, the very thing represented by the tribe of
Levi in outward relation to the nation, holds good, in all
its deep spiritual significance, of every believer. It is not
anything earthly, visible, created, and material, that is
allotted to him as his possession and his sustenance, but
Jahve and Him only; but in Him is perfect contentment.

In ver. 5*b*, תּוֹמִיךְ, as it stands, looks at first sight as though it were the *Hiph.* of a verb יָמַךְ (וְמַךְ). But such a verb is not to be found anywhere else, we must therefore seek some other explanation of the word. It cannot be a substantive in the signification of possession (Maurer, Ewald), for such a substantival form does not exist. It might more readily be explained as a participle = תּוֹמֵךְ, somewhat like יוֹסִיף, Isa. xxix. 4, xxxviii. 5, Eccl. i. 18, = יוֹסֵף, — a comparison which has been made by Aben-Ezra (*Sefath Jether* No. 421) and Kimchi (*Michlol* 11*a*), — a form of the participle to which, in writing at least, סוֹבֵיב, 2 Kings viii. 21, forms a transition; but there is good reason to doubt the existence of such a form. Had the poet intended to use the *part.* of תמך, it is more probable he would have written אתה תוֹמְכִי גורלי, just as the LXX. translators might have had it before them, taking the *Chirek compaginis* as a suffix: σὺ εἶ ὁ ἀποκαθιστῶν τὴν κληρονομίαν μου ἐμοί (Böttcher). For the conjecture of Olshausen and Thenius, תּוֹסִיף in the sense: "thou art continually my portion" halts both in thought and expression. Hitzig's conjecture תֻּמֶּיךְ "thou, thy Tummîm are my lot", is more successful and tempting. But the fact that the תֻּמִּים are never found (not even in Deut. xxxiii. 8) without the אוּרִים, is against it. Nevertheless, we should prefer this conjecture to the other explanations, if the word would not admit of being explained as *Hiph.* from יָמַךְ (וְמַךְ), which is the most natural explanation. Schultens has compared the Arabic *wamika*, to be broad, from which there is a *Hiphil* form أَوْمَكَ, to make broad, in Syro-Arabic, that is in use even in the present day among the common people.* And since we must at any rate come down to the supposition of something unusual about this תּוֹמִיךְ, it is surely not too bold to regard it as a ἅπαξ γεγραμμ.: Thou

---

* The Arabic Lexicographers are only acquainted with a noun *wamka*, breadth (*amplitudo*), but not with the verb. And even the noun does not belong to the universal and classical language. But at the present day الوَمْك (pronounced *wumk*), breadth, and *wamik* are in common use in Damascus; and it is only the verb that is shunned in the better conversational style. — Wetzstein.

makest broad my lot, *i. e.* ensurest for me a spacious habitation, a broad place, as the possession that falleth to
me,* — a thought, that is expanded in ver. 6.

Vers. 6—8. The measuring lines (חֲבָלִים) are cast
(Mic. ii. 5) and fall to any one just where and as far as his
property is assigned to him; so that נָפַל חֶבֶל (Josh. xvii.
5) is also said of the falling to any one of his allotted portion of land. נְעִמִים (according to the Masora defective as
also in ver. 11 נְעִמוֹת) is a *pluralet.*, the plural that is used
to denote a unity in the circumstances, and a similarity in
the relations of time and space, Ges. § 108, 2, *a*; and it
signifies both pleasant circumstances, Job xxxvi. 11, and,
as here, a pleasant locality, Lat. *amœna* (to which נְעִמוֹת in
ver. 11, more strictly corresponds). The lines have fallen
to him in a charming district, viz. in the pleasurable fellowship of God, this most blessed domain of love has become
his paradisaic possession. With אַף he rises from the fact
to the perfect contentment which it secures to him: such a
heritage seems to him to be fair, he finds a source of inward
pleasure and satisfaction in it. נַחֲלָת — according to Ew.
§ 173, *d*, lengthened from the construct form נַחֲלַת (like
נְגִינַת lxi. 1); according to Hupfeld, springing from נַחֲלָתִי (by
the same apocope that is so common in Syriac, perhaps like
אָמַרְתְּ ver. 1 from אָמַרְתִּי) just like זִמְרָת Exod. xv. 2 — is
rather, since in the former view there is no law for the
change of vowel and such an application of the form as we
find in lx. 13 (cviii. 13) is opposed to the latter, a stunted

---

* It is scarcely possible for two words to be more nearly identical
than גּוֹרָל and κλῆρος. The latter, usually derived from κλάω (a piece
broken off), is derived from κέλεσθαι (a determining of the divine will)
in Döderlein's *Homer. Glossar*, iii. 124. But perhaps it is one word
with גורל. Moreover κλῆρος signifies 1) the sign by which anything
whatever falls to one among a number of persons in conformity with
the decision of chance or of the divine will, a pebble, potsherd, or the
like. So in Homer, *Il.* iii. 316, vii. 175, xxiii. 351, *Od.* x. 206, where
casting lots is described with the expression κλῆρος. 2) The object
that falls to any one by lot, *patrimonium, e. g. Od.* xiv. 64, *Il.* xv. 498,
οἶκος καὶ κλῆρος, especially of lands. 3) an inheritance without the
notion of the lot, and even without any thought of inheriting, absolutely: a settled, landed property. It is the regular expression for the
allotments of land assigned to colonists (κληροῦχοι).

form of נַחֲלָתִי: the heritage = such a heritage pleases me, lit.
seems fair to me (שָׁפַר, cognate root סָפַר, צָפַר, cognate in meaning بشر, بشع, to rub, polish, make shining, intr. שָׁפֵר to be
shining, beautiful). עָלַי of beauty known and felt by him (cf.
Esth. iii. 9 with 1 Sam. xxv. 36 טוב עליו, and the later way of
expressing it Dan. iii. 32). But since the giver and the gift
are one and the same, the joy he has in the inheritance becomes of itself a constant thanksgiving to and blessing of the
Giver, that He (אשר *quippe qui*) has counselled him (lxxiii.
24) to chose the one thing needful, the good part. Even in
the night-seasons his heart keeps watch, even then his reins
admonish him (יִסַּר, here of moral incitement, as in Isa. viii.
11, to warn). The reins are conceived of as the seat of the
blessed feeling that Jahve is his possession (*vid. Psychol.*
S. 268; tr. p. 316). He is impelled from within to offer
heart-felt thanks to his merciful and faithful God. He has
Jahve always before him, Jahve is the point towards which
he constantly directs his undiverted gaze; and it is easy for
him to have Him thus ever present, for He is מִימִינִי (supply הוּא, as in xxii. 29, lv. 20, cxii. 4), at my right hand (*i. e.*
where my right hand begins, close beside me), so that he
has no need to draw upon his power of imagination. The
words בַּל־אֶמּוֹט, without any conjunction, express the natural effect of this, both in consciousness and in reality: he
will not and cannot totter, he will not yield and be overthrown.

Vers. 9—11. Thus then, as this concluding strophe,
as it were like seven rays of light, affirms, he has the most
blessed prospect before him, without any need to fear death.
Because Jahve is thus near at hand to help him, his heart
becomes joyful (שָׂמַח) and his glory, *i. e.* his soul (*vid.* on
vii. 6) rejoices, the joy breaking forth in rejoicing, as the
fut. consec. affirms. There is no passage of Scripture that
so closely resembles this as 1 Thess. v. 23. לֵב is πνεῦμα
(νοῦς), כָּבוֹד, ψυχή (*vid. Psychol.* S. 98; tr. p. 119), בָּשָׂר (according to its primary meaning, *attrectabile,* that which is frail),
σῶμα. The ἀμέμπτως τηρηθῆναι which the apostle in the
above passage desires for his readers in respect of all three
parts of their being, David here expresses as a confident
expectation; for אַף implies that he also hopes for his body

that which he hopes for his spirit-life centred in the heart,
and for his soul raised to dignity both by the work of creation and of grace. He looks death calmly and triumphantly
in the face, even his flesh shall dwell or lie securely, viz.
without being seized with trembling at its approaching
corruption. David's hope rests on this conclusion: it is
impossible for the man, who, in appropriating faith and
actual experience, calls God his own, to fall into the hands
of death. For ver. 10 shews, that what is here thought of
in connection with שָׁכַן לָבֶטַח, dwelling in safety under the
divine protection (Deut. xxxiii. 12, 28, cf. Prov. iii. 24), is
preservation from death. שַׁחַת is rendered by the LXX.
διαφθορά, as though it came from שָׁחַת διαφθείρειν, as perhaps it may do in Job xvii. 14. But in vii. 16 the LXX.
has βόθρος, which is the more correct: prop. a sinking in,
from שׁוּחַ to sink, to be sunk, like נַחַת from נוּחַ, רַחַת from
רוּחַ. To leave to the unseen world (עָזַב prop. to loosen, let
go) is equivalent to abandoning one to it, so that he becomes its prey. Ver. 10*b* — where to see the grave (xlix.
10), equivalent to, to succumb to the state of the grave, *i. e.*
death (lxxxix. 49, Lk. ii. 26, John viii. 51) is the opposite
of "seeing life", *i. e.* experiencing and enjoying it (Eccl. ix.
9, John iii. 36), the sense of sight being used as the noblest of the senses to denote the *sensus communis, i. e.* the
common sense lying at the basis of all feeling and perception, and figuratively of all active and passive experience
(*Psychol.* S. 234; tr. p. 276) — shews, that what is said
here is not intended of an abandonment by which, having
once come under the power of death, there is no coming
forth again (Böttcher). It is therefore the hope of not
dying, that is expressed by David in ver. 10. For by חֲסִידְךָ
David means himself. According to Norzi, the Spanish
MSS. have חֲסִידֶיךָ with the Masoretic note יתיר יו״ד, and the
LXX., Targ., and Syriac translate, and the Talmud and
Midrash interpret it, in accordance with this *Keri*. There
is no ground for the reading חֲסִידֶיךָ, and it is also opposed
by the personal form of expression surrounding it.*

---

* Most MSS. and the best, which have no distinction of *Keri* and
Chethib here, read חֲסִידְךָ, as also the *Biblia Ven.* 1521, the Spanish

The positive expression of hope in ver. 11 comes as a companion to the negative just expressed: Thou wilt grant me to experience (הוֹדִיעַ, is used, as usual, of the presentation of a knowledge, which concerns the whole man and not his understanding merely) אֹרַח חַיִּים, the path of life, *i. e.* the path to life (cf. Prov. v. 6, ii. 19 with *ib.* x. 17, Mat. vii. 14); but not so that it is conceived of as at the final goal, but as leading slowly and gradually onwards to life; חַיִּים in the most manifold sense, as, *e. g.*, in xxxvi. 10, Deut. xxx. 15: life from God, with God, and in God, the living God; the opposite of death, as the manifestation of God's wrath and banishment from Him. That his body shall not die is only the external and visible phase of that which David hopes for himself; on its inward, unseen side it is a living, inwrought of God in the whole man, which in its continuance is a walking in the divine life. The second part of ver. 11, which consists of two members, describes this life with which he solaces himself. According to the accentuation, — which marks חיים with *Olewejored* not with *Rebia magnum* or *Pazer,* — שֹׂבַע שְׂמָחוֹת is not a second object dependent upon תוֹדִיעֵנִי, but the subject of a substantival clause: a satisfying fulness of joy is אֶת־פָּנֶיךָ, with Thy countenance, *i. e.* connected with and naturally produced by beholding Thy face (אֶת preposition of fellowship, as in xxi. 7, cxl. 14); for joy is light, and God's countenance, or doxa, is the light of lights. And every kind of pleasurable things, נְעִמוֹת, He holds in His right hand, extending them to His saints — a gift which lasts for ever; נֶצַח equivalent to לָנֶצַח. נֶצַח, from the primary notion of conspicuous brightness, is duration extending beyond all else — an expression for לְעוֹלָם, which David has probably coined, for it appears for the first time in the Davidic Psalms. Pleasures are in Thy right hand continually — God's right hand is never empty, His fulness is inexhaustible.

The apostolic application of this Psalm (Acts ii. 29—32, xiii. 35—37) is based on the considerations that David's

----

Polyglott and other older printed copies. Those MSS. which give חֲסִידֶיךָ (without any *Keri*), on the other hand, scarcely come under consideration.

hope of not coming under the power of death was not realised in David himself, as is at once clear, to the unlimited extent in which it is expressed in the Psalm; but that it is fulfilled in Jesus, who has not been left to Hades and whose flesh did not see corruption; and that consequently the words of the Psalm are a prophecy of David concerning Jesus, the Christ, who was promised as the heir to his throne, and whom, by reason of the promise, he had prophetically before his mind. If we look into the Psalm, we see that David, in his mode of expression, bases that hope simply upon his relation to Jahve, the ever-living One. That it has been granted to him in particular, to express this hope which is based upon the mystic relation of the חסיד to Jahve in such language, — a hope which the issue of Jesus' life has sealed by an historical fulfilment, — is to be explained from the relation, according to the promise, in which David stands to his seed, the Christ and Holy One of God, who appeared in the person of Jesus. David, the anointed of God, looking upon himself as in Jahve, the God who has given the promise, becomes the prophet of Christ; but this is only indirectly, for he speaks of himself, and what he says has also been fulfilled in his own person. But this fulfilment is not limited to the condition, that he did not succumb to any peril that threatened his life so long as the kingship would have perished with him, and that, when he died, the kingship nevertheless remained (Hofmann); nor, that he was secured against all danger of death until he had accomplished his life's mission, until he had fulfilled the vocation assigned to him in the history of the plan of redemption (Kurtz) — the hope which he cherishes for himself personally has found a fulfilment which far exceeds this. After his hope has found in Christ its full realisation in accordance with the history of the plan of redemption, it receives through Christ its personal realisation for himself also. For what he says, extends on the one hand far beyond himself, and therefore refers prophetically to Christ: *in decachordo Psalterio* — as Jerome boldly expresses it — *ab inferis suscitat resurgentem.* But on the other hand that which is predicted comes back upon himself, to raise him also from death and Hades to the beholding of God. *Verus justitiæ sol* — says

Sonntag in his *Tituli Psalmorum, 1687 — e sepulcro resur-
rexit,* στήλη *seu lapis sepulcralis a monumento devolutus,
arcus triumphalis erectus, victoria ab hominibus reportata. En
vobis Michtam! En Evangelium! —*

PSALM XVII.

FLIGHT OF AN INNOCENT AND PERSECUTED MAN FOR RE-
FUGE IN THE LORD, WHO KNOWETH THEM THAT ARE HIS.

1 HEAR, O Jahve, righteousness, hearken to my cry,
  Give ear to my prayer with undeceitful lips!
2 From Thy presence let my right go forth,
  Thine eyes behold rightly.

3 Thou hast proved my heart, Thou hast visited (me)
          by night,
  Thou hast tried me — Thou findest nothing:
  If I think evil, it doth not pass my mouth.
4 In connection with the doings of men, by the words of
          Thy lips
  I have guarded myself against the paths of the destroyer;
5 My steps held fast to Thy paths,
  My footsteps have not slipped.

6 As such an one I call upon Thee, for Thou hearest me,
          O God!
  Incline Thine ear unto me, hear my speech.
7 Shew Thy marvellous lovingkindness, Helper of those
          who seek refuge
  From those that rise up [against them], at Thy right hand.

8 Keep me as the apple — the pupil — of the eye;
  Hide me in the shadow of Thy wings
9 From the wicked, who would destroy me,
  From my deadly enemies, who compass me about.

10 They have shut up their fat,
   They speak proudly with their mouth;
11 At every step they have surrounded me,
   Their purpose is to smite down to the earth.
12 He is like a lion that is greedy to ravin,
   And like a young lion lurking in the lair.

13 Arise, Jahve, go forth to meet him, cast him down,
   Deliver my soul from the wicked, with Thy sword,
14 From men, with Thy hand, Jahve — from men of this
          world,
     Whose portion is in life, and with Thy treasures Thou
          fillest their belly,
     They have plenty of children and leave their abundance
          to their young ones.
15 As for me — in righteousness shall I behold Thy face,
   I will satisfy myself, when I awake, with Thine image.

Ps. xvii. is placed after Ps. xvi., because just like the latter
(cf. xi. 7) it closes with the hope of a blessed and satisfying vision of God. In other respects also the two Psalms have
many prominent features in common: as, for instance, the
the petition שָׁמְרֵנִי, xvi. 1, xvii. 8; the retrospect on nightly
fellowship with God, xvi. 7, xvii. 3; the form of address in
prayer אֶל, xvi. 1, xvii. 6; the verb תָּמַךְ, xvi. 5, xvii. 5, &c.
(*vid. Symbolæ* p. 49), notwithstanding a great dissimilarity
in their tone. For Ps. xvi. is the first of those which we
call Psalms written in the indignant style, in the series of
the Davidic Psalms. The language of the Psalms of David,
which is in other instances so flowing and clear, becomes
more harsh and, in accordance with the subject and mood,
as it were, full of unresolved dissonances (Ps. xvii. cxl.
lviii. xxxvi. 2 sq., cf. x. 2—11) when describing the dissolute conduct of his enemies, and of the ungodly in general.
The language is then more rough and unmanageable, and
wanting in the clearness and transparency we find elsewhere. The tone of the language also becomes more dull
and, as it were, a dull murmur. It rolls on like the rumble
of distant thunder, by piling up the suffixes *mo, āmo, ēmo*,
as in xvii. 10, xxxv. 16, lxiv. 6, 9, where David speaks of
his enemies and describes them in a tone suggested by the
indignation, which is working within his breast; or in lix.
12—14, lvi. 8, xxi. 10—13, cxl. 10, lviii. 7., where, as in
prophetic language, he announces to them of the judgment
of God. The more vehement and less orderly flow of the
language which we find here, is the result of the inward
tumult of his feelings.

Thĕre are so many parallels in the thought and expression of thought of this Psalm in other Davidic Psalms (among those we have already commented on we may instance more especially Ps. vii. and xi., and also iv. and x.), that even Hitzig admits the לְדָוִד. The author of the Psalm is persecuted, and others with him; foes, among whom one, their leader, stands prominently forward, plot against his life, and have encompassed him about in the most threatening manner, eager for his death. All this corresponds, line for line, with the situation of David in the wilderness of *Maon* (about three hours and three quarters S.S.E. of Hebron), as narrated in 1 Sam. xxiii. 25 sq., when Saul and his men were so close upon the heels of David and his men, that he only escaped capture by a most fortunate incident.

The only name inscribed on this Psalm is תְּפִלָּה (a prayer), the most comprehensive name for the Psalms, and the oldest (lxxii. 20); for שִׁיר and מִזְמוֹר were only given to them when they were sung in the liturgy and with musical accompaniment. As the title of a Psalm it is found five times (xvii. lxxxvi. xc. cii. cxlii) in the Psalter, and besides that once, in Hab. iii. Habakkuk's תפלה is a hymn composed for music. But in the Psalter we do not find any indication of the Psalms thus inscribed being arranged for music. The strophe schema is 4. 7; 4. 4. 6. 7.

Vers. 1—2. צֶדֶק is the accusative of the object: the righteousness, intended by the suppliant, is his own (ver. 15*a*). He knows that he is not merely righteous in his relation to man, but also in his relation to God. In all such assertions of pious self-consciousness, that which is intended is a righteousness of life which has its ground in the righteousness of faith. True, Hupfeld is of opinion, that under the Old Testament nothing was known either of righteousness which is by faith or of a righteousness belonging to another and imputed. But if this were true, then Paul was in gross error and Christianity is built upon the sand. But the truth, that faith is the ultimate ground of righteousness, is expressed in Gen. xv. 6, and at other turning-points in the course of the history of redemption; and the truth, that the righteousness which avails before God is a gift of grace is, for instance, a thought distinctly marked out in the

expression of Jeremiah ה' צִדְקֵנוּ, "the Lord our righteousness." The Old Testament conception, it is true, looks
more to the phenomena than to the root of the matter
(*ist mehr phänomenell als wurzelhaft*), is (so to speak) more
Jacobic than Pauline; but the righteousness of life of the
Old Testament and that of the New have one and the same
basis, viz. in the grace of God, the Redeemer, towards sinful
man, who in himself is altogether wanting in righteousness
before God (cxliii. 2). Thus there is no self-righteousness,
in David's praying that the righteousness, which in him is
persecuted and cries for help, may be heard. For, on the
one hand, in his personal relation to Saul, he knows himself
to be free from any ungrateful thoughts of usurpation, and
on the other, in his personal relation to God free from מִרְמָה,
i. e. self-delusion and hypocrisy. The shrill cry for help,
רִנָּה, which he raises, is such as may be heard and answered,
because they are not lips of deceit with which he prays. The
actual fact is manifest לִפְנֵי יהוה, therefore may his right
go forth מִלְּפָנֶיו, — just what does happen, by its being
publicly proclaimed and openly maintained — from Him,
for His eyes, the eyes of Him who knoweth the hearts (xi.
4), behold מֵישָׁרִים (as in lviii. 2, lxxv. 3 = בְּמִישָׁרִים, ix. 9, and
many other passages), in uprightness, *i. e.* in accordance
with the facts of the case and without partiality. מישרים
might also be an accusative of the object (cf. 1 Chron. xxix.
17), but the usage of the language much more strongly
favours the adverbial rendering, which is made still more
natural by the confirmatory relation in which ver. 2*b* stands
to 2*a*.

Vers. 3—5. David refers to the divine testing and illu-
mination of the inward parts, which he has experienced in
himself, in support of his sincerity. The preterites in ver.
3 express the divine acts that preceded the result בַּל־תִּמְצָא,
viz. the testing He has instituted, which is referred to in
צְרַפְתַּנִי and also בְּחַנְתָּ as a trying of gold by fire, and in פָּקַד
as an investigation (Job vii. 18). The result of the close scrutiny to which God has subjected him in the night, when the
bottom of a man's heart is at once made manifest, whether
it be in his thoughts when awake or in the dream and fancies of the sleeper, was and is this, that He does not find,

viz. anything whatever to punish in him, anything that is separated as dross from the gold. To the mind of the New Testament believer with his deep, and as it were microscopically penetrating, insight into the depth of sin, such a confession concerning himself would be more difficult than to the mind of an Old Testament saint. For a separation and disunion of flesh and spirit, which was unknown in the same degree to the Old Testament, has been accomplished in the New Testament consciousness by the facts and operations of redemption revealed in the New Testament; although at the same time it must be remembered that in such confessions the Old Testament consciousness does not claim to be clear from sins, but only from a conscious love of sin, and from a self-love that is hostile to God.

With זַמֹּתִי David begins his confession of how Jahve found him to be, instead of finding anything punishable in him. This word is either an infinitive like חַנּוֹת (lxxvii. 10) with the regular *ultima* accentuation, formed after the manner of the לְ"ה verbs, — in accordance with which Hitzig renders it: my thinking does not overstep my mouth, — or even 1 *pers. præt.*, which is properly *Milel*, but does also occur as *Milra, e. g.* Deut. xxxii. 41, Isa. xliv. 16 (*vid.* on Job xix. 17), — according to which Böttcher translates: should I think anything evil, it dare not pass beyond my mouth, — or (since זָמַם may denote the determination that precedes the act, *e. g.* Jer. iv. 28, Lam. ii. 17): I have determined my mouth shall not transgress. This last rendering is opposed by the fact, that עָבַר by itself in the ethical signification "to transgress" (cf. post-biblical עֲבֵרָה πɑράβασις) is not the usage of the biblical Hebrew, and that when יַעֲבָר־פִּי stand close together, פִּי is presumptively the object. We therefore give the preference to Böttcher's explanation, which renders זַמֹּתִי as a hypothetical perfect and is favoured by Prov. xxx. 32 (which is to be translated: and if thou thinkest evil, (lay) thy hand on thy mouth!). Nevertheless בל יעבר־פי is not the expression of a fact, but of a purpose, as the combination of בל with the future requires it to be taken. The psalmist is able to testify of himself that he so keeps evil thoughts in subjection within him, even when they may arise, that they do not pass beyond his mouth,

much less that he should put them into action. But perhaps the psalmist wrote פִיךָ originally, "my reflecting does
not go beyond Thy commandment" (according to Num. xxii.
18, 1 Sam. xv. 24, Prov. viii. 29), — a meaning better suited, as a result of the search, to the nightly investigation.
The ל of לִפְעֻלּוֹת need not be the ל of reference (as to); it is
that of the state or condition, as in xxxii. 6, lxix. 22. אָדָם,
as perhaps also in Job xxxi. 33, Hos. vi. 7 (if אדם is not
there the name of the first man), means, men as they are
by nature and habit. בִּדְבַר שְׂפָתֶיךָ does not admit of being
connected with לִפְעֻלּוֹת: at the doings of the world contrary
to Thy revealed will (Hofmann and others); for פָּעַל בְּ cannot mean: to act contrary to any one, but only: to work
upon any one, Job xxxv. 6. These words must therefore
be regarded as a closer definition, placed first, of the
שָׁמַרְתִּי which follows: in connection with the doings of men,
by virtue of the divine commandment, he has taken care
of the paths of the oppressor, viz. not to go in them; 1 Sam.
xxv. 21 is an instance in support of this rendering, where
שמרתי, as in Job ii. 6, means: I have kept (Nabal's possession), not seizing upon it myself. Jerome correctly translates *vias latronis*; for פָּרִיץ signifies one who breaks in, *i. e.*
one who does damage intentionally and by violence. The
confession concerning himself is still continued in ver. 5,
for the *inf. absol.* תָּמֹךְ, if taken as imperative would express
a prayer for constancy, that is alien to the circumstances
described. The perfect after בַּל is also against such a rendering. It must therefore be taken as *inf. historicus*, and
explained according to Job xxiii. 11, cf. Ps. xli. 13. The
noun following the *inf. absol.*, which is usually the object,
is the subject in this instance, as, *e. g.* in Job xl. 2, Prov.
xvii. 12, Eccl. iv. 2, and frequently. It is אֲשׁוּרַי, and not
אֲשׁוּרִי, אשׁור (a step) never having the שׁ dageshed, except
in ver. 11 and Job xxxi. 7.

Vers. 6—7. It is only now, after his inward parts and
his walk have been laid open to Jahve, that he resumes his
petition, which is so well justified and so soundly based,
and enters into detail. The אני* found beside קְרָאתִיךָ (the

----

* The word is pointed אֲנִי in correct texts, as אני always is when

perfect referring to that which has just now been put into
execution) is meant to imply: such an one as he has described
himself to be according to the testimony of his conscience, may call upon God, for God hears such and will
therefore also hear him. הַט אָזְנְךָ exactly corresponds to
the Latin *au-di* (*aus-cul-ta*). The *Hiph.* הִפְלָה (הִפְלִיא, xxxi.
22, cf. iv. 4) signifies here to work in an extraordinary and
marvellous manner. The danger of him who thus prays
is great, but the mercies of God, who is ready and able to
help, are still greater. Oh that He may, then, exhibit all
its fulness on his behalf. The form of the address resembles the Greek, which is so fond of participles. If it is translated as Luther translates it: "Shew Thy marvellous loving-
kindness, Thou Saviour of those who trust in Thee, Against
those who so set themselves against Thy right hand", then
חוֹסִים is used just as absolutely as in Prov. xiv. 32, and
the right hand of God is conceived of as that which arranges
and makes firm. But "to rebel against God's right (not
statuta, but *dexteram*)" is a strange expression. There are
still two other constructions from which to choose, viz. "Thou
Deliverer of those seeking protection from adversaries, with
Thy right hand" (Hitz.), or: "Thou Helper of those seeking
protection from adversaries, at Thy right hand" (Aben-Ezra,
Tremell.). This last rendering is to be preferred to the two
others. Since, on the one hand, one says מחסה מן, refuge
from . . . , and on the other, חָסָה בְ to hide one's self in
any one, or in any place, this determining of the verbal
notion by the preposition (on this, see above on ii. 12) must
be possible in both directions. מִפְתְקוֹמְמִים is equivalent to
מִמְתְקוֹמְמֵיהֶם Job. xxvii. 7; and חוֹסִים בִּימִינֶךָ, those seeking
protection at the strong hand of Jahve. The force of the
בְ is just the same as in connection with הִסְתַּתֵּר, 1 Sam.
xxiii. 19. In Damascus and throughout Syria — Wetzstein observes on this passage — the weak make use of
these words when they surrender themselves to the strong:

---

it has *Munach* and *Dechi* follows, *e. g.* also cxvi. 16. This *Gaja* demands an emphatic intonation of the secondary word in its relation
to the principal word (which here is קראתיך).

انا بِقَبْضَة يدك "I am in the grasp of thy hand (in thy closed hand) *i. e.* I give myself up entirely to thee".*

Vers. 8—9. The covenant relationship towards Himself in which Jahve has placed David, and the relationship of love in which David stands to Jahve, fully justified the oppressed one in his extreme request. The apple of the eye, which is surrounded by the iris, is called אִישׁוֹן, the man (Arabic *insân*), or in the diminutive and endearing sense of the termination *on:* the little man of the eye, because a picture in miniature of one's self is seen, as in a glass, when looking into another person's eye. בַּת־עַיִן either because it is as if born out of the eye and the eye has, as it were, concentrated itself in it, or rather because the little image which is mirrored in it is, as it were, the little daughter of the eye (here and Lam. ii. 18). To the Latin *pupilla* (*pupula*), Greek κόρη, corresponds most closely בָּבַת עַיִן, Zech. ii. 12, which does not signify the gate, aperture, sight, but, as בַּת shews, the little boy, or more strictly, the little girl of the eye. It is singular that אִישׁוֹן here has the feminine בַּת־עַיִן as the expression in apposition to it. The construction might be genitival: "as the little man of the apple of the eye", inasmuch as the saint knows himself to be so near to God, that, as it were, his image in miniature is mirrored in the great eye of God. But (1) the more ordinary name for the pupil of the eye is not בַּת עַיִן, but אִישׁוֹן; and (2) with that construction the proper point of the comparison, that the apple of the eye is an object of the most careful self-preservation, is missed. There is, consequently, a combination of two names of the pupil or apple of the eye, the usual one and one more select, without reference to the gender of the former, in order to give greater definition

---

* Cognate in meaning to חסה ב are استتر ب and تَذَرَّى ب, *e. g.* تذرّى بالحايط من الريح he shelters (hides) himself by the wall from the wind, or بالعضاة من البرد by a fire against the cold, and عان, which is often applied in like manner to God's protection. Thus, *e. g.* (according to Bochâri's *Sunna*) a woman, whom Muhammed wanted to seize, cried out: أَعُوذُ بِاللهِ منك I place myself under God's protection against thee, and he replied: عُذْتِ بِمَعَانٍ thou hast taken refuge in an (inaccessible) *asylum* (cf. *Job*, i. 310 n. and ii. 22 n. 2).

and emphasis to the figure. The primary passage for this
bold figure, which is the utterance of loving entreaty, is
Deut. xxxii. 10, where the dazzling anthropomorphism is
effaced by the LXX. and other ancient versions;* cf. also Sir.
xvii. 22. Then follows another figure, taken from the eagle,
which hides its young under its wings, likewise from Deut.
xxxii, viz. ver. 11, for the figure of the hen (Mat. xxiii. 37)
is alien to the Old Testament. In that passage, Moses, in
his great song, speaks of the wings of God; but the double
figure of the shadow of God's wings (here and in xxxvi. 8,
lvii. 2, lxiii. 8) is coined by David. "God's wings" are the
spreadings out, *i. e.* the manifestations of His love, taking
the creature under the protection of its intimate fellowship,
and the "shadow" of these wings is the refreshing rest and
security which the fellowship of this love affords to those,
who hide themselves beneath it, from the heat of outward
or inward conflict.

From ver. 9 we learn more definitely the position in
which the psalmist is placed. שָׁדַד signifies to use violence,
to destroy the life, continuance, or possession of any one.
According to the accentuation בְּנֶפֶשׁ is to be connected with
אֹיְבַי, not with יַקִּיפוּ, and to be understood according to Ez.
xxv. 6: "enemies with the soul" are those whose enmity is
not merely superficial, but most deep-seated (cf. ἐκ ψυχῆς,
Eph. vi. 6, Col. iii. 23). The soul (viz. the hating and
eagerly longing soul, xxvii. 12, xli. 3) is just the same as
if בנפש is combined with the verb, viz. the soul of the enemies; and איבי נפשי would therefore not be more correct, as
Hitzig thinks, than איבי בנפש, but would have a different
meaning. They are eager to destroy him (*perf. conatus*),
and form a circle round about him, as ravenous ones, in
order to swallow him up.

Vers. 10—12 tell what sort of people these persecutors are. Their heart is called fat, *adeps,* not as though
חֵלֶב could in itself be equivalent to לֵב, more especially as
both words are radically distinct (חֵלֶב from the root לב,
λιπ; לֵב from the root לב, לף to envelope: that which is enveloped, the kernel, the inside), but (without any need for

---

* *Vid.* Geiger, *Urschrift und Uebersetzungen der Bibel*, S. 324.

von Ortenberg's conjecture חֵלֶב לְבָּמוֹ סָגְרוּ "they close their
heart with fat") because it is, as it were, entirely fat (cxix.
70, cf. lxxiii. 7), and because it is inaccessible to any feeling
of compassion, and in general incapable of the nobler emotions. To shut up the fat = the heart (cf. κλείειν τὰ
σπλάγχνα 1 John iii. 17), is equivalent to: to fortify one's
self wilfully in indifference to sympathy, tender feeling, and
all noble feelings (cf. הִשְׁמִין לֵב = to harden, Isa. vi. 10).
The construction of פִּימוֹ (which agrees in sound with פִּימָה,
Job xv. 27) is just the same as that of קוֹלִי, iii. 5. On the
other hand, אַשּׁוּרֵנוּ (after the form עַמּוּד and written *plene*) is
neither such an accusative of the means or instrument, nor
the second accusative, beside the accusative of the object,
of that by which the object is surrounded, that is usually
found with verbs of surrounding (*e. g.* v. 13, xxxii. 7); for
"they have surrounded me (us) with our step" is unintelligible. But אשורנו can be the accusative of the member, as
in iii. 8, cf. xxii. 17, Gen. iii. 15, for "it is true the step is
not a member" (Hitz.), but since "step" and "foot" are interchangeable notions, lxxiii. 2, the σχῆμα καθ᾽ ὅλον καὶ μέρος
is applicable to the former, and as, *e. g.* Homer says, *Iliad*
vii. 355: σὲ μάλιστα πόνος φρένας ἀμφιβέβηκεν, the Hebrew
poet can also say: they have encompassed us (and in fact)
our steps, each of our steps (so that we cannot go forwards
or backwards with our feet). The *Kerî* סְבָבוּנוּ gets rid of the
change in number which we have with the *Chethîb* סבבוני;
the latter, however, is admissible according to parallels like
lxii. 5, and corresponds to David's position, who is hunted
by Saul and at the present time driven into a strait at the
head of a small company of faithful followers. Their eyes
— he goes on to say in ver. 11*b* — have they set to fell,
viz. us, who are encompassed, to the earth, *i. e.* so that we
shall be cast to the ground. נָטָה is transitive, as in xviii.
10, lxii. 4, in the transitively applied sense of lxxiii. 2 (cf.
xxxvii. 31): to incline to fall (whereas in xliv. 19, Job xxxi.
7, it means to turn away from); and בָּאָרֶץ (without any need
for the conjecture בָּאֹרַח) expresses the final issue, instead
of לָאָרֶץ, vii. 6. By the expression דִּמְיוֹנוֹ one is prominently
singled out from the host of the enemy, viz. its chief, the
words being: his likeness is as a lion, according to the pecu-

liarity of the poetical style, of changing verbal into substantival clauses, instead of דָּמָה כְּאַרְיֵה. Since in Old Testament Hebrew, as also in Syriac and Arabic, כְ is only a
preposition, not a connective conjunction, it cannot be rendered: as a lion longs to prey, but: as a lion that is greedy
or hungry (cf. كسف used of sinking away, decline, obscuring or eclipsing, growing pale, and خسف more especially
of enfeebling, hunger, distinct from הָשַׂף = كشف to peel off,
make bare) to ravin. In the parallel member of the verse
the participle alternates with the attributive clause. כְּפִיר is
(according to Meier) the young lion as being covered with
thicker hair.

Vers. 13—15. The phrase קִדֵּם פְּנֵי, *antevertere faciem
alicujus*, means both to appear before any one with reverence, xcv. 2 (post-biblical: to pay one's respects to any one)
and to meet any one as an enemy, rush on him. The foe
springs like a lion upon David, may Jahve — so he prays
— as his defence cross the path of the lion and intercept
him, and cast him down so that he, being rendered harmless, shall lie there with bowed knees (כָּרַע, of the lion, Gen.
xlix. 9, Num. xxiv. 9). He is to rescue his soul from the
ungodly חַרְבֶּךָ. This חרבך, and also the יָדְךָ which follows,
can be regarded as a permutative of the subject (Böttcher,
Hupfeld, and Hitzig), an explanation which is commended
by xliv. 3 and other passages. But it is much more probably that more exact definitions of this kind are treated as
accusatives, *vid.* on iii. 5. At any rate "sword" and "hand"
are meant as the instruments by which the פַּלֵּט, rescuing,
is effected. The force of פְּלֵטָה extends into ver. 14, and
מְמֵתִים (with a *Chateph* under the letter that is freed from
reduplication, like מְמַכּוֹן, xxxiii. 14) corresponds to מֵרָשָׁע,
as יָדְךָ to חַרְבֶּךָ. The word ממתים (plural of מַת, men, Deut.
ii. 34, whence מְתָם, each and every one), which of itself gives
no complete sense, is repeated and made complete after the
interruption caused by the insertion of יָדְךָ ה', — a remarkable manner of obstructing and then resuming the thought,
which Hofmann (*Schriftbeweis* ii. 2. 495) seeks to get over
by a change in the division of the verse and in the interpunction. חֶלֶד, either from חָלַד Syriac to creep, glide, slip
away (whence חֻלְדָּה a weasel, a mole) or from חָלַד Talmudic

to cover, hide, signifies: this temporal life which glides by unnoticed (distinct from the Arabic *chald, chuld,* an abiding stay, endless duration); and consequently חֶדֶל, limited existence, from חָדַל to have an end, alternates with חֶלֶד as a play upon the letters, comp. xlix. 2 with Isa. xxxviii. 11. The combination מְתִים מֵחֶלֶד resembles x. 18, xvi. 4. What is meant, is: men who have no other home but the world, which passeth away with the lust thereof, men ἐκ τοῦ κόσμου τούτου, or υἱοὶ τοῦ αἰῶνος τούτου. The meaning of the further description חֶלְקָם בַּחַיִּים (cf. Eccl. ix. 9) becomes clear from the converse in xvi. 5. Jahve is the חֵלֶק of the godly man; and the sphere within which the worldling claims his חלק is הַחַיִּים, this temporal, visible, and material life. This is everything to him; whereas the godly man says: טוֹב חַסְדְּךָ מֵחַיִּים, lxiii. 4. The contrast is not so much between this life and the life to come, as between the world (life) and God. Here we see into the inmost nature of the Old Testament faith. To the Old Testament believer, all the blessedness and glory of the future life, which the New Testament unfolds, is shut up in Jahve. Jahve is his highest good, and possessing Him he is raised above heaven and earth, above life and death. To yield implicitly to Him, without any explicit knowledge of a blessed future life, to be satisfied with Him, to rest in Him, to hide in Him in the face of death, is the characteristic of the Old Testament faith. חלקם בחיים expresses both the state of mind and the lot of the men of the world. Material things which are their highest good, fall also in abundance to their share. The words "whose belly Thou fillest with Thy treasure" (*Chethîb:* וּצְפִינְךָ the usual participial form, but as a participle an Aramaising form) do not sound as though the poet meant to say that God leads them to repentance by the riches of His goodness, but on the contrary that God, by satisfying their desires which are confined to the outward and sensuous only, absolutely deprives them of all claim to possessions that extend beyond the world and this present temporal life. Thus, then, צָפִין in this passage is used exactly as צְפוּנִים is used in Job xx. 26 (from צָפַן to hold anything close to one, to hold back, to keep by one). Moreover, there is not the slightest alloy of murmur or envy in the words. The godly man who lacks

these good things out of the treasury of God, has higher
delights; he can exclaim, xxxi. 20: "how great is Thy goodness which Thou hast laid up (צָפַנְתָּ) for those who fear
Thee!" Among the good things with which God fills the belly
and house of the ungodly (Job xxii. 17 sq.) are also children in abundance; these are elsewhere a blessing upon piety
(cxxvii. 3 sq., cxxviii. 3 sq.), but to those who do not
acknowledge the Giver they are a snare to self-glorifying,
Job xxi. 11 (cf. Wisdom iv. 1). בָּנִים is not the subject, but
an accusative, and has been so understood by all the old
translators from the original text, just as in the phrase
שָׂבַע יָמִים to be satisfied with, or weary of, life. On עוֹלָלִים
vid. on viii. 3. יֶתֶר (from יָתַר to stretch out in length, then
to be overhanging, towering above, projecting, superfluous,
redundant) signifies here, as in Job xxii. 20, riches and the
abundance of things possessed.

Ver. 15. With אֲנִי he contrasts his incomparably greater
prosperity with that of his enemies. He, the despised and
persecuted of men, will behold God's face בְּצֶדֶק, in righteousness, which will then find its reward (Mat. v. 8, Hebr.
xii. 14), and will, when this hope is realised by him, thoroughly refresh himself with the form of God. It is not sufficient to explain the vision of the divine countenance here as
meaning the experience of the gracious influences which
proceed from the divine countenance again unveiled and
turned towards him. The parallel of the next clause requires
an actual vision, as in Num. xii. 8, according to which Jahve
appeared to Moses in the true form of His being, without
the intervention of any self-manifestation of an accommo-
dative and visionary kind; but at the same time, as in Exod.
xxxiii. 20, where the vision of the divine countenance is
denied to Moses, according to which, consequently, the self-
manifestation of Jahve in His intercourse with Moses is not
to be thought of without some veiling of Himself which
might render the vision tolerable to him. Here, however,
where David gives expression to a hope which is the final
goal and the very climax of all his hopes, one has no right
in any way to limit the vision of God, who in love permits
him to behold Him (*vid.* on xi. 7), and to limit the being
satisfied with His תְּמוּנָה (LXX. τὴν δόξαν σου, *vid. Psychol.*

S. 49; transl. p. 61). If this is correct, then בְּהָקִיץ cannot
mean "when I wake up from this night's sleep" as Ewald,
Hupfeld and others explain it; for supposing the Psalm
were composed just before falling asleep what would be the
meaning of the postponement of so transcendent a hope to
the end of his natural sleep? Nor can the meaning be to
"awake to a new life of blessedness and peace through the
sunlight of divine favour which again arises after the night
of darkness and distress in which the poet is now to be
found" (Kurtz); for to awake from a night of affliction is
an unsuitable idea and for this very reason cannot be supported. The only remaining explanation, therefore, is the
waking up from the sleep of death (cf. Böttcher, *De inferis*
§ 365—367). The fact that all who are now in their graves
shall one day hear the voice of Him that wakes the dead,
as it is taught in the age after the Exile (Dan. xii. 2), was
surely not known to David, for it was not yet revealed to
him. But why may not this truth of revelation, towards
which prophecy advances with such giant strides (Isa. xxvi.
19. Ezek. xxxvii. 1—14), be already heard even in the
Psalms of David as a bold demand of faith and as a hope
that has struggled forth to freedom out of the comfortless
conception of Sheôl possessed in that age, just as it is heard
a few decades later in the master-work of a cotemporary of
Solomon, the Book of Job? The morning in Ps. xlix. 15 is
also not any morning whatever following upon the night,
but that final morning which brings deliverance to the
upright and inaugurates their dominion. A sure knowledge
of the fact of the resurrection such as, according to Hofmann (*Schriftbeweis* ii. 2, 490), has existed in the Old Testament from the beginning, is not expressed in such passages.
For laments like vi. 6, xxx. 10, lxxxviii. 11—13, shew that
no such certain knowledge was then in existence; and when
the Old Testament literature which we now possess allows
us elsewhere an insight into the history of the perception
of redemption, it does not warrant us in concluding anything more than that the perception of the future resurrection of the dead did not pass from the prophetic word into
the believing mind of Israel until about the time of the Exile,
and that up to that period faith made bold to hope for a

redemption from death, but only *by means of an inference drawn from that which was conceived and existed within itself,* without having an express word of promise in its favour.* Thus it is here also. David certainly gives full expression to the hope of a vision of God, which, as righteous before God, will be vouchsafed to him; and vouchsafed to him, even though he should fall asleep in death in the present extremity (xiii. 4), as one again awakened from the sleep of death, and, therefore (although this idea does not directly coincide with the former), as one raised from the dead. But this hope is not a believing appropriation of a "certain knowledge", but a view that, by reason of the already existing revelation of God, lights up out of his consciousness of fellowship with Him.

PSALM XVIII.

DAVID'S HYMNIC RETROSPECT OF A LIFE CROWNED WITH
MANY MERCIES.

2 FERVENTLY do I love Thee, Jahve, my strength,
3 Jahve, my rock, and my fortress, and my Deliverer,
  My God, my fastness wherein I hide myself,
  My shield, and the horn of my salvation, my high tower!
4 As worthy to be praised do I call upon Jahve,
  And against mine enemies shall I be helped.

5 The bands of death had compassed me
  And the floods of the abyss came upon me.
6 The bands of hades had surrounded me,
  The snares of death assaulted me.

---

* To this Hofmann, *loc. cit.* S. 496, replies as follows: "We do not find that faith indulges in such boldness elsewhere, or that the believing ones cherish hopes which are based on such insecure grounds." But the word of God is surely no insecure ground, and to draw bold conclusions from that which is intimated only from afar, was indeed, even in many other respects (for instance, respecting the incarnation, and respecting the abrogation of the ceremonial law), the province of the Old Testament faith.

7 In my distress I called upon Jahve,
  And unto my God did I cry;
  He heard my call out of His temple,
  And my cry before Him came into His ears.

8 The earth shook and quaked,
  And the foundations of the mountains trembled,
  And they swung to and fro, for He was wroth.
9 There went up a smoke in His nostrils,
  And fire out of His mouth devoured,
  Coals were kindled by it.
10 Then He bowed the heavens and came down,
  And thick darkness was under His feet

11 And He rode upon a cherub and did fly,
  And floated upon the wings of the wind;
12 He made darkness His covering, His pavilion round about
      Him
  Darkness of waters, thick clouds of the skies.
13 Out of the brightness before Him there broke through His
      clouds
  Hail-stones and coals of fire.

14 Then Jahve thundered in the heavens,
  And the Highest made His voice to sound forth.
  [Hail-stones and coals of fire.]
15 And He sent forth His arrows and scattered them,
  And lightnings in abundance and discomfited them.
16 And the channels of the waters became visible,
  And the foundations of the earth were laid bare,
  At Thy threatening, Jahve,
  At the snorting of the breath of Thy wrath.

17 He reached from the height, He seized me,
  He drew me up out of great waters;
18 He delivered me from my grim foe,
  And from them that hated me, because they were too
      strong for me.
19 They came upon me in the day of my calamity,
  Then Jahve was a stay to me,

20 And brought me forth into a large place;
    He delivered me, for He delighted in me.

21 Jahve rewarded me according to my righteousness,
    According to the cleanness of my hands did He recom-
        pense me.
22 For I have kept the ways of Jahve,
    And have not wickedly departed from my God.
23 Far from this, all His judgments are my aim,
    And His statutes I do not put away from me.
24 And I was spotless towards Him,
    And I have kept myself from mine iniquity.

25 Therefore Jahve recompensed me according to any righ-
        teousness,
    According to the cleanness of my hands, which was
        manifest in His eyes.
26 Towards the good Thou shewest Thyself good
    Towards the man of perfect submission Thou shewest
        Thyself yielding.
27 Towards him who sanctifies himself Thou shewest Thy-
        self pure,
    And towards the perverse Thou shewest Thyself fro-
        ward.
28 For Thou, Thou savest the afflicted people,
    And high looks Thou bringest down.

29 For Thou makest my lamp light;
    Jahve, my God, enlighteneth my darkness.
30 For by Thee do I scatter a troop,
    And by my God do I leap walls.
31 As for God — spotless is His way,
    The word of Jahve is tried;
    A shield is He to all who hide in Him.

32 For who is a divine being, but Jahve alone,
    And who is a rock save our God?
33 The God, who girded me with strength,
    And made my way perfect,

34 Making my feet like hinds' feet,
   And who set me upon my high places,
35 Training my hands for war,
   And mine arms bent a bow of brass.

36 And Thou gavest me also the shield of Thy salvation,
   And Thy right hand upheld me,
   And Thy lowliness made me great.
37 Thou madest room for my footsteps under me,
   And mine ankles have not slipped.

38 I pursued mine enemies and overtook them,
   And turned not back, till they were consumed.
39 I smote them, so that they could not rise,
   They fell under my feet
40 And Thou didst gird me with strength for the battle,
   Thou madest my foes to bow down under me,
41 Thou gavest me the necks of mine enemies,
   And those that hated me, I utterly destroyed.

42 They cried, but there was no helper,
   Even to Jahve, but He answered them not.
43 And I crushed them as dust before the wind,
   Like the dirt of the streets I emptied them out.

44 Thou didst deliver me from the strivings of the people,
   Thou didst make me Head of the nations;
   A people that I knew not, served me.
45 At the hearing of the ear, they obeyed me,
   Strangers submitted to me,
46 Strangers faded away,
   And came forth trembling from their strongholds.

47 Jahve liveth, and blessed be my Rock,
   And let the God of my salvation be exalted;
48 The God, who gave me revenges
   And bent back peoples under me,
49 My Deliverer from mine enemies,
   Yea, Thou who liftest me up above my foes,
   Who rescuest me from the violent man.

50 Therefore will I praise Thee among the nations, O Jahve,
 And I will sing praises unto Thy name,
51 As He, who giveth great deliverance to His king
 And sheweth favour to His anointed,
 To David and his seed for ever.

Next to a תְּפִלָּה of David comes a שִׁירָה (*nom. unitatis* from שִׁיר), which is in many ways both in words and thoughts (*Symbolae* p. 49) interwoven with the former. It is the longest of all the hymnic Psalms, and bears the inscription: *To the Precentor, by the servant of Jahve, by David, who spake unto Jahve the words of this song in the day that Jahve had delivered him out of the hand of all his enemies and out of the hand of Saûl: then he said.* The original inscription of the Psalm in the primary collection was probably only למנצח לעבד ה' לדוד, like the inscription of Ps. xxxvi. The rest of the inscription resembles the language with which songs of this class are wont to be introduced in their connection in the historical narrative, Ex. xv. 1, Num. xxi. 17, and more especially Deut. xxxi. 30. And the Psalm before us is found again in 2 Sam. xxii., introduced by words, the manifestly unaccidental agreement of which with the inscription in the Psalter, is explained by its having been incorporated in one of the histories from which the Books of Samuel are extracted, — probably the Annals (*Dibre ha-Jamim*) of David. From this source the writer of the Books of Samuel has taken the Psalm, together with that introduction; and from this source also springs the historical portion of the inscription in the Psalter, which is connected with the preceding by אֲשֶׁר.

David may have styled himself in the inscription עֶבֶד ה', just as the apostles call themselves δοῦλοι 'Ιησοῦ Χριστοῦ. He also in other instances, in prayer, calls himself "the servant of Jahve", xix. 12, 14, cxliv. 10, 2 Sam. vii. 20, as every Israelite might do; but David, who is the first after Moses and Joshua to bear this designation or by-name, could do so in an especial sense. For he, with whom the kingship of promise began, marks an epoch in his service of the work of God no less than did Moses, through whose mediation Israel received the Law, and Joshua, through whose instrumentality they obtained the Land of promise.

The terminology of psalm-poesy does not include the word שִׁירָה, but only שִׁיר. This at once shews that the historical portion of the inscription comes from some other source. בְּיוֹם is followed, not by the *infin.* הַצִּיל: on the day of deliverance, but by the more exactly *plusquamperf.* הִצִּיל: on the day (בְּיוֹם = at the time, as in Gen. ii. 4, and frequently) when he had delivered — a genitival (Ges. § 116, 3) relative clause, like cxxxviii. 3, Ex. vi. 28, Num. iii.1, cf. Ps. lvi. 10. מִיַּד alternates with מִכַּף in this text without any other design than that of varying the expression. The deliverance out of the hand of Saul is made specially prominent, because the most prominent portion of the Psalm, vers. 5—20, treats of it. The danger in which David then was placed, was of the most personal, the most perilous, and the most protracted kind. This prominence was of great service to the collector, because the preceding Psalm bears the features of this time, the lamentations over which are heard there and further back, and now all find expression in this more extended song of praise.

Only a fondness for doubt can lead any one to doubt the Davidic origin of this Psalm, attested as it is in two works, which are independent of one another. The twofold testimony of tradition is supported by the fact that the Psalm contains nothing that militates against David being the author; even the mention of his own name at the close, is not against it (cf. 1 Kings ii. 45). We have before us an Israelitish counterpart to the cuneiform monumental inscriptions, in which the kings of worldly monarchies recapitulate the deeds they have done by the help of their gods. The speaker is a king; the author of the Books of Samuel found the song already in existence as a Davidic song; the difference of his text from that which lies before us in the Psalter, shews that at that time it had been transmitted from some earlier period; writers of the later time of the kings here and there use language which is borrowed from it or are echoes of it (comp. Prov. xxx. 5 with ver. 31; Hab. iii. 19 with ver. 34); it bears throughout the mark of the classic age of the language and poetry, and "if it be not David's, it must have been written in his name and by some one imbued with his spirit, and who could have been this cotemporary poet and twin-genius?" (Hitzig). All this irresistibly points us to David himself, to whom really belong also all the other songs in the Second Book of Samuel, which are introduced as Davidic (over Saul and Jonathan, over Abner, &c.). This, the greatest of all, springs entirely from the new self-consciousness to which he was raised by the promises recorded in 2 Sam. vii.; and towards the end, it closes with express retrospective reference to these promises; for David's certainty of the everlasting duration of his house, and God's covenant of mercy with his house, rests upon the announcement made by Nathan.

The Psalm divides into two halves; for the strain of praise begins anew with ver. 32, after having run its first course and come to a beautiful close in ver. 31. The two halves are also distinct in respect of their artificial form. The strophe schema of the first is: 6. 8. 8. 6. 8 (not 9). 8. 8. 8. 7. The mixture of six and eight line strophes is symmetrical, and the seven of the last strophe is nothing strange. The mixture in the second half on the contrary is varied. The art of the strophe system appears here, as is also seen in other instances in the Psalms, to be relaxed; and the striving after form at the commencement has given way to the pressure and crowding of the thoughts.

The traditional mode of writing out this Psalm, as also the *Cantica*, 2 Sam. xxii. and Judges v., is "a half-brick upon a brick, and a brick upon a half-brick" (אירח על גבי לבנה ולבנה על גבי אריח): *i. e.* one line consisting of two, and one of three parts of a verse, and the line consisting of the three parts has only one word on the right and on the left; the whole consequently forms three columns. On the other hand, the song in Deut. xxxii. (as also Josh. xii. 9 sqq., Esth. ix. 7—10) is to be written "a half-brick upon a half-brick and a brick upon a brick", *i. e.* in only two columns, cf. *infra* p. 269.

Vers. 2—4. The poet opens with a number of endearing names for God, in which he gratefully comprehends the results of long and varied experience. So far as regards the parallelism of the members, a monostich forms the beginning of this Psalm, as in Ps. xvi. xxiii. xxv. and many

others. Nevertheless the matter assumes a somewhat different aspect, if ver. 3 is not, with Maurer, Hengstenberg
and Hupfeld, taken as two predicate clauses (Jahve is . . .,
my God is . . .), but as a simple vocative — a rendering
which alone corresponds to the intensity with which this
greatest of the Davidic hymns opens — God being invoked
by 'ה, 'ה, אֵלִי, and each of these names being followed by a
predicative expansion of itself, which increases in fulness
of tone and emphasis. The אֶרְחָמְךָ (with *ā*, according to
Ew. § 251, *b*), which carries the three series of the names
of God, makes up in depth of meaning what is wanting in
compass. Elsewhere we find only the *Piel* רִחַם of tender
sympathising love, but here the *Kal* is used as an Aramaism.
Hence the Jalkut on this passage explains it by רחמאי יתך
"I love thee", of ardent, heartfelt love and attachment. The
primary signification of softness (root רח, נךְ יךְ, to be
soft, lax, loose), whence רֶחֶם, *uterus*, is transferred in both
cases to tenderness of feeling or sentiment. The most general
predicate חִזְקִי (from חֹזֶק according to a similar inflexion to
עֹמֶק, בֹּסֶר, אֹמֶר, *plur.* עָמְקֵי Prov. ix. 18) is followed by those
which describe Jahve as a protector and deliverer in persecution on the one hand, and on the other as a defender and the
giver of victory in battle. They are all typical names sym-
bolising what Jahve is in Himself; hence instead of וּמְפַלְטִי it
would perhaps have been more correct to point וּמִפְלָטִי (and
my refuge). God had already called Himself a shield to
Abram, Gen. xv. 1; and He is called צוּר (cf. אֶבֶן Gen. xlix.
24) in the great Mosaic song, Deut. xxxii. 4, 37 (the latter
verse is distinctly echoed here). סֶלַע from סָלַע, سلع, *findere*,
means properly a cleft in a rock (Arabic סֶלַע*), then a cleft

---

* Neshwân defines thus: السَّلع is a cutting in a mountain after
the manner of a gorge; and Jâkût, who cites a number of places that
are so called: a wide plain (فضاء) enclosed by steep rocks, which is
reached through a narrow pass (شِعب), but can only be descended
on foot. Accordingly, in סַלְעִי the idea of a safe (and comfortable)
hiding-place preponderates; in צוּרִי that of firm ground and inac-
cessibility. The one figure calls to mind the (well-watered) Edomitish
סֶלַע surrounded with precipitous rocks, Isa. xvi. 1, xlii. 11, the Πέτρα

rock, and צוּר, like the Arabic صَخْر, a great and hard mass
of rock (Aramaic טוּר, a mountain). The figures of the
מְצוּדָה (מְצוֹדָה, מְצָד) and the מִשְׂגָּב are related; the former
signifies properly *specula*, a watch-tower*, and the latter,
a steep height. The horn, which is an ancient figure of
victorious and defiant power in Deut. xxxiii. 17, 1 Sam. ii. 1,
is found here applied to Jahve Himself: "horn of my salvation" is that which interposes on the side of my feebleness,
conquers, and saves me. All these epithets applied to God
are the fruits of the affliction out of which David's song
has sprung, viz. his persecution by Saul, when, in a country
abounding in rugged rocks and deficient in forest, he betook himself to the rocks for safety, and the mountains
served him as his fortresses. In the shelter which the
mountains, by their natural conformations, afforded him at

---

described by Strabo, xvi. 4, 21; the other calls to mind the Phœnician
rocky island צוֹר, *Ṣûr* (Tyre), the refuge in the sea.

* In Arabic مَصَاد signifies (1) a high hill (a signification that
is wanting in Freytag), (2) the summit of a mountain, and according
to the original lexicons it belongs to the root مَصَد, which in outward appearance is supported by the synonymous forms مَصَد and
مَصَد, as also by their plurals أَمْصِدَة and مُصْدَان, since these
can only be properly formed from those singulars on the assumption
of the *m* being part of the root. Nevertheless, since the meanings of
مَصَد all distinctly point to its being formed from the root مص
contained in the reduplicated stem مَصّ to suck, but the meanings of
مَصَاد, مَصَد, and مَصْد do not admit of their being referred to it,
and moreover there are instances in which original *nn. loci* from *vv.*
med. و and ى admit of the prefixed *m* being treated as the first
radical through forgetfulness or disregard of their derivation, and with
the retention of it form secondary roots (as مَصَّر, مَكَن, مَكَّن),
it is highly probable that in *maṣâd*, *maṣad* and *maṣd* we have an
original מְצָד, מְצוֹדָה, מְצוּדָה. These Hebrew words, however, are to be
referred to a צוּד in the signification to look out, therefore properly
specula. — Fleischer.

that time, and in the fortunate accidents, which sometimes
brought him deliverance when in extreme peril, David
recognises only marvellous phenomena of which Jahve Himself was to him the final cause. The confession of the God
tried and known in many ways is continued in ver. 4 by a
general expression of his experience. מְהֻלָּל is a predicate
accusative to יהוה: As one praised (worthy to be praised)
do I call upon Jahve, — a rendering that is better suited
to the following clause, which expresses confidence in the
answer coinciding with the invocation, which is to be thought
of as a cry for help, than Olshausen's, "Worthy of praise,
do I cry, is Jahve", though this latter certainly is possible
so far as the style is concerned (*vid.* on Isa. xlv. 24, cf. also
Gen. iii. 3, Mic. ii. 6). The proof of this fact, viz. that
calling upon Him who is worthy to be praised, who, as the
history of Israel shews, is able and willing to help, is immediately followed by actual help, as events that are coincident, forms the further matter of the Psalm.

Vers. 5—7. In these verses David gathers into one
collective figure all the fearful dangers to which he had
been exposed during his persecution by Saul, together with
the marvellous answers and deliverances he experienced,
that which is unseen, which stands in the relation to that
which is visible of cause and effect, rendering itself visible
to him. David here appears as passive throughout; the
hand from out of the clouds seizes him and draws him out
of mighty waters: while in the second part of the Psalm, in
fellowship with God and under His blessing, he comes forward as a free actor.

The description begins in vers. 5—7 with the danger
and the cry for help which is not in vain. The verb אָפַף
according to a tradition not to be doubted (cf. אוֹפָן a wheel)
signifies to go round, surround, as a poetical synonym of
הִקִּיף, כִּתֵּר, סָבַב, and not, as one might after the Arabic have
thought: to drive, urge. Instead of "the bands of death,"
the LXX. (cf. Acts ii. 24) renders it ὠδῖνες (constrictive
pains) θανάτου; but ver. 6*b.* favours the meaning bands, cords,
cf. cxix. 61 (where it is likewise חֶבְלֵי instead of the חַבְלֵי,
which one might have expected, Josh. xvii. 5, Job xxxvi. 8),
death is therefore represented as a hunter with a cord and

net, xci. 3. בְּלִיַּעַל, compounded of בְּלִי and יַעַל (from וְעַל, יָעַל,
root עַל), signifies unprofitableness, worthlessness, and in
fact both deep-rooted moral corruption and also abysmal
destruction (cf. 2 Cor. vi. 15, Βελίαρ = Βελίαλ as a name
of Satan and his kingdom). Rivers of destruction are those,
whose engulfing floods lead down to the abyss of destruction
(Jon. ii. 7). Death, *Belîjáal,* and *Sheôl* are the names of
the weird powers, which make use of David's persecutors
as their instruments. *Futt.* in the sense of imperfects alternate with *prætt.* בָּעֵת (= بغت) signifies to come suddenly
upon any one (but compare also بعث, to startle, *excitare,*
to alarm), and קִדֵּם, to rush upon; the two words are distinguished from one another like *überfallen* and *anfallen.* The
הֵיכָל out of which Jahve hears is His heavenly dwelling-
place, which is both palace and temple, inasmuch as He sits
enthroned there, being worshipped by blessed spirits. לְפָנָיו
belongs to וְשַׁוְעָתִי: my cry which is poured forth before Him
(as *e. g.* in cii. 1), for it is tautological if joined with תָּבֹא
beside בְּאָזְנָיו. Before Jahve's face he made supplication and
his prayer urged its way into His ears.

Vers. 8—10. As these verses go on to describe, the
being heard became manifest in the form of deliverance. All
nature stands to man in a sympathetic relationship, sharing
his curse and blessing, his destruction and glory, and to
God in a (so to speak) synergetic relationship, furnishing the
harbingers and instruments of His mighty deeds. Accordingly in this instance Jahve's interposition on behalf of David is accompanied by terrible manifestations in nature.
Like the deliverance of Israel out of Egypt, Ps. lxviii. lxxvii.,
and the giving of the Law on Sinai, Exod. xix., and like
the final appearing of Jahve and of Jesus Christ according
the words of prophet and apostle (Hab. iii., 2 Thess. i. 7
sq.), the appearing of Jahve for the help of David has also
extraordinary natural phenomena in its train. It is true
we find no express record of any incident in David's life of
the kind recorded in 1 Sam. vii. 10, but it must be some
real experience which David here idealises (*i. e.* seizes at
its very roots, and generalises and works up into a grand
majestic picture of his miraculous deliverance). Amidst
earthquake, a black thunderstorm gathers, the charging of

which is heralded by the lightning's flash, and its thick clouds descend nearer and nearer to the earth. The aorists in ver. 8 introduce the event, for the introduction of which, from ver. 4 onwards, the way has been prepared and towards which all is directed. The inward excitement of the Judge, who appears to His servant for his deliverance, sets the earth in violent oscillation. The foundations of the mountains (Isa. xxiv. 18) are that upon which they are supported beneath and within, as it were, the pillars which support the vast mass. נָּעַשׁ (rhyming with רָעַשׁ) is followed by the *Hithpa.* of the same verb: the first impulse having been given they, viz. the earth and the pillars of the mountains, continue to shake of themselves. These convulsions occur, because "it is kindled with respect to God"; it is unnecessary to supply אַפּוֹ, חָרָה לוֹ is a synonym of חַם לוֹ. When God is wrath, according to Old Testament conception, the power of wrath which is present in Him is kindled and blazes up and breaks forth. The panting of rage may accordingly also be called the smoke of the fire of wrath (lxxiv. 1, lxxx. 5). The smoking is as the breathing out of the fire, and the vehement hot breath which is inhaled and exhaled through the nose of one who is angry (cf. Job xli. 12), is like smoke rising from the internal fire of anger. The fire of anger itself "devours out of the mouth", *i. e.* flames forth out of the mouth, consuming whatever it lays hold of, — in men in the form of angry words, with God in the fiery forces of nature, which are of a like kind with, and subservient to, His anger, and more especially in the lightning's flash. It is the lightning chiefly, that is compared here to the blazing up of burning coals. The power of wrath in God, becoming manifest in action, breaks forth into a glow, and before it entirely discharges its fire, it gives warning of action like the lightning's flash heralding the outburst of the storm. Thus enraged and breathing forth His wrath, Jahve bowed the heavens, *i. e.* caused them to bend towards the earth, and came down, and darkness of clouds (עֲרָפֶל similar in meaning to ὄρφνη, cf. ἔρεβος) was under His feet: black, low-hanging clouds announced the coming of Him who in His wrath was already on His way downwards towards the earth.

Vers. 11—13. The storm, announcing the approaching

outburst of the thunderstorm, was also the forerunner of
the Avenger and Deliverer. If we compare ver. 11 with civ.
3, it is natural to regard כְּרוּב as a transposition of רְכוּב (a
chariot, Ew. § 153,*a*). But assuming a relationship between
the biblical *Cherub* and (according to Ctesias) the Indo-Per-
sian griffin, the word (from the Zend *grab, garew, garefsh,*
to seize) signifies a creature seizing and holding irrecoverably fast whatever it seizes upon; perhaps in Semitic language the strong creature, from כָּרַב = كرب *torquere, constringere,* (whence *mukrab,* tight, strong). It is a passive
form like לְבוּשׁ, יְסֻד, גְּבוּל. The cherubim are mentioned in
Gen. iii. 24 as the guards of Paradise (this alone is enough
to refute the interpretation recently revived in the *Evang.
Kirchen-Zeit.*, 1866, No. 46, that they are a symbol of the
unity of the living One, כְּרוּב = כרוב "like a multitude"!),
and elsewhere, as it were, as the living mighty rampart and
vehicle of the approach of the inaccessible majesty of God;
and they are not merely in general the medium of God's
personal presence in the world, but more especially of the
presence of God as turning the fiery side of His doxa towards the world. As in the Prometheus of Æschylus, Oce-
anus comes flying τὸν πτερυγωκῇ τόνδ' οἰωνὸν γνώμῃ στομίων
ἄτερ εὐθύνων, so in the present passage Jahve rides upon the
cherub, of which the heathenish griffin is a distortion; or,
if by a comparison of passages like civ. 3, Isa. lxvi. 15, we
understand David according to Ezekiel, He rides upon the
cherub as upon His living throne-chariot (מֶרְכָּבָה). The
throne floats upon the cherubim, and this cherub-throne
flies upon the wings of the wind; or, as we can also say: the
cherub is the celestial spirit working in this vehicle formed
of the spirit-like elements. The Manager of the chariot is
Himself hidden behind the thick thunder-clouds. יָשֶׁת is an
aorist without the consecutive ו (cf. יַךְ Hos. vi. 1). חֹשֶׁךְ is
the accusative of the object to it; and the accusative of the
predicate is doubled: His covering, His pavilion round about
Him. In Job xxxvi. 29 also the thunder-clouds are called
God's סֻכָּה, and also in xcvii. 2 they are סְבִיבָיו, concealing
Him on all sides and announcing only His presence when
He is wroth. In ver. 12*b* the accusative of the object, הֹשֶׁךְ, is
expanded into "darkness of waters", *i. e.* swelling with

waters* and billows of thick vapour, thick, and therefore
dark, masses (עָב in its primary meaning of denseness, or a
thicket, Exod. xix. 9, cf. Jer. iv. 29) of שְׁחָקִים, which is here
a poetical name for fleecy clouds. The dispersion and discharge, according to ver. 13, proceeded from נֹגַהּ נֶגְדּוֹ. Such
is the expression for the doxa of God as being a mirroring
forth of His nature, as it were, over against Him, as being
therefore His brightness, or the reflection of His glory. The
doxa is fire and light. On this occasion the forces of wrath
issue from it, and therefore it is the fiery forces: heavy and
destructive hail (cf. Exod. ix. 23 sq., Isa. xxx. 30) and fiery
glowing coals, *i. e.* flashing and kindling lightning. The
object עָבָיו stands first, because the idea of clouds, behind
which, according to ver. 11, the doxa in concealed, is prominently connected with the doxa. It might be rendered:
before His brightness His clouds turn into hail ... , a
rendering which would be more in accordance with the
structure of the stichs, and is possible according to Ges.
§ 138, rem. 2. Nevertheless, in connection with the com-
binᵗ ᵢon of עבר with clouds, the idea of breaking through
(Lam. iii. 44) is very natural. If עביו is removed, then עברו
signifies "thence came forth hail ... " But the mention of
the clouds as the medium, is both natural and appropriate.

Vers. 14—16. Amidst thunder, Jahve hurled lightnings
as arrows upon David's enemies, and the breath of His anger
laid bare the beds of the flood to the very centre of the
earth, in order to rescue the sunken one. Thunder is the
rumble of God, and as it were the hollow murmur of His
mouth, Job xxxvii. 2. עֶלְיוֹן, the Most High, is the name of
God as the inapproachable Judge, who governs all things.
The third line of ver. 14 is erroneously repeated from the
preceding strophe. It cannot be supported on grammatical
grounds by Ex. ix. 23, since נָתַן קוֹל, *edere vocem,* has a different meaning from the נָתַן קֹלֹת, *dare tonitrua,* of that passage. The symmetry of the strophe structure is also against
it; and it is wanting both in 2 Sam. and in the LXX. רָב,

---

* Rab Dimi, *B. Taanîth* 10a, for the elucidation of the passage
quotes a Palestine proverb: נהור ענני זעירין מוהי חשוך ענני סגיין מוהי
i. e. if the clouds are transparent they will yield but little water, if they
are dark they will yield a quantity.

which, as the opposite of מְעַט Neh. ii. 12, Isa. x. 7, means adverbially "in abundance", is the parallel to וַיִּשְׁלַח. It is generally taken, after the analogy of Gen. xlix. 23, in the sense of בְּרַק, cxliv. 6: רָב in pause = רֹב (the *ō* passing over into the broader *a* like עֲי instead of עֹי in Gen. xlix. 3) = רָבַב, cognate with רָבָה, רָמָה; but the forms סַב, סַבּוּ, here, and in every other instance, have but a very questionable existence, as *e. g.* רַב, Isa. liv. 13, is more probably an adjective than the third person *præt.* (cf. Böttcher, *Neue Aehrenlese* No. 635, 1066). The suffixes *ēm* do not refer to the arrows, *i. e.* lightnings, but to David's foes. הָמַם means both to put in commotion and to destroy by confounding, Exod. xiv. 24, xxiii. 27. In addition to the thunder, the voice of Jahve, comes the stormwind, which is the snorting of the breath of His nostrils. This makes the channels of the waters visible and lays bare the foundations of the earth. אָפִיק (collateral form to אָפֵק) is the bed of the river and then the river or brook itself, *a continendo aquas* (Ges.), and exactly like the Arabic *mesîk*, *mesâk*, *mesek* (from مسك, the VI. form of which, *tamâsaka,* corresponds to הִתְאַפֵּק), means a place that does not admit of the water soaking in, but on account of the firmness of the soil preserves it standing or flowing. What are here meant are the water-courses or river beds that hold the water. It is only needful for Jahve to threaten (ἐπιτιμᾶν Mat. viii. 26) and the floods, in which he, whose rescue is undertaken here, is sunk, flee (civ. 7) and dry up (cvi. 9, Nah. i. 4). But he is already half engulfed in the abyss of Hades, hence not merely the bed of the flood is opened up, but the earth is rent to its very centre. From the language being here so thoroughly allegorical, it is clear that we were quite correct in interpreting the description as ideal. He, who is nearly overpowered by his foes, is represented as one engulfed in deep waters and almost drowning.

Vers. 17—20. Then Jahve stretches out His hand from above into the deep chasm and draws up the sinking one. The verb שָׁלַח occurs also in prose (2 Sam. vi. 6) without יָד (lvii. 4, cf. on the other hand the borrowed passage, cxliv. 7) in the signification to reach (after anything). The verb מָשָׁה, however, is only found in one other instance, viz.

Exod. ii. 10, as the root (transferred from the Egyptian
into the Hebrew) of the name of Moses, and even Luther
saw in it an historical allusion, "He hath made a Moses of
me", He hath drawn me out of great (many) waters, which
had well nigh swallowed me up, as He did Moses out of the
waters of the Nile, in which he would have perished. This
figurative language is followed, in ver. 18, by its interpretation, just as in cxliv. 7 the "great waters" are explained
by מִיַּד בְּנֵי נֵכָר, which, however, is not suitable here, or at
least is too limited.

With ver. 17 the hymn has reached the climax of epic
description, from which it now descends in a tone that becomes more and more lyrical. In the combination אֹיְבִי עָז,
עָז is not an adverbial accusative, but an adjective, like
רוּחֲךָ טוֹבָה cxliii. 10, and ὁ ἀνὴρ ἀγαθός (Hebräerbrief S. 353).
כִּי introduces the reason for the interposition of the divine
omnipotence, viz. the superior strength of the foe and the
weakness of the oppressed one. On the day of his אֵיד, i. e.
(vid. on xxxi. 12) his load or calamity, when he was altogether a homeless and almost defenceless fugitive, they came
upon him (קִדַּם xvii. 13), cutting off all possible means of
delivering himself, but Jahve became the fugitive's staff
(xxiii. 4) upon which he leaned and kept himself erect. By
the hand of God, out of straits and difficulties he reached a
broad place, out of the dungeon of oppression to freedom,
for Jahve had delighted in him, he was His chosen and beloved one.   חָפֵץ has the accent on the penult here, and
Metheg as a sign of the lengthening (הֶעֱמָדָה) beside the ē,
that it may not be read ĕ.* The following strophe tells
the reason of his pleasing God and of His not allowing
him to perish. This כִּי חָפֵץ בִּי (for He delighted in me) now
becomes the primary thought of the song.

Vers. 21—24. On גָּמַל (like שִׁלֵּם with the accusative not
merely of the thing, but also of the person, e. g. 1 Sam.
xxiv. 18), εὖ or κακῶς πράττειν τινά, vid. on vii. 5. שָׁמַר, to
observe = to keep, is used in the same way in Job xxii. 15.

---

* In like manner Metheg is placed beside the ē of the final closed
syllable that has lost the tone in חָפֵץ xxii. 9, וַתְּחוֹלֵל xc. 2., vid. Isaiah
S. 594 note.

רָשַׁע מִן is a pregnant expression of the *malitiosa desertio.* "From God's side", *i. e.* in His judgment, would be contrary to the general usage of the language (for the מִן in Job iv. 17 has a different meaning) and would be but a chilling addition. On the poetical form מֶנִּי, in pause מֶנִּי, *vid.* Ew. § 263,*b*. The *fut.* in ver. 23*b*, close after the substantival clause ver. 23*a*, is not intended of the habit in the past, but at the present time: he has not wickedly forsaken God, but (כִּי = *imo, sed*) always has God's commandments present before him as his rule of conduct, and has not put them far away out of his sight, in order to be able to sin with less compunction; and thus then (*fut. consec.*) in relation (עִם, as in Deut. xviii. 13, cf. 2 Sam. xxiii. 5) to God he was תָּמִים, with his whole soul undividedly devoted to Him, and he guarded himself against his iniquity (עָוֹן, from עָוָה, عوى, to twist, pervert, cf. غوى of error, delusion, self-enlightenment), *i. e.* not: against acquiescence in his in-dwelling sin, but: against iniquity becoming in any way his own; מֵעֲוֹנִי equivalent to מֵעֲוֹתִי (Dan. ix. 5), cf. מֵחַיַּי = than that I should live, Jon. iv. 8. In this strophe, this Psalm strikes a cord that harmonises with Ps. xvii., after which it is therefore placed. We may compare David's own testimony concerning himself in 1 Sam. xxvi. 23 sq., the testimony of God in 1 Kings xiv. 8, and the testimony of history in 1 Kings xv. 5, xi. 4.

Vers. 25.—28. What was said in ver. 21 is again expressed here as a result of the foregoing, and substantiated in vers. 26, 27. חָסִיד is a friend of God and man, just as *pius* is used of behaviour to men as well as towards God. גְּבַר תָּמִים the man (construct of גֶּבֶר) of moral and religious completeness (*integri = integritatis,* cf. xv. 2), *i. e.* of undivided devotion to God. נָבָר (instead of which we find בַּר לֵבָב elsewhere, xxiv. 4, lxxiii. 1) not one who is purified, but, in accordance with the reflexive primary meaning of *Niph.,* one who is purifying himself, ἁγνίζων ἑαυτόν, 1 John iii. 3. עִקֵּשׁ (the opposite of יָשָׁר) one who is morally distorted, perverse. Freely formed *Hithpaels* are used with these attributive words to give expression to the corresponding self-manifestation: הִתְחַסֵּד, הִתַּמֵּם (Ges. § 54, 2,*b*), הִתְבָּרֵר, and הִתְפַּתֵּל (to shew one's self נִפְתָּל or פְּתַלְתֹּל). The fervent

love of the godly man God requites with confiding love, the
entire submission of the upright with a full measure of
grace, the endeavour after purity by an unbeclouded charity (cf. lxxiii. 1), moral perverseness by paradoxical judgments, giving the perverse over to his perverseness (Rom. i.
28) and leading him by strange ways to final condemnation
(Isa. xxix. 14, cf. Lev. xxvi. 23 sq.). The truth, which is
here enunciated, is not that the conception which man forms
of God is the reflected image of his own mind and heart,
but that God's conduct to man is the reflection of the relation in which man has placed himself to God; cf. 1 Sam.
ii. 30, xv. 23. This universal truth is illustrated and substantiated in ver. 28. The people who are bowed down by
affliction experience God's condescension, to their salvation;
and their haughty oppressors, God's exaltation, to their
humiliation. Lofty, proud eyes are among the seven things
that Jahve hateth, according to Prov. vi. 17. The judgment
of God compels them to humble themselves with shame, Isa.
ii. 11.

Vers. 29—31. The confirmation of what has been asserted is continued by David's application of it to himself.
Hitzig translates the futures in vers. 29 sq. as imperfects;
but the sequence of the tenses, which would bring this rendering with it, is in this instance interrupted, as it has been
even in ver. 28, by כִּי. The lamp, נֵר (contracted from *na-
wer*), is an image of life, which as it were burns on and on,
including the idea of prosperity and high rank; in the form
נִיר (from *niwr, nijr*) it is the usual figurative word for the
continuance of the house of David, 1 Kings xi. 36, and frequently. David's life and dominion, as the covenant king,
is the lamp which God's favour has lighted for the well-
being of Israel, and His power will not allow this lamp
(2 Sam. xxi. 17) to be quenched. The darkness which breaks
in upon David and his house is always lighted up again by
Jahve. For His strength is mighty in the weak; in, with, and
by Him he can do all things. The *fut.* אָרֻץ may be all the
more surely derived from רָצַץ (= אָרֵץ), inasmuch as this verb
has the changeable *u* in the future also in Isa. xlii. 4, Eccl.
xii. 6. The text of 2 Sam. xxii., however, certainly seems
to put "rushing upon" in the stead of "breaking down". With

ver. 31 the first half of the hymn closes epiphonematically. הָאֵל is a *nom. absol.*, like הַצּוּר, Deut. xxxii. 4. This old Mosaic utterance is re-echoed here, as in 2 Sam. vii. 22, in the mouth of David. The article of הָאֵל points to God as being manifest in past history. His way is faultless and blameless. His word is צְרוּפָה, not slaggy ore, but purified solid gold, xii. 7. Whoever retreats into Him, the God of the promise, is shielded from every danger. Prov. xxx. 5 is borrowed from this passage.

Vers. 32—35. The grateful description of the tokens of favour he has experienced takes a new flight, and is continued in the second half of the Psalm in a more varied and less artificial mixture of the strophes. What is said in ver. 31 of the way and word of Jahve and of Jahve Himself, is confirmed in ver. 32 by the fact that He alone is אֱלוֹהַּ, a divine being to be reverenced, and He alone is צוּר, a rock, *i. e.* a ground of confidence that cannot be shaken. What is said in ver. 31 consequently can be said only of Him. מִבַּלְעֲדֵי and זוּלָתִי alternate; the former (with a negative intensive מִן) signifies "without reference to" and then absolutely "without" or besides, and the latter (with *î* as a connecting vowel, which elsewhere has also the function of a suffix), from זוּלַת (זוּלָה), "exception". The verses immediately following are attached descriptively to אֱלֹהֵינוּ, our God (*i. e.* the God of Israel), the God, who girded me with strength; and accordingly (*fut. consec.*) made my way תָּמִים, "perfect", *i. e.* absolutely smooth, free from stumblings and errors, leading straight forward to a divine goal. The idea is no other than that in ver. 31, cf. Job xxii. 3, except that the freedom from error here is intended to be understood in accordance with its reference to the way of a man, of a king, and of a warrior; cf., moreover, the other text. The verb

שִׁוָּה signifies, like سوّى, to make equal (*æquare*), to arrange, to set right; the dependent passage Hab. iii. 19 has, instead of this verb, the more uncoloured שִׂים. The hind, אַיָּלָה or אַיֶּלֶת, is the perfection of swiftness (cf. ἔλαφος and ἐλαφρός) and also of gracefulness among animals. "Like the hinds" is equivalent to like hinds' feet; the Hebrew style leaves it to the reader to infer the appropriate point of comparison from the figure. It is not swiftness in flight (De Wette), but in attack and pursuit that is meant, — the latter being a prominent characteristic of warriors, according to 2 Sam. i. 23, ii. 18, 1 Chron. xii. 8. David does not call the high places of the enemy, which he has made his own by conquest "my high places", but those heights of the Holy Land which belong to him as king of Israel: upon these Jahve preserves him a firm position, so that from them he may rule the land far and wide, and hold them victoriously (cf. passages like Deut. xxxii. 13, Isa. lviii. 14). The verb לִמֵּד, which has a double accusative in other instances, is here combined with לְ of the subject taught, as the aim of the teaching. The verb נִחֵת (to press down = to bend a bow) precedes the subject "my arms" in the singular; this inequality is admissible even when the subject stands first (e. g. Gen. xlix. 22, Joel i. 20, Zech. vi. 14). קֶשֶׁת נְחוּשָׁה a bow of brazen = of brass, as in Job xx. 24. It is also the manner of heroes in Homer and in the Ramâjana to press down and bend with their hand a brazen bow, one end of which rests on the ground.

Vers. 36—37. Yet it is not the brazen bow in itself that makes him victorious, but the helpful strength of his God. "Shield of Thy salvation" is that consisting of Thy salvation. מָגֵן has an unchangeable ă, as it has always. The salvation of Jahve covered him as a shield, from which every stroke of the foe rebounded; the right hand of Jahve supported him that his hands might not become feeble in the conflict. In its ultimate cause it is the divine עֲנָוָה, to which he must trace back his greatness, i. e. God's lowliness, by virtue of which His eyes look down upon that which is on the earth (cxiii. 6), and the poor and contrite ones are His favourite dwelling-place (Isa. lvii. 15, lxvi. 1 sq.); cf. B. Megilla 31a, "wherever Scripture testifies of the גבורה of the Holy One, blessed be He, it gives prominence also, in connection with it, to His condescension, עִנְוְתָנוּתוֹ, as in Deut. x. 17 and in connection with it ver. 18, Isa. lvii. 15a and 15b, Ps. lxviii. 5 and 6". The rendering of Luther, who follows the LXX. and Vulgate, "When Thou humblest me, Thou makest me great" is opposed by the fact that עֲנָוָה means the bending of one's self, and not of another. What is intended is, that condescension of God to mankind, and especially to the house of David, which was in operation, with an ultimate view to the incarnation, in the life of the son of Jesse from the time of his anointing to his death, viz. the divine χρηστότης καὶ φιλανθρωπία (Tit. iii. 4), which elected the shepherd boy to be king, and did not cast him off even when he fell into sin and his infirmities became manifest. To enlarge his steps under any one is equivalent to securing him room for freedom of motion (cf. the opposite form of expression in Prov. iv. 12). Jahve removed the obstacles of his course out of the way, and steeled his ankles so that he stood firm in fight and endured till he came off victorious. The *præt.* מֵעַד substantiates what, without any other indication of it, is required by the *consecutio temporum,* viz. that everything here has a retrospective meaning.

Vers. 38—41. Thus in God's strength, with the armour of God, and by God's assistance in fight, he smote, cast down, and utterly destroyed all his foes in foreign and in civil wars. According to the Hebrew syntax the whole of this passage is a retrospect. The imperfect signification of the futures in vers. 38, 39 is made clear from the aorist which appears in ver. 40, and from the perfects and futures in what follows it. The strophe begins with an echo of Exod. xv. 9 (cf. *supra* vii. 6). The poet calls his opponents קָמַי, as in ver. 49, xliv. 6, lxxiv. 23, cf. קִימָנוּ Job xxii. 20, inasmuch as קוּם by itself has the sense of rising up in hostility and consequently one can say קָמֵי instead of קָמִים עָלַי (קוֹמִים 2 Kings xvi. 7).* The frequent use of this phrase (*e. g.* xxxvi. 13, Lam. i. 14) shews that קוּם in ver. 39*a* does not mean "to stand (resist)", but "to rise (again)." The phrase נָתַן עֹרֶף, however, which in other passages has those fleeing as its subject (2 Chron. xxix. 6), is here differently applied: Thou gavest, or madest me mine enemies a

------

* In the language of the Beduins *ḳôm* is war, feud, and *ḳômānî* (denominative from *ḳôm*) my enemy (*hostis*); *ḳôm* also has the signification of a collective of *ḳômānî*, and one can equally well say: *entum wa-ijânâ ḳôm*, you and we are enemies, and: *bênâtnâ ḳôm*, there is war between us.

back, *i. e.* those who turn back, as in Exod. xxiii. 27. From xxi. 13 (תְּשִׁיתֵמוֹ שֶׁכֶם, Symm. τάξεις αὐτοὺς ἀποστρόφους) it becomes clear that עֹרֶף is not an accusative of the member beside the accusative of the person (as *e. g.* in Deut. xxxiii. 11), but an accusative of the factitive object according to Ges. § 139, 2.

Vers. 42—43. Their prayer to their gods, wrung from them by their distress, and even to Jahve, was in vain, because it was for their cause, and too late put up to Him. עַל = אֶל; in xlii. 2 the two prepositions are interchanged. Since we do not pulverize dust, but to dust, כְּעָפָר is to be taken as describing the result: so that they became as dust (cf. Job xxxviii. 30, כָּאֶבֶן, so that it is become like stone, and the extreme of such pregnant brevity of expression in Isa. xli. 2) before the wind (עַל־פְּנֵי as in 2 Chron. iii. 17, before the front). The second figure is to be explained differently: I emptied them out (אֲרִיקֵם from הֵרִיק) like the dirt of the streets, *i. e.* not merely: so that they became such, but as one empties it out, — thus contemptuously, ignominiously and completely (cf. Isa. x. 6, Zech. x. 5). The LXX. renders it λεανῶ from הֵרַק (root רק to stretch, make thin, cf. *tendo tenuis, dehnen dünn*); and the text of 2 Sam. xxii. presents the same idea in אֲדִיקֵם.

Vers. 44—46. Thus victorious in God, David became what he now is, viz. the ruler of a great kingdom firmly establish both in home and foreign relations. With respect to the גּוֹיִם and the verb תְּפַלְּטֵנִי which follows, רִיבֵי עָם can only be understood of the conflicts among his own people, in which David was involved by the persecution of Saul and the rebellions of Absolom and Sheba the son of Bichri; and from which Jahve delivered him, in order to preserve him for his calling of world-wide dominion in accordance with the promise. We therefore interpret the passage according to בְּרִית עָם in Isa. xlix. 8., and קְנָאַת־עָם in Isa. xxvi. 11; whereas the following עַם comes to have a foreign application by reason of the attributive clause לֹא־יָדַעְתִּי (Ges. § 123, 3). The *Niph.* נִשְׁמַע in ver. 45 is the reflexive of שָׁמַע, to obey (*e. g.* Ex. xxiv. 7), and is therefore to be rendered: shew themselves obedient (= *Ithpa.* in Dan. vii. 27). לְשֵׁמַע אֹזֶן implies more than that they obeyed at the word; שֵׁמַע means information, rumour, and שֵׁמַע אֹזֶן is the opposite of personal observation (Job xlii. 5), it is therefore to be rendered: they submitted even at the tidings of my victories; and 2 Sam. viii. 9 sq. is an example of this. כִּחֵשׁ to lie, disown, feign, and flatter, is used here, as it is frequently, of the extorted humility which the vanquished shew towards the conqueror. Ver. 46 completes the picture of the reason of the sons of a foreign country "putting a good face on a bad game". They faded away, *i. e.* they became weak and faint-hearted (Ex xviii. 18), incapable of holding out against or breaking through any siege by David, and trembled, surrendering at discretion, out of their close places, *i. e.* out of their strongholds behind which they had shut themselves in (cf. cxlii. 8). The signification of being alarmed, which in this instance, being found in combination with a local מִן, is confined to the sense of terrified flight, is secured to the verb חָרַג by the Arabic خَرَج (root خر, of audible pressure, crowding, and the like) to be pressed, crowded, tight, or narrow, to get in a strait, and the Targumic אֵימְתָא דְמוֹתָא = חַרְגְנָא דְמוֹתָא (*vid.* the Targums on Deut. xxxii. 25). خَجِل to limp, halt, which is compared by Hitzig, is far removed as to the sound; and the most natural, but colourless خرج, to go out of (according to its radical meaning — cf. خرق, خرع &c. —: to break forth, *erumpere*), cannot be supported in Hebrew or Aramaic. The יִרְגְּזוּ found in the borrowed passage in Micah, ch. vii. 17, favours our rendering.

Vers. 47—49. The hymn now draws towards the end with praise and thanksgiving for the multitude of God's mighty deeds, which have just been displayed. Like the בָּרוּךְ (צוּרִי) which is always doxological, חי ה׳ (*vivus Jahve*) is meant as a predicate clause, but is read with the accent of an exclamation just as in the formula of an oath, which is the same expression; and in the present instance it has a doxological meaning. Accordingly וְיָרוּם also signifies "exalted be," in which sense it is written וירם (וְיָרֵם = וְיָרֹם) in the other text. There are three doxological utterances drawn from the events which have just been celebrated in

song. That which follows, from הָאֵל onwards, describes
Jahve once more as the living, blessed (εὐλογητόν), and exalted One, which He has shewn Himself to be. From וַיַּדְבֵּר
we see that הַנּוֹתֵן is to be resolved as an imperfect. The
proofs of vengeance, נְקָמוֹת, are called God's gift, insofar as
He has rendered it possible to him to punish the attacks
upon his own dignity and the dignity of his people, or to
witness the punishment of such insults (*e. g.* in the case of
Nabal); for divine vengeance is a securing by punishment
(*vindicatio*) of the inviolability of the right. It is questionable whether הִדְבִּיר (synonym רָדַד, cxliv. 2) here and in
xlvii. 4 means "to bring to reason" as an intensive of דָּבַר,
to drive (Ges.); the more natural meaning is "to turn the
back" according to the Arabic *adbara* (Hitzig), cf. *dabar,
dabre*, flight, retreat; *dabira* to be wounded behind; *medbûr,*
wounded in the back. The idea from which הדביר gains the
meaning "to subdue" is that of flight, in which hostile nations, overtaken from behind, sank down under him (xlv.
6); but the idea that is fully worked out in cxxix. 3, Isa.
li. 23, is by no means remote. With מְפַלְּטִי the assertion takes
the form of an address. רוֹמֵם מִן does not differ from ix. 14:
Thou liftest me up away from mine enemies, so that I hover
above them and triumph over them. The climactic אַף, of
which poetry is fond, here unites two thoughts of a like import to give intensity of expression to the one idea. The
participle is followed by futures: his manifold experience is
concentrated in one general ideal expression.

Vers. 50—51. The praise of so blessed a God, who acts
towards David as He has promised him, shall not be confined within the narrow limits of Israel. When God's
anointed makes war with the sword upon the heathen, it is,
in the end, the blessing of the knowledge of Jahve for which
he opens up the way, and the salvation of Jahve, which he
thus mediatorially helps on. Paul has a perfect right to
quote ver. 50 of this Psalm (Rom. xv. 9), together with Deut.
xxxii. 43 and Ps. cxvii. 1, as proof that salvation belongs
to the Gentiles also, according to the divine purpose of
mercy. What is said in ver. 51 as the reason and matter of
the praise that shall go forth beyond Israel, is an echo of
the Messianic promises in 2 Sam. vii. 12—16 which is per-

fectly reconcileable with the Davidic authorship of the
Psalm, as Hitzig acknowledges. And Theodoret does not
wrongly appeal to the closing words עַד־עוֹלָם against the
Jews. In whom, but in Christ, the son of David, has the
fallen throne of David any lasting continuance, and in whom,
but in Christ, has all that has been promised to the seed
of David eternal truth and reality? The praise of Jahve,
the God of David, His anointed, is, according to its ultimate
import, a praising of the Father of Jesus Christ.

PSALM XVIII. ACCORDING TO THE TEXT OF 2 SAM. XXII.

On the differences of the introductory superscription,
see on xviii. 1. The relation of the prose accentuation of
the Psalm in 2 Sam. xxii. to the poetical accentuation in
the Psalter is instructive. Thus, for example, instead of
Mercha mahpach. (*Olewejored*) in the Psalter we here find
Athnach; instead of the *Athnach* following upon *Mercha mahpach.,* here is *Zakeph* (cf. xviii. 7, 16, 31 with 2 Sam. xxii.
7, 16, 31); instead of *Rebia mugrash*, here *Tiphcha* (cf. xviii.
4 with 2 Sam. xxii. 4); instead of *Pazer* at the beginning of
a verse, here *Athnach* (cf. Ps. xviii. 2 with 2 Sam. xxii. 2).*
The peculiar mode of writing the stichs, in which we find
this song in our editions, is the old traditional mode. If
a half-line is placed above a half-line, so that they form
two columns, it is called לבנה על־גבי לבנה אריח על־גבי אריח,
brick upon brick, a half-brick upon a half-brick, as the song
Haazinu in Deut. xxxii. is set out in our editions. On the
other hand if the half-lines appear as they do here divided
and placed in layers one over another, it is called אריח
על־גבי לבנה ולבנה על־גבי אריח. According to *Megilla* 16*b* all
the *cantica* in the Scriptures are to be written thus; and
according to *Sofrim* xiii., Ps. xviii. has this form in common
with 2 Sam. xxii.

Vers. 2—4. This strophe is stunted by the falling away
of its monostichic introit, xviii. 2. In consequence of this,
the vocatives in vers. 2 sq. are deprived of their support

------

* *Vid.* Baer's *Accentsystem* xv., and *Thorath Emeth* iii. 2 together
with S. 44, Anm.

and lowered to substantival clauses: *Jahve is my Rock*, &c., which form no proper beginning for a hymn. Instead of וּמְפַלְּטִי we have, as in cxliv. 2, וּמפלטי־לי; and instead of אֵלִי צוּרִי we find אֱלֹהֵי צוּרִי, which is contrary to the usual manner of arranging these emblematical names. The loss the strophe sustains is compensated by the addition: *and my Refuge, my Saviour, who savest me from violence.* In ver. 4*b* as in ver. 49*b* the non-assimilated מִן (cf. ver. 14, xxx. 4, lxxiii. 19) is shortened into an assimilated one. May לִי perhaps be the remains of the obliterated אֵלִי, and אֱלֹהֵי, as it were, the clothing of the צוּרִי which was then left too bare?

Vers. 5—7. The connection of this strophe with the preceding by כִּי accords with the sense, but is tame. On the other hand, the reading מְשַׁבְּרֵי instead of חֶבְלֵי (even though the author of cxvi. 3 may have thus read it) is commended by the parallelism, and by the fact, that now the latter figure is not repeated in vers. 5, 6. משברי are not necessarily waves that break upon the shore, but may also be such as break one upon another, and consequently אֲפָפוּנִי is not inadmissible. The ו of וְנַחֲלֵי, which is not wanted, is omitted. Instead of the fuller toned form סְבָבוּנִי, which is also more commensurate with the closing cadence of the verse, we have here the usual syncopated סַבּוּנִי (cf. cxviii. 11). The repetition of the אֶקְרָא (instead of אֲשַׁוֵּעַ) is even more unpoetical than the repetition of חבלי would be. On the other hand, it might originally have been וַיִּשְׁמַע instead of יִשְׁמַע; without ו it is an expression (intended retrospectively) of what takes place simultaneously, with ו it expresses the principal fact. The concluding line וְשַׁוְעָתִי בְאָזְנָיו is stunted: the brief substantival clause is not meaningless (cf. Job xv. 21, Isa. v. 9), but is only a fragment of the more copious, fuller toned conclusion of the strophe which we find in the Psalter.

Vers. 8—10. The *Kerî* here obliterates the significant alternation of the *Kal* and *Hithpa.* of גָּעַשׁ. Instead of וּמוֹסְדֵי we have the feminine form of the plural מוֹסְדוֹת (as in both texts in ver. 16) without ו. Instead of the genitive הָרִים, by an extension of the figure, we have הַשָּׁמַיִם (cf. the pillars, Job xxvi. 11), which is not intended of the mountains as of Atlasses, as it were, supporting the heavens, but of the points of support and central points of the heavens themselves: the whole universe trembles.

Vers. 11—13. Instead of the pictorial וַיֵּרָא (Deut. xxviii. 49, and hence in Jeremiah), which is generally used of the flight of the eagle, we have the plain, uncoloured וַיַּרְא *He appeared.* Instead of יָשֶׁת, which is intended as an aorist, we meet the more strictly regular, but here, where so many aorists with ו come together, less poetical וַיָּשֶׁת. In ver. 12*a* the rise and fall of the parallel members has grown over till it forms one heavy clumsy line: *And made darkness round about Him a pavilion* (סֻכּוֹת). But the ἅπ. λεγ. חַשְׁרַת, to which the signification of a "massive gathering together" is secured by the Arabic, is perhaps original. The word حشر, frequently used in the Koran of assembling to judgment, with the radical signification *stipare, cogere* (to crowd together, compress) which is also present in حشى, حاش, حشل, is here used like ἀγείρειν in the Homeric νεφεληγερέτα (the cloud-gatherer).* Ver. 13 is terribly mutilated. Of עָבָיו עָבְרוּ בָרָד וְ of the other text there are only the four letters בָּעֲרוּ (as in ver. 9*c*) left.

Vers. 14—16. Instead of וַיִּרְעֵם we find יִרְעֵם, which is less admissible here, where a principal fact is related and the description is drawing nearer and nearer to its goal. Instead of מִן־שָׁמַיִם the other text has בַּשָּׁמַיִם; in xxx. 4 also, מִן is retained without being assimilated before שׁ. But the fact, however, that the line בָּרָד וְגַחֲלֵי־אֵשׁ is wanting, is a proof, which we welcome, that it is accidentally repeated from the preceding strophe, in the other text. On the other hand, חִצִּים is inferior to חִצָּיו; וּבְרָקִים רָב is corrupted into a tame בָּרָק; and the *Keri* וַיְּהֻמֵּם erroneously assumes that the suffix of וַיְפִיצֵם refers to the arrows, *i. e.* lightnings. Again on the other hand, אֲפִיקֵי ים, channels *of the sea,* is perhaps

---

* Midrash and Talmud explain it according to the Aramaic "a straining of the clouds", inasmuch as the clouds, like a sieve, let the drops trickle down to the earth, falling close upon each other and yet separately (*B. Taanith* 9*b*: מחשרות מים עלי־גבי קרקע). Kimchi combines חשר with קשר. But the ancient Arabic حشر is the right key to the word. The root of חֹשֶׁךְ and חָשְׁכָה is perhaps the same (cf. Exod. x. 21).

original; מַיִם in this connection expresses too little, and, as
being the customary word in combination with אֲפִיקֵי (xlii.
2, Joel i. 20), may easily have been substituted after it. At
any rate יָם and תֵּבֵל form a more exact antithesis. יִגָּלוּ
instead of וַיִּגָּלוּ is the same in meaning. The close of the
strophe is here also weakened by the obliteration of the
address to God: *by* (בְּ instead of the מ of the other text)
the threatening of Jahve, at the snorting of His breath of anger.
The change of the preposition in this surge (so-to-speak)
of the members of the verse is rather interruptive than
pleasing.

Vers. 17—20. The variant מְשַׂנְאַי instead of וּמִשֹּׂנְאַי is
unimportant; but מִשְׁעָן instead of לְמִשְׁעָן, *for a support*, is
less pleasing both as it regards language and rhythm. The
resolution of וַיּוֹצִיאֵנִי into אֹתִי ... וַיֹּצֵא is a clumsy and needless emphasising of the *me*.

Vers. 21—24. Instead of כְּצִדְקִי, we find כְּצִדְקָתִי here
and in ver. 25, contrary to usage of the language of the
Psalms (cf. vii. 9 with 1 King viii. 32). Instead of the poetical אָסִיר מֶנִּי (Job xxvii. 5, xxiii. 12) we have אָסוּר מִמֶּנָּה
(with the *fem.* used as a neuter), according to the common
phrase in 2 Kings iii. 3, and frequently (cf. Deut. v. 32).
Instead of וָאֶהִי, the not less (*e. g.* cii. 8) usual וָאֶהְיֶה; and
instead of וָאֶשְׁתַּמֵּר, the form with *ah* of direction which
occurs very frequently with the first person of the *fut. convers.* in the later Hebrew, although it does also occur even
in the older Hebrew (iii. 6, vii. 5, Gen. xxxii. 6, Job xix.
20). And instead of עִמּוֹ we find לוֹ, which does not commend itself, either as a point of language or of rhythm; and
by comparison with vers. 26, 27, it certainly is not original.

Vers. 25—28. On כְּצִדְקָתִי see ver. 21. כְּבֹרִי is without
example, since elsewhere (כַּפִּים) בֹּר יָדַיִם is the only expression for innocence. In the equally remarkable expression
גְּבוֹר תָּמִים (*the upright "man of valour"*), גְּבוֹר is used just as
in the expression גְּבוֹר חַיִל. The form תִּתָּבָּר, has only the
sound of an assimilated *Hithpa.* like תִּתַּמָּם (= תתתמם), and
is rather a reflexive of the *Hiph.* הֵבֵר after the manner of
the Aramaic *Ittaphal* (therefore = תִּתְבָּרַר); and the form
תִּתָּפָּל sounds altogether like a *Hithpa.* from תָּפֵל (thou
shewest thyself insipid, absurd, foolish), but — since תִּפְלָה

cannot be ascribed to God (Job i. 22), and is even unseemly as an expression — appears to be treated likewise as an *Ittaphal* with a kind of inverted assimilation = תִּתְהַפָּתַל (Böttcher). They are contractions such as are sometimes allowed by the dialect of the common people, though contrary to all rules. וְאֵת instead of כִּי at the beginning of ver. 28 changes what is confirmatory into a mere continuation of the foregoing. One of the most sensible variations is the change of ועינים רמות to וְעֵינֶיךָ עַל־רָמִים. The rendering: And Thine eyes (are directed down) upon the haughty that Thou mayst bring (them) low (Stier, Hengst., and others), violates the accentuation and is harsh so far as the language is concerned (תַּשְׁפִּיל for לְהַשְׁפִּילֵם). Hitzig renders it, according to the accents: And Thou lowerest Thine eyes against the proud, הָפֵיל פנים = הִשְׁפִּיל עינים (Jer. iii. 12). But one would expect בְּ instead of עַל, if this were the meaning. It is better to render it according to Ps. cxiii. 6: *And Thou dost cast down Thine eyes upon the haughty*, in which rendering the haughty are represented as being far beneath Jahve notwithstanding their haughtiness, and the "casting down or depressing of the eyes" is an expression of the utmost contempt (*despectus*).

Vers. 29—31. Here in ver. 29*a* תָּאִיר has been lost, for Jahve is called, and really is, אוֹר in xxvii. 1, but not נֵר. The form of writing נֵיר is an incorrect wavering between נֵר and נִיר. The repetition יהוה ויהוה, by which the loss of תאיר, and of אֱלֹהַי in ver. 29*b*, is covered, is inelegant. We have בְּכָה here instead of בְּךָ, as twice besides in the Old Testament. The form of writing אָרוּץ, as Isa. xlii. 4 shews, does not absolutely require that we should derive it from רוּץ; nevertheless רוּץ can be joined with the accusative just as well as הָלַךְ, in the sense of running against, rushing upon; therefore, since the parallelism is favourable, it is to be rendered: *by Thee I rush upon a troop*. The omission of the ו before בֵּאלֹהַי is no improvement to the rhythm.

Vers. 32—35. The variety of expression in ver. 32 which has been preserved in the other text is lost here. Instead of הַמְאַזְּרֵנִי חָיִל we find, as if from a faded MS., מָעוּזִי חָיִל (according to Norzi מָעוּזִּי) my refuge (*lit.* hiding) of strength, *i. e.* my strong refuge, according to a syntactically more

elegant style of expression (= מָעוּזִי מָעוֹז חַיִל), like lxxi. 7,
Lev. vi. 3, xxvi. 42; *vid.* Nägelsbach § 63, *g*, where it is
correctly shewn, that this mode of expression is a matter of
necessity in certain instances.* The form of writing, מָעוּזִי,
seems here to recognise a מָעוֹז, a hiding-place, refuge, =
معان, which is different from מָעֹז a fortress (from עזז); but
just as in every other case the punctuation confuses the two
substantives (*vid.* on xxxi. 3), so it does even here, since
מָעֹז, from עזז, ought to be inflected מָעוּזִי, like מְנוּסִי, and not
מָעוּזִי. Nevertheless the *plena scriptio* may avail to indicate
to us, that here מעוז is intended to be a synonym of מַחֲסֶה.
Instead of (תמים דרכי) וַיִּתֵּן we have וַיַּתֵּר here; perhaps it is
He let, or caused, my way to be spotless, *i. e.* made it such.
Thus Ewald renders it by referring to the modern Arabic
خلّى to let, cause [Germ. *lassen*, French *faire*] = to make,
effect; even the classic ancient Arabic language uses ترك
(*lassen*) in the sense of جعل (to make), *e. g.* "I have made
(تركت) the sword my camp-companion", *i. e.* my inseparable
attendant (*lit.* I have caused it to be such), as it is to be
translated in Nöldecke's *Beiträge zur Kenntniss der Poesie
der alten Araber*, S. 131.** Or does הִתִּיר retain its full and

---

* In the present instance מָעוֹז חֵילִי, like מַחֲסֶה עֻזִּי in lxxi. 7 (cf.
Ezek. xvi. 27, xviii. 7, and perhaps Hab. iii. 8) would not be inadmissible, although in the other mode of expression greater prominence is
given to the fact of its being provided and granted by God. But in
cases like the following it would be absolutely inadmissible to append
the suffix to the *nom. rectum*, viz. שֹׂנְאַי שֶׁקֶר xxxviii. 20; בְּרִיתִי יַעֲקֹב
my covenant with Jacob, Lev. xxvi. 42; מַדּוֹ בַד his garment of linen,
Lev. vi. 3; כְּתָבָם הַמִּתְיַחְשִׂים their ancestral register, Ezra ii. 62; and
it is probable that this transference of the pronominal suffix to the
nom. regens originated in instances like these, where it was a logical
necessary and then became transferred to the *syntax ornata*. At the same
time it is clear from this, that in cases like שֹׂנְאַי שֶׁקֶר, and consequently also שֹׂנְאַי חִנָּם, the second notion is not conceived as an accusative of more precise definition, but as a governed genitive.

** *Ibid.* S. 133, Z. 13 is, with Fleischer, to be rendered: ye have
made (تركتم) my milk camels restless, *i. e.* caused them to be such,
by having stolen them and driven them away so that they now yearn
after home and their young ones.

proper meaning "to unfetter"? This is more probable, since the usage of Hebrew shews no example of הִתִּיר in the post-biblical signification "to allow, permit", which ought to form the transition to "to cause to be = to effect". Therefore we may compare on the contrary Koran ix. 15, *challu sebî-lahum* loose their way, *i. e.* let them go forth free, and render it: He unfettered, unbound, left to itself, *let my way go on as faultless* (unobstructed). Hitzig, following the *Chethib* דרכו, renders it differently: "and made the upright skip on his way." But תמים beside דרכו is to be regarded at the outset as its predicate, and הִתִּיר means "to cause to jump up", Hab. iii. 6, not "to skip along". Nevertheless, the *Chethîb* דרכו, which, from the following *Chethîb* רגליו, bears the appearance of being designed, at any rate seems to have understood תמים personally: *He unfettered (expedit) the up-right his way, making his feet like* &c. The reading וְנִחַת instead of וְנִחֲתָה, although admissible so far as the syntax is concerned (Ges. § 147,*a*), injures the flow of the rhythm.

Vers. 36—37. The pentastich is stunted here by the falling away of the middle line of ver. 36: *and Thy right hand supported me.* Instead of the expressive וְעַנְוַתְךָ (and Thy condescension) we find here וְעֵנֹתְךָ which, in accordance with the usage of the language, does not mean Thy being low (Hengst.), but rather: Thy labour (Böttch.), or more securely: *Thine answering,* LXX. ὑπακοή (*i. e.* the actual help, where-with Thou didst answer my prayer). Instead of תַּחְתָּי we find, as also in vers. 40, 48, תַּחְתֵּנִי with a verbal suffix, like בְּעַד in cxxxix. 11; it is perhaps an inaccuracy of the com-mon dialect, which confused the genitive and accusative suffix. But instances of this are not wanting even in the written language, Ges. § 103, rem. 3.

Vers. 38—41. The cohortative אֶרְדְּפָה, as frequently, has the sense of a hypothetical antecedent, whether it refers to the present, as in cxxxix. 8, or to the past as in lxxiii. 16 and here: *in case I pursued.* In the text in the Psalter it is וְאַשִּׂיגֵם, here it is וָאַשְׁמִידֵם, by which the echo of Exod. xv. is obliterated. And after עַד־כַּלּוֹתָם how tautological is the וָאֲכַלֵּם which is designed to compensate for the shortening of the verse! The verse, to wit, is shortened at the end, וְלֹא־יָכְלוּ קוּם being transformed into וְלֹא יְקוּמוּן. Instead of

וַיְפַלּוּ ,וַיִּכְּלוּ is not inappropriate. Instead of וַתְּאַזְּרֵנִי we find וַתְּזְרֵנִי, by a syncope that belongs to the dialect of the people, cf. תְּזְלִי for תְּאֶזְלִי Jer. ii. 36, מַלֶּף for מְאַלֵּף Job xxxv. 11. Of the same kind is נָתַתָּה = תַּתָּה, an apocope take from the mouths of the people, with which only רַד, Judg. xix. 11, if equivalent to יֵרַד, can be compared. The conjunctive ו of וּמְשַׂנְאַי stands here in connection with אצמיתם as a *consec.*: *my haters, whom I destroyed.* The other text is altogether more natural, better conceived, and more elegant in this instance.

Vers. 42—43. Instead of יְשַׁוְּעוּ we have יְשְׁעוּ, a substitution which is just tolerable: they look forth for help, or even: they look up expectantly to their gods, Isa. xvii. 8, xxxi. 1. The two figurative expressions in ver. 43, however, appear here, in contrast with the other text, in a distorted form: *And I pulverised them as the dust of the earth, as the mire of the street did I crush them, I trampled them down.* The lively and expressive figure כעפר על־פני רוח is weakened into בעפר־ארץ. Instead of אֲרִיקֵם, we have the overloaded glossarial אֲדִקֵּם אֶרְקָעֵם. The former (root דק, דך, to break in pieces) is a word that is interchanged with the אריקם of the other text in the misapprehended sense of אֲרִקֵּם. The latter (root רק, to stretch, to make broad, thin, and compact) looks like a gloss of this אדקם. Since one does not intentionally either crush or trample upon the dirt of the street nor tread it out thin or broad, we must in this instance take not merely כעפר־ארץ but also כטיט־חוצות as expressing the issue or result.

Vers. 44—46. The various reading רִיבֵי עַמִּי proceeds from the correct understanding, that רִיבֵי refers to David's contentions within his kingdom. The supposition that עַמִּי is a *plur. apoc.* and equivalent to עַמִּים, as it is to all appearance in cxliv. 2, and like מִנִּי = מִנִּים xlv. 9, has no ground here. The reasonable variation תִּשְׁמְרֵנִי harmonises with עַמִּי: *Thou hast kept me* (preserved me) *for a head of the nations,* viz. by not allowing David to become deprived of the throne by civil foes. The two lines of ver. 45 are reversed, and not without advantage. The *Hithpa.* יִתְכַּחֲשׁוּ instead of the *Piel* יְכַחֲשׁוּ (cf. lxvi. 3, lxxxi. 16) is the reflexive of the latter: they made themselves flatterers (cf. the *Niph.* Deut. xxxiii. 29: to shew themselves flattering, like the יִשְׁמְעוּ which follows here, *audientes se præstabant = obediebant*). Instead of (אֹזֶן) לִשְׁמֹעַ we have here, in a similar signification, but less elegant, (לִשְׁמוֹעַ(אֹזֶן *according to the hearing of the ear*, *i. e.* hearsay. Instead of וְיַחְרְגוּ we find וַיַּחְגְּרוּ, which is either a transposition of the letters as a solecism (cf. פַּרְץ 2 Sam. xiii. 27 for פָּצַר), or used in a peculiar signification. "They gird (*accincti prodeunt*)" does not give any suitable meaning to this picture of voluntary submission. But חָגַר (whence Talmudic חִגֵּר lame) may have signified "to limp" in the dialect of the people, which may be understood of those who drag themselves along with difficulty and reluctance (Hitz.). "*Out of their closed places (castles)*", here with the suff. *ām* instead of *êhém*.

Vers. 47—49. The צוּר thrust into ver. 47*b* is troublesome. וְיָרֻם (without any necessity for correcting it to וְיָרָם) is optative, cf. Gen. xxvii. 31, Prov. ix. 4, 16. Instead of וַיְדַבֵּר we have וּמֹרִיד *and who subdueth,* which is less significant and so far as the syntax is concerned less elegant. Also here consequently תַּחְתֵּנִי for תַּחְתָּי. Instead of מְפַלְטִי we find וּמוֹצִיאִי *and who bringeth me forth out of my enemies,* who surround me — a peculiar form of expression and without support elsewhere (for it is different in ver. 20). The poetical אַף is exchanged for the prose וְ, מִן־קָמַי for מִקָּמַי, and חָמָם (אִישׁ) for חֲמָסִים (אִישׁ); the last being a *plur.* (cxl. 2, 5, Prov. iv. 17), which is foreign to the genuine Davidic Psalms.

Vers. 50—51. The change of position of יהוה in ver. 50*a*, as well as אֲזַמֵּר for אֲזַמְּרָה, is against the rhythm; the latter, moreover, is contrary to custom, lvii. 10, cviii. 4. While מִגְדֹּל of the other text is not pointed מִגְדָּל, but מַגְדִּל, it is corrected in this text from מַגְדִּיל into מִגְדּוֹל *tower* of salvation — a figure that recalls lxi. 4, Prov. xviii. 10, but is obscure and somewhat strange in this connection; moreover, *migdol* for *migdal,* a tower, only occurs elsewhere in the Old Testament as a proper name.

If we now take one more glance over the mutual relationship of the two texts, we cannot say that both texts equally partake of the original. With the exception of the correct omission of ver. 14*c* and the readings מִשְׁבְּרֵי, חֲשֵׁרַת, and אֲפִיקֵי יָם there is scarely anything in the text of 2 Sam.

xxii. that specially commends itself to us. That this text
is a designed, and perhaps a Davidic, revision of the other
text (Hengst.), is an assumption that is devoid of reason
and appearance; for in 2 Sam. xxii. we have only a text
that varies in some instances, but not a substantially new
form of the text. The text in 2 Sam. xxii., as it has shewn
us, is founded upon careless written and oral transmission.
The rather decided tendency towards a defective form of
writing leads one to conjecture the greater antiquity of the
copy from which it is taken. It is easy to understand how
poetical passages inserted in historical works were less carefully dealt with. It is characteristic of the form of the text
of the Psalm in 2 Sam. xxii., that in not a few instances the
licences of popular expression have crept into it. There is
some truth in what Böttcher says, when he calls the text
in the Psalter the recension of the priests and that in the
Second Book of Samuel the recension of the laity.

PSALM XIX.

PRAYER TO GOD, WHOSE REVELATION OF HIMSELF IS TWOFOLD.

2 THE heavens are telling the glory of God,
   And the work of His hands doth the firmament declare.
3 Day unto day poureth forth speech,
   And night unto night sheweth knowledge —
4 There is no speech and there are no words,
   Whose voice is inaudible.

5 Into all lands is their line gone forth,
   And to the end of the world their utterances:
   To the sun hath He appointed a tabernacle there.
6 And he is like a bridegroom coming out of his chamber,
   He rejoiceth as a strong man to run his course.
7 From the end of the heaven is his going forth
   And his circuit unto the end of it,
   And nothing can hide itself from his heat.

8 The Law of Jahve is spotless,
             restoring the soul;
  The testimony of Jahve is sure,
             making wise the simple.
9 The statutes of Jahve are right,
             rejoicing the heart;
  The commandment of Jahve is pure,
             enlightening the eyes;
10 The fear of Jahve is clean
             enduring for ever;
  The decisions of Jahve are truth,
             righteous altogether.

11 More to be desired are they than gold,
             and much fine gold,
  And sweeter than honey
             and honey-comb.
12 Moreover Thy servant is instructed by them,
             in keeping them there is great reward.
13 As for errors who observeth them?! From hidden sins
             do Thou pronounce me clear!
14 Also from presumptuous sins keep Thy servant back,
             that they may not have dominion over me!
  Then shall I be guiltless and clean
             from great transgression.
15 Thus let be acceptable the words of my mouth
             and the meditation of my heart
  Before Thy face, O Jahve,
             my rock and my Redeemer!!

In the inscription of Ps. xviii. David is called עבד יהוה,
and in Ps. xix. he gives himself this name. In both Psalms,
in the former at the beginning, in the latter at the close,
he calls upon Jahve by the name צוּרִי, my rock. These and
other points of contact (*Symbolæ* p. 49) have concurred to
lead the collector to append Ps. xix., which celebrates God's
revelation of Himself in nature and in the Law, to Ps. xviii.,
which celebrates God's revelation of Himself in the history
of David. The view, that in Ps. xix. we have before us two
torsi blown together from some quarter or other, is founded
upon a defective insight into the relationship, which accords

with a definite plan, of the two halves vers. 2—7, 8—15, as Hitzig has recently shewn in opposition to that view. The poet begins with the praise of the glory of God the Creator, and rises from this to the praise of the mercy of God the Lawgiver; and thus through the praise, springing from wondering and loving adoration, he clears the way to the prayer for justification and sanctification. This prayer grows out of the praise of the mercy of the God who has revealed Himself in His word, without coming back to the first part, vers. 2—7. For, as Lord Bacon says, the heavens indeed tell of the glory of God, but not of His will, according to which the poet prays to be pardoned and sanctified. Moreover, if we suppose the Psalm to be called forth by the aspect of the heavens by day, just as Ps. viii. was by the aspect of the heavens by night, then the unity of this praise of the two revelations of God becomes still more clear. It is morning, and the psalmist rejoices on the one hand at the dawning light of day, and on the other he prepares himself for the day's work lying before him, in the light of the Tôra. The second part, just like the first part, consists of fourteen lines, and each of them is naturally divided into a six and an eight line strophe. But in the second part, in the place of the short lines comes the cæsural schema, which as it were bounds higher, draws deeper breaths and surges as the rise and fall of the waves, for the Tôra inspires the psalmist more than does the sun. And it is also a significant fact, that in the first part God is called אֵל according to his relationship of power to the world, and is only mentioned once; whereas in the second part, He is called by His covenant name יהוה, and mentioned seven times, and the last time by a threefold name, which brings the Psalm to a close with a full toned יהוה צורי וגאלי. What a depth of meaning there is in this distinction of the revelation of God, the Redeemer, from the revelation of God, the Creator!

The last strophe presents us with a sharply sketched soteriology *in nuce*. If we add Ps. xxxii., then we have the whole of the way of salvation in almost Pauline clearness and definiteness. Paul, moreover, quotes both Psalms; they were surely his favourites.

Vers. 2—4.   The heavens, *i. e.* the superterrestrial spheres, which, so far as human vision is concerned, are lost in infinite space, declare how glorious is God, and indeed אֵל, as the Almighty; and what His hands have made, *i. e.* what He has produced with a superior power to which everything is possible, the firmament, *i. e.* vault of heaven stretched out far and wide and as a transparency above the earth (Græco-Veneta τάμα = ἔκταμα, from רָקַע, root רק, to stretch, τείνειν), distinctly expresses.   The sky and firmament are not conceived of as conscious beings which the middle ages, in dependence upon Aristotle (*vid.* Maimonides, *More Nebuchim* ii. 5), believed could be proved from this passage, cf. Neh. ix. 6, Job xxxviii. 7.   Moreover, Scripture knows nothing of the "music of the spheres" of the Pythagoreans.   What is meant is, as the old expositors correctly say, *objectivum vocis non articulatæ præconium.*   The doxa, which God has conferred upon the creature as the reflection of His own, is reflected back from it, and given back to God as it were in acknowledgment of its origin.   The idea of perpetuity, which lies even in the participle, is expanded in ver. 3.   The words of this discourse of praise are carried forward in an uninterrupted line of transmission. הַבִּיעַ (fr. נָבַע, نبع, root נב, to gush forth, nearly allied to which, however, is also the root בע, to spring up) points to the rich fulness with which, as from an inexhaustible spring, the testimony passes on from one day to the next. The parallel word חָוָּה is an unpictorial, but poetic, word that is more Aramaic than Hebrew (= הִגִּיד).   אָמַר also belongs to the more elevated style; the γνωστὸν τοῦ Θεοῦ deposited in the creature, although not reflected, is here called דַּעַת.   The poet does not say that the tidings proclaimed by the day, if they gradually die away as the day declines, are taken up by the night, and the tidings of the night by the day; but (since the knowledge proclaimed by the day concerns the visible works of God by day, and that proclaimed by the night, His works by night), that each dawning day continues the speech of that which has declined, and each approaching night takes up the tale of that which has passed away (*Psychol.* S. 347, tr. p. 408).   If ver. 4 were to be rendered "there is no speech and there are no words, their voice is inaudible", *i. e.* they are silent, speechless witnesses, uttering no sound, but yet speaking aloud (Hengst.), only inwardly audible but yet intelligible everywhere (Then.): then, ver. 5 ought at least to begin with a *Waw adversativum*, and, moreover, the poet would then needlessly check his fervour, producing a tame thought and one that interrupts the flow of the hymn. To take ver. 4 as a circumstantial clause to ver. 5, and made to precede it, as Ewald does, "without loud speech ... their sound has resounded through all the earth" (§ 341, *d*), is impossible, even apart from the fact of אֹמֶר not meaning "loud speech" and קַוָּם hardly "their sound". Ver. 4 is in the form of an independent sentence, and there is nothing whatever in it to betray any designed subordination to ver. 5. But if it be made independent in the sense "there is no loud, no articulate speech, no audible voice, which proceeds from the heavens", then ver. 5 would form an antithesis to it; and this, in like manner, there is nothing to indicate, and it would at least require that the verb יָצָא should be placed first. Luther's rendering is better: There is no language nor speech, where their voice is not heard, *i. e.*, as Calvin also renders it, the testimony of the heavens to God is understood by the peoples of every language and tongue. But this ought to be אֵין לָשׁוֹן or אֵין שָׂפָה (Gen. xi. 1). Hofmann's rendering is similar, but more untenable: "There is no speech and there are no words, that their cry is not heard, *i. e.* the language of the heavens goes forth side by side with all other languages; and men may discourse ever so, still the speech or sound of the heavens is heard therewith, it sounds above them all." But the words are not בְּלִי נִשְׁמָע (after the analogy of Gen. xxxi. 20), or rather בְּלִי יִשָּׁמַע (as in Job xli. 18, Hos. viii. 7). בְּלִי with the *part.* is a poetical expression for the *Alpha privat.* (2 Sam. i. 21), consequently בְּלִי נשְׁמָע is "unheard" or "inaudible", and the opposite of נִשְׁמָע, audible, Jer. xxxi. 15. Thus, therefore, the only rendering that remains is that of the LXX, Vitringa, and Hitzig: There is no language and no words, whose voice is unheard, *i. e.* inaudible. Hupfeld's assertion that this rendering destroys the parallelism is unfounded. The structure of the distich resembles cxxxix.

4. The discourse of the heavens and the firmament, of the day (of the sky by day) and of the night (of the sky by night), is not a discourse uttered in a corner, it is a discourse in speech that is everywhere audible, and in words that are understood by all, a φανερόν, Rom. i. 19.

Vers. 5—7. Since אֹמֶר and דְּבָרִים are the speech and words of the heavens, which form the ruling principal notion, comprehending within itself both יוֹם and לַיְלָה, the suffixes of קַוָּם and מִלֵּיהֶם must unmistakeably refer to הַשָּׁמַיִם in spite of its being necessary to assign another reference to קוֹלָם in ver. 4. Jer. xxxi. 39 shews how we are to understand קָו in connection with יָצָא. The measuring line of the heavens is gone forth into all the earth, *i. e.* has taken entire possession of the earth. Ver. 5*b* tells us what kind of measuring line is intended, viz. that of their heraldship: their words (from מִלָּה, which is more Aramaic than Hebrew, and consequently more poetic) reach to the end of the world, they fill it completely, from its extreme boundary inwards. Isaiah's קָו, ch. xxviii. 10, is inapplicable here, because it does not mean commandment, but rule, and is there used as a word of derision, rhyming with צָו. The ὁ φθόγγος αὐτῶν of the LXX. (ὁ ἦχος αὐτῶν Symm.) might more readily be justified, inasmuch as קָו might mean a harpstring, as being a cord in tension, and then, like τόνος (cf. τοναία), a tone or sound (Gesenius in his *Lex.*, and Ewald), if the reading קוֹלָם does not perhaps lie at the foundation of that rendering. But the usage of the language presents the signification of a measuring line for קָו when used with יָצָא (Aq. κανών, cf. 2 Cor. x. 13); and this gives a new thought, whereas in the other case we should merely have a repetition of what has been already expressed in ver. 4. Paul makes use of these first two lines of the strophe in order, with its very words, to testify to the spread of the apostolic message over the whole earth. Hence most of the older expositors have taken the first half of the Psalm to be an allegorical prediction, the heavens being a figure of the church and the sun a figure of the gospel. The apostle does not, however, make a formal citation in the passage referred to, he merely gives a New Testament application to Old Testament language, by taking the all-penetrating *præconium cœlorum* as figure of the all-penetrating *præco-nium evangelii;* and he is fully justified in so doing by the parallel which the psalmist himself draws between the reve-lation of God in nature and in the written word.

The reference of בָּהֶם to הַשָּׁמִים is at once opposed by the tameness of the thought so obtained. The tent, viz. the retreat (אֹהֶל, according to its radical meaning a dwell-ing, from אהל, cogn. אול, to retire from the open country) of the sun is indeed in the sky, but it is more naturally at the spot where the sky and the קְצֵה תֵבֵל meet. Accordingly בהם has the neuter signification "there" (cf. Isa. xxx. 6); and there is so little ground for reading שָׁם instead of שָׂם, as Ewald does, that the poet on the contrary has written בהם and not שָׁם, because he has just used שָׁם (Hitzig). The name of the sun, which is always feminine in Arabic, is predominantly masculine in Hebrew and Aramaic (cf. on the other hand Gen. xv. 17, Nah. iii. 17, Isa. xlv. 6, Mal. iii. 20); just as the Sabians and heathen Arabs had a sun-god (*masc.*). Accordingly in ver. 6 the sun is compared to a bridegroom, who comes forth in the morning out of his חֻפָּה. Joel ii. 16 shews that this word means a bride-chamber; properly (from חָפַף to cover) it means a canopy (Isa. iv. 5), whence in later Hebrew the bridal or portable canopy (Tal-mud. בֵּית גַּנְנָא), which is supported by four poles and borne by four boys, at the consecration of the bridal pair, and then also the marriage itself, is called *chuppa.* The morn-ing light has in it a freshness and cheerfulness, as it were a renewed youth. Therefore the morning sun is compared to a bridegroom, the desire of whose heart is satisfied, who stands as it were at the beginning of a new life, and in whose youthful countenance the joy of the wedding-day still shines. And as at its rising it is like a bridegroom, so in its rapid course (Sir. xliii. 5) it is like a hero (*vid.* on xviii. 34), inasmuch as it marches on its way ever anew, light-giving and triumphant, as often as it comes forth, with גְּבוּרָה (Judges v. 31). From one end of heaven, the extreme east of the horizon, is its going forth, *i. e.* rising (cf. Hos. vi. 3; the opposite is מָבוֹא going in = setting), and its circuit (תְּקוּפָה, from קוּף = נָקַף, Isa. xxix. 1, to revolve) עַל־קְצוֹתָם, to their (the heavens') end (= עַד Deut. iv. 32), cf.

1 Esdr. iv. 34: ταχὺς τῷ δρόμῳ ὁ ἥλιος, ὅτι στρέφεται ἐν τῷ κύκλῳ τοῦ οὐρανοῦ καὶ πάλιν ἀποτρέχει εἰς τὸν ἑαυτοῦ τόπον ἐν μιᾷ ἡμέρᾳ. On this open way there is not נִסְתָּר, anything hidden, *i. e.* anything that remains hidden, before its heat. חַמָּה is the enlightening and warming influence of the sun, which is also itself called חַמָּה in poetry.

Vers. 8—10. No sign is made use of to mark the transition from the one part to the other, but it is indicated by the introduction of the divine name יהוה instead of אֵל. The word of nature declares אֵל (God) to us, the word of Scripture יהוה (Jahve); the former God's power and glory, the latter also His counsel and will. Now follow twelve encomiums of the Law, of which every two are related as antecedent and consequent, rising and falling according to the cæsural schema, after the manner of waves. One can discern how now the heart of the poet begins to beat with redoubled joy as he comes to speak of God's word, the revelation of His will. תּוֹרָה does not in itself mean the law, but a pointing out, instruction, doctrine or teaching, and more particularly such as is divine, and therefore positive; whence it is also used of prophecy, Isa. i. 10, viii. 16, and prophetically of the New Testament gospel, Isa. ii. 3. But here no other divine revelation is meant than that given by the mediation of Moses, which is become the law, *i. e.* the rule of live (νόμος), of Israel; and this law, too, as a whole not merely as to its hortatory and disciplinary character, but also including the promises contained in it. The praises which the poet pronounces upon the Law, are accurate even from the standpoint of the New Testament. Even Paul says, Rom. vii. 12, 14, "The Law is holy and spiritual, and the commandment holy, and just, and good." The Law merits these praises in itself; and to him who is in a state of favour, it is indeed no longer a law bringing a curse with it, but a mirror of the God merciful in holiness, into which he can look without slavish fear, and is a rule for the direction of his free and willing obedience. And how totally different is the affection of the psalmists and prophets for the Law, — an affection based upon the essence and universal morality of the commandments, and upon a spiritual realisation of the letter, and the consolation

of the promises, — from the pharisaical rabbinical service
of the letter and the ceremonial in the period after the
Exile!

The divine Law is called תְּמִימָה, "perfect", *i. e.* spotless
and harmless, as being absolutely well-meaning, and altogether directed towards the well-being of man. And מְשִׁיבַת
נֶפֶשׁ restoring, bringing back, *i. e.* imparting newness of life,
quickening the soul (cf. *Pil.* שׁוֹבֵב, xxiii. 3), to him, viz., who
obeys the will of God graciously declared therein, and enters
upon the divine way or rule of salvation. Then in the place
of the word תורה we find עֵדוּת, — as the tables of the Ten
Commandments (לֻחוֹת הָעֵדוּת) are called, — from עוּד (הֵעִיד),
which signifies not merely a corroborative, but also a warning and instructive testimony or attestation. The testimony
of Jahve is נֶאֱמָנָה, made firm, sure, faithful, *i. e.* raised
above all doubt in its declarations, and verifying itself in
its threatenings and promises; and hence מַחְכִּימַת פֶּתִי, making wise simplicity, or the simple, *lit.* openness, the open
(root פתה to spread out, open, Indo-Germ. *prat*, πετ, *pat*,
pad), *i. e.* easily led astray; to such an one it gives a solid
basis and stability, σοφίζει αὐτόν, 2 Tim. iii. 15. The Law
divides into פִּקּוּדִים, precepts or declarations concerning
man's obligation; these are יְשָׁרִים, straight or upright, as
a *norma normata*, because they proceed from the upright,
absolutely good will of God, and as a *norma normans* they
lead along a straight way in the right track. They are therefore מְשַׂמְּחֵי לֵב, their educative guidance, taking one as
it were by the hand, frees one from all tottering, satisfies a
moral want, and preserves a joyous consciousness of being
in the right way towards the right goal. מִצְוַת יהוה, Jahve's
statute (from צִוָּה *statuere*), is the tenour of His commandments. The statute is a lamp — it is said in Prov. vi. 23
— and the law a light. So here: it is בָּרָה, clear, like the
light of the sun (Cant. vi. 10), and its light is imparted to
other objects: מְאִירַת עֵינָיִם, enlightening the eyes, which
refers not merely to the enlightening of the understanding,
but of one's whole condition; it makes the mind clear, and
body as well as mind healthy and fresh, for the darkness
of the eyes is sorrow, melancholy, and bewilderment. In
this chain of names for the Law, יִרְאַת ה׳ is not the fear of

God as an act performed, but as a precept, it is what God's revelation demands, effects, and maintains; so that it is the revealed way in which God is to be feared (xxxiv. 12), — in short, it is the religion of Jahve (cf. Prov. xv. 33 with Deut. xvii. 19). This is טְהוֹרָה, clean, pure, as the word which is like to pure gold, by which it is taught, xii. 7, cf. Job xxviii. 19; and therefore עֹמֶדֶת לָעַד, enduring for ever in opposition to all false forms of reverencing God, which carry their own condemnation in themselves. מִשְׁפְּטֵי ה׳ are the *jura* of the Law as a *corpus juris divini*, everything that is right and constitutes right according to the decision of Jahve. These judgments are אֱמֶת, truth, which endures and verifies itself; because, in distinction from most others and those outside Israel, they have an unchangeable moral foundation: צָדְקוּ יַחְדָּו, *i. e.* they are צַדִּיקִים, in accordance with right and appropriate (Deut. iv. 8), altogether, because no reproach of inappositeness and sanctioned injustice or wrong clings to them. The eternal will of God has attained a relatively perfect form and development in the Law of Jahve according to the standard set up as the law of the nation.

Vers. 11—15. With הַנֶּחֱמָדִים (for which, preferring a simple *Shebâ* with the gutturals, Ben-Naphtali writes הַנֶּחֱמָדִים) the poet sums up the characteristics enumerated; the article is summative, as in הַשִּׁשִּׁי at the close of the hexahemeron, Gen. i. 31. פָּז is the finest purified gold, cf. 1 Kings x. 18 with 2 Chron. ix. 17. נֹפֶת צוּפִים "the discharge (from נפת = نفث) of the honeycombs" is the virgin honey, *i. e.* the honey that flows of itself out of the cells. To be desired are the revealed words of God, to him who possesses them as an outward possession; and to him who has received them inwardly they are sweet. The poet, who is himself conscious of being a servant of God, and of striving to act as such, makes use of these words for the end for which they are revealed: he is נִזְהָר, one who suffers himself to be enlightened, instructed, and warned by them. גַּם belongs to נזהר (according to the usual arrangement of the words, *e. g.* Hos. vi. 11), just as in ver. 14 it belongs to חֲשׂךְ. He knows that בְּשָׁמְרָם (with a subjective suffix in an objective sense, cf. Prov. xxv. 7, just as we may also say:) in their observance is, or is included, great reward. עֵקֶב is that

which follows upon one's heels (עָקֵב), or comes immediately
after anything, and is used here of the result of conduct.
Thus, then, inasmuch as the Law is not only a copy of the
divine will, but also a mirror of self-knowledge, in which a
man may behold and come to know himself, he prays for
forgiveness in respect of the many sins of infirmity, —
though for the most part unperceived by him, — to which,
even the pardoned one succumbs. שְׁגִיאָה (in the terminology
of the Law, שְׁגָגָה, ἀγνόημα) comprehends the whole province
of the *peccatum involuntarium*, both the *peccatum ignorantiæ*
and the *peccatum infirmitatis*. The question *delicta quis
intelligit* is equivalent to the negative clause: no one can
discern his faults, on account of the heart of man being
unfathomable and on account of the disguise, oftentimes so
plausible, and the subtlety of sin. Hence, as an inference,
follows the prayer: pronounce me free also מִנִּסְתָּרוֹת, *ab
occultis* (*peccatis*, which, however, cannot be supplied on
grammatical grounds), equivalent to מֵעֲלָמִים (xc. 8), *i. e.*
all those sins, which even he, who is most earnestly striving
after sanctification, does not discern, although he may desire
to know them, by reason of the ever limited nature of his
knowledge both of himself and of sin.* נָקָה, δικαιοῦν, is a
vox judicialis, to declare innocent, pronounce free from, to
let go unpunished. The prayer for justification is followed
in ver. 14 by the prayer for sanctification, and indeed for
preservation against deliberate sins. From זִיד, זוּד, to seethe,
boil over, *Hiph.* to sin wilfully, deliberately, insolently, —
opp. of sin arising from infirmity, Exod. xxi. 14, Deut.
xviii. 22, xvii. 12, — is formed זֵד an insolent sinner, one
who does not sin בִּשְׁגָגָה, but בְּזָדוֹן (cf. 1 Sam. xvii. 28, where
David's brethren bring this reproach against him), or בְּיָד
רָמָה, and the neuter collective זֵדִים (cf. סֵטִים, ci. 3, Hos. v. 2)
peccata proæretica or *contra conscientiam,* which cast one
out of the state of grace or favour, Num. xv. 27—31. For
if זֵדִים had been intended of arrogant and insolent possessors

---

* In the Arab proverb, "no sin which is persisted in is small, no
sin great for which forgiveness is sought of God," صغيرة directly
means a little and كبيرة a great sin, *vid. Allgem. Literar. Zeitschr.*
1844, No. 46, p. 363.

of power (Ewald), the prayer would have taken some other form than that of "keeping back" (חָשַׂךְ as in 1 Sam. xxv. 39 in the mouth of David). זֵדִים, presumptuous sins, when they are repeated, become dominant sins, which irresistibly enslave the man (מָשַׁל with a non-personal subject, as in Isa. iii. 4b, cf. Ps. ciii. 19); hence the last member of the climax (which advances from the *peccatum involuntarium* to the *prœreticum*, and from this to the *regnans*): let them not have dominion over me (בִי with *Dechi* in Baer; generally wrongly marked with *Munach*).

Then (אָז), when Thou bestowest this twofold favour upon me, the favour of pardon and the grace of preservation, shall I be blameless (אֵיתָם 1 *fut. Kal*, instead of אֶתָּם, with י as a characteristic of *ē*) and absolved (וְנִקֵּיתִי not *Piel*, as in ver. 13, but *Niph.*, to be made pure, absolved) from great transgression. פֶּשַׁע* from פָּשַׁע (root פש), to spread out, go beyond the bounds, break through, trespass, is a collective name for deliberate and reigning, dominant sin, which breaks through man's relation of favour with God, and consequently casts him out of favour, — in one word, for apostasy. Finally, the psalmist supplicates a gracious acceptance of his prayer, in which both mouth and heart accord, supported by the faithfulness, stable as the rock (צוּרִי), and redeeming love (גּוֹאֲלִי *redemptor, vindex*, root גל, חל, to loose, redeem) of his God. הָיָה לְרָצוֹן is a standing expression of the sacrificial tôra, *e. g.* Lev. i. 3 sq. The לְפָנֶיךָ, which, according to Exod. xxviii. 38, belongs to לרצון, stands in the second member in accordance with the "parallelism by postponement." Prayer is a sacrifice offered by the inner man. The heart meditates and fashions it; and the mouth presents it, by uttering that which is put into the form of words.

---

* The *Gaja* with מַפְשִׁיעַ is intended in this instance, where מפשע רב are to be read in close connection, to secure distinctness of pronunciation for the unaccented ע, as *e. g.* is also the case in lxxviii. 13, בָּקַע יָם (*báḳa' jām*).

PSALM XX.

PRAYER FOR THE KING IN TIME OF WAR.

2 JAHVE answer thee in the day of distress,
The name of the God of Jacob set thee up on high,
3 Send thee help from the sanctuary,
And uphold thee out of Zion!

4 Remember all thy meat-offerings,
And graciously accept thy burnt offerings! (*Sela*).
5 Give thee according to thine own heart,
And fulfil all thy counsel!

6 We will shout for joy because of Thy help,
And in the name of our God will we raise our
     banners —
Jahve fulfil all thy wishes.
7 Now know I that Jahve giveth help to His Anointed;
He will answer him from His holy heaven
With the helpful mighty deeds of His right hand.

8 Some [praise] chariots and some horses,
And we, we praise the name of Jahve, our God.
9 If those have bowed down and fallen,
Then we have risen up and stand firm.

10 Jahve, Oh help the king! —
May He hear us in the day we call.

To Ps. xix. is closely attached Ps. xx., because its
commencement is as it were the echo of the prayer with
which the former closes; and to Ps. xx. is closely attached
Ps. xxi., because both Psalms refer to the same event
relatively, as prayer and thanksgiving. Ps. xx. is an intercessory psalm of the nation, and Ps. xxi. a thanksgiving
psalm of the nation, on behalf of its king. It is clearly
manifest that the two Psalms form a pair, being connected
by unity of author and subject. They both open somewhat
uniformly with a synonymous parallelism of the members,

xx. 2—6, xxi. 2—8; they then increase in fervour and assume a more vivid colouring as they come to speak of the foes of the king and the empire, xx. 7—9, xxi. 9—13; and they both close with an ejaculatory cry to Jahve, xx. 10, xxi. 14. In both, the king is apostrophised through the course of several verses, xx. 2—6, xxi. 9—13; and here and there this is done in a way that provokes the question whether the words are not rather addressed to Jahve, xx. 6, xxi. 10. In both Psalms the king is referred to by הַמֶּלֶךְ, xx. 10, xxi. 8; both comprehend the goal of the desires in the word יְשׁוּעָה, xx. 6, cf. 7, xxi. 2, 6; both delight in rare forms of expression, which are found only in these instances in the whole range of Old Testament literature, viz. נדגל xx. 6, נתעדד xx. 9, ארשת xxi. 3, תחדרהו xxi. 7.

If, as the לדוד indicates, they formed part of the oldest Davidic Psalter, then it is notwithstanding more probable that their author is a cotemporary poet, than that it is David himself. For, although both as to form of expression (cf. xxi. 12 with x. 2) and as to thoughts (cf. xxi. 7 with xvi. 11), they exhibit some points of contact with Davidic Psalms, they still stand isolated by their peculiar character. But that David is their subject, as the inscription לדוד, and their position in the midst of the Davidic Psalms, lead one to expect, is capable of confirmation. During the time of the Syro-Ammonitish war comes David's deep fall, which in itself and in its consequences made him sick both in soul and in body. It was not until he was again restored to God's favour out of this self-incurred peril, that he went to his army which lay before Rabbath Ammon, and completed the conquest of the royal city of the enemy. The most satisfactory explanation of the situation referred to in this couplet of Psalms is to be gained from 2 Sam. xi. xii. Ps. xx. prays for the recovery of the king, who is involved in war with powerful foes; and Ps. xxi. gives thanks for his recovery, and wishes him a victorious issue to the approaching campaign. The "chariots and horses" (xx. 8) are characteristic of the military power of Aram (2 Sam. x. 18, and frequently), and in xxi. 4 and 10 we perceive an allusion to 2 Sam. xii. 30, 31, or at least a remarkable agreement with what is there recorded.

Vers. 2—6. Litany for the king in distress, who offers
sacrifices for himself in the sanctuary. The futures in vers.
2—5, standing five times at the head of the climactic members
of the parallelism, are optatives. יְמַלֵּא, ver. 6, also continues
the chain of wishes, of which even נְרַנְּנָה (cf. lxix. 15) forms
one of the links. The wishes of the people accompany both
the prayer and the sacrifice. "The Name of the God of Jacob"
is the self-manifesting power and grace of the God of Israel.
יעקב is used in poetry interchangeably with ישראל, just like
אלהים with יהוה. Alshêch refers to Gen. xxxv. 3; and it
is not improbable that the desire moulds itself after the
fashion of the record of the fact there handed down to us.
May Jahve, who, as the history of Jacob shews, hears (and
answers) in the day of distress, hear the king; may the
Name of the God of Jacob bear him away from his foes to
a triumphant height. שַׂגֵּב alternates with רוֹמֵם (xviii. 49)
in this sense. This intercession on the behalf of the praying one is made in the sanctuary on the heights of Zion,
where Jahve sits enthroned. May He send him succour from
thence, like auxiliary troops that decide the victory. The
king offers sacrifice. He offers sacrifice according to custom
before the commencement of the battle (1 Sam. xiii. 9 sq.,
and cf. the phrase קִדֵּשׁ מִלְחָמָה), a whole burnt-offering and
at the same time a meat or rather meal offering also,
מְנָחוֹת;* for every whole offering and every *shelamim*- or
peace-offering had a meat-offering and a drink-offering as
its indispensable accompaniment. The word זָכַר is perfectly familiar in the ritual of the meal-offering. That
portion of the meal-offering, only a part of which was placed
upon the altar (to which, however, according to traditional
practice, does not belong the accompanying meal-offering
of the מנחת נסכים, which was entirely devoted to the altar),
which ascended with the altar fire is called אַזְכָּרָה, μνημόσυνον

---

* This, though not occurring in the Old Testament, is the principal
form of the plural, which, as even David Kimchi recognises in his
Lexicon, points to a verb מָנַח (just as שְׂמָלוֹת, גְּבָעוֹת, שְׁפָחוֹת point to
שִׂמְלָ, גֶּבַע, שִׁפְחָ); whereas other old grammarians supposed נָחָה to be
the root, and were puzzled with the traditional pronunciation m^enachôth,
but without reason.

(cf. Acts x. 4), that which brings to remembrance with God
him for whom it is offered up (not "incense", as Hupfeld
renders it); for the designation of the offering of jealousy,
Num. v. 15, as "bringing iniquity to remembrance before
God" shews, that in the meal-offering ritual זְכָר retains the
very same meaning that it has in other instances. Every
meal-offering is in a certain sense a מִנְחַת זִכָּרוֹן. Hence here
the prayer that Jahve would graciously remember them is
combined with the meal-offerings.

As regards the ʿolah, the wish "let fire from heaven (Lev.
ix. 24, 1 Kings xviii. 38, 1 Chron. xxi. 26) turn it to ashes",
would not be vain. But the language does not refer to anything extraordinary; and in itself the consumption of the
offering to ashes (Böttcher) is no mark of gracious acceptance. Moreover, as a denominative from דֶּשֶׁן, fat ashes,
דִּשֵׁן means "to clean from ashes", and not: to turn into
ashes. On the other hand, דִּשֵׁן also signifies "to make fat",
xxiii. 5, and this effective signification is applied declaratively in this instance: may He find thy burnt-offering fat,
which is equivalent to: may it be to Him a רֵיחַ נִיחֹם [an odour
of satisfaction, a sweet-smelling savour]. The voluntative
ah only occurs here and in Job xi. 17 (which see) and Isa.
v. 19, in the 3 pers.; and in this instance, just as with the
cohortative in 1 Sam. xxviii. 15, we have a change of the
lengthening into a sharpening of the sound (cf. the exactly
similar change of forms in 1 Sam. xxviii. 15, Isa. lix. 5,
Zech. v. 4, Prov. xxiv. 14, Ezek. xxv. 13) as is very frequently the case in מֶה for מָה. The alteration to יְדַשְּׁנֶה or
יְדַשְּׁנָה (Hitzig) is a felicitous but needless way of getting rid
of the rare form. The explanation of the intensifying of
the music here is, that the intercessory song of the choir is
to be simultaneous with the presentation upon the altar
(הַקְטָרָה). עֵצָה is the resolution formed in the present war-
time. "Because of thy salvation", i. e. thy success in war,
is, as all the language is here, addressed to the king, cf.
xxi. 2, where it is addressed to Jahve, and intended of the
victory accorded to him. It is needless to read נַגְדִּל instead
of נִדְגֹּל, after the rendering of the LXX. μεγαλυνθησόμεθα.
נִדְגֹּל is a denominative from דֶּגֶל: to wave a banner. In the
closing line, the rejoicing of hope goes back again to the

present and again assumes the form of an intercessory
desire.

Vers. 7—9. While vers. 2—6 were being sung the offering of the sacrifice was probably going on. Now, after a
lengthened pause, there ascends a voice, probably the voice
of one of the Levites, expressing the cheering assurance of
the gracious acceptance of the offering that has been presented
by the priest. With עַתָּה or וְעַתָּה, the usual word to indicate
the turning-point, the instantaneous entrance of the result
of some previous process of prolonged duration, whether
hidden or manifest (*e. g.* 1 Kings xvii. 24, Isa. xxix. 22), is
introduced. הוֹשִׁיעַ is the perfect of faith, which, in the
certainty of being answered, realises the fulfilment in anticipation. The exuberance of the language in ver. 7 corresponds to the exuberance of feeling which thus finds expression.

In ver. 3 the answer is expected out of Zion, in the
present instance it is looked for from God's holy heavens;
for the God who sits enthroned in Zion is enthroned for
ever in the heavens. His throne on earth is as it were the
vestibule of His heavenly throne; His presence in the sanctuary of Israel is no limitation of His omnipresence; His
help out of Zion is the help of the Celestial One and Him
who is exalted above the heaven of heavens. גְּבוּרוֹת does not
here mean the fulness of might (cf. xc. 10), but the displays of power (cvi. 2, cxlv. 4, cl. 2, Isa. lxiii. 15), by which
His right hand procures salvation, *i. e.* victory, for the
combatant. The glory of Israel is totally different from
that of the heathen, which manifests itself in boastful talk.
In ver. 8*a* הַזְכִּירוּ or יַזְכִּירוּ must be supplied from the נַזְכִּיר
in ver. 8*b* (LXX. μεγαλυνθησόμεθα = נגביר, xii. 5); הַזְכִּיר בְּ,
to make laudatory mention of any matter, to extol, and
indirectly therefore to take credit to one's self for it, to
boast of it (cf. הִלֵּל בְּ, xliv. 9). According to the Law Israel
was forbidden to have any standing army; and the law
touching the king (Deut. xvii. 16) speaks strongly against
his keeping many horses. It was also the same under the
judges, and at this time under David; but under Solomon,
who acquired for himself horses and chariots in great
number (1 Kings x. 26—29), it was very different. It is

therefore a confession that must belong to the time of David which is here made in ver. 8, viz. that Israel's glory in opposition to their enemies, especially the Syrians, is the sure defence and protection of the Name of their God alone. The language of David to Goliath is very similar, 1 Sam. xvii. 45. The preterites in ver. 9 are *præt. confidentiæ.* It is, as Luther says, "a song of triumph before the victory, a shout of joy before succour." Since קוּם does not mean to stand, but to rise, קַמְנוּ assumes the present superiority of the enemy. But the position of affairs changes: those who stand fall, and those who are lying down rise up; the former remain lying, the latter keep the field. The *Hithpa.* הִתְעוֹדֵד signifies to shew one's self firm, strong, courageous; like עוֹדֵד, cxlvi. 9, clxvii. 6, to strengthen, confirm, recover, from עוּד to be compact, firm, cogn. اد *f. i.*, inf. *aid*, strength; as, *e. g.*, the Koran (*Sur.* xxxviii. 16) calls David *dhâ-l-aidi*, possessor of strength, II. *ajjada*, to strengthen, support, and اد, inf. *add*, strength, superiority, V. *taaddada,* to shew one's self strong, brave, courageous.

Ver. 10. After this solo voice, the chorus again come on. The song is closed, as it was opened, by the whole congregation; and is rounded off by recurring to its primary note, praying for the accomplishment of that which is sought and pledged. The accentuation construes הַמֶּלֶךְ with יַעֲנֵנוּ as its subject, perhaps in consideration of the fact, that הוֹשִׁיעָה is not usually followed by a governed object, and because thus a medium is furnished for the transition from address to direct assertion. But if in a Psalm, the express object of which is to supplicate salvation for the king, הוֹשִׁיעָה הַמֶּלֶךְ stand side by side, then, in accordance with the connection, הַמֶּלֶךְ must be treated as the object; and more especially since Jahve is called מֶלֶךְ רָב, in xlviii. 3, and the like, but never absolutely הַמֶּלֶךְ. Wherefore it is, with Hupfeld, Hitzig, and others, to be rendered according to the LXX. and Vulgate, *Domine salvum fac regem.* The New Testament cry Ὡσαννὰ τῷ υἱῷ Δαυίδ is a peculiar application of this Davidic "God bless the king (God save the king)", which is brought about by means of cxviii. 25. The closing line, ver. 10*b*, is an expanded Amen.

PSALM XXI.

PSALM XXI.

THANKSGIVING FOR THE KING IN TIME OF WAR.

2 JAHVE, on account of Thy strength is the king glad,
   And on account of Thy succour how greatly doth he
       rejoice!
3 The wish of his heart hast Thou granted him,
   And the desire of his lips hast Thou not refused. (*Sela.*)

4 For Thou dost meet him bringing blessings of good,
   Thou settest upon his head a crown of fine gold.
5 He asked life of Thee, — Thou grantedst it to him,
   Length of days, for ever and ever.

6 Great is his glory through Thy help,
   Praise and glory dost Thou lay upon him.
7 For Thou makest him blessings for ever,
   Thou dost delight him with joy in Thy presence.

8 For the king trusted in Jahve,
   And through the favour of the Most High he shall not
      be moved.
9 Thy hand will reach to all thine enemies
   Thy right hand will reach all those that hate thee.

10 Thou shalt make them as a fiery oven,
         when thou art angry,
   Jahve in His wrath shall swallow them up,
         and a fire shall devour them.
11 Their fruit shalt thou destroy from the earth,
   And their seed from among the children of men.

12 For they intend evil against thee,
   They devise mischief: they shall accomplish nothing.
13 For thou wilt make them turn back,
   With thy strings wilt thou aim at their faces.

  4 Be Thou exalted, Jahve, in Thy might;
   We will celebrate with voice and harp Thy strength.

"*Jahve fulfil all thy desires*" cried the people in the preceding Psalm, as they interceded on behalf of their king; and in this Psalm they are able thankfully to say to God "*the desire of his heart hast Thou granted.*" In both Psalms the people come before God with matters that concern the welfare of their king; in the former, with their wishes and prayers, in the latter, their thanksgivings and hopes; in the latter as in the former when in the midst of war, but in the latter after the recovery of the king, in the certainty of a victorious termination of the war.

The Targum and the Talmud, *B. Succa* 52a, understand this 21st Psalm of the king Messiah. Rashi remarks that this Messianic interpretation ought rather to be given up for the sake of the Christians. But even the Christian exposition cannot surely mean to hold fast this interpretation so directly and rigidly as formerly. This pair of Psalm treats of David; David's cause, however, in its course towards a triumphant issue — a course leading through suffering — is certainly figuratively the cause of Christ.

Vers. 2—3. The Psalm begins with thanksgiving for the bodily and spiritual blessings which Jahve has bestowed and still continues to bestow upon the king, in answer to his prayer. This occupies the three opening tetrastichs, of which these verses form the first. עֹז (whence עָזְּךָ, as in lxxiv. 13, together with עֻזְּךָ, lxiii. 3, and frequently) is the power that has been made manifest in the king, which has turned away his affliction; יְשׁוּעָה is the help from above which has freed him out of his distress. The יָגִיל, which follows the מַה of the exclamation, is naturally shortened by the *Keri* into יָגֶל (with the retreat of the tone); cf. on the contrary Prov. xx. 24, where מַה is interrogative and, according to the sense, negative). The ἅπ. λεγ. אֲרֶשֶׁת has the signification eager desire, according to the connection, the LXX. δέησιν, and the perhaps also cognate רוּשׁ, to be poor; the Arabic ورش, *avidum esse,* must be left out of consideration according to the laws of the interchange of consonants, whereas יָרַשׁ, ورث, *capere, captare* (cf. إِرْث = ورث an inheritance), but not רוּשׁ (*vid.* xxxiv. 11), belongs apparently to

the same root. Observe the strong negation בַּל: no, thou
hast not denied, but done the very opposite. The fact of
the music having to strike up here favours the supposition,
that the occasion of the Psalm is the fulfilment of some
public, well-known prayer.

Vers. 4—5. "Blessings of good" (Prov. xxiv. 25) are
those which consist of good, *i. e.* true good fortune. The
verb קִדֵּם, because used of the favour which meets and
presents one with some blessing, is construed with a double
accusative, after the manner of verbs of putting on and
bestowing (Ges. § 139). Since ver. 4*b* cannot be intended
to refer to David's first coronation, but to the preservation
and increase of the honour of his kingship, this parti-
cularisation of ver. 4*a* sounds like a prediction of what is
recorded in 2 Sam. xii. 30: after the conquest of the Ammonitish royal city Rabbah David set the Ammonitish crown
(עֲטֶרֶת), which is renowned for the weight of its gold and its
ornamentation with precious stones, upon his head. David
was then advanced in years, and in consequence of heavy
guilt, which, however, he had overcome by penitence and
laying hold on the mercy of God, was come to the brink
of the grave. He, worthy of death, still lived; and the
victory over the Syro-Ammonitish power was a pledge to
him of God's faithfulness in fulfilling his promises. It is
contrary to the tenour of the words to say that ver. 5*b* does
not refer to length of life, but to hereditary succession to
the throne. To wish any one that he may live לְעוֹלָם, and
especially a king, is a usual thing, 1 Kings i. 31, and frequently. The meaning is, may the life of the king be prolonged to an indefinitely distant day. What the people have
desired elsewhere, they here acknowledge as bestowed upon
the king.

Vers. 6—7. The help of God turns to his honour, and
paves the way for him to honour, it enables him — this is
the meaning of ver. 6*b* — to maintain and strengthen his
kingship with fame and glory. שִׁוָּה עַל used, as in lxxxix.
20, of divine investiture and endowment. To make blessings,
or a fulness of blessing, is a stronger form of expressing
God's words to Abram, Gen. xii. 2: thou shalt be a blessing
i. e. a possessor of blessing thyself, and a medium of blessing

to others. Joy in connection with (אֶת as in xvi. 11) the
countenance of God, is joy in delightful and most intimate
fellowship with Him. חִדְּה, from חָדָה, which occurs once
in Exod. xviii. 9, has in Arabic, with reference to nomad
life, the meaning "to cheer the beasts of burden with a song
and urge them on to a quicker pace", and in Hebrew, as in
Aramaic, the general signification "to cheer, enliven."

Vers. 8—9. With this strophe the second half of the
Psalm commences. The address to God is now changed
into an address to the king; not, however, expressive of
the wishes, but of the confident expectation, of the speakers.
Hengstenberg rightly regards ver. 8 as the transition to the
second half; for by its objective utterance concerning the
king and God, it separates the language hitherto addressed
to God, from the address to the king, which follows. We
do not render ver. 8*b*: and [trusting] in the favour of the
Most High — he shall not be moved; the mercy is the response of the trust, which (trust) does not suffer him to be
moved; on the expression, cf. Prov. x. 30. This inference
is now expanded in respect to the enemies who desire to
cause him to totter and fall. So far from any tottering, he,
on the contrary, makes a victorious assault upon his foes.
If the words had been addressed to Jahve, it ought, in order
to keep up the connection between vers. 9 and 8, at least
to have been אִיביו and שׂנאיו (his, *i. e.* the king's, enemies).
What the people now hope on behalf of their king, they here
express beforehand in the form of a prophecy. מָצָא לְ (as
in Isa. x. 10) and מָצָא *seq. acc.* (as in 1 Sam. xxiii. 17) are
distinguished as: to reach towards, or up to anything, and
to reach anything, attain it. Supposing לְ to represent the
accusative, as *e. g.* in lxix. 6, ver. 9*b* would be a useless
repetition.

Vers. 10—11. Hitherto the Psalm has moved uniformly
in synonymous dipodia, now it becomes agitated; and one
feels from its excitement that the foes of the king are also
the people's foes. True as it is, as Hupfeld takes it, that
לְעֵת פָּנֶיךָ sounds like a direct address to Jahve, ver. 10*b*
nevertheless as truly teaches us quite another rendering.
The destructive effect, which in other passages is said to
proceed from the face of Jahve, xxxiv. 17, Lev. xx. 6, Lam.

iv. 16 (cf. ἔχει θεὸς ἔκδικον ὄμμα), is here ascribed to the face,
i. e. the personal appearing (2 Sam. xvii. 11) of the king.
David's arrival did actually decide the fall of Rabbath Ammon, of whose inhabitants some died under instruments of
torture and others were cast into brick-kilns, 2 Sam. xii.
26 sqq. The prospect here moulds itself according to this
fate of the Ammonites. כְּתַנּוּר אֵשׁ is a second accusative to
תְּשִׁיתֵמוֹ, thou wilt make them like a furnace of fire, *i. e.* a
burning furnace, so that like its contents they shall entirely
consume by fire (*synecdoche continentis pro contento*). The
figure is only hinted at, and is differently applied to what
it is in Lam. v. 10, Mal. iii. 19. Ver. 10*a* and 10*b* are
intentionally two long rising and falling wave-like lines, to
which succeed, in ver. 11, two short lines; the *latter* describe
the peaceful gleaning after the fiery judgment of God that
has been executed by the hand of David. פִּרְיָמוֹ, as in Lam.
ii. 20, Hos. ix. 16, is to be understood after the analogy of
the expression פְּרִי הַבֶּטֶן. It is the fate of the Amalekites
(cf. ix. 6 sq.), which is here predicted of the enemies of
the king.

Vers. 12—13. And this fate is the merited frustration
of their evil project. The construction of the sentences in
ver. 12 is like xxvii. 10, cxix. 83; Ew. § 362, *b.* נָטָה רָעָה
is not to be understood according to the phrase נָטָה רֶשֶׁת
(= פָּרַשׂ), for this phrase is not actually found; we have
rather, with Hitzig, to compare lv. 4, 2 Sam. xv. 14: to
incline evil down upon any one is equivalent to: to put it
over him, so that it may fall in upon him. נָטָה signifies "to
extend lengthwise", to unfold, but also to bend by drawing tight. שִׁית שְׁכֶם to make into a back, *i. e.* to make them
into such as turn the back to you, is a more choice expression than נָתַן עֹרֶף, xviii. 41, cf. 1 Sam. x. 9; the half
segolate form שְׁכֶם, (= שֶׁכֶם) becomes here, in pause, the
full segolate form שֶׁכֶם. חִצִּים must be supplied as the object
to תְּכוֹנֵן, as it is in other instances after יָדָה, הִשְׁלִיךְ, הוֹרָה;
כּוֹנֵן חֵץ, xi. 2, cf. vii. 14, signifies to set the swift arrow upon
the bow-string (יֶתֶר = מֵיתָר) = to aim. The arrows hit the
front of the enemy, as the pursuer overtakes them.

Ver. 14. After the song has spread abroad its wings in
twice three tetrastichs, it closes by, as it were, soaring aloft

and thus losing itself in a distich. It is a cry to God for
victory in battle, on behalf of the king. "Be Thou exalted",
i. e. manifest Thyself in Thy supernal (lvii. 6, 12) and judicial (vii. 7 sq.) sovereignty. What these closing words long
to see realised is that Jahve should reveal for world-wide
conquest this גְּבוּרָה, to which everything that opposes Him
must yield, and it is for this they promise beforehand a
joyous gratitude.

PSALM XXII.

ELI ELI LAMA ASABTANI.

2 MY God, my God, why hast Thou forsaken me?!
  Far from my help is my entreating cry,
3 O my God, I cry in the daytime, but Thou answerest not,
  And in the night season, but I have no rest.

4 Yet Thou art holy, sitting enthroned above the praises
        of Israel.
5 In Thee our fathers trusted,
  They trusted, and Thou didst deliver them.
6 Unto Thee they cried and were freed,
  In Thee trusting, they were not put to shame.

7 But I am a worm, and not a man;
  A reproach of men and despised of the people.
8 All they that see me laugh me to scorn;
  They shoot out the lip, they shake the head:
9 "Roll it upon Jahve — let Him deliver him,
  "Let Him rescue him, when He delighteth in him."

10 Yea Thou art He that took me out of the womb
   That inspired me with trust at my mother's breasts.
11 On Thee was I cast from my birth,
   From my mother's womb Thou art my God.
12 Be not far from me, for trouble is near,
   For there is no helper at hand.

13 Mighty bulls have compassed me,
   Strong ones of Bashan have beset me round.

14 They open their mouth against me —
   A lion ravening and roaring.

15 Like water am I poured out,
   And out of joint are all my bones.
   My heart is become like wax,
   Melted in the midst of my bowels.
16 Dried up like a potsherd is my strength,
   And my tongue cleaveth to my jaws,
   And Thou layest me in the dust of death.

17 For dogs have compassed me,
   A band of wicked men encircles me,
   Like a lion, my hands and my feet.
18 I can count all my bones,
   They look, they stare upon me.
19 They part my garments among them,
   And upon my vesture they cast lots.

20 And Thou, Jahve, remain not afar off!
   My strength, haste Thee to help me!
21 Rescue my soul from the sword,
   My only one from the paw of the dog.
22 Save me from the lion's jaws,
   And from the horns of the antilopes — Thou wilt
      answer me.

23 I will declare Thy name among my brethren,
   In the midst of the congregation will I praise Thee:
24 "Ye that fear Jahve, praise Him;
   "All ye the seed of Jacob, glorify Him,
   "And stand in awe of Him, all ye seed of Israel!"

25 "For He hath not despised nor abhorred the affliction
      of the afflicted,
   "Neither hath He hid His face from him,
   "And when he cried, He hath hearkened to him."

26 From Thee cometh my praise in the great congregation —
   My vows will I pay before them that fear Him.
27 The meek shall eat and be satisfied,
   They shall praise Jahve that seek Him:
   "Let your heart refresh itself for ever!"

28 Remember and turn unto Jahve shall all the ends of
        the earth,
   And all the families of the nations shall bow down
        before Thee.
29 For Jahve's is the kingship, and He ruleth among the
        nations.
30 All the thriving of the earth shall eat and bow down,
   Before Him shall all they that go down to the dust sink
        down and they that cannot prolong their life.
31 A seed shall serve Him: it shall be told to the generation
        concerning the Lord;
32 They shall come and declare His righteousness to a
        future people, that He hath finished it.

We have here a plaintive Psalm, whose deep complaints,
out of the midst of the most humiliating degradation and
most fearful peril, stand in striking contrast to the cheerful tone of Ps. xxi. — starting with a disconsolate cry of
anguish, it passes on to a trustful cry for help, and ends in
vows of thanksgiving and a vision of world-wide results,
which spring from the deliverance of the sufferer. In no
Psalm do we trace such an accumulation of the most ex-
cruciating outward and inward suffering pressing upon the
complainant, in connection the most perfect innocence. In
this respect Ps. lxix. is its counterpart; but it differs from
it in this particular, that there is not a single sound of
imprecation mingled with its complaints.

It is David, who here struggles upward out of the
gloomiest depth to such a bright height. It is a Davidic
Psalm belonging to the time of the persecution by Saul.
Ewald brings it down to the time preceding the destruction

of Jerusalem, and Bauer to the time of the Exile. Ewald
says it is not now possible to trace the poet more exactly.
And Maurer closes by saying: *illud unum equidem pro certo
habeo, fuisse vatem hominem opibus præditum atque illustrem,
qui magna auctoritate valeret non solum apud suos, verum etiam
apud barbaros.* Hitzig persists in his view, that Jeremiah
composed the first portion when cast into prison as an
apostate, and the second portion in the court of the prison,
when placed under this milder restraint. And according to
Olshausen, even here again, the whole is appropriate to the
time of the Maccabees. But it seems to us to be confirmed
at every point, that David, who was so persecuted by Saul,
is the author. The cry of prayer אל־תרחק (xxii. 12, 20,
xxxv. 22, xxxviii. 22, borrowed in lxxi. 12); the name given
to the soul, יחידה (xxii. 21, xxxv. 17); the designation of
quiet and resignation by דומיה (xxii. 3, xxxix. 3, lxii. 2, cf.
lxv. 2), are all regarded by us, since we do not limit the
genuine Davidic Psalms to Ps. iii. — xix. as Hitzig does, as
Davidic idioms. Moreover, there is no lack of points of
contact in other respects with genuine old Davidic hymns
(cf. xxii. 30 with xxviii. 1, those that go down to the dust,
to the grave; then in later Psalms as in cxliii. 7, in Isaiah
and Ezekiel), and more especially those belonging to the
time of Saul, as Ps. lxix. (cf. xxii. 27 with lxix. 33) and lix.
(cf. xxii. 17 with lix. 15). To the peculiar characteristics
of the Psalms of this period belong the figures taken from
animals, which are heaped up in the Psalm before us. The
fact that Ps. xxii. is an ancient Davidic original is also
confirmed by the parallel passages in the later literature of
the *Shîr* (lxxi. 5 sq. taken from xxii. 10 sq.; cii. 18 sq. in
imitation xxii. 25, 31 sq.), of the *Chokma* (Prov. xvi. 3,
גֹּל אל־ה׳ taken from Ps. xxii. 9, xxxvii. 5), and of prophecy
(Isaiah, ch. xlix. liii.; Jeremiah, in Lam. iv. 4; cf. Ps. xxii.
15, and many other similar instances). In spite of these
echoes in the later literature there are still some expressions
that remain unique in the Psalm and are not found elsewhere, as the hapaxlegomena אֱיָלוּת and עֱנוּת. Thus, then,
we entertain no doubts respecting the truth of the לדוד. David speaks in this Psalm, — he and not any other, and that

out of his own inmost being. In accordance with the nature
of lyric poetry, the Psalm has grown up on the soil of his
individual life and his individual sensibilities.

There is also in reality in the history of David, when
persecuted by Saul, a situation which may have given occasion to the lifelike picture drawn in this Psalm, viz. 1 Sam.
xxiii. 25 sq. The detailed circumstances of the distress at
that time are not known to us, but they certainly did not
coincide with the rare and terrible sufferings depicted in
this Psalm in such a manner that these can be regarded as
an historically faithful and literally exact copy of those
circumstances; cf. on the other hand Ps. xvii. which was
composed at the same period. To just as slight a degree
have the prospects, which he connects in this Psalm with his
deliverance, been realised in David's own life. On the other
h and, the first portion exactly coincides with the sufferings
of Jesus Christ, and the second with the results that have
sprung from His resurrection. It is the agonising situation of
the Crucified One which is presented before our eyes in vers.
15—18 with such artistic faithfulness: the spreading out
of the limbs of the naked body, the torturing pain in hands
and feet, and the burning thirst which the Redeemer, in
order that the Scripture might be fulfilled, announced in
the cry διψῶ, John xix. 28. Those who blaspheme and
those who shake their head at Him passed by His cross,
Mat. xxvii. 39, just as ver. 8 says; scoffers cried out to Him:
let the God in whom He trusts help Him, Mat. xxvii. 43,
just as ver. 9 says; His garments were divided and lots were
cast for His coat, John xix. 23 sq., in order that ver. 19 of
our Psalm might be fulfilled. The fourth of the seven sayings of the dying One, Ἠλί, Ἠλί κ. τ. λ., Mat. xxvii. 46,
Mark xv. 34, is the first word of our Psalm and the appropriation of the whole. And the Epistle to the Hebrews, ch. ii.
11 sq., cites ver. 23 as the words of Christ, to shew that
He is not ashamed to call them brethren, whose sanctifier
God has appointed Him to be, just as the risen Redeemer
actually has done, Mat. xxviii. 10, John xx. 17. This has
by no means exhausted the list of mutual relationships.
The Psalm so vividly sets before us not merely the sufferings
of the Crucified One, but also the salvation of the world

arising out of His resurrection and its sacramental efficacy, that it seems more like history than prophecy, *ut
non tam prophetia, quam historia videatur* (Cassiodorus).
Accordingly the ancient Church regarded Christ, not David,
as the speaker in this Psalm; and condemned Theodore of
Mopsuestia who expounded it as cotemporary history.
Bakius expresses the meaning of the older Lutheran expositors when he says: *asserimus, hunc Psalmum ad literam primo,
proprie et absque ulla allegoria, tropologia et* ἀναγωγῇ *integrum
et per omnia de solo Christo exponendum esse.* Even the synagogue, so far as it recognises a suffering Messiah, hears
Him speak here; and takes the "hind of the morning" as a
name of the *Shechina* and as a symbol of the dawning
redemption.

To ourselves, who regard the whole Psalm as the words
of David, it does not thereby lose anything whatever of its
prophetic character. It is a typical Psalm. The same God
who communicates His thoughts of redemption to the mind
of men, and there causes them to develope into the word of
prophetic announcement, has also moulded the history itself
into a prefiguring representation of the future deliverance;
and the evidence for the truth of Christianity which is derived from this factual prophecy (*Thatweissagung*) is as grand
as that derived from the verbal prediction (*Wortweissagung*).
That David, the anointed of Samuel, before he ascended the
throne, had to traverse a path of suffering which resembles
the suffering path of Jesus, the Son of David, baptized of
John, and that this typical suffering of David is embodied
for us in the Psalms as in the images reflected from a mirror, is an arrangement of divine power, mercy, and wisdom.
But Ps. xxii. is not merely a typical Psalm. For in the
very nature of the type is involved the distance between it
and the antitype. In Ps. xxii., however, David descends,
with his complaint, into a depth that lies beyond the depth
of his affliction, and rises, with his hopes, to a height that
lies far beyond the height of the reward of his affliction.

In other words: the rhetorical figure hyperbole (مُبَالَغة, *i. e.*
depiction, with colours thickly laid on), without which, in
the eyes of the Semite, poetic diction would be flat and

faded, is here made use of by the Spirit of God. By this Spirit the hyperbolic element is changed into the prophetic. This elevation of the typical into the prophetic is also capable of explanation on psychological grounds. Since David has been anointed with the oil of royal consecration, and at same time with the Holy Spirit, the Spirit of the kingship of promise, he regards himself also as the messiah of God, towards whom the promises point; and by virtue of this view of himself, in the light of the highest calling in connection with the redemptive history, the historical reality of his own experiences becomes idealised to him, and thereby both what he experiences and what he hopes for acquire a depth and height of background which stretches out into the history of the final and true Christ of God. We do not by this maintain any overflowing of his own consciousness to that of the future Christ, an opinion which has been shewn by Hengstenberg, Tholuck and Kurtz to be psychologically impossible. But what we say is, that looking upon himself as the Christ of God, — to express it in the light of the historical fulfilment, — he looks upon himself in Jesus Christ. He does not distinguish himself from the Future One, but in himself he sees the Future One, whose image does not free itself from him till afterwards, and whose history will coincide with all that is excessive in his own utterances. For as God the Father moulds the history of Jesus Christ in accordance with His own counsel, so His Spirit moulds even the utterances of David concerning himself the type of the Future One, with a view to that history. Through this Spirit, who is the Spirit of God and of the future Christ at the same time, David's typical history, as he describes it in the Psalms and more especially in this Psalm, acquires that ideal depth of tone, brilliancy, and power, by virtue of which it (the history) reaches far beyond its typical facts, penetrates to its very root in the divine counsels, and grows to be the word of prophecy: so that, to a certain extent, it may rightly be said that Christ here speaks through David, insofar as the Spirit of Christ speaks through him, and makes the typical suffering of His ancestor the medium for the representation of His own future sufferings. Without recognising this incontestable relation of the matter Ps. xxii. cannot be understand nor can we fully enter into its sentiments.

The inscription runs: *To the precentor, upon (after) the hind of the morning's dawn, a Psalm of David.* Luther, with reference to the fact that Jesus was taken in the night and brought before the Sanhedrim, renders it *"of the hind, that is early chased,"* for

> *Patris Sapientia, Veritas divina,*
> *Deus homo captus est horâ matutinâ.*

This interpretation is certainly a well-devised improvement of the ὑπὲρ τῆς ἀντιλήψεως τῆς ἑωθινῆς of the LXX. (Vulg. *pro susceptione matutina*), which is based upon a confounding of אֶיֶלֶת with אֱיָלוּת (ver. 20), and is thus explained by Theodoret: ἀντίληψις ἑωθινὴ ἡ τοῦ σωτῆρος ἡμῶν ἐπιφάνεια. Even the Midrash recalls Cant. ii. 8, and the Targum the lamb of the morning sacrifice, which was offered as soon as the watchman on the pinnacle of the Temple cried: בְּרַק בִּרְקָאִי (the first rays of the morning burst forth). אַיֶּלֶת הַשַּׁחַר is in fact, according to traditional definition, the early light preceding the dawn of the morning, whose first rays are likened to the horns of a hind.* But natural as it may be to assign to the inscription a symbolical meaning in the case of this Psalm, it certainly forms no exception to the technical meaning, in connection with the music, of the other inscriptions. And Melissus (1572) has explained it correctly "concerning the melody of a common song, whose commencement was *Ajéleth Hasháhar,* that is, The hind of the morning's dawn." And it may be that the choice of the melody bearing this name was designed to have reference to the glory which bursts forth in the night of affliction.

According to the course of the thoughts the Psalm falls into three divisions, vers. 2—12, 13—22, 23—32, which are

---

* There is a determination of the time to this effect, which is found both in the Jerusalem and in the Babylonian Talmud "from the hind of the morning's dawn till the east is lighted up." In *Jer. Berachoth, ad init.*, it is explained: אילת השחר כמין תרתי קרני דנהורא סלקין ממדינחא ומנהרין לעלמא, "like two horns of light, rising from the east and filling the world with light."

of symmetrical compass, consisting of 21, 24, and 21 lines.
Whether the poet has laid out a more complete strophic
arrangement within these three groups or not, must remain
undecided. But the seven long closing lines are detached
from the third group and stand to the column of the whole,
in the relation of its base.

Vers. 2—3. In the first division, vers. 2—12, the disconsolate cry of anguish, beginning here in ver. 2 with the
lamentation over prolonged desertion by God, struggles
through to an incipient, trustfully inclined prayer. The
question beginning with לְמָה (instead of לָמָּה before the
guttural, and perhaps to make the exclamation more piercing, *vid.* on vi. 5, x. 1) is not an expression of impatience
and despair, but of alienation and yearning. The sufferer
feels himself rejected of God; the feeling of divine wrath
has completely enshrouded him; and still he knows himself to be joined to God in fear and love; his present condition belies the real nature of his relationship to God; and
it is just this contradiction that urges him to the plaintive
question, which comes up from the lowest depths: Why
hast Thou forsaken me? But in spite of this feeling of desertion by God, the bond of love is not torn asunder; the
sufferer calls God אֵלִי (*my* God), and urged on by the longing desire that God again would grant him to feel this love,
he calls Him, אֵלִי אֵלִי. That complaining question: why
hast Thou forsaken me? is not without example even elsewhere in the Psalms, lxxxviii. 15, cf. Isa. xlix. 14. The
forsakenness of the Crucified One, however, is unique; and
may not be judged by the standard of David or of any other
sufferers who thus complain when passing through trial.
That which is common to all is here, as there, this, viz.
that behind the wrath that is felt, is hidden the love of God,
which faith holds fast; and that he who thus complains
even on account of it, is, considered in itself, not a subject
of wrath, because in the midst of the feeling of wrath he
keeps up his communion with God. The Crucified One is
to His latest breath the Holy One of God; and the reconciliation for which He now offers himself is God's own eternal purpose of mercy, which is now being realised in the

fulness of times. But inasmuch as He places himself under the judgment of God with the sin of His people and of the whole human race, He cannot be spared from experiencing God's wrath against sinful humanity as though He were himself guilty. And out of the infinite depth of this experience of wrath, which in His case rests on no mere appearance, but the sternest reality*, comes the cry of His complaint which penetrates the wrath and reaches to God's love, ἠλὶ ἠλὶ λαμὰ σαβαχθανί, which the evangelists, omitting the additional πρόσχες μοι** of the LXX., render: Θεέ μου, Θεέ μου, ἵνα τί με ἐγκατέλιπες. He does not say עֲזַבְתָּנִי, but שְׁבַקְתַּנִי, which is the Targum word for the former. He says it in Aramaic, not in order that all may understand it, — for such a consideration was far from His mind at such a time, — but because the Aramaic was His mother tongue, for the same reason that He called God אַבָּא in prayer. His desertion by God, as ver. 2*b* says, consists in God's help and His cry for help being far asunder. שְׁאָגָה, prop. of the roar of the lion (Aq. βρύχημα), is the loud cry extorted by the greatest agony, xxxviii. 9; in this instance, however, as דִּבְרֵי shews, it is not an inarticulate cry, but a cry bearing aloft to God the words of prayer. רָחוֹק is not to be taken as an apposition of the subject of עזבתני: far from my help, (from) the words of my crying (Riehm); for דברי שאגתי would then also, on its part, in connection with the non-repetition of the מן, be in apposition to מישועתי. But to this it is not adapted on account of its heterogeneousness; hence Hitzig seeks to get over the difficulty by the conjecture מִשַּׁוְעָתִי ("from my cry, from the words of my groaning"). Nor can it be explained, with Olshausen and Hupfeld, by adopting Aben-Ezra's interpretation, "My God, my God, why hast Thou forsaken me, far from my help? are the words of my crying." This violates the structure of the

---

* Eusebius observes on ver. 2 of this Psalm, δικαιοσύνης ὑπάρχων πηγὴ τὴν ἡμετέραν ἁμαρτίαν ἀνέλαβε καὶ εὐλογίας ὢν πέλαγος τὴν ἐπικειμένην ἡμῖν ἐδέξατο κατάραν, and: τὴν ὡρισμένην ἡμῖν παιδείαν ὑπῆλθεν ἑκών, παιδεία γὰρ εἰρήνης ἡμῶν ἐπ' αὐτόν, ᾗ φησὶν ὁ προφήτης.

** *Vid.* Jerome's *Ep. ad Pammachium de optimo genere interpretandi,* where he cries out to his critics, sticklers for tradition, *Reddant rationem, cur septuaginta translatores interposuerunt "respice in me"!*

verse, the rhythm, and the custom of the language, and gives
to the Psalm a flat and unlyrical commencement. Thus,
therefore, רָחוֹק in the primary form, as in cxix. 155, according to Ges. § 146, 4, will be the predicate to דברי and
placed before it: far from my salvation, *i. e.* far from my
being rescued, are the words of my cry; there is a great
gulf between the two, inasmuch as God does not answer
him though he cries unceasingly. In ver. 3 the reverential
name of God אֱלֹהַי takes the place of אֵלִי the name that
expresses His might; it is likewise vocative and accordingly
marked with *Rebia magnum.* It is not an accusative of the
object after xviii. 4 (Hitzig), in which case the construction
would be continued with וְלֹא יַעֲנֶה. That it is, however, God
to whom he calls is implied both by the direct address אלהי,
and by ולא תענה, since he from whom one expects an answer is most manifestly the person addressed. His uninterrupted crying remains unanswered, and unappeased. The
clause וְלֹא־דְמִיָּה לִי is parallel to ולא תענה, and therefore does
not mean: without allowing me any repose (Jer. xiv. 17,
Lam. iii. 49), but: without any rest being granted to me,
without my complaint being appeased or stilled. From the
sixth to the ninth hour the earth was shrouded in darkness.
About the ninth hour Jesus cried, after a long and more
silent struggle, ἠλί, ἠλί. The ἀνεβόησεν φωνῇ μεγάλῃ, Mat.
xxvii. 46, and also the κραυγὴ ἰσχυρά of Hebr. v. 7, which
does not refer exclusively to the scene in Gethsemane, calls
to mind the שַׁאֲגָתִי of ver. 2*b*. When His passion reached
its climax, days and nights of the like wrestling had preceded it, and what then becomes audible was only an outburst of the second David's conflict of prayer, which grows
hotter as it draws near to the final issue.

Vers. 4—6. The sufferer reminds Jahve of the contradiction between the long season of helplessness and His
readiness to help so frequently and so promptly attested.
וְאַתָּה opens an adverbial clause of the counterargument:
although Thou art . . . Jahve is קָדוֹשׁ, absolutely pure, *lit.*
separated (root קד, قَدّ, to cut, part, just as *ṭahura*, the
synonym of *kadusa,* is the intransitive of *ṭahara* = *abʿada,* to
remove to a distance, and בַּר pure, clean, radically distinct
from *pû-rus,* goes back to בָּרַר to sever), viz. from that

which is worldly and common, in one word: holy. Jahve
is holy, and has shewn Himself such as the תְּהִלּוֹת of Israel
solemnly affirm, upon which or among which He sits
enthroned. תהלות are the songs of praise offered to God
on account of His attributes and deeds, which are worthy
of praise (these are even called תהלות in lxxviii. 4, Exod.
xv. 11, Isa. lxiii. 7), and in fact presented in His sanctuary
(Isa. lxiv. 10). The combination יוֹשֵׁב תְּהִלּוֹת (with the accusative of the verbs of dwelling and tarrying) is like יוֹשֵׁב
כְּרֻבִים, xcix. 1, lxxx. 2. The songs of praise, which resounded
in Israel as the memorials of His deeds of deliverance, are
like the wings of the cherubim, upon which His presence
hovered in Israel. In vers. 5, 6, the praying one brings to
remembrance this graciously glorious self-attestation of God,
who as the Holy One always, from the earliest times,
acknowledged those who fear Him in opposition to their
persecutors and justified their confidence in Himself.   In
ver. 5 trust and rescue are put in the connection of cause
and effect; in ver. 6 in reciprocal relation. פָּלַט and מָלַט
are only distinguished by the harder and softer sibilants,
cf. xvii. 13 with cxvi. 4. It need not seem·strange that such
thoughts were at work in the soul of the Crucified One,
since His divine-human consciousness was, on its human
side, thoroughly Israelitish; and the God of Israel is also
the God of salvation; redemption is that which He himself
determined, why, then, should He not speedily deliver the
Redeemer?

Vers. 7—9. The sufferer complains of the greatness of
his reproach, in order to move Jahve, who is Himself involved therein, to send him speedy succour. Notwithstanding his cry for help, he is in the deepest affliction
without rescue. Every word of ver. 7 is echoed in the second
part of the Book of Isaiah. There, as here, Israel is called
a worm, ch. xli. 14; there all these traits of suffering are
found in the picture of the Servant of God, ch. xlix. 7, liii.
3, cf. l. 6, and especially lii. 14 "so marred was His appearance, that He no longer looked like a man." תּוֹלַעַת is more
particularly the kermes, or cochineal (*vermiculus*, whence
color vermiculi, *vermeil*, *vermiglio*); but the point of comparison in the present instance is not the blood-red appear-

ance, but the suffering so utterly defenceless and even ignominious. עָם is *gen. subj.*, like גּוֹי, Isa. xlix. 7. Jerome well renders the ἐξουθένωμα λαοῦ of the LXX. by *abjectio* (Tertullian: *nullificamen*) *plebis,* not *populi.* The ἐξεμυκτήρισάν με, by which the LXX. translates ילְעִיגוּ לִי, is used by Luke, ch. xxiii. 35, cf. xvi. 14, in the history of the Passion; fulfilment and prediction so exactly coincide, that no more adequate expressions can be found in writing the gospel history than those presented by prophecy. In הִפְטִיר בְּשָׂפָה, what appears in other instances as the object of the action (to open the mouth wide, *diducere labia*), is regarded as the means of its execution; so that the verbal notion being rendered complete has its object in itself: to make an opening with the mouth, cf. פָּעַר בְּפֶה, Job xvi. 10, נָתַן בְּקוֹל lxviii. 34; Ges. § 138, 1, rem. 3. The shaking of the head is, as in cix. 25, cf. xliv. 15, lxiv. 9, a gesture of surprise and astonishment at something unexpected and strange, not a προσνεύειν approving the injury of another, although נוּעַ, נוּד, נוּט, νεύ-ω, nu-t-o, nic-to, *neigen, nicken,* all form one family of roots. In ver. 9 the words of the mockers follow without לֵאמֹר. גֹּל is not the 3 *præt.* (LXX., cf. Mat. xxvii. 43) like בּוֹשׁ, אוֹר; it is not only in *Piel* (Jer. xi. 20, xx. 12, where גַּלַּתִי = גִּלִּיתִי, Ew. § 121,*a*) that it is transitive, but even in *Kal*; nor is it *inf. absol.* in the sense of the imperative (Hitz., Böttch.), although this infinitive form is found, but always only as an *inf. intens.* (Numb. xxiii. 25, Ruth ii. 16, cf. Isa. xxiv. 19); but, in accordance with the parallels xxxvii. 5 (where it is written גּוֹל), Prov. xvi. 3, cf. Ps. lv. 23, 1 Pet. v. 7, it is *imperat.:* roll, viz. thy doing and thy suffering to Jahve, *i. e.* commit it to Him. The mockers call out this גֹּל to the sufferer, and the rest they say of him with malicious looks askance. כִּי in the mouth of the foes is not confirmatory as in xviii. 20, but a conditional ἐάν (in case, provided that).

Vers. 10—12. The sufferer pleads that God should respond to his trust in Him, on the ground that this trust is made an object of mockery. With כִּי he establishes the reality of the loving relationship in which he stands to God, at which his foes mock. The intermediate thought, which is not expressed, "and so it really is", is confirmed; and thus

כִּי comes to have an affirmative signification. The verb גּוּחַ (גִּיחַ) signifies both intransitive: to break forth (from the womb), Job xxxviii. 8, and transitive: to push forward (cf. جَحَّ), more especially, the fruit of the womb, Mic. iv. 10. It might be taken here in the first signification: my breaking forth, equivalent to "the cause of my breaking forth" (Hengstenberg, Baur, and others); but there is no need for this metonymy. גֹּחִי is either *part.* equivalent to גֹּחִי, my pusher forth, *i. e.* he who causes me to break forth, or, — since גוח in a causative signification cannot be supported, and participles like בּוּס stamping and לוֹט veiling (Ges. § 72, rem. 1) are nowhere found with a suffix, — participle of a verb גָּחָה, to draw forth (Hitz.), which perhaps only takes the place, *per metaplasmum,* of the *Pil.* גִּחֵחַ with the uneuphonic מְגִחֵחִי (Ewald S. 859, *Addenda*). Ps. lxxi. has גוֹזִי (ver. 6) instead of גֹחִי, just as it has מִבְטָחִי (ver. 5) instead of מַבְטִיחִי. The *Hiph.* הִבְטִיחַ does not merely mean to make secure (Hupf.), but to cause to trust. According to biblical conception, there is even in the new-born child, yea in the child yet unborn and only living in the womb, a glimmering consciousness springing up out of the remotest depths of unconsciousness (*Psychol.* S. 215; transl. p. 254). Therefore, when the praying one says, that from the womb he has been cast* upon Jahve, *i. e.* directed to go to Him, and to Him alone, with all his wants and care (lv. 23, cf. lxxi. 6), that from the womb onwards Jahve was his God, there is also more in it than the purely objective idea, that he grew up into such a relationship to God. Twice he mentions his mother. Throughout the Old Testament there is never any mention made of a human father, or begetter, to the Messiah, but always only of His mother, or her who bare Him. And the words of the praying one here also imply that the beginning of his life, as regards its outward circumstances, was amidst poverty, which like-

---

* The *Hoph.* has *o*, not *u*, perhaps in a more neuter sense, more closely approximating to the reflexive (cf. Ezek. xxxii. 19 with xxxii. 32), rather than a purely passive. Such is apparently the feeling of the language, *vid. B. Megilla* 13*a* (and also the explanation in *Tosefoth*).

wise accords with the picture of Christ as drawn both in the Old and New Testaments. On the ground of his fellowship with God, which extends so far back, goes forth the cry for help (ver. 12), which has been faintly heard through all the preceding verses, but now only comes to direct utterance for the first time. The two כִּי are alike. That the necessity is near at hand, *i. e.* urgent, refers back antithetically to the prayer, that God would not remain afar off; no one doth, nor can help except He alone. Here the first section closes.

Vers. 13—14. Looking back upon his relationship to God, which has existed from the earliest times, the sufferer has become somewhat more calm, and is ready, in vers. 13—22, to describe his outward and inner life, and thus to unburden his heart. Here he calls his enemies פָּרִים, bullocks, and in fact אַבִּירֵי בָשָׁן (cf. l. 13 with Deut. xxxii. 14), strong ones of Bashan, the land rich in luxuriant oak forests and fat pastures (בִּשָׁן = *buthêne,* which in the Beduin dialect means rich, stoneless meadow-land, *vid. Job* S. 509 f.; tr. ii. pp. 399 sq.) north of Jabbok extending as far as to the borders of Hermon, the land of Og and afterwards of Manasseh (Num. xxx. 1). They are so called on account of their robustness and vigour, which, being acquired and used in opposition to God is brutish rather than human (cf. Amos iv. 1). Figures like these drawn from the animal world and applied in an ethical sense are explained by the fact, that the ancients measured the instincts of animals according to the moral rules of human nature; but more deeply by the fact, that according to the indisputable conception of Scripture, since man was made to fall by Satan through the agency of an animal, the animal and Satan are the two dominant powers in Adamic humanity. כִּתֵּר is a climacticsynonym of סָבַב. On ver. 14*a* compare the echoes in Jeremiah, Lam. ii. 16, iii. 46. Finally, the foes are all comprehended under the figure of a lion, which, as soon as he sights his prey, begins to roar, Amos iii. 4. The Hebrew טָרַף, *discerpere,* according to its root, belongs to חָרַף, *carpere.* They are *instar leonis dilaniaturi et rugientis.*

Vers. 15—16. Now he describes, how, thus encompassed round, he is still just living, but already as it were dead.

The being poured out like water reminds us of the ignominious abandonment of the Crucified One to a condition of weakness, in which His life, deprived of its natural support, is in the act of dissolution, and its powers dried up (2 Sam. xiv. 14); the bones being stretched out, of the forcible stretching out of His body (הִתְפָּרֵד, from פָּרַד to separate, cf. فرق according to its radical signification, which has been preserved in the common Arabic dialect: so to spread out or apart that the thing has no bends or folds,* Greek ἐξαπλοῦν); the heart being melted, recalls His burning anguish, the inflammation of the wounds, and the pressure of blood on the head and heart, the characteristic cause of death by crucifixion. נָמֵס, in pause נָמָס, is 3 *præt.*; wax, דּוֹנַג, receives its name from its melting (דנג, root דג, τήκω). In ver. 16 the comparison כַּחֶרֶשׂ has reference to the issue or result (*vid.* xviii. 43): my strength is dried up, so that it is become like a potsherd. חִכִּי (Saadia) instead of כֹּחִי commends itself, unless, כֹּח perhaps, like the Talmudic כֵּיחַ, also had the signification "spittle" (as a more dignified word for רק). לָשׁוֹן, with the exception perhaps of Prov. xxvi. 28, is uniformly feminine; here the predicate has the masculine ground-form without respect to the subject. The *part. pass.* has a tendency generally to be used without reference to gender, under the influence of the construction laid down in Ges. § 143, 1, *b*, according to which לְשׁנִי may be treated as an accusative of the object; מַלְקוֹחָי, however, is *acc. loci* (cf. לְ cxxxvii. 6, Job xxix. 10; אֶל Lam. iv. 4, Ezek. iii. 26): my tongue is made to cleave to my jaws, *fauces meas.* Such is his state in consequence of outward distresses. His enemies, however, would not have power to do all this, if God had not given it to them. Thus it is, so to speak, God Himself who lays him low in death. שָׁפַת to put anywhere, to lay, with the accompanying idea of firmness and duration, ثبات, Isa. xxvi. 12; the future is used of that which is just taking place. Just in like manner, in Isa. liii., the death of the Servant of God is spoken of not merely as happening thus, but as decreed; and not merely as permitted by God, but as being in accordance with the divine will. David is per-

---

* *vid.* Bocthor, *Dict. franç.-arabe, s. v. Etendre* and *Déployer.*

secuted by Saul, the king of His people, almost to the death; Jesus, however, is delivered over by the Sanhedrim, the authority of His people, to the heathen, under whose hands He actually dies the death of the cross: it is a judicial murder put into execution according to the conditions and circumstances of the age; viewed, however, as to its final cause, it is a gracious dispensation of the holy God, in whose hands all the paths of the world's history run parallel, and who in this instance makes sin subservient to its own expiation.

Vers. 17—19. A continuation, referring back to ver. 12, of the complaint of him who is dying and is already as it were dead. In the animal name כְּלָבִים, figuratively descriptive of character, beside shamelessness and meanness, special prominence is given to the propensity for biting and worrying, *i. e.* for persecuting; hence Symmachus and Theodotion render it θηράται, κυνηγέται. In ver. 17*b* עֲדַת מְרֵעִים takes the place of כלבים; and this again is followed by הִקִּיף in the *plur.* (to do anything in a circle, to surround by forming a circle round, a climactic synonym, like כִּתֵּר to סָבַב) either *per attractionem* (cf. cxl. 10, 1 Sam. ii. 4), or on account of the collective עֵדָה. Tertullian renders it *synagoga maleficorum,* Jerome *concilium pessimorum.* But a faction gathered together for some evil purpose is also called עֵדָה, *e. g.* עֲדַת קֹרַח. In ver. 17*c* the meaning of כָּאֲרִי, *instar leonis,* is either that, selecting a point of attack, they make the rounds of his hands and feet, just as a lion does its prey upon which it springs as soon as its prey stirs; or, that, standing round about him like lions, they make all defence impossible to his hands, and all escape impossible to his feet. But whether we take this יָדַי וְרַגְלָי as accusative of the members beside the accusative of the person (*vid.* xvii. 11), or as the object of the הִקִּיפוּ to be supplied from ver. 17*b*, it still remains harsh and drawling so far as the language is concerned. Perceiving this, the Masora on Isa. xxxviii. 13 observes, that כָּאֲרִי, in the two passages in which it occurs (Ps. xxii. 17, Isa. xxxviii. 13), occurs in two different meanings (בתרי לישני); just as the Midrash then also understands כארי in the Psalm as a verb used of marking with conjuring, magic characters.* Is the meaning of the Masora that כָּאֲרִי, in the passage before us, is equivalent to כָּאֵרִים? If so the form would be doubly Aramaic: both the participial form כָּאֵר (which only occurs in Hebrew in verbs *med. E*) and the apocopated plural, the occurrence of which in Hebrew is certainly, with Gesenius and Ewald, to be acknowledged in rare instances (*vid.* xlv. 9, and compare on the other hand 2 Sam. xxii. 44), but which would here be a capricious form of expression most liable to be misapprehended. If כארי is to be understood as a verb, then it ought to be read כָּאֵרִי. Tradition is here manifestly unreliable. Even in MSS. the readings כָּאֵרוּ and כָּאֵרִי are found. The former is attested both by the Masora on Num. xxiv. 9 and by Jacob ben Chajim in the *Masora finalis* as a MS. *Chethîb*.** Even the Targum, which renders *mordent sicut leo manus et pedes meos,* bears witness to the ancient hesitancy between the substantival and verbal rendering of the כארי. The other ancient versions have, without any doubt, read כארו. Aquila in the 1st edition of his translation rendered it ἤσχυαν (from the Aramaic and Talmudic כָּאֵר = כָּעַר to soil, *part.* כָּאוּר, dirty, nasty); but this is not applicable to hands and feet, and therefore has nothing to stand upon. In the 2nd edition of his translation the same Aquila had instead of

---

* Hupfeld suspects this Masoretic remark (כָּאֵרִי ב' קמצין בתרי לישני) as a Christian interpolation, but it occurs in the alphabetical Masōreth register ב' ב' ותרויהון בתרי לישני. Even Elias Levita speaks of it with astonishment (in his מסרת המסרה [*ed. Ginsburg*, p. 253]) without doubting its genuineness, which must therefore have been confirmed, to his mind, by MS. authority. Heidenheim also cites it in his edition of the Pentateuch, מאור עינים, on Num. xxiv. 9; and down to the present time no suspicion has been expressed on the part of Jewish critics, although all kinds of unsatisfactory attempts have been made to explain this Masoretic remark (*e. g.* in the periodical *Biccure ha-'Ittim*).

** The authenticity of this statement of the Masora כארי ידי ורגלי כארו כתיב may be disputed, especially since Jacob ben Chajim became a convert to Christianity, and other Masoretic testimonies do not mention a כארי קרי וכתיב to; nevertheless, in this instance, it would be premature to say that this statement is interpolated. Ant. Hulsius in his edition of the Psalter (1650) has written כארו in the margin according to the text of the Complutensis.

this, like Symmachus, "they have bound",* after כָּר, כָּר, to
twist, lace; but this rendering is improbable since the Hebrew has other words for "to bind", *constringere*. On the
other hand nothing of any weight can be urged against the
rendering of the LXX. ὤρυξαν (Peshito בזעו, Vulg. *foderunt*,
Jer. *fixerunt*); for (1) even if we do not suppose any special
verb בָּאַר, כָּארוּ can be expanded from (כּוּר) = (כּוּר) כָּרוּ כָּרוּ (כָּרָה)
just in the same manner as רָאֲמָה, Zech. xiv. 10 from רָמָה,
cf. קָאֲמַיָּא Dan. vii. 16. And (2) that כּוּר and כָּרָה can
signify not merely to dig out and dig into, engrave, but
also to dig through, pierce, is shewn, — apart from the
derivative מְכֵרָה (the similarity of the sound of which to
μάχαιρα from the root μαχ, *maksh, mraksh,* is only accidental), — by the double meaning of the verbs נָקַר,
ὀρύσσειν (*e. g.* ὀρύσσειν τὸν ἰσθμόν Herod. i. 174), *fodere*
(*hastâ*); the LXX. version of Ps. xl. 7 would also support
this meaning, if κατετρήσω (from κατατιτρᾶν) in that passage
had been the original reading instead of κατηρτίσω. If
כָּארוּ be read, then ver. 17c, applied to David, perhaps
under the influence of the figure of the attacking dogs
(Böhl), says that the wicked bored into his hands and feet,
and thus have made him fast, so that he is inevitably
abandoned to their inhuman desires. The fulfilment in
the nailing of the hands and (at least, the binding fast) of
the feet of the Crucified One to the cross is clear. This is
not the only passage in which it is predicted that the future
Christ shall be murderously pierced; but it is the same in
Isa. liii. 5 where He is said to be pierced (מְחֹלָל) on account
of our sins, and in Zech. xii. 10, where Jahve describes
Himself as ἐκκεντηθείς in Him.

Thus, therefore, the reading כָּארוּ might at least have an
equal right to be recognised with the present *recepta*, for which
Hupfeld and Hitzig demand exclusive recognition; while
Böttcher, — who reads כָּארִי, and gives this the meaning

---

* Also in Jerome's independent translation the reading *vinxerunt* is
found by the side of *fixerunt,* just as Abraham of Zante paraphrases
it in his paraphrase of the Psalter in rhyme גַּם כָּארִי יָדִי וְרַגְלַי אָסְרוּ.
The want of a verb is too perceptible. Saadia supplies it in a different
way "they compass me as a lion, to crush my hands and feet."

"springing round about (after the manner of dogs)", —
regards the *sicut leo* as "a production of meagre Jewish
wit"; and also Thenius after taking all possible pains to
clear it up gives it up as hopeless, and with Meier, adopting a different division of the verse, renders it: "a mob of
the wicked has encompassed me like lions. On my hands
and feet I can count all my bones." But then, how כָּאֲרִי
comes limping on after the rest! And how lamely does
יָדַי וְרַגְלַי precede ver. 18! How unnaturally does it limit
עַצְמוֹתַי, with which one chiefly associates the thought of the
breast and ribs, to the hands and feet! אֲסַפֵּר is *potientialis*.
Above in ver. 15 he has said that his bones are out of joint.
There is no more reason for regarding this "I can count
&c." as referring to emaciation from grief, than there is
for regarding the former as referring to writhing with
agony. He can count them because he is forcibly stretched out, and thereby all his bones stand out. In this
condition he is a mockery to his foes. הִבִּיט signifies the
turning of one's gaze to anything, רָאָה בְ the fixing of one's
sight upon it with pleasure. In ver. 19 a new feature is
added to those that extend far beyond David himself: they
part my garments among them . . . It does not say they
purpose doing it, they do it merely in their mind, but they
do it in reality. This never happened to David, or at least
not in the literal sense of his words, in which it has happened to Christ. In Him ver. 19*a* and 19*b* are literally fulfilled. The parting of the בְּגָדִים by the soldiers dividing
His ἱμάτια among them into four parts; the casting lots upon
the לְבוּשׁ by their not dividing the χιτὼν ἄῤῥαφος, but casting
lots for it, John xix. 23 sq. לְבוּשׁ is the garment which is put
on the body that it may not be bare; בְּגָדִים the clothes,
which one wraps around one's self for a covering; hence
לְבוּשׁ is punningly explained in *B. Sabbath* 77*b* by לא בושה
(with which one has no need to be ashamed of being naked)
in distinction from גלימא, a mantle (that through which one
appears בגולם, because it conceals the outline of the body).
In Job xxiv. 7, and frequently, לבוש is an undergarment, or
shirt, what in Arabic is called absolutely ثوب *thôb* "the
garment", or expressed according to the Roman distinction:
the *tunica* in distinction from the *toga,* whose exact desig-

nation is מְעִיל. With ver. 19 of this Psalm it is exactly as
with Zech. ix. 9, cf. Mat. xxi. 5; in this instance also, the
fulfilment has realised that which, in both phases of the
synonymous expression, is seemingly identical.*

Vers. 20—22. In ver. 19 the description of affliction
has reached its climax, for the parting of, and casting lots
for, the garments assumes the certain death of the sufferer
in the mind of the enemies. In ver. 20, with וְאַתָּה the looks
of the sufferer, in the face of his manifold torments, concentrate themselves all at once upon Jahve. He calls Him
אֱיָלוּתִי *nom. abstr.* from אֱיָל, lxxxviii. 5: the very essence of
strength, as it were the idea, or the ideal of strength; *le-
ʿezrāthi* has the accent on the *penult.*, as in lxxi. 12 (cf. on
the other hand xxxviii. 23), in order that two tone syllables
may not come together. In ver. 21, חֶרֶב means the deadly
weapon of the enemy and is used exemplificatively. In the
expression מִיַּד כֶּלֶב, מִיַּד is not merely equivalent to מִן, but
יָד is, according to the sense, equivalent to "paw" (cf. כַּף,
Lev. xi. 27), as פִּי is equivalent to jaws; although elsewhere
not only the expression "hand of the lion and of the bear",
1 Sam. xvii. 37, but also "hands of the sword", Ps. lxiii. 11,
and even "hand of the flame", Isa. xlvii. 14 are used, inasmuch as יד is the general designation of that which acts,
seizes, and subjugates, as the instrument of the act. Just
as in connection with the dog יד, and in connection with the
lion פי (cf., however, Dan. vi. 28) is mentioned as its weapon of attack, the horns, not the *horn* (also not in Deut.
xxxiii. 17), are mentioned in connection with antilopes,
רֵמִים (a shorter form, occurring only in this passage, for
רְאֵמִים, xxix. 6, Isa. xxxiv. 7). Nevertheless, Luther following the LXX. and Vulgate, renders it "rescue me from the
unicorns" (*vid.* thereon on xxix. 6). יְחִידָה, as the parallel
member here and in xxxv. 17 shews, is an epithet of נֶפֶשׁ.
The LXX. in both instances renders it correctly τὴν μονογενῆ
μου, Vulg. *unicam meam*, according to Gen. xxii. 2, Judges
xi. 34, the one soul besides which man has no second, the

---

* On such fulfilments of prophecy, literal beyond all expectation,
vid. Saat auf Hoffnung iii., 3, 47—51.

one life besides which man has no second to lose, applied
subjectively, that is, soul or life as the dearest and most
precious thing, cf. Homer's φίλον κῆρ. It is also interpreted
according to xxv. 16, lxviii. 7: my solitary one, *solitarium,*
the soul as forsaken by God and man, or at least by man,
and abandoned to its own self (Hupfeld, Kamphausen, and
others). But the parallel נַפְשִׁי, and the analogy of כְּבוֹדִי
(= נַפְשִׁי), stamp it as an universal name for the soul: the
single one, *i. e.* that which does not exist in duplicate, and
consequently that which cannot be replaced, when lost. The
præt. עֲנִיתָנִי might be equivalent to עֲנֵנִי, provided it is a
perf. consec. deprived of its *Waw convers.* in favour of the
placing of מִקַּרְנֵי רֵמִים first for the sake of emphasis; but
considering the turn which the Psalm takes in ver. 23, it
must be regarded as *perf. confidentiæ,* inasmuch as in the
very midst of his supplication there springs up in the mind
of the suppliant the assurance of being heard and answered.
To answer from the horns of the antilope is equivalent to
hearing and rescuing from them; cf. the equally pregnant
expression עָנָה בְ cxviii. 5, perhaps also Hebr. v. 7.*

Vers. 23—24. In the third section, vers. 23—32, the
great plaintive prayer closes with thanksgiving and hope.
In certainty of being answered, follows the vow of thanksgiving. He calls his fellow-country men, who are connected
with him by the ties of nature, but, as what follows, viz.
"ye that fear Jahve" shews, also by the ties of spirit, "brethren". קָהָל (from קָהַל = קָל, καλ-έω, *cal-o,* Sanscr. *kal,* to
resound) coincides with ἐκκλησία. The sufferer is conscious
of the significance of his lot of suffering in relation to the
working out of the history of redemption. Therefore he
will make that salvation which he has experienced common
property. The congregation or church shall hear the
evangel of his rescue. In ver. 24 follows the introduction
to this announcement, which is addressed to the whole of
Israel, so far as it fears the God of revelation. Instead of
וגורו the text of the Orientals (מדנחאי), *i. e.* Babylonians,

---

* Thrupp in his *Emendations on the Psalms* (*Journal of Classic and
Sacred Philology,* 1860) suggests עֲנִיָּתִי, my poverty (my poor soul),
instead of עניתני.

had here the *Chethîb* יגורו with the *Kerî* וְגוּרוּ; the introduction of the jussive (xxxiii. 8) after the two imperatives would not be inappropriate. גּוּר מִן (= יָגֹר) is a stronger form of expression for יָרֵא מִן, xxxiii. 8.

Ver. 25. This tristich is the evangel itself. The *materia laudis* is introduced by כִּי . עֱנוּת (principal form עֲנוּת) bending, bowing down, affliction, from עָנָה, the proper word to denote the Passion. For in Isaiah, ch. liii. 4, 7, the Servant of God is also said to be מְעֻנֶּה and נַעֲנֶה, and Zechariah, ch. ix. 9, also introduces Him as עָנִי and נוֹשָׁע. The LXX., Vulgate, and Targum erroneously render it "cry". עָנָה does not mean to cry, but to answer, ἀμείβεσθαι; here, however, as the stem-word of עֱנוּת, it means to be bent. From the שִׁקַּץ (to regard as an abhorrence), which alternates with בָּזָה, we see that the sufferer felt the wrath of God, but this has changed into a love that sends help; God did not long keep His countenance hidden, He hearkened to him, for his prayer was well-pleasing to Him. שָׁמֵעַ is not the verbal adjective, but, since we have the definite fact of the rescue before us, it is a pausal form for שָׁמַע, as in xxxiv. 7, 18, Jer. xxxvi. 13.

Vers. 26—27. The call to thanksgiving is now ended; and there follows a grateful upward glance towards the Author of the salvation; and this grateful upward glance grows into a prophetic view of the future. This fact, that the sufferer is able thus to glory and give thanks in the great congregation (xl. 10), proceeds from Jahve (מֵאֵת as in cxviii. 23, cf. lxxi. 6). The first half of the verse, according to Baer's correct accentuation, closes with בְּקָהָל רָב. יְרֵאָיו does not refer to קָהָל, but, as everywhere else, is meant to be referred to Jahve, since the address of prayer passes over into a declarative utterance. It is not necessary in this passage to suppose, that in the mind of David the paying of vows is purely ethical, and not a ritualistic act. Being rescued he will bring the שַׁלְמֵי נֶדֶר, which it is his duty to offer, the thank-offerings, which he vowed to God when in the extremest peril. When the sprinkling with blood (זְרִיקָה) and the laying of the fat pieces upon the altar (הַקְטָרָה) were completed, the remaining flesh of the shelamim was used by the offerer to make a joyous meal;

and the time allowed for this feasting was the day of offering and on into the night in connection with the tôda-she-
lamim offering, and in connection with the shelamim of
vows even the following dày also (Lev. vii. 15 sq.). The
invitation of the poor to share in it, which the law does not
command, is rendered probable by these appointments of
the law, and expressly commended by other and analogous
appointments concerning the second and third tithes.
Ver. 27 refers to this: he will invite the עניים, those who
are outwardly and spiritually poor, to this "eating before
Jahve"; it is to be a meal for which they thank God, who
has bestowed it upon them through him whom He has thus
rescued. Ver. 27c is as it were the host's blessing upon his
guests, or rather Jahve's guests through him: "your heart live
for ever", *i. e.* may this meal impart to you ever enduring
refreshment. יְחִי optative of חָיָה, here used of the reviving
of the heart, which is as it were dead (1 Sam. xxv. 37), to
spiritual joy. The referrence to the ritual of the peace
offerings is very obvious. And it is not less obvious, that
the blessing, which, for all who can be saved, springs from
the salvation that has fallen to the lot of the sufferer, is
here set forth. But it is just as clear, that this blessing
consists in something much higher than the material advantage, which the share in the enjoyment of the animal sacrifice imparts; the sacrifice has its spiritual meaning, so that
its outward forms are lowered as it were to a mere figure of
its true nature; it relates to a spiritual enjoyment of spiritual
and lasting results. How natural, then, is the thought of
the sacramental eucharist, in which the second David, like
to the first, having attained to the throne through the
suffering of death, makes us partakers of the fruits of
His suffering!

Vers. 28—32. The long line closing strophe, which
forms as it were the pedestal to the whole, shews how far
not only the description of the affliction of him who is speaking here, but also the description of the results of his rescue, transcend the historical reality of David's experience.
The sufferer expects, as the fruit of the proclamation of
that which Jahve has done for him, the conversion of all
peoples. The heathen have become forgetful and will again

recollect themselves; the object, in itself clear enough in ix. 18, becomes clear from what follows: there is a γνῶσις τοῦ θεοῦ (*Psychol.* S. 346 ff.; tr. pp. 407 sqq.)᾽ among the heathen, which the announcement of the rescue of this afflicted one will bring back to their consciousness.* This prospect (Jer. xvi. 19 sqq.) is, in ver. 29 (cf. Jer. x. 7), based upon Jahve's right of kingship over all peoples. A ruler is called מֹשֵׁל as being exalted above others by virtue of his office (מָשַׁל according to its primary meaning = مَثُلَ, *erectum stare*, synonymous with כָּהֵן, *vid.* on cx. 4, cf. עָמַד Mic. v. 3). In וּמֹשֵׁל we have the *part.*, used like the 3 *præt.*, without any mark of the person (cf. vii. 10, lv. 20), to express the pure *præs.*, and, so to speak, as *tempus durans:* He rules among the nations (ἔθνη). The conversion of the heathen by that sermon will, therefore, be the realisation of the kingdom of God.

Ver. 30. The eating is here again brought to mind. The perfect, אָכְלוּ, and the future of sequence, וַיִּשְׁתַּחֲווּ, stand to one another in the relation of cause and effect. It is, as is clear from ver. 27, an eating that satisfies the soul, a spiritual meal, that is intended, and in fact, one that is brought about by the mighty act of rescue God has wrought. At the close of Ps. lxix, where the form of the ritual thank-offering is straightway ignored, רָאוּ (ver. 33) takes the place of the אָכְלוּ. There it is the view of one who is rescued and who thankfully glorifies God, which leads to others sharing with him in the enjoyment of the salvation he has experienced; here it is an actual enjoyment of it, the joy, springing from thankfulness, manifesting itself not merely in words but in a thank-offering feast, at which, in Israel, those who long for salvation are the invited quests, for with them it is an acknowledgment of the mighty act of a God whom they already know; but among the heathen, men of the most diversified conditions, the richest and the poorest, for to them it is a favour unexpectedly brought to them, and which is all the more gratefully embraced by them on that account. So magnificent shall be the feast, that all דִּשְׁנֵי־אֶרֶץ, *i. e.*

---

* Augustin *De trinitate* xiv. 13, *Non igitur sic erant oblitæ istæ gentes Deum, ut ejus nec commemoratæ recordarentur.*

those who stand out prominently before the world and
before their own countrymen by reason of the abundance
of their temporal possessions (compare on the ascensive use
of ארץ, lxxv. 9, lxxvi. 10, Isa. xxiii. 9), choose it before this
abundance, in which they might revel, and, on account of
the grace and glory which the celebration includes within
itself, they bow down and worship. In antithesis to the "fat
ones of the earth" stand those who go down to the dust
(עָפָר, always used in this formula of the dust of the grave,
like the Arabic *turâb*) by reason of poverty and care. In
the place of the participle יוֹרְדֵי we now have with וְנַפְשׁוֹ (=
וַאֲשֶׁר נַפְשׁוֹ) a clause with וְלֹא, which has the value of a
relative clause (as in xlix. 21, lxxviii. 39, Prov. ix. 13, and
frequently): and they who have not heretofore prolonged and
could not prolong their life (Ges. § 123, 3, *c*). By comparing Phil. ii. 10 Hupfeld understands it to be those who are
actually dead; so that it would mean, His kingdom extends
to the living and the dead, to this world and the nether
world. But any idea of a thankful adoration of God on the
part of the dwellers in Hades is alien to the Old Testament;
and there is nothing to force us to it here, since יוֹרְדֵי עָפָר,
can just as well mean *descensuri* as *qui descenderunt*, and
חִיָּה נַפְשׁוֹ (also in Ezek. xviii. 27) means to preserve his own
life, — a phrase which can be used in the sense of *vitam
sustentare* and of *conservare* with equal propriety. It is,
therefore, those who are almost dead already with care and
want, these also (and how thankfully do these very ones)
go down upon their knees, because they are accounted
worthy to be guests at this table. It is the same great feast,
of which Isaiah, ch. xxv. 6, prophesies, and which he there
accompanies with the music of his words. And the result
of this evangel of the mighty act of rescue is not only of
boundless universality, but also of unlimited duration: it
propagates itself from one generation to another.

Formerly we interpreted ver. 31 "a seed, which shall
serve Him, shall be reckoned to the Lord for a generation;"
taking יְסֻפַּר as a metaphor applying to the census, 2 Chron.
ii. 16, cf. Ps. lxxxvii. 6, and לְדוֹר, according to xxiv. 6 and
other passages, as used of a totality of one kind, as זֶרַע of
the whole body of those of the same race. But the connec-

tion makes it more natural to take דּוֹר in a genealogical
sense; and, moreover, with the former interpretation it
ought to have been לְדוֹר instead of לַדּוֹר. We must therefore retain the customary interpretation: "a seed (posterity)
shall serve Him, it shall be told concerning the Lord to
the generation (to come)". Decisive in favour of this interpretation is לַדּוֹר with the following יָבֹאוּ, by which דּוֹר
acquires the meaning of the future generation, exactly as
in lxxi. 18, inasmuch as it at once becomes clear, that three
generations are distinctly mentioned, viz. that of the fathers
who turn unto Jahve, ver. 30, that of the coming דּוֹר, ver.
31, and עַם נוֹלָד, to whom the news of the salvation is propagated by this דּוֹר, ver. 32: "They shall come (בּוֹא as in
lxxi. 18: to come into being), and shall declare His righteousness to the people that shall be born, that He hath
finished." Accordingly זרע is the principal notion, which
divides itself into דּוֹר (יבאו) and עַם נוֹלד; from which it is
at once clear, why the expression could be thus general, "a
posterity", inasmuch as it is defined by what follows. עַם
נוֹלד is the people which shall be born, or whose birth is
near at hand (lxxviii. 6); the LXX. well renders it: λαῷ τῷ
τεχθησομένῳ (cf. cii. 19 עַם נִבְרָא populus creandus). צִדְקָתוֹ is
the δικαιοσύνη of God, which has become manifest in the
rescue of the great sufferer. That He did not suffer him
to come down to the very border of death without snatch-
ing him out of the way of his murderous foes and raising
him to a still greater glory, this was divine צְדָקָה. That He
did not snatch him out of the way of his murderous foes
without suffering him to be on the point of death — even
this wrathful phase of the divine צְדָקָה, is indicated in ver.
16c, but then only very remotely. For the fact, that the
Servant of God, before spreading the feast accompanying
the shelamim (thank-offering) in which He makes the whole
world participants in the fruit of His suffering, offered Himself as an asham (sin-offering), does not become a subject of
prophetic revelation until later on, and then under other
typical relationships. The nature of the עֲשָׂה, which is in
accordance with the determinate counsel of God, is only
gradually disclosed in the Old Testament. This one word,
so full of meaning (as in lii. 11, xxxvii. 5, Isa. xliv. 23),

implying the carrying through of the work of redemption,
which is prefigured in David, comprehends everything within itself. It may be compared to the לַעֲשׂוֹת, Gen. ii. 3, at
the close of the history of the creation. It is the last word
of the Psalm, just as τετέλεσται is the last word of the Crucified One. The substance of the gospel in its preparatory
history and its fulfilment, of the declaration concerning God
which passes from generation to generation, is this, that God
has accomplished what He planned when He anointed the
son of Jesse and the Son of David as mediator in His work
of redemption; that He accomplished it by leading the former through affliction to the throne, and making the cross
to the latter a ladder leading up to heaven.

PSALM XXIII.

PRAISE OF THE GOOD SHEPHERD.

1 JAHVE is my Shepherd, I shall not want.
2 In green pastures He maketh me to lie down,
  Beside still waters He leadeth me.
3 My soul He restoreth,
  He leadeth me in right paths —
  For His Name's sake.

4 Yea, though I walk in the valley of the shadow of
          death:
  I will fear no evil, for Thou art with me,
  Thy rod and Thy staff — they comfort me.
5 Thou preparest me a table in the presence of mine
          oppressors,
  Thou anointest my head with oil,
  My cup is fulness.

6 Only prosperity and mercy shall follow me
  All the days of my life,
  And again shall I dwell in the house of Jahve
  For length of days.

The arrangement, by which a Psalm that speaks of a great feast of mercy prepared for mankind is followed by a Psalm that praises Jahve as the Shepherd and Host of His own people, could not possibly be more sensible and appropriate. If David is the author, and there is no reason for doubting it, then this Psalm belongs to the time of the rebellion under Absolom, and this supposition is confirmed on every hand. It is like an amplification of iv. 8; and iii. 7 is also echoed in it. But not only does it contain points of contact with this pair of Psalms of the time mentioned, but also with other Psalms belonging to same period, as xxvii. 4, and more especially lxiii., which is said to have been composed when David had retreated with his faithful followers over Kidron and the Mount of Olives into the plains of the wilderness of Judah, whither Hushai sent him tidings, which counselled him to pass over Jordan with all possible haste. It is characteristic of all these Psalms, that in them David yearns after the house of God as after the peculiar home of his heart, and, that all his wishes centre in the one wish to be at home again. And does not this short, tender song, with its depth of feeling and its May-like freshness, accord with David's want and wanderings to and fro at that time?

It consists of two hexastichs with short closing lines, resembling (as also in Isa. xvi. 9, 10) the Adonic verse of the strophe of Sappho, and a tetrastich made up of very short and longer lines intermixed.

Vers. 1—3. The poet calls Jahve רֹעִי, as He who uniformly and graciously provides for and guides him and all who are His. Later prophecy announces the visible appearing of this Shepherd, Isa. xl. 11, Ezek. xxxiv. 37, and other passages. If this has taken place, the ה' רֹעִי from the mouth of man finds its cordial response in the words ἐγὼ εἰμὶ ὁ ποιμὴν ὁ καλός. He who has Jahve, the possessor of all things, himself has all things, he lacks nothing; viz. בָּל־טוֹב, whatever is good in itself and would be good for him, xxxiv. 11, lxxxiv. 12. נְאוֹת דֶּשֶׁא are the pastures of fresh and tender grass, where one lies at ease, and rest and enjoyment are combined. נָאָה (נָוֶה), according to its primary meaning, is a resting- or dwelling-place, specifically an oasis, *i. e.* a verdant spot in the desert. מֵי מְנוּחֹת are waters, where the weary finds a most pleasant resting-place (according to Hitzig, it is a plural brought in by the plural of the governing word, but it is at any rate a superlative plural), and can at the same time refresh himself. נַהֵל is suited to this as being a pastoral word used of gentle leading, and more especially of guiding the herds to the watering-places, just as הַרְבִּיץ is used of making them to rest, especially at noon-tide, Cant. i. 7; cf. ὁδηγεῖν, Apoc. vii. 17. שׁוֹבֵב נֶפֶשׁ (elsewhere הֵשִׁיב) signifies to bring back the soul that is as it were flown away, so that it comes to itself again, therefore to impart new life, *recreare.* This He does to the soul, by causing it amidst the dryness and heat of temptation and trouble, to taste the very essence of life which refreshes and strengthens it. The *Hiph.* הִנְחָה (Arabic: to put on one side, as perhaps in Job xii. 23) is, as in cxliii. 10 the intensive of נָחָה (lxxvii. 21). The poet glories that Jahve leads him carefully and without risk or wandering in מַעְגְּלֵי־צֶדֶק, straight paths and leading to the right goal, and this לְמַעַן שְׁמוֹ (for His Name's sake). He has revealed Himself as the gracious One, and as such He will prove and glorify Himself even in the need of him who submits to His guidance.

Vers. 4—5. Rod and staff are here not so much those of the pilgrim, which would be a confusing transition to a different figure, but those of Jahve, the Shepherd (שֵׁבֶט, as in Mic. vii. 14, and in connection with it, cf. Num. xxi. 18, מִשְׁעֶנֶת as the filling up of the picture), as the means of guidance and defence. The one rod, which the shepherd holds up to guide the flock and upon which he leans and anxiously watches over the flock, has assumed a double form in the conception of the idea. This rod and staff in the hand of God comfort him, *i. e.* preserve to him the feeling of security, and therefore a cheerful spirit. Even when he passes through a valley dark and gloomy as the shadow of death, where surprises and calamities of every kind threaten him, he fears no misfortune. The LXX. narrows the figure, rendering בגיא according to the Aramaic בְּגוֹא, Dan. iii. 25, ἐν μέσῳ. The noun צלמות, which occurs in this passage for the first time in the Old Testament literature,

is originally not a compound word; but being formed from a
verb צלם, ظلم (root צל, ظل), to overshadow, darken, after
the form עֲבָדוֹת, but pronounced צַלְמָוֶת (cf. חֲצַרְמָוֶת, *Hadra-
môt* = the court of death, בְּצַלְאֵל in-God's-shadow), it signifies the shadow of death as an epithet of the most fearful
darkness, as of Hades, Job x. 21 sq., but also of a shaft of
a mine, Job xxviii. 3, and more especially of darkness such
as makes itself felt in a wild, uninhabited desert, Jer. ii. 6.

After the figure of the shepherd fades away in ver. 4,
that of the host appears. His enemies must look quietly
on (נֶגֶד as in xxxi. 20), without being able to do anything,
and see how Jahve provides bountifully for His guest, an-
oints him with sweet perfumes as at a joyous and magnificent
banquet (xcii. 11), and fills his cup to excess. What is
meant thereby, is not necessarily only blessings of a spiritual kind. The king fleeing before Absolom and forsaken by
the mass of his people was, with his army, even outwardly
in danger of being destroyed by want; it is, therefore, even
an abundance of daily bread streaming in upon them, as
in 2 Sam. xvii. 27—29, that is meant; but even this, spiritually regarded, as a gift from heaven, and so that the satisfying, refreshing and quickening is only the outside phase
of simultaneous inward experiences.* The future תַּעֲרֹךְ is
followed, according to the customary return to the perfect
ground-form, by דִּשַּׁנְתָּ, which has, none the less, the signification of a present. And in the closing assertion, כּוֹסִי,
my cup, is metonymically equivalent to the contents of my
cup. This is רְוָיָה, a fulness satiating even to excess.

Ver. 6. Foes are now pursuing him, but prosperity and
favour alone shall pursue him, and therefore drive his present pursuers out of the field. אַךְ, originally affirmative,
here restrictive, belongs only to the subject-notion in its
signification *nil nisi* (xxxix. 6, 12, cxxxix. 11). The expression is remarkable and without example elsewhere: as good
spirits Jahve sends forth טוֹב and חֶסֶד to overtake David's
enemies, and to protect him against them to their shame,

---

* In the mouth of the New Testament saint, especially on the *dies
viridium*, it is the table of the Lord's supper, as Apollinaris also hints when
he applies to it the epithet ῥιγεδανῶν βρίθουσαν, *horrendorum onustam.*

and that all his life long (accusative of continuance). We
have now no need, in connection with our reference of the
Psalm to the persecution under Absolom, either to persuade
ourselves that וְשַׁבְתִּי is equivalent to וְשִׁבְתִּי xxvii. 4, or that
it is equivalent to וְיָשַׁבְתִּי. The infinitive is logically inadmissible here, and unheard of with the vowel *ă* instead of *i*,
which would here (cf. on the other hand קָחְתִּי) be confusing and arbitrary. Nor can it be shewn from Jer. xlii. 10
to be probable that it is contracted from וישבתי, since in
that passage שׁוּב signifies *redeundo* = *rursus*. The LXX.,
certainly, renders it by καθίσαντες, as in 1 Sam. xii. 2 by
καὶ καθήσομαι; but (since so much uncertainty attaches to
these translators and their text) we cannot draw a safe inference as to the existing usage of the language, which
would, in connection with such a contraction, go out of the
province of one verb into that of another, which is not the
case with תָּתָּה = נָתַתָּה in 2 Sam. xxii. 41. On the contrary
we have before us in the present passage a *constructio
prægnans*: "and I shall return (*perf. consec.*) in the house of
Jahve", *i. e.* again, having returned, dwell in the house of
Jahve. In itself וְשַׁבְתִּי בּ might also even mean *et revertam
ad* (cf. vii. 17, Hos. xii. 7), like עָלָה בְּ, xxiv. 3, *adscendere
ad* (*in*). But the additional assertion of continuance, לְאֹרֶךְ
יָמִים (as in xciii. 5, Lam. v. 20, אֹרֶךְ, root רךְ, extension,
lengthening = length) favours the explanation, that בּ is to
be connected with the idea of וישבתי, which is involved in
וְשַׁבְתִּי as a natural consequence.

PSALM XXIV.

PREPARATION FOR THE RECEPTION OF THE LORD WHO IS ABOUT TO COME.

A. Psalm on going up (below, on the hill of Zion).

Chorus of the festive procession.

1 JAHVE's is the earth, and its fulness,
 The world, and they that dwell therein.
2 For He, He hath founded it upon the seas,
 And upon streams did He set it fast.

A voice.

3 Who may ascend the hill of Jahve,
  Who may stand in His holy place?

Another voice.

4 He that is of innocent hands and of pure heart,
  He that doth not lift up his soul to vanity,
  And doth not swear deceitfully —

Chorus.

5 He shall receive a blessing from Jahve,
  And righteousness from the God of his salvation.
6 This is the generation of those who aspire after Him,
  Who seek Thy face — Jacob. (*Sela*)

B. Psalm on entering (above, on the citadel of Zion).

Chorus of the festive procession.

7 Lift up, ye gates, your heads,
  And raise yourselves, ye ancient doors,
  That the King of Glory may come in.

A voice, as it were, from the gates.

8 Who is, then, the King of Glory?

Chorus.

Jahve, a mighty one and a hero,
Jahve, a hero in battle.
9 Lift up, ye gates, your heads,
  And raise yourselves, ye ancient doors,
  That the King of Glory may come in.

As it were, from the gates.

10 Who is He, then, the King of Glory?

Chorus.

Jahve of Hosts,
He is the King of Glory. (*Sela*)

Ps. xxiii. expressed a longing after the house of Jahve on Zion; Ps. xxiv. celebrates Jahve's entrance into Zion, and the true character of him who may enter with Him. It was composed when the Ark was brought from Kirjath Jearim to Mount Zion, where David had caused it to be set up in a tabernacle built expressly for it, 2 Sam. vi. 17, cf. xi. 11, 1 Kings i. 39; or else, which is rendered the more probable by the description of Jahve as a warrior, at a time when the Ark was brought back to Mount Zion, after having been taken to accompany the army to battle (*vid.* Ps. lxviii.). Ps. xv. is very similar. But only xxiv. 1—6 is the counterpart of that Psalm; and there is nothing wanting to render the first part of Ps. xxiv. complete in itself. Hence Ewald divides Ps. xxiv. into two songs, belonging to different periods, although both old Davidic songs, viz. Ps. xxiv. 7—10, the song of victory sung at the removal of the Ark to Zion; and xxiv. 1—6, a purely di-dactic song pre-supposing this event which forms an era in their history. And it is relatively more natural to regard this Psalm rather than Ps. xix., as two songs combined and made into one; but these two songs have an internal coher-ence; in Jahve's coming to His temple is found that which occasioned them and that towards which They point; and consequently they form a whole consisting of two divisions. To the inscription לדוד מזמור the LXX. adds τῆς μιᾶς σαββά-του* (= של אחד בשבת, for the first day of the week), accord-ing to which this Psalm was a customary Sunday Psalm. This addition is confirmed by *B. Tamîd extr.*, *Rosh ha-Shana* 31*a*, *Sofrim* xviii. (cf. *supra* p. 32). In the second of these passages cited from the Talmud, R. Akiba seeks to determine the reasons for this choice by reference to the history of the creation.

Incorporated in Israel's hymn-book, this Psalm became, with a regard to its original occasion and purpose, an Old Testament Advent hymn in honour of the Lord who should come into His temple, Mal. iii. 1; and the cry: Lift up, ye

---

* The London Papyrus fragments, in Tischendorf *Monum.* i. 247, read ΤΗ ΜΙΑ ΤΩΝ ΣΑΒΒΑΤΩΝ. In the Hexaplarian text, this addi-tion to the inscription was wanting.

. gates, your heads, obtained a meaning essentially the same
as that of the voice of the crier in Isaiah xl. 3: Prepare ye
Jahve's way, make smooth in the desert a road for our God!
In the New Testament consciousness, the second appearing
takes the place of the first, the coming of the Lord of Glory
to His church, which is His spiritual temple; and in this
Psalm we are called upon to prepare Him a worthy reception. The interpretation of the second half of the Psalm
of the entry of the Conqueror of death into Hades, — an
interpretation which has been started by the Gospel of
Nicodemus (*vid.* Tischendorf's *Evv. apocrypha* p. 306 sq.)
and still current in the Greek church, — and the patristic
interpretation of it of the εἰς οὐρανοὺς ἀνάληψις τοῦ κυρίου,
do as much violence to the rules of exegesis as to the
parallelism of the facts of the Old and New Testaments.

Vers. 1—6. Jahve, whose throne of grace is now set
upon Zion, has not a limited dominion, like the heathen
deities: His right to sovereignty embraces the earth and
its fulness (l. 12, lxxxix. 12), *i. e.* everything that is to be
found upon it and in it.* For He, הוּא, is the owner of the
world, because its Creator. He has founded it upon seas,
i. e. the ocean and its streams, נְהָרוֹת, ῥέεθρα (Jon. ii. 4); for
the waters existed before the dry land, and this has been
cast up out of them at God's word, so that consequently the
solid land, — which indeed also conceals in its interior a תְּהוֹם
רַבָּה (Gen. vii. 11), — rising above the surface of the sea,
has the waters, as it were, for its foundation (cxxxvi. 6),
although it would more readily sink down into them than
keep itself above them, if it were not in itself upheld by the
creative power of God. Hereupon arises the question, who

---

* In 1 Cor. x. 26, Paul founds on this verse (cf. l. 12) the doctrine
that a Christian (apart from a charitable regard for the weak) may
eat whatever is sold in the shambles, without troubling himself to
enquire whether it has been offered to idols or not. A Talmudic
teacher, *B. Berachoth* 35a, infers from this passage the duty of prayer
before meat: He who eats without giving thanks is like one who lays
hands upon קָדְשֵׁי שָׁמַיִם (the sacred things of God); the right to eat
is only obtained by prayer.

may ascend the mountain of Jahve, and stand above in His
holy place? The futures have a potential signification: who
can have courage to do it? what, therefore, must he be,
whom Jahve receives into His fellowship, and with whose
worship He is well-pleased? Answer: he must be one innocent in his actions and pure in mind, one who does not lift
up his soul to that which is vain (לַשָּׁוְא, according to the
Masora with *Waw minusculum*). (לְ) נָשָׂא נֶפֶשׁ אֶל, to direct
one's soul, xxv. 1, or longing and striving, towards anything, Deut. xxiv. 15, Prov. xix. 18, Hos. iv. 8. The *Kerî*
נַפְשִׁי is old and acknowledged by the oldest authorities.*
Even the LXX. *Cod. Alex.* translates: τὴν ψυχήν μου; whereas *Cod. Vat.* (Eus., Apollin., Theodor., et al.): τὴν ψυχὴν αὐτοῦ.
Critically it is just as intangible, as it is exegetically incomprehensible; נַפְשִׁי might then be equivalent to שְׁמִי, Exod.
xx. 7, an explanation, however, which does not seem possible
even from Amos vi. 8, Jer. li. 14. We let this *Kerî* alone
to its undisturbed critical rights. But that the poet did
actual write thus, is incredible.

In ver. 5 (just as at the close of Ps. xv.), in continued
predicates, we are told the character of the man, who is
worthy of this privilege, to whom the question in ver. 3
refers. Such an one shall bear away, or acquire (נשׂא, as
e. g. Esth. ii. 17) blessing from Jahve and righteousness from

---

* The reading נַפְשִׁי is adopted by Saadia (in *Emunoth* ii, where
נפשי is equivalent to שְׁמִי), Juda ha-Levi (*Cuzari* iii. 27), Abulwalid
(*Rikma* p. 180), Rashi, Kimchi, the Sohar, the Codices (and among others
by that of the year 1294) and most editions (among which, the *Complutensis* has נפשי in the text). Nor does Aben-Ezra, whom Norzi has
misunderstood, by any means reverse the relation of the *Chethib* and
Kerî; to him נפשי is the *Kerî*, and he explains it as a metaphor (an
anthropomorphism): וכהוב נפשי דרך כנוי. Elias Levita is the only
one who rejects the *Kerî* נפשי; but he does so through misunderstand-
ing a Masora (*vid.* Baer's *Psalterium* p. 130) and not without admitting
Masoretic testimony in favour of it (וכן ראיתי ברוב נוסחאות המסורה).
He is the only textual critic who rejects it. For Jacob b. Chajim is
merely astonished that נַפְשׁוּ is not to be found in the Masoreth register
of words written with *Waw* and to be read with *Jod*. And even Norzi
does not reject this *Kerî*, which he is obliged to admit has greatly
preponderating testimony in its favour, and he would only too gladly
get rid of it.

the God of his salvation (xxv. 5, xxvii. 9). Righteousness,
i. e. conformity to God and that which is well-pleasing to
God, appears here as a gift, and in this sense it is used
interchangeably with יֶשַׁע (*e. g.* cxxxii. 9, 16). It is the
righteousness of God after which the righteous, but not the
self-righteous, man hungers and thirsts; that moral perfection which is the likeness of God restored to him and at
the same time brought about by his own endeavours; it is
the being changed, or transfigured, into the image of the
Holy One Himself. With ver. 5 the answer to the question
of ver. 3 is at an end; ver. 6 adds that those thus qualified, who may accordingly expect to receive God's gifts of
salvation, are the true church of Jahve, the Israel of God.
דּוֹר (lit. a revolution, Arabic *dahr*, root דר, to turn, revolve)
is used here, as in xiv. 5, lxxiii. 15, cxii. 2, of a collective
whole, whose bond of union is not cotemporaneousness, but
similarity of disposition; and it is an alliteration with the
דֹּרְשָׁיו (*Chethîb* דרשו, without the *Jod plur.*) which follows.
מְבַקְשֵׁי פָנֶיךָ is a second genitive depending on דּוֹר, as in
xxvii. 8. Here at the close the predication passes into the
form of invocation (Thy face). And יַעֲקֹב is a summarising
predicate: in short, these are Jacob, not merely after the
flesh, but after the spirit, and thus in truth (Isa. xliv. 2,
cf. Rom. ix. 6, Gal. vi. 16). By interpolating אלהי, as is
done in the LXX. and Peshîto, and adopted by Ewald, Olshausen, Hupfeld, and Böttcher, the nerve, as it were, of the
assertion is cut through. The predicate, which has been
expressed in different ways, is concentrated intelligibly
enough in the one word יעקב, towards which it all along
tends. And here the music becomes *forte*. The first part
of this double Psalm dies away amidst the playing of the
instruments of the Levitical priests; for the Ark was brought
in בְּכָל־עֹז וּבְשִׁירִים, as 2 Sam. vi. 5 (cf. 14) is to be read.

Vers. 7—10. The festal procession has now arrived
above at the gates of the citadel of Zion. These are called
פִּתְחֵי עוֹלָם, doors of eternity (not "of the world" as Luther
renders it contrary to the Old Testament usage of the language) either as doors which pious faith hopes will last for
ever, as Hupfeld and Hitzig explain it, understanding them,
in opposition to the inscription of the Psalm, to be the

gates of Solomon's Temple; or, what seems to us much more appropriate in the mouth of those who are now standing before the gates, as the portals dating back into the hoary ages of the past (עוֹלָם as *e. g.* in Gen. xlix. 26, Isa. lviii. 12), the time of the Jebusites, and even of Melchizedek, through which the King of Glory, whose whole being and acts is glory, is now about to enter. It is the gates of the citadel of Zion, to which the cry is addressed, to expand themselves in a manner worthy of the Lord who is about to enter, for whom they are too low and too strait. Rejoicing at the great honour, thus conferred upon them, they are to raise their heads (Job x. 15, Zech. ii. 4), *i. e.* lift up their portals (lintels); the doors of antiquity are to open high and wide.* Then the question echoes back to the festal procession from Zion's gates which are wont only to admit mighty lords: who, then (זֶה giving vividness to the question, Ges. § 122, 2), is this King of Glory; and they describe Him more minutely: it is the Hero-god, by whom Israel has wrested this Zion from the Jebusites with the sword, and by whom he has always been victorious in time past. The adjectival climactic form עִזּוּז (like לִמּוּד, with *i* instead of the *ă* in חַנּוּן, קָשׁוּב) is only found in one other passage, viz. Isa. xliii. 17. גִּבּוֹר מִלְחָמָה refers back to Exod. xv. 3. Thus then shall the gates raise their heads and the ancient doors lift themselves, *i. e.* open high and wide; and this is expressed here by *Kal* instead of *Niph.* (נָשָׂא to lift one's self up, rise, as in Nah. i. 5, Hos. xiii. 1, Hab. i. 3), according to the well-known order in which recurring verses and refrain-like repetitions move gently onwards. The gates of Zion ask once more, yet now no longer hesitatingly, but in order to hear more in praise of the great King. It is now the enquiry seeking fuller information; and the heaping up of the pronouns (as in Jer. xxx. 21, cf. xlvi. 7, Esth. vii. 5) expresses its urgency (*quis tandem, ecquisnam*). The answer runs, "Jahve Tsebaoth, He is the King of Glory (now making His entry)". ה' צְבָאוֹת is the proper name of Jahve as King, which had become His customary name in the time

---

of the kings of Israel. צְבָאוֹת is a genitive governed by 'ה;
and, while it is otherwise found only in reference to human
hosts, in this combination it gains, of itself, the reference
to the angels and the stars, which are called צְבָאָיו in ciii.
21, cxlviii. 2: Jahve's hosts consisting of celestial heroes,
Joel ii. 11, and of stars standing on the plain of the heavens
as it were in battle array, Isa. xl. 26, — a reference for
which experiences and utterances like those recorded in Gen.
xxxii. 2 sq., Deut. xxxiii. 2, Judges v. 20, have prepared
the way. It is, therefore, the Ruler commanding innumerable and invincible super-terrestrial powers, who desires
admission. The gates are silent and open wide; and Jahve,
sitting enthroned above the Cherubim of the sacred Ark,
enters into Zion.

PSALM XXV.

PRAYER FOR GRACIOUS PROTECTION AND GUIDANCE.

1 א UNTO Thee, Jahve, do I lift up my soul.
2 ב My God in Thee do I trust, let me not be ashamed,
   Let not mine enemies triumph over me.
3 ג Yea none that wait on Thee shall be ashamed,
   They shall be ashamed who are faithless without cause.
4 ד Thy ways, Jahve, make known to me,
   Thy paths teach Thou me.
5 ה Lead me in Thy truth, and teach me;
   For Thou art the God of my salvation,
   On Thee do I hope continually.
6 ו Remember, Jahve, Thy tender mercies and Thy loving-
      kindnesses,
   For they are ever of old.
7 ח The sins of my youth and my transgressions re-
      member not,
   According to Thy mercy remember Thou me
   For Thy goodness' sake, Jahve!
8 ט Good and upright is Jahve;
   Therefore He instructeth sinners in the right way.
9 י He leadeth the humble in that which is right,
   And teacheth the humble His way.

10 ‫ כ‬All the paths of Jahve are mercy and truth,
    To such as keep His covenant and His testimonies.
11 ‫ ל‬For Thy name's sake, Jahve, pardon my sin,
    For it is great.
12 ‫ מ‬What man is he that feareth Jahve?
    Him shall He teach in the way of right choice.
13 ‫ נ‬His soul shall dwell in prosperity,
    And his seed shall inherit the land.
14 ‫ ס‬The secret of Jahve is with them that fear Him,
    And His covenant doth He make them know.
15 ‫ ע‬Mine eyes are ever towards Jahve,
    For He will pluck my feet out of the net.
16 ‫ פ‬Turn Thee unto me and be gracious unto me,
    For I am desolate and needy.
17 ‫ צ‬Troubles have spread over my heart,
    Out of my distresses bring Thou me forth!
18 ‫ ר‬Look upon mine affliction and my trouble,
    And forgive all my sins.
19 ‫ ר‬Look upon mine enemies, that they are many,
    And with cruel hatred they hate me.
20 ‫ שׁ‬Keep my soul, and deliver me,
    Let me not be ashamed, for I trust in Thee.
21 ‫ ת‬Let integrity and uprightness preserve me,
    For I hope in Thee.
22 ‫ פ‬Redeem Israel, Elohim,
    Out of all his troubles.

A question similar to the question, *Who may ascend the mountain of Jahve?* which Ps. xxiv. propounded, is thrown out by Ps. xxv., *Who is he that feareth Jahve?* in order to answer it in great and glorious promises. It is a calmly confident prayer for help against one's foes, and for God's instructing, pardoning, and leading grace. It is without any definite background indicating the history of the times in which it was composed; and also without any clearly marked traits of individuality. But it is one of the nine alphabetical Psalms of the whole collection, and the companion to Ps. xxxiv., to which it corresponds even in many peculiarities of the acrostic structure. For both Psalms

have no ו strophe; they are parallel both as to sound and
meaning in the beginnings of the מ, ע, and the first פ
strophes; and both Psalms, after having gone through the
alphabet, have a פ strophe added as the concluding one,
whose beginning and contents are closely related. This
homogeneousness points to one common author. We see
nothing in the alphabetical arrangement at least, which
even here as in Ps. ix—x. is handled very freely and not
fully carried out, to hinder us from regarding David as
this author. But, in connection with the general ethical
and religious character of the Psalm, it is wanting in positive proofs of this. In its universal character and harmony
with the plan of redemption Ps. xxv. coincides with many
post-exilic Psalms. It contains nothing but what is common to the believing consciousness of the church in every
age; nothing specifically belonging to the Old Testament
and Israelitish, hence Theodoret says: ἁρμόζει μάλιστα τοῖς ἐξ
ἐθνῶν κεκλημένοις. The introits for the second and third
Quadragesima Sundays are taken from vers. 6 and 15; hence
these Sundays are called *Reminiscere* and *Oculi*. Paul Gerhardt's hymn "*Nach dir, o Herr, verlanget mich*" is a beautiful poetical rendering of this Psalm.

Vers. 1—2. The Psalm begins, like Ps. xvi. xxiii.,
with a monostich. Ver. 2 is the ב strophe, אֱלֹהַי (unless
one is disposed to read בך אלהי according to the position of
the words in xxxi. 2), after the manner of the interjections
in the tragedians, *e. g.* ὤμοι, not being reckoned as
belonging to the verse (J. D. Köhler). In need of help and
full of longing for deliverance he raises his soul, drawn
away from earthly desires, to Jahve (lxxxvi. 4, cxliii. 8),
the God who alone can grant him that which shall truly
satisfy his need. His ego, which has the soul within itself,
directs his soul upwards to Him whom he calls אֱלֹהַי, because
in believing confidence he clings to Him and is united with
Him. The two אַל declare what Jahve is not to allow him
to experience, just as in xxxi. 2, 18. According to xxxv.
19, 24, xxxviii. 17, it is safer to construe לִי with יַעַלְצוּ (cf.
lxxi. 10), as also in xxvii. 2, xxx. 2, Mic. vii. 8, although it

would be possible to construe it with אֹיְבַי (cf. cxliv. 2). In
ver. 3 the confident expectation of the individual is generalised.

Ver. 3. That wherewith the praying one comforts
himself is no peculiar personal prerogative, but the certain,
joyous prospect of all believers: ἡ ἐλπὶς οὐ καταισχύνει, Rom.
v. 5. These are called קֹוֶיךָ (קֹוֶה participle to קָוָה, just as
דֹּבֵר is the participle to דִּבֶּר). Hope is the eye of faith
which looks forth clear and fixedly into the future. With
those who hope in Jahve, who do not allow themselves to
be in any way disconcerted respecting Him, are contrasted
those who act treacherously towards Him (cxix. 158, Aq.,
Symm., Theodot., οἱ ἀποστατοῦντες), and that רֵיקָם, i. e. —
and it can only mean this — from vain and worthless
pretexts, and therefore from wanton unconscientiousness.

Ver. 4. Recognising the infamy of such black ingratitude,
he prays for instruction as to the ways which he must take
according to the precepts of God (xviii. 22). The will of
God, it is true, lies before us in God's written word, but
the expounder required for the right understanding of that
word is God Himself. He prays Him for knowledge; but
in order to make what he knows a perfect and living reality, he still further needs the grace of God, viz. both His
enlightening and also His guiding grace.

Ver. 5. His truth is the lasting and self-verifying fact
of His revelation of grace. To penetrate into this truth
and to walk in it (xxvi. 3, lxxxvi. 11) without God, is a
contradiction in its very self. Therefore the psalmist prays,
as in cxix. 35, ὁδήγησόν με ἐν τῇ ἀληθείᾳ σου (LXX. *Cod.
Alex.*; whereas *Cod. Vat.* ἐπὶ τὴν . . . , cf. John xvi. 13). He
prays thus, for his salvation comes from Jahve, yea Jahve
is his salvation. He does not hope for this or that, but for
Him, all the day, *i. e.* unceasingly,* for everything worth
hoping for, everything that can satisfy the longing of the
soul, is shut up in Him. All mercy or grace, however,

---

* Hupfeld thinks the accentuation inappropriate; the first half of
the verse, however, really extends to יְשַׁעִי, and consists of two parts,
of which the second is the confirmation of the first: the second half
contains a relatively new thought. The sequence of the accents: *Rebia
magnum, Athnach,* therefore fully accords with the matter.

which proceeds from Him, has its foundation in His compassion and condescension.

Ver. 6. The supplicatory *reminiscere* means, may God never forget to exercise His pity and grace towards him, which are (as the plurals imply) so rich and superabundant. The ground on which the prayer is based is introduced with כִּי (*nam,* or even *quoniam*). God's compassion and grace are as old in their operation and efficacy as man's feebleness and sin; in their counsels they are eternal, and therefore have also in themselves the pledge of eternal duration (c. 5, ciii. 17).

Ver. 7. May Jahve not remember the faults of his youth (הַטֹּאות), into which lust and thoughtlessness have precipitated him, nor the transgressions (פְּשָׁעִים), by which even in maturer and more thoughtful years he has turned the grace of God into licentiousness and broken off his fellowship with Him (בְּ פֶּשַׁע, of defection); but may He, on the contrary, turn His remembrance to him (זְכָר לְ as in cxxxvi. 23) in accordance with His grace or loving-kindness, which אַתָּה challenges as being the form of self-attestation most closely corresponding to the nature of God. *Memor esto quidem mei,* observes Augustine, *non secundum iram, qua ego dignus sum, sed secundum misericordiam tuam, quae te digna est.* For God is טוֹב, which is really equivalent to saying, He is ἀγάπη. The next distich shews that טוּב is intended here of God's goodness, and not, as *e. g.* in Neh. ix. 35, of His abundance of possessions.

Ver. 8. The בְּ with הוֹרָה denotes the way, *i. e.* the right way (Job xxxi. 7), as the sphere and subject of the instruction, as in xxxii. 8, Prov. iv. 11, Job xxvii. 11. God condescends to sinners in order to teach them the way that leads to life, for He is טוֹב־וְיָשָׁר; well-doing is His delight, and, if His anger be not provoked (xviii. 27*b*), He has only the sincerest good intention in what He does.

Ver. 9. The shortened form of the future stands here, according to Ges. § 128, 2, rem., instead of the full form (which, viz. יַדְרִךְ, is perhaps meant); for the connection which treats of general facts, does not admit of its being taken as optative. The בְּ (cf. ver. 5, cvii. 7, cxix. 35) denotes the sphere of the guidance. מִשְׁפָּט is the right so far as it is traversed, *i. e.* practised or carried out. In this course of right He leads the עֲנָוִים, and teaches them the way that is pleasing to Himself. עֲנָוִים is the one word for the gentle, *mansueti,* and the humble, *modesti.* Jerome uses these words alternately in ver. 9*a* and 9*b*; but the poet designedly repeats the one word — the cardinal virtue of עֲנָוָה — here with the preponderating notion of lowliness. Upon the self-righteous and self-sufficient He would be obliged to force Himself even against their will. He wants disciples eager to learn; and how richly He rewards those who guard what they have learnt!

Ver. 10. The paths intended, are those which He takes with men in accordance with His revealed will and counsel. These paths are חֶסֶד [loving-kindness, mercy, or grace], for the salvation of men is their goal, and אֶמֶת [truth], for they give proof at every step of the certainty of His promises. But only they who keep Hiᶜ covenant and His testimonies faithfully and obediently shall share in this mercy and truth. To the psalmist the name of Jahve, which unfolds itself in mercy and truth, is precious. Upon it he bases the prayer that follows.

Ver. 11. The *perf. consec.* is attached to the יְהִי, which is, according to the sense, implied in לְמַעַן שִׁמְךָ, just as in other instances it follows adverbial members of a clause, placed first for the sake of emphasis, when those members have reference to the future, Ges. § 126, rem. 1. Separate and manifold sins (ver. 7) are all comprehended in עָוֹן, which is in other instances also the collective word for the corruption and the guilt of sin. כִּי gives the ground of the need and urgency of the petition. A great and multiform load of sin lies upon him, but the name of God, *i. e.* His nature that has become manifest in His mercy and truth, permits him to ask and to hope for forgiveness, not for the sake of anything whatever that he has done, but just for the sake of this name (Jer. xiv. 7, Isa. xliii. 25). How happy therefore is he who fears God, in this matter!

Ver. 12. The question: *quisnam est vir,* which resembles xxxiv. 13, cvii. 43, Isa. l. 10, is only propounded in order to draw attention to the person who bears the character described, and then to state what such an one has to expect.

In prose we should have a relative antecedent clause instead, viz. *qui* (*quisquis*) *talis est qui Dominum vereatur.** The attributive יִבְחָר, (*viam*) *quam eligat* (cf. Isa. xlviii. 17), might also be referred to God: in which He takes delight (LXX.); but parallels like cxix. 30, 173, favour the rendering: which he should chose. Among all the blessings which fall to the lot of him who fears God, the first place is given to this, that God raises him above the vacillation and hesitancy of human opinion.

Ver. 13. The verb לִין (לוּן), probably equivalent to לִיל (from לִיל) signifies to tarry the night, to lodge. Good, *i. e.* inward and outward prosperity, is like the place where such an one turns in and finds shelter and protection. And in his posterity will be fulfilled what was promised to the patriarchs and to the people delivered from Egypt, viz. possession of the land, or as this promise runs in the New Testament, of the earth, Mat. v. 5 (cf. Ps. xxxvii. 11), Apoc. v. 10.

Ver. 14. The LXX. renders סוֹד, κραταίωμα, as though it were equivalent to יְסוֹד. The reciprocal נוֹסַד, ii. 2 (which see), leads one to the right primary signification. Starting from the primary meaning of the root סד, " to be or to make tight, firm, compressed", סוֹד signifies a being closely pressed together for the purpose of secret communication and converse, confidential communion or being together, lxxxix. 8, cxi. 1 (Symm. ὁμιλία), then the confidential communication itself, lv. 15, a secret (Aquila ἀπόρρητον, Theod. μυστήριον). So here: He opens his mind without any reserve, speaks confidentially with those who fear Him; cf. the derivative passage Prov. iii. 32, and an example of the thing itself in Gen. xviii. 17. In ver. 14*b* the infinitive with לְ, according to Ges. § 132, rem. 1, as in Isa. xxxviii. 20, is an expression for the *fut. periphrast.: fœdus suum notum facturus est iis;* the position of the words is like Dan. ii. 16, 18, iv. 15. הוֹדִיעַ is used of the imparting of not merely intellectual, but experimental knowledge. Hitzig renders it differently, viz.

---

* The verb *ver-eri*, which signifies "to guard one's self, defend one's self from anything" according to its radical notion, has nothing to do with יָרֵא (וְרָא).

to enlighten them. But the *Hiph.* is not intended to be used thus absolutely even in 2 Sam. vii. 21. בְּרִיתוֹ is the object; it is intended of the rich and deep and glorious character of the covenant revelation. The poet has now on all sides confirmed the truth, that every good gift comes down from above, from the God of salvation; and he returns to the thought from which he started.

Ver. 15. He who keeps his eyes constantly directed towards God (cxli. 8, cxxiii. 1), is continually in a praying mood, which cannot remain unanswered. תָּמִיד corresponds to ἀδιαλείπτως in 1 Thess. v. 17. The aim of this constant looking upwards to God, in this instance, is deliverance out of the enemy's net. He can and will pull him out (xxxi. 5) of the net of complicated circumstances into which he has been ensnared without any fault of his own.

Ver. 16. The rendering "regard me", so far as פְּנֵה אֵל means God's observant and sympathising turning to any one (LXX. ἐπιβλέπειν), corresponds to lxxxvi. 16, Lev. xxvi. 9. For this he longs, for men treat him as a stranger and refuse to have anything to do with him. יָחִיד is the only one of his kind, one who has no companion, therefore the isolated one. The recurrence of the same sounds עָנִי אָנִי is designedly not avoided. To whom could he, the isolated one, pour forth his affliction, to whom could he unveil his inmost thoughts and feelings? to God alone! To Him he can bring all his complaints, to Him he can also again and again always make supplication.

Ver. 17. The *Hiph.* הִרְחִיב signifies to make broad, and as a transitive denominative applied to the mind and heart: to make a broad space = to expand one's self (cf. as to the idea, Lam. ii. 13, "great as the sea is thy misfortune"), LXX. ἐπληθύνθησαν, perhaps originally it was ἐπλατύνθησαν. Accordingly הִרְחִיבוּ is admissible so far as language is concerned; but since it gives only a poor antithesis to צָרוֹת it is to be suspected. The original text undoubtedly was הַרְחִיב וּמִמְּצוּקוֹתַי (הַרְחִיבָה, as in lxxvii. 2, or הַרְחֵיב, as *e. g.* in 2 Kings viii. 6): the straits of my heart do Thou enlarge (cf. cxix. 32, 2 Cor. vi. 11) and bring me out of my distresses (Hitzig and others).

Vers. 18—19. The falling away of the ק is made up for

by a double ר strophe. Even the LXX. has ἴδε twice over.
The seeing that is prayed for, is in both instances a seeing
into his condition, with which is conjoined the notion of
interposing on his behalf, though the way and manner thereof is left to God. נָשָׂא לְ, with the object in the dative instead
of the accusative (*tollere peccata*), signifies to bestow a taking away, *i. e.* forgiveness, upon any one (synon. סָלַח לְ).
It is pleasing to the New Testament consciousness that God's
vengeance is not expressly invoked upon his enemies. כִּי is
an expansive *quod* as in Gen. i. 4. שִׂנְאַת חָמָס with an attributive genitive is hatred, which springs from injustice and
ends in injustice.

Ver. 20. He entreats for preservation and deliverance
from God; and that He may not permit his hope to be disappointed (אַל־אֵבוֹשׁ, cf. 1 Chron. xxi. 13, instead of אַל־אֵבוֹשָׁה,
which is usual in other instances). This his hope rests indeed in Him: he has taken refuge in Him and therefore He
cannot forsake him, He cannot let him be destroyed.

Ver. 21. Devoutness that fills the whole man, that is
not merely half-hearted and hypocritical, is called תֹּם; and
uprightness that follows the will of God without any by-
paths and forbidden ways is called יֹשֶׁר. These two radical
virtues (cf. Job i. 1) he desires to have as his guardians on
his way which is perilous not only by reason of outward
foes, but also on account of his own sinfulness. These
custodians are not to let him pass out of their sight, lest
he should be taken away from them (cf. xl. 12, Prov. xx.
28). He can claim this for himself, for the cynosure of
his hope is God, from whom proceed תֹּם and יֹשֶׁר like good
angels.

Ver. 22. His experience is not singular, but the enmity
of the world and sin bring all who belong to the people of
God into straits just as they have him. And the need of
the individual will not cease until the need of the whole
undergoes a radical remedy. Hence the intercessory prayer
of this meagre closing distich, whose connection with what
precedes is not in this instance so close as in xxxiv. 23. It
looks as though it was only added when Ps. xxv. came to
be used in public worship; and the change of the name of
God favours this view. Both Psalms close with a פ in excess

of the alphabet. Perhaps the first פ represents the π, and
the second the φ; for xxv. 16, xxxiv. 17 follow words ending
in a consonant, and xxv. 22, xxxiv. 23, words ending in a
vowel. Or is it a propensity for giving a special representation of the final letters, just as these are sometimes represented, though not always perfectly, at the close of the
hymns of the synagogue (*pijutim*)?

PSALM XXVI.

THE LONGING OF ONE WHO IS PERSECUTED INNOCENTLY, TO GIVE THANKS TO GOD IN HIS HOUSE.

1   VINDICATE my cause, Jahve, for I have walked in
          mine integrity,
     And in Jahve have I trusted without wavering.
2   Prove me, Jahve, and try me,
     Purify my reins and my heart.
3   For Thy loving-kindness is before mine eyes,
     And I walk in Thy truth.

4   I have not sat with vain persons,
     And with dissemblers I have no intercourse.
5   I hate the congregation of the wicked,
     And I sit not with the ungodly.

6   I will wash my hands in innocency,
     And I desire to compass Thine altar, Jahve;
7   That I may join in with the voice of thanksgiving,
     And tell of all Thy wondrous works.
8   Jahve, I love the habitation of Thy house,
     And the place where Thy glory dwelleth.

9   Gather not my soul with sinners,
     Nor my life with men of blood,
10   In whose hands is infamy,
     And whose right hand is full of bribery.
11   I, however, do walk in mine integrity —
     Deliver me and be gracious unto me!

12   My foot is come to stand in a wide plain,
     In the choirs of the congregation will I praise Jahve.

Ps. xxv. and xxvi. are bound together by similarity of thought and expression. In the former as in this Psalm, we find the writer's testimony to his trust in God (בָּטַחְתִּי, xxv. 2, xxvi. 1); there as here, the cry coming forth from a distressed condition for deliverance (פְּדֵה, xxv. 22, xxvi. 11), and for some manifestation of mercy (חָנֵּנִי xxvi. 11, xxv. 16); and in the midst of these, other prominent points of contact (xxvi. 11, xxv. 21; xxvi. 3., xxv. 5). These are grounds sufficient for placing these two Psalms close together. But in Ps. xxvi. there is wanting the self-accusation that goes hand in hand with the self-attestation of piety, that confession of sin which so closely corresponds to the New Testament consciousness (*vid. supra* p. 72), which is thrice repeated in Ps. xxv. The harshness of the contrast in which the psalmist stands to his enemies, whose character is here more minutely described, does not admit of the introduction of such a lament concerning himself. The description applies well to the Absolomites. They are hypocrites, who, now that they have agreed together in their faithless and bloodly counsel, have thrown off their disguise and are won over by bribery to their new master; for Absolom had stolen the hearts of the men of Israel, 2 Sam. xv. 6. David at that time would not take the Ark with him in his flight, but said: If I shall find favour in the eyes of Jahve, He will bring me back, and grant me to see both it and His habitation, 2 Sam. xv. 25. The love for the house of God, which is expressed herein, is also the very heart of this Psalm.

Vers. 1—3. The poet, as one who is persecuted, prays for the vindication of his rights and for rescue; and bases this petition upon the relation in which he stands to God. שָׁפְטֵנִי, as in vii. 9, xxxv. 24, cf. xliii. 1. תֹּם (synon. תָּמִים, which, however, does not take any suffix) is, according to Gen. xx. 5 sq., 1 Kings xxii. 34, perfect freedom from all sinful intent, purity of character, pureness, guilelessness (ἀκακία, ἀπλότης). Upon the fact, that he has walked in a

harmless mind, without cherishing or provoking enmity,
and trusted unwaveringly (לֹא אֶמְעָד, an adverbial circumstantial clause, cf. xxi. 8) in Jahve, he bases the petition
for the proving of his injured right. He does not self-
righteously hold himself to be morally perfect, he appeals
only to the fundamental tendency of his inmost nature, which
is turned towards God and to Him only. Ver. 2 also is
not so much a challenge for God to satisfy Himself of his
innocence, as rather a request to prove the state of his
mind, and, if it be not as it appears to his consciousness,
to make this clear to him (cxxxix. 23 sq). בָּחַן is not used in
this passage of proving by trouble, but by a penetrating
glance into the inmost nature (xi. 5, xvii. 3). נִסָּה, not in
the sense of πειράζειν, but of δοκιμάζειν. צָרַף, to melt down,
i. e. by the agency of fire, the precious metal, and separate
the dross (xii. 7, lxvi. 10). The *Chethîb* is not to be read
צְרוּפָה (which would be in contradiction to the request), but
צְרוּפָה, as it is out of pause also in Isa. xxxii. 11, cf. Judges
ix. 8, 12, 1 Sam. xxviii. 8. The reins are the seat of the
emotions, the heart is the very centre of the life of the mind
and soul.

Ver. 3 tells how confidently and cheerfully he would
set himself in the light of God. God's grace or loving-
kindness is the mark on which his eye is fixed, the desire
of his eye, and he walks in God's truth. חֶסֶד is the divine
love, condescending to His creatures, and more especially to
sinners (xxv. 7), in unmerited kindness; אֱמֶת is the truth
with which God adheres to and carries out the determination of His love and the word of His promise. This lovingkindness of God has been always hitherto the model
of his life, this truth of God the determining line and the
boundary of his walk.

Vers. 4—5. He still further bases his petition upon his
comportment towards the men of this world; how he has
always observed a certain line of conduct and continues still
to keep to it. With ver. 4*a* compare Jer. xv. 17. מְתֵי שָׁוְא
(Job xi. 11, cf. xxxi. 5, where the parallel word is מִרְמָה)
are "not-real," unreal men, but in a deeper stronger sense
than we are accustomed to use this word. שָׁוְא (= שָׁוְא, from
שׁוּא) is aridity, hollowness, worthlessness, and therefore

badness (شَرّ) of disposition; the chaotic void of alienation from God; untruth white-washed over with the lie of dissimulation (xii. 3), and therefore nothingness: it is the very opposite of being filled with the fulness of God and with that which is good, which is the morally real (its synonym is אָוֶן, *e. g.* Job xxii. 15). נֶעֱלָמִים, the veiled, are those who know how to keep their worthlessness and their mischievous designs secret and to mask them by hypocrisy; post-biblical צְבוּעִים, dyed (cf. ἀνυπόκριτος, Luther *"ungefärbt"*, undyed). בּוֹא עִם (אֶת), to go in with any one, is a short expression for: to go in and out with, *i. e.* to have intercourse with him, as in Prov. xxii. 24, cf. Gen. xxiii. 10. מֵרַע (from רָעַע) is the name for one who plots that which is evil and puts it into execution. On רָשָׁע see i. 1.

Vers. 6—8. The poet supports his petition by declaring his motive to be his love for the sanctuary of God, from which he is now far removed, without any fault of his own. The coloured future וַאֲסֹבְבָה, distinct from וְאסבבה (*vid.* on iii. 6 and lxxiii. 16), can only mean, in this passage, *et ambiam,* and not *et ambibam* as it does in a different connection (Isa. xliii. 26, cf. Judges vi. 9); it is the emotional continuation (cf. xxvii. 6, Cant. vii. 12, Isa. i. 24, v. 19, and frequently) of the plain and uncoloured expression אֶרְחַץ. He wishes to wash his hands in innocence (בְּ of the state that is meant to be attested by the action), and compass (lix. 7) the altar of Jahve. That which is elsewhere a symbolic act (Deut. xxi. 6, cf. Mat. xxvii. 24), is in this instance only a rhetorical figure made use of to confess his consciousness of innocence; and it naturally assumes this form (cf. lxxiii. 13) from the idea of the priest washing his hands preparatory to the service of the altar (Exod. xxxii. 20 sq.) being associated with the idea of the altar. And, in general, the expression of vers. 6 sq. takes a priestly form, without exceeding that which the ritual admits of, by virtue of the consciousness of being themselves priests which appertained even to the Israelitish laity (Exod. xix. 16). For סבב can be used even of half encompassing as it were like a semicircle (Gen. ii. 11, Num. xxi. 4), no matter whether it be in the immediate vicinity of, or at a prescribed distance

from, the central point. לְשִׁמֵעַ is a syncopated and defectively written *Hiph.*, for לְהַשְׁמִיעַ, like לַשְׁמֵד, Isa. xxiii. 11.
Instead of לַשְׁמֵעַ קוֹל תּוֹדָה, "to cause the voice of thanksgiving
to be heard", since הִשְׁמִיעַ is used absolutely (1 Chron. xv.
19, 2 Chron. v. 13) and the object is conceived of as the
instrument of the act (Ges. § 138, 1, rem. 3), it is "in order
to strike in with the voice of thanksgiving". In the expression "all Thy wondrous works" is included the latest of
these, to which the voice of thanksgiving especially refers,
viz. the bringing of him home from the exile he had suffered from Absolom. Longing to be back again he longs most
of all for the gorgeous services in the house of his God,
which are performed around the altar of the outer court;
for he loves the habitation of the house of God, the place,
where His doxa, — revealed on earth, and in fact revealed
in grace, — has taken up its abode. מָעוֹן does not mean
refuge, shelter (Hupfeld), — for although it may obtain
this meaning from the context, it has nothing whatever to
do with عان, *med. Waw*, in the signification to help (whence
ma'ûn, ma'ûne, ma'âne, help, assistance, succour or support),
— but place, dwelling, habitation, like the Arabic *ma'ân*,
which the Kamus explains by *menzil*, a place to settle down
in, and explains etymologically by محلّ العين, *i. e.* "a
spot on which the eye rests as an object of sight"; for in
the Arabic *ma'ân* is traced back to عان *med. Je*, as is seen
from the phrase *hum minka bi-ma'ânin, i. e.* they are from
thee on a point of sight (= on a spot where thou canst see
them from the spot on which thou standest). The signification place, sojourn, abode (Targ. מְדוֹר) is undoubted; the
primary meaning of the root is, however, questionable.

Vers. 9—11. It is now, for the first time, that the
petition compressed into the one word שָׁפְטֵנִי (ver. 1) is
divided out. He prays (as in xxviii. 3), that God may not
connect him in one common lot with those whose fellowship of sentiment and conduct he has always shunned.
אַנְשֵׁי דָמִים, as in v. 7, cf. ἄνθρωποι αἱμάτων, Sir. xxxi. 25.
Elsewhere זִמָּה signifies purpose, and more particularly in a
bad sense; but in this passage it means infamy, and not
unnatural unchastity, to which בִּידֵיהֶם is inappropriate, but

scum of whatever is vicious in general: they are full of cunning and roguery, and their right hand, which ought to uphold the right — David has the lords of his people in his eye — is filled (מָלְאָה, not מִלְאָה) with accursed (Deut. xxvii. 25) bribery to the condemnation of the innocent. He, on the contrary, now, as he always has done, walks in his uprightness, so that now he can with all the more joyful conscience intreat God to interpose judicially in his behalf.

Ver. 12. The epilogue. The prayer is changed into rejoicing which is certain of the answer that shall be given. Hitherto shut in, as it were, in deep trackless gorges, he even now feels himself to be standing בְּמִישׁוֹר,* upon a pleasant plain commanding a wide range of vision (cf. בַּמֶּרְחָב, xxxi. 9), and now blends his grateful praise of God with the song of the worshipping congregation, קָהָל (LXX. ἐν ἐκκλησίαις), and its full-voiced choirs.

PSALM XXVII.

TAKING HEART IN GOD, THE ALL-RECOMPENSING ONE.

1 JAHVE is my light and my salvation,
            whom shall I fear?
  Jahve is the defence of my life,
            of whom shall I be afraid?
2 When the wicked come against me,
            to eat up my flesh,
  My oppressors and my enemies to me —
            they have stumbled and fallen.
3 Though a host should encamp against me,
            my heart shall not fear,
  Though war should rise up against me,
            in spite of it I will be confident.

---

* The first labial of the combination בְמ, בְפ, when the preceding word ends with a vowel and the two words are closely connected, receives the *Dagesh* contrary to the general rule; on this orthophonic *Dag. lene, vid. Luth. Zeitschr.*, 1863, S. 414.

4 One thing have I asked of Jahve,

             that do I desire:

  That I may dwell in the house of Jahve

              all the days of my life,

  To behold the graciousness of Jahve,

             and to meditate in His temple.

5 For He concealeth me in His pavilion

             in the day of evil,

  He hideth me in the shelter of His tabernacle,

  Upon a rock doth He raise me up.

6 Thus then shall my head be exalted above

          mine enemies round about me,

  And I will offer in His tabernacle sacrifices

      of thankful joy.

  I will sing and play the harp to Jahve.

7 Hear, Jahve, when I cry aloud; be gracious unto

          me and answer me.

8 To Thee saith my heart: Seek ye My face —

  This Thy face, Jahve, will I seek.

9 Hide not Thy face from me,

  Put not Thy servant away in anger;

  Thou art my help, cast me not away,

  And forsake me not, O God of my salvation.

10 For my father and mother have forsaken me,

  But Jahve taketh me up.

11 Teach me, Jahve, Thy way,

  And lead me in an even path because of my liers

      in wait.

12 Give me not over into the will of mine oppressors,

  For false witnesses rise up against me and such as

      breathe out violence.

13 Did I not believe to see Jahve's goodness in the land

         of the living — !

14 Hope in Jahve,

  Be of good courage, and let thine heart be strong,

  And hope in Jahve.

The same longing after Zion meets us sounding forth from this as from the preceding Psalm. To remain his whole life long in the vicinity of the house of God, is here his only prayer; and that, rescued from his enemies, he shall there offer sacrifices of thanksgiving, is his confident expectation. The הֵיכַל of God, the King, is at present only a אֹהֶל which, however, on account of Him who sits enthroned therein, may just as much be called הֵיכָל as the הֵיכַל which Ezekiel beheld in remembrance of the Mosaic tabernacle, אֹהֶל, Ezek. xli. 1. Cut off from the sanctuary, the poet is himself threatened on all sides by the dangers of war; but he is just as courageous 'in God as in iii. 7, where the battle is already going on: "*I do not fear the myriads of people, who are encamped against me.*" The situation, therefore, resembles that of David during the time of Absolom. But this holds good only of the first half, vers. 1—6. In the second half, ver. 10 is not in favour of its being composed by David. In fact the two halves are very unlike one another. They form a *hysteron-proteron,* inasmuch as the *fides triumphans* of the first part changes into *fides supplex* in the second, and with the beginning of the δέησις in ver. 7, the style becomes heavy and awkward, the strophic arrangement obscure, and even the boundaries of the lines of the verses uncertain; so that one is tempted to regard vers. 7—14 as the appendage of another writer. The compiler, however, must have had the Psalm before him exactly as we now have it; for the grounds for his placing it to follow Ps. xxvi. are to be found in both portions, cf. ver. 7 with xxvi. 11; ver. 11 with xxvi. 12.

Vers. 1—3. In this first strophe is expressed the bold confidence of faith. It is a hexastich in the cæsural schema. Let darkness break in upon him, the darkness of night, of trouble, and of spiritual conflict, yet Jahve is his Light, and if he is in Him, he is in the light and there shines upon him a sun, that sets not and knows no eclipse. This sublime, infinitely profound name for God, אוֹרִי, is found only in this passage; and there is only one other expression that can be compared with it, viz. בָּא אוֹרֵךְ in Isa. lx. 1; cf. φῶς ἐλήλυθα, John xii. 46. יִשְׁעִי does not stand beside אוֹרִי

as an unfigurative, side by side with a figurative expression;
for the statement that God is light, is not a metaphor.
David calls Him his "salvation" in regard to everything that
oppresses him, and the "stronghold (מָעוֹז from עָזַז, with an
unchangeable *â*) of his life" in regard to everything that
exposes him to peril. In Jahve he conquers far and wide; in
Him his life is hidden as it were behind a fortress built upon
a rock (xxxi. 3). When to the wicked who come upon him in
a hostile way (קָרַב עַל differing from קָרַב אֶל), he attributes the
intention of devouring his flesh, they are conceived of as wild
beasts. To eat up any one's flesh signifies, even in Job xix. 22,
the same as to pursue any one by evil speaking (in Aramaic
by slander, back-biting) to his destruction. In בִּקְרֹב the *Shebâ*
of the only faintly closed syllable is raised to a *Chateph*, as
in וְלִשְׁכֵנִי, xxxi. 12, לִשְׁאוֹל, and the like. The לִי of אֹיְבַי לִי may,
as also in xxv. 2 (cf. cxliv. 2), be regarded as giving intensity to the notion of special, personal enmity; but a mere
repetition of the subject (the enemy) without the repetition
of their hostile purpose would be tame in the parallel
member of the verse: לִי is a variation of the preceding עָלַי,
as in Lam. iii. 60 sq. In the apodosis הֵמָּה כָּשְׁלוּ וְנָפָלוּ, the
overthrow of the enemy is regarded beforehand as an
accomplished fact. The holy boldness and imperturbable
repose are expressed in ver. 3 in the very rhythm. The
thesis or downward movement in ver. 3*a* is spondaic: he
does not allow himself to be disturbed; the thesis in ver. 3*b*
is iambic: he can be bold. The rendering of Hitzig (as of
Rashi): "in this do I trust, viz. that Jahve is my light, &c.,"
is erroneous. Such might be the interpretation, if בֹּאת אֲנִי
בוֹטֵחַ closed ver. 2; but it cannot refer back over ver. 2 to
ver. 1; and why should the poet have expressed himself
thus materially, instead of saying בַּיהוָה? The fact of the
case is this, בוֹטֵחַ signifies even by itself "of good courage",
e. g. Prov. xi. 15; and בֹּאת "in spite of this" (Coccejus: *hoc
non obstante*), Lev. xxvi. 27, cf. Ps. lxxviii. 32, begins the apodosis, at the head of which we expect to find an adversative
conjunction.

Vers. 4—5. There is only one thing, that he desires,
although he also has besides full satisfaction in Jahve in
the midst of strangers and in trouble. The future is used

side by side with the perfect in ver. 4a, in order to express an ardent longing which extends out of the past into the future, and therefore runs through his whole life. The one thing sought is unfolded in שִׁבְתִּי וגו׳. A life-long dwelling in the house of Jahve, that is to say intimate spiritual intercourse with the God, who has His dwelling (בית), His palace (היכל) in the holy tent, is the one desire of David's heart, in order that he may behold and feast upon (חֲזֹה בְ of a clinging, lingering, chained gaze, and consequently a more significant form of expression than חָזָה with an accusative, lxiii. 3) נֹעַם ה׳ (xc. 17), the pleasantness (or gracefulness) of Jahve, i. e. His revelation, full of grace, which is there visible to the eye of the spirit. The interpretation which regards *amœnitas* as being equivalent to *amœnus cultus* takes hold of the idea from the wrong side. The assertion that בְּקֵּר בְּ is intended as a synonym of חֲזֹה בְ, of a pleased and lingering contemplation (Hupf., Hitz.), is contrary to the meaning of the verb, which signifies "to examine (with לְ to seek or spie about after anything, Lev. xiii. 36), to reflect on, or consider"; even the post-biblical signification to visit, more especially the sick (whence בִּקּוּר חֹלִים), comes from the primary meaning *investigare*. An appropriate sense may be obtained in the present instance by regarding it as a denominative from בֹּקֶר and rendering it as Dunash and Rashi have done, "and to appear early in His temple"; but it is unnecessary to depart from the general usage of the language. Hengstenberg rightly retains the signification "to meditate on". בְּהֵיכָלוֹ is a designation of the place consecrated to devotion, and לְבַקֵּר is meant to refer to contemplative meditation that loses itself in God who is there manifest. In ver. 5 David bases the justification of his desire upon that which the sanctuary of God is to him; the futures affirm what Jahve will provide for him in His sanctuary. It is a refuge in which he may hide himself, where Jahve takes good care of him who takes refuge therein from the storms of trouble that rage outside: there he is far removed from all dangers, he is lifted high above them and his feet are upon rocky ground. The *Chethîb* may be read בְּסֻכָּה, as in xxxi. 21 and with Ewald § 257,d; but, in this passage, with אֹהֶל alternates סֹךְ, which takes the place

of סֻכָּה in the poetic style (lxxvi. 3, Lam. ii. 6), though it
does not do so by itself, but always with a suffix.*

Ver. 6. With וְעַתָּה the poet predicts inferentially (cf.
ii. 10) the fulfilment of what he fervently desires, the guarantee of which lies in his very longing itself. זִבְחֵי תְרוּעָה
do not mean sacrifices in connection with which the trumpets are blown by the priests; for this was only the case in
connection with the sacrifices of the whole congregation
(Num. x. 10), not with those of individuals. תְּרוּעָה is a
synonym of תּוֹדָה, xxvi. 7; and זִבְחֵי תְרוּעָה is a stronger form
of expression for זבחי תודה (cvii. 22), i. e. (cf. זִבְחֵי צֶדֶק, iv. 6,
li. 21) sacrifices of jubilant thanksgiving: he will offer sacrifices in which his gratitude plays a prominent part, and will
sing songs of thanksgiving, accompanied by the playing of
stringed instruments, to his Deliverer, who has again and so
gloriously verified His promises.

Vers. 7—8. Vows of thanksgiving on the assumption
of the answering of the prayer and the fulfilment of the
thing supplicated, are very common at the close of Psalms.
But in this Psalm the prayer is only just beginning at this
stage. The transition is brought about by the preceding
conception of the danger that threatens him from the side
of his foes who are round about him. The reality, which,
in the first part, is overcome and surmounted by his faith,
makes itself consciously felt here. It is not to be rendered,
as has been done by the Vulgate, *Exaudi Domine vocem qua
clamavi* (rather, *clamo*) *ad te* (the introit of the *Dominica
exspectationis* in the interval of preparation between Ascension and Pentecost). שְׁמַע has *Dechî*, and accordingly קוֹלִי
אֶקְרָא, *voce mea* (as in iii. 5) *clamo*, is an adverbial clause
equivalent to *voce mea clamante me*. In ver. 8 לְךָ cannot

---

* Just in like manner they say in poetic style צֵידָה, cxxxii. 15;
פִּנָּה, Prov. vii. 8; מִדָּה, Job xi. 9; גֻּלָּה, Zech. iv. 2; and perhaps even
נִצָּה, Gen. xl. 10; for גֻּלָּתָה, מִדְּתָה, פִּנָּתָה, צֵידָתָה, and נִצָּתָה; as, in
general, shorter forms are sometimes found in the inflexion, which do
not occur in the corresponding principal form, e. g. צוּרָם, xlix. 15, for
צוּרָתָם; מְגוּרָם, lv. 16, for מְגוּרָתָם; בְּעָרְמָם, Job v. 13, for בְּעָרְמָתָם;
בִּתְבוּנָם, Hos. xiii. 2, for בִּתְבוּנָתָם; פֶּחָם; Neh. v. 14, for פֶּחָתָם; cf.
Hitzig on Hos. xiii. 2, and Böttcher's *Neue Aehrenlese*, No. 693.

possibly be so rendered that לְ is treated as *Lamed auctoris*
(Dathe, Olshausen): Thine, saith my heart, is (the utterance:) seek ye my face. The declaration is opposed to this
sense, thus artificially put upon it. לְךָ אָמַר are undoubtedly
to be construed together; and what the heart says to Jahve
is not: Seek ye my face, but by reason of this, and as its
echo (Calvin: *velut Deo succinens*): I will therefore seek Thy
face. Just as in Job xlii. 3, a personal inference is drawn
from a directly quoted saying of God. In the periodic style
it would be necessary to transpose בַּקְּשׁוּ פָנַי thus: since
Thou hast permitted and exhorted us, or in accordance with
Thy persuasive invitation, that we should seek Thy face, I
do seek Thy face (Hupfeld). There is no retrospective reference to any particular passage in the Tôra, such as Deut.
iv. 29. The prayer is not based upon any single passage of
Scripture, but upon God's commands and promises in
general.

Vers. 9—10. The requests are now poured forth with
all the greater freedom and importunity, that God may be
willing to be entreated and invoked. The *Hiph.* הִטָּה signifies in this passage standing by itself (cf. Job xxiv. 4): to
push aside. The clause עֶזְרָתִי הָיִיתָ does not say: be Thou
my help (which is impossible on syntactical grounds), nor
is it to be taken relatively: Thou who wast my help (for
which there is no ground in what precedes); but on the
contrary the *præt.* gives the ground of the request that
follows "Thou art my help (lit. Thou has become, or hast
ever been) — cast me, then, not away", and it is, moreover,
accented accordingly. Ver. 10, as we have already observed,
does not sound as though it came from the lips of David,
of whom it is only said during the time of his persecution
by Saul, that at that time he was obliged to part from his
parents, 1 Sam. xxii. 3 sq. The words certainly might be
David's, if ver. 10*a* would admit of being taken hypothetically, as is done by Ewald, § 362,*b*: should my father and
my mother forsake me, yet Jahve will &c. But the entreaty "forsake me not" is naturally followed by the reason:
for my father and my mother have forsaken me; and just
as naturally does the consolation: but Jahve will take me
up, prepare the way for the entreaties which begin anew in

ver. 11. Whereas, if כִּי is taken hypothetically, ver. 11 stands disconnectedly in the midst of the surrounding requests. On יְאַסְפֵנִי cf. Josh. xx. 4.

Vers. 11—12. He is now wandering about like a hunted deer; but God is able to guide him so that he may escape all dangers. And this is what he prays for. As in cxliii. 10, מִישׁוֹר is used in an ethical sense; and differs in this respect from its use in xxvi. 12. On שֹׁרְרִים, see the primary passage v. 9, of which this is an echo. Wily spies dodge his every step and would gladly see what they have invented against him and wished for him, realised. Should he enter the way of sin leading to destruction, it would tend to the dishonour of God, just as on the contrary it is a matter of honour with God not to let His servant fall. Hence he prays to be led in the way of God, for a oneness of his own will with the divine renders a man inaccessible [to evil]. נֶפֶשׁ, ver. 12, is used, as in xvii. 9, and in the similar passage, which is genuinely Davidic, xli. 3, in the signification passion or strong desire; because the soul, in its natural state, is selfishness and inordinate desire. יָפֵחַ is a collateral form of יָפִיחַ; they are both adjectives formed from the future of the verb פּוּחַ (like יָרִיב, יָרֵב): accustomed to breathe out (exhale), i.e. either to express, or to snort, breathe forth (cf. πνεῖν, or ἐμπνεῖν φόνον and φόνου, θυμοῦ, and the like, Acts ix. 1). In both Hitzig sees participles of יָפַח (Jer. iv. 31); but x. 5 and Hab. ii. 3 lead back to פּוּחַ (פִּיחַ); and Hupfeld rightly recognises such nouns formed from futures to be, according to their original source, circumlocutions of the participle after the manner of an elliptical relative clause (the صِفَة of the Arabic syntax), and explains יָפִיחַ כְּזָבִים, together with יָפֵחַ חָמָם, from the verbal construction which still continues in force.

Vers. 13—14. Self-encouragement to firmer confidence of faith. Joined to ver. 12 (Aben-Ezra, Kimchi), ver. 13 trails badly after it. We must, with Geier, Dachselt, and others, suppose that the apodosis is wanting to the protasis with its לוּלֵא pointed with three points above,* and four

---

* The ו has not any point above it, because it might be easily mistaken for a *Cholem*, *vid.* Baer's *Psalterium* p. 130.

below, according to the Masora (cf. *B. Berachoth* 4*a*), but a word which is indispensably necessary, and is even attested by the LXX. (ἑαυτῇ) and the Targum (although not by any other of the ancient versions); cf. the protasis with לוּ, which has no apodosis, in Gen. l. 15, and the apodoses with כִּי after לוּלֵי in Gen. xxxi. 42, xliii. 10, 1 Sam. xxxv. 34, 2 Sam. ii. 27 (also Num. xxii. 33, where לוּלֵי‎ = אִם לֹא‎ = אוּלַי), which are likewise to be explained *per aposiopesin*. The perfect after לוּלֵא (לוּלֵי) has sometimes the sense of a *plusquamperfectum* (as in Gen. xliii. 10, *nisi cunctati essemus*), and sometimes the sense of an *imperfect*, as in the present passage (cf. Deut. xxxii. 29, *si saperent*). The poet does not speak of a faith that he once had, a past faith, but, in regard to the danger that is even now abiding and present, of the faith he now has, a present faith. The apodosis ought to run something like this (cxix. 92, xciv. 17): did I not believe, were not confidence preserved to me . . . then (אָז or כִּי אָז) I should perish; or: then I had suddenly perished. But he has such faith, and he accordingly in ver. 14 encourages himself to go on cheerfully waiting and hoping; he speaks to himself, it is, as it were, the believing half of his soul addressing the despondent and weaker half. Instead of וֶאֱמָץ (Deut. xxxi. 7) the expression is, as in xxxi. 25, וְיַאֲמֵץ לִבֶּךָ, let thy heart be strong, let it give proof of strength. The rendering "May He (Jahve) strengthen thy heart" would require יְאַמֵּץ; but הֶאֱמִיץ, as *e.g.* הִרְחִיב xxv. 17, belongs to the transitive denominatives applying to the mind or spirit, in which the Hebrew is by no means poor, and in which the Arabic is especially rich.

PSALM XXVIII.

CRY FOR HELP AND THANKSGIVING, IN A TIME OF REBELLION.

1 TO Thee, O Jahve, do I cry;
   My Rock, remain not deaf to me,
   Lest, if Thou be silent to me, I be like them that go down
      to the pit.
2 Hear the voice of my supplication, when I cry unto Thee,
   When I lift up my hands to Thy holy sanctuary.
3 Carry me not away with the ungodly and with the workers
      of iniquity,

>   Who speak peace with their neigbbours,
>   While evil is in their hearts.
> 4 Give to them according to their work and the wickedness
>   of their deeds;
>   According to the work of their hands give to them,
>   Requite them what they have done!
> 5 For they regard not the doings of Jahve,
>   Nor the work of His hands —
>   He shall pull them down, not build them up.
>
> 6 Blessed be Jahve,
>   Because He hath heard my loud supplication!
> 7 Jahve is my defence and my shield,
>   In Him my heart trusted and I was helped —
>   Therefore my heart exulteth, and with my song do I
>   praise Him.
> 8 Jahve is a defence to them,
>   And the saving defence of His anointed one is He.
> 9 O help Thy people
>   And bless Thy heritage,
>   And feed them, and bear them up for ever!

To Ps. xxvi. and xxvii. a third Psalm is here added, belonging to the time of the persecution by Absolom. In this Psalm, also, the drawing towards the sanctuary of God cannot be lost sight of; and in addition thereto we have the intercession of the anointed one, when personally imperilled, on behalf of the people who are equally in need of help, — an intercession which can only be rightly estimated in connection with the circumstances of that time. Like Ps. xxvii. this, its neighbour, also divides into two parts; these parts, however, though their lines are of a different order, nevertheless bear a similar poetic impress. Both are composed of verses consisting of two and three lines. There are many points of contact between this Psalm and Ps. xxvii.; *e. g.* in the epithet applied to God, מעוז; but compare also ver. 3 with xxvi. 9; ver. 2 with xxxi. 23; ver. 9 with xxix. 11. The echoes of this Psalm in Isaiah are very many, and also in Jeremiah.

Vers. 1—5. This first half of the Psalm (vers. 1—5) is supplicatory. The preposition מִן in connection with the verbs חָרַשׁ, to be deaf, dumb, and חָשָׁה, to keep silence, is a pregnant form of expression denoting an aversion or turning away which does not deign to give the suppliant an answer. Jahve is his צוּר, his ground of confidence; but if He continues thus to keep silence, then he who confides in Him will become like those who are going down (xxii. 30), or are gone down (Isa. xiv. 19) to the pit. The participle of the past answers better to the situation of one already on the brink of the abyss. In the double sentence with פֶּן, the chief accent falls upon the second clause, for which the first only paratactically opens up the way (cf. Isa. v. 4, xii. 1); in Latin it would be *ne, te mihi non respondente, similis fiam.* Olshausen, and Baur with him, believes that because וְנִמְשַׁלְתִּי has not the accent on the *ultima* as being *perf. consec.*, it must be interpreted according to the accentuation thus, "in order that Thou mayst no longer keep silence, whilst I am already become like . ." But this ought to be וַאֲנִי נִמְשַׁל, or at least וַאֲנִי נִמְשַׁלְתִּי. And if ונמשלתי were to be taken as a real perfect, it would then rather have to be rendered "and I should then be like." But, notwithstanding וְנִמְשַׁלְתִּי is *Milel*, it is still *perf. consecutivum* ("and I am become like"); for if, in a sentence of more than one member following upon פֶּן, the *fut.*, as is usually the case (*vid.* on xxxviii. 17), goes over into the *perf.*, then the latter, in most instances, has the tone of the *perf. consec.* (Deut. iv. 19, Judges xviii. 25, Prov. v. 9—12, Mal. iii. 24), but not always. The *penultima*-accentuation is necessarily retained in connection with the two great pausal accents, *Silluk* and *Athnach*, Deut. viii. 12, Prov. xxx. 9; in this passage in connection with *Rebia mugrash*, just as we may say, in general, the *perf. consec.* sometimes retains its *penultima*-accentuation in connection with distinctives instead of being accented on the *ultima*; e. g. in connection with *Rebia mugrash*, Prov. xxx. 9; with *Rebia*, xix. 14 (cf. Prov. xxx. 9 with Ezek. xiv. 17); with *Zakeph.* 1 Sam. xxix. 8; and even with *Tiphcha* Obad. ver. 10, Joel iv. 21. The national grammarians are ignorant of any law on this subject.*

---

* Aben-Ezra (*Moznajim* 36*b*) explains the perfect accented on the

The point towards which the psalmist stretches forth his hands in prayer is Jahve's holy דְּבִיר. Such is the word (after the form בְּרִיחַ, כְּלִיא, עֶטִין) used only in the Books of Kings and Chronicles, with the exception of this passage, to denote the Holy of Holies, not as being χρηματιστήριον (Aquila and Symmachus), or λαλητήριον, *oraculum* (Jerome), as it were, Jahve's audience chamber (Hengstenberg) — a meaning that is not in accordance with the formation of the word, — but as the hinder part of the tent, from דָּבַר, Arabic *dabara*, to be behind, whence *dubr* (Talmudic דּוּבֶר), that which is behind (opp. *kubl, kibal*, that which is in the front), cf. *Jesurun* p. 87 sq. In vers. 3, 4 the prayer is expanded. מָשַׁךְ (instead of which we find אָסַף in xxvi. 9), to draw any one down forcibly to destruction, or to drag him to the place of judgment, Ezek. xxxii. 20. cf. x. 9, Job. xxiv. 22. The delineation of the ungodly David borrows from his actual foes. Should he succumb to them, then his fate would be like that which awaits them, to whom he is conscious that he is radically unlike. He therefore prays that God's recompensing justice may anticipate him, *i. e.* that He may requite them according to their desert, before he succumbs, to whom they have feigned שָׁלוֹם, a good understanding, or being on good terms, whereas they cherished in their heart the רָעָה that is now unmasked (cf. Jer. ix. 7). נָתַן, used of an official adjudication, as in Hos. ix. 14, Jer. xxxii. 19. The *epanaphora* of תֵּן־לָהֶם is like xxvii. 14.* The phrase הֵשִׁיב גְּמוּל (שִׁלֵּם), which occurs frequently in the prophets, signifies to recompense or repay to any one his accomplishing, his manifestation, that is to say, what he has done and merited; the thoughts and expression call to mind more particularly Isa. iii. 8—11, i. 16. The right to pray for recompense (vengeance) is grounded, in ver. 5, upon their blindness to God's just and merciful rule as it is to be seen in human history (cf. Isa. v. 12, xxii. 11). The contrast of בָּנָה and הָרַם, to pull down (with a personal object, as in

---

penult. in Prov. xxx. 9 from the conformity of sound, and Kimchi (*Michlol* 6b) simply records the phenomenon.

    * This repetition, at the end, of a significant word that has been used at the beginning of a verse, is a favourite custom of Isaiah's (*Comment.* S. 387; transl. ii. 134).

Exod. xv. 7), is like Jeremiah's style (ch. xlii. 10, cf. i. 10, xviii. 9, and frequently, Sir. xlix. 7). In ver. 5*a*, the prominent thought in David's mind is, that they shamefully fail to recognise how gloriously and graciously God has again and again acknowledged him as His anointed one. He has (2 Sam. vii.) received the promise, that God would build him a house, *i.e.* grant perpetual continuance to his kingship. The Absolomites are in the act of rebellion against this divine appointment. Hence they shall experience the very reverse of the divine promise given to David: Jahve will pull them down and not build them up, He will destroy, at its very commencement, this dynasty set up in opposition to God.

Vers. 6—9. The first half of the Psalm prayed for deliverance and for judgment; this second half gives thanks for both. If the poet wrote the Psalm at one sitting then at this point the certainty of being answered dawns upon him. But it is even possible that he added this second part later on, as a memorial of the answer he experienced to his prayer (Hitzig, Ewald). It sounds, at all events, like the record of something that has actually taken place. Jahve is his defence and shield. The conjoined perfects in ver. 7*b*. denote that which is closely united in actual realisation; and in the *fut. consec.*, as is frequently the case, *e. g.* in Job. xiv. 2, the historical signification retreats into the background before the more essential idea of that which has been produced. In מִשִּׁירִי, the song is conceived as the spring whence the הוֹדוֹת bubble forth; and instead of אוֹדֶנּוּ we have the more impressive form אֲהוֹדֶנּוּ, as in xlv. 18, cxvi. 6, 1 Sam. xvii. 47, the syncope being omitted. From suffering (*Leid*) springs song (*Lied*), and from song springs the praise (*Lob*) of Him, who has "turned" the suffering, just as it is attuned in vers. 6 and 8.*The αὐτοί, who are intended by לָמוֹ in ver. 8*a*, are those of Israel, as in xii. 8, Isa. xxxiii. 2 (Hitzig). The LXX. (κραταίωμα τοῦ λαοῦ αὐτοῦ) reads לְעַמּוֹ, as in xxix. 11, which is approved by Böttcher, Olshausen and Hupfeld; but לְמוֹ yields a similar sense. First of all

---

* There is a play of words and an alliteration in this sentence which we cannot fully reproduce in the English. — TR.

David thinks of the people, then of himself; for his
private character retreats behind his official, by virtue of
which he is the head of Israel. For this very reason his
deliverance is the deliverance of Israel, to whom, so far as
they have become unfaithful to His anointed, Jahve has
not requited this faithlessness, and to whom, so far as they
have remained true to him, He has rewarded this fidelity.
Jahve is a עֹז to them, inasmuch as He preserves them by
His might from the destruction into which they would have
precipitated themselves, or into which others would have
precipitated them; and He is the מָעוֹז יְשׁוּעוֹת of His anointed
inasmuch as He surrounds him as an inaccessible place of
refuge which secures to him salvation in all its fulness
instead of the destruction anticipated. Israel's salvation
and blessing were at stake; but Israel is in fact God's people
and God's inheritance — may He, then, work salvation for
them in every future need and bless them. Apostatised
from David, it was a flock in the hands of the hireling —
may He ever take the place of shepherd to them and carry
them in His arms through the destruction. The נַשְּׂאֵם
coupled with וּרְעֵם (thus it is to be pointed according to
Ben-Asher) calls to mind Deut. i. 31, "Jahve carried Israel
as a man doth carry his son", and Exod. xix. 4, Deut. xxxii.
11, "as on eagles' wings." The *Piel*, as in Isa. lxiii. 9, is used
of carrying the weak, whom one lifts up and thus removes
out of its helplessness and danger. Ps. iii. closes just in
the same way with an intercession; and the close of Ps. xxix.
is similar, but promissory, and consequently it is placed
next to Ps. xxviii.

PSALM XXIX.

THE PSALM OF THE SEVEN THUNDERS.

1 GIVE unto Jahve, ye sons of God,
   Give unto Jahve glory and might!
2 Give unto Jahve the glory of His name,
   Do homage to Jahve in holy attire!

3 The voice of Jahve is upon the waters,
   The God of Glory thundereth,

Jahve is upon the great waters.
4 The voice of Jahve goeth forth in power,
  The voice of Jahve goeth forth in majesty.

5 The voice of Jahve breaketh the cedars,
  Yea, Jahve breaketh the cedars of Lebanon.
6 And He maketh them to skip like a calf,
  Lebanon and Sirion like a young antelope.
7 The voice of Jahve flameth forth quivering fire.

8 The voice of Jahve shaketh the wilderness,
  Jahve shaketh the wilderness of Kadesh.
9 The voice of Jahve maketh the hinds to travail,
  He strippeth the forest —
  And in His temple everything saith: "Glory!"

10 Jahve hath sat at the Flood,
   And Jahve sitteth a King for ever.
11 Jahve will give power to His people,
   Jahve will bless His people with peace.

The occasion of this Psalm is a thunderstorm; it is not, however, limited to the outward natural phenomena, but therein is perceived the self-attestation of the God of the redemptive history. Just as in the second part of Ps. xix. the God of the revelation of salvation is called יהוה seven times in distinction from the God revealed in nature, so in this Psalm of thunders, קול ה׳ is repeated seven times, so that it may be called the Psalm of the ἑπτὰ βρονταί (Apoc. x. 3 sq.). During the time of the second Temple, as the addition to the inscription by the LXX. ἐξοδίου (ἐξόδου) σκηνῆς (= σκηνοπηγίας) seems to imply *, it was sung on the *Shemini Azereth*, the last day (ἐξόδιον, Lev. xxiii. 36) of the feast of tabernacles. Between two tetrastichs, in each of which the name

------

* The שיר of the Temple liturgy of the *Shemini Azereth* is not stated in the Talmud (*vid. Tosefoth* to *B. Succa* 47a, where, according to *Sofrim* xix. § 2 and a statement of the Jerusalem Talmud, Ps. vi., or xii, is guessed at). We only know, that Ps. xxix. belongs to the Psalm-portions for the intervening days of the feast of tabernacles, which are

יהוה occurs four times, lie three pentastichs, which, in their sevenfold קול ה', represent the peals of thunder which follow in rapid succession as the storm increases in its fury.

Vers. 1—2. The opening strophe calls upon the celestial spirits to praise Jahve; for a revelation of divine glory is in preparation, which, in its first movements, they are accounted worthy to behold, for the roots of everything that takes place in this world are in the invisible world. It is not the mighty of the earth, who are called in lxxxii. 6 בְּנֵי עֶלְיוֹן, but the angels, who are elsewhere called בְּנֵי אֱלֹהִים (e.g. Job ii. 1), that are here, as in lxxxix. 7, called בְּנֵי אֵלִים. Since אֵלִים never means God, like אלהים (so that it could be rendered sons of the deity), but gods, Exod. xv. 11, Dan. ix. 36, the expression בְּנֵי אֵלִים must be translated as a double plural from בֶּן־אֵל, after the analogy of בָּתֵּי כְלָאִים, Isa. xlii. 22, from בֵּית כְּלָא (Ges. § 108, 3), "sons of God", not "sons of gods." They, the God-begotten, i.e. created in the image of God, who form with God their Father as it were one family (vid. Genesis S. 121), are here called upon to give unto God glory and might (the primary passage is Deut. xxxii. 3), i.e. to render back to Him cheerfully and joyously in a laudatory recognition, as it were by an echo, His glory and might, which are revealed and to be revealed in the created world, and to give unto Him the glory of His name, i.e. to praise His glorious name (lxxii. 19) according its deserts. הָבוּ in all three instances has the accent on the ultima according to rule (cf., on the other hand, Job vi. 22). הַדְרַת קֹדֶשׁ is holy vestments, splendid festal attire, 2 Chron.

comprehended in the *vox memorialis* הומ"בהי (*Succa* 55a, cf. Rashi on *Joma* 3a), viz. Ps. xxix. (ה); l. 16 (ו); xciv. 16 (מ); xciv. 8 (ב); lxxxi. 7 (ה); lxxxii. 5b (י). Besides this the treatise *Sofrim* xviii. § 3 mentions Ps. xxix. as the Psalm for the festival of Pentecost and the tradition of the synagogue which prevails even at the present day recognises it only as a festival Psalm of the first day of Shabuoth [Pentecost]; the Psalm for Shemini Azereth is the 65th. The only confirmation of the statement of the LXX. is to be found in the Sohar; for there (section צ) Ps. xxix. is referred to the pouring forth of the water on the seventh day of the feast of tabernacles (*Hosianna rabba*), since it is said, that by means of the seven קוֹלוֹת (corresponding to the seven compassings of the altar) seven of the *Sephiroth* open the flood-gates of heaven.

xx. 21, cf. Ps. cx. 3.* A revelation of the power of God is near at hand. The heavenly spirits are to prepare themselves for it with all the outward display of which they are capable. If ver. 2 were a summons to the church on earth, or, as in xcvi. 9, to the dwellers upon the earth, then there ought to be some expression to indicate the change in the parties addressed; it is, therefore, in ver. 2 as in ver. 1, directed to the priests of the heavenly היכל. In the Apocalypse, also, the songs of praise and trumpeting of the angels precede the judgments of God.

Vers. 3—9. Now follows the description of the revelation of God's power, which is the ground of the summons, and is to be the subject-matter of their praise. The All-glorious One makes Himself heard in the language (Apoc. x 3 sq.) of the thunder, and reveals Himself in the storm. There are fifteen lines, which naturally arrange themselves into three five-line strophes. The chief matter with the poet, however, is the sevenfold קול ה׳. Although קול is sometimes used almost as an ejaculatory "Hark!" (Gen. iv. 10, Isa. lii. 8), this must not, with Ewald (§ 286, *f*), be applied to the קול ה׳ of the Psalm before us, the theme of which is the voice of God, who announces Himself from heaven, — a voice which moves the world. The dull sounding קול serves not merely to denote the thunder of the storm, but even the thunder of the earthquake, the roar of the tempest, and in general, every low, dull, rumbling sound, by which God makes Himself audible to the world, and more especially from the wrathful side of His doxa. The waters in ver. 3 are not the lower waters. Then the question arises what are they? Were the waters of the Mediterranean intended, they would be more definitely denoted in such a vivid description. It is, however, far more appropriate to the commencement of this description to understand them to mean the mass of water gathered together in the thick, black storm-clouds (*vid.* xviii. 12, Jer. x. 13). The rumb-

---

* The reading proposed in *B. Berachoth* 30*b* בְּחֶרְדַּת (with holy trembling) has never been a various reading; nor has בְּחַצְרֹת, after which the LXX. renders it ἐν αὐλῇ ἁγίᾳ αὐτοῦ.

ling* of Jahve is, as the poet himself explains in ver. 3*b*, the thunder produced on high by the אֵל הַכָּבוֹד (cf. מלך הכבוד, xxiv. 7 sqq.), which rolls over the sea of waters floating above the earth in the sky. Ver. 4*a* and 4*b*, just like ver. 3*a* and 3*b*, are independent substantival clauses. The rumbling of Jahve is, issues forth, or passes by; בְּ with the abstract article as in lxxvii. 14, Prov. xxiv. 5 (cf. Prov. viii. 8, Luke iv. 32, ἐν ἰσχύϊ Apoc. xviii. 2), is the בְּ of the distinctive attribute. In ver. 3 the first peals of thunder are heard; in ver. 4 the storm is coming nearer, and the peals become stronger, and now it bursts forth with its full violence: ver. 5*a* describes this in a general form, and ver. 5*b* expresses by the *fut. consec.*, as it were inferentially, that which is at present taking place: amidst the rolling of the thunder the descending lightning flashes rive the cedars of Lebanon (as is well-known, the lightning takes the outermost points). The suffix in ver. 6*a* does not refer proleptically to the mountains mentioned afterwards, but naturally to the cedars (Hengst., Hupf., Hitz.), which bend down before the storm and quickly rise up again. The skipping of Lebanon and Sirion, however, is not to be referred to the fact, that their wooded summits bend down and rise again, but, according to cxiv. 4, to their being shaken by the crash of the thunder, — a feature in the picture which certainly does not rest upon what is actually true in nature, but figuratively describes the apparent quaking of the earth during a heavy thunderstorm. שריון, according to Deut. iii. 9, is the Sidonian name of Hermon, and therefore side by side with Lebanon it represents Anti-Lebanon. The word, according to the Masora, has שׁ *sinistrum*, and consequently is שִׂרְיוֹן, wherefore Hitzig correctly derives it from شرى, *fut. i.*, to gleam, sparkle, cf. the passage from an Arab poet at cxxxiii. 3. The lightning makes these mountains bound (Luther, *lecken, i.e.* according to his

---

explanation: to spring, skip) like young antelopes. רְאֵם*,
like βούβαλος, βούβαλις, is a generic name of the antelope,
and of the buffalo that roams in herds through the forests
beyond the Jordan even at the present day; for there are antelopes that resemble the buffalo and also (except in the formation of the head and the cloven hoofs) those that resemble the
horse. The LXX. renders: ὡς υἱὸς μονοκερώτων. Does this
mean the unicorn [Germ. one-horn] depicted on Persian and
African monuments? Is this unicorn distinct from the one
horned antelope? Neither an unicorn nor an one horned antelope have been seen to the present day by any traveller.
Both animals, and consequently also their relation to one
another, are up to the present time still undefinable from a
scientific point of view.**

Each peal of thunder is immediately followed by a flash
of lightning; Jahve's thunder cleaveth flames of fire, *i. e.*
forms (as it were λατομεῖ) the fire-matter of the storm-clouds
into cloven flames of fire, into lightnings that pass swiftly
along; in connection with which it must be remembered
that קוֹל ה׳ denotes not merely the thunder as a phenomenon,
but at the same time it denotes the omnipotence of God
expressing itself therein. The brevity and threefold division
of ver. 7 depicts the incessant, zigzag, quivering movement

---

* On رَمٌ *vid.* Seetzen's *Reisen* iii. 339 and also iv. 496.

** By רְאֵם Ludolf in opposition to Bochart understands the rhinoceros; but this animal, belonging to the swine tribe, is certainly not
meant, or even merely associated with it. Moreover, the rhinoceros
[Germ. nose-horn] is called in Egypt *charnin* (from خُرْن = قُرْن), but
the unicorn, *charnit.* "In the year 1862 the French archæologist, M. Waddington, was with me in Damascus when an antiquary brought me an
ancient vessel on which a number of animals were engraved, their
names being written 'on their bellies. Among the well known animals
there was also an unicorn, exactly like a zebra or a horse, but with a
long horn standing out upon its forehead; on its body was the word
خُرْنِيت. M. Waddington wished to have the vessel and I gave it up
to him; and he took it with him to Paris. We talked a good deal
about this unicorn, and felt obliged to come to the conclusion that the
form of the fabulous animal might have become known to the Arabs at
the time of the crusades, when the English coat of arms came to
Syria." — Wetzstein.

of the lightning (*tela trisulca, ignes trisulci*, in Ovid). From
the northern mountains the storm sweeps on towards the
south of Palestine into the Arabian desert, viz. as we are
told in ver. 8*b* (cf. ver. 5, according to the schema of "parallelism by reservation"), the wilderness region of *Kadesh*
(*Kadesh Barnea*), which, however we may define its position,
must certainly have lain near the steep western slope of the
mountains of Edom toward the Arabah. Jahve's thunder,
viz. the thunderstorm, puts this desert in a state of whirl,
inasmuch as it drives the sand (חוּל) before it in whirlwinds;
and among the mountains it, viz. the strong lightning and
thundering, makes the hinds to writhe, inasmuch as from
fright they bring forth prematurely. Both the *Hiph.* יָחִיל
and the *Pil.* יְחוֹלֵל are used with a causative meaning (root
חוּ, חִי, to move in a circle, to encircle). The poet continues
with וַיֶּחֱשֹׂף, since he makes one effect of the storm to develope from another, merging as it were out of its chrysalis
state. יְעָרוֹת is a poetical plural form; and חָשַׂף describes
the effect of the storm which "shells" the woods, inasmuch
as it beats down the branches of the trees, both the tops
and the foliage. While Jahve thus reveals Himself from
heaven upon the earth in all His irresistible power, בְּהֵיכָלוֹ, in
His heavenly palace (xi. 4, xviii. 7), כֻּלּוֹ (note how בהיכלו
resolves this כלו out of itself), *i. e.* each of the beings therein,
says: כָּבוֹד. That which the poet, in vers. 1—2, has called
upon them to do, now takes place. Jahve receives back
His glory, which is immanent in the universe, in the thousand-
voiced echo of adoration.

Vers. 10—11. Luther renders it: "The Lord sitteth to
prepare a Flood", thus putting meaning into the unintelligible rendering of the Vulgate and LXX.; and in fact a
meaning that accords with the language — for יָשַׁב לְ is
most certainly intended to be understood after the analogy
of ישב למשפט, cxxii. 5, cf. ix. 8 — just as much as with the
context; for the poet has not thus far expressly referred to
the torrents of rain, in which the storm empties itself. Engel-
hardt also (*Lutherische Zeitschrift*, 1861, 216 f.), Kurtz (*Bibel
und Astronomie*, S. 568, Aufl. 4), Riehm (*Liter.-Blatt* of the
Allgem. Kirchen-Zeit., 1864, S. 110), and others understand
by מבול the quasi-flood of the torrent of rain accompanying

the lightning and thunder. But the word is not לְמַבּוּל, but
לַמַּבּוּל, and הַמַּבּוּל (Syr. *momûl*) occurs exclusively in Gen.
vi.—xi. as the name of the great Flood. Every tempest,
however, calls to mind this judgment and its merciful
issue, for it comes before us in sacred history as the first
appearance of rain with lightning and thunder, and of the
bow in the clouds speaking its message of peace (*Genesis*,
S. 276). The retrospective reference to this event is also
still further confirmed by the aorist וַיֵּשֶׁב which follows the
perfect יָשַׁב (Hofmann, *Schriftbeweis* i. 208). Jahve — says
the poet — sat (upon His throne) at the Flood (to execute
it), and sits (enthroned) in consequence thereof, or since
that time, as this present revelation of Him in the tempest
shews, as King for ever, inasmuch as He rules down here
upon earth from His throne in the heavens (cxv. 16) in wrath
and in mercy, judging and dispensing blessing. Here upon
earth He has a people, whom from above He endows with
a share of His own might and blesses with peace, while the
tempests of His wrath burst over their foes. How expressive
is בְּשָׁלוֹם as the closing word of this particular Psalm! It
spans the Psalm like a rain-bow. The opening of the Psalm
shews us the heavens opened and the throne of God in the
midst of the angelic songs of praise, and the close of the
Psalm shews us, on earth, His people victorious and blessed with peace (בְּ as in Gen. xxiv. 1*), in the midst of
Jahve's voice of anger, which shakes all things. *Gloria in
excelsis* is its beginning, and *pax in terris* its conclusion.

PSALM XXX.

SONG OF THANKSGIVING AFTER RECOVERY FROM DANGEROUS SICKNESS.

2 I WILL extol Thee, Jahve, that Thou hast raised me up,
   And hast not made mine enemies to rejoice over me.
3 Jahve, my God, I cried to Thee, then Thou didst heal me;

---

* The Holy One, blessed be He — says the Mishna, *Uksin* iii. 12,
with reference to this passage in the Psalms — has not found any
other vessel (כלי) to hold the blessing specially allotted to Israel
but peace.

4 Jahve, Thou hast brought up my soul from Hades,
  Thou hast revived me, that I should not go down to
      the grave.

5 Sing unto Jahve, ye saints of His,
  And give thanks to His holy name.
6 For His anger endureth but for a moment, His favour
      for a life long;
  At eventide weeping cometh in for the night —
  And in the morning cometh a shout of joy.

7 I, however, thought in my security:
  "I shall not totter for ever."
8 Jahve, by Thy favour hadst Thou made my mountain
      to stand strong;
  Thou hast hidden Thy face, — I became troubled.

9 To Thee, Jahve, did I cry,
  And to Jahve, made I supplication:
10 "What profit is there in my blood, in my going down to
      the grave?
  "Shall the dust praise Thee? shall it declare Thy truth?
11 "Hear, Jahve, and be gracious unto me!
  "Jahve, be Thou my helper!"

12 Thou hast turned for me my mourning into dancing,
  Thou hast put off my sackcloth and didst gird me
      with joy;
13 To the end that my glory might sing of Thee, and not
      be silent —
  Jahve, my God, for ever will I praise Thee.

The summons to praise God which is addressed to the
angels above in Ps. xxix., is directed in Ps. xxx. to the
pious here below. There is nothing against the adoption of
the לדוד. Hitzig again in this instance finds all kinds of indications of Jeremiah's hand; but the parallels in Jeremiah
are echoes of the Psalms, and דִלִּיתָנִי in ver. 2 does not need
to be explained of a lowering into a tank or dungeon, it is
a metaphorical expression for raising up out of the depths

of affliction. Even Hezekiah's song of thanksgiving in Isa. xxxviii. has grown out of the two closing strophes of this Psalm under the influence of an intimate acquaintance with the Book of Job. We are therefore warranted in supposing that it is David, who here, having in the midst of the stability of his power come to the verge of the grave, and now being roused from all carnal security, as one who has been rescued, praises the Lord, whom he has made his refuge, and calls upon all the pious to join with him in his song. The Psalm bears the inscription: *A Song-Psalm at the Dedication of the House, by David.* This has been referred to the dedication of the site of the future Temple, 2 Sam. xxiv., 1 Chron. xxi.; but although the place of the future Temple together with the altar then erected on it, can be called בֵּית יהוה (1 Chron. xxii. 1), and might also at any rate be called absolutely הַבַּיִת (as הֹר הבית, the Temple hill); yet we know that David did not himself suffer (2 Sam. xxiv. 17) from the pestilence, which followed as a punishment upon the numbering of the people which he instituted in his arrogant self-magnification. The Psalm, however, also does not contain anything that should point to a dedication of a sanctuary, whether Mount Moriah, or the tabernacle, 2 Sam. vi. 17. It might more naturally be referred to the re-consecration of the palace, that was defiled by Absolom, after David's return; but the Psalm mentions some imminent peril, the gracious averting of which does not consist in the turning away of bloodthirsty foes, but in recovery from some sickness that might have proved fatal. Thus then it must be the dedication of the citadel on Zion, the building of which was just completed. From 2 Sam. v. 12 we see that David regarded this building as a pledge of the stability and exaltation of his kingdom; and all that is needed in order to understand the Psalm is, with Aben-Ezra, Flaminius, Crusius, and Vaihinger, to infer from the Psalm itself, that David had been delayed by some severe illness from taking possession of the new building. The situation of Ps. xvi. is just like it. The regular official title אֲשֶׁר עַל־הַבַּיִת (majordomo) shews, that הבית, used thus absolutely, may denote the palace just as well as the Temple. The LXX. which renders it τοῦ ἐγκαινισμοῦ τοῦ οἴκου (τοῦ) Δαυίδ, understands the palace, not the Temple. In the Jewish ritual, Ps. xxx. is certainly, as is even stated in the Tractate *Sofrim* xviii. § 2, the Psalm for the feast of *Chanucca*, or Dedication, which refers to 1 Macc. iv. 52 sqq.

Vers. 2—4. The Psalm begins like a hymn. The *Piel* דִּלָּה (from דָּלָה, Arab. دَلا, to hold anything long, loose and pendulous, whether upwards or downwards, conj. V. تَدَلَّى, to dangle) signifies to lift or draw up, like a bucket (דְּלִי, Greek ἀντλίον, Latin *tollo, tolleno* in Festus). The poet himself says what that depth is into which he had sunk and out of which God had drawn him up without his enemies rejoicing over him (לִי as in xxv, 2), *i. e.* without allowing them the wished for joy at his destruction: he was brought down almost into Hades in consequence of some fatal sickness. חִיָּה (never: to call into being out of nothing) always means to restore to life that which has apparently or really succumbed to death, or to preserve anything living in life. With this is easily and satisfactorily joined the *Kerî* מִיָּרְדִי בוֹר (without *Makkeph* in the correct text), *ita ut non descenderem*; the infinitive of יָרַד in this instance following the analogy of the strong verb is יְרֹד, like יָבֵשׁ, יָשׁוֹן, and with suffix *jordi* (like *josdi*, Job xxxviii. 4) or *jār^edi*, for here it is to be read thus, and not *jordi* (*vid.* on xvi. 1, lxxxvi. 2).* The *Chethîb* מיורדי might also be the infinitive, written with *Cholem plenum*, as an infinitive Gen. xxxii. 20, and an imperative Num. xxiii. 8, is each pointed with *Cholem* instead of *Kametz chatuph*; but it is probably intended to be read as a participle, מִיּוֹרְדִי: Thou hast revived me from those who sink away into the grave (xxviii. 1), or out of the state of such (cf. xxii. 22*b*) — a perfectly admissible and pregnant construction.

Vers. 5—6 call upon all the pious to praise this God, who after a short season of anger is at once and henceforth gracious. Instead of שֵׁם of Jahve, we find the expression

---

* The Masora does not place the word under אלין תיבותא יתירין ו"יו וחטפין קמצין (Introduction 28*b*), as one would expect to find it if it were to be read *mijordi*, and proceeds on the assumption that *mijārdi* is infinitive like עֲמָדְךָ (read *'amādcha*) Obad. ver. 11, not participle (Ewald, S. 533).

זֵכֶר in this instance, as in xcvii. 12 after Exod. iii. 15. Jahve, by revealing Himself, renders Himself capable of being both named and remembered, and that in the most illustrious manner. The history of redemption is, as it were, an unfolding of the Name of Jahve and at the same time a setting up of a monument, an establishment of a memorial, and in fact the erection of a זֵכֶר קֹדֶשׁ; because all God's self-attestations, whether in love or in wrath, flow from the sea of light of His holiness. When He manifests Himself to His own love prevails; and wrath is, in relation to them, only a vanishing moment: *a moment passes in His anger, a* (whole) *life in His favour, i. e.* the former endures only for a moment, the latter the whole life of a man. "*Alles Ding währt seine Zeit, Gottes Lieb' in Ewigkeit.*" All things last their season, God's love to all eternity. The preposition בְּ does not here, as in the beautiful parallel Isa. liv. 7 sq., cf. lx. 10, denote the time and mode of that which takes place, but the state in which one spends the time. Ver. 6 *bc* portrays the rapidity with which love takes back wrath (cf. Isa. xvii. 14): in the evening weeping takes up its abode with us for the night, but in the morning another guest, viz. רִנָּה, appears, like a rescuing angel, before whom בְּכִי disappears. The predicate יָלִין does not belong to ver. 6*c* as well (Hupfeld, Hitzig). The substantival clause: and in the morning joy = joy is present, depicts the unexpectedness and surprise of the help of Him who sends בכי and רנה.

Vers. 7—8. David now relates his experience in detail, beginning with the cause of the chastisement, which he has just undergone. In וַאֲנִי אָמַרְתִּי (as in xxxi. 23, Psa. xlix. 4) he contrasts his former self-confidence, in which (like the רשע, x. 6) he thought himself to be immoveable, with the God-ward trust he has now gained in the school of affliction. Instead of confiding in the Giver, he trusted in the gift, as though it had been his own work. It is uncertain, — but it is all the same in the end, — whether שַׁלְוִי is the inflected infinitive שְׁלוֹ of the verb שָׁלָו (which we adopt in our translation), or the inflected noun שֶׁלְוִ (שַׁלְוֹ) = שַׁלְוָ, after the form שָׂחוּ, a swimming, Ezek. xlvii. 5, = שַׁלְוָה, Jer. xxii. 21. The inevitable consequence of such carnal security, as it is more minutely described in Deut. viii. 11—18, is some humbling divine chastisement. This intimate connection is expressed by the perfects in ver. 8, which represent God's pardon, God's withdrawal of favour, which is brought about by his self-exaltation, and the surprise of his being undeceived, as synchronous. הֶעֱמִיד עֹז, to set up might is equivalent to: to give it as a lasting possession; cf. 2 Chron. xxxiii. 8, which passage is a varied, but not (as Riehm supposes) a corrupted, repetition of 2 Kings xxi. 8. It is, therefore, unnecessary, as Hitzig does, to take לְ as accusatival and עֹז as adverbial: in Thy favour hadst Thou made my mountain to stand firm. The mountain is Zion, which is strong by natural position and by the additions of art (2 Sam. v. 9); and this, as being the castle-hill, is the emblem of the kingdom of David: Jahve had strongly established his kingdom for David, when on account of his trust in himself He made him to feel how all that he was he was only by Him, and without Him he was nothing whatever. The form of the inflexion הַרְרִי, instead of הֲרִי = harri, is defended by Gen. xiv. 6 and Jer. xvii. 3 (where it is הַרְרִי as if from הָרָר). The reading להדרי (LXX., Syr.), i. e. to my kingly dignity is a happy substitution; whereas the reading of the Targum לְהַרְרֵי, "placed (me) on firm mountains", at once refutes itself by the necessity for supplying "me."

Vers. 9—11. Nevertheless he who is thus chastened prayed fervently. The futures in ver. 9, standing as they do in the full flow of the narration, have the force of imperfects, of "the present in the past" as the Arabian grammarians call it. From the question "What profit is there (the usual expression for τί ὄφελος, quid lucri) in my blood?", it is not to be inferred that David was in danger of death by the hand of a foe; for וַתִּרְפָּאֵנִי in ver. 3 teaches us very different, "what profit would there be in my blood?" is therefore equivalent to (cf. Job xvi. 18) what advantage would there be in Thy slaying me before my time? On the contrary God would rob Himself of the praise, which the living one would render to Him, and would so gladly render. His request that his life may be prolonged was not, therefore, for the sake of worldly possessions and enjoyment, but for the glory of God. He feared death as being the end of the praise of God. For beyond the grave there will be no more psalms

sung, vi. 6. In the Old Testament, Hades was as yet un-
vanquished, Heaven was not yet opened. In Heaven are the
בני אלים, but as yet no blessed בני אדם.

Vers. 12—13. In order to express the immediate sequence of the fulfilling of the prayer upon the prayer itself,
the otherwise (*e.g.* xxxii. 5) usual ו of conjunction is omitted;
on הָפַכְתָּ וגו׳ cf. the echoes in Jer. xxxi. 13, Lam. v. 15. According to our interpretation of the relation of the Psalm
to the events of the time, there is as little reason for thinking of 2 Sam. vi. 14 in connection with מָחוֹל, as of 1 Chron.
xxi. 16 in connection with שַׂקִּי. In place of the garment of
penitence and mourning (cf. מַחֲגֹרֶת שָׂק, Isa. iii. 24) slung
round the body (perhaps fastened only with a cord) came a
girding up (אָזַר, synon. חָגַר lxv. 13, whence חֲגֹרָה, אֵזוֹר) with
joy. The designed result of such a speedy and radical
change in his affliction, after it had had the salutary effect
of humbling him, was the praise of Jahve: in order that
my glory (כָּבוֹד for כְּבוֹדִי = נַפְשִׁי, as in vii. 6, xvi. 9, cviii. 2)
may sing Thy praises without ceasing (יִדֹּם *fut. Kal*). And
the praise of Jahve for ever is moreover his resolve, just as
he vows, and at the same time carries it out, in this Psalm.

PSALM XXXI.

SURRENDER OF ONE SORELY PERSECUTED INTO THE HAND OF GOD.

2 IN Thee, Jahve, have I hidden —
   Let me not be ashamed for ever;
   In Thy righteousness set me free.
3 Bow down Thine ear to me, deliver me speedily;
   Be Thou to me a rock of refuge,
   A house of fortresses, to save me.
4 For my rock and my fortress art Thou,
   And for Thy Name's sake wilt Thou lead me and guide me.
5 Thou wilt pull me out of the net they have laid privily
      for me,
   For Thou art my defence.
6 Into Thy hand do I commend my spirit,
   Thou redeemest me, Jahve, God of truth!

 7 Hateful to me are the worshippers of vain idols,
    Whereas I cleave to Jahve.
 8 I will exult and rejoice in Thy mercy,
    That Thou hast regarded my poverty,
    That Thou hast taken knowledge of the distresses of
        my soul.
 9 And hast not shut me up in the hand of the enemy,
    Thou hast set my feet in a broad place.

10 Be gracious unto me, Jahve, for I am straitened:
    Consumed with grief is mine eye, and my soul, and
        my body.
11 For spent is my life with sorrow,
    And my years with sighing;
    My strength has failed by reason of mine iniquity,
    And my bones are consumed.
12 Because of all mine adversaries I am become a reproach,
    And a burden to my neighbours, and a terror to my
        friends;
    Those who see me in the streets flee from me.
13 I am forgotten as a dead man out of mind;
    I am become like a broken vessel.
14 For I hear the slander of many,
    Fear on every side;
    While they take counsel together against me—
    They devise to take away my life.

15 But I — in Thee do I trust, Jahve,
    I say: Thou art my God.
16 In Thy hand are my times,
    Deliver me out of the hand of mine enemies, and from
        my persecutors!
17 Make Thy face to shine upon Thy servant,
    Save me in Thy mercy.
18 Jahve, I shall not be ashamed, for on Thee do I call;
    The wicked shall be ashamed, they shall be silent in
        Hades.
19 Lying lips shall be put to silence,
    Which speak insolently of the righteous,
    With pride and contempt.

20 How great is Thy goodness, which Thou hast reserved
         for them that fear Thee,
    Which Thou dost effect for them that hide in Thee in
         the presence of the children of men.
21 Thou protectest them in the hiding-place of Thy presence
         from the factions of man;
    Thou keepest them in a pavilion from the strife of
         tongues.
22 Blessed be Jahve,
    That He hath shewed me marvellous lovingkindness in
         a strong city,
23 Whilst I said in my feeble faith:
    "I am cut off from the vision of Thine eyes."—
    Nevertheless Thou heardest the cry of my supplication
         when I cried to Thee.
24 O love Jahve, all ye His saints;
    The faithful doth Jahve preserve,
    And plentifully rewardeth the proud doer.
25 Be strong and let your heart take courage,
    All ye that wait on Jahve!

In Ps. xxxi. the poet also, in וַאֲנִי אָמַרְתִּי (ver. 23), looks
back upon a previous state of mind, viz. that of conflict,
just as in xxx. 7 upon that of security. And here, also, he
makes all the חֲסִידִים partakers with him of the healthful
fruit of his deliverance (cf. xxxi. 24 with xxx. 5). But in
other respects the situation of the two Psalms is very different. They are both Davidic. Hitzig, however, regards
them both as composed by Jeremiah. With reference to
Ps. xxxi., which Ewald also ascribes to "Jéremjá", this view
is well worthy of notice. Not only do we find ver. 14a recurring in Jeremiah, ch. xx. 10, but the whole Psalm, in its
language (cf., *e. g.*, ver. 10 with Lam. i. 20; ver. 11 with
Jer. xx. 18; ver. 18 with Jer. xvii. 18; ver. 23 with Lam.
iii. 54) and its plaintive tenderness, reminds one of Jeremiah.
But this relationship does not decide the question. The
passage Jer. xx. 10, like many other passages of this prophet,
whose language is so strongly imbued with that of the Psalter, may be just as much a reminiscence as Jon. ii. 5, 9;
and as regards its plaintive tenderness there are no two

characters more closely allied naturally and in spirit than David and Jeremiah; both are servants of Jahve, whose noble, tender spirits were capable of strong feeling, who cherished earnest longings, and abounded in tribulations. We abide, though not without some degree of hesitation, by the testimony of the inscription; and regard the Psalm as a song springing from the outward and inward conflict (LXX. ἐκστάσεως, probably by a combination of ver. 23, ἐν ἐκστάσει, בחפזי, with Sam. xxiii. 26) of the time of Saul. While ver. 12c is not suited to the mouth of the captive Jeremiah (Hitzig), the Psalm has much that is common not only to Ps. lxix. (more especially lxix. 9, 33), a Psalm that sounds much like Jeremiah's, but also to others, which we regard as Davidic; viz. the figures corresponding to the life of warfare which David then lived among the rocks and caves of the wilderness; the cheering call, xxxi. 25, cf. xxii. 27, xxvii. 14; the rare use of the *Hiph.* הִפְלִיא xxxi. 22, xvii. 7; the desire to be hidden by God, xxxi. 21, cf. xvii. 8, lxiv. 3; etc. In common with Ps. xxii. this may be noted, that the crucified Christ takes His last word from this Psalm, just as He takes His last utterance but three from that Psalm. But in xxxi. 10—14, the prefigurement of the Passion is confined within the limits of the type and does not undergo the same prophetical enhancement as it does in that unique Ps. xxii., to which only Ps. lxix. is in any degree comparable. The opening, vers. 2—4, is repeated in the centonic Ps. lxxi., the work of a later anonymous poet, just as ver. 23 is in part repeated in cxvi. 11. The arrangement of the strophes is not very clear.

Vers 2—9. The poet begins with the prayer for deliverance, based upon the trust which Jahve, to whom he surrenders himself, cannot possibly disappoint; and rejoices beforehand in the protection which he assumes will, without any doubt, be granted. Out of his confident security in God (הָסִיתִי) springs the prayer: may it never come to this with me, that I am put to confusion by the disappointment of my hope. This prayer in the form of intense desire is followed by prayers in the direct form of supplication. The supplicatory פַּלְּטֵנִי is based upon God's righteousness, which cannot refrain from repaying conduct consistent with the order of redemption, though after prolonged trial, with the longed for tokens of deliverance. In the second paragraph, the prayer is moulded in accordance with the circumstances of him who is chased by Saul hither and thither among the mountains and in the desert, homeless and defenceless. In the expression צוּר מָעוֹז, מָעוֹז is *genit. appositionis*: a rock of defence (מָעוֹז from עָזַז, as in xxvii. 1), or rather: of refuge (מָעוֹז = معاذ, from עוֹז, עוּז = عاذ, as in xxxvii. 39, lii. 9, and probably also in Isa. xxx. 2 and elsewhere);* a rock-castle, *i. e.* a castle upon a rock, would be called מָעוֹז צוּר, reversing the order of the words. צוּר מָעוֹז in lxxi. 3, a rock of habitation, *i. e.* of safe sojourn, fully warrants this interpretation. מְצוּדָה, prop. *specula*, signifies a mountain height or the summit of a mountain; a house on the mountain height is one that is situated on some high mountain

---

* It can hardly be doubted, that, in opposition to the pointing as we have it, which only recognises one מָעוֹז (מָעֹז) from עָזַז, to be strong, there are two different substantives having this principal form, viz. מָעוֹז a fortress, secure place, bulwark, which according to its derivation is inflected מָעֻזִּי, etc., and מָעוֹז equivalent to the Arabic *ma‘âdh*, a hiding-place, defence, refuge, which ought to have been declined מְעוֹזִי or מָעוֹזִי like the synonymous מְנוּסִי (Olshausen § 201, 202). Moreover עוּז, عاذ, like חָסָה, of which it is the parallel word in Isa. xxx. 2, means to hide one's self anywhere (*Piel* and *Hiph.*, Hebrew הֵעִיז, according to the Kamus, Zamachshari and Neshwân: to hide any one, *e. g.* Koran iii. 31); hence عائذ, a plant that grows among bushes (*bên esh-shôk* according to the Kamus) or in the crevices of the rocks (*fi-l-ḥazn* according to Neshwân) and is thus inaccessible to the herds; عُوَّذ, gazelles that are invisible, *i. e.* keep hidden, for seven days after giving birth, also used of pieces of flesh of which part is hidden among the bones; عُوَذَة, an amulet with which a man covers himself (*protegit*), and so forth. — Wetzstein.

Consequently מָעוֹז (formed like معاذ, according to Neshwân equivalent to مَعْوَذ) is prop. a place in which to hide one's self, synonymous with מַחֲסֶה, מָנוֹס, ملاذ, مَلْجَأ, and the like. True, the two substantives from עוּז and עָזַז meet in their meanings like *praesidium* and *asylum*, and according to passages like Jer. xvi. 19 appear to be blended in the genius of the language, but they are radically distinct.

top and affords a safe asylum (*vid.* on xviii. 3). The thought
"shew me Thy salvation, for Thou art my Saviour", underlies the connection expressed by כִּי in vers. 4 and 5*b*. Köster
considers it to be illogical, but it is the logic of every believing prayer. The poet prays that God would become to him,
actu reflexo, that which to the *actus directus* of his faith He
is even now. The futures in vers. 4, 5 express hopes which
necessarily arise out of that which Jahve is to the poet. The
interchangeable notions הִנְחָה and נִהֵל , with which we are
familiar from Ps. xxiii., stand side by side, in order to give
urgency to the utterance of the longing for God's gentle
and safe guidance. Instead of translating it "out of the net,
which etc.," according to the accents (cf. x. 2, xii. 8) it should
be rendered "out of the net there", so that טָמְנוּ לִי is a relative clause without the relative.

Into the hand of this God, who is and will be all this
to him, he commends his spirit; he gives it over into His
hand as a trust or deposit (פִּקָּדוֹן); for whatsoever is deposited there is safely kept, and freed from all danger and all
distress. The word used is not נַפְשִׁי , which Theodotion
substitutes when he renders it τὴν ἐμαυτοῦ ψυχὴν τῇ σῇ παρα-
τίθημι προμηθείᾳ, but רוּחִי ; and this is used designedly. The
language of the prayer lays hold of life at its root, as springing directly from God and as also living in the believer from
God and in God; and this life it places under His protection,
who is the true life of all spirit-life (Isa. xxxviii. 16) and
of all life. It is the language of prayer with which the dying
Christ breathed forth His life, Luke xxiii. 46. The period
of David's persecution by Saul is the most prolific in types
of the Passion; and this language of prayer, which proceeded
from the furnace of affliction through which David at that
time passed, denotes, in the mouth of Christ, a crisis in
the history of redemption in which the Old Testament
receives its fulfilment. Like David, He commends His spirit
to God; but not, that He may not die, but that dying He
may not die, *i. e.* that He may receive back again His
spirit-corporeal life, which is hidden in the hand of God, in
imperishable power and glory. That which is so ardently
desired and hoped for is regarded by him, who thus in faith
commends himself to God, as having already taken place,

"Thou hast redeemed me, Jahve, God of truth." The perfect פָּדִיתָה is not used here, as in iv. 2, of that which is past, but of that which is already as good as past; it is not precative (Ew. § 223,*b*), but, like the perfects in vers. 8, 9, an expression of believing anticipation of redemption. It is the *præt. confidentiæ* which is closely related to the *præt. prophet.*; for the spirit of faith, like the spirit of the prophets, speaks of the future with historic certainty. In the notion of אֵל אֱמֶת it is impossible to exclude the reference to false gods which is contained in אֱלֹהֵי אֱמֶת, 2 Chron. xv. 3, since, in ver. 7, "vain illusions" are used as an antithesis. הֲבָלִים, ever since Deut. xxxii. 21, has become a favourite name for idols, and more particularly in Jeremiah (*e. g.* ch. viii. 19). On the other hand, according to the context, it may also not differ very greatly from אֵל אֱמוּנָה, Deut. xxxii. 4; since the idea of God as a depositary or trustee still influences the thought, and אֱמֶת and אֱמוּנָה are used interchangeably in other passages as personal attributes. We may say that אמת is being that lasts and verifies itself, and אמונה is sentiment that lasts and verifies itself. Therefore אל אמת is the God, who as the true God, maintains the truth of His revelation, and more especially of His promises, by a living authority or rule.

In ver. 7, David appeals to his entire and simple surrender to this true and faithful God: hateful to him are those, who worship vain images, whilst he, on the other hand, cleaves to Jahve. It is the false gods, which are called הַבְלֵי־שָׁוְא, as beings without being, which are of no service to their worshippers and only disappoint their expectations. Probably (as in v. 6) it is to be read שָׂנֵאתָ with the LXX., Vulgate, Syriac, and Arabic versions (Hitzig, Ewald, Olshausen, and others). In the text before us, which gives us no corrective *Keri* as in 2 Sam. xiv. 21, Ruth iv. 5, וַאֲנִי is not an antithesis to the preceding clause, but to the member of that clause which immediately precedes it. In Jonah's psalm, ch. ii. 9, this is expressed by מְשַׁמְּרִים הַבְלֵי־שָׁוְא; in the present instance the *Kal* is used in the signification *observare, colere,* as in Hos. iv. 10, and even in Prov. xxvii. 18. In the waiting of service is included, according to lix. 10, the waiting of trust. The word בָּטַח which denotes the *fiducia fidei* is usually construed with בְּ of adhering to, or עַל of resting upon; but here it is combined with אֶל of hanging on. The cohortatives in ver. 8 express intentions. Olshausen and Hitzig translate them as optatives: may I be able to rejoice; but this, as a continuation of ver. 7, seems less appropriate. Certain that he will be heard, he determines to manifest thankful joy for Jahve's mercy, that (אֲשֶׁר as in Gen. xxxiv. 27) He has regarded (ἐπέβλεψε, Luke i. 48) his affliction, that He has known and exerted Himself about his soul's distresses. The construction יָדַע בְּ, in the presence of Gen. xix. 33, 35, Job xii. 9, xxxv. 15, cannot be doubted (Hupfeld); it is more significant than the expression "to know of anything"; בְּ is like ἐπί in ἐπιγιγνώσκειν used of the perception or comprehensive knowledge, which grasps an object and takes possession of it, or makes itself master of it. הִסְגִּיר, ver. 9, συγκλείειν, as in 1 Sam. xxiii. 11 (in the mouth of David) is so to abandon, that the hand of another closes upon that which is abandoned to it, *i. e.* has it completely in its power. מֶרְחָב, as in xviii. 20, cf. xxvi. 12. The language is David's, in which the language of the Tôra, and more especially of Deuteronomy (xxxii. 30, xxiii. 16), is re-echoed.

Vers. 10—14. After the pæan before victory, which he has sung in the fulness of his faith, in this second part of the Psalm (with groups, or strophes, of diminishing compass: 6. 5. 4) there again breaks forth the petition, based upon the greatness of the suffering which the psalmist, after having strengthened himself in his trust in God, now all the more vividly sets before Him. צַר־לִי, *angustum est mihi*, as in lxix. 18, cf. xviii. 7. Ver. 10*b* is word for word like vi. 8, except that in this passage to עֵינִי, the eye which mirrors the state of suffering in which the sensuous perception and objective receptivity of the man are concentrated, are added נֶפֶשׁ, the soul forming the *nexus* of the spirit and the body, and בֶּטֶן, the inward parts of the body reflecting the energies and feelings of the spirit and the soul. חַיִּים, with which is combined the idea of the organic intermingling of the powers of soul and body, has the predicate in the plural, as in lxxxviii. 4. The fact that the poet makes mention of his iniquity as that by which his physical strength has be-

come tottering (כָּשַׁל as in Neh. iv. 4), is nothing surprising
even in a Psalm that belongs to the time of his persecution
by Saul; for the longer this persecution continued, the more
deeply must David have felt that he needed this furnace of
affliction.

The text of ver. 12*ab* upon which the LXX. rendering is
based, was just the same as ours: παρὰ πάντας τοὺς ἐχθρούς
μου ἐγενήθην ὄνειδος, καὶ τοῖς γείτοσί μου σφόδρα καὶ φόβος τοῖς
γνωστοῖς μου. But this σφόδρα (Jerome *nimis*) would certainly
only be tolerable, if it could be rendered, "I am become a
reproach even to my neighbours exceedingly" — in favour
of this position of מְאֹד we might compare Judges xii. 2, —
and this rendering is not really an impossible one; for not
only has ן frequently the sense of "even" as in 2 Sam. i. 23,
but (independently of passages, in which it may even be
explained as "and that", an expression which takes up what
has been omitted, as in Amos iv. 10) it sometimes has this
meaning direct (like καί, *et* = *etiam*), Isa. xxxii. 7, Hos. viii.
6 (according to the accents), 2 Chron. xxvii. 5, Eccl. v. 5
(cf. Ew. § 352,*b*). Inasmuch, however, as this usage, in Hebrew, was not definitely developed, but was only as it were
just developing, it may be asked whether it is not possible
to find a suitable explanation without having recourse to this
rendering of the ן as equivalent to גַּם, a rendering which is
always hazardous. Olshausen places ולשׁבני after למידעי, a
change which certainly gets rid of all difficulty. Hitzig alters
מְאֹד into מְנַד, frightened, scared. But one naturally looks
for a parallel substantive to הֶרְפָּה, somewhat like "terror"
(Syriac) or "burden". Still מָגוֹר (dread) and מַשְׂאֵת (a burden)
do not look as though מאד could be a corruption of either
of those words. Is it not perhaps possible for מאד itself to be
equivalent in meaning to משׂאת? Since in the signification
σφόδρα it is so unsuited to this passage, the expression would
not be ambiguous, if it were here used in a special sense.

J. D. Michaelis has even compared the Arabic اوْر (اوْر) in
the sense of *onus*. We can, without the hesitation felt by
Maurer and Hupfeld, suppose that מאד has indeed this meaning in this passage, and without any necessity for its being
pointed מָאֹר; for even the adverb מְאֹד is originally a sub-

stantive derived from אוּד, öͤ (after the form מֶצַד from צוּד)
gravitas, firmitas, which is then used in the sense of *graviter,*
firmiter (cf. the French *ferme*). אוּד, öͤ, however, has the
radical signification to be compressed, compact, firm, and
solid, from which proceed the significations, which are divided between *âda, jaîdu,* and *âda, jaûdu,* to be strong, powerful, and to press upon, to burden, both of which meanings
öͤ unites within itself (cf. on xx. 9).

The number of opponents that David had, at length
made him a reproach even in the eyes of the better disposed
of his people, as being a revolter and usurper. Those among
whom he found friendly shelter began to feel themselves
burdened by his presence because they were thereby imperilled; and we see from the sad fate of Abimelech and the
other priests of Nob what cause, humanly speaking, they,
who were not merely slightly, but even intimately acquainted with him (מְיֻדָּעִים as in lv. 14, lxxxviii. 9, 19), had for
avoiding all intercourse with him. Thus, then, he is like one
dead, whom as soon as he is borne out of his home to the
grave, men are wont, in general, to put out of mind also (נִשְׁכַּח
מִלֵּב, *oblivione extingui ex corde;* cf. מָפֶה, Deut. xxxi. 21). All
intimate connection with him is as it were sundered, he is
become כִּכְלִי אֹבֵד, — a phrase, which, as we consider the
confirmation which follows in ver. 14, has the sense of *vas
periens* (not *vas perditum*), a vessel that is in the act of אֹבֵד,
i. e. one that is set aside or thrown away, being abandoned
to utter destruction and no more cared for (cf. Hos. viii. 8,
together with Jer. xlviii. 38, and Jer. xxii. 28). With כִּי he
gives the ground for his comparison of himself to a household vessel that has become worthless. The insinuations
and slanders of many brand him as a transgressor, dread
surrounds him on every side (this is word for word the same
as in Jer. xx. 10, where the prophet, with whom in other
passages also מָגוֹר מִסָּבִיב is a frequent and standing formula,
under similar circumstances uses the language of the psalmist); when they come together to take counsel concerning him
(according to the accents the second half of the verse begins
with בְּהִוָּסְדָם), they think only how they may get rid of him.
If the construction of בְּ with its infinitive were intended to be

continued in ver. 14*d*, it would have been וְזָמְמוּ לָקַחַת נַפְשִׁי or
לָקַחַת נַפְשִׁי יָזְמוּ.

Vers. 15—19. But, although a curse of the world and
an offscouring of all people, he is confident in God, his Deliverer and Avenger. By וַאֲנִי prominence is given to the
subject by way of contrast, as in ver. 7. It appears as though
Jahve had given him up in His anger; but he confides in
Him, and in spite of this appearance, he even confides in
Him with the prayer of appropriating faith. עִתּוֹת or עִתִּים
(1 Chron. xxix. 30) are the appointed events and circumstances, the vicissitudes of human life; like the Arabic *'idât*
(like עֵת from וָעַד), the appointed rewards and punishments.
The times, with whatsoever they bring with them, are in the
Lord's hand, every lot is of His appointment or sending. The
Vulgate follows the LXX., *in manibus tuis sortes meæ*. The
petitions of vers. 16*b*, 17, spring from this consciousness that
the almighty and faithful hand of God has moulded his life.
There are three petitions; the middle one is an echo of the
Aaronitish blessing in Num. vi. 25. כִּי קְרָאתִיךָ, which gives
the ground of his hope that he shall not be put to shame
(cf. ver. 2), is to be understood like אָמַרְתִּי in ver. 15, according to Ges. § 126, 3. The expression of the ground for
אַל־אֵבוֹשָׁה, favours the explanation of it not so much as the
language of petition (let me not be ashamed) as of hope.
The futures which follow might be none the less regarded
as optatives, but the order of the words does not require
this. And we prefer to take them as expressing hope, so that
the three petitions in vers. 16, 17, correspond to the three
hopes in vers. 18, 19. He will not be ashamed, but the
wicked shall be ashamed and silenced for ever. The form
יִדְּמוּ, from דָּמַם, is, as in Jer. viii. 14, the plural of the *fut.*
Kal יִדֹּם, with the doubling of the first radical, which is
customary in Aramaic (other examples of which we have in
יִקֹּד, יִשֹּׁם, יִתֹּם), not of the *fut. Niph.* יִדַּם, the plural of which
would be יִדַּמּוּ, as in 1 Sam. ii. 9; *conticescere in orcum* is
equivalent to: to be silent, *i. e.* being made powerless to
fall a prey to hades. It is only in accordance with the connection, that in this instance נֶאֱלָם, ver. 19, just like דָּמַם, denotes
that which is forcibly laid upon them by the judicial intervention of God: all lying lips shall be dumb, *i. e.* made dumb.

עָתָק prop. that which is unrestrained, free, insolent (cf. Arabic ʿâtik, ʿatîk, unrestrained, free*) is the accusative of the
object, as in xciv. 4, and as it is the nominative of the subject in 1 Sam. ii. 3.

Vers. 20—25. In this part well-grounded hope expands
to triumphant certainty; and this breaks forth into grateful
praise of the goodness of God to His own, and an exhortation
to all to wait with steadfast faith on Jahve. The thought:
how gracious hath Jahve been to me, takes a more universal form in ver. 20. It is an exclamation (מָה, as in xxxvi. 8)
of adoring admiration. טוּב יהוה is the sum of the good which
God has treasured up for the constant and ever increasing
use and enjoyment of His saints. צָפַן is used in the same
sense as in xvii. 14; cf. τὸ μάννα τὸ κεκρυμμένον, Apoc. ii. 17.
Instead of פָּעַלְתָּ it ought strictly to be נָתַתָּ; for we can say
פָּעַל טוֹב, but not פָּעַל טוֹב. What is meant is, the doing or
manifesting of טוֹב springing from this טוּב, which is the
treasure of grace. Jahve thus makes Himself known to His
saints for the confounding of their enemies and in defiance
of all the world besides, xxiii. 5. He takes those who are His
under His protection from the רֻכְסֵי אִישׁ, confederations
of men (from רֹכֶם, رَكْس, magna copia), from the wrangling,
i. e. the slanderous scourging, of tongues. Elsewhere it is
said, that God hides one in סֵתֶר אֹהֲלוֹ (xxvii. 5), or in סֵתֶר
כְּנָפָיו (lxi. 5), or in His shadow (צֵל, xci. 1); in this passage
it is: in the defence and protection of His countenance, i. e.
in the region of the unapproachable light that emanates from
His presence. The סֻכָּה is the safe and comfortable protection of the Almighty which spans over the persecuted one
like an arbour of rich foliage. With בָּרוּךְ ה׳ David again
passes over to his own personal experience. The unity of
the Psalm requires us to refer the praise to the fact of the
deliverance which is anticipated by faith. Jahve has shewn
him wondrous favour, inasmuch as He has given him a עִיר
מָצוֹר as a place of abode. מָצוֹר, from צוּר to shut in (Arabic
misr with the denominative verb massara, to found a fortified
city), signifies both a siege, i. e. a shutting in by siege-

---

* But these Arabic words do not pass over into the signification
'insolent'.

works, and a fortifying (cf. lx. 11 with cviii. 11), *i. e.* a shutting in by fortified works against the attack of the enemy, 2 Chron. viii. 5. The fenced city is mostly interpreted as God Himself and His powerful and gracious protection. We might then compare Isa. xxxiii. 21 and other passages. But why may not an actual city be intended, viz. Ziklag? The fact, that after long and troublous days David there found a strong and sure resting-place, he here celebrates beforehand, and unconsciously prophetically, as a wondrous token of divine favour. To him Ziklag was indeed the turning-point between his degradation and exaltation. He had already said in his trepidation (חָפַז, *trepidare*), cf. cxvi. 11: I am cut away from the range of Thine eyes. נִגְרַזְתִּי is explained according to גַּרְזֶן, an axe; Lam. iii. 54, נִגְרַזְתִּי, and Jonah ii. 5, נִגְרַשְׁתִּי, favour this interpretation. He thought in his fear and despair, that God would never more care about him. אָכֵן, *verum enim vero*, but Jahve heard the cry of his entreaty, when he cried unto Him (the same words as in xxviii. 2). On the ground of these experiences he calls upon all the godly to love the God who has done such gracious things, *i. e.* to love Love itself. On the one hand, He preserves the faithful (אֱמוּנִים, from אָמוּן = אֵמוּן, πιστοί, as in xii. 2), who keep faith with Him, by also proving to them His faithfulness by protection in every danger; on the other hand, not scantily, but plentifully (עַל as in Isa. lx. 7, Jer. vi. 14: κατὰ περισσείαν) He rewardeth those that practise pride — in the sight of God, the Lord, the sin of sins. An animating appeal to the godly (metamorphosed out of the usual form of the expression חֲזַק יֶאֱמַץ, *macte esto*), resembling the animating call to his own heart in xxvii. 14, closes the Psalm. The godly and faithful are here called "those who wait upon Jahve". They are to wait patiently, for this waiting has a glorious end; the bright, spring sun at length breaks through the dark, angry aspect of the heavens, and the *esto mihi* is changed into *halleluja*. This eye of hope patiently directed towards Jahve is the characteristic of the Old Testament faith. The substantial unity, however, of the Old Testament order of grace, or mercy, with that of the New Testament, is set before us in Ps. xxxii.,

which, in its New Testament and Pauline character, is the
counterpart of Ps. xix.

PSALM XXXII.

THE WAY TO THE FORGIVENESS OF SINS.

1 BLESSED is he whose transgression is taken away,
    whose sin is covered.
2 Blessed is the man to whom Jahve doth not reckon ini-
    quity,
And in whose spirit there is no guile.

3 When I kept silence, my bones rotted
Through my constant groaning.
4 For day and night Thy hand was heavy upon me,
My moisture was changed with the drought of summer.
    (*Sela*)
5 I acknowledged my sin unto Thee and did not cover my
    guilt;
I said: "I will confess my transgressions unto Jahve" —
And Thou, Thou hast taken away the guilt of my sin.
    (*Sela*)

6 For this cause let every godly man pray unto Thee in
    a time when Thou mayest be found;
Surely, when the great waters rise —
They shall not reach him.
7 Thou art my hiding-place, from trouble Thou wilt
    guard me,
With songs of deliverance wilt Thou compass me about.
    (*Sela*)

8 I will instruct thee and teach thee concerning the way
    thou shalt go.
I will give counsel, keeping mine eye upon thee.
9 Be ye not as horses, as mules without understanding,
With bit and bridle is their mouth to be curbed,
Otherwise they will not come near unto thee.

10 Many sorrows are to the ungodly,
　　But whoso trusteth in Jahve, with favour doth He com-
　　　　pass him about.

11 Be glad in Jahve, and rejoice, ye righteous,
　　And shout for joy all ye that are upright in heart!

There are several prominent marks by which this Psalm is coupled with the preceding (*vid. Symbolæ* § 52). In both Psalms, with the word אָמַרְתִּי, the psalmist looks back upon some fact of his spiritual life; and both close with an exhortation to the godly, which stands in the relation of a general inference to the whole Psalm. But in other respects the two Psalms differ. For Ps. xxxi. is a prayer under circumstances of outward distress, and Ps. xxxii. is a didactic Psalm, concerning the way of penitence which leads to the forgiveness of sins; it is the second of the seven *Psalmi pœnitentiales* of the church, and Augustine's favourite Psalm. We might take Augustine's words as its motto: *intelligentia prima est ut te noris peccatorem.* The poet bases it upon his own personal experience, and then applies the general teaching which he deduces from it, to each individual in the church of God. For a whole year after his adultery David was like one under sentence of condemnation. In the midst of this fearful anguish of soul he composed Ps. li., whereas Ps. xxxii. was composed after his deliverance from this state of mind. The former was written in the very midst of the penitential struggle; the latter after he had recovered his inward peace. The theme of this Psalm is the precious treasure which he brought up out of that abyss of spiritual distress, viz. the doctrine of the blessedness of forgiveness, the sincere and unreserved confession of sin as the way to it, and the protection of God in every danger, together with joy in God, as its fruits.

In the signification *psalmus dīdascalicus s. informatorius* (Reuchlin: *ut si liceret dicere intellectificum vel resipiscentificum*), מַשְׂכִּיל would after all be as appropriate a designation as we could have for this Psalm which teaches the way of salvation. This meaning, however, cannot be sustained. It is improbable that מַשְׂכִּיל, which, in all other instances, signifies *intelligens,* should, as a technical term, mean *intelligentem faciens;* because the *Hiph.* הִשְׂכִּיל, in the causative meaning "to impart understanding", occurs only in solitary instances (ver. 8, Prov. xxi. 11) in the Hebrew of the period before the Exile, and only came into common use in the later language (in Daniel, Chronicles, and Nehemiah). But, that which is decisive against the meaning "a didactic poem" is the fact, that among the thirteen Psalms which are inscribed מַשְׂכִּיל, there are only two (xxxii. and lxxviii.) which can be regarded as didactic poems. Ps. xlv. is called, in addition, שִׁיר יְדִדֹת, and Ps. cxlii., תְּפִלָּה, two names which ill accord with a didactic intention and plan. Even Ps. xlvii. 8, a passage of importance in the determining of the right idea of the word, in which מַשְׂכִּיל occurs as an accusative of the object, excludes the meaning "didactic poem". Ewald observes (*Dichter des Alten Bundes*, i, 31) that "in Ps. xlvii. 8 we have the safest guide to the correct meaning of the word; in this passage מַשְׂכִּיל stands side by side with זַמֵּר as a more exact definition of the singing and there can be no doubt, that an *intelligent,* melodious song must be equivalent to a *choice* or *delicate*, skillfully composed song". But in all other cases, מַשְׂכִּיל is only found as an attribute of persons, because it is not that which makes prudent, but that which is in itself intelligent, that is so named. Even in 2 Chron. xxx. 22, where allusion is made to the *Maskîl* Psalms, it is the Levite musicians themselves who are called (שֵׂכֶל טוֹב) הַמַּשְׂכִּילִים (*i. e.* those who play skillfully with delicate tact). Thus then we are driven to the Hiphil meaning of pensive meditation in cvi. 7, cf. xli. 2, Prov. xvi. 20; so that מַשְׂכִּיל signifies that which meditates, then meditation, just like מַכְבִּיר, that which multiplies, and then fulness; מַשְׁחִית, that which destroys, and then destruction. From the *Maskîl* Psalms, as *e. g.* from liv. and cxlii., we cannot discover anything special as to the technical meaning or use of the word. The word means just *pia meditatio*, a devout meditation, and nothing more.

Vers. 1—2. The Psalm begins with the celebration of the happiness of the man who experiences God's justifying grace, when he gives himself up unreservedly to Him. Sin is called פֶּשַׁע, as being a breaking loose or tearing away from God; חֲטָאָה, as a deviation from that which is well-pleasing to God; עָוֹן, as a perversion, distortion, misdeed. The forgiveness of sin is styled נָשָׂא (Exod. xxxiv. 7), as a lifting up and taking away, αἴρειν and ἀφαιρεῖν, Exod. xxxiv. 7; כִּסָּה (lxxxv. 3, Prov. x. 12, Neh. iii. 37), as a covering, so that it becomes invisible to God, the Holy One, and is as though it had never taken place; לֹא חָשַׁב (2 Sam. xix. 20, cf. حسب, to number, reckon, οὐ λογίζεσθαι, Rom. iv. 6—9), as a non-imputing; the δικαιοσύνη χωρὶς ἔργων is here distinctly expressed. The justified one is called נְשׂוּי־פֶּשַׁע, as being one who is exempted from transgression, *prævaricatione levatus* (Ges. § 135, 1); נְשׂוּי, instead of נָשָׂא, Isa. xxxiii. 24, is intended to rhyme with כְּסוּי (which is the *part.* to כִּסָּה, just as בָּרוּךְ is the participle to בֵּרַךְ); *vid.* on Isa. xxii. 13. One "covered of sin" is one over whose sin lies the covering of expiation (כִּפֶּר, root כף, to cover, cogn. غفر, غمر, خمر, خفر) before the holy eyes of God. The third designation is an attributive clause: "to whom Jahve doth not reckon misdeed", inasmuch as He, on the contrary, regards it as discharged or as settled. He who is thus justified, however, is only he in whose spirit there is no רְמִיָּה, no deceit, which denies and hides, or extenuates and excuses, this or that favourite sin. One such sin designedly retained is a secret ban, which stands in the way of justification.

Vers. 3—5. For, as his own experience has taught the poet, he who does not in confession pour out all his corruption before God, only tortures himself until he unburdens himself of his secret curse. Since ver. 3 by itself cannot be regarded as the reason for the proposition just laid down, כִּי signifies either "because, *quod*" (*e. g.* Prov. xxii. 22) or "when, *quum*" (Judges xvi. 16, Hos. xi. 1). The שְׁאָגָה was an outburst of the tortures which his accusing conscience prepared for him. The more he strove against confessing, the louder did conscience speak; and while it was not in his power to silence this inward voice, in which the wrath of God found utterance, he cried the whole day, viz. for help; but while his heart was still unbroken, he cried yet received no answer. He cried all day long, for God's punishing right hand (xxxviii. 3, xxxix. 11) lay heavy upon him day and night; the feeling of divine wrath left him no rest, cf. Job xxxiii. 14 sqq. A fire burned within him which threatened completely to devour him. The expression is בְּחַרְבֹנֵי (like בעשן in xxxvii. 20, cii. 4), without כ, inasmuch as the fears which burn fiercely within him even to his heart and, as it were, scorch him up, he directly calls the droughts of summer. The בְּ is the *Beth* of the state or condition, in connection with which the change, *i. e.* degeneration (Job xx. 14), took place; for *mutare in aliquid* is expressed by הָפַךְ לְ. The לְ (which Saadia and other have mistaken) in לְשַׁדִּי is part of the root; לָשָׁד (from לָשַׁד, لسد, to suck), inflected after the analogy of גָּמָל and the like, signifies *succus*. In the summer-heat of anxiety his vital moisture underwent a change: it burned and dried up. Here the music becomes louder and does its part in depicting these torments of the awakened conscience in connecuion with a heart that still remains un-broken. In spite of this διάψαλμα, however, the historical connection still retains sufficient intluence to give אוֹדִיעֲךָ the force of the imperfect (cf. xxx. 9): "I made known my sin and my guilt did I not cover up (כִּסָּה used here as in Prov. xxviii. 13, Job xxxi. 33); I made the resolve: I will confess my transgressions to the Lord (הוֹדָה = הִתְוַדָּה, Neh. i. 6, ix. 2; elsewhere construed with the accusative, *vid.* Prov. xxviii. 13) — then Thou forgavest", etc. Hupfeld is inclined to place אמרתי before חטאתי אודיעך, by which אודיעך and אודה would become futures; but וַעֲוֹנִי לא כסיתי sounds like an assertion of a fact, not the statement of an intention, and וְאַתָּה נָשָׂאתָ is the natural continuation of the אמרתי which immediately precedes. The form וְאַתָּה נָשָׂאתָ is designedly used instead of וַתִּשָּׂא. Simultaneously with his confession of sin, made *fide supplice,* came also the absolution: then Thou forgavest the guilt (עָוֹן, misdeed, as a deed and also as a matter of fact, *i. e.* guilt contracted, and penance or punishment, cf. Lam. iv. 6, Zech. xiv. 19) of my sin. *Vox nondum est in ore,* says Augustine, *et vulnus sanatur in corde.* The סלה here is the antithesis of the former one. There we have a shrill lament over the sinner who tortures himself in vain, here the clear tones of joy at the blessed experience of one who pours forth his soul to God — a musical Yea and Amen to the great truth of justifying grace.

Vers. 6—7. For this mercy, which is provided for every sinner who repents and confesses his sin, let then, every חָסִיד, who longs for חֶסֶד, turn in prayer to Jahve לְעֵת מְצֹא, at the time (xxi. 10, 1 Chron. xii. 22; cf. בְּעֵת, Isa. xlix. 8) when He, and His mercy, is to be found (cf. Deut. iv. 29 with Jer. xxix. 13, Isa. lv. 6, בְּהִמָּצְאוֹ). This hortatory wish is followed by a promissory assurance. The fact of לְשֵׁטֶף מַיִם רַבִּים being virtually a protasis: *quum inundant aquæ magnæ* (לְ of the time), which separates רַק from אֵלָיו, prohibits our regarding רק as belonging to אֵלָיו in this instance, although like אַף, אַךְ, גַּם, and כֵּן, רַק is also placed *per hypallage* at the head of the clause (as in Prov. xiii. 10: with pride there is only contention), even when belonging to a part of the clause that follows further on. The restrictive meaning of רק here, as is frequently the case (Deut. iv. 6, Judges xiv. 16, 1 Kings xxi. 25, cf. Ps. xci. 8), has passed over to the affirmative: *certo quum,* etc. Inundation or flooding is an exemplificative description of the divine judgment (cf. Nah. i. 8); ver. 6*bc* is a brief form of expressing the promise which is expanded in Ps. xci. In ver. 7, David confirms it from his own experience. The assonance in מֵצַר תִּצְּרֵנִי (Thou wilt preserve me, so that צַר, *angustum* = *angustiæ*, does not come upon me, cxix. 143) is not undesigned; and after תצרני comes רני, just like כלו after בהיכלו in xxix. 9. There is no sufficient ground for setting aside רני, with Houbigant and others, as a repetition of the half of the word תצרני. The infinitive רֹן (Job xxxviii. 7) might, like רֹב, *plur.* רִבֵּי, חֹק, *plur.* חֻקֵּי, with equal right be inflected as a substantive; and פַּלֵּט (as in lvi. 8), which is likewise treated as a substantive, cf. נַפֵּץ, Dan. xii. 7, presents, as a genitive, no more difficulty than does דַּעַת in the expression אִישׁ דַּעַת. With songs of deliverance doth Jahve surround him, so that they encompass him on all sides, and an occasion of exulting meets him in whatever direction he turns. The music here again for the third time becomes *forte,* and that to express the highest feeling of delight.

Vers. 8—10. It is not Jahve, who here speaks in answer to the words that have been thus far addressed to Him. In this case the person addressed must be the poet, who, however, has already attained the knowledge here treated of.

It is he himself who now directly adopts the tone of the teacher (cf. xxxiv. 12). That which David, in Ps. li. 15, promises to do, he here takes in hand, viz. the instruction of sinners in the way of salvation. It is unnecessary to read אִיעָצֵךְ instead of אִיעֲצָה, as Olshausen does; the suffix of אַשְׂכִּילְךָ and אוֹרְךָ (for אֹרְךָ) avails also for this third verb, to which עָלֶיךָ עֵינִי, equivalent to שָׂם עָלֶיךָ עֵינִי עֵינִי (fixing my eye upon thee, *i. e.* with sympathising love taking an interest in thee), stands in the relation of a subordinate relative clause. The LXX. renders it by ἐπιστηριῶ ἐπὶ σὲ τοὺς ὀφθαλμούς μου, so that it takes יָעַץ, in accordance with its radical signification *firmare*, as the *regens* of עֵינִי (I will fix my eye steadfastly upon thee); but for this there is no support in the general usage of the language. The accents give a still different rendering; they apparently make עֵינִי an *accus. adverb.* (since איעֲצָה עָלֶיךָ עֵינִי is transformed from (אִיעֲצָה עָלֶיךָ עֵינִי: I will counsel thee with mine eye; but in every other instance, יָעַץ עַל means only a hostile determination against any one, *e. g.* Isa. vii. 5. The form of address, without changing its object, passes over, in ver. 9, into the plural and the expression becomes harsh in perfect keeping with the perverted character which it describes. The sense is on the whole clear: not constrained, but willing obedience is becoming to man, in distinction from an irrational animal which must be led by a bridle drawn through its mouth. The asyndeton clause: like a horse, a mule (פֶּרֶד as an animal that is isolated and does not pair;

cf. فَرْد alone of its kind, single, unlike, the opposite of which is زَوْج, a pair, equal number), has nothing remarkable about it, cf. xxxv. 14, Isa. xxxviii. 14. But it is not clear what עֶדְיוֹ is intended to mean. We might take it in its usual signification "ornament", and render "with bit and bridle, its ornament", and perhaps at once recognise therein an allusion to the senseless servility of the animal, viz. that its ornament is also the means by which it is kept in check, unless עֲדִי, ornament, is perhaps directly equivalent to "harness". Still the rendering of the LXX. is to be respected: *in camo et fræno* — as Jerome reproduces it — *maxillas eorum constringere qui non approximant ad te.* If עֲדִי means jaw, mouth or cheek, then עֶדְיוֹ לִבְלוֹם is equivalent to *ora eorum obturanda sunt* (Ges. § 132, rem. 1), which the LXX. expresses by ἄγξαι, *constringe*, or, following the *Cod. Alex.*, ἄγξις (ἄγξεις), *constringes*. Like Ewald and Hitzig (on Ezek. xvi. 7), we may compare with עֶדְי, the cheek, the Arabic خَلّ, which, being connected with גְּדוּד, a furrow, signifies properly the furrow of the face, *i. e.* the indented part running downwards from the inner corners of the eyes to both sides of the nose, but then by synecdoche the cheek. If עֶדְיו refers to the mouth or jaws, then it looks as if בַּל קְרֹב אֵלֶיךָ must be translated: in order that they may not come too near thee, viz. to hurt thee (Targ., Syriac, Rashi, etc.); but this rendering does not produce any point of comparison corresponding to the context of this Psalm. Therefore, it is rather to be rendered: otherwise there is no coming near to thee. This interpretation takes the emphasis of the בל into account, and assumes that, according to a usage of the language that is without further support, one might, for instance, say: בַּל לֶכְתִּי שָׁמָּה, "I will never go thither." In Prov. xxiii. 17, בל also includes within itself the verb to be. So here: by no means an approaching to thee, *i. e.* there is, if thou dost not bridle them, no approaching or coming near to thee. These words are not addressed to God, but to man, who is obliged to use harsh and forcible means in taming animals, and can only thus keep them under his control and near to him. In the antitype, it is the sinner, who will not come to God, although God only is his help, and who, as David has learned by experience, must first of all endure inward torture, before he comes to a right state of mind. This agonising life of the guilty conscience which the ungodly man leads, is contrasted in ver. 10 with the mercy which encompasses on all sides him, who trusts in God. רַבִּים, in accordance with the treatment of this adjective as if it were a numeral (*vid.* lxxxix. 51), is an attributive or adjective placed before its noun. The final clause might be rendered: mercy encompasses him; but the *Poel* and ver. 7 favour the rendering: with mercy doth He encompass him.

Ver. 11. After the doctrine of the Psalm has been unfolded in three unequal groups of verses, there follows, corresponding to the brief introduction, a still shorter close, which calls upon those whose happy state is there celebrated, to join in songs of exultant joy.

PSALM XXXIII.

PRAISE OF THE RULER OF THE WORLD AS BEING THE DEFENDER OF HIS PEOPLE.

1 SHOUT for joy, O ye righteous, in Jahve,
  For the upright praise is comely.
2 Praise Jahve with cithern,
  With a ten-stringed nabla play unto Him.
3 Sing unto Him a new song,
  Play merrily with a joyful noise.

4 For upright is the word of Jahve,
  And all His working is in faithfulness.
5 He loveth righteousness and judgment;
  The earth is full of the mercy of Jahve.

6 By the word of Jahve were the heavens made,
  And by the breath of His mouth all their host.
7 He gathereth the waters of the sea together as a heap,
  He layeth up the depths in storehouses.

8 Let all the earth fear before Jahve,
  Let all the inhabitants of the world stand in awe of
     Him.
9 For He spake, and it was done;
  He commanded, and it stood fast.

10 Jahve hath brought the counsel of the heathen to nought,
  He hath made the thoughts of the people of none effect.
11 The counsel of Jahve standeth for ever,
  The thoughts of His heart to all generations.

12 Blessed is the nation whose God is Jahve,
  The people whom He chooseth for His own inheritance.

13 From heaven Jahve looketh down,
   He seeth all the children of men.

14 From the place of His habitation He looketh
   Upon all the inhabitants of the earth,
15 He, who fashioneth their heart together,
   Who considereth all their works.

16 A king doth not triumph by great strength,
   A mighty man is not delivered by great power.
17 A vain thing is a horse for victory,
   And its great strength cannot deliver.

18 Behold, the eye of Jahve is upon them that fear Him,
   Upon them that hope in His mercy,
1ꞌ To deliver their soul from death,
   And to keep them alive in famine.

20 Our soul waiteth for Jahve,
   Our help and our shield is He.
21 For in Him shall our heart rejoice,
   Because we trust in His holy Name
22 Let, then, Thy mercy, O Jahve, be upon us,
   According as we hope in Thee!

The Davidic Maskîl, Ps. xxxii., is followed by an anonymous congregational song of a hymnic character, which begins just like the former closes. It owes its composition apparently to some deliverance of the nation from heathen oppression, which had resulted from God's interposition and without war. Moreover it exhibits no trace of dependence upon earlier models, such as might compel us to assign a late date to it; the time of Jeremiah, for instance, which Hitzig adopts. The structure is symmetrical. Between the two hexastichs, vers. 1—3, 20—22, the *materia laudis* is set forth in eight tetrastichs.

Vers. 1—3. The call contained in this hexastich is addressed to the righteous and upright, who earnestly seek to live a godly and God-pleasing life, and the sole determining rule of whose conduct is the will and good pleasure of God. These alone know God, whose true nature finds in them a clear mirror; so on their part they are joyfully to confess what they possess in Him. For it is their duty, and at the same time their honour, to praise him, and make their boast in Him. נָאוָה is the feminine of the adjective נָאֶה (formed out of נַאֲוִי), as in cxlvii. 1, cf. Prov. xix. 10. On כִּנּוֹר (LXX. κιθάρα, κινύρα) and נֶבֶל (LXX. ψαλτήριον, νάβλα, ναῦλα, etc.) vid. Introduction § II. נֶבֶל is the name given to the harp or lyre on account of its resemblance to a skin bottle or flask (root נב, to swell, to be distended), and נֵבֶל עָשׂוֹר, "harp of the decade", is the ten-stringed harp, which is also called absolutely עָשׂוֹר, and distinguished from the customary נֶבֶל, in xcii. 4. By a comparison of the asyndeton expressions in xxxv. 14, Jer. xi. 19, Aben-Ezra understands by נבל עשור twoinstruments, contrary to the tenour of the words. Gecatilia, whom he controverts, is only so far in error as that he refers the ten to holes (נקבים) instead of to strings. The בְּ is *Beth instrum.*, just like the expression κιθαρίζειν ἐν κιθάραις, Apoc. xiv. 2. A "new song" is one which, in consequence of some new mighty deeds of God, comes from a new impulse of gratitude in the heart, xl. 4, and frequently in the Psalms, Isa. xlii. 10, Judith vi. 13, Apoc. v. 9. In הֵיטִיבוּ the notions of *scite* and *strenue*, *suaviter* and *naviter,* blend. With בִּתְרוּעָה, referring back to רננו, the call to praise forms, as it were, a circle as it closes.

Vers. 4—5. Now begins the body of the song. The summons to praise God is supported (1) by a setting forth of His praiseworthiness* (*a*) as the God of revelation in the kingdom of Grace. His word is יָשָׁר, upright in intention, and, without becoming in any way whatever untrue to itself, straightway fulfilling itself. His every act is an act in אֱמוּנָה, truth, which verifies the truth of His word, and one which accomplishes itself. On אָהֵב, equivalent to אָהֵב הוּא, *vid.* vii. 10, xxii. 29. צְדָקָה is righteousness as

---

* We have adopted the word "praiseworthiness" for the sake of conciseness of expression, in order to avoid an awkward periphrasis, in the sense of being worthy to be praised. — TR.

conduct; מִשְׁפָּט is right as a rule of judgment and a state
or condition. חֶסֶד is an accusative, as in cxix. 64: *miseri-
cordiâ Domini plena est terra* (the introit for Misercordias
Sunday or the second Sunday after Easter).

Vers. 6—9. God's praiseworthiness (*b*) as the Creator
of the world in the kingdom of Nature. Jahve's דְּבַר is
His almighty "Let there be"; and רוּחַ פִּיו (inasmuch as
the breath is here regarded as the material of which the
word is formed and the bearer of the word) is the command,
or in general, the operation of His commanding omnipotence
(Job xv. 30, cf. iv. 9; Isa. xxxiv. 16, cf. xi. 4). The heavens
above and the waters beneath stand side by side as miracles
of creation. The display of His power in the waters of the
sea consists in His having confined them within fixed bounds
and keeping them within these. נֵד is a pile, *i. e.* a piled up
heap (Arabic *nadd*), and more especially in reference to
harvest: like such a heap do the convex waters of the sea,
being firmly held together, rise above the level of the con-
tinents. The expression is like that in Josh. iii. 13, 16, cf.
Exod. xv. 8; although there the reference is to a miracle
occurring in the course of history, and in this passage to a
miracle of creation. כְּנֵס refers to the heap itself, not to the
walls of the storehouses as holding together. This latter
figure is not introduced until ver. 7*b*: the bed of the sea
and those of the rivers are, as it were, אוֹצָרוֹת, treasuries or
storehouses, in which God has deposited the deep, foaming
waves or surging mass of waters. The inhabitants (יֹשְׁבֵי, not
יוֹשְׁבֵי) of the earth have cause to fear God who is thus omnipotent (מִן, in the sense of falling back *from* in terror); for
He need only speak the word and that which He wills comes
into being out of nothing, as we see from the hexaëmeron
or history of Creation, but which is also confirmed in human
history (Lam. iii. 37). He need only command and it stands
forth like an obedient servant, that appears in all haste at
the call of his lord, cxix. 91.

Vers. 10—11. His praiseworthiness (*c*) as the irresistible
Ruler in the history of men. Since in 2 Sam. xv. 34, xvii.
14, and frequently, הֵפֵר עֵצָה is a common phrase, therefore
הֵפִיר as in lxxxix. 34, Ezek. xvii. 19, is equivalent to הֵפֵר
(Ges. § 67, rem. 9). The perfects are not used in the abstract,

but of that which has been experienced most recently, since
the "new song" presupposes new matter. With ver. 11 compare Prov. xix. 21. The עֵצַת of God is the unity of the
"thoughts of His heart," *i. e.* of the ideas, which form the
inmost part, the ultimate motives of everything that takes
place. The whole history of the world is the uninterrupted
carrying out of a divine plan of salvation, the primary
object of which is His people, but in and with these are
included humanity at large.

Vers. 12—19. Hence the call to praise God is supported
(2) by a setting forth of that which His people possess in
Him. This portion of the song is like a paraphrase of the
אַשְׁרֵי in Deut. xxxiii. 29. The theme in ver. 12 is proved in
vers. 13—15 by the fact, that Jahve is the omniscient Ruler,
because He is the Creator of men, without whose knowledge
nothing is undertaken either secretly or openly, and especially
if against His people. Then in vers. 16—19 it is supported
by the fact, that His people have in Jahve a stronger defence
than the greatest worldly power would be. Jahve is called
the fashioner of all the hearts of men, as in Zech. xii. 1, cf.
Prov. xxiv. 12, as being their Maker. As such He is also
the observer of all the works of men; for He is acquainted
with their origin in the laboratory of the heart, which He
as Creator has formed. Hupfeld takes יַחַד as an equalisation
(*pariter ac*) of the two appositions; but then it ought to be
וּמֵבִין (cf. xlix. 3, 11). The LXX. correctly renders it κατα-
μόνας, *singillatim*. It is also needless to translate it, as Hupfeld does: He who formed, *qui finxit*; for the hearts of men
were not from the very first created all at one time, but the
primeval impartation of spirit-life is continued at every birth
in some mysterious way. God is the Father of spirits, Hebr.
xii. 9. For this very reason everything that exists, even to
the most hidden thing, is encompassed by His omniscience
and omnipotence. He exercises an omniscient control over
all things, and makes all things subservient to the designs
of His plan of the universe, which, so far as His people are
concerned, is the plan of salvation. Without Him nothing
comes to pass; but through Him everything takes place.
The victory of the king, and the safety of the warrior, are
not their own works. Their great military power and bodily

strength can accomplish nothing without God, who can also
be mighty in the feeble. Even for purposes of victory
(תְּשׁוּעָה, cf. יְשׁוּעָה, xxi. 2) the war-horse is שֶׁקֶר, *i. e.* a thing
that promises much, but can in reality do nothing; it is not
its great strength, by which it enables the trooper to escape
(יְמַלֵּט). "The horse", says Solomon in Prov. xxi. 31, "is equipped for the day of battle, but לה׳ הַתְּשׁוּעָה, Jahve's is the victory", He giveth it to whomsoever He will. The ultimate
ends of all things that come to pass are in His hands, and —
as vers. 18 sq. say, directing special attention to this important truth by הִנֵּה — the eye of this God, that is to say the
final aim of His government of the world, is directed towards
them that fear Him, is pointed at them that hope in His
mercy (לַמְיַחֲלִים). In ver. 19, the object, לְחַסְדּוֹ, is expanded
by way of example. From His mercy or loving-kindness,
not from any acts of their own, conscious of their limited
condition and feebleness, they look for protection in the
midst of the greatest peril, and for the preservation of their
life in famine. Ps. xx. 8 is very similar; but the one passage
sounds as independent as the other.

Vers. 20—22. Accordingly, in this closing hexastich,
the church acknowledges Him as its help, its shield, and
its source of joy. Besides the passage before us, חִכָּה occurs
in only one other instance in the Psalter, viz. cvi. 13. This
word, which belongs to the group of words signifying hoping
and waiting, is perhaps from the root חכ (حكى، حكأ،
firmiter constringere sc. *nodum*), to be firm, compact, like קַוֶּה
from קָוָה, to pull tight or fast, cf. the German *harren* (to
wait) and *hart* (hard, compact). In ver. 20*b* we still hear the
echo of the primary passage Deut. xxxiii. 29 (cf. ver. 26).
The emphasis, as in cxv. 9—11, rests upon הוּא, into which
בּוֹ, in ver. 21, puts this thought, viz. He is the unlimited
sphere, the inexhaustible matter, the perennial spring of
our joy. The second כִּי confirms this subjectively. His holy
Name is His church's ground of faith, of love, and of hope;
for from thence comes its salvation. It can boldly pray
that the mercy of the Lord may be upon it, for it waits
upon Him, and man's waiting or hoping and God's giving
are reciprocally conditioned. This is the meaning of the

כַּאֲשֶׁר. God is true to His word. The *Te Deum laudamus*
of Ambrose closes in the same way.

PSALM XXXIV.

THANKSGIVING AND TEACHING OF ONE WHO HAS EXPERIENCED DELIVERANCE.

2 א I WILL bless Jahve at all times,
    Continually let His praise be in my mouth.

3 ב In Jahve shall my soul make her boast,
    The patient shall hear thereof and be glad.

4 ג O magnify Jahve with me,
    And let us exalt His name together.

5 ד I sought Jahve, and He answered me,
    And out of all my fears did He deliver me.

6 ה Looking unto Him they are lightened,
    And their faces shall not be ashamed.

7 ז This afflicted one cried, and Jahve heard,
    And saved him out of all his troubles.

8 ח The Angel of Jahve encampeth round about them that
       fear Him,
    And delivereth them.

9 ט Taste and see, that Jahve is good —
    Blessed is the man that trusteth in Him.

10 י Fear Jahve, ye His saints!
    For there is no want to them that fear Him.

11 כ Young lions do lack and suffer hunger,
    But they that seek Jahve do not want any good thing.

12 ל Come, ye children, hearken unto me!
    The fear of Jahve will I teach you.

13 מ Whosoever thou art, dost thou desire long life,
    Dost thou love days that thou mayst see good —:

14 נ Keep thy tongue from evil,
    And thy lips from deceitful speaking.

15 ס Depart from evil and do good,
    Seek peace, and pursue it.

16 ע The eyes of Jahve observe the righteous,
    And His ears their cry.

17 פ The face of Jahve is against the evil doers,
    To cut off their remembrance from the earth.
18 צ The former cry unto Jahve, and He heareth,
    And out of all their troubles He delivereth them.
19 ק Jahve is nigh unto them that are of a broken heart,
    And saveth such as be of a contrite spirit.
20 ר Many are the afflictions of the righteous,
    But out of them all doth Jahve deliver him.
21 ש He preserveth all his bones,
    Not one of them is broken.
22 ת Evil shall slay the wicked,
    And they that hate the righteous shall be punished.
23 פ Jahve redeemeth the soul of His servant,
    And they shall not be punished who trust in Him.

In Ps. xxxiii. 18 we heard the words, *"Behold, the eye of Jahve is directed towards them that fear Him"*, and in xxxiv. 16 we hear this same grand thought, *"the eyes of Jahve are directed towards the righteous"*. Ps. xxxiv. is one of the eight Psalms which are assigned, by their inscriptions, to the time of David's persecution by Saul, and were composed upon that weary way of suffering extending from Gibea of Saul to Ziklag. (The following is an approximation to their chronological order: vii., lix., lvi., xxxiv., lii., lvii., cxlii., liv.). The inscription runs: *Of David, when he disguised his understanding* (טַעְמוֹ with *Dag.*, lest it should be pronounced טַעֲמוֹ) *before Abimelech, and he drove him away* (וַיְגָרֲשֵׁהוּ, with *Chateph Pathach*, as is always the case with verbs whose second radical is ר, if the accent is on the third radical) *and he departed.* David, being pressed by Saul, fled into the territory of the Philistines; here he was recognised as the man who had proved such a dangerous enemy to them years since and he was brought before Achish, the king. Ps. lvi. is a prayer which implores help in the trouble of this period (and its relation to Ps. xxiv. resembles that of Ps. li. to xxxii.). David's life would have been lost had not his desperate attempt to escape by playing the part of a madman been successful. The king commanded him to depart, and David betook himself to a place of concealment in his own country, viz. the cave of Adullam in the wilderness of Judah.

The correctness of the inscription has been disputed.
Hupfeld maintains that the writer has blindly taken it from
1 Sam. xxi. 14. According to Redslob, Hitzig, Olshausen,
and Stähelin, he had reasons for so doing, although they
are invalid. The טַעֲמוּ of the Psalm (ver. 9) seemed to him
to accord with טַעְמוֹ, 1 Sam. xxi. 14; and in addition to this,
he combined תִּתְהַלֵּל, *gloriaris,* of the Psalm (ver. 3) with
וַיִּתְהֹלָל, *insanivit,* 1 Sam. xxi 14. We come to a different conclusion. The Psalm does not contain any express reference
to that incident in Philistia, hence we infer that the writer
of the inscription knew of this reference from tradition. His
source of information is not the Books of Samuel; for there
the king is called אָכִישׁ, whereas he calls him אֲבִימֶלֶךְ, and
this, as even Basil has perceived (*vid.* Euthymius Zigadenus'
introduction to this Psalm), is the title of the Philistine kings,
just as *Pharaoh* is title of the Egyptian, *Agag* of the Ama-
lekite, and *Lucumo* of the Etruscan kings. His source of
information, as a comparison of 2 Sam. xxii. 1 with Ps.
xviii. 1 shews, is a different work, viz. the Annals of David,
in which he has traced the Psalm before us and other Psalms
to their historical connection, and then indicated it by an
inscription in words taken from that source. The fact of
the Psalm being alphabetical says nothing against David as
its author (*vid.* on Ps. ix.—x.). It is not arranged for music; for although it begins after the manner of a song of
praise, it soon passes into the didactic tone. It consists of
verses of two lines, which follow one another according to
the order of the letters of the alphabet. The ו is wanting,
just as the נ is wanting in Ps. cxlv.; and after ת, as in Ps.
xxv., which is the counterpart to xxxiv., follows a second
supernumerary פ.

Vers. 2—4. The poet begins with the praise of Jahve,
and calls upon all the pious to unite with him in praising
Him. The substantival clause ver. 2*b*, is intended to have
just as much the force of a cohortative as the verbal clause
ver. 2*a*. אֲבָרְכָה, like וִיגָרְשֻׁהוּ, is to be written with *Chateph-
Pathach* in the middle syllable. In distinction from עֲנִיִּים,
afflicti, עֲנָוִים signifies *submissi,* those who have learnt endurance or patience in the school of affliction. The praise of

the psalmist will greatly help to strengthen and encourage such; for it applies to the Deliverer of the oppressed. But in order that this praise may sound forth with strength and fulness of tone, he courts the assistance of companions in ver. 4. To acknowledge the divine greatness with the utterance of praise is expressed by גִּדֵּל with an accusative in lxix. 31; in this instance with לְ: to offer גְּדֻלָּה unto Him, cf. xxix. 2. Even רוֹמֵם has this subjective meaning: with the heart and in word and deed, to place the exalted Name of God as high as it really is in itself. In accordance with the rule, that when in any word two of the same letters follow one another and the first has a *Sh⁰bâ*, this *Sh⁰bâ* must be an audible one, and in fact *Chateph Pathach* preceded by *Gaja* (*Metheg*), we must write וּנְרוֹמֲמָה.

Vers. 5—7. The poet now gives the reason for this praise by setting forth the deliverance he has experienced. He longed for God and took pains to find Him (such is the meaning of דָּרַשׁ in distinction from בִּקֵּשׁ), and this striving, which took the form of prayer, did not remain without some actual answer (עָנָה is used of the being heard and the fulfilment as an answer to the petition of the praying one). The perfects, as also in vers. 6, 7, describe facts, one of which did not take place without the other; whereas וַיַּעֲנֵנִי would give them the relation of antecedent and consequent. In ver. 6, his own personal experience is generalised into an experimental truth, expressed in the historical form: they look unto Him and brighten up, *i. e.* whosoever looketh unto Him (הִבִּיט אֶל of a look of intense yearning, eager for salvation, as in Num. xxi. 9, Zech. xii. 10) brightens up. It is impracticable to make the עֲנָוִים from ver. 3 the subject; it is an act and the experience that immediately accompanies it, that is expressed with an universal subject and in gnomical perfects. The verb נָהַר, here as in Isa. lx. 5, has the signification to shine, glitter (whence נְהָרָה, light). Theodoret renders it: Ὁ μετὰ πίστεως τῷ θεῷ προσιὼν φωτὸς ἀκτῖνας δέχεται νοεροῦ, the gracious countenance of God is reflected on their faces; to the *actus directus* of *fides supplex* succeeds the *actus reflexus* of *fides triumphans*. It never comes to pass that their countenances must be covered with shame on account of disappointed hope: this shall not and cannot be, as the sympathetic force of אֶל implies. In all the three dialects חָפֵר (חָפַר) has the signification of being ashamed and scared; according to Gesenius and Fürst (root פר) it proceeds from the primary signification of reddening, blushing; in reality, however, since it is to be combined, not with حمر, but with خمر (cf. غمر, غفر, كفر, כפר), it proceeds from the primary signification of covering, hiding, veiling (Arabic *chafira*, *tachaffara*, used of a woman, cf. *chamara*, to be ashamed, to blush, to be modest, used of both sexes), so that consequently the shame-covered countenance is contrasted with that which has a bright, bold, and free look. In ver. 7, this general truth is again individualised. By זֶה עָנִי (like זֶה סִינַי in lxviii. 9) David points to himself. From the great peril in which he was placed at the court of the Philistines, from which God has rescued him, he turns his thoughts with gratitude and praise to all the deliverances which lie in the past.

Vers. 8—11. This praise is supported by a setting forth of the gracious protection under which God's saints continually are. The מַלְאַךְ יהוה, is none other than He who was the medium of Jahve's intercourse with the patriarchs, and who accompanied Israel to Canaan. This name is not collective (Calvin, Hupfeld, Kamphausen, and others). He, the One, encampeth round about them, in so far as He is the Captain of the host of Jahve (Josh. v. 14), and consequently is accompanied by a host of inferior ministering angels; or insofar as He can, as being a spirit not limited by space, furnish protection that covers them on every side. חֹנֶה (cf. Zech. ix. 8) is perhaps an allusion to מַחֲנַיִם in Gen. xxxii. 2 sq., that angel-camp which joined itself to Jacob's camp, and surrounded it like a barricade or *carrago*. On the *fut. consec.* וַיְחַלְּצֵם, *et expedit eos*, as a simple expression of the sequence, or even only of a weak or loose internal connection, *vid.* Ewald, § 343, *a*. By reason of this protection by the Angel of God arises (ver. 9) the summons to test the graciousness of God in their own experience. Tasting (γεύσασθαι, Hebr. vi. 4 sq., 1 Pet. ii. 3) stands before seeing; for spiritual experience leads to spiritual perception or knowledge, and not *vice versâ*. *Nisi gustaveris*, says Bernard, *non videbis*.

David is desirous that others also should experience what he has experienced in order that they may come to know what he has come to know, viz. the goodness of God.* Hence, in ver. 10, the call to the saints to fear Jahve (יִרְאוּ instead of יִרְאוּ, in order to preserve the distinction between *veremini* and *videbunt*, as in Josh. xxiv. 14, 1 Sam. xii. 24); for whoso fears Him, possesses everything in Him. The young mature lions may sooner lack and suffer hunger, because they have no prey, than that he should suffer any want whatsoever, the goal of whose striving is fellowship with God. The verb רוּשׁ (to lack, be poor, once by metaplasm יָרַשׁ, 1 Sam. ii. 7, root רשׁ, to be or to make loose, lax), elsewhere used only of men, is here, like civ. 21 בִּקֵּשׁ מֵאֵל, transferred to the lions, without כְּפִירִים being intended to refer emblematically (as in xxxv. 17, lvii. 5, xvii. 12) to his powerful foes at the courts of Saul and of Achish.

Vers. 12—15. The first main division of the Psalm is ended; the second (much the same as in Ps. xxxii.) assumes more the tone of a didactic poem; although even vers. 6, 9—11 have something of the didactic style about them. The poet first of all gives a direction for fearing God. We may compare xxxii. 8, li. 15 — how thoroughly Davidic is the turn which the Psalm here takes! בָּנִים are not children in years or in understanding; but it is a tender form of address of a master experienced in the ways of God to each one and to all, as in Prov. i. 8, and frequently. In ver. 13 he throws out the question, which he himself answers in vers. 14 sq. This form of giving impressiveness to a truth by setting it forth as a solution of some question that has been propounded is a habit with David: xv. 1, xxiv. 8, 10, xxv. 12. In the use made of this passage from the Psalms in 1 Pet. iii. 10—12 (= vers. 13—17 *a* of the Psalm) this form of the question is lost sight of. To חָפֵץ חַיִּים, as being just as exclusive in sense, corresponds אֹהֵב יָמִים, so that consequently לִרְאוֹת is a definition of the purpose. יָמִים signifies days in the mass, just as חַיִּים means long-enduring life. We see from James

---

* On account of this ver. 9, Γεύσασθε καὶ ἴδετε, κ. τ. λ., Ps. xxxiii. (xxxiv.) was the Communion Psalm of the early church, *Constit. Apost.* viii. 13, Cyril, *Catech. Myst.* v. 17.

iii. 2 sqq., where ver. 13 also, in its form, calls to mind the
Psalm before us, why the poet give the pre-eminence to the
avoiding of sins of the tongue. In ver. 15, from among what
is good peace is made prominent, — peace, which not only
are we not to disturb, but which we are to seek, yea, pursue
it like as the hunter pursues the finest of the herds. Let us
follow, says the apostle Paul also, Rom. xiv. 19 (cf. Hebr.
xii. 14), after those things which make for peace. שָׁלוֹם is
a relationship, harmonious and free from trouble, that is
well-pleasing to the God of love. The idea of the bond of
fellowship is connected with the corresponding word εἰρήνη,
according to its radical notion.

Vers. 17—22. The poet now recommends the fear of
God, to which he has given a brief direction, by setting forth
its reward in contrast with the punishment of the ungodly.
The prepositions אֶל and בְּ, in vers 16a and 17a, are a well
considered interchange of expression: the former, of gracious
inclination (xxxiii. 18), the latter, of hostile intention or
determining, as in Job vii. 8, Jer. xxi. 10, xliv. 11, after the
phrase in Lev. xvii. 10. The evil doers are overwhelmed by
the power of destruction that proceeds from the countenance of Jahve, which is opposed to them, until there is not
the slightest trace of their earthly existence left. The subjects to ver. 18 are not, according to cvii. 17—19, the עֹשֵׂי רָע
(evil doers), since the indispensable characteristic of penitence is in this instance wanting, but the צַדִּיקִים (the righteous). Probably the פ strophe stood originally before the
ע strophe, just as in Lam. ii—iv. the פ precedes the ע
(Hitzig). In connection with the present sequence of the
thoughts, the structure of ver. 18 is just like ver. 6: *Clamant
et Dominus audit = si qui (quicunque) clamant.* What is
meant is the cry out the depth of a soul that despairs of
itself. Such crying meets with a hearing with God, and in
its realisation, an answer that bears its own credentials.
"The broken in heart" are those in whom the egotistical, *i.
e.* self-loving, life, which encircles its own personality,
is broken at the very root; "the crushed or contrite (דַּכְאֵי,
from דָּכָא, with a changeable *ā*, after the form אַיָּלוֹת from
אַיָּל) in spirit" are those whom grievous experiences, leading
to penitence, of the false eminence to which their proud self-

consciousness has raised them, have subdued and thoroughly
humbled. To all such Jahve is nigh, He preserves them
from despair, He is ready to raise up in them a new life
upon the ruins of the old and to cover or conceal their infinitive deficiency; and, they, on their part, being capable
of receiving, and desirous of, salvation, He makes them
partakers of His salvation. It is true these afflictions come
upon the righteous, but Jahve rescues him out of them all,
מְבַּלָּן = מִכֻּלָּם (the same *enallage generis* as in Ruth i. 19, iv.
11). He is under the most special providence, "He keepeth
all his bones, not one of them (*ne unum quidem*) is broken"
— a pictorial exemplification of the thought that God does
not suffer the righteous to come to the extremity, that He
does not suffer him to be severed from His almighty protecting love, nor to become the sport of the oppressors.
Nevertheless we call to mind the literal fulfilment which
these words of the psalmist received in the Crucified One;
for the Old Testament prophecy, which is quoted in John
xix. 33—37, may be just as well referred to our Psalm as
to Exod. xii. 46. Not only the Paschal lamb, but in a comparative sense even every affliction of the righteous, is a
type. Not only is the essence of the symbolism of the worship
of the sanctuary realised in Jesus Christ, not only is the history
of Israel and of David repeated in Him, not only does human
suffering attain in connection with Him its utmost intensity,
but all the promises given to the righteous are fulfilled in
Him κατ' ἐξοχήν; because He is the righteous One in the most
absolute sense, the Holy One of God in a sense altogether
unique (Isa. liii. 11, Jer. xxiii. 5, Zach. ix. 9, Acts iii. 14,
xxii. 14). — The righteous is always preserved from extreme
peril, whereas evil (רָעָה) slays (מוֹתֵת stronger than הֵמִית)
the ungodly: evil, which he loved and cherished, becomes
the executioner's power, beneath which he falls. And they
that hate the righteous must pay the penalty. Of the meanings
to incur guilt, to feel one's self guilty, and to undergo
punishment as being guilty, אָשֵׁם (*vid.* on iv. 11) has the
last in this instance.

Ver. 23. The order of the alphabet having been gone
through, there now follows a second פ exactly like xxv. 22.
Just as the first פ, xxv. 16, is פְּנֵה, so here in ver. 17 it is

פָנַי; and in like manner the two supernumerary *Phe*'s correspond to one another — the Elohimic in the former
Psalm, and the Jehovic in this latter.

PSALM XXXV.

CALL TO ARMS AGAINST UNGRATEFUL PERSECUTORS, ADDRESSED TO GOD.

1 CONTEND, Jahve, with those who contend with me,
  Fight Thou against those who fight against me.
2 Lay hold of shield and buckler,
  And stand up as my help.
3 And draw forth the spear and shut up the way against
      my persecutors,
  Say unto my soul: I am thy salvation.

4 Let those be confounded and ashamed who seek after
      my soul,
  Let those fall back and be covered with shame who de-
      vise my hurt.
5 Let them become as chaff before the wind,
  The Angel of Jahve thrusting them away.
6 Let their way become darkness and slipperinesses,
  The Angel of Jahve pursuing them.

7 For without cause have they hid for me their net,
  Without cause a pit have they digged for my soul.
8 Let destruction come upon him at unawares,
  And let his net, which he hath hid, catch himself,
  With a crash let him fall into it.

9 So shall my soul exult in Jahve,
  It shall rejoice in His salvation.
10 All my bones shall say: Jahve, who is like unto Thee,
  Who deliverest the afflicted from him who is too strong
      for him,
  The afflicted and the poor from him who robbeth him!

11 Unjust witnesses rise up;
  That which I know not, they ask of me.
12 They reward me evil for good,
  Bereavement hath come upon my soul.
13 And I — when they were sick, my clothing was sack-
      cloth,
  I mortified my soul with fasting,
  And my prayer returned into my own bosom.

14 As for a friend, a brother to me, did I go about,
  As one who sorroweth for a mother, I went softly about
      in mourning attire.
15 And now when I halt they are joyous and gather them-
      selves together,
  The abjects gather themselves together against me, and
      those whom I do not know,
  They mock and cease not.
16 After the manner of common parasites,
  They gnash upon me with their teeth.

17 O Lord, how long wilt Thou look on?!
  Bring back my soul from their destructions,
  My only one from the lions.
18 I will praise Thee in a great congregation,
  Among much people will I sing praise unto Thee.

19 Let not mine enemies falsely rejoice over me,
  Let not those who hate me without a cause wink the
      eye.
20 For they utter not peaceful words,
  But against those who are quiet in the land they devise
      deceitful matters.
21 And they open their mouth wide concerning me,
  They say: Aha, aha, now our eye sees it.

22 Thou seest it, Jahve, therefore keep not silence;
  O Lord, remain not far from me.
23 Stir up Thyself and awake to my right,
  My God and my Lord, to my cause.

24 Do justice to me according to Thy righteousness, Jahve,
        my God,
   And let them not rejoice over me.

25 Let them not say in their heart: Aha, it is our desire!
   Let them not say: We have swallowed him up.
26 Let those be ashamed and be covered with confusion
        together
   Who rejoice at my hurt,
   Let those be clothed with shame and dishonour
   Who magnify themselves against me.

27 Let those shout for joy and rejoice who do not envy me
        my right.
   And let them say continually: Jahve be magnified,
   Who hath pleasure in the prosperity of His servant.
28 And my tongue shall declare Thy righteousness,
   Thy praise at all times.

This Ps. xxxv. and Ps. xxxiv. form a pair. They are
the only Psalms in which the name מלאך יהוה is mentioned.
The Psalms that belong to the time of David's persecution
by Saul are the Psalms which are more especially pervaded
by such retrospective references to the Tôra. And in fact
this whole Psalm is, as it were, the lyrical expansion of that
which David expresses before Saul in 1 Sam. xxiv. 16 [15,
Engl.]. The critical opinion as to the authorship of this
Psalm is closely allied with that respecting the author of
Ps. xl. and lxix. to which Ps. xxxv. is nearly related; cf.
vers. 21, 27 with xl. 16 sq.; ver. 13 with lxix. 11 sq.; whereas
the relation of Ps. lxxi. to Ps. xxxv. is decidedly a secondary one. Hitzig conjectures it to be Jeremiah; but vers.
1—3 are appropriate in the lips of a persecuted king, and
not of a persecuted prophet. The points of contact of the
writings of Jeremiah with our Psalm (Jer. xviii. 19 sq.,
xxiii. 12, Lam. ii. 16), may therefore in this instance be
more safely regarded as reminiscences of an earlier writer
than in Ps. lxix. Throughout the whole Psalm there
prevails a deep vexation of spirit (to which corresponds
the suffix ־ָמוֹי, as in Ps. lix. lvi. xi. xvii. xxii. lxiv.)

and strong emotion; it is not until the second part, where the poet describes the base ingratitude of his enemies, that the language becomes more calm and transparent, and a more quiet sadness takes the place of indignation and rage.

Each of the three parts opens with a cry for deliverance; and closes, in the certain assumption that it will take place, with a vow of thanksgiving. The divisions cannot therefore be mistaken, viz. vers. 1—10, 11—18, 19—28. The relative numbers of the stichs in the separate groups is as follows: 6. 6. 5. 5. | 7. 7. 5. | 6. 6. 6. 5.

There are only a few Psalms of David belonging to the time of Saul's persecution, which, like Ps. xxii., keep within the limits of deep inward grief; and in scarcely a single instance do we find him confining himself to the expression of the accursed fate of his enemies with prophetic certainty, as that which he confidently expects will be realised (as, *e. g.*, in vii. 13—17). But for the most part the objective announcement of punishment is swallowed up by the force of his inmost feelings, and changed into the most importunate prayer (as in vii. 7, xvii. 13, and frequently); and this feverish glow of feeling becomes still more harshly prominent, when the prayer for the revelation of divine judgment in punishment passes over into a wish that it may actually take place. In this respect Ps. vii. xxxv. lxix. cix. form a fearful gradation. In Ps. cix., the old expositors count as many as thirty anathemas. What explanation can we give of such language coming from the lips and heart of the poet? Perhaps as paroxysms of a desire for revenge? His advance against Nabal shews that even a David was susceptible of such feelings; but 1 Sam. xxv. 32 sq. also shews that only a gentle stirring up of his conscience was needed to dissuade him from it. How much more natural — we throw out this consideration in agreement with Kurtz — that the preponderance of that magnanimity peculiar to him should have maintained its ascendancy in the moments of the highest religious consecration in which he composed his Psalms! It is inconceivable that the unholy fire of personal passion could be here mingled with the holy fire of his love to God. It is in fact the Psalms more especially, which are the purest and most faithful mirror of the piety of the Old Testament:

the duty of love towards one's enemies, however, is so little
alien to the Old Testament (Exod. xxiii. 4 sq., Lev. xix. 18,
Prov. xx. 22, xxiv. 17, xxv. 21 sq., Job xxxi. 29 sq.), that
the very words of the Old Testament are made use of even
in the New to inculcate this love. And from Ps. vii., in its
agreement with the history of his conduct towards Saul, we
have seen that David was conscious of having fulfilled this
duty. All the imprecatory words in these Psalms come,
therefore, from the pure spring of unself-seeking zeal for
the honour of God. That this zeal appears in this instance
as zeal for his own person or character arises from the fact,
that David, as the God-anointed heir of the kingdom, stands
in antagonism to Saul, the king alienated from God; and,
that to his mind the cause of God, the continuance of the
church, and the future of Israel, coincide with his own
destiny. The fire of his anger is kindled at this focus (so to
speak) of the view which he has of his own position in the
course of the history of redemption. It is therefore a holy
fire; but the spirit of the New Testament, as Jesus Himself
declares in Luke ix. 55, is in this respect, nevertheless, a
relatively different spirit from that of the Old. That act of
divine love, redemption, out of the open fountain of which
there flowed forth the impulse of a love which embraces
and conquers the world, was then as yet not completed;
and a curtain then still hung before eternity, before heaven
and hell, so that imprecations like lxix. 20 were not understood, even by him who uttered them, in their infinite depth
of meaning. Now that this curtain is drawn up, the New
Testament faith shrinks back from invoking upon any one
a destruction that lasts לְעוֹלָם; and love seeks, so long as a
mere shadow of possibility exists, to rescue everything human from the perdition of an unhappy future, — a perdition the full meaning of which cannot be exhausted by human thought.

In connection with all this, however, there still remains
one important consideration. The curses, which are contained
in the Davidic Psalms of the time of Saul's persecution, are
referred to in the New Testament as fulfilled in the enemies of
Jesus Christ, Acts i. 20, Rom. xi. 7—10. One expression found
in our Psalm, ἐμίσησάν με δωρεάν (cf. lxix. 5) is used by Jesus

(John xv. 25) as fulfilled in Him; it therefore appears as
though the whole Psalm ought to be, or at least may be,
taken typically as the words of Christ. But nowhere in the
Gospels do we read an imprecation used by Jesus against
His own and the enemies of the kingdom of God; David's
imprecations are not suited to the lips of the Saviour, nor
do the instances in which they are cited in the New Testament give them the impress of being His direct words: they
are treated as the language of prophecy by virtue of the
Spirit, whose instrument David was, and whose work the
Scriptures are. And it is only in this sense that the Christian adopts them in prayer. For after the pattern of his
Lord, who on the cross prayed "Father forgive them", he
desires that even his bitterest enemies may not be eternally
lost, but, though it be only when *in articulo mortis*, that
they may come to their right mind. Even the anathemas of
the apostle against the Judaising false teachers and against
Alexander the smith (Gal. i. 9, v. 12, 2 Tim. iv. 14), refer
only to temporal removal and chastisement, not to eternal
perdition. They mark the extreme boundary where, in extraordinary instances, the holy zeal of the New Testament comes
in contact with the holy fervour of the Old Testament.

Vers. 1—3. The psalmist begins in a martial and an-
thropomorphical style such as we have not hitherto met
with. On the ultima-accentuation of רִיבָה, *vid*. on iii. 8.
Both את are signs of the accusative. This is a more natural
rendering here, where the psalmist implores God to subjugate his foes, than to regard את as equivalent to עִם (cf.
Isa. xlix. 25 with *ib*. xxvii. 8, Job x. 2); and, moreover, for
the very same reason the expression in this instance is לָחֶם
(in the *Kal*, which otherwise only lends the *part*. לֹחֵם, lvi.
2 sq., to the *Niph*. נלחם) instead of the reciprocal form
הִלָּחֵם. It is usually supposed that לָחַם means properly
vorare, and war is consequently conceived of as a devouring
of men; but the Arabic offers another primary meaning: to
press close and compact (*Niph*. to one another), consequently מִלְחָמָה means a dense crowd, a dense bustle and
tumult (cf. the Homeric κλόνος). The summons to Jahve to

arm, and that in a twofold manner, viz. with the מָגֵן for warding off the hostile blow and צִנָּה (*vid.* v. 13) which covers the body like a *testudo* — by which, inasmuch as it is impossible to hold both shields at the same time, the figure is idealised — is meant to express, that He is to make Himself felt by the foes, in every possible way, to their own confounding, as the unapproachable One. The בְּ of בְּעֶזְרָתִי (in the character of help turned towards me) is the so-called *Beth essentiæ*,* as in Exod. xviii. 4, Prov. iii. 26, Isa. xlviii. 10 (*tanquam argentum*), and frequently. הָרִיק has the same meaning as in Exod. xv. 9, cf. Gen. xiv. 14, viz. to bring forth, draw forth, to draw or unsheath (a sword); for as a sword is sheathed when not in use, so a spear is kept in the δουροδόχη (*Odyss.* i. 128). Even Parchon understands סְגֹר to mean a weapon; and the word σάγαρις, in Herodotus, Xenophon, and Strabo, a northern Asiatic, more especially a Scythian, battle-axe, has been compared here;** but the battle-axe was not a Hebrew weapon, and סְגֹר, which, thus defectively written, has the look of an imperative, also gives the best sense when so taken (LXX. σύγκλεισον, Targ. וּטְרוֹק), viz. close, *i. e.* cut off, *interclude* scil. *viam.* The word has *Dechî*, because לִקְרַאת רֹדְפָי, "casting Thyself against my per-

---

* The Hebrew *Beth essentiæ* is used much more freely and extensively than the Arabic, which is joined exclusively to the predicate of a simple clause, where in our language the verb is "to be", and as a rule only to the predicate of negative clauses: *laisa bi-ḥakîmin*, he is not wise, or *laisa bi-l-ḥakîmi*, he is not the wise man. The predicate can accordingly be indeterminate or determinate. Moreover, in Hebrew, where this בְּ is found with the predicate, with the complement of the subject, or even, though only as a solecism (*vid.* Gesenius' Thesaurus p. 175), with the subject itself, the word to which it is prefixed may be determinate, whether as an attribute determined by itself (Exod. vi. 3. בְּאֵל שַׁדַּי), by a suffix (as above, xxxv. 2, cf. cxlvi. 5, Exod. xviii. 4, Prov. iii. 26), or even by the article. At all events no syntactic objection can be brought against the interpretations of בְּעָשָׁן, "in the quality of smoke", xxxvii. 20; cf. כַּהֶבֶל, lxxviii. 33, and of בַּנֶּפֶשׁ, "in the character of the soul", Lev. xvii. 11.

** Probably one and the same word with the Armenian *sakr*, to which are assigned the (Italian) meanings *mannaja, scure, brando ferro*, in Ciakciak's Armenian Lexicon; cf. Lagarde's *Gesammelte Abhandlungen*, 1866, S. 203.

secutors", belongs to both the preceding summonses. Dach-selt rightly directs attention to the similar sequence of the accents in lv. 19, lxvi. 15. The Mosaic figure of Jahve as a man of war (אִישׁ מִלְחָמָה, Exod. xv. 3, Deut. xxxii. 41 sq.) is worked out here with brilliant colours, under the impulse of a wrathful spirit. But we see from ver. 3*b* what a spiritual meaning, nevertheless, the whole description is intended to convey. In God's intervention, thus manifested in facts, he would gladly hear His consolatory utterance to himself. The burden of his cry is that God's love may break through the present outward appearance of wrath and make itself felt by him.

Vers. 4—8. Throughout the next two strophes follow terrible imprecations. According to Fürst and others the relation of בּוֹשׁ and חָפֵר is like that of *erblassen*, to turn pale (cf. Isa. xxix. 22 with Ps. xxxiv. 6), and *erröthen*, to turn red, to blush. בּוֹשׁ has, however, no connection with בּוּץ, nor has חָפֵר, خفر, خمر, any connection with حمر, to be red; but, according to its radical notion, בּוֹשׁ means *disturbari* (*vid.* vi. 11), and חָפֵר, *obtegere, abscondere* (*vid.* xxxiv. 6). יִסֹּגוּ, properly "let them be made to fall back" (cf., *e. g.*, Isa. xlii. 17). On the figure in ver. 5*a* cf. lxxxiii. 14. The clauses respecting the Angel of Jahve, vers. 5*b* and 6*b*, are circumstantial clauses, viz. clauses defining the manner. דֹּחֶה (giving, viz. them, the push that shall cause their downfall, equivalent to דֹּחֶם or דְּחֵם, lxviii. 28) is closely connected with the figure in ver. 6*a*, and רֹדְפָם, with the figure in ver. 5*a*; consequently it seems as though the original position of these two clauses respecting the Angel of Jahve had been disturbed; just as in Ps. xxxiv., the ע strophe and the פ strophe have changed their original places. It is the Angel, who took off Pharaoh's chariot wheels so that they drave them heavily (Exod. xiv. 25) that is intended here. The fact that this Angel is concerned here, where the point at issue is whether the kingship of the promise shall be destroyed at its very beginning or not, harmonises with the appearing of the מַלְאַךְ ה׳ at all critical junctures in the course of the history of redemption. חֲלַקְלַקּוֹת, *loca passim lubrica*, is an intensive form of expression for חֲלָקוֹת, lxxiii. 18. Just as דֹּחֶה recalls to mind Exod.

xv., so רֹדְפָם recalls Judges v. In this latter passage the Angel of Jahve also appears in the midst of the conquerors who are pursuing the smitten foe, incarnate as it were in Deborah.

Ver. 7 also needs re-organising, just as in vers. 5 sq. the original positions of דחה and רדפם are exchanged. שַׁחַת רִשְׁתָּם would be a pit deceptively covered over with a net concealed below; but, as even some of the older critics have felt, שחת is without doubt to be brought down from ver. 7a into 7b: without cause, i. e. without any provocation on my part, have they secretly laid their net for me (as in ix. 16, xxxi. 5), without cause have they digged a pit for my soul. In ver. 8 the foes are treated of collectively. לֹא יֵדַע is a negative circumstantial clause (Ew. § 341, b): improviso, as in Prov. v. 6, Isa. xlvii. 11 extrem. Instead of תְּלַכְּדֶנּוּ, the expression is תִּלְכְּדוּ, as in Hos. viii. 3; the sharper form is better adapted to depict the suddenness and certainty of the capture. According to Hupfeld, the verb שָׁאָה signifies a wild, dreary, confused noise or crash, then devastation and destruction, a transition of meaning which — as follows from שׁוֹאָה (cf. תֹהוּ) as a name of the desolate steppe, from שָׁוְא, a waste, emptiness, and from other indications — is solely brought about by transferring the idea of a desolate confusion of tones to a desolate confusion of things, without any intermediate notion of the crashing in of ruins. But it may be asked whether the reverse is not rather the case, viz. that the signification of a waste, desert, emptiness or void is the primary one, and the meaning that has reference to sound (cf. هوى, to gape, be empty; to drive along, fall down headlong, then also: to make a dull sound as of something falling, just like *rumor* from *ruere, fragor* from *frangi*) the derived one. Both etymology (cf. תָּהָה, whence תֹהוּ) and the preponderance of other meanings, favour this latter view. Here the two significations are found side by side, inasmuch as שׁוֹאָה in the first instance means a waste = devastation, desolation, and in the second a waste = a heavy, dull sound, a rumbling (δουπεῖν). In the Syriac version it is rendered: "into the pit which he has digged let him fall", as though it were שַׁחַת in the second instance instead of שׁוֹאָה; and from this Hupfeld, with J. H. Michaelis, Stier, and others, is of opinion that it must be rendered: "into the destruction which he himself has prepared let him fall". But this *quam ipse paravit* is not found in the text, and to mould the text accordingly would be a very arbitrary proceeding.

Vers. 9—10. This strophe, with which the first part of the song closes, contains the logical apodosis· of those imprecatory jussives. The downfall of the power that is opposed to God will be followed by the joy of triumph. The bones of the body, which elsewhere are mentioned as sharing only in the anguish of the soul (vi. 3, xxxi. 11, xxxii. 3, li. 10), are here made to share (as also in li. 10) in the joy, into which the anxiety, that agitated even the marrow of the bones, is changed. The joy which he experiences in his soul shall throb through every member of his body and multiply itself, as it were, into a choir of praiseful voices. כָּל with a conjunctive accent and without *Makkeph*, as also in Prov. xix. 7 (not ־כָּל, *vid.* the Masora in Baer's *Psalterium* p. 133), is to be read *cāl* (with קְמָץ רחב, *opp.* קְמָץ הטוף) according to Kimchi. According to Lonzano, however, it is to be read *col*, the conjunctive accent having an equal power with *Makkeph*; but this view is false, since an accent can never be placed against *Kametz chatuph*. The exclamation מִי כָמוֹךְ is taken from Exod. xv. 11, where, according to the Masora, it is to be pointed מִי כָּמוֹךְ, as Ben Naphtali also points it in the passage before us. The *Dagesh*, which is found in the former passage and is wanting here, sharpens and hardens at the same time; it requires that the expression should be emphatically pronounced (without there being any danger in this instance of its being slurred over); it does not serve to denote the closer connection, but to give it especial prominence. חָזָק מִמֶּנּוּ, stronger than he, is equivalent to: strong, whereas the other is weak, just as in Jer. xxxi. 11, cf. Hab. i. 13, צַדִּיק מִמֶּנּוּ, righteous, whereas he is ungodly. The repetition of וְעָנִי is meant to say: He rescues the עָנִי, who is אֶבְיוֹן (poor) enough already, from him who would take even the few goods that he possesses.

Vers. 11—16. The second part begins with two strophes of sorrowful description of the wickedness of the enemy. The futures in vers. 11, 12 describe that which at present takes place. עֵדֵי חָמָם are μάρτυρες ἄδικοι (LXX.). They demand from him

a confession of acts and things which lie entirely outside
his consciousness and his way of acting (cf. lxix. 5): they
would gladly brand him as a perjurer, as an usurper, and
as a plunderer. What David complains of in ver. 12*a*, we
hear Saul confess in 1 Sam. xxiv. 18; the charge of ingratitude is therefore well-grounded. שְׁכוֹל לְנַפְשִׁי is not dependent on יְשַׁלְּמוּנִי, in which case one would have looked for
כְּשׁוֹל rather than שְׁכוֹל, but a substantival clause: "bereavement is to my soul", its condition is that of being forsaken
by all those who formerly shewed me marks of affection;
all these have, as it were, died off so far as I am concerned.
Not only had David been obliged to save his parents by
causing them to flee to Moab, but Michal was also torn
from him, Jonathan removed, and all those at the court of
Saul, who had hitherto sought the favour and friendship of the
highly-gifted and highly-honoured son-in-law of the king,
were alienated from him. And how sincerely and sympathis-
ingly had he reciprocated their leanings towards himself!
By וַאֲנִי in ver. 13, he contrasts himself with the ungrateful
and unfeeling ones. Instead of לְבַשְׁתִּי שָׂק, the expression is
לְבוּשִׁי שָׂק; the tendency of poetry for the use of the substantival clause is closely allied to its fondness for well-conceived
brevity and pictorial definition. He manifested towards them a
love which knew no distinction between the *ego* and *tu,* which
regarded their sorrow and their guilt as his own, and joined
with them in their expiation for it; his head was lowered upon
his breast, or he cowered, like Elijah (1 Kings xviii. 42), upon
the ground with his head hanging down upon his breast even
to his knees, so that that which came forth from the inmost
depths of his nature returned again as it were in broken accents into his bosom. Riehm's rendering, "at their ungodliness
and hostility my prayer for things not executed came back",
is contrary to the connection, and makes one look for אֵלַי
instead of אֶל־חֵיקִי. Perret-Gentil correctly renders it, *Je
priai la tête penchée sur la poitrine.*

The psalmist goes on to say in ver. 14, I went about
as for a friend, for a brother to me, *i. e.* as if the sufferer
had been such to me. With הִתְהַלֵּךְ, used of the solemn
slowness of gait, which corresponds to the sacredness of
pain, alternates שָׁחַח used of the being bowed down very

low, in which the heavy weight of pain finds expression. כְּאֵבֶל־אֵם, not: like the mourning (from אָבֵל, like הֶבֶל from הֶבֶל) of a mother (Hitzig), but, since a personal אֵבֶל is more natural, and next to the mourning for an only child the loss of a mother (cf. Gen. xxiv. 67) strikes the deepest wound: like one who mourns (אֲבֵל־[*], like לְבֶן־, Gen. xlix. 12, from אָבֵל, construct state, like טְמֵא) for a mother (the objective genitive, as in Gen. xxvii. 41, Deut. xxxiv. 8, Amos viii. 10, Jer. vi. 26). קֹדֵר signifies the colours, outward appearance, and attire of mourning: with dark clothes, with tearful unwashed face, and with neglected beard. But as for them — how do they act at the present time, when he finds himself in צֶלַע (xxxviii. 17, Job. xviii. 12), a sideway direction, *i. e.* likely to fall (from צָלַע, ظلع, to incline towards the side)?

They rejoice and gather themselves together, and this assemblage of ungrateful friends rejoicing over another's misfortune, is augmented by the lowest rabble that attach themselves to them. The verb נָכָה means to smite; *Niph.* נִכָּא, Job xxx. 6, to be driven forth with a whip, after which the LXX. renders it μάστιγες, Symm. πλῆκται, and the Targum *conterentes me verbis suis;* cf. הִכָּה בַלָּשׁוֹן, Jer. xviii. 18. But נֵכִים cannot by itself mean smiters with the tongue. The adjective נָכֶה signifies elsewhere with רַגְלַיִם, one who is smitten in the feet, *i. e.* one who limps or halts, and with רוּחַ, but also without any addition, in Isa. xvi. 7, one smitten in spirit, *i. e.* one deeply troubled or sorrowful. Thus, therefore, נֵכִים from נָכָה, like גֵּאִים from גָּאָה, may mean smitten men, *i. e.* men who are brought low or reduced (Hengstenberg). It might also, after the Arabic *nawika*, to be injured in mind, *anwak*, stupid, silly (from the same root נך, to prick, smite, wound, cf. *ichtalla*, to be pierced through = mad), be understood as those mentally deranged, enraged at nothing or without cause. But the former definition of the notion of the word is favoured by the continua-

---

[*] According to the old Babylonian reading (belonging to a period when *Pathach* and *Segol* were as yet not distinguished from one another), כְּאֵבֶל (with the sign of *Pathach* and the stroke for *Raphe* below = ä); *vid.* Pinsker, *Zur Geschichte des Karaismus,* S. 141, and *Einleitung,* S. 118.

tion of the idea of the verbal adjective נבים by וְלֹא יָדַעְתִּי,
persons of whom I have hitherto taken no notice because
they were far removed from me, *i. e.* men belonging to the
dregs of the people (cf. Job xix. 18, xxx. 1). The addition
of ולא ידעתי certainly makes Olshausen's conjecture that we
should read נָבְרִים somewhat natural; but the expression
then becomes tautological, and there are other instances
also in which psalm-poesy goes beyond the ordinary range
of words, in order to find language to describe that which
is loathsome, in the most glaring way. קָרַע, to tear, rend
in pieces, viz. with abusive and slanderous words (like قرع II.)
also does not occur anywhere else. And what remarkable
language we now meet with in ver. 16*a*! מָעוֹג does not
mean scorn or buffoonery, as Böttcher and Hitzig imagine*,
but according to 1 Kings xvii. 12, a cake of a round formation (like the Talmudic עֻגָּה, a circle); לָעֵג, jeering,
jesting. Therefore לְעַגֵי מָעוֹג means: mockers for a cake, *i. e.*
those who for a delicate morsel, for the sake of dainty fare,
make scornful jokes, viz. about me, the persecuted one, vile
parasites; German *Tellerlecker, Bratenriecher,* Greek κνισ-
σοκόλακες, ψωμοκόλακες, Mediæval Latin *buccellarii.* This
לְעַגֵי מָעוֹג, which even Rashi interprets in substantially the
same manner, stands either in a logical co-ordinate relation
(*vid.* on Isa. xix. 11) or in a logical as well as grammatical
subordinate relation to its *regens* חַנְפֵי. In the former case,
it would be equivalent to: the profane, viz. the cake-jesters;
in the latter, which is the more natural, and quite suitable:
the profane (= the profanest, *vid.* xlv. 13, Isa. xxix. 19,
Ezek. vii. 24) among cake-jesters. The בְּ is not the *Beth* of
companionship or fellowship, to express which עַם or אֵת
(Hos. vii. 5) would have been used, but *Beth essentiæ* or the
Beth of characterisation: in the character of the most abject
examples of this class of men do they gnash upon him with
their teeth. The gerund חָרֹק (of the noise of the teeth being
pressed together, like حرق of the crackling of a fire and the
grating of a file), which is used according to Ges. § 131,

---

* The Talmudic עגה (לִשׁוֹן), *B. Sanhedrin* 101*b*, which is said to
mean "a jesting way of speaking", has all the less place here, as the
reading wavers between עגה (עגא) and אגא.

4, *b*, carries its subject in itself. They gnash upon him with their teeth after the manner of the profanest among those, by whom their neighbour's honour is sold for a delicate morsel.

Vers. 17—18. Just as the first part of the Psalm closed with wishes, and thanksgiving for their fulfilment, so the second part also closes with prayer and thanksgiving. כַּמָּה (compounded of כְּ, *instar*, and the interrogative מָה which is drawn into the genitive by it; Aramaic כְּמָא, Arabic *kam*, Hebrew, like בַּמָּה, with *Dag. forte conjunct.*, properly: the total of what?), which elsewhere means *quot*, here has the signification of *quousque*, as in Job vii. 19. מִשֹּׁאֵיהֶם from שֹׁאָ, the plural of which may be both שֹׁאִים and שֹׁאוֹת (this latter, however, does not occur), like the plural of אֵימָה, terror, אֵימִים and אֵימוֹת. The suffix, which refers to the enemies as the authors of the destructions (Prov. iii. 25), shews that it is not to be rendered "from their destroyers" (Hitzig). If God continues thus to look on instead of acting, then the destructions, which are passing over David's soul, will utterly destroy it. Hence the prayer: lead it back, bring that back, which is already well nigh borne away to destruction. On יְחִידָה *vid.* xxii. 21. The כְּפִירִים, which is intended literally in xxxiv. 11, is here emblematical. אוֹדְךָ is the cohortative. עָצוּם as a parallel word to רַב always refers, according to the context, to strength of numbers or to strength of power.

Vers. 19—21. In the third part, vers. 19—28 the description of the godlessness of his enemies is renewed; but the soul of the praying psalmist has become more tranquil, and accordingly the language also is more clear and moves on with its accustomed calmness. שֶׁקֶר and חִנָּם are genitives, having an attributive sense (*vid.* on 2 Sam. xxii. 23). The verb קָרַץ signifies both to pinch = nip, Job xxxiii. 6 (cf. the Arabic *karaḍa*, to cut off), and to pinch together, compress = to wink, generally used of the eyes, but also of the lips, Prov. xvi. 30, and always as an insidiously malicious gesture. אַל rules over both members of the verse as in lxxv. 6, and frequently. שָׁלוֹם in ver. 20 is the word for whatever proceeds from good intentions and aims at the promotion or restoration of a harmonious relationship.

רִגְעֵי־אָרֶץ (from רָגַע, cf. עַנְוֵי־אָרֶץ, lxxvi. 10, Zeph. ii. 3,
צְפוּנֶיךָ, lxxxiii. 4) are those who quietly and unostentatiously
walk in the ways of God. Against such they devise mischievous, lying slanders and accusations. And with wide-
opened mouth, *i. e.* haughty scorn, they cry, as they
carouse in sight of the misfortune of those they have persecuted: now we have that which we have longed to see.
הֶאָח (composed of הֵה and אָח) is a cry of joy, and more
especially of malignant joy at another's hurt (cf. Ezek. xxv. 3).

Vers. 22—24. The poet takes up this malignant "now
our eye sees it" and gives another turn to it. With יהוה,
alternates in vers. 22, 23, cf. ver. 17, אֲדֹנָי, the pronominal
force of which is revived in the combination אֱלֹהַי וַאדֹנָי (*vid.*
xvi. 2). הֵעִיר, carrying its object within itself, signifies to
stir, rouse up, and הֵקִיץ, to break off, tear one's self away,
gather one's self up from, sleep. "To my right", viz. to prove
it by facts; "to my cause", to carry it on in my defence.

Vers. 25—26. On the metonymical use of נפשׁ, like
τὸ ὀρεκτικόν for ὄρεξις, *vid. Psychol.* S. 203 [tr. p. 239]. The
climax of desire is to swallow David up, *i. e.* to overpower
him and clear him out of the way so that there is not a
trace of him left. בִּלַּעֲנוּהוּ with עַ before נ, as in cxxxii. 6,
and frequently; on the law of the vowels which applies to
this, *vid.* Ewald, § 60, *a.* שְׂמֵחֵי רָעָתִי is a short form of expression for שְׂמֵחִים עַל (בְּ) רָעָתִי To put on shame and dishonour (cix. 29, cf. 18), so that these entirely cover them,
and their public external appearance corresponds with their
innermost nature.

Vers. 27—28. Those who wish that David's righteousness may be made manifest and be avenged are said to take
delight in it. When this takes place, Jahve's righteousness
is proved. יִגְדַּל, let Him be acknowledged and praised as
great, *i. e.* let Him be magnified! David desires that all who
remain true to him may thus speak; and he, on his part,
is determined to stir up the revelation of God's righteousness in his heart, and to speak of that of which his heart
is full (lxxi. 24).

BIBLICAL COMMENTARY

ON

THE OLD TESTAMENT

BIBLICAL COMMENTARY

ON

THE PSALMS

BY

FRANZ DELITZSCH, D.D.,

PROFESSOR OF OLD AND NEW TESTAMENT EXEGESIS, LEIPSIC.

Translated from the German

(FROM THE SECOND EDITION, REVISED THROUGHOUT)

BY THE

REV. FRANCIS BOLTON, B.A.,

PRIZEMAN IN HEBREW AND NEW TESTAMENT GREEK IN THE UNIVERSITY OF LONDON.

TABLE OF CONTENTS

EXCURSUS BY J. G. WETZSTEIN.

PSALM XXXVI.

THE CURSE OF ALIENATION FROM GOD, AND THE BLESSING
OF FELLOWSHIP WITH HIM.

2 AN oracle of transgression hath the ungodly within his
     heart:
  There is no fear of God before his eyes.
3 For it flattereth him in his own eyes,
  In order that he may become guilty, that he may hate.

4 The words of his mouth are evil and deceit;
  He hath ceased to act wisely and well.
5 Evil doth he devise upon his bed,
  He taketh his stand in a way that is not good,
  He abhorreth not evil.

6 O Jahve, to the heavens doth Thy mercy extend,
  Thy faithfulness unto the clouds.
7 Thy righteousness is like the mountains of God,
  Thy judgments are a great deep,
  Man and beast dost Thou preserve, O Jahve.

8 How precious is Thy mercy, Elohim,
  That the children of men find refuge in the shadow of Thy
     wings!

    9 They become drunk with the fatness of Thy house,
       And Thou givest them to drink of the river of Thy
   10 For with Thee is the fountain of life,   [pleasures.
       And in Thy light do we see light.

   11 Lengthen out Thy mercy to those who know Thee,
       And Thy righteousness to those who are upright in heart.
   12 Let not the foot of pride overtake me,
       And let not the hand of the wicked scare me away.
   13 Behold, there have the workers of evil fallen,
       They are thrust down and are not able to rise.

The preceding Psalm, in the hope of speedy deliverance, put into the lips of the friends of the new kingship, who were now compelled to keep in the background, the words: "Jahve, be magnified, who hath pleasure in the well-being of *His servant*." David there calls himself the servant of Jahve, and in the inscription to Ps. xxxvi. he bears the very same name: *To the Precentor, by the servant of Jahve, by David.* The *textus receptus* accents למנצח with a conjunctive *Illuj*; Ben-Naphtali accents it less ambiguously with a disjunctive *Legarme* (*vid. Psalter*, ii. 462), since David is not himself the מנצח. Ps. xii., xiv. (liii.), xxxvi., xxxvii., form a group. In these Psalms David complains of the moral corruption of his generation. They are all merely reflections of the character of the time, not of particular occurrences. In common with Ps. xii., the Psalm before us has a prophetic colouring; and, in common with Ps. xxxvii., allusions to the primeval history of the Book of Genesis. The strophe schema is 4. 5. 5. 6. 6.

Vers. 2–5. At the outset the poet discovers to us the wickedness of the children of the world, which has its roots in alienation from God. Supposing it were admissible to render ver. 2: "A divine word concerning the evil-doing of the ungodly is in the inward parts of my heart" (נאם with a genitive of the object, like משׂא, which is compared by Hofmann), then the difficulty of this word, so much complained of, might find the desired relief in some much more easy way than by means of the conjecture proposed by Diestel, נָעֵם (נָעֵם), "Pleasant is transgression to the evil-doer," etc. But the genitive after נאם

(which in cx. 1, Num. xxiv. 3 sq., 15 sq., 2 Sam. xxiii. 1, Prov. xxx. 1, just as here, stands at the head of the clause) always denotes the speaker, not the thing spoken. Even in Isa. v. 1 שִׁירַת דּוֹדִי לְכַרְמוֹ is not a song concerning my beloved in relation to His vineyard, but a song of my beloved (such a song as my beloved has to sing) touching His vineyard. Thus, therefore, פֶּשַׁע must denote the speaker, and לָרָשָׁע, as in cx. 1 לַאדֹנִי, the person or thing addressed; transgression is personified, and an oracular utterance is attributed to it. But the predicate בְּקֶרֶב לִבִּי, which is intelligible enough in connection with the first rendering of פשע as *genit. obj.*, is difficult and harsh with the latter rendering of פשע as *gen. subj.*, whatever way it may be understood: whether, that it is intended to say that the utterance of transgression to the evil-doer is inwardly known to him (the poet), or it occupies and affects him in his inmost parts. It is very natural to read לִבּוֹ, as the LXX., Syriac, and Arabic versions, and Jerome do. In accordance therewith, while with Von Lengerke he takes נְאֻם as part of the inscription, Thenius renders it: "Sin is to the ungodly in the midst of his heart," *i. e.* it is the inmost motive or impulse of all that he thinks and does. But this isolation of נְאֻם is altogether at variance with the usage of the language and custom. The rendering given by Hupfeld, Hitzig, and at last also by Böttcher, is better: "The suggestion of sin dwells in the ungodly in the inward part of his heart;" or rather, since the idea of בקרב is not central, but circumferential, in the realm of (within) his heart, altogether filling up and absorbing it. And in connection with this explanation, it must be observed that this combination בקרב לבו (instead of בקרבו, or בלבבו, בלבו) occurs only here, where, together with a personification of sin, an incident belonging to the province of the soul's life, which is the outgrowth of sin, is intended to be described. It is true this application of נְאֻם does not admit of being further substantiated; but נְאֻם (cognate הָמָה, נָהַם), as an onomatopoetic designation of a dull, hollow sound, is a suitable word for secret communication (cf. Arabic *nemmâm*, a tale-bearer), or even— since the genius of the language does not combine with it the idea of that which is significantly secretly, and solemnly silently communicated, but spoken out—a suitable word for that which transgression says to the ungodly with all the solemn mien of the prophet or the philosopher, inasmuch as it has set itself within his heart in the place of God and of the voice of his conscience. לָרָשָׁע does not, however, denote the person addressed, but, as in xxxii. 10, the possessor. He possesses this inspiration of iniquity as the contents of his heart, so that the fear of God has no place therein, and to him God has no existence (objectivity), that He should command his adoration.

Since after this נְאֻם פֶּשַׁע we expect to hear further. what and how transgression speaks to him, so before all else the most probable thing is, that transgression is the subject to הֶחֱלִיק. We do not interpret: He flatters God in His eyes (with eye-service), for this rendering is contrary both to what precedes and to what follows; nor with Hupfeld (who follows Hofmann): " God deals smoothly (gently) with him according to his delusions," for the assumption that הֶחֱלִיק must, on account of בְּעֵינָיו, have some other subject than the evil-doer himself, is indeed correct. It does not, however, necessarily point to God as the subject, but, after the solemn opening of ver. 2a, to transgression, which is personified. This addresses flattering words to him (אֶל like עַל in Prov. xxix. 5) in his eyes, *i.e.* such as are pleasing to him; and to what end? For the finding out, *i.e.* establishing (מָצָא עָוֹן, as in Gen. xliv. 16, Hos. xii. 9), or—since this is not exactly suited to פֶּשַׁע as the subject, and where it is a purpose that is spoken of, the meaning *assequi*, originally proper to the verb מצא, is still more natural—*to the attainment of his culpability*, *i.e.* in order that he may inculpate himself, *to hating*, *i.e.* that he may hate God and man instead of loving them. לִשְׂנֹא is designedly used without an object just as in Eccles. iii. 8, in order to imply that the flattering words of פֶּשַׁע incite him to turn into an object of hatred everything that he ought to love, and to live and move in hatred as in his own proper element. Thenius endeavours to get rid of the harshness of the expression by the following easy alteration of the text: לִמְצֹא עָוֹן וְלִשְׂנֹא; and interprets it: Yea, it flatters him in his own eyes (it tickles his pride) to discover faults in others and to make them suffer for them. But there is no support in the general usage of the language for the impersonal rendering of the הֶחֱלִיק; and the בְּעֵינָיו, which in this case is not only pleonastic, but out of place, demands a distinction between the flatterer and the person who feels himself flattered. The expression in ver. 3*b*, in whatever way it may be explained, is harsh; but David's language, whenever he describes the corruption of sin with deep-seated indignation, is wont to envelope itself in such clouds, which, to our difficult comprehension, look like corruptions of the text. In the second strophe the whole language is more easy. לְהַשְׂכִּיל לְהֵיטִיב is just such another asyndeton as למצא עונו לשׂנא. A man who has thus fallen a prey to the dominion of sin, and is alienated from God, has ceased (חָדַל לְ, as in 1 Sam. xxiii. 13) to act wisely and well (things which essentially accompany one another). His words when awake, and even his thoughts in the night-time, run upon אָוֶן (Isa. lix. 7), evil, wickedness, the absolute opposite of that which alone is truly good. Most diligently does he take up his position in the way which leads in the opposite direction to that which is good (Prov. xvi. 29, Isa. lxv. 2); and his conscience is deadened against evil: there is not a trace of aversion to it to be found in him, he loves it with all his soul.

Vers. 6–10. The poet now turns from this repulsive prospect to one that is more pleasing. He contemplates, and praises, the infinite, ever sure mercy of God, and the salvation, happiness, and light which spring from it. Instead of בַּשָּׁמַיִם, the expression is בְּהַשָּׁמַיִם, the syncope of the article not taking place. בְּ alternating with עַד, cf. lvii. 11, has here, as in xix. 5, lxxii. 16, the sense of touching or reaching to the spot that is denoted in connection with it. The poet describes the exaltation and super-eminence of divine mercy and faithfulness figuratively, after earthly standards. They reveal themselves on earth in a height that reaches to the heavens and extends to שְׁחָקִים, *i.e.* the thin veil of vapour which spreads itself like a veil over the depths of the heavens; they transcend all human thought, desire, and comprehension (ciii. 11, and cf. Eph. iii. 18). The צדקה (righteousness) is distinguished from the אמונה (faithfulness) thus: the latter is governed by the promises of God, the former by His holiness; and further, the latter has its being in the love of God, the former, on the other hand, manifests itself partly as justifying in mercies, and partly as avenging in wrath. Concerning the righteousness, the poet says that it is like the mountains of God, *i.e.* (cf. cedars of God, lxxx. 11) unchangeably firm (cxi. 3), like the giant primeval mountains which bear witness to the greatness and glory of God; concerning God's judgments, that they are "a great deep," incomprehensible and unsearchable (ἀνεξερεύ-νηται, Rom. xi. 33) as the great, deep-surging mass of waters in the lower parts of the earth, which becomes visible in the seas and in the rivers. God's punitive righteousness, as at length becomes evident, has His compassion for its reverse side; and this, as in the case of the Flood (cf. Jon. iv. 11), embraces the animal world, which is most closely involved, whether for weal or for woe, with man, as well as mankind.

Lost in this depth, which is so worthy of adoration, the Psalmist exclaims: How precious (cf. cxxxix. 17) is Thy mercy, Elohim! *i.e.* how valuable beyond all treasures, and how precious to him who knows how to prize it! The *Waw* of וּבְנֵי is the explicative *Waw* = *et hoc ipsum quod.* The energetic form of the future, יֶחֱסָיוּן, has the pre-tonic Kametz, here in pause, as in xxxvi. 8, xxxix. 7, lxxviii. 44. The shadow of God's wings is the protection of His love, which hides against temptation and persecution. To be thus hidden in God is the most unspeakable blessedness, ver. 9: they satiate themselves, they drink full draughts of "the fatness of Thy house." The house of God is His sanctuary, and in general the domain of His mercy and grace. דֶּשֶׁן (cf. טוּב, lxv. 5) is the expression for the abundant, pleasant, and powerful gifts and goods and recreations with which God entertains those who are His; and רָוָה (whence יִרְוְיֻן, as in Deut. viii. 13, Isa. xl. 18) is the spiritual joy of the soul that experiences God's mercy to overflowing. The abundant fare of the priests from Jahve's table (*vid.* Jer. xxxi. 14), and the festive joy of the guests at the shelamim-offering, *i.e.* the communion-offering,—these outward rites are here treated according to their spiritual significance, receive the depth of meaning which radically belongs to them, and are ideally generalized. It is a stream of pleasures (עֲדָנִים) with which He irrigates and fertilizes them, a paradisaic river of delights. This, as the four arms of the river of Paradise had one common source (Gen. ii. 10), has its spring in God, yea, God is the fountain itself. He is "the fountain of life" (Jer. ii. 13); all life flows forth from Him, who is the absolutely existing and happy One. The more inwardly, therefore, one is joined to Him, the fuller are the draughts of life which he drinks from this first fountain of all life. And as God is the fountain of life, so also is He the fountain of light: "In Thy light do we see light;" out of God, seeing we see only darkness, whereas immersed in God's sea of light we are illumined by divine knowledge, and lighted up with spiritual joy. The poet, after having taken a few glimpses into the chaos of evil, here moves in the blessed depths of holy mysticism [*Mystik, i.e.* mysticism in the good sense—true religion, vital godliness], and in proportion as in the former case his language is obscure, so here it is clear as crystal.

Vers. 11–13. Now for the first time, in the concluding hexastich, after complaint and commendation comes the language of prayer. The poet prays that God would lengthen out, *i.e.* henceforth preserve (מְשֹׁךְ, as in cix. 12), such mercy to His saints; that the foot of arrogance, which is conceived of as a tyrant, may not come suddenly upon him (בּוֹא, as in xxxv. 8), and that the hand of the wicked may not drive him from his home into exile (cf. x. 18). With חֶסֶד alternates צְדָקָה, which, on its merciful side, is turned towards them that know God, and bestows upon them the promised gracious reward. Whilst the Psalmist is thus praying, the future all at once becomes unveiled to him. Certain in his own mind that his prayer will be heard, he sees the adversaries of God and of His saints for ever overthrown. שָׁם, as in xiv. 5, points to the place where the judgment is executed. The preterites are prophetic, as in xiv. 5, lxiv. 8–10. The poet, like Isaiah (ch. xxvi. 14), beholds the whole tribe of the oppressors of Jahve's Church changed into a field of corpses, without hope of any rising again.

PSALM XXXVII.

THE SEEMING PROSPERITY OF THE WICKED, AND THE REAL PROSPERITY OF THE GODLY.

1 א BE not incensed at the evil-doers,
    Be not envious of the workers of iniquity.
2   For like grass they are soon cut down,
    And like a green herb they wither away.
3 ב Trust in Jahve and do good,
    Dwell in the land and cultivate faithfulness.

4   And delight thyself in Jahve,
    So shall He give thee the desires of thy heart.

5 ג Commit thy way unto Jahve,
    And trust in Him; and He will bring it to pass.

6   He will bring forth like the light thy righteousness,
    And thy right like the noon-day brightness.

7 ד Resign thyself to Jahve and wait for Him;
    Fret not thyself over him who prospereth in his
        way,
    Over the man who bringeth wicked devices to pass.

8 ה Cease from anger and let go wrath,
    Be not incensed, it leads only to evil-doing.

9   For evil-doers shall be cut off,
    But they who hope in Jahve—they inherit the land.

10 ו Yet a little while and the wicked is no more,
    And if thou observest his place, he is gone.

11   But the meek shall inherit the land,
    And delight themselves in the abundance of peace.

12 ז The wicked deviseth evil against the righteous,
    And gnasheth upon him with his teeth—

13   The Lord laugheth at him,
    For He seeth that his day is coming.

14 ח The wicked draw the sword and bend their bow,
    To cast down the poor and needy,
    To slay them that are of upright walk.

15   Their sword shall enter into their own heart,
    And their bows shall be broken.

16 ט Better is the little that a righteous man hath,
    Than the riches of many wicked.

17   For the arms of the wicked shall be broken,
    And Jahve upholdeth the righteous.

18 י Jahve observeth the days of the perfect,
    And their inheritance shall endure for ever.

19   They are not ashamed in the evil time,
    And in the days of famine they are satisfied.

20 כ But the wicked perish,
    And the enemies of Jahve are like the glory of the
        meadows,
    They vanish away like smoke, they disappear.

21 ל The wicked is obliged to borrow and cannot pay,
    But the righteous is liberal and can give.
22   For they that are blessed of Him shall inherit the
        land,
    And they that are cursed of Him shall be cut off.
23 מ With Jahve are a man's steps established,
    And He hath delight in his way.
24   When he falls, he shall not be utterly cast down,
    For Jahve upholdeth his hand.
25 נ I have been young, and now am old,
    Yet have I not seen a righteous man forsaken,
    And his seed begging bread.
26   He continually giveth and lendeth,
    And his seed is a blessing.
27 ס Depart from evil and do good,
    And dwell for evermore.
28   For Jahve loveth the right,
    And will not forsake His saints.
    For ever are they preserved,
    But the seed of the wicked is cut off.
29   The righteous shall inherit the land,
    And dwell therein for ever.
30 פ The mouth of the righteous uttereth wisdom,
    And his tongue speaketh what is right.
31   The law of his God is in his heart,
    His steps do not slip.

32 צ The wicked lieth in wait for the righteous,
    And seeketh to slay him.
33   Jahve doth not give him over into his hand,
    Nor condemn him when he is judged.
34 ק Wait on Jahve and keep His way,
    So shall He exalt thee to inherit the land;
    With the cutting off the wicked shalt thou delight thine
        eyes.
35 ר I have seen a violent wicked man,
    And he spread himself like an indigenous tree of luxuriant
        foliage.
36   And one passed by, and lo he was not,
    And I sought him and he was not to be found.

37 שׁ Mark the perfect man, and observe the upright;
    That the man of peace hath a posterity.
38   But the transgressors are destroyed together,
    The posterity of the wicked is cut off.
39 ת And the salvation of the righteous is from Jahve,
    Who is their hiding-place in the time of trouble.
40   And Jahve helpeth them and rescueth them,
    He rescueth them from the wicked and saveth them,
    Because they trust in Him.

The bond of connection between Ps. xxxvi. and xxxvii. is their similarity of contents, which here and there extends even to accords of expression. The fundamental thought running through the whole Psalm is at once expressed in the opening verses: Do not let the prosperity of the ungodly be a source of vexation to thee, but wait on the Lord; for the prosperity of the ungodly will suddenly come to an end, and the issue determines between the righteous and the unrighteous. Hence Tertullian calls this Psalm *providentiæ speculum;* Isodore, *potio contra murmur;* and Luther, *vestis piorum, cui adscriptum: Hic Sanctorum patientia est* (Apoc. xiv. 12). This fundamental thought the poet does not expand in strophes of ordinary compass, but in shorter utterances of the proverbial form following the order of the letters of the alphabet, and not without some repetitions and recurrences to a previous thought, in order to impress it still more convincingly and deeply upon the mind. The Psalm belongs therefore to the series Ps. ix. and x., xxv., xxxiv.,—all alphabetical Psalms of David, of whose language, cheering, high-flown, thoughtful, and at the same time so easy and unartificial, and withal elegant, this Psalm is fully worthy. The structure of the proverbial utterances is almost entirely tetrastichic; though ר, כ, and ק are tristichs, and ח (which is twice represented, though perhaps unintentionally), ג, and ת are pentastichs. The ע is apparently wanting; but, on closer inspection, the originally separated strophes ס and ע are only run into one another by the division of the verses. The ע strophe begins with לְעוֹלָם, ver. 28*b*, and forms a tetrastich, just like the ס. The fact that the preposition לְ stands before the letter next in order need not confuse one. The ת, ver. 39, also begins with וּתְשׁוּעַת. The homogeneous beginnings,

צוֹפֶה רֹשׁע, לְוֶה רֹשׁע, וְזֹמֵם רָשָׁע, vers. 12, 21, 32, seem, as Hitzig re-marks, to be designed to give prominence to the pauses in the succession of the proverbial utterances.

Vers. 1, 2. Olshausen observes, "The poet keeps entirely to the standpoint of the old Hebrew doctrine of recompense, which the Book of Job so powerfully refutes." But, viewed in the light of the final issue, all God's government is really in a word righteous recompense; and the Old Testament theodicy is only inadequate in so far as the future, which adjusts all present inconsistencies, is still veiled. Meanwhile the punitive justice of God does make itself manifest, as a rule, in the case of the ungodly even in the present world; even their dying is usually a fearful end to their life's prosperity. This it is which the poet means here, and which is also expressed by Job him-self in the Book of Job, ch. xxvii. With הִתְחָרָה, to grow hot or angry (distinct from תִּחֲרֶה, to emulate, Jer. xii. 5, xxii. 15), alternates קִנֵּא, to get into a glow, *excandescentia*, whether it be the restrained heat of sullen envy, or the incontrollable heat of impetuous zeal which would gladly call down fire from heaven. This first distich has been transferred to the Book of Proverbs, ch. xxiv. 19, cf. xxiii. 17, xxiv. 1, iii. 31; and in general we may remark that this Psalm is one of the Davidic patterns for the Salomonic gnome system. The form יִמָּלוּ is, according to Gesenius, Olshausen, and Hitzig, *fut. Kal* of מָלַל, cognate אָמֵל, they wither away, pausal form for יִמְּלוּ like יִתַּמּוּ, cii. 28; but the signification to cut off also is secured to the verb מָלַל by the *Niph.* נָמַל, Gen. xvii. 11, whence *fut.* יִמּוֹל = יִמַּלּוּ; *vid.* on Job xiv. 2, xviii. 16. יֶרֶק דֶּשֶׁא is a genitival combination: the green (*viror*) of young vigorous vegetation.

Vers. 3, 4. The "land" is throughout this Psalm the promised possession (*Heilsgut*), viz. the land of Jahve's pre-sence, which has not merely a glorious past, but also a future rich in promises; and will finally, more perfectly than under Joshua, become the inheritance of the true Israel. It is there-fore to be explained: enjoy the quiet sure habitation which God gives thee, and diligently cultivate the virtue of faithful-ness. The two imperatives in ver. 3b, since there are two of them (cf. ver. 27) and the first is without any conjunctive *Waw*, have the appearance of being continued admonitions, not pro-

mises; and consequently אֱמוּנָה is not an adverbial accusative as
in cxix. 75 (Ewald), but the object to רְעֵה, to pasture, to pursue,
to practise (Syriac רְדַף, Hos. xii. 2); cf. רֵעֶה, רֵעַ, one who interests himself in any one, or anything; Beduin صاحب = راعى
of every kind of closer relationship (*Deutsch. Morgenländ.
Zeitschr.* v. 9). In ver. 4, וְיִתֶּן is an apodosis: delight in Jahve
(cf. Job xxii. 26, xxvii. 10, Isa. lviii. 14), so will He grant thee
the desire (מִשְׁאֲלֹת, as in xx. 6) of thy heart; for he who,
entirely severed from the creature, finds his highest delight in
God, cannot desire anything that is at enmity with God, but
he also can desire nothing that God, with whose will his own is
thoroughly blended in love, would refuse him.

Vers. 5, 6. The LXX. erroneously renders גּוֹל (= גֹּל, xxii.
9) by ἀποκάλυψον instead of ἐπίρριψον, 1 Pet. v. 7: roll the
burden of cares of thy life's way upon Jahve, leave the guidance of thy life entirely to Him, and to Him alone, without
doing anything in it thyself: He will gloriously accomplish (all
that concerns thee): עָשָׂה, as in xxii. 32, lii. 11; cf. Prov. xvi. 3,
and Paul Gerhardt's *Befiehl du deine Wege,* "Commit thou all
thy ways," etc. The perfect in ver. 6 is a continuation of the
promissory יַעֲשֶׂה. הוֹצִיא, as in Jer. li. 10, signifies to set forth:
He will bring to light thy misjudged righteousness like the
light (the sun, Job xxxi. 26, xxxvii. 21, and more especially the
morning sun, Prov. iv. 18), which breaks through the darkness;
and thy down-trodden right (מִשְׁפָּטֶךָ is the pausal form of the
singular beside *Mugrash*) like the bright light of the noon-day:
cf. Isa. lviii. 10, as on ver. 4, Isa. lviii. 14.

Ver. 7. The verb דָּמַם, with its derivatives (lxii. 2, 6, Lam.
iii. 28), denotes resignation, *i.e.* a quiet of mind which rests on
God, renounces all self-help, and submits to the will of God.
הִתְחוֹלֵל (from חוּל, to be in a state of tension, to wait) of the inward gathering of one's self together in hope intently directed
towards God, as in *B. Berachoth* 30b as a synonym of התחונן,
and as it were reflexive of חִלָּה of the collecting one's self to
importunate prayer. With ver. 7b the primary tone of the
whole Psalm is struck anew. On ver. 7c compare the definition of the mischief-maker in Prov. xxiv. 8.

Vers. 8, 9. On הֶרֶף (let alone), *imper. apoc. Hiph.,* instead
of הַרְפֵּה, *vid.* Ges. § 75, rem. 15. אַךְ לְהָרֵעַ is a clause to itself

(cf. Prov. xi. 24, xxi. 5, xxii. 16): it tends only to evil-doing, it ends only in thy involving thyself in sin. The final issue, without any need that thou shouldst turn sullen, is that the מְרֵעִים, like to whom thou dost make thyself by such passionate murmuring and displeasure, will be cut off, and they who, turning from the troublous present, make Jahve the ground and aim of their hope, shall inherit the land (*vid.* xxv. 13). It is the end, the final and consequently eternal end, that decides the matter.

Vers. 10, 11. The protasis in ver. 10*a* is literally: *adhuc parum (temporis superest)*, עוֹד מְעַט וְ, as *e.g.* Ex. xxiii. 30, and as in a similar connection מְעַט וְ, Job xxiv. 24. וְהִתְבּוֹנַנְתָּ also is a protasis with a hypothetical perfect, Ges. § 155, 4, *a*. This promise also runs in the mouth of the Preacher on the Mount (Matt. v. 5) just as the LXX. renders ver. 11*a*: οἱ δὲ πρᾳεῖς κληρονομήσουσι γῆν. Meekness, which is content with God, and renounces all earthly stays, will at length become the inheritor of the land, yea of the earth. Whatever God-opposed self-love may amass to itself and may seek to acquire, falls into the hands of the meek as their blessed possession.

Vers. 12, 13. The verb זָמַם is construed with לְ of that which is the object at which the evil devices aim. To gnash the teeth (elsewhere also: with the teeth) is, as in xxxv. 16, cf. Job xvi. 9, a gesture of anger, not of mockery, although anger and mockery are usually found together. But the Lord, who regards an assault upon the righteous as an assault upon Himself, laughs (ii. 4) at the enraged schemer; for He, who orders the destinies of men, sees beforehand, with His omniscient insight into the future, his day, *i.e.* the day of his death (2 Sam. xxvi. 10), of his visitation (cxxxvii. 7, Obad. ver. 12, Jer. l. 27, 31).

Vers. 14, 15. That which corresponds to the "treading" or stringing of the bow is the drawing from the sheath or unsheathing of the sword: פָּתַח, Ezek. xxi. 33, cf. Ps. lv. 22. The combination יִשְׁרֵי־דָרֶךְ is just like תְּמִימֵי־דֶרֶךְ, cxix. 1. The emphasis in ver. 15 is upon the suffix of בְּלִבָּם: they shall perish by their own weapon. קַשְּׁתוֹתָם has (in Baer) a *Shebâ dirimens*, as also in Isa. v. 28 in correct texts.

Vers. 16, 17. With ver. 16 accord Prov. xv. 16, xvi. 8, cf. Tobit xii. 8. The לְ of לַצַּדִּיק is a periphrastic indication of the

genitive (Ges. § 115).   הָמוֹן is a noisy multitude, here used of
earthly possessions.   רַבִּים is not *per attract.* (cf. xxxviii. 11,
הֵם for הוּא) equivalent to רָב, but the one righteous man is contrasted with many unrighteous.   The arms are here named
instead of the bow in ver. 15*b*.   He whose arms are broken can
neither injure others nor help himself.   Whereas Jahve does
for the righteous what earthly wealth and human power cannot
do: He Himself upholds them.

Vers. 18, 19.   The life of those who love Jahve with the
whole heart is, with all its vicissitudes, an object of His loving
regard and of His observant providential care, i. 6, xxxi. 8, cf.
16.   He neither suffers His own to lose their heritage nor to
be themselves lost to it.   The αἰώνιος κληρονομία is not as yet
thought of as extending into the future world, as in the New
Testament.   In ver. 19 the surviving refers only to this present life.

Ver. 20.   With כִּי the preceding assertion is confirmed by
its opposite (cf. cxxx. 4).   בִּיקַר כָּרִים forms a fine play in sound;
יְקַר is a substantivized adjective like גֹּדֶל, Ex. xv. 16.   Instead
of בֶּעָשָׁן, it is not to be read כְּעָשָׁן, Hos. xiii. 3; the ב is secured
by cii. 4, lxxviii. 33.   The idea is, that they vanish into smoke,
i.e. are resolved into it, or also, that they vanish in the manner
of smoke, which is first thick, but then becomes thinner and
thinner till it disappears (Rosenmüller, Hupfeld, Hitzig); both
expressions are admissible as to fact and as to the language,
and the latter is commended by בַּהֶבֶל, lxxviii. 33, cf. בְּצֶלֶם,
xxxix. 7.   בֶּעָשָׁן belongs to the first, regularly accented כָּלוּ; for
the *Munach* by בעשן is the substitute for *Mugrash*, which never
can be used where at least two syllables do not precede the
Silluk tone (*vid. Psalter* ii. 503).   The second כָּלוּ has the
accent on the *penult.* for a change (Ew. § 194, *c*), *i.e.* variation
of the rhythm (cf. לָמָה · · לָמָּה, xlii. 10, xliii. 2; עוֹרִי · · עוּרִי,
Judg. v. 12, and on cxxxvii. 7), and in particular here on
account of its pausal position (cf. עָרוּ, cxxxvii. 7).

Vers. 21, 22.   It is the promise expressed in Deut. xv. 6,
xxviii. 12, 44, which is rendered in ver. 21 in the more universal, sententious form.   לָוָה signifies to be bound or under obligation to any one = to borrow and to owe (*nexum esse*).   The
confirmation of ver. 22 is not inappropriate (as Hitzig considers
it, who places ver. 22 after ver. 20): in that ever deeper

downfall of the ungodly, and in that charitableness of the
righteous, which becomes more and more easy to him by reason
of his prosperity, the curse and blessing of God, which shall
be revealed in the end of the earthly lot of both the righteous
and the ungodly, are even now foretold. Whilst those who
reject the blessing of God are cut off, the promise given to the
patriarchs is fulfilled in the experience of those who are blessed
of God, in all its fulness.

Vers. 23, 24. By Jahve (מֵ, ἀπό, almost equivalent to ὑπό
with the passive, as in Job xxiv. 1, Eccles. xii. 11, and in a few
other passages) are a man's steps made firm, established; not:
ordered or directed (LXX., Jerome, κατευθύνεται), which,
according to the extant usage of the language, would be הוּכְנוּ
(passive of הֵכִין, Prov. xvi. 9, Jer. x. 23, 2 Chron. xxvii. 6),
whereas כּוֹנָנוּ, the *Pulal* of כּוֹנֵן, is to be understood according to
xl. 3. By גֶּבֶר is meant man in an emphatic sense (Job xxxviii.
3), and in fact in an ethical sense; compare, on the other hand,
the expression of the more general saying, "Man proposes, and
God disposes," Prov. xvi. 9, xx. 24, Jer. x. 23. Ver. 23*b* shows
that it is the upright man that is meant in ver. 23*a*: to the way,
i.e. course of life, of such an one God turns with pleasure (יֶחְפָּץ
pausal change of vowel for יַחְפֹּץ): supposing he should fall,
whether it be a fall arising from misfortune or from error, or
both together, he is not prostrated, but Jahve upholds his
hand, affords it a firm point of support or fulcrum (cf. תָּמַךְ בְּ,
lxiii. 9, and frequently), so that he can raise himself again,
rise up again.

Vers. 25, 26. There is an old theological rule: *promissiones
corporales intelligendæ sunt cum exceptione crucis et castigationis.*
Temporary forsakenness and destitution the Psalm does not
deny: it is indeed even intended to meet the conflict of doubt
which springs up in the minds of the God-fearing out of certain
conditions and circumstances that are seemingly contradictory
to the justice of God; and this it does, by contrasting that
which in the end abides with that which is transitory, and in
fact without the knowledge of any final decisive adjustment in
a future world; and it only solves its problem, in so far as it
is placed in the light of the New Testament, which already
dawns in the Book of Ecclesiastes.

Vers. 27, 28*a*. The round of the exhortations and promises

is here again reached as in ver. 3.   The imperative שְׁכֹן, which
is there hortatory, is found here with the ו of sequence in the
sense of a promise: and continue, doing such things, to dwell
for ever = so shalt thou, etc. (שָׁכַן, pregnant as in cii. 29, Isa.
lvii. 15).   Nevertheless the imperative retains its meaning even
in such instances, inasmuch as the exhortation is given to share
in the reward of duty at the same time with the discharge of
it.   On ver. 28*a* compare xxxiii. 5.

Vers. 28*b*, 29.   The division of the verses is wrong; for the
ס strophe, without any doubt, closes with חֲסִידָיו, and the ע
strophe begins with לְעוֹלָם, so that, according to the text which
we possess, the ע of this word is the acrostic letter.   The
LXX., however, after εἰς τὸν αἰῶνα φυλαχθήσονται has
another line, which suggests another commencement for the
ע strophe, and runs in *Cod. Vat.*, incorrectly, ἄμωμοι ἐκδική-
σονται, in *Cod. Alex.*, correctly, ἄνομοι δὲ ἐκδιωχθήσονται
(Symmachus, ἄνομοι ἐξαρθήσονται).   By ἄνομος the LXX.
translates עָרִיץ in Isa. xxix. 20; by ἄνομα, עַוְלָה in Job xxvii. 4;
and by ἐκδιώκειν, הִצְמִית, the synonym of הִשְׁמִיד, in Ps. ci. 5; so
that consequently this line, as even Venema and Schleusner
have discerned, was עַוָּלִים נִשְׁמָדוּ.   It will at once be seen
that this is only another reading for לעולם נשמרו; and, since it
stands side by side with the latter, that it is an ancient attempt
to produce a correct beginning for the ע strophe, which has
been transplanted from the LXX. into the text.   It is, however, questionable whether this reparation is really a restoration
of the original words (Hupfeld, Hitzig); since עַוָּל (עֲוִיל) is not
a word found in the Psalms (for which reason Böttcher's conjecture of עֹשֵׂי עַוְלָה more readily commends itself, although it is
critically less probable), and לְעוֹלָם נשמרו forms a continuation
that is more naturally brought about by the context and perfectly logical.

Vers. 30, 31.   The verb הָגָה unites in itself the two meanings of meditating and of meditative utterance (*vid.* ii. 1),
just as אָמַר those of thinking and speaking.   Ver. 31*b* in this
connection affirms the stability of the moral nature.   The walk
of the righteous has a fixed inward rule, for the Tôra is to him
not merely an external object of knowledge and a compulsory
precept; it is in his heart, and, because it is the Tôra of his God
whom he loves, as the motive of his actions closely united with

his own will. On תִּמְעַד, followed by the subject in the plural, compare xviii. 35, lxxiii. 2 *Chethîb*.

Vers. 32, 33. The Lord as ἀνακρίνων is, as in 1 Cor. iv. 3 sq., put in contrast with the ἀνακρίνειν of men, or of human ἡμέρα. If men sit in judgment upon the righteous, yet God, the supreme Judge, does not condemn him, but acquits him (cf. on the contrary cix. 7). *Si condemnamur a mundo*, exclaimed Tertullian to his companions in persecution, *absolvimur a Deo*.

Ver. 34. Let the eye of faith directed hopefully to Jahve go on its way, without suffering thyself to be turned aside by the persecution and condemnation of the world, then He will at length raise thee out of all trouble, and cause thee to possess (לָרֶשֶׁת, *ut possidas et possideas*) the land, as the sole lords of which the evil-doers, now cut off, conducted themselves.

Vers. 35, 36. עָרִיץ (after the form צַדִּיק) is coupled with רָשָׁע, just as these two words alternate in Job xv. 20: a terror-inspiring, tyrannical evil-doer; cf. besides also Job v. 3. The participle in ver. 35*b* forms a clause by itself: *et se diffundens*, scil. *erat*. The LXX. and Jerome translate as though it were כארז הלבנן, "like the cedars of Lebanon," instead of כאזרח רענן. But אֶזְרָח רַעֲנָן is the expression for an oak, terebinth, or the like, that has grown from time immemorial in its native soil, and has in the course of centuries attained a gigantic size in the stem, and a wide-spreading overhanging head. וַיַּעֲבֹר does not mean: then he vanished away (Hupfeld and others); for עָבַר in this sense is not suitable to a tree. Luther correctly renders it: *man ging vorüber*, one (they) passed by, Ges. § 137, 3. The LXX., Syriac, and others, by way of lightening the difficulty, render it: then I passed by.

Vers. 37, 38. תָּם might even be taken as neuter for תֹּם, and יָשָׁר for יֹשֶׁר; but in this case the poet would have written רְעֵה instead of רְאֵה; שָׁמַר is therefore used as, *e.g.*, in 1 Sam. i. 12. By כִּי that to which attention is specially called is introduced. The man of peace has a totally different lot from the evil-doer who delights in contention and persecution. As the fruit of his love of peace he has אַחֲרִית, a future, Prov. xxiii. 18, xxiv. 14, viz. in his posterity, Prov. xxiv. 20; whereas the apostates are altogether blotted out; not merely they themselves, but even the posterity of the ungodly is cut off, Amos

iv. 2, ix. 1, Ezek. xxiii. 25. To them remains no posterity to carry forward their name, their אַחֲרִית is devoted to destruction (cf. cix. 13 with Num. xxiv. 20).

Vers. 39, 40. The salvation of the righteous cometh from Jahve; it is therefore characterized, in accordance with its origin, as sure, perfect, and enduring for ever. מָעוּזָּם is an apposition; the *plena scriptio* serves, as in 2 Sam. xxii. 33, to indicate to us that מעוז is meant in this passage to signify not a fortress, but a hiding-place, a place of protection, a refuge, in which sense معان الله (the protection of God) and معان وجه الله (the protection of God's presence) is an Arabic expression (also used as a formula of an oath); *vid.* moreover on xxxi. 3. The moods of sequence in ver. 40 are *aoristi gnomici.* The parallelism in ver. 40*ab* is progressive after the manner of the Psalms of degrees. The short confirmatory clause *ki chǎ'su bo* forms an expressive closing cadence.

PSALM XXXVIII.

PRAYER FOR THE CHANGING OF MERITED WRATH INTO RESCUING LOVE.

2 JAHVE, do not in Thy wrath rebuke me,
  And in Thy hot displeasure chasten me.
3 For Thine arrows have entered deep into me,
  And Thy hand hath sunk down upon me.

4 There is no soundness in my flesh because of Thine anger,
  There is no health in my bones because of my sin.
5 For mine iniquities are gone over my head,
  Like a heavy burden they are too heavy for me.

6 My wounds stink and fester
  Because of my foolishness.
7 I am bent, I am sore bowed down,
  All the day long do I go mourning.

8 For my loins are full of burning,
  And there is no soundness in my flesh.

 9 I am benumbed and sore crushed,
   I roar by reason of the groaning of my heart.

10 O Lord, to Thee is all my desire manifest,
   And my sighing is not hidden from Thee.
11 My heart beateth quickly, my strength hath failed me,
   And the light of mine eyes, even of these, is gone from me.

12 My lovers and friends stand aloof from my stroke,
   [And my kinsmen stand afar off,]
13 And they lay snares for me who seek after my soul,
   And they who strive after my misfortune speak mischievous
   And utter falsehoods continually.   [things,

14 But I am like a deaf man, as though I heard not,
   And like one dumb that openeth not his mouth;
15 I am become like a man that heareth not,
   And in whose mouth are no replies.

16 For in Thee, Jahve, do I hope;
   Thou, Thou wilt answer, O Lord my God.
17 For I say: Let them not rejoice over me
   Who, when my foot tottereth, would magnify themselves
            against me.

18 For I am ready to fall,
   And my great sorrow is ever before me.
19 For mine iniquity must I confess,
   I must tremble on account of my sin.

20 But mine enemies are vigorous, they are numerous,
   And many are my lying haters.
21 And requiting evil for good,
   They are hostile towards me for my following that which
            is good.

22 Forsake me not, Jahve;
   My God, be not far from me.
23 Make haste to help me,
   O Lord, who art my salvation!

The penitential Psalm, xxxviii., is placed immediately after
Ps. xxxvii. on account of the similarity of its close to the ת
strophe of that Psalm. It begins like Ps. vi. If we regard
David's adultery as the occasion of it (cf. more especially 2 Sam.
xii. 14), then Ps. vi., xxxviii., li., xxxii. form a chronological series.
David is distressed both in mind and body, forsaken by his friends,
and regarded by his foes as one who is cast off for ever. The fire
of divine anger burns within him like a fever, and the divine
withdrawal as it were rests upon him like darkness. But he
fights his way by prayer through this fire and this darkness to
the bright confidence of faith. The Psalm, although it is the
pouring forth of such elevated and depressed feelings, is nevertheless symmetrically and skilfully laid out. It consists of
three main paragraphs, which divide into four (vers. 2–9), three
(vers. 10–15), and four (vers. 16–23) tetrastichs. The way in
which the names of God are brought in is well conceived.
The first word of the first group or paragraph is יהוה, the first
word of the second אֲדֹנָי, and in the third יהוה and אֲדֹנָי are used
interchangeably twice. The Psalm, in common with Ps. lxx.,
bears the inscription לְהַזְכִּיר. The chronicler, in 1 Chron. xvi.
4, refers to these *Hazkir* Psalms together with the *Hodu* and
Halleluja Psalms. In connection with the presentation of
meat-offerings, מְנָחוֹת, a portion of the meat-offering was cast
into the altar fire, viz. a handful of the meal mixed with oil
and the whole of the incense. This portion was called אַזְכָּרָה,
ἀνάμνησις, and to offer it הִזְכִּיר (a denominative), because the
ascending smoke was intended to bring the owner of the offering into remembrance with God. In connection with the
presentation of this memorial portion of the *mincha*, the two
Psalms are appointed to be used as prayers; hence the inscription: *at the presentation of the Azcara* (the portion taken from
the meal-offering). The LXX. adds here περὶ (τοῦ) σαββάτου; perhaps equivalent to לְשַׁבֵּת.

In this Psalm we find a repetition of a peculiarity of the
penitential Psalms, viz. that the praying one has to complain
not only of afflictions of body and soul, but also of outward
enemies, who come forward as his accusers and take occasion
from his sin to prepare the way for his ruin. This arises from
the fact that the Old Testament believer, whose perception of
sin was not as yet so spiritual and deep as that of the New

Testament believer, almost always calls to mind some sinful act that has become openly known. The foes, who would then prepare for his ruin, are the instruments of the Satanic power of evil (cf. ver. 21, יִשְׂטְנוּנִי), which, as becomes perceptible to the New Testament believer even without the intervention of outward foes, desires the death of the sinning one, whereas God wills that he should live.

Vers. 2–9. David begins, as in Ps. vi., with the prayer that his punitive affliction may be changed into disciplinary. Bakius correctly paraphrases ver. 2: *Corripe sane per legem, castiga per crucem, millies promerui, negare non possum, sed castiga, quæso, me ex amore ut pater, non ex furore et fervore ut judex; ne punias justitiæ rigore, sed misericordiæ dulcore* (cf. on vi. 2). The negative is to be repeated in ver. 2*b*, as in i. 5, ix. 19, lxxv. 6. In the description, which gives the ground of the cry for pity, נִחַת is not the *Piel*, as in xviii. 35, but the *Niphal* of the *Kal* נָחַת immediately following (root נח). קֶצֶף is anger as a breaking forth, *fragor* (cf. Hos. x. 7, LXX. φρύγανον), with ĕ instead of ĭ in the first syllable, vowels which alternate in this word; and חֵמָה, as a glowing or burning. חִצִּים (in Homer, κῆλα), God's wrath-arrows, *i.e.* lightnings of wrath, are His judgments of wrath; and יָד, as in xxxii. 4, xxxix. 11, God's punishing hand, which makes itself felt in dispensing punishment, hence תִּנְחַת might be attached as a mood of sequence. In ver. 4 wrath is called זַעַם as a boiling up. Sin is the cause of this experiencing wrath, and the wrath is the cause of the bodily derangement; sin as an exciting cause of the wrath always manifests itself outwardly even on the body as a fatal power. In ver. 5*a* sin is compared to waters that threaten to drown one, as in ver. 5*b* to a burden that presses one down. יִכְבְּדוּ מִמֶּנִּי, they are heavier than I, *i.e.* than my power of endurance, too heavy for me. In ver. 6 the effects of the operation of the divine hand (as punishing) are wounds, חַבּוּרֹת (properly, suffused variegated marks from a blow or wheals, Isa. i. 6; from חָבַר, حبر, to be or make striped, variegated), which הִבְאִישׁוּ, send forth an offensive smell, and נָמַקּוּ, suppurate. Sin, which causes this, is called אִוֶּלֶת, because, as it is at last manifest, it is always the destruction of itself.

With emphasis does מִפְּנֵי אִוַּלְתִּי form the second half of the verse. To take נַעֲוֵיתִי out of ver. 7 and put it to this, as Meier and Thenius propose, is to destroy this its proper position. On the three מִפְּנֵי, *vid.* Ewald, § 217, *l.* Thus sick in soul and body, he is obliged to bow and bend himself in the extreme. נֵעֱוָה is used of a convulsive drawing together of the body, Isa. xxi. 3 ; שָׁחַח, of a bowed mien, Ps. xxxv. 14 ; הִלֵּךְ, of a heavy, lagging gait. With כִּי in ver. 8 the grounding of the petition begins for the third time. His כְּסָלִים, *i.e.* internal muscles of the loins, which are usually the fattest parts, are full of נִקְלֶה, that which is burnt, *i.e.* parched. It is therefore as though the burning, starting from the central point of the bodily power, would spread itself over the whole body : the wrath of God works commotion in this latter as well as in the soul. Whilst all the energies of life thus yield, there comes over him a partial, almost total lifelessness. פּוּג is the proper word for the coldness and rigidity of a corpse; the *Niphal* means to be brought into this condition, just as נִדְכָּא means to be crushed, or to be brought into a condition of crushing, *i.e.* of violent dissolution. The מִן of מִנַּהֲמַת is intended to imply that the loud wail is only the utterance of the pain that is raging in his heart, the outward expression of his ceaseless, deep inward groaning.

Vers. 10–15. Having thus bewailed his suffering before God, he goes on in a somewhat calmer tone : it is the calm of weariness, but also of the rescue which shows itself from afar. He has complained, but not as if it were necessary for him first of all to make God acquainted with his suffering; the Omniscient One is directly cognisant of (has directly before Him, נֶגֶד, like לְנֶגֶד in xviii. 25) every wish that his suffering extorts from him, and even his softer sighing does not escape His knowledge. The sufferer does not say this so much with the view of comforting himself with this thought, as of exciting God's compassion. Hence he even goes on to draw the piteous picture of his condition : his heart is in a state of violent rotary motion, or only of violent, quickly repeated contraction and expansion (*Psychol.* S. 252; tr. p. 297), that is to say, a state of violent palpitation (סְחַרְחַר, *Pealal* according to Ges. § 55, 3). Strength of which the heart is the centre (xl. 13) has left him, and the light of his eyes, even of these (by attraction for גַּם־הוּא,

since the light of the eyes is not contrasted with anything else),
is not with him, but has become lost to him by weeping, watching, and fever. Those who love him and are friendly towards
him have placed themselves far from his stroke (נֶגַע, the touch
of God's hand of wrath), merely looking on (Obad. ver. 11),
therefore, in a position hostile (2 Sam. xviii. 13) rather than
friendly. מִנֶּגֶד, far away, but within the range of vision,
within sight, Gen. xxi. 16, Deut. xxxii. 52. The words וּקְרוֹבַי
מֵרָחֹק עָמָדוּ, which introduce a pentastich into a Psalm that is
tetrastichic throughout, have the appearance of being a gloss
or various reading: מֵרָחֹק = מִנֶּגֶד, 2 Kings ii. 7. His enemies,
however, endeavour to take advantage of his fall and helplessness, in order to give him his final death-blow. וַיְנַקְשׁוּ (with
the ק dageshed*) describes what they have planned in consequence of the position he is in. The substance of their words
is הַוּוֹת, utter destruction (vid. v. 10); to this end it is מִרְמוֹת,
deceit upon deceit, malice upon malice, that they unceasingly
hatch with heart and mouth. In the consciousness of his sin
he is obliged to be silent, and, renouncing all self-help, to
abandon his cause to God. Consciousness of guilt and resignation close his lips, so that he is not able, nor does he wish, to
refute the false charges of his enemies; he has no תּוֹכָחוֹת,
counter-evidence wherewith to vindicate himself. It is not to
be rendered: "just as one dumb opens not his mouth;" כְּ is
only a preposition, not a conjunction, and it is just here, in
vers. 14, 15, that the manifest proofs in support of this are
found.†

------

* The various reading וַיְנַקְשׁוּ in Norzi rests upon a misapprehended
passage of Abulwalîd (Rikma, p. 166).

† The passages brought forward by Hupfeld in support of the use of כְּ
as a conjunction, viz. xc. 5, cxxv. 1, Isa. liii. 7, lxi. 11, are invalid; the
passage that seems most to favour it is Obad. ver. 16, but in this instance
the expression is elliptical, כְּלֹא being equivalent to כַּאֲשֶׁר לֹא, like כְּלֹא,
Isa. lxv. 1, = לַאֲשֶׁר לֹא. It is only כְּמוֹ (كَما) that can be used as a conjunction; but כְּ (كَ) is always a preposition in ancient Hebrew just as in
Syriac and Arabic (vid. Fleischer in the Hallische Allgem. Lit. Zeitschr.
1843, Bd. iv. S. 117 ff.). It is not until the mediæval synagogal poetry
(vid. Zunz, Synagogal-poesie des Mittelalters, S. 121, 381 f.) that it is
admissible to use it as a conjunction (e.g. כְּמָצָא, when he had found), just
as it also occurs in Himjaritic, according to Osiander's deciphering of the

Vers. 16–23. Become utterly useless in himself, he renounces all self-help, for (כִּי) he hopes in Jahve, who alone can help him. He waits for His answer, for (כי) he says, etc. —he waits for an answer, for the hearing of this his petition which is directed towards the glory of God, that God would not suffer his foes to triumph over him, nor strengthen them in their mercilessness and injustice. Ver. 18*b* appears also to stand under the government of the פֶּן;* but, since in this case one would look for a *Waw relat.* and a different order of the words, ver. 18*b* is to be regarded as a subject clause: "who, when my foot totters, *i.e.* when my affliction changes to entire downfall, would magnify themselves against me." In ver. 18, כִּי connects what follows with בְּמוֹט רַגְלִי by way of confirmation: he is נָכוֹן לְצֶלַע, ready for falling (xxxv. 15), he will, if God does not graciously interpose, assuredly fall headlong. The fourth כִּי in ver. 19 is attached confirmatorily to ver. 18*b*: his intense pain or sorrow is ever present to him, for he is obliged to confess his guilt, and this feeling of guilt is just the very sting of his pain. And whilst he in the consciousness of well-deserved punishment is sick unto death, his foes are numerous and withal vigorous and full of life. Instead of חַיִּים, probably חִנָּם, as in xxxv. 19, lxix. 5, is to be read (Houbigant, Hitzig, Köster, Hupfeld, Ewald, and Olshausen). But even the LXX. read חיים; and the reading which is so old, although it does not very well suit עָצְמוּ (instead of which one would look for וְעָצוּמִים), is still not without meaning: he looks upon himself, according to ver. 9, more as one dead than living; his foes, however, are חַיִּים, living, *i.e.* vigorous. The verb frequently has this pregnant meaning, and the adjective can also

---

inscriptions. The verbal clause appended to the word to which this כְּ, *instar*, is prefixed is for the most part an attributive clause as above, but sometimes even a circumstantial clause (حَال), as in xxxviii. 14; cf. *Sur.* lxii. 5: "as the likeness of an ass carrying books."

* The following are the constructions of פֶּן when a clause of more than one member follows it: (1) *fut.* and *perf.*, the latter with the tone of the *perf. consec.*, *e.g.* Ex. xxxiv. 15 sq., or without it, *e.g.* xxviii. 1 (which see); (2) *fut.* and *fut.* as in ii. 12, Jer. li. 46. This construction is indispensable where it is intended to give special prominence to the subject notion or a secondary notion of the clause, *e.g.* Deut. xx. 6. In one instance פֶּן is even followed (3) by the *perf.* and *fut. consec.*, viz. 2 Kings ii. 1C.

have it. Just as the accentuation of the form סַבּוּ varies elsewhere out of pause, וְרַבּוּ here has the tone on the *ultima*, although it is not *perf. consec.** Ver. 21*a* is an apposition of the subject, which remains the same as in ver. 20. Instead of רֹדְפִי (Ges. § 61, rem. 2) the *Kerî* is רָדְפִי, *rād⁰phî* (without any *Makkeph* following), or רֹדְפִי, *rād⁰phî*; cf. on this pronunciation, lxxxvi. 2, xvi. 1, and with the *Chethîb* רדופי, the *Chethîb* צרופה, xxvi. 2, also מיורדי, xxx. 4. By the "following of that which is good" David means more particularly that which is brought into exercise in relation to his present foes.† He closes in vers. 22 sq. with sighs for help. No lighting up of the darkness of wrath takes place. The *fides supplex* is not changed into *fides triumphans*. But the closing words, "O Lord, my salvation" (cf. li. 16), show where the repentance of Cain and that of David differ. True repentance has faith within itself, it despairs of itself, but not of God.

PSALM XXXIX.

PRAYERS OF ONE SORELY TRIED AT THE SIGHT OF THE PROSPERITY OF THE UNGODLY.

2 I SAID: "I will keep my ways against sinning with my
  tongue;
  I will keep a bridle on my mouth,
  So long as the wicked is before me."
3 I was dumb in silence,

---

* As *perf. consec.* the following have the accent on the *ultima*:—וְחַתּוּ, Isa. xx. 5, Obad. ver. 9, and וְרַבּוּ, Isa. lxvi. 16; perhaps also וְקַלּוּ וְחַדּוּ, Hab. i. 8, and וְרַבּוּ (*perf. hypoth.*), Job xxxii. 15. But there is no special reason for the *ultima*-accentuation of רָכּוּ, lv. 22; רַבּוּ, lxix. 5; דַּלּוּ, Isa. xxxviii. 14; קַלּוּ, Jer. iv. 13; שָׂחוּ, Prov. xiv. 19, Hab. iii. 6; חַתּוּ, Job xxxii. 15; זַכּוּ, צָחוּ, Lam. iv. 7.

† In the Greek and Latin texts, likewise in all the Æthiopic and several Arabic texts, and in the Syriac *Psalterium Medilanense*, the following addition is found after ver. 21: *Ce aperripsan me ton agapeton osi necron ebdelygmenon, Et projecerunt me dilectum tanquam mortuum abominatum* (so the *Psalt. Veronense*). Theodoret refers it to Absalom's relation to David. The words ὡσεὶ νεκρὸν ἐβδελυγμένον are taken from Isa. xiv. 19.

I held my peace taking no note of prosperity,
Yet my pain became violent.
4 My heart was hot within me,
While I mused the fire burned—
I spake with my tongue.

5 Make me to know, O Jahve, mine end,
And the measure of my days how short it is;
Oh that I might know, how frail I am!
6 Behold, Thou hast made my days as a handbreadth,
And my lifetime is as nothing before Thee.
Only a mere breath is every man, however firm he may
      stand. (*Sela.*)
7 Only as a shadow doth man wander to and fro,
Only for a breath do they make an uproar;
He heapeth up and knoweth not who will gather it.

8 And now for what shall I wait, Lord!
My hope is towards Thee.
9 From all my transgressions rescue me,
Make me not a reproach of the profane!
10 I am dumb, I open not my mouth,
For Thou, Thou hast done it.
11 Take away from me Thy stroke,
Before the blow of Thy hand I must perish.
12 When Thou with rebukes dost chasten a man for iniquity,
Thou makest his beauty melt away, like the damage of the
      moth—
Only a breath are all men. (*Sela.*)

13 O hear my prayer, Jahve,
And hearken to my cry!
At my tears be not silent,
For I am a guest with Thee,
A sojourner, like all my fathers.
14 Look away from me, that I may rally,
Before I go hence and am no more.

In xxxviii. 14 the poet calls himself a dumb person, who
opens not his mouth; this submissive, resigned keeping of

silence he affirms of himself in the same words in xxxix. 3 also. This forms a prominent characteristic common to the two Psalms, which fully warranted their being placed together as a pair. There is, however, another Psalm, which is still more closely related to Ps. xxxix., viz. Ps. lxii., which, together with Ps. iv., has a similar historical background. The author, in his dignity, is threatened by those who from being false friends have become open enemies, and who revel in the enjoyment of illegitimately acquired power and possessions. From his own experience, in the midst of which he commits his safety and his honour to God, he derives the general warnings, that to trust in riches is deceptive, and that power belongs alone to God the Avenger—two doctrines, in support of which the issue of the affair with Absalom was a forcible example. Thus it is with Ps. lxii., and in like manner Ps. xxxix. also. Both Psalms bear the name of Jeduthun side by side with the name of David at their head; both describe the nothingness of everything human in the same language; both delight more than other Psalms in the use of the assuring, confident אַךְ; both have סלה twice; both coincide in some points with the Book of Job; the form of both Psalms, however, is so polished, transparent, and classic, that criticism is not authorized in assigning to this pair of Psalms any particular poet other than David. The reason of the redacteur not placing Ps. lxii. immediately after Ps. xxxix. is to be found in the fact that Ps. lxii. is an Elohim-Psalm, which could not stand in the midst of Jahve-Psalms.

To the inscribed לַמְנַצֵּחַ, לִידִיתוּן is added in this instance. The name is also written thus in lxxvii. 1, 1 Chron. xvi. 38, Neh. xi. 17, and always with the *Kerî* יְדוּתוּן, which, after the analogy of זְבוּלֻן, is the more easily pronouncible pointing (lxii. 1). It is an offshoot of the form יְדוּת or יְדִית; cf. שְׁבוּת and שְׁבִית, חִפְשׁוּת and חָפְשִׁית. It is the name of one of David's three choir-masters or precentors—the third in conjunction with Asaph and Heman, 1 Chron. xvi. 41 sq., xxv. 1 sqq., 2 Chron. v. 12, xxxv. 15, and is, without doubt, the same person as אֵיתָן, 1 Chron. ch. xv., a name which is changed into ידותן after the arrangement in Gibeon, 1 Chron. ch. xvi. Consequently side by side with למנצח, לידותן will be the name of the מנצח himself, *i.e.* the name of the person to whom the

song was handed over to be set to music. The fact that in
two inscriptions (lxii. 1, lxxvii. 1) we read עַל instead of the לְ of
לִידִיתוּן, does not militate against this. By לְ Jeduthun is denoted
as the person to whom the song was handed over for performance; and by עַל, as the person to whom the performance
was assigned. The rendering: "to the director of the Jedi-
thunites," adopted by Hitzig, is possible regarding the ידותן as
used as a generic name like אהרן in 1 Chron. xii. 27, xxvii. 17;
but the customary use of the לְ in inscriptions is against it.

The Psalm consists of four stanzas without any strophic
symmetry. The first three are of only approximately the
same compass, and the final smaller stanza has designedly the
character of an epilogue.

Vers. 2–4. The poet relates how he has resolved to bear
his own affliction silently in the face of the prosperity of the
ungodly, but that his smart was so overpowering that he was
compelled involuntarily to break his silence by loud complaint.
The resolve follows the introductory אָמַרְתִּי in cohortatives. He
meant to take heed to his ways, i.e. his manner of thought and
action, in all their extent, lest he should sin with his tongue,
viz. by any murmuring complaint concerning his own misfortune, when he saw the prosperity of the ungodly. He was
resolved to keep (i.e. cause invariably to press) a bridling (cf.
on the form, Gen. xxx. 37), or a bridle (capistrum), upon his
mouth, so long as he should see the ungodly continuing and
sinning in the fulness of his strength, instead of his speedy
ruin which one ought to expect. Then he was struck dumb
דּוּמִיָּה, in silence, i.e. as in lxii. 2, cf. Lam. iii. 26, in resigned
submission, he was silent מִטּוֹב, turned away from (vid. xxviii.
1, 1 Sam. vii. 8, and frequently) prosperity, i.e. from that in
which he saw the evil-doer rejoicing; he sought to silence for
ever the perplexing contradiction between this prosperity and
the righteousness of God. But this self-imposed silence gave
intensity to the repressed pain, and this was thereby נֶעְכָּר, stirred
up, excited, aroused; the inward heat became, in consequence
of restrained complaint, all the more intense (Jer. xx. 9): "and
while I was musing a fire was kindled," i.e. the thoughts and
emotions rubbing against one another produced a blazing fire,
viz. of irrepressible vexation, and the end of it was: "I spake

with my tongue," unable any longer to keep in my pain. What now follows is not what was said by the poet when in this condition. On the contrary, he turns away from his purpose, which has been proved to be impracticable, to God Himself with the prayer that He would teach him calm submission.

Vers. 5–7. He prays God to set the transitoriness of earthly life clearly before his eyes (cf. xc. 12); for if life is only a few spans long, then even his suffering and the prosperity of the ungodly will last only a short time. Oh that God would then grant him to know his end (Job vi. 11), *i.e.* the end of his life, which is at the same time the end of his affliction, and the measure of his days, how it is with this (מֶה, *interrog. extenuantis*, as in viii. 5), in order that he may become fully conscious of his own frailty! Hupfeld corrects the text to מַה־חֶלֶד אָנִי, after the analogy of lxxxix. 48, because חָדֵל c nnot signify "frail." But חָדֵל signifies that which leaves off and ceases, and consequently in this connection, finite and transitory or frail. מה, *quam*, in connection with an adjective, as in viii. 2, xxxi. 20, xxxvi. 8, lxvi. 3, cxxxiii. 1. By הֵן (the customary form of introducing the *propositio minor*, Lev. x. 18, xxv. 20) the preceding petition is supported. God has, indeed, made the days, *i.e.* the lifetime, of a man טְפָחוֹת, handbreadths, *i.e.* He has allotted to it only the short extension of a few handbreadths (cf. יָמִים, a few days, *e.g.* Isa. lxv. 20), of which nine make a yard (cf. πήχυιος χρόνος in Mimnermus, and 1 Sam. xx. 3); the duration of human life (on חֶלֶד *vid.* xvii. 14) is as a vanishing nothing before God the eternal One. The particle אַךְ is originally affirmative, and starting from that sense becomes restrictive; just as רַק is originally restrictive and then affirmative. Sometimes also, as is commonly the case with אָכֵן, the affirmative signification passes over into the adversative (cf. *verum, verum enim vero*). In our passage, agreeably to the restrictive sense, it is to be explained thus: nothing but mere nothingness (cf. xlv. 14, Jas. i. 2) is every man נִצָּב, standing firmly, *i.e.* though he stand never so firmly, though he be never so stedfast (Zech. xi. 16). Here the music rises to tones of bitter lament, and the song continues in ver. 7 with the same theme. צֶלֶם, belonging to the same root as צֵל, signifies a shadow-outline, an image; the בְּ is, as in xxxv. 2, *Beth essentiæ*: he walks about consisting only of an unsubstantial shadow.

Only הֶבֶל, breath-like, or after the manner of breath (cxliv. 4),
from empty, vain motives and with vain results, do they make a
disturbance (pausal *fut. energicum*, as in xxxvi. 8); and he who
restlessly and noisily exerts himself knows not who will suddenly snatch together, *i.e.* take altogether greedily to himself,
the many things that he heaps up (צָבַר, as in Job xxvii. 16);
cf. Isa. xxxiii. 4, and on —*ām* = αὐτά, Lev. xv. 10 (in connection with which אלה הדברים, cf. Isa. xlii. 16, is in the mind of
the speaker).

Vers. 8–12. It is customary to begin a distinct turning-
point of a discourse with וְעַתָּה: and now, *i.e.* in connection
with this nothingness or vanity of a life which is so full of
suffering and unrest, what am I to hope, *quid sperem* (concerning the perfect, *vid.* on xi. 3)? The answer to this question
which he himself throws out is, that Jahve is the goal of his
waiting or hoping. It might appear strange that the poet is
willing to make the brevity of human life a reason for being
calm, and a ground of comfort. But here we have the explanation. Although not expressly assured of a future life of
blessedness, his faith, even in the midst of death, lays hold on
Jahve as the Living One and as the God of the living. It is
just this which is so heroic in the Old Testament faith, that in
the midst of the riddles of the present, and in the face of the
future which is lost in dismal night, it casts itself unreservedly
into the arms of God. While, however, sin is the root of all
evil, the poet prays in ver. 9*a* before all else, that God would
remove from him all the transgressions by which he has fully
incurred his affliction; and while, given over to the consequences of his sin, he would become, not only to his own
dishonour but also to the dishonour of God, a derision to the
unbelieving, he prays in ver. 9*b* that God would not permit it
to come to this. כָּל, ver. 9*a*, has *Mercha*, and is consequently,
as in xxxv. 10, to be read with *ā* (not *ŏ*), since an accent can
never be placed by *Kametz chatûph*. Concerning נָבָל, ver. 9*b*,
see on xiv. 1. As to the rest he is silent and calm; for God
is the author, viz. of his affliction (עָשָׂה, used just as absolutely
as in xxii. 32, xxxvii. 5, lii. 11, Lam. i. 21). Without ceasing
still to regard intently the prosperity of the ungodly, he recognises the hand of God in his affliction, and knows that he
has not merited anything better. But it is permitted to him to

pray that God would suffer mercy to take the place of right. נִגְעֶךָ is the name he gives to his affliction, as in xxxviii. 12, as being a stroke (blow) of divine wrath; תִּגְרַת יָדֶךָ, as a quarrel into which God's hand has fallen with him; and by אֲנִי, with the almighty (punishing) hand of God, he contrasts himself the feeble one, to whom, if the present state of things continues, ruin is certain. In ver. 12 he puts his own personal experience into the form of a general maxim: when with rebukes (תּוֹכָחוֹת from תּוֹכַחַת, collateral form with תּוֹכַחָה, תּוֹכֵחוֹת) Thou chastenest a man on account of iniquity (*perf. conditionale*), Thou makest his pleasantness (Isa. liii. 3), *i.e.* his bodily beauty (Job xxxiii. 21), to melt away, moulder away (וַתֶּמֶם, *fut. apoc.* from הִמְסָה, to cause to melt, vi. 7), like the moth (Hos. v. 12), so that it falls away, as a moth-eaten garment falls into rags. Thus do all men become mere nothing. They are sinful and perishing. The thought expressed in ver. 6*c* is here repeated as a refrain. The music again strikes in here, as there.

Vers. 13, 14. Finally, the poet renews the prayer for an alleviation of his sufferings, basing it upon the shortness of this earthly pilgrimage. The urgent שִׁמְעָה is here fuller toned, being שָׁמְעָה.* Side by side with the language of prayer, tears even appear here as prayer that is intelligible to God; for when the gates of prayer seem to be closed, the gates of tears still remain unclosed (שערי דמעות לא ננעלו), *B. Berachoth* 32*b*. As a reason for his being heard, David appeals to the instability and finite character of this earthly life in language which we also hear from his own lips in 1 Chron. xxix. 15. גֵּר is the stranger who travels about and sojourns as a guest in a country that is not his native land; תּוֹשָׁב is a sojourner, or one enjoying the protection of the laws, who, without possessing any hereditary title, has settled down there, and to whom a settlement is allotted by sufferance. The earth is God's; that which may be said of the Holy Land (Lev. xxv. 23) may be said of the

---

* So Heidenheim and Baer, following Abulwalîd, Efodi, and Mose ha-Nakdan. The Masoretic observation לית קמץ חטף, "only here with *Kametz chateph*," is found appended in codices. This *Chateph kametz* is euphonic, as in לְקָחָה, Gen. ii. 23, and in many other instances that are obliterated in our editions, *vid.* Abulwalîd, חרקמה ס׳, p. 198, where even מְטָהֲרוֹ = מְטַהֲרוֹ, lxxxix. 45, is cited among these examples (Ges. § 10, 2 rem.)

whole earth ; man has no right upon it, he only remains there
so long as God permits him. כְּכָל־אֲבוֹתַי glances back even to
the patriarchs (Gen. xlvii. 9, cf. xxiii. 4). Israel is, it is true,
at the present time in possession of a fixed dwelling-place, but
only as the gift of his God, and for each individual it is only
during his life, which is but a handbreadth long. May Jahve,
then—so David prays—turn away His look of wrath from him,
in order that he may shine forth, become cheerful or clear up,
before he goes hence and it is too late. הָשַׁע is *imper. apoc.*
Hiph. for הַשְׁעֵה (in the signification of *Kal*), and ought, according to the form הֶרֶב, properly to be הֶשַׁע ; it is, however, pointed
just like the *imper. Hiph.* of שָׁעַע in Isa. vi. 10, without any
necessity for explaining it as meaning *obline (oculos tuos)* =
connive (Abulwalîd), which would be an expression unworthy
of God. It is on the contrary to be rendered: look away
from me; on which compare Job vii. 19, xiv. 6; on אַבְלִיגָה cf.
ib. x. 20, ix. 27 ; on בְּטֶרֶם אֵלֵךְ, *ib.* x. 21 ; on וְאֵינֶנִּי, *ib.* vii. 8, 21.
The close of the Psalm, consequently, is re-echoed in many
ways in the Book of Job. The Book of Job is occupied with
the same riddle as that with which this Psalm is occupied.
But in the solution of it, it advances a step further. David
does not know how to disassociate in his mind sin and suffering,
and wrath and suffering. The Book of Job, on the contrary,
thinks of suffering and love together; and in the truth that
suffering also, even though it be unto death, must serve the
highest interests of those who love God, it possesses a satisfactory solution.

PSALM XL.

THANKSGIVING, AN OFFERING UP OF ONE'S SELF,
AND PRAYER.

2 I WAITED patiently upon Jahve,
 And He inclined unto me, and heard my cry.
3 And He drew me up out of a pit of destruction, out of the
  mire of the swamp,
 And set my feet upon a rock, made my footsteps firm.
4 And put into my mouth a new song, praise unto our God—
 Many see it and fear, and put their trust in Jahve.

5 Blessed is the man who maketh Jahve his trust,
  And doth not turn to the proud and to lying apostates.
6 Much hast Thou done, Jahve, my God, in Thy wonders
        and Thy thoughts on our behalf;
  Nothing can be compared unto Thee,
  Else would I declare and speak—
  They are too numerous to be numbered.

7 Sacrifice and meat-offering dost Thou not desire,
  Ears hast Thou digged for me,
  Burnt-offering and sin-offering dost Thou not require.
8 Then said I: " Lo, I come with the roll of the book which
        is written concerning me.
9 To do Thy will, my God, do I desire,
  And Thy Law is in my inward part."

10 I brought glad tidings of righteousness in the great con-
   Lo, I closed not my lips;   [gregation,
   Jahve, Thou, even Thou knowest it.
11 Thy righteousness did I not hide within my heart,
   Thy faithfulness and Thy salvation did I declare,
   I concealed not Thy loving-kindness and Thy truth from
        the great congregation.

12 Do Thou, then, Jahve, not shut up Thy tender mercies
        from me,
   Let Thy loving-kindness and Thy truth continually pro-
        tect me.
13 For evils have surrounded me without number,
   Mine iniquities have taken hold upon me and I am not able
        to see;
   They are more numerous than the hairs of my head,
   And my heart hath failed me.

14 Be pleased, O Jahve, to deliver me;
   Jahve, to my help make haste!
15 Let those be ashamed and confounded together who seek .
        my soul to destroy it;
   Let those fall back and be put to shame who desire my
        misfortune.

16 Let those be struck dumb on account of the merited
          punishment of their shame,
   Who say to me: Aha, aha!

17 Let all those heartily rejoice in Thee who seek Thee,
   Let those continually say " Jahve be magnified " who love
          Thy salvation.
18 Though I be both needy and poor,
   The Lord will care for me.
   My help and my deliverer art Thou!
   My God, make no tarrying!

Ps. xxxix. is followed by Ps. xl., because the language of
thanksgiving with which it opens is, as it were, the echo of the
language of prayer contained in the former. If Ps. xl. was
composed by David, and not rather by Jeremiah—a question
which can only be decided by including Ps. lxix. (which see)
in the same investigation—it belongs to the number of those
Psalms which were composed between Gibea of Saul and
Ziklag. The mention of the roll of the book in ver. 8 harmonizes with the retrospective references to the Tôra, which
abound in the Psalms belonging to the time of Saul. And to
this we may add the vow to praise Jahve בְּקָהָל, vers. 10 sq.,
cf. xxii. 26, xxxv. 18; the expression, " more in number than
the hairs of my head," ver. 13, cf. lxix. 5; the wish יִצְּרוּנִי, ver.
12, cf. xxv. 21; the mocking הֶאָח הֶאָח, ver. 16, cf. xxxv. 21,
25; and much besides, on which *vid.* my *Commentary on the
Epistle to the Hebrews,* S. 457 [transl. vol. ii. p. 149]. The
second half has an independent form in Ps. lxx. It is far
better adapted to form an independent Psalm than the first
half, which merely looks back into the past, and for this very
reason contains no prayer.

   The long lines, more in keeping with the style of prayer
than of song, which alternate with disproportionately shorter
ones, are characteristic of this Psalm. If with these long lines
we associate a few others, which are likewise more or less
distinctly indicated, then the Psalm can be easily divided into
seven six-line strophes.

   In the Epistle to the Hebrews, ch. x. 5–10, vers. 7–9 of this
Psalm are, by following the LXX., taken as the language of

the Christ at His coming into the world. There can be no
doubt in this particular instance that, as we look to the second
part of the Psalm, this rendering is brought about typically.
The words of David, the anointed one, but only now on the
way to the throne, are so moulded by the Holy Spirit, the
Spirit of prophecy, that they sound at the same time like the
words of the second David, passing through suffering to glory,
whose offering up of Himself is the close of the animal
sacrifices, and whose person and work are the very kernel and
star of the roll of the Law. We are not thereby compelled to
understand the whole Psalm as typically predictive. It again
descends from the typically prophetic height to which it has
risen even from ver. 10 onwards ; and from ver. 13 onwards,
the typically prophetic strain which still lingers in vers. 10 and
11 has entirely ceased.

Vers. 1–4. David, whom, though not without some hesitation, we regard as the author, now finds himself in a situation
in which, on the one hand, he has just been rescued from
danger, and, on the other, is still exposed to peril. Under
such circumstances praise rightly occupies the first place, as in
general, according to l. 23, gratitude is the way to salvation.
His hope, although תּוֹחֶלֶת מְמֻשָּׁכָה (Prov. xiii. 12), has not deceived him ; he is rescued, and can now again sing a new song
of thanksgiving, an example for others, strengthening their
trust.   קַוֹּה קִוִּיתִי, I waited with constancy and perseverance.
יהוה is the accusative as in xxv. 5, cxxx. 5, and not the vocative as in xxxix. 8. אֲזְנוֹ is to be supplied in thought to וַיֵּט,
although after the analogy of xvii. 6, xxxi. 3, one might have
looked for the *Hiph.* וַיַּט instead of the *Kal.* בּוֹר שָׁאוֹן does not
mean a pit of roaring (of water), since שָׁאוֹן standing alone
(see, on the other hand, lxv. 8, Isa. xvii. 12 sq.) has not this
meaning ; and, moreover, " rushing, roaring " (Hengstenberg),
tumultuous waters of a pit or a cistern does not furnish any
idea that is true to nature ; neither does it mean a pit of falling
in, since שָׁאָה does not exhibit the signification *deorsum labi ;*
but the meaning is : a pit of devastation, of destruction, of ruin
(Jer. xxv. 31, xlvi. 17), *vid. supra* on xxxv. 8. Another figure
is " mire of the marsh " (יָוֵן found only here and in lxix. 3),
i.e. water, in the miry bottom of which one can find no firm

footing—a combination like מְטַר־גֶּשֶׁם, Zech. x. 1, אַדְמַת־עָפָר,
Dan. xii. 2, explained in the Mishna, *Mikvaoth* ix. 2, by טיט
הבורות (mire of the cisterns). Taking them out of this, Jahve
placed his feet upon a rock, established his footsteps, *i.e.*
removed him from the danger which surrounded him, and gave
him firm ground under his feet. The high rock and the firm
footsteps are the opposites of the deep pit and the yielding miry
bottom. This deliverance afforded him new matter for thanksgiving (cf. xxxiii. 3), and became in his mouth " praise to our
God ;" for the deliverance of the chosen king is an act of the
God of Israel on behalf of His chosen people. The futures in
ver. 4*b* (with an alliteration similar to lii. 8) indicate, by their
being thus cumulative, that they are intended of the present
and of that which still continues in the future.

Vers. 5, 6. He esteems him happy who puts his trust (מִבְטַחוֹ,
with a latent *Dagesh*, as, according to Kimchi, also in lxxi. 5,
Job xxxi. 24, Jer. xvii. 7) in Jahve, the God who has already
made Himself glorious in Israel by innumerable wonderful
works. Jer. xvii. 7 is an echo of this אַשְׁרֵי. Ps. lii. 9 (cf.
xci. 9) shows how Davidic is the language. The expression is
designedly not הָאִישׁ, but הַגֶּבֶר, which is better adapted to designate
the man as being tempted to put trust in himself. רְהָבִים from
רָהָב (not from רַהַב) are the impetuous or violent, who in their
arrogance cast down everything. שָׂטֵי כָזָב, " turners aside of
falsehood" (שׂוּט = שָׂטָה, cf. ci. 3), is the expression for apostates
who yield to falsehood instead of to the truth : to take כָזָב as
accusative of the aim is forbidden by the *status construct.*; to
take it as the genitive in the sense of the accusative of the
object (like הֹלְכֵי תֹם, Prov. ii. 7) is impracticable, because שׂוּט
(שׂטה) does not admit of a transitive sense ; כזב is, therefore,
genit. qualit. like אָוֶן in lix. 6. This second strophe contains
two practical applications of that which the writer himself has
experienced. From this point of view, he who trusts in God
appears to the poet to be supremely happy, and a distant view
of God's gracious rule over His own people opens up before
him. נִפְלְאֹת are the thoughts of God realized, and מַחֲשָׁבֹת those
that are being realized, as in Jer. li. 29, Isa. lv. 8 sq. רַבּוֹת is
an accusative of the predicate : in great number, in rich abundance ; אֵלֵינוּ, " for us," as *e.g.* in Jer. xv. 1 (Ew. § 217, *c*). His
doings towards Israel were from of old a fulness of wondrous

deeds and plans of deliverance, which was ever realizing and
revealing itself. There is not עֲרֹךְ אֵלֶיךָ, a possibility of comparison with Thee, οὐκ ἔστι (Ew. § 321, c) ἰσοῦν τί σοι—עֲרָךְ
as in lxxxix. 7, Isa. xl. 18—they are too powerful (עָצֵם of a
powerful sum, as in lxix. 5, cxxxix. 17, cf. Jer. v. 6) for one to
enumerate. According to Rosenmüller, Stier, and Hupfeld,
אֵין עֵרֶךְ אֵלֶיךָ even affirms the same thing in other words: it is
not possible to lay them forth to Thee (before Thee); but that
man should "lay forth" (Symmachus ἐκθέσθαι) before God
His marvellous works and His thoughts of salvation, is an
unbecoming conception. The cohortative forms, which follow,
אַגִּידָה וַאֲדַבֵּרָה, admit of being taken as a protasis to what follows,
after the analogy of Job xix. 18, xvi. 6, xxx. 26, Ps. cxxxix. 8:
if I wish to declare them and speak them forth, they are too
powerful (numerous) to be enumerated (Ges. § 128, 1, d).
The accentuation, however, renders it as a parenthetical clause:
I would (as in li. 18, lv. 13, Job vi. 10) declare them and
speak them forth. He would do this, but because God, in the
fulness of His wondrous works and thoughts of salvation, is
absolutely without an equal, he is obliged to leave it undone—
they are so powerful (numerous) that the enumeration of them
falls far short of their powerful fulness. The words *alioqui
pronunciarem et eloquerer* have the character of a parenthesis,
and, as ver. 7 shows, this accords with the style of this Psalm.

Vers. 7–9. The connection of the thoughts is clear: great
and manifold are the proofs of Thy loving-kindness, how am
I to render thanks to Thee for them? To this question he
first of all gives a negative answer: God delights not in outward sacrifices. The sacrifices are named in a twofold way:
(a) according to the material of which they consist, viz. זֶבַח, the
animal sacrifice, and מִנְחָה, the meal or meat offering (including
the נֶסֶךְ, the wine or drink offering, which is the inalienable
accessory of the accompanying *mincha*); (b) according to their
purpose, in accordance with which they bring about either the
turning towards one of the good pleasure of God, as more
especially in the case of the עוֹלָה, or, as more especially in the
case of the חַטָּאת (in this passage חֲטָאָה), the turning away of the
divine displeasure. The fact of the זֶבַח and עוֹלָה standing first,
has, moreover, its special reason in the fact that זֶבַח specially
designates the *shelamîm* offerings, and to the province of these

latter belongs the thank-offering proper, viz. the *tôda-shelamîm*
offering; and that עוֹלָה as the sacrifice of adoration ($\pi\rho o\sigma\epsilon v\chi\acute{\eta}$),
which is also always a general thanksgiving ($\epsilon\dot{v}\chi\alpha\rho\iota\sigma\tau\acute{\iota}\alpha$), is
most natural, side by side with the shelamim, to him who gives
thanks. When it is said of God, that He does not delight in
and desire such non-personal sacrifices, there is as little intention as in Jer. vii. 22 (cf. Amos v. 21 sqq.) of saying that the
sacrificial Tôra is not of divine origin, but that the true, essential
will of God is not directed to such sacrifices.

Between these synonymous utterances in ver. 7*a* and 7*c*
stands the clause אָזְנַיִם כָּרִיתָ לִּי. In connection with this position it is natural, with Rosenmüller, Gesenius, De Wette, and
Stier, to explain it "ears hast Thou pierced for me" = this
hast Thou engraven upon my mind as a revelation, this disclosure hast Thou imparted to me. But, although כָּרָה, to dig,
is even admissible in the sense of digging through, piercing
(*vid.* on xxii. 17), there are two considerations against this
interpretation, viz.: (1) that then one would rather look for אֹזֶן
instead of אָזְנַיִם after the analogy of the phrases הֵעִיר אֹזֶן, גָּלָה אֹזֶן,
and פָּתַח אֹזֶן, since the inner sense, in which the external organs
of sense, with their functions, have their basis of unity, is commonly denoted by the use of the singular; (2) that according
to the syntax, כָּרִיתָ, חָפַצְתָּ, and שָׁאַלְתָּ are all placed on the same
level. Thus, therefore, it is with this very אזנים כרית לי that
the answer is intended, in its positive form, to begin; and the
primary passage, 1 Sam. xv. 22, favours this view: "*Hath
Jahve delight in whole burnt-offerings and sacrifices as in one's
obeying the voice of Jahve? Behold, to obey is better than sacrifice, to attend better than the fat of rams!*" The assertion of
David is the echo of this assertion of Samuel, by which the
sentence of death was pronounced upon the kingship of Saul,
and consequently the way of that which is well-pleasing to God
was traced out for the future kingship of David. God—says
David—desires not outward sacrifices, but obedience; ears
hath He digged for me, *i.e.* formed the sense of hearing,
bestowed the faculty of hearing, and given therewith the
instruction to obey.* The idea is not that God has given

---

* There is a similar expression in the Tamul Kural, Graul's translation,
S. 63, No. 418: "An ear, that was not hollowed out by hearing, has, even

him ears in order to hear that disclosure concerning the true will of God (Hupfeld), but, in general, to hear the word of God, and to obey that which is heard. God desires not sacrifices but hearing ears, and consequently the submission of the person himself in willing obedience. To interpret it "Thou hast appropriated me to Thyself לְעֶבֶד עוֹלָם," after Ex. xxi. 6, Deut. xv. 17, would not be out of harmony with the context; but it is at once shut out by the fact that the word is not אֹזֶן, but אָזְנַיִם. Concerning the generalizing rendering of the LXX., σῶμα δὲ κατηρτίσω μου, following which Apollinaris renders it αὐτὰρ ἐμοὶ βροτέης τεκτήναο σάρκα γενέθλης, and the Italic (which is also retained in the *Psalterium Romanum*), *corpus autem perfecisti mihi; vide* on Heb. x. 5, *Commentary*, S. 460 sq. [transl. vol. ii. p. 153].

The אָז אָמַרְתִּי, which follows, now introduces the expression of the obedience, with which he placed himself at the service of God, when he became conscious of what God's special will concerning him was. With reference to the fact that obedience and not sacrifice has become known to him as the will and requirement of God, he has said: "Lo, I come," etc. By the words "Lo, I come," the servant places himself at the call of his master, Num. xxii. 38, 2 Sam. xix. 21. It is not likely that the words בִּמְגִלַּת סֵפֶר כָּתוּב עָלָי then form a parenthesis, since ver. 9 is not a continuation of that "Lo, I come," but a new sentence. We take the *Beth*, as in lxvi. 13, as the *Beth* of the accompaniment; the roll of the book is the Tôra, and more especially Deuteronomy, written upon skins and rolled up together, which according to the law touching the king (Deut. xvii. 14–20) was to be the vade-mecum of the king of Israel. And עָלָי cannot, as synonymous with the following בְּמֵעַי, signify as much as "written upon my heart," as De Wette and Thenius render it—a meaning which, as Maurer has already correctly replied, עַל obtains elsewhere by means of a conception that is altogether inadmissible in this instance. On the contrary, this preposition here, as in 2 Kings xxii. 13, denotes the object of the contents; for כָּתַב עַל signifies to write anything concerning any one, so that he is the subject one has specially in view (*e.g.*

---

if hearing, the manner of not hearing." The "hollowing out" meaning in this passage an opening of the inward sense of hearing by instruction.

of tne judicial decision recorded in writing, Job xiii. 26).
Because Jahve before all else requires obedience to His will,
David comes with the document of this will, the Tôra, which
prescribes to him, as a man, and more especially as the king,
the right course of conduct. Thus presenting himself to the
God of revelation, he can say in ver. 9, that willing obedience
to God's Law is his delight, as he then knows that the written
Law is written even in his heart, or, as the still stronger expression used here is, in his bowels. The principal form of מֵעַי
does not occur in the Old Testament; it was מֵעִים (from מֵעַ,
מֵעֶה, or even מְעִי), according to current Jewish pronunciation
מֵעַיִם (which Kimchi explains as dual); and the word properly
means (vid. on Isa. xlviii. 19) the soft parts of the body, which
even elsewhere, like רַחֲמִים, which is synonymous according to
its original meaning, appear pre-eminently as the seat of
sympathy, but also of fear and of pain. This is the only
passage in which it occurs as the locality of a mental acquisition, but also with the associated notion of loving acceptance
and cherishing protection (cf. the Syriac phrase סם בגו מעיא,
som b⁰gau m⁰ajo, to shut up in the heart = to love). That the
Tôra is to be written upon the tables of the heart is even indicated by the Deuteronomion, Deut. vi. 6, cf. Prov. iii. 3, vii. 3.
This reception of the Tôra into the inward parts among the
people hitherto estranged from God is, according to Jer. xxxi.
33, the characteristic of the new covenant. But even in the
Old Testament there is among the masses of Israel " a people
with My law in their heart" (Isa. li. 7), and even in the Old
Testament, " he who hath the law of his God in his heart" is
called righteous (Ps. xxxvii. 31). As such an one who has
the Tôra within him, not merely beside him, David presents
himself on the way to the throne of God.

Vers. 10, 11. The self-presentation before Jahve, intro-
duced by אָז אָמַרְתִּי, extends from הנה to מֵעִי; consequently בִּשַּׂרְתִּי
joins on to אמרתי, and the אֶכְלָא which stands in the midst of
perfects describes the synchronous past. The whole is a retrospect. בִּשֵּׂר, بشر (root בש), starting from its sensible primary
signification to scrape off, scratch off, rub smooth, means: tc
smooth any one (glätten), Engl. to gladden one, i.e. vultum ejus
diducere, to make him joyful and glad, more especially to cheer

one by good news (*e.g. basharahu* or *bashsharuhu bi-maulûdin*, he has cheered him by the intelligence of the birth of a son), in Hebrew directly equivalent to εὐαγγελίζειν (εὐαγγελίζεσθαι). He has proclaimed to all Israel the evangel of Jahve's justifying and gracious rule, which only changes into retribution towards those who despise His love; and he can appeal to the Omniscient One (Jer. xv. 15), that neither through fear of men, nor through shame and indolence, has he restrained his lips from confessing Him. God's conduct, in accordance with the prescribed order of redemption, is as a matter of fact called צֶדֶק, and as an attribute of His holy love, צְדָקָה; just as אֱמוּנָה is His faithfulness which fulfils the promises made and which does not suffer hope to be put to shame, and תְּשׁוּעָה is His salvation as it is manifested in facts. This rich matter for the preaching of the evangel, which may be comprehended in the two words חֶסֶד וֶאֱמֶת, the Alpha and Omega of God's self-attestation in the course of the redemptive history, he has not allowed to slumber as a dead, unfruitful knowledge hidden deep down in his heart. The new song which Jahve put into his mouth, he has also really sung. Thus far we have the first part of the song, which renders thanks for past mercies.

Vers. 12, 13. Now, in accordance with the true art of prayer, petition developes itself out of thanksgiving. The two כְלֹא, ver. 10 and here, stand in a reciprocal relation to one another: he refrained not his lips; therefore, on His part, let not Jahve withhold His tender mercies so that they should not be exercised towards him (מִמֶּנִּי). There is just the same correlation of mercy and truth in ver. 11 and here: he wishes continually to stand under the protection of these two saving powers, which he has gratefully proclaimed before all Israel. With כִּי, ver. 13, he bases these desires upon his own urgent need. רָעוֹת are the evils, which come even upon the righteous (xxxiv. 20) as trials or as chastenings. אָפְפוּ עָלַי is a more circumstantial form of expression instead of אֲפָפוּנִי, xviii. 5. His misdeeds have taken hold upon him, *i.e.* overtaken him in their consequences (הִשִּׂיג, as in Deut. xxviii. 15, 45; cf. לְכַד, Prov. v. 22), inasmuch as they have changed into decrees of suffering. He cannot see, because he is closely encompassed on all sides, and a free and open view is thereby altogether taken from him (the expression is used elsewhere of loss of sight, 1 Sam. iii. 2, iv. 15, 1 Kings xiv. 4). The interpretation adopted by Hupfeld and Hitzig: I am not able to survey, viz. their number, puts into the expression more than it really expresses in the common usage of the language. His heart, *i.e.* the power of vital consistence, has forsaken him, he is disconcerted, dejected, as it were driven to despair (xxxviii. 11). This feeling of the misery of sin is not opposed to the date of the Psalm being assigned to the time of Saul, *vid.* on xxxi. 11.

Vers. 14–16. In the midst of such sufferings, which, the longer they last, discover him all the more to himself as a sinner, he prays for speedy help. The cry for help in ver. 14 turns with רְצֵה towards the will of God; for this is the root of all things. As to the rest, it resembles xxii. 20 (xxxviii. 23). The persecuted one wishes that the purpose of his deadly foes may as it were rebound against the protection of God and miserably miscarry. לְסִפּוֹתָהּ, *ad abripiendam eam* (with *Dagesh* in the ס according to Ges. § 45, 2, Ew. § 245, *a*, and not as Gesenius, *Thesaurus*, p. 1235, states, aspirated*), is added to מְבַקְשֵׁי נַפְשִׁי by way of explanation and definiteness. יָשֹׁמּוּ from שָׁמֵם, to become torpid, here used of outward and inward paralysis, which is the result of overpowering and as it were bewitching surprise or fright, and is called by the Arabs *ro'b* or *ra'b* (paralysis through terror) [cf. *Job*, i. 322, note]. An עַל following upon יָשֹׁמּוּ looks at first sight as though it introduced the object and reason of this fright; it is therefore not: as a reward, in consequence of their infamy, which would not be עַל־עֵקֶב, but merely the accusative עֵקֶב (Isa. v. 23, Arabic عقيب), it is rather: on account of the reward (xix. 12) of their disgrace (cf., as belonging to the same period, cix. 29, xxxv. 26), *i.e.* of the reward which consists in their being put to shame (Hitzig). לִ as in iii. 3, xli. 6: with reference to me. הֶאָח הֶאָח (Aquila, *àà*

---

* After לְ the aspirate usually disappears, as here and in cxviii. 13; but there are exceptions, as לִנְתוֹשׁ וְלִנְתוֹץ, Jer. i. 10, and frequently, לִשְׁדוֹד, *ib.* xlvii. 4. After בְ and כְ it usually remains, as in lxxxvii. 6, Job iv. 13, xxxiii. 15, 2 Sam. iii. 34, 1 Kings i. 21, Eccles. v. 10; but again there are exceptions, as בִּשְׁכֹּן, Gen. xxxv. 22, כִּזְכֹּר, Jer. xvii. 2. In Gen. xxiii. 2 it is pointed לִבְכֹּתָהּ according to the rule, and in my *Comment.* S. 423 it is to be read "with a Dagesh."

ἀά, αὐτῇ συγχρησάμενος, as Eusebius says, οὕτως ἐχούσῃ τῇ Ἑβραϊκῇ φωνῇ) is an exclamation of sarcastic delight, which finds its satisfaction in another's misfortune (xxxv. 25).

Vers. 17, 18. On ver. 17 compare xxxv. 27. David wishes, as he does in that passage, that the pious may most heartily rejoice in God, the goal of their longing; and that on account of the salvation that has become manifest, which they love (2 Tim. iv. 8), they may continually say: Let Jahve become great, *i.e.* be magnified or celebrated with praises! In ver. 18 with וַאֲנִי he comes back to his own present helpless state, but only in order to contrast with it the confession of confident hope. True he is עָנִי וְאֶבְיוֹן (as in cix. 22, lxxxvi. 1, cf. xxv. 16), but He who ruleth over all will care for him: *Dominus solicitus erit pro me* (Jerome). חָשַׁב in the same sense in which in ver. 6 the מַחְשְׁבוֹת, *i.e.* God's thoughts of salvation, is conceived of (cf. the corresponding North-Palestinian expression in Jonah i. 6). A sigh for speedy help (אַל־תְּאַחַר, as in Dan. ix. 19 with a transition of the merely tone-long *Tsere* into a pausal *Pathach*, and here in connection with a preceding closed syllable, Olshausen, § 91, *d*, under the accompanying influence of two final letters which incline towards the *a* sound) closes this second part of the Psalm. The first part is nothing but thanksgiving, the second is exclusively prayer.

PSALM XLI.

COMPLAINT OF A SUFFERER OF BEING SURROUNDED BY HOSTILE AND TREACHEROUS PERSONS.

2 BLESSED is he who regardeth the afflicted,
  In the day of evil Jahve will deliver him.
3 Jahve will protect him and preserve him,
  That he may be pronounced happy in the land;
  And Thou dost not give him over to the greed of his
    enemies.
4 Jahve will support him on the bed of sickness,
  All his couch dost Thou turn, when he falleth sick.

5 As for me, I say: Jahve, be merciful unto me,
  O heal my soul, for I have sinned against Thee.

6 Mine enemies, however, speak evil of me:
"When will he die and his name perish?!"
7 And if one cometh to see me, he speaketh deceit,
His heart gathereth that which is groundless to itself,
He goeth abroad, he telleth it.

8 Together against me do all those whisper one to another
who hate me,
Against me do they imagine evil for me:
9 "An incurable evil is welded to him,
And when once he lieth down he will not rise up again."
10 Even the man of my friendship in whom I trusted,
Who did eat of my bread, lifteth his heel high against me.

11 And Thou, Jahve, be merciful unto me and raise me up,
Then will I requite them.
12 By this I should like to know, that Thou hast pleasure in
me:
That mine enemy cannot exult over me.
13 And as for me, in mine integrity dost Thou uphold me,
And dost set me before Thine eyes for ever.
14 BLESSED BE JAHVE THE GOD OF ISRAEL FROM EVER-
LASTING TO EVERLASTING.
AMEN, AMEN.

After a Psalm with אשרי follows one beginning with אשרי;
so that two Psalms with אשרי close the First Book of the
Psalms, which begins with אשרי. Ps. xli. belongs to the time
of the persecution by Absalom. Just as the Jahve-Psalm xxxix.
forms with the Elohim-Psalm lxii. a coherent pair belonging to
this time, so does also the Jahve-Psalm xli. with the Elohim-
Psalm lv. These two Psalms have this feature in common, viz.
that the complaint concerning the Psalmist's foes dwells with
especial sadness upon some faithless bosom-friend. In Ps. xli.
David celebrates the blessing which accompanies sincere sympathy, and depicts the hostility and falseness which he himself
experiences in his sickness, and more especially from a very
near friend. It is the very same person of whom he complains
in Ps. lv., that he causes him the deepest sorrow—no ideal
character, as Hengstenberg asserts; for these Psalms have the

most distinctly impressed individual physiognomy of the writer's own times. In Ps. lv. the poet wishes for the wings of a dove, in order that, far away from the city, he might seek for himself a safe spot in the wilderness; for in the city deceit, violence, and mischief prevail, and the storm of a wide-spread conspiracy is gathering, in which he himself sees his most deeply attached friend involved. We need only supplement what is narrated in the second Book of Samuel by a few features drawn from these two Psalms, and these Psalms immediately find a satisfactory explanation in our regarding the time of their composition as the period of Absalom's rebellion. The faithless friend is that Ahithophel whose counsels, according to 2 Sam. xvi. 23, had with David almost the appearance of being divine oracles. Absalom was to take advantage of a lingering sickness under which his father suffered, in order to play the part of the careful and impartial judge and to steal the heart of the men of Israel. Ahithophel supported him in this project, and in four years after Absalom's reconciliation with his father the end was gained. These four years were for David a time of increasing care and anxiety; for that which was planned cannot have remained altogether concealed from him, but he had neither the courage nor the strength to smother the evil undertaking in the germ. His love for Absalom held him back; the consciousness of his own deed of shame and bloodshed, which was now notorious, deprived him of the alacrity essential to energetic interference; and the consciousness of the divine judgments, which ought to follow his sin, must have determined him to leave the issue of the conspiracy that was maturing under his very eyes entirely to the compassion of his God, without taking any action in the matter himself. From the standpoint of such considerations, Ps. xli. and lv. lose every look of being alien to the history of David and his times. One confirmation of their Davidic origin is the kindred contents of Ps. xxviii.

Jesus explains (John xiii. 18) that in the act of Judas Iscariot Ps. xli. 10 is fulfilled, ὁ τρώγων μετ' ἐμοῦ τὸν ἄρτον, ἐπῆρεν ἐπ' ἐμὲ τὴν πτέρναν αὐτοῦ (not following the LXX.), and John xvii. 12, Acts i. 16 assume in a general way that the deed and fate of the traitor are foretold in the Old Testament Scriptures, viz. in the Davidic Psalms of the time of

Absalom—the treachery and the end of Ahithophel belong to
the most prominent typical features of David's affliction in
this second stage of persecution (*vid.* Hofmann, *Weissagung
und Erfüllung,* ii. 122).

Vers. 2–4. The Psalm opens by celebrating the lot, so rich
in promises, of the sympathetic man. דַּל is a general designation of the poor (*e.g.* Ex. xxx. 15), of the sick and weakly
(Gen xli. 19), of the sick in mind (2 Sam. xiii. 4), and of that
which outwardly or inwardly is tottering and consequently
weak, frail. To show sympathising attention, thoughtful consideration towards such an one (הִשְׂכִּיל אֶל as in Neh. viii. 13,
cf. עַל Prov. xvii. 20) has many promises. The verb חִיָּה, which
elsewhere even means to call to life again (lxxi. 20), in this
instance side by side with preserving, viz. from destruction, has
the signification of preserving life or prolonging life (as in
xxx. 4, xxii. 30). The *Pual* אֻשַּׁר signifies to be made happy
(Prov. iii. 18), but also declaratively: to be pronounced happy
(Isa. ix. 15); here, on account of the בָּאָרֶץ that stands with it,
it is the latter. The *Chethîb* יְאֻשַּׁר sets forth as an independent
promise that which the *Kerî* וְאֻשַּׁר joins on to what has gone
before as a consequence. אַל, ver. 3c (cf. xxxiv. 6 and frequently), expresses a negative with full sympathy in the utterance. נָתַן בְּנֶפֶשׁ as in xxvii. 12. The supporting in ver. 4a is a
keeping erect, which stops or arrests the man who is sinking
down into death and the grave. דְּוַי (= *davj*, similar form to
מֵעַי, שְׁמַי, but wanting in the syllable before the tone) means
sickness. If ver. 4a is understood of the supporting of the
head after the manner of one who waits upon the sick (cf.
Cant. ii. 6), then ver. 4 must, with Mendelssohn and others, be
understood of the making of the couch or bed. But what then
is meant by the word כל ? מִשְׁכָּב is a sick-bed in Ex. xxi. 18
in the sense of being bedridden; and הָפַכְתָּ (cf. xxx. 12) is a
changing of it into convalescence. By כל־מִשְׁכָבוֹ is not meant
the constant lying down of such an one, but the affliction that
casts him down, in all its extent. This Jahve turns or changes,
so often as such an one is taken ill (בְּחָלְיוֹ, at his falling sick,
parallel with עַל־עֶרֶשׂ דְּוָי). He gives a complete turn to the
"sick-bed" towards recovery, so that not a vestige of the sickness remains behind.

Vers. 5–7. He, the poet, is treated in his distress of soul in a manner totally different from the way just described which is so rich in promises of blessing. He is himself just such a דַּל, towards whom one ought to manifest sympathising consideration and interest. But, whilst he is addressing God in the language of penitential prayer for mercy and help, his enemies speak evil to him, *i.e.* with respect to him, wishing that he might die and that his name might perish. רְפָאָה is as an exception *Milra*, inasmuch as א draws the tone to its own syllable; cf. on the other hand רְגְזָה, Isa. xxxii. 11 (Hitzig). מָתַי (prop. extension, length of time) has only become a Semitic interrogative in the signification *quando* by the omission of the interrogative אֵי (common Arabic in its full form ايمتى, *êmata*). וְאָבַד is a continuation of the future. In ver. 7 one is singled out and made prominent, and his hypocritically malicious conduct described. רָאוֹת of a visit to a sick person as in 2 Sam. xiii. 5 sq., 2 Kings viii. 29. אָם is used both with the *perf.* (l. 18, lxiii. 7, lxxviii. 34, xciv. 18, Gen. xxxviii. 9, Amos vii. 2, Isa. xxiv. 13, xxviii. 25) and with the *fut.* (lxviii. 14, Job xiv. 14), like *quum*, as a blending together of *si* and *quando*, Germ. *wenn* (if) and *wann* (when). In ידבר לבו two *Rebias* come together, the first of which has the greater value as a distinctive, according to the rule laid down in Baer's *Psalterium*, p. xiv. Consequently, following the accents, it must not be rendered: "falsehood doth his heart speak." The LXX., Vulgate, and Targum have discerned the correct combination of the words. Besides, the accentuation, as is seen from the Targum and expositors, proceeds on the assumption that לִבּוֹ is equivalent to בְּלִבּוֹ. But why may it not be the subject-notion? "His heart gathereth" is an expression of the activity of his mind and feelings, concealed beneath a feigned and friendly outward bearing. The asyndeton portrays the despatch with which he seeks to make the material for slander, which has been gathered together, public both in the city and in the country.

Vers. 8–10. Continuation of the description of the conduct of the enemies and of the false friend. הִתְלַחֵשׁ, as in 2 Sam. xii. 19, to whisper to one another, or to whisper among themselves; the *Hithpa.* sometimes (cf. Gen. xlii. 1) has a reciprocal meaning like the *Niphal*. The intelligence brought out by hypocritical visitors of the invalid concerning his critical condition is spread from mouth to mouth by all who wish him ill as satisfactory news; and in fact in whispers, because at that time caution was still necessary. עָלַי stands twice in a prominent position in the sense of *contra me*. רָעָה לִי belong together: they maliciously invent what will be the very worst for him (going beyond what is actually told them concerning him). In this connection there is a feeling in favour of בְּלִיַּעַל being intended of an evil fate, according to xviii. 5, and not according to ci. 3 (cf. Deut. xv. 9) of pernicious or evil thought and conduct. And this view is also supported by the predicate יָצוּק בּוֹ: "a matter of destruction, an incurable evil (Hitzig) is poured out upon him," *i.e.* firmly cast upon him after the manner of casting metal (Job xli. 15 sq.), so that he cannot get free from it, and he that has once had to lie down will not again rise up. Thus do we understand אֲשֶׁר in ver. 9*b*; there is no occasion to take it as an accusative by departing from the most natural sense, as Ewald does, or as a conjunction, as Hitzig does. Even the man of his peace, or literally of his harmonious relationship (אִישׁ שְׁלוֹם as in Obad. ver. 7, Jer. xx. 10, xxxviii. 22), on whom he has depended with fullest confidence, who did eat his bread, *i.e.* was his messmate (cf. lv. 15), has made his heel great against him, LXX. ἐμεγάλυνεν ἐπ' ἐμὲ πτερνισμόν. The combination הִגְדִּיל עָקֵב is explained by the fact that עָקֵב is taken in the sense of a thrust with the heel, a kick: to give a great kick, *i.e.* with a good swing of the foot.

Vers. 11–13. Having now described their behaviour towards him, sick in soul and body as he is, so devoid of affection, yea, so malignantly hostile and so totally contrary to the will and promise of God, David prays that God would raise him up, for he is now lying low, sick in soul and in body. The prayer is followed, as in xxxix. 14 and many other passages, by the future with *ah*: that I may be able to requite them, or: then will I requite them. What is meant is the requiting which it was David's duty as a duly constituted king to exercise, and which he did really execute by the power of God, when he subdued the rebellion of Absalom and maintained his ground in opposition to faithlessness and meanness. Instead of בְּזֹאת אֵדַע (Gen. xlii. 33, cf. xv. 8, Ex. vii. 17, Num. xvi.

28, Josh. iii. 10) the expression is בְּזֹאת יָדַעְתִּי in the sense of (*ex hoc*) *cognoverim*. On חָפַצְתָּ בִּי cf. xviii. 20, xxii. 9, xxxv. 27. By the second כִּי, the בְּזֹאת, which points forwards, is explained. The adversatively accented subject וַאֲנִי stands first in ver. 13*a* as a *nom. absol.*, just as in xxxv. 13. Ver. 13 states, retrospectively from the standpoint of fulfilment, what will then be made manifest and assure him of the divine good pleasure, viz. Jahve upholds him (תָּמַךְ as in lxiii. 9), and firmly sets him as His chosen one before Him (cf. xxxix. 6) in accordance with the Messianic promise in 2 Sam. vii. 16, which speaks of an unlimited future.

Ver. 14. The closing doxology of the First Book, *vid.* Introduction, p. 15. Concerning בָּרוּךְ *vid.* xviii. 47. The expression "from æon to æon" is, according to *Berachoth* ix. 5, directed against those who deny the truth of the future world. אָמֵן וְאָמֵן (a double ἀληθές or ἀληθῶς) seals it in a climactic form.

SECOND BOOK OF THE PSALTER.

Ps. XLII.–LXXII.

~~~~~~

PSALM XLII.–XLIII.

LONGING FOR ZION IN A HOSTILE COUNTRY

2 AS a hind, which panteth after the water-brooks,
So panteth my soul after Thee, Elohim.
3 My soul thirsteth for Elohim, for the living God:
When shall I come and appear before Elohim ?!
4 My tears have been my food by day and night,
While they say continually unto me: Where is thy God?
5 I think thereon, pouring out my soul within me:
How I passed along among the throng, how I accompanied
them to the house of Elohim
Among the sound of rejoicing and thanksgiving,—a multitude keeping holy-day.
6 Why art thou bowed down, O my soul, and why groanest
thou within me?
Hope in Elohim, for I shall yet give thanks to Him,
That He is the health of my countenance and my God.

7 Within me is my soul bowed down, therefore do I remember Thee
From the land of Jordan and of the Hermôns, from the
mountain of Miz‘ar.
8 Flood calleth to flood at the sound of Thy cataracts,
All Thy breakers and Thy billows have passed over me.
~~~~~~

 9 By day Jahve will command His loving-kindness,
   And at night a song concerning Him is with me, prayer to
      the God of my life.
10 Therefore say I to God, my rock: Why dost Thou forget
      me?
   Why must I go mourning under the oppression of the
      enemy?
11 Like a crushing in my bones my oppressors scoff at me,
   While they say to me continually: Where is thy God?
12 Why art thou bowed down, O my soul, and why groanest
      thou within me?
   Hope in Elohim, for I shall yet give thanks to Him,
   That He is the health of my countenance and my God.

 1 JUDGE me, Elohim, and plead my cause against an un-
      merciful people,
   From the man of deceit and roguery be Thou pleased to
      rescue me;
 2 For Thou art God, my fortress, why dost Thou spurn me?
   Why must I go about mourning under the oppression of
      the enemy?
 3 Send Thy light and Thy truth, let them lead me,
   Let them bring me to Thy holy mountain and to Thy
      tabernacles—
 4 Then will I go in unto the altar of Elohim,
   To the God of my exultant joy,
   And give thanks to Thee with the cithern, Elohim my God.
 5 Why art thou bowed down, O my soul, and why groanest
      thou within me?
   Hope in Elohim, for I shall yet give thanks to Him,
   That He is the health of my countenance and my God.

The Second Book of Psalms consists entirely of Elohimic
Psalms (*vid.* Introduction, p. 22); for whilst in the First Book
יהוה occurred 272 times and אלהים only 15 times, the relation is
here reversed: אלהים occurs 164 times, and יהוה only 30 times,
and in almost every instance by a departure from the customary mode of expression for reasons that lie close at hand.

   At the head of these Psalms written in the Elohimic style
there stand seven inscribed לִבְנֵי־קֹרַח. That here as in לְאָסָף the

ל is *Lamed auctoris*, is made clear by the fact that none of these Psalms, as might be expected, have לדוד in addition to the name of the author. The LXX. renders it τοῖς υἱοῖς Κορέ, just as it does τῷ Δαυίδ, without distinguishing the one ל from the other indicating the authorship, and even in the Talmud a similar meaning to the *Lamed* of לדוד is assumed. It is certainly remarkable that instead of an author it is always the family that is named, a rule from which Ps. lxxxviii. (which see) is only a seeming departure. The designation "*Bohmische Brüder*" in the hymnology of the German church is very similar. Probably the Korahitic songs originally formed a book of themselves, which bore the title שירי בני קרח or something similar; and then the בני קרח of this title passed over to the inscription of each separate song of those incorporated in two groups in the Psalm-collection, just as appears also to be the case with the inscription שיר המעלות, which is repeated fifteen times. Or we must suppose that it had become a family custom in the circle of the singers among the Korahites to allow the individual to retreat behind the joint responsibility of family unity, and, vying together, to expiate the name of their unfortunate ancestor by the best liturgical productions.

For Korah, the great-grandson of Levi, and grandson of Kehāth, is the same as he who perished by a divine judgment on account of his rebellion against Moses and Aaron (Num. ch. xvi.), whose sons, however, were not involved with him in this judgment (Num. xxvi. 11). In David's time the בני קרח were one of the most renowned families of the Levite race of the Kehathites. The kingship of the promise very soon found valiant adherents and defenders in this family. Korahites gathered together to David to Ziklag, in order to aid in defending him and his title to the throne with the sword (1 Chron. xii. 6); for הַקָּרְחִים in this passage can hardly (as Bertheau is of opinion) be descendants of the קרח of the family of Judah mentioned in 1 Chron. ii. 43, but otherwise unrenowned, since that name is elsewhere, viz. in ch. ix. 19, 31, a Levitic family name. In Jerusalem, after the Exile, Korahites were keepers of the temple gates (1 Chron. ix. 17, Neh. xi. 19), and the chronicler there informs us that even in David's time they were keepers of the threshold of the אהל (erected over the Ark on Zion); and still earlier, in the time of Moses, in the camp of

Jahve they were appointed as watchers of the entrance. They retained this ancient calling, to which allusion is made in Ps. lxxxiv. 11, in connection with the new arrangements instituted by David. The post of door-keeper in the temple was assigned to two branches of the Korahite families together with one Merarite (1 Chron. xxvi. 1–19). But they also even then served as musicians in the sanctuary. Heman, one of the three precentors (to be distinguished from Heman the wise man mentioned in 1 Kings v. 11 [Engl. iv. 31]), was a Korahite (1 Chron. vi. 18–23); his fourteen sons belonged, together with the four sons of Asaph and the six sons of Ethan, to the twenty-four heads of the twenty-four divisions of the musicians (1 Chron. ch. xxv.). The Korahites were also renowned even in the days of Jehoshaphat as singers and musicians; see 2 Chron. xx. 19, where a plural בְּנֵי הַקֹּרְחִים (cf. Ges. § 108, 3) is formed from בני־קרח, which has as it were become smelted together as one word. Whereas in the period after the Exile there is no longer any mention of them in this character. We may therefore look for Korahitic Psalms belonging to the post-Davidic time of the kings; whereas we ought at the outset to be less inclined to find any post-exilic Psalms among them. The common feature of this circle of songs consists herein,—they delight in the praise of Elohim as the King who sits enthroned in Jerusalem, and join in the services in His temple with the tenderest and most genuine emotion. And this impress of unity which they bear speaks strongly in favour of taking לבני־קרח in the sense of denoting authorship.

The composer of the מַשְׂכִּיל, Ps. xlii., finds himself, against his will, at a great distance from the sanctuary on Zion, the resting-place of the divine presence and manifestation, surrounded by an ungodly people, who mock at him as one forsaken of God, and he comforts his sorrowful soul, looking longingly back upon that which it has lost, with the prospect of God's help which will soon appear. All the complaints and hopes that he expresses sound very much like those of David during the time of Absalom. David's yearning after the house of God in Ps. xxiii., xxvi., lv., lxiii., finds its echo here: the conduct and outlines of the enemies are also just the same; even the sojourn in the country east of Jordan agrees with

David's settlement at that time at Mahanaim in the mountains
of Gilead. The Korahite, however, as is to be assumed in
connection with a lyric poem, speaks out of the depth of his
own soul, and not, as Hengstenberg and Tholuck maintain,
" as from the soul of David." He merely shares David's
vexation, just as he then in lxxxiv. 10 prays for the anointed
one. This Ps. lxxxiv. breathes forth the same feelings, and even
in other respects bears traces of the same author; cf. אֶל חַי,
lxxxiv. 3, xlii. 3 ; מִשְׁכְּנוֹתֶיךָ, lxxxiv. 2, xliii. 3 ; מִזְבְּחוֹתֶיךָ, lxxxiv.
4, xliii. 4 ; and the similar use of עוֹד, lxxxiv. 5, xlii. 6, cf. Isa.
xlix. 20, Jer. xxxii. 15. The distinguishing features of the
Korahitic type of Psalm meet us in both Psalms in the most
strong and vivid manner, viz. the being joyous and weeping
with God's anointed, the praise of God the King, and the yearning after the services in the holy place. And there are, it is
true, thoughts that have been coined by David which we here
and there distinctly hear in them (cf. xlii. 2 sq., lxxxiv. 3, with
lxiii. 2) ; but they are reproduced with a characteristic beauty
peculiar to the author himself. We do not, therefore, in the
least doubt that Ps. xlii. is the poem of a Korahitic Levite, who
found himself in exile beyond the Jordan among the attendants
of David, his exiled king.

Concerning Ps. xliii. Eusebius has said : ὅτι μέρος ἔοικεν
εἶναι τοῦ πρὸ αὐτοῦ δεδήλωται ἔκ τε τῶν ὁμοίων ἐν ἀμφοτέροις
λόγων καὶ ἐκ τῆς ἐμφεροῦς διανοίας, and an old Midrash reckons
147 Psalms, taking Ps. xlii.–xliii. together as one, just as with
ix.–x., xxxii.–xxxiii. The similarity of the situation, of the
general impress, of the structure, and of the refrain, is decisive
in favour of these Psalms, which are commonly reckoned as
two, being one. The one Psalm consists of three parts : thrice
his pain breaks forth into complaint, and is each time again
overcome by the admonitory voice of his higher consciousness.
In the depicting of the past and the future there is unmistakeable progress. And it is not until the third part (Ps. xliii.)
that complaint, resignation, and hope are perfected by the
language of confident prayer which supervenes. The unity of
the Psalms is not affected by the repetition of xlii. 10*b* in xliii.
2*b*, since xlii. 11*b* is also a repetition of xlii. 4*b*. Beside an
edging in by means of the refrain, the poet is also fond of such
internal links of connection. The third part has thereby come

to consist of thirteen lines, whereas the other two parts consist of twelve lines each.

What a variegated pattern card of hypotheses modern criticism opens out before us in connection with this Psalm (xlii.–xliii.)! Vaihinger regards it as a song composed by one of the Levites who was banished by Athaliah. Ewald thinks that King Jeconiah, who was carried away to Babylon, may have composed the Psalm; and in fact, when (and this is inferred from the Psalm itself) on the journey to Babylon, he may have been detained just a night in the vicinity of Hermon. Reuss (in the *Nouvelle Revue de Théologie*, 1858) prefers to suppose it is one of those who were carried off with Jeconiah (among whom there were also priests, as Ezekiel). Hitzig, however, is no less decisive in his view that the author is a priest who was carried off in the direction of Syria at the time of the wars of the Seleucidæ and Ptolemies; probably Onias III., high priest from 199 B.C., the collector of the Second Book of the Psalms, whom the Egyptians under the general Skopas carried away to the citadel of Paneas. Olshausen even here, as usual, makes Antiochus Epiphanes his watchword. In opposition to this positive criticism, Maurer adheres to the negative; he says: *quærendo elegantissimi carminis scriptore frustra se fatigant interpretes.*

Ps. xlii. 2–6. The poet compares the thirsting of his soul after God to the thirsting of a stag. אַיָּל (like other names of animals is epicœne, so that there is no necessity to adopt Böttcher's emendation כְּאַיֶּלֶת תַּעֲרֹג) is construed with a feminine predicate in order to indicate the stag (hind) as an image of the soul. עָרַג is not merely a quiet languishing, but a strong, audible thirsting or panting for water, caused by prevailing drought, lxiii. 2, Joel i. 20; the signification *desiderare* refers back to the primary notion of *inclinare* (cf. الميل, the act of inclining), for the primary meaning of the verb عرج is to be slanting, inclined or bent, out of which has been developed the signification of ascending and moving upwards, which is transferred in Hebrew to an upward-directed longing. Moreover, it is not with Luther (LXX., Vulgate [and authorized version]) to be rendered: *as the* (a) *stag crieth*, etc., but (and

it is accented accordingly): as a stag, which, etc.   אָפֵק = אָפִיק is,
according to its primary signification, a watercourse holding
water (*vid.* xviii. 16). By the addition of מַיִם the full and
flowing watercourse is distinguished from one that is dried up.
עַל and אֶל point to the difference in the object of the longing,
viz. the hind has this object beneath herself, the soul above
itself ; the longing of the one goes *deorsum*, the longing of the
other *sursum*. The soul's longing is a thirsting לְאֵל חָי. Such
is the name here applied to God (as in lxxxiv. 3) in the sense
in which flowing water is called living, as the spring or fountain of life (xxxvi. 10) from which flows forth a grace that
never dries up, and which stills the thirst of the soul. The
spot where this God reveals Himself to him who seeks Him is
the sanctuary on Zion : when shall I come and appear in the
presence of Elohim ? ! The expression used in the Law for
the three appearings of the Israelites in the sanctuary at
solemn feasts is נִרְאָה אֶל־פְּנֵי ה' or אֶת־פְּנֵי, Ex. xxiii. 17, xxxiv. 23.
Here we find instead of this expression, in accordance with the
licence of poetic brevity, the bare *acc. localis* (which is even
used in other instances in the definition of localities, *e.g.* Ezek.
xl. 44). Böttcher, Olshausen, and others are of opinion that
אראה in the mind of the poet is to be read אֶרְאֶה, and that it has
only been changed into אֵרָאֶה through later religious timidity;
but the avoidance of the phrase רָאָה פְּנֵי ה' is explained from
the fundamental assumption of the Tôra that a man could not
behold God's פנים without dying, Ex. xxxiii. 20. The poet
now tells us in ver. 4 what the circumstances were which drove
him to such intense longing. His customary food does not
revive him, tears are his daily bread, which day and night run
down upon his mouth (cf. lxxx. 6, cii. 20), and that בֶּאֱמֹר, when
say to him, viz. the speakers, all day long, *i.e.* continually :
Where is thy God ? Without cessation, these mocking words
are continually heard, uttered again and again by those who
are round about him, as their thoughts, as it were, in the soul
of the poet. This derision, in the Psalms and in the Prophets,
is always the keenest sting of pain : lxxix. 10, cxv. 2 (cf. lxxi.
11), Joel ii. 17, Mic. vii. 10.

In this gloomy present, in which he is made a mock of, as
one who is forsaken of God, on account of his trust in the
faithfulness of the promises, he calls to remembrance the

bright and cheerful past, and he pours out his soul within him (on the עָלַי used here and further on instead of בִּי or בְּקִרְבִּי, and as distinguishing between the *ego* and the soul, vid. *Psychol.* S. 152; tr. p. 180), inasmuch as he suffers it to melt entirely away in pain (Job xxx. 16). As in lxxvii. 4, the cohortatives affirm that he yields himself up most thoroughly to this bitter-sweet remembrance and to this free outward expression of his pain. אֵלֶּה (*hœcce*) points forwards; the כִּי (*quod*) which follows opens up the expansion of this word. The futures, as expressing the object of the remembrance, state what was a habit in the time past. עָבַר frequently signifies not *prœterire*, but, without the object that is passed over coming into consideration, *porro ire*. סָךְ (a collateral form of סֹךְ), properly a thicket, is figuratively (cf. Isa. ix. 17, x. 34) an interwoven mass, a mixed multitude. The rendering therefore is: that I moved on in a dense crowd (here the distinctive *Zinnor*). The form אֶדַּדֵּם is *Hithpa.*, as in Isa. xxxviii. 15, after the form הִדַּמָּה from the verb דָּדָה, "to pass lightly and swiftly along,"

derived by reduplication from the root דא (cf. ﺩﺍﺩﺍ), which has the primary meaning to push, to drive (ἐλαύνειν, *pousser*), and

in various combinations of the ד (דא, גצ, דח, גצ, דב, דף)

expresses manifold shades of onward motion in lighter or heavier thrusts or jerks. The suffix, as in גְּדֵלַנִי = גְּדֵל עִמִּי, Job xxxi. 18 (Ges. § 121, 4), denotes those in reference to whom, or connection with whom, this moving onwards took place, so that consequently אֶדַּדֵּם includes within itself, together with the subjective notion, the transitive notion of אַדֵּם, for the singer of the Psalm is a Levite; as an example in support of this אֶדַּדֵּם, vid. 2 Chron. xx. 27 sq., cf. ver. 21. הָמוֹן חוֹגֵג is the apposition to the personal suffix of this אדדם: with them, a multitude keeping holy-day. In ver. 6 the poet seeks to solace and encourage himself at this contrast of the present with the past: Why art thou thus cast down . . . (LXX. ἵνα τί περίλυπος εἶ, κ.τ.λ., cf. Matt. xxvi. 38, John xii. 27). It is the spirit which, as the stronger and more valiant part of the man, speaks to the soul as to the σκεῦος ἀσθενέστερον; the spiritual man soothes the natural man. The *Hithpa.* הִשְׁתּוֹחַח, which occurs only here and in Ps. xliii., signifies to bow one's self very low, to sit down upon the ground like a mourner (xxxv 14, xxxviii. 7), and to bend one's self downwards (xliv. 26). הָמָה (the future of which Ben-Asher here points וַתֶּהֱמִי, but Ben-Naphtali וַתֶּהֱמִי), to utter a deep groan, to speak quietly and mumbling to one's self. Why this gnawing and almost desponding grief? I shall yet praise Him with thanksgiving, praise יְשׁוּעוֹת פָּנָיו, the ready succour of His countenance turned towards me in mercy. Such is the text handed down to us. Although it is, however, a custom with the psalmists and prophets not to express such refrainlike thoughts in exactly the same form and words (cf. xxiv. 7, 9, xlix. 13, 21, lvi. 5, 11, lix. 10, 18), nevertheless it is to be read here by a change in the division both of the words and the verses, according to ver. 12 and xliii. 5, יְשׁוּעוֹת פָּנַי וֵאלֹהָי, as is done by the LXX. (*Cod. Alex.*), Syriac, Vulgate, and most modern expositors. For the words יְשׁוּעוֹת פָּנָיו, though in themselves a good enough sense (*vid. e.g.* xliv. 4, Isa. lxiv. 9), produce no proper closing cadence, and are not sufficient to form a line of a verse.*

Vers. 7–12. The poet here continues to console himself with God's help. God Himself is indeed dishonoured in him; He will not suffer the trust he has reposed in Him to go unjustified. True, עָלַי seems at the beginning of the line to be tame, but from עָלַי and אֶזְכָּרְךָ, the beginning and end of the line, standing in contrast, עָלַי is made emphatic, and it is at the same time clear that עַל־כֵּן is not equivalent to עַל־כֵּן אֲשֶׁר — which Gesenius asserts in his *Lexicon*, erroneously referring to i. 5, xlv. 3, is a poetical usage of the language; an assertion for which, however, there is as little support as that כִּי עַל־כֵּן in Num. xiv. 43 and other passages is equivalent to עַל־כֵּן כִּי. In all such passages, *e.g.* Jer. xlviii. 36, עַל־כֵּן means "therefore," and the relationship of reason and consequence is reversed. So even here: within him his soul is bowed very low, and on account of this downcast condition he thinks continually of God, from whom he is separated. Even in Jonah ii. 8 this thinking upon God does not appear as the cause but as the consequence of pain. The "land of Jordan and of Hermonim" is not necessarily the northern mountain range together

---

* Even an old Hebrew MS. directs attention to the erroneousness of the Soph pasuk here; *vid.* Pinsker, *Einleitung*, S. 133 l.

with the sources of the Jordan. The land beyond the Jordan is so called in opposition to אֶרֶץ לְבָנוֹן, the land on this side. According to Dietrich (*Abhandlungen*, S. 18), חֶרְמוֹנִים is an amplificative plural: the Hermon, as a peak soaring far above all lower summits. John Wilson (*Lands of the Bible*, ii. 161) refers the plural to its two summits. But the plural serves to denote the whole range of the Antilebanon extending to the south-east, and accordingly to designate the east Jordanic country. It is not for one moment to be supposed that the psalmist calls Hermon even, in comparison with his native Zion, the chosen of God, הַר מִצְעָר, *i.e.* the mountain of littleness: the other member of the antithesis, the majesty of Zion, is wanting, and the מִ which is repeated before הר is also opposed to this. Hitzig, striking out the מ of מהר, makes it an address to Zion: "because I remember thee out of the land of Jordan and of summits of Hermon, thou little mountain;" but, according to ver. 8, these words are addressed to Elohim. In the vicinity of *Mitz'ar*, a mountain unknown to us, in the country beyond Jordan, the poet is sojourning; from thence he looks longingly towards the district round about his home, and just as there, in a strange land, the wild waters of the awe-inspiring mountains roar around him, there seems to be a corresponding tumult in his soul. In ver. 8*a* he depicts the natural features of the country round about him — and it may remind one quite as much of the high and magnificent waterfalls of the lake of *Muzêrîb* (vid. *Job*, ii. 422) as of the waterfall at the source of the Jordan near Paneas and the waters that dash headlong down the mountains round about— and in ver. 8*b* he says that he feels just as though all these threatening masses of water were rolling like so many waves of misfortune over his head (Tholuck, Hitzig, and Riehm). Billow follows billow as if called by one another (cf. Isa. vi. 3 concerning the continuous antiphon of the seraphim) at the roar (לְקוֹל as in Hab. iii. 16) of the cataracts, which in their terrible grandeur proclaim the Creator, God (LXX. τῶν καταῤῥακτῶν σου)—all these breaking, sporting waves of God pass over him, who finds himself thus surrounded by the mighty works of nature, but taking no delight in them; and in them all he sees nothing but the mirrored image of the many afflictions which threaten to involve him in utter destruction (cf. the borrowed passage in that mosaic work taken from the Psalms, Jon. ii. 4).

He, however, calls upon himself in ver. 9 to take courage in the hope that a morning will dawn after this night of affliction (xxx. 6), when Jahve, the God of redemption and of the people of redemption, will command His loving-kindness (cf. xliv. 5, Amos ix. 3 sq.); and when this by day has accomplished its work of deliverance, there follows upon the day of deliverance a night of thanksgiving (Job xxxv. 10): the joyous excitement, the strong feeling of gratitude, will not suffer him to sleep. The suffix of שִׁירֹה is the suffix of the object: a hymn in praise of Him, prayer (viz. praiseful prayer, Hab. iii. 1) to the God of his life (cf. Sir. xxiii. 4), *i.e.* who is his life, and will not suffer him to come under the dominion of death. Therefore will he say (אוֹמְרָה), in order to bring about by prayer such a day of loving-kindness and such a night of thanksgiving songs, to the God of his rock, *i.e.* who is his rock (*gen. appos.*): Why, etc.? Concerning the different accentuation of למה here and in xliii. 2, *vid.* on xxxvii. 20 (cf. x. 1). In this instance, where it is not followed by a guttural, it serves as a "variation" (Hitzig); but even the retreating of the tone when a guttural follows is not consistently carried out, *vid.* xlix. 6, cf. 1 Sam. xxviii. 15 (Ew. § 243, *b*). The view of Vaihinger and Hengstenberg is inadmissible, viz. that vers. 10 to 11 are the "prayer," which the psalmist means in ver. 9; it is the prayerful sigh of the yearning for deliverance, which is intended to form the burthen of that prayer. In some MSS. we find the reading כְּרֶצַח instead of בְּרֶצַח; the בְּ is here really synonymous with the כְּ, it is the *Beth essentiæ* (*vid.* xxxv. 2): after the manner of a crushing (cf. Ezek. xxi. 27, and the verb in lxii. 4 of overthrowing a wall) in my bones, *i.e.* causing me a crunching pain which seethes in my bones, mine oppressors reproach me (חֵרֲף with the transfer of the primary meaning *carpere*, as is also customary in the Latin, to a plucking and stripping one of his good name). The use of בּ here differs from its use in ver. 10*b*; for the reproaching is not added to the crushing as a continuing state, but is itself thus crushing in its operation (*vid.* ver. 4). Instead of בֶּאֱמֹר we have here the easier form of expression בְּאָמְרָם; and in the refrain פְּנֵי וֵאלֹהָי, which is also to be restored in ver. 6.

Ps. xliii. 1–3. The Elohimic *Judica* (the introit of the so-called Cross or Passion Sunday which opens the *celebritas Passionis*), with which the supplicatory and plaintive first strophe of the Psalm begins, calls to mind the Jehovic *Judica* in vii. 9, xxvi. 1, xxxv. 1, 24: judge me, *i.e.* decide my cause (LXX. κρῖνόν με, Symmachus κρῖνόν μοι). רִיבָה has the tone upon the *ultima* before the רִיבִי which begins with the half-guttural ר, as is also the case in lxxiv. 22, cxix. 154. The second prayer runs: *vindica me a gente impia;* מִן standing for *contra* in consequence of a *constr. prægnans.* לֹא־חָסִיד is here equivalent to one practising no חֶסֶד towards men, that is to say, one totally wanting in that חסד, by which God's חסד is to be imitated and repaid by man in his conduct towards his fellow-men. There is some uncertainty whether by אִישׁ one chief enemy, the leader of all the rest, is intended to be men-tioned side by side with the unloving nation, or whether the special manner of his enemies is thus merely individualized. עַוְלָה means roguish, mischievous conduct, utterly devoid of all sense of right. In ver. 2 the poet establishes his petition by a twofold Why. He loves God and longs after Him, but in the mirror of his present condition he seems to himself like one cast off by Him. This contradiction between his own con-sciousness and the inference which he is obliged to draw from his afflicted state cannot remain unsolved. אֱלֹהֵי מָעֻזִּי, God of my fortress, is equivalent to who is my fortress. Instead of אֵלֵךְ we here have the form אֶתְהַלֵּךְ, of the slow deliberate gait of one who is lost in his own thoughts and feelings. The sting of his pain is his distance from the sanctuary of his God. In con-nection with ver. 3 one is reminded of lvii. 4 and Ex. xv. 13, quite as much as of xlii. 9. "Light and truth" is equivalent to mercy and truth. What is intended is the light of mercy or loving-kindness which is coupled with the truth of fidelity to the promises; the light, in which the will or purpose of love, which is God's most especial nature, becomes outwardly mani-fest. The poet wishes to be guided by these two angels of God; he desires that he may be brought (according to the *Chethîb* of the Babylonian text יבואוני, "let come upon me;" but the אל which follows does not suit this form) to the place where his God dwells and reveals Himself. "Tabernacles" is, as in lxxxiv. 2, xlvi. 5, an amplificative designation of the tent, magnificent in itself and raised to special honour by Him who dwells therein

Vers. 4, 5. The poet, in anticipation, revels in the thought of that which he has prayed for, and calls upon his timorous soul to hope confidently for it. The cohortatives in ver. 4 are, as in xxxix. 14 and frequently, an apodosis to the petition. The poet knows no joy like that which proceeds from God, and the joy which proceeds from Him he accounts as the very highest; hence he calls God אֶל שִׂמְחַת גִּילִי, and therefore he knows no higher aim for his longing than again to be where the fountainhead of this exultant joy is (Hos. ix. 5), and where it flows forth in streams (xxxvi. 9). Removed back thither, he will give thanks to Him with the cithern (*Beth instrum.*). He calls Him אֱלֹהִים אֱלֹהָי, an expression which, in the Elohim-Psalms, is equivalent to יהוה אלהי in the Jahve-Psalms. The hope expressed in ver. 4 casts its rays into the prayer in ver. 3. In ver. 5, the spirit having taken courage in God, holds this picture drawn by hope before the distressed soul, that she may therewith comfort herself. Instead of ותהמי, xlii. 6, the expression here used, as in xlii. 12, is וּמַה־תֶּהֱמִי. Variations like these are not opposed to a unity of authorship.

PSALM XLIV.

A LITANY OF ISRAEL, HARD PRESSED BY THE ENEMY, AND YET FAITHFUL TO ITS GOD.

2 ELOHIM, with our own ears have we heard,
  Our fathers have declared to us:
  A work hast Thou wrought in their days, in the days of old.
3 Thou,—Thine own hand did drive out peoples and did
      plant them,
  Did destroy nations and did spread them out.
4 For not by their own sword did they acquire the land,
  And their own arm did not obtain for them the victory;
  But Thy right hand, Thine arm, the light of Thy counte-
      nance, because Thou didst love them.

5 Thou, Thou art my King, Elohim:
  Command the full salvation of Jacob!

6 By Thee do we push down our oppressors,
  In Thy name do we tread down those who rise up against
      us.
7 For not in mine own bow do I trust,
  And my sword doth not obtain for me the victory.
8 No indeed, Thou givest us the victory over our oppressors,
  And dost put to shame those who hate us.
9 In Elohim do we make our boast continually,
  And to Thy name will we ever give thanks.   (*Sela.*)

10 Nevertheless Thou hast cast off and put us to confusion,
  And wentest not forth with our armies ;
11 Thou madest us to turn back before the oppressor,
  And those who hate us spoiled just as they liked.
12 Thou gavest us up like sheep for consumption,
  And among the heathen didst Thou scatter us,
13 Thou didst sell Thy people for a mere nothing,
  And didst not set a high price upon them.

14 Thou didst make us a reproach to our neighbours,
  A scorn and a derision to those who are round about us.
15 Thou didst make us a proverb among the heathen,
  A shaking of the head among the peoples.
16 Continually is my confusion before me,
  And the shame of my face covereth me ;
17 Because of the voice of him who reproacheth and blas-
     phemeth,
  Because of the sight of the enemy and the revengeful.

18 All this is come upon us and we have not forgotten
     Thee,
  And have not become faithless to Thy covenant.
19 Our heart has not turned back,
  That our step should have declined from Thy path,
20 That Thou hast crushed us in the place of jackals,
  And didst cover us with the shadow of death.
21 If we had forgotten the name of our God,
  And stretched out our hands to a strange god :
22 Would not Elohim have searched it out?
  For He knoweth the hidden things of the heart.

23 No indeed, for Thy sake are we slain continually,
   We are counted as sheep for the slaughter.
24 Awake then, why sleepest Thou, O Lord?
   Arouse Thyself, cast not off for ever!
25 Wherefore hidest Thou Thy face,
   Why forgettest Thou our affliction and oppression?
26 For our soul is bowed down to the dust,
   Our body cleaveth to the earth.
27 Oh arise for our help,
   And redeem us, for Thy loving-kindness' sake.

The Korahitic *Maskîl* Ps. xlii., with its counterpart Ps. xliii., is followed by a second, to which a place is here assigned by manifold accords with Ps. xlii.–xliii., viz. with its complaints (cf. xliv. 26 with the refrain of xliii., xlii.; xliv. 10, 24 sq. with xliii. 2, xlii. 10), and prayers (cf. xliv. 5 with xliii. 3, xlii. 9). The counterpart to this Psalm is Ps. lxxxv. Just as Ps. xlii.–xliii. and lxxxiv. form a pair, so do Ps. xliv. and lxxxv. as being Korahitic plaintive and supplicatory Psalms of a national character. Moreover, Ps. lx. by David, Ps. lxxx. by Asaph, and Ps. lxxxix. by Ethan, are nearest akin to it. In all these three there are similar lamentations over the present as contrasting with the former times and with the promise of God; but they do not contain any like expression of consciousness of innocence, a feature in which Ps. xliv. has no equal.

In this respect the Psalm seems to be most satisfactorily explained by the situation of the חסידים (saints), who under the leadership of the Maccabees defended their nationality and their religion against the Syrians and fell as martyrs by thousands. The war of that period was, in its first beginnings at least, a holy war of religion; and the nation which then went forth on the side of Jahve against Jupiter Olympius, was really, in distinction from the apostates, a people true to its faith and confession, which had to lament over God's doom of wrath in 1 Macc. i. 64, just as in this Psalm. There is even a tradition that it was a stated lamentation Psalm of the time of the Maccabees. The Levites daily ascended the pulpit (דוכן) and raised the cry of prayer: Awake, why sleepest Thou, O Lord?! These Levite criers praying for the interposition of God were called מְעוֹרְרִים (wakers). It is related in *B. Sota* 48a of

Jochanan the high priest, *i.e.* John Hyrcanus (135–107 B.C.), that he put an end to these מעוררים, saying to them : " Doth the Deity sleep ? Hath not the Scripture said : Behold the Keeper of Israel slumbereth not and sleepeth not !? Only in a time when Israel was in distress and the peoples of the world in rest and prosperity, only in reference to such circumstances was it said : Awake, why sleepest Thou, O Lord ?"

Nevertheless many considerations are opposed to the composition of the Psalm in the time of the Maccabees. We will mention only a few. In the time of the Maccabees the nation did not exactly suffer any overthrow of its " armies" (ver. 10) after having gathered up its courage : the arms of Judah, of Jonathan, and of Simon were victorious, and the one defeat to which Hitzig refers the Psalm, viz. the defeat of Joseph and Azaria against Gorgias in Jamnia (1 Macc. v. 55 sqq.), was a punishment brought upon themselves by an indiscreet enterprise. The complaints in vers. 10 sq. are therefore only partially explained by the events of that time ; and since a nation is a unit and involved as a whole, it is also surprising that no mention whatever is made of the apostates. But Ewald's reference of the Psalm to the time of the post-exilic Jerusalem is still more inadmissible ; and when, in connection with this view, the question is asked, What disaster of war is then intended ? no answer can be given ; and the reference to the time of Jehoiachin, which Tholuck in vain endeavours to set in a more favourable light—a king who did evil in the eyes of Jahve, 2 Chron. xxxvi. 9, with which the descriptions of character drawn by Jeremiah, ch. xxii. 20–30, and by Ezekiel, ch. xix., fully accord—is also inadmissible. On the other hand, the position of the Psalm in the immediate neighbourhood of Psalms belonging to the time of Jehoshaphat, and also to a certain extent its contents, favours the early part of the reign of king Joash, in which, as becomes evident from the prophecy of Joel, there was no idolatry on the part of the people to be punished, and yet there were severe afflictions of the people to be bewailed. It was then not long since the Philistines and Arabs from the neighbourhood of the Cushites had broken in upon Judah, ransacked Jerusalem and sold the captive people of Judah for a mere song to the Greeks (2 Chron. xxi. 16 sq., Joel iv. 2–8). But this reference to cotemporary history is also untenable. That unhappy event, together with others, belongs to the category of well-merited judgments, which came upon king and people in the reign of Jehoram; nor does the Psalm sound like a retrospective glance at the time of Jehoram from the standpoint of the time of Joash: the defeat of which it complains, is one that is now only just experienced.

Thus we seem consequently driven back to the time of David; and the question arises, whethei the Psalm does not admit, with Ps. lx., with which it forms a twin couple, of being understood as the offspring of a similar situation, viz. of the events which resulted from the Syro-Ammonitish war. The fact that a conflict with the foes of the kingdom in the south, viz. with the Edomites, was also mixed up with the wars with the Ammonites and their Syrian allies at that period, becomes evident from lx. 1 sq. when compared with 2 Sam. viii. 13, where the words ἐπάταξε τὴν Ἰδουμαίαν (LXX.) have fallen out. Whilst David was contending with the Syrians, the Edomites came down upon the country that was denuded of troops. And from 1 Kings xi. 15 it is very evident that they then caused great bloodshed; for, according to that passage, Joab buried the slain and took fearful revenge upon the Edomites: he marched, after having slain them in the Valley of Salt, into Idumæa and there smote every male. Perhaps, with Hengstenberg, Keil, and others, the Psalm is to be explained from the position of Israel before this overthrow of the Edomites. The fact that in ver. 12 the nation complains of a dispersion among the heathen may be understood by means of a deduction from Amos i. 6, according to which the Edomites had carried on a traffic in captive Israelites. And the lofty self-consciousness, which finds expression in the Psalm, is after all best explained by the times of David; for these and the early part of the times of Solomon are the only period in the history of Israel when the nation as a whole could boast of being free and pure of all foreign influence in its worship. In the kindred Ps. lx., lxxx. (also lxxxix.), it is true this self-consciousness does not attain the same lofty expression; in this respect Ps. xl. stands perfectly alone: it is like the national mirroring of the Book of Job, and by reason of this takes a unique position in the range of Old Testament literature side by side with Lam. ch. iii. and the deutero-Isaiah. Israel's affliction, which could not possibly be of a punitive character, resembles the affliction of Job; in this Psalm, Israel stands in exactly the same relation to God as Job and the "Servant of Jahve" in Isaiah, if we except all that was desponding in Job's complaint and all that was expiatory in the affliction of the Servant of Jahve. But this very self-consciousness does somewhat approximately find expression even in lx. 6 [4]. In that passage also no distinction is made between Israel and the God-fearing ones in Israel; but the psalmist calls Israel absolutely the God-fearing ones, and the battle, in which Israel is defeated, but not without hope of final victory, is a battle for the truth.

The charge has been brought against this Psalm, that it manifests a very superficial apprehension of the nature of sin, in consequence of which the writer has been betrayed into accusing God of unfaithfulness, instead of seeking for guilt in the congregation of Israel. This judgment is unjust. The writer certainly cannot mean to disown the sins of individuals, nor even this or that transgression of the whole people. But any apostasy on the part of the nation from its God, such as could account for its rejection, did not exist at that time. The supremacy granted to the heathen over Israel is, therefore, an abnormal state of things, and for this very reason the poet, on the ground of Israel's fidelity and of God's loving-kindness, prays for speedy deliverance. A Psalm born directly out of the heart of the New Testament church would certainly sound very differently. For the New Testament church is not a national community; and both as regards the relation between the reality and idea of the church, and as regards the relation between its afflictions and the motive and design of God, the view of the New Testament church penetrates far deeper. It knows that it is God's love that makes it conformable to the passion of Christ, in order that, being crucified unto the world, it may become through suffering partaker of the glory of its Lord and Head.

Vers. 2–4. The poet opens with a tradition coming down from the time of Moses and of Joshua which they have heard with their own ears, in order to demonstrate the vast distance between the character of the former times and the present, just

as Asaph, also, in lxxviii. 3, appeals not to the written but to
the spoken word. That which has been heard follows in the
oratio directa. Ver. 3 explains what kind of "work" is intended : it is the granting of victory over the peoples of
Canaan, the work of God for which Moses prays in xc. 16.
Concerning יָדְךָ, *vid.* on iii. 5, xvii. 14. The position of the
words here, as in lxix. 11, lxxxiii. 19, leads one to suppose that
יָדְךָ is treated as a permutative of אַתָּה, and consequently in the
same case with it. The figure of "planting" (after Ex. xv. 17)
is carried forward in וַתְּשַׁלְּחֵם ; for this word means to send forth
far away, to make wide-branching, a figure which is wrought
up in Ps. lxxx. It was not Israel's own work, but (כִּי, no indeed, for [Germ. *nein, denn*] = *imo*) God's work : "Thy right
hand and Thine arm and the light of Thy countenance," they
it was which brought Israel salvation, *i.e.* victory. The combination of synonyms יְמִינְךָ וּזְרוֹעֲךָ is just as in lxxiv. 11, Sir.
xxxiii. 7, χεῖρα καὶ βραχίονα δεξιόν, and is explained by both
the names of the members of the body as applied to God being
only figures : the right hand being a figure for energetic interposition, and the arm for an effectual power that carries through
the thing designed (cf. *e.g.* lxxvii. 16, Isa. liii. 1), just as the
light of His countenance is a figure for His loving-kindness
which lights up all darkness. The final cause was His purpose
of love : for (inasmuch as) Thou wast favourable to them (רָצָה
as in lxxxv. 2). The very same thought, viz. that Israel owes
the possession of Canaan to nothing but Jahve's free grace,
runs all through Deut. ch. ix.

Vers. 5–9. Out of the retrospective glance at the past, so
rich in mercy, springs up (ver. 5) the confident prayer concerning the present, based upon the fact of the theocratic
relationship which began in the time of the deliverance wrought
under Moses (Deut. xxxiii. 5). In the substantival clause אַתָּה
הוּא מַלְכִּי, הוּא is neither logical copula nor predicate (as in cii.
28, Deut. xxxii. 39, there equivalent to אַתָּה הוּא אֲשֶׁר, cf. 1
Chron. xxi. 17), but an expressive resumption of the subject,
as in Isa. xliii. 25, Jer. xlix. 12, Neh. ix. 6 sq., Ezra v. 11, and
in the frequently recurring expression יהוה הוּא האלהים ; it is
therefore to be rendered : Thou—He who (such an one) is my
King. May He therefore, by virtue of His duty as king
which He has voluntarily taken upon Himself, and of the

kingly authority and power indwelling in Him, command the salvation of Jacob, full and entire (xviii. 51, liii. 7). צַוֵּה as in xlii. 9. *Jacob* is used for *Israel* just as *Elohim* is used instead of *Jahve*. If Elohim, Jacob's King, now turns graciously to His people, they will again be victorious and invincible, as ver. 6 affirms. נְגַּח with reference to קֶרֶן as a figure and emblem of strength, as in lxxxix. 25 and frequently; קָמֵינוּ equivalent to קָמִים עָלֵינוּ. But only in the strength of God (בְּךָ as in xviii. 30); for not in my bow do I trust, etc., ver. 7. This teaching Israel has gathered from the history of the former times; there is no bidding defiance with the bow and sword and all the carnal weapons of attack, but Thou, etc., ver. 8. This "Thou" in הוֹשַׁעְתָּנוּ is the emphatic word; the preterites describe facts of experience belonging to history. It is not Israel's own might that gives them the supremacy, but God's gracious might in Israel's weakness. Elohim is, therefore, Israel's glory or pride: "In Elohim do we praise," *i.e.* we glory or make our boast in Him; cf. הִלֵּל עַל, x. 3. The music here joins in after the manner of a hymn. The Psalm here soars aloft to the more joyous height of praise, from which it now falls abruptly into bitter complaint.

Vers. 10–13. Just as אַף signifies *imo vero* (lviii. 3) when it comes after an antecedent clause that is expressly or virtually a negative, it may mean "nevertheless, ὅμως," when it opposes a contrastive to an affirmative assertion, as is very frequently the case with גַּם or וְגַם. True, it does not mean this in itself, but in virtue of its logical relation: we praise Thee, we celebrate Thy name unceasingly—also (= nevertheless) Thou hast cast off. From this point the Psalm comes into closest connection with Ps. lxxxix. 39, on a still more extended scale, however, with Ps. lx., which dates from the time of the Syro-Ammonitish war, in which Psalm ver. 10 recurs almost word for word. The צְבָאוֹת are not exactly standing armies (an objection which has been raised against the Maccabean explanation), they are the hosts of the people that are drafted into battle, as in Ex. xii. 41, the hosts that went forth out of Egypt. Instead of leading these to victory as their victorious Captain (2 Sam. v. 24), God leaves them to themselves and allows them to be smitten by the enemy. The enemy spoil לָמוֹ, *i.e.* just as they like, without meeting with any resistance, to their hearts' content. And whilst He gives over (נָתַן as in Mic. v. 2, and the first יִתֵּן in Isa. xli. 2) one portion of the people as "sheep appointed for food," another becomes a *diaspora* or dispersion among the heathen, viz. by being sold to them as slaves, and that בְּלֹא־הוֹן, "for not-riches," *i.e.* for a very low price, a mere nothing. We see from Joel iv. [iii.] 3 in what way this is intended. The form of the litotes is continued in ver. 13*b*: Thou didst not go high in the matter of their purchase-money; the rendering of Maurer is correct: *in statuendis pretiis eorum.* The בּ is in this instance not the *Beth* of the price as in ver. 13*a*, but, as in the phrase הֵלֵל בְּ, the *Beth* of the sphere and thereby indirectly of the object. רִבָּה in the sense of the Aramaic רַבִּי (cf. Prov. xxii. 16, and the derivatives מַרְבִּית, תַּרְבִּית), to make a profit, to practise usury (Hupfeld), produces a thought that is unworthy of God; *vid.* on the other hand, Isa. lii. 3. At the head of the strophe stands (ver. 10*a*) a perfect with an aorist following; וְלֹא חָצָא is consequently a negative וַתֵּצֵא. And ver. 18, which sums up the whole, shows that all the rest is also intended to be retrospective.

Vers. 14–17. To this defeat is now also added the shame that springs out of it. A distinction is made between the neighbouring nations, or those countries lying immediately round about Israel (סְבִיבוֹת, as in the exactly similar passage lxxix. 4, cf. lxxx. 7, which closely resembles it), and the nations of the earth that dwell farther away from Israel. מָשָׁל is here a jesting, taunting proverb, and one that holds Israel up as an example of a nation undergoing chastisement (*vid.* Hab. ii. 6). The shaking of the head is, as in xxii. 8, a gesture of malicious astonishment. In נֶגְדִּי תָמִיד (as in xxxviii. 18) we have both the permanent aspect or look and the perpetual consciousness. Instead of "shame covers my face," the expression is "the shame of my face covers me," *i.e.* it has overwhelmed my entire inward and outward being (cf. concerning the radical notions of בּוֹשׁ, vi. 11, and חָפֵר, xxxiv. 6). The juxtaposition of "enemy and revengeful man" has its origin in viii. 3. In ver. 17 מִקּוֹל and מִפְּנֵי alternate; the former is used of the impression made by the jeering voice, the other of the impression produced by the enraged mien.

Vers. 18–22. If Israel compares its conduct towards God with this its lot, it cannot possibly regard it as a punishment

that it has justly incurred. Construed with the accusative,
בּוֹא signifies, as in xxxv. 8, xxxvi. 12, to come upon one, and
more especially of an evil lot and of powers that are hostile.
שִׁקֵּר, to lie or deceive, with בְּ of the object on whom the decep-
tion or treachery is practised, as in lxxxix. 34. In ver. 19*b*
אֲשׁוּר is construed as *fem.*, exactly as in Job xxxi. 7; the *fut.
consec.* is also intended as such (as *e.g.* in Job iii. 10, Num.
xvi. 14) : that our step should have declined from, etc.; inward
apostasy is followed by outward wandering and downfall. This
is therefore not one of the many instances in which the לֹא of
one clause also has influence over the clause that follows (Ges.
§ 152, 3). כִּי, ver. 20, has the sense of *quod :* we have not
revolted against Thee, that Thou shouldest on that account
have done to us the thing which is now befallen us. Concerning תַּנִּים *vid.* Isa. xiii. 22. A "place of jackals" is, like
a habitation of dragons (Jer. x. 22), the most lonesome and
terrible wilderness ; the place chosen was, according to this, an
inhospitable מדבר, far removed from the dwellings of men. כִּפָּה
is construed with עַל of the person covered, and with בְּ of that with
which (1 Sam. xix. 13) he is covered : Thou coveredst us over
with deepest darkness (*vid.* xxiii. 4). אִם, ver. 21, is not that
of asseveration (verily we have not forgotten), but, as the
interrogatory apodosis ver. 22*a* shows, conditional : if we have
(= should have) forgotten. This would not remain hidden
from Him who knoweth the heart, for the secrets of men's
hearts are known to Him. Both the form and matter here
again strongly remind one of Job ch. xxxi., more especially
ver. 4; cf. also on תַּעֲלֻמוֹת, Job xi. 6, xxviii. 11.

Vers. 23–27. The church is not conscious of any apostasy,
for on the contrary it is suffering for the sake of its fidelity.
Such is the meaning intended by כִּי, ver. 23 (cf. xxxvii. 20).
The emphasis lies on עָלֶיךָ, which is used exactly as in lxix. 8.
Paul, in Rom. viii. 36, transfers this utterance to the sufferings
of the New Testament church borne in witnessing for the truth,
or I should rather say he considers it as a divine utterance
corresponding as it were prophetically to the sufferings of the
New Testament church, and by anticipation, coined concerning
it and for its use, inasmuch as he cites it with the words καθὼς
γέγραπται. The suppliant cries עוּרָה and הָקִיצָה are Davidic,
and found in his earlier Psalms, vii. 7, xxxv. 23, lix. 5 sq., cf.

lxxviii. 65. God is said to sleep when He does not interpose in whatever is taking place in the outward world here below; for the very nature of sleep is a turning in into one's own self from all relationship to the outer world, and a resting of the powers which act outwardly. The writer of our Psalm is fond of couplets of synonyms like עֲנֵינוּ וְלַחֲצֵנוּ in ver. 25; cf. ver. 4, יְמִינֶךָ וּזְרוֹעֶךָ. Ps. cxix. 25 is an echo of ver. 26. The suppliant cry קוּמָה (in this instance in connection with the עזרתה which follows, it is to be accented on the *ultima*) is Davidic, iii. 8, vii. 7; but originally it is Mosaic. Concerning the *ah* of עֶזְרָתָה, here as also in lxiii. 8 of like meaning with לְעֶזְרָתִי, xxii. 20, and frequently, *vid.* on iii. 3.

PSALM XLV.

MARRIAGE SONG IN HONOUR OF THE PEERLESS KING.

2 MY heart overflows with goodly speech,
   I say to myself: "My production is concerning a king,"
   My tongue is the pen of a quick writer.
3 With beauty art thou arrayed beyond the children of
      men,
   Gracefulness is shed upon thy lips;
   Therefore hath Elohim blessed thee for ever.

4 Gird thy sword upon thy thigh, O mighty one,
   Thy brightness and thy majesty.
5 And in thy majesty press through, ride on,
   For the sake of truth and of the suffering of innocence,
   And thy right hand shall teach thee terrible deeds.
6 Thine arrows are sharp,—peoples shall fall under thee,—
   In the heart of the king's enemies!

7 Thy throne, Elohim, endureth for ever and ever,
   An upright sceptre is the sceptre of thy kingdom.
8 Loving righteousness, thou hatest wickedness;
   Therefore hath Elohim thy God anointed thee
   With the oil of joy above thy fellows.

9 Myrrh and aloes, cassia are all thy garments;
　Out of ivory palaces doth the music of stringed instruments
　　　make thee glad.
10 Kings' daughters are among thy beloved ones,
　The queen hath set herself at thy right hand
　In ornaments of gold of Ophir.

11 Hearken, O daughter, and see and incline thine ear,
　And forget thine own people and thy father's house;
12 And if the king desireth thy beauty,—
　For he is thy Lord,—then do thou do homage to him.
13 And the daughter of Tyre, with gifts shall they conciliate
　　　thy face,
　The richest among the peoples.

14 All glory is the king's daughter in the inner chamber,
　Of gold-woven textures is her clothing.
15 In variegated embroidered garments is she escorted to the
　　　king;
　Virgins after her, her companions,
　Are brought unto thee—
16 They are escorted with joy and exultation,
　They enter into the king's palace.—

17 Instead of thy fathers shall be thy sons,
　Thou shalt set them as princes in all lands.
18 Thy name will I remember in every generation,
　Therefore shall the peoples praise thee for ever and ever.

To a Korahitic *Maskîl* is appended a song of the same
name, and likewise bearing a royal impress after the style of
the Korahitic productions. But whilst in xliv. 5 the words
" *Thou, Thou art my King, Elohim,*" are addressed in prayer
to the God of Israel, in this Psalm the person of the king who
is celebrated is a matter of doubt and controversy. The Epistle
to the Hebrews (ch. i. 8) proceeds on the assumption that it is
the future Christ, the Son of God. It is supported in this
view by a tradition of the ancient synagogue, in accordance
with which the Targumist renders ver. 3, " *Thy beauty, O King
Messiah, is greater than that of the children of men.*" This

Messianic interpretation must be very ancient. Just as Ezek. xxi. 32 refers back to שִׁילֹה, Gen. xlix. 10, אֵל גִּבּוֹר among the names of the Messiah in Isa. ix. 5 (cf. Zech. xii. 8) refers back in a similar manner to Ps. xlv. And whilst the reception of the Song of Songs into the canon admits of being understood even without the assumption of any prophetically allegorical meaning in it, the reception of this Psalm without any such assumption is unintelligible. But this prophetically Messianic sense is therefore not the original meaning of the Psalm. The Psalm is a poem composed for some special occasion the motive of which is some cotemporary event. The king whom it celebrates was a cotemporary of the poet. If, however, it was a king belonging to David's family, then he was a possessor of a kingship to which were attached, according to 2 Sam. ch. vii., great promises extending into the unlimited future, and on which, consequently, hung all the prospects of the future prosperity and glory of Israel; and the poet is therefore fully warranted in regarding him in the light of the Messianic idea, and the church is also fully warranted in referring the song, which took its rise in some passing occasion, as a song for all ages, to the great King of the future, the goal of its hope. Moreover, we find only such poems of an occasional and individual character received into the Psalter, as were adapted to remain in constant use by the church as prayers and spiritual songs.

With respect to the historical occasion of the song, we adhere to the conjecture advanced in our commentary on Canticles and on the Epistle to the Hebrews, viz. that it was composed in connection with the marriage of Joram of Judah with Athaliah. The reference to the marriage of Ahab of Israel with Jezebel of Tyre, set forth by Hitzig, is at once set aside by the fact that the poet idealizes the person celebrated, as foreshadowing the Messiah, in a way that can only be justified in connection with a *Davidic* king. It could more readily be Solomon the king of Israel, whose appearance was fair as that of a woman, but majestic as that of a hero.* Even to the present day several interpreters† explain the Psalm of Solo-

---

* So Disraeli in his romance of *Alroy* (1845).
† So even Kurtz in the *Dorpater Zeitschrift* for 1865, S. 1–24.

mon's marriage with the daughter of Pharaoh; but the entire absence of any mention of Egypt is decisive against this view. Hence Hupfeld imagines a daughter of Hiram to be the bride, by reference to the Zidonian Ashtôreth which is mentioned among Solomon's strange gods (1 Kings xi. 5, 33). But the fact that the king here celebrated is called upon to go forth to battle, is also strange, whilst the glory of Solomon consists in his being, in accordance with his name, the Prince of Peace, or אִישׁ מְנוּחָה, 1 Chron. xxii. 9. Further, the wish is expressed for him that he may have children who shall take the place of his ancestors: Solomon, however, had a royal father, but not royal fathers; and there is the less ground for any retrospective reference to the princes of Judah as Solomon's ancestors (which Kurtz inclines to), since of these only one, viz. Nahshon, occurs among the ancestry of David.

All this speaks against Solomon, but just with equal force in favour of Joram, as being the king celebrated. This Joram is the son of Jehoshaphat, the second Solomon of the Israelitish history. He became king even during the lifetime of his pious father, under whom the Salomonic prosperity of Israel was revived (cf. 2 Chron. xviii. 1 with xxi. 3, 2 Kings viii. 16, and Winer's *Realwörterbuch* under *Jehoram*); he was also married to Athaliah during his father's lifetime; and it is natural, that just at that time, when Judah had again attained to the height of the glory of the days of Solomon, the highest hopes should be gathered around these nuptials. This explains the name שֵׁגָל which the queen bears,—a name that is elsewhere Chaldæan (Dan. v. 2 sq.) and Persian (Neh. ii. 6), and is more North-Palestinian * than Jewish; for Athaliah sprang from the royal family of Tyre, and was married by Joram out of the royal family of Israel. If she is the queen, then the exhortation to forget her people and her father's house has all the greater force. And it becomes intelligible why the homage of Tyre in particular, and only of Tyre, is mentioned. The Salomonic splendour of Asiatic perfumes and costly things is thus quite as easily explained as by referring the Psalm to Solomon. For even Jehoshaphat had turned his attention to

---

* In Deborah's song (Judg. v. 30) probably שֵׁגָל is to be read instead of לְצַוְּארֵי שָׁלָל.

foreign wares, more especially Indian gold; he even prepared
a fleet for the purpose of going to Ophir, but, ere it started,
it was wrecked in the harbour of Ezion-geber (1 Kings xxii.
48–50, 2 Chron. xx. 35 sqq.).   And Solomon, it is true, had a
throne of ivory (1 Kings x. 18), and the Salomonic Song of
Songs (vii. 5) makes mention of a tower of ivory; but he had
no ivory palace; whereas the mention of הֵיכְלֵי־שֵׁן in our Psalm
harmonizes surprisingly with the fact that Ahab, the father
of Athaliah, built a palace of ivory (בֵּית־שֵׁן), which the Book
of Kings, referring to the annals, announces as something
especially worthy of note, 1 Kings xxii. 39 (cf. Amos iii. 15,
בָּתֵּי הַשֵּׁן).

But why should not even Joram, at a crisis of his life so
rich in hope, have been a type of the Messiah?   His name is
found in the genealogy of Jesus Christ, Matt. i. 8.   Joram
and Athaliah are among the ancestors of our Lord.   This
significance in relation to the history of redemption is still left
them, although they have not realized the good wishes expressed
by the poet at the time of their marriage, just as in fact Solomon also began in the spirit and ended in the flesh.   Joram
and Athaliah have themselves cut away all reference of the
Psalm to them by their own godlessness.   It is with this Psalm
just as it is with the twelve thrones upon which, according to
the promise, Matt. xix. 28, the twelve apostles shall sit and
judge the twelve tribes of Israel.   This promise was uttered
even in reference to Judas Iscariot.   One of the twelve seats
belonged to him, but he has fallen away from it.   Matthias
became heir to the throne of Judas Iscariot, and who has
become the heir to the promises in this Psalm?   All the glorious
things declared in the Psalm depend upon this as the primary
assumption, as essential to their being a blessing and being
realized, viz. that the king whom it celebrates should carry out
the idea of the theocratic kingship.   To the Old Testament
prophecy and hope, more especially since the days of Isaiah,
the Messiah, and to the New Testament conception of the fulfilment of prophecy Jesus Christ, is the perfected realization
of this idea.

The inscription runs: *To the Precentor, upon Lilies, by the
Benē-Korah, a meditation, a song of that which is lovely.*   Concerning *Maskîl, vid.* on xxxii. 1.   שׁוֹשַׁן is the name for the (six-

leafed) lily,* that is wide-spread in its use in the East ; it is not the (five-leafed) rose, which was not transplanted into Palestine until a much later period. In עַל־שֹׁשַׁנִּים Hengstenberg sees a symbolical reference to the "lovely brides" mentioned in the Psalm. Luther, who renders it "concerning the roses," understands it to mean the *rosæ futuræ* of the united church of the future. We would rather say, with Bugenhagen, Joh. Gerhard, and other old expositors, "The heavenly Bridegroom and the spiritual bride, they are the two roses or lilies that are discoursed of in this Psalm." But the meaning of עַל־שֹׁשַׁנִים must be such as will admit of the inscribed עַל־שׁוּשַׁן עֵדוּת, lx. 1, and אֶל־שֹׁשַׁנִּים עֵדוּת (which is probably all one expression notwithstanding the *Athnach*), lxxx. 1, being understood after the analogy of it. The preposition עַל (אֶל) forbids our thinking of a musical instrument, perhaps lily-shaped bells.† There must therefore have been some well-known popular song, which began with the words "A lily is the testimony . . ." or "Lilies are the testimonies (עֵדוֹת) . . . ;" and the Psalm is composed and intended to be sung after the melody of this song in praise of the Tôra.‡ It is questionable whether יְדִידֹת (Origen ιδιδωθ, Jerome *ididoth*) in the last designation of the Psalm is to be taken as a collateral form of יְדִידוּת (love, and metonymically an object of love, Jer. xii. 7), or whether we are to explain it after the analogy of צַחוֹת, Isa. xxxii. 4, and נְכֹחוֹת, Isa. xxvi. 10 : it is just on this neuter use of the *plur. fem.* that the interchange which sometimes occurs of *óth* with *ûth* in an abstract signification (Ew. § 165, *c*) is based. In the former case it ought to be rendered a song of love (Aquila ᾆσμα προσφιλίας) ; in the latter, a song of that which is beloved, *i.e.* lovely, or lovable, and this is the more natural rendering. The adjective יָדִיד signified beloved, or even (lxxxiv. 2) lovable. It is things that are loved, because exciting love, therefore lovely,

---

* This name is also ancient Egyptian, *vid.* the *Book of the Dead*, lxxxi. 2 : *nuk seshni pir am t.ah-en-Phrā*, *i.e.* I am a lily, sprung from the fields of the sun-god.

† *Vide* C. Jessen, On the lily of the Bible, in Hugo von Mohl's *Botanische Zeitung*, 1861, No. 12. Thrupp in his *Introduction* (1860) also understands שׁוּשַׁנִּים to mean cymbals in the form of a lily.

‡ The point of comparison, then, to adopt the language of Gregory of Nyssa, is τὸ λαμπρόν τε καὶ χιονῶδες εἶδος of the lily.

most pleasing things, which, as שִׁיר יְדִידֹת says, form the contents of the song. שִׁיר יְדִידֹת does not signify a marriage-song; this would be called שִׁיר חֲתֻנָּה (cf. xxx. 1). Nor does it signify a secular erotic song, instead of which the expression שִׁיר עֲגָבִים, Ezek. xxxiii. 32, or even (after Ezek. xvi. 8 and other passages) שִׁיר דּוֹדִים, would have been used. יָדִיד is a noble word, and used of holy love.

Vers. 2, 3. The verb רָחַשׁ, as מַרְחֶשֶׁת shows, signifies originally to bubble up, boil, and is used in the dialects generally of excited motion and lively excitement; it is construed with the accusative after the manner of verbs denoting fulness, like the synonymous נָבַע, cxix. 171 (cf. Talmudic לְשׁוֹנְךָ תַּרְחִישׁ רְנָנוֹת, let thy tongue overflow with songs of praise). Whatever the heart is full of, with that the mouth overflows; the heart of the poet gushes over with a "good word." דָּבָר is a matter that finds utterance and is put into the form of words; and טוֹב describes it as good with the collateral idea of that which is cheerful, pleasing, and rich in promise (Isa. lii. 7, Zech. i. 13). The fact that out of the fulness and oppression of his heart so good a word springs forth, arises from the subject in which now his whole powers of mind are absorbed: I am saying or thinking (אָנִי pausal form by *Dechî*, in order that the introductory formula may not be mistaken), *i.e.* my purpose is: מַעֲשַׂי לְמֶלֶךְ, my works or creations (not *sing.*, but *plur.*, just as also מִקְנַי in Ex. xvii. 3, Num. xx. 19, where the connection leads one to expect the plural) shall be dedicated to the king; or even: the thought completely fills me, quite carries me away, that they concern or have reference to the king. In the former case לְמֶלֶךְ dispenses with the article because it is used after the manner of a proper name (as in xxi. 2, lxxii. 1); in the latter, because the person retires before the office or dignity belonging to it: and this we, in common with Hitzig, prefer on account of the self-conscious and reflecting אֹמֵר אָנִי by which it is introduced. He says to himself that it is a king to whom his song refers; and this lofty theme makes his tongue so eloquent and fluent that it is like the style of a γραμματεὺς ὀξύγραφος. Thus it is correctly rendered by the LXX.; whereas סוֹפֵר מָהִיר as an epithet applied to Ezra (ch. vii. 6) does not denote a rapid writer, but a learned or skilled scribe.

Rapidly, like the style of an agile writer, does the tongue of the poet move; and it is obliged to move thus rapidly because of the thoughts and words that flow forth to it out of his heart. The chief thing that inspires him is the beauty of the king. The form יָפְיָפִ֫יתָ, which certainly ought to have a passive sense (Aquila κάλλει ἐκαλλίωθης), cannot be explained as formed by reduplication of the first two radicals of the verb יָפָה (יְפִי); for there are no examples to be found in support of quinqueliterals thus derived. What seems to favour this derivation is this, that the legitimately formed *Pealal* יְפֵיפָה (cf. the adjective יְפֵיפִי = יְפֵהפִי, Jer. xlvi. 20) is made passive by a change of vowels in a manner that is altogether peculiar, but still explicable in connection with this verb, which is a twofold weak verb. The meaning is: Thou art beyond compare beautifully fashioned, or endowed with beauty beyond the children of men. The lips are specially singled out from among all the features of beauty in him. Over his lips is poured forth, viz. from above, חֵן (gracefulness or benevolence), inasmuch as, even without his speaking, the form of his lips and each of their movements awakens love and trust; it is evident, however, that from such lips, full of χάρις, there must proceed also λόγοι τῆς χάριτος (Luke iv. 22, Eccles. x. 12). In this beauty of the king and this charm of his lips the psalmist sees a manifestation of the everlasting blessing of God, that is perceptible to the senses. It is not to be rendered: because Elohim hath blessed thee for ever. The assertion that עַל־כֵּן is used in some passages for עַל־כֵּן אֲשֶׁר cannot be proved (*vid.* on xlii. 7). But the meaning of the psalmist is, moreover, not that the king, because he is so fair and has such gracious lips, is blessed of God. If this were the idea, then the noble moral qualities of which the beauty of this king is the transparent form, ought to be more definitely expressed. Thus personally conceived, as it is here, beauty itself is a blessing, not a ground for blessing. The fact of the matter is this, beauty is denoted by עַל־כֵּן as a reason for the blessing being known or recognised, not as a reason why the king should be blessed. From his outward appearance it is at once manifest that the king is one who is blessed by God, and that blessed for ever. The psalmist could not but know that " grace is deceitful and beauty vain " (Prov. xxxi. 30), therefore the beauty of this king was in his eyes more than mere earthly beauty; it appears to him in the light of a celestial transfiguration, and for this very reason as an imperishable gift, in which there becomes manifest an unlimited endless blessing.

Vers. 4–6. In the ever blessed one the greatest strength and vigour are combined with the highest beauty. He is a hero. The praise of his heroic strength takes the form of a summons to exert it and aid the good in obtaining the victory over evil. Brightness and majesty, as the objects to חֲגוֹר, alternating with the sword, are not in apposition to this which is their instrument and symbol (Hengstenberg), but permutatives, inasmuch as חֲגוֹר is zeugmatically referable to both objects: the king is (1) to gird himself with his sword, and (2) to surround himself with his kingly, God-like doxa. הוֹד וְהָדָר is the brilliancy of the divine glory (xcvi. 6), of which the glory of the Davidic kingship is a reflection (xxi. 6); mentioned side by side with the sword, it is, as it were, the panoply that surrounds the king as bright armour. In ver. 5 והדרך, written accidentally a second time, is probably to be struck out, as Olshausen and Hupfeld are of opinion. Hitzig points it וְהִדְרֵךְ, "and step forth;" but this is not Hebrew. As the text runs, wa-hadārcha (with *Legarme* preceded by *Illuj, vid. Accentsystem* xiii. § 8c, 9) looks as though it were repeated out of ver. 4 in the echo-like and interlinked style that we frequently find in the songs of degrees, *e.g.* cxxi. 1, 2; and in fact repeated as an accusative of more exact definition (in the same bold manner as in xvii. 13, 14) to צְלַח, which, like صلح, starting from the primary notion of cleaving, breaking through, pressing forward, comes to have the notion of carrying anything through prosperously, of being successful, *pervadere et bene procedere* (cf. the corresponding development of signification in فلح, افلح), and, according to Ges. § 142, rem. 1, gives to רְכַב the adverbial notion of that which is effectual (victorious) or effective and successful. We cannot determine whether רְכַב is here intended to say *vehi curru* or *vehi equo;* but certainly not upon a mule or an ass (1 Kings i. 44, Zech. ix. 9), which are the beasts ridden in a time of peace. The king going forth to battle either rides in a war-chariot (like Ahab and Jehoshaphat, 1 Kings ch. xxii.), or upon a war-horse, as in Apoc. xix. 11

the Logos of God is borne upon a white horse. That which
he is to accomplish as he rides forth in majesty is introduced
by עַל־דְּבַר (for the sake of, on account of), which is used just
as in lxxix. 9, 2 Sam. xviii. 5. The combination עֲנָוה־צֶדֶק is very
similar to עֶרְיָה־בֹשֶׁת, Mic. i. 11 (nakedness-ignominy = ignominious nakedness), if עֲנָוה = עֲנָוה is to be taken as the name of a
virtue. The two words are then the names of virtues, like
אֱמֶת (truth = veracity, which loves and practises that which is
true and which is hostile to lying, falseness, and dissimulation);
and whereas צֶדֶק עֲנָוה would signify meek righteousness, and
עֲנַות צֶדֶק, righteous meekness, this conjunction standing in the
middle between an addition and an asyndeton denotes meekness
and righteousness as twin-sisters and reciprocally pervasive.
The virtues named, however, stand for those who exemplify
them and who are in need of help, on whose behalf the king is
called upon to enter the strife: the righteous, if they are at
the same time עֲנָוִים (עֲנִיִּים), are doubly worthy and in need of
his help. Nevertheless another explanation of עֲנָוה presents
itself, and one that is all the more probable as occurring just
in this Psalm which has such a North-Palestinian colouring.
The observation, that North-Palestinian writers do not always
point the construct state with *ath*, in favour of which Hitzig,
on lxviii. 29, wrongly appeals to Hos. x. 6, Job xxxix. 13, but
rightly to Judg. vii. 8, viii. 32 (cf. Deut. xxxiii. 4, 27), is perfectly correct. Accordingly עֲנָוה may possibly be equivalent to
עֲנַות, but not in the signification business, affair = עִנְיָן, parallel
with דָּבָר, but in the signification *afflictio* (after the form רְאֶה,
Ezek. xxviii. 17); so that it may be rendered: in order to put
a stop to the oppression of righteousness or the suffering of
innocence. The jussive וְתוֹרְךָ, like וְיִתְאָו in ver. 12, begins the
apodosis of a hypothetical protasis that is virtually there (Ew.
§ 347, *b*): so shall thy right hand teach thee, *i.e.* lead thee forth
and cause thee to see terrible things, *i.e.* awe-inspiring deeds.
But in ver. 6 both summons and desire pass over into the
expression of a sure and hopeful prospect and a vision, in
which that which is to be is present to the mind: thine arrows
are sharpened, and therefore deadly to those whom they hit;
peoples shall fall (יִפְּלוּ)* under thee, *i.e.* so that thou passest

---

* It is not יִפֹּלוּ; for the pause falls upon שְׁנוּנִים, and the *Athnach* of

over them as they lie upon the ground; in the heart of the
enemies of the king, viz. they (*i.e.* the arrows) will stick.　The
harsh ellipse is explained by the fact of the poet having the
scene of battle before his mind as though he were an eye-
witness of it.　The words "in the heart of the king's enemies"
are an exclamation accompanied by a pointing with the finger.
Thither, he means to say, those sharp arrows fly and smite.
Crusius' explanation is similar, but it goes further than is
required: *apostrophe per prosopopœiam directa ad sagittas quasi
jubens, quo tendere debeant.*　We are here reminded of cx. 2,
where a similar בְּקֶרֶב occurs in a prophetico-messianic connection.　Moreover, even according to its reference to cotemporary
history the whole of this strophe sounds Messianic.　The poet
desires that the king whom he celebrates may rule and triumph
after the manner of the Messiah; that he may succour truth
and that which is truly good, and overcome the enmity of the
world, or, as Ps. ii. expresses it, that the God-anointed King of
Zion may shatter everything that rises up in opposition with
an iron sceptre.　This anointed One, however, is not only the
Son of David, but also of God.　He is called absolutely בֵּר,
ὁ υἱός.　Isaiah calls Him, even in the cradle, אֵל גִּבּוֹר, ch. ix. 5,
cf. x. 21.　We shall not, therefore, find it to be altogether
intolerable, if the poet now addresses him as אֱלֹהִים, although
the picture thus far sketched is thoroughly human in all its
ideality.

Vers. 7, 8.　In order to avoid the addressing of the king
with the word *Elohim*, ver. 6*a* has been interpreted, (1) "Thy
throne of God is for ever and ever,"—a rendering which is
grammatically possible, and, if it were intended to be expressed,
must have been expressed thus (Nagelsbach, § 64, *g*); (2) "Thy
throne is God (= divine) for ever and ever;" but it cannot
possibly be so expressed after the analogy of "the altar of wood
= wooden" (cf. ver. 9), or "the time is showers of rain =
rainy" (Ezra x. 13), since God is neither the substance of
the throne, nor can the throne itself be regarded as a representation or figure of God: in this case the predicative *Elohim*

יִפְלוּ stands merely in the place of *Zakeph* (Num. vi. 12).　The *Athnach*
after *Olewejored* does not produce any pausal effect; *vid.* l. 23, lxviii. 9, 14,
lxix. 4, cxxix. 1, and cf. *supra*, vol. i. p. 95, note 2.

would require to be taken as a genitive for כְּסֵא אלהים, which, however, cannot possibly be supported in Hebrew by any syntax, not even by 2 Kings xxiii. 17, cf. Ges. § 110, 2, *b*. Accordingly one might adopt the first mode of interpretation, which is also commended by the fact that the earthly throne of the theocratic king is actually called כסא יהוה in 1 Chron. xxix. 23. But the sentence "thy throne of God is an everlasting one" sounds tautological, inasmuch as that which the predicate asserts is already implied in the subject; and we have still first of all to try whether אלהים cannot, with the LXX. ὁ θρόνος σου, ὁ Θεός, εἰς αἰῶνα αἰῶνος, be taken as a vocative. Now, since before everything else God's throne is eternal (x. 16, Lam. v. 19), and a love of righteousness and a hatred of evil is also found elsewhere as a description of divine holiness (v. 5, Isa. lxi. 8), אלהים would be obliged to be regarded as addressed to God, if language addressed to the king did not follow with עַל־כֵּן. But might אלהים by any possibility be even addressed to the king who is here celebrated? It is certainly true that the custom with the Elohim-Psalms of using *Elohim* as of equal dignity with *Jahve* is not favourable to this supposition; but the following surpassing of the אלהים by אלהים אלהיך renders it possible. And since elsewhere earthly authorities are also called אלהים, Ex. xxi. 6, xxii. 7 sq., Ps. lxxxii., cf. cxxxviii. 1, because they are God's representatives and the bearers of His image upon earth, so the king who is celebrated in this Psalm may be all the more readily styled *Elohim*, when in his heavenly beauty, his irresistible doxa or glory, and his divine holiness, he seems to the psalmist to be the perfected realization of the close relationship in which God has set David and his seed to Himself. He calls him אֱלֹהִים, just as Isaiah calls the exalted royal child whom he exultingly salutes in ch. ix. 1–6, אֵל־גִּבּוֹר. He gives him this name, because in the transparent exterior of his fair humanity he sees the glory and holiness of God as having attained a salutary or merciful conspicuousness among men. At the same time, however, he guards this calling of the king by the name *Elohim* against being misapprehended by immediately distinguishing the God, who stands above him, from the divine king by the words "Elohim, thy God," which, in the Korahitic Psalms, and in the Elohimic Psalms in general, is equivalent to "Jahve, thy God" (xliii. 4, xlviii. 15, l. 7); and the two words are accordingly united by *Munach*.* Because the king's sceptre is a "sceptre of uprightness" (cf. Isa. xi. 4), because he loves righteousness and consequently (*fut. consec.*) hates iniquity, therefore God, his God, has anointed him with the oil of joy (Isa. lxi. 3; cf. on the construction Amos vi. 6) above his fellows. What is intended is not the anointing to his office (cf. lxxxix. 21 with Acts x. 38) as a dedication to a happy and prosperous reign, but that God has poured forth upon him, more especially on this his nuptial day, a superabundant joy, both outwardly and in his spirit, such as He has bestowed upon no other king upon the face of the earth. That he rises high above all those round about him is self-evident; but even among his fellows of royal station, kings like himself, he has no equal. It is a matter of question whether the writer of the Epistle to the Hebrews (ch. i. 8) has taken the first ὁ Θεός of the expression ὁ Θεὸς ὁ Θεός σου as a vocative. Apollinaris does not seem so to have understood him; for he renders it τοὔνεκά σοι Θεὸς αὐτὸς ἐὴν περίχευεν ἀλοιφήν χρίσας τερπωλῆς μετόχοις παρὰ πάντας ἐλαίῳ, and the Greek expositors also take ὁ Θεός here as a nominative.

Vers. 9, 10. The song of that which is lovely here reaches the height towards which it aspires from the beginning. It has portrayed the lovely king as a man, as a hero, and as a divine ruler; now it describes him as a bridegroom on the day of his nuptials. The sequence of the thoughts and of the figures corresponds to the history of the future. When Babylon is fallen, and the hero riding upon a white horse, upon whom is inscribed the name "King of kings and Lord of lords," shall have smitten the hostile nations with the sword that goeth out of His mouth, there then follows the marriage of the Lamb, for which the way has been prepared by these avenging victories (Apoc. xix. 7 sq.). It is this final γάμος

---

* The view that the *Munach* is here *vicarius Tiphchæ anterioris* (Dachselt in his *Biblia Accentuata*) is erroneous, *vid. Accentuationssystem*, xviii. § 4. It is the conjunctive to אֱלֹהֶיךָ, which, in Heidenheim and Baer, on the authority of the Codices, has *Tiphcha anterior*, not *Athnach* as in the editions heretofore published. The proper place for the *Athnach* would at first be by שָׂשׂוֹן; but according to *Accentuationssystem*, xix. § 6, it cannot stand there.

which the Psalm, as a song of the congregation, when the light
was dawning upon the Old Testament church, sees by anticipation, and as it were goes forth to meet it, rejoicing to behold
it afar off. The king's garments are so thoroughly scented
with costly spices that they seem to be altogether woven out
of them. And מִנִּי out of the ivory palaces enchant him. This
מִנִּי has been taken mostly, according to Isa. lix. 18 (cf. also
Isa. lii. 6), as a repetition of the מִן: "out of ivory palaces,
whence they enchant thee." But this repetition serves no
special purpose. Although the apocopated plural in *î*, instead
of *îm*, is controvertible in Biblical Hebrew (*vid.* on xxii. 17,
2 Sam. xxii. 44), still there is the venture that in this instance
מִנִּי is equivalent to מִנִּים, the music of stringed instruments
(cl. 4); and if in connection with any Psalm at all, surely we
may venture in connection with this Psalm, which in other respects has such an Aramaic or North-Palestinian colouring, to
acknowledge this apocope, here perhaps chosen on account of
the rhythm. In accordance with our historical rendering of the
Psalm, by the ivory palaces are meant the magnificent resi-
dences of the king, who is the father of the bride. Out of the
inner recesses of these halls, inlaid within with ivory and
consequently resplendent with the most dazzling whiteness, the
bridegroom going to fetch his bride, as he approaches and
enters them, is met by the sounds of festive music: viewed in
the light of the New Testament, it is that music of citherns or
harps which the seer (Apoc. xiv. 2) heard like the voice of
many waters and of mighty thunder resounding from heaven.
The Old Testament poet imagines to himself a royal citadel
that in its earthly splendour far surpasses that of David and
of Solomon. Thence issues forth the sound of festive music
zealous, as it were, to bid its welcome to the exalted king.

Even the daughters of kings are among his precious ones.
יָקָר is the name for that which is costly, and is highly prized
and loved for its costliness (Prov. vi. 26). The form בִּיקְרוֹתֶיךָ
resembles the form לִיקְּהַת, Prov. xxx. 17, in the appearance of
the *i* and supplanting the *Sheba mobile*, and also in the *Dag.*
dirimens in the ק (cf. עֲקְבִי, Gen. xlix. 17; מִקְּדֹשׁ, Ex. xv. 17).*

---

* It is the reading of Ben-Naphtali that has here, as an exception,
become the *receptus;* whereas Ben-Asher reads בְּיִקְרוֹתָיִךְ. Saadia, Rashi,

Now, however, he has chosen for himself his own proper wife,
who is here called by a name commonly used of Chaldæan and
Persian queens, and, as it seems (cf. on Judg. v. 30), a North-
Palestinian name, שֵׁגָל,* instead of גְּבִירָה. From the fact that,
glittering with gold of Ophir, she has taken the place of honour
at the right hand of the king (נִצְּבָה, 3d *præt.*, not *part.*), it is
evident that her relationship to the king is at this time just in
the act of being completed. Who are those daughters of kings
and who is this queen standing in closest relationship to the
king? The former are the heathen nations converted to Christ,
and the latter is the Israel which is remarried to God in Christ,
after the fulness of the heathen is come in. It is only when
Israel is won to Him, after the fulness of the heathen is come
in (Rom. xi. 25), that the morning of the great day will dawn,
which this Psalm as a song of the church celebrates. בְּנוֹת
מְלָכִים cannot certainly, like בַּת־צֹר, be a personificative designation of heathen kingdoms, although שֵׁגָל is the believing Israel
conceived of as one person. It is actually kings' daughters as
the representatives of their nations that are intended; and the
relation of things is just the same here as in Isa. xlix. 23, where,
of the Israelitish church of the future, it is predicted that kings
shall be its foster-fathers and their princesses its nursing-
mothers.

Vers. 11–13. The poet next turns to address the one
bride of the king, who is now honoured far above the kings'
daughters. With שִׁמְעִי he implores for himself a hearing; by
רְאִי he directs her eye towards the new relationship into which

---

Simson ha-Nakdan and others, who derive the word from בָּקַר (to visit,
wait on), follow the *receptus*, comparing מְשִׁיסָה, Isa. xlii. 24, in support of
the form of writing. Also in לִיקֲהַת, Prov. xxx. 17; וַיְלֲלַת, Jer. xxv. 36;
כִּיתְרוֹן, Eccles. ii. 13, the otherwise rejected orthography of Ben-Naphtali
(who pointed וְיַחֲלוּ, Job xxix. 21, לְיִשְׂרָאֵל, וַיִּתֵּן, and the like) is retained,
as quite an exception, in the *textus receptus*. *Vide* S. D. Luzzatto, *Prole-
gomeni*, § cxcix., and *Grammatica della Lingua Ebraica*, § 193.

* Bar-Ali says that in Babylonia Venus is called שׁגל ודלפת, *vid.* Lagarde,
Gesammelte Abhandl. S. 17. Windischmann (*Zoroastrische Studien*, S. 161)
erroneously compares *ćagar* (pronounced *tshagar*) as a name of one of the
two wives of Zarathustra; but it happens that this is not the name of the
wife who holds the first rank (Neo-Persic *padishâh-zen*), but of the second
(*ćakir-zen*, bond-woman).

she is just entering; by הַקְשִׁי אָזְנֵךְ he bespeaks her attention to the exhortation that follows; by בַּת he puts himself in a position in relation to her similar to that which the teacher and preacher occupies who addresses the bridal pair at the altar. She is to forget her people and her father's house, to sever her natural, inherited, and customary relationships of life, both as regards outward form and inward affections; and should the king desire her beauty, to which he has a right,—for he, as being her husband (1 Pet. iii. 6), and more especially as being king, is her lord,—she is to show towards him her profoundest, reverent devotion. וְיִתְאָו is a hypothetical protasis according to Ges. § 128, 2, c. The reward of this willing submission is the universal homage of the nations. It cannot be denied on the ground of syntax that וּבַת־צֹר admits of being rendered "and O daughter of Tyre" (Hitzig),—a rendering which would also give additional support to our historical interpretation of the Psalm,—although, apart from the one insecure passage, Jer. xx. 12 (Ew. § 340, c), there is no instance to be found in which a vocative with ו occurs (Prov. viii. 5, Joel ii. 23, Isa. xliv. 21), when another vocative has not already preceded it. But to what purpose would be, in this particular instance, this apostrophe with the words בַּת־צֹר, from which it looks as though she were indebted to her ancestral house, and not to the king whose own she is become, for the acts of homage which are prospectively set before her? Such, however, is not the case; "daughter of Tyre" is a subject-notion, which can all the more readily be followed by the predicate in the plural, since it stands first almost like a *nomin. absol.* The daughter, *i.e.* the population of Tyre—approaching with presents shall they court (*lit.* stroke) thy face, *i.e.* meeting thee bringing love, they shall seek to propitiate thy love towards themselves. (פָּנִי) חִלָּה corresponds to the Latin *mulcere* in the sense of *delenire;* for חָלָה, حَلَا (root חל, whence חָלַל, حَلَّ, *solvit, laxavit*), means properly to be soft and tender, of taste to be sweet (in another direction: to be lax, weak, sick); the *Piel* consequently means to soften, conciliate, to make gentle that which is austere. Tyre, however, is named only by way of example; עֲשִׁירֵי עָם is not an apposition, but a continuation of the subject: not only Tyre, but in general those who are the richest among each separate people or

nation.   Just as אֶבְיוֹנֵי אָדָם (Isa. xxix. 19) are the poorest of mankind, so עֲשִׁירֵי עָם are the richest among the peoples of the earth.

As regards the meaning which the congregation or church
has to assign to the whole passage, the correct paraphrase of
the words "and forget thy people" is to be found even in the
Targum : "Forget the evil deeds of the ungodly among thy
people, and the house of the idols which thou hast served in
the house of thy father."   It is not indeed the hardened mass
of Israel which enters into such a loving relationship to God
and to His Christ, but, as prophecy from Deut. ch. xxxii.
onward declares, a remnant thoroughly purged by desolating
and sifting judgments and rescued, which, in order to belong
wholly to Christ, and to become the holy seed of a better
future (Isa. vi. 13), must cut asunder all bonds of connection
with the stiff-neckedly unbelieving people and paternal house,
and in like manner to Abram secede from them.   This church
of the future is fair; for she is expiated (Deut. xxxii. 43),
washed (Isa. iv. 4), and adorned (Isa. lxi. 3) by her God.
And if she does homage to Him, without looking back, He
not only remains her own, but in Him everything that is glorious belonging to the world also becomes her own.   Highly
honoured by the King of kings, she is the queen among the
daughters of kings, to whom Tyre and the richest among
peoples of every order are zealous to express their loving and
joyful recognition.   Very similar language to that used here
of the favoured church of the Messiah is used in lxxii. 10 sq.
of the Messiah Himself.

Vers. 14–16.   Now follows the description of the manner
in which she absolutely leaves her father's house, and richly
adorned and with a numerous train is led to the king and makes
her entry into his palace; and in connection therewith we
must bear in mind that the poet combines on the canvas of one
picture (so to speak) things that lie wide apart both as to time
and place.   He sees her first of all in her own chamber (פְּנִימָה,
prop. towards the inside, then also in the inside, Ges. § 90, 2, b),
and how there* she is nothing but splendour (כָּל־כְּבוּדָּה, prop.

---

* In Babylonia these words, according to *B. Jebamoth* 77a, are cited
in favour of domesticity as a female virtue; in Palestine (במערבא) more
appropriately, Gen. xviii. 9.   The LXX. *Codd. Vat. et Sinait.* has Ἐσεβών

mere splendour, *fem.* of כָּבוֹד as in Ezek. xxiii. 41; cf. כָּל־הֶבֶל,
xxxix. 6, mere nothingness), her clothing is gold-interwoven
textures (*i.e.* such as are interwoven with threads of gold, or
woven in squares or diamond patterns and adorned with gold
in addition). She, just like Esther (Esth. ii. 12), is being led
to the king, her husband, and this takes place לִרְקָמוֹת, in variegated, embroidered garments (לְ used just as adverbially as in
2 Chron. xx. 21, לְהַדְרַת), with a retinue of virgins, her companions, who at the same time with herself become the property
of her spouse. According to the accents it is to be rendered:
virgines post eam, sociæ ejus, adducuntur tibi, so that רֵעוֹתֶיהָ is
an apposition. This is also in harmony with the allegorical
interpretation of the Psalm as a song of the church. The
bride of the Lamb, whom the writer of the Apocalypse beheld,
arrayed in shining white linen (*byssus*), which denotes her
righteousness, just as here the variegated, golden garments
denote her glory, is not just one person nor even one church,
but the church of Israel together with the churches of the
Gentiles united by one common faith, which have taken a
hearty and active part in the restoration of the daughter of
Zion. The procession moves on with joy and rejoicing; it is
the march of honour of the one chosen one and of the many
chosen together with her, of her friends or companions; and
to what purpose, is shown by the hopes which to the mind of
the poet spring up out of the contemplation of this scene.

Vers. 17, 18. All this has its first and most natural meaning
in relation to cotemporary history, but without being at variance with the reference of the Psalm to the King Messiah, as
used by the church. Just as the kings of Judah and of Israel
allowed their sons to share in their dominion (2 Sam. viii. 18,
1 Kings iv. 7, cf. 2 Chron. xi. 23; 1 Kings xx. 15), so out of
the loving relationship of the daughter of Zion and of the
virgins of her train to the King Messiah there spring up
children, to whom the regal glory of the house of David
which culminates in Him is transferred,—a royal race among
which He divides the dominion of the earth (*vid.* Ps. cxlix.);
for He makes His own people "kings and priests, and they

(Eusebius), which is meaningless; *Cod. Alex.* correctly, ἔσωθεν (Italic, Jerome,
Syriac, Chrysostom, Theodoret, Apollinaris).

shall reign on the earth" (Apoc. v. 10). Those children are to be understood here which, according to Ps. cx., are born to Him as the dew out of the womb of the morning's dawn—the ever-youthful nation, by which He conquers and rules the world. When, therefore, the poet says that he will remember the name of the king throughout all generations, this is based upon the twofold assumption, that he regards himself as a member of an imperishable church (Sir. xxxvii. 25), and that he regards the king as a person worthy to be praised by the church of every age. Elsewhere Jahve's praise is called a praise that lives through all generations (cii. 13, cxxxv. 13); here the king is the object of the everlasting praise of the church, and, beginning with the church, of the nations also. On יְהוֹדוּךְ (as in the name יְהוּדָה) cf. the forms in cxvi. 6, lxxxi. 6. First of all Israel, whom the psalmist represents, is called upon to declare with praise the name of the Messiah from generation to generation. But it does not rest with Israel alone. The nations are thereby roused up to do the same thing. The end of the covenant history is that Israel and the nations together praise this love-worthy, heroic, and divine King: "His name shall endure for ever; as long as the sun shall His name bud, and all nations shall be blessed in Him (and) shall praise Him" (lxxii. 17).

PSALM XLVI.

A SURE STRONGHOLD IS OUR GOD.*

2 ELOHIM is unto us a refuge and safe retreat,
   As a help in distresses He is thoroughly proved.
3 Therefore do we not fear when the earth changeth,
   And the mountains fall into the heart of the ocean;
4 Let the waters thereof roar, let them foam,
   Let mountains shake at the swelling thereof. (*Sela.*)

5 There is a river—the streams whereof make glad the city
     of Elohim,
   The holy place of the tabernacles of the Most High.

---

* " *Ein feste Burg ist unser Gott.*"

6 Elohim is in the midst of her, she tottereth not,
 Elohim helpeth her, when the morning dawneth.
7 The peoples rage, the kingdoms totter—
 He raiseth His voice, and the earth melteth.
8 Jahve of Hosts is with us,
 A stronghold unto us is the God of Jacob. (*Sela.*)

9 Go, behold the deeds of Jahve,
 Who maketh desolations upon the earth,
10 Who maketh wars to cease unto the ends of the earth,
 Who breaketh the bow and cutteth the spear in sunder,
 Who destroyeth the chariots by fire.
11 "Cease ye, and know that I am Elohim!
 I will be exalted among the peoples, I will be exalted upon
   the earth."
12 Jahve of Hosts is with us,
 A stronghold unto us is the God of Jacob. (*Sela.*)

When, during the reign of Jehoshaphat, the Moabites, Ammonites, and Edomites (more particularly the Maonites, for in 2 Chron. xx. 1 it is to be read מֵהַמְּעוּנִים) carried war into the kingdom of David and threatened Jerusalem, the Spirit of the Lord came upon Jahaziël the Asaphite in the temple congregation which the king had called together, and he prophesied a miraculous deliverance on the morrow. Then the Levite singers praised the God of Israel with jubilant voice, viz. singers of the race of Kohāth, and in fact out of the family of Korah. On the following day Levite singers in holy attire and with song went forth before the army of Jehoshaphat. The enemy, surprised by the attack of another plundering band of the sons of the desert, had turned their weapons against one another, being disbanded in the confusion of flight, and the army of Jehoshaphat found the enemy's camp turned into a field of corpses. In the feast of thanksgiving for victory which followed in *Emek ha-Beracha* the Levite singers again also took an active part, for the spoil-laden army marched thence in procession to Jerusalem and to the temple of Jahve, accompanied by the music of the nablas, citherns, and trumpets. Thus in the narrative in 2 Chron. xxii. does the chronicler give us the key to the Asaphic Psalm lxxxiii. (lxxvi. ?) and to the

Korahitic Psalms xlvi., xlvii., xlviii. It is indeed equally admissible to refer these three Korahitic Psalms to the defeat of Sennacherib's army under Hezekiah, but this view has not the same historical consistency. After the fourteenth year of Hezekiah's reign the congregation could certainly not help connecting the thought of the Assyrian catastrophe so recently experienced with this Psalm; and more especially since Isaiah had predicted this event, following the language of this Psalm very closely. For Isaiah and this Psalm are remarkably linked together.

Just as Ps. ii. is, as it were, the quintessence of the book of Immanuel, Isa. ch. vii.–xii., so is Ps. xlvi. of Isa. ch. xxxiii., that concluding discourse to Isa. ch. xxviii.–xxxii., which is moulded in a lyric form, and was uttered before the deliverance of Jerusalem at a time of the direst distress. The fundamental thought of the Psalm is expressed there in ver. 2 in the form of a petition; and by a comparison with Isa. xxv. 4 sq. we may see what a similarity there is between the language of the psalmist and of the prophet. Isa. xxxiii. 13 closely resembles the concluding admonition; and the image of the stream in the Psalm has suggested the grandly bold figure of the prophet in ver. 21, which is there more elaborately wrought up: "*No indeed, there dwells for us a glorious One, Jahve—a place of streams, of canals of wide extent, into which no fleet of rowing vessels shall venture, and which no mighty man-of-war shall cross.*" The divine determination expressed in אָרוּם we also hear in Isa. xxxiii. 10. And the prospect of the end of war reminds us of the familiar prediction of Isaiah (ch. ii.), closely resembling Micah's in its language, of eternal peace; just as vers. 8, 12 remind us of the watch-word עמנו אל in Isa. vii.–xii. The mind of Isaiah and that of Jeremiah have, each in its own peculiar way, taken germs of thought (*lit.* become impregnated) from this Psalm.

We have already incidentally referred to the inscribed words עַל־עֲלָמוֹת, on vi. 1. Böttcher renders them *ad voces puberes,* "for tenor voices," a rendering which certainly accords with the fact that, according to 1 Chron. xv. 20, they were accustomed to sing בִּנְבָלִים עַל־עֲלָמוֹת, and the Oriental sounds, according to Villoteau (*Description de l'Egypte*), correspond *aux six sons vers l'aigu de l'octave du medium de la voix de* *tenor.* But עֲלָמוֹת does not signify *voces puberes,* but *puellæ puberes* (from עלם, غلم, cogn. חלם, حلم, to have attained to puberty); and although certainly no eunuchs sang in the temple, yet there is direct testimony that Levite youths were among the singers in the second temple;* and Ps. lxviii. mentions the עֲלָמוֹת who struck the timbrels at a temple festival. Moreover, we must take into consideration the facts that the compass of the tenor extends even into the soprano, that the singers were of different ages down to twenty years of age, and that Oriental, and more particularly even Jewish, song is fond of falsetto singing. We therefore adopt Perret-Gentil's rendering, *chant avec voix de femmes,* and still more readily Armand de Mestral's, *en soprano;* whereas Melissus' rendering, "upon musical instruments called *Alamoth* (the Germans v ould say, upon the virginal)," has nothing to commend it.

Vers. 2–4. The congregation begins with a general declaration of that which God is to them. This declaration is the result of their experience. Luther, after the LXX. and Vulg., renders it, "in the great distresses which have come upon us." As though נִמְצָא could stand for הַנִּמְצָאוֹת, and that this again could mean anything else but "at present existing," to which מְאֹד is not at all appropriate. God Himself is called נמצא מאד as being one who allows Himself to be found in times of distress (2 Chron. xv. 4, and frequently) exceedingly; *i.e.* to those who then seek Him He reveals Himself and verifies His word beyond all measure. Because God is such a God to them, the congregation or church does not fear though a still greater distress than that which they have just withstood, should break in upon them: if the earth should change, *i.e.* effect, enter upon, undergo or suffer a change (an inwardly transitive *Hiphil,* Ges. § 53, 2); and if the mountains should sink down

---

* The Mishna, *Erachin* 13*b*, expressly informs us, that whilst the Levites sang to the accompanying play of the nablas and citherns, their youths, standing at their feet below the pulpit, sang with them in order to give to the singing the harmony of high and deep voices (תֶּבֶל, *condimentum*). These Levite youths are called צֹעֲרֵי or סוֹעֲדֵי הַלְוִיִּים, *parvuli* (although the Gemara explains it otherwise) or *adjutores Levitarum.*

into the heart (בְּלֵב exactly as in Ezek. xxvii. 27, Jon. ii. 4) of the sea (ocean), *i.e.* even if these should sink back again into the waters out of which they appeared on the third day of the creation, so that consequently the old chaos should return. The church supposes the most extreme case, viz. the falling in of the universe which has been creatively set in order. We are no more to regard the language as being allegorical here (as Hengstenberg interprets it, the mountains being = the kingdoms of the world), than we would the language of Horace: *si fractus illabatur orbis* (*Carm.* iii. 3, 7). Since יַמִּים is not a numerical but amplificative plural, the singular suffixes in ver. 4 may the more readily refer back to it. גַּאֲוָה, pride, self-exaltation, used of the sea as in lxxxix. 10 גֵּאוּת, and in Job xxxviii. 11 גָּאוֹן are used. The futures in ver. 4 do not continue the infinitive construction: if the waters thereof roar, foam, etc.; but they are, as their position and repetition indicate, intended to have a concessive sense. And this favours the supposition of Hupfeld and Ewald that the refrain, vers. 8, 12, which ought to form the apodosis of this concessive clause (cf. cxxxix. 8–10, Job xx. 24, Isa. xl. 30 sq.) has accidentally fallen out here. In the text as it lies before us ver. 4 attaches itself to לֹא־נִירָא: (we do not fear), let its waters (*i.e.* the waters of the ocean) rage and foam continually; and, inasmuch as the sea rises high, towering beyond its shores, let the mountains threaten to topple in. The music, which here becomes *forte*, strengthens the believing confidence of the congregation, despite this wild excitement of the elements.

Vers. 5–8. Just as, according to Gen. ii. 10, a stream issued from Eden, to water the whole garden, so a stream makes Jerusalem as it were into another paradise: a river— whose streams make glad the city of Elohim (lxxxvii. 3, xlviii. 9, cf. ci. 8); פְּלָגָיו (used of the windings and branches of the main-stream) is a second permutative subject (xliv. 3). What is intended is the river of grace, which is also likened to a river of paradise in xxxvi. 9. When the city of God is threatened and encompassed by foes, still she shall not hunger and thirst, nor fear and despair; for the river of grace and of her ordinances and promises flows with its rippling waves through the holy place, where the dwelling-place or tabernacle of the Most High is pitched. קְדֹשׁ, *Sanctum* (cf. *El-Ḳuds* as a name of

Jerusalem), as in lxv. 5, Isa. lvii. 15; גְּדֹל, Ex. xv. 16. מִשְׁכְּנֵי, dwellings, like מִשְׁכָּנוֹת, xliii. 3, lxxxiv. 2, cxxxii. 5, 7, equivalent to "a glorious dwelling." In ver. 6 in the place of the river we find Him from whom the river issues forth. Elohim helps her לִפְנוֹת בֹּקֶר—there is only a night of trouble, the return of the morning is also the sunrise of speedy help. The preterites in ver. 7 are hypothetical: if peoples and kingdoms become enraged with enmity and totter, so that the church is in danger of being involved in this overthrow—all that God need do is to make a rumbling with His almighty voice of thunder (נָתַן בְּקוֹלוֹ, as in lxviii. 34, Jer. xii. 8, cf. הֵרִים בַּמַּטֶּה, to make a lifting with the rod, Ex. vii. 20), and forthwith the earth melts (מוּג, as in Amos ix. 5, Niph. Isa. xiv. 31, and frequently), i.e. their titanic defiance becomes cowardice, the bonds of their confederation slacken, and the strength they have put forth is destroyed—it is manifest that *Jahve Tsebaoth* is with His people. This name of God is, so to speak, indigenous to the Korahitic Psalms, for it is the proper name of God belonging to the time of the kings (*vid.* on xxiv. 10, lix. 6), on the very verge of which it occurs first of all in the mouth of Hannah (1 Sam. i. 11), and the Korahitic Psalms have a royal impress upon them. In the God, at whose summons all created powers are obliged to marshal themselves like the hosts of war, Israel has a steep stronghold, מִשְׂגָּב, which cannot be scaled by any foe—the army of the confederate peoples and kingdoms, ere it has reached Jerusalem, is become a field of the dead.

Vers. 9–12. The mighty deeds of Jahve still lie visibly before them in their results, and those who are without the pale of the church are to see for themselves and be convinced. In a passage founded upon this, lxvi. 5, stands מפעלות אלהים; here, according to Targum and Masora (*vid. Psalter*, ii. 472), מפעלות יהוה.* Even an Elohimic Psalm gives to the God of Israel in opposition to all the world no other name than יהוה. שַׁמּוֹת does not here signify *stupenda* (Jer. viii. 21), but in

---

* Nevertheless מפעלות אֱלֹהִים is also found here as a various reading that goes back to the time of the Talmud. The oldest Hebrew Psalter of 1477 reads thus, *vide Repertorium für Bibl. und Morgenländ. Liter.* v. (1779), 148. Norzi decides in favour of it, and Biesenthal has also adopted it in his edition of the Psalter (1837), which in other respects is a reproduction of Heidenheim's text.

accordance with the phrase שׂוּם לְשַׁמָּה, Isa. xiii. 9, and frequently: devastations, viz. among the enemies who have kept the field against the city of God. The participle מַשְׁבִּית is designedly used in carrying forward the description. The annihilation of the worldly power which the church has just now experienced for its rescue, is a prelude to the ceasing of all war, Mic. iv. 3 (Isa. ii. 4). Unto the ends of the earth will Jahve make an end of waging war; and since He has no pleasure in war in general, much less in war waged against His own people, all the implements of war He in part breaks to pieces and in part consigns to the flames (cf. Isa. liv. 16 sq.). Cease, cries He (ver. 12) to the nations, from making war upon my people, and know that I am God, the invincible One,—invincible both in Myself and in My people,—who will be acknowledged in My exaltation by all the world. A similar inferential admonition closes Ps. ii. With this admonition, which is both warning and threatening at the same time, the nations are dismissed; but the church yet once more boasts that Jahve Tsebaoth is its God and its stronghold.

PSALM XLVII.

EXULTATION AT THE LORD'S TRIUMPHANT ASCENSION.

2 ALL ye peoples, clap your hands,
　　Shout unto Elohim with loud rejoicing.
3 For Jahve is highly exalted, terrible,
　　A great King over all the earth.
4 He subdued peoples under us,
　　And nations under our feet.
5 He chose for us our inheritance,
　　The pride of Jacob, whom He hath loved.　　(*Sela.*)

6 Elohim is gone up with a shout,
　　Jahve with the sound of a trumpet.
7 Harp ye to Elohim, harp,
　　Harp ye to our King, harp!
8 For the King of all the earth is Elohim—
　　Harp ye songs of praise.

9 Elohim ruleth as king over the nations,
  Elohim hath set Himself upon His holy throne.

10 The princes of the peoples gather themselves together—
  A people of the God of Abraham.
  For the shields of the earth are Elohim's,
  Very highly exalted is He.

Whilst between Ps. xlv. and xlvi. scarcely any other bond of relationship but the similar use of the significant עֶלְיוֹן can be discovered, Ps. xlvii. has, in common with Ps. xlvi., not only the thought of the kingly exaltation of Jahve over the peoples of the earth, but also its historical occasion, viz. Jehoshaphat's victory over the allied neighbouring nations,—a victory without a conflict, and consequently all the more manifestly a victory of Jahve, who, after having fought for His people, ascended again amidst the music of their celebration of victory; an event that was outwardly represented in the conducting of the Ark back to the temple (2 Chron. xx. 28). Ps. xlvii. has grown out of this event. The strophe schema cannot be mistaken, viz. 8. 8. 4.

On account of the blowing of the trumpet* mentioned in ver. 6, this Psalm is the proper new year's Psalm in the synagogue (together with Ps. lxxxi., the Psalm of the second new year's feast day); and on account of the mention of the ascension of Jahve, it is the Psalm for Ascension day in the church. Luther styles it, the "Christ ascended to Heaven of the sons of Korah." Paulus Burgensis quarrels with Lyra because he does not interpret it directly of the Ascension; and Bakius says: *Lyranus a Judæis seductus, in cortice hæret.* The whole truth here, as is often the case, is not to be found on either side. The Psalm takes its occasion from an event in the reign of Jehoshaphat. But was the church of the ages succeeding required to celebrate, and shall more especially the New Testament church still celebrate, that defeat of the

---

* In connection with which, עָלָה then is intended to point to the fact that, when the sound of the trumpets of Israel begins, God rises from the throne of justice and takes His seat upon the throne of mercy: *vid.* Buxtorf, *Lex. Talmud.* col. 2505.

allied neighbouring peoples? This defeat brought the people
of God repose and respect for a season, but not true and lasting
peace; and the ascent at that time of Jahve, who had fought
here on earth on behalf of His people, was not as yet the ascent
above the powers that are most hurtful to His people, and that
stand most in the way of the progress of salvation, viz. those
powers of darkness which form the secret background of everything that takes place upon earth that is in opposition to God.
Hence this Psalm in the course of history has gained a prophetic meaning, far exceeding its first occasion, which has only
been fully unravelled by the ascension of Christ.

Vers. 2–5. "*Thereupon the fear of Elohim*"—so closes the
chronicler (2 Chron. xx. 29) the narrative of the defeat of the
confederates—"*came upon all kingdoms of the countries, when
they heard that Jahve had fought against the enemies of Israel.*"
The psalmist, however, does not in consequence of this particular event call upon them to tremble with fear, but to rejoice;
for fear is an involuntary, extorted inward emotion, but joy a
perfectly voluntary one. The true and final victory of Jahve
consists not in a submission that is brought about by war and
bloodshed and in consternation that stupefies the mind, but in
a change in the minds and hearts of the peoples, so that they
render joyful worship unto Him. In order that He may thus
become the God of all peoples, He has first of all become the
God of Israel; and Israel longs that this the purpose of its
election may be attained. Out of this longing springs the call
in ver. 2. The peoples are to show the God of revelation their
joy by their gestures and their words; for Jahve is absolutely
exalted (עֶלְיוֹן, here it is a predicate, just as in lxxviii. 56 it is an
attribute), terrible, and the sphere of His dominion has Israel
for its central point, not, however, for its limit, but it extends
over the whole earth. Everything must do homage to Him in
His own people, whether willingly or by constraint. According
to the tenses employed, what is affirmed in ver. 4 appears to be
a principle derived from their recent experience, inasmuch as
the cotemporary fact is not expressed in an historical form,
but generalized and idealized. But יִבְחַר, ver. 5a, is against
this, since the choosing (election) is an act done once for all
and not a continued act; we are therefore driven to regard the

futures, as in Num. xxiii. 7, Judg. ii. 1, as a statement of historical facts. Concerning יְדַבֵּר, He bent, made to stoop, *vid.* xviii. 48. There is now no necessity for altering יִבְחַר into יַרְחֵב, and more especially since this is not suited to the fact which has given occasion to the Psalm. On the contrary, יבחר presupposes that in the event of the day God has shown Himself to be a faithful and powerful Lord [*lit.* feudal Lord] of the land of Israel; the hostile confederation had thought of nothing less than driving Israel entirely out of its inheritance (2 Chron. xx. 11). The Holy Land is called the pride (גְּאוֹן) of Jacob, as being the gift of grace of which this, the people of God's love, can boast. In Amos vi. 8 גאון יעקב has a different meaning (of the sin of pride), and again another sense in Nah. ii. 3 (of the glory of all Israel in accordance with the promise); here it is similar to Isa. xiii. 19. אֶת has a conjunctive accent instead of being followed by *Makkeph*, as in lx. 2, Prov. iii. 12 (these are the only three instances). The strophe which follows supports the view that the poet, in ver. 5, has a recent act of God before his mind.

Vers. 6–9. The ascent of God presupposes a previous descent, whether it be a manifestation of Himself in order to utter some promise (Gen. xvii. 22, Judg. xiii. 20) or a triumphant execution of judgment (vii. 8, lxviii. 19). So here: God has come down to fight on behalf of His people. They return to the Holy City and He to His throne, which is above on Zion, and higher still, is above in heaven. On בִּתְרוּעָה and קוֹל שׁוֹפָר cf. xcviii. 6, 1 Chron. xv. 28, but more especially Amos ii. 2; for the "shout" is here the people's shout of victory, and "the sound of the horn" the clear sound of the horns announcing the victory, with reference to the celebration of the victory in the Valley of praise and the homeward march amidst the clanging music (2 Chron. xx. 26 sq.). The poet, who has this festival of victory before his mind as having recently taken place, desires that the festive sounds may find an unending and boundless echo unto the glory of God. זַמֵּר is first construed with the accusative as in lxviii. 33, then with the dative. Concerning מַשְׂכִּיל = ᾠδὴ πνευματική (Eph. v. 19, Col. iii. 16), *vid.* on xxxii. 1. That which excites to songs of praise is Jahve's dominion of the world which has just been made manifest. מָלַךְ is to be taken in just the same historical

sense as ἐβασίλευσας, Apoc. xi. 15–18.   What has taken place
is a prelude of the final and visible entering upon the kingdom,
the announcement of which the New Testament seer there
hears.   God has come down to earth, and after having obtained
for Himself a recognition of His dominion by the destruction
of the enemies of Israel, He has ascended again in visible
kingly glory.   *Imago conscensi a Messia throni gloriæ*, says
Chr. Aug. Crusius, *tunc erat deportatio arcæ fœderis in sedem
regni.*

Ver. 10.   In the mirror of the present event, the poet reads
the great fact of the conversion of all peoples to Jahve which
closes the history of the world.   The nobles of the peoples
(נְדִיבֵי with the twofold meaning of *generosi*), the "shields (*i.e.*
the lords who are the defenders of their people) of the earth"
(Hos. iv. 18), enter into the society of the people of the God
of Abraham; πέρας αἱ πρὸς τὸν πατριάρχην Ἀβραὰμ ἔλαβον
ὑποσχέσεις, as Theodoret observes.   The promise concerning
the blessing of the tribes of the nations in the seed of the
patriarch is being fulfilled; for the nobles draw the peoples
who are protected by them after themselves.   It is unnecessary
to read עַם instead of עָם with Ewald, and following the LXX.
and Syriac; and it is also inadmissible, since one does not say
נֶאֱסַף עָם, but לְ or אֶל.   Even Eusebius has rightly praised Symmachus and Theodotion, because they have translated the
ambiguous ἀμ by λαὸς (τοῦ Θεοῦ Ἀβραάμ), viz. as being a
nominative of the effect or result, as it is also understood by
the Targum, Jerome, Luther, and most of the Jewish expositors, and among modern expositors by Crusius, Hupfeld, and
Hitzig: They gather and band themselves together as a people
or into a people of the God of Abraham, they submit themselves with Israel to the one God who is proved to be so
glorious.*   The conclusion (ver. 11) reminds one of the song
of Hannah, 1 Sam. ii. 8.   Thus universal homage is rendered
to Him: He is gone up in triumph, and is in consequence
thereof highly exalted (נַעֲלָה, 3d *præt.*, the result or consequence
of the עָלָה in ver. 6).

---

* It is also accented accordingly, viz. נֶאֶסְפוּ with *Rebia magnum*, which
(and in this respect it is distinguished from *Mugrash*) makes a pause; and
this is then followed by the supplementing clause with *Zinnor*, *Galgal*, and
Olewejored.

PSALM XLVIII.

THE INACCESSIBLENESS OF THE CITY OF GOD.

2 GREAT is Jahve and greatly to be praised
  In the city of our God, His holy mountain.
3 Beautifully elevated, a joy of the whole earth
  Is mount Zion, the angle of the north.
  The city of the great King.

4 Elohim in her palaces   became known as a stronghold.
5 For, lo, the kings allied   advanced together;
6 Yet they beheld, they were amazed immediately,
                          bewildered they fled away.
7 Trembling hath seized upon them there,
                          pangs as of travail.
8 With an east wind didst Thou break
                          the ships of Tarshish,

9 As we have heard, so have we seen
  In the city of Jahve of Hosts, the city of our God—
  Elohim upholdeth her for ever.   (*Sela.*)

10 We thought, Elohim, upon Thy loving-kindness
  In the midst of Thy temple.
11 As is Thy name, Elohim, so is Thy praise
  Unto the ends of the earth;
  Full of righteousness is Thy right hand.

12 Let mount Zion rejoice,
  Let the daughters of Judah exult
  Because of Thy judgments.

13 Walk ye about Zion and go round about her,
  Tell her towers,
14 Mark well her bulwark,
  March through her palaces,
  That ye may tell it the next generation.

15 That such an one is Elohim our God for ever—
He will guide us

*   *   *   *

After " Mûth."

Ps. xlviii. is also a song of thanksgiving for victory. It is connected with Ps. xlvi. and xlvii. by the fundamental thought of the exaltation of Jahve above the peoples of the earth; but is distinguished from them both in this respect, viz. that, in accordance with the favourite characteristic of Korahitic poetry, the song of thanksgiving for victory has become a song in praise of Jerusalem, the glorious and strong city, protected by God who sits enthroned in it. The historical occasion is the same. The mention of the kings points to an army of confederates; ver. 10 points to the gathering held in the temple before the setting out of the army; and the figurative representation of the hostile powers by the shattered ships of Tarshish does not apply to any period so well as to the time of Jehoshaphat. The points of coincidence between this Psalm (cf. ver. 7 with Isa. xxxiii. 14; ver. 8 with Isa. xxxiii. 21; ver. 13 with Isa. xxxiii. 18; ver. 15 with Isa. xxxiii. 22), as well as Ps. xlvi., and Isaiah do not prove that he is its author.

Vers. 2–9. Viewed as to the nature of its subject-matter, the Psalm divides itself into three parts. We begin by considering the three strophes of the first part. The middle strophe presents an instance of the rising and falling cæsural schema. Because Jahve has most marvellously delivered Jerusalem, the poet begins with the praise of the great King and of His Holy City. Great and praised according to His due (מְהֻלָּל as in xviii. 4) is He in her, is He upon His holy mountain, which there is His habitation. Next follow, in ver. 3, two predicates of a threefold, or fundamentally only twofold, subject; for יַרְכְּתֵי צָפוֹן, in whatever way it may be understood, is in apposition to הַר־צִיּוֹן. The predicates consequently refer to Zion-Jerusalem; for קִרְיַת מֶלֶךְ רָב is not a name for Zion, but, inasmuch as the transition is from the holy mountain to the Holy City (just as the reverse is the case in ver. 2*b*), Jerusalem; ὅτι πόλις ἐστὶ τοῦ μεγάλου βασιλέως, Matt. v. 35. Of Zion-Jerusalem it is therefore said, it is יְפֵה נוֹף, beautiful in prominence or elevation (נוֹף from נוּף, Arabic *nâfa, nauf,* root נָף, the stronger force of נב, نب, to raise one's self, to mount, to come sensibly forward; just as יפה also goes back to a root יְף, يف, وف, which signifies "to rise, to be high," and is transferred in the Hebrew to eminence, perfection, beauty of form), a beautifully rising terrace-like height;[*] and, in the second place, it is the joy (מְשׂוֹשׂ) of the whole earth. It is deserving of being such, as the people who dwell there are themselves convinced (Lam. ii. 15); and it is appointed to become such, it is indeed such even now in hope,—hope which is, as it were, being anticipatorily verified. But in what sense does the appositional יַרְכְּתֵי צָפוֹן follow immediately upon הַר־צִיּוֹן? Hitzig, Ewald, Hengstenberg, Caspari (*Micha*, p. 359), and others, are of opinion that the hill of Zion is called the extreme north with reference to the old Asiatic conception of the mountain of the gods—old Persic *Ar-burg'* (*Al-burg'*), also called absolutely *hara* or *haraiti,*[†] old Indian *Kailâsa* and *Mêru*[‡]—forming the connecting link between heaven and earth, which lay in the inaccessible, holy distance and concealment of the extreme north. But the poet in no way betrays the idea that he applies this designation to Zion in an ideal sense only, as being not inferior to the extreme north (Bertheau, *Lage des Paradieses*, S. 50, and so also S. D. Luzzatto on Isa. xiv. 13), or as having taken the place of it (Hitzig). That notion is found, it is true, in Isa. xiv. 13, in the mouth of the king of the Chaldeans; but, with the exception of the passage before us, we have no trace of the Israelitish mind having blended this foreign mythological style of speech with its own. We therefore take the expression "sides of the north" to be a topographical designation, and intended literally. Mount Zion is thereby more definitely designated as the Temple-hill; for the Temple-hill, or Zion in the narrower sense, formed in reality the north-eastern angle

---

[*] Luther with Jerome (departing from the LXX. and Vulgate) renders it: "Mount Zion is like a beautiful branch," after the Mishna-Talmudic נוֹף, a branch, *Maccoth* 12a, which is compared also by Saadia and Dunash. The latter renders it "beautiful in branches," and refers it to the Mount of Olives.

[†] *Vide* Spiegel, *Erân*, S. 287 f.

[‡] *Vide* Lassen, *Indische Alterthumskunde*, ii. 847.

or corner of ancient Jerusalem. It is not necessarily the extreme north (Ezek. xxxviii. 6, xxxix. 2), which is called יַרְכְּתֵי צָפוֹן; for יַרְכָּתַיִם are the two sides, then the angle in which the two side lines meet, and just such a northern angle was Mount Moriah by its position in relation to the city of David and the lower city.

Ver. 4, where the pointing is rightly נוֹדַע, not נוֹדָע, shows that the praise sung by the poet is based upon an event in cotemporary history. Elohim has made Himself known by the loftily built parts* of Jerusalem (cxxii. 7) לְמִשְׂגָּב (the לְ that is customary with verbs of becoming and making), *i.e.* as an inaccessible fortress, making them secure against any hostile attack. The fact by which He has thus made Himself known now immediately follows. הַמְּלָכִים points to a definite number of kings known to the poet; it therefore speaks in favour of the time of peril and war in the reign of Jehoshaphat and against that in the reign of Hezekiah. נוֹעַד is reciprocal: to appoint themselves a place of meeting, and meet together there. עָבַר, as in Judg. xi. 29, 2 Kings viii. 21, of crossing the frontier and invasion (Hitzig), not of perishing and destruction, as in xxxvii. 36, Nah. i. 12 (De Wette); for נעברו requires further progress, and the declaration respecting their sudden downfall does not follow till later on. The allies encamped in the desert of Tekoa, about three hours distant from Jerusalem. The extensive view at that point extends even to Jerusalem: as soon as they saw it they were amazed, *i.e.* the seeing and astonishment, panic and confused flight, occurred all together; there went forth upon them from the Holy City, because Elohim dwells therein, a חֶרְדַּת אֱלֹהִים (1 Sam. xiv. 15), or as we should say, a panic or a panic-striking terror. Concerning כֵּן as expressive of simultaneousness, *vid.* on Hab. iii. 10. כַּאֲשֶׁר in the correlative protasis is omitted, as in Hos. xi. 2, and frequently; cf. on Isa. lv. 9. Trembling seized upon them there (שָׁם, as in xiv. 5), pangs as of a woman in travail. In ver. 8, the description passes over emotionally into the form of address. It moulds itself according to the remembrance of a recent event

---

* LXX.: ἐν ταῖς βάρεσιν αὐτῆς, on which Gregory of Nyssa remarks (*Opera, Ed. Paris*, t. i. p. 333): βάρεις λέγει τὰς τῶν οἰκοδομημάτων περιγραφὰς ἐν τετραγώνῳ τῷ σχήματι.

of the poet's own time, viz. the destruction of the merchant
fleet fitted out by Jehoshaphat in conjunction with Ahaziah,
king of Israel (1 Kings xxii. 49, 2 Chron. xx. 36 sq.). The
general meaning of ver. 8 is, that God's omnipotence is irresistible. Concerning the "wind of the east quarter," which
here, as in Ezek. xxvii. 26, ·causes shipwreck, *vid.* on Job
xxvii. 21. The "ships of Tarshish," as is clear from the context both before and after, are not meant literally, but used as
a figure of the worldly powers; Isaiah (ch. xxxiii.) also compares Assyria to a gallant ship. Thus, then, the church can
say that in the case of Jerusalem it has, as an eye-witness,
experienced that which it has hitherto only heard from the
tradition of a past age (רָאָה and שָׁמַע as in Job xlii. 5), viz.
that God holds it erect, establishes it, *for ever.* Hengstenberg
observes here, "The Jerusalem that has been laid in ruins is
not that which the psalmist means; it is only its outward form
which it has put off" [*lit.* its broken and deserted pupa]. It is
true that, according to its inner and spiritual nature, Jerusalem
continues its existence in the New Testament church; but it is
not less true that its being trodden under foot for a season in
the καιροὶ ἐθνῶν no more annuls the promise of God than
Israel's temporary rejection annuls Israel's election. The
Holy City does not fall without again rising up.

Vers. 10–12. Now follows grateful praise to God, who
hears prayer and executes justice, to the joy of His city and
of His people. By דִּמִּינוּ the poet refers back to the service
held in the temple before the army set out, as narrated in
2 Chron. ch. xx., to the prayers offered in the time of their
impending danger, and to the remembrance of the favour
hitherto shown towards Jerusalem, from which source they
drew the comfort of hope for the present time. דִּמָּה, to compare, to hold one thing over against another, in this instance
by causing the history of the past to pass before one's mind.
To God's mighty deeds of old is now added a new one. The
Name of God, *i.e.* the sum of His self-attestations hitherto,
was the subject of the דמינו in the temple, and more particularly of the Korahitic songs (2 Chron. xx. 19); and this name
has gloriously verified itself by a new deed of righteousness.
His fame extends even to the ends of the earth (2 Chron. xx.
29) He has proved Himself to be One whose right hand is

full of righteousness, and who practises righteousness or justice where it is necessary.   Let, then, the Holy City, let the country cities of Judah (Isa. xl. 9, cf. xvi. 2) rejoice.   The whole inheritance of Israel was threatened.   Now it is most gloriously delivered.

Vers. 13–15.   The call is addressed not to the enemies of Jerusalem—for it would be absurd to invite such to look round about upon Jerusalem with joy and gladness—but to the people of Jerusalem itself.   From the time of the going forth of the army to the arrival of the news of victory, they have remained behind the walls of the city in anxious expectation.   Now they are to make the circuit of the city (הַקִּיף, still more definite than סָבַב, Josh. vi. 3) outside the walls, and examine them and see that its towers are all standing, its bulwark is intact, its palaces are resplendent as formerly.   לְחֵילָה, "upon its bulwark," = לְחֵילָה (Zech. ix. 4), with softened suffix as in Isa. xxiii. 17, xlv. 6, and frequently; Ew. § 247, d.   פְּסַג (according to another reading, הִפְסִיג) signifies, in B. *Baba kamma* 81b, to cut through (a vineyard in a part where there is no way leading through it); the signification "to take to pieces and examine, to contemplate piece by piece," has no support in the usage of the language, and the signification "to extol" (*erhöhen*, Luther following Jewish tradition) rests upon a false deduction from the name פִּסְגָּה.   Louis de Dieu correctly renders it: *Dividite palatia, h. e. obambulate inter palatia ejus, secando omnes palatiorum vias, quo omnia possitis commode intueri.*   They are to convince themselves by all possible means of the uninjured state of the Holy City, in order that they may be able to tell to posterity, that זֶה, such an one, such a marvellous helper as is now manifest to them, is Elohim our God.   He will also in the future guide us. . . . Here the Psalm closes; for, although נָהַג is wont to be construed with עַל in the signification ἄγειν ἐπί (xxiii. 2, Isa. xlix. 10), still "at death" [*lit.* dying], *i.e.* when it comes to dying (Hengstenberg), or "even unto (עַל as in ver. 11, xix. 7) death" [*lit.* dying] (Hupfeld), forms no suitable close to this thoroughly national song, having reference to a people of whom the son of Sirach says (ch. xxxvii. 25): ζωὴ ἀνδρὸς ἐν ἀριθμῷ ἡμερῶν καὶ αἱ ἡμέραι τοῦ Ἰσραὴλ ἀναρίθμητοι.   The rendering of Mendelssohn, Stier, and others, "over death," *i.e.* beyond death (Syriac), would be better; more accurately:

beyond dying = destruction (Bunsen, *Bibelwerk*, Th. i. S. clxi.). But the expression does not admit of this extension, and the thought comes upon one unexpectedly and as a surprise in this Psalm belonging to the time before the Exile. The Jerusalem Talmud, *Megilla*, ch. ii. (fol. 73, col. *b*, ed. *Venet.*), presents a choice of the following interpretations: (1) עֲלָמוֹת = בְּעֲלִימוֹת, in youthfulness, adopting which, but somewhat differently applied, the Targum renders, "in the days of youth;" (2) בְּאִילִין עֲלָמוֹת, like virgins, with which Luther's rendering coincides: like youth (*wie die Jugent*); (3) according to the reading עֲלָמוֹת, which the LXX. also reproduces: in this and the future world, noting at the same time that Akilas (Aquila) translates the word by ἀθανασία: "in a world where there is no death." But in connection with this last rendering one would rather expect to find אַל־מוֹת (Prov. xii. 28) instead of עַל־מוֹת. עֲלָמוֹת, however, as equivalent to αἰῶνες is Mishnic, not Biblical; and a Hebrew word עֲלָמוֹת (עֲלִימוֹת) in the sense of the Aramaic עֲלִימוֹת cannot be justified elsewhere. We see from the wavering of the MSS., some of which give עַל־מוֹת, and others עֲלָמוֹת, and from the wavering of expositors, what little success is likely to follow any attempt to gain for עַל־מוֹת, as a substantial part of the Psalm, any sense that is secure and in accordance both with the genius of the language and with the context. Probably it is a marginal note of the melody, an abbreviation for עַל־מוֹת לַבֵּן, ix. 1. And either this note, as in Hab. iii. 19 לַמְנַצֵּחַ בִּנְגִינוֹתָי, stands in an exceptional manner at the end instead of the beginning (Hitzig, Reggio), or it belongs to the למנצח of the following Psalm, and is to be inserted there (Böttcher, *De inferis*, § 371). If, however, עַל־מוֹת does not belong to the Psalm itself, then it must be assumed that the proper closing words are lost. The original close was probably more full-toned, and somewhat like Isa. xxxiii. 22.

PSALM XLIX.

OF THE VANITY OF EARTHLY PROSPERITY AND GOOD:

A DIDACTIC POEM.

2 HEAR ye this, all ye peoples
   Observe, all ye inhabitants of the world,

3 Both low and high,
  Rich and poor together!
4 My mouth shall utter wisdom
  And the meditation of my heart is understanding.
5 I will incline mine ear to the maxim,
  I will disclose my riddle with the accompaniment of the
          cithern.

6 Wherefore should I fear in the days of misfortune,
  When the evil-doing of my supplanters encompasseth me,
7 Who trust in their wealth
  And boast themselves in the abundance of their riches?
8 A man is not able by any means to redeem his brother,
  Nor can he give to God a ransom for him,
9 (Too costly is the redemption of their soul,
  And he must give it up for ever);
10 That he should live continually,
  [And] not see the grave.
11 No indeed, he must see, that wise men the,
  Likewise the fool and the stupid man perish,
  And leave to others their wealth.
12 Their thought is that their houses are for ever,
  Their dwellings from generation to generation;
  They proclaim their names over lands.
13 *But man in pomp hath no abiding,*
  He is like to the beasts that are destroyed.

14 This is the lot of those who are full of self-confidence,
  And who following them yield assent to their mouth. (*Sela.*)
15 Like sheep gathered to Hades death doth shepherd them,
  And the upright shall triumph over them on that morning,
  Whereas their form, falling a prey to the devouring of
          Hades, becomes habitationless.
16 Yet Elohim will redeem my soul from the power of
          Hades,
  For He will take me up. (*Sela.*)
17 Be not thou afraid, when a man becometh rich,
  When the glory of his house is increased.
18 For when he dieth he shall take nothing away with him,
  His glory doth not go down after him.

19 Though a man blesseth his soul during his life—
   And they praise thee that thou dost enjoy thyself—
20 It shall come to the generation of his fathers:
   In eternity they shall never see the light.
21 *Man in pomp, and yet having no understanding,*
   Is like to the beasts that are destroyed.

To the pair of Psalms xlvii. and xlviii. is appended Ps. xlix., which likewise begins with an appealing " all ye peoples;" in other respects, being a didactic song, it has nothing in common with the national and historical Psalms, xlvi.–xlviii. The poet here steps forward as a preacher in the midst of men. His theme is the transitoriness of the prosperity of the ungodly, and, on the other hand, the hope of the upright which rests on God. Accordingly the Psalm falls into the following divisions: an introduction, vers. 2–5, which by its very promissory tone reminds one of the speeches of Elihu in the Book of Job, and the two parts of the sermon following thereupon, vers. 6–13, 14–21, which are marked out by a refrain, in which there is only a slight variation of expression. In its dogmatic character it harmonizes with the Psalms of the time of David, and by its antique and bold form takes rank with such Psalms as Ps. xvii. by David and lxxiii. by Asaph. Since also in the didactic Psalms of David and Asaph we meet with a style differing from that of their other Psalms, and, where the doings of the ungodly are severely rebuked, we find a harsher and more concise mode of expression and a duller, heavier tone, there is nothing at variance with the assumption that Ps. xlix. was composed by the writer of Ps. xlii.–xliii. and lxxxiv.; and more especially since David has composed Psalms of a kindred character (xxxix. and lxii.) in the time of the persecution by Absalom. Nothing, however, is involved in this unity of the author.

Vers. 2–5. Introduction. Very similarly do the elder (in the reign of Jehoshaphat) and the younger Micha (Micah) introduce their prophecies (1 Kings xxii. 28, Mic. i. 2), and Elihu in the Book of Job his didactic discourses (ch. xxxiv. 2, cf. xxxiii. 2). It is an universal theme which the poet intends to take up, hence he calls upon all peoples and all the inhabi-

tants of the חֶלֶד. Such is the word first of all for this temporal
life, which glides by unnoticed, then for the present transitory
world itself (*vid.* on xvii. 14). It is his intention to declare to
the rich the utter nothingness or vanity of their false ground
of hope, and to the poor the superiority of their true ground of
hope; hence he wishes to have as hearers both בני אדם, children
of the common people, who are men and have otherwise nothing
distinctive about them, and בְּנֵי־אִישׁ, children of men, *i.e.* of
rank and distinction (*vid.* on iv. 3)—rich and poor, as he adds
to make his meaning more clear. For his mouth will, or shall,
utter חָכְמוֹת, not: all sorts of wise teachings, but: weighty
wisdom. Just in like manner תְּבוּנוֹת signifies profound insight
or understanding; cf. plurals like בִּינוֹת, Isa. xxvii. 11, יְשׁוּעֹת,
Ps. xlii. 12 and frequently, שַׁלְוֹת, Jer. xxii. 21. The parallel
word תְּבוּנוֹת in the passage before us, and the plural predicate
in Prov. xxiv. 7, show that חָכְמוֹת, here and in Prov. i. 20, ix. 1,
cf. xiv. 1, is not to be regarded, with Hitzig, Olshausen, and
others, as another form of the singular חָכְמוֹת. Side by side
with the speaking of the mouth stands הָגוּת לֵב (with an unchangeable *Kametz* before the tone-syllable, Ew. § 166, *c*): the
meditation (LXX. μελέτη) of the heart, and in accordance
therewith the well-thought-out discourse. What he intends to
discourse is, however, not the creation of his own brain, but
what he has received. A מָשָׁל, a saying embodying the wisdom
of practical life, as God teaches men it, presents itself to his
mind demanding to be heard; and to this he inclines his ear in
order that, from being a diligent scholar of the wisdom from
above, he may become a useful teacher of men, inasmuch as
he opens up, *i.e.* unravels, the divine *Mashal*, which in the
depth and fulness of its contents is a חִידָה, *i.e.* an involved
riddle (from חוּד, cogn. אָגַר, עָקַד), and plays the cithern thereby
(בְּ of the accompaniment). The opening of the riddle does not
consist in the solving of it, but in the setting of it forth. פָּתַח,
to open = to propound, deliver [of a discourse], comes from
the phrase פָּתַח אֶת־פִּיו, Prov. xxxi. 26; cf. cxix. 130, where
פֶּתַח, an opening, is equivalent to an unlocking, a revelation.

Vers. 6–13. First division of the sermon. Those who
have to endure suffering from rich sinners have no need to
fear, for the might and splendour of their oppressors is hastening towards destruction. יְמֵי רָע are days in which one experi-

ences evil, as in xciv. 13, cf. Amos vi. 3. The genitive רֵע is continued in ver. 6*b* in a clause that is subordinate to the בִּימֵי of ver. 6*a* (cf. 1 Sam. xxv. 15, Job xxix. 2, Ps. xc. 15). The poet calls his crafty and malicious foes עֲקֵבַי. There is no necessity for reading עֹקְבַי as Böttcher does, since without doubt a participial noun עָקֵב, *supplantator*, can be formed from עָקַב, *supplantare*; and although in its branchings out it coincides with עָקֵב, *planta*, its meaning is made secure by the connection. To render the passage: "when wickedness surrounds me about my heels," whether with or without changing עֲוֹן into עָוֹן (Hupfeld, von Ortenberg), is proved on all sides to be inadmissible: it ought to have been עַל instead of עָוֹן; but even then it would still be an awkward expression, "to *surround* any one's heels,"* and the הַבֹּטְחִים, which follows, would be unconnected with what precedes. This last word comes after עֲקֵבַי, giving minuteness to the description, and is then continued quite regularly in ver. 7*b* by the finite verb. Up to this point all is clear enough; but now the difficulties accumulate. One naturally expects the thought, that the rich man is not able to redeem himself from death. Instead of this it is said, that no man is able to redeem another from death. Ewald, Böttcher, and others, therefore, take אָח, as in Ezek. xviii. 10, xxi. 20 (*vid.* Hitzig), to be a careless form of writing for אַךְ, and change יִפְדֶּה into the reflexive יִפָּדֶה; but the thought that is sought thus to be brought out is only then arrived at with great difficulty: the words ought to be אַךְ אִישׁ לֹא יִפְדֶה נַפְשׁוֹ. The words as they stand assert: a brother (אָח, as a prominently placed object, with *Rebia magnum*, = אָחִיו, cf. Ezek. v. 10, xviii. 18, Mic. vii. 6, Mal. i. 6) can a man by no means redeem, *i.e.* men cannot redeem one another. Hengstenberg and Hitzig find the thought that is to be expected in ver. 8*b*: the rich ungodly man can with all his riches not even redeem another (אָח), much less then can he redeem himself, offer a כֹּפֶר for himself.

---

* This might be avoided if it were possible for עֲוֹן עֲקֵבִי to mean "the sin that follows my heels, that follows me at the heels;" but apart from עָוֹן being unsuitable with this interpretation, an impossible meaning is thereby extorted from the genitive construction. This, however, is perhaps what is meant by the expression of the LXX., ἡ ἀνομία τῆς πτέρνης μου, so much spoken of in the Greek Church down to the present day.

But if the poet meant to be so understood, he must have
written וְלֹא and בֹּפֶּר נַפְשׁוֹ. Vers. 8*a* and 8*b* bear no appearance
of referring to different persons; the second clause is, on the
contrary, the necessary supplement of the first: Among men
certainly it is possible under some circumstances for one who
is delivered over to death to be freed by money, but no כֹּפֶּר
(= פִּדְיוֹן נפשׁ, Ex. xxi. 30 and frequently) can be given to God
(לֵאלֹהִים).

All idea of the thought one would most naturally look for
must therefore be given up, so far as it can be made clear why
the poet has given no direct expression to it. And this can be
done. The thought of a man's redeeming himself is far from
the poet's mind; and the contrast which he has before his
mind is this: no man can redeem another, Elohim only can
redeem man. That one of his fellow-men cannot redeem a
man, is expressed as strongly as possible by the words לֹא־פָדֹה
יִפְדֶּה; the negative in other instances stands after the intensive
infinitive, but here, as in Gen. iii. 4, Amos ix. 8, Isa. xxviii.
28, before it. By an easy flight of irony, ver. 9 says that the
λύτρον which is required to be paid for the souls of men is too
precious, *i.e.* exorbitant, or such as cannot be found, and that
he (whoever might wish to lay it down) lets it alone (is obliged
to let it alone) for ever. Thus much is clear enough, so far
as the language is concerned (וְחָדַל according to the *consec.*
temp. = וַיֶּחְדַּל)), and, although somewhat fully expressed, is perfectly in accordance with the connection. But how is ver. 10
attached to what precedes? Hengstenberg renders it, " he
must for ever give it up, that he should live continually and
not see the grave." But according to the syntax, וִיחִי cannot be
attached to וְחָדַל, but only to the futures in ver. 8, ranking
with which the voluntative וִיחִי, *et vivat*, is equivalent to the
consequential *ut vivat* (Ew. § 347, *a*). Thus, therefore, nothing
remains but to take ver. 9 (which von Ortenberg expunges as
a gloss upon ver. 8) as a parenthesis; the principal clause
affirms that no man can give to God a ransom that shall pro
tect another against death, so that this other should still continue (עוֹד) to live, and that without end (לָנֶצַח), without seeing
the grave, *i.e.* without being obliged to go down into the grave.
The כִּי in ver. 11 is now confirmatory of what is denied by its
opposite; it is, therefore, according to the sense, *imo* (cf. 1 Kings

xxi. 15) : . . . that he may not see the grave—no indeed, without being able to interpose and alter it, he must see how all men, without distinction, succumb to death. Designedly the word used of the death of wise men is מוּת, and of the death of the fool and the stupid man, אָבַד. Kurtz renders : " together with the fool and the slow of understanding ;" but יַחַד as a pro- position cannot be supported ; moreover, וְעָזְבוּ would then have " the wise" as its subject, which is surely not the intention of the poet. Everything without distinction, and in mingled con- fusion, falls a prey to death ; the rich man must see it, and yet he is at the same time possessed by the foolish delusion that he, with his wealth, is immortal. The reading קִבְרָם (LXX., Targ., Syr.), preferred by Ewald, and the conjecture קְבָרִם, adopted by Olshausen and Riehm, give a thought that is not altogether contrary to the connection, viz. the narrow grave is the eternal habitation of those who called broad lands their own ; but this thought appears here, in view of ver. 12c, too early. קֶרֶב denotes the inward part, or that which is within, described according to that which encircles or contains it : that which is within them is, " their houses (pronounce *báttēmo*) are for ever" (Hengstenberg, Hitzig) ; *i.e.* the contents of their inward part is the self-delusion that their houses are everlast- ing, and their habitations so durable that one generation after another will pass over them ; cf. the similar style of expression in x. 4b, Esth. v. 7. Hitzig further renders : men celebrate their names in the lands ; קָרָא בְשֵׁם, to call with a name = solemnly to proclaim it, to mention any one's name with honour (Isa. xliv. 5). But it is unlikely that the subject of קָרְאוּ should now again be any other than the rich men them- selves ; and עֲלֵי אֲדָמוֹת for בְּכָל־הָאָרֶץ or בַּאֲרָצוֹת is contrary to the usage of the language. אֲדָמָה is the earth as tillage, אֲדָמוֹת (only in this passage) in this connection, fields, estates, lands ; the proclaiming of names is, according to 2 Sam. xii. 28, 1 Kings viii. 43, Amos ix. 12, equivalent to the calling of the lands or estates after their (the possessors') names (Böttcher, Hupfeld, Kurtz). The idea of the rich is, their houses and dwelling-places (and they themselves who have grown up to- gether with them) are of eternal duration ; accordingly they solemnly give their own names to their lands, as being the names of immortals. But, adds the poet, man בִּיקָר, in the pomp of his riches and outward show, abideth not (*non per-noctat = non permanet*). בִּיקָר is the complement of the subject, although it logically (cf. xxv. 13) also belongs to בַּל־יָלִין. Böttcher has shown the impropriety of reading בַּל־יָבִין here according to ver. 21. There are other instances also of refrains that are not exact repetitions; and this correction is moreover at once overthrown by the fact that בל will not suit יבין, it would stamp each man of rank, as such, as one deficient in intelligence. On the other hand, this emotional negative בל is admirably suitable to ילין: no indeed, he has no abiding. He is compared (נִמְשַׁל like the New Testament ὡμοιώθη), of like kind and lot, to cattle (כְּ as in Job xxx. 19). נִדְמוּ is an attributive clause to כַּבְּהֵמוֹת: like heads of cattle which are cut off or destroyed. The verb is so chosen that it is appropriate at the same time to men who are likened to the beasts (Hos. x. 7, 15, Obad. ver. 5, Isa. vi. 5).

Vers. 14–21. Second part of the discourse, of equal compass with the first. Those who are thought to be immortal are laid low in Hades; whilst, on the other hand, those who cleave to God can hope to be redeemed by Him out of Hades. Olshausen complains on this passage that the expression is abrupt, rugged, and in part altogether obscure. The fault, however, lies not, as he thinks, in a serious corruption of the text, but in the style, designedly adopted, of Psalms like this of a gloomy turn. זֶה דַרְכָּם refers back to ver. 13, which is the proper *mashal* of the Psalm: this is their way or walk (דֶּרֶךְ as in xxxvii. 5, cf. Hag. i. 5). Close upon this follows כֶּסֶל לָמוֹ (their way), of those (cf. lxix. 4) who possess self-confidence; כֶּסֶל signifies confidence both in a good and bad sense, self-confidence, impudence, and even (Eccles. vii. 25) in general, folly. The attributive clause is continued in ver. 14*b*: and of those who after them (*i.e.* when they have spoken, as Hitzig takes it), or in a more universal sense: after or behind them (*i.e.* treading in their footsteps), have pleasure in their mouth, *i.e.* their haughty, insolent, rash words (cf. Judg. ix. 38). If the meaning were "and after them go those who," etc., then one would expect to find a verb in connection with אַחֲרֵיהֶם (cf. Job xxi. 33). As a collateral definition, "after them = after their death," it would, however, without any reason, exclude the idea of the assent given by their cotemporaries. It is therefore to be explained according to Job xxix. 22, or more universally according to Deut. xii. 30. It may seem remarkable that the music here strikes in *forte;* but music can on its part, in mournfully shrill tones, also bewail the folly of the world.

Ver. 15, so full of eschatological meaning, now describes what becomes of the departed. The subject of שַׁתּוּ (as in lxxiii. 9, where it is *Milra,* for שָׁתוּ) is not, as perhaps in the case of ἀπαιτοῦσιν, Luke xii. 20, higher powers that are not named; but שׁוּת (here שָׁתַת), as in iii. 7, Hos. vi. 11, Isa. xxii. 7, is used in a semi-passive sense : like a herd of sheep they lay themselves down or they are made to lie down לִשְׁאוֹל (thus it is pointed by Ben-Asher; whereas Ben-Naphtali points לִשְׁאוֹל, with a silent *Shebâ*), to Hades = down into Hades (cf. lxxxviii. 7), so that they are shut up in it like sheep in their fold. And who is the shepherd there who rules these sheep with his rod ? מָוֶת יִרְעֵם. Not the good Shepherd (xxiii. 1), whose pasture is the land of the living, but Death, into whose power they have fallen irrecoverably, shall pasture them. Death is personified, as in Job xviii. 14, as the king of terrors. The *modus consecutivus,* וַיִּרְדּוּ, now expresses the fact that will be realized in the future, which is the reverse side of that other fact. After the night of affliction has swiftly passed away, there breaks forth, for the upright, a morning; and in this morning they find themselves to be lords over these their oppressors, like conquerors, who put their feet upon the necks of the vanquished (the LXX. well renders it by κατακυριεύσουσιν). Thus shall it be with the upright, whilst the rich at their feet beneath, in the ground, are utterly destroyed. לַבֹּקֶר has *Rebia magnum,* יְשָׁרִים has *Asla-Legarme;* accordingly the former word does not belong to what follows (in the morning, then vanishes . . .), but to what precedes. צוּר or צִיר (as in Isa. xlv. 16) signifies a form or image, just as צוּרָה (صورة) is generally used; properly, that which is pressed in or pressed out, *i.e.* primarily something moulded or fashioned by the pressure of the hand (as in the case of the potter, יָצַר) or by means of some instrument that impresses and cuts the material. Here the word is used to denote materiality or corporeity, including the whole outward appearance (φαντασία, Acts xxv. 23). The לֹו which refers to

this, shows that וְצוּרָם is not a contraction of וְצוּרָתָם (*vid.* on
xxvii. 5). Their materiality, their whole outward form belonging to this present state of being, becomes (falls away)
לְבַלּוֹת שְׁאוֹל. The *Lamed* is used in the same way as in הָיָה לְבָעֵר,
Isa. vi. 13; and שְׁאוֹל is subject, like, *e.g.*, the noun that follows
the infinitive in lxviii. 19, Job xxxiv. 22. The same idea is
obtained if it is rendered: and their form Hades is ready to
consume (*consumturus est*); but the order of the words, though
not making this rendering impossible (cf. xxxii. 9, so far as
עֵדְיוֹ there means " its cheek "), is, however, less favourable to
it (cf. Prov. xix. 8, Esth. iii. 11). בִּלָּה was the most appropriate word for the slow, but sure and entire, consuming away
(Job xiii. 28) of the dead body which is gnawed or destroyed
in the grave, this gate of the lower world. To this is added
מִזְּבֻל לֹו as a negative definition of the effect: so that there no
longer remains to it, *i.e.* to the pompous external nature of the
ungodly, any dwelling-place, and in general any place whatever; for whatever they had in and about themselves is destroyed, so that they wander to and fro as bare shadows in the
dreary waste of Hades. To them, who thought to have built
houses for eternity and called great districts of country after
their own names, there remains no longer any זְבֻל of this corporeal nature, inasmuch as Hades gradually and surely destroys
it; it is for ever freed from its solid and dazzling shell, it wastes
away lonesome in the grave, it perishes leaving no trace behind.
Hupfeld's interpretation is substantially the same, and that of
Jerome even is similar: *et figura eorum conteretur in infero
post habitaculum suum*; and Symmachus: τὸ δὲ κρατερὸν αὐτῶν
παλαιώσει ᾅδης ἀπὸ τῆς οἰκήσεως τῆς ἐντίμου αὐτῶν.

Other expositors, it is true, solve the riddle of the half-verse
in a totally different way. Mendelssohn refers צוּרָם to the
upright: whose being lasts longer than the grave (survives it),
hence it cannot be a habitation (eternal dwelling) to it; and
adds, " the poet could not speak more clearly of the resurrection (immortality)." * A modern Jewish Christian, Isr. Pick,
looked upon in Jerusalem as dead, sees here a prediction of
the breaking through of the realm of the dead by the risen

----

* In the fragments of a commentary to his translation of Psalms, contributed by David Friedländer

One: "Their Rock is there, to break through the realm of the dead, that it may no longer serve Him as an abode."*   Von Hofmann's interpretation (last of all in his *Schriftbeweis* ii. 2, 499, 2d edition) lays claim to a more detailed consideration, because it has been sought to maintain it against all objections. By the morning he understands the end of the state or condition of death both of the righteous and of the ungodly.   "In the state of death have they both alike found themselves: but now the dominion of death is at an end, and the dominion of the righteous begins."   But those who have, according to ver. 15, died are only the ungodly, not the righteous as well.   Hofmann then goes on to explain: their bodily form succumbs to the destruction of the lower world, so that it no longer has any abode; which is said to convey the thought, that the ungodly, "by means of the destruction of the lower world, to which their corporeal nature in common with themselves becomes subject, lose its last gloomy abode, but thereby lose their corporeal nature itself, which has now no longer any continuance:" "their existence becomes henceforth one absolutely devoid of possessions and of space, [the exact opposite of the time when they possessed houses built for eternity, and broad tracts of country bore their name."]   But even according to the teaching of the Old Testament concerning the last things, in the period after the Exile, the resurrection includes the righteous and the unrighteous (Dan. xii. 2); and according to the teaching of the New Testament, the damned, after Death and Hades are cast into the lake of fire, receive another זְבֻל, viz. Gehenna, which stands in just the same relation to Hades as the transformed world does to the old heavens and the old earth.   The thought discovered in ver. 15, therefore, will not bear being put to the proof.   There is, however, this further consideration, that nothing whatever is known in any other part of the Old Testament of such a destruction of Sheôl; and לְבַלּוֹת found in the Psalm before us would be a most inappropriate word to express it, instead of which it ought to have been לְכַלּוֹת; for the figurative language in cii. 27, Isa. li. 6, is worthless as a justification of this word, which signifies a gradual wearing out and

---

* In a fugitive paper of the so-called Amen Congregation, which now unhappily exists no longer, in München-Gladbach.

using up or consuming, and must not, in opposition to the
usage of the language, be explained according to בַּל and בְּלִי.
For this reason we refrain from making this passage a *locus
classicus* in favour of an eschatological conception which cannot
be supported by any other passage in the Old Testament. On
the other side, however, the meaning of לַבֹּקֶר is limited if it be
understood only of the morning which dawns upon the righteous
one after the night of affliction, as Kurtz does. What is, in
fact, meant is a morning which not merely for individuals, but
for all the upright, will be the end of oppression and the dawn
of dominion : the ungodly are totally destroyed, and they (the
upright) now triumph above their graves. In these words is
expressed, in the manner of the Old Testament, the end of all
time. Even according to Old Testament conception human
history closes with the victory of good over evil. So far ver.
15 is really a " riddle " of the last great day ; expressed in New
Testament language, of the resurrection morn, on which οἱ ἅγιοι
τὸν κόσμον κρινοῦσι (1 Cor. vi. 2).

With אַךְ, in ver. 16 (used here adversatively, as *e.g.* in Job
xiii. 15, and as אָכֵן is more frequently used), the poet contrasts
the totally different lot that awaits him with the lot of the rich
who are satisfied in themselves and unmindful of God. אַךְ belongs logically to נַפְשִׁי, but (as is moreover frequently the case
with רַק, גַּם, and אַף) is, notwithstanding this relation to a following member of the sentence, placed at the head of the sentence :
yet Elohim will redeem my soul out of the hand of Sheôl
(lxxxix. 49, Hos. xiii. 14). In what sense the poet means this
redemption to be understood is shown by the allusion to the
history of Enoch (Gen. v. 24) contained in כִּי יִקָּחֵנִי. Böttcher
shrewdly remarks, that this line of the verse is all the more
expressive by reason of its relative shortness. Its meaning
cannot be : He will take me under His protection ; for לָקַח does
not mean this. The true parallels are lxxiii. 24, Gen. v. 24.
The removals of Enoch and Elijah were, as it were, finger-
posts which pointed forward beyond the cheerless idea they
possessed of the way of all men, into the depth of Hades.
Glancing at these, the poet, who here speaks in the name of
all upright sufferers, gives expression to the hope, that God
will wrest him out of the power of Sheôl and take him to
Himself. It is a hope that possesses no direct word of God

upon which it could rest; it is not until later on that it receives the support of divine promise, and is for the present only a "bold flight" of faith. Nor can we, for this very reason, attempt to define in what way the poet conceived of this redemption and this taking to Himself. In this matter he himself has no fully developed knowledge; the substance of his hope is only a dim inkling of what may be. This dimness that is only gradually lighted up, which lies over the last things in the Old Testament, is the result of a divine plan of education, in accordance with which the hope of eternal life was gradually to mature, and to be born as it were out of this wrestling faith itself. This faith is expressed in ver. 16; and the music accompanies his confidence in cheerful and rejoicing strains.

After this, in vers. 17 sqq., there is a return from the lyric strain to the gnomic and didactic. It must not, with Mendelssohn, be rendered: let it (my soul) not be afraid; but, since the psalmist begins after the manner of a discourse: fear thou not. The increasing כָּבוֹד, *i.e.* might, abundance, and outward show (all these combined, from כָּבֵד, *grave esse*), of the prosperous oppressor is not to make the saint afraid: he must after all die, and cannot take hence with him הַכֹּל, the all = anything whatever (cf. לַכֹּל, for anything whatever, Jer. xiii. 7). כִּי, ver. 17, like ἐάν, puts a supposable case; כִּי, ver. 18, is confirmatory; and כִּי, ver. 19*a*, is concessive, in the sense of גַּם־כִּי, according to Ew. § 362, *b*: even though he blessed his soul during his life, *i.e.* called it fortunate, and flattered it by cherished voluptuousness (cf. Deut. xxix. 18, הִתְבָּרֵךְ בְּנַפְשׁוֹ, and the soliloquy of the rich man in Luke xii. 19), and though they praise thee, O rich man, because thou dost enjoy thyself (Luke xvi. 25), wishing themselves equally fortunate, still it (the soul of such an one) will be obliged to come or pass עַד־דּוֹר אֲבוֹתָיו There is no necessity for taking the noun דּוֹר here in the rare signification dwelling (Arabic *dâr*, synonym of *menzîl*), and it appears the most natural way to supply נַפְשׁוֹ as the subject to תָּבוֹא (Hofmann, Kurtz, and others), seeing that one would expect to find אֲבוֹתֶיךָ in the case of תבוא being a form of address. And there is then no need, in order to support the synallage, which is at any rate inelegant, to suppose that the suffix יו‑ takes its rise from the formula בּוֹא (נֶאֱסַף) אֶל־אֲבֹתָיו, and is, in

spite of the unsuitable grammatical connection, retained, just
as יַחְדָּו and כֻּלָּם, without regard to the suffixes, signify " together" and "all together" (Böttcher). Certainly the poet
delights in difficulties of style, of which quite sufficient remain
to him without adding this to the list. It is also not clear
whether ver. 20*b* is intended to be taken as a relative clause
intimately attached to אֲבוֹתָיו, or as an independent clause. The
latter is admissible, and therefore to be preferred: there are
the proud rich men together with their fathers buried in darkness for ever, without ever again seeing the light of a life
which is not a mere shadowy life.

The didactic discourse now closes with the same proverb as
the first part, ver. 13. But instead of בַּל־יָלִין the expression
here used is וְלֹא יָבִין, which is co-ordinate with בִּיקָר as a second
attributive definition of the subject (Ew. § 351, *b*): a man in
glory and who has no understanding, viz. does not distinguish
between that which is perishable and that which is imperishable, between time and eternity. The proverb is here more
precisely expressed. The gloomy prospect of the future does
not belong to the rich man as such, but to the worldly and
carnally minded rich man.

PSALM L.

DIVINE DISCOURSE CONCERNING THE TRUE SACRIFICE
AND WORSHIP.

1 EL ELOHIM JAHVE speaketh,
　　And summoneth the earth from the rising of the sun to its
　　　　going down.
2 Out of Zion, the perfection of beauty, Elohim shineth.
3 Our God will come and shall not keep silence;
　　Fire devoureth before Him,
　　And round about Him it is very tempestuous.

4 He calleth to the heavens above
　　And to the earth to come to judge His people.
5 " Gather My saints together unto Me,
　　Who make a covenant with Me over sacrifice!"—

6 And the heavens proclaim His righteousness,
  For Elohim purposeth to sit in judgment.   (*Sela.*)

7 Hear, then, My people, and I will speak;
  O Israel, and I will testify to thee—
  Elohim, thy God am I.
8 Not for thy sacrifices do I reprove thee,
  And thy burnt-offerings are continually before Me.
9 I have no need to take bullocks out of thy house,
  Nor he-goats out of thy folds.
10 For Mine is every beast of the forest,
  The cattle upon a thousand hills.
11 I know every bird of the mountains,
  And that which moveth on the meadows is with Me.
12 If I were hungry I would not tell thee,
  For Mine is the world and its fulness.
13 Should I eat the flesh of bulls?
  And the blood of he-goats should I drink?
14 Offer unto God thanksgiving,
  And pay to the Most High thy vows.
15 And call upon Me in the day of trouble—
  I will deliver thee, and thou shalt honour Me.

16 But to the evil-doer Elohim saith:
  How dost thou dare to tell My statutes,
  And that thou takest My covenant into thy mouth;
17 Whereas thou nevertheless hatest instruction,
  And castest My words behind thee?!
18 When thou seest a thief, thou takest pleasure in him,
  And with adulterers dost thou make thyself familiar.
19 Thou lettest thy mouth loose to wickedness,
  And thy tongue frameth deceit.
20 Thou sittest and slanderest thy brother,
  Upon thy mother's son thou bringest reproach.
21 These things doest thou, and, because I keep silence,
  Thou thinkest I am exactly like thee—
  I will show thee and set it before thine eyes.

22 Consider, now, this, ye who forget God,
  Lest I tear in pieces and there be none to rescue.

23 Whoso offereth thanksgiving, honoureth Me truly,
   And prepareth a way, in which I may show him the salva-
      tion of Elohim.

With the preceding Psalm the series of the Korahitic
Elohim-Psalms of the primary collection (Ps. i.–lxxii.) closes.
There are, reckoning Ps. xlii. and xliii. as one Psalm, seven of
them (Ps. xlii.–xlix.).   They form the principal group of the
Korahitic Psalms, to which the third book furnishes a supplement, bearing in part an Elohimic (Ps. lxxxiv.) and in part a
Jehovic impress (Ps. lxxxv., lxxxvii., lxxxviii.).   The Asaphic
Psalms, on the contrary, belong exclusively to the Elohimic
style of Psalms, but do not, however, all stand together: the
principal group of them is to be found in the third book (Ps.
lxxiii.–lxxxiii.), and the primary collection contains only one
of them, viz. Ps. l., which is here placed immediately after Ps.
xlix. on account of several points of mutual relationship, and
more especially because the prominent *Hear then, My people*
(l. 7), is in accord with the beginning of Ps. xlix., *Hear, all ye
peoples.*
     According to 1 Chron. xxiii. 2–5, the whole of the thirty-
eight thousand Levites were divided by David into four
divisions (24,000 + 6000 + 4000 + 4000).   To the fourth
division (4000) was assigned the music belonging to divine
worship.   Out of this division, however, a select company of
two hundred and eighty-eight singers was further singled out,
and divided into twenty-four classes.   These last were placed
under three leaders or precentors (*Sangmeister*), viz. fourteen
classes under Heman the Kehathite and his fourteen sons;
four classes under Asaph the Gersonite and his four sons;
and six classes under Ethan (Jeduthun) and his six sons
(1 Chron. ch. xxv., cf. ch. xv. 17 sqq.).   The instruments
played by these three leaders, which they made use of on
account of their clear, penetrating sound, were the cymbals
(1 Chron. xv. 19).   Also in 1 Chron. xvi. 5, where Asaph is
described as the chief (הָרֹאשׁ) of the sacred music in the tent
where the Ark was placed, he strikes the cymbals.   That he
was the chief, first leader, cannot be affirmed.   The usual
order of the names is "Heman, Asaph, and Ethan."   The
same order is also observed in the genealogies of the three in

1 Chron. vi. 16–32. Heman takes the prominent place, and at his right hand stands Asaph, and on his left Ethan.

History bears witness to the fact that Asaph was also a Psalm-writer. For, according to 2 Chron. xxix. 30, Hezekiah brought " the words of David and of Asaph the seer" into use again in the service of the house of God. And in the Book of Nehemiah, ch. xii. 46, David and Asaph are placed side by side as רָאשֵׁי הַמְשֹׁרְרִים in the days of old in Israel.

The twelve Psalms bearing the inscription לְאָסָף are all Elohimic. The name of God יהוה does not occur at all in two (lxxvii., lxxxii.), and in the rest only once, or at the most twice. Side by side with אלהים, אֲדֹנָי and אֵל are used as favourite names, and especial preference is also given to עֶלְיוֹן. Of compounded names of God, אֵל אֱלֹהִים יְהֹוָה (only besides in Josh. xxii. 22) in the Psalter, and אֱלֹהִים צְבָאוֹת in the Old Testament Scriptures generally (vid. Symbolæ, pp. 14–16), are exclusively peculiar to them. So far as concerns their contents, they are distinguished from the Korahitic Psalms by their prophetically judicial character. As in the prophets, God is frequently introduced as speaking; and we meet with detailed prophetical pictures of the appearing of God the Judge, together with somewhat long judicial addresses (Ps. l., lxxv., lxxxii.). The appellation הַחֹזֶה, which Asaph bears in 2 Chron. xxix. 30, accords with this; notwithstanding the chronicler also applies the same epithet to both the other precentors. The ground of this, as with נִבָּא, which is used by the chronicler of the singing and playing of instruments in the service of the house of God, is to be found in the intimate connection between the sacred lyric and prophecy as a whole. The future visionary character of the Asaphic Psalms has its reverse side in the historical past. We frequently meet with descriptive retrospective glances at facts of the primeval history (lxxiv. 13–15, lxxvii. 15 sqq., lxxx. 9–12, lxxxi. 5–8, lxxxiii. 10–12), and Ps. lxxviii. is entirely taken up with holding up the mirror of the ancient history of the nation to the people of the present. If we read the twelve Psalms of Asaph in order one after the other, we shall, moreover, observe this striking characteristic, that mention is made of Joseph and the tribes descended from him more frequently than anywhere else (lxxvii. 16, lxxviii. 9, 67 sq., lxxxi. 6, lxxx. 2 sq.). Nor is another feature less remarkable, viz. that the mutual relationship of Jahve to Israel is set forth under the figure of the shepherd and his flock rather than any other (lxxiv. 1, lxxvii. 21, lxxviii. 52, cf. lxx.-lxxii., lxxix. 13, lxxx. 2). Moreover these Psalms delight in other respects to vary the designations for the people of God as much as possible.

In Ps. l., lxxiii.-lxxxiii., we have before us a peculiar type of Psalms. The inscription לְאָסָף has, so to speak, deep-lying internal grounds in its support. But it does not follow from this inscription that all these Psalms were composed by the aged Asaph, who, as lxxviii. 69 shows, lived until the early part of Solomon's reign. The outward marks peculiar to Asaph were continued in his posterity even into the period after the Exile. History mentions Asaphites under Jehoshaphat (2 Chron. xx. 14), under Hezekiah (2 Chron. xxix. 13), and among the exiles who returned (Ezra ii. 41, cf. iii. 10, one hundred and twenty-eight Asaphites; Neh. vii. 44, cf. xi. 22, a hundred and forty-eight of them). Since down to the period after the Exile even the cymbals (מְצִלְתַּיִם) descended to them from their ancestor, the poetic talent and enthusiasm may also have been hereditary among them. The later "Psalms of Asaph," whether composed by later Asaphites or some other person, are inscribed לְאָסָף because, by whomsoever, they are composed in the style of Asaph and after Asaphic models. Ps. l., however, is an original Psalm of Asaph.

After the manner of the prophets the twofold truth is here advanced, that God has no delight in animal sacrifice without the sacrifice of prayer in which the heart is engaged, and that the confession of His word without a life that accords with His word is an abomination to Him. It is the very same fundamental thought which is expressed in xl. 7–9, lxix. 31 sq., li. 18 sq., and underlies Ps. xxiv. (1–6) and xv.; they are all echoes of the grand utterance of Samuel (1 Sam. xv. 22), the father of the poetry of the Psalms. It cannot surprise one that stress is laid on this denunciation of a heartless service of works by so many voices during the Davidic age. The nothingness of the *opus operatum* is also later on the watchword of the prophets in times when religious observances, well ordered and in accordance with legal prescription, predominate in Judah. Nor should it seem strange that Asaph the Levite, who was appointed to the sanctuary on Zion, ex-

presses himself thus; for Jeremiah was also a Levite and even
a priest (*cohen*), and yet no one has spoken a bolder, and more
cutting word against the outward and formal service of sacrifice
than he (Jer. vii. 22 sq.).   Both these objections being removed,
there is nothing else that stands in the way of our ascribing
this Psalm to Asaph himself.   This is favoured by echoes of
the Psalm in the prophets (cf. ver. 2 with Lam. ii. 15, and the
verse-ending ver. 8, xxxviii. 18, with Isa. xlix. 16), and there
is nothing opposed to it in the form of the language.

Vers. 1–3.   The theophany.   The names of God are heaped
up in ver. 1 in order to gain a thoroughly full-toned exordium
for the description of God as the Judge of the world.   Hupfeld
considers this heaping up cold and stiff; but it is exactly in
accordance with the tasto of the Elohimic style.   The three
names are co-ordinate with one another; for אֵל אֱלֹהִים does not
mean "God of gods," which would rather be expressed by
אֱלֹהֵי הָאֱלֹהִים or אֵל אֵלִים.   אֵל is the name for God as the Almighty;
אֱלֹהִים as the Revered One; יְהֹוָה as the Being, absolute in His
existence, and who accordingly freely influences and moulds history after His own plan—this His peculiar proper-name is the
third in the triad.   Perfects alternate in vers. 1–6 with futures,
at one time the idea of that which is actually taking place, and
at another of that which is future, predominating.   Jahve summons the earth to be a witness of the divine judgment upon
the people of the covenant.   The addition "from the rising of
the sun to its going down," shows that the poet means the earth
in respect of its inhabitants.   He speaks, and because what He
speaks is of universal significance He makes the earth in all
its compass His audience.   This summons precedes His self-
manifestation.   It is to be construed, with Aquila, the Syriac,
Jerome, Tremellius, and Montanus, " out of Zion, the perfection of beauty, Elohim shineth."   Zion, the perfect in beauty
(cf. the dependent passage Lam. ii. 15, and 1 Macc. ii. 12, where
the temple is called ἡ καλλονὴ ἡμῶν), because the place of
the presence of God the glorious One, is the bright spot whence
the brightness of the divine manifestation spreads forth like the
rising sun.   In itself certainly it is not inappropriate, with the
LXX., Vulgate, and Luther, to take מִכְלַל־יֹפִי as a designation
of the manifestation of Elohim in His glory, which is the *non*

pius ultra of beauty, and consequently to be explained according to Ezek. xxviii. 12, cf. Ex. xxxiii. 19, and not according to Lam. ii. 15 (more particularly since Jeremiah so readily gives a new turn to the language of older writers). But, taking the fact into consideration that nowhere in Scripture is beauty (יְפִי) thus directly predicated of God, to whom peculiarly belongs a glory that transcends all beauty, we must follow the guidance of the accentuation, which marks מכלל־יפי by *Mercha* as in apposition with צִיּוֹן (cf. *Psychol.* S. 49; tr. p. 60). The poet beholds the appearing of God, an appearing that resembles the rising of the sun (הוֹפִיעַ, as in the Asaph Psalm lxxx. 2, after Deut. xxxiii. 2, from יָפַע, with a transition of the primary notion of rising, يفع ,وفع, to that of beaming forth and lighting up far and wide, as in سطع); for "our God will come and by no means keep silence." It is not to be rendered: Let our God come (Hupfeld) and not keep silence (Olshausen). The former wish comes too late after the preceding הופיע (יָבֹא is consequently *veniet*, and written as *e.g.* in xxxvii. 13), and the latter is superfluous. אַל, as in xxxiv. 6, xli. 3, Isa. ii. 9, and frequently, implies in the negative a lively interest on the part of the writer: He cannot, He dare not keep silence, His glory will not allow it. He who gave the Law, will enter into judgment with those who have it and do not keep it; He cannot long look on and keep silence. He must punish, and first of all by word in order to warn them against the punishment by deeds. Fire and storm are the harbingers of the Lawgiver of Sinai who now appears as Judge. The fire threatens to consume the sinners, and the storm (viz. a tempest accompanied with lightning and thunder, as in Job xxxviii. 1) threatens to drive them away like chaff. The expression in ver. 3*b* is like xviii. 9. The *fem. Niph.* נִשְׂעֲרָה does not refer to אֵשׁ, but is used as neuter: it is stormed, *i.e.* a storm rages (Apollinaris, ἐλαιλαπίσθη σφόδρα). The fire is His wrath; and the storm the power or force of His wrath.

Vers. 4–6. The judgment scene. To the heavens above (מֵעָל, elsewhere a preposition, here, as in Gen. xxvii. 39, xlix. 25, an adverb, *desuper*, *superne*) and to the earth God calls (קָרָא אֶל as, *e.g.*, Gen. xxviii. 1), to both לָדִין עַמּוֹ, in order to sit in judgment upon His people in their presence, and with them as witnesses of His doings. Or is it not that they are summoned to attend, but that the commission, ver. 5, is addressed to them (Olshausen, Hitzig)? Certainly not, for the act of gathering is not one that properly belongs to the heavens and the earth, which, however, because they exist from the beginning and will last for ever, are suited to be witnesses (Deut. iv. 26, xxxii. 1, Isa. i. 2, 1 Macc. ii. 37). The summons אִסְפוּ is addressed, as in Matt. xxiv. 31, and frequently in visions, to the celestial spirits, the servants of the God here appearing. The accused who are to be brought before the divine tribunal are mentioned by names which, without their state of mind and heart corresponding to them, express the relationship to Himself in which God has placed them (cf. Deut. xxxii. 15, Isa. xlii. 19). They are called חֲסִידִים, as in the Asaph Psalm lxxix. 2. This contradiction between their relationship and their conduct makes an undesigned but bitter irony. In a covenant relationship, consecrated and ratified by a covenant sacrifice (עֲלֵי־זֶבַח similar to xcii. 4, Num. x. 10), has God placed Himself towards them (Ex. xxiv.); and this covenant relationship is also maintained on their part by offering sacrifices as an expression of their obedience and of their fidelity. The participle כֹּרְתֵי here implies the constant continuance of that primary covenant-making. Now, while the accused are gathered up, the poet hears the heavens solemnly acknowledge the righteousness of the Judge beforehand. The participial construction שֹׁפֵט הוּא, which always, according to the connection, expresses the present (Nah. i. 2), or the past (Judg. iv. 4), or the future (Isa. xxv. 31), is in this instance an expression of that which is near at hand (*fut. instans*). הוּא has not the sense of *ipse* (Ew. § 314, *a*), for it corresponds to the "I" in אֲנִי שֹׁפֵט or הִנְנִי שֹׁפֵט; and כִּי is not to be translated by *nam* (Hitzig), for the fact that God intends to judge requires no further announcement. On the contrary, because God is just now in the act of sitting in judgment, the heavens, the witnesses most prominent and nearest to Him, bear witness to His righteousness. The earthly music, as the סלה directs, is here to join in with the celestial praise. Nothing further is now wanting to the completeness of the judgment scene; the action now begins.

Vers. 7–15. Exposition of the sacrificial Tôra for the good of those whose holiness consists in outward works. The forms strengthened by *ah*, in ver. 7, describe God's earnest desire to have Israel for willing hearers as being quite as strong as His desire to speak and to bear witness. הָעִיד בְּ, *obtestari aliquem*, to come forward as witness, either solemnly assuring, or, as here and in the Psalm of Asaph, lxxxi. 9, earnestly warning and punishing (cf. شَهِدَ with بِ, to bear witness against any one). On the *Dagesh forte conjunctive* in בָּךְ, *vid.* Ges. § 20, 2, *a*. He who is speaking has a right thus to stand face to face with Israel, for he is Elohim, the God of Israel—by which designation reference is made to the words אנכי יהוה אלהיך (Ex. xx. 2), with which begins the Law as given from Sinai, and which here take the Elohimic form (whereas in lxxxi. 11 they remain unaltered) and are inverted in accordance with the context. As ver. 8 states, it is not the material sacrifices, which Israel continually, without cessation, offers, that are the object of the censuring testimony. וְעוֹלֹתֶיךָ, even if it has *Mugrash*, as in Baer, is not on this account, according to the interpretation given by the accentuation, equivalent to וְעַל־עוֹלוֹתֶיךָ (cf. on the other hand xxxviii. 18); it is a simple assertory substantival clause: thy burnt-offerings are, without intermission, continually before Me. God will not dispute about sacrifices in their outward characteristics; for—so vers. 9–11 go on to say—He does not need sacrifices for the sake of receiving from Israel what He does not otherwise possess. His is every wild beast (חַיְתוֹ, as in the Asaph Psalm, lxxix. 2) of the forest, His the cattle בְּהַרְרֵי אָלֶף, upon the mountains of a thousand, *i.e.* upon the thousand (and myriad) mountains (similar to מְתֵי מִסְפָּר or מְתֵי מְעָט), or: where they live by thousands (a similar combination to נֵבֶל עָשׂוֹר). Both explanations of the genitive are unsupported by any perfectly analogous instance so far as language is concerned; the former, however, is to be preferred on account of the singular, which is better suited to it. He knows every bird that makes its home on the mountains; יָדַע, as usually, of a knowledge which masters a subject, compasses it and makes it its own. Whatever moves about the fields is with Him, *i.e.* is within the range of His knowledge (cf. Job xxvii. 11, x. 13), and therefore of His power; זִיז (here and in the Asaph Psalm lxxx. 14) from זָאָא = זָעַע, to move to and fro, like טִיט from טִיטָא, to sweep out, cf. κινώπετον, κνώδαλον, from κινεῖν. But just as little as God requires sacrifices in order thereby to enrich Himself, is there any need on His part that might be satisfied by sacrifices, vers. 12 sq. If God should hunger, He would not stand in need of man's help in order to satisfy Himself; but He is never hungry, for He is the Being raised above all carnal wants. Just on this account, what God requires is not by any means the outward worship of sacrifice, but a spiritual offering, the worship of the heart, ver. 14. Instead of the שְׁלָמִים, and more particularly זֶבַח תּוֹדָה, Lev. vii. 11–15, and שַׁלְמֵי נֶדֶר, Lev. vii. 16 (under the generic idea of which are also included, strictly speaking, vowed thank-offerings), God desires the thanksgiving of the heart and the performance of that which has been vowed in respect of our moral relationship to Himself and to men; and instead of the עוֹלָה in its manifold forms of devotion, the prayer of the heart, which shall not remain unanswered, so that in the round of this λογικὴ λατρεία everything proceeds from and ends in εὐχαριστία. It is not the sacrifices offered in a becoming spirit that are contrasted with those offered without the heart (as, *e.g.*, Sir. xxxii. [xxxv.] 1–9), but the outward sacrifice appears on the whole to be rejected in comparison with the spiritual sacrifice. This entire turning away from the outward form of the legal ceremonial is, in the Old Testament, already a predictive turning towards that worship of God in spirit and in truth which the new covenant makes alone of avail, after the forms of the Law have served as swaddling clothes to the New Testament life which was coming into being in the old covenant. This "becoming" begins even in the Tôra itself, especially in Deuteronomy. Our Psalm, like the Chokma (Prov. xxi. 3), and prophecy in the succeeding age (cf. Hos. vi. 6, Mic. vi. 6–8, Isa. i. 11–15, and other passages), stands upon the standpoint of this concluding book of the Tôra, which traces back all the requirements of the Law to the fundamental command of love.

Vers. 16–21. The accusation of the manifest sinners. It is not those who are addressed in vers. 7 sqq., as Hengstenberg thinks, who are here addressed. Even the position of the words וְלָרָשָׁע אָמַר clearly shows that the divine discourse is now turned to another class, viz. to the evil-doers, who, in connection with open and manifest sins and vices, take the word of God upon

their lips, a distinct class from those who base their sanctity
upon outward works of piety, who outwardly fulfil the commands of God, but satisfy and deceive themselves with this
outward observance. מַה־לְּךָ, what hast thou, that thou = it
belongs not to thee, it does not behove thee. With וְאַתָּה, in
ver. 17, an adversative subordinate clause begins: since thou
dost not care to know anything of the moral ennobling which
it is the design of the Law to give, and my words, instead of
having them as a constant test-line before thine eyes, thou
castest behind thee and so turnest thy back upon them (cf.
Isa. xxxviii. 17). וַתִּרֶץ is not from רוּץ (LXX., Targum, and
Saadia), in which case it would have to be pointed וַתָּרָץ, but
from רָצָה, and is construed here, as in Job xxxiv. 9, with עִם:
to have pleasure in intercourse with any one. In ver. 18a the
transgression of the eighth commandment is condemned, in
ver. 18b that of the seventh, in vers. 19 sq. that of the ninth
(concerning the truthfulness of testimony). שָׁלַח פֶּה בְרָעָה, to
give up one's mouth unrestrainedly to evil, *i.e.* so that evil
issues from it. תֵּשֵׁב, ver. 20a, has reference to gossiping company (cf. i. 1). דֹּפִי signifies a thrust, a push (cf. הָדַף), after
which the LXX. renders it ἐτίθεις σκάνδαλον (cf. Lev. xix.
14), but it also signifies vexation and mockery (cf. גָּדַף); it is
therefore to be rendered: to bring reproach (Jerome, *oppro-
brium*) upon any one, to cover him with dishonour. The preposition בְּ with דִּבֶּר has, just as in Num. xii. 1, and frequently,
a hostile signification. "Thy mother's son" is he who is born
of the same mother with thyself, and not merely of the same
father, consequently thy brother after the flesh in the fullest
sense. What Jahve says in this passage is exactly the same
as that which the apostle of Jesus Christ says in Rom. ii. 17-24.
This contradiction between the knowledge and the life of men
God must, for His holiness' sake, unmask and punish, ver. 21.
The sinner thinks otherwise: God is like himself, *i.e.* that is
also not accounted by God as sin, which he allows himself to
do under the cloak of his dead knowledge. For just as a man
is in himself, such is his conception also of his God (*vid.* xviii.
26 sq.). But God will not encourage this foolish idea: "I will
therefore reprove thee and set (it) in order before thine eyes"
(וְאֶעֶרְכָה, not וְאַעַרְכֶה, in order to give expression, the second time
at least, to the mood, the form of which has been obliterated

by the suffix); He will set before the eyes of the sinner, who
practically and also in theory denies the divine holiness, the
real state of his heart and life, so that he shall be terrified at
it.   Instead of הָיֹה, the *infin. intensit.* here, under the influence
of the close connection of the clauses (Ew. § 240, *c*), is הֱיוֹת;
the *oratio obliqua* begins with it, without כִּי (*quod*).   כָּמוֹךָ
exactly corresponds to the German *deines Gleichen*, thine
equal.

Vers. 22, 23.   Epilogue of the divine discourse.   Under the
name שֹׁכְחֵי אֱלוֹהַּ are comprehended the decent or honourable
whose sanctity relies upon outward works, and those who know
better but give way to licentiousness; and they are warned of
the final execution of the sentence which they have deserved.
In dead works God delighteth not, but whoso offereth thanksgiving (viz. not *shelamim-tôda*, but the *tôda* of the heart), he
praises Him* and שָׂם דֶּרֶךְ.   It is unnecessary with Luther,
following the LXX., Vulgate, and Syriac versions, to read שָׁם.
The Talmudic remark אל תקרי וְשָׁם אלא וְשָׁם [do not read וְשָׁם,
but וְשָׁם] assumes ושם to be the traditional reading.   If we take
שָׂם דֶּרֶךְ as a thought complete in itself,—which is perfectly
possible in a certain sense (*vid.* Isa. xliii. 19),—then it is best
explained according to the Vulgate (*qui ordinat viam*), with
Böttcher, Maurer, and Hupfeld: *viam h. e. recta incedere* (*lege
agere*) *parans*; but the expression is inadequate to express this
ethical sense (cf. Prov. iv. 26), and consequently is also without
example.   The LXX. indicates the correct idea in the rendering καὶ ἐκεῖ ὁδὸς ᾗ δείξω αὐτῷ τὸ σωτήριον Θεοῦ.   The ושם דרך
(designedly not pointed דֶּרֶךְ), which standing entirely by itself
has no definite meaning, receives its requisite supplement by
means of the attributive clause that follows.   Such an one
prepares a way along which I will grant to him to see the salvation of Elohim, *i.e.* along which I will grant him a rapturous
vision of the full reality of My salvation.   The form יְכַבְּדָנְנִי is
without example elsewhere.   It sounds like the likewise epen-
thetical יִקְרָאֻנְנִי, Prov. i. 28, cf. viii. 17, Hos. v. 15, and may
be understood as an imitation of it as regards sound.   יְכַבְּדָנְנִי
(= יְכַבְּדֵנִי) is in the writer's mind as the form out of pause

---

* In Vedic *jag′*, old Bactrian *jaz* (whence *jag′jas*, the primitive word of
ἅγιος), the notions of offering and of praising lie one within the other.

Ges. § 58, 4). With ver. 23 the Psalm recurs to its central point and climax, ver. 14 sq. What Jahve here discourses in a post-Sinaitic appearing, is the very same discourse concerning the worthlessness of dead works and concerning the true will of God that Jesus addresses to the assembled people when He enters upon His ministry. The cycle of the revelation of the Gospel is linked to the cycle of the revelation of the Law by the Sermon on the Mount; this is the point at which both cycles touch.

PSALM LI.

PENITENTIAL PRAYER AND INTERCESSION FOR RESTORATION TO FAVOUR.

3 BE merciful to me, Elohim, according to Thy loving-
    kindness,
  According to the greatness of Thy compassion blot out my
    transgressions!
4 Wash me thoroughly from mine iniquity,
  And from my sin make me clean.

5 For of my transgressions I am conscious,
  And my sin is ever present to me.
6 Against Thee only have I sinned,
  And done that which is evil in Thine eyes;
  That Thou mayest appear just when Thou speakest,
  Clear when Thou judgest.

7 Behold, in iniquity was I born,
  And in sin did my mother conceive me.
8 Behold, truth dost Thou desire in the reins,
  And in the hidden part do Thou make me to know wisdom.

9 Oh purge me with hyssop, and I shall be clean;
  Wash me, and I shall be whiter than snow.
10 Make me to hear joy and gladness,
  That the bones which Thou hast crushed may exult.
11 Hide Thy face from my sins,
  And all my iniquities do Thou blot out.

12 Create me a clean heart, Elohim,
    And renew a stedfast spirit in my inward part.
13 Cast me not from Thy presence,
    And Thy Holy Spirit take not from me.

14 Turn again upon me the joy of Thy salvation,
    And with a spirit of willingness uphold me.
15 Then will I teach transgressors Thy ways,
    And sinners shall be converted to Thee.

16 Deliver me from blood-guiltiness, Elohim, God of my
        salvation,
    Then shall my tongue exult over Thy righteousness.
17 O Lord, open Thou my lips,
    And my mouth shall declare Thy praise.
18 For Thou delightest not in sacrifice, else would I give it,
    Burnt-offering Thou desirest not.
19 The sacrifices of Elohim are a broken spirit,
    A heart broken and contrite, Elohim, Thou dost not
        despise !—

20 Do good in Thy good pleasure unto Zion,
    Build Thou the walls of Jerusalem;
21 Then shalt Thou delight in true sacrifices, burnt-offering
        and whole-burnt-offering;
    Then shall bullocks be offered on Thine altar.

The same depreciation of the external sacrifice that is expressed in Ps. l. finds utterance in Ps. li., which supplements the former, according as it extends the spiritualizing of the sacrifice to the offering for sin (cf. xl. 7). This Psalm is the first of the Davidic Elohim-Psalms. The inscription runs: *To the Precentor, a Psalm by David, when Nathan the prophet came to him, after he had gone in to Bathsheba.* The carelessness of the Hebrew style shows itself in the fact that one and the same phrase is used of Nathan's coming in an official capacity to David (cf. 2 Sam. xii. 1) and of David's going in unto Bathsheba (בּוֹא אֶל, as in Gen. vi. 4, xvi. 2, cf. 2 Sam. xi. 4). The comparative כַּאֲשֶׁר, as a particle of time in the whole compass of the Latin *quum,* holds together that which precedes and

that which subsequently takes place. Followed by the perfect
(2 Sam. xii. 21, 1 Sam. xii. 8), it has the sense of *postquam*
(cf. the confusing of this כאשר with אחרי אשר, Josh. ii. 7). By
בְּבוֹא the period within which the composition of the Psalm
falls is merely indicated in a general way. The Psalm shows
us how David struggles to gain an inward and conscious certainty of the forgiveness of sin, which was announced to him
by Nathan (2 Sam. xii. 13). In Ps. vi. and xxxviii. we have
already heard David, sick in soul and body, praying for forgiveness; in Ps. li. he has even become calmer and more
cheerful in his soul, and there is nothing wanting to him except
the rapturous realization of the favour within the range of
which he already finds himself. On the other hand, Ps. xxxii.
lies even beyond Ps. li. For what David promises in li. 15,
viz. that, if favour is again shown to him, he will teach the
apostate ones the ways of God, that he will teach sinners how
they are to turn to God, we heard him fulfil in the sententious
didactic Ps. xxxii.

Hitzig assigns Ps. li., like Ps. l., to the writer of Isa. ch.
xl.–lxvi. But the manifold coincidences of matter and of style
only prove that this prophet was familiar with the two Psalms.
We discern in Ps. li. four parts of decreasing length. The
first part, vers. 3–11, contains the prayer for remission of sin;
the second, vers. 12–15, the prayer for renewal; the third,
vers. 16–19, the vow of spiritual sacrifices; the fourth, vers.
20, 21, the intercession for all Jerusalem. The divine name
Elohim occurs five times, and is appropriately distributed
throughout the Psalm.

Vers. 3, 4. Prayer for the remission of sin. Concerning
the interchangeable names for sin, *vid.* on xxxii. 1 sq. Although
the primary occasion of the Psalm is the sin of adultery, still
David says פְּשָׁעַי, not merely because many other sins were developed out of it, as his guilt of blood in the case of Uriah, the
scandal put into the mouths of the enemies of Jahve, and his
self-delusion, which lasted almost a whole year; but also because
each solitary sin, the more it is perceived in its fundamental
character and, as it were, microscopically discerned, all the
more does it appear as a manifold and entangled skein of sins,
and stands forth in a still more intimate and terrible relation,

as of cause and effect, to the whole corrupt and degenerated condition in which the sinner finds himself. In מְחֵה sins are conceived of as a cumulative debt (according to Isa. xliv. 22, cf. xliii. 25, like a thick, dark cloud) written down (Jer. xvii. 1) against the time of the payment by punishment. In כַּבְּסֵנִי (from כִּבֵּס, πλύνειν, to wash by rubbing and kneading up, distinguished from רָחַץ, λούειν, to wash by rinsing) iniquity is conceived of as deeply ingrained dirt. In טַהֲרֵנִי, the usual word for a declarative and *de facto* making clean, sin is conceived of as a leprosy, Lev. xiii. 6, 34. The *Kerî* runs הֶרֶב כַּבְּסֵנִי (*imperat. Hiph.*, like הֶרֶף, xxxvii. 8), "make great or much, wash me," *i.e.* (according to Ges. § 142, 3, *b*) wash me altogether, *penitus et totum*, which is the same as is expressed by the *Chethîb* הַרְבֵּה (prop. *multum faciendo = multum, prorsus*, Ges. § 131, 2). In כְּרֹב (Isa. lxiii. 7) and הֶרֶב is expressed the depth of the consciousness of sin; *profunda enim malitia*, as Martin Geier observes, *insolitam raramque gratiam postulat.*

Vers. 5, 6. Substantiation of the prayer by the consideration, that his sense of sin is more than superficial, and that he is ready to make a penitential confession. True penitence is not a dead knowledge of sin committed, but a living sensitive consciousness of it (Isa. lix. 12), to which it is ever present as a matter and ground of unrest and pain. This penitential sorrow, which pervades the whole man, is, it is true, no merit that wins mercy or favour, but it is the condition, without which it is impossible for any manifestation of favour to take place. Such true consciousness of sin contemplates sin, of whatever kind it may be, directly as sin against God, and in its ultimate ground as sin against Him alone (חָטָא with לְ of the person sinned against, Isa. xlii. 24, Mic. vii. 9); for every relation in which man stands to his fellow-men, and to created things in general, is but the manifest form of his fundamental relationship to God; and sin is " that which is evil in the eyes of God" (Isa. lxv. 12, lxvi. 4), it is contradiction to the will of God, the sole and highest Lawgiver and Judge. Thus it is, as David confesses, with regard to his sin, in order that . . . This לְמַעַן must not be weakened by understanding it to refer to the result instead of to the aim or purpose. If, however, it is intended to express intention, it follows close upon the moral relationship of man to God expressed in הָרַע בְּעֵינֶיךָ and לְךָ לְבַדְּךָ,

—a relationship, the aim of which is, that God, when He now condemns the sinner, may appear as the just and holy One, who, as the sinner is obliged himself to acknowledge, cannot do otherwise than pronounce a condemnatory decision concerning him. When sin becomes manifest to a man as such, he must himself say Amen to the divine sentence, just as David does to that passed upon him by Nathan. And it is just the nature of penitence so to confess one's self to be in the wrong in order that God may be in the right and gain His cause. If, however, the sinner's self-accusation justifies the divine righteousness or justice, just as, on the other hand, all self-justification on the part of the sinner (which, however, sooner or later will be undeceived) accuses God of unrighteousness or injustice (Job xl. 8): then all human sin must in the end tend towards the glorifying of God. In this sense ver. 6*b* is applied by Paul (Rom. iii. 4), inasmuch as he regards what is here written in the Psalter—ὅπως ἄν δικαιωθῇς ἐν τοῖς λόγοις σου, καὶ νικήσῃς ἐν τῷ κρίνεσθαί σε (LXX.)—as the goal towards which the whole history of Israel tends. Instead of בְּדָבְרֶךָ (*infin.* like שָׁלְחֶךָ, Gen. xxxviii. 17, in this instance for the sake of similarity of sound* instead of the otherwise usual form דַּבֵּר), *in Thy speaking*, the LXX. renders ἐν τοῖς λόγοις σου = בִּדְבָרֶיךָ; instead of בְּשָׁפְטֶךָ, ἐν τῷ κρίνεσθαί σε = בְּהִשָּׁפְטֶךָ (*infin. Niph.*), provided κρίνεσθαι is intended as passive and not (as in Jer. ii. 9 LXX., cf. Matt. v. 40) as middle. The thought remains essentially unchanged by the side of these deviations; and even the taking of the verb זָכָה, to be clean, pure, in the Syriac signification νικᾶν, does not alter it. That God may be justified in His decisive speaking and judging; that He, the Judge, may gain His cause in opposition to all human judgment, towards this tends David's confession of sin, towards this tends all human history, and more especially the history of Israel.

Vers. 7, 8. David here confesses his hereditary sin as the root of his actual sin. The declaration moves backwards from his birth to conception, it consequently penetrates even to the most remote point of life's beginning. חוֹלַלְתִּי stands instead of

---

* Cf. the following forms, chosen on account of their accord:—נָשׂוּי, xxxii. 1; הִנָּדֹף, lxviii. 3; צְאֶינָה, Cant. iii. 11 ; שְׁתוֹת, Isa. xxii. 13 ; מְמַחִים, *ib.* xxv. 6 ; הַלּוֹט, *ib.* xxv. 7.

נוֹלַדְתִּי, perhaps (although elsewhere, *e.g.* in xc. 2, the idea of painfulness is kept entirely in the background) with reference to the decree, "with pain shalt thou bring forth children," Gen. iii. 16 (Kurtz); and instead of הֹרַתָה אֹתִי, with still more definite reference to that which precedes conception, the expression is יֶחֱמַתְנִי (for יִחֲמַתְנִי, following the same interchange of vowel as in Gen. xxx. 39, Judg. v. 28). The choice of the verb decides the question whether by עָוֹן and חֵטְא is meant the guilt and sin of the child or of the parents. יָחַם (to burn with desire) has reference to that, in coition, which partakes of the animal, and may well awaken modest sensibilities in man, without עון and חטא on that account characterizing birth and conception itself as sin; the meaning is merely, that his parents were sinful human beings, and that this sinful state (*habitus*) has operated upon his birth and even his conception, and from this point has passed over to him. What is thereby expressed is not so much any self-exculpation, as on the contrary a self-accusation which glances back to the ultimate ground of natural corruption. He is sinful מִלֵּדָה וּמֵהֵרָיוֹן (lviii. 4, Gen. viii. 21), is טָמֵא מִטָּמֵא, an unclean one springing from an unclean (Job xiv. 4), flesh born of flesh. That man from his first beginning onwards, and that this beginning itself, is tainted with sin; that the proneness to sin with its guilt and its corruption is propagated from parents to their children; and that consequently in the single actual sin the sin-pervaded nature of man, inasmuch as he allows himself to be determined by it and himself resolves in accordance with it, becomes outwardly manifest—therefore the fact of hereditary sin is here more distinctly expressed than in any other passage in the Old Testament, since the Old Testament conception, according to its special character, which always fastens upon the phenomenal, outward side rather than penetrates to the secret roots of a matter, is directed almost entirely to the outward manifestation only of sin, and leaves its natural foundation, its issue in relation to primeval history, and its demonic background undisclosed. The הֵן in ver. 7 is followed by a correlative second הֵן in ver. 8 (cf. Isa. lv. 4 sq., liv. 15 sq.). Geier correctly says: *Orat ut sibi in peccatis concepto veraque cordis probitate carenti penitiorem ac mysticam largiri velit sapientiam, cujus medio liberetur a peccati tum reatu tum dominio.* אֱמֶת is the nature and life of man as conformed

to the nature and will of God (cf. ἀλήθεια, Eph. iv. 21). חָכְמָה,
wisdom which is most intimately acquainted with (*eindringlich
weiss*) such nature and life and the way to attain it.　God
delights in and desires truth בַּטֻּחוֹת.　The *Beth* of this word is
not a radical letter here as it is in Job xii. 6, but the preposition.　The reins *utpote adipe obducti*, here and in Job xxxviii.
36, according to the Targum, Jerome, and Parchon, are called
טֻחוֹת (*Psychol.* S. 269; tr. p. 317).　Truth in the reins (cf. xl.
9, God's law *in visceribus meis*) is an upright nature in man's
deepest inward parts; and in fact, since the reins are accounted
as the seat of the tenderest feelings, in man's inmost experience
and perception, in his most secret life both of conscience and
of mind (xvi. 7).　In the parallel member סָתֻם denotes the
hidden inward part of man.　Out of the confession, that
according to the will of God truth ought to dwell and rule in
man even in his reins, comes the wish, that God would impart
to him (*i.e.* teach him and make his own),—who, as being born
and conceived in sin, is commended to God's mercy,—that
wisdom in the hidden part of his mind which is the way to
such truth.

Vers. 9–11.　The possession of all possessions, however,
most needed by him, the foundation of all other possessions, is
the assurance of the forgiveness of his sins.　The second
futures in ver. 9 are consequents of the first, which are used
as optatives.　Ver. 9*a* recalls to mind the sprinkling of the
leper, and of one unclean by reason of his contact with a dead
body, by means of the bunch of hyssop (Lev. ch. xiv., Num.
ch. xix.), the βοτάνη καθαρτική (Bähr, *Symbol.* ii. 503); and
ver. 9*b* recalls the washings which, according to priestly directions, the unclean person in all cases of uncleanness had to
undergo.　Purification and washing which the Law enjoins,
are regarded in connection with the idea implied in them, and
with a setting aside of their symbolic and carnal outward side,
inasmuch as the performance of both acts, which in other
cases takes place through priestly mediation, is here supplicated directly from God Himself.　Manifestly בְּאֵזוֹב (not
כְּבְאֵזוֹב) is intended to be understood in a spiritual sense.　It
is a spiritual medium of purification without the medium itself
being stated.　The New Testament believer confesses, with
Petrarch in the second of his seven penitential Psalms: *omnes*

sordes meas una gutta, vel tenuis, sacri sanguinis absterget. But there is here no mention made of atonement by blood; for the antitype of the atoning blood was still hidden from David. The operation of justifying grace on a man stained by the blood-red guilt of sin could not, however, be more forcibly denoted than by the expression that it makes him whiter than snow (cf. the dependent passage Isa. i. 18). And history scarcely records a grander instance of the change of blood-red sin into dazzling whiteness than this, that out of the subsequent marriage of David and Bathsheba sprang Solomon, the most richly blessed of all kings. At the present time David's very bones are still shaken, and as it were crushed, with the sense of sin. דִּכִּיתָ is an attributive clause like יִפְעַל in vii. 16. Into what rejoicing will this smitten condition be changed, when he only realizes within his soul the comforting and joyous assuring utterance of the God who is once more gracious to him! For this he yearns, viz. that God would hide His face from the sin which He is now visiting upon him, so that it may as it were be no longer present to Him; that He would blot out all his iniquities, so that they may no longer testify against him. Here the first part of the Psalm closes; the close recurs to the language of the opening (ver. 3*b*).

Vers. 12, 13. In the second part, the prayer for justification is followed by the prayer for renewing. A clean heart that is not beclouded by sin and a consciousness of sin (for לֵב includes the conscience, *Psychology*, S. 134; tr. p. 160); a stedfast spirit (נָכוֹן, cf. lxxviii. 37, cxii. 7) is a spirit certain respecting his state of favour and well-grounded in it. David's prayer has reference to the very same thing that is promised by the prophets as a future work of salvation wrought by God the Redeemer on His people (Jer. xxiv. 7, Ezek. xi. 19, xxxvi. 26); it has reference to those spiritual facts of experience which, it is true, could be experienced even under the Old Testament relatively and anticipatively, but to the actual realization of which the New Testament history, fulfilling ancient prophecy, has first of all produced effectual and comprehensive grounds and motives, viz. μετάνοια (לֵב = νοῦς), καινὴ κτίσις, παλιγγενεσία καὶ ἀνακαίνωσις πνεύματος (Tit. iii. 5). David, without distinguishing between them, thinks of himself as king, as Israelite, and as man. Consequently we are not at liberty to say that רוּחַ הַקֹּדֶשׁ (as in Isa. lxiii. 16), πνεῦμα ἁγιωσύνης = ἅγιον, is here the Spirit of grace in distinction from the Spirit of office. If Jahve should reject David as He rejected Saul, this would be the extreme manifestation of anger (2 Kings xxiv. 20) towards him as king and as a man at the same time. The Holy Spirit is none other than that which came upon him by means of the anointing, 1 Sam. xvi. 13. This Spirit, by sin, he has grieved and forfeited. Hence he prays God to show favour rather than execute His right, and not to take this His Holy Spirit from him.

Vers. 14, 15. In connection with רוּחַ נְדִיבָה, the old expositors thought of נָדִיב, a noble, a prince, and נְדִיבָה, nobility, high rank, Job xxx. 15, LXX. πνεύματι ἡγεμονικῷ (*spiritu princi-pali*) στήριξόν με,—the word has, however, without any doubt, its ethical sense in this passage, Isa. xxxii. 8, cf. נְדָבָה, Ps. liv. 8; and the relation of the two words רוח נדיבה is not to be taken as adjectival, but genitival, since the poet has just used רוח in the same personal sense in ver. 12a. Nor are they to be taken as a nominative of the subject, but—what corresponds more closely to the connection of the prayer—according to Gen. xxvii. 37, as a second accusative of the object: with a spirit of willingness, of willing, noble impulse towards that which is good, support me; *i.e.* imparting this spirit to me, uphold me constantly in that which is good. What is meant is not the Holy Spirit, but the human spirit made free from the dominion of sin by the Holy Spirit, to which good has become an inward, as it were instinctive, necessity. Thus assured of his justification and fortified in new obedience, David will teach transgressors the ways of God, and sinners shall be converted to Him, viz. by means of the testimony concerning God's order of mercy which he is able to bear as the result of his own rich experience.

Vers. 16–19. The third part now begins with a doubly urgent prayer. The invocation of God by the name *Elohim* is here made more urgent by the addition of אֱלֹהֵי תְּשׁוּעָתִי; inasmuch as the prayers for justification and for renewing blend together in the "deliver me." David does not seek to lessen his guilt; he calls it in דָּמִים by its right name,—a word which signifies blood violently shed, and then also a deed of blood and blood-guiltiness (ix. 13, cvi. 38, and frequently). We have

also met with הִצִּיל construed with מִן of the sin in xxxix. 9. He
had given Uriah over to death in order to possess himself of
Bathsheba. And the accusation of his conscience spoke not
merely of adultery, but also of murder. Nevertheless the
consciousness of sin no longer smites him to the earth, Mercy
has lifted him up; he prays only that she would complete her
work in him, then shall his tongue exultingly praise (רִנֵּן with
an accusative of the object, as in lix. 17) God's righteousness,
which, in accordance with the promise, takes the sinner under
its protection. But in order to perform what he vowed he
would do under such circumstances, he likewise needs grace,
and prays, therefore, for a joyous opening of his mouth. In
sacrifices God delighteth not (xl. 7, cf. Isa. i. 11), otherwise he
would bring some (וְאֶתֵּנָה, darem, sc. si velles, vid. on xl. 6);
whole-burnt-offerings God doth not desire: the sacrifices that
are well-pleasing to Him and most beloved by Him, in comparison with which the flesh and the dead work of the עולות and
the זבחים (שלמים) is altogether worthless, are thankfulness (l. 23)
out of the fulness of a penitent and lowly heart. There is
here, directly at least, no reference to the spiritual antitype of
the sin-offering, which is never called זבח. The inward part of
a man is said to be broken and crushed when his sinful nature
is broken, his ungodly self slain, his impenetrable hardness
softened, his haughty vainglorying brought low,—in fine, when
he is in himself become as nothing, and when God is everything to him.   Of such a spirit and heart, panting after grace
or favour, consist the sacrifices that are truly worthy God's
acceptance and well-pleasing to Him (cf. Isa. lvii. 15, where
such a spirit and such a heart are called God's earthly temple).*

Vers. 20, 21. From this spiritual sacrifice, well-pleasing to
God, the Psalm now, in vers. 20 sq., comes back to the material
sacrifices that are offered in a right state of mind; and this is

---

* The Talmud finds a significance in the plural זְבָחֵי. Joshua ben Levi
(*B. Sanhedrin* 43*b*) says: At the time when the temple was standing, whoever brought a burnt-offering received the reward of it, and whoever
brought a meat-offering, the reward of it; but the lowly was accounted
by the Scriptures as one who offered every kind of sacrifice at once (כאילו
הקריב כל הקרבנות כולן). In Irenæus, iv. 17, 2, and Clemens Alexandrinus,
Pædag. iii. 12, is found to θυσία τῷ Θεῷ καρδία συντετριμμένη the addition :
ὀσμὴ εὐωδίας τῷ Θεῷ καρδία δοξάζουσα τὸν πεπλακότα αὐτήν.

to be explained by the consideration that David's prayer for himself here passes over into an intercession on behalf of all Israel: Do good in Thy good pleasure unto Zion. אֶת־ may be a sign of the accusative, for הֵיטִיב (הֵטִיב) does take the accusative of the person (Job xxiv. 21); but also a preposition, for as it is construed with לְ and עִם, so also with אֵת in the same signification (Jer. xviii. 10, xxxii. 41). זִבְחֵי־צֶדֶק are here, as in iv. 6, Deut. xxxiii. 19, those sacrifices which not merely as regards their outward character, but also in respect of the inward character of him who causes them to be offered on his behalf, are exactly such as God the Lawgiver will have them to be. By כָּלִיל beside עוֹלָה might be understood the priestly vegetable whole-offering, Lev. vi. 15 sq. (מִנְחַת חֲבִתִּין, *Epistle to the Hebrews*, ii. 8), since every עוֹלָה as such is also כָּלִיל; but Psalm-poetry does not make any such special reference to the sacrificial tôra. וְכָלִיל is, like כליל in 1 Sam. vii. 9, an explicative addition, and the combination is like ימינך וזרוער, xliv. 4, ארץ ותבל, xc. 2, and the like. A שֶׁלֶם כָּלִיל (Hitzig, after the Phœnician sacrificial tables) is unknown to the Israelitish sacrificial worship. The prayer: *Build Thou the walls of Jerusalem,* is not inadmissible in the mouth of David; since בָּנָה signifies not merely to build up what has been thrown down, but also to go on and finish building what is in the act of being built (lxxxix. 3); and, moreover, the wall built round about Jerusalem by Solomon (1 Kings iii. 1) can be regarded as a fulfilment of David's prayer.

Nevertheless what even Theodoret has felt cannot be denied: τοῖς ἐν Βαβυλῶνι . . . ἁρμόττει τὰ ῥήματα. Through penitence the way of the exiles led back to Jerusalem. The supposition is very natural that vers. 20 sq. may be a liturgical addition made by the church of the Exile. And if the origin of Isa. ch. xl.–lxvi. in the time of the Exile were as indisputable as the reasons against such a position are forcible, then it would give support not merely to the derivation of vers. 20 sq. (cf. Isa. lx. 10, 5, 7), but of the whole Psalm, from the time of the Exile; for the general impress of the Psalm is, according to the accurate observation of Hitzig, thoroughly deutero-Isaianic. But the writer of Isa. xl.–lxvi. shows signs in other respects also of the most familiar acquaintance with the earlier literature of the *Shîr* and the *Mashal;* and that he is none

other than Isaiah reveals itself in connection with this Psalm
by the echoes of this very Psalm, which are to be found not
only in the second but also in the first part of the Isaianic
collection of prophecy (cf. on vers. 9, 18).   We are therefore
driven to the inference, that Ps. li. was a favourite Psalm of
Isaiah's, and that, since the Isaianic echoes of it extend equally
from the first verse to the last, it existed in the same complete
form even in his day as in ours; and that consequently the
close, just like the whole Psalm, so beautifully and touchingly
expressed, is not the mere addition of a later age.

PSALM LII.

THE PUNISHMENT THAT AWAITS THE EVIL TONGUE.

3 WHY boastest thou thyself of wickedness, O thou mighty
        one ?!—
  The mercy of God endureth continually.
4 Destruction doth thy tongue devise,
  Like a sharpened razor, O worker of guile!
5 Thou lovest evil rather than good,
  Lying instead of speaking that which is right.   (*Sela.*)
6 Thou lovest only destroying words, O deceitful tongue!

7 Thus then will God smite thee down for ever,
  He will seize thee and pluck thee out of the tent,
  And root thee out of the land of the living.   (*Sela.*)
8 The righteous shall see it and fear,
  And over him shall they laugh :
9 "Behold there the man who made not Elohim his hiding-
        place,
  And boasted of the abundance of his riches, trusted in his
        self-devotedness !"

10 I, however, am like a green olive-tree in the house of Elohim,
   I trust in the mercy of Elohim for ever and ever.
11 I will give thanks to Thee for ever, that Thou hast accom-
        plished it;
   And I will wait on Thy name, because it is so gracious, in
        the presence of Thy saints.

With Ps. lii., which, side by side with Ps. li., exhibits the contrast between the false and the right use of the tongue, begins a series of Elohimic *Maskîls* (Ps. lii.–lv.) by David. It is one of the eight Psalms which, by the statements of the inscriptions, of which some are capable of being verified, and others at least cannot be replaced by anything that is more credible, are assigned to the time of his persecution by Saul (vii., lix., lvi., xxxiv., lii., lvii., cxlii., liv.). Augustine calls them *Psalmos fugitivos*. The inscription runs: *To the Precentor, a meditation* (vid. xxxii. 1), *by David, when Doeg the Edomite came and told Saul and said to him: David is gone in to the house of Ahimelech.* By בְּבוֹא, as in li. 2, liv. 2, the writer of the inscription does not define the exact moment of the composition of the Psalm, but only in a general way the period in which it falls. After David had sojourned a short time with Samuel, he betook himself to Nob to Ahimelech the priest; and he gave him without hesitation, as being the son-in-law of the king, the shew-bread that had been removed, and the sword of Goliath that had been hung up in the sanctuary behind the ephod. Doeg the Edomite was witness of this; and when Saul, under the tamarisk in Gibea, held an assembly of his serving men, Doeg, the overseer of the royal mules, betrayed what had taken place between David and Ahimelech to him. Eighty-five priests immediately fell as victims of this betrayal, and only Abiathar (*Ebjathar*) the son of Ahimelech escaped and reached David, 1 Sam. xxii. 6–10 (where, in ver. 9, פרדי is to be read instead of עבדי, cf. ch. xxi. 8).

Vers. 3–6. It is bad enough to behave wickedly, but bad in the extreme to boast of it at the same time as an heroic act. Doeg, who causes a massacre, not, however, by the strength of his hand, but by the cunning of his tongue, does this. Hence he is sarcastically called גִּבּוֹר (cf. Isa. v. 22). David's cause, however, is not therefore lost; for it is the cause of God, whose loving-kindness endures continually, without allowing itself to be affected, like the favour of men, by calumny. Concerning הַוּוֹת *vid.* on v. 10. לָשׁוֹן is as usual treated as *fem.*; עֹשֵׂה רְמִיָּה (according to the Masora with *Tsere*) is consequently addressed to a person. In ver. 5 רָע after אָהַבְתָּ has the *Dagesh* that is usual also in other instances according to the rule of the אתי

מַרְחִיק, especially in connection with the letters בגד'כפת (with which *Resh* is associated in the Book of Jezira, *Michlol* 96*b*, cf. 63*b*).* The מִן of מִטּוֹב and מִדַּבֵּר is not meant to affirm that he loves good, etc., less than evil, etc., but that he does not love it at all (cf. cxviii. 8 sq., Hab. ii. 16). The music which comes in after ver. 5 has to continue the accusations *con amarezza* without words. Then in ver. 6 the singing again takes them up, by addressing the adversary with the words "thou tongue of deceit" (cf. cxx. 3), and by reproaching him with loving only such utterances as swallow up, *i.e.* destroy without leaving a trace behind (בִּלַּע, pausal form of בִּלֵּע, like בֶּצַע in cxix. 36, cf. the verb in xxxv. 25, 2 Sam. xvii. 16, xx. 19 sq.), his neighbour's life and honour and goods. Hupfeld takes ver. 6*b* as a second object; but the figurative and weaker expression would then follow the unfigurative and stronger one, and "to love a deceitful tongue" might be said with reference to this character of tongue as belonging to another person, not with reference to his own.

Vers. 7–9. The announcement of the divine retribution begins with גַּם as in Isa. lxvi. 4, Ezek. xvi. 43, Mal. ii. 9. The אֹהֶל is not, as one might suppose, the holy tent or tabernacle, that he has desecrated by making it the lurking-place of the betrayer (1 Sam. xxi. 8 [7]), which would have been expressed by מֵאָהֳלִי, but his own dwelling. God will pull him, the lofty and

---

* אָתֵי מֵרָחִיק is the name by which the national grammarians designate a group of two words, of which the first, ending with *Kametz* or *Segol*, has the accent on the *penult.*, and of which the second is a monosyllable, or likewise is accented on the *penult.* The initial consonant of the second word in this case receives a *Dagesh*, in order that it may not, in consequence of the first *ictus* of the group of words "coming out of the distance," *i.e.* being far removed, be too feebly and indistinctly uttered. This dageshing, however, only takes place when the first word is already of itself *Milel*, or at least, as *e.g.* מָצְאָה בַיִת, had a half-accented *penult.*, and not when it is from the very first *Milra* and is only become *Milel* by means of the retreating of the accent, as עָשָׂה פֶלֶא, lxxviii. 12, cf. Deut. xxiv. 1. The penultima-accent has a greater lengthening force in the former case than in the latter; the following syllables are therefore uttered more rapidly in the first case, and the *Dagesh* is intended to guard against the third syllable being too hastily combined with the second. Concerning the rule, *vid.* Baer's *Thorath Emeth*, p. 29 sq.

imperious one, down (נָתַץ, like a tower perhaps, Judg. viii. 9, Ezek. xxvi. 9) from his position of honour and his prosperity, and drag him forth out of his habitation, much as one rakes a coal from the hearth (חָתָה Biblical and Talmudic in this sense), and tear him out of this his home (נָסַח, cf. נָתַק, Job xviii. 14) and remove him far away (Deut. xxviii. 63), because he has betrayed the homeless fugitive; and will root him out of the land of the living, because he has destroyed the priests of God (1 Sam. xxii. 18). It then proceeds in vers. 8 sq. very much like xl. 4*b*, 5, just as the figure of the razor also coincides with Psalms belonging to exactly the same period (li. 8, lvii. 5, cf. לְמַשׁ, vii. 13). The excitement and indignant anger against one's foes which expresses itself in the rhythm and the choice of words, has been already recognised by us since Ps. vii. as a characteristic of these Psalms. The hope which David, in ver. 8, attaches to God's judicial interposition is the same as *e.g.* in Ps. lxiv. 10. The righteous will be strengthened in the fear of God (for the play of sounds cf. xl. 4) and laugh at him whom God has overthrown, saying: Behold there the man, etc. According to lviii. 11, the laughing is joy at the ultimate breaking through of justice long hidden and not discerned; for even the moral teaching of the Old Testament (Prov. xxiv. 17) reprobates the low malignant joy that glories at the overthrow of one's enemy. By וַיִּבְטַח the former trust in mammon on the part of the man who is overtaken by punishment is set forth as a consequence of his refusal to put trust in God, in Him

who is the true מָעוֹז = معاذ, hiding-place or place of protection

(*vid.* on xxxi. 3, xxxvii. 39, cf. xvii. 7, 2 Sam. xxii. 33). הַוָּה is here the passion for earthly things which rushes at and falls upon them (*animo fertur*).

Vers. 10, 11. The gloomy song now brightens up, and in calmer tones draws rapidly to a close. The betrayer becomes like an uprooted tree; the betrayed, however, stands firm and is like to a green-foliaged olive (Jer. xi. 16) which is planted in the house of Elohim (xc. 14), that is to say, in sacred and inaccessible ground; cf. the promise in Isa. lx. 13. The weighty expression כִּי עָשִׂיתָ refers, as in xxii. 32, to the gracious and just carrying out of that which was aimed at in the election of David. If this be attained, then he will for ever give thanks and further wait on the Name, *i.e.* the self-attestation, of God, which is so gracious and kind, he will give thanks and "wait" in the presence of all the saints. This "waiting," וַאֲקַוֶּה, is open to suspicion, since what he intends to do in the presence of the saints must be something that is audible or visible to them. Also "hoping in the name of God" is, it is true, not an unbiblical notional combination (Isa. xxvi. 8); but in connection with שִׁמְךָ כִי טוֹב which follows, one more readily looks for a verb expressing a thankful and laudatory proclamation (cf. liv. 8). Hitzig's conjecture that we should read וְאַחֲוֶּה is therefore perfectly satisfactory. נֶגֶד חֲסִידֶיךָ does not belong to טוֹב, which would be construed with בְּעֵינֵי, and not נגד, but to the two votive words; cf. xxii. 26, cxxxviii. 1, and other passages. The whole church (xxii. 23 sq., xl. 10 sq.) shall be witness of his thankfulness to God, and of his proclamation of the proofs which God Himself has given of His love and favour.

PSALM LIII.

ELOHIMIC VARIATION OF THE JAHVE-PSALM XIV.

2 THE fool hath said in his heart: " There is no God; "
Corruptly and abominably do they carry on their iniquity,
There is none that doeth good.

3 Elohim looketh down from heaven upon the children of
    men,
To see if there be any that have understanding,
If any that seek after God.

4 Every one of them is gone back, altogether they are corrupt,
There is none that doeth good,
Not even one.

5 Are the workers of iniquity so utterly devoid of under-
    standing,
Who eating up my people eat up bread,
(And) call not on Elohim?

6 Then were they in great fear, when there was no fear;
  For Elohim scattered the bones of him that encamped
      round about thee;
  Thou didst put them to shame, for Elohim had despised
      them.

7 Oh that the salvation of Israel were come out of Zion!
  When Elohim turneth the captivity of His people,
  Jacob shall rejoice, Israel shall be glad.

Psalms lii. and liv., which are most closely related by
occasion, contents, and expression, are separated by the insertion of Ps. liii., in which the individual character of Ps. lii., the
description of moral corruption and the announcement of the
divine curse, is generalized. Ps. liii. also belongs to this series
according to its species of poetic composition; for the inscription runs: *To the Precentor, after Machalath, a Maskîl of David.*
The formula עַל־מָחֲלַת recurs in lxxxviii. 1 with the addition of
לְעַנּוֹת. Since Ps. lxxxviii. is the gloomiest of all the Psalms,
and Ps. liii., although having a bright border, is still also a
dark picture, the signification of מַחֲלָה, laxness (root חל, *opp.*
מר), sickness, sorrow, which is capable of being supported by
Ex. xv. 26, must be retained. עַל־מחלת signifies *after a sad
tone* or *manner;* whether it be that מָחֲלַת itself (with the ancient
dialectic feminine termination, like נְגִינַת, lxi. 1) is a name for
such an elegiac kind of melody, or that it was thereby designed
to indicate the initial word of some popular song. In the
latter case מָחֲלַת is the construct form, the standard song
beginning מָחֲלַת לֵב or some such way. The signification to be
sweet (Aramaic) and melodious (Æthiopic), which the root חלי
obtains in the dialects, is foreign to Hebrew. It is altogether
inadmissible to combine מחלת with ﺔَﻠﻬﻣ, ease, comfort (Germ.
Gemächlichkeit, cf. *mächlich,* easily, slowly, with *mählich,* by
degrees), as Hitzig does; since מחל, Rabbinic, to pardon, coincides more readily with מָחָה, li. 3, 11. So that we may regard
machalath as equivalent to *mesto,* not *piano* or *andante.*
  That the two texts, Ps. xiv. and liii., are "vestiges of an
original identity" (Hupfeld) is not established: Ps. liii. is a
later variation of Ps. xiv. The musical designation, common

only to the earlier Psalms, at once dissuades one from coming down beyond the time of Jehoshaphat or Hezekiah. Moreover, we have here a manifest instance that even Psalms which are composed upon the model of, or are variations of Davidic Psalms, were without any hesitation inscribed לְדָוִד.

Beside the critical problem, all that remains here for the exegesis is merely the discussion of anything peculiar in the deviations in the form of the text.

Ver. 2. The well-grounded asyndeton הִשְׁחִיתוּ הִתְעִיבוּ is here dismissed; and the expression is rendered more bombastic by the use of עָוֶל instead of עֲלִילָה. עָוֶל (the masculine to עַוְלָה), *pravitas*, is the accusative of the object (cf. Ezek. xvi. 52) to both verbs, which give it a twofold superlative attributive notion. Moreover, here הִשְׁחִיתוּ is accented with *Mugrash* in our printed texts instead of *Tarcha*. One *Mugrash* after another is contrary to all rule.

Ver. 3. In both recensions of the Psalm the name of God occurs seven times. In Ps. xiv. it reads three times *Elohim* and four times *Jahve;* in the Psalm before us it is all seven times *Elohim*, which in this instance is a proper name of equal dignity with the name *Jahve*. Since the mingling of the two names in Ps. xiv. is perfectly intentional, inasmuch as *Elohim* in vers. 1, 2c describes God as a Being most highly exalted and to be reverentially acknowledged, and in ver. 5 as the Being who is present among men in the righteous generation and who is mighty in their weakness, it becomes clear that David himself cannot be the author of this levelling change, which is carried out more rigidly than the Elohimic character of the Psalm really demands.

Ver. 4. Instead of הַכֹּל, the totality, we have כֻּלּוֹ, which denotes each individual of the whole, to which the suffix, that has almost vanished (xxix. 9) from the genius of the language, refers. And instead of סָר, the more elegant סָג, without any distinction in the meaning.

Ver. 5. Here in the first line the word בַּל, which, as in v. 6, vi. 9, is in its right place, is wanting. In Ps. xiv. there then follow, instead of two tristichs, two distichs, which are perhaps each mutilated by the loss of a line. The writer who has retouched the Psalm has restored the tristichic symmetry that had been lost sight of, but he has adopted rather violent means : inasmuch as he has fused down the two distichs into a single tristich, which is as closely as possible adapted to the sound of their letters.

Ver. 6.   The last two lines of this tristich are in letters so similar to the two distichs of Ps. xiv., that they look like an attempt at the restoration of some faded manuscript.   Nevertheless, such a close following of the sound of the letters of the original, and such a changing of the same by means of an interchange of letters, is also to be found elsewhere (more especially in Jeremiah, and *e.g.* also in the relation of the Second Epistle of Peter to Jude).   And the two lines sound so complete in themselves and full of life, that this way of accounting for their origin takes too low an estimate of them. A later poet, perhaps belonging to the time of Jehoshaphat or Hezekiah, has here adapted the Davidic Psalm to some terrible catastrophe that has just taken place, and given a special character to the universal announcement of judgment.   The addition of לֹא־הָיָה פָחַד (supply אֲשֶׁר שָׁם = אֲשֶׁר, lxxxiv. 4) is meant to imply that fear of judgment had seized upon the enemies of the people of God, when no fear, *i.e.* no outward ground for fear, existed ; it was therefore חֶרְדַּת אלהים (1 Sam. xiv. 15), a God-wrought panic.   Such was the case with the host of the confederates in the days of Jehoshaphat (2 Chron. xx. 22–24) ; such also with the army of Sennacherib before Jerusalem (Isa. xxxvii. 36).   כִּי gives the proof in support of this fright from the working of the divine power.   The words are addressed to the people of God : *Elohim hath scattered the bones* (so that unburied they lie like dirt upon the plain a prey to wild beasts, cxli. 7, Ezek. vi. 5) *of thy besieger, i.e.* of him who had encamped against thee.   חֹנָךְ instead of חֹנֵךְ = עָלֶיךָ חָנָה.*   By the might of his God, who has overthrown them, the enemies of

---

* So it has been explained by Menachem ; whereas Dunash wrongly takes the ךְ of חֹנֵךְ as part of the root, overlooking the fact that with the suffix it ought rather to have been חֹנֶךָ instead of חֹנָךְ.   It is true that within the province of the verb *âch* does occur as a pausal masculine suffix nstead of *écha*, with the preterite (Deut. vi. 17, Isa. xxx. 19, lv. 5, and even out of pause in Jer. xxiii. 37), and with the infinitive (Deut. xxviii. 24, Ezek. xxviii. 15), but only in the passage before us with the participle.

His people, Israel has put them to shame, *i.e.* brought to
nought in a way most shameful to them, the project of those
who were so sure of victory, who imagined they could devour
Israel as easily and comfortably as bread. It is clear that in
this connection even ver. 5 receives a reference to the foreign
foes of Israel originally alien to the Psalm, so that consequently Mic. iii. 3 is no longer a parallel passage, but passages
like Num. xiv. 9, *our bread are they* (the inhabitants of
Canaan); and Jer. xxx. 16, *all they that devour thee shall be
devoured.*

Ver. 7. The two texts now again coincide. Instead of
יְשׁוּעַת, we here have יְשׁוּעוֹת; the expression is strengthened, the
plural signifies entire, full, and final salvation.

PSALM LIV.

CONSOLATION IN THE PRESENCE OF BLOODTHIRSTY ADVERSARIES.

3 ELOHIM, by Thy name save me,
    And by Thy strength maintain my cause!
4 Elohim, hear my prayer,
    Hearken to the words of my mouth:
5 For strangers are risen up against me,
    And violent men seek after my life;
    They set not Elohim before their eyes.   (*Sela.*)

6 Behold, Elohim is my helper,
    The Lord it is who upholdeth my soul.
7 He will requite the evil to mine enemies—
    By virtue of Thy truth cut Thou them off.

Attached to the participle this masculine suffix closely approximates to the
Aramaic; with proper substantives there are no examples of it found in
Hebrew. Simson ha-Nakdan, in his חבור הקונים (a MS. in Leipzig University Library, fol. 29*b*), correctly observes that forms like שְׁמָךְ, עֲמָךְ, are
not biblical Hebrew, but Aramaic, and are only found in the language of
the Talmud, formed by a mingling of the Hebrew and Aramaic.

8 With willing mind will I sacrifice unto Thee,
  I will give thanks to Thy name, Jahve, that it is gracious.
9 For out of all distress hath it delivered me,
  And upon mine enemies doth mine eye delight itself.

Here again we have one of the eight Psalms dated from the time of Saul's persecution,—a *Maskîl*, like the two preceding Psalms, and having points of close contact both with Ps. liii. (cf. ver. 5 with liii. 3) and with Ps. lii. (cf. the resemblance in the closing words of ver. 8 and lii. 11): *To the Precentor, with the accompaniment of stringed instruments (vid. on iv. 1), a meditation, by David, when the Ziphites came and said to Saul: Is not David hidden among us?* Abiathar, the son of Ahimelech, had escaped to David, who with six hundred men was then in the fortified town of Keïla (Keilah), but received through Abiathar the divine answer, that the inhabitants would give him up if Saul should lay siege to the town. Thereupon we find him in the wilderness of Zîph; the Ziphites betray him and pledge themselves to capture him, and thereby he is in the greatest straits, out of which he was only rescued by an invasion of the Philistines, which compelled Saul to retreat (1 Sam. xxiii. 19 sqq.). The same history which the earlier narrator of the Books of Samuel relates here, we meet with once more in 1 Sam. ch. xxvi., related with fuller colouring. The form of the inscription of the Psalm is word for word the same as both in 1 Sam. xxiii. 19 and in 1 Sam. xxvi. 1; the annals are in all three passages the ultimate source of the inscription.

Vers. 3—5. This short song is divided into two parts by *Sela*. The first half prays for help and answer. The Name of God is the manifestation of His nature, which has mercy as its central point (for the Name of God is טוֹב, ver. 8, lii. 11), so that בְּשִׁמְךָ (which is here the parallel word to בִּגְבוּרָתְךָ) is consequently equivalent to בְּחַסְדֶּךָ. The obtaining of right for any one (דִּין like שָׁפַט, vii. 9, and frequently, עָשָׂה דִין, ix. 5) is attributed to the all-conquering might of God, which is only one side of the divine Name, *i.e.* of the divine nature which manifests itself in the diversity of its attributes. הַאֲזִין (ver. 4*b*) is construed with לְ (cf. אֶל, lxxvii. 2) like הִטָּה אֹזֶן, lxxviii. 1.

The Targum, misled by lxxxvi. 14, reads זֵרִים instead of זָרִים in
ver. 5. The inscription leads one to think of the Ziphites in
particular in connection with "strangers" and "violent men."
The two words in most instances denote foreign enemies, Isa.
xxv. 2 sq., xxix. 5, Ezek. xxxi. 12; but זָר is also a stranger in
the widest sense, regulated in each instance according to the
opposite, *e.g.* the non-priest, Lev. xxii. 10; and one's fellow-
countrymen can also turn out to be עָרִיצִים, Jer. xv. 21. The
Ziphites, although Judæans like David, might be called
"strangers," because they had taken the side against David;
and "violent men," because they pledged themselves to seize
and deliver him up. Under other circumstances this might
have been their duty as subjects. In this instance, however,
it was godlessness, as ver. 5c (cf. lxxxvi. 14) says. Any one
at that time in Israel who feared God more than man, could
not lend himself to be made a tool of Saul's blind fury. God
had already manifestly enough acknowledged David.

Vers. 6–9. In this second half, the poet, in the certainty
of being heard, rejoices in help, and makes a vow of thanksgiving. The בְּ of בְּסֹמְכֵי is not meant to imply that God is one
out of many who upheld his threatened life; but rather that
He comes within the category of such, and fills it up in Himself
alone, cf. cxviii. 7; and for the origin of this *Beth essentiæ*,
xcix. 6, Judg. xi. 35. In ver. 7 the *Kerî* merits the preference over the *Chethîb* (evil shall "revert" to my spies), which
would at least require עַל instead of לְ (cf. vii. 17). Concerning
שֹׁרְרָי, *vid.* on xxvii. 11. In the rapid transition to invocation
in ver. 7b the end of the Psalm announces itself. The truth
of God is not described as an instrumental agent of the cutting
off, but as an impelling cause. It is the same *Beth* as in the
expression בִּנְדָבָה (Num. xv. 3): by or out of free impulse.
These free-will sacrifices are not spiritual here in opposition to
the ritual sacrifices (l. 14), but ritual as an outward representation of the spiritual. The subject of הִצִּילֵנִי is the Name of God;
the post-biblical language, following Lev. xxiv. 11, calls God
straightway הַשֵּׁם, and passages like Isa. xxx. 27 and the one
before us come very near to this usage. The præterites mention the ground of the thanksgiving. What David now still
hopes for, will then lie behind him in the past. The closing
line, ver. 9b, recalls xxxv. 21, cf. lix. 11, xcii. 12; the invoking

of the curse upon his enemies in ver. 7 recalls xvii. 13, lvi. 8,
lix. 12 sqq.; and the vow of thanksgiving in ver. 8 recalls xxii.
26, xxxv. 18, xl. 10 sqq.

PSALM LV.

PRAYER OF ONE WHO IS MALICIOUSLY BESET AND BETRAYED BY HIS FRIEND.

2 GIVE ear, Elohim, to my prayer,
  And veil not Thyself from my supplication;
3 Oh hearken to me and answer me!
  I toss to and fro in my thoughts and must groan,
4 Because of the voice of the enemy, because of the oppression
    of the evil-doer.

  For they roll iniquity upon me,
  And in anger do they pursue me.
5 My heart writhes within me,
  And the terrors of death have fallen upon me.
6 Fear and trembling come upon me,
  And horror hath covered me.

7 I thought: Oh that I had wings like a dove,
  Then would I fly away and be at rest!
8 Yea, I would flee afar off,
  I would lodge in the wilderness.   (*Sela.*)
9 I would soar to my place of refuge
  From the raging wind, from the tempest.

10 Destroy, O Lord, divide their tongues,
  For I see violence and strife in the city.
11 Day and night they go their rounds upon its walls,
  And evil and trouble are in the midst of it.
12 Destruction is in the midst of it,
  And oppression and guile depart not from its market-place.

13 For it is not an enemy that reproacheth me, then I would
    bear it;

Neither is it he that hateth me that exalteth himself
    against me,
Then I could indeed hide myself from him.
14 But thou wast a man on an equality with me, my companion
    and familiar friend,
15 We who were wont to have sweet intercourse together,
To the house of Elohim we walked in the festive throng.

16 Let death surprise them,
    Let them go down alive to Hades;
    For wickedness is in their dwelling, in their inward part.
17 As for me, to Elohim do I cry,
    And Jahve will save me.

18 Evening and morning and at noon will I meditate and groan,
    And He will hear my voice,
19 He will deliver, in peace, my soul, so that they come not
      at me;
    For they are very many against me.
20 God will hear, and answer them—
    Yea, He sitteth enthroned from the very beginning—(*Sela*)

Even them, who think nothing of another,
And who fear not Elohim.
21 He layeth his hand upon those who are at peace with him,
    He violateth his covenant.
22 Smooth are the butter-words of his mouth,
                and war is his heart;
    Soft are his words as oil,   and yet are sword-blades.

23 Cast thy burden upon Jahve,
    He, He will sustain thee;
    He will never suffer the righteous to be moved.
24 And Thou, Elohim, shalt cast them down into the abyss of
      the pit,
    Bloody and deceitful men shall not live out half their lives;
    But I trust in Thee.

Ps. liv. is followed by another Davidic Psalm bearing the
same inscription: *To the Precentor, with accompaniment of*

stringed instruments, a meditation, by David. It also accords with the former in the form of the prayer with which it opens (cf. ver. 2 with liv. 3 sq.); and it is the Elohimic counterpart of the Jahve-Psalm xli. If the Psalm is by David, we require (in opposition to Hengstenberg) an assignable occasion for it in the history of his life. For how could the faithless bosom friend, over whom the complaint concerning malicious foes here, as in Ps. xli., lingers with special sadness, be a mere abstract personage; since it has in the person of Judas Iscariot its historical living antitype in the life and passion of the second David? This Old Testament Judas is none other than Ahithôphel, the right hand of Absalom. Ps. lv. belongs, like Ps. xli., to the four years during which the rebellion of Absalom was forming; only to a somewhat later period, when Absalom's party were so sure of their cause that they had no need to make any secret of it. How it came to pass that David left the beginnings and progressive steps of the rebellion of Absalom to take their course without bringing any other weapon to bear against it than the weapon of prayer, is discussed on Ps. xli.

Hitzig also holds this Psalm to be Jeremianic. But it contains no coincidences with the language and thoughts of Jeremiah worth speaking of, excepting that this prophet, in ch. ix. 1, gives utterance to a similar wish to that of the psalmist in vers. 7–9, and springing from the same motive. The argument in favour of Jeremiah in opposition to David is consequently referred to the picture of life and suffering which is presented in the Psalm; and it becomes a question whether this harmonizes better with the persecuted life of Jeremiah or of David. The exposition which follows here places itself—and it is at least worthy of being attempted—on the standpoint of the writer of the inscription.

Vers. 2–9. In this first group sorrow prevails. David spreads forth his deep grief before God, and desires for himself some lonely spot in the wilderness far away from the home or lurking-place of the confederate band of those who are compassing his overthrow. "Veil not Thyself" here, where what is spoken of is something audible, not visible, is equivalent to "veil not Thine ear," Lam. iii. 56, which He designedly does, when the right state of heart leaves the praying one, and consequently that which makes it acceptable and capable of being answered is wanting to the prayer (cf. Isa. i. 15). שִׂיחַ signifies a shrub (Syriac *shucho*, Arabic شدّ), and also reflection and care (Arabic, carefulness, attention; Aramaic, סח, to babble, talk, discourse). The *Hiph.* הֵרִיד, which in Gen. xxvii. 40 signifies to lead a roving life, has in this instance the signification to move one's self backwards and forwards, to be inwardly uneasy; root רד, رَدَّ, to totter, whence *râda, jarûda*, to run up and down (IV. to desire, will); *raïda*, to shake (said of a soft bloated body); *radda*, to turn (whence *taraddud*, a moving to and fro, doubting); therefore: I wander hither and thither in my reflecting or meditating, turning restlessly from one thought to another. It is not necessary to read וְאֶהֱמָיָה after lxxvii. 4 instead of וְאָהִימָה, since the verb הָמָה = הוּם, xlii. 6, 12, is secured by the derivatives. Since these only exhibit הוּם, and not הִים (in Arabic used more particularly of the raving of love), וְאָהִימָה, as also אָרִיד, is *Hiph.*, and in fact like this latter used with an inward object: I am obliged to raise a tumult or groan, break out into the dull murmuring sounds of pain. The cohortative not unfrequently signifies "I have to" or "I must" of incitements within one's self which are under the control of outward circumstances. In this restless state of mind he finds himself, and he is obliged to break forth into this cry of pain on account of the voice of the foe which he cannot but hear; by reason of the pressure or constraint (עָקַת) of the evil-doer which he is compelled to feel. The conjecture צַעֲקַת (Olshausen and Hupfeld) is superfluous. עָקָה is a more elegant Aramaizing word instead of צָרָה.

The second strophe begins with a more precise statement of that which justifies his pain. The *Hiph.* הֵמִיט signifies here, as in cxl. 11 (*Chethîb*), *declinare*: they cast or roll down evil (calamity) upon him and maliciously lay snares for him בְּאַף, breathing anger against him, who is conscious of having manifested only love towards them. His heart turns about in his body, it writhes (יָחִיל); cf. on this, xxxviii. 11. Fear and trembling take possession of his inward parts; יָבֹא in the expression יָבֹא בִי, as is always the case when followed by a tone syllable, is a so-called נסוג אחור, *i.e.* it has the tone that has retreated to the *penult*. (Deut. i. 38, Isa. vii. 24, lx. 20), although this is only with difficulty discernible in our printed copies, and is therefore (*vid. Accentsystem*, vi. § 2) noted with *Mercha.* The *fut. consec.* which follows introduces the heightened state of terror which proceeds from this crowding on of fear and trembling. Moreover, the wish that is thereby urged from him, which David uttered to himself, is introduced in the third strophe by a *fut. consec.** "Who will give me?" is equivalent to "Oh that I had!" Ges. § 136, 1. In וְאֶשְׁכֹּנָה is involved the self-satisfying signification of settling down (Ezek. xxxi. 13), of coming to rest and remaining in a place (2 Sam. vii. 10). Without going out of our way, a sense perfectly in accordance with the matter in hand may be obtained for אָחִישָׁה מִפְלָט לִי, if אחישה is taken not as *Kal* (lxxi. 12), but after Isa. v. 19, lx. 12, as *Hiph.*: I would hasten, *i.e.* quickly find for myself a place which might serve me as a shelter from the raging wind, from the storm. רוּחַ סֹעָה is equivalent to the Arabic *rîhin sâijat-in*, inasmuch as سعى, "to move one's self quickly, to go or run swiftly," can be said both of light (Koran, lxvi. 8) and of water-brooks (*vid.* Jones, *Comm. Poes. Asiat.*, ed. *Lipsiæ*, p. 358), and also of strong currents of air, of winds, and such like. The correction סְעָרָה, proposed by Hupfeld, produces a disfiguring tautology. Among those about David there is a wild movement going on which is specially aimed at his overthrow. From this he would gladly flee and hide himself, like a dove taking refuge in a cleft of the rock from the approaching storm, or from the talons of the bird of prey, fleeing with its noiseless but persevering flight.†

Vers. 10–17. In the second group anger is the prevailing feeling. In the city all kinds of party passions have broken loose; even his bosom friend has taken a part in this hostile

---

* That beautiful old song of the church concerning Jesus has grown out of this strophe:—

> *Ecquis binas columbinas*
> *Alas dabit animæ?*
> *Et in almam crucis palmam*
> *Evolat citissime,* etc.

† Kimchi observes that the dove, when she becomes tired, draws in one wing and flies with the other, and thus the more surely escapes. Aben-Ezra finds an allusion here to the carrier-pigeon.

rising. The retrospective reference to the confusion of tongues at Babel which is contained in the word פַּלַּג (cf. Gen. x. 25), also in remembrance of בָּלַל (Gen. xi. 1–9), involves the choice of the word בַּלַּע, which here, after Isa. xix. 3, denotes a swallowing up, *i.e.* annihilation by means of confounding and rendering utterly futile. לְשׁוֹנָם is the object to both imperatives, the second of which is פַּלַּג (like the pointing usual in connection with a final guttural) for the sake of similarity of sound. Instead of חָמָס וָרִיב, the pointing is חמס וְרִיב, which is perfectly regular, because the וריב with a conjunctive accent logically hurries on to בָּעִיר as its supplement.* The subjects to ver. 11*a* are not violence and strife (Hengstenberg, Hitzig), for it is rather a comical idea to make these personified run round about upon the city walls; but (cf. lix. 7, 15) the Absalomites, and in fact the spies who incessantly watch the movements of David and his followers, and who to this end roam about upon the heights of the city. The narrative in 2 Sam. ch. xv. shows how passively David looked on at this movement, until he abandoned the palace of his own free will and quitted Jerusalem. The espionage in the circuit of the city is contrasted with the movements going on within the city itself by the word בְּקֶרֶב. We are acquainted with but few details of the affair; but we can easily fill in the details for ourselves in accordance with the ambitious, base, and craftily malicious character of Absalom. The assertion that deceit (מִרְמָה) and the extremest madness had taken possession of the city is confirmed in ver. 13 by כִּי. It is not open enemies who might have had cause for it that are opposed to him, but faithless friends, and among them that Ahithophel of Giloh, the scum of perfidious ingratitude. The futures וְאֶשָּׂא and וְאֶסָּתֵר are used as subjunctives, and וְ is equivalent to *alioqui*, as in li. 18, cf. Job vi. 14. He tells him to his face, to his shame, the relationship in which he had stood to him whom he now betrays. Ver. 14 is not to be rendered: and thou art, etc., but: *and thou* (who dost act thus) *wast,* etc.; for it is only because the principal clause has a

---

* Certain exceptions, however, exist, inasmuch as וְ sometimes remains even in connection with a disjunctive accent, Isa. xlix. 4, Jer. xl. 10, xli. 16; and it is pointed וְ in connection with a conjunctive in Gen. xlv. 23, xlvi. 12, Lev. ix. 3, Mic. ii. 11, Job iv. 16, Eccles. iv. 8.

retrospective meaning that the futures נַמְתִּיק and נְהַלֵּךְ describe
what was a custom in the past. The expression is designedly
אֱנוֹשׁ כְּעֶרְכִּי and not אִישׁ כערכי; David does not make him feel
his kingly eminence, but places himself in the relation to him
of man to man, putting him on the same level with himself
and treating him as his equal. The suffix of כערכי is in this
instance not subjective as in the כערכך of the law respecting the
asham or trespass-offering: according to my estimation, but
objectively: equal to the worth at which I am estimated, that
is to say, equally valued with myself. What heart-piercing
significance this word obtains when found in the mouth of the
second David, who, although the Son of God and peerless King,
nevertheless entered into the most intimate human relationship
as the Son of man to His disciples, and among them to that
Iscariot! אַלּוּף from אָלַף, Arabic *alifa*, to be accustomed to
anything, *assuescere*, signifies one attached to or devoted to any
one; and מְיֻדָּע, according to the Hebrew meaning of the verb
יָדַע, an intimate acquaintance. The first of the relative clauses
in ver. 15 describes their confidential private intercourse; the
second the unrestrained manifestation of it in public. סוֹד here,
as in Job xix. 19 (*vid. supra* on xxv. 14). הַמְתִּיק סוֹד, to make
friendly intercourse sweet, is equivalent to cherishing it. רֶגֶשׁ
stands over against סוֹד, just like סוֹד, secret counsel, and רִגְשָׁה,
loud tumult, in lxiv. 3. Here רֶגֶשׁ is just the same as that
which the Korahitic poet calls הָמוֹן חוֹגֵג in xlii. 5.

In the face of the faithless friend who has become the head
of the Absalomite faction David now breaks out, in ver. 16,
into fearful imprecations. The *Chethîb* is יְשִׁימוֹת, *desolationes*
(*super eos*); but this word occurs only in the name of a place
("House of desolations"), and does not well suit such direct
reference to persons. On the other hand, the *Kerî* יַשִּׁיא מָוֶת,
let death ensnare or impose upon them, gives a sense that is
not to be objected to; it is a pregnant expression, equivalent to:
let death come upon them unexpectedly. To this יַשִּׁיא corresponds the חַיִּים of the second imprecation: let them go down
alive into Hades (שְׁאוֹל, perhaps originally שְׁאוֹלָה, the ה of which
may have been lost beside the ח that follows), *i.e.* like the company of Korah, while their life is yet vigorous, that is to say,
let them die a sudden, violent death. The drawing together of
the *decipiat* (*opprimat*) *mors* into one word is the result of the

ancient *scriptio continua* and of the defective mode of writing,
יִשִּׁי, like יֵנִי, cxli. 5, אָבִי, 1 Kings xxi. 29. Böttcher renders it
differently: let death crash in upon them; but the future form
יְשַׁי = יִשָּׁאֶה from שָׁאָה = שָׁאַי is an imaginary one, which cannot
be supported by Num. xxi. 30. Hitzig renders it: let death
benumb them (יַשִּׁים); but this gives an inconceivable figure,
with the turgidity of which the *trepidantes Manes* in Virgil,
Æneid viii. 246, do not admit of comparison. In the confirmation, ver. 16*c*, בִּמְגוּרָם, together with the בְּקִרְבָּם which follows,
does not pretend to be any advance in the thought, whether
מָגוּר be rendered a settlement, dwelling, παροικία (LXX.,
Targum), or an assembly (Aquila, Symmachus, Jerome).
Hence Hitzig's rendering: in their shrine, in their breast
(= ἐν τῷ θησαυρῷ τῆς καρδίας αὐτῶν, Luke vi. 45), מְגוּרָם being
short for מְגוּרָתָם in accordance with the love of contraction
which prevails in poetry (on xxv. 5). But had the poet intended to use this figure he would have written בִּמְגוּרַת קרבם,
and is not the assertion that wickedness is among them, that it
is at home in them, really a climax? The change of the names
of God in ver. 17 is significant. He calls upon Him who is
exalted above the world, and He who mercifully interposes in
the history of the world helps him.

Vers. 18–24. In the third group confidence prevails, the
tone that is struck up in ver. 17 being carried forward. Evening, morning, and noon, as the beginning, middle, and close of
the day, denote the day in its whole compass or extent: David
thus gives expression to the incessancy with which he is determined to lay before God, both in the quiet of his spirit and in
louder utterances, whatsoever moves him. The *fut. consec.* וַיִּשְׁמַע
connects the hearing (answer) with the prayer as its inevitable
result. Also in the *præt.* פָּדָה expression is given to the certainty of faith; and בְּשָׁלוֹם side by side with it denotes, with the
same pregnancy of meaning as in cxviii. 5, the state of undisturbed outward and inward safety and prosperity, into which
God removes his soul when He rescues him. If we read
mi-kᵉrob, then קרב is, as the ancient versions regard it, the
infinitive: *ne appropinquent mihi;* whereas since the time of
J. H. Michaelis the preference has been given to the pronunciation *mi-kᵉrāb: a conflictu mihi sc. parato*, in which case
it would be pointed מִקְּרָב־ (with *Metheg*), whilst the MSS., in

order to guard against the reading with *ă*, point it מִקְּרָב־.
Hitzig is right when he observes, that after the negative מִן the
infinitive is indicated beforehand, and that לִי‎ = עָלַי, xxvii. 2, is
better suited to this. Moreover, the confirmatory clause ver.
19*b* is connected with what precedes in a manner less liable to
be misunderstood if מקרב is taken as infinitive: that they may
not be able to gain any advantage over me, cannot come near
me to harm me (xci. 10). For it is not until now less precari-
ous to take the enemies as the subject of הָיוּ, and to take עִמָּדִי in
a hostile sense, as in Job x. 17, xiii. 19, xxiii. 6, xxxi. 13, cf. עַ‎
xciv. 16, and this is only possible where the connection suggests
this sense. Heidenheim's interpretation: among the magnates
were those who succoured me (viz. Hushai, Zadok, and Abiathar, by whom the counsel of Ahithophel was frustrated), does
not give a thought characteristic of the Psalms. And with
Aben-Ezra, who follows *Numeri Rabba* 294*a*, to think of the
assistance of angels in connection with בְּרַבִּים, certainly strongly
commends itself in view of 2 Kings vi. 16 (with which Hitzig
also compares 2 Chron. xxxii. 7); here, however, it has no
connection, whereas the thought, " as many (consisting of
many) are they with me, *i.e.* do they come forward and fight
with me," is very loosely attached to what has gone before.
The *Beth essentiæ* serves here, as it does frequently, *e.g.* xxxix.
17, to denote the qualification of the subject. The preterite
of confidence is followed in ver. 20 by the future of hope.
Although side by side with יִשְׁמַע, ענה presumptively has the
signification to answer, *i.e.* to be assured of the prayer being
heard, yet this meaning is in this instance excluded by the fact
that the enemies are the object, as is required by ver. 20*d*
(even if ver. 19*b* is understood of those who are on the side of
the poet). The rendering of the LXX.: εἰσακούσεται ὁ Θεὸς
καὶ ταπεινώσει αὐτοὺς ὁ ὑπάρχων πρὸ τῶν αἰώνων, is appropriate, but requires the pronunciation to be וְיַעֲנֵם, since the
signification to bow down, to humble, cannot be proved to
belong either to *Kal* or *Hiphil*. But even granted that יַעֲנֵם
might, according to 1 Kings viii. 35 (*vid.* Keil), signify ταπεινώσει αὐτούς, it is nevertheless difficult to believe that ויענם is
not intended to have a meaning correlative with יִשְׁמַע, of which
it is the continuation. Saadia has explained יַעֲנֵם in a manner
worthy of attention, as being for יַעֲנֶה בָם, he will testify against

them; an interpretation which Aben-Ezra endorses. Hengstenberg's is better: "God will hear (the tumult of the enemies) and answer them (judicially)." The original text may have been וְיַעֲנֵמוֹ יֹשֵׁב קֶדֶם. But as it now stands, וְיֹשֵׁב קֶדֶם represents a subordinate clause, with the omission of the הוּא, pledging that judicial response: since He it is who sitteth enthroned from earliest times (*vid.* on vii. 10). The bold expression יֹשֵׁב קֶדֶם is an abbreviation of the view of God expressed in lxxiv. 12, Hab. i. 12, cf. Deut. xxxiii. 27, as of Him who from primeval days down to the present sits enthroned as King and Judge, who therefore will be able even at the present time to maintain His majesty, which is assailed in the person of His anointed one.

Ver. 20c. In spite of this interruption and the accompanying clashing in of the music, אֲשֶׁר with its dependent clause continues the ויענם, more minutely describing those whom God will answer in His wrath. The relative clause at the same time gives the ground for this their fate from the character they bear: they persevere in their course without any regard to any other in their godlessness. The noun חֲלִיפָה, which is used elsewhere of a change of clothes, of a reserve in time of war, of a relief of bands of workmen, here signifies a change of mind (Targum), as in Job xiv. 14 a change of condition; the plural means that every change of this kind is very far from them. In ver. 21 David again has the one faithless foe among the multitude of the rebels before his mind. שְׁלֹמָיו is equivalent to שְׁלֵמִים אִתּוֹ, Gen. xxxiv. 21, those who stood in peaceful relationship to him (שָׁלוֹם, xli. 10). David classes himself with his faithful adherents. בְּרִית is here a defensive and offensive treaty of mutual fidelity entered into in the presence of God. By שָׁלַח and חִלֵּל is meant the intention which, though not carried out as yet, is already in itself a violation and profanation of the solemn compact. In ver. 22 the description passes into the tone of the cæsural schema. It is impossible for מַחֲמָאֹת, so far as the vowels are concerned, to be equivalent to מֵחֶמְאוֹת, since this change of the vowels would obliterate the preposition; but one is forbidden to read מֵחֶמְאוֹת (Targum, Symmachus, Jerome) by the fact that פִּיו (LXX. τοῦ προσώπου αὐτοῦ, as in Prov. ii. 6) cannot be the subject to חָלְקוּ. Consequently מ belongs to the noun itself, and the denominative מַחְמָאוֹת (from חֶמְאָה), like מַעֲדַנּוֹת (from עֵדֶן), dainties, signifies articles of food prepared from curdled milk; here it is used figuratively of "milk-words" or butter-words" which come from the lips of the hypocrite softly, sweetly, and supplely as cream: *os nectar promit, mens aconita vomit.* In the following words וְקָרְב־לִבּוֹ (וְקָרַב) the *Makkeph* (in connection with which it would have to be read *uk^erob* just the same as in ver. 19, since the ־ַ has not a *Metheg*) is to be crossed out (as in fact it is even wanting here and there in MSS. and printed editions). The words are an independent substantival clause: war (קְרָב, a pushing together, assault, battle, after the form כְּתָב with an unchangeable *â*) is his inward part and his words are swords; these two clauses correspond. רַכּוּ (properly like

رَكَّ, to be thin, weak, then also: to be soft, mild; root רק, רך, *tendere, tenuare*) has the accent on the *ultima, vid.* on xxxviii. 20. פְּתִיחָה is a drawn, unsheathed sword (xxxvii. 14).

The exhortation, ver. 23, which begins a new strophe and is thereby less abrupt, is first of all a counsel which David gives to himself, but at the same time to all who suffer innocently, cf. xxvii. 14. Instead of the obscure ἅπαξ γεγραμ. יְהָבְךָ, we read in xxxvii. 5 דרכך, and in Prov. xvi. 3 מעשׂיך, according to which the word is not a verb after the form יְדָעֲךָ (Chajug', Gecatilia, and Kimchi), but an accusative of the object (just as it is in fact accented; for the *Legarme* of יהוה has a lesser disjunctive value than the *Zinnor* of יהבך). The LXX. renders it ἐπίρριψον ἐπὶ κύριον τὴν μέριμνάν σου. Thus are these words of the Psalm applied in 1 Pet. v. 7. According to the Talmud יְהָב (the same form as קְרָב) signifies a burden. " One day," relates Rabba bar-Chana, *B. Rosh ha-Shana,* 26*b*, and elsewhere, " I was walking with an Arabian (Nabatæan?) tradesman, and happened to be carrying a heavy pack. And he said to me, שׁקיל יהביך ושׁדי אגמלאי, Take thy burden and throw it on my camel." Hence it is wiser to refer יְהָב to יְהַב, to give, apportion, than to a stem יְהַב = יָאַב, cxix. 131 (root אב, או), to desire; so that it consequently does not mean desiring, longing, care, but that which is imposed, laid upon one, assigned or allotted to one (Böttcher), in which sense the Chaldee derivatives of יְהַב (Targum Ps. xi. 6, xvi. 5, for מְנָת) do actually occur. On whomsoever one casts what is allotted to him to

carry, to him one gives it to carry. The admonition proceeds
on the principle that God is as willing as He is able to bear
even the heaviest burden for us; but this bearing it for us is
on the other side our own bearing of it in God's strength, and
hence the promise that is added runs: He will sustain thee
(כִּלְכֵּל), that thou mayest not through feebleness succumb. Ver.
23c also favours this figure of a burden: He will not give, *i.e.*
suffer to happen (lxxviii. 66), tottering to the righteous for
ever, He will never suffer the righteous to totter. The righteous shall never totter (or be moved) with the overthrow that
follows; whereas David is sure of this, that his enemies shall
not only fall to the ground, but go down into Hades (which is
here, by a combination of two synonyms, בְּאֵר שַׁחַת, called a well,
i.e. an opening, of a sinking in, *i.e.* a pit, as *e.g.* in Prov. viii.
31, Ezek. xxxvi. 3), and that before they have halved their
days, *i.e.* before they have reached the half of the age that
might be attained under other circumstances (cf. cii. 25, Jer.
xvi. 11). By וְאַתָּה אֱלֹהִים prominence is given to the fact that
it is the very same God who will not suffer the righteous to fall
who casts down the ungodly; and by וַאֲנִי David contrasts himself with them, as being of good courage now and in all time
to come.

PSALM LVI.

CHEERFUL COURAGE OF A FUGITIVE.

2 BE gracious unto me, Elohim, for man is greedy after me,
   All the day he, fighting, oppresseth me.
3 Mine adversaries are greedy after me all the day,
   For many are they who proudly war against me.
4 In the day that I fear do I cling confidingly to Thee.
5 Through Elohim will I praise His word,
   In Elohim do I trust, without fearing:
   What can flesh do unto me?

6 All the day long they wrest my words,
   Against me are all their thoughts for evil.
7 They band together, they set spies—
   They watch my heels, because seeking after my life.

8 By such evil-doing shall they escape?—
  In wrath cast down the peoples, Elohim!

9 My fugitive life Thou hast told,
  My tears are laid up in Thy bottle—
  Are they not in Thy book?
10 Then must mine enemies fall back in the day that I call;
  This I know: that Elohim is for me.
11 Through Elohim do I praise the word,
  Through Jahve do I praise the word.
12 In Elohim do I trust without fearing:
  What can men do unto me?

13 Binding upon me, Elohim, are Thy vows;
  I will pay thank-offerings unto Thee.
14 For Thou hast delivered my soul from death,
  Yea my feet from falling,
  That I might walk before Elohim in the light of life.

To Ps. lv., which in vers. 7 sq. gives utterance to the wish: "*Oh that I had wings like a dove*," etc., no Psalm could be more appropriately appended, according to the mode of arrangement adopted by the collector, than Ps. lvi., the musical inscription of which runs: *To the Precentor, after "The silent dove among the far off," by David, a Michtam.* רְחֹקִים is a second genitive, cf. Isa. xxviii. 1, and either signifies distant men or *longiqua*, distant places, as in lxv. 6, cf. נַעֲיִמִים, xvi. 6. Just as in lviii. 2, it is questionable whether the punctuation אֵלֶם has lighted upon the correct rendering. Hitzig is anxious to read אֵלֶם, "Dove of the people in the distance;" but אֵלֶם, people, in spite of Egli's commendation, is a word unheard of in Hebrew, and only conjectural in Phœnician. Olshausen's אֵלֶם more readily commends itself, "Dove of the distant terebinths." As in other like inscriptions, עַל does not signify *de* (as Joh. Campensis renders it in his paraphrase of the Psalms (1532 and frequently): *Præfecto musices, de columba muta quæ procul avolaverat*), but *secundum*; and the coincidence of the defining of the melody with the situation of the writer of the Psalm is explained by the consideration that the melody is chosen with reference to that situation. The LXX. (cf. the Targum),

interpreting the figure, renders: ὑπὲρ τοῦ λαοῦ τοῦ ἀπὸ τῶν
ἁγίων (from the sanctuary) μεμακρυμμένου, for which Symmachus has: φύλου ἀπωσμένου. The rendering of Aquila is
correct: ὑπὲρ περιστερᾶς ἀλάλου μακρυσμῶν. From Ps. lv.
(vers. 7 sq., cf. xxxviii. 14) we may form an idea of the standard
song designated by the words יונת אלם רחקים; for Ps. lv. is not
this song itself, and for this reason, that it belongs to the time
of Absalom, and is therefore of later date than Ps. lvi., the
historical inscription of which, "*when the Philistines assaulted
him in Gath*" (cf. בְּיָדָם, 1 Sam. xxi. 14), carries us back into
the time of Saul, to the same time of the sojourn in Philistia
to which Ps. xxxiv. is assigned. Ps. lvi. exhibits many points
of the closest intermingling with the Psalms of this period, and
thus justifies its inscription. It is a characteristic possessed in
common by these Psalms, that the prospect of the judgment
that will come upon the whole of the hostile world is combined
with David's prospect of the judgment that will come upon his
enemies: lvi. 8, vii. 9, lix. 6 (12). The figure of the bottle in
which God preserves the tears of the suffering ones corresponds
to the sojourn in the wilderness. As regards technical form,
Ps. lvi. begins the series of Davidic Elohimic *Michtammîm*, Ps.
lvi.–lx. Three of these belong to the time of Saul. These
three contain refrains, a fact that we have already recognised
on xvi. 1 as a peculiarity of these "favourite-word-poems."
The favourite words of this Ps. lvi. are (ו)באלהים אהלל דבר and
מַה-יַּעֲשֶׂה בָשָׂר (אָדָם) לִי.

Vers. 2–5. אֱלֹהִים and אֱנוֹשׁ, ver. 2 (ix. 20, x. 18), are anti-
theses: over against God, the majestic One, men are feeble
beings. Their rebellion against the counsel of God is ineffec-
tive madness. If the poet has God's favour on his side, then
he will face these pigmies that behave as though they were
giants, who fight against him מָרוֹם, moving on high, *i.e.* proudly
(cf. מִמָּרוֹם, lxxiii. 8), in the invincible might of God. שָׁאַף,
inhiare, as in lvii. 4; לָחַם, as in xxxv. 1, with לְ like אֶל, *e.g.* in
Jer. i. 19. Thus, then, he does not fear; in the day when (Ges.
§ 123, 3, *b*) he might well be afraid (conjunctive future, as *e.g.*
in Josh. ix. 27), he clings trustfully to (אֶל as in iv. 6, and
frequently, Prov. iii. 5) his God, so that fear cannot come near
him. He has the word of His promise on his side (דְּבָרוֹ as *e.g.*

cxxx. 5); בֵּאלֹהִים, through God will he praise this His word, inasmuch as it is gloriously verified in him. Hupfeld thus correctly interprets it; whereas others in part render it "in Elohim do I praise His word," in part (and the form of this favourite expression in ver. 11*ab* is opposed to it): "Elohim do I celebrate, His word." Hitzig, however, renders it: "Of God do I boast in matter," *i.e.* in the present affair; which is most chillingly prosaic in connection with an awkward brevity of language. The exposition is here confused by x. 3 and xliv. 9. הִלֵּל does not by any means signify *gloriari* in this passage, but *celebrare;* and באלהים is not intended in any other sense than that in lx. 14. בָּטַח בְּ is equivalent to the New Testament phrase πιστεύειν ἐν. לֹא אִירָא is a circumstantial clause with a finite verb, as is customary in connection with לֹא, xxxv. 8, Job xxix. 24, and בַּל, Prov. xix. 23.

Vers. 6–8. This second strophe describes the adversaries, and ends in imprecation, the fire of anger being kindled against them. Hitzig's rendering is: "All the time they are injuring my concerns," *i.e.* injuring my interests. This also sounds unpoetical. Just as we say חָמַס תורה, to do violence to the Tôra (Zeph. iii. 4, Ezek. xxii. 26), so we can also say: to torture any one's words, *i.e.* his utterances concerning himself, viz. by misconstruing and twisting them. It is no good to David that he asseverates his innocence, that he asserts his filial faithfulness to Saul, God's anointed; they stretch his testimony concerning himself upon the rack, forcing upon it a false meaning and wrong inferences. They band themselves together, they place men in ambush. The verb גּוּר signifies sometimes to turn aside, turn in, dwell (= جَار); sometimes, to be afraid (= יָגֹר, وَجَرَ); sometimes, to stir up, excite, cxl. 3 (= גֵּרָה); and sometimes, as here, and in lix. 4, Isa. liv. 15: to gather together (= אָגַר). The *Keri* reads יָצֹפוּנוּ (as in x. 8, Prov. i. 11), but the *scriptio plena* points to *Hiph.* (cf. Job xxiv. 6, and also Ps. cxxvi. 5), and the following הֵמָּה leads one to the conclusion that it is the causative יַצְפִּינוּ that is intended: they cause one to keep watch in concealment, they lay an ambush (synon. הֶאֱרִיב, 1 Sam. xv. 5); so that המה refers to the liers-in-wait told off by them: as to these—they observe my heels or (like the feminine plural in lxxvii. 20, lxxxix. 52) footprints (Rashi: *mes traces*), *i.e.* all my footsteps or movements, because (properly, "in accordance with this, that," as in Mic. iii. 4) they now as formerly (which is implied in the perfect, cf. lix. 4) attempt my life, *i.e.* strive after, lie in wait for it (קִוָּה like שָׁמַר, lxxi. 10, with the accusative = קִוָּה לְ in cxix. 95). To this circumstantial representation of their hostile proceedings is appended the clause עַל־אָוֶן פַּלֶּט־לָמוֹ, which is not to be understood otherwise than as a question, and is marked as such by the order of the words (2 Kings v. 26, Isa. xxviii. 28): *In spite of iniquity [is there] escape for them?* *i.e.* shall they, the liers-in-wait, notwithstanding such evil good-for-nothing mode of action, escape? At any rate פַּלֶּט is, as in xxxii. 7, a substantivized infinitive, and the "by no means" which belongs as answer to this question passes over forthwith into the prayer for the overthrow of the evil ones. This is the customary interpretation since Kimchi's day. Mendelssohn explains it differently: "In vain be their escape," following Aben-Jachja, who, however, like Saadia, takes פלט to be imperative. Certainly adverbial notions are expressed by means of עַל,—*e.g.* עַל־יֶתֶר, abundantly, xxxi. 24; עַל־שֶׁקֶר, falsely, Lev. v. 22 (*vid.* Gesenius, *Thesaurus*, p. 1028),— but one does not say עַל־הֶבֶל, and consequently also would hardly have said עַל־אָוֶן (by no means, for nothing, in vain); moreover the connection here demands the prevailing ethical notion for אָוֶן. Hupfeld alters פלט to פַּלֵּס, and renders it: "recompense to them for wickedness," which is not only critically improbable, but even contrary to the usage of the language, since פלס signifies to weigh out, but not to requite, and requires the accusative of the object. The widening of the circle of vision to the whole of the hostile world is rightly explained by Hengstenberg by the fact that the special execution of judgment on the part of God is only an outflow of His more general and comprehensive execution of judgment, and the belief in the former has its root in a belief in the latter. The meaning of הוֹרֵד becomes manifest from the preceding Psalm (lv. 24), to which the Psalm before us is appended by reason of manifold and closely allied relation.

Vers. 9–12. What the poet prays for in ver. 8, he now expresses as his confident expectation with which he solaces himself. נֹד (ver. 9) is not to be rendered "flight," which certainly is not a thing that can be numbered (Olshausen); but

" a being fugitive," the unsettled life of a fugitive (Prov. xxvii.
8), can really be numbered both by its duration and its many
temporary stays here and there.   And upon the fact that God,
that He whose all-seeing eye follows him into every secret
hiding-place of the desert and of the rocks, counteth (telleth)
it, the poet lays great stress; for he has long ago learnt to despair
of man.   The accentuation gives special prominence to נֹדִי as
an emphatically placed object, by means of *Zarka;* and this
is then followed by סָפַרְתָּה with the conjunctive *Galgal* and the
pausal אָתָּה with *Olewejored* (the ⌣ of which is placed over the
final letter of the preceding word, as is always the case when
the word marked with this double accent is monosyllabic, or
dissyllabic and accented on the first syllable).   He who counts
(Job xxxi. 4) all the steps of men, knows how long David has
already been driven hither and thither without any settled home,
although free from guilt.   He comforts himself with this fact,
but not without tears, which this wretched condition forces
from him, and which he prays God to collect and preserve.
Thus it is according to the accentuation, which takes שִׂימָה as
imperative, as *e.g.* in 1 Sam. viii. 5; but since שִׂימָה, שִׂים, is also
the form of the passive participle (1 Sam. ix. 24, and frequently,
2 Sam. xiii. 32), it is more natural, in accordance with the
surrounding thoughts, to render it so even in this instance
(*posita est lacrima mea*), and consequently to pronounce it as
Milra (Ewald, Hupfeld, Böttcher, and Hitzig). דמעתי (Eccles.
iv. 1) corresponds chiastically (crosswise) to נֹדִי, with which
בְנֹאדֶךָ forms a play in sound; and the closing clause הֲלֹא בְּסִפְרָתֶךָ
unites with סָפַרְתָּה in the first member of the verse.   Both ver.
9*b* and ver. 9*c* are wanting in any particle of comparison.   The
fact thus figuratively set forth, viz. that God collects the tears
of His saints as it were in a bottle, and notes them together
with the things which call them forth as in a memorial (Mal.
iii. 16), the writer assumes; and only appropriatingly applies it to
himself.   The אָז which follows may be taken either as a logical
" in consequence of so and so" (as *e.g.* xix. 14, xl. 8), or as a
" then" fixing a turning-point in the present tearful wandering
life (viz. when there have been enough of the "wandering" and
of the "tears"), or "at a future time" (more abruptly, like שָׁם
in xiv. 5, xxxvi. 13, *vid.* on ii. 5).   בְּיוֹם אֶקְרָא is not an expansion
of this אָז, which would trail awkwardly after it.   The poet says

that one day his enemies will be obliged to retreat, inasmuch as a day will come when his prayer, which is even now heard, will be also outwardly fulfilled, and the full realization of the succour will coincide with the cry for help. By זֶה־יָדַעְתִּי in ver. 10*b* he justifies this hope from his believing consciousness. It is not to be rendered, after Job xix. 19: "I who know," which is a trailing apposition without any proper connection with what precedes; but, after 1 Kings xvii. 24: this I know (of this I am certain), that Elohim is for me. זֶה as a neuter, just as in connection with יָדַע in Prov. xxiv. 12, and also frequently elsewhere (Gen. vi. 15, Ex. xiii. 8, xxx. 13, Lev. xi. 4, Isa. xxix. 11, cf. Job xv. 17); and לִי as *e.g.* in Gen. xxxi. 42. Through Elohim, ver. 11 continues, will I praise דָּבָר: thus absolutely is the word named; it is therefore the divine word, just like בַּר in ii. 12, the Son absolutely, therefore the divine Son. Because the thought is repeated, *Elohim* stands in the first case and then *Jahve*, in accordance with the Elohimic Psalm style, as in lviii. 7. The refrain in ver. 12 (cf. ver. 5*b*) indicates the conclusion of the strophe. The fact that we read אָדָם instead of בָּשָׂר in this instance, just as in ver. 11 דָּבָר instead of דְּבָרוֹ (ver. 5*a*), is in accordance with the custom in the Psalms of not allowing the refrain to recur in exactly the same form.

Vers. 13, 14. In prospect of his deliverance the poet promises beforehand to fulfil the duty of thankfulness. עָלַי, incumbent upon me, as in Prov. vii. 14, 2 Sam. xviii. 11. נְדָרֶיךָ, with an objective subject, are the vows made to God; and תּוֹדוֹת are distinguished from them, as *e.g.* in 2 Chron. xxix. 31. He will suffer neither the pledged שַׁלְמֵי נֶדֶר nor the שַׁלְמֵי תּוֹדָה to be wanting; for—so will he be then able to sing and to declare—Thou hast rescued, etc. The perfect after כִּי denotes that which is then past, as in lix. 17, cf. the dependent passage cxvi. 8 sq. There the expression is אַרְצוֹת הַחַיִּים instead of אוֹר הַחַיִּים (here and in Elihu's speech, Job xxxiii. 30). Light of life (John viii. 12) or of the living (LXX. τῶν ζώντων) is not exclusively the sun-light of this present life. Life is the opposite of death in the deepest and most comprehensive sense; light of life is therefore the opposite of the night of Hades, of this seclusion from God and from His revelation in human history.

PSALM LVII.

BEFORE FALLING ASLEEP IN THE WILDERNESS.

2 BE gracious unto me, Elohim, be gracious unto me,
 For in Thee hath my soul hidden;
 And in the shadow of Thy wings do I seek refuge,
 Until the destruction passeth by.

3 I call upon Elohim, the Most High,
 Upon God who performeth it for me:
4 He will send from heaven and save me.
 If he who is greedy for me doth slander—(*Sela.*)
 Elohim will send His mercy and truth.

5 My soul is in the midst of lions,
 I will lie down among those who breathe forth fire.
 The children of men—their teeth are spears and
        arrows,
 And their tongue is a sharp sword.
6 Oh show Thyself exalted above the heavens, Elohim,
 Above the whole earth Thy glory!

7 They had laid a net for my steps,
 They had bowed down my soul,
 They had digged out a pit before me—
 They themselves fall therein.   (*Sela.*)

8 Confident is my heart, Elohim, confident is my heart,
 I will sing and play upon the harp.
9 Awake up, my glory,
 Awake up, O harp and cithern,
 I will awake the morning dawn!

10 I will praise Thee among the peoples, O Lord,
 I will praise Thee upon the harp among the nations.
11 For great unto the heavens is thy mercy,
 And unto the clouds Thy truth.

12 Oh show Thyself exalted above the heavens, Elohim,
   Above the whole earth Thy glory.

The Psalms that are to be sung after the melody אַל־תַּשְׁחֵת (lvii., lviii., lix. Davidic, lxxv. Asaphic) begin here. The direction referring to the musical execution of the Psalm ought properly to be עַל אל־תשחת (אֶל); but this is avoided as being unmelodious, and harsh so far as the syntax is concerned. The Geneva version is correct: *pour le chanter sur Al taschchet.* There is no actual reference in the words to Deut. ix. 26, or 1 Sam. xxvi. 9 (why not also to Isa. lxv. 8?).

The historical inscription runs: *when he fled from Saul, in the cave.* From the connection in the history from which this statement is extracted, it will have been clear whether the Psalm belongs to the sojourn in the cave of Adullam (1 Sam. ch. xxii.) or in the labyrinthine cave upon the alpine heights of Engedi, " by the sheep-folds" (1 Sam. ch. xxiv.), described in Van de Velde's *Journey,* ii. 74–76.

How manifold are the points in which these Psalms belonging to the time of Saul run into one another! Ps. lvii. has not merely the supplicatory " Be gracious unto me, Elohim," at the beginning, but also שָׁאַף applied in the same way (lvii. 4, lvi. 2 sq.), in common with Ps. lvi; in common with Ps. vii., נפשׁי = כבודי (lvii. 9, vii. 6); the comparison of one's enemies to lions and lionesses (lvii. 5, vii. 3); the figure of the digging of a pit (lvii. 7, vii. 16); with Ps. lix. the figure of the sword of the tongue (lvii. 5, lix. 8, cf. lii. 4); with Ps. lii. the poetical expression הוות (lvii. 2, lii. 4); with Ps. xxii. the relation of the deliverance of the anointed one to the redemption of all peoples (lvii. 10, xxii. 28 sqq.). Also with Ps. xxxvi. it has one or two points of contact, viz. the expression " refuge under the shadow of God's wings" (ver. 2, xxxvi. 8), and in the measuring of the mercy and truth of God by the height of the heavens (ver. 11, xxxvi. 6). Yet, on the other hand, it has a thoroughly characteristic impress. Just as Ps. lvi. delighted in confirming what was said by means of the interrogatory הֲלֹא (vers. 9, 14), so Ps. lvii. revels in the figure epizeuxis, or an emphatic repetition of a word (vers. 2, 4, 8, 9). Ps. cviii. (which see) is a cento taken out of Ps. lvii. and lx.

The strophe-schema of Ps. lvii. is the growing one: 4. 5. 6;

4. 5. 6.* Here also the *Michtam* is not wanting in its prominent favourite word. A refrain of a lofty character closes the first and second parts. In the first part cheerful submission rules, in the second a certainty of victory, which by anticipation takes up the song of praise.

Vers. 2–6. By means of the two distinctive tense-forms the poet describes his believing flight to God for refuge as that which has once taken place (חָסָיָה from חָסָה = חָסִי out of pause, like the same forms in lxxiii. 2, cxxii. 6), and still, because it is a living fact, is ever, and now in particular, renewed (אֶחְסֶה). The shadow of the wings of God is the protection of His gentle, tender love; and the shadow of the wings is the quickening, cordial solace that is combined with this protection. Into this shadow the poet betakes himself for refuge now as he has done before, until הַוּוֹת, *i.e.* the abysmal danger that threatens him, be overpast, *præteriverit* (cf. Isa. xxvi. 20, and on the *enallage numeri* x. 10, Ges. § 147, *a*). Not as though he would then no longer stand in need of the divine protection, but he now feels himself to be specially in need of it; and therefore his chief aim is an undaunted triumphant resistance of the impending trials. The effort on his own part, however, by means of which he always anew takes refuge in this shadow, is prayer to Him who dwells above and rules the universe. עֶלְיוֹן is without the article, which it never takes; and גֹּמֵר (ver. 3*b*) is the same, because it is regularly left out before the participle, which admits of being more fully defined, Amos ix. 12, Ezek. xxi. 19 (Hitzig). He calls upon God who accomplisheth concerning, *i.e.* for him (Esth. iv. 16), who carrieth out his cause, the cause of the persecuted one; גָּמַר is transitive as in cxxxviii. 8. The LXX. renders τὸν εὐεργετήσαντά με, as though it were גָּמַל עָלַי (xiii. 6, and frequently); and even Hitzig and Hupfeld hold that the meaning is exactly the same. But although גמל and גמר fall back upon one and the same radical notion, still it is just their distinctive final letters that serve to indicate a difference of signification

---

that is strictly maintained. In ver. 4 follow futures of hope. In this instance "that which brings me deliverance" is to be supplied in thought to יִשְׁלַח (cf. xx. 3) and not יָדוֹ as in xviii. 17, cf. cxliv. 7; and this general and unmentioned object is then specialized and defined in the words "His mercy and His truth" in ver. 4c. Mercy and truth are as it were the two good spirits, which descending from heaven to earth (cf. xliii. 3) bring the divine יְשׁוּעָה to an accomplishment. The words חֵרֵף שֹׁאֲפִי standing between a and c have been drawn by the accentuators to the first half of the verse, they probably interpreting it thus: He (God) reproacheth my devourers for ever (*Sela*). But חֵרֵף always (*e.g.* Isa. xxxvii. 23) has God as its object, not as its subject. חרף שאפי is to be connected with what follows as a hypothetical protasis (Ges. § 155, 4, *a*): supposing that he who is greedy or pants for me (*inhians mihi*) slandereth, then Elohim will send His mercy and His truth. The music that becomes *forte* in between, introduces and accompanies the throbbing confidence of the apodosis.

In ver. 5, on the contrary, we may follow the interpretation of the text that is handed down and defined by the accentuation, natural as it may also be, with Luther and others, to take one's own course. Since לְבָאִם has *Zarka* (*Zinnor*) and לֹהֲטִים *Olewejored*, it is accordingly to be rendered: "My soul is in the midst of lions, I will (must) lie down with flaming ones; the children of men—their teeth are a spear and arrows." The rendering of the LXX., of Theodotion, and of the Syriac version accords with the interpunction of our text so far as both begin a new clause with ἐκοιμήθην (ודמכת, and I slept); whereas Aquila and Symmachus (taking נפשי, as it seems, as a periphrastic expression of the subject-notion placed in advance) render all as far as להטים as one clause, at least dividing the verse into two parts, just as the accentuators do, at להטים. The rendering of Aquila is ἐν μέσῳ λεαινῶν κοιμηθήσομαι λάβρων; that of Symmachus: ἐν μέσῳ λεόντων εὐθαρσῶν ἐκοιμήθην, or according to another reading, μεταξὺ λεόντων ἐκοιμήθην φλεγόντων. They are followed by Jerome, who, however, in order that he may be able to reproduce the נפשי, changes אשכבה into שכבה: *Anima mea in medio leonum dormivit ferocientium.* This construction, however, can be used in Greek and Latin, but not in Hebrew. We therefore follow the accents even in reference to the *Zarka* above לְבָאִים (a plural form that only occurs in this one passage in the Psalter, = לְבָיִם). In a general way it is to be observed that this לבאים in connection with אֶשְׁכְּבָה is not so much the accusative of the object as the accusative of the place, although it may even be said to be the customary local accusative of the object with verbs of dwelling; on שׁכב cf. Ruth iii. 8, 14, and Ps. lxxxviii. 6, Mic. vii. 5 (where at least the possibility of this construction of the verb is presupposed). But in particular it is doubtful (1) what לֹהֲטִים signifies. The rendering "flaming ones" is offered by the Targum, Saadia, and perhaps Symmachus. The verb להט obtains this signification apparently from the fundamental notion of licking or swallowing; and accordingly Theodotion renders it by ἀναλισκόντων, and Aquila most appropriately by λάβρων (a word used of a ravenous furious longing for anything). But להט nowhere means "to devour;" the poet must, therefore, in connection with להטים, have been thinking of the flaming look or the fiery jaws of the lions, and this attributive will denote figuratively their strong desire, which snorts forth as it were flames of fire. The question further arises, (2) how the cohortative אשכבה is meant to be taken. Since the cohortative sometimes expresses that which is to be done more by outward constraint than inward impulse — never, however, without willing it one's self (Ew. § 228, a)—the rendering "I must," or "therefore must I lie down," commends itself. But the contrast, which has been almost entirely overlooked, between the literal beasts of prey and the children of men, who are worse than these, requires the simple and most natural rendering of the cohortative. We need only picture to ourselves the situation. The verb שׁכב here has the sense of *cubitum ire* (iv. 9). Starting from this אשכבה we look to ver. 9, and it at once becomes clear that we have before us an evening or nightly song. David the persecuted one finds himself in the wilderness and, if we accept the testimony of the inscription, in a cave: his soul is in the midst of lions, by which he means to say that his life is exposed to them. Here bold in faith, he is resolved to lie down to sleep, feeling himself more secure among lions than among men; for the children of men, his deadly foes both in word and in deed, are worse than beasts of prey : teeth and tongue are murderous weapons. This more than brutal joy at the destruction of one's neighbour * which prevails among men, urges him to put forth the prayer that God, who in Himself is exalted above the heavens and the whole earth, would show Himself by some visible manifestation over the heavens above as the exalted One, and the prayer that His glory may be, *i.e.* may become manifest (or even: exalted be His glory, יָרוּם), over the whole earth beneath,—His glory which to His saints is a health-diffusing light, and to the heartless foes of men and God a consuming fire,—so that the whole world shall be compelled to acknowledge this glory in which His holiness manifests itself, and shall become conformed to it after everything that is hostile is overthrown.

Vers. 7–12. In this second half of the Psalm the poet refreshes himself with the thought of seeing that for which he longs and prays realized even with the dawning of the morning after this night of wretchedness. The perfect in ver. 7*d* is the perfect of certainty; the other perfects state what preceded and is now changed into the destruction of the crafty ones themselves. If the clause כָּפַף נַפְשִׁי is rendered: my soul was bowed down (cf. חָלַל, cix. 22), it forms no appropriate corollary to the crafty laying of snares. Hence כפף must be taken as transitive: he had bowed down my soul; the change of number in the mention of the enemies is very common in the Psalms relating to these trials, whether it be that the poet has one enemy κατ' ἐξοχήν before his mind or comprehends them all in one. Even the LXX. renders καὶ κατέκαμψαν τὴν ψυχήν μου, it is true, as though it were וכפפו, but can scarcely have read it thus. This line is still remarkable; one would expect for ver. 7*b* a thought parallel with ver. 7*d*, and perhaps the poet wrote כפף נפשו, his (the net-layer's) own soul bends (viz. in order to fall into the net). Then כפף like נפל would be *præt. confidentiæ*. In this certainty, to express which the music here becomes triumphantly *forte*, David's heart is confident, cheerful (Symmachus ἑδραία), and a powerful inward impulse urges him to song and harp. Although נָכוֹן may signify ready, equipped (Ex. xxxiv. 2, Job xii. 5), yet this meaning is to be

---

* Cf. Sir. xxv. 15, in the Hebrew: אין ראש מעל ראש פתן ואין חמה מעל חמה אויב (no poison exceeds the poison of the serpent, and no wrath exceeds the wrath of an enemy).

rejected here in view of li. 12, lxxviii. 37, cxii. 7: it is not appropriate to the emphatic repetition of the word. His evening mood which found expression in ver. 4, was hope of victory; the morning mood into which David here transports himself, is certainty of victory. He calls upon his soul to awake (כְּבוֹדִי as in xvi. 9, xxx. 13), he calls upon harp and cithern to awake (הַנֵּבֶל וְכִנּוֹר with one article that avails for both words, as in Jer. xxix. 3, Neh. i. 5; and עוּרָה with the accent on the *ultima* on account of the coming together of two aspirates), from which he has not parted even though a fugitive; with the music of stringed instruments and with song he will awake the not yet risen dawn, the sun still slumbering in its chamber: אָעִירָה, *expergefaciam* (not *expergiscar*), as *e.g.* in Cant. ii. 7, and as Ovid (*Metam.* xi. 597) says of the cock, *evocat auroram.** His song of praise, however, shall not resound in a narrow space where it is scarcely heard; he will step forth as the evangelist of his deliverance and of his Deliverer in the world of nations (בַעַמִּים; and the parallel word, as also in cviii. 4, cxlix. 7, is to be written בַּלְאֻמִּים with *Lamed raphatum* and *Metheg* before it); his vocation extends beyond Israel, and the events of his life are to be for the benefit of mankind. Here we perceive the self-consciousness of a comprehensive mission, which accompanied David from the beginning to the end of his royal career (*vid.* xviii. 50). What is expressed in ver. 11 is both motive and theme of the discourse among the peoples, viz. God's mercy and truth which soar high as the heavens (xxxvi. 6). That they extend even to the heavens is only an earthly conception of their infinity (cf. Eph. iii. 18). In the refrain, ver. 12, which only differs in one letter from ver. 6, the Psalm comes back to the language of prayer. Heaven and earth have a mutually involved history, and the blessed, glorious end of this history is the sunrise of the divine doxa over both, here prayed for.

---

* With reference to the above passage in the Psalms, the Talmud, *B. Berachoth* 3*b*, says, " A cithern used to hang above David's bed; and when midnight came, the north wind blew among the strings, so that they sounded of themselves; and forthwith he arose and busied himself with the Tôra until the pillar of the dawn (עַמּוּד הַשַּׁחַר) ascended." Rashi observes, " The dawn awakes the other kings; but I, said David, will awake the dawn (אֲנִי מְעוֹרֵר אֶת הַשַּׁחַר)."

PSALM LVIII.

CRY FOR VENGEANCE UPON THOSE WHO PERVERT JUSTICE.

2 DO ye really, O ye gods, speak righteousness,
  Do ye in uprightness judge the children of men?
3 Nay, in heart ye work iniquities,
  In the land ye weigh out the violence of your hands.

4 Apostate are the ungodly from the womb,
  Gone astray from the birth are the speakers of lies.
5 Poison have they after the likeness of the poison of the
        serpent,
  Like a deaf adder which stoppeth her ear,
6 That she may not hear the voice of the charmers,
  The skilful practiser of sorcery.

7 Elohim, break their teeth in their mouth,
  The teeth of the lions do Thou wrench out, Jahve!
8 They must melt away as running water;
  When he shooteth his arrows they are as though cut off.
9 (Let them be) as a snail that goes along dissolving as it goes,
  (As) the untimely birth of a woman, that hath not seen the
        sun.
10 Before, then, your pots feel the thorn,
  Whether it be raw or at boiling heat—He whirleth it away.

11 The righteous shall rejoice that he seeth vengeance,
  He shall bathe his footsteps in the blood of the ungodly.
12 And men shall confess: Verily the righteous findeth fruit,
  Verily there is a deity judging in the earth.

Their teeth, said Ps. lvii., *are spear and arrows, and their
tongue a sharp sword;* Ps. lviii. prays: *crush their teeth in
their mouth.* This prominent common thought has induced the
collector to append the one *Michtam* of David, to be sung *al-
tashcheth*, to the other. Ps. lviii., however, belongs to another
period, viz. to the time of Absalom. The incomparable boldness
of the language does not warrant us in denying it to David.

In no one Psalm do we meet with so many high-flown figures coming together within the same narrow compass. But that it is David who speaks in this Psalm is to a certain extent guaranteed by Ps. lxiv. and cxl. These three Psalms, of which the closing verses so closely resemble one another that they at once invite comparison, show that the same David who writes elsewhere so beautifully, tenderly, and clearly, is able among his manifold transitions to rise to an elevation at which his words as it were roll along like rumbling thunder through the gloomy darkness of the clouds, and more especially where they supplicate (lviii. 7) or predict (cxl. 10) the judgment of God.

The cumulative use of כְּמוֹ in different applications is peculiar to this Psalm. Its *Michtam* character becomes clearly defined in the closing verse.

Vers. 2, 3. The text of ver. 2a runs: *Do ye really dictate the silence of righteousness?* *i.e.* that before which righteousness must become silent, as the collector (cf. lvi. 1) appears to have read it (אֵלֶם = אִלּוּם, *B. Chullin* 89a). But instead of אֵלֶם it is, with Houbigant, J. D. Michaelis, Mendelssohn, and others, to be read אֵלִם (= אֵלִים, as in Ex. xv. 11), as an apostrophe of those who discharge the godlike office of rulers and judges. Both the interrogative הַאֻמְנָם (with *ŭ* as is always the case at the head of interrogative clauses), *num vere*, which proceeds from doubt as to the questionable matter of fact (Num. xxii. 37, 1 Kings viii. 27, 2 Chron. vi. 18), and the parallel member of the verse, and also the historical circumstances out of which the Psalm springs, demand this alteration. Absalom with his followers had made the administration of justice the means of stealing from David the heart of his people; he feigned to be the more impartial judge. Hence David asks: Is it then really so, ye gods (אֵלִם like אֱלֹהִים, lxxxii. 1, and here, as there, not without reference to their superhumanly proud and assumptive bearing), that ye speak righteousness, that ye judge the children of men in accordance with justice? Nay, on the contrary (אַף, *imo*, introducing an answer that goes beyond the first No), in heart (*i.e.* not merely outwardly allowing yourselves to be carried away) ye prepare villanies (פָּעַל, as in Mic. ii. 1; and עוֹלֹת, as in lxiv. 7, from עוֹלָה = עַוְלָה, xcii. 16, Job v. 16, with *ô* = *ă* + *w*), in the land ye weigh out the violence of your hands (so that consequently violence fills the balances of your pretended justice). בְּנֵי אָדָם in ver. 2b is the accusative of the object; if it had been intended as a second vocative, it ought to have been בְּנֵי־אִישׁ (iv. 3). The expression is inverted in order to make it possible to use the heavy energetic futures. בָּאָרֶץ (mostly errously marked with *Pazer*) has *Athnach*, cf. xxxv. 20, lxxvi. 12.

Vers. 4–6. After this bold beginning the boldest figures follow one another rapidly; and the first of these is that of the serpent, which is kept up longer than any of the others. The verb זוּר (cogn. סוּר) is intentionally written זוֹר in this instance in a neuter, not an active sense, plural זֹרוּ, like בֹּשׁוּ, טֹבוּ. Bakius recognises a retrospective reference to this passage in Isa. xlviii. 8. In such passages Scripture bears witness to the fact, which is borne out by experience, that there are men in whom evil from childhood onwards has a truly diabolical character, *i.e.* a selfish character altogether incapable of love. For although hereditary sinfulness and hereditary sin (guilt) are common to all men, yet the former takes the most manifold combinations and forms; and, in fact, the inheriting of sin and the complex influence of the power of evil and of the power of grace on the propagation of the human race require that it should be so. The Gospel of John more particularly teaches such a dualism of the natures of men. חֲמַת־לָמוֹ (with *Rĕbia*, as in xviii. 18a) is not the subject: the poison belonging to them, etc., but a clause by itself: poison is to them, they have poison; the construct state here, as in Lam. ii. 18, Ezek. i. 27, does not express a relation of actual union, but only a close connection. יַאְטֵם (with the orthophonic *Dagesh* which gives prominence to the *Teth* as the commencement of a syllable) is an optative future form, which is also employed as an indicative in the poetic style, *e.g.* xviii. 11. The subject of this attributive clause, continuing the adjective, is the deaf adder, such an one, viz., as makes itself deaf; and in this respect (as in their evil serpent nature) it is a figure of the self-hardening evil-doer. Then with אֲשֶׁר begins the more minute description of this adder. There is a difference even among serpents. *They* belong to the worst among them that are inaccessible to any kind of human influence. All the arts of sorcery are lost upon them. מְלַחֲשִׁים are the whisperers of magic formulæ (cf. Arabic *naffathât*, adjurations), and חוֹבֵר חֲבָרִים is one who works binding by spells, exorcism, and tying fast by magic knots (cf. חָבַר, to bind = to bewitch, cf. عقّ‎, عنّ‎, Persic *bend* = κατάδεσμος, *vid. Isaiah*, i. 118, ii. 242). The most inventive affection and the most untiring patience cannot change their mind. Nothing therefore remains to David but to hope for their removal, and to pray for it.

Vers. 7–10. The verb הָרַס is used much in the same way in ver. 7*a* as ἀράσσειν (*e.g. Iliad*, xiii. 577, ἀπὸ δὲ τρυφάλειαν ἄραξεν), which presents a similar onomatope. The form יִמָּאֲסוּ is, as in Job vii. 5, = יִמַּסוּ. The Jewish expositors, less appropriately, compare צְנַאֲכֶם, Num. xxxii. 24, and בְּזֹאוּ = בָּזְזוּ, Isa. xviii. 2, 7; שָׁאֲסָיִךְ, *Chethîb*, Jer. xxx. 16, and רָאֲמָה, Zech. xiv. 10, more nearly resemble it. The treading (bending) of the bow is here, as in lxiv. 4, transferred to the arrows (= כּוֹנֵן, xi. 2): he bends and shoots off his arrows, they shall be as though cut off in the front, *i.e.* as inoperative as if they had no heads or points (כְּמוֹ as in Isa. xxvi. 18). In ver. 9 follow two figures to which the apprecatory "let them become" is to be supplied. Or is it perhaps to be rendered: As a snail, which Thou causest to melt away, *i.e.* squashest with the foot (תֶּמֶס, as in xxxix. 12, *fut. Hiph.* of מָסָה = מָסַס), let him perish? The change of the number does not favour this; and according to the usage of the language, which is fond of construing הָלַךְ with gerunds and participles, and also with abstract nouns, *e.g.* הָלֹךְ קָרִי, הָלֹךְ תָּם, the words תֶּמֶס יַהֲלֹךְ belong together, and they are also accented accordingly: as a snail or slug which goes along in dissolution, goes on and dissolves as it goes (תֶּמֶס after the form תֵּבֵל from בָּלַל*). The snail has received its name from this apparent dissolving into slime. For שַׁבְּלוּל (with *Dag. dirimens* for שְׁבְלוּל) is the naked slimy snail or slug (Targum, according to ancient conception, זְחִיל תִּבְלָלָא "the slime-worm"), from שַׁבְלֵל, to make wet, moist.† In the second figure,

---

* In the Phœnician, the Cyprian copper mine Ταμασσός appears to have taken its name from תמם, *liquefactio* (Levy, *Phönizische Studien*, iii. 7).

† "God has created nothing without its use," says the Talmud, *B. Shabbath* 77*b*; "He has created the snail (שבלול לכתית) to heal bruises by laying it upon them:" cf. *Genesis Rabba*, ch. li. *init.*, where שבלול is explained by לימצא, סיליי, ביליי, κοχχύλη, σέσιλος, *limax*. Abraham b. David

the only sense in which נֵפֶל אֵשֶׁת belong together is "the untimely birth of a woman;" and rather than explain with the Talmud (*B. Môed katan* 6*b*) and Targum (contrary to the accents): as an abortion, a mole,* one would alter אֵשֶׁת into אִשָּׁה. But this is not necessary, since the construct form אֵשֶׁת is found also in other instances (Deut. xxi. 11, 1 Sam. xxviii. 7) out of the genitival relation, in connection with a close coordinate construction. So here, where בַּל־חָזוּ שָׁמֶשׁ, according to Job iii. 16, Eccles. vi. 3–5, is an attributive clause to נֵפֶל אֵשֶׁת (the falling away of a woman = abortions), which is used collectively (Ew. § 176, *b*). The accentuation also harmonizes here with the syntactic relation of the words. In ver. 10, אָטָד (plural in African, *i.e.* Punic, in Dioscorides ἀταδίν) is the rhamnus or buckthorn, which, like רֹתֶם, the broom, not only makes a cheerful crackling fire, but also produces an ash that retains the heat a long time, and is therefore very useful in cooking. The alternative כְּמוֹ—כְּמוֹ signifies *sive, sive,* whether the one or the other. חַי is that which is living, fresh, viz. the fresh, raw meat still having the blood in it, the opposite of מְבֻשָּׁל (1 Sam. ii. 15); חָרוֹן, a fierce heat or fire, here a boiling heat. There is no need to understand חרון metonymically, or perhaps as an adjective = *charrôn,* of boiled meat: it is a statement of the condition. The suffix of יִשְׂעָרֶנּוּ, however, refers, as being neuter, to the whole cooking apparatus, and more especially to the contents of the pots. The rendering therefore is: whether raw or in a state of heat, *i.e.* of being cooked through, He (Jahve) carries it away as with a whirlwind. Hengstenberg

---

of Fez, the cotemporary of Saadia, has explained it in his Arabico-Hebrew Lexicon by אלחלזון, the slug. Nevertheless this is properly the name of the snail with a house (נרתיק), Talmudic חִלָּזוֹן, and even at the present day in Syria and Palestine حلزون (which is pronounced *ḥalezôn*); whereas שַׁבְלוּל, in conformity with the etymon and with the figure, is the naked snail or slug. The ancient versions perhaps failed to recognise this, because the slug is not very often to be seen in hot eastern countries; but שבלול in this signification can be looked upon as traditional. The rendering "a rain-brook or mountain-torrent (Arabic *seil sâbil*) which running runs away," would, to say nothing more, give us, as Rosenmüller has already observed, a figure that has been made use of already in ver. 8.

* The mole, which was thought to have no eyes, is actually called in post-biblical Hebrew אֵשֶׁת, plur. אִישׁוֹת (*vid. Kēlim* xxi. 3).

rightly remarks, " To the raw meat correspond the immature
plots, and to the cooked the mature ones."   To us, who regard
the Psalm as belonging to the time of Absalom, and not, like
Hengstenberg, to the time of Saul, the meat in the pots is the
new kingship of Absalom.   The greater the self-renunciation
with which David at that time looked on at the ripening revolt,
disclaiming all action of his own, the stronger the confidence
with which he expected the righteous interposition of God that
did actually follow, but (as he here supposes possible) not until
the meat in the pot was almost done through; yet, on the
other side, so quickly, that the pots had scarcely felt the crackling heat which should fully cook the meat.

Vers. 11, 12.   Finally, we have a view of the results of the
judicial interposition of God.   The expression made use of to
describe the satisfaction which this gives to the righteous is
thoroughly Old Testament and warlike in its tone (cf. lxviii.
24).   David is in fact king, and perhaps no king ever remained
so long quiet in the face of the most barefaced rebellion, and
checked the shedding of blood, as David did at that time.   If,
however, blood must nevertheless flow in streams, he knows
full well that it is the blood of the partisans of his deluded son;
so that the men who were led the further astray in their judgment concerning him, the more inactive he remained, will at
last be compelled to confess that it does really repay one to be
just, and that there is really one higher than the high ones
(Eccles. v. 7 [8]), a deity (אֱלֹהִים) above the gods (אֵלִים) who,
though not forthwith, will nevertheless assuredly execute judgment in the earth.   אַךְ here, as in Job xviii. 21, Isa. xlv. 14,
retains its originally affirmative signification, which it has in
common with אָכֵן.   אֱלֹהִים is construed with the plural (Ges. §
112, rem. 3), as is frequently the case, e.g. 2 Sam. vii. 23 (where,
however, the chronicler, in 1 Chron. xvii. 21, has altered the
older text).   This is not because the heathen are speaking
(Baur), but in order to set the infinite majesty and omnipotence of the heavenly Judge in contrast with these puffed-
up " gods."

PSALM LIX.

PRAYER OF AN INNOCENT MAN WHOM MEN ARE TRYING TO TAKE.

2 DELIVER me from mine enemies, O my God,
   From those who rise up against me bear me away!
3 Deliver me from the workers of iniquity,
   And from men of blood save me!
4 For, lo, they lie in wait for my soul,
   The shameless gather themselves together against me—
   Not on account of transgression on my part and on account
      of sin, Jahve!
5 Without sin they run and make themselves ready;
   Awake to meet me, and examine!
6 And do Thou, Jahve Elohim of hosts, God of Israel,
   Stir Thyself to visit all the heathen,
   Spare not all those who are atrociously faithless.   (*Sela.*)

7 They come again at evening, they howl like dogs,
   And go the rounds in the city.
8 Lo they foam at their mouth;
   Swords are in their lips,
   For " who doth hear it?!"
9 And Thou, Jahve, laughest at them,
   Thou mockest at all the heathen.
10 *My strength, upon Thee will I wait,*
   For Elohim is my fortress.

11 My God will come to meet me with His mercy,
   Elohim will cause me to rejoice over those who lie in wait
      for me.
12 Slay them not, lest my people forget it,
   Cause them to go astray by Thy power and cast them down;
   Thou art our shield, O Lord!
13 The sin of their mouth is the word of their lips,
   Therefore let them be ensnared in their pride,
   And on account of the curse and the deceit which they
      utter.

14 Destroy in wrath, destroy, that they may be no more,
   And that they may know that Elohim is Ruler in Jacob
   Unto the ends of the earth!   (*Sela.*)

15 They come again at evening, they howl like dogs,
   And go the rounds in the city.
16 They wander to and fro in order to eat;
   If they are not satisfied, they stay over night—
17 But as for me, I shall sing of Thy strength,
   And exult, in the morning, over Thy mercy;
   That Thou hast been a fortress to me,
   And a refuge in the day when I was afraid.
18 *My strength, to Thee will I harp,*
   For Elohim is my fortress, my merciful God.

This *Michtam*, after the melody *Al-tashcheth*, coinciding witn lvii. 5 and lviii. 7 in the figure used in ver. 8, is the earliest among the Davidic Psalms which are dated from the time of Saul's persecution. *When Saul sent and they* (those who were sent by him) *watched the house in order to slay him* (David); it therefore belongs to the time spoken of in 1 Sam. xix. 11 sqq This inscription is no more intended to imply that the Psalm was composed on that night before the flight, which was rendered possible by the artifice of Michal, than the inscription of Ps. li. is meant to imply that the origin of the Psalm was coincident with the arrival of Nathan. The בְּ of such inscriptions only sets forth in a general way the historical groundwork of the song. If we consider the contents of the Psalm from this point of view, we shall obtain a tolerably distinct picture of the situation. We must imagine that Saul, even before he issued that command to watch David's house the night through and to slay him in the morning, *i.e.* to assassinate him behind Michal's back (1 Sam. xix. 11), sought to get rid of him in some more secret way; that the venal men of his court, themselves not less ill-disposed towards David, had offered him their hand for the deed; and that in consequence of this, great activity, which was probably seen through by him whose life was threatened, was observable in Gibea, and that more especially every evening, when the bandits strolled through the city in order to meet with the dreaded rival and give him his death-blow. The Psalms and the Prophets are often the medium through which we gain a deeper insight into events which are only sketched in the historical books after their most prominent outward features.

In consideration of the fact that the description of the nightly proceedings of the enemies is repeated after the manner of a refrain, and that the poet in ver. 17 contrasts his believingly joyous prospects for the coming morning with the ineffectual ardour with which they pass the night patrolling the streets, Psalm lix. seems to be an evening song belonging to those perilous days spent in Gibea.

Vers. 2—10. First part. As far as ver. 4 we recognise strains familiar in the Psalms. The enemies are called מִתְקוֹמְמַי as in Job xxvii. 7, cf. Ps. xvii. 7; עַזִּים as shameless, עַזֵּי פָנִים or עַזֵּי נֶפֶשׁ; as in Isa. lvi. 11, on account of their bold shameless greediness, dogs. On לֹא in a subordinate clause, *vid.* Ewald, § 286, *g*: without there being transgression or sin on my side, which might have caused it. The suffix (transgression on my part) is similar to xviii. 24. בְּלִי־עָוֹן (cf. Job xxxiv. 6) is a similar adverbial collateral definition: without there existing any sin, which ought to be punished. The energetic future *jeruzûn* depicts those who servilely give effect to the king's evil caprice; they run hither and thither as if attacking and put themselves in position. הִתְכּוֹנֵן = הִכּוֹנֵן, like the *Hithpa.* הִכַּפָּה, Prov. xxvi. 26, the *Hothpa.* הֻכַּבֵּס, Lev. xiii. 55 sq., and the *Nithpa.* נִכַּפֵּר, Deut. xxi. 8. Surrounded by such a band of assassins, David is like one besieged, who sighs for succour; and he calls upon Jahve, who seems to be sleeping and inclined to abandon him, with that bold עוּרָה לִקְרָאתִי וּרְאֵה, to awake to meet him, *i.e.* to join him with His help like a relieving army, and to convince Himself from personal observation of the extreme danger in which His charge finds himself. The continuation was obliged to be expressed by וְאַתָּה, because a special appeal to God interposes between עוּרָה and הָקִיצָה. In the emphatic "Thou," however, after it has been once expressed, is implied the conditional character of the deliverance by the absolute One. And each of the divine names made use of in this lengthy invocation, which corresponds to the deep anxiety of the poet, is a challenge, so to speak, to the ability and will-

ingness, the power and promise of God.   The juxtaposition
Jahve Elohim Tsebaoth (occurring, besides this instance, in
lxxx. 5, 20, lxxxiv. 9), which is peculiar to the Elohimic Psalms,
is to be explained by the consideration that *Elohim* had become
a proper name like *Jahve*, and that the designation *Jahve
Tsebaoth*, by the insertion of *Elohim* in accordance with the
style of the Elohimic Psalms, is made still more imposing and
solemn; and now צבאות is a genitive dependent not merely
upon יהוה but upon יהוה אלהים (similar to lvi. 1*a*, Isa. xxviii. 1*b*;
Symbolæ, p. 15).   אֱלֹהֵי יִשְׂרָאֵל is in apposition to this threefold
name of God.   The poet evidently reckons himself as belonging to an Israel from which he excludes his enemies, viz. the
true Israel which is in reality the people of God.   Among the
heathen, against whom the poet invokes God's interposition,
are included the heathen-minded in Israel; this at least is the
view which brings about this extension of the prayer.   Also in
connection with the words כָּל־בֹּגְדֵי אָוֶן the poet, in fact, has chiefly
before his mind those who are immediately round about him
and thus disposed.   It is those who act treacherously from
extreme moral nothingness and worthlessness (אָוֶן *genit. epexeg.*).
The music, as *Sela* directs, here becomes more boisterous; it
gives intensity to the strong cry for the judgment of God; and
the first unfolding of thought of this *Michtam* is here brought
to a close.

The second begins by again taking up the description of
the movements of the enemy which was begun in vers. 4, 5.
We see at a glance how here ver. 7 coincides with ver. 5, and
ver. 8 with ver. 4, and ver. 9 with ver. 6.   Hence the imprecatory rendering of the futures of ver. 7 is not for a moment
to be entertained.   By day the emissaries of Saul do not
venture to carry out their plot, and David naturally does not
run into their hands.   They therefore come back in the evening, and that evening after evening (cf. Job xxiv. 14); they
snarl or howl like dogs (הָמָה, used elsewhere of the growling of
the bear and the cooing of the dove; it is distinct from נבח,

نَبَّ, نبح, to bark, and כלב, to yelp), because they do not want
to betray themselves by loud barking, and still cannot altogether
conceal their vexation and rage; and they go their rounds in
the city (like סוֹבֵב בָּעִיר, Cant. iii. 2, cf. *supra* lv. 11), in order

to cut off their victim from flight, and perhaps, what would be
very welcome to them, to run against him in the darkness.
The further description in ver. 8 follows them on this patrol.
What they belch out or foam out is to be inferred from the
fact that swords are in their lips, which they, as it were, draw
so soon as they merely move their lips. Their mouth overflows
with murderous thoughts and with slanders concerning David,
by which they justify their murderous greed to themselves as
if there were no one, viz. no God, who heard it. But Jahve,
from whom nothing, as with men, can be kept secret, laughs
at them, just as He makes a mockery of all heathen, to whom
this murderous band, which fears the light and is unworthy of
the Israelitish name, is compared. This is the primary passage
to xxxvii. 13, ii. 4; for Ps. lix. is perhaps the oldest of the
Davidic Psalms that have come down to us, and therefore also
t‹ e earliest monument of Israelitish poetry in which the divine
name *Jahve Tsebaoth* occurs; and the chronicler, knowing that
it was the time of Samuel and David that brought it into use,
uses this name only in the life of David. Just as this strophe
opened in ver. 7 with a distich that recurs in ver. 15, so it also
closes now in ver. 10 with a distich that recurs below in ver.
18, and that is to be amended according to the text of that
passage. For all attempts to understand עֻזּוֹ as being genuine
prove its inaccuracy. With the old versions it has to be read
עֻזִּי; but as for the rest, אֶשְׁמֹרָה must be retained in accordance
with the usual variation found in such refrains: my strength,
Thee will I regard (1 Sam. xxvi. 15; observe, 2 Sam. xi. 16),
or upon Thee will I wait (cf. לְ, cxxx. 6); *i.e.* in the consciousness of my own feebleness, tranquil and resigned, I will look
for Thine interposition on my behalf.

Vers. 11–18. In this second half of the Psalm the cry of
fear is hushed. Hope reigns, and anger burns more fiercely.
The *Kerî* says that ver. 11a is to be read: אֱלֹהֵי חַסְדִּי יְקַדְּמֵנִי, my
gracious God will anticipate me,—but with what? This ques-
tion altogether disappears if we retain the *Chethîb* and point
אֱלֹהֵי חַסְדּוֹ: my God will anticipate me with His mercy (cf. xxi.
4), *i.e.* will meet me bringing His mercy without any effort of
mine. Even the old translators have felt that חסדו must belong to the verb as a second object. The LXX. is perfectly
correct in its rendering, ὁ Θεός μου τὸ ἔλεος αὐτοῦ προφθάσει

με. The *Keri* has come into existence in looking to ver. 18, according to which it seems as though אֱלֹהֵי חַסְדִּי ought to be added to the refrain, ver. 10 (cf. a similar instance in xlii. 6, 7). But ver. 11*a* would be stunted by doing this, and it accords with Biblical poetic usage that the refrain in ver. 18 should be climactic in comparison with ver. 10 (just as it also does not altogether harmonize in its first half); so that Olshausen's proposal to close ver. 10 with אלהי חסדי and to begin ver. 11 with חסדו (cf. lxxix. 8) is only just to be put on record. The prayer "slay them not" does not contradict the prayer that follows for their destruction. The poet wishes that those who lie in wait for him, before they are totally swept away, may remain for a season before the eyes of his people as an example of punishment. In accordance with this, הֲנִיעֵמוֹ, by a comparison of the *Hiph.* in Num. xxxii. 13, and of the *Kal* in ver. 16, cix. 10, is to be rendered: cause them to wander about (Targum, cf. *Genesis Rabba*, ch. xxxviii. *init.*, טַלְטְלֵמוֹ); and in connection with בְּחֵילְךָ one is involuntarily reminded of x. 10, 14, and is tempted to read בְּחֶלְךָ or בְּחָלְךָ: cause them to wander

about in adversity or wretchedness, = عُمْر حَالِك, *vita caliginosa h. e. misera*), and more especially since בחיל occurs nowhere else instead of בִּזְרֹעֶךָ or בִּימִינְךָ. But the *Jod* in בחילך is unfavourable to this supposition; and since the martial apostrophe of God by "our shield" follows, the choice of the word is explained by the consideration that the poet conceives of the power of God as an army (Joel ii. 25), and perhaps thinks directly of the heavenly host (Joel iv. [iii.] 11), over which the Lord of Hosts holds command (Hitzig). By means of this He is first of all to cause them to go astray (נָע וָנָד, Gen. iv. 12), then utterly to cast them down (lvi. 8). The Lord (אֲדֹנָי) is to do this, as truly as He is Israel's shield against all the heathen and all pseudo-Israelites who have become as heathen. The first member of ver. 13 is undoubtedly meant descriptively: "the sin of their mouth (the sin of the tongue) is the word of their lips" (with the dull-toned suffix *mo*, in the use of which Ps. lix. associates itself with the Psalms of the time of Saul, lvi., xi., xvii., xxii., xxxv., lxiv.). The combination וְיִלָּכְדוּ בִגְאוֹנָם, however, more readily suggests parallel passages like Prov. xi. 6 than Prov. vi. 2; and moreover the מִן of the expression וּמֵאָלָה וּמִכַּחַשׁ, which is without example in connection with סִפֵּר, and, taken as expressing the motive (Hupfeld), ought to be joined with some designations of the disposition of mind, is best explained as an appended statement of the reason for which they are to be ensnared, so that consequently יְסַפֵּרוּ (cf. lxix. 27, lxiv. 6) is an attributive clause; nor is this contrary to the accentuation, if one admits the *Munach* to be a transformation of *Mugrash*. It is therefore to be rendered: "let them, then, be taken in their pride, and on account of the curse and deceit which they wilfully utter." If, by virtue of the righteousness of the Ruler of the world, their sin has thus become their fall, then, after they have been as it were a warning example to Israel, God is utterly to remove them out of the way, in order that they (it is unnecessary to suppose any change of subject), while perishing, may perceive that Elohim is Ruler in Jacob (בְּ, used elsewhere of the object, *e.g.* Mic. v. 1, is here used of the place of dominion), and as in Jacob, so from thence unto the ends of the earth (לְ like עַל, xlviii. 11) wields the sceptre. Just like the first group of the first part, this first group of the second part also closes with *Sela*.

The second group opens like the second group in the first part, but with this exception, that here we read וַיָּשֻׁבוּ, which loosely connects it with what precedes, whereas there it is יָשׁוּבוּ. The poet's gaze is again turned towards his present straitened condition, and again the pack of dogs by which Saul is hunting him present themselves to his mind. הֵמָּה points towards an antithesis that follows, and which finds its expression in וַאֲנִי. וַיָּלִינוּ and לַבֹּקֶר stand in direct contrast to one another, and in addition to this לָעֶרֶב has preceded. The reading of the LXX. (Vulgate, Luther, [and authorized version]), καὶ γογγύσουσιν = וַיָּלִּינוּ or וַיַּלִּינוּ, is thereby proved to be erroneous. But if וַיָּלִינוּ is the correct reading, then it follows that we have to take ver. 16 not as foretelling what will take place, but as describing that which is present; so that consequently the *fut. consec.* (as is frequently the case apart from any historical connection) is only a consecutive continuation of יְנוּעוּן (for which the *Keri* has יְנִיעוּן; the form that was required in ver. 12, but is inadmissible here): they wander up and down (נוּעַ as in cix. 10, cf. נוּד, Job xv. 23) to eat (that is to say, seeking after food); and if they are not satisfied, they pass the night, *i.e.* remain, eager for food

and expecting it, over night on the spot. This interpretation
is the most natural, the simplest, and the one that harmonizes
best not only with the text before us (the punctuation יִשְׂבְּעוּ,
not יִשְׂבָּעוּ, gives the member of the clause the impress of being
a protasis), but also with the situation. The poet describes
the activity of his enemies, and that by completing or re-
touching the picture of their comparison to dogs : he himself
is the food or prey for which they are so eager, and which they
would not willingly allow to escape them, and which they
nevertheless cannot get within their grasp. Their morbid
desire remains unsatisfied : he, however, in the morning, is
able to sing of the power of God, which protects him, and
exultantly to praise God's loving-kindness, which satiates and
satisfies him (xc. 14) ; for in the day of fear, which to him is
now past, God was his inaccessible stronghold, his unapproachable asylum. To this God, then, even further the play of his
harp shall be directed (אֲזַמְּרָה), just as was his waiting or hoping
(אֶשְׁמֹרָה, ver. 10).

PSALM LX.

DRILL PSALM AFTER A LOST BATTLE.

3 ELOHIM, Thou hast cast us off, Thou hast scattered us,
 Thou hast been angry, restore us again !
4 Thou hast made the land to tremble, Thou hast torn it
  asunder,
 Heal its breaches, for it tottereth !!
5 Thou hast made Thy people experience a hard thing,
 Thou hast given us wine to drink to intoxication.
6 Thou hast given those who fear Thee a banner
 To lift themselves up on account of the truth.   (*Sela.*)
7 In order that Thy beloved may be delivered,
 Save now with Thy right hand and answer me !!!

8 Elohim hath promised in His holiness :
 I shall rejoice, I shall portion out Shechem,
 And measure out the valley of Succoth.

9 Mine is Gilead and mine Manasseh,
  And Ephraim is the helm of my head,
  Judah is my sceptre,
10 Moab is my wash-pot,
  Upon Edom I cast my shoe.
  Cry out concerning me, O Philistia!

11 Who will conduct me to the fortified city?
  Who will bring me to Edom?!
12 Hast not Thou, Elohim, cast us off,
  And goest not forth, Elohim, with our armies?—
13 Grant us deliverance from the oppressor;
  Yea, vain is the help of man.
14 In Elohim shall we obtain the victory,
  And He will tread down our oppressors.

This last of the Elohimic *Michtammîm* of David is dated from the time of the Syro-Ammonitish war: *When he* (David) *waged war* (*Hiph.* of נצה, to pull, to seize by the hair) *with* (אֶת like עַל in Num. xxvi. 9; according to Ben-Asher, with *Segol* instead of *Makkeph* here, as in xlvii. 5, Prov. iii. 12, three passages which are noted by the Masora) *Aram of the two rivers* (the people of the land of the twin streams, Μεσοποταμία) *and with Aram Zobah* (probably between the Euphrates and Orontes north-east of Damascus), *and Joab returned* (וַיָּשָׁב, transition from the infinitive to the finite verb, Ges. § 132, rem. 2) *and smote Edom in the Valley of Salt* (the Edomitish *Ghor*, i.e. the salt plain, some ten miles wide, at the southern extremity of the Dead Sea) *with twelve thousand men*. This historical inscription comes from an historical work which gave the Psalm in this connection. It is not taken out of any of the histories that have been preserved to us. For both in 2 Sam. viii. 13 and in 1 Chron. xviii. 12 we find the number eighteen thousand instead of twelve. In the former passage, in which עָשָׂה שֵׁם is substantially equivalent to the Roman *triumphum agere*, we have to read אֶת־אֱדֹם after the inscription of our Psalm instead of אֶת־אֲרָם. It is, however, still more probable that the words וַיַּךְ אֶת־אֱדֹם (LXX. ἐπάταξε τὴν Ἰδουμαίαν) have accidentally fallen out. The fact that here in the Psalm the victory over the Edomites is ascribed to Joab, in the Chronicles to Abshai

(Abishai), and in 2 Sam. ch. viii. to David, is a difference which may easily be reconciled by the consideration that the army of David was under the supreme command of Joab, and this battle in the Valley of Salt was fought against the Edomites by Joab indirectly through his brother (cf. 2 Sam. x. 10).

The inscription carries us into the time of the greatest, longest, and most glorious of David's wars, that with the Ammonites, which, so far as these were concerned, ended in the second year in the conquest of Rabbah (*vid.* Ps. xxi.), and with their Aramæan allies, among whom Hadadezer, the ruler of the powerful kingdom of Zobah, was defeated in the first year at Chêlam on the other side the Jordan. Then when, in the second year, he endeavoured to fortify himself anew in the districts on the banks of the Euphrates, he was completely subjugated together with the Syrians who had come to his assistance. Thus are the accounts of Aramæan wars related in 2 Sam. ch. viii. and x.–xii. to be combined. Whilst, now, the arms of David were making such triumphant progress in the north, the Edomites in the south had invaded the land which was denuded of troops, and here a new war, which jeopardized all the results that had been gained in the north, awaited the victorious army. Ps. lx. refers more especially to this Edomitish war. Hengstenberg is wrong when he infers from the inscription that it was composed after the victory in the Valley of Salt and before the conquest of Idumæa. The inscription only in a general way gives to the Psalm its historical setting. It was composed before the victory in the Valley of Salt, and presupposes the Israelitish south had been at that time grievously laid waste by the Edomites, against whom they were unable to oppose an adequate force. We may also infer from other indications how the occupation of the neighbouring and brother-country by the Edomites called for vengeance against them; *vid.* on Ps. xliv. That Korahitic Psalm may have been composed after the Davidic Psalm, and is designedly, by ver. 10, brought into relationship with it. In the cento Ps. cviii. vers. 7–14 correspond to lx. 7–14.

The *Michtam* character of the Psalm manifests itself both in the fact that a divine oracle is unfolded in it, and also in the fact that the language of complaint, " Elohim, Thou hast cast us off" (cf. xliv. 10), is repeated as its favourite utterance. Concerning עַל־שׁוּשַׁן עֵדוּת, after "*A Lily is the testimony*" (or "*The Lily of the testimony*"), vid. on xlv. 1. The addition of לְלַמֵּד is to be interpreted according to לְלַמֵּד בְּנֵי־יְהוּדָה קָשֶׁת, 2 Sam. i. 18: the song is thereby appointed to be sung in connection with the practice of the bow. The elegy on Saul and Jonathan was suited to this by reason of the praise which is therein given to the bow of Jonathan, the favourite weapon of that brave warrior, and by the indirect remembrance of the skilful Philistine archers, who brought a disgrace upon the name of Israel in the battle on Gilboa, that needed as speedily as possible to be wiped out. Ps. lx., this most martial of all the Psalms, is also a song at the practice of arms, which was designed to inflame and to hallow the patriotic martial ardour of the young men when they were being exercised.

Hengstenberg and others, who reckon according to the Masoretic verses, divide the Psalm into three strophes of four Masoretic verses each. The fact that the use made of Ps. lx. in Ps. cviii. begins with ver. 7, למען יחלצון, lends some colour to this division, which is also strengthened by the *Sela*. Nevertheless vers. 6 and 7 belong inseparably together.

Vers. 3–7. This first strophe contains complaint and prayer; and establishes the prayer by the greatness of the need and Israel's relationship to God. The sense in which פְּרַצְתָּנוּ is intended becomes clear from 2 Sam. v. 20, where David uses this word of the defeat of the Philistines, and explains it figuratively. The word signifies to break through what has hitherto been a compact mass, to burst, blast, scatter, disperse. The prayer is first of all timidly uttered in תְּשׁוֹבֵב לָנוּ in the form of a wish; then in רְפָה (ver. 4b) and הוֹשִׁיעָה (ver. 7b) it waxes more and more eloquent. שׁוֹבֵב ל here signifies to grant restoration (like הֵנִיחַ ל, to give rest; xxiii. 3, Isa. lviii. 12). The word also signifies to make a turn, to turn one's self away, in which sense, however, it cannot be construed with ל.

On פְּצַמְתָּהּ Dunash has already compared فصم, *rumpere, scindere*, and Mose ha-Darshan the Targumic פְּצַם = קְרַע, Jer. xxii. 14. The deep wounds which the Edomites had inflicted upon the country, are after all a wrathful visitation of God Himself—

reeling or intoxicating wine, or as יֵין תַּרְעֵלָה (not יַיִן), properly
conceived of, is : wine which is sheer intoxication (an apposition
instead of the genitive attraction, *vid.* on Isa. xxx. 20), is reached
out by Him to His people. The figure of the intoxicating cup
has passed over from the Psalms of David and of Asaph to the
prophets (*e.g.* Isa. li. 17, 21). A kindred thought is expressed
in the proverb : *Quem Deus perdere vult, eum dementat.* All
the preterites as far as הִשְׁקִיתָנוּ (ver. 5*b*) glance back plaintively
at that which has been suffered. But ver. 6 cannot be thus
intended ; for to explain with Ewald and Hitzig, following the
LXX., "Thou hast set up a banner for those who reverence
Thee, not for victory, but for flight," is inadmissible, notwithstanding the fact that נוּס מִפְּנֵי קֶשֶׁת is a customary phrase and
the inscribed לְלַמֵּד is favourable to the mention of the bow.
For (1) The words, beginning with נָתַתָּ, do not sound like an
utterance of something worthy of complaint,—in this case it
ought at least to have been expressed by אַךְ לְהִתְנוֹסֵס (only for
flight, not for victory) ; (2) it is more than improbable that the
bow, instead of being called קֶשֶׁת (feminine of the Arabic masculine *kaus*), is here, according to an incorrect Aramaic form of
writing, called קֹשֶׁט, whereas this word in its primary form קֹשְׁטְ
(Prov. xxii. 21) corresponds to the Aramaic קוּשְׁטָא not in the
signification "a bow," but (as it is also intended in the Targum
of our passage) in the signification "truth" (Arabic *kist* of
strict unswerving justice, root קשׁ, to be hard, strong, firm ; just
as, *vice versâ*, the word *sidk*, coming from a synonymous root, is
equivalent to "truth"). We therefore take the perfect predication, like ver. 4*a*, as the foundation of the prayer which
follows : Thou hast given those who fear Thee a banner to
muster themselves (*sich aufpanieren*), *i.e.* to raise themselves as
around a standard or like a standard, on account of the truth
—help then, in order that Thy beloved ones may be delivered,
with Thy right hand, and answer me. This rendering, in
accordance with which ver. 6 expresses the good cause of Israel
in opposition to its enemies, is also favoured by the heightened
effect of the music, which comes in here, as *Sela* prescribes.
The reflexive התנוסס here therefore signifies not, as *Hithpal.* of
נוס, "to betake one's self to flight," but "to raise one's self "—
a signification on behalf of which we cannot appeal to Zech.
ix. 16, where מִתְנוֹסְסוֹת is apparently equivalent to מִתְנוֹצְצוֹת,

"sparkling," but which here results from the juxtaposition with

נֵס (cf. נָסָה, iv. 7), inasmuch as נֵס itself, like نَصّ, is so called

from נָסַס, نَصّ, to set up, raise, whether it be that the *Hithpo.*
falls back upon the *Kal* of the verb or that it is intended as a
denominative (to raise one's self as a banner, *sich aufpanieren*).*
It is undeniable that not merely in later (*e.g.* Neh. v. 15), but
also even in older Hebrew, מִפְּנֵי denotes the reason and motive
(*e.g.* Deut. xxviii. 20).   Moreover Ps. xliv. is like a commentary on this מִפְּנֵי קֹשֶׁט, in which the consciousness of the
people of the covenant revelation briefly and comprehensively
expresses itself concerning their vocation in the world.   Israel
looks upon its battle against the heathen, as now against Edom,
as a rising for the truth in accordance with its mission.   By
reason of the fact and of the consciousness which are expressed
in ver. 6, arises the prayer in ver. 7, that Jahve would interpose to help and to rescue His own people from the power
of the enemy.   יְמִינְךָ is instrumental (*vid.* on iii. 5).   It is to
be read עֲנֵנִי according to the *Kerî*, as in cviii. 7, instead of
עֲנֵנוּ; so that here the king of Israel is speaking, who, as he
prays, stands in the place of his people.

Vers. 8–10.   A divine utterance, promising him victory,
which he has heard, is expanded in this second strophe.   By
reason of this he knows himself to be in the free and inalienable possession of the land, and in opposition to the neighbouring nations, Moab, Edom, and Philistia, to be the victorious
lord to whom they must bow.   The grand word of promise in
2 Sam. vii. 9 sq. is certainly sufficient in itself to make this
feeling of certainty intelligible, and perhaps vers. 8–10 are only

---

* [This expression well illustrates the power of the German language
in coining words, so that the language critically dealt with may be exactly
reproduced to the German mind.   The meaning will at once be clear when
we inform our readers that *Panier* is a banner or standard; the reflexive
denominative, therefore, in imitation of the Hebrew, *sich aufpanieren* signifies to " up-standard one's self," to raise one's self up after the manner of a
standard, which being " done into English" may mean to rally (as around
a standard).   We have done our best above faithfully to convey the meaning of the German text, and we leave our readers to infer from this illustration the difficulties with which translators have not unfrequently to
contend.—Tr.]

a pictorial reproduction of that utterance; but it is also possible that at the time when Edom threatened the abandoned bordering kingdom, David received an oracle from the high priest by means of the Urim and Thummim, which assured him of the undiminished and continued possession of the Holy Land and the sovereignty over the bordering nations. That which God speaks "in His holiness" is a declaration or a promise for the sure fulfilment and inviolability of which He pledges His holiness; it is therefore equal to an oath "by His holiness" (lxxxix. 36, Amos iv. 2). The oracle does not follow in a direct form, for it is not God who speaks (as Olshausen thinks), to whom the expression אֶעְלֹזָה is unbecoming, nor is it the people (as De Wette and Hengstenberg), but the king, since what follows refers not only to the districts named, but also to their inhabitants. כִּי might have stood before אעלזה, but without it the mode of expression more nearly resembles the Latin *me exultaturum esse* (cf. xlix. 12). Shechem in the centre of the region on this side the Jordan, and the valley of Succoth in the heart of the region on the other side, form the beginning; for

there is not only a ساكوت (the name both of the eminence and of the district) on the west side of the Jordan south of Beisân (Scythopolis), but there must also have been another on the other side of the Jordan (Gen. xxxiii. 17 sq., Judg. viii. 4 sq.) which has not as yet been successfully traced. It lay in the vicinity of Jabbok (*ez-Zerka*), about in the same latitude with Shechem (Sichem), south-east of Scythopolis, where Estori ha-Parchi contends that he had found traces of it not far from the left bank of the Jordan. Josh. xiii. 27 gives some information concerning the עֵמֶק (valley) of Succoth. The town and the valley belonged to the tribe of Gad. Gilead, side by side with Manasseh, ver. 9*a*, comprehends the districts belonging to the tribes of Gad and Reuben. As far as ver. 9*c*, therefore, free dominion in the cis- and trans-Jordanic country is promised to David. The proudest predicates are justly given to Ephraim and Judah, the two chief tribes; the former, the most numerous and powerful, is David's helmet (the protection of his head), and Judah his staff of command (מְחֹקֵק, the command-giving = staff of command, as in Gen. xlix. 10, Num. xxi. 18); for Judah, by virtue of the ancient promise, is the royal tribe of the people

who are called to the dominion of the world. This designation
of Judah as the king's staff or sceptre and the marshal's baton
shows that it is the king who is speaking, and not the people.
To him, the king, who has the promise, are Moab, Edom, and
Philistia subject, and will continue so. Moab the boastful
serves him as a wash-basin;* Edom the crafty and malicious
is forcibly taken possession of by him and obliged to submit;
and Philistia the warlike is obliged to cry aloud concerning
him, the irresistible ruler. סִיר רַחַץ is a wash-pot or basin in
distinction from a seething-pot, which is also called סִיר. The
throwing of a shoe over a territory is a sign of taking forcible
possession, just as the taking off of the shoe (חֲלִיצָה) is a sign of
the renunciation of one's claim or right: the shoe is in both
instances the symbol of legal possession.† The rendering of
the last line, with Hitzig and Hengstenberg: "exult concerning me, O Philistia," i.e. hail me, though compelled to do so, as
king, is forbidden by the עָלַי, instead of which we must have
looked for לִי. The verb רוּעַ certainly has the general signification "to break out into a loud cry," and like the *Hiph.* (e.g.

---

* A royal attendant, the *tasht-dâr*, cup- or wash-basin-bearer, carried
the wash-basin for the Persian king both when in battle and on a journey
(*vid.* Spiegel, *Avesta* ii. LXIX.). Moab, says the Psalmist, not merely
waits upon him with the wash-basin, but himself serves as such to him.

† The sandal or the shoe, I. as an *object* of وَطِئ, of treading down,
oppressing, signifies metaphorically, (1) a man that is weak and incapable
of defending himself against oppression, since one says, *ma kuntu naʿlan,*
I am no shoe, *i.e.* no man that one can tread under his feet; (2) a wife
(*quæ subjicitur*), since one says, *gʾalaaʿ naʿlahu,* he has taken off his shoe,
i.e. cast off his wife (cf. Lane under حَذَآءَ, which even signifies a shoe
and a wife). II. As an *instrument* of وَطِئ, tropically of the act of oppressing and of reducing to submission, the نَعْل serves as a symbol of subjugation to the dominion of another. Rosenmüller (*Das alte und neue
Morgenland,* No. 483) shows that the Abyssinian kings, at least, cast a shoe
upon anything as a sign of taking forcible possession. Even supposing
this usage is based upon the above passage of the Psalms, it proves, however, that a people thinking and speaking after the Oriental type associated
this meaning with the casting of a shoe upon anything.—FLEISCHER. Cf.
Wetzstein's Excursus at the end of this volume

Isa. xv. 4) the *Hithpal.* can also be used of a loud outcry at
violence.

Vers. 11–14. The third strophe reverts to prayer; but
the prayer now breathes more freely with a self-conscious
courage for the strife. The fortified city (עִיר מָצוֹר) is not
Rabbath Ammon; but, as becomes evident from the parallel
member of the verse and 2 Kings xiv. 7, the Idumæan chief
city of Selaʿ (סֶלַע) or Petra (*vid.* Knobel on Gen. xxxvi. 42,
cf. Ps. xxxi. 22, 2 Chron. viii. 5, xi. 5 together with xiv. 5).
The wish: who will conduct me = Oh that one would conduct
me (Ges. § 136, 1)! expresses a martial desire, joyful at the prospect of victory; concerning מִי נָחַנִי, *quis perduxerit me,* vid. on
xi. 3. What follows is not now to be rendered: Not Thou (who
but Thou), Elohim, who . . . (Hitzig)—for in order to have been
understood thus and not as in ver. 3, xliv. 10, the poet could
not have omitted אֲשֶׁר—on the contrary, the interrogatory הֲלֹא
is the foundation on which the supplicatory הָבָה is raised. The
king of Israel is hard pressed in the battle, but he knows that
victory comes from above, from the God who has hitherto in
anger refused it to His people, inasmuch as He has given
power to Edom to break through the defensive forces of Israel
(*vid.* xliv. 10). עֶזְרָת (not עֶזְרָת = עֶזְרָה) is, as in cviii. 13, equivalent to עֶזְרָתָה The view that it is equal to עֶזְרָתִי, the suffix being
cast away, is not confirmed in this instance, *vid.* on xvi. 6, cf.
iii. 3. How vain is human succour, has been seen only very
recently in the case of the kings of Zobah and Ammon, who
have succumbed in spite of their confederates. Israel prays
for its victorious power from above, and also obtains it thence,
as is most confidently expressed in ver. 14. עָשָׂה חַיִל, to do
valiantly, to show valour, is equivalent to: to be victorious, as
in cxviii. 16. In God does Israel conquer, and God, who is
in Israel, will by means of Israel tread down Edom in accordance with its deserts.

PSALM LXI.

PRAYER AND THANKSGIVING OF AN EXPELLED KING ON HIS WAY BACK TO THE THRONE.

2 OH hear, Elohim, my plaintive cry,
 Oh hearken to my prayer!
3 From the end of the earth I cry to Thee when my heart
    languisheth,
 Up a rock too high for me do Thou lead me;
4 For Thou hast become a refuge for me,
 A strong tower, hiding me from the enemy.
5 I shall dwell in Thy tabernacle for æons,
 I shall find refuge in the protection of Thy wings.   (*Sela.*)

6 For Thou, Elohim, hast hearkened to my vows,
 Thou hast given back the heritage of those who fear Thy
    name.
7 Days to the days of the king do Thou add,
 Let his years be as a generation and a generation.
8 Let him remain for ever in the presence of Elohim—
 Mercy and truth do Thou appoint to preserve him—
9 So will I harp unto Thy name for it for ever,
 That I may pay my vows day by day.

The Davidic *Michtammîm* are now ended, and there follows a short Davidic song עַל־נְגִינַת. Does this expression mean "with the accompaniment of stringed instruments?" Not strictly, for this is expressed by the inscription בִּנְגִינוֹת (iv. 1, cf. Isa. xxx. 29, 32). But the formula may signify "*upon the music of stringed instruments,*" *i.e.* upon stringed instruments. And this is more probable than that נְגִינַת is the beginning of a standard song. The termination *ath* is not necessarily the construct state. It was the original feminine termination; and the prevailing one in Phœnician.

Some expositors, like Köster, Ewald, Hitzig, and Olshausen, feel themselves here also bound, by reason of the לדוד of the inscription, to seek a place for this Psalm as far down as the Babylonian Exile and the times of the Ptolemies and the

Seleucidæ.   Hupfeld deals somewhat more kindly with the
לדוד in this instance, and Böttcher (*De Inferis*, p. 204) refutes
the hypotheses set up in its stead in order finally to decide in
favour of the idea that the king of whom the Psalm speaks is
Cyrus—which is only another worthless bubble.   We abide
by the proudly ignored לדוד, and have as our reward a much
more simple interpretation of the Psalm, without being obliged
with Ewald to touch it up by means of a verse of one's own
invention interwoven between verses 5 and 6.   It is a Psalm
of the time of Absalom, composed in Mahanaim or elsewhere
in Gilead, when the army of the king had smitten the rebels
in the wood of Ephraim.   It consists of two parts of eight
lines.

Vers. 2–5.   Hurled out of the land of the Lord in the
more limited sense* into the country on the other side of the
Jordan, David felt only as though he were banished to the
extreme corner of the earth (not: of the land, cf. xlvi. 10,
Deut. xxviii. 49, and frequently), far from the presence of God
(Hengstenberg).   It is the feeling of homelessness and of
separation from the abode of God by reason of which the
distance, in itself so insignificant (just as was the case with the
exiles later on), became to him immeasurably great.   For he
still continually needed God's helpful intervention; the enveloping, the veiling, the faintness of his heart still continues

(עָטַף, عطف, according to its radical signification: to bend and

lay anything round so that it lies or draws over something else
and covers it, here of a self-enveloping); a rock of difficulties
still ever lies before him which is too high for his natural
strength, for his human ability, therefore insurmountable.
But he is of good courage: God will lead him up with a sure
step, so that, removed from all danger, he will have rocky

---

* Just as in Num. xxxii. 29 sq. the country east of Jordan is excluded
from the name "the land of Canaan" in the stricter sense, so by the
Jewish mind it was regarded from the earliest time to a certain extent as
a foreign country (חוצה לארץ), although inhabited by the two tribes and a
half; so that not only is it said of Moses that he died in a foreign land,
but even of Saul that he is buried in a foreign land (*Numeri Rabba*, ch.
viii. and elsewhere).

ground under his feet. He is of good courage, for God has already proved Himself to be a place of refuge to him, to be a strong tower, defying all attack, which enclosed him, the persecuted one, so that the enemy can gain no advantage over him (cf. Prov. xviii. 10). He is already on the way towards his own country, and in fact his most dearly loved and proper home: he will or he has to (in accordance with the will of God) dwell (cf. the cohortative in Isa. xxxviii. 10, Jer. iv. 21) in God's tabernacle (*vid.* on xv. 1) throughout æons (an utterance which reminds one of the synchronous Ps. xxiii. ver. 6). With גּוּר is combined the idea of the divine protection (cf. Arabic *g'âr ollah*, the charge or protegé of God, and Beduinic *g'aur*, the protecting hearth; *g'awir*, according to its form = גֵּר, one who flees for refuge to the hearth). A bold figure of this protection follows: he has to, or will trust, *i.e.* find refuge, beneath the protection of God's wings. During the time the tabernacle was still being moved from place to place we hear no such mention of dwelling in God's tabernacle or house. It was David who coined this expression for loving fellowship with the God of revelation, simultaneously with his preparation of a settled dwelling-place for the sacred Ark. In the Psalms that belong to the time of his persecution by Saul such an expression is not yet to be found; for in Ps. lii. 7, when it is desired that Doeg may have the opposite of an eternal dwelling-place, it is not the sacred tent that is meant. We see also from its second part that this Ps. lxi. does not belong to the time of Saul; for David does not speak here as one who has drawn very near to his kingly office (cf. xl. 8), but as one who is entering upon a new stage in it.

Vers. 6–9. The second part begins with a confirmation of the gracious purpose of God expressed in ver. 5. David believes that he shall experience what he gives expression to in ver. 5; for God has already practically shown him that neither his life nor his kingship shall come to an end yet; He has answered the prayers of His chosen one, that, blended with vows, resulted from the lowly, God-resigned spirit which finds expression in 2 Sam. xv. 25 sq., and He has given or delivered up to him the land which is his by inheritance, when threatened by the rebels as robbers,—the land to which those who fear the covenant God have a just claim. It is clear enough that the receivers are "those who fear the name of Jahve;" the genitive relation describes the יְרֻשָּׁה as belonging to them in opposition to those who had usurped it.   Or does יְרֻשָּׁה here perhaps mean the same as אֲרֶשֶׁת in xxi. 3?   Certainly not.   נָתַן יְרֻשָּׁה לְ is a customary phrase, the meaning of which, "to give anything to any one as his inheritance or as his own property," is to be retained (*e.g.* Deut. ii. 19).   God has acknowledged David's cause; the land of Israel is again wrested from those to whom it does not belong; and now begins a new era in the reign of its rightful king.   In view of this the king prays, in vers. 7, 8, that God would add another goodly portion to the duration of his life.   The words sound like intercession, but the praying one is the same person as in vers. 2–5.   The expression מַלְכָּא מְשִׁיחָא (the King Messiah) of the Targum shows to whom the church referred the word "king" after the extinction of the Davidic dynasty.   The exalted tone of the wish expressed in ver. 7*b* (cf. Joel ii. 2) favours this without absolutely requiring it (cf. עוֹלָמִים, ver. 5, xxi. 5, and the royal salutation, 1 Kings i. 31, Dan. ii. 4, and frequently).   There ought (as also *e.g.* in ix. 8) not to be any question whether יֵשֵׁב in ver. 8 signifies "to sit enthroned," or "to sit" = "to abide;" when the person spoken of is a king it means "to remain enthroned," for with him a being settled down and continuous enthronement are co-incident.   מַן in ver. 8*b* is *imperat. apoc.* for מַנֵּה (after the form צַו, נַס, הַס).   The poet prays God to appoint mercy and truth as guardian angels to the king (xl. 12, Prov. xx. 28, where out of pause it is יִצְּרוּ; cf. on the other hand lxxviii. 7, Prov. ii. 11, v. 2).   Since the poet himself is the king for whom he prays, the transition to the first person in ver. 9 is perfectly natural. כֵּן signifies, as it always does, so or thus = in accordance therewith, corresponding to the fulfilment of these my petitions, thankfully responding to it.   לְשַׁלְּמִי is the infinitive of the aim or purpose.   Singing praise and accompanying it with music, he will make his whole life one continuous paying of vows.

PSALM LXII.

RESIGNATION TO GOD WHEN FOES CROWD IN UPON ONE.

2 VERILY resignation to Elohim is my soul,
From Him cometh my salvation.
3 Verily He is my rock and my salvation,
My fortress, I shall not be greatly moved.
4 How long will ye rush in upon a man,
How long will ye thrust him in all of you as a bowing wall,
a tottering fence?!—

5 Only from his exaltation have they determined to thrust
him down,
Seeing they love lies, each one blesseth with his mouth,
And in their inward part they curse.   (*Sela.*)

6 Verily to Elohim resign thyself, my soul;
For from Him cometh my hope.
7 Verily He is my rock and my salvation,
My fortress, I shall not be moved.
8 Upon Elohim dependeth my salvation and my glory;
The rock of my defence, and my refuge, have I in Elohim.

9 Trust in Him at all times, ye people!
Pour out your heart before Him,
Elohim is a refuge for us!   (*Sela.*)

10 Only a breath are the children of men, the sons of nobles a
lie ;
Going swiftly upward in the balance, they are altogether
like a breath.
11 Trust not in oppression, and through plunder become not
vain,
Increase of wealth do not deign to regard !
12 One thing hath Elohim spoken,
These two have I heard :
That power is of Elohim,
13 And Thine, O Lord, is mercy—
For Thou recompensest every man according to his work.

Concerning this Psalm, which is placed next to the preceding Psalm by reason of several points of mutual relationship (cf. lxii. 8*b* with lxi. 4, 8; lxii. 9*b* with lxi. 4; lxii. 13*b* with lxi. 9), as being a product of the time of the persecution by Absalom, and also concerning עַל־יְדוּתוּן, we have spoken already in the introduction to Ps. xxxix., which forms with it a twin pair. The particle אַךְ occurs there four times, and in this Psalm even as many as six times. The strophic structure somewhat resembles that of Ps. xxxix., in that here we also have longer strophes which are interspersed by tristichs.

Vers. 2–5. The poet, although apparently irrecoverably lost, does not nevertheless despair, but opposes one thing to the tumultuous crowding in upon him of his many foes, viz. quiet calm submission,—not, however, a fatalistic resignation, but that which gives up everything to God, whose hand (*vid.* 2 Sam. xii. 7–13) can be distinctly recognised and felt in what is now happening to him. אַךְ (yea, only, nevertheless) is the language of faith, with which, in the face of all assault, established truths are confessed and confirmed; and with which, in the midst of all conflict, resolutions, that are made and are to be firmly kept, are deliberately and solemnly declared and affirmed. There is no necessity for regarding דּוּמִיָּה (not דּוּמִיָה), which is always a substantive (not only in xxii. 3, xxxix. 3, but also in this instance and in lxv. 2), and which is related to דּוּמָה, silence, xciv. 17, cxv. 17, just as עֲלִילִיָּה, Jer. xxxii. 19, is related to עֲלִילָה, as an *accus. absol.*: in silent submission (Hupfeld). Like תְּפִלָּה in cix. 4, it is a predicate: his soul is silent submission, *i.e.* altogether resigned to God without any purpose and action of its own. His salvation comes from God, yea, God Himself is his salvation, so that, while God is his God, he is even already in possession of salvation, and by virtue of it stands imperturbably firm. We see clearly from xxxvii. 24, what the poet means by רַבָּה. He will not greatly, very much, particularly totter, *i.e.* not so that it should come to his falling and remaining down. רַבָּה is an adverb like רַבַּת, cxxiii. 4, and הַרְבֵּה, Eccles. v. 19.

There is some difficulty about the ἅπαξ λεγομ. תְּהוֹתְתוּ (ver. 4*a*). Abulwalîd, whom Parchon, Kimchi, and most others follow, compares the Arabic هتّ الرّجل, the man brags; but

this هَتّ (intensive form هَنّهَتّ) signifies only in a general
way to speak fluently, smoothly and rapidly one word after
another, which would give too poor an idea here. There is
another هَتّ (cogn. هَتَكَ, *proscindere*) which has a meaning
that is even better suited to this passage, and one which is still
retained in the spoken language of Syria at the present day:
hattani is equivalent to "he compromised me" (= *hataka
es-sitra 'annî*, he has pulled my veil down), dishonoured me
before the world by speaking evil concerning me; whence in
Damascus *el-hettât* is the appellation for a man who without
any consideration insults a person before others, whether he be
present or absent at the time. But this هَتّ only occurs in *Kal*
and with an accusative of the object. The words עַד־אָנָה תְּהוֹתְתוּ
עַל־אִישׁ find their most satisfactory explanation in the هَوَّت
in common use in Damascus at the present day, which is not
used in *Kal*, but only in the intensive form. The *Piel* هَوَّت
عَلَى فُلَان signifies to rush upon any one, viz. with a shout and
raised fist in order to intimidate him.* From this הַוֵּת, of which
even the construction with عَلَى together with the intensive form
is characteristic, we here read the *Pil.* הוֹתֵת, which is not badly
rendered by the LXX. ἐπιτίθεσθε, Vulgate *irruitis*. In ver.
4*b* it is a question whether the reading תְּרָצְּחוּ of the school of
Tiberias or the Babylonian תְּרַצְּחוּ is to be preferred. Certainly
the latter; for the former (to be rendered, "may you" or
"ye shall be broken in pieces, slain") produces a thought that
is here introduced too early, and one that is inappropriate to
the figures that follow. Standing as it still does under the

---

* Neshwân and the Kâmûs say: "*hawwata* and *hajjata bi-fulân-in*
signifies to call out to any one in order to put him in terror (صاح بِهِ);"
"but in Syria," as Wetzstein goes on to say, "the verb does not occur
as *med. Jod*, nor is *hawwata* there construed with بِ, but only with عَلَى.
A very ready phrase with the street boys in Damascus is هَوَّت شَىْ لَّى
عَلَى, 'why dost thou threaten me?'"

regimen of עַד־אָנָה, תְּרָצְּחוּ is to be read as a *Piel;* and, as the following figures show, is to be taken, after xlii. 11, in its primary signification *contundere* (root רץ).* The sadness of the poet is reflected in the compressed, obscure, and peculiar character of the expression. אִישׁ and כֻּלְּכֶם (a single one— ye all) stand in contrast. כְּקִיר וגו׳, *sicut parietem = similem parieti* (cf. lxiii. 6), forms the object to תְּרָצְּחוּ. The transmitted reading גָּדֵר הַדְּחוּיָה, although not incorrect in itself so far as the gender (Prov. xxiv. 31) and the article are concerned (Ges. § 111, 2, *a*), must apparently be altered to גְּדֵרָה דְחוּיָה (Olshausen and others) in accordance with the parallel member of the verse, since both גְּדֵרָה and גָּדֵר are words that can be used of every kind of surrounding or enclosure. To them David seems like a bent, overhanging wall, like a wall of masonry that has received the thrust that must ultimately cause its fall; and yet they rush in upon him, and all together they pursue against the one man their work of destruction and ruin. Hence he asks, with an indignation that has a somewhat sarcastic tinge about it, how long this never-satiated self-satisfying of their lust of destruction is meant to last. Their determination (יָעַץ as in Isa. xiv. 24) is clear. It aims only or entirely (אַךְ, here *tantummodo, prorsus*) at thrusting down from his high position, that is to say from the throne, viz. him, the man at whom they are always rushing (לְהַדִּיחוּ = לְהַדִּיחַ). No means are too base for them in the accomplishment of their object, not even the mask of the hypocrite. The clauses which assume a future form of expression are, logically at least, subordinate clauses (Ew. § 341, *b*). The Old Testament language allows itself a change of number like בְּפִיו instead of בְּפִיהֶם, even to the very extreme, in the hurry of emotional utterance. The singular is distributive in this instance: *suo quisque ore*, like לוֹ

---

* The reading of Ben-Asher תְּרָצְּחוּ is followed by Aben-Ezra, Kimchi, and others, taking this form (which could not possibly be anything else) as *Pual.* The reading of Ben-Naphtali תְּרָצְּחוּ is already assumed in *B. Sanhedrin* 119a. Besides these the reading תְּרָצְחוּ (without *Dag.*) is also found, which cannot be taken as a resolved *Piel*, since the *Metheg* is wanting, but is to be read *terotzchu*, and is to be taken (as also the reading מַלְּשְׁנִי, ci. 5, and וַיְחַלְּקֵם, 1 Chron. xxiii. 6, xxiv. 3) as *Poal* (*vid.* on xciv. 20, cix. 10).

in Isa. ii. 20, מִמֶּנּוּ, Isa. v. 23, cf. xxx. 22, Zech. xiv. 12. The pointing יְקַלְלוּ follows the rule of יהַלְלוּ, xxii. 27, יְרַנְּנוּ, cxlix. 5, and the like (to which the only exceptions are רִנַּת, חִקְקֵי, הִנְנִי).

Vers. 6–9. The beginning of the second group goes back and seizes upon the beginning of the first. אַךְ is affirmative both in ver. 6 and in ver. 7. The poet again takes up the emotional affirmations of vers. 2, 3, and, firm and defiant in faith, opposes them to his masked enemies. Here what he says to his soul is very similar to what he said of his soul in ver. 2, inasmuch as he makes his own soul objective and exalts himself above her; and it is just in this that the secret of personality consists. He here admonishes her to that silence which in ver. 2 he has already acknowledged as her own; because all spiritual existence as being living remains itself unchanged only by means of a perpetual "becoming" (*mittelst steten Werdens*), of continuous, self-conscious renovation. The "hope" in ver. 6*b* is intended to be understood according to that which forms its substance, which here is nothing more nor less than salvation, ver. 2*b*. That for which he who resigns himself to God hopes, comes from God; it cannot therefore fail him, for God the Almighty One and plenteous in mercy is surety for it. David renounces all help in himself, all personal avenging of his own honour—his salvation and his honour are עַל־אֱלֹהִים (*vid.* on vii. 11). The rock of his strength, *i.e.* his strong defence, his refuge, is בֵּאלֹהִים; it is where Elohim is, Elohim is it in person (בְּ as in Isa. xxvi. 4). By עָם, ver. 9, the king addresses those who have remained faithful to him, whose feeble faith he has had to chide and sustain in other instances also in the Psalms belonging to this period. The address does not suit the whole people, who had become for the most part drawn into the apostasy. Moreover it would then have been עַמִּי (my people). עַם frequently signifies the people belonging to the retinue of a prince (Judg. iii. 18), or in the service of any person of rank (1 Kings xix. 21), or belonging to any union or society whatever (2 Kings iv. 42 sq.). David thus names those who cleave to him; and the fact that he cannot say "my people" just shows that the people as a body had become alienated from him. But those who have remained to him of the people are not therefore to despair; but they are to pour out before God, who will know how to protect both

them and their king, whatever may lie heavily upon their
heart.

Vers. 10–13. Just as all men with everything earthly
upon which they rely are perishable, so also the purely earthly
form which the new kingship has assumed carries within itself
the germ of ruin ; and God will decide as Judge, between the
dethroned and the usurpers, in accordance with the relationship
in which they stand to Him. This is the internal connection
of the third group with the two preceding ones. By means of
the strophe vers. 10–13, our Psalm is brought into the closest
reciprocal relationship with Ps. xxxix. Concerning בְּנֵי־אָדָם and
בְּנֵי־אִישׁ vid. on xlix. 3, iv. 3. The accentuation divides ver. 10
quite correctly. The *Athnach* does not mark בְּמֹאזְנַיִם לַעֲלוֹת as
an independent clause : they are upon the balance לַעֲלוֹת, for a
going up ; they must rise, so light are they (Hengstenberg).
Certainly this expression of the periphrastic future is possible
(*vid.* on xxv. 14, Hab. i. 17), still we feel the want here of the
subject, which cannot be dispensed with in the clause as an
independent one. Since, however, the combining of the words
with what follows is forbidden by the fact that the infinitive
with לְ in the sense of the *ablat. gerund.* always comes after the
principal clause, not before it (Ew. § 280, *d*), we interpret :
upon the balances *ad ascendendum = certo ascensuri,* and in
fact so that this is an attributive that is co-ordinate with כָּזָב.
Is the clause following now meant to affirm that men, one and
all, belong to nothingness or vanity (מִן *partitivum*), or that they
are less than nothing (מִן *comparat.*) ? Umbreit, Stier, and
others explain Isa. xl. 17 also in the latter way ; but parallels
like Isa. xli. 24 do not favour this rendering, and such as Isa.
xliv. 11 are opposed to it. So also here the meaning is not
that men stand under the category of that which is worthless
or vain, but that they belong to the domain of the worthless or
vain.

The warning in ver. 11 does not refer to the Absalomites,
but, pointing to these as furnishing a salutary example, to
those who, at the sight of the prosperous condition and joyous
life on that side, might perhaps be seized with envy and covetousness. Beside בָּטַח בְּ the meaning of הָבַל בְּ is nevertheless
not : to set a vain hope upon anything (for the idea of hoping
does not exist in this verb in itself, Job xxvii. 12, Jer. ii. 5, nor

in this construction of the verb), but: to be befooled, blinded
by something vain (Hitzig). Just as they are not to suffer
their heart to be befooled by their own unjust acquisition, so
also are they not, when the property of others increases (נוּב,
root נב, to raise one's self, to mount up; cf. Arabic *nabata*, to
sprout up, grow; *nabara*, to raise; intransitive, to increase, and
many other verbal stems), to turn their heart towards it, as
though it were something great and fortunate, that merited
special attention and commanded respect. Two great truths
are divinely attested to the poet. It is not to be rendered:
once hath God spoken, now twice (Job xl. 5, 2 Kings vi. 10)
have I heard this; but after lxxxix. 36: One thing hath God
spoken, two things (it is) that I have heard; or in accordance
with the interpunction, which here, as in xii. 8 (cf. on ix. 16),
is not to be called in question: these two things have I heard.
Two divine utterances actually do follow. The two great
truths are: (1) that God has the power over everything earthly,
that consequently nothing takes place without Him, and that
whatever is opposed to Him must sooner or later succumb;
(2) that of this very God, the sovereign Lord (אֲדֹנָי), is mercy
also, the energy of which is measured by His omnipotence,
and which does not suffer him to succumb upon whom it is
bestowed. With כִּי the poet establishes these two revealed
maxims which God has impressed upon his mind, from His
righteous government as displayed in the history of men. He
recompenses each one in accordance with his doing, κατὰ τὰ
ἔργα αὐτοῦ, as Paul confesses (Rom. ii. 6) no less than David,
and even (*vid.* LXX.) in the words of David. It shall be
recompensed unto every man according to his conduct, which
is the issue of his relationship to God. He who rises in opposition to the will and order of God, shall feel God's power (עֹז)
as a power for punishment that dashes in pieces; and he who,
anxious for salvation, resigns his own will to the will of God,
receives from God's mercy or loving-kindness (חֶסֶד), as from
an overflowing fulness, the promised reward of faithfulness:
his resignation becomes experience, and his hoping attainment.

PSALM LXIII.

MORNING HYMN OF ONE WHO IS PERSECUTED, IN A WATERLESS DESERT.

2 ELOHIM, Thou art my God, early do I seek Thee;
   My soul thirsteth after Thee, my flesh pineth for Thee
   In a land of dryness, and is wearied without water.
3 Thus have I looked after Thee in the sanctuary,
   To see Thy power and Thy glory.
4 For Thy loving-kindness is better than life,
   My lips shall praise Thee.

5 Thus will I bless Thee while I live,
   In Thy name will I lift up my hands.
6 As with marrow and fat is my soul satisfied,
   And with jubilant lips doth my mouth sing praise.
7 When I remember Thee upon my bed,
   Throughout the night-watches do I meditate upon Thee.
8 For Thou hast become a help to me,
   And in the shadow of Thy wings can I shout for joy.
9 My soul followeth hard after Thee,
   Thy right hand holdeth me fast.

10 But they, to destruction do they seek my soul:
   They shall go into the abysses of the earth.
11 They deliver him into the power of the sword,
   A portion of jackals do they become.
12 Nevertheless the king shall rejoice in Elohim,
   Every one shall glory who sweareth by Him;
   For the mouth of those who speak lies shall be stopped.

Now follows Ps. lxiii., the morning Psalm of the ancient church with which the singing of the Psalms was always introduced at the Sunday service.*   This Psalm is still more closely

---

* *Constitutiones Apostolicæ*, ii. 59 : Ἑκάστης ἡμέρας συναθροίζεσθε ὄρθρου καὶ ἑσπέρας ψάλλοντες καὶ προσευχόμενοι ἐν τοῖς κυριακοῖς· ὄρθρου μὲν λέγοντε; ψαλμὸν τὸν ξβ′ (lxiii), ἑσπέρας δὲ τὸν ρμ′ (cxli.).   Athanasius says just the

related to Ps. lxi. than Ps. lxii. Here, as in Ps. lxi., David gives utterance to his longing for the sanctuary; and in both Psalms he speaks of himself as king (*vid. Symbolæ*, p. 56). All the three Psalms, lxi.–lxiii., were composed during the time of Absalom; for we must not allow ourselves to be misled by the inscription, *A Psalm, by David, when he was in the wilderness of Judah* (also LXX., according to the correct reading and the one preferred by Euthymius, τῆς Ἰουδαίας, not τῆς Ἰδουμαίας), into transferring it, as the old expositors do, to the time of Saul. During that period David could not well call himself "the king;" and even during the time of his persecution by Absalom, in his flight, before crossing the Jordan, he tarried one or two days בערבות המדבר, in the steppes of the desert (2 Sam. xv. 23, 28, xvii. 16), *i.e.* of the wilderness of Judah lying nearest to Jerusalem, that dreary waste that extends along the western shore of the Dead Sea. We see clearly from 2 Sam. xvi. 2 (הַיָּעֵף בַּמִּדְבָּר) and xvi. 14 (עֲיֵפִים), that he there found himself in the condition of a עָיֵף. The inscription, when understood thus, throws light upon the whole Psalm, and verifies itself in the fact that the poet is a king; that he longs for the God on Zion, where he has been so delighted to behold Him, who is there manifest; and that he is persecuted by enemies who have plotted his ruin. The assertion that he is in the wilderness (ver. 2) is therefore no mere rhetorical figure; and when, in ver. 11, he utters the imprecation over his enemies, "*let them become a portion for the jackals*," the influence of the desert upon the moulding of his thoughts is clearly seen in it.

We have here before us the Davidic original, or at any rate the counterpart, to the Korahitic pair of Psalms, xlii., xliii. It is a song of the most delicate form and deepest spiritual contents; but in part very difficult of exposition. When we have, approximately at least, solved the riddle of

---

same in his *De virginitate*: πρὸς ὄρθρον τὸν ψαλμὸν τοῦτον λέγετε, κ.τ.λ. Hence Ps. lxiii. is called directly ὁ ὀρθρινός (the morning hymn) in *Constit. Apostol.* viii. 37. Eusebius alludes to the fact of its being so *in Ps. xci.* (*xcii.*), p. 608, ed. Montfaucon. In the Syrian order of service it is likewise the morning Psalm κατ᾽ ἐξοχήν, *vid.* Dietrich, *De psalterii usu publico et divisione in Ecclesia Syriaca*, p. 3. The LXX. renders אֲשַׁחֲרֶךָ in ver. 2, πρός σε ὀρθρίζω, and באשמרות in ver. 7, ἐν τοῖς ὄρθροις (*in matutinis*).

one Psalm, the second meets us with new riddles. It is not
merely the poetical classic character of the language, and the
spiritual depth, but also this half-transparent and half-opaque
covering which lends to the Psalms such a powerful and un-
varying attractiveness. They are inexhaustible, there always
remains an undeciphered residue; and therefore, though the
work of exposition may progress, it does not come to an end.
But how much more difficult is it to adopt this choice spiritual
love-song as one's own prayer! For this we need a soul that
loves after the same manner, and in the main it requires such
a soul even to understand it rightly; for, as the saintly Bernard
says, *lingua amoris non amanti barbara est.*

Vers. 2–4. If the words in ver. 2 were אֱלֹהִים אַתָּה אֲשַׁחֲרֶךָ,
then we would render it, with Böttcher, after Gen. xlix. 8:
Elohim, Thee do I seek, even Thee! But אֵלִי forbids this
construction; and the assertion that otherwise it ought to be,
"Jahve, my God art Thou" (cxl. 7), rests upon a non-recognition of the Elohimic style. *Elohim* alone by itself is a vocative, and accordingly has *Mehupach legarme.* The verb שַׁחַר
signifies earnest, importunate seeking and inquiring (*e.g.* lxxviii.
34), and in itself has nothing to do with שַׁחַר, the dawn; but
since ver. 7 looks back upon the night, it appears to be chosen
with reference to the dawning morning, just as in Isa. xxvi. 9
also, שַׁחַר stands by the side of אִוָּה בַלַּיְלָה. The LXX. is therefore not incorrect when it renders it: πρὸς σὲ ὀρθρίζω (cf. ὁ
λαὸς ὤρθριζεν πρὸς αὐτόν, Luke xxi. 38); and Apollinaris
strikes the right note when he begins his paraphrase,

Νύκτα μετ' ἀμφιλύκην σὲ μάκαρ μάκαρ ἀμφιχορεύσω—
    At night when the morning dawns will I exult around Thee,
        most blessed One.

The supposition that בְּאֶרֶץ is equivalent to כַּאֲשֶׁר בְּאֶרֶץ, or even
that the *Beth* is *Beth essentiæ* (" as a," etc.), are views that have
no ground whatever, except as setting the inscription at defiance. What is meant is the parched thirsty desert of sand in
which David finds himself. We do not render it: in a dry
and languishing land, for צִיָּה is not an adjective, but a substantive,—the transition of the feminine adjective to the masculine
primary form, which sometimes (as in 1 Kings xix. 11) occurs,
therefore has no application here; nor: in the land of drought

and of weariness, for who would express himself thus? וְעָיֵף,
referring to the nearest subject בְּשָׂרִי, continues the description
of the condition (cf. Gen. xxv. 8). In a region where he is
surrounded by sun-burnt aridity and a nature that bears only
one uniform ash-coloured tint, which casts its unrefreshing
image into his inward part, which is itself in much the same
parched condition, his soul thirsts, his flesh languishes, wearied
and in want of water (*languidus deficiente aqua*), for God, the
living One and the Fountain of life. כָּמַהּ (here with the tone
drawn back, כָּ֫מַהּ, like בָּ֫חַר, 1 Chron. xxviii. 10, עָ֫מַד, Hab. iii.
11) of ardent longing which consumes the last energies of a
man (root כם, whence כָּמֵן and כָּמַס to conceal, and therefore
like עָטַף, עָלַף, proceeding from the idea of enveloping; Arabic

كَمِهَ, to be blind, dark, pale, and disconcerted). The LXX.

and Theodotion erroneously read כַּמָּה (how frequently is this
the case!); whereas Aquila renders it ἐπετάθη, and Symmachus still better, ἱμείρεται (the word used of the longing of love).
It is not a small matter that David is able to predicate such
languishing desire after God even of his flesh; it shows us
that the spirit has the mastery within him, and not only forcibly
keeps the flesh in subjection, but also, so far as possible, draws
it into the realm of its own life—an experience confessedly
more easily attained in trouble, which mortifies our carnal
nature, than in the midst of the abundance of outward prosperity. The God for whom he is sick [*lit.* love-sick] in soul
and body is the God manifest upon Zion.

Now as to the כֵּן in ver. 3—a particle which is just such
a characteristic feature in the physiognomy of this Psalm as
אַךְ is in that of the preceding Psalm—there are two notional
definitions to choose from: thus = so, as my God (Ewald),
and: with such longing desire (as *e.g.* Oettinger). In the
former case it refers back to the confession, "Elohim, my God
art Thou," which stands at the head of the Psalm; in the
latter, to the desire that has just been announced, and that not
in its present exceptional character, but in its more general
and constant character. This reference to what has immediately gone before, and to the modality, not of the object, but
of the disposition of mind, deserves the preference. "Thus"
is accordingly equivalent to "longing thus after Thee." The

two כִּן in vers. 3 and 5 are parallel and of like import. The
alternation of the perfect (ver. 3) and of the future (ver. 5)
implies that what has been the Psalmist's favourite occupation
heretofore, shall also be so in the future. Moreover, בארץ ציה
and בַּקֹּרֶשׁ form a direct antithesis. Just as he does now in a
dry land, so formerly in the sanctuary he looked forth longingly
towards God (חָזָה with the conjoined idea of solemnity and
devotion). We have now no need to take לראות as a gerundive
(*videndo*), which is in itself improbable; for one looks, peers,
gazes at anything just for the purpose of seeing what the
nature of the object is (xiv. 2, Isa. xlii. 18). The purpose of
his gazing upon God was to gain an insight into the nature of
God, so far as it is disclosed to the creature; or, as it is expressed here, to see His power and glory, *i.e.* His majesty on its
terrible and on its light and loving side, to see this, viz., in its
sacrificial appointments and sacramental self-attestations. Such
longing after God, which is now all the more intense in the
desert far removed from the sanctuary, filled and impelled him;
for God's loving-kindness is better than life, better than this
natural life (*vid.* on xvii. 14), which is also a blessing, and as
the prerequisite of all earthly blessings a very great blessing.
The loving-kindness of God, however, is a higher good, is in
fact the highest good and the true life: his lips shall praise this
God of mercy, his morning song shall be of Him; for that
which makes him truly happy, and after which he even now,
as formerly, only and solely longs, is the mercy or loving-kindness (חֶסֶד) of this God, the infinite worth of which is measured by
the greatness of His power (עֹז) and glory (כָּבוֹד). It might also
be rendered, "Because Thy loving-kindness is better than life,
my lips shall praise Thee;" but if כִּי is taken as demonstrative
(for), it yields a train of thought that that is brought about not
merely by what follows (as in the case of the relative because),
but also by what precedes: "for Thy loving-kindness . . . my
lips shall then praise Thee" (יְשַׁבְּחוּנְךָ with the suffix appended to
the energetic plural form *ûn*, as in Isa. lx. 7, 10, Jer. ii. 24).

Vers. 5–9. This strophe again takes up the כִּן (ver. 3):
thus ardently longing, for all time to come also, is he set
towards God, with such fervent longing after God will he
bless Him in his life, *i.e.* entirely filling up his life therewith
(בְּחַיָּי as in civ. 33, cxlvi. 2; cf. Baruch iv. 20, ἐν ταῖς ἡμέραις

μου), and in His name, *i.e.* invoking it and appealing to it, will
he lift up his hands in prayer. The being occupied with God
makes him, even though as now in the desert he is obliged to
suffer bodily hunger, satisfied and cheerful like the fattest and
most marrowy food : *velut adipe et pinguedine satiatur anima
mea.* From Lev. iii. 17, vii. 25, Grussetius and Frisch infer
that *spirituales epulæ* are meant. And certainly the poet cannot have had the sacrificial feasts (Hupfeld) in his mind; for
the חֵלֶב of the *shelamim* is put upon the altar, and is removed
from the part to be eaten. Moreover, however, even the Tôra
does not bind itself in its expression to the letter of that prohibition of the fat of animals, *vid.* Deut. xxxii. 14, cf. Jer. xxxi.
14. So here also the expression "with marrow and fat" is the
designation of a feast prepared from well-fed, noble beasts.
He feels himself satisfied in his inmost nature just as after a
feast of the most nourishing and dainty meats, and with lips of
jubilant songs (*accus. instrum.* according to Ges. § 138, rem. 3),
i.e. with lips jubilant and attuned to song, shall his mouth sing
praise. What now follows in ver. 7 we no longer, as formerly,
take as a protasis subsequently introduced (like Isa. iv. 3 sq.) :
" when I remembered . . . meditated upon Thee," but so that
ver. 7*a* is the protasis and ver. 7*b* the apodosis, cf. xxi. 12, Job
ix. 16 (Hitzig) : When I remember Thee (*meminerim,* Ew. §
355, *b*) upon my bed (*stratis meis,* as in cxxxii. 3, Gen. xlix. 4,
cf. 1 Chron. v. 1)—says he now as the twilight watch is passing
gradually into the morning—I meditate upon Thee in the
night-watches (Symmachus, καθ' ἑκάστην φυλακήν), or during,
throughout the night-watches (like בְּחַיָּי in ver. 5); *i.e.* it is no
passing remembrance, but it so holds me that I pass a great
part of the night absorbed in meditation on Thee. He has no
lack of matter for his meditation; for God has become a help
(*auxilio, vid.* on iii. 3) to him : He has rescued him in this
wilderness, and, well concealed under the shadow of His wings
(*vid.* on xvii. 8, xxxvi. 8, lvii. 2), which affords him a cool
retreat in the heat of conflict and protection against his persecutors, he is able to exult (אֲרַנֵּן, the potential). Between
himself and God there subsists a reciprocal relationship of
active love. According to the schema of the crosswise position
of words (*chiasmus*), אַחֲרֶיךָ and בִּי intentionally jostle close
against one another: he depends upon God, following close

behind Him, *i.e.* following Him everywhere and not leaving
Him when He wishes to avoid him; and on the other side
God's right hand holds him fast, not letting him go, not aban-
doning him to his foes.

Vers. 10–12. The closing strophe turns towards these foes.
By וְהֵמָּה he contrasts with his own person, as in lix. 16 sq., lvi.
7 sq., the party of the enemy, before which he has retreated
into the desert. It is open to question whether לְשׁוֹאָה is intended to be referred, according to xxxv. 17, to the persecuted
one (to destroy my life), or, with Hupfeld, to the persecutors
(to their own destruction, they themselves for destruction). If
the former reference to the persecuted be adopted, we ought, in
order to give prominence to the evidently designed antithesis to
ver. 9, to translate: those, however, who . . . , shall go down
into the depths of the earth (Böttcher, and others); a rendering
which is hazardous as regards the syntax, after הֵמָּה and in connection with ,this position of the words. Therefore translate:
On the other hand, those, to (their own) ruin do they seek my
soul. It is true this ought properly to be expressed by לְשׁוֹאָתָם,
but the absence of the suffix is less hazardous than the above
relative rendering of יְבַקְשׁוּ. What follows in ver. 10*b*–11 is
the expansion of לְשׁוֹאָה. The futures from יָבֹאוּ onwards are to
be taken as predictive, not as imprecatory; the former accords
better with the quiet, gentle character of the whole song. It
shall be with them as with the company of Korah. תַּחְתִּיּוֹת
הָאָרֶץ is the interior of the earth down into its deepest bottom;
this signification also holds good in cxxxix. 15, Isa. xliv. 23.*
The phrase הִגִּיר עַל־יְדֵי חֶרֶב here and in Jer. xviii. 21, Ezek.
xxxv. 5 (*Hiph.*, not of גָּרַר, to drag, tear away, but נָגַר, to draw
towards, flow), signifies properly to pour upon = into the hands
(Job xvi. 11), *i.e.* to give over (הִסְגִּיר) into the power of the
sword; *effundent eum* is (much the same as in Job iv. 19, xviii.
18, and frequently) equivalent to *effundetur*. The enallage is

---

* In this passage in Isaiah are meant the depths of the earth (LXX.
θεμέλια τῆς γῆς), the earth down to its inmost part, with its caverns,
abysses, and subterranean passages. The apostle, however, in Eph. iv. 9
by τὰ κατώτερα τῆς γῆς means exactly the same as what in our passage is
called in the LXX. τὰ κατώτατα τῆς γῆς: the interior of the earth = the
under world, just as it is understood by all the Greek fathers (so far as my
knowledge extends); the comparative κατώτερος is used just like ἐνέρτερος.

like v. 10, vii. 2 sq., and frequently: the singular refers to each individual of the homogeneous multitude, or to this multitude itself as a concrete *persona moralis*. The king, however, who is now banished from Jerusalem to the habitation of jackals, will, whilst they become a portion (מָנָה = מְנָת), *i.e.* prey, of the jackals (*vid.* the fulfilment in 2 Sam. xviii. 7 sq.), rejoice in Elohim. Every one who sweareth by Him shall boast himself. Theodoret understands this of swearing κατὰ τὴν τοῦ βασιλέως σωτηρίαν. Hengstenberg compares the oath חֵי פַרְעֹה, Gen. xlii. 15. Ewald also (§ 217, *f*) assumes this explanation to be unquestionable. But the Israelite is to swear by the name of Jahve and by no other, Deut. vi. 13, Isa. lxv. 16, cf. Amos viii. 14. If the king were meant, why was it not rather expressed by הַנִּשְׁבַּע לוֹ, he who swears allegiance to him? The syntax does not help us to decide to what the בּוֹ refers. Heinrich Moeller (1573) says of the בּו as referred to the king: *peregrinum est et coactum;* and A. H. Franke in his *Introductio in Psalterium* says of it as referred to Elohim: *coactum est.* So far as the language is concerned, both references are admissible; but as regards the subject-matter, only the latter. The meaning, as everywhere else, is a swearing by God. He who, without allowing himself to turn from it, swore by Elohim, the God of Israel, the God of David His anointed, and therefore acknowledged Him as the Being exalted above all things, shall boast himself or "glory," inasmuch as it shall be practically seen how well-founded and wise was this recognition. He shall glory, for the mouth of those who speak lies shall be stopped, forcibly closed, viz. those who, together with confidence in the Christ of God, have by falsehood also undermined the reverence which is due to God Himself. Ps. lxiv. closes very similarly, and hence is placed next in order.

PSALM LXIV.

INVOCATION OF DIVINE PROTECTION AGAINST THE FALSENESS OF MEN.

2 HEAR, Elohim, my voice in my complaint,
From the terror of the enemy do Thou preserve my life;

3 Hide me from the conspiracy of evil-doers,
  From the tumultuous throng of the workers of iniquity,
4 Who whet their tongue like a sword,
  Who aim their arrows, bitter words,
5 To shoot, in lurking-places, at the virtuous—
  Suddenly they shoot at him, and fear not.

6 They make firm for themselves an evil agreement,
  They decide to lay snares,
  They ask, who can observe them?
7 They search out knavish things—
  They are ready with a cunningly-wrought-out plan—
  And the inward part of a man, and the heart, is deep!

8 But Elohim will shoot them with an arrow,
  Suddenly do their wounds come.
9 And they are obliged to fall, upon them cometh their own
        tongue;
  All who see them shall shake the head.
10 Then all men shall fear and declare the deed of Elohim,
   And His work shall they consider well.
11 The righteous shall rejoice in Jahve and trust in Him,
   And all the upright in heart shall glory.

Even Hilary begins the exposition of this Psalm with the
words *Psalmi superscriptio historiam non continet*, in order at
the outset to give up all attempt at setting forth its historical
connection. The Midrash observes that it is very applicable
to Daniel, who was cast into the lions' den by the satraps by
means of a delicately woven plot. This is indeed true; but
only because it is wanting in any specially defined features and
cannot with any certainty be identified with one or other of the
two great periods of suffering in the life of David.

Vers. 2–5. The Psalm opens with an octostich, and closes
in the same way. The infinitive noun שִׂיחַ signifies a complaint,
expressed not by the tones of pain, but in words. The rendering of the LXX. (here and in lv. 3) is too general, ἐν τῷ
θέεσθαί με. The "terror" of the enemy is that proceeding
from him (*gen. obj.* as in Deut. ii. 15, and frequently). The

generic singular אֹיֵב is at once particularized in a more detailed description with the use of the plural.   סוֹד is a club or clique; רִגְשָׁה (Targumic = הָמוֹן, *e.g.* Ezek. xxx. 10) a noisy crowd.   The perfects after אֲשֶׁר affirm that which they now do as they have before done; cf. cxl. 4 and lviii. 8, where, as in this passage, the treading or bending of the bow is transferred to the arrow. דָּבָר מָר is the interpretation added to the figure, as in cxliv. 7 That which is bitter is called מַר, root מר, *stringere*, from the harsh astringent taste; here it is used tropically of speech that wounds and inflicts pain (after the manner of an arrow or a stiletto), πικροὶ λόγοι.   With the *Kal* לִירוֹת (xi. 2) alternates the *Hiph.* יִרְהוּ.   With פִּתְאֹם the description takes a new start. וְלֹא יִירָאוּ, forming an assonance with the preceding word, means that they do it without any fear whatever, and therefore also without fear of God (lv. 20, Deut. xxv. 18).

Vers. 6, 7.   The evil speech is one with the bitter speech in ver. 4, the arrow which they are anxious to let fly.   This evil speech, here agreement or convention, they make firm to themselves (*sibi*), by securing, in every possible way, its effective execution.   סַפֵּר (frequently used of the cutting language of the ungodly, lix. 13, lxix. 27; cf. Talmudic סִפֵּר לָשׁוֹן שְׁלִישִׁי, to speak as with three tongues, *i.e.* slanderously) is here construed with לְ of that at which their haughty and insolent utterances aim.   In connection therewith they take no heed of God, the all-seeing One: they say (ask), *quis conspiciat ipsis.* There is no need to take לָמוֹ as being for לוֹ (Hitzig); nor is it the dative of the object instead of the accusative, but it is an ethical dative: who will see or look to them, *i.e.* exerting any sort of influence upon them?   The form of the question is not the direct (lix. 8), but the indirect, in which מִי, *seq. fut.*, is used in a simply future (Jer. xliv. 28) or potential sense (Job xxii. 17, 1 Kings i. 20).   Concerning עֹלֹת, *vid.* lviii. 3.   It is doubtful whether תַּמְנוּ* is the first person (=תַּמּוֹנוּ) as in Num. xvii. 28, Jer. xliv. 18, or the third person as in Lam. iii. 22 (=תַּמּוּ, which first of all resolved is תַּנְמוּ, and then transposed תַּמְנוּ, like מָעֻזֶּיהָ = מָעֻנְזֶיהָ = מָעֻזֶּיהָ, Isa. xxiii. 11).   The reading טָמְנוּ, from which Rashi proceeds, and which Luther follows in

---

* תַּמֻּנוּ in Baer's *Psalterium* is an error that has been carried over from Heidenheim's.

his translation, is opposed by the LXX and Targum; it does not suit the governing subject, and is nothing but an involuntary lightening of the difficulty. If we take into consideration, that תָּמַם signifies not to make ready, but to be ready, and that consequently חֵפֶשׂ מְחֻפָּשׂ is to be taken by itself, then it must be rendered either: they excogitate knavish tricks or villanies, "we are ready, a clever stroke is concocted, and the inward part of man and the heart is deep!" or, which we prefer, since there is nothing to indicate the introduction of any soliloquy: they excogitate knavish tricks, they are ready—a delicately devised, clever stroke (nominative of the result), and (as the poet ironically adds) the inward part of man and the heart is (verily) deep. There is nothing very surprising in the form תַּמְנוּ for תַּמּוּ, since the Psalms, whenever they depict the sinful designs and doings of the ungodly, delight in singularities of language. On וְלֵב (not וְלֶב) = (אִישׁ) וְלֵב = וְלִבּוֹ, cf. cxviii. 14a.

Vers. 8–11. Deep is man's heart and inward part, but not too deep for God, who knoweth the heart (Jer. xvii. 9 sq.). And He will just as suddenly surprise the enemies of His anointed with their death-blow, as they had plotted it for him. The *futt. consec.* that follow represent that which is future, with all the certainty of an historical fact as a retribution springing from the malicious craftiness of the enemies. According to the accentuation, ver. 8 is to be rendered: "then will Elohim shoot them, a sudden arrow become their wounds." Thus at length Hupfeld renders it; but how extremely puzzling is the meaning hidden behind this sentence! The Targum and the Jewish expositors have construed it differently: "Then will Elohim shoot them with arrows suddenly;" in this case, however, because ver. 8b then becomes too blunt and bald, פִּתְאֹם has to be repeated in thought with this member of the verse, and this is in itself an objection to it. We interpunctuate with Ewald and Hitzig thus: then does Elohim shoot them with an arrow, suddenly arise (become a reality) their wounds (cf. Mic. vii. 4), namely, of those who had on their part aimed the murderous weapon against the upright for a sudden and sure shot. Ver. 9a is still more difficult. Kimchi's interpretation, which accords with the accents: *et corruere facient eam super se, linguam suam*, is intolerable; the proleptic suffix, having reference to לְשׁוֹנָם (Ex. iii. 6, Job xxxiii. 20), ought to have been feminine (*vid.* on xxii. 16), and "to make their own tongue fall upon themselves" is an odd fancy. The objective suffix will therefore refer *per enallagen* to the enemy. But not thus (as Hitzig, who now seeks to get out of the difficulty by an alteration of the text, formerly rendered it): "and they cause those to fall whom they have slandered [*lit.* upon whom their tongue came]." This form of retribution does not accord with the context; and moreover the gravely earnest עֲלֵימוֹ, like the הוּ—, refers more probably to the enemies than to the objects of their hostility. The interpretation of Ewald and Hengstenberg is better: "and one overthrows him, inasmuch as their tongue, *i.e.* the sin of their tongue with which they sought to destroy others, comes upon themselves." The subject to וַיַּכְשִׁילֵהוּ, as in lxiii. 11, Job iv. 19, vii. 3, Luke xii. 20, is the powers which are at the service of God, and which are not mentioned at all; and the thought עֲלֵימוֹ לְשׁוֹנָם (a circumstantial clause) is like cxl. 10, where in a similar connection the very same singularly rugged lapidary, or terse, style is found. In ver. 9*b* we must proceed on the assumption that רָאָה בְ in such a connection signifies the gratification of looking upon those who are justly punished and rendered harmless. But he who tarries to look upon such a scene is certainly not the person to flee from it; הִתְנוֹדֵד does not here mean "to betake one's self to flight" (Ewald, Hitzig), but to shake one's self, as in Jer. xlviii. 27, viz. to shake the head (xliv. 15, Jer. xviii. 16)—the recognised (*vid.* xxii. 8) gesture of malignant, mocking astonishment. The approbation is awarded, according to ver. 10, to God, the just One. And with the joy at His righteous interposition,—viz. of Him who has been called upon to interpose,—is combined a fear of the like punishment. The divine act of judicial retribution now set forth becomes a blessing to mankind. From mouth to mouth it is passed on, and becomes an admonitory *nota bene*. To the righteous in particular it becomes a consolatory and joyous strengthening of his faith. The judgment of Jahve is the redemption of the righteous. Thus, then, does he rejoice in his God, who by thus judging and redeeming makes history into the history of redemption, and hide himself the more confidingly in Him; and all the upright boast themselves, viz. in God, who looks into the heart and practically acknowledges them whose heart is directed unswervingly

towards Him, and conformed entirely to Him.   In place of
the *futt. consec.*, which have a prophetic reference, simple *futt.*
come in here, and between these a *perf. consec.* as expressive of
that which will then happen when that which is prophetically
certain has taken place.

PSALM LXV.

THANKSGIVING SONG FOR VICTORY AND BLESSINGS BESTOWED.

2 TO Thee resignation is as praise, Elohim, in Zion,
   And to Thee is the vowed paid.
3 O Thou who answerest prayer! to Thee doth all flesh come.
4 If instances of iniquity have overpowered me—
   Our transgressions Thou, Thou expiatest them.
5 Blessed is he who is chosen to dwell near Thee
                    in Thy courts!
   We will enjoy the good of Thy house,
                    of Thy holy Temple!!

6 In terrible deeds of righteousness dost Thou answer us,
                  O God of our salvation,
   The confidence of all the ends of the earth
                  and of the farthest sea,
7 Who setteth fast the mountains by His strength,
                  girded with might,
8 Who stilleth the roar of the seas,   the roar of their waves,
   And the tumult of the nations.
9 Therefore the dwellers at the boundaries of the earth are
      afraid at Thy tokens,
   The outgoings of the morning and of the evening Thou
      makest to sing for joy.

10 Thou hast visited the land, that it should overflow,
   Abundantly didst Thou enrich it.
   The fountain of Elohim was full of water—
   Thou didst prepare their corn, for Thou didst thus pre-
      pare it;

11 Watering the furrows of the land, softening the ridges
     thereof.
  By showers of rain Thou madest it loose;
  Its increase didst Thou bless.

12 Thou hast crowned the year of Thy goodness,
  And Thy tracks drop with fat.
13 The pastures of the steppe drop,
  And with rejoicing do the hills gird themselves.
14 The meadows are clothed with flocks,
  And the valleys are covered over with corn—
  Everything shouts for joy, everything sings.

In this Psalm, the placing of which immediately after the
preceding is at once explicable by reason of the וַיִּירְאוּ so prominent in both (lxiv. 10, lxv. 9), we come upon the same intermingling of the natural and the historical as in Ps. viii., xix.,
xxix. The congregation gathered around the sanctuary on
Zion praises its God, by whose mercy its imperilled position
in relation to other nations has been rescued, and by whose
goodness it again finds itself at peace, surrounded by fields rich
in promise. In addition to the blessing which it has received in
the bounties of nature, it does not lose sight of the answer to
prayer which it has experienced in its relation to the world of
nations. His rule in human history and His rule in nature
are, to the church, reflected the one in the other. In the latter,
as in the former, it sees the almighty and bountiful hand of
Him who answers prayer and expiates sins, and through judgment opens up a way for His love. The deliverance which
it has experienced redounds to the acknowledgment of the
God of its salvation among the most distant peoples; the
beneficial results of Jahve's interposition in the events trans-
piring in the world extend temporally as well as spiritually
far beyond the bounds of Israel; it is therefore apparently the
relief of Israel and of the peoples in general from the oppression of some worldly power that is referred to. The spring of
the third year spoken of in Isa. xxxvii. 30, when to Judah the
overthrow of Assyria was a thing of the past, and they again
had the fields ripening for the harvest before their eyes, offers
the most appropriate historical basis for the twofold purport of

the Psalm. The inscription, *To the Precentor, a Psalm, by David, a song* (cf. lxxv. 1, lxxvi. 1), does not mislead us in this matter. For even we regard it as uncritical to assign to David all the Psalms bearing the inscription לדוד. The Psalm in many MSS. (Complutensian, Vulgate), beside the words Εἰς τὸ τέλος ψαλμὸς τῷ Δαυίδ ᾠδή, has the addition ᾠδὴ Ἰερεμίου καὶ Ἰεζεκιήλ, (ἐκ) τοῦ λαοῦ τῆς παροικίας ὅτε ἔμελλον ἐκπορεύεσθαι. At the head of the following Psalm it might have some meaning,—here, however, it has none.

Vers. 2–5. The praise of God on account of the mercy with which He rules out of Zion. The LXX. renders σοὶ πρέπει ὕμνος, but דּוּמִיָּה, *tibi par est, h. e. con(v)enit laus* (Ewald), is not a usage of the language (cf. xxxiii. 1, Jer. x. 7). דְּמִיָּה signifies, according to xxii. 3, silence, and as an ethical notion, resignation, lxii. 2. According to the position of the words it looks like the subject, and תְּהִלָּה like the predicate. The accents at least (*Illuj, Shalsheleth*) assume the relationship of the one word to the other to be that of predicate and subject; consequently it is not: To Thee belongeth resignation, praise (Hengstenberg), but: To Thee is resignation praise, *i.e.* resignation is (given or presented) to Thee as praise. Hitzig obtains the same meaning by an alteration of the text: לך דמיה תְהַלֵּל; but opposed to this is the fact that הִלֵּל לְ is not found anywhere in the Psalter, but only in the writings of the chronicler. And since it is clear that the words לך תהלה belong together (xl. 4), the poet had no need to fear any ambiguity when he inserted דמיה between them as that which is given to God as praise in Zion. What is intended is that submission or resignation to God which gives up its cause to God and allows Him to act on its behalf, renouncing all impatient meddling and interference (Ex. xiv. 14). The second member of the sentence affirms that this praise of pious resignation does not remain unanswered. Just as God in Zion is praised by prayer which resigns our own will silently to His, so also to Him are vows paid when He fulfils such prayer. That the answers to prayer are evidently thought of in connection with this, we see from ver. 3, where God is addressed as the " Hearer or Answerer of prayer." To Him as being the Hearer and Answerer of prayer all flesh comes, and in fact, as עָדֶיךָ implies (cf. Isa. xlv. 24), without finding help anywhere else, it clears a way for itself until it gets to Him; *i.e.* men, absolutely dependent, impotent in themselves and helpless, both collectively and individually (those only excepted who are determined to perish or despair), flee to Him as their final refuge and help. Before all else it is the prayer for the forgiveness of sin which He graciously answers. The perfect in ver. 4*a* is followed by the future in ver. 4*b*. The former, in accordance with the sense, forms a hypothetical protasis: granted that the instances of faults have been too powerful for me, *i.e.* (cf. Gen. iv. 13) an intolerable burden to me, our transgressions are expiated by Thee (who alone canst and also art willing to do it). דְּבָרֵי is not less significant than in xxxv. 20, cv. 27, cxlv. 5, cf. 1 Sam. x. 2, 2 Sam. xi. 18 sq.: it separates the general fact into its separate instances and circumstances. How blessed therefore is the lot of that man whom (supply אֲשֶׁר) God chooses and brings near, *i.e.* removes into His vicinity, that he may inhabit His courts (future with the force of a clause expressing a purpose, as *e.g.* in Job xxx. 28, which see), *i.e.* that there, where He sits enthroned and reveals Himself, he may have his true home and be as if at home (*vid.* xv. 1)! The congregation gathered around Zion is esteemed worthy of this distinction among the nations of the earth; it therefore encourages itself in the blessed consciousness of this its privilege flowing from free grace (בחר), to enjoy in full draughts (שָׂבַע with בְּ as in ciii. 5) the abundant goodness or blessing (טוּב) of God's house, of the holy (ἅγιον) of His temple, *i.e.* of His holy temple (קֹדֶשׁ as in xlvi. 5, cf. Isa. lvii. 15). For for all that God's grace offers us we can give Him no better thanks than to hunger and thirst after it, and satisfy our poor soul therewith.

Vers. 6–9. The praise of God on account of the loving-kindness which Israel as a people among the peoples has experienced. The future תַּעֲנֵנוּ confesses, as a present, a fact of experience that still holds good in all times to come. נוֹרָאוֹת might, according to xx. 7, as in cxxxix. 14, be an accusative of the more exact definition; but why not, according to 1 Sam. xx. 10, Job ix. 3, a second accusative under the government of the verb? God answers the prayer of His people superabundantly. He replies to it נוֹראות, terrible deeds, viz. בְּצֶדֶק, by a rule which stringently executes the will of His righteousness

(*vid.* on Jer. xlii. 6); in this instance against the oppressors of
His people, so that henceforth everywhere upon earth He is a
ground of confidence to all those who are oppressed. "The
sea (יָם construct state, as is frequently the case, with the retention of the *â*) of the distant ones" is that of the regions lying
afar off (cf. lvi. 1). Venema observes, *Significatur, Deum esse
certissimum præsidium, sive agnoscatur ab hominibus et ei fidatur,
sive non* (therefore similar to γνόντες, Rom. i. 21; *Psychol.* S.
347; tr. p. 408). But according to the connection and the
subjective colouring the idea seems to have, מִבְטָח וגו׳ is to be
understood of the believing acknowledgment which the God of
Israel attains among all mankind by reason of His judicial and
redemptive self-attestation (cf. Isa. xxxiii. 13, 2 Chron. xxxii.
22 sq.). In the natural world and among men He proves
Himself to be the Being girded with power to whom everything
must yield. He it is who setteth fast the mountains (cf. Jer
x. 12) and stilleth the raging of the ocean. In connection with
the giant mountains the poet may have had even the worldly
powers (*vid.* Isa. xli. 15) in his mind; in connection with the
seas he gives expression to this allegorical conjunction of
thoughts. The roaring of the billows and the wild tumult of
the nations as a mass in the empire of the world, both are
stilled by the threatening of the God of Israel (Isa. xvii.
12–14). When He shall overthrow the proud empire of the
world, whose tyranny the earth has been made to feel far and
wide, then will reverential fear of Him and exultant joy at the
end of the thraldom (*vid.* Isa. xiv. 3–8) become universal.
אוֹתֹת (from the originally feminine אוֹת = *ăwăjat*, from אָוָה, to
mark, Num. xxxiv. 10), σημεῖα, is the name given here to His
marvellous interpositions in the history of our earth. קַצְוֵי,
ver. 6 (also in Isa. xxvi. 15), out of construction is קְצָוֹת. "The
exit places of the morning and of the evening" are the East
and West with reference to those who dwell there. Luther
erroneously understands מוֹצָאֵי as directly referring to the creatures which at morning and evening "sport about (*webern*),
i.e. go safely and joyfully out and in." The meaning is,
the regions whence the morning breaks forth and where the
evening sets. The construction is zeugmatic so far as בּוֹא, not
יָצָא, is said of the evening sun, but only to a certain extent, for
neither does one say מבוא ערב (Ewald). Perret-Gentil ren-

ders it correctly: *les lieux d'où surgissent l'aube et le crepuscule.*
God makes both these to shout for joy, inasmuch as He commands a calm to the din of war.

Vers. 10–14. The praise of God on account of the present year's rich blessing, which He has bestowed upon the land of His people. In vers. 10, 11 God is thanked for having sent down the rain required for the ploughing (*vid. Commentary on Isaiah,* ii. 522) and for the increase of the seed sown, so that, as vers. 12–14 affirm, there is the prospect of a rich harvest. The harvest itself, as follows from ver. 14*b*, is not yet housed. The whole of vers. 10, 11 is a retrospect; in vers. 12–14 the whole is a description of the blessing standing before their eyes, which God has put upon the year now drawing to a close. Certainly, if the forms רַוֵּה and נַחֵת were supplicatory imperatives, then the prayer for the early or seed-time rain would attach itself to the retrospect in ver. 11, and the standpoint would be not about the time of the Passover and Pentecost, both festivals belonging to the beginning of the harvest, but about the time of the feast of Tabernacles, the festival of thanksgiving for the harvest, and vers. 12–14 would be a glance into the future (Hitzig). But there is nothing to indicate that in ver. 11 the retrospect changes into a looking forward. The poet goes on with the same theme, and also arranges the words accordingly, for which reason רַוֵּה and נַחֵת are not to be understood in any other way. שֹׁקֵק beside הֶעֱשִׁיר (to enrich) signifies to cause to run over, overflow, *i.e.* to put anything in a state of plenty or abundance, from שׁוּק (*Hiph.* Joel ii. 24, to yield in abundance),

ساق, to push, impel, to cause to go on in succession and to follow in succession. רַבַּת (for which we find רַבָּה in lxii. 3) is an adverb, copiously, richly (cxx. 6, cxxiii. 4, cxxix. 1), like מֵאַת, a hundred times (Eccles. viii. 12). תַּעְשְׁרֶנָּה is *Hiph.* with the middle syllable shortened, Ges. § 53, 3, rem. 4. The fountain (פֶּלֶג) of God is the name given here to His inexhaustible stores of blessing, and more particularly the fulness of the waters of the heavens from which He showers down fertilizing rain. כֵּן, "thus thoroughly," forms an alliteration with הֵכִין, to prepare, and thereby receives a peculiar twofold colouring. The meaning is: God, by raising and tending, prepared the produce of the field which the inhabitants of the land needed; for He thus thoroughly prepared the land in conformity with the fulness of His fountain, viz. by copiously watering (רַוֵּה *infin. absol.* instead of רַוֵּה, as in 1 Sam. iii. 12, 2 Chron. xxiv. 10; Ex. xxii. 22, Jer. xiv. 19, Hos. vi. 9) the furrows of the land and pressing down, *i.e.* softening by means of rain, its ridges (גְּדוּדֶהָ, defective plural, as *e.g.* in Ruth ii. 13), which the ploughshare has made. תֶּלֶם (related by root with تَلّ, *tell*, a hill, prop. that which is thrown out to a place, that which is thrown up, a mound) signifies a furrow as being formed by casting up or (if from ثَلَم, *ébrécher*, to make a fracture, rent, or notch in anything) by tearing into, breaking up the ground; גְּדוּד (related by root with *uchdûd* and *chatt*, the usual Arabic words for a furrow*) as being formed by cutting into the ground. In ver. 12 the year in itself appears as a year of divine goodness (טוֹבָה, *bonitas*), and the prospective blessing of harvest as the crown which is set upon it. For Thou hast crowned " the

---

* Fürst erroneously explains תֶּלֶם as a bed or strip of ground between two deep furrows, in distinction from מַעֲנָה or מַעֲנִית (*vid.* on cxxix. 3), a furrow. Beds such as we have in our potato fields are unknown to Syrian agriculture. There is a mode which may be approximately compared with it called *ketif* (כָּתֵף), another far wider called *meskeba* (מְשִׂכְּבָה). The Arabic *tilm* (تِلْم, Hebrew תֶּלֶם = *talm*), according to the Ḳamûs (as actually in Magrebinish Arabic) *talam* (תֶּלֶם), corresponds exact to our furrow, *i.e.* (as the Turkish Ḳamûs explains) a ditch-like fissure which the iron of the plough cuts into the field. Neshwân (i. 491) says: " The verb *talam*, fut. *jatlum* and *jatlim*, signifies in Jemen and in the Ghôr (the land on the shore of the Red Sea) the crevices (الشُّقُوق) which the ploughman forms, and *tilm*, collective plural *tilâm*, is, in the countries mentioned, a furrow of the corn-field. Some persons pronounce the word even *thilm*, collective plural *thilâm*." Thus it is at the present day universally in *Ḥaurân; in Edre'ât* I heard the water-furrow of a corn-field called *thilm el-ḳanâh* (تلم القناة). But this pronunciation with ث is certainly not the original one, but has arisen through a substitution of the cognate and more familiar verbal stem ثَلَم, cf. شَرَم, to slit (*shurêm*, a harelip). In other parts of Syria and Palestine, also where the distinction between the sounds ت and ث is carefully observed, I have only heard the pronunciation *tilm*.—WETZSTEIN.

year of Thy goodness" and " with Thy goodness" are different
assertions, with which also different (although kindred as to
substance) ideas are associated.   The futures after עֲטַרְתָּ depict
its results as they now lie out to view.   The chariot-tracks
(*vid.* Deut. xxxiii. 26) drop with exuberant fruitfulness, even
the meadows of the uncultivated and, without rain, unproduc-
tive pasture land (Job xxxviii. 26 sq.).   The hills are personified in ver. 13*b* in the manner of which Isaiah in particular is
so fond (*e.g.* ch. xliv. 23, xlix. 13), and which we find in the
Psalms of his type (xcvi. 11 sqq., xcviii. 7 sqq., cf. lxxxix. 13).
Their fresh, verdant appearance is compared to a festive garment, with which those which previously looked bare and
dreary gird themselves ; and the corn to a mantle in which the
valleys completely envelope themselves (עָטַף with the accusa-

tive, like تَعَطَّفَ with بِ of the garment : to throw it around
one, to put it on one's self).   The closing words, locking themselves as it were with the beginning of the Psalm together,
speak of joyous shouting and singing that continues into the
present time.   The meadows and valleys (Böttcher) are not the
subject, of which it cannot be said that they sing ; nor can the
same be said of the rustling of the waving corn-fields (Kimchi).
The expression requires men to be the subject, and refers to
men in the widest and most general sense.   Everywhere there is
shouting coming up from the very depths of the breast (*Hithpal.*), everywhere songs of joy ; for this is denoted by שִׁיר in
distinction from קִנֵן.

PSALM LXVI.

THANKSGIVING FOR A NATIONAL AND PERSONAL
DELIVERANCE.

1 RAISE a joyful shout unto Elohim, all ye lands,
2 Harp the glory of His name,
  Give glory as praise unto Him.
3 Say unto Elohim : " How terrible are Thy works !
  By reason of Thine omnipotence must Thy foes submit
      to Thee.

4 All lands shall do homage to Thee and harp to Thee,
　 They shall harp to Thy name." (*Sela.*)

5 Come ye and see the mighty deeds of Elohim,
　 Who ruleth terribly over the children of men !
6 He hath turned the sea into dry land,
　 Through the river they passed on foot—
　 Then we rejoiced in Him !
7 He who ruleth in His strength for ever—
　 His eyes keep watch upon the nations.
　 Let not the rebellious thus exalt themselves ! (*Sela.*)

8 Bless, O ye peoples, our God,
　 And make His praise to sound aloud—
9 Who putteth our soul in life,
　 And hath not given our feet over to stumbling.
10 For Thou hast proved us, Elohim,
　 Thou hast smelted us as the smelting of silver.
11 Thou didst bring us into the mountain-hold,
　 Thou didst lay an oppressive burden upon our loins;
12 Thou didst cause men to ride over our head,
　 We fell into fire and into water—
　 Yet Thou didst bring us out into rich abundance.

13 I will enter Thy house with burnt-offerings,
　 I will pay Thee my vows,
14 Which my lips have uttered,
　 And which my mouth hath spoken, when I was straitened.
15 Burnt-offerings of fat sheep will I bring to Thee,
　 Together with the incense of rams,
　 I will offer bullocks with kids. (*Sela.*)

16 Come, hear, and I will tell, all ye who fear Elohim,
　 What He hath done for my soul.
17 Unto Him with my mouth did I cry—
　 And a hymn was under my tongue.
18 If I had purposed evil in my heart,
　 The Lord would not hear.
19 Elohim hath, however, heard,
　 He hath hearkened to the cry of my prayer.

20 Blessed be Elohim,
   Who hath not turned away my prayer
   And His mercy from me.

From Ps. lxv. onwards we find ourselves in the midst of a series of Psalms which, with a varying arrangement of the words, are inscribed both מזמור and שׁיר (lxv.–lxviii.). The two words שׁיר מִזְמוֹר stand according to the accents in the *stat. constr.* (lxxxviii. 1), and therefore signify a *Psalm-song.** This series, as is universally the case, is arranged according to the community of prominent watchwords. In Ps. lxv. 2 we read: "*To Thee is the vow paid,*" and in lxvi. 13: "*I will pay Thee my vows;*" in Ps. lxvi. 20: "*Blessed be Elohim,*" and in lxvii. 8: "*Elohim shall bless us.*" Besides, Ps. lxvi. and lxvii. have this feature in common, that למנצח, which occurs fifty-five times in the Psalter, is accompanied by the name of the poet in every instance, with the exception of these two anonymous Psalms. The frequently occurring *Sela* of both Psalms also indicates that they were intended to have a musical accompaniment. These annotations referring to the temple-music favour the pre-exilic rather than the post-exilic origin of the two Psalms. Both are purely Elohimic; only in one instance (lxvi. 18) does אֲדֹנָי, equally belonging to this style of Psalm, alternate with *Elohim.*

On the ground of some deliverance out of oppressive bondage that has been experienced by Israel arises in Ps. lxvi. the summons to the whole earth to raise a shout of praise unto God. The congregation is the subject speaking as far as ver. 12. From ver. 13 the person of the poet appears in the foreground; but that which brings him under obligation to present a thank-offering is nothing more nor less than that which the whole congregation, and he together with it, has experienced. It is hardly possible to define this event more minutely. The lofty consciousness of possessing a God to whom all the world must bow, whether cheerfully or against its will, became strong among the Jewish people more especially after the overthrow

---

* If it were meant to be rendered *canticum psalmus* (not *psalmi*) it would surely have been accented לַמְנַצֵּחַ שִׁיר מִזְמוֹר (for למנצח שִׁיר מִזְמוֹר, according to section xviii. of the *Accentuationssystem*).

of Assyria in the reign of Hezekiah. But there is no ground
for conjecturing either Isaiah or Hezekiah to be the composer
of this Psalm. If עולם in ver. 7 signified the world (Hitzig),
then he would be (*vid.* xxiv. 9) one of the latest among the
Old Testament writers; but it has the same meaning here that
it has everywhere else in Old Testament Hebrew.

In the Greek Church this Psalm is called Ψαλμὸς ἀναστάσεως; the LXX. gives it this inscription, perhaps with
reference to ver. 12, ἐξήγαγες ἡμᾶς εἰς ἀναψυχήν.

Vers. 1–4. The phrase שִׂים כָּבוֹד לְ signifies "to give glory
to God" in other passages (Josh. vii. 19, Isa. xlii. 12), here with
a second accusative, either (1) if we take תְּהִלָּתוֹ as an accusative of the object: *facite laudationem ejus gloriam = gloriosam*
(Maurer and others), or (2) if we take כָּבוֹד as an accusative
of the object and the former word as an accusative of the
predicate: *reddite honorem laudem ejus* (Hengstenberg), or (3)
also by taking תהלתו as an apposition: *reddite honorem, scil.
laudem ejus* (Hupfeld). We prefer the middle rendering:
give glory as His praise, *i.e.* to Him as or for praise. It is
unnecessary, with Hengstenberg, to render: How terrible art
Thou in Thy works! in that case אַתָּה ought not to be wanting.
מַעֲשֶׂיךָ might more readily be singular (Hupfeld, Hitzig); but
these forms with the softened *Jod* of the root dwindle down to
only a few instances upon closer consideration. The singular
of the predicate (what a terrible affair) here, as frequently, *e.g.*
cxix. 137, precedes the plural designating things. The song
into which the Psalmist here bids the nations break forth, is
essentially one with the song of the heavenly harpers in Apoc.
xv. 3 sq., which begins, Μεγάλα καὶ θαυμαστὰ τὰ ἔργα σου.

Vers. 5–7. Although the summons: Come and see . . .
(borrowed apparently from xlvi. 9), is called forth by cotemporary manifestations of God's power, the consequences of
which now lie open to view, the rendering of ver. 6*c*, "then
will we rejoice in Him," is nevertheless unnatural, and, rightly
looked at, neither grammar nor the matter requires it. For
since שָׁם in this passage is equivalent to אָז, and the future after
אָז takes the signification of an aorist; and since the cohortative
form of the future can also (*e.g.* after עַד, lxxiii. 7, and in
clauses having a hypothetical sense) be referred to the past,

and does sometimes at least occur where the writer throws himself back into the past (2 Sam. xxii. 38), the rendering: Then did we rejoice in Him, cannot be assailed on syntactical grounds. On the "we," cf. Josh. v. 1, *Chethîb*, Hos. xii. 5 [4]. The church of all ages is a unity, the separate parts being jointly involved in the whole. The church here directs the attention of all the world to the mighty deeds of God at the time of the deliverance from Egypt, viz. the laying of the Red Sea and of Jordan dry, inasmuch as it can say in ver. 7, by reason of that which it has experienced in the present, that the sovereign power of God is ever the same: its God rules in His victorious might עוֹלָם, *i.e.* not "over the world," because that ought to be בָּעוֹלָם, but "in eternity" (accusative of duration, as in lxxxix. 2 sq., xlv. 7), and therefore, as in the former days, so also in all time to come. His eyes keep searching watch among the peoples; the rebellious, who struggle against His yoke and persecute His people, had better not rise, it may go ill with them. The *Chethîb* runs יָרִימוּ, for which the *Kerî* is יָרוּמוּ. The meaning remains the same; הֵרִים can (even without יָד, רֹאשׁ, קֶרֶן, lxv. 5) mean "to practise exaltation," *superbire.* By means of לָמוֹ this proud bearing is designated as being egotistical, and as unrestrainedly boastful. Only let them not imagine themselves secure in their arrogance! There is One more exalted, whose eye nothing escapes, and to whose irresistible might whatever is not conformed to His gracious will succumbs.

Vers. 8–12. The character of the event by which the truth has been verified that the God who redeemed Israel out of Egypt still ever possesses and exercises to the full His ancient sovereign power, is seen from this reiterated call to the peoples to share in Israel's *Gloria.* God has averted the peril of death and overthrow from His people: He has put their soul in life (בַּחַיִּים, like בִּישַׁע in xii. 6), *i.e.* in the realm of life; He has not abandoned their foot to tottering unto overthrow (מוֹט the substantive, as in cxxi. 3; cf. the reversed construction in lv. 23). For God has cast His people as it were into a smelting-furnace or fining-pot in order to purify and to prove them by suffering;—this is a favourite figure with Isaiah and Jeremiah, but is also found in Zech. xiii. 9, Mal. iii. 3. Ezek. xix. 9 is decisive concerning the meaning of מְצוּדָה, where הֵבִיא

בִּמְצוּדוֹת signifies "to bring into the holds or prisons;" besides, the figure of the fowling-net (although this is also called מְצוּדָה as well as מְצוֹדָה) has no footing here in the context. מְצוּדָה (*vid.* xviii. 3) signifies *specula,* and that both a natural and an artificial watch-post on a mountain; here it is the mountain-hold or prison of the enemy, as a figure of the total loss of freedom. The laying on of a heavy burden mentioned by the side of it in ver. 11*b* also accords well with this.   מוּעָקָה, a being oppressed, the pressure of a burden, is a *Hophal* formation, like מֻטֶּה, a being spread out, Isa. viii. 8; cf. the similar masculine forms in lxix. 3, Isa. viii. 13, xiv. 6, xxix. 3.   The loins are mentioned because when carrying heavy loads, which one has to stoop down in order to take up, the lower spinal region is called into exercise.   אֱנוֹשׁ is frequently (ix. 20 sq., x. 18, lvi. 2, Isa. li. 12, 2 Chron. xiv. 10) the word used for tyrants as being wretched mortals, perishable creatures, in contrast with their all the more revolting, imperious, and self-deified demeanour. God so ordered it, that "wretched men" rode upon Israel's head.   Or is it to be interpreted: He caused them to pass over Israel (cf. cxxix. 3, Isa. li. 23)?   It can scarcely mean this, since it would then be *in dorso nostro,* which the Latin versions capriciously substitute.   The preposition לְ instead of עַל is used with reference to the phrase יָשַׁב לְ : sitting upon Israel's head, God caused them to ride along, so that Israel was not able to raise its head freely, but was most ignominiously wounded in its self-esteem.   Fire and water are, as in Isa. xliii. 2, a figure of vicissitudes and perils of the most extreme character.   Israel was nigh to being burnt up and drowned, but God led it forth לָרְוָיָה, to an abundant fulness, to abundance and superabundance of prosperity.   The LXX., which renders εἰς ἀναψυχήν (Jerome absolutely: *in refrigerium*), has read לִרְוָחָה; Symmachus, εἰς εὐρυχωρίαν, probably reading לָרְחָבָה (cxix. 45, xviii. 20).   Both give a stronger antithesis. But the state of straitness or oppression was indeed also a state of privation.

Vers. 13–15.   From this point onwards the poet himself speaks, but, as the diversity and the kind of the sacrifices show, as being a member of the community at large.   The עֹלוֹת stand first, the gifts of adoring homage; בְּ is the *Beth* of the accompaniment, as in Lev. xvi. 3, 1 Sam. i. 24, cf. Heb. ix. 25.

" My vows" refer more especially to שַׁלְמֵי נֶדֶר. פָּצָה פֶה also occurs elsewhere of the involuntary vowing to do extraordinary things urged from one by great distress (Judg. xi. 35). אֲשֶׁר is an accusative of the object relating to the vows, *quæ aperue-runt = aperiendo nuncupaverunt labia mea* (Geier). In ver. 15 עָשָׂה, used directly (like the Aramaic and Phœnician עבד) in the signification "to sacrifice" (Ex. xxix. 36–41, and frequently), alternates with הֶעֱלָה, the synonym of הִקְטִיר. The sacrifices to be presented are enumerated. מֵיחִים (incorrect for מֵחִים) are marrowy, fat lambs; lambs and bullocks (בָּקָר) have the most universal appropriation among the animals that were fit for sacrifices. The ram (אַיִל), on the contrary, is the animal for the whole burnt-offering of the high priest, of the princes of the tribes, and of the people; and appears also as the animal for the shelamim only in connection with the shelamim of Aaron, of the people, of the princes of the tribes, and, in Num. vi. 14, of the Nazarite. The younger he-goat (עַתּוּד) is never mentioned as an animal for the whole burnt-offering; but, indeed, as an animal for the shelamim of the princes of the tribes in Num. ch. vii. It is, therefore, probable that the shelamim which were to be offered in close connection with the whole burnt-offerings are introduced by עִם, so that קְטֹרֶת signifies the fat portions of the shelamim upon the altar smoking in the fire. The mention of "rams" renders it necessary that we should regard the poet as here comprehending himself among the people when he speaks thus.

Vers. 16–20. The words in ver. 16 are addressed in the widest extent, as in vers. 5 and 2, to all who fear God, wheresoever such are to be found on the face of the earth. To all these, for the glory of God and for their own profit, he would gladly relate what God has made him to experience. The individual-looking expression לְנַפְשִׁי is not opposed to the fact of the occurrence of a marvellous answering of prayer, to which he refers, being one which has been experienced by him in common with the whole congregation. He cried unto God with his mouth (that is to say, not merely silently in spirit, but audibly and importunately), and a hymn (רוֹמַם,* something

---

* Kimchi (*Michlol* 146*a*) and Parchon (under רמם) read רוֹמַם with *Pathach;* and Heidenheim and Baer have adopted it.

that rises, collateral form to רוֹמֵם, as עוֹלֵל and שׁוֹבֵב to עוֹלֵל and שׁוֹבֵב) was under my tongue; *i.e.* I became also at once so sure of my being heard, that I even had the song of praise in readiness (*vid.* x. 7), with which I had determined to break forth when the help for which I had prayed, and which was assured to me, should arrive. For the purpose of his heart was not at any time, in contradiction to his words, אָוֶן, God-abhorred vileness or worthlessness; רָאָה with the accusative, as in Gen. xx. 10, Ps. xxxvii. 37: to aim at, or design anything, to have it in one's eye. We render: If I had aimed at evil in my heart, the Lord would not hear; not: He would not have heard, but: He would not on any occasion hear. For a hypocritical prayer, coming from a heart which has not its aim sincerely directed towards Him, He does not hear. The idea that such a heart was not hidden behind his prayer is refuted in ver. 19 from the result, which is of a totally opposite character. In the closing doxology the accentuation rightly takes תְּפִלָּתִי וְחַסְדּוֹ as belonging together. Prayer and mercy stand in the relation to one another of call and echo. When God turns away from a man his prayer and His mercy, He commands him to be silent and refuses him a favourable answer. The poet, however, praises God that He has deprived him neither of the joyfulness of prayer nor the proof of His favour. In this sense Augustine makes the following practical observation on this passage: *Cum videris non a te amotam deprecationem tuam, securus esto, quia non est a te amota misericordia ejus.*

PSALM LXVII.

HARVEST THANKSGIVING SONG.

2 ELOHIM be merciful unto us and bless us,
   May He cause His face to shine among us—(*Sela.*)

3 That Thy way may be known upon earth,
   Among all the heathen Thy salvation.

4 *Peoples shall praise Thee, Elohim,*
   The peoples shall praise Thee, all of them.

5 Nations shall rejoice and shout for joy,
   For Thou wilt judge peoples in uprightness,
   And the nations upon earth Thou wilt lead.   (*Sela.*)

6 *Peoples shall praise Thee, Elohim,*
   The peoples shall praise Thee, all of them.

7 The earth hath yielded her fruit,
   Elohim our God doth bless us.

8 Elohim shall bless us,
   And all the ends of the earth shall fear Him.

Like Ps. lxv., this Psalm, inscribed *To the Precentor, with accompaniment of stringed instruments, a song-Psalm* (מזמור שיר), also celebrates the blessing upon the cultivation of the ground. As Ps. lxv. contemplated the corn and fruits as still standing in the fields, so this Psalm contemplates, as it seems, the harvest as already gathered in, in the light of the redemptive history. Each plentiful harvest is to Israel a fulfilment of the promise given in Lev. xxvi. 4, and a pledge that God is with His people, and that its mission to the whole world (of peoples) shall not remain unaccomplished. This mission-tone referring to the end of God's work here below is unfortunately lost in the church's closing strain, "God be gracious and merciful unto us," but it sounds all the more distinctly and sweetly in Luther's hymn, "*Es woll uns Gott genädig sein,*" throughout.

There are seven stanzas: twice three two-line stanzas, having one of three lines in the middle, which forms the clasp or spangle of the septiad, a circumstance which is strikingly appropriate to the fact that this Psalm is called "the Old Testament Paternoster" in some of the old expositors.* The second half after the three-line stanza begins in ver. 6 exactly as the first closed in ver. 4. יברכנו is repeated three times, in order that the whole may bear the impress of the blessing of the priest, which is threefold.

-----

* *Vid.* Sonntag's *Tituli Psalmorum* (1687), where it is on this account laid out as the Rogate Psalm.

Vers. 2, 3. The Psalm begins (ver. 2) with words of the priest's benediction in Num. vi. 24–26. By אָתָּנוּ the church desires for itself the unveiled presence of the light-diffusing loving countenance of its God. Here, after the echo of the holiest and most glorious benediction, the music strikes in. With ver. 3 the *Beracha* passes over into a *Tephilla*. לָדַעַת is conceived with the most general subject: that one may know, that may be known Thy way, etc. The more graciously God attests Himself to the church, the more widely and successfully does the knowledge of this God spread itself forth from the church over the whole earth. They then know His דֶּרֶךְ, *i.e.* the progressive realization of His counsel, and His יְשׁוּעָה, the salvation at which this counsel aims, the salvation not of Israel merely, but of all mankind.

Vers. 4, 5. Now follows the prospect of the entrance of all peoples into the kingdom of God, who will then praise Him in common with Israel as their God also. His judging (שׁפט) in this instance is not meant as a judicial punishment, but as a righteous and mild government, just as in the christological parallels lxxii. 12 sq., Isa. xi. 3 sq. מִישׁוֹר in an ethical sense for מֵישָׁרִים, as in xlv. 7, Isa. xi. 4, Mal. ii. 6. הִנְחָה as in xxxi. 4 of gracious guidance (otherwise than in Job xii. 23).

Vers. 6–8. The joyous prospect of the conversion of heathen, expressed in the same words as in ver 4, here receives as its foundation a joyous event of the present time: the earth has just yielded its fruit (cf. lxxxv. 13), the fruit that had been sown and hoped for. This increase of corn and fruits is a blessing and an earnest of further blessing, by virtue of which (Jer. xxxiii. 9, Isa. lx. 3; cf. on the contrary Joel ii. 17) it shall come to pass that all peoples unto the uttermost bounds of the earth shall reverence the God of Israel. For it is the way of God, that all the good that He manifests towards Israel shall be for the well-being of mankind.

PSALM LXVIII.

HYMN OF WAR AND VICTORY IN THE STYLE OF DEBORAH.

2 LET Elohim arise, let His enemies be scattered,
And let those who hate Him flee before His face.

3 As smoke is driven away, do Thou drive them away;
  As wax melteth before the fire,
  Let the wicked perish before Elohim.

4 And let the righteous rejoice, let them exult before Elohim,
  And let them be glad with joy.
5 Sing unto Elohim, harp His name,
  Pave a highway for Him who rideth along through the
      steppes;
  Jāh is His name, and exult ye before Him.

6 A Father of the fatherless and an Advocate of the widows
  Is Elohim in His holy habitation.
7 Elohim maketh a household for the solitary,
  He leadeth forth prisoners into prosperity;
  Yet the rebellious abide in a land of drought.

8 Elohim, when Thou wentest forth before Thy people,
  When Thou didst march along in the wilderness—(*Sela.*)
9 The earth shook,
  The heavens also dropped before Elohim,
  Yon Sinai before Elohim, the God of Israel.

10 With plentiful rain didst Thou, Elohim, water Thine in-
      heritance,
  And when it was parched, THOU hast confirmed it.
11 Thy creatures have settled down therein,
  Thou didst provide with Thy goodness for the poor,
      Elohim.

12 The Lord will sound forth the mandate;
  Of the women who herald victory there is a great army.
13 The kings of hosts shall flee, shall flee,
  And she that tarrieth at home shall divide the spoil.

14 If ye encamp among the sheep-folds,
  The dove's wings are covered with silver
  And her feathers with glistening gold.
15 When the Almighty scattereth kings therein,
  It becometh snow-white upon Zalmon.

16 A mountain of Elohim is the mountain of Bashan,
   A mountain full of peaks is the mountain of Bashan.
17 Why look ye enviously, ye many-peaked mountains,
   Upon the mountain which Elohim hath chosen, to dwell
        thereon?
   Yea, Jahve will dwell [there] for ever.

18 The war-chariots of Elohim are myriads, a thousand thou-
        sands,
   The Lord is among them, it is a Sinai in holiness.
19 Thou hast ascended up to the height, Thou hast led captives
        captive,
   Thou hast received gifts among men,
   Even from the rebellious, that Jāh Elohim might dwell
        [there].

20 Blessed be the Lord:
   Day by day doth He bear our burden,
   He, God, is our salvation.   (*Sela.*)
21 He, God, is to us a God for deeds of deliverance,
   And Jahve the Lord hath ways of escape for death.

22 Yea, Elohim will smite the head of His enemies,
   The hairy scalp of him who stalketh along in his trespasses.
23 The Lord hath said: Out of Bashan will I bring back,
        I will bring back out of the depths of the sea,
24 That thou mayest bathe thy foot in blood,
   That the tongue of thy dogs may have its share of the
        enemy.

25 They behold Thy splendid procession, Elohim,
   The splendid procession of my God, my King in holiness.
26 Before went the singers, behind the players on stringed in-
        struments,
   In the midst of damsels striking timbrels.
27 In the choirs of the congregation bless ye Elohim,
   The Lord, ye who are out of the fountain of Israel.
28 There is Benjamin the youngest, their ruler;
   The princes of Judah—their motley band,
   The princes of Zebulun, the princes of Naphtali.

29 Thy God hath commanded thy supreme power—
    Uphold in power, Elohim, what Thou hast wrought for us!—
30 From Thy temple above Jerusalem
    Let kings present offerings into Thee.
31 Threaten the wild beast of the reed, the troops of bulls with
            the calves of the people,
    That they may prostrate themselves with ingots of silver!—
    He hath scattered the peoples that delight in wars.
32 Magnates come out of Egypt,
    Cush—quickly do his hands stretch out unto Elohim.

33 Ye kingdoms of the earth, sing unto Elohim,
    Praising the Lord with stringed instruments—(*Sela.*)
34 To Him who rideth in the heaven of heavens of the
            primeval time—
    Lo, He made Himself heard with His voice, a mighty voice.
35 Ascribe ye might unto Elohim!

    Over Israel is His majesty,
    And His omnipotence in the heights of the heavens.
36 Terrible is Elohim out of thy sanctuaries;
    "The God of Israel giveth might and abundant strength
            to the people!"
    Blessed be Elohim!

Is it not an admirably delicate tact with which the collec-
tor makes the מזמור שיר lxviii. follow upon the מזמור שיר lxvii.?
The latter began with the echo of the benediction which
Moses puts into the mouth of Aaron and his sons, the former
with a repetition of those memorable words in which, at the
breaking up of the camp, he called upon Jahve to advance
before Israel (Num. x. 35). "It is in reality," says Hitzig of
Ps. lxviii., "no easy task to become master of this Titan."
And who would not agree with him in this remark? It is a
Psalm in the style of Deborah, stalking along upon the highest
pinnacle of hymnic feeling and recital; all that is most glorious
in the literature of the earlier period is concentrated in it:
Moses' memorable words, Moses' blessing, the prophecies of
Balaam, the Deuteronomy, the Song of Hannah re-echo here.
But over and above all this, the language is so bold and so

peculiarly its own, that we meet with no less than thirteen
words that do not occur anywhere else. It is so distinctly
Elohimic in its impress, that the simple *Elohim* occurs twenty-
three times; but in addition to this, it is as though the whole
cornucopia of divine names were poured out upon it: יהוה in
ver. 17; אדני six times; הָאֵל twice; שַׁדַּי in ver. 15; יָהּ in ver. 5;
יהוה אדני in ver. 21; יה אלהים in ver. 19; so that this Psalm
among all the Elohimic Psalms is the most resplendent. In
connection with the great difficulty that is involved in it, it is
no wonder that expositors, more especially the earlier expositors, should differ widely in their apprehension of it as a whole
or in separate parts. This circumstance has been turned to
wrong account by Ed. Reuss in his essay, "*Der acht-und-
sechzigste Psalm, Ein Denkmal exegetischer Noth und Kunst zu
Ehren unsrer ganzen Zunft*, Jena, 1851," for the purpose of
holding up to ridicule the uncertainty of Old Testament exegesis, as illustrated in this Psalm.

The Psalm is said, as Reuss ultimately decides, to have
been written between the times of Alexander the Great and
the Maccabees, and to give expression to the wish that the
Israelites, many of whom were far removed from Palestine and
scattered abroad in the wide earth, might soon be again united
in their fatherland. But this apprehension rests entirely upon
violence done to the exegesis, more particularly in the supposition that in ver. 23 the exiles are the persons intended by those
whom God will bring back. Reuss makes out those who are
brought back out of Bashan to be the exiles in Syria, and those
who are brought back out of the depths of the sea he makes
out to be the exiles in Egypt. He knows nothing of the
remarkable concurrence of the mention of the Northern tribes
(including Benjamin) in ver. 28 with the Asaphic Psalms:
Judah and Benjamin, to his mind, is Judæa; and Zebulun and
Naphtali, Galilee in the sense of the time after the return from
exile. The "wild beast of the reed" he correctly takes to be an
emblem of Egypt; but he makes use of violence in order to
bring in a reference to Syria by the side of it. Nevertheless
Olshausen praises the services Reuss has rendered with respect
to this Psalm; but after incorporating two whole pages of the
"*Denkmal*" in his commentary he cannot satisfy himself with
the period between Alexander and the Maccabees, and by

means of three considerations arrives, in this instance also, at the common refuge of the Maccabæan period, which possesses such an irresistible attraction for him.

In opposition to this transplanting of the Psalm into the time of the Maccabees we appeal to Hitzig, who is also quick-sighted enough, when there is any valid ground for it, in find-ing out Maccabæan Psalms. He refers the Psalm to the victorious campaign of Joram against faithless Moab, under-taken in company with Jehoshaphat. Böttcher, on the other hand, sees in it a festal hymn of triumph belonging to the time of Hezekiah, which was sung antiphonically at the great fra-ternizing Passover after the return home of the young king from one of his expeditions against the Assyrians, who had even at that time fortified themselves in the country east of the Jordan (Bashan). Thenius (following the example of Rödiger) holds a different view. He knows the situation so very defi-nitely, that he thinks it high time that the discussion concern-ing this Psalm was brought to a close. It is a song composed to inspirit the army in the presence of the battle which Josiah undertook against Necho, and the prominent, hateful character in ver. 22 is Pharaoh with his lofty artificial adornment of hair upon his shaven head. It is, however, well known what a memorably tragical issue for Israel that battle had; the Psalm would therefore be a memorial of the most lamentable disap-pointment.

All these and other recent expositors glory in not advanc-ing any proof whatever in support of the inscribed לדוד. And yet there are two incidents in David's life, with regard to which the Psalm ought first of all to be accurately looked at, before we abandon this לדוד to the winds of conjecture. The first is the bringing home of the Ark of the covenant to Zion, to which, *e.g.*, Franz Volkmar Reinhard (in vol. ii. of the Velt-husen *Commentationes Theol.* 1795), Stier, and Hofmann refer the Psalm. But the manner in which the Psalm opens with a paraphrase of Moses' memorable words is at once opposed to this; and also the impossibility of giving unity to the explana-tion of its contents by such a reference is against it. Jahve has long since taken up His abode upon the holy mountain; the poet in this Psalm, which is one of the Psalms of war and victory describes how the exalted One, who now, however, as

in the days of old, rides along through the highest heavens at
the head of His people, casts down all powers hostile to Him
and to His people, and compels all the world to confess that
the God of Israel rules from His sanctuary with invincible
might. A far more appropriate occasion is, therefore, to be
found in the Syro-Ammonitish war of David, in which the
Ark was taken with them by the people (2 Sam. xi. 11); and
the hymn was not at that time first of all composed when, at
the close of the war, the Ark was brought back to the holy
mountain (Hengstenberg, Reinke), but when it was set in
motion from thence at the head of Israel as they advanced
against the confederate kings and their army (2 Sam. x. 6).
The war lasted into the second year, when a second campaign
was obliged to be undertaken in order to bring it to an end;
and this fact offers at least a second possible period for the
origin of the Psalm. It is clear that in vers. 12–15, and still
more clear that in vers. 20–24 (and from a wider point of view,
vers. 29–35), the victory over the hostile kings is only hoped
for, and in vers. 25–28, therefore, the pageantry of victory is
seen as it were beforehand. It is the spirit of faith, which here
celebrates beforehand the victory of Jahve, and sees in the
single victory a pledge of His victory over all the nations of
the earth. The theme of the Psalm, generalized beyond its
immediate occasion, is the victory of the God of Israel over the
world. Regarded as to the nature of its contents, the whole
divides itself into two halves, vers. 2–19, 20–35, which are on
the whole so distinct that the first dwells more upon the mighty
deed God has wrought, the second upon the impressions it produces upon the church and upon the peoples of the earth; in both
parts it is viewed now as future, now as past, inasmuch as the
longing of prayer and the confidence of hope soar aloft to the
height of prophecy, before which futurity lies as a fulfilled fact.
The musical *Sela* occurs three times (vers. 8, 20, 33). These
three *forte* passages furnish important points of view for the
apprehension of the collective meaning of the Psalm.

But is David after all the author of this Psalm? The
general character of the Psalm is more Asaphic than Davidic
(*vid. Habakkuk*, S. 122). Its references to Zalmon, to Benjamin and the Northern tribes, to the song of Deborah, and in
general to the Book of Judges (although not in its present

form), give it an appearance of being Ephraimitish. Among the Davidic Psalms it stands entirely alone, so that criticism is quite unable to justify the לדוד. And if the words in ver. 29a are addressed to the king, it points to some other poet than David. But is it to a cotemporary poet? The mention of the sanctuary on Zion in vers. 30, 36, does not exclude such an one. Only the threatening of the " wild beast of the sedge" (ver. 31) seems to bring us down beyond the time of David; for the inflammable material of the hostility of Egypt, which broke out into a flame in the reign of Rehoboam, was first gathering towards the end of Solomon's reign. Still Egypt was never entirely lost sight of from the horizon of Israel; and the circumstance that it is mentioned in the first rank, where the submission of the kingdoms of this world to the God of Israel is lyrically set forth in the prophetic prospect of the future, need not astonish one even in a poet of the time of David. And does not ver. 28 compel us to keep on this side of the division of the kingdom? It ought then to refer to the common expedition of Jehoram and Jehoshaphat against Moab (Hitzig), the indiscriminate celebration of which, however, was no suitable theme for a psalmist.

Vers. 2–7. The Psalm begins with the expression of a wish that the victory of God over all His foes and the triumphant exultation of the righteous were near at hand. Ewald and Hitzig take יקום אלהים hypothetically: If God arise, His enemies will be scattered. This rendering is possible in itself so far as the syntax is concerned, but here everything conspires against it; for the futures in vers. 2–4 form an unbroken chain; then a glance at the course of the Psalm from ver. 20 onwards shows that the circumstances of Israel, under which the poet writes, urged forth the wish: let God arise and humble His foes; and finally the primary passage, Num. x. 35, makes it clear that the futures are the language of prayer transformed into the form of the wish. In ver. 3 the wish is addressed directly to God Himself, and therefore becomes petition. הִנְדֹּף is inflected (as *vice versâ* יִרְדֹּף, vii. 6, from יִרְדֹּף) from הִנָּדֵף (like הִנָּתֹן, Jer. xxxii. 4); it is a violation of all rule in favour of the confor-mity of sound (cf. הִקְצֹת for הַקְצֹת, Lev. xiv. 43, and *supra* on li. 6) with תִּנְדֹּף, the object of which is easily supplied (*dispellas*, *sc. hostes tuos*), and is purposely omitted in order to direct attention more stedfastly to the omnipotence which to every creature is so irresistible.   Like smoke, wax (דּוֹנָג, root דג, τηκ, Sanscrit *tak*, to shoot past, to run, Zend *tak'*, whence *vitak'ina*, dissolving, Neo-Persic *gudâchten;* causative: to cause to run in different directions = to melt or smelt) is an emblem of human feebleness.   As Bakius observes, *Si creatura creaturam non fert, quomodo creatura creatoris indignantis faciem ferre possit?*   The wish expressed in ver. 4 forms the obverse of the preceding.   The expressions for joy are heaped up in order to describe the transcendency of the joy that will follow the release from the yoke of the enemy.   לִפְנֵי is expressively used in alternation with מפני in vers. 2, 3 : by the wrathful action, so to speak, that proceeds from His countenance [just as the heat radiating from the fire melts the wax] the foes are dispersed, whereas the righteous rejoice before His gracious countenance.

As the result of the challenge that has been now expressed in vers. 2–4, Elohim, going before His people, begins His march; and in ver. 5 an appeal is made to praise Him with song, His name with the music of stringed instruments, and to make a way along which He may ride בַּעֲרָבוֹת.   In view of ver. 34 we cannot take ערבות, as do the Targum and Talmud (*B. Chagiga* 12*b*), as a name of one of the seven heavens, a meaning to which, apart from other considerations, the verb עָרַב, to be effaced, confused, dark, is not an appropriate stem-word; but it must be explained according to Isa. xl. 3.   There Jahve calls in the aid of His people, here He goes forth at the head of His people; He rides through the steppes in order to fight against the enemies of His people.   Not merely the historical reference assigned to the Psalm by Hitzig, but also the one adopted by ourselves, admits of allusion being made to the "steppes of Moab;" for the way to Mêdebâ, where the Syrian mercenaries of the Ammonites had encamped (1 Chron. xix. 7), lay through these steppes, and also the way to Rabbath Ammon (2 Sam. x. 7 sq.).   סֹלּוּ calls upon them to make a way for Him, the glorious, invincible King (cf. Isa. lvii. 14, lxii. 10); סָלַל signifies to cast up, heap up or pave, viz. a raised and suitable street or highway, Symmachus καταστρώσατε.   He who thus rides along makes the salvation of His people His aim: "Jāh is His name, therefore shout with joy before Him."   The *Beth* in בְּיָהּ (Symmachus, Quinta: ἴα) is the *Beth essentiæ*, which here, as in Isa. xxvi. 4, stands beside the subject: His name is (exists) in יה, *i.e.* His essential name is יה, His self-attestation, by which He makes Himself capable of being known and named, consists in His being the God of salvation, who, in the might of free grace, pervades all history. This Name is a fountain of exultant rejoicing to His people.

This Name is exemplificatively unfolded in vers. 6 sq. The highly exalted One, who sits enthroned in the heaven of glory, rules in all history here below and takes an interest in the lowliest more especially, in all circumstances of their lives following after His own to succour them. He takes the place of a father to the orphan. He takes up the cause of the widow and contests it to a successful issue. Elohim is one who makes the solitary or isolated to dwell in the house; בַּיְתָה with *He locale*, which just as well answers the question where? as whither? בַּיִת, a house = family bond, is the opposite of יָחִיד, *solitarius*, recluse, xxv. 16. Dachselt correctly renders it, *in domum, h.e. familiam numerosam durabilemque eos ut patres-familias plantabit.* He is further One who brings forth (out of the dungeon and out of captivity) those who are chained into abundance of prosperity. כּוֹשָׁרוֹת, occurring only here, is a *pluralet.* from כָּשַׁר, synonym אָשֵׁר, to be straight, fortunate. Ver. 7c briefly and sharply expresses the reverse side of this His humanely condescending rule among mankind. אַךְ is here (cf. Gen. ix. 4, Lev. xi. 4) restrictive or adversative (as is more frequently the case with אָכֵן); and the preterite is the preterite of that which is an actual matter of experience. The סוֹרְרִים, *i.e.* (not from סוּר, the apostate ones, Aquila ἀφιστάμενοι, but as in lxvi. 7, from סָרַר) the rebellious, Symmachus ἀπειθεῖς, who were not willing to submit to the rule of so gracious a God, had ever been excluded from these proofs of favour. These must inhabit צְחִיחָה (accusative of the object), a sun-scorched land; from צָחַח, to be dazzlingly bright, sunny, dried or parched up. They remain in the desert without coming into the land, which, fertilized by the waters of grace, is resplendent with a fresh verdure and with rich fruits. If the poet has before his mind in connection with this the bulk of the people delivered out of Egypt, ὧν τὰ κῶλα ἔπεσαν ἐν τῇ ἐρήμῳ (Heb. iii. 17), then the transition to what follows is much more easily effected. There is, however, no necessity for any such intermediation. The poet had the march through the desert to Canaan under the guidance of Jahve, the irresistible Conqueror, in his mind even from the beginning, and now he expressly calls to mind that marvellous divine leading in order that the present age may take heart thereat.

Vers. 8–11. In vers. 8 sq. the poet repeats the words of Deborah (Judg. v. 4 sq.), and her words again go back to Deut. xxxiii. 2, cf. Ex. xix. 15 sqq.; on the other hand, our Psalm is the original to Hab. ch. iii. The martial verb יָצָא represents Elohim as, coming forth from His heavenly dwelling-place (Isa. xxvi. 21), He places Himself at the head of Israel. The stately verb צָעַד represents Him as He accompanies the hosts of His people with the step of a hero confident of victory; and the terrible name for the wilderness, יְשִׁימוֹן, is designedly chosen in order to express the contrast between the scene of action and that which they beheld at that time. The verb to זֶה סִינַי is easily supplied; Dachselt's rendering according to the accents is correct: *hic mons Sinai* (sc. *in specie ita tremuit*). The description fixes our attention upon Sinai as the central point of all revelations of God during the period of deliverance by the hand of Moses, as being the scene of the most glorious of them all (*vid.* on Hab. p. 136 sq.). The majestic phenomena which proclaimed the nearness of God are distributed over the whole journeying, but most gloriously concentrated themselves at the giving of the Law on Sinai. The earth trembled throughout the extended circuit of this vast granite range, and the heavens dropped, inasmuch as the darkness of thunder clouds rested upon Sinai, pierced by incessant lightnings (Ex. ch. xix.). There, as the original passages describe it, Jahve met His people; He came from the east, His people from the west; there they found themselves together, and shaking the earth, breaking through the heavens, He gave them a pledge of the omnipotence which should henceforth defend and guide them. The poet has a purpose in view in calling Elohim in this passage "the God of Israel;" the covenant relationship of God to Israel dates from Sinai, and from this period onwards, by reason of the Tôra, He became Israel's King (Deut. xxxiii. 5). Since the statement of a fact of earlier history has preceded, and since the preterites alternate with

them, the futures that follow in vers. 10, 11 are to be understood as referring to the synchronous past; but hardly so that
ver. 10 should refer to the miraculous supply of food, and more
especially the rain of manna, during the journeyings through
the wilderness. The giving of the Law from Sinai has a view
to Israel being a settled, stationary people, and the deliverance
out of the land of bondage only finds its completion in the
taking and maintaining possession of the Land of Promise.
Accordingly vers. 10, 11 refer to the blessing and protection
of the people who had taken up their abode there.

The נַחֲלָה of God (*genit. auctoris*, as in 2 Macc. ii. 4) is the
land assigned by Him to Israel as an inheritance; and גֶּשֶׁם
נְדָבוֹת an emblem of the abundance of gifts which God has
showered down upon the land since Israel took up its abode
in it. נְדָבָה is the name given to a deed and gift springing
from an inward impulse, and in this instance the intensive idea
of richness and superabundance is associated therewith by
means of the plural; גֶּשֶׁם נְדָבוֹת is a shower-like abundance of
good gifts descending from above. The *Hiphil* הֵנִיף here governs
a double accusative, like the *Kal* in Prov. vii. 17, in so far, that
is, as נחלתך is drawn to ver. 10*a*; for the accentuation, in opposition to the Targum, takes נחלתך ונלאה together: Thine inheritance and that the parched one (*Waw epexeget.* as in 1 Sam.
xxviii. 3, Amos iii. 11, iv. 10). But this "and that" is devoid of
aim; why should it not at once be read הַנִּלְאָה? The rendering
of Böttcher, "Thy sickened and wearied," is inadmissible, too,
according to the present pointing; for it ought to be נַחֲלָתֵךְ or
נַחֲלָתֵךְ. And with a suffix this *Niphal* becomes ambiguous, and
more especially so in this connection, where the thought of נַחֲלָה,
an inherited possession, a heritage, lies so naturally at hand.
נַחֲלָתֵךְ is therefore to be drawn to ver. 10*a*, and ver. 10*b* must
begin with וְנִלְאָה, as in the LXX., καὶ ἠσθένησε, σὺ δὲ κατηρτίσω αὐτήν. It is true נִלְאָה is not a hypothetical preterite
equivalent to וְנִלְאָתָה; but, as is frequently the case with the
anarthrous participle (Ew. § 341, *b*), it has the value of a
hypothetical clause: "and if it (Israel's inheritance) were in a
parched, exhausted condition (cf. the cognate root לָהָה, Gen.
xlvii. 13), then hast Thou always made it again firm" (viii. 4,
Ex. xv. 17), *i.e.* strengthened, enlivened it. Even here the
idea of the inhabitants is closely associated with the land itself;

in ver. 11 they are more especially thought of : "Thy creatures dwelt therein." Nearly all modern expositors take חַיָּה either according to 2 Sam. xxiii. 11, 13 (cf. 1 Chron. xi. 15), in the signification tent-circle, ring-camp (root חו, حو, to move in a circle, to encircle, to compass), or in the signification of حَى (from حيى = חַיָּה, חַיּ), a race or tribe, *i.e.* a collection of living beings (cf. חַי, 1 Sam. xviii. 18). But the Asaphic character of this Psalm, which is also manifest in other points, is opposed to this rendering. This style of Psalm is fond of the comparison of Israel to a flock, so that also in lxxiv. 19 חית ענייך signifies nothing else than "the creatures [*Gethier*, collective] of Thy poor, Thy poor creatures." This use of חַיָּה is certainly peculiar; but not so remarkable as if by the "creatures of God" we had to understand, with Hupfeld, the quails (Ex. ch. xvi.). The avoiding of בְּהֵמָה on account of the idea of *brutum* (lxxiii. 22) which is inseparable from this word, is sufficient to account for it; in חיה, ζῶον, there is merely the notion of moving life. We therefore are to explain it according to Mic. vii. 14, where Israel is called a flock dwelling in a wood in the midst of Carmel: God brought it to pass, that the flock of Israel, although sorely persecuted, nevertheless continued to inhabit the land. בָּהּ, as in ver. 15, refers to Canaan. עָנִי in ver. 11*b* is the *ecclesia pressa* surrounded by foes on every side: Thou didst prepare for Thy poor with Thy goodness, Elohim, *i.e.* Thou didst regale or entertain Thy poor people with Thy possessions and Thy blessings. הֵכִין לְ, as in Gen. xliii. 16, 1 Chron. xii. 39, to make ready to eat, and therefore to entertain; טוֹבָה as in lxv. 12, טוּב ה', Jer. xxxi. 12. It would be quite inadmissible, because tautological, to refer תָּכִין to the land according to lxv. 10 (Ewald), or even to the desert (Olshausen), which the description has now left far behind.

Vers. 12–15. The futures that now follow are no longer to be understood as referring to previous history; they no longer alternate with preterites. Moreover the transition to the language of address in ver. 14 shows that the poet here looks forth from his present time and circumstances into the future; and the introduction of the divine name אֲדֹנָי, after *Elohim* has been used eleven times, is an indication of a new commencement. The prosperous condition in which God places His church by giving it the hostile powers of the world as a spoil is depicted. The noun אֹמֶר, never occurring in the genitival relationship, and never with a suffix, because the specific character of the form would be thereby obliterated, always denotes an important utterance, more particularly God's word of promise (lxxvii. 9), or His word of power (Hab. iii. 9), which is represented elsewhere as a mighty voice of thunder (lxviii. 34, Isa. xxx. 30), or a trumpet-blast (Zech. ix. 14); in the present instance it is the word of power by which the Lord suddenly changes the condition of His oppressed church. The entirely new state of things which this omnipotent behest as it were conjures into existence is presented to the mind in ver. 12*b*: the women who proclaim the tidings of victory—a great host. Victory and triumph follow upon God's אֹמֶר, as upon His creative יְהִי. The deliverance of Israel from the army of Pharaoh, the deliverance out of the hand of Jabin by the defeat of Sisera, the victory of Jephthah over the Ammonites, and the victorious single combat of David with Goliath were celebrated by singing women. God's decisive word shall also go forth this time, and of the evangelists, like Miriam (Mirjam) and Deborah, there shall be a great host.

Ver. 13 describes the subject of this triumphant exultation. Hupfeld regards vers. 13–15 as the song of victory itself, the fragment of an ancient triumphal ode (*epinikion*) reproduced here; but there is nothing standing in the way that should forbid our here regarding these verses as a direct continuation of ver. 12. The "hosts" are the numerous well-equipped armies which the kings of the heathen lead forth to the battle against the people of God. The unusual expression "kings of hosts" sounds very much like an ironically disparaging antithesis to the customary "Jahve of Hosts" (Böttcher). He, the Lord, interposes, and they are obliged to flee, staggering as they go, to retreat, and that, as the anadiplosis (cf. Judg. v. 7, xix. 20) depicts, far away, in every direction. The *fut. energicum* with its *ultima*-accentuation gives intensity to the pictorial expression. The victors then turn homewards laden with rich spoils. נְוַת בַּיִת, here in a collective sense, is the wife who stays at home (Judg. v. 24) while the husband goes forth to battle. It is not: the ornament (נָוֶה as in Jer. vi. 2) of the house, which Luther, with the LXX., Vulgate, and Syriac, adopts in his version,* but: the dweller or homely one (cf. נָוֶת, a dwelling-place, Job viii. 6) of the house, ἡ οἰκουρός. The dividing of the spoil elsewhere belongs to the victors; what is meant here is the distribution of the portions of the spoil that have fallen to the individual victors, the further distribution of which is left for the housewife (Judg. v. 30 sq., 2 Sam. i. 24). Ewald now recognises in vers. 14 sq. the words of an ancient song of victory; but ver. 13*b* is unsuitable to introduce them. The language of address in ver. 14 is the poet's own, and he here describes the condition of the people who are victorious by the help of their God, and who again dwell peaceably in the land after the war. אִם passes out of the hypothetical signification into the temporal, as *e.g.* in Job xiv. 14 (*vid.* on lix. 16.) The lying down among the sheep-folds (שְׁפַתַּיִם = מִשְׁפְּתַיִם, cf. שֶׁפֶט, מִשְׁפָּט, the staked-in folds or pens consisting of hurdles standing two by two over against one another) is an emblem of thriving peace, which (like vers. 8, 28) points back to Deborah's song, Judg. v. 16, cf. Gen. xlix. 14. Just such a time is now also before Israel, a time of peaceful prosperity enhanced by rich spoils. Everything shall glitter and gleam with silver and gold. Israel is God's turtle-dove, lxxiv. 19, cf. lvi. 1, Hos. vii. 11, xi. 11. Hence the new circumstances of ease and comfort are likened to the varied hues of a dove disporting itself in the sun. Its wings are as though overlaid with silver (נֶחְפָּה, not 3. *præt.*, but *part. fem. Niph.* as predicate to כַּנְפֵי, cf. 1 Sam. iv. 15, Mic. iv. 11, i. 9; Ew. § 317, *a*), therefore like silver wings (cf. Ovid, *Metam.* ii. 537: *Niveis argentea pennis Ales*); and its pinions with gold-green,† and that, as the reduplicated

---

* "*Hausehre,*" says he, is the housewife or matron as being the adornment of the house; *vid.* F. Dietrich, *Frau und Dame*, a lecture bearing upon the history of language (1864), S. 13.

† Ewald remarks, "Arabian poets also call the dove الوَرْقَاء, the greenish yellow, golden gleaming one, *vid.* Kosegarten, *Chrestom.* p. 156, 5." But this Arabic poetical word for the dove signifies rather the ash-green, whity blackish one. Nevertheless the signification greenish for the Hebrew יְרַקְרַק is established. Bartenoro, on *Negaim* xi. 4, calls the colour of the wings of the peacock ירקרק; and I am here reminded of what Wetzstein once told me, that, according to an Arab proverb, the surface of good coffee ought to be "like the neck of the dove," *i.e.* so oily that it gleams

form implies, with the iridescent or glistering hue of the finest gold (חָרוּץ, not dull, but shining gold). Side by side with this bold simile there appears in ver. 15 an equally bold but contrastive figure, which, turning a step or two backward, likewise vividly illustrates the results of their God-given victory. The suffix of בָּהּ refers to the land of Israel, as in Isa. viii. 21, lxv. 9. צַלְמוֹן, according to the usage of the language so far as it is now preserved to us, is not a common noun: deep darkness (Targum = צַלְמָוֶת), it is the name of a mountain in Ephraim, the trees of which Abimelech transported in order to set fire to the tower of Shechem (Judg. ix. 48 sqq.). The Talmudic literature was acquainted with a river taking its rise there, and also somewhat frequently mentions a locality bearing a similar name to that of the mountain. The mention of this mountain may in a general way be rendered intelligible by the consideration that, like Shiloh (Gen. xlix. 10), it is situated about in the centre of the Holy Land.* הִשְׁלִיג signifies to bring forth snow, or even, like اثلج, to become snow-white; this *Hiph.* is not a word descriptive of colour, like הִלְבִּין. Since the protasis is בְּפָרֵשׂ, and not בְּפָרְשָׂךְ, תַּשְׁלֵג is intended to be impersonal (cf. l. 3, Amos iv. 7, Mic. iii. 6); and the voluntative form is explained from its use in apodoses of hypothetical protases (Ges. § 128, 2). It indicates the issue to which, on the supposition of the other, it must and shall come. The words are therefore to be

---

like the eye of a peacock. A way for the transition from green to grey in *aurak* as the name of a colour is already, however, opened up in post-biblical Hebrew, when to frighten any one is expressed by הוריק פנים, *Genesis Rabba*, 47*a*. The intermediate notion is that of fawn colour, *i.e.* yellowish grey. In the Talmud the plumage of the full-grown dove is called זהוב and צהוב, *Chullin*, 22*b*.

* In *Tosifta Para*, ch. viii., a river of the name of יורדת הצלמון is mentioned, the waters of which might not be used in preparing the water of expiation (מי חטאת), because they were dried up at the time of the war, and thereby hastened the defeat of Israel (viz. the overthrow of Barcochba). Grätz (*Geschichte der Juden*, iv. 157, 459 f.) sees in it the *Nahar Arsuf*, which flows down the mountains of Ephraim past Bethar into the Mediterranean. The village of *Zalmon* occurs in the Mishna, *Jebamoth* xvi. 6, and frequently. The Jerusalem Gemara (*Maaseroth* i. 1) gives pre-eminence to the carob-trees of Zalmona side by side with those of Shitta and Gadara.

rendered: then it snows on Zalmon; and the snowing is either
an emblem of the glistening spoil that falls into their hands in
such abundance, or it is a figure of the becoming white, whether
from bleached bones (cf. Virgil, *Æn.* v. 865: *albi ossibus
scopuli;* xii. 36: *campi ossibus albent;* Ovid, *Fasti* i. 558:
humanis ossibus albet humus) or even from the naked corpses
(2 Sam. i. 19, עַל־בָּמוֹתֶיךָ חָלָל). Whether we consider the point
of comparison to lie in the spoil being abundant as the flakes
of snow, and like to the dazzling snow in brilliancy, or in the
white pallid corpses, at any rate בְּצַלְמוֹן is not equivalent to
כְּבְצַלְמוֹן, but what follows "when the Almighty scatters kings
therein" is illustrated by Zalmon itself. In the one case
Zalmon is represented as the battle-ground (cf. cx. 6), in the
other (which better corresponds to the nature of a wooded
mountain) as a place of concealment. The protasis בפרש וגו׳
favours the latter; for פֵּרֵשׂ signifies to spread wide apart, to
cause a compact whole—and the host of "the kings" is conceived of as such—to fly far asunder into many parts (Zech. ii.
10, cf. the *Niph.* in Ezek. xvii. 21). The hostile host disperses
in all directions, and Zalmon glitters, as it were with snow,
from the spoil that is dropped by those who flee. Homer also
(*Iliad,* xix. 357–361) likens the mass of assembled helmets,
shields, armour, and lances to the spectacle of a dense fall of
snow. In this passage of the Psalm before us still more than
in Homer it is the spectacle of the fallen and far seen glistening snow that also is brought into the comparison, and not
merely that which is falling and that which covers everything
(*vid. Iliad,* xii. 277 sqq.). The figure is the pendant of the
figure of the dove.*

---

* Wetzstein gives a different explanation (*Reise in den beiden Trachonen
und um das Haurângebirge* in the *Zeitschrift für allgem. Erdkunde,* 1859, S.
198). "*Then fell snow on Zalmon, i.e.* the mountain clothed itself in a
bright garment of light in celebration of this joyous event. Any one who
has been in Palestine knows how very refreshing is the spectacle of the
distant mountain-top capped with snow. The beauty of this poetical
figure is enhanced by the fact that Zalmon (ظلمان), according to its etymology, signifies a mountain range dark and dusky, either from shade,
forest, or black rock. The last would well suit the mountains of Haurân,
among which Ptolemæus (p. 365 and 370, *Ed. Wilberg*) mentions a mountain (according to one of the various readings) ʼΑσαλμανος."

Vers. 16–19. This victory of Israel over the kings of the
Gentiles gives the poet the joyful assurance that Zion is the
inaccessible dwelling-place of Elohim, the God of the heavenly
hosts. The mention of Zalmon leads him to mention other
mountains. He uses the mountains of Bashan as an emblem
of the hostile powers east of Jordan. These stand over
against the people of God, as the mighty mountains of Bashan
rising in steep, only slightly flattened peaks, to little hill-like
Zion. In the land on this side Jordan the limestone and
chalk formation with intermingled strata of sandstone predominates; the mountains of Bashan, however, are throughout
volcanic, consisting of slag, lava, and more particularly basalt
(*basanites*), which has apparently taken its name from Bashan
(Basan).* As a basalt range the mountains of Bashan are
conspicuous among other creations of God, and are therefore
called "the mountain of Elohim:" the basalt rises in the form
of a cone with the top lopped off, or even towers aloft like so
many columns precipitous and rugged to sharp points; hence
the mountains of Bashan are called הַר גַּבְנֻנִּים, *i.e.* a mountain
range (for הַר, as is well known, signifies both the single eminence
and the range of summits) of many peaks = a many-peaked
mountain; גַּבְנֹן is an adjective like רַעֲנָן, אֻמְלָל. With this boldly
formed mass of rock so gloomily majestic, giving the impression
of antiquity and of invincibleness, when compared with the
ranges on the other side of unstable porous limestone and softer
formations, more particularly with Zion, it is an emblem of the
world and its powers standing over against the people of God
as a threatening and seemingly invincible colossus. The poet
asks these mountains of Bashan "why," etc.? רָצַד is explained
from the Arabic رصد, which, in accordance with its root رص,
signifies to cleave firmly to a place (*firmiter inhæsit loco*), properly used of a beast of prey couching down and lying in wait
for prey, of a hunter on the catch, and of an enemy in ambush;
hence then: to lie in wait for, lurk, ἐνεδρεύειν, craftily, *insidiose*
(whence *râsid*, a lier-in-wait, *tarrassud*, an ambush), here: to
regard enviously, *invidiose*. In Arabic, just as in this instance,
it is construed as a direct transitive with an accusative of the

---

* This is all the more probable as Semitism has no proper word for
basalt; in Syria it is called *ḥag'ar aswad*, "black stone."

object, whereas the original signification would lead one to look for a dative of the object (רְצַד לְ), which does also really occur in the common Arabic. *Olewejored* is placed by גבנים, but what follows is not, after all, the answer: "the mountain— Elohim has chosen it as the seat of His throne," but הָהָר is the object of the interrogative clause: *Quare invidiose observatis, montes cacuminosi, hunc montem* (δεικτικῶς : that Zion yonder), *quem*, etc. (an attributive clause after a determinate substantive, as in lii. 9, lxxxix. 50, and many other instances, contrary to the Arabic rule of style). Now for the first time, in ver. 17c, follows that which is boastfully and defiantly contrasted with the proud mountains: "Jahve will also dwell for ever;" not only that Elohim has chosen Zion as the seat of His throne, it will also continue to be the seat of His throne, Jahve will continue to dwell [there] for ever. Grace is superior to nature, and the church superior to the world, powerful and majestic as this may seem to be. Zion maintains its honour over against the mountains of Bashan.

Ver. 18 now describes the kind of God, so to speak, who sits enthroned on Zion. The war-chariots of the heavenly hosts are here collectively called רֶכֶב, as in 2 Kings vi. 17. רִבֹּתַיִם (with *Dechî*, not *Olewejored*) is a dual from רִבּוֹת; and this is either an abstract noun equivalent to רִבּוּת (from which comes the apocopated רִבּוּ = רִבּוֹ), a myriad, consequently רִבֹּתַיִם, two myriads, or a contracted plural out of רִבָּאוֹת, Ezra ii. 69, therefore the dual of a plural (like לְהוֹתַיִם, חוֹמֹתַיִם) : an indefinite plurality of myriads, and this again doubled (Hofmann). With this sense, in comparison with which the other is poor and meagre, also harmonizes the expression אַלְפֵי שִׁנְאָן, thousands of repetition (ἅπαξ λεγομ. = שִׁנְיָן), *i.e.* thousands and again thousands, numberless, incalculable thousands; cf. the other and synonymous expression in Dan. vii. 10.* It is intended to

---

* Tradition (Targum, Saadia, and Abulwalîd) takes שִׁנְאָן forthwith as a synonym of מַלְאָךְ, an angel. So also the LXX. (Jerome): χιλιάδες εὐθηνούντων (שִׁנְאָן = שַׁאֲנַן), and Symmachus, χιλιάδες ἠχούντων (from שָׁאָה?). The stem-word is, however, שָׁנָה, just as שְׁנַיִם, Arabic *thinân, ithnân,* is also formed from a singular that is to be assumed, viz. שֵׁן, ثِن (اِثْن), and this from שָׁנָה, ثَنَى (cf. בֵּן from בָּנָה, بَنَى).

give a conception of the "hosts" which Elohim is to set in array against the "kings of hosts," *i.e.* the martial power of the kingdom of the world, for the protection and for the triumph of His own people. Chariots of fire and horses of fire appear in 2 Kings ii. 11, vi. 17 as God's retinue; in Dan. vii. 10 it is angelic forces that thus make themselves visible. They surround Him on both sides in many myriads, in countless thousands. אֲדֹנָי בָם (with *Beth raphatum*[*]), the Lord is among them (cf. Isa. xlv. 14), *i.e.* they are round about Him, He has them with Him (Jer. xli. 15), and is present with them. It now becomes clear why Sinai is mentioned, viz. because at the giving of the Law Jahve revealed Himself on Sinai surrounded by "ten thousands of saints" (Deut. xxxiii. 2 sq.). But in what sense is it mentioned? Zion, the poet means, presents to the spiritual eye now a spectacle such as Sinai presented in the earlier times, although even Sinai does not belong to the giants among the mountains:[†] God halts there with His angel host as a protection and pledge of victory to His people. The conjectures בא מסיני and בם מסיני (Hitzig) are of no use to us. We must either render it: Sinai is in the sanctuary, *i.e.* as it were transferred into the sanctuary of Zion; or: a Sinai is it in holiness, *i.e.* it presents a spectacle such as Sinai presented when God by His appearing surrounded it with holiness. The use of the expression בַּקֹּדֶשׁ in ver. 25, lxxvii. 14, Ex. xv. 11, decides in favour of the latter rendering.

With ver. 19 the Psalm changes to prayer. According to vii. 8, xlvii. 6, לַמָּרוֹם appears to be the height of heaven; but since in vers. 16—18 Zion is spoken of as Jahve's inaccessible dwelling-place, the connection points to מְרוֹם צִיּוֹן, Jer. xxxi. 12, cf. Ezek. xvii. 23, xx. 40. Moreover the preterites, which

---

[*] This is one of the three passages (the others being Isa. xxxiv. 11, Ezek. xxiii. 42; cf. Ew. § 93, *b*) in which the dageshing of the opening mute of the following word is given up after a soft final consonant, when the words are connected by a conjunctive accent or *Makkeph*.

[†] Cf. the epigram in Sadi's *Garden of Roses*, "Of all mountains Sinai is the smallest, and yet the greatest in rank and worth in the estimation of God," etc. On the words סיני בקדש which follow we may to a certain extent compare the name of honour given to it in Arabic, *ṭûr m'ana*, "Sinai of pensiveness" (Pertsch, *Die persischen Handschriften der Gothaer Bibliotkek*, 1859, S. 24).

under other circumstances we should be obliged to take as prophetic, thus find their most natural explanation as a retrospective
glance at David's storming of "the stronghold of Zion" (2 Sam.
v. 6–10) as the deed of Jahve Himself. But we should exceed
the bounds of legitimate historical interpretation by referring
לָקַחְתָּ מַתָּנוֹת בָּאָדָם to the *Nethînim*, Ezra viii. 20 (cf. Num. xvii.
6), those bondmen of the sanctuary after the manner of the
Gibeonites, Josh. ix. 23. The *Beth* of באדם is not *Beth sub-*
stantiæ: gifts consisting of men, so that these themselves are
the thing given (J. D. Michaelis, Ewald), but the expression
signifies *inter homines*, as in lxxviii. 60, 2 Sam. xxiii. 3, Jer.
xxxii. 20. עָלִיתָ לַמָּרוֹם mentions the ascending of the triumphant
One; שָׁבִיתָ שֶּׁבִי (cf. Judg. v. 12), the subjugation of the enemy;
לָקַחְתָּ וגו', the receiving of the gifts betokening homage and
allegiance (Deut. xxviii. 38, and frequently), which have been
presented to Him since He has taken possession of Zion,—there
He sits enthroned henceforth over men, and receives gifts like
to the tribute which the vanquished bring to the victor. These
He has received among men, and even (וְאַף, *atque etiam*, as in
Lev. xxvi. 39–42) among the rebellious ones. Or does a new
independent clause perhaps begin with וְאַף סוֹרֲרִים? This point
will be decided by the interpretation of the words that follow.
Side by side with an infinitive with ל expressing a purpose, the
one following noun (here a twofold name) has the assumption
against it of being the subject. Is יה אלהים then consequently
the object, or is it an apostrophe? If it be taken as the language of address, then the definition of the purpose, לשכן,
ought, as not being suited to what immediately precedes, to
refer back to עלית; but this word is too far off. Thus, therefore, the construction of יה אלהים with לשכן, as its object, is
apparently intended (Ewald, Hupfeld): and even the rebellious
are to dwell (Ges. § 132, rem. 1) with Jāh Elohim (*accus.* as
in v. 5, and frequently). This interpretation is also the one
most generally adopted among the old expositors. The Targum
renders: and even the rebellious who turn and repent, even
upon them will the Shechîna of the glory of Jāh Elohim
descend and dwell; the Syriac version: and even the rebellious
will ("not" is probably to be crossed out) dwell before God
(יעמדון קדם אלהא); and Jerome: *insuper et non credentes inhabi-*
tare Dominum Deum. Thus Theodoret also understands the

versions of the LXX. and of Aquila: "Thou hast not regarded their former disobedience, but notwithstanding their rebellion hast Thou continually been gracious to them ἕως αὐτοὺς οἰκητήριον οἰκεῖον ἀπέφηνας." The expression, however, sounds too grand to have "the rebellious ones" as its subject, and more particularly in view of ver. 7. Hence we take וְאַף סוֹרְרִים with בָּאָדָם: and even among rebellious ones (hast Thou received gifts), or: and even rebellious ones (give Thee); and לִשְׁכֹּן as a clause denoting the purpose, followed by the subject (as e.g. in 2 Sam. xix. 20): in order that Jāh Elohim may dwell, i.e. continue to dwell (as in ver. 17, cf. Isa. lvii. 15).

The first half of the Psalm ends here. With the words Jāh Elohim the Psalm has reached a summit upon which it takes its rest. God has broken forth on behalf of His people against their enemies, and He now triumphs over and on behalf of men. The circumstance of Elohim arising is the rise of the final glory, and His becoming manifest as Jāh Elohim is its zenith. Paul (Eph. iv. 8) gathers up the meaning of ver. 19, without following the LXX., in the following manner: ἀναβὰς εἰς ὕψος ᾐχμαλώτευσεν αἰχμαλωσίαν καὶ ἔδωκε δόματα τοῖς ἀνθρώποις. Might he perhaps have had the Targum, with which the Syriac version agrees, in his mind at the time: יְהַבְתָּא לְהוֹן מַתְּנָן לִבְנֵי נְשָׁא? He interprets in the light and in the sense of the history that realizes it. For the ascension of Elohim in its historical fulfilment is none other than the ascension of Christ. This latter was, however, as the Psalm describes it, a triumphal procession (Col. ii. 15); and what the Victor has gained over the powers of darkness and of death, He has gained not for His own aggrandisement, but for the interests of men. It is מַתָּנוֹת בָּאָדָם, gifts which He now distributes among men, and which benefit even the erring ones. So the apostle takes the words, inasmuch as he changes ἔλαβες into ἔδωκε. The gifts are the *charismata* which come down from the Exalted One upon His church.* It is a distribution of gifts, a dispensing of blessing, which stands related to His victory as its primary cause; for as Victor He is also the possessor of blessing, His

---

* In this respect Ps. lxviii. is the most appropriate Psalm for the *Dominica Pentecostes*, just as it is also, in the Jewish ritual, the Psalm of the second Shabuoth day.

gifts are as it were the spoils of the victory He has gained over sin, death, and Satan.* The apostle is the more warranted in this interpretation, since Elohim in what follows is celebrated as the Lord who also brings out of death. This praise in the historical fulfilment applies to Him, who, as Theodoret observes on ver. 21, has opened up the prison-house of death, which for us had no exit, and burst the brazen doors, and broken asunder the iron bolts,† viz. to Jesus Christ, who now has the keys of Death and of Hades.

Vers. 20–28. Now begins the second circuit of the hymn. Comforted by the majestic picture of the future that he has beheld, the poet returns to the present, in which Israel is still oppressed, but yet not forsaken by God. The translation follows the accentuation, regular and in accordance with the sense, which has been restored by Baer after Heidenheim, viz. אֲדֹנָי has *Zarka*, and יַעֲמָס־לָנוּ *Olewejored* preceded by the sub-distinctive *Rebia parvum;* it is therefore: *Benedictus Dominator: quotidie bajulat nobis,*—with which the Targum, Rashi, and Kimchi agree.‡ עָמַס, like נָשָׂא and סָבַל, unites the significations to lay a burden upon one (Zech. xii. 3, Isa. xlvi. 1, 3), and to carry a burden; with עַל it signifies to lay a burden upon any one, here with לְ to take up a burden for any one and to bear it for him. It is the burden or pressure of the hostile world that is meant, which the Lord day by day helps His church to bear, inasmuch as He is mighty by His strength in her who of herself is so feeble. The divine name אֵל, as being the subject of the sentence, is הָאֵל: God is our salvation. The music here again strikes in *forte,* and the same thought that is emphasized

---

* Just so Hölemann in the second division of his *Bibelstudien* (1861); whereas to Hofmann (*Schriftbeweis,* ii. 482 ff.) the New Testament application of the citation from the Psalm is differently brought about, because he refers neither ᾐχμαλώτευσεν αἰχμαλωσίαν nor κατέβη εἰς τὰ κατώτερα μέρη τῆς γῆς to the descent of the Lord into Hades.

† Just so that portion of the Gospel of Nicodemus that treats of Christ's descent into Hades; *vid.* Tischendorf, *Evangelia Apocryph.* (1853), p. 307.

‡ According to the customary accentuation the second יוֹם has *Mercha* or *Olewejored,* and יַעֲמָס־לָנוּ, *Mugrash.* But this *Mugrash* has the position of the accents of the *Silluk*-member against it; for although it does exceptionally occur that two conjunctives follow Mugrash (*Accentsystem,* xvii. § 5), yet these cannot in any case be *Mahpach sarkatum* and *Illui.*

by the music in its turn, is also repeated in ver. 21*a* with heightened expression: God is to us a God לְמוֹשָׁעוֹת, who grants us help in rich abundance. The *pluralet.* denotes not so much the many single proofs of help, as the riches of rescuing power and grace. In ver. 21*b* לַמָּוֶת corresponds to the לָנוּ; for it is not to be construed תּוֹצָאוֹת לַמָּוֶת: Jahve's, the Lord, are the outgoings to death (Böttcher), *i.e.* He can command that one shall not fall a prey to death. תוצאות, the parallel word to מוֹשָׁעוֹת, signifies, and it is the most natural meaning, the escapings; יָצָא, *evadere*, as in 1 Sam. xiv. 41, 2 Kings xiii. 5, Eccles. vii. 18. In Jahve's power are means of deliverance for death, *i.e.* even for those who are already abandoned to death. With אַךְ a joyously assuring inference is drawn from that which God is to Israel. The parallelism of the correctly divided verse shows that ראֹשׁ here, as in cx. 6, signifies *caput* in the literal sense, and not in the sense of *princeps*. The hair-covered scalp is mentioned as a token of arrogant strength, and unhumbled and impenitent pride, as in Deut. xxxii. 42, and as the Attic κομᾶν directly signifies to strut along, give one's self airs. The genitival construction is the same as in Isa. xxviii. 1*b*, xxxii. 13*b*. The form of expression refers back to Num. xxiv. 17, and so to speak inflects this primary passage very similarly to Jer. xlviii. 45. If קָדְקֹד שֵׂעָר be an object, then ראֹשׁ ought also to be a second object (that of the member of the body); the order of the words does not in itself forbid this (cf. iii. 8 with Deut. xxxiii. 11), but would require a different arrangement in order to avoid ambiguity. In ver. 23 the poet hears a divine utterance, or records one that he has heard: "From Bashan will I bring back, I will bring back from the eddies of the sea (from צוּל = צָלַל, to whiz, rattle; to whirl, eddy), *i.e.* the depths or abysses of the sea." Whom? When after the destruction of Jerusalem a ship set sail for Rome with a freight of distinguished and well-formed captives before whom was the disgrace of prostitution, they all threw themselves into the sea, comforting themselves with this passage of Scripture (*Gittin* 57*b*, cf. *Echa Rabbathi* 66*a*). They therefore took ver. 23 to be a promise which has Israel as its object;* but the clause expressing a

---

* So also the Targum, which understands the promise to refer to the restoration of the righteous who have been eaten by wild beasts and

purpose, ver. 24, and the paraphrase in Amos ix. 2 sq., show
that the foes of Israel are conceived of as its object. Even if
these have hidden themselves in the most out-of-the-way places,
God will fetch them back and make His own people the execu-
tioners of His justice upon them. The expectation is that the
flight of the defeated foes will take a southernly direction, and
that they will hide themselves in the primeval forests of Bashan,
and still farther southward in the depths of the sea, *i.e.* of the
Dead Sea (יָם as in Isa. xvi. 8, 2 Chron. xx. 2). Opposite to
the hiding in the forests of the mountainous Bashan stands the
hiding in the abyss of the sea, as the extreme of remoteness,
that which is in itself impossible being assumed as possible.
The first member of the clause expressing the purpose, ver. 24,
becomes more easy and pleasing if we read תִּרְחַץ (LXX.,
Syriac, and Vulgate, *ut intingatur*), according to lviii. 11. So
far as the letters are concerned, the conjecture תֶּחְמַץ (from
which תמחץ, according to Chajug′, is transposed), after Isa. lxiii.
1, is still more natural (Hitzig): that thy foot may redden itself
in blood. This is certainly somewhat tame, and moreover מִדָּם
would be better suited to this rendering than בְּדָם. As the text
now stands, תֶּמְחַץ* is equivalent to תִּמְחָצֵם (them, viz. the
enemies), and רַגְלְךָ בְּדָם is an adverbial clause (setting or plung-
ing thy foot in blood). It is, however, also possible that מָחַץ

is used like مَخَضَ (*vehementer commovere*): *ut concutias s.*

agites pedem tuam in sanguine. Can it now be that in ver. 24*b*
from among the number of the enemies the one who goes about
glorying in his sins, the רָשָׁע κατ' ἐξοχήν (cf. Isa. xi. 4, Hab. iii.
13, and other passages), is brought prominently forward by מִנֵּהוּ?
Hardly so; the absence of תִּלֹק (*lambat*) cannot be tolerated, cf.

----

drowned in the sea (Midrash: מבין שני אריות = מבשן); cf. also the things
related from the time of the Khaliphs in Jost's *Geschichte des Judenthums*,
ii. 399, and Grätz' *Gesch. der Juden*, v. 347.

    * The *Gaja* of the first closed syllable warns one to make a proper pause
upon it, in order that the guttural of the second, so apt to be slurred over,
may be distinctly pronounced; cf. תִּבְחַר, lxv. 5; הַרְחִיק, ciii. 12. So also
with the sibilants at the beginning of the second syllable, *e.g.* תַּדְשֵׁא, Gen.
i. 11, in accordance with which, in xiv. 1, liii. 2, we must write הִשְׁחִיתוּ
וְהִתְעִיבוּ.

1 Kings xxi. 19, xxii. 38. It is more natural, with Simonis, to refer מִנֵּהוּ back to לָשׁוֹן (a word which is usually *fem.*, but sometimes perhaps is *masc.*, xxii. 16, Prov. xxvi. 28); and, since side by side with מִמֶּנּוּ only מִנֵּהוּ occurs anywhere else (Ew. § 263, *b*), to take it in the signification *pars ejus* (מֶן from מָנַן = מָנָה, after the form גֵּו, חֵן, קֵץ, of the same meaning as מְנָה, מְנָת, lxiii. 11), in favour of which Hupfeld also decides.

What is now described in vers. 25-28, is not the rejoicing over a victory gained in the immediate past, nor the rejoicing over the earlier deliverance at the Red Sea, but Israel's joyful celebration when it shall have experienced the avenging and redemptive work of its God and King. According to lxxvii. 14, Hab. iii. 6, הֲלִיכוֹת appears to be God's march against the enemy; but what follows shows that the *pompa magnifica* of God is intended, after He has overcome the enemy. Israel's festival of victory is looked upon as a triumphal procession of God Himself, the King, who governs in holiness, and has now subjugated and humbled the unholy world; בַּקֹּדֶשׁ as in ver. 18. The rendering "in the sanctuary" is very natural in this passage, but Ex. xv. 11, Ps. lxxvii. 14, are against it. The subject of רָאוּ is all the world, more especially those of the heathen who have escaped the slaughter. The perfect signifies: they have seen, just as קִדְּמוּ, they have occupied the front position. Singers head the procession, after them (אַחַר,* an adverb as in Gen. xxii. 13, Ex. v. 1) players upon citherns and harps (נֹגְנִים, participle to נֵגֵּן), and on either side virgins with timbrels (Spanish *adufe*); תּוֹפֵפוֹת, apocopated *part. Poel* with the retention of *ē* (cf. שׁוֹקֵקָה, cvii. 9), from תָּפַף, to strike the תֹּף (دَفّ).

It is a retrospective reference to the song at the Sea, now again come into life, which Miriam and the women of Israel sang amidst the music of timbrels. The deliverance which is now being celebrated is the counterpart of the deliverance out of Egypt. Songs resound as in ver. 27, " in gatherings of the

---

* This אַחַר, according to *B. Nedarim* 37*b*, is a so-called עִטּוּר סוֹפְרִים (*ablatio scribarum*), the sopherim (sofrim) who watched over the faithful preservation of the text having removed the reading וְאַחַר, so natural according to the sense, here as in Gen. xviii. 5, xxiv. 55, Num. xxxi. 2, and marked it as not genuine.

congregation (and, so to speak, in full choirs) praise ye Elohim."
מַקְהֵלוֹת (מַקְהֵלִים, xxvi. 12) is the plural to קָהָל (xxii. 23), which
forms none of its own (cf. post-biblical קְהִלּוֹת from קְהִלָּה).   Ver.
27b is abridged from בָּרְכוּ אֲדֹנָי אֲשֶׁר אַתֶּם מִמָּקוֹר יִשְׂרָאֵל, praise ye
the Lord, ye who have Israel for your fountainhead.   אֲדֹנָי, in
accordance with the sense, has *Mugrash*. *Israel* is here the
name of the patriarch, from whom as from its fountainhead
the nation has spread itself abroad; cf. Isa. xlviii. 1, li. 1, and
as to the syntax מִמְּךָ, those who descend from thee, Isa. lviii.
12.   In the festive assembly all the tribes of Israel are represented by their princes. Two each from the southern and
northern tribes are mentioned. Out of Benjamin was Israel's
first king, the first royal victor over the Gentiles; and in Benjamin, according to the promise (Deut. xxxiii. 12) and according to the accounts of the boundaries (Josh. xviii. 16 sq., xv. 7
sq.), lay the sanctuary of Israel. Thus, therefore, the tribe
which, according both to order of birth (Gen. xliii. 29 sqq.)
and also extent of jurisdiction and numbers (1 Sam. ix. 21),
was "little," was honoured beyond the others.*   Judah, however, came to the throne in the person of David, and became for
ever the royal tribe.   Zebulun and Naphtali are the tribes highly
praised in Deborah's song of victory (Judg. v. 18, cf. iv. 6) on
account of their patriotic bravery.   רֹדֵם, giving no sense when
taken from the well-known verb רָדַם, falls back upon רָדָה, and
is consequently equivalent to רֹדָם (cf. Lam. i. 13), subduing or
ruling them; according to the sense, equivalent to רֹדֶה בָם (1
Kings v. 30, ix. 23, 2 Chron. viii. 10), like הַמַּעֲלֶם, not "their
leader up," but ὁ ἀναγαγὼν αὐτούς, Isa. lxiii. 11, not = רֹדֵיהֶם
(like רֹאֵיהֶם, עֹשֵׂיהֶם), which would signify their subduer or their
subduers.   The verb רָדָה, elsewhere to subjugate, oppress, hold
down by force, Ezek. xxxiv. 4, Lev. xxv. 53, is here used of
the peaceful occupation of the leader who maintains the order
of a stately and gorgeous procession.   For the reference to the
enemies, "their subduer," is without any coherence. But to
render the parallel word רִגְמָתָם "their (the enemies') stoning"
(Hengstenberg, Vaihinger, and others, according to Böttcher's

---

* Tertullian calls the Apostle Paul, with reference to his name and his
Benjamitish origin, *parvus Benjamin*, just as Augustine calls the poetess of
the *Magnificat*, *nostra tympanistria*.

"*Proben*"), is, to say nothing more, devoid of taste; moreover רָגַם does not mean to throw stones with a sling, but to stone as a judicial procedure. If we assign to the verb רָגַם the primary signification *congerere, accumulare*, after رجم VIII., and ركم, then רִגְמָתָם signifies their closely compacted band, as Jewish expositors have explained it (קהלם או קבוצם). Even if we connect רָגַם with רָקַם, *variegare*, or compare the proper name רֶגֶם = رجم, *socius* (Böttcher), we arrive at much the same meaning. Hupfeld's conjecture רִגְשָׁתָם is consequently unnecessary.

Vers. 29—36. The poet now looks forth beyond the domain of Israel, and describes the effects of Jahve's deed of judgment and deliverance in the Gentile world. The language of ver. 29*a* is addressed to Israel, or rather to its king (lxxxvi. 16, cx. 2): God, to whom everything is subject, has given Israel עֹז, victory and power over the world. Out of the consciousness that He alone can preserve Israel upon this height of power upon which it is placed, who has placed it thereon, grows the prayer: establish (עוּזָּה with וּ for *ŭ*, as is frequently the case, and with the accent on the *ultima* on account of the following *Aleph*, *vid.* on vi. 5), Elohim, that which Thou hast wrought for us; עָזַז, *roborare*, as in Prov. viii. 28, Eccles. vii. 19, LXX. δυνάμωσον, Symmachus ἐνίσχυσον. It might also be interpreted: show Thyself powerful (cf. רוּמָה, xxi. 14), Thou who (Isa. xlii. 24) hast wrought for us (פָּעַל as in Isa. xliii. 13, with לְ, like עָשָׂה לְ, Isa. lxiv. 3); but in the other way of taking it the prayer attaches itself more sequentially to what precedes, and lxii. 12 shows that זוּ can also represent the neuter. Hitzig has a still different rendering: the powerful divine help, which Thou hast given us; but although ה— instead of ת— in the *stat. construct.* is Ephraimitish style (*vid.* on xlv. 5), yet עוּזָּה for עֹז is an unknown word, and the expression "from Thy temple," which is manifestly addressed to Elohim, shows that פָּעַלְתָּ is not the language of address to the king (according to Hitzig, to Jehoshaphat). The language of prayerful address is retained in ver. 30. From the words מהיכלך על ירושלם there is nothing to be transported to ver. 29*b* (Hupfeld); for ver. 30 would thereby become stunted. The words together are the statement of the starting-point of the oblations belonging to יוֹבִילוּ: starting from Thy temple, which soars aloft over Jerusalem, may kings bring Thee, who sittest enthroned there in the Holy of holies, tributary gifts (שַׁי as in lxxvi. 12, Isa. xviii. 7).   In this connection (of prayer) it is the expression of the desire that the Temple may become the zenith or cynosure, and Jerusalem the metropolis, of the world.   In this passage, where it introduces the seat of religious worship, the taking of מִן as expressing the primary cause, " because or on account of Thy Temple" (Ewald), is not to be entertained. In ver. 31 follows a summons, which in this instance is only the form in which the prediction clothes itself.   The " beast of the reed" is not the lion, of which sojourn among the reeds is not a characteristic (although it makes its home *inter arundineta Mesopotamiæ*, Ammianus, xviii. 7, and in the thickets of the Jordan, Jer. xlix. 19, l. 44, Zech. xi. 3).   The reed is in itself an emblem of Egypt (Isa. xxxvi. 6, cf. xix. 6), and it is therefore either the crocodile, the usual emblem of Pharaoh and of the power of Egypt (Ezek. xxix. 3, cf. Ps. lxxiv. 13 sq.) that is meant, or even the hippopotamus (Egyptian *p-ehe-môut*), which also symbolizes Egypt in Isa. xxx. 6 (which see), and according to Job. xl. 21 is more appropriately than the crocodile (הַתַּנִּין אֲשֶׁר בַּיָּם, Isa. xxvii. 1) called חַיַּת קָנֶה.   Egypt appears here as the greatest and most dreaded worldly power. Elohim is to check the haughty ones who exalt themselves over Israel and Israel's God.   אַבִּירִים, strong ones, are bulls (xxii. 13) as an emblem of the kings; and עֶגְלֵי explains itself by the *genit. epexeg.* עַמִּים: together with (*Beth* of the accompaniment as in ver. 31*b*, lxvi. 13, and beside the *plur. humanus*, Jer. xli. 15) the calves, viz. the peoples, over whom those bulls rule. With the one emblem of Egypt is combined the idea of defiant self-confidence, and with the other the idea of comfortable security (*vid.* Jer. xlvi. 20 sq.).   That which is brought prominently forward as the consequence of the menace is moulded in keeping with these emblems.   מִתְרַפֵּס, which has been explained by Flaminius substantially correctly: *ut supplex veniat*, is intended to be taken as a *part. fut.* (according to the Arabic grammar, حال مقدّر, *lit.* a predisposed condition).   It thus comprehensively in the singular (like עֹבֵר in viii. 9) with one stroke depicts thoroughly humbled pride; for רָפַס (cf. רָמַס) signifies to stamp, pound, or trample, to knock down, and the *Hithpa.* either to behave as a trampling one, Prov. vi. 3, or to trample upon one's self, *i.e.* to cast one's self violently upon the ground. Others explain it as *conculcandum se præbere;* but such a meaning cannot be shown to exist in the sphere of the Hebrew *Hithpael;* moreover this "suffering one's self to be trampled upon" does not so well suit the words, which require a more active sense, viz. בְּרַצֵּי־כָסֶף, in which is expressed the idea that the riches which the Gentiles have hitherto employed in the service of God-opposed worldliness, are now offered to the God of Israel by those who both in outward circumstances and in heart are vanquished (cf. Isa. lx. 9). רַץ־כֶּסֶף (from רָצַץ, *confringere*) is a piece of uncoined silver, a bar, wedge, or ingot of silver. In בַּזַּר there is a wide leap from the call גְּעַר to the language of description. This rapid change is also to be found in other instances, and more especially in this dithy-rambic Psalm we may readily give up any idea of a change in the pointing, as בַּזֵּר or בַּזַּר (LXX. διασκόρπισον); בִּזַּר, as it stands, cannot be imperative (Hitzig), for the final vowel essential to the *imperat. Piel* is wanting. God hath scattered the peoples delighting in war; war is therefore at an end, and the peace of the world is realized.

In ver. 32, the contemplation of the future again takes a different turn: futures follow as the most natural expression of that which is future. The form יֶאֱתָיוּ, more usually found in pause, here stands pathetically at the beginning, as in Job xii. 6. חַשְׁמַנִּים, compared with the Arabic خشم (whence خَشْم, a nose, a word erroneously denied by Gesenius), would signify the supercilious, contemptuous (cf. أَشَمُ, *nasutus*, as an appella-tion of a proud person who will put up with nothing). On the other hand, compared with حشم, it would mean the fat ones, inasmuch as this verbal stem (root حشك, cf. חַשְׁרַת, 2 Sam. xxii. 12), starting from the primary signification "to be pressed together," also signifies "to be compressed, become compact," *i.e.* to regain one's plumpness, to make flesh and fat, applied, according to the usage of the language, to wasted men and

animals. The commonly compared حَشَم, *vir magni famulitii,*
is not at all natural,—a usage which is brought about by the
intransitive signification proper to the verb starting from its
radical signification, "to become or be angry, to be zealous
about any one or anything," inasmuch as the *nomen verbale*
حَشَم signifies in the concrete sense a person, or collectively
persons, for whose maintenance, safety, and honour one is
keenly solicitous, such as the members of the family, household attendants, servants, neighbours, clients or protégés,
guest-friends; also a thing which one ardently seeks, and over
the preservation of which one keeps zealous watch (Fleischer).
Here there does not appear to be any connecting link whatever
in the Arabic which might furnish some hold for the Hebrew;
hence it will be more advisable, by comparison of הַשְׁמַל and
חֹשֶׁן, to understand by הֹשְׁמַנִּים, the resplendent, most distinguished ones, *perillustres.* The dignitaries of Egypt come to
give glory to the God of Israel, and Æthiopia, disheartened
by fear before Jahve (cf. Hab. iii. 7), causes his hands to run
to Elohim, *i.e.* hastens to stretch them out. Thus it is interpreted by most expositors. But if it is יָדָיו, why is it not also
יָרִיץ? We reply, the Hebrew style, even in connection with
words that stand close beside one another, does not seek to
avoid either the *enallage generis* (*e.g.* Job xxxix. 3, 16), or the
enall. numeri (*e.g.* lxii. 5). But "to cause the hands to run"
is a far-fetched and easily misunderstood figure. We may
avoid it, if, with Böttcher and Olshausen, we disregard the
accentuation and interpret thus, "Cush—his hands cause to
hasten, *i.e.* bring on in haste (1 Sam. xvii. 17, 2 Chron.
xxxv. 13), to Elohim," viz. propitiating gifts; תָּרִיץ being the
predicate to יָדָיו, according to Ges. § 146, 3.

Ver. 33. The poet stands so completely in the midst of this
glory of the end, that soaring onwards in faith over all the
kingdoms of the world, he calls upon them to render praise to
the God of Israel. לָרֹכֵב attaches itself to the dominating
notion of שִׁירוּ in ver. 33*a*. The heavens of heavens (Deut. x.
14) are by קֶדֶם described as primeval (perhaps, following the
order of their coming into existence, as extending back beyond
the heavens that belong to our globe, of the second and fourth

day of Creation). God is said to ride along in the primeval heavens of the heavens (Deut. xxxiii. 26), when by means of the cherub (xviii. 11) He extends His operations to all parts of these infinite distances and heights. The epithet "who rideth along in the heavens of heavens of the first beginning" denotes the exalted majesty of the superterrestrial One, who on account of His immanency in history is called "He who rideth along through the steppes" (רֹכֵב בָּעֲרָבוֹת, ver. 5). In יִתֵּן בְּקוֹלוֹ we have a repetition of the thought expressed above in ver. 12 by יִתֵּן אֹמֶר; what is intended is God's voice of power, which thunders down everything that contends against Him. Since in the expression נָתַן בְּקוֹל (xlvi. 7, Jer. xii. 8) the voice, according to Ges. § 138, rem. 3, note, is conceived of as the medium of the giving, *i.e.* of the giving forth from one's self, of the making one's self heard, we must take קוֹל עֹז not as the object (as in the Latin phrase *sonitum dare*), but as an apposition:* behold, He maketh Himself heard with His voice, a powerful voice. Thus let them then give God עֹז, *i.e.* render back to Him in praise that acknowledges His omnipotence, the omnipotence which He hath, and of which He gives abundant proof. His glory (גַּאֲוָה) rules over Israel, more particularly as its guard and defence; His power (עֹז), however, embraces all created things, not the earth merely, but also the loftiest regions of the sky. The kingdom of grace reveals the majesty and glory of His redemptive work (cf. Eph. i. 6), the kingdom of nature the universal dominion of His omnipotence. To this call to the kingdoms of the earth they respond in ver. 36: "Awful is Elohim out of thy sanctuaries." The words are addressed to Israel, consequently מִקְדָּשִׁים is not the heavenly and earthly sanctuary (Hitzig), but the one sanctuary in Jerusalem (Ezek. xxi. 7 [2]) in the manifold character of its holy places (Jer. li. 51, cf. Am. vii. 9). Commanding reverence—such is the confession of the Gentile world—doth Elohim rule from thy most holy places, O Israel, the God who hath chosen thee as His mediatorial people. The second part of the confession runs: the God of Israel giveth power and abundant strength to the people, viz. whose God He is, equivalent to

---

* The accentuation does not decide; it admits of our taking it in both ways. Cf. xiv. 5, xli. 2, lviii. 7, lxviii. 28, Prov. xiii. 22, xxvii. 1.

לְעֻמּוֹ, xxix. 11. Israel's might in the omnipotence of God it is
which the Gentile world has experienced, and from which it
has deduced the universal fact of experience, ver. 36*b*. All
peoples with their gods succumb at last to Israel and its God.
This confession of the Gentile world closes with בָּרוּךְ אֱלֹהִים
(which is preceded by *Mugrash* transformed out of *Athnach*).
That which the psalmist said in the name of Israel in ver. 20,
"Blessed be the Lord," now re-echoes from all the world,
"Blessed be Elohim." The world is overcome by the church
of Jahve, and that not merely in outward form, but spiritually.
The taking up of all the kingdoms of the world into the kingdom of God, this the great theme of the Apocalypse, is also
after all the theme of this Psalm. The first half closed with
Jahve's triumphant ascension, the second closes with the
results of His victory and triumph, which embrace the world
of peoples.

PSALM LXIX.

PRAYER OUT OF THE DEPTH OF AFFLICTION BORNE
FOR THE SAKE OF THE TRUTH.

2 SAVE me, Elohim, for the waters press upon my life.
3 I have sunk in the mud of the abyss, and there is no standing;
   I am fallen into the depths of the waters and a flood over-
      floweth me.

4 I am wearied by my calling, my throat is parched,
   Mine eyes have failed, I who wait for my God.
5 More than the hairs of my head are those who hate me
      without a cause,
   Numerous are my destroyers, mine enemies falsely—
   That which I stole not, I must then restore.

6 Elohim, Thou knowest of my folly,
   And my guiltinesses are not hidden from Thee.
7 Let not those be ashamed, in me, who wait on Thee, O
      Lord, Jahve of hosts,
   Let not those be confounded, in me, who seek Thee, O God
      of Israel!

8 For for Thy sake have I borne reproach,
   Shame hath covered my face.

9 I am become estranged from my brethren,
   And an alien to my mother's children.
10 For the zeal of Thy house hath consumed me,
   And the reproaches of those who reproach Thee are fallen
      upon me.
11 As for me, my soul wept fasting,
   And it became reproaches to me.

12 I made sackcloth my garment,
   And became a satire to them.
13 Those who sit in the gate talk of me.
   And the music of the carousers.
14 Yet I, I pray to Thee, Jahve, in a time of favour,
   Elohim, by reason of Thy great mercy;
   Answer me with the truth of Thy salvation!

15 Rescue me out of the mud, that I sink not;
   Let me be rescued from my haters and out of the depths of
      the waters.
16 Let not the flood of waters overflow me,
   And let not the abyss swallow me up,
   And let not the well close its mouth upon me.

17 Answer me, Jahve, for good is Thy loving-kindness;
   According to the abundance of Thy compassion turn Thou
      unto me.
18 And hide not Thy face from Thy servant,
   For I am afraid, speedily answer me.
19 Draw near to my soul, redeem it,
   Because of mine enemies deliver me.

20 Thou knowest my reproach, and my shame, and my dis-
      honour;
   Present to Thee are all mine adversaries.
21 Reproach hath broken my heart, and I became sick unto
   I hoped for pity, but in vain,   [death,
   And for comforters—finding none.

22 They gave me for my meat gall,
    And for my thirst they gave me vinegar to drink.

23 Let their table before them become a snare,
    And to the unconcerned a trap.
24 Let their eyes be darkened that they see not,
    And make their loins continually to shake.
25 Pour out upon them Thine indignation,
    And let the burning of Thine anger seize them.

26 Let their village be desolate,
    In their tents let there be no dweller.
27 For him who is smitten of Thee they persecute,
    And of the pain of Thy pierced ones do they tell.
28 Add Thou iniquity to their iniquity,
    And let them not enter into Thy righteousness.

29 Let them be blotted out of the book of life,
    And with the righteous let them not be written down!
30 I, however, am afflicted and in pain,
    Thy help, Elohim, shall set me up on high.
31 I will praise the name of Elohim with song,
    And extol it with thanksgiving.

32 And it shall please Jahve better than young bullocks,
    Having horns, cleaving the hoof.
33 The afflicted seeing it, shall rejoice;
    Ye who seek after Elohim—let your heart revive!
34 For observant of the needy is Jahve,
    And His captives doth He not despise.

35 Let heaven and earth praise Him,
    The seas and everything that moveth therein.
36 For Elohim will save Zion and build the cities of Judah,
    That they may dwell there and possess them.
37 And the seed of His servants shall inherit them,
    And those who love His name shall dwell therein.

This Psalm follows Ps. lxviii. because in vers. 36 sq. the very same thought is expressed in unfigurative language, that we found in lxviii. 11 represented under a figure, viz. *Thy creatures dwelt therein.* In other respects the two Psalms are as different as day and night. Ps. lxix. is not a martial and triumphal Psalm, but a Psalm of affliction which does not brighten until near the close; and it is not the church that is the speaker here, as in the preceding Psalm, but an individual. This individual, according to the inscription, is David; and if David, it is not the ideal righteous man (Hengstenberg), but David the righteous, and that when he was unjustly persecuted by Saul. The description of suffering harmonizes in many points with the Psalms belonging to the time of Saul, even the estrangement of his nearest adherents, lxix. 9, xxxi. 12 (cf. xxvii. 10); the fasting till he is thoroughly enfeebled, lxix. 11, cix. 24; the curse upon his foes, in which respect Ps. xxxv., lxix., and cix. form a fearful gradation; and the inspiriting call to the saints who are his companions in suffering, lxix. 33, xxii. 27, xxxi. 25. Were there no doubt about Ps. xl. being Davidic, then the Davidic origin of Ps. lxix. would at the same time be firmly established; but instead of their inscriptions לדוד being mutually confirmatory, they tend, on the contrary, to shake our confidence. These two Psalms are closely related as twin-Psalms: in both the poet describes his suffering as a sinking into a miry pit; in both we meet with the same depreciation of ceremonial sacrifice; the same method of denoting a great multitude, "more than the hairs of my head," lxix. 5, xl. 13; and the same prospect of the faith of the saints being strengthened, lxix. 33, 7, xl. 17, 4.

But whilst in Ps. xl. it is more the style and in general the outward form than the contents that militate against its Davidic authorship, in Ps. lxix. it is not so much in form as in subject-matter that we find much that does not accord with David's authorship. For this reason Clericus and Vogel (in his dissertation *Inscriptiones Psalmorum serius demum additas videri*, 1767) have long ago doubted the correctness of the לדוד; and Hitzig has more fully supported the conjecture previously advanced by Seiler, von Bengel, and others, that Ps. lxix., as also Ps. xl., is by Jeremiah. The following points favour this view: (1) The martyrdom which the author endured in his zeal for the house of God, in his self-mortification, and in this consuming of himself with the scorn and deadly hostility of his foes; we may compare more particularly Jer. xv. 15–18, a confession on the part of the prophet very closely allied in spirit to both these Psalms.   (2) The murderous animosity which the prophet had to endure from the men of Anathoth, Jer. xi. 18 sq., with which the complaint of the psalmist in ver. 9 fully accords.   (3) The close of the Psalm, vers. 35–37, which is like a summary of that which Jeremiah foretells in the Book of the Restoration, ch. xxx.–xxxiii. (4) The peculiar character of Jeremiah's sufferings, who was cast by the princes, as being an enemy to his country, into the waterless but muddy cistern of prince Malchiah (Malkîja) in the court of the guard, and there as it were buried alive.   It is true, in Jer. xxxviii. 6 it is said of this cistern that there was "no water, but only mire," which seems to contradict the language of the Psalm; but since he sank into the mud, the meaning is that just then there was no water standing in it as at other times, otherwise he must at once have been drowned. Nevertheless, that he was in peril of his life is clear to us from the third *kînah* (Lam. ch. iii.), which in other respects also has many points of close contact with Ps. lxix.; for there in vers. 53–58 he says: "*They cut off my life in the pit and cast stones at me.   Waters flowed over my head; I thought: I am undone. I called upon Thy name, Jahve, out of the lowest pit.   Thou didst hear my cry: Hide not Thine ear from the outpouring of my heart, from my cry for help!   Thou didst draw near in the day that I cried, Thou saidst: Fear not.*"   The view of Hitzig, that in Ps. lxix. we have this prayer out of the pit, has many things in its favour, and among them, (5) the style, which on the whole is like that of Jeremiah, and the many coincidences with the prophet's language and range of thought visible in single instances.   But how could this Psalm have obtained the inscription לדוד?   Could it be on account of the similarity between the close of Ps. lxix. and the close of Ps. xxii.?   And why should not Ps. lxxi., which is to all appearance by Jeremiah, also have the inscription לדוד?   Ps. lxix. is wanting in that imitative character by which Ps. lxxi. so distinctly points to Jeremiah.   Therefore we duly recognise the instances and considerations brought forward against the Jeremianic authorship by Keil (*Luth. Zeitschrift*, 1860, S. 485 f.) and Kurtz (*Dorpater Zeitschrift*, 1865, S. 58 ff.), whilst, on the contrary, we still maintain, as formerly, that the Psalm admits of being much more satisfactorily explained from the life of Jeremiah than that of David.

The passion Psalms are the part of the Old Testament Scriptures most frequently cited in the New Testament; and after Ps. xxii. there is no Psalm referred to in so many ways as Ps. lxix. (1) The enemies of Jesus hated Him without a cause: this fact, according to John xv. 25, is foretold in ver. 5. It is more probable that the quotation by John refers to lxix. 5 than to xxxv. 19. (2) When Jesus drove the buyers and sellers out of the Temple, ver. 10a received its fulfilment, according to John ii. 17: the fierce flame of zeal against the profanation of the house of God consumes Him, and because of this zeal He is hated and despised. (3) He willingly bore this reproach, being an example to us; ver. 10b of our Psalm being, according to Rom. xv. 3, fulfilled in Him. (4) According to Acts i. 20, the imprecation in ver. 26a has received its fulfilment in Judas Iscariot. The suffixes in this passage are plural; the meaning can therefore only be that indicated by J H. Michaelis, *quod ille primus et præ reliquis hujus maledictionis se fecerit participem.* (5) According to Rom. xi. 9 sq., vers. 23 sq. of the Psalm have been fulfilled in the present rejection of Israel. The apostle does not put these imprecations directly into the mouth of Jesus, just as in fact they are not appropriate to the lips of the suffering Saviour; he only says that what the psalmist there, in the zealous ardour of the prophetic Spirit—a zeal partaking of the severity of Sinai and of the spirit of Elias—invokes upon his enemies, has been completely fulfilled in those who wickedly have laid violent hands upon the Holy One of God. The typically prophetic hints of the Psalm are far from being exhausted by these New Testament quotations. One is reminded, in connection with ver. 13, of the mockery of Jesus by the soldiers in the prætorium, Matt. xxvii. 27–30; by ver. 22, of the offer of vinegar mingled with gall (according to Mark xv. 23, wine mingled with myrrh) which Jesus refused, before the crucifixion, Matt. xxvii. 34, and of the sponge dipped in vinegar which they put to the mouth of the crucified One by means of a stalk of hyssop, John xix. 29 sq. When John there says that Jesus, freely and consciously preparing Himself to die, only desired a drink in order that, according to God's appointment, the Scripture might receive its utmost fulfilment, he thereby points back to Ps. xxii. 16 and lxix. 22. And what an amount of New Testament light, so to speak, falls upon ver. 27a when we compare with it Isa. ch. liii. and Zech. xiii. 7! The whole Psalm is typically prophetic, in as far as it is a declaration of a history of life and suffering moulded by God into a factual prediction concerning Jesus the Christ, whether it be the story of a king or a prophet; and in as far as the Spirit of prophecy has even moulded the declaration itself into the language of prophecy concerning the future One.

The Psalm falls into three parts, consisting of the following strophes: (1) 3. 5. 6. 6. 7; (2) 5. 6. 7; (3) 6. 6. 6. 6. 6. Does שׁוֹשַׁנִּים perhaps point to the preponderating six-line strophes under the emblem of the six-leaved lily? This can hardly be the case. The old expositors said that the Psalm was so inscribed because it treats of the white rose of the holy innocence of Christ, and of the red rose of His precious blood. שׁוֹשָׁן properly does not signify a rose; this flower was altogether unknown in the Holy Land at the time this Psalm was written. The rose was not transplanted thither out of Central Asia until much later, and was called וֶרֶד (ῥόδον); שׁוֹשָׁן, on the other hand, is the white, and in the Holy Land mostly red, lily—certainly, as a plant, a beautiful emblem of Christ. *Propter me*, says Origen, *qui in convalle eram, Sponsus descendit et fit lilium.*

Vers. 2–14. Out of deep distress, the work of his foes, the complaining one cries for help; he thinks upon his sins, which his sufferings bring to his remembrance, but he is also distinctly conscious that he is an object of scorn and hostility for God's sake, and from His mercy he looks for help in accordance with His promises. The waters are said to rush in unto the soul (עַד־נָפֶשׁ), when they so press upon the imperilled one that the soul, *i.e.* the life of the body, more especially the breath, is threatened; cf. Jonah ii. 6, Jer. iv. 10. Waters are also a figure of calamities that come on like a flood and drag one into their vortex, xviii. 17, xxxii. 6, cxxiv. 5, cf. lxvi. 12, lxxxviii. 8, 18; here, however, the figure is cut off in such a way that it conveys the impression of reality expressed in a poetical form, as in Ps. xl., and much the same as in Jonah's psalm. The soft, yielding morass is called יָוֵן, and the eddying deep מְצוּלָה. The *nomen Hophal.* מָעֳמָד signifies properly a being placed, then a standing-place, or firm standing (LXX. ὑπόστασις), like מַטֶּה, that which is stretched out, extension, Isa. viii. 8. שִׁבֹּלֶת (Ephraimitish סִבֹּלֶת) is a streaming, a flood, from שׁבל, سبل, to stream, flow (cf. note on lviii. 9a). בּוֹא בְ, to fall into, as in lxvi. 12, and שָׁטַף with an accusative, to overflow, as in cxxiv. 4. The complaining one is nearly drowned in consequence of his sinking down, for he has long cried in vain for help: he is wearied by continual crying (יָגֵעַ בְּ, as in vi. 7, Jer. xlv. 3), his throat is parched (נִחַר from חָרַר; LXX. and Jerome: it is become hoarse), his eyes have failed (Jer. xiv. 6) him, who waits upon his God. The participle מְיַחֵל, equal to a relative clause, is, as in xviii. 51, 1 Kings xiv. 6, attached to the suffix of the preceding noun (Hitzig). Distinct from this use of the participle without the article is the adverbially qualifying participle in Gen. iii. 8, Cant. v. 2, cf חַי, 2 Sam. xii. 21, xviii. 14. There is no necessity for the correction of the text מְיַחֵל (LXX. ἀπὸ τοῦ ἐλπίζειν με). Concerning the accentuation of רַבּוּ *vid.* on xxxviii. 20. Apart from the words "more than the hairs of my head" (xl. 13), the complaint of the multitude of groundless enemies is just the same as in xxxviii. 20, xxxv. 19, cf. cix. 3, both in substance and expression. Instead of מַצְמִיתַי, my destroyers, the Syriac version has the reading מֵעַצְמוֹתַי (more numerous than my bones), which is approved by Hupfeld; but to reckon the multitude of the enemy by the number of one's own bones is both devoid of taste and unheard of. Moreover the reading of our text finds support, if it need any, in Lam. iii. 52 sq. The words, "what I have not taken away, I must then restore," are intended by way of example, and perhaps, as also in Jer. xv. 10, as a proverbial expression: that which I have not done wrong, I must suffer for (cf. Jer. xv. 10, and the similar complaint in Ps. xxxv. 11). One is tempted to take אָז in the sense of "nevertheless" (Ewald), a meaning, however, which it is by no means intended to convey. In this passage it takes the place of זֹאת (cf. οὕτως for ταῦτα, Matt. vii. 12), inasmuch as it gives prominence to the restitution desired, as an inference from a false assumption: then, although I took it not away, stole it not.

The transition from the bewailing of suffering to a confession of sin is like xl. 13. In the undeserved persecution which he endures at the hand of man, he is obliged nevertheless to recognise well-merited chastisement from the side of God. And whilst by אַתָּה יָדַעְתָּ (cf. xl. 10, Jer. xv. 15, xvii. 16, xviii. 23, and on לְ as an exponent of the object, Jer. xvi. 16, xl. 2) he does not acknowledge himself to be a sinner after the standard of his own shortsightedness, but of the divine omniscience, he at the same time commends his sinful need, which with self-accusing modesty he calls אִוֶּלֶת (xxxviii. 6) and אַשְׁמוֹת (2 Chron. xxviii. 10), to the mercy of the omniscient One. Should he, the sinner, be abandoned by God to destruction, then all those who are faithful in their intentions towards the Lord would be brought to shame and confusion in him, inasmuch as they would be taunted with this example. קוֶֹיךָ designates the godly from the side of the πίστις, and מְבַקְשֶׁיךָ from the side of the ἀγάπη. The multiplied names of God are so many appeals to God's honour, to the truthfulness of His covenant relationship. The person praying here is, it is true, a sinner, but that is no justification of the conduct of men towards him; he is suffering for the Lord's sake, and it is the Lord Himself who is reviled in him. It is upon this he bases his prayer in ver. 8. עָלֶיךָ, for Thy sake, as in xliv. 23, Jer. xv. 15. The reproach that he has to bear, and ignominy that has covered his face and made it quite unrecognisable (xliv. 16, cf. lxxxiii. 17), have totally estranged (xxxviii. 12, cf. lxxxviii. 9, Job xix. 13–15, Jer. xii. 6) from him even his own brethren (אֶחָי, parallel word בְּנֵי אִמִּי, as in l. 20; cf., on the other hand, Gen. xlix. 8, where the interchange designedly takes another form of expression); for the glow of his zeal (קִנְאָה from קָנָא, according to the Arabic, to be a deep or bright red) for the house of Jahve, viz. for the sanctity of the sanctuary and of the congregation gathered about it (which is never directly called "the house of Jahve" in the Old Testament, vid. Köhler on Zech. ix. 8, but here, as in Num. xii. 7, Hos. viii. 1, is so called in conjunction with the sanctuary), as also for the honour of Him who sits enthroned therein, consumes him, like a fire burning in his bones which incessantly breaks forth and rages all through him (Jer. xx. 9, xxiii. 9), and therefore all the malice of those who are estranged from God is concentrated upon and against him.

He now goes on to describe how sorrow for the sad condition of the house of God has brought nothing but reproach to him (cf. cix. 24 sq.). It is doubtful whether נַפְשִׁי is an alternating subject to וָאֶבְכֶּה (*fut. consec.* without being apocopated), cf. Jer. xiii. 17, or a more minutely defining accusative as in Isa. xxvi. 9 (*vid.* on iii. 5), or whether, together with בַּצּוֹם, it forms a circumstantial clause (*et flevi dum in jejunio esset anima mea*), or even whether it is intended to be taken as an accusative of the object in a pregnant construction (= בָּכָה וְיִשְׁפַּךְ נַפְשׁוֹ, xlii. 5, 1 Sam. i. 15): I wept away my soul in fasting. Among all these possible renderings, the last is the least probable, and the first, according to xliv. 3, lxxxiii. 19, by far the most probable, and also that which is assumed by the accentuation.* The reading of the LXX. וָאֲעַנֶּה, καὶ συνέκαψα (Olshausen, Hupfeld, and Böttcher), is a very natural (xxxv. 13) exchange of the poetically bold expression for one less choice and less expressive (since עִנָּה נֶפֶשׁ is a phrase of the Pentateuch equivalent to צוּם). The garb of mourning, like the fasting, is an expression of sorrow for public distresses, not, as in xxxv. 13, of personal condolence; concerning וָאֶתְּנָה, *vid.* on iii. 6. On account of this mourning, reproach after reproach comes upon him, and they fling gibes and raillery at him; everywhere, both in the gate, the place where the judges sit and where business is transacted, and also at carousals, he is jeered at and traduced (Lam. iii. 14, cf. v. 14, Job xxx. 9). שִׂיחַ בְּ signifies in itself *fabulari de . . .* without any bad secondary meaning (cf. Prov. vi. 22, *confabulabitur tecum*); here it is construed first with a personal and then a neuter subject (cf. Amos viii. 5), for in ver 13*b* neither בִּי (Job xxx. 9, Lam. iii. 14) nor אֲנִי (Lam. iii. 63) is to be supplied. Ver. 14 tells us how he acts in the face of such hatred and scorn; וַאֲנִי, as in cix. 4, *sarcasmis hostium suam opponit in precibus constantiam* (Geier). As for himself, his prayer is directed towards Jahve at the present time, when his affliction

---

* The *Munach* of בצום is a transformation of *Dechî* (just as the *Munach* of לחרפות is a transformation of *Mugrash*), in connection with which נפשי might certainly be conceived of even as object (cf. xxvi. 6*a*); but this after וָאֶבְכֶּה (not וָאֶבְכָּה), and as being without example, could hardly have entered the minds of the punctuists.

as a witness for God gives him the assurance that He will be well-pleased to accept it (בְּעֵת רָצוֹן = עֵת רָצוֹן, Isa. xlix. 8). It is addressed to Him who is at the same time *Jahve* and *Elohim,*—the revealed One in connection with the history of redemption, and the absolute One in His exaltation above the world,—on the ground of the greatness and fulness of His mercy: may He then answer him with or in the truth of His salvation, *i.e.* the infallibility with which His purpose of mercy verifies itself in accordance with the promises given. Thus is ver. 14 to be explained in accordance with the accentuation. According to Isa. xlix. 8, it looks as though עת רצון must be drawn to עֵנֵני (Hitzig), but xxxii. 6 sets us right on this point; and the fact that ברב־חסדך is joined to ver. 14*a* also finds support from v. 8. But the repetition of the divine name perplexes one, and it may be asked whether or not the accent that divides the verse into its two parts might not more properly stand beside רצון, as in xxxii. 6 beside מְצֹא; so that ver. 14*b* runs: *Elohim, by virtue of the greatness of Thy mercy hear me, by virtue of the truth of Thy salvation.*

Vers. 15–22. In this second part the petition by which the first is as it were encircled, is continued; the peril grows greater the longer it lasts, and with it the importunity of the cry for help. The figure of sinking in the mire or mud and in the depths of the pit (בְּאֵר, lv. 24, cf. בּוֹר, xl. 3) is again taken up, and so studiously wrought out, that the impression forces itself upon one that the poet is here describing something that has really taken place. The combination "from those who hate me and from the depths of the waters" shows that "the depths of the waters" is not a merely rhetorical figure; and the form of the prayer: let not the pit (the well-pit or covered tank) close (תֶּאְטַר with *Dagesh* in the *Teth,* in order to guard against its being read תֶּאֱטַר; cf. on the signification of אָטַר, *clausus = claudus,* scil. *manu*) its mouth (*i.e.* its upper opening) upon me, exceeds the limits of anything that can be allowed to mere rhetoric. "Let not the water-flood overflow me" is intended to say, since it has, according to ver. 3, already happened, let it not go further to my entire destruction. The "answer me" in ver. 17*a* is based upon the plea that God's loving-kindness is טוֹב, *i.e.* good, absolutely good (as in the kindred passion-Psalm, cix. 21), better than all besides (lxiii. 4),

the means of healing or salvation from all evil. On ver. 17*b*
cf. li. 3, Lam. iii. 32. In ver. 18 the prayer is based upon the
painful situation of the poet, which urgently calls for speedy
help (מַהֵר beside the imperative, cii. 3, cxliii. 7, Gen. xix. 22,
Esth. vi. 10, is certainly itself not an imperative like הֶרֶב, li. 4,
but an adverbial infinitive as in lxxix. 8). קָרְבָה, or, in order to
ensure the pronunciation *korbah* in distinction from *kārbah*,
Deut. xv. 9, קָרְבָה (in Baer*), is *imperat. Kal;* cf. the fulfilment
in Lam. iii. 57. The reason assigned, "because of mine
enemies," as in v. 9, xxvii. 11, and frequently, is to be understood according to xiii. 5: the honour of the all-holy One
cannot suffer the enemies of the righteous to triumph over
him.† The accumulation of synonyms in ver. 20 is Jeremiah's
custom, ch. xiii. 14, xxi. 5, 7, xxxii. 37, and is found also in
Ps. xxxi. (ver. 10) and xliv. (vers. 4, 17, 25). On חֶרְפָּה שָׁבְרָה
לִבִּי, cf. li. 19, Jer. xxiii. 9. The ἅπαξ γεγραμ. וָאָנוּשָׁה (historical
tense), from נוּשׁ, is explained by אָנוּשׁ from אָנַשׁ, sickly, danger-
ously ill, evil-disposed, which is a favourite word in Jeremiah.
Moreover נוּד in the signification of manifesting pity, not found
elsewhere in the Psalter, is common in Jeremiah, *e.g.* ch. xv.
5; it signifies originally to nod to any one as a sign of a pity
that sympathizes with him and recognises the magnitude of the
evil. "To give wormwood for meat and מֵי־רֹאשׁ to drink" is a
Jeremianic (ch. viii. 14, ix. 14, xxiii. 15) designation for inflicting the extreme of pain and anguish upon one. רֹאשׁ (רוֹשׁ)
signifies first of all a poisonous plant with an umbellated head
of flower or a capitate fruit; but then, since bitter and poisonous are interchangeable notions in the Semitic languages, it
signifies gall as the bitterest of the bitter. The LXX. renders:
καὶ ἔδωκαν εἰς τὸ βρῶμά μου χολήν, καὶ εἰς τὴν δίψαν μου
ἐπότισάν με ὄξος. Certainly נָתַן בְּ can mean to put something
into something, to mix something with it, but the parallel word

---

* Originally — was the sign for every kind of ŏ, hence the Masora includes the חָטוּף also under the name קָמִץ חָטֻף; *vid. Luther. Zeitschrift,*
1863, S. 412 f., cf. Wright, *Genesis,* p. xxix.

† Both נַפְשִׁי and אֹיְבַי, contrary to logical interpunction, are marked
with *Munach;* the former ought properly to have *Dechî,* and the latter
Mugrash. But since neither the *Athnach*-word nor the *Silluk*-word has
two syllables preceding the tone syllable, the accents are transformed
according to *Accentuationssystem,* xviii. § 2, 4.

לְצִמְאִי (for my thirst, *i.e.* for the quenching of it, Neh. ix. 15, 20) favours the supposition that the בְּ of בִּבְרוּתִי is *Beth essentiæ*, after which Luther renders : " they give me gall to eat."   The ἅπαξ γεγραμ. בְּרוּת (Lam. iv. 10 בָּרוֹת) signifies βρῶσις, from בָּרָה, βιβρώσκειν (root βορ, Sanscrit *gar*, Latin *vor-are*).

Vers. 23–37.   The description of the suffering has reached its climax in ver. 22, at which the wrath of the persecuted one flames up and bursts forth in imprecations.   The first imprecation joins itself upon ver. 22.   They have given the sufferer gall and vinegar ; therefore their table, which was abundantly supplied, is to be turned into a snare to them, from which they shall not be able to escape, and that לִפְנֵיהֶם, in the very midst of their banqueting, whilst the table stands spread out before them (Ezek. xxiii. 41).   שְׁלוֹמִים (collateral form of שְׁלֵמִים) is the name given to them as being carnally secure ; the word signifies the peaceable or secure in a good (lv. 21) and in a bad sense.   Destruction is to overtake them suddenly, " when they say : Peace and safety" (1 Thess. v. 3).   The LXX. erroneously renders : καὶ εἰς ἀνταπόδοσιν = וּלְשִׁלּוּמִים.   The association of ideas in ver. 24 is transparent.   With their eyes they have feasted themselves upon the sufferer, and in the strength of their loins they have ill-treated him.   These eyes with their bloodthirsty malignant looks are to grow blind.   These loins full of defiant self-confidence are to shake (הַמְעַד, imperat. *Hiph.* like הַרְחַק, Job xiii. 21, from הִמְעִיד, for which in Ezek. xxix. 7, and perhaps also in Dan. xi. 14, we find העמיד).   Further : God is to pour out His wrath upon them (lxxix. 6, Hos. v. 10, Jer. x. 25), *i.e.* let loose against them the cosmical forces of destruction existing originally in His nature.   זַעְמְּךָ has the *Dagesh* in order to distinguish it in pronunciation from זַעֲמְךָ. In ver. 26 טִירָה (from טוּר, to encircle) is a designation of an encamping or dwelling-place (LXX. ἔπαυλις) taken from the circular encampments (Arabic صيرات, *sirât*, and دوار, *duâr*) of the nomads (Gen. xxv. 16).   The laying waste and desolation of his own house is the most fearful of all misfortunes to the Semite (*Job*, i. 327).   The poet derives the justification of such fearful imprecations from the fact that they persecute him, who is besides smitten of God. God has smitten him on account of his sins, and that by having placed him in the midst of a time in which he must be consumed with zeal and solicitude for the house of God. The suffering decreed for him by God is therefore at one and the same time suffering as a chastisement and as a witnessing for God ; and they heighten this suffering by every means in their power, not manifesting any pity for him or any indulgence, but imputing to him sins that he has not committed, and requiting him with deadly hatred for benefits for which they owed him thanks.

There are also some others, although but few, who share this martyrdom with him. The psalmist calls them, as he looks up to Jahve, חֲלָלֶיךָ, Thy fatally smitten ones; they are those to whom God has appointed that they should bear within themselves a pierced or wounded heart (*vid.* cix. 22, cf. Jer. viii. 18) in the face of such a godless age. Of the deep grief (אֶל, as in ii. 7) of these do they tell, viz. with self-righteous, self-blinded mockery (cf. the Talmudic phrase ספר בלשון הרע or ספר לשון הרע, of evil report or slander). The LXX. and Syriac render יֹסִיפוּ (προσέθηκαν): they add to the anguish; the Targum, Aquila, Symmachus, and Jerome follow the traditional text. Let God therefore, by the complete withdrawal of His grace, suffer them to fall from one sin into another—this is the meaning of the *da culpam super culpam eorum*—in order that accumulated judgment may correspond to the accumulated guilt (Jer. xvi. 18). Let the entrance into God's righteousness, *i.e.* His justifying and sanctifying grace, be denied to them for ever. Let them be blotted out of סֵפֶר חַיִּים (Ex. xxxii. 32, cf. Isa. iv. 3, Dan. xii. 1), that is to say, struck out of the list of the living, and that of the living in this present world; for it is only in the New Testament that we meet with the Book of Life as a list of the names of the heirs of the ζωὴ αἰώνιος. According to the conception both of the Old and of the New Testament the צַדִּיקִים are the heirs of life. Therefore ver. 29*b* wishes that they may not be written by the side of the righteous, who, according to Hab. ii. 4, "live," *i.e.* are preserved, by their faith. With וַאֲנִי the poet contrasts himself, as in xl. 18, with those deserving of execration. They are now on high, but in order to be brought low; he is miserable and full of poignant pain, but in order to be exalted; God's salvation will remove him from his enemies on to a height that is too steep for them (lix. 2, xci. 14). Then will he praise (הִלֵּל) and magnify (גִּדֵּל) the

Name of God with song and thankful confession. And such spiritual תּוֹדָה, such thank-offering of the heart, is more pleasing to God than an ox, a bullock, *i.e.* a young ox (= פַּר הַשּׁוֹר, an ox-bullock, Judg. vi. 25, according to Ges. § 113), one having horns and a cloven hoof (Ges. § 53, 2). The attributives do not denote the rough material animal nature (Hengstenberg), but their legal qualifications for being sacrificed. מַקְרִין is the name for the young ox as not being under three years old (cf. 1 Sam. i. 24, LXX. ἐν μόσχῳ τριετίζοντι); מַפְרִים as belonging to the clean four-footed animals, viz. those that are cloven-footed and chew the cud, Lev. ch. xi. Even the most stately, full-grown, clean animal that may be offered as a sacrifice stands in the sight of Jahve very far below the sacrifice of grateful praise coming from the heart.

When now the patient sufferers (עֲנָוִים) united with the poet by community of affliction shall see how he offers the sacrifice of thankful confession, they will rejoice. רָאוּ is a hypothetical preterite; it is neither וְרָאוּ (*perf. consec.*), nor יִרְאוּ (xl. 4, lii. 8, cvii. 42, Job xxii. 19). The declaration conveying information to be expected in ver. 33*b* after the *Waw apodoseos* changes into an apostrophe of the "seekers of Elohim:" their heart shall revive, for, as they have suffered in company with him who is now delivered, they shall now also refresh themselves with him. We are at once reminded of xxii. 27, where this is as it were the exhortation of the entertainer at the thank-offering meal. It would be rash to read שָׁמַע in ver. 34, after xxii. 25, instead of שֹׁמֵעַ (Olshausen); the one object in that passage is here generalized: Jahve is attentive to the needy, and doth not despise His bound ones (cvii. 10), but, on the contrary, He takes an interest in them and helps them. Starting from this proposition, which is the clear gain of that which has been experienced, the view of the poet widens into the prophetic prospect of the bringing back of Israel out of the Exile into the Land of Promise. In the face of this fact of redemption of the future he calls upon (cf. Isa. xliv. 23) all created things to give praise to God, who will bring about the salvation of Zion, will build again the cities of Judah, and restore the land, freed from its desolation, to the young God-fearing generation, the children of the servants of God among the exiles. The feminine suffixes refer to עָרֵי (cf. Jer. ii. 15, xxii. 6 *Chethîb*).

The tenor of Isa. lxv. 9 is similar. If the Psalm were written by David, the closing turn from ver. 34 onwards might be more difficult of comprehension than xiv. 7, li. 20 sq. If, however, it is by Jeremiah, then we do not need to persuade ourselves that it is to be understood not of restoration and re-peopling, but of continuance and completion (Hofmann and Kurtz). Jeremiah lived to experience the catastrophe he foretold; but the nearer it came to the time, the more comforting were the words with which he predicted the termination of the Exile and the restoration of Israel. Jer. xxxiv. 7 shows us how natural to him, and to him in particular, was the distinction between Jerusalem and the cities of Judah. The predictions in Jer. ch. xxxii., xxxiii., which sound so in accord with vers. 36 sq., belong to the time of the second siege. Jerusalem was not yet fallen; the strong places of the land, however, already lay in ruins.

PSALM LXX.

CRY OF A PERSECUTED ONE FOR HELP.

2 ELOHIM, to deliver me—
  Jahve to my help, make haste!
3 Let those be ashamed and confounded who seek my soul,
  Let those fall back and be put to shame who desire my
      misfortune,
4 Let those turn back as a reward of their shame,
  Who say: Aha, aha!

5 Let all those heartily rejoice in Thee who seek Thee,
  And let those continually say " Elohim be magnified" who
      love Thy salvation.
6 I, however, am needy and poor—
  Elohim, make haste unto me!
  My help and my Deliverer art Thou,
  Jahve, make no tarrying!

This short Psalm, placed after Ps. lxix. on account of the kindred nature of its contents (cf. more especially ver. 6 with lxix. 30), is, with but few deviations, a repetition of Ps. xl. 14

sqq. This portion of the second half of Ps. xl. is detached
from it and converted into the Elohimic style. Concerning
לְהַזְכִּיר, *at the presentation of the memorial portion of the mincha,*
vid. xxxviii. 1. It is obvious that David himself is not the
author of the Psalm in this stunted form. The לדוד is moreover justified, if he composed the original Psalm which is here
modified and appropriated to a special liturgical use.

Vers. 2–4. We see at once at the very beginning, in the
omission of the רְצֵה (xl. 14), that what we have here before us
is a fragment of Ps. xl., and perhaps a fragment that only accidentally came to have an independent existence. The לְהַצִּילֵנִי,
which was under the government of רצה, now belongs to חוּשָׁה,
and the construction is without example elsewhere. In ver. 3
(= xl. 15) יַחַד and לְסִפּוֹתָהּ are given up entirely; the original is
more full-toned and soaring. Instead of יִשֹּׁמּוּ, *torpescant,* ver.
4a has יָשׁוּבוּ, *recedant* (as in vi. 11, cf. ix. 18), which is all the
more flat for coming after יסֹּגוּ אחור. In ver. 4b, after האמרים
the לִּי, which cannot here (cf., on the contrary, xxxv. 21) be
dispensed with, is wanting.

Vers. 5, 6. וְיֹאמְרוּ instead of יאמרו is unimportant. But
since the divine name *Jahve* is now for once chosen side by
side with *Elohim,* it certainly had a strong claim to be retained
in ver. 5b. Instead of תְּשׁוּעָתֶךָ we have יְשׁוּעָתֶךָ here; instead of
עֶזְרָתִי, here עֶזְרִי. And instead of אֲדֹנָי יַחֲשָׁב לִי we have here
אֱלֹהִים חוּשָׁה־לִּי,—the hope is turned into petition : *make haste*
unto me, is an innovation in expression that is caused by the
taking over of the לִּי.

PSALM LXXI.

PRAYER OF A GREY-HEADED SERVANT OF GOD FOR
FURTHER DIVINE AID.

1 IN Thee, Jahve, have I hidden, let me not be ashamed
    for ever.
2 Through Thy righteousness deliver me and rescue me,
    Incline Thou Thine ear unto me and save me.

  3 Be Thou to me a rock of habitation to take me up alway;
    Thou hast given commandment to save me,
    For my rock and my fortress art Thou.

  4 My God, rescue me out of the hand of the wicked,
    Out of the grasp of the evil-doer and the violent man.
  5 For Thou art my hope, O Lord Jahve,
    My trust from my youth.
  6 Upon Thee have I been supported from the womb,
    Thou art He who didst separate me from my mother's
            bowels,
    Of Thee is my song of praise continually.

  7 As a wonder am I to many,
    But Thou art my refuge, a strong one.
  8 My mouth shall be filled with Thy praise,
    All the day long with Thy glorification.
  9 Cast me not away in the time of old age;
    Now when my strength faileth, forsake me not!

 10 For mine enemies speak concerning me,
    And those who lie in wait for my soul take counsel together,
 11 Saying: " Elohim hath forsaken him;
    Persecute and seize him, for he cannot be rescued."
 12 Elohim, be not far from me,
    My God, to my help make haste!

 13 Let be ashamed, let vanish away, the adversaries of my soul;
    Let those be covered with reproach and dishonour who seek
            my hurt.
 14 But I will hope continually,
    And will yet praise Thee more and more.
 15 My mouth shall tell of Thy righteousness,
    Of Thy salvation continually, for I know not the numbers
            thereof.

 16 I will come with the mighty deeds of the Lord Jahve,
    I will praise Thy righteousness, Thee alone.
 17 Elohim, Thou hast taught me from my youth up,
    And until now do I declare Thy wondrous works.

18 Even to old age and white hairs, Elohim, forsake me not,
    Till I declare Thine arm to posterity, to all that shall come
        Thy strength.

19 And Thy righteousness, Elohim, reacheth to the sky;
    Thou who doest great things—Elohim, who is like Thee?!
20 Who hast caused us to see distresses many and sore,
    Thou wilt quicken us again,
    And out of the abysses of the earth Thou wilt bring us up
        again;
21 Thou wilt increase my dignity and turn Thyself to com-
        fort me.

22 I will also praise Thee upon the nabla, Thy truth, my God;
    I will play to Thee upon the cithern, O Holy One of Israel.
23 My lips shall exult, when I shall harp to Thee,
    And my soul, which Thou hast redeemed.
24 Also my tongue shall continually make known Thy right-
        eousness,
    That those are ashamed, that those are put to the blush
        who seek my hurt.

The Davidic Psalm lxx. is followed by an anonymous
Psalm which begins like Ps. xxxi. and closes like Ps. xxxv., in
which ver. 12, just like lxx. 2, is an echo of xl. 14. The
whole Psalm is an echo of the language of older Psalms, which
is become the mental property, so to speak, of the author, and
is revived in him by experiences of a similar character. Notwithstanding the entire absence of any thorough originality, it
has an individual, and in fact a Jeremianic, impress.

The following reasons decide us in considering the Psalm
as coming from the pen of Jeremiah :—(1) Its relationship to
Psalms of the time of David and of the earlier times of the
kings, but after David, leads us down to somewhere about the
age of Jeremiah. (2) This anthological weaving together of
men's own utterances taken from older original passages, and this
skilful variation of them by merely slight touches of his own, is
exactly Jeremiah's manner. (3) In solitary instances the style
of Psalm lxix., slow, loose, only sparingly adorned with figures,
and here and there prosaic, closely resembles Jeremiah; also

to him corresponds the situation of the poet as one who is persecuted; to him, the retrospect of a life rich in experience and full of miraculous guidings; to him, whose term of active service extended over a period of more than thirty years under Zedekiah, the transition to hoary age in which the poet finds himself; to him, the reference implied in ver. 21 to some high office; and to him, the soft, plaintive strain that pervades the Psalm, from which it is at the same time clearly seen that the poet has attained a degree of age and experience, in which he is accustomed to self-control and is not discomposed by personal misfortune. To all these correspondences there is still to be added an historical testimony. The LXX. inscribes the Psalm τῷ Δαυίδ, υἱῶν 'Ιωναδάβ καὶ τῶν πρώτων αἰχμαλωτισθέντων. According to this inscription, the τῷ Δαυίδ of which is erroneous, but the second part of which is so explicit that it must be based upon tradition, the Psalm was a favourite song of the Rechabites and of the first exiles. The Rechabites are that tribe clinging to a homely nomad life in accordance with the will of their father, which Jeremiah (ch. xxxv.) holds up before the men of his time as an example of self-denying faithful adherence to the law of their father which puts them to shame. If the Psalm is by Jeremiah, it is just as intelligible that the Rechabites, to whom Jeremiah paid such a high tribute of respect, should appropriate it to their own use, as that the first exiles should do so. Hitzig infers from ver. 20, that at the time of its composition Jerusalem had already fallen; whereas in Ps. lxix. it is only the cities of Judah that as yet lie in ashes. But after the overthrow of Jerusalem we find no circumstances in the life of the prophet, who is no more heard of in Egypt, that will correspond to the complaints of the psalmist of violence and mockery. Moreover the foe in ver. 4 is not the Chaldæan, whose conduct towards Jeremiah did not merit these names. Nor can ver. 20 have been written at the time of the second siege and in the face of the catastrophe.

Vers. 1–6. Stayed upon Jahve, his ground of trust, from early childhood up, the poet hopes and prays for deliverance out of the hand of the foe. The first of these two strophes (vers. 1–3) is taken from xxxi. 2–4, the second (vers. 4–6, with the exception of vers. 4 and 6c) from xxii. 10, 11; both, how-

ever, in comparison with Ps. lxx. exhibit the far more encroach-
ing variations of a poet who reproduces the language of others
with a freer hand.   Olshausen wishes to read מָעוֹן in ver. 3, xc.
1, xci. 9, instead of מָעוֹן, which he holds to be an error in writing.   But this old Mosaic, Deuteronomial word (*vid.* on xc. 1)
—cf. the post-biblical oath המעון (by the Temple!)—is unassailable.   Jahve, who is called a rock of refuge in xxxi. 3, is here
called a rock of habitation, *i.e.* a high rock that cannot be
stormed or scaled, which affords a safe abode; and this figure
is pursued still further with a bold remodelling of the text of
xxxi. 3: לָבוֹא תָמִיד, constantly to go into, *i.e.* whither I can
constantly, and therefore always, as often as it is needful,
betake myself for refuge.   The additional צִוִּיתָ is certainly not
equivalent to צַוֵּה; it would more likely be equivalent to אֲשֶׁר
צִוִּית; but probably it is an independent clause: Thou hast (in
fact) commanded, *i.e.* unalterably determined (xliv. 5, lxviii. 29,
cxxxiii. 3), to show me salvation, for my rock, etc.   To the
words לבוא תמיד צוית corresponds the expression לבית מצודות in
xxxi. 3, which the LXX. renders καὶ εἰς οἶκον καταφυγῆς,
whereas instead of the former three words it has καὶ εἰς τόπον
ὀχυρόν, and seems to have read לבית מבצרות, cf. Dan. xi. 15 (Hitzig).   In ver. 5, *Thou art my hope* reminds one of the divine
name מִקְוֵה יִשְׂרָאֵל in Jer. xvii. 13, l. 7 (cf. ἡ ἐλπὶς ἡμῶν used of
Christ in 1 Tim. i. 1, Col. i. 27).   נִסְמַכְתִּי is not less beautiful
than הָשְׁלַכְתִּי in xxii. 11.   In its incipient slumbering state (cf.
iii. 6), and in its self-conscious continuance, He was and is the
upholding prop and the supporting foundation, so to speak, of
my life.   And גוֹזִי instead of גֹּחִי in xxii. 10, is just such another
felicitous modification.   It is impracticable to define the mean-

ing of this גוֹזִי according to גָּזָה = גְּזָא, جَزَى, *retribuere* (prop. to cut

up, distribute), because גָּמַל is the representative of this Aramæo-
Arabic verb in the Hebrew.   Still less, however, can it be
derived from גּוּז, *transire*, the participle of which, if it would
admit of a transitive meaning = מוֹצִיאִי (Targum), ought to be
גוֹזִי.   The verb גָּזָה, in accordance with its radical signification
of *abscindere* (root גז, synon. קץ, קד, קט, and the like), denotes
in this instance the separating of the child from the womb of
the mother, the retrospect going back from youth to childhood,
and even to his birth.   The LXX. σκεπαστής (μου) is an

erroneous reading for ἐκσπαστής, as is clear from xxii. 10, ὁ ἐκσπάσας με. הִלֵּל בְּ, xliv. 9 (cf. שִׂיחַ בְּ, lxix. 13), is at the bottom of the expression in ver. 6c. The God to whom he owes his being, and its preservation thus far, is the constant, inexhaustible theme of his praise.

Vers. 7–12. Brought safely through dangers of every kind, he is become כְּמוֹפֵת, as a wonder, a miracle (Arabic أَفَت from أَفَت, cognate أَفَك, הָפַךְ, to bend, distort: a turning round, that which is turned round or wrenched, *i.e.* that which is contrary to what is usual and looked for) to many, who gaze upon him as such with astonishment (xl. 4). It is his God, however, to whom, as hitherto so also in time to come, he will look to be thus wonderfully preserved: מַחֲסִי־עֹז, as in 2 Sam. xxii. 33. עֹז is a genitive, and the suffix is thrown back (*vid. supra*, vol. i. 274) in order that what God is to, and does for, the poet may be brought forward more clearly and independently [*lit.* unalloyed]. Ver. 8 tells us what it is that he firmly expects on the ground of what he possesses in God. And on this very ground arises the prayer of ver. 9 also: Cast me not away (viz. from Thy presence, li. 13, Jer. vii. 15, and frequently) in the time (לְעֵת, as in Gen. viii. 11) of old age—he is therefore already an old man (זָקֵן), though only just at the beginning of the זִקְנָה. He supplicates favour for the present and for the time still to come: now that my vital powers are failing, forsake me not! Thus he prays because he, who has been often wondrously delivered, is even now threatened by foes. Ver. 11, introduced by means of ver. 10, tells us what their thoughts of him are, and what they purpose doing. לְ, ver. 10a, does not belong to אוֹיְבַי, as it does not in xxvii. 2 also, and elsewhere. The לְ is that of relation or of reference, as in xli. 6. The unnecessary לֵאמֹר betrays a poet of the later period; cf. cv. 11, cxix. 82 (where it was less superfluous), and on the contrary, lxxxiii. 5 sq. The later poet also reveals himself in ver. 12, which is an echo of very similar prayers of David in xxii. 12, 20 (xl. 14, cf. lxx. 2), xxxv. 22, xxxviii. 22 sq. The Davidic style is to be discerned here throughout in other points also. In place of חִישָׁה the *Keri* substitutes חוּשָׁה, which is the form exclusively found elsewhere.

Vers. 13–18. In view of xl. 15 (lxx. 3), xxxv. 4, 26, cix.

29, and other passages, the reading of יַכְלְמוּ, with the Syriac,
instead of יִכְלוּ in ver. 13*a* commends itself; but there are also
other instances in this Psalm of a modification of the original
passages, and the course of the thoughts is now climactic: confusion, ruin (cf. vi. 11), and in fact ruin accompanied by reproach and shame. This is the fate that the poet desires for
his deadly foes. In prospect of this he patiently composes
himself, ver. 14*a* (cf. xxxi. 25); and when righteous retribution appears, he will find new matter and ground and motive
for the praise of God in addition to all such occasion as he has
hitherto had. The late origin of the Psalm betrays itself
again here; for instead of the *præt. Hiph.* הוֹסִיף (which is found
only in the Books of Kings and in Ecclesiastes), the older
language made use of the *præt. Kal.* Without ceasing shall
his mouth tell (סָפַּר, as in Jer. li. 10) of God's righteousness,
of God's salvation, for he knows not numbers, *i.e.* the counting
over or through of them (cxxxix. 17 sq.); * the divine proofs of
righteousness or salvation עָצְמוּ מִסַּפֵּר (xl. 6), they are in themselves endless, and therefore the matter also which they furnish
for praise is inexhaustible. He will tell those things which
cannot be so reckoned up; he will come with the mighty deeds
of the Lord Jahve, and with praise acknowledge His righteousness, Him alone. Since גְּבֻרוֹת, like the New Testament
δυνάμεις, usually signifies the proofs of the divine גְּבוּרָה (*e.g.*
xx. 7), the *Beth* is the *Beth* of accompaniment, as *e.g.* in xl. 8,
lxvi. 13. בּוֹא בְ, *venire cum*, is like جآءَ بِ (أتَى), equivalent
to *afferre*, he will bring the proofs of the divine power, this
rich material, with him. It is evident from vers. 18 sq. that
בגברות does not refer to the poet (in the fulness of divine
strength), but, together with צדקתך, forms a pair of words that
have reference to God. לְבַדֶּךָ, according to the sense, joins
closely upon the suffix of צִדְקָתֶךָ (cf. lxxxiii. 19): Thy righteousness (which has been in mercy turned towards me), Thine
alone (*te solum = tui solius*). From youth up God has in-

---

* The LXX. renders οὐκ ἔγνων πραγματείας; the Psalterium Romanum,
non cognovi negotiationes; Psalt. Gallicum (Vulgate), non cognovi literaturam
(instead of which the Psalt. Hebr., literaturas). According to Böttcher,
the poet really means that he did not understand the art of writing.

structed him, viz. in His ways (xxv. 4), which are worthy of all praise, and hitherto (עַד־הֵנָּה, found only in this passage in the Psalter, and elsewhere almost entirely confined to prose) has he, " the taught of Jahve " (לִמּוּד ה'), had to praise the wonders of His rule and of His leadings. May God, then, not forsake him even further on עַד־זִקְנָה וְשֵׂיבָה. The poet is already old (זָקֵן), and is drawing ever nearer to שֵׂיבָה, silvery, hoary old age (cf. 1 Sam. xii. 2). May God, then, in this stage of life also to which he has attained, preserve him in life and in His favour, until (עַד־אֲשֶׁר = עַד, as in cxxxii. 5, Gen. xxxviii. 11, and frequently) he shall have declared His arm, *i.e.* His mighty interposition in human history, to posterity (דּוֹר), and to all who shall come (supply אֲשֶׁר), *i.e.* the whole of the future generation, His strength, *i.e.* the impossibility of thwarting His purposes. The primary passage for this is xxii. 31 sq.

Vers. 19–24. The thought of this proclamation so thoroughly absorbs the poet that he even now enters upon the tone of it; and since to his faith the deliverance is already a thing of the past, the tender song with its uncomplaining prayer dies away into a loud song of praise, in which he pictures it all to himself. Without vers. 19–21 being subordinate to עַד־אַגִּיד in ver. 18, וְצִדְקָתְךָ is coupled by close connection with גְּבוּרָתְךָ. Ver. 19*a* is an independent clause; and עַד־מָרוֹם takes the place of the predicate: the righteousness of God exceeds all bounds, is infinite (xxxvi. 6 sq., lvii. 11). The cry מִי כָמוֹךָ, as in xxxv. 10, lxxxix. 9, Jer. x. 6, refers back to Ex. xv. 11. According to the *Chethîb*, the range of the poet's vision widens in ver. 20 from the proofs of the strength and righteousness of God which he has experienced in his own case to those which he has experienced in common with others in the history of his own nation. The *Kerî* (cf. on the other hand lx. 5, lxxxv. 7, Deut. xxxi. 17) rests upon a failing to discern how the experience of the writer are interwoven with those of the nation. תָּשׁוּב in both instances supplies the corresponding adverbial notion to the principal verb, as in lxxxv. 7 (cf. li. 4). תְּהוֹם, prop. a rumbling, commonly used of a deep heaving of waters, here signifies an abyss. "The abysses of the earth" (LXX. ἐκ τῶν ἀβύσσων τῆς γῆς, just as the old Syriac version renders the New Testament ἄβυσσος, *e.g.* in Luke viii. 31, by ܬܗܘܡܐ) are,

like the gates of death (ix. 14), a figure of extreme perils and
dangers, in the midst of which one is as it were half hidden in
the abyss of Hades. The past and future are clearly distinguished in the sequence of the tenses. When God shall again
raise His people out of the depth of the present catastrophe,
then will He also magnify the גְּדֻלָּה of the poet, *i.e.* the dignity
of his office, by most brilliantly vindicating him in the face of
his foes, and will once more (תָּסֹוב, *fut. Niph.* like תָּשׁוּב above)
comfort him. He on his part will also (cf. Job xl. 14) be
grateful for this national restoration and this personal vindication: he will praise God, will praise His truth, *i.e.* His fidelity
to His promises. בִּכְלִי־נֶבֶל instead of בְּנֶבֶל sounds more circumstantial than in the old poetry. The divine name " The Holy
One of Israel" occurs here for the third time in the Psalter; the
other passages are lxxviii. 41, lxxxix. 19, which are older in time,
and older also than Isaiah, who uses it thirty times, and Habakkuk, who uses it once. Jeremiah has it twice (ch. l. 29, li. 5),
and that after the example of Isaiah. In vers. 23, 24*a* the
poet means to say that lips and tongue, song and speech, shall
act in concert in the praise of God. תְּרַנֵּנָּה with *Dagesh* also in
the second *Nun*, after the form תִּקֹונֵנָּה, תִּשְׁכֹּבְנָה, side by side with
which we also find the reading תְּרַנֵּנָה, and the reading תְּרַנֶּנָה,
which is in itself admissible, after the form תֶּאֱמַנָה, תֵּעָגֵנָה, but
is here unattested.* The cohortative after כִּי (LXX. ὅταν) is
intended to convey this meaning: when I feel myself impelled
to harp unto Thee. In the perfects in the closing line that
which is hoped for stands before his soul as though it had
already taken place. כי is repeated with triumphant emphasis.

---

* Heidenheim reads תְּרַנֶּנָּה with *Segol*, following the statement of Ibn-
Bil'am in his טעמי המקרא and of Mose ha-Nakdan in his דרכי הנקוד, that
Segol always precedes the ending נָּה, with the exception only of הִנֵּה and
הַאֲזֵנָּה. Baer, on the other hand, reads תרננה, following Aben-Ezra and
Kimchi (*Michlol* 66*b*).

PSALM LXXII.

PRAYER FOR THE DOMINION OF PEACE OF THE ANOINTED ONE OF GOD.

1 ELOHIM, give Thy rights unto the king,
And Thy righteousness unto the king's son.
2 May he govern Thy people with uprightness,
And Thine afflicted with justice.
3 May the mountains bring peace to the people,
And the hills by righteousness.
4 May he judge the afflicted among the people,
Save the children of the needy, and crush the oppressor.

5 May they fear Thee as long as the sun,
And before the moon to all generations.
6 May he come down like rain upon the meadow-grass,
As showers, a heavy rain upon the earth.
7 In his days may the righteous flourish,
And abundance of peace, till the moon be no more.
8 And may he have dominion from sea to sea,
And from the river unto the ends of the earth.

9 Before him shall the inhabitants of the wilderness bow,
And his enemies shall lick the dust.
10 The kings of Tarshish and of the isles shall bring gifts,
The kings of Saba and Meroë shall offer tribute.
11 And all kings shall do homage to him,
All peoples shall serve him.

12 For he shall deliver the needy who crieth,
And the afflicted who have no succour.
13 He shall deal gently with the poor and needy,
And help the souls of the needy;
14 From oppression and violence he shall redeem their soul,
And precious is their blood in his eyes:
15 And he shall live, and he will present him with gold of Saba,
And he will pray for him always, bless him continually.

16 May there be abundance of corn in the land unto the top
        of the mountains,
    May its fruit wave like Lebanon,
    And may they blossom out of cities like the herbs of the
        earth.
17 May his name endure for ever,
    Before the sun may his name throw out shoots.
    And may they bless themselves in him, may all peoples call
        him blessed.
18 Blessed be Jahve Elohim the God of Israel,
    Who alone doeth wondrous things.
19 And blessed be His glorious name for ever,
    And let the whole earth be filled with His
        glory.
            Amen, and Amen.
20 *Ended are the prayers of David the son of Jesse.*

This last Psalm of the primary collection, united to Ps.
lxxi. by community of the prominent word צדקתך, appears, as
we look to the superscription, lxxii. 20, to be said to be a
Psalm of David; so that consequently לִשְׁלֹמֹה designates Solomon as the subject, not the author. But the *Lamed* of לשלמה
here and in cxxvii. 1 cannot have any other meaning than that
which the *Lamed* always has at the head of the Psalms when
it is joined to proper names; it is then always the expression
denoting that the Psalm belongs to the person named, as its
author. Then in style and general character the Psalm has
not the least kinship with the Psalms of David. Characteristic of Solomon, on the other hand, are the movement
proverb-like, and for the most part distichic, which has less of
original freshness and directness than of an artificial, reflective,
and almost sluggish manner, the geographic range of view, the
richness in figures drawn from nature, and the points of contact with the Book of Job, which belongs incontrovertibly to
the circle of the Salomonic literature: these are coincident
signs which are decisive in favour of Solomon. But if Solomon
is the author, the question arises, who is the subject of the
Psalm? According to Hitzig, Ptolemy Philadelphus; but no
true Israelite could celebrate him in this manner, and there is
no reliable example of carmina of this character having found

their way into the song-book of Israel. The subject of the Psalm is either Solomon (LXX. εἰς Σαλωμών) or the Messiah (Targum, "O God, give Thy regulations of right to the King Messiah, לְמַלְכָּא מְשִׁיחָא"). Both are correct. It is Solomon himself to whom the intercession and desires of blessing of this Psalm refer. Solomon, just as David with Psalms xx. and xxi., put it into the heart and mouth of the people, probably very soon after his accession, it being as it were a church-prayer on behalf of the new, reigning king. But the Psalm is also none the less Messianic, and with perfect right the church has made it the chief Psalm of the festival of Epiphany, which has received its name of *festum trium regum* out of it.

Solomon was in truth a righteous, benign, God-fearing ruler; he established and also extended the kingdom; he ruled over innumerable people, exalted in wisdom and riches above all the kings of the earth; his time was the most happy, the richest in peace and joy that Israel has ever known. The words of the Psalm were all fulfilled in him, even to the one point of the universal dominion that is wished for him. But the end of his reign was not like the beginning and the middle of it. That fair, that glorious, that pure image of the Messiah which he had represented waxed pale; and with this fading away its development in relation to the history of redemption took a new turn. In the time of David and of Solomon the hope of believers, which was attached to the kingship of David, had not yet fully broken with the present. At that time, with few exceptions, nothing was known of any other Messiah than the Anointed One of God, who was David or Solomon himself. When, however, the kingship in these its two most glorious impersonations had proved itself unable to bring to full realization the idea of the Messiah or of the Anointed One of God, and when the line of kings that followed thoroughly disappointed the hope which clung to the kingship of the present,—a hope which here and there, as in the reign of Hezekiah, blazed up for a moment and then totally died out, and men were driven from the present to look onward into the future,—then, and not until then, did any decided rupture take place between the Messianic hope and the present. The image of the Messiah is now painted on the pure ethereal sky of the future (though of the immediate future) in colours which were furnished by older unfulfilled prophecies, and by the contradiction between the existing kingship and its idea; it becomes more and more, so to speak, an image, super-earthly, super-human, belonging to the future, the invisible refuge and invisible goal of a faith despairing of the present, and thereby rendered relatively more spiritual and heavenly (cf. the Messianic image painted in colours borrowed from our Psalm in Isa. ch. xi., Mic. v. 3, 6, Zech. ix. 9 sq.). In order rightly to estimate this, we must free ourselves from the prejudice that the centre of the Old Testament proclamation of salvation [or gospel] lies in the prophecy of the Messiah. Is the Messiah, then, anywhere set forth as the Redeemer of the world? The Redeemer of the world is Jahve. The appearing (*parusia*) of Jahve is the centre of the Old Testament proclamation of salvation. An allegory may serve to illustrate the way in which the Old Testament proclamation of salvation unfolds itself. The Old Testament in relation to the Day of the New Testament is Night. In this Night there rise in opposite directions two stars of Promise. The one describes its path from above downwards: it is the promise of Jahve who is about to come. The other describes its path from below upwards: it is the hope which rests on the seed of David, the prophecy of the Son of David, which at the outset assumes a thoroughly human, and merely earthly character. These two stars meet at last, they blend together into one star; the Night vanishes and it is Day. This one Star is Jesus Christ, Jahve and the Son of David in one person, the King of Israel and at the same time the Redeemer of the world,—in one word, the God-man.

Vers. 1–4. The name of God, occurring only once, is *Elohim;* and this is sufficient to stamp the Psalm as an Elohimic Psalm. מֶלֶךְ (cf. xxi. 2) and בֶּן־מֶלֶךְ are only used without the article according to a poetical usage of the language. The petition itself, and even the position of the words, show that the king's son is present, and that he is king; God is implored to bestow upon him His מִשְׁפָּטִים, *i.e.* the rights or legal powers belonging to Him, the God of Israel, and צְדָקָה, *i.e.* the official gift in order that he may exercise those rights in accordance with divine righteousness. After the supplicatory תֵּן the futures which now follow, without the *Waw apodoseos,* are

manifestly optatives.   Mountains and hills describe synecdochically the whole land of which they are the high points visible
afar off.   נָשָׂא is used in the sense of נָשָׂא פְּרִי Ezek. xvii. 8 :
may שָׁלוֹם be the fruit which ripens upon every mountain and
hill; universal prosperity satisfied and contented within itself.
The predicate for ver. 3*b* is to be taken from ver. 3*a*, just as,
on the other hand, בִּצְדָקָה, "in or by righteousness," the fruit
of which is indeed peace (Isa. xxxii. 17), belongs also to ver.
3*a*; so that consequently both members supplement one
another.   The wish of the poet is this: By righteousness,
may there in due season be such peaceful fruit adorning all the
heights of the land.   Ver. 3*b*, however, always makes one feel
as though a verb were wanting, like תִּפְרַחְנָה suggested by
Böttcher.   In ver. 4 the wishes are continued in plain unfigurative language.   הוֹשִׁיעַ in the signification to save, to obtain
salvation for, has, as is frequently the case, a dative of the
object.   בְּנֵי־אֶבְיוֹן are those who are born to poverty, just like
בֶּן־מֶלֶךְ, one who is born a king.   Those who are born to poverty
are more or less regarded, by an unrighteous government, as
having no rights.

Vers. 5–8.   The invocation of ver. 1 is continued in the
form of a wish: may they fear Thee, Elohim, עִם־שָׁמֶשׁ, with
the sun, *i.e.* during its whole duration (עִם in the sense of cotemporary existence, as in Dan. iii. 33).   לִפְנֵי־יָרֵחַ, in the moonlight
(cf. Job viii. 16, לִפְנֵי־שֶׁמֶשׁ, in the sunshine), *i.e.* so long as the
moon shines.   דּוֹר דּוֹרִים (accusative of the duration of time,
cf. cii. 25), into the uttermost generation which outlasts the
other generations (like שְׁמֵי הַשָּׁמַיִם of the furthest heavens
which surround the other heavens).   The first two periphrastic
expressions for unlimited time recur in Ps. lxxxix. 37 sq., a
Psalm composed after the time of Solomon; cf. the unfigurative expression in Solomon's prayer at the dedication of the
Temple in 1 Kings viii. 40.   The continuance of the kingship,
from the operation of which such continuance of the fear of
God is expected, is not asserted until ver. 17.   It is capricious
to refer the language of address in ver. 5 to the king (as
Hupfeld and Hitzig do), who is not directly addressed either
in ver. 4, or in ver. 6, or anywhere in the Psalm.   With respect
to God the desire is expressed that the righteous and benign
rule of the king may result in the extension of the fear of God

from generation to generation into endless ages. The poet in
ver. 6 delights in a heaping up of synonyms in order to give
intensity to the expression of the thoughts, just as in ver. 5 ;
the last two expressions stand side by side one another without
any bond of connection as in ver. 5. רְבִיבִים (from רָבַב, رَبَّ,
densum, spissum esse, and then, starting from this signification,
sometimes *multum* and sometimes *magnum esse*) is the shower
of rain pouring down in drops that are close together ; nor is
זַרְזִיף a synonym of גֵּז, but (formed from זָרַף, ذَرَفَ, to flow, by
means of a rare reduplication of the first two letters of the
root, Ew. § 157, *d*) properly the water running from a roof
(cf. *B. Joma* 87*a :* "when the maid above poured out water,
זרזיפי דמיא came upon his head"). גֵּז, however, is not the
meadow-shearing, equivalent to a shorn, mown meadow, any
more than גֵּז, גִּזָּה, Arabic *g'izza,* signifies a shorn hide, but, on
the contrary, a hide with the wool or feathers (*e.g.* ostrich
feathers) still upon it, rather a meadow, *i.e.* grassy plain, that
is intended to be mown. The closing word אָרֶץ (*accus. loci* as
in cxlvii. 15) unites itself with the opening word יֵרֵד : *descendat
in terram.* In his last words (2 Sam. ch. xxiii.) David had
compared the effects of the dominion of his successor, whom
he beheld as by vision, to the fertilizing effects of the sun and of
the rain upon the earth. The idea of ver. 6 is that Solomon's
rule may prove itself thus beneficial for .the country. The
figure of the rain in ver. 7 gives birth to another : under his
rule may the righteous blossom (expanding himself unhindered
and under the most favourable circumstances), and (may there
arise) salvation in all fulness עַד־בְּלִי יָרֵחַ, until there is no more
moon (cf. the similar expression in Job xiv. 12). To this
desire for the uninterrupted prosperity and happiness of the
righteous under the reign of this king succeeds the desire for
an unlimited extension of his dominion, ver. 8. The sea (the
Mediterranean) and the river (the Euphrates) are geographi-
cally defined points of issue, whence the definition of boundary
is extended into the unbounded. Solomon even at his accession ruled over all kingdoms from the Euphrates as far as the
borders of Egypt ; the wishes expressed here are of wider
compass, and Zechariah repeats them predictively (ch. ix. 10)
with reference to the King Messiah.

Vers. 9–11.   This third strophe contains prospects, the ground of which is laid down in the fourth.   The position of the futures here becomes a different one.   The contemplation passes from the home relations of the new government to its foreign relations, and at the same time the wishes are changed into hopes.   The awe-commanding dominion of the king shall stretch even into the most distant corners of the desert.   צִיִּים is used both for the animals and the men who inhabit the desert, to be determined in each instance by the context; here they are men beyond all dispute, but in lxxiv. 14, Isa. xxiii. 13, it is matter of controversy whether men or beasts are meant.   Since the LXX., Aquila, Symmachus, and Jerome here, and the LXX. and Jerome in lxxiv. 14, render Αἰθίοπες, the nomadic tribes right and left of the Arabian Gulf seem traditionally to have been associated in the mind with this word, more particularly the so-called Ichthyophagi.   These shall bend the knee reverentially before him, and those who contend against him shall be compelled at last to veil their face before him in the dust.   The remotest west and south become subject and tributary to him, viz. the kings of Tartessus in the south of Spain, rich in silver, and of the islands of the Mediterranean and the countries on its coasts, that is to say, the kings of the Polynesian portion of Europe, and the kings of the Cushitish or of the Joktanitish שְׁבָא and of the Cushitish סְבָא, as, according to Josephus, the chief city of Meroë was called (vid. Genesis, S. 206).   It was a queen of that Joktanitish, and therefore South Arabian Sheba,—perhaps, however, more correctly (vid. Wetzstein in my Isaiah, ii. 529) of the Cushitish (Nubian) Sheba,— whom the fame of Solomon's wisdom drew towards him, 1 Kings ch. x.   The idea of their wealth in gold and in other precious things is associated with both peoples.   In the expression הֵשִׁיב מִנְחָה (to pay tribute, 2 Kings xvii. 3, cf. iii. 4) the tribute is not conceived of as rendered in return for protection afforded (Maurer, Hengstenberg, and Olshausen), nor as an act repeated periodically (Rödiger, who refers to 2 Chron. xxvii. 5), but as a bringing back, i.e. repayment of a debt, referre s. reddere debitum (Hupfeld), after the same idea according to which obligatory incomings are called reditus (revenues). In the synonymous expression הִקְרִיב אֶשְׁכָּר the presentation appears as an act of sacrifice.   אֶשְׁכָּר signifies in Ezek. xxvii. 15

a payment made in merchandise, here a rent or tribute due, from שָׂכָר, which in blending with the *Aleph prostheticum* has passed over into שֶׂכֶר by means of a shifting of the sound after the Arabic manner, just as in אֶשְׁבֹּל the verb שָׂבַל, to interweave, passes over into שָׁבַל (Rödiger in Gesenius' *Thesaurus*). In ver. 11 hope breaks through every bound: everything shall submit to his world-subduing sceptre.

Vers. 12–15. The confirmation of these prospects is now given. Voluntative forms are intermingled because the prospect extending into the future is nevertheless more lyrical than prophetic in its character. The elevation of the king to the dominion of the world is the reward of his condescension; he shows himself to be the helper and protecting lord of the poor and the oppressed, who are the especial object upon which God's eye is set. He looks upon it as his task to deal most sympathizingly and most considerately (יָחֹם) just with those of reduced circumstances and with the poor, and their blood is precious in his eyes. Ver. 12 is re-echoed in Job xxix. 12. The meaning of ver. 14*b* is the same as cxvi. 15. Instead of יֵקַר, by a retention of the *Jod* of the stem it is written יִיקַר. Just as in xlix. 10, ייקר here also is followed by וִיחִי. The assertion is individualized: and he (who was threatened with death) shall live (voluntative, having reference to the will of the king). But who is now the subject to וְיִתֶּן־? Not the rescued one (Hitzig), for after the foregoing designations (vers. 11 sq.) we cannot expect to find "the gold of Sheba" (gold from Jeman or Æthiopia) in his possession. Therefore it is the king, and in fact Solomon, of whom the disposal of the gold of Sheba (Saba) is characteristic. The king's thought and endeavour are directed to this, that the poor man who has almost fallen a victim shall live or revive, and not only will he maintain his cause, he will also bestow gifts upon him with a liberal hand, and he (the poor one who has been rescued and endowed from the riches of the king) shall pray unceasingly for him (the king) and bless him at all times. The poor one is he who is restored to life and endowed with gifts, and who intercedes and blesses; the king, however, is the beneficent giver. It is left for the reader to supply the right subjects in thought to the separate verbs. That clearly marked precision which we require in rhetorical recital is alien to the Oriental

style (*vid.* my *Geschichte der jüdischen Poesie,* S. 189).   Maurer
and Hofmann also give the same interpretation as we have done.

Vers. 16, 17.   Here, where the futures again stand at the
head of the clauses, they are also again to be understood as
optatives.   As the blessing of such a dominion after God's
heart, not merely fertility but extraordinary fruitfulness may
be confidently desired for the land.   פִּסַּה (*ἅπ. λεγ.*), rendered by
the Syriac version *sugo,* abundance, is correctly derived by the
Jewish lexicographers from פָּשָׂה = פָּסַם (in the law relating to
leprosy), Mishnic פָּסָה, Aramaic פְּסָא, Arabic لشا, but also فش
(*vid. Job,* ii. 275), to extend, *expandere;* so that it signifies
an abundance that occupies a broad space.   בְּרֹאשׁ, unto the
summit, as in xxxvi. 6, xix. 5.   The idea thus obtained is the
same as when Hofmann (*Weissagung und Erfüllung,* i. 180 f.)
takes פִּסַּה (from אָפֵס = פָּסַם) in the signification of a boundary
line : "close upon the summit of the mountain shall the last
corn stand," with reference to the terrace-like structure of
the heights.   פִּרְיוֹ does not refer back to בארץ (Hitzig, who
misleads one by referring to Joel ii. 3), but to בַּר : may the
corn stand so high and thick that the fields, being moved
by the wind, shall shake, *i.e.* wave up and down, like the
lofty thick forest of Lebanon.   The LXX., which renders
ὑπεραρθήσεται, takes ירעשׁ for יראשׁ, as Ewald does : may its
fruit rise to a summit, *i.e.* rise high, like Lebanon.   But a
verb רָאַשׁ is unknown ; and how bombastic is this figure in
comparison with that grand, but beautiful figure, which we
would not willingly exchange even for the conjecture יֶעְשַׁר
(may it be rich) !   The other wish refers to a rapid, joyful increase of the population : may men blossom out of this city and
out of that city as the herb of the earth (cf. Job v. 25, where
צֶאֱצָאֶיךָ also accords in sound with יְצִיצוּ), *i.e.* fresh, beautiful,
and abundant as it.   Israel actually became under Solomon's
sceptre as numerous " as the sand by the sea" (1 Kings iv.
20), but increase of population is also a settled feature in the
picture of the Messianic time (cx. 3, Isa. ix. 2, xlix. 20, Zech.
ii. 8 [4] ; cf. Sir. xliv. 21).   If, however, under the just and
benign rule of the king, both land and people are thus blessed,
eternal duration may be desired for his name.   May this name,
is the wish of the poet, ever send forth new shoots (יִנִּין *Chethib*),

or receive new shoots (יְפֻוֹן *Kerî*, from *Niph.* נִנֹּון), as long as the sun turns its face towards us, inasmuch as the happy and blessed results of the dominion of the king ever afford new occasion for glorifying his name. May they bless themselves in him, may all nations call him blessed, and that, as *וְיִתְבָּרְכוּ בוֹ implies, so blessed that his abundance of blessing appears to them to be the highest that they can desire for themselves. To *et benedicant sibi in eo* we have to supply in thought the most universal, as yet undefined subject, which is then more exactly defined as *omnes gentes* with a second synonymous predicate. The accentuation (*Athnach, Mugrash, Silluk*) is blameless.

Vers. 18, 19. Closing *Beracha* of the Second Book of the Psalter. It is more full-toned than that of the First Book, and God is intentionally here called *Jahve Elohim the God of Israel* because the Second Book contains none but Elohim-Psalms, and not, as there, *Jahve the God of Israel*. "Who alone doeth wonders" is a customary praise of God, lxxxvi. 10, cxxxvi. 4, cf. Job ix. 8. שֵׁם כְּבוֹדוֹ is a favourite word in the language of divine worship in the period after the Exile (Neh. ix. 5); it is equivalent to the שֵׁם כְּבוֹד מַלְכוּתוֹ in the liturgical *Beracha*, God's glorious name, the name that bears the impress of His glory. The closing words: and let the whole earth be full, etc., are taken from Num. xiv. 21. Here, as there, the construction of the active with a double accusative of that which fills and that which is to be filled is retained in connection with the passive; for כְּבוֹדוֹ is also accusative: let be filled with His glory the whole earth (let one make it full of it). The אָמֵן coupled by means of *Waw* is, in the Old Testament, exclusively peculiar to these doxologies of the Psalter.

Ver. 20. Superscription of the primary collection. The origin of this superscription cannot be the same as that of the doxology, which is only inserted between it and the Psalm, because it was intended to be read with the Psalm at the reading in the course of the service (*Symbolæ*, p. 19). כָּלּוּ = כָּלוּ, like דֹּחוּ in xxxvi. 13, כָּסוּ, lxxx. 11, all being *Pual* forms, as is

---

* Pronounce *wejithbārchu*, because the tone rests on the first letter of the root; whereas in ver. 15 it is *jebārᵃchenhu* with *Chateph*. *vid.* the rule in the *Luther. Zeitschrift*, 1863, S. 412.

manifest in the accented *ultima*. A parallel with this verse is
the superscription "*are ended the words of Job*" in Job xxxi.
40, which separates the controversial speeches and Job's mono-
logue from the speeches of God. No one taking a survey of
the whole Psalter, with the many Psalms of David that follow
beyond Ps. lxxii., could possibly have placed this key-stone
here. If, however, it is more ancient than the doxological
division into five books, it is a significant indication in relation
to the history of the rise of the collection. It proves that
the collection of the whole as it now lies before us was at
least preceded by one smaller collection, of which we may say
that it extended to Ps. lxxii., without thereby meaning to maintain that it contained all the Psalms up to that one, since several
of them may have been inserted into it when the redaction of
the whole took place. But it is possible for it to have contained
Ps. lxxii., since at the earliest it was only compiled in the time
of Solomon. The fact that the superscription following directly
upon a Psalm of Solomon is thus worded, is based on the same
ground as the fact that the whole Psalter is quoted in the New
Testament as Davidic. David is the father of the שִׁיר ה', 2
Chron. xxix. 27, and hence all Psalms may be called Davidic,
just as all מְשָׁלִים may be called Salomonic, without meaning
thereby that they are all composed by David himself.

PSALM LXXIII.

TEMPTATION TO APOSTASY OVERCOME.

1 VERILY good to Israel is Elohim,
  To those who are of a clean heart.
2 But as for me—my feet had almost tottered,
  My steps had well-nigh slipped.

3 For I was incensed at the boastful,
  When I saw the prosperity of the wicked.
4 For they suffer no pangs,
  Healthy and fat is their belly.
5 In the trouble of men they are not,
  And not as other men are they plagued.
6 Therefore pride encircleth their neck,
  Violence covereth them round about as a garment.

7 Their eyes stand out with fat,
  The imaginations of the heart appear outwardly.
8 They mock and speak oppression in wickedness,
  They speak from on high.
9 They set their mouth in the heavens,
  And their tongue stalketh along upon the earth.
10 Therefore their people turn hither,
  And water in abundance is swallowed down by them.

11 And they say: "How should God know,
   And knowledge dwell in the Most High?!
12 Behold those are godless,
   And always reckless have they attained to great power!
13 Only in vain have I cleansed my heart,
   And washed my hands in innocence,
14 And yet was plagued all the day long,
   And my chastisement was present every morning."—

15 Had I thought: I will speak thus,
   Behold, I should have dealt faithlessly with the generation
           of Thy children.
16 Yet when I mused in order to solve the riddle,
   It was too difficult in mine eyes—
17 Until I went into the sanctuary of God,
   Until I gave good heed unto their end:
18 Surely in slippery places dost Thou set them,
   Thou castest them down to ruins.

19 How are they become a desolation as in a moment,
   Brought to an end, gone by reason of terrors!
20 As a dream, as soon as one awaketh,
   O Lord, being aroused, Thou dost get rid of their image.
21 If my heart should grow bitter,
   And I should be pricked in my reins:
22 Then I should be a stupid one and without understanding,
   A behēmôth should I be in comparison with Thee.

23 But I remain continually with Thee,
   Thou hast taken hold of my right hand.
24 According to Thy counsel wilt Thou lead me,
   And afterward receive me to honour.
25 Whom have I in the heavens?
   And if Thou art mine, the earth doth not delight me!
26 My flesh and my heart may fail—
   The refuge of my heart and my portion is Elohim for
           ever.

27 For, lo, those who are estranged from Thee shall perish,
   Thou destroyest all those who wantonly forsake Thee.

28 But as for me—to be united to Elohim is my happiness,
  I make in the Lord, Jahve, my refuge,
  That I may declare all Thy works.

After the one Asaph Psalm of the Second Book, Ps. l.,
follow eleven more of them from Ps. lxxiii. to lxxxiii. They
are all Elohimic, whereas the Korah Psalms divide into an
Elohimic and a Jehovic group. Ps. lxxxiv. forms the transition from the one to the other. The Elohim-Psalms extend
from Ps. xlii.–lxxxiv., and are fenced in on both sides by Jahve-
Psalms.

In contents Ps. lxxiii. is the counterpart or pendant of Ps. l.
As in that Psalm the semblance of a sanctity based upon works
is traced back to its nothingness, so here the seeming good
fortune of the ungodly, by which the poet felt himself tempted
to fall away, not into heathenism (Hitzig), but into that free-
thinking which in the heathen world does not less cast off the
δεισιδαιμονία than it does the belief in Jahve within the pale
of Israel. Nowhere does there come to light in the national
history any background that should contradict the לְאִסָף, and the
doubts respecting the moral order of the world are set at rest
in exactly the same way as in Ps. xxxvii., xlix., and in the Book
of Job. Theodicy, or the vindication of God's ways, does not
as yet rise from the indication of the retribution in this present
time which the ungodly do not escape, to a future solution of
all the contradictions of this present world; and the transcendent glory which infinitely outweighs the suffering of this
present time, still remains outside the range of vision. The
stedfast faith which, gladly renouncing everything, holds fast to
God, and the pure love to which this possession is more than
heaven and earth, is all the more worthy of admiration in connection with such defective knowledge.

The strophe schema of the Psalm is predominantly octa-
stichic: 4. 8. 8. 8; 8. 8. 5. Its two halves are vers. 1–14,
15–28.

Vers. 1, 2. אַךְ, belonging to the favourite words of the
faith that bids defiance to assault, signifies originally "thus =
not otherwise," and therefore combines an affirmative and restrictive, or, according to circumstances, even an adversative

signification (*vid.* on xxxix. 6).   It may therefore be rendered: yea good, assuredly good, or: only good, nothing but good; both renderings are an assertion of a sure, infallible relation of things.   God appears to be angry with the godly, but in reality He is kindly disposed towards them, though He send affliction after affliction upon them (Lam. iii. 25).   The words ישראל אלהים are not to be taken together, after Gal. vi. 16 (τὸν Ἰσραὴλ τοῦ Θεοῦ); not, "only good is it with the Israel of Elohim," but "only good to Israel is Elohim," is the right apprehension of the truth or reality that is opposed to what seems to be the case.   The Israel which in every relationship has a good and loving God is limited in ver. 1*b* to the pure in heart (xxiv. 4, Matt. v. 8).   Israel in truth are not all those who are descended from Jacob, but those who have put away all impurity of disposition and all uncleanness of sin out of their heart, *i.e.* out of their innermost life, and by a constant striving after sanctification (ver. 13) maintain themselves in such purity.   In relation to this, which is the real church of God, God is pure love, nothing but love.   This it is that has been confirmed to the poet as he passed through the conflict of temptation, but it was through conflict, for he almost fell by reason of the semblance of the opposite.   The *Chethîb* נטוי רַגְלָי (cf. Num. xxiv. 4) or נָטוּי (cf. 2 Sam. xv. 32) is erroneous. The narration of that which is past cannot begin with a participial clause like this, and בִּמְעַט, in such a sense (*non multum abfuit quin*, like כִּאַיִן, *nihil abfuit quin*), always has the perfect after it, *e.g.* xciv. 17, cxix. 87.   It is therefore to be read נָטְיוּ (according to the fuller form for נָטוּ, which is used not merely with great distinctives, as in xxxvi. 8, cxxii. 6, Num. xxiv. 6, but also with conjunctives out of pause, *e.g.* lvii. 2, cf. xxxvi. 9, Deut. xxxii. 37, Job xii. 6): my feet had almost inclined towards, had almost slipped backwards and towards the side. On the other hand the *Chethîb* שֻׁפְּכָה is unassailable; the feminine singular is frequently found as predicate both of a plural subject that has preceded (xviii. 35, cf. Deut. xxi. 7, Job xvi. 16) and also more especially of one that is placed after it, *e.g.* xxxvii. 31, Job xiv. 19.   The footsteps are said to be poured out when one "flies out or slips" and falls to the ground.

Vers. 3–6.   Now follows the occasion of the conflict of temptation: the good fortune of tnose who are estranged from

God. In accordance with the gloominess of the theme, the style is also gloomy, and piles up the dull-toned suffixes *amo* and *emo* (*vid.* lxxviii. 66, lxxx. 7, lxxxiii. 12, 14); both are after the example set by David. קִנֵּא with *Beth* of the object on which the zeal or warmth of feeling is kindled (xxxvii. 1, Prov. iii. 31) here refers to the warmth of envious ill-feeling. Concerning הוֹלְלִ *vid.* v. 6. Ver. 3*b* tells under what circumstances the envy was excited; cf. so far as the syntax is concerned, xlix. 6, lxxvi. 11. In ver. 4 חַרְצֻבּוֹת (from חַרְצֹב = חַצֹב from חָצַב, cognate עָצַב, whence עֶצֶב, pain, Arabic *'asábe*, a snare, cf. חֶבֶל, ὠδίς, and חֶבֶל, σχοινίον), in the same sense as the Latin *tormenta* (from *torquere*), is intended of pains that produce convulsive contractions. But in order to give the meaning "they have no pangs (to suffer) till their death," לָהֶם (לְמוֹ) could not be omitted (that is, assuming also that לְ, which is sometimes used for עַד, *vid.* lix. 14, could in such an exclusive sense signify the *terminus ad quem*). Also " there are no pangs for their death, *i.e.* that bring death to them," ought to be expressed by לָהֶם לָמֶוֶת. The clause as it stands affirms that their dying has no pangs, *i.e.* it is a painless death; but not merely does this assertion not harmonize with vers. 18 sq., but it is also introduced too early here, since the poet cannot surely begin the description of the good fortune of the ungodly with the painlessness of their death, and then for the first time come to speak of their healthy condition. We may therefore read, with Ewald, Hitzig, Böttcher, and Olshausen:

כי אין חרצבות לָמוֹ
תָּם ובריא אולם

i.e. they have (suffer) *no pangs, vigorous* (תָּם like הֹם, Job xxi. 23, תָּמִים, Prov. i. 12) *and well-nourished is their belly;* by which means the difficult לְמוֹתָם is got rid of, and the gloomy picture is enriched by another form ending with *mo*. אוּל, here in a derisive sense, signifies the body, like the Arabic آلّ, آل (from آل, *coaluit, cohæsit,* to condense inwardly, to gain consistency).*

---

* Hitzig calls to mind οὖλος, " corporeal;" but this word is Ionic and equivalent to ὅλος, *solidus*, the ground-word of which is the Sanscrit *sarvas*, whole, complete.

The observation of ver. 4*a* is pursued further in ver. 5 : whilst one would have thought that the godly formed an exception to the common wretchedness of mankind, it is just the wicked who are exempt from all trouble and calamity. It is also here to be written אֵינֵמוֹ, as in lix. 14, not אֵינֵימוֹ. Therefore is haughtiness their neck-chain, and brutishness their mantle. עָנַק is a denominative from עֲנָק = αὐχήν : to hang round the neck ; the neck is the seat of pride (αὐχεῖν) : haughtiness hangs around their neck (like עֲנָק, a neck-ornament). Accordingly in ver. 6*b* חָמָס is the subject, although the interpunction construes it differently, viz. "they wrap round as a garment the injustice belonging to them," in order, that is, to avoid the construction of יַעֲטֹף (*vid.* lxv. 14) with לָמוֹ ; but active verbs can take a dative of the object (*e.g.* רָפָא לְ, אָהֵב לְ, כִּסָּה לְ) in the sense : to be or to grant to any one that which the primary notion of the verb asserts. It may therefore be rendered : they put on the garment of violence (שִׁית חָמָס like בִּגְדֵי נָקָם, Isa. lix. 17), or even by avoiding every *enallage numeri :* violence covers them as a garment ; so that שִׁית is an apposition which is put forth in advance.

Vers. 7–10. The reading עוֹנֵמוֹ, ἡ ἀδικία αὐτῶν LXX. (cf. in Zech. v. 6 the עינם, which is rendered by the LXX. in exactly the same way), in favour of which Hitzig, Böttcher, and Olshausen decide, "their iniquity presses forth out of a fat heart, out of a fat inward part," is favoured by xvii. 10, where חֵלֶב obtains just this signification by combination with סָגַר, which it would obtain here as being the place whence sin issues ; cf. ἐξέρχεσθαι ἐκ τῆς καρδίας, Matt. xv. 18 sq. ; and the parallelism decides its superiority. Nevertheless the traditional reading also gives a suitable sense ; not (since fat tends to make the eyes appear to be deeper in) "their eyes come forward *præ adipe*," but "they stare forth *ex adipe*, out of the fat of their bloated visage," מֵחֵלֶב being equivalent to מחלב פְּנֵיהֶם, Job xv. 27. This is a feature of character faithfully drawn after nature. Further, just as in general τὸ περίσσευμα τῆς καρδίας wells over in the gestures and language (Matt. xii. 34), so is it also with their "views or images of the heart" (from שָׂכָה, like שֶׂכְוִי, the cock with its gift of divination as *speculator*) : the illusions of their unbounded self-confidence come forth out-

wardly, they overflow after the manner of a river,* viz., as ver.
8 says, in words that are proud beyond measure (Jer. v. 28).
Luther: "they destroy everything" (synon. they make it as or
into rottenness, from מָקַק).   But הֵמִיק is here equivalent to the
Aramaic מַיֵּק (μωκᾶσθαι): they mock and openly speak בְּרָע
(with *ā* in connection with *Munach* transformed from *Dechî*),
with evil disposition (cf. Ex. xxxii. 12), oppression; *i.e.* they
openly express their resolve which aims at oppression.   Their
fellow-man is the sport of their caprice; they speak or dictate
מִמָּרוֹם, down from an eminence, upon which they imagine themselves to be raised high above others.   Even in the heavens
above do they set (שַׁתּוּ as in xlix. 15 instead of שָׁתוּ,—there, in
accordance with tradition, *Milel;* here at the commencement of
the verse *Milra*) their mouth; even these do not remain untouched by their scandalous language (cf. Jude ver. 16); the
Most High and Holy One, too, is blasphemed by them, and
their tongue runs officiously and imperiously through the earth
below, everywhere disparaging that which exists and giving new
laws.   תִּהֲלַךְ, as in Ex. ix. 23, a *Kal* sounding much like *Hithpa.,*
in the signification *grassari.*   In ver. 10 the *Chethîb* יָשִׁיב
(therefore he, this class of man, turns a people subject to him
hither, *i.e.* to himself) is to be rejected, because הֲלֹם is not
appropriate to it.   עַמּוֹ is the subject, and the suffix refers not
to God (Stier), whose name has not been previously mentioned,
but to the kind of men hitherto described: what is meant is
the people which, in order that it may turn itself hither (שׁוּב,
not: to turn back, but to turn one's self towards, as *e.g.* in Jer.
xv. 19†), becomes his, *i.e.* this class's people (cf. for this sense of

---

* On the other hand, Redslob (*Deutsch. Morgenländ. Zeitschr.* 1860, S.
675) interprets it thus: they run over the fencings of the heart, from שָׂבָה in
the signification to put or stick through, to stick into (*infigere*), by comparing
קִירוֹת לִבִּי, Jer. iv. 19, and ἕρκος ὀδόντων. He regards מַשְׂבִית and mosaic as
one word, just as the Italian *ricamare* (to stitch) and רָקַם is one word.
Certainly the root זך, زكّ, ذكّ, has the primary notion of piercing (cf.
זכר), and also the notion of purity, which it obtains, proceeds from the idea
of the brilliance which pierces into the eye; but the primary notion of שָׂבָה
is that of cutting through (whence שַׂבִּין, like מַחֲלָף, a knife, from חָלַף,
Judg. v. 26).

† In general שׁוּב does not necessarily signify to turn back, but, like the
Arabic ʿâda, Persic *gashʻen*, to enter into a new (active or passive) state.

the suffix as describing the issue or event, xviii. 24, xlix. 6, lxv. 12).   They gain adherents (xlix. 14) from those who leave the fear of God and turn to them; and מֵי מָלֵא, water of fulness, *i.e.* of full measure (cf. lxxiv. 15, streams of duration = that do not dry up), which is here an emblem of their corrupt principles (cf. Job xv. 16), is quaffed or sucked in (מָצָה, root

מץ, whence first of all מָצַץ, مصّ, to suck) by these befooled

ones (לָמוֹ, αὐτοῖς = ὑπ' αὐτῶν).   This is what is meant to be further said, and not that this band of servile followers is in fulness absorbed by them (Sachs).   Around the proud free-thinkers there gathers a rabble submissive to them, which eagerly drinks in everything that proceeds from them as though it were the true water of life.   Even in David's time (x. 4, xiv. 1, xxxvi. 2) there were already such stout spirits (Isa. xlvi. 12) with a *servûm imitatorum pecus*.   A still far more favourable soil for these לֵצִים was the worldly age of Solomon.

Vers. 11–14.   The persons speaking are now those apostates who, deluded by the good fortune and free-thinking of the ungodly, give themselves up to them as slaves.   Concerning the modal sense of יָדַע, *quomodo sciverit, vid.* xi. 3, cf. Job xxii. 13.   With וְיֵשׁ the doubting question is continued.   Böttcher renders thus: nevertheless knowledge is in the Most High (a circumstantial clause like Prov. iii. 28, Mal. i. 14, Judg. vi. 13); but first of all they deny God's actual knowledge, and then His attributive omniscience.   It is not to be interpreted: behold, such are (according to their moral nature) the ungodly (אֵלֶּה, *tales*, like זֶה, xlviii. 15, Deut. v. 26, cf. הֵמָּה, Isa. lvi. 11); nor, as is more in accordance with the parallel member ver. 12*b* and the drift of the Psalm: behold, thus it befalleth the ungodly (such are they according to their lot, as in Job xviii. 21, cf. Isa. xx. 6); but, what forms a better connection as a statement of the ground of the scepticism in ver. 11, either, in harmony with the accentuation: behold, the ungodly, etc., or, since it is not הרשעים: behold, these are ungodly, and, ever reckless (Jer. xii. 1), they have acquired great power.   With the bitter הִנֵּה, as Stier correctly observes, they bring forward the obvious proof to the contrary.   How can God be said to be the omniscient Ruler of the world?—the ungodly in their carnal security become very powerful and mighty, but piety, very far from being rewarded, is joined with nothing but misfortune. My striving after sanctity (cf. Prov. xx. 9), my abstinence from all moral pollution (cf. Prov. xxvi. 6), says he who has been led astray, has been absolutely (אַךְ as in 1 Sam. xxv. 21) in vain; I was notwithstanding (Ew. § 345, a) incessantly tormented (cf. ver. 5), and with every morning's dawn (לַבְּקָרִים, as in ci. 8, cf. לִבְקָרִים in Job vii. 18) my chastitive suffering was renewed. We may now supply the conclusion in thought in accordance with ver. 10: Therefore have I joined myself to those who never concern themselves about God and at the same time get on better.

Vers. 15–18. To such, doubt is become the transition to apostasy. The poet has resolved the riddle of such an unequal distribution of the fortunes of men in a totally different way. Instead of כְּמוֹ in ver. 15, to read כְּמוֹהֶם (Böttcher), or better, by taking up the following הנה, which even Saadia allows himself to do, contrary to the accents (مثل هذا), כְּמוֹ הֵנָּה (Ewald), is unnecessary, since prepositions are sometimes used elliptically (בְּעַל, Isa. lix. 18), or even without anything further (Hos. vii. 16, xi. 7) as adverbs, which must therefore be regarded as possible also in the case of כְּמוֹ (Aramaic, Arabic כְּמָא, Æthiopic *kem*). The poet means to say, If I had made up my mind to the same course of reasoning, I should have faithlessly forsaken the fellowship of the children of God, and should consequently also have forfeited their blessings. The subjunctive signification of the perfects in the hypothetical protasis and apodosis, ver. 15 (cf. Jer. xxiii. 22), follows solely from the context; futures instead of perfects would signify *si dicerem . . . perfide agerem*. דּוֹר בָּנֶיךָ is the totality of those, in whom the filial relationship in which God has placed Israel in relation to Himself is become an inward or spiritual reality, the true Israel, ver. 1, the "righteous generation," xiv. 5. It is an appellative, as in Deut. xiv. 1, Hos. ii. 1. For on the point of the υἱοθεσία the New Testament differs from the Old Testament in this way, viz. that in the Old Testament it is always only as a people that Israel is called בֵּן, or as a whole בנים, but that the individual, and that in his direct relationship to God, dared not as yet call himself "child of God." The individual character is not as yet freed from its absorption in the species, it is not

as yet independent; it is the time of the minor's νηπιότης, and
the adoption is as yet only effected nationally, salvation is as
yet within the limits of the nationality, its common human
form has not as yet appeared. The verb בָּגַד with בְּ signifies to
deal faithlessly with any one, and more especially (whether
God, a friend, or a spouse) faithlessly to forsake him; here, in
this sense of malicious desertion, it contents itself with the simple
accusative.

On the one side, by joining in the speech of the free-
thinkers he would have placed himself outside the circle of the
children of God, of the truly pious; on the other side, however, when by meditation he sought to penetrate it (לְדַעַת), the
doubt-provoking phenomenon (זֹאת) still continued to be to him
עָמָל, trouble, *i.e.* something that troubled him without any
result, an unsolvable riddle (cf. Eccles. viii. 17). Whether we
read הוּא or הִיא, the sense remains the same; the *Keri* הוּא prefers, as in Job xxxi. 11, the attractional gender. Neither here
nor in Job xxx. 26 and elsewhere is it to be supposed that וָאחשׁבה
is equivalent to וָאחשׁבה (Ewald, Hupfeld). The cohortative form
of the future here, as frequently (Ges. § 128, 1), with or without
a conditional particle (cxxxix. 8, 2 Sam. xxii. 38, Job xvi. 6,
xi. 17, xix. 18, xxx. 26), forms a hypothetical protasis: and
(yet) when I meditated; Symmachus (according to Montfaucon),
εἰ ἐλογιζόμην. As Vaihinger aptly observes, "thinking alone
will give neither the right light nor true happiness." Both are
found only in faith. The poet at last struck upon the way of
faith, and there he found light and peace. The future after
עַד frequently has the signification of the imperfect subjunctive,
Job xxxii. 11, Eccles. ii. 3, cf. Prov. xii. 19 (*donec nutem* = only
a moment); also in an historical connection like Josh. x. 13,
2 Chron. xxix. 34, it is conceived of as subjunctive (*donec
ulcisceretur, se sanctificarent*), sometimes, however, as indicative,
as in Ex. xv. 16 (*donec transibat*) and in our passage, where עַד
introduces the objective goal at which the riddle found its
solution: until I went into the sanctuary of God, (purposely)
attended to (לְ as in the primary passage Deut. xxxii. 29, cf.
Job xiv. 21) their life's end. The cohortative is used here
exactly as in וָאָבִינָה, but with the collateral notion of that which
is intentional, which here fully accords with the connection.
He went into God's dread sanctuary (plural as in lxviii. 36, cf.

מִקְדָּשׁ in the Psalms of Asaph, lxvii. 7, lxxviii. 69); here he prayed for light in the darkness of his conflict, here were his eyes opened to the holy plans and ways of God (lxxvii. 14), here the sight of the sad end of the evil-doers was presented to him. By "God's sanctuaries" Ewald and Hitzig understand His secrets; but this meaning is without support in the usage of the language. And is it not a thought perfectly in harmony with the context and with experience, that a light arose upon him when he withdrew from the bustle of the world into the quiet of God's dwelling-place, and there devoutly gave his mind to the matter?

The strophe closes with a summary confession of the explanation received there. שִׁית is construed with *Lamed* inasmuch as *collocare* is equivalent to *locum assignare* (*vid.* ver. 6*b*). God makes the evil-doers to stand on smooth, slippery places, where one may easily lose one's footing (cf. xxxv. 6, Jer. xxiii. 12). There, then, they also inevitably fall; God casts them down לְמַשּׁוּאוֹת, into ruins, *fragores = ruinæ*, from שׁוֹא = שָׁאָה, to be confused, desolate, to rumble. The word only has the appearance of being from נָשָׁא: ensnarings, sudden attacks (Hitzig), which is still more ill suited to lxxiv. 3 than to this passage; desolation and ruin can be said even of persons, as הָרַם, xxviii. 5, וְנִשְׁבָּרוּ, Isa. viii. 15, נֶפֶץ, Jer. li. 21–23. The poet knows no other theodicy but this, nor was any other known generally in the pre-exilic literature of Israel (*vid.* Ps. xxxvii., xxxix., Jer. ch. xii., and the Book of Job). The later prophecy and the Chokma were much in advance of this, inasmuch as they point to a last universal judgment (*vid.* more particularly Mal. iii. 13 sqq.), but not one that breaks off this present state; the present state and the future state, time and eternity, are even there not as yet thoroughly separated.

Vers. 19–22. The poet calms himself with the solution of the riddle that has come to him; and it would be beneath his dignity as a man to allow himself any further to be tempted by doubting thoughts. Placing himself upon the standpoint of the end, he sees how the ungodly come to terrible destruction in a moment: they come to an end (סָפוּ from סוּף, not סָפָה), it is all over with them (תַּמּוּ) in consequence of (מִן as in lxxvi. 7, and unconnected as in xviii. 4, xxx. 4, 2 Sam. xxii. 14) frightful occurrences (בַּלָּהוֹת, a favourite word, especially in the Book of Job), which clear them out of the way. It is with them as with a dream, after (מִן as in 1 Chron. viii. 8) one is awoke. One forgets the vision on account of its nothingness (Job xx. 8). So the evil-doers who boast themselves μετὰ πολλῆς φαντασίας (Acts xxv. 23) are before God a צֶלֶם, phantom or unsubstantial shadow. When He, the sovereign Lord, shall awake, *i.e.* arouse Himself to judgment after He has looked on with forbearance, then He will despise their shadowy image, will cast it contemptuously from Him. Luther renders, *So machstu HERR jr Bilde in der Stad verschmecht* (So dost Thou, Lord, make their image despised in the city). But neither has the *Kal* בָּזָה this double transitive signification, "to give over to contempt," nor is the mention of the city in place here. In Hos. xi. 9 also בְּעִיר in the signification *in urbem* gives no right sense; it signifies heat of anger or fury, as in Jer. xv. 8, heat of anguish, and Schröder maintains the former signification (*vid.* on Ps. cxxxix. 20), *in fervore* (*iræ*), here also; but the pointing בָּעִיר is against it. Therefore בְּעִיר is to be regarded, with the Targum, as syncopated from בְּהָעִיר (cf. לְבִיא, Jer. xxxix. 7, 2 Chron. xxxi. 10; בְּכִשְׁלוֹ, Prov. xxiv. 17, and the like); not, however, to be explained, "when they awake," viz. from the sleep of death (Targum*), or after lxxviii. 38, "when Thou awakest them," viz. out of their sleep of security (De Wette, Kurtz), but after xxxv. 23, "when Thou awakest," viz. to sit in judgment.

Thus far we have the divine answer, which is reproduced by the poet after the manner of prayer. Hengstenberg now goes on by rendering it, " for my heart was incensed;" but we cannot take יִתְחַמֵּץ according to the sequence of tenses as an imperfect, nor understand כִּי as a particle expressing the reason. On the contrary, the poet, from the standpoint of the explanation he has received, speaks of a possible return (כִּי *seq. fut.* = ἐάν) of his temptation, and condemns it beforehand: *si exacerbaretur animus meus atque in renibus meis pungerer.*

---

* The Targum version is, "As the dream of a drunken man, who awakes out of his sleep, wilt Thou, O Lord, on the day of the great judgment, when they awake out of their graves, in wrath abandon their image to contempt." The text of our editions is to be thus corrected according to Bechai (on Deut. xxxiii. 29) and Nachmani (in his treatise שַׁעַר הַגְּמוּל).

הִתְחַמֵּץ, to become sour, bitter, passionate; הִשְׁתּוֹנֵן, with the more exactly defining accusative כִּלְיוֹתַי, to be pricked, piqued, irritated. With וַאֲנִי begins the apodosis: then should I be . . . I should have become (perfect as in ver. 15, according to Ges. § 126, 5). Concerning לֹא יֵדַע, *non sapere*, *vid*. xiv. 4. בְּהֵמוֹת can be taken as *compar. decurtata* for כַּבהמות; nevertheless, as apparently follows from Job xl. 15, the poet surely has the *p-ehe-mou*, the water-ox, *i.e.* the hippopotamus, in his mind, which being Hebraized is בְּהֵמוֹת,* and, as a plump colossus of flesh, is at once an emblem of colossal stupidity (Maurer, Hitzig). The meaning of the poet is, that he would not be a man in relation to God, over against God (עָם, as in lxxviii. 37, Job ix. 2, cf. عِنْدَ, in comparison with), if he should again give way to the same doubts, but would be like the most stupid animal, which stands before God incapable of such knowledge as He willingly imparts to earnestly inquiring man.

Vers. 23–26. But he does not thus deeply degrade himself: after God has once taken him by the right hand and rescued him from the danger of falling (ver. 2), he clings all the more firmly to Him, and will not suffer his perpetual fellowship with Him to be again broken through by such seizures which estrange him from God. Confidently does he yield up himself to the divine guidance, though he may not see through the mystery of the plan (עֵצָה) of this guidance. He knows that afterwards (אַחַר with *Mugrash:* adverb as in lxviii. 26), *i.e.* after this dark way of faith, God will כָּבוֹד receive him, *i.e.* take him to Himself and take him from all suffering (לָקַח as in xlix. 16, and of Enoch, Gen. v. 24). The comparison of Zech. ii. 12 [8] is misleading; there אַחַר is rightly accented as a preposition: after glory hath He sent me forth (*vid.* Köhler), and here as an adverb; for although the adverbial sense of אחר would more readily lead one to look for the arrangement of the words ואחר תקחני כבוד, still "to receive after glory" (cf. the reverse Isa. lviii. 8) is an awkward thought. כבוד, which as an

---

* The Egyptian *p* frequently passes over into the Hebrew *b*, and *vice versâ*, as in the name *Aperiu* = עברים; *p*, however, is retained in פרעה = *phar-aa*, grand-house (οἶκος μέγας in Horapollo), the name of the Egyptian rulers, which begins with the sign of the plan of a house = *p*.

adjective "glorious" (Hofmann) is alien to the language, is
either accusative of the goal (Hupfeld), or, which yields a form
of expression that is more like the style of the Old Testament,
accusative of the manner (Luther, "with honour"). In אַחַר the
poet comprehends in one summary view what he looks for at
the goal of the present divine guidance. The future is dark to
him, but lighted up by the one hope that the end of his earthly
existence will be a glorious solution of the riddle. Here, as
elsewhere, it is faith which breaks through not only the darkness of this present life, but also the night of Hades. At that
time there was as yet no divine utterance concerning any
heavenly triumph of the church, militant in the present world,
but to faith the Jahve-Name had already a transparent depth
which penetrated beyond Hades into an eternal life. The
heaven of blessedness and glory also is nothing without God;
but he who can in love call God his, possesses heaven upon
earth, and he who cannot in love call God his, would possess
not heaven, but hell, in the midst of heaven. In this sense the
poet says in ver. 25: whom have I in heaven? *i.e.* who there
without Thee would be the object of my desire, the stilling of
my longing? without Thee heaven with all its glory is a vast
waste and void, which makes me indifferent to everything, and
with Thee, *i.e.* possessing Thee, I have no delight in the earth,
because to call Thee mine infinitely surpasses every possession
and every desire of earth. If we take בָּאָרֶץ still more exactly
as parallel to בַּשָּׁמַיִם, without making it dependent upon חָפַצְתִּי:
and possessing Thee I have no desire upon the earth, then the
sense remains essentially the same; but if we allow בארץ to be
governed by חפצתי in accordance with the general usage of the
language, we arrive at this meaning by the most natural way.
Heaven and earth, together with angels and men, afford him no
satisfaction—his only friend, his sole desire and love, is God.
The love for God which David expresses in xvi. 2 in the brief
utterance, "Thou art my Lord, Thou art my highest good," is
here expanded with incomparable mystical profoundness and
beauty. Luther's version shows his master-hand. The church
follows it in its "*Herzlich lieb hab' ich dich*" when it sings—

> "The whole wide world delights me not,
>   For heaven and earth, Lord, care I not,
>   If I may but have Thee;"

and following it, goes on in perfect harmony with the text of
our Psalm—

> " Yea, though my heart be like to break,
> Thou art my trust that nought can shake ; " *

or with Paul Gerhard, [in his Passion-hymn *" Ein Lämmlein
geht und trägt die Schuld der Welt und ihrer Kinder,"*]

> " Light of my heart, that shalt Thou be ;
> And when my heart in pieces breaks,
> Thou shalt my heart remain."

For the hypothetical perfect כָּלָה expresses something in spite of
which he upon whom it may come calls God his God : *licet defe-
cerit.*   Though his outward and inward man perish, nevertheless
God remains ever the rock of his heart as the firm ground upon
which he, with his *ego*, remains standing when everything else
totters ; He remains his portion, *i.e.* the possession that cannot
be taken from him, if he loses all, even his spirit-life pertaining
to the body,—and God remains to him this portion לְעוֹלָם, he
survives with the life which he has in God the death of the old
life.   The poet supposes an extreme case,—one, that is, it is true,
impossible, but yet conceivable,—that his outward and inward
being should sink away ; even then with the *merus actus* of his
ego he will continue to cling to God.   In the midst of the
natural life of perishableness and of sin, a new, individual life
which is resigned to God has begun within him, and in this
he has the pledge that he cannot perish, so truly as God, with
whom it is closely united, cannot perish.   It is just this that is
also the nerve of the proof of the resurrection of the dead which
Jesus advances in opposition to the Sadducees (Matt. xxii. 32).

Vers. 27, 28.   The poet here once more gives expression
to the great opposites into which good fortune and misfortune
are seemingly, but only seemingly, divided in a manner so contradictory to the divine justice.   The central point of the confirmation that is introduced with כִּי lies in ver. 28.   " Thy far
removing ones" was to be expressed with רָחֵק, which is distinct
from רָחוֹק.   זָנָה has מִן instead of מִתַּחַת or מֵאַחֲרֵי after it.   Those
who remove themselves far from the primary fountain of life
fall a prey to ruin ; those who faithlessly abandon God, and

---

* [Miss Winkworth's translation.]

choose the world with its idols rather than His love, fall a prey
to destruction.   Not so the poet; the nearness of God, *i.e.* a
state of union with God, is good to him, *i.e.* (cf. cxix. 71 sq.)
he regards as his good fortune.   קִרְבָה is *nom. act.* after the
form יְקָהָה, وَقَه, obedience, and נִצְרָה, a watch, cxli. 3, and of
essentially the same signification with *kurba* (קִרְבָה), the Arabic
designation of the *unio mystica;* cf. Jas. iv. 8, ἐγγίσατε τῷ
Θεῷ καὶ ἐγγιεῖ ὑμῖν.   Just as קרבת אלהים stands in antithesis
to רחקיך, so לִי טוֹב stands in antithesis to יאבדו and הצמתה.   To
the former their alienation from God brings destruction; he
finds in fellowship with God that which is good to him for the
present time and for the future.   Putting his confidence (מַחְסִי,
not מְחַסִי) in Him, he will declare, and will one day be able to
declare, all His מַלְאֲכוֹת, *i.e.* the manifestations or achievements
of His righteous, gracious, and wise government.   The language of assertion is quickly changed into that of address.
The Psalm closes with an upward look of grateful adoration to
God beforehand, who leads His own people, ofttimes wondrously indeed, but always happily, viz. through suffering to
glory.

PSALM LXXIV.

APPEAL TO GOD AGAINST RELIGIOUS PERSECUTION, IN WHICH THE TEMPLE IS VIOLATED.

1 WHY, Elohim, hast Thou cast off for ever,
  Why doth Thine anger smoke against the flock of Thy
      pasture?
2 Remember Thy congregation which Thou hast purchased
     of old,
  Which Thou hast ransomed for the tribe of Thy possession—
  Of Mount Zion whereon Thou dwellest.
3 Oh lift up Thy footsteps unto the perpetual ruins,
  Everything hath the enemy destroyed in the sanctuary.

4 Thine adversaries roared in the midst of Thy place of
     assembly,
  They set up their signs as signs.

 5 It looked as when one lifteth up on high
   Axes in the thicket of the wood:
 6 And now—at its carved work altogether
   With hatchet and mattocks they hewed right and left;
 7 They have set on fire Thy Temple,
   To the earth they have defiled the dwelling-place of Thy
      name;
 8 They said in their hearts: we will crush them altogether;
   They have burnt up all the houses of God in the land.

 9 Our signs we see not.
   There is no longer any prophet,
   And among us there is no one who knoweth: until when?—
10 How long, Elohim, shall the oppressor blaspheme?
   Shall the enemy scoff at Thy name for ever?
11 Why dost Thou draw back Thy hand and Thy right hand?
   Out of the midst of Thy bosom bring it forth, destroy!—

12 And yet Elohim is my King from the days of old,
   Working deliverances in the midst of the earth.
13 Thou hast divided the sea by Thy power,
   Thou hast broken the heads of the dragons upon the waters.
14 Thou hast broken in pieces the heads of leviathan,
   Thou gavest him as food to a people: to the creatures of
      the desert.

15 Thou hast cleft fountains and brooks,
   Thou hast dried up never-failing rivers.
16 Thine is the day, also Thine the night,
   Thou hast prepared the star of night and the sun.
17 Thou hast established all the borders of the earth,
   Summer and winter hast Thou formed.

18 Remember this: the enemy revileth Jahve,
   And a foolish people scoffeth at Thy name.
19 Give not over to the wild beast the soul of Thy turtle-dove,
   Thy poor creatures forget not for ever.
20 Look upon the covenant,
   For the corners of the land are full of the habitations of
      violence.

21 Let not the disheartened turn back ashamed,
　Let the afflicted and the needy praise Thy name.
22 Arise, Elohim, fight out Thy cause,
　Remember Thy reproach from the foolish continually !
23 Forget not the cry of Thine adversaries,
　The tumult of those who rise up against Thee which ascend-
　　eth ever !!

The מִזְמוֹר lxxiii. is here followed by a *Maskîl* (*vid.* xxxii. 1)
which, in common with the former, has the prominent, rare
word מַשּׁוּאוֹת (lxxiv. 3, lxxiii. 18), but also the old Asaphic impress. We here meet with the favourite Asaphic contemplation
of Israel as a flock, and the predilection of the Asaphic Psalms
for retrospective references to Israel's early history (lxxiv.
13–15). We also find the former of these two characteristic
features in Ps. lxxix., which reflects the same circumstances of
the times.

Moreover Jeremiah stands in the same relationship to both
Psalms. In Jer. x. 25, Ps. lxxix. 6 sq. is repeated almost word
for word. And one is reminded of Ps. lxxiv. by Lam. ii. 2
(cf. lxxiv. 7), ii. 7 (cf. lxxiv. 4), and other passages. The
lament " there is no prophet any more " (lxxiv. 9) sounds very
much like Lam. ii. 9. In connection with Jeremiah's reproductive manner, and his habit of allowing himself to be
prompted to new thoughts by the original passages by means
of the association of ideas (cf. כְּיוֹם מוֹעֵד, Lam. ii. 7, with
בְּקֶרֶב מוֹעֲדֶךָ of the Psalm), it is natural to assign the priority
in age to the two Asaphic national lamentation Psalms.

But the substance of both Psalms, which apparently brings
us down not merely into the Chaldæan, but even into the
Maccabæan age, rises up in opposition to it. After his return
from the second Egyptian expedition (170 B.C.) Antiochus
Epiphanes chastised Jerusalem, which had been led into revolt
by Jason, in the most cruel manner, entered the Temple accompanied by the court high priest Menalaus, and carried away
the most costly vessels, and even the gold of the walls and
doors, with him. Myriads of the Jews were at that time massacred or sold as slaves. Then during the fourth Egyptian
expedition (168) of Antiochus, when a party favourably disposed towards the Ptolemies again arose in Jerusalem, he sent

Apollonius to punish the offenders (167), and his troops laid
the city waste with fire and sword, destroyed houses and walls,
burnt down several of the Temple-gates and razed many of its
apartments.   Also on this occasion thousands were slain and
led away captive.   Then began the attempt of Antiochus to
Hellenize the Jewish nation.   An aged Athenian was entrusted
with the carrying out of this measure.   Force was used to
compel the Jews to accept the heathen religion, and in fact to
serve Olympian Zeus (Jupiter): on the 15th of Chislev a
smaller altar was erected upon the altar of burnt-offering in
the Temple, and on the 25th of Chislev the first sacrifice was
offered to Olympian Zeus in the Temple of Jahve, now dedicated to him.   Such was the position of affairs when a band of
faithful confessors rallied around the Asmonæan (Hasmonæan)
priest Mattathias.

How strikingly does much in both Psalms, more particularly in Ps. lxxiv., harmonize with this position of affairs!   At
that time it was felt more painfully than ever that prophecy
had become dumb, 1 Macc. iv. 46, ix. 27, xiv. 41.   The confessors and martyrs who bravely declared themselves were
called, as in Ps. lxxix. 2, חסידים, 'Ασιδαῖοι.   At that time " they
saw," as 1 Macc. iv. 38 says, " the sanctuary desolate, and the
altar profaned, and the gates burnt up, and shrubs growing in
the courts as in a forest, or as in one of the mountains, yea, and
the priests' chambers pulled down."   The doors of the Temple-
gates were burned to ashes (cf. 2 Macc. viii. 33, i. 8).   The
religious אותות (lxxiv. 4) of the heathen filled the place where
Jahve was wont to reveal Himself.   Upon the altar of the
court stood the βδέλυγμα ἐρημώσεως; in the courts they had
planted trees, and likewise the " signs" of heathendom; and
the לִשָׁכוֹת (παστοφόρια) lay in ruins.   When later on, under
Demetrius Soter (161), Alcimus (an apostate whom Antiochus
had appointed high priest) and Bacchides advanced with
promises of peace, but with an army at the same time, a band
of scribes, the foremost of the 'Ασιδαῖοι of Israel, went forth
to meet them to intercede for their nation.   Alcimus, however,
seized sixty of them, slaughtered them in one day, and that, as
it is added in 1 Macc. vii. 16 sq., " according to the word
which he wrote: The flesh of Thy saints and their blood
have they shed round about Jerusalem, and there was none to

bury them." The formula of citation κατὰ τὸν λόγον ὃν (τοὺς λόγους οὓς) ἔγραψε, and more particularly the ἔγραψε,—which as being the aorist cannot have the Scripture (ἡ γραφή), and, since the citation is a prayer to God, not God, but only the anonymous psalmist, as its subject (*vid.*, however, the various readings in Grimm on this passage),—sounds as though the historian were himself conscious that he was quoting a portion of Scripture that had taken its rise among the calamities of that time. In fact, no age could be regarded as better warranted in incorporating some of its songs in the Psalter than the Maccabæan, the sixty-third week predicted by Daniel, the week of suffering bearing in itself the character of the time of the end, this strictly martyr age of the Old Covenant, to which the Book of Daniel awards a high typical significance in relation to the history of redemption.

But unbiassed as we are in the presence of the question whether there are Maccabæan Psalms, still there is, on the other hand, much, too, that is against the referring of the two Psalms to the Maccabæan age. In Ps. lxxix. there is nothing that militates against referring it to the Chaldæan age, and lxxix. 11 (cf. cii. 21, lxix. 34) is even favourable to this. And in Ps. lxxiv., in which vers. 4*b*, 8*b*, 9*b* are the most satisfactorily explained from the Maccabæan age, there are, again, other parts which are better explained from the Chaldæan. For what is said in ver. 7*a*, " *they have set Thy Temple on fire*," applies just as unconditionally as it runs to the Chaldæans, but not to the Syrians. And the cry of prayer, lxxiv. 3, " *lift up Thy footsteps to the eternal ruins*," appears to assume a laying waste that has taken place within the last few years at least, such as the Maccabæan age cannot exhibit, although at the exaltation of the Maccabees Jerusalem was ἀοίκητος ὡς ἔρημος (1 Macc. iii. 45). Hitzig, it is true, renders: *raise Thy footsteps for sudden attacks without end;* but both the passages in which מַשֻּׁאוֹת occurs mutually secure to this word the signification " desolations " (Targum, Symmachus, Jerome, and Saadia). If, however, the Chaldæan catastrophe were meant, then the author of both Psalms, on the ground of Ezra ii. 41, Neh. vii. 44 (cf. xi. 22), might be regarded as an Asaphite of the time of the Exile, although they might also be composed by any one in the Asaphic style. And as regards their relation to Jeremiah, we ought to be contented with the fact that Jeremiah, whose peculiarity as a writer is otherwise so thoroughly reproductive, is, notwithstanding, also reproduced by later writers, and in this instance by the psalmist.

Nothing is more certain than that the physiognomy of these Psalms does not correspond to any national misfortune prior to the Chaldæan catastrophe. Vaihinger's attempt to comprehend them from the time of Athaliah's reign of terror, is at issue with itself. In the history of Israel instances of the sacking of Jerusalem and of the Temple are not unknown even prior to the time of Zedekiah, as in the reign of Jehoram, but there is no instance of the city being reduced to ashes. Since even the profanation of the Temple by the Persian general Bagoses (Josephus, *Ant.* xi. 7), to which Ewald formerly referred this Psalm, was not accompanied by any injury of the building itself, much less its reduction to ashes, there remains only the choice between the laying waste of Jerusalem and of the Temple in the year 588 and in the year 167. We have reserved to ourselves the liberty of acknowledging some insertions from the time of the Maccabees in the Psalter; *supra,* vol. i. pp. 11–14. Now since in both Psalms, apart from the מִשּׁאות נצח, everything accords with the Maccabæan age, whilst when we refer them to the Chaldæan period the scientific conscience is oppressed by many difficulties (more especially in connection with lxxiv. 4, 8, 9, lxxix. 2, 3), we yield to the force of the impression and base both Psalms upon the situation of the Jewish nation under Antiochus and Demetrius. Their contents coincide with the prayer of Judas Maccabæus in 2 Macc. viii. 1–4.

Vers. 1–3. The poet begins with the earnest prayer that God would again have compassion upon His church, upon which His judgment of anger has fallen, and would again set up the ruins of Zion. Why for ever (ver. 10, lxxix. 5, lxxxix. 47, cf. xiii. 2)? is equivalent to, why so continually and, as it seems, without end? The preterite denotes the act of casting off, the future, ver. 1*b*, the lasting condition of this casting off. למה, when the initial of the following word is a guttural, and particularly if it has a merely half-vowel (although in other instances also, Gen. xii. 19, xxvii. 45, Cant. i. 7), is deprived of its *Dagesh* and accented on the *ultima*, in order (as Mose ha-Nakdan expressly observes) to guard against the swallowing up of the *ah;* cf. on x. 1. Concerning the smoking of anger, *vid.* xviii. 9. The characteristically Asaphic expression צֹאן מַרְעִיתוֹ is not less Jeremianic, Jer. xxiii. 1. In ver. 2 God is reminded of what He has once done for the congregation of His people. קֶדֶם, as in xliv. 2, points back into the Mosaic time of old, to the redemption out of Egypt, which is represented in קנה (Ex. xv. 17) as a purchasing, and in גאל (lxxvii. 16, lxxviii. 35, Ex. xv. 13) as a ransoming (*redemptio*). שֵׁבֶט נַחֲלָתֶךָ is a factitive object; שֵׁבֶט is the name given to the whole nation in its distinctness of race from other peoples, as in Jer. x. 16, li. 19, cf. Isa. lxiii. 17. זֶה (ver. 2*b*) is rightly separated from הר־צִיּוֹן (*Mugrash*); it stands directly for אֲשֶׁר, as in civ. 8, 26, Prov. xxiii. 22, Job xv. 17 (Ges. § 122, 2). The congregation of the people and its central abode are, as though forgotten of God, in a condition which sadly contrasts with their election. מַשֻּׁאוֹת נֶצַח are ruins (*vid.* lxxiii. 18) in a state of such total destruction, that all hope of their restoration vanishes before it; נֶצַח here looks forward, just as עוֹלָם (חרבות), Isa. lviii. 12, lxi. 4, looks backwards. May God then lift His feet up high (פְּעָמִים poetical for רַגְלַיִם, cf. lviii. 11 with lxviii. 24), *i.e.* with long hurried steps, without stopping, move towards His dwelling-place that now lies in ruins, that by virtue of His interposition it may rise again. Hath the enemy made merciless havoc—he hath ill-treated (הֵרַע, as in xliv. 3) everything (כֹּל, as in viii. 7, Zeph. i. 2, for הַכֹּל or אֶת־כֹּל) in the sanctuary—how is it possible that this sacrilegious vandalism should remain unpunished!

Vers. 4–8. The poet now more minutely describes how the enemy has gone on. Since קֹדֶשׁ in ver. 3 is the Temple, מוֹעֲדֶיךָ in ver. 4 ought likewise to mean the Temple with reference to the several courts; but the plural would here (cf. ver. 8*b*) be misleading, and is, too, only a various reading. Baer has rightly decided in favour of מוֹעֲדֶךָ;* מוֹעֵד, as in Lam. ii. 6 sq., is the instituted (Num. xvii. 19 [4]) place of God's inter-

----

* The reading מְעוֹדֶיךָ is received, *e.g.*, by Elias Hutter and Nissel; the Targum translates it, Kimchi follows it in his interpretation, and Abraham of Zante follows it in his paraphrase; it is tolerably widely known, but, according to the LXX. and Syriac versions and MSS., it is to be rejected.

course with His congregation (cf. مَعِيدٌ, a rendezvous).   What Jeremiah says in Lam. ii. 7 (cf. שָׁאַג, Jer. ii. 15) is here more briefly expressed.   By אוֹתֹתָם (ver. 4*b*) we must not understand military insignia; the scene of the Temple and the supplanting of the Israelitish national insignia to be found there, by the substitution of other insignia, requires that the word should have the religious reference in which it is used of circumcision and of the Sabbath (Ex. xxxi. 13); such heathen אֹתוֹת, which were thrust upon the Temple and the congregation of Jahve as henceforth the lawful ones, were those which are set forth in 1 Macc. i. 45–49, and more particularly the so-called abomination of desolation mentioned in ver. 54 of the same chapter. With יִוָּדַע (ver. 5) the terrible scene which was at that time taking place before their eyes (lxxix. 10) is introduced.   כְּמֵבִיא is the subject; it became visible, tangible, noticeable, *i.e.* it looked, and one experienced it, as if a man caused the axe to enter into the thicket of the wood, *i.e.* struck into or at it right and left.   The plural קַרְדֻּמּוֹת forces itself into the simile because it is the many heathen warriors who are, as in Jer. xlvi. 22 sq., likened to these hewers of wood.   Norzi calls the *Kametz* of בִּסְבָךְ־עֵץ *Kametz chatuph*; the combining form would then be a contraction of סְבֹךְ (Ewald, Olshausen), for the long *ā* of סְבָךְ does not admit of any contraction.   According to another view it is to be read *bi-sbāch-etz*, as in Esth. iv. 8 *kethāb-hadāth* (with counter-tone *Metheg* beside the long vowel, as *e.g.* עֵץ־הַגָּן, Gen. ii. 16).   The poet follows the work of destruction up to the destroying stroke, which is introduced by the ועת (perhaps וְעֵת, *Keri* וְעַתָּה), which arrests one's attention.   In ver. 5 the usual, unbroken quiet is depicted, as is the heavy Cyclopean labour in the Virgilian *illi inter sese*, etc.; in *jaha-lomûn*, ver. 6*b* (now and then pointed *jahlomûn*), we hear the stroke of the uplifted axes, which break in pieces the costly carved work of the Temple.   The suffix of פִּתּוּחֶיהָ (the carved works thereof) refers, according to the sense, to מוֹעֵד.   The LXX., favouring the Maccabæan interpretation, renders: ἐξέ-κοψαν τὰς θύρας αὐτῆς (פְּתָחֶיהָ).   This shattering of the panelling is followed in ver. 7 by the burning, first of all, as we may suppose, of this panelling itself so far as it consists of wood. The guaranteed reading here is מִקְדָּשֶׁךָ, not מִקְדָּשֶׁיךָ.   שִׁלַּח בָּאֵשׁ signifies to set on fire, *immittere igni*, differing from שִׁלַּח אֵשׁ בְּ,

to set fire to, *immittere ignem.* On לָאָרֶץ חִלְּלוּ, cf. Lam. ii. 2, Jer. xix. 13. Hitzig, following the LXX., Targum, and Jerome, derives the exclamation of the enemies נִינָם from נִין: their whole generation (viz. we will root out)! But נִין is posterity, descendants; why therefore only the young and not the aged? And why is it an expression of the object and not rather of the action, the object of which would be self-evident? נִינָם is *fut. Kal* of יָנָה, here = *Hiph.* הוֹנָה, to force, oppress, tyrannize over, and like אָנַס, to compel by violence, in later Hebrew. נִינָם (from יָנָה, like יִיפָּה) is changed in pause into נִינָם; cf. the future forms in Num. xxi. 30, Ex. xxxiv. 19, and also in Ps. cxviii. 10–12. Now, after mention has been made of the burning of the Temple framework, מוֹעֲדֵי־אֵל cannot denote the place of the divine manifestation after its divisions (Hengstenberg), still less the festive assemblies (Böttcher), which the enemy could only have burnt up by setting fire to the Temple over their heads, and כל does not at all suit this. The expression apparently has reference to synagogues (and this ought not to be disputed), as Aquila and Symmachus render the word. For there is no room for thinking of the separate services conducted by the prophets in the northern kingdom (2 Kings iv. 23), because this kingdom no longer existed at the time this Psalm was written; nor of the בָּמוֹת, the burning down of which no pious Israelite would have bewailed; nor of the sacred places memorable from the early history of Israel, which are nowhere called מוֹעֲדִים, and after the founding of the central sanctuary appear only as the seats of false religious rites. The expression points (like בֵּית וַעַד, *Sota* ix. 15) to places of assembly for religious purposes, to houses for prayer and teaching, that is to say, to synagogues—a weighty instance in favour of the Maccabæan origin of the Psalm.

Vers. 9–11. The worst thing the poet has to complain of is that God has not acknowledged His people during this time of suffering as at other times. "Our signs" is the direct antithesis to "their signs" (ver. 4), hence they are not to be understood, after lxxxvi. 17, as signs which God works. The suffix demands, besides, something of a perpetual character; they are the instituted ordinances of divine worship by means of which God is pleased to stand in fellowship with His people, and which are now no longer to be seen because the enemies have set them aside. The complaint "there is no prophet any more" would seem strange in the period immediately after the destruction of Jerusalem, for Jeremiah's term of active service lasted beyond this. Moreover, a year before (in the tenth year of Zedekiah's reign) he had predicted that the Babylonian domination, and relatively the Exile, would last seventy years; besides, six years before the destruction Ezekiel appeared, who was in communication with those who remained behind in the land. The reference to Lam. ii. 9 (cf. Ezek. vii. 26) does not satisfy one; for there it is assumed that there were prophets, a fact which is here denied. Only perhaps as a voice coming out of the Exile, the middle of which (cf. Hos. iii. 4, 2 Chron. xv. 3, and besides *Canticum trium puerorum*, ver. 14: καὶ οὐκ ἔστιν ἐν τῷ καιρῷ τούτῳ ἄρχων καὶ προφήτης καὶ ἡγούμενος) was truly thus devoid of signs or miracles, and devoid of the prophetic word of consolation, can ver. 9 be comprehended. The seventy years of Jeremiah were then still a riddle without any generally known solution (Dan. ch. ix.). If, however, synagogues are meant in ver. 8*b*, ver. 9 now too accords with the like-sounding lament in the calamitous times of Antiochus (1 Macc. iv. 46, ix. 27, xiv. 41). In ver. 10 the poet turns to God Himself with the question "How long?" how long is this (apparently) endless blaspheming of the enemy to last? Why dost Thou draw back (viz. מִמֶּנּוּ, from us, not עָלֵינוּ, lxxxi. 15) Thy hand and Thy right hand? The conjunction of synonyms "Thy hand and Thy right hand" is, as in xliv. 4, Sirach xxxiii. 7, a fuller expression for God's omnipotent energy. This is now at rest; ver. 11*b* calls upon it to give help by an act of judgment. "Out of the midst of Thy bosom, destroy," is a pregnant expression for, "drawing forth out of Thy bosom the hand that rests inactive there, do Thou destroy." The *Chethîb* הוקך has perhaps the same meaning; for חוֹק, حَوق, signifies, like חֵיק, حَيق, the act of encompassing, then that which encompasses. Instead of מֵחֵיקֶךָ (Ex. iv. 7) the expression is מִקֶּרֶב חֵיקךָ, because there, within the realm of the bosom, the punitive justice of God for a time as it were slumbers. On the כַלֵּה, which outwardly is without any object, cf. lix. 14.

Vers. 12–17. With this prayer for the destruction of the enemies by God's interposition closes the first half of the

Psalm, which has for its subject-matter the crying contradiction between the present state of things and God's relationship to Israel. The poet now draws comfort by looking back into the time when God as Israel's King unfolded the rich fulness of His salvation everywhere upon the earth, where Israel's existence was imperilled. בְּקֶרֶב הָאָרֶץ, not only within the circumference of the Holy Land, but, *e.g.*, also within that of Egypt (Ex. viii. 18 [22]). The poet has Egypt directly in his mind, for there now follows first of all a glance at the historical (vers. 13–15), and then at the natural displays of God's power (vers. 16, 17). Hengstenberg is of opinion that vers. 13–15 also are to be understood in the latter sense, and appeals to Job xxvi. 11–13. But just as Isaiah (ch. li. 9, cf. xxvii. 1) transfers these emblems of the omnipotence of God in the natural world to His proofs of power in connection with the history of redemption which were exhibited in the case of a worldly power, so does the poet here also in vers. 13–15. The תַּנִּין (the extended saurian) is in Isaiah, as in Ezekiel (הַתַּנִּים, ch. xxix. 3, xxxii. 2), an emblem of Pharaoh and of his kingdom; in like manner here the *leviathan* is the proper natural wonder of Egypt. As a water-snake or a crocodile, when it comes up with its head above the water, is killed by a powerful stroke, did God break the heads of the Egyptians, so that the sea cast up their dead bodies (Ex. xiv. 30). The צִיִּים, the dwellers in the steppe, to whom these became food, are not the Æthiopians (LXX., Jerome), or rather the Ichthyophagi (Bochart, Hengstenberg), who according to Agatharcides fed ἐκ τῶν ἐκριπτομένων εἰς τὴν χέρσον κητῶν, but were no cannibals, but the wild beasts of the desert, which are called עַם, as in Prov. xxx. 25 sq. the ants and the rock-badgers. לְצִיִּים is a permutative of the notion לְעָם, which was not completed: to a (singular) people, viz. to the wild animals of the steppe. Ver. 15 also still refers not to miracles of creation, but to miracles wrought in the course of the history of redemption; ver. 15*a* refers to the giving of water out of the rock (lxxviii. 15), and ver. 15*b* to the passage through the Jordan, which was miraculously dried up (הוֹבַשְׁתָּ, as in Josh. ii. 10, iv. 23, v. 1). The object מַעְיָן וָנָחַל is intended as referring to the result: so that the water flowed out of the cleft after the manner of a fountain and a brook. נְהָרוֹת are the several streams of the one Jordan; the attributive genitive אֵיתָן describes them as streams having an abundance that does not dry up, streams of perennial fulness. The God of Israel who has thus marvellously made Himself known in history is, however, the Creator and Lord of all created things. Day and night and the stars alike are His creatures. In close connection with the night, which is mentioned second, the moon, the מָאוֹר of the night, precedes the sun; cf. viii. 4, where כּוֹנֵן is the same as הֵכִין in this passage. It is an error to render thus: bodies of light, and more particularly the sun; which would have made one expect מְאוֹרוֹת before the specializing *Waw*. גְּבוּלוֹת are not merely the bounds of the land towards the sea, Jer. v. 22, but, according to Deut. xxxii. 8, Acts xvii. 26, even the boundaries of the land in themselves, that is to say, the natural boundaries of the inland country. קַיִץ וָחֹרֶף are the two halves of the year: summer including spring (אָבִיב), which begins in Nisan, the spring-month, about the time of the vernal equinox, and autumn including winter (סְתָו), after the termination of which the strictly spring vegetation begins (Cant. ii. 11). The seasons are personified, and are called God's formations or works, as it were the angels of summer and of winter.

Vers. 18–23. The poet, after he has thus consoled himself by the contemplation of the power of God which He has displayed for His people's good as their Redeemer, and for the good of the whole of mankind as the Creator, rises anew to prayer, but all the more cheerfully and boldly. Since ever present facts of creation have been referred to just now, and the historical mighty deeds of God only further back, זֹאת refers rather forwards to the blaspheming of the enemies which He suffers now to go on unpunished, as though He took no cognizance of it. חֵרֵף has *Pasek* after it in order to separate the word, which signifies reviling, from the most holy Name. The epithet עַם־נָבָל reminds one of Deut. xxxii. 21. In ver. 19*a* according to the accents חַיַּת is the absolute state (the primary form of חַיָּה, *vid.* on lxi. 1): give not over, abandon not to the wild beast (beasts), the soul of Thy turtle-dove. This is probably correct, since לְחַיַּת נֶפֶשׁ, "to the eager wild beast," this inversion of the well-known expression נֶפֶשׁ חַיָּה, which on the contrary yields the sense of *vita animæ*, is an improbable and exampleless expression. If נפשׁ were intended to be thus understood, the poet might have written אל־תתן לנפשׁ חיה תורך,

"give not Thy turtle-dove over to the desire of the wild beast."
Hupfeld thinks that the "old, stupid reading" may be set
right at one stroke, inasmuch as he reads אל תתן לנפש חית תורך,
and renders it "give not to rage the life Thy turtle-dove;"
but where is any support to be found for this לנפש, "to rage,"
or rather (*Psychology*, S. 202; tr. p. 239) "to eager desire?"
The word cannot signify this in such an isolated position.
Israel, which is also compared to a dove in lxviii. 14, is called
a turtle-dove (תּוֹר). In ver. 19*b* חַיַּת has the same signification
as in ver. 19*a*, and the same sense as lxviii. 11 (cf. lxix. 37):
the creatures of Thy miserable ones, *i.e.* Thy poor, miserable
creatures—a figurative designation of the *ecclesia pressa*. The
church, which it is the custom of the Asaphic Psalms to designate with emblematical names taken from the animal world,
finds itself now like sheep among wolves, and seems to itself as
if it were forgotten by God. The cry of prayer הַבֵּט לַבְּרִית
comes forth out of circumstances such as were those of the
Maccabæan age. בְּרִית is the covenant of circumcision (Gen.
ch. xvii.); the persecution of the age of the Seleucidæ put
faith to the severe test, that circumcision, this sign which was
the pledge to Israel of God's gracious protection, became just
the sign by which the Syrians knew their victims. In the
Book of Daniel, ch. xi. 28, 30, cf. Ps. xxii. 32, ברית is used
directly of the religion of Israel and its band of confessors.
The confirmatory clause ver. 20*b* also corresponds to the
Maccabæan age, when the persecuted confessors hid themselves
far away in the mountains (1 Macc. ii. 26 sqq., 2 Macc. vi. 11),
but were tracked by the enemy and slain,—at that time the
hiding-places (κρύφοι, 1 Macc. i. 53) of the land were in reality
full of the habitations of violence. The combination נְאוֹת חָמָס
is like נְאוֹת הַשָּׁלוֹם, Jer. xxv. 37, cf. Gen. vi. 11. From this
point the Psalm draws to a close in more familiar Psalm-strains.
אַל־יָשֹׁב, ver. 21, viz. from drawing near to Thee with their supplications. "The reproach of the foolish all the day" is that
which incessantly goes forth from them. עֹלֶה תָמִיד, "going up
(1 Sam. v. 12, not: increasing, 1 Kings xxii. 35) perpetually,"
although without the article, is not a predicate, but attributive
(*vid.* on lvii. 3). The tone of the prayer is throughout tem-
perate; this the ground upon which it bases itself is therefore
all the more forcible.

PSALM LXXV.

THE NEARNESS OF THE JUDGE WITH THE CUP OF WRATH.

2 WE give thanks unto Thee, Elohim, we give thanks,
And near is Thy Name:
Men declare Thy wondrous works.

3 For "I will seize the moment,
I, in uprightness will I judge.
4 If the earth and all its inhabitants are dissolving—
I, even I set up its pillars."   (*Sela.*)
5 "I say to the boastful: Boast not!
And to the evil-doers: Lift not up the horn!
6 Lift not up on high your horn,
Speak not impudence with a stiff neck!'

7 For not from the rising and not from the setting,
And not from the desert of the mountain-heights—
8 Nay, Elohim judgeth the cause,
He putteth down one, and setteth up another.
9 For a cup is in the hand of Jahve,
And it foameth with wine, it is full of mixture;
And He poureth out from it, yea the dregs thereof
Must all the wicked of the earth sip, drink up.

10 And I, even I will proclaim for ever,
I will sing praises to the God of Jacob;
11 And all the horns of the wicked will I smite down,
The horns of the righteous shall be exalted.

That for which Ps. lxxiv. prays: *Arise, Jahve, plead Thine own cause* (vers. 22 sq.), Ps. lxxv. beholds; the judgment of God upon the proud sinners becomes a source of praise and of a triumphant spirit to the psalmist. The prophetic picture stands upon a lyrical groundwork of gold; it emerges out of the depth of feeling, and it is drawn back again into it. The inscription: *To the Precentor,* (after the measure:) *Destroy not* (*vid.* on lvii. 1), *a Psalm by Asaph, a Song,* is fully borne out.

The *Sela* shows that the Psalm, as שִׁיר מִזְמוֹר says, is appointed
to be sung with musical accompaniment; and to the לְאָסָף corresponds its thoroughly Asaphic character, which calls Ps. l. to
mind with especial force. But from this Psalm Ps. lxxv.
differs, however, in this particular, viz. that a more clearly
defined situation of affairs manifests itself through the hope of
the judicial interposition of God which is expressed in it with
prophetic certainty. According to appearances it is the time
of the judgment of the nations in the person of Assyria; not,
however, the time immediately following the great catastrophe,
but prior to this, when Isaiah's prophecy concerning the shattering of the Assyrian power against Jerusalem had gone forth,
just as Hengstenberg also regards this Psalm as the lyrical
companion of the prophecies which Isaiah uttered in the presence of the ruin which threatened from Assyria, and as a
testimony to the living faith with which the church at that
time received the word of God. Hitzig, however, assigns both
Ps. lxxv. and lxxvi. to Judas Maccabæus, who celebrates the
victory over Apollonius in the one, and the victory over Seron
in the other: " we may imagine that he utters the words of
lxxv. 11 whilst he brandishes the captured sword of the fallen
Apollonius." But the probability that it refers to the Assyrian
period is at least equally balanced with the probability that it
refers to the Maccabæan (*vid.* lxxv. 7, lxxvi. 5–7); and if the
time of Hezekiah were to be given up, then we might sooner
go back to the time of Jehoshaphat, for both songs are too
original to appear as echoes and not much rather as models of
the later prophecy. The only influence that is noticeable in
Ps. lxxv. is that of the Song of Hannah.

Vers. 2–6. The church in anticipation gives thanks for
the judicial revelation of its God, the near approach of which
He Himself asserts to it. The connection with וְ in וְקָרוֹב שְׁמֶךָ
presents a difficulty. Neither here nor anywhere else is it to
be supposed that וְ is synonymous with כִּי; but at any rate
even כי might stand instead of it. For Hupfeld's attempt
to explain it: and "near is Thy name" Thy wonders have
declared; and Hitzig's: and Thou whose Name is near, they
declare Thy wondrous works,—are past remedy. Such a personification of wonders does not belong to the spirit of Hebrew

poetry, and such a relative clause lies altogether beyond the bounds of syntax. If we would, however, take וקרוב שמך, after l. 23, as a result of the thanksgiving (Campensis), then that for which thanks are rendered would remain undefined; neither will it do to take קרוב as referring to the being inwardly present (Hengstenberg), since this, according to Jer. xii. 2 (cf. Deut. xxx. 14), would require some addition, which should give to the nearness this reference to the mouth or to the heart. Thus, therefore, nothing remains for us but to connect the nearness of the Name of God as an outward fact with the earnest giving of thanks. The church has received the promise of an approaching judicial, redemptive revelation of God, and now says, "We give Thee thanks, we give thanks and near is Thy Name;" it welcomes the future act of God with heartfelt thanksgiving, all those who belong to it declare beforehand the wonders of God. Such was really the position of matters when in Hezekiah's time the oppression of the Assyrians had reached its highest point—Isaiah's promises of a miraculous divine deliverance were at that time before them, and the believing ones saluted beforehand, with thanksgiving, the " coming Name of Jahve" (Isa. xxx. 27). The כִּי which was to be expected after הודינו (cf., *e.g.*, c. 4 sq.) does not follow until ver. 3. God Himself undertakes the confirmation of the forthcoming thanksgiving and praise by a direct announcement of the help that is hailed and near at hand (lxxxv. 10). It is not to be rendered, "when I shall seize," etc., for ver. 3*b* has not the structure of an apodosis. כִּי is confirmatory, and whatever interpretation we may give to it, the words of the church suddenly change into the words of God. מוֹעֵד in the language of prophecy, more especially of the apocalyptic character, is a standing expression for the appointed time of the final judgment (*vid.* on Hab. ii. 3). When this moment or juncture in the lapse of time shall have arrived, then God will seize or take possession of it (לָקַח in the unweakened original sense of taking hold of with energy, cf. xviii. 17, Gen. ii. 15): He Himself will then interpose and hold judgment according to the strictly observed rule of right (מֵישָׁרִים, adverbial accusative, cf. במישרים, ix. 9, and frequently). If it even should come to pass that the earth and all its inhabitants are melting away (cf. Isa. xiv. 31, Ex. xv. 15, Josh. ii. 9), *i.e.* under the pressure of injustice (as is to be inferred from ver. 3*b*), are disheartened, scattered asunder, and are as it were in the act of dissolution, then He (the absolute I, אָנֹכִי) will restrain this melting away; He setteth in their places the pillars, *i.e.* the internal shafts (Job ix. 6), of the earth, or without any figure: He again asserts the laws which lie at the foundation of its stability. תִּכַּנְתִּי is a mood of certainty, and ver. 4*a* is a circumstantial clause placed first, after the manner of the Latin ablative absolute. Hitzig appropriately compares Prov. xxix. 9; Isa. xxiii. 15 may also be understood according to this bearing of the case.

The utterance of God is also continued after the *Sela*. It is not the people of God who turn to the enemies with the language of warning on the ground of the divine promise (Hengstenberg); the poet would then have said אָמַרְנוּ, or must at least have said עַל־כֵּן אָמַרְתִּי. God Himself speaks, and His words are not yet peremptorily condemning, as in l. 16 sqq., cf. xlvi. 11, but admonitory and threatening, because it is not He who has already appeared for the final judgment who speaks, but He who announces His appearing. With אָמַרְתִּי He tells the braggarts who are captivated with the madness of supposed greatness, and the evil-doers who lift up the horn or the head,[*] what He will have once for all said to them, and what they are to suffer to be said to them for the short space of time till the judgment. The poet, if we have assigned the right date to the Psalm, has Rabshakeh and his colleagues before his mind, cf. Isa. xxxvii. 23. The לְ, as in that passage, and like אֶל in Zech. ii. 4 (*vid.* Köhler), has the idea of a hostile tendency. אַל rules also over ver. 6*b*: "speak not insolence with a raised neck." It is not to be construed בְּצַוָּאר עָתָק, with a stiff neck. Parallel passages like xxxi. 19, xciv. 4, and more especially the primary passage 1 Sam. v. 3, show that עָתָק is an object-notion, and that בְּצַוָּאר by itself (with which, too, the accentuation harmonizes, since *Munach* here is the *vicarius* of a distinctive), according to Job xv. 26, has the sense of τραχηλιῶτες or ὑπεραυχοῦντες.

---

[*] The head is called in Sanscrit *çiras*, in Zend *çaranh*, = κάρα; the horn in Sanscrit, *çrĭnga*, *i.e.* (according to Burnouf, *Etudes*, p. 19) that which proceeds from and projects out of the head (*çiras*), Zend *çrva* = κέρας, קֶרֶן (*karn*).

Vers. 7–9. The church here takes up the words of God, again beginning with the כִּי of ver. 3 (cf. the כִּי in 1 Sam. ii. 3). A passage of the Midrash says כל הרים שבמקרא הרים חוץ מזה (everywhere where *harim* is found in Scripture it signifies *harim*, mountains, with the exception of this passage), and accordingly it is explained by Rashi, Kimchi, Alshêch, and others, that man, whithersoever he may turn, cannot by strength and skill attain great exaltation and prosperity.* Thus it is according to the reading מִמִּדְבָּר, although Kimchi maintains that it can also be so explained with the reading מִמְּדַבֵּר, by pointing to מְרַמֵּס (Isa. x. 6) and the like. It is, however, difficult to see why, in order to express the idea "from any-where," three quarters of the heavens should be used and the north left out. These three quarters of the heavens which are said to represent the earthly sources of power (Hupfeld), are a frame without the picture, and the thought, "from no side (viz. of the earth) cometh promotion"—in itself whimsical in expression—offers a wrong confirmation for the dissuasive that has gone before. That, however, which the church longs for is first of all not promotion, but redemption. On the other hand, the LXX., Targum, Syriac, and Vulgate render: *a deserto montium* (*desertis montibus*); and even Aben-Ezra rightly takes it as a Palestinian designation of the south, when he supplements the aposiopesis by means of מי שיושיעם (more biblically יָבֹא עֶזְרֵנוּ, cf. cxxi. 1 sq.). The fact that the north is not mentioned at all shows that it is a northern power which arrogantly, even to blasphemy, threatens the small Israelitish nation with destruction, and against which it looks for help neither from the east and west, nor from the reed-staff of Egypt (Isa. xxxvi. 6) beyond the desert of the mountains of Arabia Petræa, but from Jahve alone, according to the watchword of Isaiah: ה' שְׁפָטֵנוּ (Isa. xxxiii. 22). The negative thought is left unfinished, the discourse hurrying on to the opposite affirmative thought. The close connection of the two thoughts is strik-ingly expressed by the rhymes הָרִים and יָרִים. The כִּי of ver. 8 gives the confirmation of the negation from the opposite, that which is denied; the כִּי of ver. 9 confirms this confirmation.

---

* *E.g. Bamidbar Rabba* ch. xxii.; whereas according to *Berêshith Rabba* ch. lii. הָרִים is equivalent to דָּרוֹם.

If it were to be rendered, "and the wine foams," it would then have been הַיַּיִן; מֶסֶךְ, which is undoubtedly accusative, also shows that יַיִן is also not considered as anything else: and it (the cup) foams (חָמַר like اختمر, to ferment, effervesce) with wine, is full of mixture. According to the ancient usage of the language, which is also followed by the Arabic, this is wine mixed with water in distinction from *merum*, Arabic *chamr memzûg'e*. Wine was mixed with water not merely to dilute it, but also to make it more pleasant; hence מָסַךְ signifies directly as much as to pour out (*vid.* Hitzig on Isa. v. 22). It is therefore unnecessary to understand spiced wine (Talmudic קונדיטן, *conditum*), since the collateral idea of weakening is also not necessarily associated with the admixture of water. מִזֶּה refers to כּוֹס, which is used as masculine, as in Jer. xxv. 15; the word is feminine elsewhere, and changes its gender even here in שְׁמָרֶיהָ (cf. Ezek. xxiii. 34). In the *fut. consec.* וַיַּגֵּר the historical signification of the consecutive is softened down, as is frequently the case. אַךְ affirms the whole assertion that follows. The dregs of the cup—a *dira necessitas*—all the wicked of the earth shall be compelled to sip (Isa. li. 17), to drink out: they shall not be allowed to drink and make a pause, but, compelled by Jahve, who has appeared as Judge, they shall be obliged to drink it out with involuntary eagerness even to the very last (Ezek. xxiii. 34). We have here the primary passage of a figure, which has been already hinted at in lx. 5, and is filled in on a more and more magnificent and terrible scale in the prophets. Whilst Obadiah (ver. 16, cf. Job xxi. 20) contents himself with a mere outline sketch, it is found again, in manifold applications, in Isaiah, Habakkuk, and Ezekiel, and most frequently in Jeremiah (ch. xxv. 27 sq., xlviii. 26, xlix. 12), where in ch. xxv. 15 sqq. it is embodied into a symbolical act. Jahve's cup of intoxication (inasmuch as חֵמָה and חֶמֶר, the burning of anger and intoxicating, fiery wine, are put on an equality) is the judgment of wrath which is meted out to sinners and given them to endure to the end.

Vers. 10, 11. The poet now turns back thankfully and cheerfully from the prophetically presented future to his own actual present. With וַאֲנִי he contrasts himself as a member of the now still oppressed church with its proud oppressors: he will be a perpetual herald of the ever memorable deed of redemption. לְעוֹלָם, says he, for, when he gives himself up so entirely to God the Redeemer, for him there is no dying. If he is a member of the *ecclesia pressa,* then he will also be a member of the *ecclesia triumphans ;* for εἰ ὑπομένομεν, καὶ συμβασιλεύσομεν (2 Tim. ii. 12). In the certainty of this συμβασιλεύειν, and in the strength of God, which is even now mighty in the weak one, he measures himself in ver. 11 by the standard of what he expresses in ver. 8 as God's own work. On the figure compare Deut. xxxiii. 17, Lam. ii. 3, and more especially the four horns in the second vision of Zechariah, ch. ii. 1 sq. [i. 18 sq.]. The plural is both קַרְנוֹת and קַרְנֵי, because horns that do not consist of horn are meant. Horns are powers for offence and defence. The spiritual horns maintain the sovereignty over the natural. The Psalm closes as subjectively as it began. The prophetic picture is set in a lyric frame.

PSALM LXXVI.

PRAISE OF GOD AFTER HIS JUDGMENT HAS GONE FORTH.

2 IN Judah is Elohim become known,
　In Israel is His name great.
3 He pitched His tabernacle in Salem,
　And His dwelling-place in Zion.
4 There brake He the lightnings of the bow,
　Shield and sword and weapons of war.　(*Sela.*)

5 Brilliant art Thou, glorious before the mountains of prey !
6 Spoiled were the stout-hearted ;
　They fell asleep in their sleep,
　And none of the valiant ones found their hands.
7 Before Thy rebuke, O God of Jacob,
　Both chariot and horse became deeply stupefied.

8 Thou, terrible art Thou,
　And who can stand before Thee when Thy wrath beginneth?
9 From heaven didst Thou cause judgment to sound forth—
　The earth feared and became silent,
10 At the rising of Elohim to judgment,
　To save all the afflicted of the land.　(*Sela.*)

11 For the wrath of man is to Thee as praise,
    Seeing Thou with the remainder of the fulness of wrath
        dost gird Thyself.
12 Vow and pay unto Jahve, your God,
    Let all who are round about Him bring offerings to the
        terrible One.
13 He cutteth down the snorting of despots,
    He is terrible to the kings of the earth.

No Psalm has a greater right to follow Ps. lxxv. than this, which is inscribed *To the Precentor, with accompaniment of stringed instruments* (*vid.* iv. 1), *a Psalm by Asaph, a song.* Similar expressions (*God of Jacob*, lxxv. 10, lxxvi. 7; *saints, wicked of the earth*, lxxv. 9, lxxvi. 10) and the same impress throughout speak in favour of unity of authorship. In other respects, too, they form a pair: Ps. lxxv. prepares the way for the divine deed of judgment as imminent, which Ps. lxxvi. celebrates as having taken place. For it is hardly possible for there to be a Psalm the contents of which so exactly coincide with an historical situation of which more is known from other sources, as the contents of this Psalm confessedly (LXX. πρὸς τὸν ᾿Ασσύριον) does with the overthrow of the army of Assyria before Jerusalem and its results. The Psalter contains very similar Psalms which refer to a similar event in the reign of Jehoshaphat, viz. to the defeat at that time of the allied neighbouring peoples by a mutual massacre, which was predicted by the Asaphite Jahaziel (*vid.* on Ps. xlvi. and lxxxiii.). Moreover in Ps. lxxvi. the "mountains of prey," understood of the mountains of Seir with their mounted robbers, would point to this incident. But just as in Ps. lxxv. the reference to the catastrophe of Assyria in the reign of Hezekiah was indicated by the absence of any mention of the north, so in Ps. lxxvi. both the שָׁמָּה in ver. 4 and the description of the catastrophe itself make this reference and no other natural. The points of contact with Isaiah, and in part with Hosea (cf. ver. 4 with Hos. ii. 20) and Nahum, are explicable from the fact that the lyric went hand in hand with the prophecy of that period, as Isaiah predicts for the time when Jahve shall discharge His fury over Assyria, ch. xxx. 29, "*Your song shall re-echo as in the night, in which the feast is celebrated.*"

The Psalm is hexastichic, and a model of symmetrical strophe-structure.

Vers. 2–4. In all Israel, and more especially in Judah, is Elohim known (here, according to ver. 2*b*, participle, whereas in ix. 17 it is the finite verb), inasmuch as He has made Himself known (cf. דֵּעוֹ, Isa. xxxiii. 13). His Name is great in Israel, inasmuch as He has proved Himself to be a great One and is praised as a great One. In Judah more especially, for in Jerusalem, and that upon Zion, the citadel with the primeval gates (xxiv. 7), He has His dwelling-place upon earth within the borders of Israel. שָׁלֵם is the ancient name of Jerusalem; for the Salem of Melchizedek is one and the same city with the Jerusalem of Adonizedek, Josh. x. 1. In this primeval Salem God has סֻכּוֹ, His tabernacle (= שֻׂכּוֹ, Lam. ii. 6, = סֻכָּתוֹ, as in xxvii. 5), there מְעוֹנָתוֹ, His dwelling-place,—a word else-where used of the lair of the lion (civ. 22, Am. iii. 4); cf. on the choice of words, Isa. xxxi. 9. The future of the result וַיְהִי is an expression of the fact which is evident from God's being known in Judah and His Name great in Israel. Ver. 4 tells what it is by which He has made Himself known and glorified His Name. שָׁמָּה, thitherwards, in that same place (as in fact the accusative, in general, is used both in answer to the question where? and whither?), is only a fuller form for שָׁם, as in Isa. xxii. 18, lxv. 9, 2 Kings xxiii. 8, and frequently; ثَمَّ (ثُمَّ) and תַּמָּן (from תַּמָּה) confirm the accusative value of the *ah*. רִשְׁפֵי־קָשֶׁת (with *Phe raphatum*, cf. on the other hand, Cant. viii. 6*) are the arrows swift as lightning that go forth (Job xli. 20 [28]) from the bow; side by side with these, two other weapons are also mentioned, and finally everything that pertains to war is gathered up in the word מִלְחָמָה (cf. Hos. ii. 20 [18]). God has broken in pieces the weapons of the worldly power directed against Judah, and therewith this power itself (Isa. xiv. 25), and consequently (in accordance with the prediction Hos. i. 7, and Isa. ch. x., xiv. xvii., xxix., xxxi., xxxiii., xxxvii., and more particularly xxxi. 8) has rescued His people

---

* The pointing is here just as inconsistent as in יַלְדוּת, and on the contrary מַרְדוּת.

by direct interposition, without their doing anything in the matter.

Vers. 5–7. The "mountains of prey," for which the LXX. has ὀρέων αἰωνίων (טֶרֶם?), is an emblematical appellation for the haughty possessors of power who also plunder every one that comes near them,* or the proud and despoiling worldly powers. Far aloft beyond these towers the glory of God. He is נָאוֹר, *illustris*, prop. illumined; said of God: light-encircled, fortified in light, in the sense of Dan. ii. 22, 1 Tim. vi. 16. He is the אַדִּיר, to whom the Lebanon of the hostile army of the nations must succumb (Isa. x. 34). According to Solinus (*ed. Mommsen*, p. 124) the Moors call Atlas *Addirim*. This succumbing is described in vers. 6 sq. The strong of heart or stout-hearted, the lion-hearted, have been despoiled, disarmed, *exuti*; אֶשְׁתּוֹלֲלוּ† is an Aramaizing *præt. Hithpo.* (like אֶתְחַבַּר, 2 Chron. xx. 35, cf. Dan. iv. 16, Isa. lxiii. 3) with a passive signification. From ver. 6*ac* we see that the beginning of the catastrophe is described, and therefore נָמוּ (perhaps on that account accented on the *ult.*) is meant inchoatively: they have fallen into their sleep, viz. the eternal sleep (Jer. li. 39, 57), as Nahum says (ch. iii. 18): *thy shepherds sleep, O king of Assyria, thy valiant ones rest.* In ver. 6*c* we see them lying in the last throes of death, and making a last effort to spring up again. But they cannot find their hands, which they have lifted up threateningly against Jerusalem: these are lamed, motionless, rigid and dead; cf. the phrases in Josh. viii. 20, 2 Sam. vii. 27, and the Talmudic phrase, "he did not find his hands and feet in the school-house," *i.e.* he was entirely disconcerted and stupefied.‡ This field of corpses is the effect of the omnipotent energy of the word of the God of Jacob; cf. וְגָעַר בּוֹ, Isa. xvii. 13. Before His threatening both war-chariot and horse (ן—ן) are sunk into motionlessness and unconscious-

---

* One verse of a beautiful poem of the *Muḥammel* which *Ibn Dûchî*, the phylarch of the *Beni Zumeir*, an honoured poet of the steppe, dictated to Consul Wetzstein runs thus: The noble are like a very lofty hill-side upon which, when thou comest to it, thou findest an evening meal and protection (العشا وندرى).

† With orthophonic *Gaja*, vid. Baer's *Metheg-Setzung*, § 45.

‡ Dukes, *Rabbinische Blumenlese*, S. 191.

ness—an allusion to Ex. ch. xv., as in Isa. xliii. 17: *who bringeth out chariot and horse, army and heroes—together they faint away, they shall never rise; they have flickered out, like a wick they are extinguished.*

Vers. 8–10.   Nahum also (ch. i. 6) draws the same inference from the defeat of Sennacherib as the psalmist does in ver. 8.   מֵאָז אַפֶּךָ (cf. Ruth ii. 7, Jer. xliv. 18), from the decisive turning-point onwards, from the אָז in ii. 5, when Thine anger breaks forth.   God sent forth His judiciary word from heaven into the midst of the din of war of the hostile world: immediately (cf. on the sequence of the tenses xlviii. 6, and on Hab. iii. 10) it was silenced, the earth was seized with fear, and its tumult was obliged to cease, when, namely, God arose on behalf of His disquieted, suffering people, when He spoke as we read in Isa. xxxiii. 10, and fulfilled the prayer offered in extreme need in Isa. xxxiii. 2.

Vers. 11–13.   The fact that has just been experienced is substantiated in ver. 11 from a universal truth, which has therein become outwardly manifest.   The rage of men shall praise Thee, *i.e.* must ultimately redound to Thy glory, inasmuch as to Thee, namely (ver. 11*b* as to syntax like lxxiii. 3*b*), there always remains a שְׁאֵרִית, *i.e.* a still unexhausted remainder, and that not merely of חֵמָה, but of חֵמֹת, with which Thou canst gird, *i.e.* arm, Thyself against such human rage, in order to quench it.   שְׁאֵרִית חֵמֹת is the infinite store of wrath still available to God after human rage has done its utmost.   Or perhaps still better, and more fully answering to the notion of שְׁאֵרִית: it is the store of the infinite fulness of wrath which still remains on the side of God after human rage (חֵמָה) has spent itself, when God calmly, and laughing (ii. 4), allows the Titans to do as they please, and which is now being poured out.   In connection with the interpretation: with the remainder of the fury (of hostile men) wilt Thou gird Thyself, *i.e.* it serves Thee only as an ornament (Hupfeld), the alternation of חֵמָה and חֵמֹת is left unexplained, and תַּחְגֹּר is alienated from its martial sense (Isa. lix. 17, li. 9, Wisd. v. 21 [20]), which is required by the context.   Ewald, like the LXX., reads תְּחָגֶּךָ, ἑορτάσει σοι, in connection with which, apart from the high-sounding expression, שארית חמת (ἐγκατάλειμμα ἐνθυμίου) must denote the remainder of malignity that is suddenly converted into its

opposite; and one does not see why what ver. 11a says concerning rage is here limited to its remainder. Such an inex-
haustiveness in the divine wrath-power has been shown in what
has just recently been experienced. Thus, then, are those who
belong to the people of God to vow and pay, *i.e.* (inasmuch as
the preponderance falls upon the second imperative) to pay
their vows; and all who are round about Him, *i.e.* all peoples
dwelling round about Him and His people (כָּל־סְבִיבָיו, the subject to what follows, in accordance with which it is also
accented), are to bring offerings (lxviii. 30) to God, who is
מוֹרָא, *i.e.* the sum of all that is awe-inspiring. Thus is He
called in Isa. viii. 13; the summons accords with Isaiah's prediction, according to which, in consequence of Jahve's deed of
judgment upon Assyria, Æthiopia presents himself to Him as
an offering (ch. xviii.), and with the fulfilment in 2 Chron.
xxxii. 23. Just so does ver. 13a resemble the language of
Isaiah; cf. Isa. xxv. 1–5, xxxiii. 11, xviii. 5: God treats the
snorting of the princes, *i.e.* despots, as the vine-dresser does the
wild shoots or branches of the vine-stock: He lops it, He cuts
it off, so that it is altogether ineffectual. It is the figure that
is sketched by Joel iv. [iii.] 13, then filled in by Isaiah, and
embodied as a vision in Apoc. xiv. 17–20, which is here indicated. God puts an end to the defiant, arrogant bearing of
the tyrants of the earth, and becomes at last the feared of all
the kings of the earth—all kingdoms finally become God's and
His Christ's.

PSALM LXXVII.

COMFORT DERIVED FROM THE HISTORY OF THE PAST
DURING YEARS OF AFFLICTION.

2 I CALL unto Elohim, and will cry,
  I call unto Elohim, that He may hearken unto me.
3 In the day of my distress do I seek the Lord;
  My hand is stretched out in the night without ceasing,
  My soul refuseth to be comforted.
4 If I remember Elohim, I must groan;
  If I muse, my spirit languisheth. (*Sela.*)

5 Thou holdest mine eyelids open,
  I am tossed to and fro, and I am speechless.
6 I consider the days of old,
  The years of ancient times;
7 I will remember my music in the night,
  I will commune with my own heart, and my spirit maketh
     diligent search.
8 Will the Lord cast off for ever,
  And will He be favourable no more?
9 Is, then, His mercy passed away for ever,
  Is it at an end with His promise to all generations?
10 Hath God forgotten to be gracious,
  Or hath He drawn in in anger His tender mercies?!   (*Sela.*)

11 Thereupon say I to myself: my decree of affliction is this,
  The years of the right hand of the Most High.
12 With praise do I remember the deeds of Jāh,
  Yea, I will call to mind Thy wondrous doing from olden
     times,
13 And meditate on all Thy work,
  And will muse over Thy doings.
14 Elohim, in holiness is Thy way:
  Where is there a God, great as Elohim?
15 Thou art God alone, doing wonders,
  Thou hast revealed Thy might among the peoples.
16 Thou hast with uplifted arm redeemed Thy people,
  The sons of Jacob and Joseph.   (*Sela.*)

17 The waters saw Thee, Elohim,
  The waters saw Thee, they writhed,
  The depths also trembled.
18 The clouds poured out waters,
  The skies rumbled,
  Thine arrows also went to and fro.
19 Thy thunder resounded in the whirlwind,
  The lightnings lightened the world,
  The earth trembled and shook.
20 In the sea was Thy way,
  And Thy path in great waters,
  And Thy footsteps were not to be discerned.

21 Thou hast led Thy people like a flock
By the hand of Moses and Aaron.

"*The earth feared and became still*," says Ps. lxxvi. 9; *the earth trembled and shook*, says Ps. lxxvii. 19: this common thought is the string on which these two Psalms are strung. In a general way it may be said of Ps. lxxvii., that the poet flees from the sorrowful present away into the memory of the years of olden times, and consoles himself more especially with the deliverance out of Egypt, so rich in wonders. As to the rest, however, it remains obscure what kind of national affliction it is which drives him to find his refuge from the God who is now hidden in the God who was formerly manifest. At any rate it is not a purely personal affliction, but, as is shown by the consolation sought in the earlier revelations of power and mercy in connection with the national history, an affliction shared in company with the whole of his people. In the midst of this hymnic retrospect the Psalm suddenly breaks off, so that Olshausen is of opinion that it is mutilated, and Tholuck that the author never completed it. But as Ps. lxxvii. and lxxxi. show, it is the Asaphic manner thus to close with an historical picture without the line of thought recurring to its commencement. Where our Psalm leaves off, Hab. ch. iii. goes on, taking it up from that point like a continuation. For the prophet begins with the prayer to revive that deed of redemption of the Mosaic days of old, and in the midst of wrath to remember mercy; and in expression and figures which are borrowed from our Psalm, he then beholds a fresh deed of redemption by which that of old is eclipsed. Thus much, at least, is therefore very clear, that Ps. lxxvii. is older than Habakkuk. Hitzig certainly calls the psalmist the reader and imitator of Hab. ch. iii.; and Philippson considers even the mutual relationship to be accidental and confined to a general similarity of certain expressions. We, however, believe that we have proved in our *Commentary on Habakkuk* (1843), S. 118–125, that the mutual relationship is one that is deeply grounded in the prophetic type of Habakkuk, and that the Psalm is heard to re-echo in Habakkuk, not Habakkuk in the language of the psalmist; just as in general the Asaphic Psalms are full of boldly sketched outlines to be filled in by later pro-

phetic writers.   We also now further put this question: how
was it possible for the gloomy complaint of Ps. lxxvii., which
is turned back to the history of the past, to mould itself after
Hab. ch. iii., that joyous looking forward into a bright and
blessed future?   Is not the prospect in Hab. ch. iii. rather the
result of that retrospect in Ps. lxxvii., the confidence in being
heard which is kindled by this Psalm, the realizing as present,
in the certainty of being heard, of a new deed of God in which
the deliverances in the days of Moses are antitypically revived?

More than this, viz. that the Psalm is older than Habakkuk,
who entered upon public life in the reign of Josiah, or even as
early as in the reign of Manasseh, cannot be maintained.   For
it cannot be inferred from ver. 16 and ver. 3, compared with
Gen. xxxvii. 35, that one chief matter of pain to the psalmist
was the fall of the kingdom of the ten tribes which took place
in his time.   Nothing more, perhaps, than the division of the
kingdom which had already taken place seems to be indicated
in these passages.   The bringing of the tribes of Joseph prominently forward is, however, peculiar to the Asaphic circle of
songs.

The task of the precentor is assigned by the inscription to
Jeduthun (*Chethîb*: Jedithun), for ל (xxxix. 1) alternates with
עַל (lxii. 1); and the idea that יְדוּתוּן denotes the whole of the
Jeduthunites (“overseer over . . .”) might be possible, but
is without example.

The strophe schema of the Psalm is 7. 12. 12. 12. 2.   The
first three strophes or groups of stichs close with *Sela.*

Vers. 2–4.   The poet is resolved to pray without intermission, and he prays; for his soul is comfortless and sorely tempted
by the vast distance between the former days and the present
times.   According to the pointing, וְהַאֲזִין appears to be meant
to be imperative after the form הַקְטִיל, which occurs instead of
הַקְטֵל and הַקְטִילָה, cf. xciv. 1, Isa. xliii. 8, Jer. xvii. 18, and the
mode of writing הַקְמֵיל, cxlii. 5, 2 Kings viii. 6, and frequently;
therefore *et audi* = *ut audias* (cf. 2 Sam. xxi. 3).   But such
an isolated form of address is not to be tolerated; וְהַאֲזִין has
been regarded as *perf. consec.* in the sense of *ut audiat*, although
this modification of הַאֲזִין into הַאֲזִין in connection with the appearing of the *Waw consec.* cannot be supported in any other

instance (Ew. § 234, *e*), and Kimchi on this account tries to persuade himself to that which is impossible, viz. that וְהָאֲזִין in respect of sound stands for וְיַאֲזִין. The preterites in ver. 3 express that which has commenced and which will go on. The poet labours in his present time of affliction to press forward to the Lord, who has withdrawn from him; his hand is diffused, *i.e.* stretched out (not: poured out, for the radical meaning of נגר, as the Syriac shows, is *protrahere*), in the night-time without wearying and leaving off; it is fixedly and stedfastly (אֱמוּנָה, as it is expressed in Ex. xvii. 12) stretched out towards heaven. His soul is comfortless, and all comfort up to the present rebounds as it were from it (cf. Gen. xxxvii. 35, Jer. xxxi. 15). If he remembers God, who was once near to him, then he is compelled to groan (cf. lv. 18, 3; and on the cohortative form of a *Lamed He* verb, cf. Ges. § 75, 6), because He has hidden Himself from him; if he muses, in order to find Him again, then his spirit veils itself, *i.e.* it sinks into night and feebleness (הִתְעַטֵּף as in cvii. 5, cxlii. 4, cxliii. 4). Each of the two members of ver. 4 are protasis and apodosis; concerning this emotional kind of structure of a sentence, *vid.* Ewald, § 357, *b.*

Vers. 5–10. He calls his eyelids the "guards of my eyes." He who holds these so that they remain open when they want to shut together for sleep, is God; for his looking up to Him keeps the poet awake in spite of all overstraining of his powers. Hupfeld and others render thus: "Thou hast held, *i.e.* caused to last, the night-watches of mine eyes,"—which is affected in thought and expression. The preterites state what has been hitherto and has not yet come to a close. He still endures, as formerly, such thumps and blows within him, as though he lay upon an anvil (פָּעַם), and his voice fails him. Then silent soliloquy takes the place of audible prayer; he throws himself back in thought to the days of old (cxliii. 5), the years of past periods (Isa. li. 9), which were so rich in the proofs of the power and loving-kindness of the God who was then manifest, but is now hidden. He remembers the happier past of his people and his own, inasmuch as he now in the night purposely calls back to himself in his mind the time when joyful thankfulness impelled him to the song of praise accompanied by the music of the harp (בַּלַּיְלָה belongs according to the accents to the verb, not to נגינתי, although that construction certainly is

strongly commended by parallel passages like xvi. 7, xlii. 9,
xcii. 3, cf. Job xxxv. 10), in place of which, crying and sighing
and gloomy silence have now entered. He gives himself up to
musing "with his heart," *i.e.* in the retirement of his inmost
nature, inasmuch as he allows his thoughts incessantly to hover
to and fro between the present and the former days, and in
consequence of this (*fut. consec.* as in xlii. 6) his spirit betakes
itself to scrupulizing (what the LXX. reproduces with σκάλ-
λειν, Aquila with σκαλεύειν)—his conflict of temptation grows
fiercer. Now follow the two doubting questions of the tempted
one: he asks in different applications, vers. 8–10 (cf. lxxxv. 6),
whether it is then all at an end with God's loving-kindness and
promise, at the same time saying to himself, that this nevertheless is at variance with the unchangeableness of His nature
(Mal. iii. 6) and the inviolability of His covenant. אָפֵס (only
occurring as a 3. *præt.*) alternates with גָּמַר (xii. 2). חַנּוֹת is an
infinitive construct formed after the manner of the *Lamed He*
verbs, which, however, does also occur as infinitive absolute
(שַׁמּוֹת, Ezek. xxxvi. 3, cf. on xvii. 3); Gesenius and Olshausen
(who doubts this infinitive form, § 245, *f*) explain it, as do
Aben-Ezra and Kimchi, as the plural of a substantive חַנָּה, but
in the passage cited from Ezekiel (*vid.* Hitzig) such a substantival plural is syntactically impossible. קָפַץ רַחֲמִים is to draw
together or contract and draw back one's compassion, so that
it does not manifest itself outwardly, just as he who will not
give shuts (יִקְפֹּץ) his hand (Deut. xv. 7; cf. *supra*, xvii. 10).

Vers. 11–16. With וָאֹמַר the poet introduces the self-encouragement with which he has hitherto calmed himself when
such questions of temptation were wont to intrude themselves
upon him, and with which he still soothes himself. In the
rendering of חַלּוֹתִי (with the tone regularly drawn back before
the following monosyllable) even the Targum wavers between
מַרְעוּתִי (my affliction) and בָּעוּתִי (my supplication); and just in
the same way, in the rendering of ver. 11*b*, between אִשְׁתַּנִי
(have changed) and שְׁנִין (years). שְׁנוֹת cannot possibly signify
"change" in an active sense, as Luther renders: "The right
hand of the Most High can change everything," but only a
having become different (LXX. and the *Quinta* ἀλλοίωσις,
Symmachus ἐπιδευτέρωσις), after which Maurer, Hupfeld, and
Hitzig render thus: my affliction is this, that the right hand of

the Most High has changed.   But after we have read שְׁנוֹת in
ver. 6 as a poetical plural of שָׁנָה, a year, we have first of all to
see whether it may not have the same signification here.   And
many possible interpretations present themselves.   It can be
interpreted: "my supplication is this: years of the right hand
of the Most High" (viz. that years like to the former ones may
be renewed); but this thought is not suited to the introduction
with וָאֹמַר.   We must either interpret it: my sickness, viz.
from the side of God, *i.e.* the temptation which befalls me from
Him, the affliction ordained by Him for me (Aquila ἀῤῥωστία
μου), is this (cf. Jer. x. 19); or, since in this case the unam-
biguous חַלּוֹתִי would have been used instead of the *Piel*: my
being pierced, my wounding, my sorrow is this (Symmachus
τρῶσίς μου, *inf. Kal* from חָלַל, cix. 22, after the form חַנּוֹת
from חָנַן)—they are years of the right hand of the Most High,
i.e. those which God's mighty hand, under which I have to
humble myself (1 Pet. v. 6), has formed and measured out to
me.   In connection with this way of taking ver. 11*b*, ver. 12*a*
is now suitably and easily attached to what has gone before.
The poet says to himself that the affliction allotted to him
has its time, and will not last for ever.   Therein lies a hope
which makes the retrospective glance into the happier past a
source of consolation to him.   In ver. 12*a* the *Chethîb* אזכיר is
to be retained, for the כי in ver. 12*b* is thus best explained:
"I bring to remembrance, *i.e.* make known with praise or celebrate (Isa. lxiii. 7), the deeds of Jāh, for I will remember Thy
wondrous doing from days of old."   His sorrow over the
distance between the present and the past is now mitigated by
the hope that God's right hand, which now casts down, will
also again in His own time raise up.   Therefore he will now,
as the advance from the indicative to the cohortative (cf. xvii.
15) imports, thoroughly console and refresh himself with God's
work of salvation in all its miraculous manifestations from the
earliest times.   יָהּ is the most concise and comprehensive
appellation for the God of the history of redemption, who, as
Habakkuk prays, will revive His work of redemption in the
midst of the years to come, and bring it to a glorious issue.
To Him who then was and who will yet come the poet now
brings praise and celebration.   The way of God is His historical
rule, and more especially, as in Hab. iii. 6, הֲלִיכוֹת, His redemp-

tive rule. The primary passage Ex. xv. 11 (cf. Ps. lxviii. 25) shows that בַּקֹּדֶשׁ is not to be rendered "in the sanctuary" (LXX. ἐν τῷ ἁγίῳ), but "in holiness" (Symmachus ἐν ἁγιασμῷ). Holy and glorious in love and in anger, God goes through history, and shows Himself there as the incomparable One, with whose greatness no being, and least of all any one of the beingless gods, can be measured. He is הָאֵל, the God, God absolutely and exclusively, a miracle-working (עֹשֵׂה פֶלֶא, not עֹשֵׂה פְלָא, cf. Gen. i. 11*) God, and a God who by these very means reveals Himself as the living and supra-mundane God. He has made His omnipotence known among the peoples, viz., as ver. 16 says, by the redemption of His people, the tribes of Jacob and the double tribe of Joseph, out of Egypt,—a deed of His arm, *i.e.* the work of His own might, by which He has proved Himself to all peoples and to the whole earth to be the Lord of the world and the God of salvation (Ex. ix. 16, xv. 14). בִּזְרוֹעַ, *brachio* scil. *extenso* (Ex. vi. 6, Deut. iv. 34, and frequently), just as in lxxv. 6, בְּצַוָּאר, *collo* scil. *erecto*. The music here strikes in; the whole strophe is an overture to the following hymn in celebration of God, the Redeemer out of Egypt.

Vers. 17–20. When He directed His glance towards the Red Sea, which stood in the way of His redeemed, the waters immediately fell as it were into pangs of travail (יָחִילוּ, as in Hab. iii. 10, not וַיָּחִילוּ), also the billows of the deep trembled; for before the omnipotence of God the Redeemer, which creates a new thing in the midst of the old creation, the rules of the ordinary course of nature become unhinged. There now follow in vers. 18, 19 lines taken from the picture of a thunder-storm. The poet wishes to describe how all the powers of nature became the servants of the majestic revelation of Jahve, when He executed judgment on Egypt and delivered Israel. זֹרֶם, *Poel* of זָרַם (cognate זָרַב, זָרַף, Æthiopic זנם, to rain), signifies inten-

---

* The joining of the second word, accented on the first syllable and closely allied in sense, on to the first, which is accented on the *ultima* (the tone of which, under certain circumstances, retreats to the *penult.*, נסוג אחור) or monosyllabic, by means of the hardening *Dagesh* (the so-called דהיק), only takes place when that first word ends in הָ— or הֶ—, not when it ends in הֶ—.

sively: to stream forth in full torrents. Instead of this line,
Habakkuk, with a change of the letters of the primary passage,
which is usual in Jeremiah more especially, has זֶרֶם מַיִם עָבָר.
The rumbling which the שְׁחָקִים* cause to sound forth (נָתְנוּ, cf.
lxviii. 34) is the thunder. The arrows of God (חֲצָצֶיךָ, in
Habakkuk חִצֶּיךָ) are the lightnings. The *Hithpa.* (instead of
which Habakkuk has יְהַלֵּכוּ) depicts their busy darting hither
and thither in the service of the omnipotence that sends them
forth. It is open to question whether גַּלְגַּל denotes the roll of
the thunder (Aben-Ezra, Maurer, Böttcher): the sound of Thy
thunder went rolling forth (cf. xxix. 4),—or the whirlwind
accompanying the thunder-storm (Hitzig); the usage of the
language (lxxxiii. 14, also Ezek. x. 13, Syriac *golgolo*) is in
favour of the latter. On ver. 19*bc* cf. the echo in xcvii. 4.
Amidst such commotions in nature above and below Jahve
strode along through the sea, and made a passage for His redeemed. His person and His working were invisible, but the
result which attested His active presence was visible. He took
His way through the sea, and cut His path (*Chethîb* plural,
שְׁבִילָיךָ, as in Jer. xviii. 15) through great waters (or, according
to Habakkuk, caused His horses to go through), without the

----

* We have indicated on xviii. 12, xxxvi. 6, that the שְׁחָקִים are so called
from their thinness, but passages like xviii. 12 and the one before us do
not favour this idea. One would think that we have more likely to go
back to سَحِقَ, to be distant (whence *suḥk*, distance; *saḥîk*, distant), and
that שְׁחָקִים signifies the distances, like שָׁמַיִם, the heights, from שְׁחָק =
suḥk, in distinction from שַׁחַק, an atom (Wetzstein). But the Hebrew
affords no trace of this verbal stem, whereas שָׁחַק, سَحَقَ, *contundere*,
comminuere (Neshwân: to pound to dust, used *e.g.* of the apothecary's
drugs), is just as much Hebrew as Arabic. And the word is actually associated with this verb by the Arabic mind, inasmuch as سَحَاب سَاحِق
(*nubes tenues, nubila tenuia*) is explained by سَحَاب رَقِيق. Accordingly
שְׁחָקִים, according to its primary notion, signifies that which spreads itself
out thin and fine over a wide surface, and, according to the usage of the
language, in contrast with the thick and heavy פְּנֵי הָאָרֶץ, the uppermost
stratum of the atmosphere, and then the clouds, as also أَعْنَان, and the
collective عَنَن and عَنَان (*vid. Isaiah*, i. 156, note 1), is not first of all
the clouds, but the surface of the sky that is turned to us (Fleischer).

footprints (עִקְּבוֹת with *Dag. dirimens*) of Him who passes and passed through being left behind to show it.

Ver. 21. If we have divided the strophes correctly, then this is the refrain-like close. Like a flock God led His people by Moses and Aaron (Num. xxxiii. 1) to the promised goal. At this favourite figure, which is as it were the monogram of the Psalms of Asaph and of his school, the poet stops, losing himself in the old history of redemption, which affords him comfort in abundance, and is to him a prophecy of the future lying behind the afflictive years of the present.

PSALM LXXVIII.

THE WARNING-MIRROR OF HISTORY FROM MOSES
TO DAVID.

1 GIVE ear, O my people, to my teaching,
  Incline your ear to the utterances of my mouth.
2 I will open my mouth with a parable,
  I will pour forth riddles out of the days of old.
3 What we have heard, and become conscious of,
  And our fathers have told us,
4 We will not hide from their children;
  Telling to the generation to come the glorious deeds of
    Jahve,
  And His proof of power and His wonders, which He hath
    done.

5 He hath established a testimony in Jacob
  And laid down a law in Israel,
  Which He hath commanded our fathers
  To make it known unto their children;
6 In order that the generation to come might know it, the
    children born afterwards,
  That they might arise and tell it again to their children,
7 And might place their confidence in Elohim,
  And might not forget the deeds of God,
  And might keep His commandments—

8 And might not become as their fathers a stubborn and re-
    bellious generation,
  A generation that set not its heart aright,
  And whose spirit was not faithful towards God.
9 The sons of Ephraim, the bow-equipped archers,
  Turned back in the day of battle.
10 They kept not the covenant of Elohim,
  And in His law they refused to walk.
11 And they forgot His works
  And His wonders, which He showed them.

12 In the sight of their fathers He proved Himself to be a
    miracle-worker,
  In the land of Egypt, in the field of Zoan.
13 He divided the sea, and led them through,
  And piled the waters up as a heap ;
14 And led them in the cloud by day,
  And the whole night in a fiery light.
15 He clave rocks in the desert,
  And gave them as it were the floods of the sea to drink
    abundantly,
16 And brought forth streams out of the rock,
  And caused the waters to flow down like rivers.

17 They, however, continued further to sin against Him,
  To act rebelliously towards the Most High in a parched land.
18 They tempted God in their heart
  To desire food for their soul,
19 And spake against Elohim, they said :
  " Will God be able to prepare a table in the desert ?
20 Behold He smote rock, and waters gushed out,
  And streams dashed along—
  Will He also be able to give bread,
  Or to provide flesh for His people ? "

21 Therefore, hearing this, Jahve was wroth,
  And fire kindled in Jacob,
  And anger also ascended against Israel
22 For they believed not in Elohim,
  And trusted not in His salvation.

23 Nevertheless He commanded the clouds above,
And the doors of heaven He opened;
24 He rained upon them manna to eat,
And corn of heaven gave He unto them.
25 Bread of angels did man eat,
Meat He sent them in superabundance.

26 He caused the east wind to blow in the heaven,
And by His power brought on the south wind,
27 And rained flesh upon them like the dust,
And winged fowls as the sand of the seas.
28 And it fell within the circuit of its camp,
Round about its tents.
29 Then they did eat and were well filled,
And their desire He fulfilled to them.

30 Still they were not estranged from their desire,
The food was still in their mouth,
31 Then the anger of Elohim went up against them,
And slew among their fat ones,
And smote down the young men of Israel.
32 For all this they sinned still more,
And believed not in His wonders.
33 Then He made their days vanish in a breath,
And their years in sudden haste.

34 When He slew them, they inquired after Him,
They turned back and sought God diligently,
35 And remembered that Elohim was their rock,
And God the Most High their Redeemer.
36 They appeased Him with their mouth,
And with their tongue they lied unto Him;
37 But their heart was not stedfast with Him,
And they did not prove faithful in His covenant.

38 Nevertheless He is full of compassion—
He forgiveth iniquity and doth not destroy,
And hath ofttimes restrained His anger,
And stirred not up all His fury.

39 He remembered that they were flesh,
   A breath of wind that passeth by and returneth not.
40 How oft did they provoke Him in the desert,
   Did they grieve Him in the wilderness!

41 And again and again they sought God,
   And vexed the Holy One of Israel.
42 They remembered not His hand,
   The day when He delivered them from the oppressor,
43 When He set His signs in Egypt
   And His remarkable deeds in the field of Zoan.
44 He turned their Niles into blood,
   And their running waters they could not drink.

45 He sent gad-flies against them, which devoured them,
   And frogs, which brought destruction upon them.
46 He gave the fruit of their field to the cricket,
   And their labour to the locust;
47 He smote down their vine with hail,
   And their sycamore-trees with hail-stones;
48 And He gave over their cattle to the hail,
   And their flocks to the lightnings.

49 He let loose upon them the burning of His anger,
   Indignation and fury and distress,
   An embassy of angels of misfortune;
50 He made plain a way for His anger,
   He spared not their soul from death,
   And their life He gave over to the pestilence.
51 He smote all the first-born in Egypt,
   The firstlings of manly strength in the tents of Ham.

52 Then He made His own people to go forth like sheep,
   And guided them like a flock in the desert;
53 And He led them safely without fear,
   But their enemies the sea covered.
54 He brought them to His holy border,
   To the mountain, which His right hand had acquired;
55 He drove out nations before them,

And allotted them as a marked out inheritance,
And settled the tribes of Israel in their tents.

56 Nevertheless they tempted and provoked Elohim the Most
   High,
And His testimonies they kept not.
57 They turned back and fell away like their fathers,
They turned aside like a deceitful bow.
58 They incensed Him by their high places,
And by their idols they excited His jealousy.
59 Elohim heard and was wroth,
And became greatly wearied with Israel.

60 Then He cast off the tabernacle of Shiloh,
The tent which He had pitched among men;
61 He gave His might into captivity,
And His glory into the oppressor's hand.
62 He gave over His people to the sword,
And was wroth concerning His inheritance.
63 Their young men fire devoured,
And for their maidens they sang no bridal song.
64 Their priests, by the sword they fell,
And their widows could not mourn.

65 Then the Lord awaked as one sleeping,
As a hero, shouting from wine,
66 And smote their oppressors behind,
Eternal reproach did He put upon them—
67 And He despised the tent of Joseph,
And the tribe of Ephraim He chose not.
68 He chose the tribe of Judah,
The mount Zion, which He hath loved.

69 And He built, as the heights of heaven, His sanctuary,
Like the earth which He hath founded for ever.
70 And He chose David His servant,
And took him from the sheep-folds;
71 Following the ewes that gave suck He took him away
To pasture Jacob His people,
And Israel His inheritance.

72 And he pastured them according to the integrity of his
    heart,
And with judicious hands he led them.

In the last verse of Ps. lxxvii. Israel appears as a flock
which is led by Moses and Aaron; in the last verse of Ps.
lxxviii. as a flock which is led by David, of a pure heart, with
judicious hands. Both Psalms also meet in thoughts and expressions, just as the לְאָסָף of both leads one to expect. Ps.
lxxviii. is called *Maskîl, a meditation.* The word would also be
appropriate here in the signification "a didactic poem." For
the history of Israel is recapitulated here from the leading
forth out of Egypt through the time of the Judges down to
David, and that with the practical application for the present
age that they should cleave faithfully to Jahve, more faithfully than the rebellious generation of the fathers. After the
manner of the Psalms of Asaph the Ephraimites are made
specially prominent out of the whole body of the people, their
disobedience as well as the rejection of Shiloh and the election
of David, by which it was for ever at an end with the supremacy
of Ephraim and also of his brother-tribe of Benjamin.

The old Asaphic origin of the Psalm has been contested:—
(1) Because ver. 9 may be referred to the apostasy of Ephraim
and of the other tribes, that is to say, to the division of the
kingdom. But this reference is capriciously imagined to be
read in ver. 9. (2) Because the Psalm betrays a malice, indeed
a national hatred against Ephraim, such as is only explicable
after the apostasy of the ten tribes. But the alienation and
jealousy between Ephraim and Judah is older than the rupture
of the kingdom. The northern tribes, in consequence of their
position, which was more exposed to contact with the heathen
world, had already assumed a different character from that of
Judah living in patriarchal seclusion. They could boast of a
more excited, more martial history, one richer in exploit; in the
time of the Judges especially, there is scarcely any mention of
Judah. Hence Judah was little thought of by them, especially
by powerful Ephraim, which regarded itself as the foremost
tribe of all the tribes. From the beginning of Saul's persecution of David, however, when the stricter principle of the south
came first of all into decisive conflict for the mastery with the

more lax principle of the Ephraimites, until the rebellion of
Jeroboam against Solomon, there runs through the history of
Israel a series of facts which reveal a deep reft between Judah
and the other tribes, more especially Benjamin and Ephraim.
Though, therefore, it were true that a tone hostile to Ephraim
is expressed in the Psalm, this would not be any evidence
against its old Asaphic origin, since the psalmist rests upon
facts, and, without basing the preference of Judah upon merit,
he everywhere contemplates the sin of Ephraim, without any
Judæan boasting, in a connection with the sin of the whole
nation, which involves all in the responsibility. Nor is ver.
69 against Asaph the cotemporary of David; for Asaph may
certainly have seen the building of the Temple of Solomon as
it towered upwards to the skies, and Caspari in his Essay on
the Holy One of Israel (*Luther. Zeitschrift*, 1844, 3) has
shown that even the divine name קְדוֹשׁ יִשְׂרָאֵל does not militate
against him. We have seen in connection with Ps. lxxvi. how
deeply imbued Isaiah's language is with that of the Psalms of
Asaph. It cannot surprise us if Asaph is Isaiah's predecessor
in the use of the name "the Holy One of Israel." The fact,
however, that the writer of the Psalm takes the words and
colours of his narration from all five books of the Pentateuch,
with the exception of Leviticus, is not opposed to our view of
the origin of the Pentateuch, but favourable to it. The author
of the Book of Job, with whom in ver. 64 he verbally coincides, is regarded by us as younger; and the points of contact
with other Psalms inscribed "by David," "by the sons of
Korah," and "by Asaph," do not admit of being employed for
ascertaining his time, since the poet is by no means an unin-
dependent imitator.

The manner of representation which characterizes the Psalm
becomes epical in its extension, but is at the same time concise
after the sententious style. The separate historical statements
have a gnome-like finish, and a gem-like elegance. The whole
falls into two principal parts, vers. 1–37, 38–72; the second
part passes over from the God-tempting unthankfulness of the
Israel of the desert to that of the Israel of Canaan. Every
three strophes form one group.

Vers. 1–11. The poet begins very similarly to the poet of

Ps. xlix. He comes forward among the people as a preacher, and demands for his *tôra* a willing, attentive hearing. תּוֹרָה is the word for every human doctrine or instruction, especially for the prophetic discourse which sets forth and propagates the substance of the divine teaching. Asaph is a prophet, hence ver. 2 is quoted in Matt. xiii. 34 sq. as ῥηθὲν διὰ τοῦ προφήτου.* He here recounts to the people their history מִנִּי־קֶדֶם, from that Egyptæo-Sinaitic age of yore to which Israel's national independence and specific position in relation to the rest of the world goes back. It is not, however, with the external aspect of the history that he has to do, but with its internal teachings. מָשָׁל is an allegory or parable, παραβολή, more particularly the apophthegm as the characteristic species of poetry belonging to the *Chokma*, and then in general a discourse of an elevated style, full of figures, thoughtful, pithy, and rounded. חִידָה is that which is entangled, knotted, involved, *perplexe dictum*. The poet, however, does not mean to say that he will literally discourse gnomic sentences and propound riddles, but that he will set forth the history of the fathers after the manner of a parable and riddle, so that it may become as a parable, *i.e.* a didactic history, and its events as marks of interrogation and nota-bene's to the present age. The LXX. renders thus: ἀνοίξω ἐν παραβολαῖς τὸ στόμα μου, φθέγξομαι προβλήματα ἀπ᾿ ἀρχῆς. Instead of this the Gospel by Matthew has: ἀνοίξω ἐν παραβολαῖς τὸ στόμα μου, ἐρεύξομαι κεκρυμμένα ἀπὸ καταβολῆς (κόσμου), and recognises in this language of the Psalm a prophecy of Christ; because it is moulded so appropriately for the mouth of Him who is the Fulfiller not only of the Law and of Prophecy, but also of the vocation of the prophet. It is the object-clause to נְכַחֵד, and not a relative clause belonging to the "riddles out of the age of yore," that follows in ver. 3 with אֲשֶׁר, for that which has been heard only becomes riddles by the appropriation and turn the poet gives to it. Ver. 3 begins a new period (cf. lxix. 27, Jer. xiv. 1, and frequently): What we have heard, and in consequence thereof known, and what our fathers have told us (word for word, like xliv. 2,

---

* The reading διὰ Ἡσαΐου τοῦ προφήτου is, although erroneous, nevertheless ancient; since even the Clementine Homilies introduce this passage as the language of Isaiah.

Judg. vi. 13), that will we not hide from their children (cf. Job xv. 18). The accentuation is perfectly correct. The *Rebîa* by מבניהם has a greater distinctive force than the *Rebîa* by אחרון (לדור); it is therefore to be rendered: telling to the later generation (which is just what is intended by the offspring of the fathers) the glorious deeds of Jahve, etc. The *fut. consec.* וַיָּקֶם joins on to אֲשֶׁר עָשָׂה. Glorious deeds, proofs of power, miracles hath He wrought, and in connection therewith set up an admonition in Jacob, and laid down an order in Israel, which He commanded our fathers, viz. to propagate by tradition the remembrance of those mighty deeds (Ex. xiii. 8, 14, Deut. iv. 9, and other passages). לְהוֹדִיעָם has the same object as וְהוֹדַעְתָּם in Deut. iv. 9, Josh. iv. 22. The matter in question is not the giving of the Law in general, as the purpose of which, the keeping of the laws, ought then to have been mentioned before anything else, but a precept, the purpose of which was the further proclamation of the *magnalia Dei*, and indirectly the promotion of trust in God and fidelity to the Law; cf. lxxxi. 5 sq., where the special precept concerning the celebration of the Feast of the Passover is described as a עֵדוּת laid down in Joseph. The following generation, the children, which shall be born in the course of the ages, were to know concerning His deeds, and also themselves to rise up (יָקוּמוּ, not: come into being, like the יָבֹאוּ of the older model-passage xxii. 32) and to tell them further to their children, in order that these might place their confidence in God (שִׂים כֶּסֶל, like שִׁית מַחְסֶה in lxxiii. 28), and might not forget the mighty deeds of God (lxxvii. 12), and might keep His commandments, being warned by the disobedience of the fathers. The generation of the latter is called סוֹרֵר וּמֹרֶה, just as the degenerate son that is to be stoned is called in Deut. xxi. 18. הֵכִין לִבּוֹ, to direct one's heart, *i.e.* to give it the right direction or tendency, to put it into the right state, is to be understood after ver. 37, 2 Chron. xx. 33, Sir. ii. 17.

Ver. 9, which comes in now in the midst of this description, is awkward and unintelligible. The supposition that " the sons of Ephraim " is an appellation for the whole of Israel is refuted by vers. 67 sq. The rejection of Ephraim and the election of Judah is the point into which the historical retrospect runs out; how then can " the sons of Ephraim " denote Israel as a whole? And yet what is here said of the Ephraimites also holds good of the Israelites in general, as ver. 57 shows. The fact, however, that the Ephraimites are made specially conspicuous out of the "generation" of all Israel, is intelligible from the special interest which the Psalms of Asaph take in the tribes of Joseph, and here particularly from the purpose of practically preparing the way for the rejection of Shiloh and Ephraim related further on. In vers. 10 and 11 the Ephraimites are also still spoken of; and it is not until ver. 12, with the words "in sight of their fathers," that we come back again to the nation at large. The Ephraimites are called נֹשְׁקֵי רוֹמֵי־קָשֶׁת in the sense of נושקי קשת רומי קשת; the two participial construct forms do not stand in subordination but in co-ordination, as in Jer. xlvi. 9, Deut. xxxiii. 19, 2 Sam. xx. 19, just as in other instances also two substantives, of which one is the explanation of the other, are combined by means of the construct, Job xx. 17, cf. 2 Kings xvii. 13 *Kerî*. It is therefore: those who prepare the bow, *i.e.* those arming themselves therewith (נָשַׁק as in 1 Chron. xii. 2, 2 Chron. xvii. 17), those who cast the bow, *i.e.* those shooting arrows from the bow (Jer. iv. 29), cf. Böttcher, § 728. What is predicated of them, viz. "they turned round" (הָפַךְ as in Judg. xx. 39, 41), stands in contrast with this their ability to bear arms and to defend themselves, as a disappointed expectation. Is what is meant thereby, that the powerful warlike tribe of Ephraim grew weary in the work of the conquest of Canaan (Judg. ch. i.), and did not render the services which might have been expected from it? Since the historical retrospect does not enter into details until ver. 12 onwards, this special historical reference would come too early here; the statement consequently must be understood more generally and, according to ver. 57, figuratively: Ephraim proved itself unstable and faint-hearted in defending and in conducting the cause of God, it gave it up, it abandoned it. They did not act as the covenant of God required of them, they refused to walk (לָלֶכֶת, cf. לָלֶכֶת, Eccles. i. 7) within the limit and track of His Tôra, and forgat the deeds of God of which they had been eye-witnesses under Moses and under Joshua, their comrades of the same family.

Vers. 12–25. It is now related how wonderfully God led the fathers of these Ephraimites, who behaved themselves so badly as the leading tribe of Israel, in the desert; how they again and again ever indulged sinful murmuring, and still He continued to give proofs of His power and of His loving-kindness. The (according to Num. xiii. 22) very ancient *Zoan* (*Tanis*), ancient Egyptian *Zane*, Coptic *G'ane*, on the east bank of the Tanitic arm of the Nile, so called therefrom—according to the researches to which the Turin Papyrus No. 112 has led, identical with *Avaris* (*vid.* on Isa. xix. 11) *—was the seat of the Hyksos dynasties that ruled in the eastern Delta, where after their overthrow Rameses ii., the Pharaoh of the bondage, in order to propitiate the enraged mass of the Semitic population of Lower Egypt, embraced the worship of Baal instituted by King Apophis. The colossal sitting figure of Rameses ii. in the pillared court of the Royal Museum in Berlin, says Brugsch (*Aus dem Orient* ii. 45), is the figure which Rameses himself dedicated to the temple of Baal in Tanis and set up before its entrance. This mighty colossus is a cotemporary of Moses, who certainly once looked upon this monument when, as Ps. lxxviii. says, he " wrought wonders in the land of Egypt, in the field of Zoan." The psalmist, moreover, keeps very close to the Tôra in his reproduction of the history of the Exodus, and in fact so close that he must have had it before him in the entirety of its several parts, the Deuteronomic, Elohimistic, and Jehovistic. Concerning the rule by which it is pointed ʿā́sa phéle, *vid.* on lii. 5. The primary passage to ver. 13*b* (cf. נֹזְלִים ver. 16) is Ex. xv. 8. נֵד is a pile, *i.e.* a piled up heap or mass, as in xxxiii. 7. And ver. 14 is the abbreviation of Ex. xiii. 21. In vers. 15 sq. the writer condenses into one the two instances of the giving of water from the rock, in the first year of the Exodus (Ex. ch. xvii.) and in the fortieth year (Num. ch. xx.). The *Piel* יְבַקַּע and the plural צְרִים correspond to this compression. רַבָּה is not an adjective (after the analogy of תְּהוֹם רַבָּה), but an adverb as in lxii. 3; for the giving to drink needs a qualificative, but תהמות does not need any enhancement. וַיּוֹצִא has *î* instead of *ē* as in cv. 43.

---

* The identity of Avaris and Tanis is in the meanwhile again become doubtful. *Tanis* was the Hyksos city, but *Pelusium* = *Avaris* the Hyksos fortress; *vid.* Petermann's *Mittheilungen*, 1866, S. 296-298.

The fact that the subject is continued in ver. 17 with וַיּוֹסִיפוּ without mention having been made of any sinning on the part of the generation of the desert, is explicable from the consideration that the remembrance of that murmuring is closely connected with the giving of water from the rock to which the names *Massah u-Merîbah* and *Merîbath-Kadesh* (cf. Num. xx. 13 with xxvii. 14, Deut. xxxii. 51) point back: they went on (עוֹד) sinning against Him, in spite of the miracles they experienced. לַמְרוֹת is syncopated from לְהַמְרוֹת as in Isa. iii. 8. The poet in ver. 18 condenses the account of the manifestations of discontent which preceded the giving of the quails and manna (Ex. ch. xvi.), and the second giving of quails (Num. ch. xi.), as he has done the two cases of the giving of water from the rock in ver. 15. They tempted God by unbelievingly and defiantly demanding (לִשְׁאָל, *postulando*, Ew. § 280, *d*) instead of trustfully hoping and praying. בִּלְבָבָם points to the evil fountain of the heart, and לְנַפְשָׁם describes their longing as a sensual eagerness, a lusting after it. Instead of allowing the miracles hitherto wrought to work faith in them, they made the miracles themselves the starting-point of fresh doubts. The poet here clothes what we read in Ex. xvi. 3, Num. xi. 4 sqq., xxi. 5, in a poetic dress. In לָעֵמוֹ the unbelief reaches its climax, it sounds like self-irony. On the co-ordinating construction " therefore Jahve heard it and was wroth," cf. Isa. v. 4, xii. 1, l. 2, Rom. vi. 17. The allusion is to the wrath-burning at Taberah (Tab‘ēra), Num. xi. 1–3, which preceded the giving of the quails in the second year of the Exodus. For it is obvious that ver. 21 and Num. xi. 1 coincide, וַיִּתְעַבֵּר וְאֵשׁ here being suggested by the וַתִּבְעַר־בָּם אֵשׁ of that passage, and אַף עָלָה being the opposite of וַתִּשְׁקַע הָאֵשׁ in ver. 2. A conflagration broke out at that time in the camp, at the same time, however, with the breaking out of God's anger. The nexus between the anger and the fire is here an outward one, whereas in Num. xi. 1 it is an internal one. The ground upon which the wrathful decree is based, which is only hinted at there, is here more minutely given in ver. 22: they believed not in Elohim (*vid.* Num. xiv. 11), *i.e.* did not rest with believing confidence in Him, and trusted not in His salvation, viz. that which they had experienced in the redemption out of Egypt (Ex. xiv. 13, xv. 2), and which was thereby guaranteed for time to come.

Now, however, when Taberah is here followed first by the giving of the manna, vers. 23–25, then by the giving of the quails, vers. 26–29, the course of the events is deranged, since the giving of the manna had preceded that burning, and it was only the giving of the quails that followed it. This putting together of the two givings out of order was rendered necessary by the preceding condensation (in vers. 18–20) of the clamorous desire for a more abundant supply of food before each of these events. Notwithstanding Israel's unbelief, He still remained faithful: He caused manna to rain down out of the opened gates of heaven (cf. "the windows of heaven," Gen. vii. 11, 2 Kings vii. 2, Mal. iii. 10), that is to say, in richest abundance. The manna is called corn (as in cv. 40, after Ex. xvi. 4, it is called bread) of heaven, because it descended in the form of grains of corn, and supplied the place of bread-corn during the forty years. לֶחֶם אַבִּירִים the LXX. correctly renders ἄρτον ἀγγέλων (אַבִּירִים = כֹּחַ גְּבֻּרֵי, ciii. 20). The manna is called "bread of angels" (Wisd. xvi. 20) as being bread from heaven (ver. 24, cv. 40), the dwelling-place of angels, as being *mann es-semâ,* heaven's gift, its Arabic name,—a name which also belongs to the vegetable manna which flows out of the *Tamarix mannifera* in consequence of the puncture of the *Coccus manniparus,* and is even at the present day invaluable to the inhabitants of the desert of Sinai. אִישׁ is the antithesis to אבירים; for if it signified "every one," אָכְלוּ would have been said (Hitzig). צֵידָה as in Ex. xii. 39; לָשֹׂבַע as in Ex. xvi. 3, cf. 8.

Vers. 26–37. Passing over to the giving of the quails, the poet is thinking chiefly of the first occasion mentioned in Ex. ch. xvi., which directly preceded the giving of the manna. But the description follows the second: יַסַּע (He caused to depart, set out) after Num. xi. 31. "East" and "south" belong together: it was a south-east wind from the Ælanitic Gulf. "To rain down" is a figurative expression for a plentiful giving or dispensing from above. "Its camp, its tents," are those of Israel, Num. xi. 31, cf. Ex. xvi. 13. The תַּאֲוָה, occurring twice, vers. 29, 30 (of the object of strong desire, as in xxi. 3), points to *Kibroth-hattaavah,* the scene of this carnal lusting; הֵבִיא is the transitive of the בּוֹא in Prov. xiii. 12. In vers. 30, 31 even in the construction the poet closely follows Num. xi.

33 (cf. also זָרִי with לְזָרָא, aversion, loathing, Num. xi. 20).
The *Waw* unites what takes place simultaneously; a construction which presents the advantage of being able to give special
prominence to the subject. The wrath of God consisted in
the breaking out of a sickness which was the result of immode-
rate indulgence, and to which even the best-nourished and
most youthfully vigorous fell a prey. When the poet goes on
in ver. 32 to say that in spite of these visitations (בְּכָל־זֹאת) they
went on sinning, he has chiefly before his mind the outbreak
of "fat" rebelliousness after the return of the spies, cf. ver.
32*b* with Num. xiv. 11. And ver. 33 refers to the judgment
of death in the wilderness threatened at that time to all who
had come out of Egypt from twenty years old and upward
(Num. xiv. 28–34). Their life devoted to death vanished from
that time onwards בַּהֶבֶל, in breath-like instability, and בַּבֶּהָלָה, in
undurable precipitancy; the mode of expression in xxxi. 11,
Job xxxvi. 1 suggests to the poet an expressive play of words.
When now a special judgment suddenly and violently thinned
the generation that otherwise was dying off, as in Num. xxi.
6 sqq., then they inquired after Him, they again sought His
favour, those who were still preserved in the midst of this dying
again remembered the God who had proved Himself to be a
"Rock" (Deut. xxxii. 15, 18, 37) and to be a "Redeemer"
(Gen. xlviii. 16) to them. And what next? Vers. 36,* 37
tell us what effect they gave to this disposition to return to
God. They appeased Him with their mouth, is meant to say:
they sought to win Him over to themselves by fair speeches,
inasmuch as they thus anthropopathically conceived of God,
and with their tongue they played the hypocrite to Him; their
heart, however, was not sincere towards Him (עִם like אֶת in
ver. 8), *i.e.* not directed straight towards Him, and they proved
themselves not stedfast (πιστοὶ, or properly βέβαιοι) in their
covenant-relationship to Him.

Vers. 38–48. The second part of the Psalm now begins.
God, notwithstanding, in His compassion restrains His anger;
but Israel's God-tempting conduct was continued, even after the

---

* According to the reckoning of the Masora this ver. 36 is the middle
verse of the 2527 verses of the Psalter (Buxtorf, *Tiberias*, 1620, p. 133).

journey through the desert, in Canaan, and the miracles of judgment amidst which the deliverance out of Egypt had been effected were forgotten. With וְהוּא in ver. 38* begins an adversative clause, which is of universal import as far as יַשְׁחִית, and then becomes historical. Ver. 38*b* expands what lies in רַחוּם: He expiates iniquity and, by letting mercy instead of right take its course, arrests the destruction of the sinner. With וְהִרְבָּה (Ges. § 142, 2) this universal truth is supported out of the history of Israel. As this history shows, He has many a time called back His anger, *i.e.* checked it in its course, and not stirred up all His glowing anger (cf. Isa. xlii. 13), *i.e.* His anger in all its fulness and intensity. We see that ver. 38*cd* is intended historically, from the fact more particularly that if the whole of ver. 38 were intended as abstract, ver. 39 would inadequately express the result which accrued to Israel from this conduct of God. If, however, ver. 38*cd* refers to His conduct towards Israel, then ver. 39 follows with the ground of the determination, and that in the form of an inference drawn from such conduct towards Israel. He moderated His anger against Israel, and consequently took human frailty and perishableness into consideration. The fact that man is flesh (which not merely affirms his physical fragility, but also his moral weakness, Gen. vi. 3, cf. viii. 21), and that, after a short life, he falls a prey to death, determines God to be long-suffering and kind; it was in fact sensuous desire and loathing by which Israel was beguiled time after time. The exclamation "how oft!" ver. 40, calls attention to the praiseworthiness of this undeserved forbearance.

But with ver. 41 the record of sins begins anew. There is nothing by which any reference of this ver. 41 to the last example of insubordination recorded in the Pentateuch, Num. xxv. 1–9 (Hitzig), is indicated. The poet comes back once more to the provocations of God by the Israel of the wilderness in order to expose the impious ingratitude which revealed itself

---

* According to *B. Kiddushin* 30*a*, this ver. 38 is the middle one of the 5896 פְּסוּקִין, στίχοι, of the Psalter. According to *B. Maccoth* 22*b*, Ps. lxxviii. 38, and previously Deut. xxviii. 58, 59, xxix. 8 [9], were recited when the forty strokes of the lash save one, which according to 2 Cor. xi. 24 Paul received five times, were being counted out to the culprit.

in this conduct. הִתְוָה is the causative of תָּוָה = ܬ݁ܘܳܐ, תְּהָא, to repent, to be grieved, LXX. παρώξυναν. The miracles of the time of redemption are now brought before the mind in detail, *ad exaggerandum crimen tentationis Dei cum summa ingratitudine conjunctum* (Venema). The time of redemption is called יוֹם, as in Gen. ii. 4 the hexahemeron. שִׂים אוֹת (synon. נָתַן, עָשָׂה) is used as in Ex. x. 2. We have already met with מִנִּי־צָר in xliv. 11. The first of the plagues of Egypt (Ex. vii. 14–25), the turning of the waters into blood, forms the beginning in ver. 44. From this the poet takes a leap over to the fourth plague, the עָרֹב (LXX. κυνόμυια), a grievous and destructive species of fly (Ex. viii. 16–28 [20–32]), and combines with it the frogs, the second plague (Ex. vii. 26 [viii. 1]–viii. 11 [15]). צְפַרְדֵּעַ is the lesser Egyptian frog, *Rana Mosaica*, which is even now called ضفدع, *ḍofda*. Next in ver. 46 he comes to the eighth plague, the locusts, חָסִיל (a more select name of the migratory locusts than אַרְבֶּה), Ex. x. 1–20; the third plague, the gnats and midges, כִּנִּים, is left unmentioned in addition to the fourth, which is of a similar kind. For the chastisement by means of destructive living things is now closed, and in ver. 47 follows the smiting with hail, the seventh plague, Ex. ix. 13–35. חֲנָמַל (with pausal *á*, not *ā*, cf. in Ezek. viii. 2 the similarly formed הַחַשְׁמַלָה) in the signification hoar-frost (πάχνη, LXX., Vulgate, Saadia, and Abulwalîd), or locusts (Targum כַּרְזוּבָא = חָגָב), or ants (J. D. Michaelis), does not harmonize with the history; also the hoar-frost is called כְּפוֹר, the ant נְמָלָה (collective in Arabic *neml*). Although only conjecturing from the context, we understand it, with Parchon and Kimchi, of hailstones or hail. With thick lumpy pieces of ice He smote down vines and sycamore-trees (*Fayum* was called in ancient Egyptian "the district of the sycamore"). הָרַג proceeds from the Biblical conception that the plant has a life of its own. The description of this plague is continued in ver. 48. Two MSS. present לִדְבֶר instead of לַבָּרָד; but even supposing that רְשָׁפִים might signify the fever-burnings of the pestilence (*vid.* on Hab. iii. 5), the mention of the pestilence follows in ver. 50, and the devastation which, according to Ex. ix. 19–22, the hail caused among the cattle of the Egyptians is in its right place here. Moreover it is expressly said in Ex. ix. 24 that there was conglomerate fire among the hail; רְשָׁפִים are therefore flaming, blazing lightnings.

Vers. 49–59. When these plagues rose to the highest pitch, Israel became free, and removed, being led by its God, into the Land of Promise; but it continued still to behave there just as it had done in the desert. The poet in vers. 49–51 brings the fifth Egyptian plague, the pestilence (Ex. ix. 1–7), and the tenth and last, the smiting of the first-born (מַכַּת בְּכֹרוֹת), Ex. ch. xi., xii., together. Ver. 49a sounds like Job xx. 23 (cf. below ver. 64). מַלְאֲכֵי רָעִים are not wicked angels, against which view Hengstenberg refers to the scriptural thesis of Jacobus Ode in his work *De Angelis, Deum ad puniendos malos homines mittere bonos angelos et ad castigandos pios usurpare malos*, but angels that bring misfortune. The mode of construction belongs to the chapter of the genitival subordination of the adjective to the substantive, like אֵשֶׁת רָע, Prov. vi. 24, cf. 1 Sam. xxviii. 7, Num. v. 18, 24, 1 Kings x. 15, Jer. xxiv. 2, and the Arabic مسجد الجامع, the mosque of the assembling one, *i.e.* the assembling (congregational) mosque, therefore: angels (not of the wicked ones = wicked angels, which it might signify elsewhere, but) of the evil ones = evil, misfortune-bringing angels (Ew. § 287, a). The poet thus paraphrases the הַמַּשְׁחִית that is collectively conceived in Ex. xii. 13, 23, Heb. xi. 28. In ver. 50a the anger is conceived of as a stream of fire, in ver. 50b death as an executioner, and in 50c the pestilence as a foe. רֵאשִׁית אוֹנִים (Gen. xlix. 3, Deut. xxi. 17) is that which had sprung for the first time from manly vigour (*plur. intensivus*). Egypt is called חָם as in Ps. cv. and cxi. according to Gen. x. 6, and is also called by themselves in ancient Egyptian *Kemi*, Coptic *Chêmi, Kême* (*vid.* Plutarch, *De Iside et Osiride*, ch. xxxiii.). When now these plagues which softened their Pharaoh went forth upon the Egyptians, God procured for His people a free departure, He guided flock-like (כַּעֵדֶר like בַּעֵדֶר, Jer. xxxi. 24, with *Dag. implicitum*), *i.e.* as a shepherd, the flock of His people (the favourite figure of the Psalms of Asaph) through the desert,—He led them safely, removing all terrors out of the way and drowning their enemies in the Red Sea, to His holy territory, to the mountain which (זֶה) His right hand had acquired, or according to the accents (cf. *supra*, vol.

i. 169): to the mountain there (זֶה), which, etc. It is not Zion that is meant, but, as in the primary passage Ex. xv. 16 sq., in accordance with the parallelism (although this is not imperative) and the usage of the language, which according to Isa. xi. 9, lvii. 13, is incontrovertible, the whole of the Holy Land with its mountains and valleys (cf. Deut. xi. 11). בְּחֶבֶל נַחֲלָה is the poetical equivalent to בְּנַחֲלָה, Num. xxxiv. 2, xxxvi. 2, and frequently. The *Beth* is *Beth essentiæ* (here in the same syntactical position as in Isa. xlviii. 10, Ezek. xx. 41, and also Job xxii. 24 surely): He made them (the heathen, viz., as in Josh. xxiii. 4 their territories) fall to them (viz., as the expression implies, by lot, בגורל) as a line of inheritance, *i.e.* (as in cv. 11) as a portion measured out as an inheritance. It is only in ver. 56 (and not so early as ver. 41) that the narration passes over to the apostate conduct of the children of the generation of the desert, that is to say, of the Israel of Canaan. Instead of עֵדְוֹתָיו from עֵדוּת, the word here is עֵדוֹתָיו from עֵדָה (a derivative of עוּד, not יָעַד). Since the apostasy did not gain ground until after the death of Joshua and Eleazar, it is the Israel of the period of the Judges that we are to think of here. קֶשֶׁת רְמִיָּה, ver. 57, is not: a bow of slackness, but: a bow of deceit; for the point of comparison, according to Hos. vii. 16, is its missing the mark: a bow that discharges its arrow in a wrong direction, that makes no sure shot. The verb רָמָה signifies not only to allow to hang down slack (cogn. רָפָה), but also, according to a similar conception to *spe dejicere*, to disappoint, deny. In the very act of turning towards God, or at least being inclined towards Him by His tokens of power and loving-kindness, they turned (Jer. ii. 21) like a bow that misses the mark and disappoints both aim and expectation. The expression in ver. 58 is like Deut. xxxii. 16, 21. שִׁמַּע refers to their prayer to the Baʿalim (Judg. ii. 11). The word הִתְעַבֵּר, which occurs three times in this Psalm, is a word belonging to Deuteronomy (ch. iii. 26). Ver. 59 is purposely worded exactly like ver. 21. The divine purpose of love spurned by the children just as by the fathers, was obliged in this case, as in the former, to pass over into angry provocation.

Vers. 60–72. The rejection of Shiloh and of the people worshipping there, but later on, when the God of Israel is again overwhelmed by compassion, the election of Judah, and of Mount Zion, and of David, the king after His own heart. In

the time of the Judges the Tabernacle was set up in Shiloh
(Josh. xviii. 1) ; there, consequently, was the central sanctuary
of the whole people,—in the time of Eli and Samuel, as follows
from 1 Sam. ch. i.-iii., it had become a fixed temple building.
When this building was destroyed is not known ; according to
Judg. xviii. 30 sq., cf. Jer. vii. 12–15, it was probably not until
the Assyrian period.   The rejection of Shiloh, however, preceded the destruction, and practically took place simultaneously
with the removal of the central sanctuary to Zion ; and was,
moreover, even previously decided by the fact that the Ark of
the covenant, when given up again by the Philistines, was not
brought back to Shiloh, but set down in Kirjath Jearîm (1
Sam. vii. 2).   The attributive clause שִׁכֵּן בָּאָדָם uses שִׁכֵּן as
הִשְׁפִּין is used in Josh. xviii. 1.   The pointing is correct, for the
words do not suffice to signify "where He dwelleth among
men" (Hitzig); consequently שִׁכֵּן is the causative of the *Kal*,
Lev. xvi. 16, Josh. xxii. 19.   In ver. 61 the Ark of the covenant is called the might and glory of God (אֲרוֹן עֻזּוֹ, cxxxii. 8,
cf. כָּבוֹד, 1 Sam. iv. 21 sq.), as being the place of their presence
in Israel and the medium of their revelation.   Nevertheless,
in the battle with the Philistines between Eben-ezer and Aphek,
Jahve gave the Ark, which they had fetched out of Shiloh,
into the hands of the foe in order to visit on the high-priesthood of the sons of Ithamar the desecration of His ordinances,
and there fell in that battle 30,000 footmen, and among them
the two sons of Eli, Hophni and Phinehas, the priests (1 Sam.
ch. iv.).   The fire in ver. 63 is the fire of war, as in Num. xxi.
28, and frequently.   The incident mentioned in 1 Sam. vi. 19
is reasonably (*vid.* Keil) left out of consideration.   By לֹא הוּלָּלוּ
(LXX. erroneously, οὐκ ἐπένθησαν = הוֹלְלוּ = הֵילִילוּ) are meant
the marriage-songs (cf. Talmudic הִלּוּלָא, the nuptial tent, and
בֵּית הִלּוּלִים the marriage-house).   "Its widows (of the people, in
fact, of the slain) weep not" (word for word as in Job xxvii.
15) is meant of the celebration of the customary ceremony of
mourning (Gen. xxiii. 2): they survive their husbands (which,
with the exception of such a case as that recorded in 1 Sam.
xiv. 19-22, is presupposed), but without being able to show
them the last signs of honour, because the terrors of the war
(Jer. xv. 8) prevent them.

  With ver. 65 the song takes a new turn.   After the punitive judgment has sifted and purified Israel, God receives His people to Himself afresh, but in such a manner that He transfers the precedence of Ephraim to the tribe of Judah. He awakes as it were from a long sleep (xliv. 24, cf. lxxiii. 20); for He seemed to sleep whilst Israel had become a servant to the heathen; He aroused Himself, like a hero exulting by reason of wine, *i.e.* like a hero whose courage is heightened by the strengthening and exhilarating influence of wine (Hengstenberg). הִתְרוֹנֵן is not the *Hithpal.* of רנן in the Arabic signification, which is alien to the Hebrew, to conquer, a meaning which we do not need here, and which is also not adapted to the reflexive form (Hitzig, without any precedent, renders thus: who allows himself to be conquered by wine), but *Hithpo.* of רָנַן: to shout most heartily, after the analogy of the reflexives הִתְאוֹנֵן, הִתְרוֹעֵעַ, הִתְנוֹדֵד. The most recent defeat of the enemy which the poet has before his mind is that of the Philistines. The form of expression in ver. 66 is moulded after 1 Sam. v. 6 sqq. God smote the Philistines most literally *in posteriora* (LXX., Vulgate, and Luther). Nevertheless ver. 66 embraces all the victories under Samuel, Saul, and David, from 1 Sam. ch. v. and onwards. Now, when they were able to bring the Ark, which had been brought down to the battle against the Philistines, to a settled resting-place again, God no longer chose Shiloh of Ephraim, but Judah and the mountain of Zion, which He had loved (xlvii. 5), of Benjamitish-Judæan (Josh. xv. 63, Judg. i. 8, 21)—but according to the promise (Deut. xxxiii. 12) and according to the distribution of the country (*vid.* on lxviii. 28) Benjamitish—Jerusalem.* There God built His Temple כְּמוֹ־רָמִים. Hitzig proposes instead of this to read כְּמְרוֹמִים; but if נְעִימִים, xvi. 6, signifies *amœna*, then רָמִים may signify *excelsa* (cf. Isa. xlv. 2 הֲדוּרִים, Jer. xvii. 6 חֲרֵרִים) and be poetically equivalent to מרומים: lasting as the heights of heaven, firm as the earth, which He hath founded for ever. Since the eternal duration of heaven and of the earth is quite consistent with a radical change in the manner of its duration, and that not less in the sense of the Old Testament than of the New (*vid. e.g.* Isa. lxv. 17), so the לְעוֹלָם applies not to the stone

---

* According to *B. Menachoth* 53*b*, Jedidiah (Solomon, 2 Sam. xii. 25) built the Temple in the province of Jedidiah (of Benjamin, Deut. xxxiii. 12).

building, but rather to the place where Jahve reveals Himself, and to the promise that He will have such a dwelling-place in Israel, and in fact in Judah. Regarded spiritually, *i.e.* essentially, apart from the accidental mode of appearing, the Temple upon Zion is as eternal as the kingship upon Zion with which the Psalm closes. The election of David gives its impress to the history of salvation even on into eternity. It is genuinely Asaphic that it is so designedly portrayed how the shepherd of the flock of Jesse (Isai) became the shepherd of the flock of Jahve, who was now to pasture old and young in Israel with the same care and tenderness as the ewe-lambs after which he went (עָלוֹת as in Gen. xxxiii. 13, and רָעָה בְּ, cf. 1 Sam. xvi. 11, xvii. 34, like מָשַׁל בְּ and the like). The poet is also able already to glory that he has fulfilled this vocation with a pure heart and with an intelligent mastery. And with this he closes. From the decease of David lyric and prophecy are retrospectively and prospectively turned towards David.

PSALM LXXIX.

SUPPLICATORY PRAYER IN A TIME OF DEVASTATION, OF BLOODSHED, AND OF DERISION.

1 ELOHIM, the heathen have pressed into Thine inheritance,
  They have defiled Thy holy Temple,
  They have turned Jerusalem into a heap of stones.
2 They have given the dead bodies of Thy servants for food
      to the birds of the heaven,
  The flesh of Thy saints to the beasts of the land;
3 They have poured out their blood like water
  Round about Jerusalem, and no one burieth them.
4 We are become a reproach to our neighbours,
  A mockery and derision to those who are round about us.

5 How long, Jahve, wilt Thou be angry for ever,
  Shall Thy jealousy burn like fire?!
6 Pour out Thy fury upon the heathen who know Thee not,
  And over the kingdoms, which call not upon Thy name!

7 For they devour Jacob,
  And have laid waste his dwelling-place.
8 Remember not against us the iniquities of the forefathers;
  Speedily let Thy tender mercies come to meet us,
  For we are brought very low.

9 Help us, O God of our salvation, for the glory of Thy
      Name,
  And deliver us, and expiate our sins for Thy Name's sake!
10 Wherefore shall the heathen say: where is now their God?—
  Let there be made known among the heathen before our
      eyes
  The avenging of the blood of Thy servants, which is shed.
11 Let the sighing of the prisoners come before Thee,
  According to the greatness of Thine arm spare the children
      of death.
12 And render unto our neighbours sevenfold into their bosom
  Their reproach, wherewith they have reproached Thee, O
      Lord!

13 And we, Thy people and the flock of Thy pasture,
  We will give Thee thanks for ever,
  In all generations will we tell forth Thy praise.

This Psalm is in every respect the pendant of Ps. lxxiv. The
points of contact are not merely matters of style (cf. lxxix. 5,
how long for ever? with lxxiv. 1, 10; lxxix. 10, יִוָּדַע, with lxxiv.
5; lxxix. 2, the giving over to the wild beasts, with lxxiv. 19,
14; lxxix. 13, the conception of Israel as of a flock, in which
respect Ps. lxxix. is judiciously appended to Ps. lxxviii. 70–72,
with Ps. lxxiv. 1, and also with lxxiv. 19). But the mutual relationships lie still deeper. Both Psalms have the same Asaphic
stamp, both stand in the same relation to Jeremiah, and both
send forth their complaint out of the same circumstances of the
time, concerning a destruction of the Temple and of Jerusalem,
such as only the age of the Seleucidæ (1 Macc. i. 31, iii. 45,
2 Macc. viii. 3) together with the Chaldæan period* can ex-

---

* According to *Sofrim* xviii. § 3, Ps. lxxix. and cxxxvii. are the Psalms
for the Kînoth-day, *i.e.* the 9th day of Ab, the day commemorative of the
Chaldæan and Roman destruction of Jerusalem.

hibit, and in conjunction with a defiling of the Temple and a massacre of the servants of God, of the *Chasîdim* (1 Macc. vii. 13, 2 Macc. xiv. 6), such as the age of the Seleucidæ exclusively can exhibit. The work of the destruction of the Temple which was in progress in Ps. lxxiv., appears in Ps. lxxix. as completed, and here, as in the former Psalm, one receives the impression of the outrages, not of some war, but of some persecution: it is straightway the religion of Israel for the sake of which the sanctuaries are destroyed and the faithful are massacred.

Apart from other striking accords, vers. 6, 7 are repeated verbatim in Jer. x. 25. It is in itself far more probable that Jeremiah here takes up the earlier language of the Psalm than that the reverse is the true relation; and, as Hengstenberg has correctly observed, this is also favoured by the fact that the words immediately before, viz. Jer. x. 24, originate out of Ps. vi. 2, and that the connection in the Psalm is a far closer one. But since there is no era of pre-Maccabæan history corresponding to the complaints of the Psalm,* Jeremiah is to be regarded in this instance as the example of the psalmist; and in point of fact the borrower is betrayed in vers. 6, 7 of the Psalm by the fact that the correct עַל of Jeremiah is changed into אֶל, the more elegant מִשְׁפָּחוֹת into מַמְלָכוֹת, and the plural אָכְלוּ into אָכַל, and the soaring exuberance of Jeremiah's expression is impaired by the omission of some of the words.

Vers. 1–4. The Psalm begins with a plaintive description, and in fact one that makes complaint to God. Its opening sounds like Lam. i. 10. The defiling does not exclude the reducing to ashes, it is rather spontaneously suggested in lxxiv. 7 in company with wilful incendiarism. The complaint in ver. 1c reminds one of the prophecy of Micah, ch. iii. 12, which in its time excited so much vexation (Jer. xxvi. 18); and ver. 2, Deut. xxviii. 26. עֲבָדֶיךָ confers upon those who were massacred the honour of martyrdom. The LXX. ren-

---

* Cassiodorus and Bruno observe: *deplorat Antiochi persecutionem tempore Machabeorum factam, tunc futuram.* And Notker adds: To those who have read the First Book of the Maccabees it (viz. the destruction bewailed in the Psalm) is familiar.

ders לעיים by εἰς ὀπωροφυλάκιον, a flourish taken from Isa. i. 8. Concerning the quotation from memory in 1 Macc. vii. 16 sq., *vid.* the introduction to Ps. lxxiv. The translator of the originally Hebrew First Book of the Maccabees even in other instances betrays an acquaintance with the Greek Psalter (cf. 1 Macc. i. 37, καὶ ἐξέχεαν αἷμα ἀθῶον κύκλῳ τοῦ ἁγιάσματος). "As water," *i.e.* (cf. Deut. xv. 23) without setting any value upon it and without any scruple about it. Ps. xliv. 14 is repeated in ver. 4. At the time of the Chaldæan catastrophe this applied more particularly to the Edomites.

Vers. 5–8. Out of the plaintive question how long? and whether endlessly God would be angry and cause His jealousy to continue to burn like a fire (Deut. xxxii. 22), grows up the prayer (ver. 6) that He would turn His anger against the heathen who are estranged from and hostile towards Him, and of whom He is now making use as a rod of anger against His people. The taking over of vers. 6 and 7 from Jer. x. 25 is not betrayed by the looseness of the connection of thought; but in themselves these four lines sound much more original in Jeremiah, and the style is exactly that of this prophet, cf. Jer. vi. 11, ii. 3, and frequently, xlix. 20. The אֶל, instead of עַל, which follows שָׁפַךְ is incorrect; the singular אָכַל gathers all up as in one mass, as in Isa. v. 26, xvii. 13. The fact that such power over Israel is given to the heathen world has its ground in the sins of Israel. From ver. 8 it may be inferred that the apostasy which raged earlier is now checked. רִאשֹׁנִים is not an adjective (Job xxxi. 28, Isa. lix. 2), which would have been expressed by עֲוֺנֹתֵינוּ הָרִאשֹׁנִים, but a genitive: the iniquities of the forefathers (Lev. xxvi. 14, cf. 39). On ver. 8c cf. Judg. vi. 6. As is evident from ver. 9, the poet does not mean that the present generation, itself guiltless, has to expiate the guilt of the fathers (on the contrary, Deut. xxiv. 16, 2 Kings xiv. 6, Ezek. xviii. 20); he prays as one of those who have turned away from the sins of the fathers, and who can now no longer consider themselves as placed under wrath, but under sin-pardoning and redeeming grace.

Vers. 9–12. The victory of the world is indeed not God's aim; therefore His own honour does not suffer that the world of which He has made use in order to chasten His people should for ever haughtily triumph. שִׁמְךָ is repeated with emphasis at the end of the petition in ver. 9, according to the figure epanaphora. עַל־דְּבַר = לְמַעַן, as in xlv. 5, cf. vii. 1, is a usage even of the language of the Pentateuch. Also the motive, "wherefore shall they say?" occurs even in the Tôra (Ex. xxxii. 12, cf. Num. xiv. 13–17, Deut. ix. 28). Here (cf. cxv. 2) it originates out of Joel ii. 17. The wish expressed in ver. 10*bc* is based upon Deut. xxxii. 43. The poet wishes in company with his cotemporaries, as eye-witnesses, to experience what God has promised in the early times, viz. that He will avenge the blood of His servants. The petition in ver. 11 runs like cii. 21, cf. xviii. 7. אָסִיר individualizingly is those who are carried away captive and incarcerated; בְּנֵי תְמוּתָה are those who, if God does not preserve them by virtue of the greatness (גֹּדֶל, cf. גְּדֹל Ex. xv. 16) of His arm, *i.e.* of His far-reaching omnipotence, succumb to the power of death as to a *patria potestas.** That the petition in ver. 12 recurs to the neighbouring peoples is explained by the fact, that these, who might most readily come to the knowledge of the God of Israel as the one living and true God, have the greatest degree of guilt on account of their reviling of God. The bosom is mentioned as that in which one takes up and holds that which is handed to him (Luke vi. 38); הֵשִׁיב (שִׁלַּם) אֶל (עַל)־חֵיק, as in Isa. lxv. 7, 6, Jer. xxxii. 18. A sevenfold requital (cf. Gen. iv. 15, 24) is a requital that is fully carried out as a criminal sentence, for seven is the number of a completed process.

Ver. 13. If we have thus far correctly hit upon the parts of which the Psalm is composed (9. 9. 9), then the lamentation closes with this tristichic vow of thanksgiving.

PSALM LXXX.

PRAYER FOR JAHVE'S VINE.

2 SHEPHERD of Israel, Oh give ear,
Thou who leadest Joseph like a flock,
Who sittest enthroned above the cherubim, Oh appear!

---

* The Arabic has just this notion in an active application, viz. *benî el-môt* = the heroes (destroyers) in the battle.

 3 Before Ephraim and Benjamin and Manasseh
   Stir up Thy warrior-strength,
   And come to our help!
 4 *Elohim, restore us,*
   And cause Thy face to shine, then shall we be helped!

 5 Jahve Elohim Tsebaôth,
   How long wilt Thou be angry when Thy people pray?!
 6 Thou gavest them to eat bread of tears,
   And gavest them to drink tears in great measure.
 7 Thou madest us a strife to our neighbours,
   And our enemies carry on their mockery.
 8 *Elohim Tsebaôth, restore us,*
   And cause Thy face to shine, then shall we be helped!

 9 Thou broughtest a vine out of Egypt,
   Thou didst drive out nations and plant it;
10 Thou hast made a space before it,
   And it struck roots and filled the earth.
11 Mountains were covered by its shadow,
   And by its boughs, the cedars of God.
12 It spread its branches unto the sea,
   And towards the river its young shoots.

13 Why hast Thou broken down its hedges,
   That all who pass by the way do pluck it?
14 The boar out of the forest doth devour it,
   And that which roameth the field doth feed upon it.
15 Elohim Tsebaôth, Oh look again from heaven and behold,
   And accept this vine!
16 And be the protection of that which Thy right hand hath
     planted,
   And over the son, whom Thou hast firmly chosen for
     Thyself.

17 Burnt with fire, swept away,
   Before the threatening of Thy countenance they perish.
18 Oh hold Thy hand over the man of Thy right hand,
   Over the son of man whom Thou hast chosen for
     Thyself;

19 And we will not go back from Thee—
   Quicken us, and we will celebrate Thy Name.
20 *Jahve Elohim Tsebaôth, restore us,*
   Cause Thy face to shine, then shall we be helped!

With the words *We are Thy people and the flock of Thy pasture*, Ps. lxxix. closes; and Ps. lxxx. begins with a cry to the Shepherd of Israel. Concerning the inscription of the Psalm: *To be practised after the " Lilies, the testimony . . .," by Asaph, a Psalm, vid.* on xlv. 1, *supra*, p. 76 sq. The LXX. renders, εἰς τὸ τέλος (unto the end), ὑπὲρ τῶν ἀλλοιωθησομένων (which is unintelligible and ungrammatical = אֶל־שֹׁשַׁנִּים), μαρτύριον τῷ Ἀσάφ (as the accentuation also unites these words closely by *Tarcha*), ψαλμὸς ὑπὲρ τοῦ Ἀσσυρίου (cf. lxxvi. 1), perhaps a translation of אֶל־אַשּׁוּר, an inscribed note which took the " boar out of the forest" as an emblem of Assyria. This hint is important. It solves the riddle why Joseph represents all Israel in ver. 2, and why the tribes of Joseph in particular are mentioned in ver. 3, and why in the midst of these Benjamin, whom like descent from Rachel and chagrin, never entirely overcome, on account of the loss of the kingship drew towards the brother-tribes of Joseph. Moreover the tribe of Benjamin had only partially remained to the house of David since the division of the kingdom,* so that this triad is to be regarded as an expansion of the " Joseph" (ver. 2). After the northern kingdom had exhausted its resources in endless feuds with Damascene Syria, it succumbed to the world-wide dominion of Assyria in the sixth year of Hezekiah, in consequence of the heavy visitations which are closely associated with the names

---

* It is true we read that Benjamin stood on the side of Rehoboam with Judah after the division of the kingdom (1 Kings xii. 21), Judah and Benjamin appear as parts of the kingdom of Judah (2 Chron. xi. 3, 23, xv. 8 sq., and frequently); but if, according to 1 Kings xi. 13, 32, 36, only שֵׁבֶט אֶחָד remains to the house of David, this is Judah, inasmuch as Benjamin did not remain entirely under the Davidic sceptre, and Simeon is to be left out of account (cf. *Genesis*, S. 603); the Benjamitish cities of Bethel, Gilgal, and Jericho belonged to the northern kingdom, but, as in the case of Rama (1 Kings xv. 21 sq.), not without being contested (cf. *e.g.* 2 Chron. xiii. 19); the boundaries were therefore fluctuating, *vid.* Ewald, *Geschichte des Volkes Israel* (3d ed.), S. 439–441.

of the Assyrian kings Pul, Tiglath-pileser, and Shalmaneser.
The psalmist, as it seems, prays in a time in which the oppression of Assyria rested heavily upon the kingdom of Ephraim,
and Judah saw itself threatened with ruin when this bulwark
should have fallen. We must not, however, let it pass without
notice that our Psalm has this designation of the nation according to the tribes of Joseph in common with other pre-exilic
Psalms of Asaph (lxxvii. 16, lxxviii. 9, lxxxi. 6). It is a
characteristic belonging in common to this whole group of
Psalms. Was Asaph, the founder of this circle of songs, a
native, perhaps, of one of the Levite cities of the province of
the tribe of Ephraim or Manasseh?

The Psalm consists of five eight-line strophes, of which the
first, second, and fifth close with the refrain, " Elohim, restore
us, let Thy countenance shine forth, then shall we be helped!"
This prayer grows in earnestness. The refrain begins the first
time with *Elohim*, the second time with *Elohim Tsebaôth*, and
the third time with a threefold *Jahve Elohim Tsebaôth*, with
which the second strophe (ver. 5) also opens.

Vers. 2–4. The first strophe contains nothing but petition.
First of all the nation is called *Israel* as springing from Jacob;
then, as in lxxxi. 6, *Joseph*, which, where it is distinct from
Jacob or *Judah*, is the name of the kingdom of the ten tribes
(*vid.* Caspari on Obad. ver. 18), or at least of the northern
tribes (lxxvii. 16, lxxviii. 67 sq.). Ver. 3 shows that it is also
these that are pre-eminently intended here. The fact that in
the blessing of Joseph, Jacob calls God a Shepherd (רֹעֶה), Gen.
xlviii. 15, xlix. 24, perhaps has somewhat to do with the choice of
the first two names. In the third, the sitting enthroned in the
sanctuary here below and in the heaven above blend together;
for the Old Testament is conscious of a mutual relationship
between the earthly and the heavenly temple (היכל) until the
one merges entirely in the other. The cherûbim, which God
enthrones, *i.e.* upon which He sits enthroned, are the bearers
of the chariot (מרכבה) of the Ruler of the world (*vid.* xviii.
11). With הוֹפִיעָה (from יפע, يفع, *eminere, emicare*, as in the
Asaph Psalm l. 2) the poet prays that He would appear in His
splendour of light, *i.e.* in His fiery bright, judging, and rescuing

doxa, whether as directly visible, or even as only recognisable
by its operation.   Both the comparison " after the manner
of a flock" and the verb נֹהֵג are Asaphic, lxxviii. 52, cf. 26.
Just so also the names given to the nation.   The designation
of Israel after the tribes of *Ephraim* and *Manasseh* attaches
itself to the name *Joseph*; and the two take the brother after
the flesh into their midst, of whom the beloved Rachel was the
mother as well as of Joseph, the father of Ephraim and
Manasseh.   In Num. ch. ii. also, these three are not separated,
but have their camp on the west side of the Tabernacle.   May
God again put into activity—which is the meaning of עוֹרֵר
(*excitare*) in distinction from הֵעִיר (*expergefacere*)—His נבורה,
the need for the energetic intervention of which now makes
itself felt, before these three tribes, *i.e.* by becoming their victorious leader.   לְכָה is a summoning imperative.*   Concerning
יְשֻׁעָתָה *vid.* on iii. 3 ; the construction with *Lamed* says as little
against the accusative adverbial rendering of the *ah* set forth
there as does the *Beth* of בַּחֹרְשָׁה (in the wood) in 1 Sam. xxiii.
15, *vid.* Böttcher's *Neue Aehrenlese*, Nos. 221, 384, 449.   It
is not a bringing back out of the Exile that is prayed for by
הֲשִׁיבֵנוּ, for, according to the whole impression conveyed by the
Psalm, the people are still on the soil of their fatherland ; but
in their present feebleness they are no longer like themselves,
they stand in need of divine intervention in order again to
attain a condition that is in harmony with the promises, in
order to become themselves again.   May God then cause His
long hidden countenance to brighten and shine upon them, then
shall they be helped as they desire (וְנִוָּשֵׁעָה).

Vers. 5–8.   In the second strophe there issues forth bitter
complaint concerning the form of wrath which the present
assumes, and, thus confirmed, the petition rises anew.   The
transferring of the smoking (עָשֵׁן) of God's nostrils = the hard
breathing of anger (lxxiv. 1, Deut. xxix. 19 [20]), to God
Himself is bold, but in keeping with the spirit of the Biblical

---

* Not a pronoun : to Thee it belongs to be for salvation for us, as the
Talmud, Midrash, and Masora (*vid.* Norzi) take it ; wherefore in *J. Succa*
54c it is straightway written לך.   Such a לְךָ=לכה is called in the language
of the Masora, and even in the Midrash (*Exod. Rabba*, fol. 121), לכה וראית
(*vid.* Buxtorf, *Tiberias*, p. 245).

view of the wrath of God (*vid.* on xviii. 9), so that there is no need
to avoid the expression by calling in the aid of the Syriac word
עָשֵׁן, to be strong, powerful (why art Thou hard, why dost Thou
harden Thyself . . .). The perfect after עַד־מָתַי has the sense of
a present with a retrospective glance, as in Ex. x. 3, cf. עַד־אָנָה,
Ex. xvi. 28, Hab. i. 2. The construction of עָשֵׁן with בְּ is not
to be understood after the analogy of חָרָה בְ (to kindle = to be
angry against any one), for the prayer of the people is not an
object of wrath, but only not a means of turning it aside.
While the prayer is being presented, God veils Himself in the
smoke of wrath, through which it is not able to penetrate. The
LXX. translators have read בתפלת עבדיך, for they render ἐπὶ
τὴν προσευχὴν τῶν δούλων σου (for which the common reading
is τοῦ δούλου σου). Bread of tears is, according to xlii. 4, bread
consisting of tears; tears, running down in streams upon the
lips of the praying and fasting one, are his meat and his drink.
הִשְׁקָה with an accusative signifies to give something to drink,
and followed by *Beth*, to give to drink by means of something,
but it is not to be translated: *potitandum das eis cum lacrymis
trientem* (De Dieu, von Ortenberg, and Hitzig). שָׁלִישׁ (Talmudic, a third part) is the accusative of more precise definition
(Vatablus, Gesenius, Olshausen, and Hupfeld): by thirds (LXX.
ἐν μέτρῳ, Symmachus μέτρῳ); for a third of an ephah is cer
tainly a very small measure for the dust of the earth (Isa. xl.
12), but a large one for tears. The neighbours are the neighbouring nations, to whom Israel is become מָדוֹן, an object, a
butt of contention. In לָמוֹ is expressed the pleasure which the
mocking gives them.

Vers. 9–20. The complaint now assumes a detailing character in this strophe, inasmuch as it contrasts the former days
with the present; and the ever more and more importunate
prayer moulds itself in accordance therewith. The retrospective description begins, as is rarely the case, with the second
modus, inasmuch as " the speaker thinks more of the bare nature
of the act than of the time" (Ew. § 136, *b*). As in the blessing
of Jacob (Gen. xlix. 22) Joseph is compared to the layer
(בֵּן) of a fruitful growth (פֹּרָת), whose shoots (בָּנוֹת) climb over
the wall: so here Israel is compared to a vine (Gen. xlix. 22;
בֶּן פֹּרִיָּה, cxxviii. 3), which has become great in Egypt and been
transplanted thence into the Land of Promise. הִפִּיעַ, LXX.

μεταίρειν, as in Job xix. 10, perhaps with an allusion to the
מסעים of the people journeying to Canaan (lxxviii. 52).* Here
God made His vine a way and a place (פִּנָּה, to clear, from פָּנָה,
to turn, turn aside, Arabic *fanija*, to disappear, pass away; root
פֹּן, to urge forward), and after He had secured to it a free soil
and unchecked possibility of extension, it (the vine) rooted its
roots, *i.e.* struck them ever deeper and wider, and filled the
earth round about (cf. the antitype in the final days, Isa.
xxvii. 6). The Israelitish kingdom of God extended itself on
every side in accordance with the promise. תְּשַׁלַּח (cf. Ezek.
xvii. 6, and vegetable שֶׁלַח, a shoot) also has the vine as its
subject, like תַּשְׁרֵשׁ. Vers. 11 and 12 state this in a continued
allegory, by the "mountains" pointing to the southern boundary, by the "cedars" to the northern, by the "sea" to the
western, and by the "river" (Euphrates) to the eastern boundary of the country (*vid.* Deut. xi. 24 and other passages). צִלָּהּ
and עֲנָפֶיהָ are accusatives of the so-called more remote object
(Ges. § 143, 1). קָצִיר is a cutting = a branch; יוֹנֶקֶת, a (vegetable) sucker = a young, tender shoot; אַרְזֵי־אֵל, the cedars of
Lebanon as being living monuments of the creative might of
God. The allegory exceeds the measure of the reality of
nature, inasmuch as this is obliged to be extended according to
the reality of that which is typified and historical. But how
unlike to the former times is the present! The poet asks
"wherefore?" for the present state of things is a riddle to him.
The surroundings of the vine are torn down; all who come in
contact with it pluck it (אָרָה, to pick off, pluck off, Talmudic
of the gathering of figs); the boar out of the wood (מִיַּעַר with
עַיִן תְּלוּיָה, suspended *Ajin†*) cuts it off (כִּרְסֵם, formed out of כַּסַם

---

* *Exod. Rabba*, ch. xliv., with reference to this passage, says: "When
husbandmen seek to improve a vine, what do they do? They root (עוקרין)
it out of its place and plant (שׁותלין) it in another." And *Levit. Rabba*,
ch. xxxvi., says: "As one does not plant a vine in a place where there
are great, rough stones, but examines the ground and then plants it, so
didst Thou drive out peoples and didst plant it," etc.

† According to *Kiddushin*, 30a, because this *Ajin* is the middle letter
of the Psalter as the *Waw* of גחון, Lev. xi. 42, is the middle letter of the
Tôra. One would hardly like to be at the pains of proving the correctness
of this statement; nevertheless in the seventeenth century there lived one
Laymarius, a clergyman, who was not afraid of this trouble, and found

= נָזֶם*), viz. with its tusks; and that which moves about the
fields (vid. concerning זִיז, l. 11), i.e. the untractable, lively wild
beast, devours it.   Without doubt the poet associates a distinct
nation with the wild boar in his mind; for animals are also in
other instances the emblems of nations, as e.g. the leviathan,
the water-serpent, the behemoth (Isa. xxx. 6), and flies (Isa.
vii. 18) are emblems of Egypt.   The Midrash interprets it of
Seïr-Edom, and זִיז שָׂדִי, according to Gen. xvi. 12, of the nomadic
Arabs.

In ver. 15 the prayer begins for the third time with threefold urgency, supplicating for the vine renewed divine providence, and a renewal of the care of divine grace.   We have
divided the verse differently from the accentuation, since שׁוּב־נָא
הַבֵּט is to be understood according to Ges. § 142.   The junction by means of וְ is at once opposed to the supposition that
וְכַנָּה in ver. 16 signifies a slip or plant, plantam (Targum, Syriac,
Aben-Ezra, Kimchi, and others), and that consequently the
whole of ver. 16 is governed by וּפְקֹד.   Nor can it mean its (the
vine's) stand or base, כַּן (Böttcher), since one does not plant a
"stand."   The LXX. renders וכנה: καὶ κατάρτισαι, which is
imper. aor. 1. med., therefore in the sense of כּוֹנְנָה.†   But the
alternation of עַל (cf. Prov. ii. 11, and جَنَّ علی, to cover over)
with the accusative of the object makes it more natural to
derive כנה, not from כָּנַן = כּוּן, but from גָּנַן = كَنَّ כָּנַן, to cover,
conceal, protect (whence كِنّ, a covering, shelter, hiding-place):

---

the calculations of the Masora (e.g. that אֲדֹנָי ה׳ occurs 222 times) in part
inaccurate; vid. Monatliche Unterredungen, 1691, S. 467, and besides, Geiger,
Urschrift und Uebersetzungen der Bibel, S. 258 f.

* Saadia appropriately renders it يَقْرِضُهَا, by referring, as does Dunash
also, to the Talmudic קִרְסֵם, which occurs of ants, like قَرَض of rodents.
So Peah ii. § 7, Menachoth 71b, on which Rashi observes, "the locust
(חגב) is accustomed to eat from above, the ant tears off the corn-stalk
from below."   Elsewhere קירסם denotes the breaking off of dry branches
from the tree, as זָרַד the removal of green branches.

† Perhaps the Caph majusculum is the result of an erasure that required to be made, vid. Geiger, Urschrift, S. 295.   Accordingly the Ajin
suspensum might also be the result of a later inserted correction, for there
is a Phœnician inscription that has יר (wood, forest); vid. Levy, Phöni-
zisches Wörterbuch, S. 22.

and protect him whom . . . or: protect what Thy right hand
has planted. The pointing certainly seems to take כנה as the
feminine of כֵּן (LXX., Dan. xi. 7, φυτόν); for an *imperat.
paragog. Kal* of the form כַּנֵּה does not occur elsewhere, although
it might have been regarded by the punctuists as possible from
the form גַּל, *volve*, cxix. 22. If it is regarded as impossible,
then one might read כֻּנָּה. At any rate the word is imperative,
as the following אֲשֶׁר, *eum quem*, also shows, instead of which,
if כנה were a substantive, one would expect to find a relative
clause without אשר, as in ver. 16*b*. Moreover ver. 16*b* requires
this, since פָּקַד עַל can only be used of visiting with punishment.
And who then would the slip (branch) and the son of man be
in distinction from the vine? If we take כנה as imperative,
then, as one might expect, the vine and the son of man are
both the people of God. The Targum renders ver. 16*b* thus:
"and upon the King Messiah, whom Thou hast established for
Thyself," after Ps. ii. and Dan. vii. 13; but, as in the latter
passage, it is not the Christ Himself, but the nation out of
which He is to proceed, that is meant. אִמֵּץ has the sense of
firm appropriation, as in Isa. xliv. 14, inasmuch as the notion
of making fast passes over into that of laying firm hold of, of
seizure. Rosenmüller well renders it: *quem adoptatum tot
nexibus tibi adstrinxisti*. The figure of the vine, which rules
all the language here, is also still continued in ver. 17; for the
partt. fem. refer to גֶּפֶן,—the verb, however, may take the plural
form, because those of Israel are this "vine," which *combusta
igne, succisa* (as in Isa. xxxiii. 12; Aramaic, to cut off, tear off,

in ver. 13 the Targum word for אָרָה; Arabic, ⟨كسح⟩, to clear

away, peel off), is just perishing, or hangs in danger of destruction (יאבֵדוּ) before the threatening of the wrathful countenance
of God. The absence of anything to denote the subject, and
the form of expression, which still keeps within the circle of
the figure of the vine, forbid us to understand this ver. 17 of
the extirpation of the foes. According to the sense תְּהִי־יָדְךָ עַל*

---

* The תְהִי has *Gaja*, like שְׂאוּ־זִמְרָה (lxxxi. 3), בְּנִי־נֵכָר (cxliv. 7), and
the like. This *Gaja* beside the *Shebâ* (instead of beside the following vowel)
belongs to the peculiarities of the metrical books, which in general, on
account of their more melodious mode of delivery, have many such a *Gaja*

coincides with the supplicatory כנה על. It is Israel that is called בֵּן in ver. 16, as being the son whom Jahve has called into being in Egypt, and then called out of Egypt to Himself and solemnly declared to be His son on Sinai (Ex. iv. 22, Hos. xi. 1), and who is now, with a play upon the name of Benjamin in ver. 3 (cf. ver. 16), called אִישׁ יְמִינֶךָ, as being the people which Jahve has preferred before others, and has placed at His right hand* for the carrying out of His work of salvation; who is called, however, at the same time בֶּן־אָדָם, because belonging to a humanity that is feeble in itself, and thoroughly conditioned and dependent. It is not the more precise designation of the "son of man" that is carried forward by וְלֹא־נָסוֹג, "and who has not drawn back from Thee" (Hupfeld, Hitzig, and others), but it is, as the same relation which is repeated in ver. 19*b* shows, the apodosis of the preceding petition: then shall we never depart from Thee; נָסוֹג being not a participle, as in xliv. 19, but a *plene* written voluntative: *recedamus*, vowing new obedience as thanksgiving for the divine preservation. To the prayer in ver. 18 corresponds, then, the prayer תְּחַיֵּנוּ, which is expressed as future (which can rarely be avoided, Ew. § 229), with a vow of thanksgiving likewise following: then will we call with Thy name, *i.e.* make it the medium and matter of solemn proclamation. In ver. 20 the refrain of this Psalm, which is laid out as a trilogy, is repeated for the third time. The name of God is here threefold.

---

beside *Shebâ*, which does not occur in the prose books. Thus, *e.g.*, יְהוָֹה and אֱלֹהִים always have *Gaja* beside the *Shebâ* when they have *Rebia magnum* without a conjunctive, probably because *Rebia* and *Dechî* had such a fulness of tone that a first stroke fell even upon the *Shebâ*-letters.

    * Pinsker punctuates thus: Let Thy hand be upon the man, Thy right hand upon the son of man, whom, etc.; but the impression that יְמִינֶךָ and אמצתה לך coincide is so strong, that no one of the old interpreters (from the LXX. and Targum onwards) has been able to free himself from it.

PSALM LXXXI.

EASTER FESTIVAL SALUTATION AND DISCOURSE.

2 CAUSE shouts of joy to resound unto Elohim, our safe
      retreat,
  Make a joyful noise unto the God of Jacob.
3 Raise a song and sound the timbrel,
  The pleasant cithern together with the harp.
4 Blow the horn at the new moon,
  At the full moon, in honour of the day of our feast.
5 For a statute for Israel is it,
  An ordinance of the God of Jacob.
6 A testimony hath He laid it down in Joseph,
  When He went forth over the land of Egypt—
  A language of one not known did I hear.

7 I have removed his back from the burden,
  His hands were freed from the task-basket.
8 In distress didst thou cry, and I delivered thee,
  I answered thee in a covering of thunder,
  I proved thee at the waters of Meribah.   (*Sela.*)
9 Hear, O my people, and I will testify unto thee;
  Israel, Oh that thou wouldst hearken unto Me!—
10 Let there be among thee no strange god,
  And do not thou worship a god of a foreign country.
11 I, I am Jahve thy God,
  Who led thee up out of the land of Egypt—
  Open wide thy mouth, and I will fill it.

12 But My people hearkened not unto My voice,
  And Israel did not obey Me.
13 Then I cast them forth to the hardness of their heart,
  They went on in their own counsels.
14 Oh that My people would be obedient unto Me,
  That Israel would walk in My ways!
15 Suddenly would I humble their enemies,
  And against their oppressors turn My hand.
16 The haters of Jahve should submit themselves to Him,

And their time should endure for ever.
17 He fed them with the fat of wheat,
   And with honey out of the rock did I satisfy thee.

Ps. lxxx., which looks back into the time of the leading forth out of Egypt, is followed by another with the very same Asaphic thoroughly characteristic feature of a retrospective glance at Israel's early history (cf. more particularly lxxxi. 11 with lxxx. 9). In Ps. lxxxi. the lyric element of Ps. lxxvii. is combined with the didactic element of Ps. lxxviii. The unity of these Psalms is indubitable. All three have towards the close the appearance of being fragmentary. For the author delights to ascend to the height of his subject and to go down into the depth of it, without returning to the point from which he started. In Ps. lxxvii. Israel as a whole was called "the sons of Jacob and Joseph;" in Ps. lxxviii. we read "the sons of Ephraim" instead of the whole nation; here it is briefly called "Joseph." This also indicates the one author. Then Ps. lxxxi., exactly like lxxix., is based upon the Pentateuchal history in Exodus and Deuteronomy. Jahve Himself speaks through the mouth of the poet, as He did once through the mouth of Moses—Asaph is κατ᾽ ἐξοχήν the prophet (חֹזֶה) among the psalmists. The transition from one form of speech to another which accompanies the rapid alternation of feelings, what the Arabs call *talwîn el-chitâb*, " a colouring of a speech by a change of the persons," is also characteristic of him, as later on of Micah (*e.g.* vi. 15 sq.).

This Ps. lxxxi. is according to ancient custom the Jewish New Year's Psalm, the Psalm of the Feast of Trumpets (Num. xxix. 1), therefore the Psalm of the first (and second) of Tishri; it is, however, a question whether the blowing of the horn (*shophar*) at the new moon, which it calls upon them to do, does not rather apply to the first of Nisan, to the ecclesiastical New Year. In the weekly liturgy of the Temple it was the Psalm for the Thursday.

The poet calls upon them to give a jubilant welcome to the approaching festive season, and in vers. 7 sqq. Jahve Himself makes Himself heard as the Preacher of the festival. He reminds those now living of His loving-kindness towards ancient Israel, and admonishes them not to incur the guilt of like

unfaithfulness, in order that they may not lose the like tokens
of His loving-kindness. What festive season is it? Either
the Feast of the Passover or the Feast of Tabernacles; for it
must be one of these two feasts which begin on the day of the
full moon. Because it is one having reference to the redemption of Israel out of Egypt, the Targum, Talmud (more particularly *Rosh ha-Shana*, where this Psalm is much discussed),
Midrash, and Sohar understand the Feast of Tabernacles;
because vers. 2–4*a* ⸗eem to refer to the new moon of the
seventh month, which is celebrated before other new moons
(Num. x. 10) as יוֹם הַתְּרוּעָה (Num. xxix. 1, cf. Lev. xxiii. 24), *i.e.*
to the first of Tishri, the civil New Year; and the blowing of
horns at the New Year is, certainly not according to Scripture, but yet according to tradition (*vid.* Maimonides, *Hilchoth
Shophar* i. 2), a very ancient arrangement. Nevertheless we
must give up this reference of the Psalm to the first of Tishri
and to the Feast of Tabernacles, which begins with the fifteenth
of Tishri:—(1) Because between the high feast-day of the
first of Tishri and the Feast of Tabernacles on the fifteenth to
the twenty-first (twenty-second) of Tishri lies the great day of
Atonement on the tenth of Tishri, which would be ignored, by
greeting the festive season with a joyful noise from the first of
Tishri forthwith to the fifteenth. (2) Because the remembrance of the redemption of Israel clings far more characteristically to the Feast of the Passover than to the Feast of
Tabernacles. This latter appears in the oldest law-giving (Ex.
xxiii. 16, xxxiv. 22) as חַג הָאָסִיף, *i.e.* as a feast of the ingathering
of the autumn fruits, and therefore as the closing festival of the
whole harvest; it does not receive the historical reference to
the journey through the desert, and therewith its character of
a feast of booths or arbours, until the addition in Lev. xxiii.
39–44, having reference to the carrying out of the celebration
of the feasts in Canaan; whereas the feast which begins with
the full moon of Nisan has, it is true, not been entirely free of
all reference to agriculture, but from the very beginning bears
the historical names פֶּסַח and חַג הַמַּצּוֹת. (3) Because in the
Psalm itself, viz. in ver. 6*b*, allusion is made to the fact which
the Passover commemorates.

Concerning עַל־הַגִּתִּית *vid.* on viii. 1. The symmetrical, stichic
plan of the Psalm is clear: the schema is 11. 12. 12.

Vers. 2–6. The summons in ver. 2 is addressed to the whole congregation, inasmuch as הָרִיעוּ is not intended of the clanging of the trumpets, but as in Ezra iii. 11, and frequently. The summons in ver. 3 is addressed to the Levites, the appointed singers and musicians in connection with the divine services, 2 Chron. v. 12, and frequently. The summons in ver. 4 is addressed to the priests, to whom was committed not only the blowing of the two (later on a hundred and twenty, *vid.* 2 Chron. v. 12) silver trumpets, but who appear also in Josh. vi. 4 and elsewhere (cf. xlvii. 6 with 2 Chron. xx. 28) as the blowers of the shophar. The Talmud observes that since the destruction of the Temple the names of instruments שׁוֹפְרָא and חֲצוֹצַרְתָּא are wont to be confounded one for the other (*B. Sabbath* 36a, *Succa* 34a), and, itself confounding them, infers from Num. x. 10 the duty and significance of the blowing of the shophar (*B. Erachin 3b*). The LXX. also renders both by σάλπιγξ; but the Biblical language mentions שׁוֹפָר and חֲצֹצְרָה, a horn (more especially a ram's horn) and a (metal) trumpet, side by side in xcviii. 6, 1 Chron. xv. 28, and is therefore conscious of a difference between them. The Tôra says nothing of the employment of the shophar in connection with divine service, except that the commencement of every fiftieth year, which on this very account is called שְׁנַת הַיּוֹבֵל, *annus buccinæ*, is to be made known by the horn signal throughout all the land (Lev. xxv. 9). But just as tradition by means of an inference from analogy derives the blowing of the shophar on the first of Tishri, the beginning of the common year, from this precept, so on the ground of the passage of the Psalm before us, assuming that בַּחֹדֶשׁ, LXX. ἐν νεομηνίᾳ, refers not to the first of Tishri but to the first of Nisan, we may suppose that the beginning of every month, but, in particular, the beginning of the month which was at the same time the beginning of the ecclesiastical year, was celebrated by a blowing of the shophar, as, according to Josephus, *Bell.* iv. 9, 12, the beginning and close of the Sabbath was announced from the top of the Temple by a priest with the salpinx. The poet means to say that the Feast of the Passover is to be saluted by the congregation with shouts of joy, by the Levites with music, and even beginning from the new moon (*neomenia*) of the Passover month with blowing of shophars, and that this is to

be continued at the Feast of the Passover itself. The Feast
of the Passover, for which Hupfeld devises a gloomy physiognomy,* was a joyous festival, the Old Testament Christmas.
2 Chron. xxx. 21 testifies to the exultation of the people and
the boisterous music of the Levite priests, with which it was
celebrated. According to Num. x. 10, the trumpeting of the
priests was connected with the sacrifices ; and that the slaying
of the paschal lambs took place amidst the *Tantaratan* of the
priests (long-drawn notes interspersed with sharp shrill ones,
תקיעה תרועה ותקיעה), is expressly related of the post-exilic service at least.†

The phrase נָתַן תֹּף proceeds from the phrase נָתַן קוֹל, according
to which נָתַן directly means: to attune, strike up, cause to be
heard. Concerning בֶּסֶה (Prov. vii. 20 כֶּסֶא) tradition is uncertain. The Talmudic interpretation (*B. Rosh ha-Shana* 8*b*,
Betza 16*a*, and the Targum which is taken from it), according
to which it is the day of the new moon (the first of the month),
on which the moon hides itself, *i.e.* is not to be seen at all in
the morning, and in the evening only for a short time immediately after sunset, and the interpretation that is adopted by a
still more imposing array of authorities (LXX., Vulgate,
Menahem, Rashi, Jacob Tam, Aben-Ezra, Parchon, and others),
according to which a time fixed by computation (from בֶּסֶה =
בֶּסֶם, *computare*) is so named in general, are outweighed by the
usage of the Syriac, in which *keso* denotes the full moon as the
moon with covered, *i.e.* filled-up orb, and therefore the fifteenth
of the month, but also the time from that point onwards, perhaps because then the moon covers itself, inasmuch as its
shining surface appears each day less large (cf. the Peshîto,
1 Kings xii. 32 of the fifteenth day of the eighth month,
2 Chron. vii. 10 of the twenty-third day of the seventh month,
in both instances of the Feast of Tabernacles), after which, too,
in the passage before us it is rendered *wa-b-kese*, which a Syro-
Arabic glossary (in Rosenmüller) explains *festa quæ sunt in
medio mensis*. The Peshîto here, like the Targum, proceeds

---

* In the first of his *Commentationes de primitiva et vera festorum apud
Hebræos ratione*, 1851, 4to.

† *Vid.* my essay on the Passover rites during the time of the second
Temple in the *Luther. Zeitschr.* 1855; and cf. Armknecht, *Die heilige
Psalmodie* (1855), S. 5.

from the reading חֲגֵּימּ, which, following the LXX. and the
best texts, is to be rejected in comparison with the singular
חַגֵּנּ. If, however, it is to be read חגנו, and כֵּסֶה (according to
Kimchi with *Segol* not merely in the second syllable, but with
double *Segol* כֶּסֶה, after the form מְנָא = מַנָּא) signifies not *inter-
lunium*, but *plenilunium* (instead of which also Jerome has *in
medio mense*, and in Prov. vii. 20, *in die plenæ lunæ*, Aquila
ἡμέρα πανσελήνου), then what is meant is either the Feast of
Tabernacles, which is called absolutely הֶחָג in 1 Kings viii. 2
(2 Chron. v. 3) and elsewhere, or the Passover, which is also
so called in Isa. xxx. 29 and elsewhere. Here, as ver. 5 will
convince us, the latter is intended, the Feast of unleavened
bread, the porch of which, so to speak, is עֶרֶב פֶּסַח together with
the לֵיל שִׁמֻּרִים (Ex. xii. 42), the night from the fourteenth to
the fifteenth of Nisan. In vers. 2, 3 they are called upon to
give a welcome to this feast. The blowing of the shophar is to
announce the commencement of the Passover month, and at
the commencement of the Passover day which opens the Feast
of unleavened bread it is to be renewed. The ל of לְיוֹם is not
meant temporally, as perhaps in Job xxi. 30: at the day = on
the day; for why was it not ביום? It is rather: towards the
day, but בכסה assumes that the day has already arrived; it is
the same *Lamed* as in ver. 2, the blowing of the shophar is to
concern this feast-day, it is to sound in honour of it.

Vers. 5 and 6 now tell whence the feast which is to be met
with singing and music has acquired such a high significance:
it is a divine institution coming from the time of the redemption by the hand of Moses. It is called חֹק as being a legally
sanctioned decree, מִשְׁפָּט as being a lawfully binding appointment, and עֵדוּת as being a positive declaration of the divine will.
The ל in לְיִשְׂרָאֵל characterizes Israel as the receiver, in לֵאלֹהֵי the
God of Israel as the Owner, *i.e.* Author and Lawgiver. By
בְּצֵאתוֹ the establishing of the statute is dated back to the time
of the Exodus; but the statement of the time of its being established, "when He went out over the land of Egypt," cannot be
understood of the exodus of the people out of Egypt, natural
as this may be here, where Israel has just been called יְהוֹסֵף
(pathetic for יוֹסֵף), by a comparison with Gen. xli. 45, where
Joseph is spoken of in the same words. For this expression
does not describe the going forth out of a country, perhaps in the

sight of its inhabitants, Num. xxxiii. 3, cf. Ex. xiv. 8 (Hengstenberg), but the going out over a country. Elohim is the
subject, and צאת is to be understood according to Ex. xi. 4
(Kimchi, De Dieu, Dathe, Rosenmüller, and others): when
He went out for judgment over the land of Egypt (cf. Mic.
i. 3). This statement of the time of itself at once decides the
reference of the Psalm to the Passover, which commemorates
the sparing of Israel at that time (Ex. xii. 27), and which was
instituted on that very night of judgment. The accentuation
divides the verse correctly. According to this, שְׂפַת לֹא־יָדַעְתִּי אֶשְׁמָע
is not a relative clause to מצרים: where I heard a language that
I understood not (cxiv. 1). Certainly ידע שׂפה, "to understand
a language," is an expression that is in itself not inadmissible
(cf. ידע ספר, to understand writing, to be able to read, Isa. xxix.
11 sq.), the selection of which instead of the more customary
phrase שׁמע לשׁון (Deut. xxviii. 49, Isa. xxxiii. 19, Jer. v. 15)
might be easily intelligible here beside אשׁמע; but the omission
of the שָׁם (אֲשֶׁר) is harsh, the thought is here purposeless, and
excluded with our way of taking בצאתו. From the speech of
God that follows it is evident that the clause is intended to
serve as an introduction of this divine speech, whether it now
be rendered *sermonem quem non novi* (cf. xviii. 44, *populus
quem non novi*), or *alicujus, quem non novi* (Ges. § 123, rem. 1),
both of which are admissible. Is it now in some way an introduction to the following speech of God as one which it has
been suddenly given to the psalmist to hear: "An unknown
language, or the language of one unknown, do I hear"? Thus
Döderlein explains it: *Subitanea et digna poetico impetu digressio,
cum vates sese divino adflatu subito perculsum sentit et oraculum
audire sibi persuadet;* and in the same way De Wette, Olshausen, Hupfeld, and others. But the oracle of God cannot
appear so strange to the Israelitish poet and seer as the spirit-
voice to Eliphaz (Job iv. 16); and moreover אשׁמע after the
foregoing historical predicates has the presumption of the imperfect signification in its favour. Thus, then, it will have to be
interpreted according to Ex. vi. 2 sq. It was the language of
a known, but still also unknown God, which Israel heard in
the redemption of that period. It was the God who had been
made manifest as יהוה only, so to speak, by way of prelude
hitherto, who now appeared at this juncture of the patriarchal

history, which had been all along kept in view, in the marvellous and new light of the judgment which was executed upon
Egypt, and of the protection, redemption, and election of Israel,
as being One hitherto unknown, as the history of salvation
actually then, having arrived at Sinai, receives an entirely new
form, inasmuch as from this time onwards the congregation or
church is a nation, and Jahve the King of a nation, and the
bond of union between them a national law educating it for
the real, vital salvation that is to come. The words of Jahve
that follow are now not the words heard then in the time of
the Exodus. The remembrance of the words heard forms only
a transition to those that now make themselves heard. For
when the poet remembers the language which He who reveals
Himself in a manner never before seen and heard of spoke to
His people at that time, the Ever-living One Himself, who is
yesterday and to-day the same One, speaks in order to remind
His people of what He was to them then, and of what He spake
to them then.

Vers. 7–11. It is a gentle but profoundly earnest festival
discourse which God the Redeemer addresses to His redeemed
people. It begins, as one would expect in a Passover speech,
with a reference to the סִבְלוֹת of Egypt (Ex. i. 11–14, v. 4,
vi. 6 sq.), and to the דּוּד, the task-basket for the transport of
the clay and of the bricks (Ex. i. 14, v. 7 sq.).* Out of such
distress did He free the poor people who cried for deliverance
(Ex. ii. 23–25); He answered them בְּסֵתֶר רַעַם, i.e. not (according to xxii. 22, Isa. xxxii. 2): affording them protection against
the storm, but (according to xviii. 12, lxxvii. 17 sqq.): out of
the thunder-clouds in which He at the same time revealed and
veiled Himself, casting down the enemies of Israel with His
lightnings, which is intended to refer pre-eminently to the
passage through the Red Sea (vid. lxxvii. 19); and He proved
them (אֶבְחָֽנְךָ with ŏ contracted from ō, cf. on Job xxxv. 6) at
the waters of Merîbah, viz. whether they would trust Him
further on after such glorious tokens of His power and loving-

---

* In the *Papyrus Leydensis* i. 346 the Israelites are called the "*Aperiu*
(עברים), who dragged along the stones for the great watch-tower of the
city of Rameses," and in the *Pap. Leyd.* i. 349, according to Lauth, the
"*Aperiu*, who dragged along the stones for the storehouse of the city of
Rameses."

kindness. The name " *Waters of Meríbah,*" which properly is borne only by *Meríbath Kadesh*, the place of the giving of water in the fortieth year (Num. xx. 13, xxvii. 14, Deut. xxxii. 51, xxxiii. 8), is here transferred to the place of the giving of water in the first year, which was named *Massah u-Meríbah* (Ex. xvii. 7), as the remembrances of these two miracles, which took place under similar circumstances, in general blend together (*vid.* on xcv. 8 sq.). It is not now said that Israel did not act in response to the expectation of God, who had so wondrously verified Himself; the music, as *Sela* imports, here rises, and makes a long and forcible pause in what is being said. What now follows further, are, as the further progress of ver. 12 shows, the words of God addressed to the Israel of the desert, which at the same time with its faithlessness are brought to the remembrance of the Israel of the present. הָעִיד בְּ, as in L 7, Deut. viii. 19, to bear testimony that concerns him against any one. אִם (according to the sense, *o si*, as in Ps. xcv. ver. 7, which is in many ways akin to this Psalm) properly opens a searching question which wishes that the thing asked may come about (whether thou wilt indeed give me a willing hearing?!). In ver. 10 the key-note of the revelation of the Law from Sinai is struck: the fundamental command which opens the decalogue demanded fidelity to Jahve and forbade idol-worship as the sin of sins. אֵל זָר is an idol in opposition to the God of Israel as the true God; and אֵל נֵכָר, a strange god in opposition to the true God as the God of Israel. To this one God Israel ought to yield itself all the more undividedly and heartily as it was more manifestly indebted entirely to Him, who in His condescension had chosen it, and in His wonder-working might had redeemed it (הַמַּעַלְךָ, *part. Hiph.* with the *eh* elided, like הַפֹּדְךָ, Deut. xiii. 6, and אֲכָלְךָ, from כָּלָה, Ex. xxxiii. 3); and how easy this submission ought to have been to it, since He desired nothing in return for the rich abundance of His good gifts, which satisfy and quicken body and soul, but only a wide-opened mouth, *i.e.* a believing longing, hungering for mercy and eager for salvation (cxix. 131)!

Vers. 12–17. The Passover discourse now takes a sorrowful and awful turn: Israel's disobedience and self-will frustrated the gracious purpose of the commandments and promises of its God. "My people" and "Israel" alternate as in the complaint

in Isa. i. 3. לֹא־אָבָה followed by the dative, as in Deut. xiii. 9
([8], οὐ συνθελήσεις αὐτῷ). Then God made their sin their
punishment, by giving them over judicially (שָׁלַּח as in Job
viii. 4) into the obduracy of their heart, which rudely shuts
itself up against His mercy (from שָׁרַר, Aramaic שְׁרַר, Arabic
سر, to make firm = to cheer, make glad), so that they went on

(cf. on the sequence of tense, lxi. 8) in *their,* *i.e.* their own,
egotistical, God-estranged determinations; the suffix is thus
accented, as *e.g.* in Isa. lxv. 2, cf. the borrowed passage Jer.
vii. 24, and the same phrase in Mic. vi. 16. And now, because
this state of unfaithfulness in comparison with God's faithfulness has remained essentially the same even to to-day, the
exalted Orator of the festival passes over forthwith to the
generation of the present, and that, as is in accordance with
the cheerful character of the feast, in a charmingly alluring
manner. Whether we take לוּ in the signification of *si* (followed by the participle, as in 2 Sam. xviii. 12), or like אִם above
in ver. 9 as expressing a wish, *o si* (if but!), vers. 15 sqq. at
any rate have the relation of the apodosis to it. From כִּמְעַט
(for a little, easily) it may be conjectured that the relation of
Israel at that time to the nations did not correspond to the
dignity of the nation of God which is called to subdue and
rule the world in the strength of God. הֵשִׁיב signifies in this
passage only to turn, not: to again lay upon. The meaning
is, that He would turn the hand which is now chastening
His people against those by whom He is chastening them (cf.
on the usual meaning of the phrase, Isa. i. 25, Amos i. 8, Jer.
vi. 9, Ezek. xxxviii. 12). The promise in ver. 16 relates to
Israel and all the members of the nation. The haters of Jahve
would be compelled reluctantly to submit themselves to Him,
and their time would endure for ever. "Time" is equivalent
to duration, and in this instance with the collateral notion of
prosperity, as elsewhere (Isa. xiii. 22) of the term of punishment.
One now expects that it should continue with וְאַאֲכִילֵהוּ, in the
tone of a promise. The Psalm, however, closes with an historical statement. For וַיַּאֲכִילֵהוּ cannot signify *et cibaret eum;*
it ought to be pronounced וְיַאֲכִילֵהוּ. The pointing, like the
LXX., Syriac, and Vulgate, takes ver. 17*a* (cf. Deut. xxxii.
13 sq.) as a retrospect, and apparently rightly so. For even

the Asaphic Psalms lxxvii. and lxxviii. break off with historical pictures. Ver. 17*b* is, accordingly, also to be taken as retrospective. The words of the poet in conclusion once more change into the words of God. The closing word runs אַשְׂבִּיעֶךָ, as in l. 8, Deut. iv. 31, and (with the exception of the *futt. Hiph.* of *Lamed He* verbs ending with *ekka*) usually. The Babylonian system of pointing nowhere recognises the suffix-form *ekka.* If the Israel of the present would hearken to the Lawgiver of Sinai, says ver. 17, then would He renew to it the miraculous gifts of the time of the redemption under Moses.

PSALM LXXXII.

GOD'S JUDGMENT UPON THE GODS OF THE EARTH.

1 ELOHIM standeth in the congregation of God,
  Among the elohim doth He judge.
2 "How long will ye judge unjustly,
  And take the side of the wicked?   (*Sela.*)

3 Do justice to the destitute and fatherless,
  Acquit the afflicted and the poor!
4 Deliver the destitute and needy,
  Rescue out of the hand of the wicked!"—

5 "They know not, and understand not,
  In darkness they walk to and fro;
  All the foundations of the land totter.

6 *I* have said: Ye are elohim,
  And sons of the Most High are ye all.
7 Yet as men shall ye die,
  And as one of the princes shall ye fall."

8 Arise, Elohim, oh judge the earth,
  For Thou hast a claim upon all nations.

As in Ps. lxxxi., so also in this Psalm (according to the Talmud the Tuesday Psalm of the Temple liturgy) God is in-

troduced as speaking after the manner of the prophets. Ps.
lviii. and xciv. are similar, but more especially Isa. iii. 13–15.
Asaph the seer beholds how God, reproving, correcting, and
threatening, appears against the chiefs of the congregation of
His people, who have perverted the splendour of majesty which
He has put upon them into tyranny. It is perfectly characteristic of Asaph (Ps. l., lxxv., lxxxi.) to plunge himself into
the contemplation of the divine judgment, and to introduce
God as speaking. There is nothing to militate against the
Psalm being written by Asaph, David's cotemporary, except the
determination not to allow to the לאסף of the inscription its
most natural sense. Hupfeld, understanding "angels" by the
elohim, as Bleek has done before him, inscribes the Psalm:
"God's judgment upon unjust judges in heaven and upon
earth." But the angels as such are nowhere called *elohim*
in the Old Testament, although they might be so called; and
their being judged here on account of unjust judging, Hupfeld
himself says, is "an obscure point that is still to be cleared up."
An interpretation which, like this, abandons the usage of the
language in order to bring into existence a riddle that it cannot
solve, condemns itself. At the same time the assertion of
Hupfeld (of Knobel, Graf, and others), that in Ex. xxi. 6,
xxii. 7 sq., 27,* אלהים denotes God Himself, and not directly
the authorities of the nation as being His earthly representatives, finds its most forcible refutation in the so-called and
mortal *elohim* of this Psalm (cf. also xlv. 7, lviii. 2).

By reference to this Psalm Jesus proves to the Jews (John
x. 34–36) that when He calls Himself the Son of God, He
does not blaspheme God, by an *argumentatio a minori ad majus*.
If the Law, so He argues, calls even those gods who are offi-
cially invested with this name by a declaration of the divine
will promulgated in time (and the Scripture cannot surely, as
in general, so also in this instance, be made invalid), then it
cannot surely be blasphemy if He calls Himself the Son of
God, whom not merely a divine utterance in this present time
has called to this or to that worldly office after the image of
God, but who with His whole life is ministering to the accom-

---

* In the English authorized version, Ex. xxi. 6, xxii. 8 sq. ("judges"),
28 ("gods," margin "judges").—Tr.

plishment of a work to which the Father had already sanctified
Him when He came into the world. In connection with ἡγίασε
one is reminded of the fact that those who are called *elohim* in
the Psalm are censured on account of the unholiness of their
conduct. The name does not originally belong to them, nor do
they show themselves to be morally worthy of it. With ἡγίασε
καὶ ἀπέστειλεν Jesus contrasts His divine sonship, prior to time,
with theirs, which began only in this present time.

Vers. 1–4. God comes forward and makes Himself heard
first of all as censuring and admonishing. The "congregation
of God" is, as in Num. xxvii. 17, xxxi. 16, Josh. xxii. 16 sq.,
"the congregation of (the sons of) Israel," which God has purchased from among the nations (lxxiv. 2), and upon which as
its Lawgiver He has set His divine impress. The psalmist and
seer sees Elohim standing in this congregation of God. The
part. Niph. (as in Isa. iii. 13) denotes not so much the suddenness and unpreparedness, as, rather, the statue-like immobility
and terrifying designfulness of His appearance. Within the
range of the congregation of God this holds good of the *elohim*.
The right over life and death, with which the administration of
justice cannot dispense, is a prerogative of God. From the
time of Gen. ix. 6, however, He has transferred the execution
of this prerogative to mankind, and instituted in mankind an
office wielding the sword of justice, which also exists in His
theocratic congregation, but here has His positive law as the
basis of its continuance and as the rule of its action. Everywhere among men, but here pre-eminently, those in authority
are God's delegates and the bearers of His image, and therefore
as His representatives are also themselves called *elohim*, "gods"
(which the LXX. in Ex. xxi. 6 renders τὸ κριτήριον τοῦ Θεοῦ,
and the Targums here, as in Ex. xxii. 7, 8, 27 uniformly, דִּינָיָא).
The God who has conferred this exercise of power upon these
subordinate elohim, without their resigning it of themselves,
now sits in judgment in their midst. יִשְׁפֹּט of that which takes
place before the mind's eye of the psalmist. How long, He
asks, will ye judge unjustly ? שָׁפַט עָוֶל is equivalent to עָשָׂה עָוֶל
בְּמִשְׁפָּט, Lev. xix. 15, 35 (the opposite is שְׁפַט מֵישָׁרִים, lviii. 2).
How long will ye accept the countenance of the wicked, *i.e.*
incline to accept, regard, favour the person of the wicked ? The

music, which here becomes *forte,* gives intensity to the terrible sternness (*das Niederdonnernde*) of the divine question, which seeks to bring the "gods" of the earth to their right mind. Then follow admonitions to do that which they have hitherto left undone. They are to cause the benefit of the administration of justice to tend to the advantage of the defenceless, of the destitute, and of the helpless, upon whom God the Lawgiver especially keeps His eye. The word רָשׁ (רָאשׁ), of which there is no evidence until within the time of David and Solomon, is synonymous with אֶבְיוֹן. דל with ויתום is pointed דָּל, and with ואביון, on account of the closer notional union, דַּל (as in lxxii. 13). They are words which are frequently repeated in the prophets, foremost in Isaiah (ch. i. 17), with which is enjoined upon those invested with the dignity of the law, and with jurisdiction, justice towards those who cannot and will not themselves obtain their rights by violence.

Vers. 5–7. What now follows in ver. 5 is not a parenthetical assertion of the inefficiency with which the divine correction rebounds from the judges and rulers. In connection with this way of taking ver. 5, the manner in which the divine language is continued in ver. 6 is harsh and unadjusted. God Himself speaks in ver. 5 of the judges, but reluctantly alienated from them; and confident of the futility of all attempts to make them better, He tells them their sentence in vers. 6 sq. The verbs in ver. 5a are designedly without any object: complaint of the widest compass is made over their want of reason and understanding; and ידעו takes the perfect form in like manner to ἐγνώκασι, *noverunt,* cf. xiv. 1, Isa. xliv. 18. Thus, then, no result is to be expected from the divine admonition: they still go their ways in this state of mental darkness, and that, as the *Hithpa.* implies, stalking on in carnal security and self-complacency. The commands, however, which they transgress are the foundations (cf. xi. 3), as it were the shafts and pillars (lxxv. 4, cf. Prov. xxix. 4), upon which rests the permanence of all earthly relationships which are appointed by creation and regulated by the Tôra. Their transgression makes the land, the earth, to totter physically and morally, and is the prelude of its overthrow. When the celestial Lord of the domain thinks upon this destruction which injustice and tyranny are bringing upon the earth, His wrath

kindles, and He reminds the judges and rulers that it is His
own free declaratory act which has clothed them with the godlike dignity which they bear. They are actually elohim, but
not possessed of the right of self-government; there is a Most
High (עֶלְיוֹן) to whom they as sons are responsible. The idea
that the appellation *elohim*, which they have given to themselves, is only sarcastically given back to them in ver. 1 (Ewald,
Olshausen), is refuted by ver. 6, according to which they are
really *elohim* by the grace of God. But if their practice is not
an Amen to this name, then they shall be divested of the
majesty which they have forfeited; they shall be divested of
the prerogative of Israel, whose vocation and destiny they
have belied. They shall die off כְּאָדָם, like common men not
rising in any degree above the mass (cf. בְּנֵי אָדָם, *opp.* בְּנֵי אִישׁ,
iv. 3, xlix. 3); they shall fall like any one (Judg. xvi. 7,
Obad. ver. 11) of the princes who in the course of history
have been cast down by the judgment of God (Hos. vii. 7).
Their divine office will not protect them. For although *justitia
civilis* is far from being the righteousness that avails before
God, yet *injustitia civilis* is in His sight the vilest abomination.

Ver. 8. The poet closes with the prayer for the realization of that which he has beheld in spirit. He implores God
Himself to sit in judgment (שָׁפְטָה as in Lam. iii. 59), since
judgment is so badly exercised upon the earth. All peoples
are indeed His נַחֲלָה, He has an hereditary and proprietary
right among (LXX. and Vulgate according to Num. xviii. 20,
and frequently), or rather in (בְּ as in מָשַׁל בְּ, instead of the
accusative of the object, Zech. ii. 16), all nations (ἔθνη)—may
He then be pleased to maintain it judicially. The inference
drawn from this point backwards, that the Psalm is directed
against the possessors of power among the Gentiles, is erroneous. Israel itself, in so far as it acts inconsistently with its
theocratic character, belies its sanctified nationality, is a גוֹי
like the גוֹים, and is put into the same category with these.
The judgment over the world is also a judgment over the
Israel that is become conformed to the world, and its God-
estranged chiefs.

PSALM LXXXIII.

BATTLE-CRY TO GOD AGAINST ALLIED PEOPLES.

2 ELOHIM, let there be no repose to Thee,
  Be not silent and rest not, O God!
3 For lo Thine enemies make a tumult,
  And Thy haters carry the head high.
4 Against Thy people they meditate a crafty design,
  And take counsel together against Thy protegés.
5 They say: "Up! we will destroy them from among the
      peoples,
  And the name of Israel shall not be remembered any
      more!"

6 For they take counsel together with one mind,
  Against Thee they make a covenant:
7 The tents of Edom and of the Ishmaelites,
  Moab and the Hagarenes;
8 Gebâl and Ammon and Amalek,
  Philistia, with the inhabitants of Tyre;
9 Also Asshur hath joined itself to them,
  They lend their arm to the sons of Lot.   (*Sela.*)

10 Do unto them as unto Midian,
  As unto Sisera, as unto Jabin at the brook Kishon!
11 They were destroyed at Endor,
  They became as dung for the land;
12 Make them, their nobles, like Oreb and Zeēb,
  And like Zebach and Zalmunna all their princes,
13 Who said:
  "Let us take possession of the habitations of Elohim!"

14 My God, make them like the whirlwind,
  As stubble before the wind!
15 As fire, burning a forest,
  And as flame, singeing mountains:
16 Thus do Thou pursue them with Thy tempest,

And with Thy hurricane overthrow them !
17 Fill their face with shame,
That they may seek Thy name, Jahve !

18 Let them be ashamed and overthrown for ever,
And let them be confounded and perish;
19 And let them know that Thou, Thy Name, Jahve, Thou
alone,
Art the Most High over all the earth.

The close of this Psalm is in accord with the close of the
preceding Psalm. It is the last of the twelve Psalms of Asaph
of the Psalter. The poet supplicates help against the many
nations which have allied themselves with the descendants of
Lot, *i.e.* Moab and Ammon, to entirely root out Israel as a
nation. Those who are fond of Maccabæan Psalms (Hitzig
and Olshausen), after the precedent of van Til and von
Bengel, find the circumstances of the time of the Psalm in 1
Macc. ch. v., and Grimm is also inclined to regard this as correct; and in point of fact the deadly hostility of the ἔθνη
κυκλόθεν which we there see breaking forth on all sides,* as it
were at a given signal, against the Jewish people, who have
become again independent, and after the dedication of the
Temple doubly self-conscious, is far better suited to explain the
Psalm than the hostile efforts of Sanballat, Tobiah, and others
to hinder the rebuilding of Jerusalem, in the time of Nehemiah
(Vaihinger, Ewald, and Dillmann). There is, however, still
another incident beside that recorded in 1 Macc. ch. v. to
which the Psalm may be referred, viz. the confederation of the
nations for the extinction of Judah in the time of Jehoshaphat
(2 Chron. ch. xx.), and, as it seems to us, with comparatively
speaking less constraint. For the Psalm speaks of a real league,
whilst in 1 Macc. ch. v. the several nations made the attack
without being allied and not jointly; then, as the Psalm
assumes in ver. 9, the sons of Lot, *i.e.* the Moabites and
Ammonites, actually were at the head at that time, whilst in

---

* Concerning the υἱοὶ Βαιάν (*Benî Baijân*), 1 Macc. v. 4, the difficulty
respecting which is to the present time unsolved, *vid.* Wetzstein's Excursus
II., at the end of this volume.

1 Macc. ch. v. the sons of Esau occupy the most prominent place; and thirdly, at that time, in the time of Jehoshaphat, as is recorded, an Asaphite, viz. Jahaziël, did actually interpose in the course of events, a circumstance which coincides remarkably with the לאסף. The league of that period consisted, according to 2 Chron. xx. 1, of Moabites, Ammonites, and a part of the מְעוּנִים (as it is to be read after the LXX.). But ver. 2 (where without any doubt מאדם is to be read instead of מארם) adds the Edomites to their number, for it is expressly stated further on (vers. 10, 22, 23) that the inhabitants of Mount Seïr were with them. Also, supposing of course that the "Ishmaelites" and "Hagarenes" of the Psalm may be regarded as an unfolding of the מעונים, which is confirmed by Josephus, *Antiq.* ix. 1. 2 ; and that Gebâl is to be understood by the Mount Seïr of the chronicler, which is confirmed by the جبال still in use at the present day, there always remains

a difficulty in the fact that the Psalm also names *Amalek, Philistia, Tyre,* and *Asshur,* of which we find no mention there in the reign of Jehoshaphat. But these difficulties are counterbalanced by others that beset the reference to 1 Macc. ch. v., viz. that in the time of the Seleucidæ the Amalekites no longer existed, and consequently, as might be expected, are not mentioned at all in 1 Macc. ch. v. ; further, that there the Moabites, too, are no longer spoken of, although some formerly Moabitish cities of Gileaditis are mentioned; and thirdly, that אשׁור = Syria (a certainly possible usage of the word) appears in a subordinate position, whereas it was, however, the dominant power. On the other hand, the mention of Amalek is intelligible in connection with the reference to 2 Chron. ch. xx., and the absence of its express mention in the chronicler does not make itself particularly felt in consideration of Gen. xxxvi. 12. Philistia, Tyre, and Asshur, however, stand at the end in the Psalm, and might also even be mentioned with the others if they rendered aid to the confederates of the south-east without taking part with them in the campaign, as being a succour to the actual leaders of the enterprise, the sons of Lot. We therefore agree with the reference of Ps. lxxxiii. (as also of Ps. xlviii.) to the alliance of the neighbouring nations against Judah in the reign of Jehoshaphat, which has been already

recognised by Kimchi and allowed by Keil, Hengstenberg, and
Movers.

Vers. 2–5. The poet prays, may God not remain an inactive looker-on in connection with the danger of destruction
that threatens His people. דֳּמִי (with which יְהִי is to be supplied) is the opposite of alertness; חָרַשׁ the opposite of speaking (in connection with which it is assumed that God's word
is at the same time deed); שָׁקַט the opposite of being agitated
and activity. The energetic future *jehemajûn* gives outward
emphasis to the confirmation of the petition, and the fact that
Israel's foes are the foes of God gives inward emphasis to it.
On נָשָׂא רֹאשׁ, cf. cx. 7. סוֹד is here a secret agreement; and
יַעֲרִימוּ, elsewhere to deal craftily, here signifies to craftily plot,
devise, bring a thing about. צְפוּנֶיךָ is to be understood according to xxvii. 5, xxxi. 21. The *Hithpa.* הִתְיָעֵץ alternates here
with the more ancient *Niph.* (ver. 6). The design of the
enemies in this instance has reference to the total extirpation
of Israel, of the separatist-people who exclude themselves from
the life of the world and condemn it. מִגּוֹי, from being a people
= so that it may no longer be a people or nation, as in Isa.
vii. 8, xvii. 1, xxv. 2, Jer. xlviii. 42. In the borrowed passage,
Jer. xlviii. 2, by an interchange of a letter it is נַכְרִיתֶנָּה. This
Asaph Psalm is to be discerned in not a few passages of the
prophets; cf. Isa. lxii. 6 sq. with ver. 2, Isa. xvii. 12 with
ver. 3.

Vers. 6–9. Instead of לֵב אֶחָד, 1 Chron. xii. 38, it is *deli-
berant corde unâ*, inasmuch as יַחְדָּו on the one hand gives
intensity to the reciprocal signification of the verb, and on the
other lends the adjectival notion to לֵב. Of the confederate
peoples the chronicler (2 Chron. ch. xx.) mentions the Moabites, the Ammonites, the inhabitants of Mount Seïr, and the
Me'unim, instead of which Josephus, *Antiq.* ix. 1. 2, says: a
great body of Arabians. This crowd of peoples comes from
the other side of the Dead Sea, מֵאֱדֹם (as it is to be read in
ver. 2 in the chronicler instead of מֵאֲרָם, cf. on lx. 2); the
territory of Edom, which is mentioned first by the poet, was
therefore the rendezvous. The tents of Edom and of the

Ishmaelites are (cf. أَهْل, people) the people themselves who

live in tents.   Moreover, too, the poet ranges the hostile
nations according to their geographical position.   The seven
first named from Edom to Amalek, which still existed at the
time of the psalmist (for the final destruction of the Amalekites by the Simeonites, 1 Chron. iv. 42 sq., falls at an indeterminate period prior to the Exile), are those out of the regions
east and south-east of the Dead Sea.   According to Gen. xxv.
18, the Ishmaelites had spread from Higâz through the penin-
sula of Sinai beyond the eastern and southern deserts as far
up as the countries under the dominion of Assyria.   The
Hagarenes dwelt in tents from the Persian Gulf as far as the
east of Gilead (1 Chron. v. 10) towards the Euphrates.   גְּבָל,

جبال, is the name of the people inhabiting the mountains

situated in the south of the Dead Sea, that is to say, the
northern Seïritish mountains.   Both Gebâl and also, as it appears, the Amalek intended here according to Gen. xxxvi. 12
(cf. Josephus, *Antiq.* ii. 1. 2 : Ἀμαληκῖτις, a part of Idumæa),
belong to the wide circuit of *Edom.*   Then follow the Philistines and Phœnicians, the two nations of the coast of the
Mediterranean, which also appear in Amos ch. i. (cf. Joel ch.
iv. [iii.]) as making common cause with the Edomites against
Israel.   Finally Asshur, the nation of the distant north-east,
here not as yet appearing as a principal power, but strengthening (*vid.* concerning זְרוֹעַ, an arm = assistance, succour, Gesenius, *Thesaurus,* p. 433*b*) the sons of Lot, *i.e.* the Moabites and
Ammonites, with whom the enterprise started, and forming a
powerful reserve for them.   The music bursts forth angrily at
the close of this enumeration, and imprecations discharge themselves in the following strophe.

Vers. 10-13.   With כְּמִדְיָן reference is made to Gideon's
victory over the Midianites, which belongs to the most glorious
recollections of Israel, and to which in other instances, too,
national hopes are attached, Isa. ix. 3 [4], x. 26, cf. Hab. iii.
7 ; and with the asyndeton כְּסִיסְרָא כְיָבִין (כְּסִיסְרָא, as Norzi states,
who does not rightly understand the placing of the *Metheg*) to the
victory of Barak and Deborah over Sisera and the Canaanitish
king Jabin, whose general he was.   The *Beth* of בְּנַחַל is like
the *Beth* of בַּדֶּרֶךְ in cx. 7 : according to Judg. v. 21 the Kishon
carried away the corpses of the slain army.   '*Endôr,* near

Tabor, and therefore situated not far distant from Taanach and Megiddo (Judg. v. 19), belonged to the battle-field. אֲדָמָה, starting from the radical notion of that which flatly covers anything, which lies in דם, signifying the covering of earth lying flat over the globe, therefore *humus* (like אֶרֶץ, *terra*, and תֵּבֵל, *tellus*), is here (cf. 2 Kings ix. 37) in accord with דֹּמֶן (from דָּמַן), which is in substance akin to it. In ver. 12 we have a retrospective glance at Gideon's victory. 'Oreb and Zeēb were שָׂרִים of the Midianites, Judg. vii. 25; *Zebach* and *Tsalmunna*', their kings, Judg. viii. 5 sqq.* The pronoun precedes the word itself in שִׁיתֵמוֹ, as in Ex. ii. 6; the heaped-up suffixes *ēmo* (*êmo*) give to the imprecation a rhythm and sound as of rolling thunder. Concerning נְסִיךְ, *vid.* on ii. 6. So far as the matter is concerned, 2 Chron. xx. 11 harmonizes with ver. 13. Canaan, the land which is God's and which He has given to His people, is called נְאוֹת אלהים (cf. lxxiv. 20).

Vers. 14–17. With the אֱלֹהַי, which constrains God in faith, the "thundering down" begins afresh. גַּלְגַּל signifies a wheel and a whirling motion, such as usually arises when the wind changes suddenly, then also whatever is driven about in the whirling, Isa. xvii. 13.† קַשׁ (from קָשַׁשׁ, قش, *aridum esse*) is the dry corn-stalks, whether as left standing or, as in this instance, as straw upon the threshing-floor or upon the field. Like a fire that spreads rapidly, laying hold of everything, which burns up the forest and singes off the wooded mountain so that only a bare cone is left standing, so is God to drive them before Him in the raging tempest of His wrath and take them unawares. The figure in ver. 15 is fully worked up by

---

* The Syriac Hexapla has (Hos. x. 14) צלמנע instead of שלמן, a substitution which is accepted by Geiger, *Deutsch. Morgenländ. Zeitschr.* 1862, S. 729 f. Concerning the signification of the above names of Midianitish princes, *vid.* Nöldeke, *Ueber die Amalekiter*, S. 9.

† Saadia, who renders the גַּלְגַּל in lxxvii. 19 as an astronomical expression with الفلك, the sphere of the heavens, here has professedly كالغرابلة, which would be a plural form expanded out of غرابيل, "sieves" or "tambourines;" it is, however, to be read, as in Isa. xvii. 13, *Codex Oxon.*, كالغربالة. The verb غربل, "to sift," is transferred to the wind, *e.g.* in *Mutanabbi* (edited with Wahidi's commentary by Dieterici), p. 29, l. 5 and 6: "it is

Isaiah, ch. x. 16–19; לְהֵט as in Deut. xxxii. 22. In the apodosis, ver. 16, the figure is changed into a kindred one: wrath is a glowing heat (חרון) and a breath (נשמה, Isa. xxx. 33) at the same time. In ver. 17*b* it becomes clear what is the final purpose towards which this language of cursing tends: to the end that all, whether willingly or reluctantly, may give the glory to the God of revelation. Directed towards this end the earnest prayer is repeated once more in the tetrastichic closing strain.

Vers. 18, 19. The aim of the wish is that they in the midst of their downfall may lay hold upon the mercy of Jahve as their only deliverance: first they must come to nought, and only by giving Jahve the glory will they not be utterly destroyed. Side by side with אַתָּה, ver. 19*a*, is placed שִׁמְךָ as a second subject (cf. xliv. 3, lxix. 11). In view of ver. 17*b* וְיֵדְעוּ (as in lix. 14) has not merely the sense of perceiving so far as the justice of the punishment is concerned; the knowledge which is unto salvation is not excluded. The end of the matter which the poet wishes to see brought about is this, that Jahve, that the God of revelation (שמך), may become the All-exalted One in the consciousness of the nations.

---

as though the dust of this region, when the winds chase one another therein, were sifted," مغربل (*i.e.* caught up and whirled round); and with other notional and constructional applications in *Makkari*, i. p. 102, l. 18: "it is as though its soil had been cleansed from dust by sifting," غربلت (*i.e.* the dust thereof swept away by a whirlwind). Accordingly غربال signifies first, as a *nom. vicis*, a whirling about (of dust by the wind), then in a concrete sense a whirlwind, as Saadia uses it, inasmuch as he makes use of it twice for גַּלְגַּל. So Fleischer in opposition to Ewald, who renders "like the sweepings or rubbish."

EXCURSUS BY J. G. WETZSTEIN.

<div align="center">~~~~~~~~~~</div>

I.—THE SYMBOLICAL MEANING OF THE WASH-POT AND OF THE SHOE.

On Ps. lx. 10 (pp. 199 sq.).

THE most natural interpretation of the words *Moab is my wash-pot, and upon Edom I cast my shoe,* seems to me, according to the conception in Syria at the present day, to be: Moab is the vessel in which I wash my face and hands clean, *i.e.* the country and people in which I acquire to myself (by its conquest) splendour and renown, and Edom I degrade to the place whither I throw my cast-off shoes,* *i.e.* I cause Edom to endure the most humiliating treatment, that of a helot. The idea is still the same, if the poet conceived of Edom as a person at whom he casts his shoe as an insult. It is surely not to be doubted that these first two members of the verse—according to the apprehension of the whole Psalm—refer to a conquest of the two nations either as already completed or as near at hand, since the third member of the verse, having reference to the Philistines, speaks with certainty of such a conquest ; התרועעי

---

* In the old Arabic נַעַל is both singular and collective; and so, too, it will be in Hebrew, and the occurrence of the dual is not opposed to this. The modern language still has the *nomen unitatis* נַעְלָה, but the Beduins are very glad to avoid both words on account of their accord with לְעָנָה, "a curse," a terrible word to them ; still they use the former when they intend the latter, and say *'alêh en-na'ᵉla,* "the shoe upon him!" (or the horse-shoe, for *na'ᵉl* also has this meaning) in the sense of "the curse upon him!" Upon this, too, is based the proverb: *el-weled el-charâ jegîb li-ah'luh en-na'ᵉla,* "the dirty child brings to his [family] the shoe," *i.e.* a bad child brings a curse upon his [family] (cf. Tantawi's *Traité,* p. 119). The word *na'ᵉl* is still found now-a-days, but almost exclusively among the nomads and the *ḳarâwina* (the inhabitants of the villages of the desert). The shoe together with the latchets or thongs is cut out of the raw hide of a slaugh-

412

may be understood of a battle-cry (when the fight is at hand) or a cry for vengeance (after the conquest).

The pregnant language of poetry is satisfied with the mention of the wash-pot in order to bring before the mind the figure so familiar to the Semite of "washing one's self white," *i.e.* to acquire a reputation. In the Arabian poets the metaphor not unfrequently is " to wash one's self white in the blood of the enemies" (بيَّض وجهه بدم العِدا). In the language of common life بيَاض الوجه (*candor faciei*) is a broad notion, for everything good and beautiful that a man does or receives makes his face white (يبيَض وجهه). Now, since the one or the other is often taking place, one also very frequently hears the expression made use of. We see from Isa. i. 16–18, Job ix. 30, and Prov. xxx. 12, that among the Hebrews too the figurative phrase of washing one's self white had a far more extended application than it might seem according to Ps. li. 9 ; and a conquest of the Moabites must have furnished an Israelitish king with the بياض الوجه before his people. The opposite is the سوَاد الوجه (*nigror faciei*), which is brought about by everything bad and ugly that one does or suffers. Since the denying of a request, unsuccessful mediation between disputants, the non-acceptance of a present, and the not returning of a greeting blackens the face (يسوِّد وجهه) of the petitioner, of the

---

tered or fallen camel, and while moist fitted on to the foot, in order that in drying it may receive the shape of the foot. The Syrian peasantry in the present day wear the red or yellow *gezma* a handbreadth high, a kind of boot ; and the poorer inhabitants of the towns the red *surmeia* reaching to the ankle, a real shoe ; whilst the more prosperous wear a yellow under-shoe (*kalshîn*) and a red over-shoe (*bâbûga*, collective *bâbûg* and *bawâbîg*). These four foreign words lead one to infer that the thing itself is of foreign origin ; yet the simple *surmeia*, which is also called *merkûb* (מַרכּוּב), is very old in the cities of Syria and of Palestine. According to Amos ii. 6, viii. 6, it is scarcely to be doubted that the real leathern shoe was also understood among the Hebrews by the word נַעַל.

mediator, of the giver, and of him who greets, it comes to pass that in a Syrian town one almost daily meets with the expression, as with the "blackened" individual himself; cf. Burckhardt, *Arabic Proverbs*, pp. 48 sq.; Freytag, *Prov. Arab.* iii. p. 239 (No. 1435 and No. 1436),[*] and p. 534.

As to the second member of the verse, the shoe, as being the commonest part of one's clothing, is the figure of vileness and despicableness; and one would no more think of mentioning the shoe than the indecent word *charâ*, "dung," without saving one's self in the presence of the hearer by the addition of the words *agellak Allâh*, "may God glorify thee!" The proverb *adhall min en-na‘âl*, "more common than the shoe," is found in Freytag, *Prov. Arab.* i. 514; the same in meaning with this is *adhall min el-hidhâ, ibid.* p. 516. On the first Meidânî quotes two verses of poetry. The one runs thus: "The cheek of the Kulêbites more easily undergoes the disgracing touch than the shoe" (which the feet tread in the dirt); the other is: "Accustomed to many years' disgrace, they accommodate themselves more easily to the footsteps than does the shoe." Here belongs, too, *jâ habbadhâ el-munta‘limûna kiâmâ* (in Freytag, iii. 513)—"Oh what a nice thing it is to draw on one's shoes standing!" *i.e.* to associate with the common people without making one's self common.[†] If it is a disgrace to be compared to the shoe, it is a still greater disgrace to be struck with one. Being warned of the presence of a foe, the Arab, in order to express the greatest possible contempt of this foe, cries: *bâbûgî ‘alâ ra'suh*,[‡] "my shoe upon his head," *i.e.* it only requires a few blows with my shoe to be rid of him. A discharged bad servant sends to ask his master to take him on again, and the master answers the intermediary: *jegî wa-ja'chodh surmeiatî ‘alâ kafâh*, "he may come if he

---

[*] Freytag has here erroneously translated the word *sawâd* by *opes.* The proverb is: misfortune upon misfortune makes the heart blind, *i.e.* breaks the spirit and energy. In Damascus they say الطفر يعمى القلب, "poverty makes the heart blind."

[†] The anecdote given on this proverb by Meidânî is one of those bad jokes such as the Arabs have on a great many of their proverbs.

[‡] Instead of *bâbûgî* they also say *surmeiatî*, and in the country always *gezmatî.* This swaggering phrase is very frequent among the common people; I have, however, never seen it put into practice.

wishes to have my shoe upon his head," *i.e.* I would drive him away again in the most disgraceful manner. The Khaliph Mutewekkil sent to the Imâm Ahmed (Ibn Hanbal) to ask him to pray for one of the maidens of his palace who had epilepsy: the imâm took off his shoe (*na'ăl*), gave it to the messenger, and saiɑ: Go, place it at the bed-head of the maiden and say, "Ahmed sends to ask whether thou wilt depart from the maiden or have seventy counted out with this shoe?" The messenger did as he was told, and the evil spirit (*el-mârid*) answered through the mouth of the maiden: "I obey! If Ahmed had commanded me to leave the 'Irâk, I would do it." And he came out of her and fled, and the maiden was made whole, etc. (MSS. in the Royal Library in Berlin, Section Wetzstein, ii. No. 355, folio 113*a*). In Damascus they say of a cunning, wicked man, proverbially: *ḍarab esh-Shêtân alf bâbûga*, "he struck Satan a thousand times with his shoe," *i.e.* Satan was his disciple, but was such a bungler in comparison with his master that he treated him in the most contemptible manner, and sought to discipline him by means of the vilest kind of punishment. Another Damascene proverb runs: *el-gehennam bên el-bawâbîg*, "Hell is among the shoes." The reception-room of houses in the city is divided into two parts; the very much larger part is furnished with carpets and divans, and here the guests sit; the lesser part, called *'ataba*, is from one to three steps lower, and here the attendants, slaves, and all contemptible people who do not dare to go up higher, stand. Here, too, stand the over-shoes of those who sit in the upper part. The proverb therefore signifies, that the feeling of being unhonoured and condemned, of being obliged to stand in the place where the others set their shoes, resembles the pains of hell.* This proverb seems to me to illustrate the *first* of the two interpretations of Ps. lx. 10*b* indicated above as possible; whilst in support of the *second* we may call to mind that enactment of *El-Hâkim bi'amr-Allah*, according to which in Syria and Egypt the Christians were compelled to hang wooden crosses and the Jews wooden shoes about their necks, which

---

* As is well known, the Arabs are not so sensitive to anything as they are to outward distinctions; and the words of the poet Abû Farrâs: *lanâ eṣ-ṣadr au el-ḳabr*, "we desire the seat of honour or the grave," are uttered by every Arab from the very soul.

they were not allowed to take off even in the bath. That this was designed solely as a mark of *disgrace,* is clear from the further points of that enactment, viz. that both parties were allowed to wear only black turbans; not to ride upon horses, but only upon donkeys without saddle-cloths; not to have any Moslem servants, etc. (MSS. in the Royal Library in Berlin, Section Wetzstein, ii. No. 351, fol. 167r).

The supposition of many expositors, that the taking possession of Edom is to be understood by the casting of the shoe upon it, I hold to be incorrect. In his work on the Psalms (ii. 33) Hitzig observes in its favour: "The shoe may be regarded as the symbol of a thing that has a master, for one says of a divorced woman, 'she was my slipper, and I have cast her off' (Burckhardt, *Notes on the Bedouins*, 1831, p. 113); to take it off may therefore mean to give up a property, according to Deut. xxv. 9, Ruth iv. 7 sq., and to cast it upon or at something may mean to take possession of it." Here I must first show that the quotation from Burckhardt is a phrase of which variations are to be met with. The figure of the shoe as symbolizing rejection is used only by the common people, and only by these when any one is aroused by offensive reproaches, or when filled with hatred against the divorced or her family. The dweller in Haurân in this case says in opposition to the reproach: *thôbî wa-shalaḫtuh,* "it was *my* shirt, and I have taken it off." A father or a brother who (and this is a custom of the country) has slain his daughter or sister that has, as a virgin, been seduced, turns aside the reproaches of strangers with the standing phrase: *iṣbaʿî wa-kataʿtuh,* "it was my own finger, and I have cut it off," or: *iṣbaʿî wa-ʿâb, kataʿtuh,* "it was my own finger, and it became unsound, so I cut it off," *i.e.* it was my own flesh and blood, not that of a stranger, what right have you therefore to call me to account? But the two Scripture passages only favour that interpretation in a very slight degree. In Deut. xxv. 9, where the despised widow takes off the shoe of her brother-in-law and spits into his face, she means simply to *disgrace* him. If the right of determining for one's self were transferred to her together with the shoe, then the act of taking off the shoe ought not to have been performed by her, but by him, since she cannot herself take this right upon herself. And when the man was called "barefoot" from this time forth, this epithet would no longer be a stigma upon him, which it is evidently intended to be, but would signify nothing more than "the possessionless one," which would have no meaning. The taking off of the shoe is, however, here designed to say: As thou despisest thy deceased brother and his widow, so shalt thou be like those despised and destitute ones who have not the meanest article of clothing, the shoe, and who are obliged to walk barefooted upon the sharp and hot stones, and in snow, in rain, and in dirt.

Ruth iv. 7, 8 is very different from this passage. Here one man delivers his shoe to another man certainly as the sign of the transfer of a right, yet without the unclean shoe as such being in general the symbol of ownership or property. For this no authenticated evidence is to be found. It is rather that his handing over the shoe is only the visible sign of the act of delivering up and taking possession (of the *teslîm* and *tesellum*), by means of which a sale, exchange, renunciation, or presentation becomes an established fact (לְקַיֵּם כָּל־דָּבָר). If an article of clothing be chosen for this purpose, because thereby one would seemingly part with an actual possession, then it might also be some other article. If, however, we may argue from the simple clothing of the inhabitants of Haurân at the present day, and of the whole of the country east of the Jordan, concerning the clothing of the ancient Scripture times, then there would frequently, especially in the country, only be the mantle besides the shoe at one's disposal; and even this a person would not always have with him in the hot season. This is apart from the consideration that the choice of the shoe was favoured by its meanness, which would say that one lightly parted with the object given up, and gave it heartily to the other.

II.—CONCERNING THE υἱοὶ Βαιάν IN 1 MACC. V. 4.

On Ps. lxxxiii. (p. 406, note).

THE υἱοὶ Βαιάν were a small tribe, by name בְּנֵי בַיָן. In the Arabian genealogies the word بَيَان not unfrequently occurs, as a name of men; even the *Ḳâmûs* under بين has an ابو على بن بيَّان. Its appellative signification is that of the proper names فاروق and فَيَصل, viz. *discernens seu ratione seu gladio.*

With respect to the abode of the *Benî Baijân,* from the fact that Judas found it to be the best opportunity of inflicting upon them the appointed chastisement for highway robberies when he had surprised and smitten the Edomites in the valley of the 'Araba, it may be inferred that they took up their abode in the neighbourhood of much-frequented highroads in the valley of the 'Araba. An important junction of the roads of that district is the *Ghamr*-well (الغَمر),* which has an abundant supply of water, and is frequently mentioned in the annals of Islam. It is situated on the western side of the 'Araba, distant two caravan marches north of *Aila,* and the same distance from the ruins of *Ṣoghar* in the south-west of the Dead Sea. For here the main road leading from Aila to Hebron and Jerusalem intersects the road which led from Egypt to Petra and farther east. The caravans going from Aila to *Ghazza* certainly did not touch at Ghamr, since, as at the present day, they used to take the more westerly direction farther south, but they were always obliged to halt at the drinking-places of the *Wâdî el-Lahjâna,* which lie scarcely ten hours south-west of Ghamr. They therefore likewise remained within the range of the robbers, if these inhabited the mountains which lie between Ghamr and that wâdî. This mountain range is, however, called *Gebel el-Baijâna* (جبل البيَّانة), which is synonymous with *Gebel Benî Baijân;* for ever since the Arabic language has given up the use of the plural in *ûn* and *în* for gentile nouns, البيَّانى, "the Baijânite," takes the form البيَّانة, "the Baijânites."† Burckhardt (*Travels in Syria and the Holy Land,* London 1822, 4to, p. 444), setting out

---

* Usually called *Ghamr el-'Arabât* in distinction from another watering-place and highroad-station of the same name between *Ma'ân* and *Têmâ.*

† For the most part, as one will be aware, the gentile noun is fond of the broken plural, *e.g.* الجوابرة (from the singular جابرى), "the Benî

from 'Ain es-Sâdika at the northern end of Gebel Sherâh
towards Egypt, crossed the 'Araba south of Ghamr. His
language in reference to the matter in hand is as follows:
"We were one hour and a half in crossing the Araba, direction W. by N. In some places the sand is very deep, but it is
firm, and the camels walk over it without sinking. . . . . There
is not the slightest appearance of a road or of any other work
of human art in this part of the valley. On the other side we
ascended the western chain of mountains. The mountain
opposite to us appeared to be the highest point of the whole

Gâbir" (Burckhardt, *Travels in Syria*, p. 405); الصوالحة (from the singular (صالحى), "the Benî Ṣâliḥ (*ibid.* p. 489); compare besides, المَقادسة,
العَناطكة, البوالتة, the inhabitants of Jerusalem, of Beirût, of Antioch.
By analogy one would expect to meet with a plural البيَائنة from البيَانى;
but such a plural is not possible on phonetic grounds, and therefore, too,
the بنى سيَال (a tribe in the Trachonitis) is called only السيَالة, and not
السيائلة. Also from a plural بيَائنة one could not with certainty infer a
singular بيَانى, since the ن of the final syllable in the *pluralis fractus* of
gentilia is very frequently a servile letter, *e.g.* in اللِيَاثِنة (from the singular
(اللِيثى), the Benî Leith (Burckhardt, *Syria*, p. 420), الغوارنة (from the
singular (الغورى), "the dwellers in the *Ghor*" (Burckhardt, *ibid.* p. 391);
cf. besides, الحَماصنة and الصوارنة (from the singular الحمصى and
(الصورى), "the inhabitants of *Emesa* and *Tyre*." Since the form فَعَالة is
become a very favourite collective of فَعَال (cf. ḥassâda, the mowers;
reggâda, the reapers; derrâsa, the threshers; keijâla, the measurers of the
corn; tarrâba, the tillers of the ground; lebbâna, the brickmakers, etc.),
it is natural simply to foist the name of ancestor of the tribe *Baijân* on the
collective *Baijâna* as the singular. This supposition is, however, unnecessary, since in connection with other word-formations too the ى of the
nisba disappears in the collective; cf. الفرجة, السبعة, الحَسنة, العنزة,
all of which are names of nomadic tribes, the singulars of which are
فريابجى, سبيعى, حسينى, عذيزى.

chain, as far as I could see N. and S.; it is called Djebel
Beyane (جبل بيانه); the height of this chain, however, is not
half that of the eastern mountains. It is intersected by
numerous broad Wadys in which the Talh tree grows; the rock
is entirely silicious, of the same species as that of the desert
which extends from hence to Suez. . . . After an hour and a
half of gentle ascent we arrived at the summit of the hills. . . ."
The article is wanting before *Beyâne* in Burckhardt; perhaps
the name given to the mountain to him by some of his attendants was *G. Beyân,* "mountain of the (*Benî*) *Baijân,*" and
by others *G. el-Beyâne,* "mountain of the Baijânites," so that
he regarded the absence of the article in the one and the form
of the other as the more correct. One of those "broad wadys,"
—perhaps the one on which was situated the fortress destroyed
by Judas,—is called, according to Robinson (*Biblical Researches
in Palestine,* 2d edition, i. 182, 1st ed. i. 269, etc.), the " *Wadî*
of the *Baijânites*" [" *el-Beyâneh*"] (وادى البيانة). Here also
belongs a statement in the Geographical Lexicon of *Abû ʿObeid
el-Bekrî* (died 487 of the Higra), which Juynboll unfortunately
gives incompletely in his edition of كتاب المراصد (vol. iv. p.
416), as follows : بيَّان بالفتح والتشديد موضع مجاور للغَمر الخ,
" *Baijân* with double *a* and a doubled *Jod* is a locality in the
neighbourhood of *Ghamr,* etc." Probably in the original text
used by Bekrî it stood خربة بيان or جبل بيان (the ruins of
Baijân, or the mountain of Baijân). Bekrî, however, imagining that in بيان he had the proper name not of a people but
of a locality, substituted for the خربة or جبل standing before it
the word موضع, which had at one time become stereotyped, and
by which those compilers described everything when possible.

BIBLICAL COMMENTARY

ON

THE OLD TESTAMENT.

BIBLICAL COMMENTARY

ON

THE PSALMS

BY

FRANZ DELITZSCH, D.D.,

PROFESSOR OF OLD AND NEW TESTAMENT EXEGESIS, LEIPSIC.

Translated from the German

(FROM THE SECOND EDITION, REVISED THROUGHOUT)

BY THE

REV. FRANCIS BOLTON, B.A.,

PRIZEMAN IN HEBREW AND NEW TESTAMENT GREEK IN THE UNIVERSITY OF LONDON.

TABLE OF CONTENTS

EXPOSITION OF THE PSALTER.

EXCURSUS BY J. G. WETZSTEIN.

THIRD BOOK OF THE PSALTER (CONTINUED)

Ps. LXXIII.–LXXXIX.

PSALM LXXXIV.

LONGING FOR THE HOUSE OF GOD, AND FOR THE
HAPPINESS OF DWELLING THERE.

2 HOW lovely are Thy dwelling-places, Jahve of Hosts!
3 My soul longeth, yea fainteth, for the courts of Jahve,
  My heart and my flesh sing for joy towards the living God.

4 Yea, the sparrow hath found a house,
  And the swallow a nest for herself,
  Where she hath sheltered her young—
  Thine altars, Jahve of Hosts,
  My King and my God.

5 Blessed are they who dwell in Thy house,
  They shall still praise Thee.   (*Sela.*)

6 Blessed is the man whose strength is in Thee—
  The pilgrims' ways are in their heart.
7 Passing through the valley of Baca,
  They make it a place of springs,
  The rain also enshroudeth it in blessings.

8 They go from strength to strength,
  There stand they before Elohim in Zion:

9 "Jahve Elohim of Hosts,
   Oh hear my prayer,
   Give ear, O God of Jacob!"   (*Sela.*)

10 Thou our Shield, look into it, Elohim,
   And look upon the face of Thine anointed!
11 For better is a day in Thy courts than a thousand;
   I had rather lie upon the threshold in the house of my God,
   Than dwell in the tents of wickedness.

12 For a sun and shield is Jahve Elohim.
   Grace and glory doth Jahve dispense,
   He doth not withhold any good thing from those who walk
       in uprightness.

13 Jahve of Hosts,
   Blessed is the man who trusteth in Thee.

With Ps. lxxxiii. the circle of the Asaphic songs is closed
(twelve Psalms, viz. one in the Second Book and eleven in the
Third), and with Ps. lxxxiv. begins the other half of the Korahitic circle of songs, opened by the last of the Korahitic Elohim-Psalms. True, Hengstenberg (transl. vol. iii. Appendix, p.
xlv) says that no one would, with my *Symbolæ*, p. 22, regard this
Ps. lxxxiv. as an Elohimic Psalm; but the marks of the Elohimic
style are obvious. Not only that the poet uses *Elohim* twice,
and that in ver. 8, where a non-Elohimic Psalm ought to have
said *Jahve;* it also delights in compound names of God, which
are so heaped up that *Jahve Tsebaoth* occurs three times, and
the specifically Elohimic *Jahve Elohim Tsebaoth* once.

The origin of this Psalm has been treated of already in
connection with its counterpart, Ps. xlii.–xliii. It is a thoroughly
heartfelt and intelligent expression of the love to the sanctuary
of Jahve which yearns towards it out of the distance, and calls
all those happy who have the like good fortune to have their
home there. The prayer takes the form of an intercession for
God's anointed; for the poet is among the followers of David,
the banished one.* He does not pray, as it were, out of his

---

* Nic. Nonnen takes a different view in his *Dissertatio de Tzippor et*

soul (Hengstenberg, Tholuck, von Gerlach), but for him; for loving Jahve of Hosts, the heavenly King, he also loves His inviolably chosen one. And wherefore should he not do so, since with him a new era for the neglected sanctuary had dawned, and the delightful services of the Lord had taken a new start, and one so rich in song? With him he shares both joy and grief. With his future he indissolubly unites his own.

To the Precentor upon the Gittith, the inscription runs, *by Benê-Korah, a Psalm.* Concerning עַל־הַגִּתִּית, *vid.* on viii. 1. The structure of the Psalm is artistic. It consists of two halves with a distichic *ashrê*-conclusion. The schema is 3. 5. 2 | 5. 5. 5. 3. 2.

Vers. 2–5. How loved and lovely (יְדִידוֹת) is the sacred dwelling-place (*plur.* as in xliii. 3) of the all-commanding, re-demptive God, viz. His dwelling-place here below upon Zion! Thither the poet is drawn by the deeply inward yearning of love, which makes him pale (נִכְסַף from כָּסַף, to grow pale, xvii. 12) and consumes him (כָּלָה as in Job xix. 27). His heart and flesh joyfully salute the living God dwelling there, who, as a never-failing spring, quenches the thirst of the soul (xlii. 3); the joy that he feels when he throws himself back in spirit into the long-denied delight takes possession even of his bodily nature, the bitter-sweet pain of longing completely fills him (lxiii. 2). The mention of the "courts" (with the exception of the Davidic Psalm lxv. 5, occurring only in the anonymous Psalms) does not preclude the reference of the Psalm to the tent-temple on Zion. The Tabernacle certainly had only one חָצֵר; the arrangement of the Davidic tent-temple, however, is indeed unknown to us, and, according to reliable traces,* it may be well assumed that it was more gorgeous and more spacious than the old Tabernacle which remained in Gibeon. In ver. 4 the preference must be given to that explanation which makes אֶת־מִזְבְּחוֹתֶיךָ dependent upon מָצְאָה, without being obliged to supply an intermediate thought like בֵּית (with hardening

---

Deror, etc., 1741. He considers one of the Ephraimites who were brought back to the fellowship of the true worship of God in the reign of Jehosha-phat (2 Chron. xix. 4) to be the subject of the Psalm.

* *Vid.* Knobel on Exodus, S. 253–257, especially S. 255.

Dagesh like בֵּן, Gen. xix. 38, *vid.* the rule at lii. 5) and קֵן as a more definite statement of the object which the poet has in view. The altars, therefore, or (what this is meant to say without any need for taking אֶת as a preposition) the realm, province of the altars of Jahve—this is the house, this the nest which sparrow and swallow have found for themselves and their young. The poet thereby only indirectly says, that birds have built themselves nests on the Temple-house, without giving any occasion for the discussion whether this has taken place in reality. By the bird that has found a comfortable snug home on the place of the altars of Jahve in the Temple-court and in the Temple-house, he means himself. צִפּוֹר (from צָפַר) is a general name for whistling, twittering birds, like the finch* and the sparrow, just as the LXX. here renders it. דְּרוֹר is not the turtle-dove (LXX., Targum, and Syriac), but the swallow, which is frequently called even in the Talmud צפור דרור (= סְנוּנִית), and appears to take its name from its straightforward darting, as it were, radiating flight (cf. Arabic *jadurru* of the horse: it darts straight forward). Saadia renders *dûrîje*, which is the name of the sparrow in Palestine and Syria (*vid.* Wetzstein's Excursus I. at the end of this volume). After the poet has said that his whole longing goes forth towards the sanctuary, he adds that it could not possibly be otherwise (גַּם standing at the head of the clause and belonging to the whole sentence, as *e.g.* in Isa. xxx. 33; Ewald, § 352, *b*): he, the sparrow, the swallow, has found a house, a nest, viz. the altars of Jahve of Hosts, his King and his God (xliv. 5, xlv. 7), who gloriously and inaccessibly protects him, and to whom he unites himself with most heartfelt and believing love. The addition "where (אֲשֶׁר as in xcv. 9, Num. xx. 13) she layeth her young," is not without its significance. One is here reminded of the fact, that at the time of the second Temple the sons of the priests were called פִּרְחֵי כְהֻנָּה, and the Levite poet means himself together with his family; God's altars secure to them shelter and sustenance. How happy, blessed, therefore, are those who enjoy this good fortune, which he now longs for again with pain in a strange country, viz. to be able to make his home in the house of such an adorable and gracious God! עוֹד here signifies, not

---

* *Vid.* Tobler, *Denkblätter aus Jerusalem*, 1853, S. 117.

"constantly" (Gen. xlvi. 29), for which תָּמִיד would have been used, but "yet," as in xlii. 6. The relation of ver. 5*b* to 5*a* is therefore like xli. 2. The present is dark, but it will come to pass even yet that the inmates of God's house (οἰκεῖοι τοῦ Θεοῦ, Eph. ii. 10) will praise Him as their Helper. The music here strikes in, anticipating this praise.

Vers. 6–13. This second half takes up the "blessed" of the distichic epode (ἐπῳδὸς) of the first, and consequently joins member to member chain-like on to it. Many hindrances must be cleared away if the poet is to get back to Zion, his true home; but his longing carries the surety within itself of its fulfilment: blessed, yea in himself blessed, is the man, who has his strength (עוֹז only here *plene*) in God, so that, consequently, the strength of Him to whom all things are possible is mighty in his weakness. What is said in ver. 6*b* is less adapted to be the object of the being called blessed than the result of that blessed relationship to God. What follows shows that the "high-roads" are not to be understood according to Isa. xl. 3 sq., or any other passage, as an ethical, notional figure (Venema, Hengstenberg, Hitzig, and others), but according to Isa. xxxiii. 8 (cf. Jer. xxxi. 21), with Aben-Ezra, Vatablus, and the majority of expositors, of the roads leading towards Zion; not, however, as referring to the return from the Exile, but to the going up to a festival: the pilgrim-high-roads with their separate halting-places (stations) were constantly present to the mind of such persons. And though they may be driven never so far away from them, they will nevertheless reach the goal of their longing. The most gloomy present becomes bright to them: passing through even a terrible wilderness, they turn it (יְשִׁיתֻהוּ) into a place of springs, their joyous hope and the infinite beauty of the goal, which is worth any amount of toil and trouble, afford them enlivening comfort, refreshing strengthening in the midst of the arid steppe. עֵמֶק הַבָּכָא does not signify the "Valley of weeping," as Hupfeld at last renders it (LXX. κοιλάδα τοῦ κλαυθμῶνος), although Burckhardt found a وادي البكا (Valley of weeping) in the neighbourhood of Sinai. In Hebrew "weeping" is בְּכִי, בְּכֶה, בְּכוּת, not בָּכָא. Rénan, in the fourth chapter of his *Vie de Jésus*, understands the expression to mean the last station of those who journey from northern

Palestine on this side of the Jordan towards Jerusalem, viz.
Ain el-Haramîje, in a narrow and gloomy valley where a black
stream of water flows out of the rocks in which graves are dug,
so that consequently עמק הבכא signifies Valley of tears or of
trickling waters. But such trickling out of the rock is also
called בְּכִי, Job xxviii. 11, and not בָּכָא. This latter is the
singular to בְּכָאִים in 2 Sam. v. 24 (cf. נְכָאִים, צְבָאִים, ciii. 21), the
name of a tree, and, according to the old Jewish lexicographers,
of the mulberry-tree (Talmudic תּוּת, توت); but according to
the designation, of a tree from which some kind of fluid flows,
and such a tree is the بَكَا, resembling the balsam-tree, which is
very common in the arid valley of Mecca, and therefore might
also have given its name to some arid valley of the Holy Land
(*vid.* Winer's *Realwörterbuch*, s.v. *Bacha*), and, according to
2 Sam. v. 22–25, to one belonging, as it would appear, to the
line of valley which leads from the coasts of the Philistines to
Jerusalem. What is spoken of in passages like Isa. xxxv. 7,
xli. 18, as being wrought by the omnipotence of God, who
brings His people home to Zion, appears here as the result of
the power of faith in those who, keeping the same end of their
journeyings in view, pass through the unfruitful sterile valley.
That other side, however, also does not remain unexpressed.
Not only does their faith bring forth water out of the sand and
rock of the desert, but God also on His part lovingly anticipates their love, and rewardingly anticipates their faithfulness:
a gentle rain, like that which refreshes the sown fields in the
autumn, descends from above and enwraps it (viz. the Valley of
Baca) in a fulness of blessing (יַעְטֶה, *Hiphil* with two accusatives, of which one is to be supplied: cf. on the figure, lxv. 14).
The arid steppe becomes resplendent with a flowery festive
garment (Isa. xxxv. 1 sq.), not to outward appearance, but
to them spiritually, in a manner none the less true and real.
And whereas under ordinary circumstances the strength of the
traveller diminishes in proportion as he has traversed more and
more of his toilsome road, with them it is the very reverse;
they go from strength to strength (cf. on the expression, Jer.
ix. 2, xii. 2), *i.e.* they receive strength for strength (cf. on the
subject-matter, Isa. xl. 31, John i. 16), and that an ever increasing strength, the nearer they come to the desired goal,

which also they cannot fail to reach. The pilgrim-band (this is the subject to יֵרָאֶה), going on from strength to (אֶל) strength, at last reaches, attains to (אֶל instead of the אֶל־פְּנֵי used in other instances) Elohim in Zion. Having reached this final goal, the pilgrim-band pours forth its heart in the language of prayer such as we have in ver. 9, and the music here strikes up and blends its sympathetic tones with this converse of the church with its God.

The poet, however, who in spirit accompanies them on their pilgrimage, is now all the more painfully conscious of being at the present time far removed from this goal, and in the next strophe prays for relief. He calls God מָגִנֵּנוּ (as in lix. 12), for without His protection David's cause is lost. May He then behold (רְאֵה, used just as absolutely as in 2 Chron. xxiv. 22, cf. Lam. iii. 50), and look upon the face of IIis anointed, which looks up to Him out of the depth of its reproach. The position of the words shows that מָגִנֵּנוּ is not to be regarded as the object to רְאֵה, according to lxxxix. 19 (cf. xlvii. 10) and in opposition to the accentuation, for why should it not then have been אלהים ראה מגננו? The confirmation (ver. 11) puts the fact that we have before us a Psalm belonging to the time of David's persecution by Absalom beyond all doubt. Manifestly, when his king prevails, the poet will at the same time (cf. David's language, 2 Sam. xv. 25) be restored to the sanctuary. A single day of his lfe in the courts of God is accounted by him as better than a thousand other days (מֵאָלֶף with *Olewejored* and preceded by *Rebia parvum*). He would rather lie down on the threshold (concerning the significance of this הִסְתּוֹפֵף in the mouth of a Korahite, *vid. supra*, vol. ii. p. 53) in the house of his God than dwell within in the tents of ungodliness (not "palaces," as one might have expected, if the house of God had at that time been a palace). For how worthless is the pleasure and concealment to be had there, when compared with the salvation and protection which Jahve Elohim affords to His saints! This is the only instance in which God is directly called a sun (שֶׁמֶשׁ) in the sacred writings (cf. Sir. xlii. 16). He is called a shield as protecting those who flee to Him and rendering them inaccessible to their foes, and a sun as the Being who dwells in an unapproachable light, which, going forth from Him in love towards men, is particularized as חֵן and

כבוד, as the gentle and overpowering light of the grace and glory (χάρις and δόξα) of the Father of Lights. The highest good is self-communicative (*communicativum sui*). The God of salvation does not refuse any good thing to those who walk בְּתָמִים (בְּדֶרֶךְ תמים, ci. 6; cf. on xv. 2). Upon all receptive ones, *i.e.* all those who are desirous and capable of receiving His blessings, He freely bestows them out of the abundance of His good things. Strophe and anti-strophe are doubled in this second half of the song. The epode closely resembles that which follows the first half. And this closing *ashrê* is not followed by any *Sela*. The music is hushed. The song dies away with an iambic cadence into a waiting expectant stillness.

PSALM LXXXV.

PETITION OF THE HITHERTO FAVOURED PEOPLE FOR A RESTORATION OF FAVOUR.

2 THOU hast been favourable, Jahve, unto Thy land,
 Thou hast turned the captivity of Jacob;
3 Thou hast taken away the iniquity of Thy people,
 Thou hast covered all their sin— (*Sela.*)
4 Thou hast drawn in all Thy wrath,
 Thou hast turned from the heat of Thine anger.

5 Turn unto us again, O God of our salvation,
 And cause Thine indignation against us to cease.
6 Wilt Thou for ever be angry with us,
 Wilt Thou draw out Thine anger to all generations?
7 Wilt Thou not quicken us again,
 That Thy people may rejoice in Thee?
8 Cause us to see, Jahve, Thy loving-kindness,
 And grant us Thy salvation.

9 I will hear what God Jahve will speak — —
 Yea, He speaketh peace to His people and to His saints;
 Only let them not again fall into folly!
10 Yea, nigh unto those who fear Him is His salvation,
 That glory may again dwell in our land.

11 Loving-kindness and truth shall meet together,
 Righteousness and peace shall kiss each other.

12 Truth shall spring out of the earth,
 And righteousness shall look down from heaven.
13 Jahve shall give every good thing,
 And our land shall again yield its increase.
14 Righteousness shall go before Him
 And attend unto the way of His steps.

The second part of the Book of Isaiah is written for the Israel of the Exile. It was the incidents of the Exile that first unsealed this great and indivisible prophecy, which in its compass is without any parallel. And after it had been unsealed there sprang up out of it those numerous songs of the Psalm-collection which remind us of their common model, partly by their allegorizing figurative language, partly by their lofty prophetic thoughts of consolation. This first Korahitic Jahve-Psalm (in ver. 13 coming into contact with Ps. lxxxiv., cf. lxxxiv. 12), which more particularly by its allegorizing figurative language points to Isa. ch. xl.–lxvi., belongs to the number of these so-called deutero-Isaianic Psalms.

The reference of Ps. lxxxv. to the period after the Exile and to the restoration of the state, says Dursch, is clearly expressed in the Psalm. On the other hand, Hengstenberg maintains that "the Psalm does not admit of any historical interpretation," and is sure only of this one fact, that vers. 2–4 do not relate to the deliverance out of the Exile. Even this Psalm, however, is not a formulary belonging to no express period, but has a special historical basis; and vers. 2–4 certainly sound as though they came from the lips of a people restored to their fatherland.

Vers. 2–4. The poet first of all looks back into the past, so rich in tokens of favour. The six perfects are a remembrance of former events, since nothing precedes to modify them. Certainly that which has just been experienced might also be intended; but then, as Hitzig supposes, vers. 5–8 would be the petition that preceded it, and ver. 9 would go back to the turning-point of the answering of the request—a retrograde move-

ment which is less probable than that in שׁוּבֵנוּ, ver. 5, we have a
transition to the petition for a renewal of previously manifested
favour. (שְׁבִית) שָׁב שְׁבוּת, here said of a cessation of a national
judgment, seems to be meant literally, not figuratively (*vid.*
xiv. 7). רָצָה, with the accusative, to have and to show pleasure
in any one, as in the likewise Korahitic lamentation-Psalm xliv.
4, cf. cxlvii. 11. In ver. 3*a* sin is conceived of as a burden of
the conscience; in ver. 3*b* as a blood-stain. The music strikes
up in the middle of the strophe in the sense of the "blessed"
in xxxii. 1. In ver. 4*a* God's עֶבְרָה (*i.e.* unrestrained wrath)
appears as an emanation; He draws it back to Himself (אָסַף as
in Joel iv. [iii.] 15, Ps. civ. 29, 1 Sam. xiv. 19) when He ceases
to be angry; in ver. 4*b*, on the other hand, the fierce anger is
conceived of as an active manifestation on the part of God
which ceases when He turns round (הֵשִׁיב, *Hiph.* as inwardly
transitive as in Ezek. xiv. 6, xxi. 35; cf. the *Kal* in Ex. xxxii.
12), *i.e.* gives the opposite turn to His manifestation.

Vers. 5–8. The poet now prays God to manifest anew the
loving-kindness He has shown formerly. In the sense of
"restore us again," שׁוּבֵנוּ does not form any bond of connection
between this and the preceding strophe; but it does if, according to Ges. § 121, 4, it is intended in the sense of שׁוּב לָנוּ (אֵלֵינוּ),
turn again to us. The poet prays that God would manifest
Himself anew to His people as He has done in former days.
Thus the transition from the retrospective perfects to the petition is, in the presence of the existing extremity, adequately
brought about. Assuming the post-exilic origin of the Psalm,
we see from this strophe that it was composed at a period in
which the distance between the temporal and spiritual condition
of Israel and the national restoration, promised together with
the termination of the Exile, made itself distinctly felt. On עִמָּנוּ
(in relation to and bearing towards us) beside בַּעֲסְךָ, cf. Job x.
17, and also on הֵפֵר, lxxxix. 34. In the question in ver. 6 reminding God of His love and of His promise, מָשַׁךְ has the
signification of constant endless continuing or pursuing, as in
xxxvi. 11. The expression in ver. 7*a* is like lxxi. 20, cf. lxxx.
19; שׁוּב is here the representative of *rursus*, Ges. § 142. יֵשַׁעֲךָ
from יֵשַׁע, like קֶצֶף in xxxviii. 2, has *ĕ* (cf. the inflexion of פְּרִי and
חֹק) instead of the *ŏ* in אֱלֹהֵי יִשְׁעֵנוּ. Here at the close of the strophe
the prayer turns back inferentially to this attribute of God.

Vers. 9–11. The prayer is followed by attention to the divine answer, and by the answer itself. The poet stirs himself up to give ear to the words of God, like Habakkuk, ch. ii. 1. Beside אֶשְׁמְעָה we find the reading אִשְׁמְעָה, *vid.* on xxxix. 13. The construction of הָאֵל ה׳ is appositional, like הַמֶּלֶךְ דָּוִד, Ges. § 113. כִּי neither introduces the divine answer in express words, nor states the ground on which he hearkens, but rather supports the fact that God speaks from that which He has to speak. Peace is the substance of that which He speaks to His people, and that (the particularizing *Waw*) to His saints; but with the addition of an admonition. אַל is dehortative. It is not to be assumed in connection with this ethical notion that the *ah* of לְכִסְלָה is the locative *ah* as in לִשְׁאוֹלָה, ix. 18. כִּסְלָה is related to כְּסַל like foolery to folly. The present misfortune, as is indicated here, is the merited consequence of foolish behaviour (playing the fool). In vers. 10 sqq. the poet unfolds the promise of peace which he has heard, just as he has heard it. What is meant by יִשְׁעוֹ is particularized first by the infinitive, and then in perfects of actual fact. The possessions that make a people truly happy and prosperous are mentioned under a charming allegory exactly after Isaiah's manner, ch. xxxii. 16 sq., xlv. 8, lix. 14 sq. The glory that has been far removed again takes up its abode in the land. Mercy or loving-kindness walks along the streets of Jerusalem, and there meets fidelity, like one guardian angel meeting the other. Righteousness and peace or prosperity, these two inseparable brothers, kiss each other there, and fall lovingly into each other's arms.*

Vers. 12–14. The poet pursues this charming picture of the future further. After God's אֱמֶת, *i.e.* faithfulness to the promises, has descended like dew, אמת, *i.e.* faithfulness to the covenant, springs up out of the land, the fruit of that fertilizing influence. And צְדָקָה, gracious justice, looks down from heaven,

---

* Concerning St. Bernard's beautiful parable of the reconciliation of the inviolability of divine threatening and of justice with mercy and peace in the work of redemption, which has grown out of this passage of the Psalms, *Misericordia et veritas obviaverunt sibi, justitia et pax osculatæ sunt,* and has been transferred to the painting, poetry, and drama of the middle ages, *vid.* Piper's *Evangelischer Kalender,* 1859, S. 24–34, and the beautiful miniature representing the ἀσπασμός of δικαιοσύνη and εἰρήνη of a Greek Psalter, 1867, S. 63.

smiling favour and dispensing blessing. נַּם in ver. 13 places
these two prospects in reciprocal relation to one another (cf.
lxxxiv. 7); it is found once instead of twice.   Jahve gives הַטּוֹב,
everything that is only and always good and that imparts true
happiness, and the land, corresponding to it, yields יְבוּלָהּ, the increase which might be expected from a land so richly blessed
(cf. lxvii. 7 and the promise in Lev. xxvi. 4).   Jahve Himself
is present in the land: righteousness walks before Him ma-
jestically as His herald, and righteousness יָשֵׂם לְדֶרֶךְ פְּעָמָיו, sets
(viz. its footsteps) upon the way of His footsteps, that is to
say, follows Him inseparably.   פְּעָמָיו stands once instead of
twice; the construct is to a certain extent attractional, as in
lxv. 12, Gen. ix. 6.   Since the expression is neither דֶּרֶךְ (l. 23,
Isa. li. 10) nor לַדֶּרֶךְ (Isa. xlix. 11), it is natural to interpret the
expression thus, and it gives moreover (cf. Isa. lviii. 8, lii. 12)
an excellent sense.   But if, which we prefer, שִׂים is taken in
the sense of שִׂים לֵב (as *e.g.* in Job iv. 20) with the following לְ,
to give special heed to anything (Deut. xxxii. 46, Ezek. xl. 4,
xliv. 5), to be anxiously concerned about it (1 Sam. ix. 20),
then we avoid the supplying in thought of a second פעמיו, which
is always objectionable, and the thought obtained by the other
interpretation is brought clearly before the mind: righteousness goes before Jahve, who dwells and walks abroad in Israel,
and gives heed to the way of His steps, that is to say, follows
carefully in His footsteps.

PSALM LXXXVI.

PRAYER OF A PERSECUTED SAINT.

1 BOW down, Jahve, Thine ear, answer me,
   For I am needy and poor.
2 Preserve my soul, for I am pious;
   Help Thy servant, O Thou my God,
   Who cleaveth confidingly to Thee.
3 Be merciful unto me, Lord,
   For unto Thee do I cry all the day.
4 Rejoice the soul of Thy servant,
   For unto Thee, Lord, do I lift up my soul.

5 For Thou, Lord, art good and ready to forgive,
  And plenteous in mercy unto all who call upon Thee.

6 Give ear, Jahve, to my prayer,
  And hearken to the cry of my importunate supplications.
7 In the day of my distress do I call unto Thee,
  For Thou wilt answer me.
8 There is none like unto Thee among the gods, O Lord,
  And Thy works have not their equal.
9 All nations which Thou hast made shall come and worship
        before Thee, Lord,
  And give glory to Thy name.
10 For Thou art great and doest wondrous things,
  Thou, Thou art God alone.
11 Teach me, Jahve, Thy way,
  I desire to walk in Thy truth;
  Unite my heart to fear Thy Name.
12 I will give thanks to Thee, O Lord my God, with all my
        heart,
  And will glorify Thy Name for ever,
13 That Thy mercy has been great over me,
  And Thou hast rescued my soul out of the deep hell.

14 Elohim, the proud are risen against me,
  And an assembly of violent men seek my soul,
  And have not set Thee before their eyes.
15 But Thou, Lord, art a God compassionate and gracious,
  Long-suffering and plenteous in mercy and truth.
16 Turn unto me and be gracious to me,
  O give strength unto Thy servant
  And save the son of Thy handmaid.
17 Show me a token for good,
  That those who hate me may see it and be ashamed,
  That Thou, Jahve, hast helped me and comforted me.

A Psalm "by David" which has points of contact with
Ps. lxxxv. (cf. lxxxvi. 2, חסיד, with lxxxv. 9; lxxxvi. 15, חסד
ואמת, with lxxxv. 11) is here inserted between Korahitic Psalms:
it can only be called a Psalm by David as having grown out
of Davidic and other model passages. The writer cannot be

compared for poetical capability either with David or with the authors of such Psalms as Ps. cxvi. and cxxx. His Psalm is more liturgic than purely poetic, and it is also only entitled תְּפִלָּה, without bearing in itself any sign of musical designation. It possesses this characteristic, that the divine name אדני occurs seven times,* just as it occurs three times in Ps. cxxx., forming the start for a later, Adonajic style in imitation of the Elohimic.

Vers. 1–5. The prayer to be heard runs like lv. 3; and the statement of the ground on which it is based, ver. 1*b*, word for word like xl. 18. It is then particularly expressed as a prayer for preservation (שָׁמְרָה, as in cxix. 167, although imperative, to be read *shām᷍rah*; cf. xxx. 4 מִיָּרְדִי, xxxviii. 21 רֹדְפִי or רֹדְפִי, and what we have already observed on xvi. 1 שָׁמְרֵנִי); for he is not only in need of God's help, but also because חָסִיד (iv. 4, xvi. 10), *i.e.* united to Him in the bond of affection (חֶסֶד, Hos. vi. 4, Jer. ii. 2), not unworthy of it. In ver. 2 we hear the strains of xxv. 20, xxxi. 7; in ver. 3, of lvii. 2 sq.: the confirmation in ver. 4*b* is taken verbally from xxv. 1, cf. also cxxx. 6. Here, what is said in ver. 4 of this shorter Adonajic Psalm, cxxx., is abbreviated in the ἅπαξ γεγραμ. סַלָּח (root סל, שׁל, to allow to hang loose, χαλᾶν, to give up, *remittere*). The Lord is good (טוב), *i.e.* altogether love, and for this very reason also ready to forgive, and great and rich in mercy for all who call upon Him as such. The beginning of the following group also accords with Ps. cxxx. in ver. 2.

Vers. 6–13. Here, too, almost everything is an echo of earlier language of the Psalms and of the Law; viz., ver. 7 follows xvii. 6 and other passages; ver. 8*a* is taken from Ex. xv. 11, cf. lxxxix. 9, where, however, אלהים, gods, is avoided; ver. 8*b* follows Deut. iii. 24; ver. 9 follows xxii. 28; ver. 11*a* is taken from xxvii. 11; ver. 11*b* from xxvi. 3; ver. 13, שְׁאוֹל תַּחְתִּיָה from Deut. xxxii. 22, where instead of this it is תַּחְתִּית, just as in cxxx. 2 תַּחֲנוּנַי (supplicatory prayer) instead of תַּחֲנוּנֹתַי

---

* For the genuine reading in ver. 4 (where Heidenheim reads יהוה) and in ver. 5 (where Nissel reads יהוה) is also אֲדֹנָי (Bomberg, Hutter, etc.). Both the divine names in vers. 4 and 5 belong to the 134 וְדָאִין. The divine name אֲדֹנָי, which is written and is not merely substituted for יהוה, is called in the language of the Masora וְדָאִי (the true and real one).

(importunate supplications); and also ver. 10 (cf. lxxii. 18) is a doxological formula that was already in existence. The construction הִקְשִׁיב בְּ is the same as in lxvi. 19. But although for the most part flowing on only in the language of prayer borrowed from earlier periods, this Psalm is, moreover, not without remarkable significance and beauty. With the confession of the incomparableness of the Lord is combined the prospect of the recognition of the incomparable One throughout the nations of the earth. This clear unallegorical prediction of the conversion of the heathen is the principal parallel to Apoc. xv. 4. "All nations, which Thou hast made"—they have their being from Thee; and although they have forgotten it (*vid.* ix. 18), they will nevertheless at last come to recognise it. כָּל־גּוֹיִם, since the article is wanting, are nations of all tribes (countries and nationalities); cf. Jer. xvi. 16 with Ps. xxii. 18; Tobit xiii. 11, ἔθνη πολλά, with *ibid.* xiv. 6, πάντα τὰ ἔθνη. And how weightily brief and charming is the petition in ver. 11: *uni cor meum, ut timeat nomen tuum!* Luther has rightly departed from the renderings of the LXX., Syriac, and Vulgate: *lœtetur* (יַחְדְּ from חָדָה). The meaning, however, is not so much "keep my heart near to the only thing," as "direct all its powers and concentrate them on the one thing." The following group shows us what is the meaning of the deliverance out of the hell beneath (שְׁאוֹל תַּחְתִּיָּה, like אֶרֶץ תַּחְתִּית, the earth beneath, the inner parts of the earth, Ezek. xxxi. 14 sqq.), for which the poet promises beforehand to manifest his thankfulness (כִּי, ver. 13, as in lvi. 14).

Vers. 14–17. The situation is like that in the Psalms of the time of Saul. The writer is a persecuted one, and in constant peril of his life. He has taken ver. 14ab out of the Elohimic Ps. liv. ver. 5, and retained the *Elohim* as a proper name of God (cf. on the other hand vers. 8, 10); he has, however, altered זָרִים to זֵדִים, which here, as in Isa. xiii. 11 (cf., however, *ibid.* xxv. 5), is the alternating word to עָרִיצִים. In ver. 15 he supports his petition that follows by Jahve's testimony concerning Himself in Ex. xxxiv. 6. The appellation given to himself by the poet in ver. 16 recurs in cxvi. 16 (cf. Wisd. ix. 5). The poet calls himself "the son of Thy handmaid" as having been born into the relation to Him of servant; it is a relationship that has come to him by birth. How beautifully does the *Adonaj* come in here for the seventh time! He is even from his mother's womb the servant of the sovereign Lord, from whose omnipotence he can therefore also look for a miraculous interposition on his behalf. A " token for good " is a special dispensation, from which it becomes evident to him that God is kindly disposed towards him. לְטוֹבָה as in the mouth of Nehemiah, ch. v. 19, xiii. 31; of Ezra, ch. viii. 22; and also even in Jeremiah and earlier. וְיֵבֹשׁוּ is just as parenthetical as in Isa. xxvi. 11.

PSALM LXXXVII.

THE CITY OF THE NEW BIRTH OF THE NATIONS.

1 HIS founded [city] upon the holy mountains—
2 Jahve loveth the gates of Zion
  More than all the dwellings of Jacob.
3 Glorious things are spoken of thee, thou city of God!
    (*Sela.*)
4 " I will proclaim Rahab and Babylon as My intimates;
  Behold Philistia and Tyre, together with Æthiopia—
  That one is born there."

5 And to Zion it shall one day be said:
  Each and every one is born in her,
  And He, the Highest, doth establish her.
6 Jahve shall reckon in the list of the nations:
  That one is born there. (*Sela.*)
7 And singing as well as dancing (they say):
  All my fountains are in thee!

The mission thought in lxxxvi. 9 becomes the ruling thought in this Korahitic Psalm. It is a prophetic Psalm in the style, boldly and expressively concise even to obscurity (Eusebius, σφόδρα αἰνιγματώδης καὶ σκοτεινῶς εἰρημένος), in which the first three oracles of the tetralogy Isa. xxi.–xxii. 14, and the passage Isa. xxx. 6, 7—a passage designed to be as it were a memorial exhibition—are also written. It also resembles these oracles in this respect, that ver. 1*b* opens the whole arsis-like

by a solemn statement of its subject, like the emblematical
inscriptions there. As to the rest, Isa. xliv. 5 is the key to its
meaning. The threefold יֻלַּד here corresponds to the threefold
זֶה in that passage.

Since Rahab and Babylon as the foremost worldly powers
are mentioned first among the peoples who come into the
congregation of Jahve, and since the prospect of the poet
has moulded itself according to a present rich in promise and
carrying such a future in its bosom, it is natural (with Tholuck,
Hengstenberg, Vaihinger, Keil, and others) to suppose that the
Psalm was composed when, in consequence of the destruction
of the Assyrian army before Jerusalem, offerings and presents
were brought from many quarters for Jahve and the king of
Judah (2 Chron. xxxii. 23), and the admiration of Hezekiah,
the favoured one of God, had spread as far as Babylon. Just
as Micah (ch. iv. 10) mentions Babylon as the place of the
chastisement and of the redemption of his nation, and as
Isaiah, about the fourteenth year of Hezekiah's reign, predicts
to the king a carrying away of his treasures and his posterity
to Babylon, so here Egypt and Babylon, the inheritress of
Assyria, stand most prominent among the worldly powers that
shall be obliged one day to bow themselves to the God of Israel.
In a similar connection Isaiah (ch. xix.) does not as yet mention
Babylon side by side with Egypt, but Assyria.

Vers. 1—4. The poet is absorbed in the contemplation of
the glory of a matter which he begins to celebrate, without
naming it. Whether we render it: His founded, or (since
מִיסָּד and מוּסָּד are both used elsewhere as *part. pass.*): His
foundation (after the form מְלוּכָה, poetically for יְסוֹד, a founding,
then that which is set fast = a foundation), the meaning remains
the same; but the more definite statement of the object with
שַׁעֲרֵי צִיּוֹן is more easily connected with what precedes by regarding it as a participle. The suffix refers to Jahve, and it is Zion,
whose praise is a favourite theme of the Korahitic songs, that
is intended. We cannot tell by looking to the accents whether
the clause is to be taken as a substantival clause (His founded
[city] is upon the holy mountains) or not. Since, however,
the expression is not יְסוּדָתוֹ הִיא בְּהַרְרֵי־קֹדֶשׁ, ‏יסודתו בהררי קדשׁ is
an object placed first in advance (which the antithesis to the

other dwellings of Jacob would admit of), and in ver. 2*a* a new synonymous object is subordinated to אֹהֵב by a similar turn of the discourse to Jer. xiii. 27, vi. 2 (Hitzig). By altering the division of the verses as Hupfeld and Hofmann do (His foundation or founded [city] upon the holy mountains doth Jahve love), ver. 2 is decapitated. Even now the God-founded city (surrounded on three sides by deep valleys), whose firm and visible foundation is the outward manifestation of its imperishable inner nature, rises aloft above all the other dwelling-places of Israel. Jahve stands in a lasting, faithful, loving relationship (אֹהֵב, not 3 *præt.* אָהֵב) to the gates of Zion. These gates are named as a periphrasis for Zion, because they bound the circuit of the city, and any one who loves a city delights to go frequently through its gates; and they are perhaps mentioned in prospect of the fulness of the heathen that shall enter into them. In ver. 3 the LXX. correctly, and at the same time in harmony with the syntax, renders: Δεδοξασμένα ἐλαλήθη περὶ σοῦ. The construction of a plural subject with a singular predicate is a syntax common in other instances also, whether the subject is conceived of as a unity in the form of the plural (*e.g.* lxvi. 3, cxix. 137, Isa. xvi. 8), or is individualized in the pursuance of the thought (as is the case most likely in Gen. xxvii. 29, cf. xii. 3) ; here the glorious things are conceived of as the sum-total of such. The operation of the construction of the active (Ew. § 295, *b*) is not probable here in connection with the participle. בְּ beside דִּבֶּר may signify the place or the instrument, substance and object of the speech (*e.g.* cxix. 46), but also the person against whom the words are spoken (*e.g.* l. 20), or concerning whom they are uttered (as the words of the suitor to the father or the relatives of the maiden, 1 Sam. xxv. 39, Cant. viii. 8 ; cf. on the construction, 1 Sam. xix. 3). The poet, without doubt, here refers to the words of promise concerning the eternal continuance and future glory of Jerusalem : Glorious things are spoken, *i.e.* exist as spoken, in reference to thee, O thou city of God, city of His choice and of His love.

The glorious contents of the promise are now unfolded, and that with the most vivid directness : Jahve Himself takes up the discourse, and declares the gracious, glorious, world-wide mission of His chosen and beloved city : it shall become the

birth-place of all nations. *Rahab* is Egypt, as in lxxxix. 11,
Isa. xxx. 7, li. 9, the southern worldly power, and *Babylon* the
northern. הַזְכִּיר, as frequently, of loud (Jer. iv. 16) and
honourable public mention or commemoration, xlv. 18. It
does not signify " to record or register in writing;" for the
official name מַזְכִּיר, which is cited in support of this meaning,
designates the historian of the empire as one who keeps in
remembrance the memorable events of the history of his time
It is therefore impossible, with Hofmann, to render: I will
add Rahab and Babylon to those who know me. In general
לְ is not used to point out to whom the addition is made as
belonging to them, but for what purpose, or as what (cf. 2 Sam.
v. 3, Isa. iv. 3), these kingdoms, hitherto hostile towards God
and His people, shall be declared: Jahve completes what He
Himself has brought about, inasmuch as He publicly and
solemnly declares them to be those who know Him, *i.e.* those
who experimentally (*vid.* xxxvi. 11) know Him as their God.
Accordingly, it is clear that זֶה יֻלַּד־שָׁם is also meant to refer to
the conversion of the other three nations to whom the finger
of God points with הִנֵּה, viz. the war-loving Philistia, the rich
and proud Tyre, and the adventurous and powerful Ethiopia
(Isa. ch. xviii.). זֶה does not refer to the individuals, nor to the
sum-total of these nations, but to nation after nation (cf. זֶה
הָעָם, Isa. xxiii. 13), by fixing the eye upon each one separately.
And שָׁם refers to Zion. The words of Jahve, which come in
without any intermediary preparation, stand in the closest connection with the language of the poet and seer. Zion appears
elsewhere as the mother who brings forth Israel again as a
numerous people (Isa. lxvi. 7, liv. 1–3): it is the children of
the dispersion (*diaspora*) which Zion regains in Isa. lx. 4 sq.;
here, however, it is the nations which are born in Zion. The
poet does not combine with it the idea of being born again in
the depth of its New Testament meaning; he means, however,
that the nations will attain a right of citizenship in Zion
(πολιτεία τοῦ Ἰσραήλ, Eph. ii. 12) as in their second mother-
city, that they will therefore at any rate experience a spiritual
change which, regarded from the New Testament point of
view, is the new birth out of water and the Spirit.

Vers. 5–7. Inasmuch now as the nations come thus into
the church (or congregation) of the children of God and of

the children of Abraham, Zion becomes by degrees a church immeasurably great. To Zion, however, or of Zion (לְ of reference to), shall it be said אִישׁ וְאִישׁ יֻלַּד־בָּהּ. Zion, the one city, stands in contrast to all the countries, the one city of God in contrast to the kingdoms of the world, and אִישׁ וְאִישׁ in contrast to זֶה. This contrast, upon the correct apprehension of which depends the understanding of the whole Psalm, is missed when it is said, " whilst in relation to other countries it is always only the whole nation that comes under consideration, Zion is not reckoned up as a nation, but by persons" (Hofmann). With this rendering the יֻלַּד retires into the background ; in that case this giving of prominence to the value of the individual exceeds the ancient range of conception, and it is also an inadmissible appraisement that in Zion each individual is as important as a nation as a whole. Elsewhere אִישׁ אִישׁ, Lev. xvii. 10, 13, or אִישׁ וְאִישׁ, Esth. i. 8, signifies each and every one; accordingly here אִישׁ וְאִישׁ (individual and, or after, individual) affirms a *progressus in infinitum,* where one is ever added to another. Of an immeasurable multitude, and of each individual in this multitude in particular, it is said that he was born in Zion. Now, too, וְהוּא יְכוֹנְנֶהָ עֶלְיוֹן has a significant connection with what precedes. Whilst from among foreign peoples more and more are continually acquiring the right of natives in Zion, and thus are entering into a new national alliance, so that a breach of their original national friendships is taking place, He Himself (cf. 1 Sam. xx. 9), the Most High, will uphold Zion (xlviii. 9), so that under His protection and blessing it shall become ever greater and more glorious. Ver. 6 tells us what will be the result of such a progressive incorporation in the church of Zion of those who have hitherto been far removed, viz. Jahve will reckon when He writeth down (כָּתוֹב as in Josh. xviii. 8) the nations ; or better,—since this would more readily be expressed by בְּכָתְבוֹ, and the book of the living (Isa. iv. 3) is one already existing from time immemorial,—He will reckon in the list (כָּתוֹב after the form חֲלוֹם, חֲלוֹף, פָּקוֹד = כָּתֹב, Ezek. xiii. 9) of the nations, *i.e.* when He goes over the nations that are written down there and chosen for the coming salvation, " this one was born there ;" He will therefore acknowledge them one after another as those born in Zion. The end of all history is that Zion shall become the metropolis of all nations. When the fulness of the Gentiles is thus come in, then shall all and each one as well singing as dancing say (supply יֹאמְרוּ) : All my fountains are in thee. Among the old translators the rendering of Aquila is the best: καὶ ᾄδοντες ὡς χοροί· πᾶσαι πηγαὶ ἐν σοί, which Jerome follows, *et cantores quasi in choris : omnes fontes mei in te.* One would rather render חֹלְלִים, "flute-players" (LXX. ὡς ἐν αὐλοῖς) ; but to pipe or play the flute is חָלַל (a denominative from חָלִיל), 1 Kings i. 40, whereas to dance is חֹלֵל (*Pilel* of חוּל) ; it is therefore = מְחוֹלְלִים, like לְצֵצִים, Hos. vii. 5. But it must not moreover be rendered, " And singers as well as dancers (will say) ;" for " singers" is מְשֹׁרְרִים, not שָׁרִים, which signifies *cantantes*, not *cantores*. Singing as dancing, *i.e.* making known their festive joy as well by the one as by the other, shall the men of all nations incorporated in Zion say : All my fountains, *i.e.* fountains of salvation (after Isa. xii. 3), are in thee (O city of God). It has also been interpreted: my looks (*i.e.* the object on which my eye is fixed, or the delight of my eyes), or : my thoughts (after the modern Hebrew עִיֵּן of spiritual meditation) ; but both are incongruous. The conjecture, too, of Böttcher, and even before him of Schnurrer (*Dissertationes*, p. 150), כָּל־מְעִיְנֵי, all who take up their abode (instead of which Hupfeld conjectures מעיני, all my near-dwellers, *i.e.* those who dwell with me under the same roof*), is not Hebrew, and deprives us of the thought which corresponds to the aim of the whole, that Jerusalem shall be universally regarded as the place where the water of life springs for the whole of man kind, and shall be universally praised as this place of fountains.

PSALM LXXXVIII.

PLAINTIVE PRAYER OF A PATIENT SUFFERER LIKE JOB.

2 JAHVE, God of my salvation,
  In the time when I cry in the night before Thee,

---

* Hupfeld cites Rashi as having thus explained it ; but his gloss is to be rendered: my whole inmost part (after the Aramaic = מְעַי) is with thee, *i.e.* thy salvation.

3 Let my prayer come before Thy face,
　Incline Thine ear to my crying.
4 For satiated with sufferings is my soul,
　And my life is come nigh unto Hades.
5 I am accounted as those who go down to the pit,
　I am become as a man that hath no strength—

6 A freed one among the dead,
　Like the slain, those buried in the grave,
　Whom Thou rememberest no more,
　And they are cut off from Thy hand.
7 Thou hast laid me in the pit of the abysses,
　In darknesses, in the depths of the sea.
8 Upon me Thy fierce anger lieth hard,
　And all Thy waves dost Thou bend down.　(*Sela.*)

9 Thou hast removed my familiar friends from me,
　Thou hast made me an abomination to them,
　Who am shut up and cannot come forth.
10 Mine eye languisheth by reason of affliction,
　I call upon Thee, Jahve, every day,
　I stretch out my hands unto Thee.

11 Wilt Thou do wonders unto the dead,
　Or shall the shades arise to give thanks unto Thee?　(*Sela.*)
12 Shall Thy loving-kindness be declared in the grave,
　Thy faithfulness in the place of destruction?
13 Shall Thy wonder-working power be made known in the
　　　darkness,
　And Thy righteousness in the land of forgetfulness?

14 And as for me—to Thee, Jahve, do I cry,
　Even in the morning my prayer cometh to meet Thee.
15 Wherefore, Jahve, dost Thou cast off my soul,
　Dost Thou hide Thy face from me?
16 Needy am I and ready to die from my youth up,
　I bear Thy terrors, I am utterly helpless.

17 Over me Thy fierce anger hath passed,
　Thy terrors have destroyed me.

18 They have surrounded me like waters all the day,
   They compassed me about altogether.
19 Thou hast removed far from me lover and friend,
   My familiar friends are darkness.

Ps. lxxxviii. is as gloomy as Ps. lxxxvii. is cheerful; they stand near one another as contrasts. Not Ps. lxxvii., as the old expositors answer to the question *quænam ode omnium tristissima*, but this Ps. lxxxviii. is the darkest, gloomiest, of all the plaintive Psalms; for it is true the name "God of my salvation," with which the praying one calls upon God, and his praying itself, show that the spark of faith within him is not utterly extinguished; but as to the rest, it is all one pouring forth of deep lament in the midst of the severest conflict of temptation in the presence of death, the gloom of melancholy does not brighten up to become a hope, the Psalm dies away in Job-like lamentation. Herein we discern echoes of the Korahitic Ps. xlii. and of Davidic Psalms: compare ver. 3 with xviii. 7; ver. 5 with xxviii. 1; ver. 6 with xxxi. 23; ver. 18 with xxii. 17; ver. 19 (although differently applied) with xxxi. 12; and more particularly the questions in vers. 11–13 with vi. 6, of which they are as it were only the amplification. But these Psalm-echoes are outweighed by the still more striking points of contact with the Book of Job, both as regards linguistic usage (דָּאַב, ver. 10, Job xli. 44; רְפָאִים, ver. 11, Job xxvi. 5; אֲבַדּוֹן, ver. 12, Job xxvi. 6, xxviii. 22; נֹעַר, ver. 16*a*, Job xxxiii. 25, xxxvi. 14; אֵמִים, ver. 16*b*, Job xx. 25; בִּעוּתִים, ver. 17, Job vi. 4) and single thoughts (cf. ver. 5 with Job xiv. 10; ver. 9 with Job xxx. 10; ver. 19 with Job xvii. 9, xix. 14), and also the suffering condition of the poet and the whole manner in which this finds expression. For the poet finds himself in the midst of the same temptation as Job not merely so far as his mind and spirit are concerned; but his outward affliction is, according to the tenor of his complaints, the same, viz. the leprosy (ver. 9), which, the disposition to which being born with him, has been his inheritance from his youth up (ver. 16). Now, since the Book of Job is a Chokma-work of the Salomonic age, and the two Ezrahites belonged to the wise men of the first rank at the court of Solomon (1 Kings v. 11 [iv. 31]), it is natural to suppose that the Book of Job has sprung out of this very Chokma-company, and that perhaps this very Heman the Ezrahite who is the author of Ps. lxxxviii. has made a passage of his own life, suffering, and conflict of soul, a subject of dramatic treatment.

The inscription of the Psalm runs: *A Psalm-song by the Korahites; to the Precentor, to be recited* (lit. *to be pressed down*, not after Isa. xxvii. 2: *to be sung*, which expresses nothing, nor: *to be sung alternatingly*, which is contrary to the character of the Psalm) *after a sad manner* (cf. liii. 1) *with muffled voice, a meditation by Heman the Ezrahite.* This is a double inscription, the two halves of which are contradictory. The bare להימן side by side with לבני־קרח would be perfectly in order, since the precentor Heman is a Korahite according to 1 Chron. vi. 18–23 [33–38]; but הימן האזרחי is the name of one of the four great Israelitish sages in 1 Kings v. 11 [iv. 31], who, according to 1 Chron. ii. 6, is a direct descendant of Zerah, and therefore is not of the tribe of Levi, but of Judah. The suppositions that Heman the Korahite had been adopted into the family of Zerah, or that Heman the Ezrahite had been admitted among the Levites, are miserable attempts to get over the difficulty. At the head of the Psalm there stand two different statements respecting its origin side by side, which are irreconcilable. The assumption that the title of the Psalm originally was either merely שיר מזמור לבני־קרח, or merely למנצח וגו', is warranted by the fact that only in this one Psalm למנצח does not occupy the first place in the inscription. But which of the two statements is the more reliable one? Most assuredly the latter; for שיר מזמור לבני־קרח is only a recurrent repetition of the inscription of Ps. lxxxvii. The second statement, on the other hand, by its precise designation oˆ the melody, and by the designation of the author, which corresponds to the Psalm that follows, gives evidence of its antiquity and its historical character.

Vers. 2–8. The poet finds himself in the midst of circumstances gloomy in the extreme, but he does not despair; he still turns towards Jahve with his complaints, and calls Him the God of his salvation. This *actus directus* of fleeing in prayer to the God of salvation, which urges its way through all tha is dark and gloomy, is the fundamental characteristic of all true f⸱ith.   Ver. 2*a* is not to be rendered, as a clause of itself: "by day I cry unto Thee, in the night before Thee" (LXX. and Targum), which ought to have been יוֹמָם, but (as it is also pointed, especially in Baer's text): by day, *i.e.* in the time (lvi. 4, lxxviii. 42, cf. xviii. 1), when I cry before Thee in the night, let my prayer come ... (Hitzig).   In ver. 3*b* he calls his piercing lamentation, his wailing supplication, רִנָּתִי, as in xvii. 1, lxi. 2.   הַטֵּה as in lxxxvi. 1, for which we find הַט in xvii. 6. The *Beth* of בְּרָעוֹת, as in lxv. 5, Lam. iii. 15, 30, denotes that of which his soul has already had abundantly sufficient.   On ver. 4*b*, cf. as to the syntax xxxi. 11.   אֱיָל (ἅπαξ λεγομ. like אֱיָלוּת, xxii. 20) signifies succinctness, compactness, vigorousness (ἁδρότης): he is like a man from whom all vital freshness and vigour is gone, therefore now only like the shadow of a man, in fact like one already dead.   חָפְשִׁי, in ver. 6*a*, the LXX. renders ἐν νεκροῖς ἐλεύθερος (Symmachus, ἀφεὶς ἐλεύθερος); and in like manner the Targum, and the Talmud which follows it in formulating the proposition that a deceased person is חפשי מן המצוות, free from the fulfilling of the precepts of the Law (cf. Rom. vi. 7).   Hitzig, Ewald, Köster, and Böttcher, on the contrary, explain it according to Ezek. xxvii. 20 (where חֹפֶשׁ signifies *stragulum*): among the dead is my couch (חפשי = יצועי, Job xvii. 13).   But in respect of Job iii. 19 the adjectival rendering is the more probable; "one set free among the dead" (LXX.) is equivalent to one released from the bond of life (Job xxxix. 5), somewhat as in Latin a dead person is called *defunctus*.   God does not remember the dead, *i.e.* practically, inasmuch as, devoid of any progressive history, their condition remains always the same; they are in fact cut away (נִגְזַר as in xxxi. 23, Lam. iii. 54, Isa. liii. 8) from the hand, viz. from the guiding and helping hand, of God.   Their dwelling-place is the pit of the places lying deep beneath (cf. on תַּחְתִּיּוֹת, lxiii. 10, lxxxvi. 13, Ezek. xxvi. 20, and more particularly Lam. iii. 55), the dark regions (מַחֲשַׁכִּים as in cxliii. 3, Lam. iii. 6), the submarine depths (בִּמְצֹלוֹת; LXX., Symmachus, the Syriac, etc.: ἐν σκιᾷ θανάτου = בצלמות, according to Job x. 21 and frequently, but contrary to Lam. iii. 54), whose open abyss is the grave for each one.   On ver. 8*b* cf. xlii. 8.   The *Mugrash* by כל־משבריך stamps it as an adverbial accusative (Targum), or more correctly, since the expression is not עניתני,

as the object placed in advance. Only those who are not con-
versant with the subject (as Hupfeld in this instance) imagine
that the accentuation marks עִנִּיתָ as a relative clause (cf. on the
contrary viii. 7*b*, xxi. 3*b*, etc.). עִנָּה, to bow down, press down;
here used of the turning or directing downwards (LXX.
ἐπήγαγες) of the waves, which burst like a cataract over the
afflicted one.

Vers. 9–13. The octastichs are now followed by hexastichs
which belong together in pairs. The complaint concerning the
alienation of his nearest relations sounds like Job xix. 13 sqq.,
but the same strain is also frequently heard in the earlier
Psalms written in times of suffering, *e.g.* xxxi. 9. He is forsaken by all his familiar friends (not: acquaintances, for מְיֻדָּע
signifies more than that), he is alone in the dungeon of wretchedness, where no one comes near him, and whence he cannot
make his escape. This sounds, according to Lev. ch. xiii., very
much like the complaint of a leper. The Book of Leviticus
there passes over from the uncleanness attending the beginning
of human life to the uncleanness of the most terrible disease.
Disease is the middle stage between birth and death, and, according to the Eastern notion, leprosy is the worst of all diseases,
it is death itself clinging to the still living man (Num. xii. 12),
and more than all other evils a stroke of the chastening hand
of God (נֶגַע), a scourge of God (צָרַעַת). The man suspected of
having leprosy was to be subjected to a seven days' quarantine
until the determination of the priest's diagnosis; and if the
leprosy was confirmed, he was to dwell apart outside the camp
(Lev. xiii. 46), where, though not imprisoned, he was nevertheless separated from his dwelling and his family (cf. *Job*, i. 347),
and if a man of position, would feel himself condemned to a
state of involuntary retirement. It is natural to refer the כְּלֻא,
which is closely connected with שַׁתַּנִי, to this separation. עֵינִי,
ver. 10, instead of עֵינַי, as in vi. 8, xxxi. 10: his eye has lan-
guished, vanished away (דָּאַב of the same root as *tabescere*,
cognate with the root of הוֹנָג, lxviii. 3), in consequence of (his)
affliction. He calls and calls upon Jahve, stretches out (שִׁטַּח,
expandere, according to the Arabic, more especially after the
manner of a roof) his hands (*palmas*) towards Him, in order to
shield himself from His wrath and to lead Him compassionately
to give ear to him. In vers. 11–13 he bases his cry for help

upon a twofold wish, viz. to become an object of the miraculous
help of God, and to be able to praise Him for it. Neither of
these wishes would be realized if he were to die; for that which
lies beyond this life is uniform darkness, devoid of any progressive history. With מֵתִים alternates רְפָאִים (sing. רָפָא), the
relaxed ones, *i.e.* shades (σκιαί) of the nether world. With
reference to יוֹדוּ instead of לְהוֹדוֹת, *vid.* Ewald, § 337, *b*. Beside
חֹשֶׁךְ (Job x. 21 sq.) stands אֶרֶץ נְשִׁיָּה, the land of forgetfulness
(λήθη), where there is an end of all thinking, feeling, and
acting (Eccles. ix. 5, 6, 10), and where the monotony of death,
devoid of thought and recollection, reigns. Such is the representation given in the Old Testament of the state beyond the
present, even in Ecclesiastes, and in the Apocrypha (Sir. xvii.
27 sq. after Isa. xxxviii. 18 sq.; Baruch ii. 17 sq.); and it was
obliged to be thus represented, for in the New Testament not
merely the conception of the state after death, but this state
itself, is become a different one.

Vers. 14–19. He who complains thus without knowing
any comfort, and yet without despairing, gathers himself up
afresh for prayer. With וַאֲנִי he contrasts himself with the
dead who are separated from God's manifestation of love.
Being still in life, although under wrath that apparently has
no end, he strains every nerve to struggle through in prayer
until he shall reach God's love. His complaints are petitions,
for they are complaints that are poured forth before God. The
destiny under which for a long time he has been more like one
dying than living, reaches back even into his youth. מִנֹּעַר
(since נֹעַר is everywhere undeclined) is equivalent to מִנְּעָרַי.
The ἐξηπορήθην of the LXX. is the right indicator for the
understanding of the ἅπαξ λεγ. אָפוּנָה. Aben-Ezra and Kimchi
derive it from פֶּן, like עָלָה from עַל,* and assign to it the signification of *dubitare*. But it may be more safely explained after

the Arabic words مافون, أفن, أفن (root افن, to urge forwards,
push), in which the fundamental notion of driving back, nar-

---

* The derivation is not contrary to the genius of the language; the
supplementing productive force of the language displayed in the liturgical
poetry of the synagogue, also changes particles into verbs: *vid.* Zunz,
Die synagogaie Poesie des Mittelalters, S. 421.

rowing and exhausting, is transferred to a weakening or weakness of the intellect. We might also compare פָּנָה, فَنِیَ, " to
disappear, vanish, pass away;" but the ἐξηπορήθην of the
LXX. favours the kinship with that أَفِنَ, *infirma mente et
consilii inops fuit*,* which has been already compared by Castell.
The aorist of the LXX., however, is just as erroneous in this
instance as in xlii. 5, lv. 3, lvii. 5. In all these instances the
cohortative denotes the inward result following from an outward
compulsion, as they say in Hebrew: I lay hold of trembling
(Isa. xiii. 8, Job xviii. 20, xxi. 6) or joy (Isa. xxxv. 10, li. 11),
when the force of circumstances drives one into such states of
mind. Labouring under the burden of divine dispensations of
a terrifying character, he finds himself in a state of mental
weakness and exhaustion, or of insensible (senseless) fright;
over him as their destined goal before many others go God's
burnings of wrath (*plur*. only in this instance), His terrible
decrees (*vid*. concerning בעת on xviii. 5) have almost anni-
hilated him. צְמַתְּתוּנִי is not an impossible form (Olshausen,
§ 251, *a*), but an intensive form of צְמַתּוּ, the last part of the
already inflected verb being repeated, as in אֲהֵבוּ הֵבוּ, Hos. iv.
18 (cf. in the department of the noun, פִּיפִיוֹת, edge-edges =
many edges, cxlix. 6), perhaps under the influence of the derivative.† The corrections צְמִתְּתֻנִי (from צָמֵתַת) or צִמְּתַתְנִי (from
צָמֵת) are simple enough; but it is more prudent to let tradition
judge of that which is possible in the usage of the language.
In ver. 18 the burnings become floods; the wrath of God can
be compared to every destroying and overthrowing element.
The billows threaten to swallow him up, without any helping
hand being stretched out to him on the part of any of his
lovers and friends. Is ver. 19*a* to be now explained according
to Job xvii. 14, viz. My familiar friends are gloomy darkness;

---

* Abulwalîd also explains אֲפוּנָה after the Arabic, but in a way that
cannot be accepted, viz. " for a long time onwards," from the Arabic *iffân*
(*ibbân, iff, afaf, ifâf, taïffah*), time, period—time conceived of in the onward rush, the constant succession of its moments.

† Heidenheim interprets: Thy terrors are become to me as צְמִתֻת (Lev.
xxv. 23), *i.e.* inalienably my own.

i.e. instead of those who were hitherto my familiars (Job xix. 14), darkness is become my familiar friend? One would have thought that it ought then to have been מְיֻדָּעִי (Schnurrer), or, according to Prov. vii. 4, מוֹדָעִי, and that, in connection with this sense of the noun, מחשך ought as subject to have the precedence, that consequently מְיֻדָּעַי is subject and מַחְשָׁךְ predicate: my familiar friends have lost themselves in darkness, are become absolutely invisible (Hitzig at last). But the regular position of the words is kept to if it is interpreted: my familiar friends are reduced to gloomy darkness as my familiar friend, and the plural is justified by Job xix. 14: *Mother and sister* (do I call) *the worm*. With this complaint the harp falls from the poet's hands. He is silent, and waits on God, that He may solve this riddle of affliction. From the Book of Job we might infer that He also actually appeared to him. He is more faithful than men. No soul that in the midst of wrath lays hold upon His love, whether with a firm or with a trembling hand, is suffered to be lost.

PSALM LXXXIX.

PRAYER FOR A RENEWAL OF THE MERCIES OF DAVID.

2 OF the loving-kindnesses of Jahve for ever will I sing,
　To remote generations will I make known Thy faithfulness
　　　with my mouth.
3 For I say: For ever is mercy being built up,
　In the heavens—there dost Thou establish Thy faithfulness.

4 "I have made a covenant with My chosen,
　I have sworn unto David My servant:
5 For ever will I establish thy seed,
　And build up thy throne to remote generations." (*Sela.*)

6 And the heavens praise Thy wondrousness, Jahve,
　Thy faithfulness also in the assembly of the holy ones.
7 For who in the sky can be compared to Jahve,
　Who among the sons of the gods is like unto Jahve?

8 A God terrible in the great council of the holy ones,
　And fearful above all those who are round about Him.

 9 Jahve, God of hosts, who is as Thou ? !
   A mighty One, Jāh, and Thy faithfulness is round about
           Thee.

10 Thou art He who restraineth the pride of the sea ;
   When its waves arise, Thou stillest them.
11 THOU hast crushed Rahab as one that is slain,
   By the arm of Thy might hast Thou scattered Thy foes.

12 Thine are the heavens, Thine also is the earth ;
   The earth and that which filleth it hast THOU founded.
13 North and south, THOU hast created them ;
   Tabor and Hermon shout for joy at Thy name.

14 Thine is an arm with heroic strength,
   Strong is Thy hand, exalted is Thy right hand.
15 Righteousness and right is the foundation of Thy throne,
   Mercy and truth stand waiting before Thee.

16 Blessed are the people who know the joyful sound,
   Who walk, O Jahve, in the light of Thy countenance !
17 In Thy name do they rejoice continually,
   And through Thy righteousness are they exalted.

18 For the glory of their mightiness art Thou,
   And through Thy favour is our horn exalted.
19 For to Jahve belongeth our shield,
   And to the Holy One of Israel our king.

20 Once Thou spakest in vision to Thy familiar one, and
           saidst :
   " I have granted help to a mighty one,
   I have raised a stripling out of the people.
21 I have found David My servant,
   With My holy oil have I anointed him ;

22 With whom My hand shall be stedfast,
   My arm also shall strengthen him.
23 An enemy shall not ensnare him,
   And the son of wantonness shall not oppress him.

24 I will break in pieces his oppressors before him,
   And I will smite those who hate him.
25 And My faithfulness and My mercy are with him,
   And in My Name shall his horn be exalted.
26 I will set his hand upon the sea,
   And his right hand upon the rivers.

27 He shall cry unto Me : My Father art Thou,
   My God, and the Rock of my salvation !
28 In return I will make him My first-born,
   The highest with respect to the kings of the earth.

29 For ever will I preserve to him My mercy,
   And My covenant shall be inviolable with him.
30 I will make his seed to endure for ever,
   And his throne like the days of heaven.

31 If his children shall forsake My law
   And walk not in My judgments ;
32 If they profane My statutes
   And keep not My commandments :

33 Then will I visit their transgression with the rod,
   And their iniquity with stripes ;
34 Nevertheless My loving-kindness will I not break off from
      him,
   And will not belie My faithfulness—

35 I will not profane My covenant
   Nor alter the vow of My lips.
36 One thing have I sworn by My holiness ;
   Verily I will not deceive David :

37 His seed shall endure to eternity,
   And his throne as the sun before Me.
38 As the moon shall it continue for ever—
   And the witness in the sky is faithful ! ”   (*Sela.*)

39 And Thou Thyself hast rejected and despised,
   Thou hast been wroth with Thine anointed ;

40 Thou hast shaken off from Thee the covenant of Thy
       servant,
  Thou hast profaned his diadem to the earth.

41 Thou hast broken down all his hedges,
  Thou hast laid his strongholds in ruins.
42 All who pass by the way spoil him,
  He is become a reproach to his neighbours.

43 Thou hast exalted the right hand of his oppressors,
  Thou hast made all his enemies to rejoice.
44 Thou didst also turn back the edge of his sword,
  And didst not hold him erect in the battle.

45 Thou hast caused him to lose his splendour,
  And hast cast his throne down to the ground.
46 Thou hast shortened the days of his youth,
  Thou hast covered him round with shame.   (*Sela.*)

47 How long, Jahve, wilt Thou hide Thyself for ever,
  Shall Thy wrath burn like fire?
48 Remember : I— how utterly perishable!
  For what vanity hast Thou created all the children of men!
49 Who is the man that should live and not see death,
  That should be able to secure his soul against the nether
      world?   (*Sela.*)

50 Where are Thy former loving-kindnesses, Lord,
  Which Thou hast sworn to David in Thy faithfulness?
51 Remember, Lord, the reproach of Thy servants,
  That I carry in my bosom the reproach of many peoples,
52 Which reproach—Thine enemies, Jahve!—
  Which reproach the footsteps of Thine anointed.

53   BLESSED BE JAHVE FOR EVERMORE!
          AMEN, AND AMEN.

After having recognised the fact that the double inscription of Ps. lxxxviii. places two irreconcilable statements concerning the origin of that Psalm side by side, we renounce the

artifices by which Ethan (אֵיתָן*) the Ezrahite, of the tribe of Judah (1 Kings v. 11 [iv. 31], 1 Chron. ii. 6), is made to be one and the same person with Ethan (Jeduthun) the son of Kushaiah the Merarite, of the tribe of Levi (1 Chron. xv. 17, vi. 29–32 [44–47]), the master of the music together with Asaph and Heman, and the chief of the six classes of musicians over whom his six sons were placed as sub-directors (1 Chron. ch. xxv.).

The collector has placed the Psalms of the two Ezrahites together. Without this relationship of the authors the juxtaposition would also be justified by the reciprocal relation in which the two Psalms stand to one another by their common, striking coincidences with the Book of Job. As to the rest, however, Ps. lxxxviii. is a purely individual, and Ps. lxxxix. a thoroughly national Psalm. Both the poetical character and the situation of the two Psalms are distinct.

The circumstances in which the writer of Ps. lxxxix. finds himself are in most striking contradiction to the promises given to the house of David. He revels in the contents of these promises, and in the majesty and faithfulness of God, and then he pours forth his intense feeling of the great distance between these and the present circumstances in complaints over the afflicted lot of the anointed of God, and prays God to be mindful of His promises, and on the other hand, of the reproach by which at this time His anointed and His people are overwhelmed. The anointed one is not the nation itself (Hitzig), but he who at that time wears the crown. The crown of the king is defiled to the ground; his throne is cast down to the earth; he is become grey-headed before his time, for all the fences of his land are broken through, his fortresses fallen, and his enemies have driven him out of the field, so that reproach and scorn follow him at every step.

There was no occasion for such complaints in the reign of Solomon; but surely in the time of Rehoboam, into the first decade of whose reign Ethan the Ezrahite may have survived king Solomon, who died at the age of sixty. In the fifth year of Rehoboam, Shishak (שִׁישַׁק = Σέσογχις = *Sheshonk I.*), the

---

* This name אֵיתָן is also Phœnician in the form יתן, *Itan*, Ἰτανός; ליתן, *litan*, is Phœnician, and equivalent to לעלם.

first Pharaoh of the twenty-second (Bubastic) dynasty, marched against Jerusalem with a large army gathered together out of many nations, conquered the fortified cities of Judah, and spoiled the Temple and Palace, even carrying away with him the golden shields of Solomon—a circumstance which the history bewails in a very especial manner. At that time Shemaiah preached repentance, in the time of the greatest calamity of war; king and princes humbled themselves; and in the midst of judgment Jerusalem accordingly experienced the gracious forbearance of God, and was spared. God did not complete his destruction, and there also again went forth דברים טובים, *i.e.* (cf. Josh. xxiii. 14, Zech. i. 13) kindly comforting words from God, in Judah. Such is the narrative in the Book of Kings (1 Kings xiv. 25-28) and as supplemented by the chronicler (2 Chron. xii. 1-12).

During this very period Ps. lxxxix. took its rise. The young Davidic king, whom loss and disgrace make prematurely old, is Rehoboam, that man of Jewish appearance whom Pharaoh Sheshonk is bringing among other captives before the god Amun in the monumental picture of Karnak, and who bears before him in his embattled ring the words *Judhmelek* (King of Judah)—one of the finest and most reliable discoveries of Champollion, and one of the greatest triumphs of his system of hieroglyphics.*

Ps. lxxxix. stands in kindred relationship not only to Ps. lxxiv., but besides Ps. lxxix., also to Ps. lxxvii., lxxviii., all of which glance back to the earliest times in the history of Israel. They are all Asaphic Psalms, partly old Asaphic (lxxvii., lxxviii.), partly later ones (lxxiv., lxxix.). From this fact we see that the Psalms of Asaph were the favourite models in that school of the four wise men to which the two Ezrahites belong.

Vers. 2–5. The poet, who, as one soon observes, is a חכם (for the very beginning of the Psalm is remarkable and ingenious), begins with the confession of the inviolability of the mercies promised to the house of David, *i.e.* of the חַסְדֵי דָוִד

---

* *Vid.* Blau, *Sisags Zug gegen Juda*, illustrated from the monument in Karnak, *Deutsche Morgenländ. Zeitschr.* xv. 233-250.

הַנֶּאֱמָנִים, Isa. lv. 3.* God's faithful love towards the house of David, a love faithful to His promises, will he sing without ceasing, and make it known with his mouth, *i.e.* audibly and publicly (cf. Job xix. 16), to the distant posterity. Instead of חַסְדֵּי, we find here, and also in Lam. iii. 22, חַסְדֵי with a not merely slightly closed syllable. The *Lamed* of לְדֹר וָדֹר is, according to ciii. 7, cxlv. 12, the datival *Lamed*. With כִּי־אָמַרְתִּי (LXX., Jerome, contrary to ver. 3*b*, ὅτι εἶπας) the poet bases his resolve upon his conviction. נִבְנֶה means not so much to be upheld in building, as to be in the course of continuous building (*e.g.* Job xxii. 23, Mal. iii. 15, of an increasingly prosperous condition). Loving-kindness is for ever (accusative of duration) in the course of continuous building, viz. upon the unshakeable foundation of the promise of grace, inasmuch as it is fulfilled in accordance therewith. It is a building with a most solid foundation, which will not only not fall into ruins, but, adding one stone of fulfilment upon another, will rise ever higher and higher. שָׁמַיִם then stands first as *casus absol.*, and בָּהֶם is, as in xix. 5, a pronoun having a backward reference to it. In the heavens, which are exalted above the rise and fall of things here below, God establishes His faithfulness, so that it stands fast as the sun above the earth, although the condition of things here below seems sometimes to contradict it (cf. cxix. 89). Now follow in vers. 4, 5 the direct words of God, the sum of the promises given to David and to his seed in 2 Sam. ch. vii., at which the poet arrives more naturally in vers. 20 sqq. Here they are strikingly devoid of connection. It is the special substance of the promises that is associated in thought with the " loving-kindness " and " truth " of ver. 3, which is expanded as it were appositionally therein. Hence also אָכִין and תָּכִין, וּבָנִיתִי and יִבְנֶה correspond to one another. David's seed, by virtue of divine faithfulness, has an eternally sure existence ; Jahve builds up David's throne " into generation and generation," inasmuch as He causes it to rise ever fresh and vigorous, never as that which is growing old and feeble.

Vers. 6–9. At the close of the promises in vers. 4, 5 the

---

* The Vulgate renders : *Misericordias Domini in æternum cantabo.* The second Sunday after Easter takes its name from this rendering.

music is to become *forte*. And וְיוֹדוּ attaches itself to this jubilant *Sela*. In vers. 6–19 there follows a hymnic description of the exalted majesty of God, more especially of His omnipotence and faithfulness, because the value of the promise is measured by the character of the person who promises. The God of the promise is He who is praised by the heavens and the holy ones above. His way of acting is פֶּלֶא, of a transcendent, paradoxical, wondrous order, and as such the heavens praise it; it is praised (יודו, according to Ges. § 137, 3) in the assembly of the holy ones, *i.e.* of the spirits in the other world, the angels (as in Job v. 1, xv. 15, cf. Deut. xxxiii. 2), for He is peerlessly exalted above the heavens and the angels. שַׁחַק, poetic singular instead of שְׁחָקִים (*vid. supra* on lxxvii. 18), which is in itself already poetical; and עָרַךְ, not, as *e.g.* in Isa. xl. 18, in the signification to co-ordinate, but in the medial sense: to rank with, be equal to. Concerning בְּנֵי אֵלִים, *vid.* on xxix. 1. In the great council (concerning סוֹד, of both genders, perhaps like כּוֹס, *vid.* on xxv. 14) of the holy ones also, Jahve is terrible; He towers above all who are about Him (1 Kings xxii. 19, cf. Dan. vii. 10) in terrible majesty. רַבָּה might, according to lxii. 3, lxxviii. 15, be an adverb, but according to the order of the words it may more appropriately be regarded as an adjective; cf. Job xxxi. 34, כִּי אֶעֱרֹץ הָמוֹן רַבָּה, " when I feared the great multitude." In ver. 9 He is apostrophized with אלהי צבאות as being the One exalted above the heavens and the angels. The question " Who is as Thou?" takes its origin from Ex. xv. 11. חֲסִין is not the construct form, but the principal form, like עֱוִיל, יָדִיד, גְּבִיר, and is a Syriasm; for the verbal stem ܚܣܝܢ is native to the Aramaic, in which ܚܣܝܢܐ = שַׁדִּי. In יָהּ, what God is is reduced to the briefest possible expression (*vid.* lxviii. 19). In the words, " Thy faithfulness compasseth Thee round about," the primary thought of the poet again breaks through. Such a God it is who has the faithfulness with which He fulfils all His promises, and the promises given to the house of David also, as His constant surrounding. His glory would only strike one with terror; but the faithfulness which encompasses Him softens the sunlike brilliancy of His glory, and awakens trust in so majestic a Ruler.

Vers. 10–15. At the time of the poet the nation of the

house of David was threatened with assault from violent foes ; and this fact gives occasion for this picture of God's power in the kingdom of nature.　He who rules the raging of the sea, also rules the raging of the sea of the peoples, lxv. 8.　גֵּאוּת, a proud rising, here of the sea, like גַּאֲוָה in xlvi. 4.　Instead of בְּשׂוֹא, Hitzig pleasantly enough reads בִּשְׂאוֹ = בְּשׂוֹא from שָׁאָה ; but שׂוֹא is also possible so far as language is concerned, either as an infinitive = נְשׂוֹא, xxviii. 2, Isa. i. 14 (instead of שְׂאֵת), or as an infinitival noun, like שִׂיא, loftiness, Job xx. 6, with a likewise rejected *Nun*.　The formation of the clause favours our taking it as a verb : when its waves rise, Thou stillest them. From the natural sea the poet comes to the sea of the peoples ; and in the doings of God at the Red Sea a miraculous subjugation of both seas took place at one and the same time.　It is clear from lxxiv. 13–17, Isa. li. 9, that Egypt is to be understood by *Rahab* in this passage as in lxxxvii. 4.　The word signifies first of all impetuosity, violence, then a monster, like " the wild beast of the reed," lxviii. 31, *i.e.* the leviathan or the dragon.　דִּכִּאתָ is conjugated after the manner of the *Lamed He* verbs, as in xliv. 20.　בְּחָלָל is to be understood as describing the event or issue (*vid.* xviii. 43) : so that in its fall the proudly defiant kingdom is like one fatally smitten.　Thereupon in vers. 12–15 again follows in the same co-ordination first the praise of God drawn from nature, then from history.　Jahve's are the heavens and the earth.　He is the Creator, and for that very reason the absolute owner, of both.　The north and the right hand, *i.e.* the south, represent the earth in its entire compass from one region of the heavens to the other.　Tabor on this side of the Jordan represents the west (cf. Hos. v. 1), and Hermon opposite the east of the Holy Land.　Both exult by reason of the name of God ; by their fresh, cheerful look they give the impression of joy at the glorious revelation of the divine creative might manifest in themselves.　In ver. 14 the praise again enters upon the province of history.　" An arm with (עֹם) heroic strength," says the poet, inasmuch as he distinguishes between the attribute inherent in God and the medium of its manifestation in history.　His throne has as its מָכוֹן, *i.e.* its immovable foundation (Prov. xvi. 12, xxv. 5), righteousness of action and right, by which all action is regulated, and which is unceasingly realized by means of the action.

And mercy and truth wait upon Him. קִדֶּם פָּנָי is not : to go before any one (הִלֵּךְ לִפְנֵי, lxxxv. 14), but anticipatingly to present one's self to any one, lxxxviii. 14, xcv. 2, Mic. vi. 6. Mercy and truth, these two genii of sacred history (xliii. 3), stand before His face like waiting servants watching upon His nod.

Vers. 16–19. The poet has now described what kind of God He is upon whose promise the royal house in Israel depends. Blessed, then, is the people that walks in the light of His countenance. הִלֵּךְ of a self-assured, stately walk. The words יֹדְעֵי תְרוּעָה are the statement of the ground of the blessing interwoven into the blessing itself : such a people has abundant cause and matter for exultation (cf. lxxxiv. 5). תְּרוּעָה is the festive sound of joy of the mouth (Num. xxiii. 21), and of trumpets or sackbuts (xxvii. 6). This confirmation of the blessing is expanded in vers. 17–19. Jahve's שֵׁם, i.e. revelation or manifestation, becomes to them a ground and object of unceasing joy ; by His צְדָקָה, i.e. the rigour with which He binds Himself to the relationship He has entered upon with His people and maintains it, they are exalted above abjectness and insecurity. He is תִּפְאֶרֶת עֻזָּמוֹ, the ornament of their strength, i.e. their strength which really becomes an ornament to them. In ver. 18b the poet declares Israel to be this happy people. Pinsker's conjecture, קַרְנָם (following the Targum), destroys the transition to ver. 19, which is formed by ver. 18b. The plural reading of Kimchi and of older editions (e.g. Bomberg's), קַרְנֵינוּ, is incompatible with the figure ; but it is immaterial whether we read תָּרִים with the *Chethîb* (Targum, Jerome), or with the *Kerî* (LXX., Syriac) תָּרוּם.* ‑ מָגִנֵּנוּ and מַלְכֵּנוּ in ver. 19 are parallel designations of the human king of Israel ; מָגֵן as in xlvii. 10, but not in lxxxiv. 10. For we are not compelled, with a total disregard of the limits to the possibilities of style (Ew. § 310, a), to render ver. 19b : and the Holy One

---

* *Zur Geschichte des Karaismus*, pp. קפא and קפב, according to which, reversely, in Josh. v. 1 עברנו is to be read instead of עברם, and Isa. xxxiii. 2 זרעֵנוּ instead of זרעם, Ps. xii. 8 תשמרֵנוּ instead of תשמרם, Mic. vii. 19 חטאתנו instead of חטאתם, Job xxxii. 8 תבינֵנוּ instead of תבינם, Prov. xxv. 27 כבודֵנוּ instead of כבודם (the limiting of our honour brings honour,—an unlikely interpretation of the חקר).

of Israel, (as to Him, He) is our King (Hitzig), since we do not bring down the Psalm beyond the time of the kings. Israel's shield, Israel's king, the poet says in the holy defiant confidence of faith, is Jahve's, belongs to the Holy One of Israel, *i.e.* he stands as His own possession under the protection of Jahve, the Holy One, who has taken Israel to Himself for a possession; it is therefore impossible that the Davidic throne should become a prey to any worldly power.

Vers. 20—23. Having thus again come to refer to the king of Israel, the poet now still further unfolds the promise given to the house of David. The present circumstances are a contradiction to it. The prayer to Jahve, for which the way is thus prepared, is for the removal of this contradiction. A long line, extending beyond the measure of the preceding lines, introduces the promises given to David. With אָז the respective period of the past is distinctly defined. The intimate friend of Jahve (חָסִיד) is Nathan (1 Chron. xvii. 15) or David, according as we translate בְּחָזוֹן " in a vision" or " by means of a vision." But side by side with the לַחֲסִידֶךָ we also find the preferable reading לַחֲסִידֶיךָ, which is followed in the renderings of the LXX., Syriac, Vulgate, Targum, Aquila, Symmachus, and the Quarta, and is adopted by Rashi, Aben-Ezra, and others, and taken up by Heidenheim and Baer. The plural refers to Samuel and Nathan, for the statement brings together what was revealed to these two prophets concerning David. עֵזֶר is assistance as a gift, and that, as the designation of the person succoured by it (שִׁוָּה עַל as in xxi. 6) with גִּבּוֹר shows, aid in battle. בָּחוּר (from בָּחַר = בָּגַר in the Mishna : to ripen, to be manly or of marriageable age, distinct from בָּחִיר in ver. 4) is a young man, *adolescens:* while yet a young man David was raised out of his humble lowly condition (lxxviii. 71) high above the people. When he received the promise (2 Sam. ch. vii.) he had been anointed and had attained to the lordship over all Israel. Hence the preterites in vers. 20, 21, which are followed by promissory futures from ver. 22 onwards. תִּכּוֹן is *fut. Niph.*, to be established, to prove one's self to be firm, unchangeable (lxxviii. 37), a stronger expression than תִּהְיֶה, 1 Sam. xviii. 12, 14, 2 Sam. iii. 10. The *Hiph.* הִשִּׁיא, derived from נָשָׁא = נָשָׁה, to credit (*vid.* on Isa. xxiv. 2 ; Gesenius, Hengstenberg), does not give any suitable sense ; it therefore

signifies here as elsewhere, " to impose upon, surprise," with בְּ,
as in lv. 16 with עַל. Ver. 23*b* is the echo of 2 Sam. vii. 10.

Vers. 24–30. What is promised in ver. 26 is world-wide
dominion, not merely dominion within the compass promised in
the primeval times (Gen. xv. 18, 2 Chron. ix. 26), in which
case it ought to have been said ובנהר (of the Euphrates). Nor
does the promise, however, sound so definite and boundless here
as in lxxii. 8, but it is indefinite and universal, without any
need for our asking what rivers are intended by נהרות. נָתַן
יָד בְּ, like שָׁלַח in Isa. xi. 14, of a giving and taking possession.
With אַף־אָנִי (with retreated tone, as in cxix. 63, 125) God tells
with what He will answer David's filial love. Him who is the
latest-born among the sons of Jesse, God makes the first-born
(בְּכוֹר from בָּכַר, to be early, *opp.* לָקַשׁ, to be late, *vid. Job*, ii.
21), and therefore the most favoured of the " sons of the Most
High," lxxxii. 6.   And as, according to Deut. xxviii. 1, Israel
is to be high (עֶלְיוֹן) above all nations of the earth, so David,
Israel's king, in whom Israel's national glory realizes itself, is
made as the high one (עליון) with respect to the kings, *i.e.* above
the kings, of the earth. In the person of David his seed is
included ; and it is that position of honour which, after having
been only prelusively realized in David and Solomon, must go
on being fulfilled in his seed exactly as the promise runs. The
covenant with David is, according to ver. 29, one that shall
stand for ever. David is therefore, as ver. 30 affirms, eternal
in his seed ; God will make David's seed and throne לָעַד, into
eternal, *i.e.* into such as will abide for ever, like the days of
heaven, everlasting. This description of eternal duration is,
as also in Sir. xlv. 15, Bar. i. 11, taken from Deut. xi. 21 ; the
whole of ver. 30 is a poetic reproduction of 2 Sam. vii. 16.

Vers. 31–38. Now follows the paraphrase of 2 Sam. vii.
14, that the faithlessness of David's line in relation to the
covenant shall not interfere with (annul) the faithfulness of
God—a thought with which one might very naturally console
one's self in the reign of Rehoboam. Because God has placed
the house of David in a filial relationship to Himself, He will
chastise the apostate members as a father chastises his son ;
cf. Prov. xxiii. 13 sq. In 1 Chron. xvii. 13 the chronicler
omits the words of 2 Sam. vii. 14 which there provide against
perverted action (הֶעֱוֹת) on the part of the seed of David ; our

Psalm proves their originality. But even if, as history shows, this means of chastisement should be ineffectual in the case of individuals, the house of David as such will nevertheless remain ever in a state of favour with Him. In ver. 34 וְחַסְדִּי לֹא־אָפִיר מֵעִמּוֹ corresponds to וְחַסְדִּי לֹא־יָסוּר מִמֶּנּוּ in 2 Sam. vii. 15 (LXX., Targum): the *fut. Hiph.* of פרר is otherwise always אָפֵר; the conjecture אָסִיר is therefore natural, yet even the LXX. translators (οὐ μὴ διασκεδάσω) had אפיר before them. שִׁקֵּר בְּ as in xliv. 18. The covenant with David is sacred with God: He will not profane it (חִלֵּל, to loose the bonds of sanctity). He will fulfil what has gone forth from His lips, *i.e.* His vow, according to Deut. xxiii. 24 [23], cf. Num. xxx. 3 [2]. One thing hath He sworn to David; not: once = once for all (LXX.), for what is introduced by ver. 36 (cf. xxvii. 4) and follows in vers. 37, 38, is in reality one thing (as in lxii. 12, two). He hath sworn it *per sanctitatem suam*. Thus, and not *in sanctuario meo*, בְקָדְשִׁי in this passage and Amos iv. 2 (cf. on lx. 8) is to be rendered, for elsewhere the expression is בִּי, Gen. xxii. 16, Isa. xlv. 23, or בְּנַפְשׁוֹ, Amos vi. 8, Jer. li. 14, or בִּשְׁמִי, Jer xliv. 26, or בִּימִינוֹ, Isa. lxii. 8. It is true we do not read any set form of oath in 2 Sam. ch. vii., 1 Chron. ch. xvii., but just as Isaiah, ch. liv. 9, takes the divine promise in Gen. viii. 21 as an oath, so the promise so earnestly and most solemnly pledged to David may be accounted by Psalm-poesy (here and in cxxxii. 11), which reproduces the historical matter of fact, as a promise attested with an oath. With אִם in ver. 36*b* God asserts that He will not disappoint David in reference to this one thing, viz. the perpetuity of his throne. This shall stand for ever as the sun and moon; for these, though they may one day undergo a change (cii. 27), shall nevertheless never be destroyed. In the presence of 2 Sam. vii. 16 it looks as if ver. 38*b* ought to be rendered: and as the witness in the clouds shall it (David's throne) be faithful (perpetual). By the witness in the clouds one would then have to understand the rainbow as the celestial memorial and sign of an everlasting covenant. Thus Luther, Geier, Schmid, and others. But neither this rendering, nor the more natural one, " and as the perpetual, faithful witness in the clouds," is admissible in connection with the absence of the כ of comparison. Accordingly Hengstenberg, following the example of Jewish exposi-

tors, renders : " and the witness in the clouds is perpetual," viz.
the moon, so that the continuance of the Davidic line would
be associated with the moon, just as the continuance of the
condemned earth is with the rainbow. But in what sense
would the moon have the name, without example elsewhere, of
witness ? Just as the Book of Job was the key to the conclusion of Ps. lxxxviii., so it is the key to this ambiguous verse
of the Psalm before us. It has to be explained according
to Job xvi. 19, where Job says : " *Behold in heaven is my
witness, and my surety in the heights.*" Jahve, the אֵל נֶאֱמָן
(Deut. vii. 9), seals His sworn promise with the words, " and
the witness in the sky (ethereal heights) is faithful" (cf. concerning this *Waw* in connection with asseverations, Ew. § 340,
c). Hengstenberg's objection, that Jahve cannot be called His
own witness, is disposed of by the fact that עֵד frequently signifies the person who testifies anything concerning himself ; in
this sense, in fact, the whole Tôra is called עֵדוּת ה׳ (the testimony of Jahve).

Vers. 39–46. Now after the poet has turned his thoughts
towards the beginnings of the house of David which were so
rich in promise, in order that he might find comfort under the
sorrowful present, the contrast of the two periods is become all
the more sensible to him. With וְאַתָּה in ver. 39 (And Thou—
the same who hast promised and affirmed this with an oath)
his Psalm takes a new turn, for which reason it might even
have been וְעַתָּה. זָנַח is used just as absolutely here as in xliv.
24, lxxiv. 1, lxxvii. 8, so that it does not require any object to
be supplied out of ver. 39*b*. נֵאַרְתָּה in ver. 40 the LXX.
renders κατέστρεψας ; it is better rendered in Lam. ii. 7 ἀπετί-
ναξε ; for נִאֵר is synonymous with נִעֵר, to shake off, push away,
cf. Arabic *el-menā'ir*, the thrusters (with the lance). עַבְדֶּךָ is a
vocational name of the king as such. His crown is sacred as
being the insignia of a God-bestowed office. God has therefore
made the sacred thing vile by casting it to the ground (חִלֵּל
לָאָרֶץ, as in lxxiv. 17, to cast profaningly to the ground). The
primary passage to vers. 41, 42 is lxxx. 13. " His hedges "
are all the boundary and protecting fences which the land of
the king has ; and מִבְצָרָיו " the fortresses " of his land (in both
instances without כֹּל, because matters have not yet come to such

a pass).* In שָׁפֻּהוּ the notions of the king and of the land blend together. עֹבְרֵי־דָרֶךְ are the hordes of the peoples passing through the land. שְׁכֵנָיו are the neighbouring peoples that are otherwise liable to pay tribute to the house of David, who sought to take every possible advantage of that weakening of the Davidic kingdom. In ver. 44 we are neither to translate "rock of his sword" (Hengstenberg), nor "O rock" (Olshausen). צוּר does not merely signify *rupes*, but also from another root (צוּר, صار,

originally of the grating or shrill noise produced by pressing and squeezing, then more particularly to cut or cut off with pressure, with a sharply set knife or the like) a knife or a blade (cf. English knife, and German *kneifen*, to nip) : God has decreed it that the edge or blade of the sword of the king has been turned back by the enemy, that he has not been able to maintain his ground in battle (הֲקֵמֹתוֹ with *ē* instead of *î*, as also when the tone is not moved forward, Mic. v. 4). In ver. 45 the *Mem* of מטהרו, after the analogy of Ezek. xvi. 41, xxxiv. 10, and other passages, is a preposition : *cessare fecisti eum a splendore suo.* A noun מְטֹהָר = מִטְהָר with *Dag. dirimens*,† like מִקְדָּשׁ Ex. xv. 17, מִנְזַר Nah. iii. 17 (Abulwalîd, Aben-Ezra, Parchon, Kimchi, and others), in itself improbable in the signification required here, is not found either in post-biblical or in biblical Hebrew. טֹהַר, like צֹהַר, signifies first of all not purity, but brilliancy. Still the form טֹהַר does not lie at the basis of it in this instance ; for the reading found here just happens not to be טֳהֳרוֹ, but מְטָהֳרוֹ ; and the reading adopted by Norzi, Heidenheim, and Baer, as also by Nissel and others, so far as form is concerned is not distinct from it, viz. מִטָּהֳרוֹ (*mittŏharo*), the character of the *Shebâ* being determined by the

---

* In the list of the nations and cities conquered by King Sheshonk ɪ. are found even cities of the tribe of Issachar, *e.g. Shen-ma-an*, Sunem; *vid.* Brugsch, *Reiseberichte*, S. 141–145, and Blau as referred to above.

† The view of Pinsker (*Einleitung*, S. 69), that this *Dag.* is not a sign of the doubling of the letter, but a diacritic point (that preceded the invention of the system of vowel-points), which indicated that the respective letter was to be pronounced with a *Chateph* vowel (*e.g. miṭŏhar*), is incorrect. The doubling *Dag.* renders the *Shebâ* audible, and having once become audible it readily receives this or that colouring according to the nature of its consonant and of the neighbouring vowel.

analogy of the *â* following (cf. בַּסְּעָרָה, 2 Kings ii. 1), which
presupposes the principal form סְעָר (Böttcher, § 386, cf. *supra*,
ii. 31, note). The personal tenor of ver. 46*a* requires that it
should be referred to the then reigning Davidic king, but not
as dying before his time (Olshausen), but as becoming prematurely old by reason of the sorrowful experiences of his reign.
The larger half of the kingdom has been wrested from him;
Egypt and the neighbouring nations also threaten the half that
remains to him; and instead of the kingly robe, shame completely covers him.

Vers. 47–52. After this statement of the present condition
of things the psalmist begins to pray for the removal of all that
is thus contradictory to the promise. The plaintive question,
ver. 47, with the exception of one word, is *verbatim* the same as
lxxix. 5. The wrath to which *quousque* refers, makes itself to
be felt, as the intensifying (*vid.* xiii. 2) לנצח implies, in the
intensity and duration of everlasting wrath. חֶלֶד is this temporal life which glides past secretly and unnoticed (xvii. 14);
and זְכָר־אֲנִי is not equivalent to זָכְרֵנִי (instead of which by way
of emphasis only זָכְרֵנִי אָנִי can be said), but אֲנִי מֶה־חָלֶד stands
for מֶה־חֶלֶד אֲנִי—according to the sense equivalent to מֶה־חָדֵל אֲנִי,
xxxix. 5, cf. 6. The conjecture of Houbigant and modern
expositors, זְכֹר אֲדֹנָי (cf. ver. 51), is not needed, since the inverted
position of the words is just the same as in xxxix. 5. In ver.
48*b* it is not pointed עַל־מָה שָׁוְא, "wherefore (Job x. 2, xiii. 14)
hast Thou in vain (cxxvii. 1) created?" (Hengstenberg), but
עַל־מַה־שָּׁוְא, on account of or for what a nothing (מַה־שָּׁוְא belonging together as adjective and substantive, as in xxx. 10, Job
xxvi. 14) hast Thou created all the children of men? (De Wette,
Hupfeld, and Hitzig.) עַל, of the ground of a matter and
direct motive, which is better suited to the question in ver. 49
than the other way of taking it: the life of all men passes on
into death and Hades; why then might not God, within this
brief space of time, this handbreadth, manifest Himself to His
creatures as the merciful and kind, and not as the always angry
God? The music strikes in here, and how can it do so otherwise than in elegiac *mesto*? If God's justice tarries and fails
in this present world, then the Old Testament faith becomes
sorely tempted and tried, because it is not able to find consolation in the life beyond. Thus it is with the faith of the poet

in the present juncture of affairs, the outward appearance of which is in such perplexing contradiction to the loving-kindness sworn to David and also hitherto vouchsafed. חֲסָדִים has not the sense in this passage of promises of favour, as in 2 Chron. vi. 42, but proofs of favour; הָרִאשֹׁנִים glances back at the long period of the reigns of David and of Solomon.* The Asaph Psalm lxxvii. and the Tephilla Isa. ch. lxiii. contain similar complaints, just as in connection with ver. 51a one is reminded of the Asaph Psalm lxxix. 2, 10, and in connection with ver. 52 of lxxix. 12. The phrase נָשָׂא בְחֵיקוֹ is used in other instances of loving nurture, Num. xi. 12, Isa. xl. 11. In this passage it must have a sense akin to חֶרְפַּת עֲבָדֶיךָ. It is impossible on syntactic grounds to regard כָּל־רַבִּים עַמִּים as still dependent upon חֶרְפַּת (Ewald) or, as Hupfeld is fond of calling it, as a " post-liminiar" genitive. Can it be that the כל is perhaps a mutilation of כְּלִמַּת, after Ezek. xxxvi. 15, as Böttcher suggests? We do not need this conjecture. For (1) to carry any one in one's bosom, if he is an enemy, may signify: to be obliged to cherish him with the vexation proceeding from him (Jer. xv. 15), without being able to get rid of him; (2) there is no doubt that רַבִּים can, after the manner of numerals, be placed before the substantive to which it belongs, xxxii. 10, Prov. xxxi. 29, 1 Chron. xxviii. 5, Neh. ix. 28; cf. the other position, *e.g.*, in Jer. xvi. 16; (3) consequently כָּל־רַבִּים עַמִּים may signify the " totality of many peoples " just as well as כֹּל גּוֹיִם רַבִּים in Ezek. xxxi. 6. The poet complains as a member of the nation, as a citizen of the empire, that he is obliged to foster many nations in his bosom, inasmuch as the land of Israel was overwhelmed by the Egyptians and their allies, the Libyans, Troglodytes, and Ethiopians. The אֲשֶׁר which follows in ver. 52 cannot now be referred back over ver. 51b to חֶרְפַּת (*quâ calumniâ*), and yet the relative sense, not the confirmatory (because, *quoniam*), is at issue. We therefore refer it to עמים, and take אוֹיְבֶיךָ as an apposition, as in cxxxix. 20: who reproach Thee, (as) Thine

---

* The *Pasek* between הראשנים and אדני is not designed merely to remove the limited predicate from the Lord, who is indeed the First and the Last, but also to secure its pronunciation to the guttural *Aleph*, which might be easily passed over after *Mem;* cf. Gen. i. 27, xxi. 17, xxx. 20, xlii. 21, and frequently.

enemies, Jahve, who reproach the footsteps (עִקְּבוֹת as in lxxvii.
20 with *Dag. dirimens*, which gives it an emotional turn) of
Thine anointed, *i.e.* they follow him everywhere, wheresoever
he may go, and whatsoever he may do.   With these significant
words, עִקְּבוֹת מְשִׁיחֶךָ, the Third Book of the Psalms dies away.
    Ver. 53.   The closing doxology of the Third Book.

FOURTH BOOK OF THE PSALTER

Ps. XC.–CVI.

~~~~~~

PSALM XC.

TAKING REFUGE IN THE LOVING-KINDNESS OF THE ETERNAL
ONE UNDER THE WRATHFUL JUDGMENT OF DEATH.

1 O LORD, Thou hast been a place of refuge for us in all
    generations!
2 Before the mountains were brought forth,
  And Thou gavest birth to the earth and the world,
  And from æon to æon Thou art God!
3 Thou turnest mortal man to dust,
  And sayest: Return, ye children of men.
4 For a thousand years in Thine eyes
  Are as yesterday when it passeth,
  And a watch in the night.

5 Thou carriest them away as with a flood, they become a sleep,
  In the morning they are as grass springing up again.
6 In the morning it flourisheth and springeth up again,
  In the evening it is cut down and it drieth up.
7 For we are consumed by Thine anger,
  And by Thy fierce anger are we scared away.
8 Thou hast set our iniquities before Thee,
  Our most secret matter in the light of Thy countenance.

9 For all our days are passed away in Thy wrath;
  We have spent our years as a whisper.
~~~~~~

10 The days of our years—their sum is seventy years,
   And, if very many, eighty years;
   And their pride is labour and vanity,
   For it passed swiftly and we fled away.
11 Who knoweth the power of Thine anger
   And the fear of Thee according to Thy wrath?
12 Teach us rightly to number our days,
   That we may gain a wise heart!

13 Turn, Jahve—how long?!—
   And have compassion upon Thy servants.
14 Satisfy us at morning-dawn with Thy mercy,
   Then will we joy and rejoice all our days.
15 Make us glad according to the days in which Thou hast
        humbled us,
   The years wherein we have seen evil.
16 Let Thy work appear unto Thy servants,
   And Thy glory upon their children.
17 And let the graciousness of the Lord our God be upon us,
   And the work of our hands do Thou establish upon us,
   Yea, the work of our hands establish Thou it!

The Fourth Book of the Psalms, corresponding to the ספר
במדבר of the Pentateuch, begins with a *Prayer of Moses the man
of God*, which comes out of the midst of the dying off of the
older generation during the march through the wilderness.
To the name, which could not be allowed to remain so bald,
because next to Abraham he is the greatest man known to the
Old Testament history of redemption, is added the title of
honour אִישׁ הָאֱלֹהִים (as in Deut. xxxiii. 1, Josh. xiv. 6), an
ancient name of the prophets which expresses the close relationship of fellowship with God, just as " servant of Jahve "
expresses the relationship of service, in accordance with the
special office and in relation to the history of redemption, into
which Jahve has taken the man and into which he himself has
entered.   There is scarcely any written memorial of antiquity
which so brilliantly justifies the testimony of tradition concerning its origin as does this Psalm, which may have been
preserved in some one or other of the older works, perhaps the
" Book of Jashar" (Josh. x. 13, 2 Sam. i. 18), until the time

of the final redaction of the Psalter. Not alone with respect to its contents, but also with reference to the form of its language, it is perfectly suitable to Moses. Even Hitzig can bring nothing of importance against this view, for the objection that the author in ver. 1 glances back upon past generations, whilst Israel was only born in the time of Moses, is removed by the consideration that the existence of Israel reaches back into the patriarchal times; and there is as little truth in the assertion that the *Piel* שַׁבְּעֵנוּ in ver. 14 instead of the *Hiphil* brings the Psalm down into very late times, as in the idea that the *Hiph.* וְהַאֲבַדְתָּ in cxliii. 12 instead of the *Piel* carries this Ps. cxliii. back into very early times. These trifling points dwindle down to nothing in comparison with the fact that Ps. xc. bears within itself distinct traces of the same origin as the song האזינו (Deut. ch. xxxii.), the blessing of Moses (Deut. ch. xxxiii.), the discourses in Deuteronomy, and in general the directly Mosaic portions of the Pentateuch. The Book of the Covenant, together with the Decalogue (Ex. ch. xix.–xxiv.) and Deuteronomy (with the exception of its supplement), are regarded by us, on very good grounds, as the largest originally Mosaic constituent parts of the Pentateuch. The Book of Deuteronomy is תּוֹרַת מֹשֶׁה in a pre-eminent sense.

Vers. 1–4. The poet begins with the confession that the Lord has proved Himself to His own, in all periods of human history, as that which He was before the world was and will be for evermore. God is designedly appealed to by the name אֲדֹנָי, which frequently occurs in the mouth of Moses in the middle books of the Pentateuch, and also in the Song at the Sea, Ex. xv. 17 and in Deut. iii. 24. He is so named here as the Lord ruling over human history with an exaltation ever the same. Human history runs on in דֹּר וָדֹר, so that one period (περίοδος) with the men living cotemporaneous with it goes and another comes; the expression is Deuteronomic (Deut. xxxii. 7). Such a course of generations lies behind the poet; and in them all the Lord has been מָעוֹן to His church, out of the heart of which the poet discourses. This expression too is Deuteronomic (Deut. xxxiii. 27). מעון signifies a habitation, dwelling-place (*vid.* on xxvi. 8), more especially God's heavenly and earthly dwelling-place, then the dwelling-place which God

Himself is to His saints, inasmuch as He takes up to Himself, conceals and protects, those who flee to Him from the wicked one and from evil, and turn in to Him (lxxi. 3, xci. 9). In order to express *fuisti* הָיִיתָ was indispensable; but just as *fuisti* comes from *fuo*, φύω, הָיָה (הָוָה) signifies not a closed, shut up being, but a being that discloses itself, consequently it is *fuisti* in the sense of *te exhibuisti*. This historical self-manifestation of God is based upon the fact that He is אֵל, *i.e.* might absolutely, or the absolutely Mighty One; and He was this, as ver. 2 says, even before the beginning of the history of the present world, and will be in the distant ages of the future as of the past. The foundation of this world's history is the creation. The combination אֶרֶץ וְתֵבֵל shows that this is intended to be taken as the object. וַתְּחוֹלֵל (with *Metheg* beside the *ē* of the final syllable, which is deprived of its accent, *vid.* on xviii. 20) is the language of address (Rashi): that which is created is in a certain sense born from God (יֻלָּד), and He brings it forth out of Himself; and this is here expressed by חוֹלֵל (as in Deut. xxxii. 18, cf. Isa. li. 2), creation being compared to travail which takes place amidst pains (*Psychology*, S. 114; tr. p. 137). If, after the example of the LXX. and Targum, one reads as passive וַתְּחוֹלַל (Böttcher, Olshausen, Hitzig) from the *Pulal* חֹלַל, Prov. viii. 24,—and this commends itself, since the pre-existence of God can be better dated back beyond facts than beyond the acts of God Himself,—then the conception remains essentially the same, since the Eternal and Absolute One is still to be thought of as מְחוֹלֵל. The fact that the mountains are mentioned first of all, harmonizes with Deut. xxxiii. 15. The *modus consecutivus* is intended to say: before the mountains were brought forth and Thou wast in labour therewith . . . The forming of the mountains consequently coincides with the creation of the earth, which is here as a body or mass called אֶרֶץ, and as a continent with the relief of mountains and lowlands is called תֵבֵל (cf. תֵבֵל אֶרֶץ, Prov. viii. 31, Job xxxvii. 12). To the double clause with טֶרֶם *seq. præt.* (cf. on the other hand *seq. fut.* Deut. xxxi. 21) is appended וּמֵעוֹלָם as a second definition of time: before the creation of the world, and from eternity to eternity. The Lord was God before the world was—that is the first assertion of ver. 2; His divine existence reaches out of the unlimited past into the unlimited future—this is the second. אֵל is not vocative, which it some-times, though rarely, is in the Psalms; it is a predicate, as *e.g.* in Deut. iii. 24.

This is also to be seen from vers. 3, 4, when ver. 3 ·now more definitely affirms the omnipotence of God, and ver. 4 the supra-temporality of God or the omnipresence of God in time. The LXX. misses the meaning when it brings over אל from ver. 2, and reads אַל־תָּשֵׁב. The shorter future form תָּשֵׁב for תָּשִׁיב stands poetically instead of the longer, as *e.g.* in xi. 6, xxv. 9; cf. the same thing in the *inf. constr.* in Deut. xxvi. 12, and both instances together in Deut. xxxii. 8. The poet intentionally calls the generation that is dying away אֱנוֹשׁ, which denotes man from the side of his frailty or perishable-ness; and the new generation בְּנֵי־אָדָם, with which is combined the idea of entrance upon life. It is clear that הֵשִׁיב עַד־דַּכָּא is intended to be understood according to Gen. iii. 19; but it is a question whether דַּכָּא is conceived of as an adjective (with mutable *ā*), as in xxxiv. 19, Isa. lvii. 15: Thou puttest men back into the condition of crushed ones (cf. on the construc-tion Num. xxiv. 24), or whether as a neutral feminine from דַּךְ (= דַּכָּה): Thou changest them into that which is crushed = dust, or whether as an abstract substantive like דִּכָּה, or according to another reading (cf. cxxvii. 2) דַּכָּא, in Deut. xxiii. 2: to crushing. This last is the simplest way of taking it, but it comes to one and the same thing with the second, since דַּכָּא signifies crushing in the neuter sense. A *fut. consec.* follows. The fact that God causes one generation to die off has as its consequence that He calls another into being (cf. the Arabic epithet of God *el-muʿîd* = הַמֵּשִׁיב, the Resuscitator). Hofmann and Hitzig take תָּשֵׁב as imperfect on account of the following וַתֹּאמֶר: Thou didst decree mortality for men; but the *fut. consec.* frequently only expresses the sequence of the thoughts or the connection of the matter, *e.g.* after a future that refers to that which is constantly taking place, Job xiv. 10. God causes men to die without letting them die out; for—so it continues in ver. 4—a thousand years is to Him a very short period, not to be at all taken into account. What now is the connection between that which confirms and that which is con-firmed here? It is not so much ver. 3 that is confirmed as ver. 2, to which the former serves for explanation, viz. this,

that God as the Almighty (אֵל), in the midst of this change of
generations, which is His work, remains Himself eternally the
same. This ever the same, absolute existence has its ground
herein, that time, although God fills it up with His working,
is no limitation to Him. A thousand years, which would make
any man who might live through them weary of life, are to
Him like a vanishing point. The proposition, as 2 Pet. iii. 8
shows, is also true when reversed: "One day is with the Lord
as a thousand years." He is however exalted above all time,
inasmuch as the longest period appears to Him very short, and
in the shortest period the greatest work can be executed by
Him. The standpoint of the first comparison, " *as yesterday*,"
is taken towards the end of the thousand of years. A whole
millennium appears to God, when He glances over it, just as
the yesterday does to us when (כִּי) it is passing by (יַעֲבֹר), and
we, standing on the border of the opening day, look back upon
the day that is gone. The second comparison is an advance
upon the first, and an advance also in form, from the fact that
the *Caph similitudinis* is wanting: a thousand years are to God
a watch in the night. אַשְׁמוּרָה is a night-watch, of which the
Israelites reckoned three, viz. the first, the middle, and the
morning watch (*vid.* Winer's *Realwörterbuch* s. v. *Nachtwache*).
It is certainly not without design that the poet says אַשְׁמוּרָה בַלַּיְלָה
instead of אַשְׁמֹרֶת הַלַּיְלָה. The night-time is the time for sleep;
a watch in the night is one that is slept away, or at any rate
passed in a sort of half-sleep. A day that is past, as we stand
on the end of it, still produces upon us the impression of a
course of time by reason of the events which we can recall;
but a night passed in sleep, and now even a fragment of the
night, is devoid of all trace to us, and is therefore as it were
timeless. Thus is it to God with a thousand years: they do
not last long to Him; they do not affect Him; at the close of
them, as at the beginning, He is the Absolute One (אֵל). Time
is as nothing to Him, the Eternal One. The changes of time
are to Him no barrier restraining the realization of His counsel
—a truth which has a terrible and a consolatory side. The
poet dwells upon the fear which it produces.

Vers. 5–8. Vers. 5, 6 tell us how great is the distance
between men and this eternal selfsameness of God. The
suffix of זְרַמְתָּם, referred to the thousand years, produces a

synallage (since שָׁנָה is feminine), which is to be avoided whenever it is possible to do so; the reference to בְּנֵי־אָדָם, as being
the principal object pointed to in what has gone before, is the
more natural, to say the very least. In connection with both
ways of applying it, זְרַם does not signify: to cause to rattle
down like sudden heavy showers of rain; for the figure that
God makes years, or that He makes men (Hitzig: the germs
of their coming into being), to rain down from above, is fanci-
ful and strange. זְרַם may also mean to sweep or wash away
as with heavy rains, *abripere instar nimbi*, as the old expositors
take it. So too Luther at one time: *Du reyssest sie dahyn*
(Thou carriest them away), for which he substituted later:
Du lessest sie dahin faren wie einen Strom (Thou causest them
to pass away as a river); but זְרֵם always signifies rain pouring
down from above. As a sudden and heavy shower of rain,
becoming a flood, washes everything away, so God's omnipotence sweeps men away. There is now no transition to another
alien figure when the poet continues: שֵׁנָה יִהְיוּ. What is meant
is the sleep of death, lxxvi. 6, שְׁנַת עוֹלָם, Jer. li. 39, 57, cf. יְשֵׁן
xiii. 4. He whom a flood carries away is actually brought
into a state of unconsciousness, he goes entirely to sleep, *i.e.*
he dies.

From this point the poet certainly does pass on to another
figure. The one generation is carried away as by a flood in
the night season, and in the morning another grows up. Men
are the subject of יַחֲלֹף, as of יִהְיוּ. The collective singular
alternates with the plural, just as in ver. 3 the collective אֱנוֹשׁ
alternates with בְּנֵי־אָדָם. The two members of ver. 5 stand in
contrast. The poet describes the succession of the generations. One generation perishes as it were in a flood, and
another grows up, and this also passes on to the same fate.
The meaning in both verses of the חלף, which has been for the
most part, after the LXX., Vulgate, and Luther, erroneously
taken to be *præterire = interire*, is determined in accordance
with this idea. The general signification of this verb, which
corresponds to the Arabic خلف, is " to follow or move after,
to go into the place of another, and in general, of passing
over from one place or state into another." Accordingly the
Hiphil signifies to put into a new condition, cii. 27, to set a

new thing on the place of an old one, Isa. ix. 9 [10], to gain new strength, to take fresh courage, Isa. xl. 31, xli. 1; and of plants: to send forth new shoots, Job xiv. 7; consequently the *Kal,* which frequently furnishes the perfect for the future *Hiphil* (Ew. § 127, *b,* and Hitzig on this passage), of plants signifies: to gain new shoots, not: to sprout (Targum, Syriac), but to sprout again or afresh, *regerminare;* cf. خَلْف, an after-growth, new wood. Perishing humanity renews its youth in ever new generations. Ver. 6*a* again takes up this thought: in the morning it grows up and shoots afresh, viz. the grass to which men are likened (a figure appropriated by Isa. ch. xl.), in the evening it is cut down and it dries up. Others trans-late מוֹלֵל to wither (root מל, properly to be long and lax, to allow to hang down long, cf. אָמֵל,אָמְלַל with أَمِلَ, to hope, *i.e.* to look forth into the distance); but (1) this *Pilel* of מוּל or *Poël* of מָלַל is not favourable to this intransitive way of taking it; (2) the reflexive in lviii. 8 proves that מוֹלֵל signifies to cut off in the front or above, after which perhaps even xxxvii. 2, Job xiv. 2, xviii. 16, by comparison with Job xxiv. 24, are to be explained. In the last passage it runs: *as the top of the stalk they are cut off* (*fut. Niph.* of מָלַל). Such a cut or plucked ear of corn is called in Deut. xxiii. 26 מְלִילָה, a Deuteronomic hapaxlegomenon which favours our way of taking the יְמוֹלֵל (with a most general subject = יְמוֹלַל). Thus, too, וְיָבֵשׁ is better attached to what precedes: the cut grass becomes parched hay. Just such an alternation of morning springing forth and evening drying up is the alternation of the generations of men.

The poet substantiates this in vers. 7 sq. from the expe-rience of those amongst whom he comprehended himself in the לָנוּ of ver. 1. Hengstenberg takes ver. 7 to be a statement of the cause of the transitoriness set forth: its cause is the wrath of God; but the poet does not begin כי באפך but כי כלינו. The chief emphasis therefore lies upon the perishing, and כי is not argumentative but explicative. If the subject of כָּלִינוּ were men in general (Olshausen), then it would be elucidating *idem per idem.* But, according to ver. 1, those who speak here are those whose refuge the Eternal One is. The poet therefore speaks in the name of the church, and confirms the lot of men

from that which his people have experienced even down to the
present time. Israel is able out of its own experience to cor-
roborate what all men pass through; it has to pass through
the very same experience as a special decree of God's wrath
on account of its sins. Therefore in vers. 7, 8 we stand altogether upon historical ground. The testimony of the inscription is here verified in the contents of the Psalm. The older
generation that came out of Egypt fell a prey to the sentence of
punishment, that they should gradually die off during the forty
years' journey through the desert; and even Moses and Aaron,
Joshua and Caleb only excepted, were included in this punishment on special grounds, Num. xiv. 26 sqq., Deut. i. 34—39.
This it is over which Moses here laments. God's wrath is here
called אַף and חֵמָה; just as the Book of Deuteronomy (in distinction from the other books of the Pentateuch) is fond of
combining these two synonyms (Deut. ix. 19, xxix. 22, 27, cf.
Gen. xxvii. 44 sq.). The breaking forth of the infinitely great
opposition of the holy nature of God against sin has swept
away the church in the person of its members, even down to
the present moment; נִבְהַל as in civ. 29, cf. בֶּהָלָה, Lev. xxvi.
16. It is the consequence of their sins. עָוֹן signifies sin as the
perversion of the right standing and conduct; עָלֻם, that which
is veiled in distinction from manifest sins, is the sum-total of
hidden moral, and that sinful, conduct. There is no necessity to
regard עֲלֻמֵנוּ as a defective plural; עֲלָמִים signifies youth (from
a radically distinct word, עֶלֶם); secret sins would therefore
be called עֲלֻמוֹת according to xix. 13. God sets transgressions
before Him when, because the measure is full and forgiveness
is inadmissible, He makes them an object of punishment. שַׁתָּ
(Kerî, as in viii. 7: שַׁתָּה, cf. vi. 4 וְאַתָּ, lxxiv. 6 וְעַתָּ) has the
accent upon the *ultima* before an initial guttural. The parallel
to לְנֶגְדֶּךָ is לִמְאוֹר פָּנֶיךָ. אוֹר is light, and מָאוֹר is either a body of
light, as the sun and moon, or, as in this passage, the circle of
light which the light forms. The countenance of God (פני ה׳)
is God's nature in its inclination towards the world, and מאור
פני ה׳ is the doxa of His nature that is turned towards the
world, which penetrates everything that is conformed to God
as a gracious light (Num. vi. 25), and makes manifest to the
bottom everything that is opposed to God and consumes it as
a wrathful fire.

Vers. 9–12. After the transitoriness of men has now been confirmed in vers. 6 sq. out of the special experience of Israel, the fact that this particular experience has its ground in a divine decree of wrath is more definitely confirmed from the facts of this experience, which, as vers. 11 sq. complain, unfortunately have done so little to urge them on to the fear of God, which is the condition and the beginning of wisdom. In ver. 9 we distinctly hear the Israel of the desert speaking. That was a generation that fell a prey to the wrath of God (דּוֹר עֶבְרָתוֹ, Jer. vii. 29). עֶבְרָה is wrath that passes over, breaks through the bounds of subjectivity. All their days (cf. ciii. 15) are passed away (פָּנָה, to turn one's self, to turn, *e.g.* Deut. i. 24) in such wrath, *i.e.* thoroughly pervaded by it. They have spent their years like a sound (כְּמוֹ־הֶגֶה), which has hardly gone forth before it has passed away, leaving no trace behind it; the noun signifies a gentle dull sound, whether a murmur (Job xxxvii. 2) or a groan (Ezek. ii. 10). With בָּהֶם in ver. 10 the sum is stated: there are comprehended therein seventy years; they include, run up to so many. Hitzig renders: the days wherein (בהם) our years consist are seventy years; but שְׁנוֹתֵינוּ side by side with ימי must be regarded as its more minute genitival definition, and the accentuation cannot be objected to. Beside the plural שָׁנִים the poetic plural שָׁנוֹת appears here, and it also occurs in Deut. xxxii. 7 (and nowhere else in the Pentateuch). That of which the sum is to be stated stands first of all as a *casus absol.* Luther's rendering: *Siebenzig Jar, wens hoch kompt so sinds achtzig* (seventy years, or at the furthest eighty years), as Symmachus also meant by his ἐν παραδόξῳ (in Chrysostom), is confirmed by the Talmudic הגיע לגבורות, " to attain to extreme old age" (*B. Moëd katan* 28a), and rightly approved of by Hitzig and Olshausen. גְּבוּרֹת signifies in lxxi. 16 full strength, here full measure. Seventy, or at most eighty years, were the average sum of the extreme term of life to which the generation dying out in the wilderness attained. וְרָהְבָּם the LXX. renders τὸ πλεῖον αὐτῶν, but רָהְבָּם is not equivalent to רֻבָּם. The verb רָהַב signifies to behave violently, *e.g.* of importunate entreaty, Prov. vi. 3, of insolent treatment, Isa. iii. 5, whence רַהַב (here רֹהַב), violence, impetuosity, and more especially a boastful vaunting appearance or coming forward, Job ix. 13, Isa. xxx. 7. The poet means to say that everything of which our life is proud (riches, outward appearance, luxury, beauty, etc.), when regarded in the right light, is after all only עָמָל, inasmuch as it causes us trouble and toil, and אָוֶן, because without any true intrinsic merit and worth. To this second predicate is appended the confirmatory clause. חִישׁ is *infin. adverb.* from חוּשׁ, חִישׁ, Deut. xxxii. 35: speedily, swiftly (Symmachus, the Quinta, and Jerome). The verb גּוּז signifies *transire* in all the Semitic dialects; and following this signification, which is applied transitively in Num. xi. 31, the Jewish expositors and Schultens correctly render: *nam transit velocissime.* Following upon the perfect גָּז, the *modus consecutivus* וַנָּעֻפָה maintains its retrospective signification. The strengthening of this mood by means of the intentional *ah* is more usual with the 1*st pers. sing., e.g.* Gen. xxxii. 6, than with the 1*st pers. plur.,* as here and in Gen. xli. 11; Ew. § 232, *g.* The poet glances back from the end of life to the course of life. And life, with all of which it had been proud, appears as an empty burden; for it passed swiftly by and we fled away, we were borne away with rapid flight upon the wings of the past.

Such experience as this ought to urge one on to the fear of God; but how rarely does this happen! and yet the fear of God is the condition (stipulation) and the beginning of wisdom. The verb יָדַע in ver. 11*a*, just as it in general denotes not merely notional but practically living and efficient knowledge, is here used of a knowledge which makes that which is known conduce to salvation. The meaning of וּכְיִרְאָתְךָ is determined in accordance with this. The suffix is here either *gen. subj.*: according to Thy fearfulness (יִרְאָה as in Ezek. i. 18), or *gen. obj.*: according to the fear that is due to Thee, which in itself is at once (cf. v. 8, Ex. xx. 20, Deut. ii. 25) more natural, and here designates the knowledge which is so rarely found, as that which is determined by the fear of God, as a truly religious knowledge. Such knowledge Moses supplicates for himself and for Israel: to number our days teach us rightly to understand. 1 Sam. xxiii. 17, where יָדַע כֵּן signifies "he does not know it to be otherwise, he is well aware of it," shows how כֵּן is meant. Hitzig, contrary to the accentuation, draws it to לִמְנוֹת יָמֵינוּ; but "to number our days" is in itself equivalent to "hourly to contemplate the fleeting character and brevity of our lifetime;" and כֵּן הוֹדַע prays for a true qualification for this, and one that accords with experience. The future that follows is well adapted to the call, as frequently aim and result. But הָבִיא is not to be taken, with Ewald and Hitzig, in the signification of bringing as an offering, a meaning this verb cannot have of itself alone (why should it not have been וְנַקְרִיב?). Böttcher also erroneously renders it after the analogy of Prov. ii. 10: "that we may bring wisdom into the heart," which ought to be בְּלֵב. הָבִיא, deriving its meaning from agriculture, signifies "to carry off, obtain, gain, prop. to bring in," viz. into the barn, 2 Sam. ix. 10, Hagg. i. 6; the produce of the field, and in a general way gain or profit, is hence called תְּבוּאָה. A wise heart is the fruit which one reaps or garners in from such numbering of the days, the gain which one carries off from so constantly reminding one's self of the end. לְבַב חָכְמָה is a poetically intensified expression for לֵב חָכָם, just as לֵב מַרְפֵּא in Prov. xiv. 30 signifies a calm easy heart.

Vers. 13–17. The prayer for a salutary knowledge, or discernment, of the appointment of divine wrath is now followed by the prayer for the return of favour, and the wish that God would carry out His work of salvation and bless Israel's undertakings to that end. We here recognise the well-known language of prayer of Moses in Ex. xxxii. 12, according to which שׁוּבָה is not intended as a prayer for God's return to Israel, but for the turning away of His anger; and the sigh עַד־מָתַי that is blended with it asks how long this being angry, which threatens to blot Israel out, is still to last. וְהִנָּחֵם is explained according to this same parallel passage: May God feel remorse or sorrow (which in this case coincide) concerning His servants, i.e. concerning the affliction appointed to them. The naming of the church by עֲבָדֶיךָ (as in Deut. ix. 27, cf. Ex. xxxii. 13 of the patriarchs) reminds one of Deut. xxxii. 36: *concerning His servants He shall feel compassion* (*Hithpa.* instead of the *Niphal*). The prayer for the turning of wrath is followed in ver. 14 by the prayer for the turning towards them of favour. In בַּבֹּקֶר there lies the thought that it has been night hitherto in Israel. "Morning" is therefore the beginning of a new season of favour. In שַׂבְּעֵנוּ (to which חַסְדֶּךָ is a second accusative of the object) is implied the thought that Israel whilst under wrath has been hungering after favour;

cf. the adjective שָׂבֵעַ in the same tropical signification in Deut. xxxiii. 23. The supplicatory imperatives are followed by two moods expressive of intention: then will we, or: in order that we may rejoice and be glad; for futures like these set forth the intention of attaining something as a result or aim of what has been expressed just before: Ew. § 325, a. בְּכָל־יָמֵינוּ is not governed by the verbs of rejoicing (cxviii. 24), in which case it would have been בְּחַיֵּינוּ, but is an adverbial definition of time (cxlv. 2, Jer. xxxv. 8): within the term of life allotted to us. We see from ver. 15 that the season of affliction has already lasted for a long time. The duration of the forty years of wrath, which in the midst of their course seemed to them as an eternity, is made the measure of the reviving again that is earnestly sought. The plural יְמוֹת instead of יְמֵי is common only to our Psalm and Deut. xxxii. 7; it is not known elsewhere to Biblical Hebrew. And the poetical שְׁנוֹת instead of שְׁנֵי, which also occurs elsewhere, appears for the first time in Deut. xxxii. 7. The meaning of עִנִּיתָנוּ, in which יְמוֹת is specialized after the manner of a genitive, is explained from Deut. viii. 2 sqq., according to which the forty years' wandering in the wilderness was designed to humble (עַנּוֹת) and to prove Israel through suffering. At the close of these forty years Israel stands on the threshold of the Promised Land. To Israel all final hopes were closely united with the taking possession of this land. We learn from Gen. ch. xlix. that it is the horizon of Jacob's prophetic benediction. This Psalm too, in vers. 16, 17, terminates in the prayer for the attainment of this goal. The psalmist has begun in ver. 1 his adoration with the majestic divine name אֲדֹנָי; in ver. 13 he began his prayer with the gracious divine name יַהֲוֶה; and now, where he mentions God for the third time, he gives to Him the twofold name, so full of faith, אֲדֹנָי אֱלֹהֵינוּ. אֵל used once alternates with the thrice repeated עַל: salvation is not Israel's own work, but the work of Jahve; it therefore comes from above, it comes and meets Israel. It is worthy of remark that the noun פֹּעַל occurs only in Deuteronomy in the whole Tôra, and that here also of the gracious rule of Jahve, ch. xxxii. 4, cf. xxxiii. 11. The church calls the work of the Lord מַעֲשֵׂה יָדֵינוּ in so far as He executes it through them. This expression מַעֲשֵׂה יָדִים as a designation of human undertakings runs through the whole of the Book of

Deuteronomy: ch. **ii.** 7, iv. 28, xi. 7, xiv. 29, xvi. 15, xxiv. 19, xxvii. 15, xxviii. 12, xxx. 9. In the work of the Lord the bright side of His glory unveils itself, hence it is called הָדָר; this too is a word not alien at least to the language of Deuteronomy, ch. xxxiii. 17. Therein is made manifest נֹעַם ה׳, His graciousness and condescension—an expression which David has borrowed from Moses in Ps. xxvii. 4. יֵרָאֶה and יְהִי are optatives. כּוֹנְנָה is an urgent request, *imperat. obsecrantis* as the old expositors say. With *Waw* the same thought is expressed over again (cf. Isa. lv. 1, וּלְכוּ, yea come)—a simple, childlike anadiplosis which vividly reminds us of the Book of Deuteronomy, which revolves in thoughts that are ever the same, and by that very means speaks deeply to the heart. Thus the Deuteronomic impression of this Psalm accompanies us from beginning to end, from מָעוֹן to מַעֲשֵׂה יָדַיִם. Nor will it now be merely accidental that the fondness for comparisons, which is a peculiarity of the Book of Deuteronomy (ch. i. 31, 44, viii. 5, xxviii. 29, 49, cf. xxviii. 13, 44, xxix. 17, 18), is found again in this Psalm.

PSALM XCI.

TALISMANIC SONG IN TIME OF WAR AND PESTILENCE.

First Voice:

1 HE who sitteth in the protection of the Most High,
  Who abideth in the shadow of the Almighty—

Second Voice:

2 I say to Jahve: My refuge and my fortress,
  My God in whom I trust.

First Voice:

3 For HE shall deliver thee from the snare of the fowler,
    from the destroying pestilence.
4 With His feathers shall He defend thee,
  And under His wings art thou hidden;
  A shield and buckler is His truth.
5 Thou shalt not be afraid for any nightly terror,
  For the arrow that flieth by day,

6 For the pestilence that walketh in the darkness,
    For the sickness that wasteth at noon-day.
7 A thousand may fall at thy side and ten thousand at thy
        right hand,
    It shall not come nigh thee—
8 Nay, with thine own eyes shalt thou look on
    And see the recompense of the wicked.

Second Voice:

9 For Thou, O Jahve, art my refuge!

First Voice:

The Most High hast thou made thy habitation.
10 The range of misfortune toucheth thee not,
    And the plague doth not come nigh thy tent.
11 For His angels hath He given charge over thee,
    To keep thee in all thy ways.
12 On their hands shall they bear thee up,
    That thou dost not dash thy foot against a stone.
13 Over lions and adders shalt thou walk,
    Thou shalt trample lions and dragons under thy feet.

Third (divine) Voice:

14 For he loveth Me, therefore will I deliver him,
    I will set him on high, for he knoweth My Name.
15 If he shall call upon Me, I will answer him,
    I will be with him in trouble;
    I will rescue him and bring him to honour.
16 With length of life will I satisfy him,
    And cause him to delight himself in My salvation.

The primeval song is followed by an anonymous song (inscribed by the LXX. without any warrant τῷ Δαυίδ), the time of whose composition cannot be determined; and it is only placed in this order because the last verse accords with the last verse but one of Ps. xc. There the revelation of Jahve's work is prayed for, and here Jahve promises: *I will grant him to see My salvation;* the "work of Jahve" is His realized "salvation." The two Psalms also have other points of contact, *e.g.* in the מָעוֹן referred to God (*vid. Symbolæ*, p. 60).

In this Psalm, the Invocavit Psalm of the church, which
praises the protecting and rescuing grace which he who believingly takes refuge in God experiences in all times of danger
and distress,* the relation of ver. 2 to ver. 1 meets us at the
very beginning as a perplexing riddle. If we take ver. 1 as a
clause complete in itself, then it is tautological. If we take אֹמַר
in ver. 2 as a participle (Jerome, *dicens*) instead of אֹמֵר, ending
with *Pathach* because a construct form (cf. xciv. 9, cxxxvi. 6),
then the participial subject would have a participial predicate:
" He who sitteth is saying," which is inelegant and also improbable, since אֹמַר in other instances is always the 1*st pers. fut.*
If we take אֹמַר as 1*st pers. fut.* and ver. 1 as an apposition of the
subject expressed in advance: as such an one who sitteth . . .
I say, then we stumble against יִתְלוֹנָן; this transition of the
participle to the finite verb, especially without the copula (וּבְצֵל),
is confusing. If, however, we go on and read further into the
Psalm, we find that the same difficulty as to the change of
person recurs several times later on, just as in the opening.
Olshausen, Hupfeld, and Hitzig get rid of this difficulty by all
sorts of conjectures. But a reason for this abrupt change of
the person is that dramatic arrangement recognised even in the
Targum, although awkwardly indicated, which, however, was
first of all clearly discerned by J. D. Michaelis and Maurer.
There are, to wit, two voices that speak (as in Ps. cxxi.), and at
last the voice of Jahve comes in as a third. His closing utterance, rich in promise, forms, perhaps not unaccidentally, a
seven-line strophe. Whether the Psalm came also to be executed
in liturgical use thus with several voices, perhaps by three
choirs, we cannot tell; but the poet certainly laid it out dra-
matically, as the translation represents it. In spite of the many
echoes of earlier models, it is one of the freshest and most
beautiful Psalms, resembling the second part of Isaiah in its
light-winged, richly coloured, and transparent diction.

----

* Hence in *J. Shabbath* 8, *col.* 2, and *Midrash Shocher tob* on xci. 1 and
elsewhere, it is called, together with Ps. iii., (פגעים) שִׁיר פְּגוּעִין, a song of
occurrences, *i.e.* a protective (or talismanic) song in times of dangers that
may befall one, just as Sebald Heyden's Psalm-song, " He who is in the
protection of the Most High and resigns himself to God," is inscribed
" Preservative against the pestilence."

Vers. 1, 2. As the concealing One, God is called עֶלְיוֹן, the inaccessibly high One; and as the shadowing One שַׁדַּי, the invincibly almighty One. Faith, however, calls Him by His covenant name (*Heilsname*) יהוה and, with the suffix of appropriation, אֱלֹהַי (*my* God). In connection with ver. 1 we are reminded of the expressions of the Book of Job, ch. xxxix. 28, concerning the eagle's building its nest in its eyrie. According to the accentuation, ver. 2a ought to be rendered with Geier, "*Dicit: in Domino meo* (or *Domini*) *latibulum*, etc." But the combination אֹמַר לה׳ is more natural, since the language of address follows in both halves of the verse.

Vers. 3–9a. יָקוֹשׁ, as in Prov. vi. 5, Jer. v. 26, is the dullest toned form for יָקֹשׁ or יוֹקֵשׁ, cxxiv. 7. What is meant is death, or "he who has the power of death," Heb. ii. 14, cf. 2 Tim. ii. 26. "The snare of the fowler" is a figure for the peril of one's life, Eccles. ix. 12. In connection with ver. 4 we have to call to mind Deut. xxxii. 11: God protects His own as an eagle with its large strong wing. אֶבְרָה is *nom. unitatis*, a pinion, to אֵבֶר, Isa. xl. 31; and the *Hiph.* הֵסֵךְ, from סָכַךְ, with the dative of the object, like the *Kal* in cxl. 8, signifies to afford covering, protection. The ἅπαξ λεγ. סֹחֵרָה, according to its stem-word, is that which encompasses anything round about, and here beside צִנָּה, a weapon of defence surrounding the body on all sides; therefore not corresponding to the Syriac ܡܣܓܪܬܐ, a stronghold (מִסְגֶּרֶת, סֹהַר), but to ܣܟܪܐ, a shield. The Targum translates צִנָּה with תְּרִיסָא, θυρεός, and סֹחֵרָה with עֲגִילָא, which points to the round *parma*. אֲמִתּוֹ is the truth of the divine promises. This is an impregnable defence (*a*) in war-times, ver. 5, against nightly surprises, and in the battle by day; (*b*) in times of pestilence, ver. 6, when the destroying angel, who passes through and destroys the people (Ex. xi. 4), can do no harm to him who has taken refuge in God, either in the midnight or the noontide hours. The future יַהֲלֹךְ is a more rhythmical and, in the signification to rage (as of disease) and to vanish away, a more usual form instead of יֵלֵךְ. The LXX., Aquila, and Symmachus erroneously associate the demon name שֵׁד with יָשׁוּד. It is a metaplastic (as if formed from שׁוּד) future for יָשֹׁד, cf. Prov. xxix. 6, יָרוּן, and Isa. xlii. 4, יָרוּץ, *frangetur*. Ver. 7a a hypothetical protasis: *si cadant;* the preterite would signify *ceciderint*, Ew. § 357, *b*. With רַק that which will solely and exclusively take place is introduced. Burk correctly renders: *nullam cum peste rem habebis, nisi ut videas*. Only a spectator shalt thou be, and that with thine own eyes, being thyself inaccessible and left to survive, conscious that thou thyself art a living one in contrast with those who are dying. And thou shalt behold, like Israel on the night of the Passover, the just retribution to which the evil-doers fall a prey. שִׁלֻּמָה, recompense, retribution, is a hapaxlegomenon, cf. שִׁלֻּמִים, Isa. xxxiv. 8. Ascribing the glory to God, the second voice confirms or ratifies these promises.

Vers. 9*b*–16. The first voice continues this ratification, and goes on weaving these promises still further: thou hast made the Most High thy dwelling-place (מְעוֹן); there shall not touch thee . . . The promises rise ever higher and higher, and sound more glorious. The *Pual* אֻנָּה, prop. to be turned towards, is equivalent to "to befall one," as in Prov. xii. 21; Aquila well renders: οὐ μεταχθήσεται πρὸς σὲ κακία. לֹא־יִקְרַב reminds one of Isa. liv. 14, where אֶל follows; here it is בְּ, as in Judg. xix. 13. The angel guardianship which is apportioned to him who trusts in God appears in vers. 11, 12 as a universal fact, not as a solitary fact and occurring only in extraordinary instances. *Hæc est vera miraculorum ratio*, observes Brentius on this passage, *quod semel aut iterum manifeste revelent ea quæ Deus semper abscondite operatur*. In יִשָּׂאוּנְךָ the suffix has been combined with the full form of the future. The LXX. correctly renders ver. 12*b*: μήποτε προσκόψῃς πρὸς λίθον τὸν πόδα σου, for נֶגֶף everywhere else, and therefore surely here too and in Prov. iii. 23, has a transitive signification, not an intransitive (Aquila, Jerome, Symmachus), cf. Jer. xiii. 16. Ver. 13 tells what he who trusts in God has power to do by virtue of this divine succour through the medium of angels. The promise calls to mind Mark xvi. 18, ὄφεις ἀροῦσι, they shall take up serpents, but still more Luke x. 19: Behold, I give you power to tread ἐπάνω ὄφεων καὶ σκορπίων καὶ ἐπὶ πᾶσαν τὴν δύναμιν τοῦ ἐχθροῦ. They are all kinds of destructive powers belonging to nature, and particularly to the spirit-world, that are meant. They are called lions and fierce lions from the side of their open power, which threatens destruction, and adders and dragons from the side

of their venomous secret malice. In ver. 13*a* it is promised
that the man who trusts in God shall walk on over these
monsters, these malignant foes, proud in God and unharmed;
in ver. 13*b*, that he shall tread them to the ground (cf. Rom.
xvi. 20). That which the divine voice of promise now says at
the close of the Psalm is, so far as the form is concerned, an
echo taken from Ps. l. Vers. 15 and 23 of that Psalm sound
almost word for word the same. Gen. xlvi. 4, and more
especially Isa. lxiii. 9, are to be compared on ver. 15*b*. In *B.
Taanith* 16*a* it is inferred from this passage that God compas-
sionates the suffering ones whom He is compelled by reason of
His holiness to chasten and prove. The " salvation of Jahve,"
as in l. 23, is the full reality of the divine purpose (or counsel)
of mercy. To live to see the final glory was the rapturous
thought of the Old Testament hope, and in the apostolic age,
of the New Testament hope also.

PSALM XCII.

SABBATH THOUGHTS.

2 IT is good to give thanks unto Jahve,
  And to harp unto Thy Name, O Most High—
3 To show forth in the morning Thy loving-kindness,
  And Thy faithfulness in the nights,
4 Upon a ten-stringed instrument and upon the nabla,
  In skilful playing with the cithern.

5 For Thou makest me glad, Jahve, through Thy rule,
  Because of the works of Thy hands can I exult.
6 How great are Thy works, Jahve!
  Very deep are Thy thoughts.
7 A brutish man remains unconscious,
  And a fool doth not discern this.

8 When the ungodly sprang up as the green herb
  And all the workers of evil flourished,
    It came to pass that they were absolutely destroyed.
9 And Thou art exaltation for ever, Jahve!

10 For lo Thine enemies, Jahve—
   For lo Thine enemies shall perish,
   All the workers of evil shall melt away.

11 And Thou exaltest, as an antelope, my horn,
   I am anointed with refreshing oil.
12 And mine eye feasteth upon those that lie in wait for me,
   Mine ears see their desire upon those who maliciously rose
                    up against me.
13 The righteous shall sprout forth as the palm,
   As a cedar on Lebanon shall he grow up.

14 Planted in the house of Jahve,
   They shall blossom in the courts of our God.
15 They shall be still vigorous in old age,
   Full of sap and green shall they remain,
16 To make known that Jahve is upright,
   My rock, and there is no unrighteousness in Him.

This *Song-Psalm for the Sabbath-day* was the Sabbath-Psalm among the week's Psalms of the post-exilic service (cf. vol. i. pp. 32, 334); and was sung in the morning at the drink-offering of the first Tamîd lamb, just as at the accompanying Sabbath-musaph-offering (Num. xxviii. 9 sq.) a part of the song Deut. ch. xxxii. (divided into six parts) was sung, and at the service connected with the Mincha or evening sacrifice one of the three pieces, Ex. xv. 1–10, 11–19, Num. xxi. 17–20 (*B. Rosh ha-Shana* 31a). 1 Macc. ix. 23 is a reminiscence from Ps. xcii. deviating but little from the LXX. version, just as 1 Macc. vii. 17 is a quotation taken from Ps. lxxix. With respect to the sabbatical character of the Psalm, it is a disputed question even in the Talmud whether it relates to the Sabbath of the Creation (R. Nehemiah, as it is taken by the Targum) or to the final Sabbath of the world's history (R. Akiba: the day that is altogether Sabbath; cf. Athanasius: αἰνεῖ ἐκείνην τὴν γενησομένην ἀνάπαυσιν). The latter is relatively more correct. It praises God, the Creator of the world, as the Ruler of the world, whose rule is pure loving-kindness and faithfulness, and calms itself, in the face of the flourishing condition of the evil-doers, with the prospect of the final issue, which will brilliantly vindicate the righteousness of God, that was at that time imperceptible to superficial observation, and will change the congregation of the righteous into a flourishing grove of palms and cedars upon holy ground. In this prospect Ps. xcii. 12 and Ps. xci. 8 coincide, just as God is also called "the Most High" at the beginning of these two Psalms. But that the *tetragrammaton* occurs seven times in both Psalms, as Hengstenberg says, does not turn out to be correct. Only the Sabbath-Psalm (and not Ps. xci.) repeats the most sacred Name seven times. And certainly the unmistakeable strophe-schema too, 6. 6. 7. 6. 6, is not without significance. The middle of the Psalm bears the stamp of the sabbatic number. It is also worthy of remark that the poet gains the number seven by means of an anadiplosis in ver. 10. Such an emphatic climax by means of repetition is common to our Psalm with xciii. 3, xciv. 3, xcvi. 13.

Vers. 2–4. The Sabbath is the day that God has hallowed, and that is to be consecrated to God by our turning away from the business pursuits of the working days (Isa. lviii. 13 sq.) and applying ourselves to the praise and adoration of God, which is the most proper, blessed Sabbath employment. It is good, *i.e.* not merely good in the eyes of God, but also good for man, beneficial to the heart, pleasant and blessed. Lovingkindness is designedly connected with the dawn of the morning, for it is morning light itself, which breaks through the night (xxx. 6, lix. 17), and faithfulness with the nights, for in the perils of the loneliness of the night it is the best companion, and nights of affliction are the " foil of its verification." עָשׂוֹר beside נֶבֶל (נֵבֶל) is equivalent to נֵבֶל עָשׂוֹר in xxxiii. 2, cxliv. 9 : the ten-stringed harp or lyre. הִגָּיוֹן is the music of stringed instruments (*vid.* on ix. 17), and that, since הגה in itself is not a suitable word for the rustling (*strepitus*) of the strings, the impromptu or phantasia playing (in Amos vi. 5, scornfully, פָּרַט), which suits both ix. 17 (where it is appended to the *forte* of the interlude) and the construction with *Beth instrumenti.*

Vers. 5–7. Statement of the ground of this commendation of the praise of God. Whilst פָּעַל is the usual word for God's historical rule (xliv. 2, lxiv. 10, xc. 16, etc.), מַעֲשֵׂי יָדֶיךָ

denotes the works of the Creator of the world, although not to the exclusion of those of the Ruler of the world (cxliii. 5). To be able to rejoice over the revelation of God in creation and the revelation of God in general is a gift from above, which the poet thankfully confesses that he has received. The Vulgate begins ver. 5 *Quia delectasti me*, and Dante in his *Purgatorio*, xxviii. 80, accordingly calls the Psalm *il Salmo Delectasti;* a smiling female form, which represents the life of Paradise, says, as she gathers flowers, she is so happy because, with the Psalm *Delectasti*, she takes a delight in the glory of God's works. The works of God are transcendently great; very deep are His thoughts, which mould human history and themselves gain form in it (cf. xl. 6, cxxxix. 17 sq., where infinite fulness is ascribed to them, and Isa. lv. 8 sq., where infinite height is ascribed to them). Man can neither measure the greatness of the divine works nor fathom the depth of the divine thoughts; he who is enlightened, however, perceives the immeasurableness of the one and the unfathomableness of the other, whilst a אִישׁ־בַּעַר, a man of animal nature, *homo brutus* (*vid.* lxxiii. 22), does not come to the knowledge (לֹא יֵדַע, used absolutely as in xiv. 4), and כְּסִיל, a blockhead, or one dull in mind, whose carnal nature outweighs his intellectual and spiritual nature, does not discern אֶת־זֹאת (cf. 2 Sam. xiii. 17), *id ipsum*, viz. how unsearchable are God's judgments and untrackable His ways (Rom. xi. 33).

Vers. 8–10. Upon closer examination the prosperity of the ungodly is only a semblance that lasts for a time. The infinitive construction in ver. 8 is continued in the historic tense, and it may also be rendered as historical. זֹאת הָיְתָה (Saadia: فانه) is to be supplied in thought before לְהִשָּׁמְדָם, as in Job xxvii. 14. What is spoken of is an historical occurrence which, in its beginning, course, and end, has been frequently repeated even down to the present day, and ever confirmed afresh. And thus, too, in time to come and once finally shall the ungodly succumb to a peremptory, decisive (עֲדֵי־עַד) judgment of destruction. Jahve is מָרוֹם לְעֹלָם, by His nature and by His rule He is " a height for ever;" *i.e.* in relation to the creature and all that goes on here below He has a nature beyond and above all this (*Jenseitigkeit*), ever the same and absolute ; He is absolutely inaccessible to the God-opposed one here below who vaunts himself in stupid pride and rebelliously exalts himself as a titan, and only suffers it to last until the term of his barren blossoming is run out. Thus the present course of history will and must in fact end in a final victory of good over evil : for lo Thine enemies, Jahve—for lo Thine enemies . . . הִנֵּה points as it were with the finger to the inevitable end ; and the emotional anadiplosis breathes forth a zealous love for the cause of God as if it were his own. God's enemies shall perish, all the workers of evil shall be disjointed, scattered, יִתְפָּרְדוּ (cf. Job iv. 11). Now they form a compact mass, which shall however fall to pieces, when one day the intermingling of good and evil has an end.

Vers. 11–13. The hitherto oppressed church then stands forth vindicated and glorious. The *futt. consec.*, as preterites of the ideal past, pass over further on into the pure expression of future time. The LXX. renders : καὶ ὑψωθήσεται (וַתָּרֶם) ὡς μονοκέρωτος τὸ κέρας μου. By רְאֵים (incorrect for רְאֵם, primary form רְאָם), μονόκερως, is surely to be understood the *oryx*, one-horned according to Aristotle and the Talmud (*vid.* on xxix. 6, Job xxxix. 9–12). This animal is called in Talmudic קרש (perhaps abbreviated from μονόκερως) ; the Talmud also makes use of ארזילא (the gazelle) as synonymous with רְאֵם (Aramaic definitive or emphatic state רֵימָא).* The primary passages for figures taken from animal life are Num. xxiii. 22, Deut. xxxiii. 17. The horn is an emblem of defensive power and at the same time of stately grace ; and the fresh, green oil an emblem of the pleasant feeling and enthusiasm, joyous in the prospect of victory, by which the church is then pervaded (Acts iii. 19). The LXX. erroneously takes בַּלֹּתִי as *infin. Piel*, τὸ γῆράς μου, my being grown old, a signification which the *Piel* cannot have. It is 1*st præt. Kal* from בָּלַל, *perfusus sum* (cf. Arabic *balla*, to be moist, *ballah* and *bullah*, moistness, good health, the freshness of youth), and the *ultima*-accentuation, which also occurs in this form of double *Ajin* verbs without *Waw convers.* (*vid.* on Job xix. 17), ought not to mislead. In the expression שֶׁמֶן רַעֲנָן, the adjective used in other instances only of the olive-tree itself is transferred to the oil,

---

* *Vid.* Lewysohn, *Zoologie des Talmud*, §§ 146 and 174.

which contains the strength of its succulent verdure as an
essence. The *ecclesia pressa* is then *triumphans*. The eye,
which was wont to look timidly and tearfully upon the persecutors, the ears, upon which even their name and the tidings
of their approach were wont to produce terror, now see their
desire upon them as they are blotted out. שָׁמַע בְּ (found only
here) follows the sense of רָאָה בְ, cf. نظر فى, to lose one's self
in the contemplation of anything. שׁוּרָי is either a substantive
after the form בּוּז, גּוּר, or a participle in the signification
" those who regarded me with hostility, those who lay in wait
for me," like נוּס, fled, Num. xxxv. 32, סוּר, having removed
themselves to a distance, Jer. xvii. 13, שׁוּב, turned back, Mic.
ii. 8 ; for this participial form has not only a passive signification (like מוּל, circumcised), but sometimes, too, a deponent
perfect signification ; and חוּשׁ in Num. xxxii. 17, if it belongs
here, may signify hurried = in haste. In שׁוּרָי, however, no
such passive colouring of the meaning is conceivable ; it is
therefore : *insidiati* (Luzatto, *Grammatica*, § 518 : *coloro che
mi guatavano*). There is no need for regarding the word,
with Böttcher and Olshausen, as distorted from שֹׁרְרָי (the apocopated participle *Pilel* of the same verb) ; one might more
readily regard it as a softening of that word as to the sound
(Ewald, Hitzig). In ver. 12*b* it is not to be rendered : upon
the wicked doers (villains) who rise up against me. The
placing of the adjective thus before its substantive must (with
the exception of רַב when used after the manner of a numeral)
be accounted impossible in Hebrew, even in the face of the
passages brought forward by Hitzig, viz. 1 Chron. xxvii. 5,
1 Sam. xxxi. 3 ;* it is therefore : upon those who as villains
rise up against. The circumstance that the poet now in ver.
13 passes from himself to speak of the righteous, is brought
about by the fact that it is the congregation of the righteous
in general, *i.e.* of those who regulate their life according to
the divine order of salvation, into whose future he here takes a
glance. When the prosperity [lit. the blossoming] of the un-

---

* In the former passage כֹּהֵן רֹאשׁ is taken as one notion (chief priest),
and in the latter אֲנָשִׁים בַּקֶּשֶׁת (men with the bow) is, with Keil, to be
regarded as an apposition.

godly comes to an end, the springing up and growth of the
righteous only then rightly has its beginning. The richness of
the inflorescence of the date-palm (תָּמָר) is clear from the fact,
that when it has attained its full size, it bears from three to four,
and in some instances even as many as six, hundred pounds
of fruit. And there is no more charming and majestic sight
than the palm of the oasis, this prince among the trees of the
plain, with its proudly raised diadem of leaves, its attitude
peering forth into the distance and gazing full into the face of
the sun, its perennial verdure, and its vital force, which constantly renews itself from the root—a picture of life in the
midst of the world of death. The likening of the righteous
to the palm, to the " blessed tree," to this " sister of man," as
the Arabs call it, offers points of comparison in abundance.
Side by side with the palm is the cedar, the prince of the trees
of the mountain, and in particular of Mount Lebanon. The
most natural point of comparison, as יִשְׂגֶּה (cf. Job viii. 11)
states, is its graceful lofty growth, then in general τὸ δασὺ καὶ
θερμὸν καὶ θρέψιμον (Theodoret), i.e. the intensity of its vegetative strength, but also the perpetual verdure of its foliage
and the perfume (Hos. xiv. 7) which it exhales.

Vers. 14–16. The soil in which the righteous are planted
or (if it is not rendered with the LXX. πεφυτευμένοι, but with
the other Greek versions μεταφυτευθέντες) into which they are
transplanted, and where they take root, a planting of the Lord,
for His praise, is His holy Temple, the centre of a family
fellowship with God that is brought about from that point as
its starting-point and is unlimited by time and space. There
they stand as in sacred ground and air, which impart to them
ever new powers of life; they put forth buds (הִפְרִיחַ as in Job
xiv. 9) and preserve a verdant freshness and marrowy vitality
(like the olive, lii. 10, Judg. ix. 9) even into their old age (נוּב
of a productive force for putting out shoots; vid. with reference
to the root נב, Genesis, S. 635 sq.), cf. Isa. lxv. 22: like the
duration of the trees is the duration of my people; they live
long in unbroken strength, in order, in looking back upon a
life rich in experiences of divine acts of righteousness and
loving-kindness, to confirm the confession which Moses, in
Deut. xxxii. 4, places at the head of his great song. There
the expression is אֵין עָוֶל, here it is אֵין עֹלָתָה בּוֹ. This 'ôlātha,

softened from ʿawlātha—so the *Kerî*—with a transition from
the *aw*, *au* into *ô*, is also found in Job v. 16 (cf. עֹלָה = עַוְלָה Ps.
lviii. 3, lxiv. 7, Isa. lxi. 8), and is certainly original in this
Psalm, which also has many other points of coincidence with
the Book of Job (like Ps. cvii., which, however, in ver. 42
transposes עֹלָתָה into עַוְלָה).

PSALM XCIII.

THE ROYAL THRONE ABOVE THE SEA OF THE PEOPLES.

1 JAHVE now is King, He hath clothed Himself with
       majesty;
  Jahve hath clothed Himself, He hath girded Himself with
       might:
  Therefore the world standeth fast without tottering.

2 Thy throne standeth fast from of old,
  From everlasting art THOU.

3 The floods have lifted up, Jahve,
  The floods have lifted up their roaring,
  The floods lift up their noise.

4 More than the rumblings of great waters,
  Of the glorious, of the breakers of the sea,
  Is Jahve glorious in the height.

5 Thy testimonies are inviolable,
  Holiness becometh Thy house,
  Jahve, unto length of days.

Side by side with those Psalms which behold in anticipation the Messianic future, whether it be prophetically or only
typically, or typically and prophetically at the same time, as
the kingship of Jahve's Anointed which overcomes and blesses
the world, there are others in which the perfected theocracy
as such is beheld beforehand, not, however, as an appearing
(*parusia*) of a human king, but as the appearing of Jahve

Himself, as the kingdom of God manifest in all its glory. These theocratic Psalms form, together with the christocratic, two series of prophecy referring to the last time which run parallel with one another. The one has for its goal the Anointed of Jahve, who rules out of Zion over all peoples; the other, Jahve sitting above the cherubim, to whom the whole world does homage. The two series, it is true, converge in the Old Testament, but do not meet; it is the history that fulfils these types and prophecies which first of all makes clear that which flashes forth in the Old Testament only in certain climaxes of prophecy and of lyric too (*vid.* on xlv. 1), viz. that the parusia of the Anointed One and the parusia of Jahve is one and the same.

Theocracy is an expression coined by Josephus. In contrast with the monarchical, oligarchical, and democratic form of government of other nations, he calls the Mosaic form θεοκρατία, but he does so somewhat timidly, ὡς ἄν τις εἴποι βιασάμενος τὸν λόγον [*c. Apion.* ii. 17]. The coining of the expression is thankworthy; only one has to free one's self from the false conception that the theocracy is a particular constitution. The alternating forms of government were only various modes of its adjustment. The theocracy itself is a reciprocal relationship between God and men, exalted above these intermediary forms, which had its first manifest beginning when Jahve became Israel's King (Deut. xxxiii. 5, cf. Ex. xv. 18), and which will be finally perfected by its breaking through this national self-limitation when the King of Israel becomes King of the whole world, that is overcome both outwardly and spiritually. Hence the theocracy is an object of prediction and of hope. And the word מָלַךְ is used with reference to Jahve not merely of the first beginning of His imperial dominion, and of the manifestation of the same in facts in the most prominent points of the redemptive history, but also of the commencement of the imperial dominion in its perfected glory. We find the word used in this lofty sense, and in relation to the last time, *e.g.* in Isa. xxiv. 23, lii. 7, and most unmistakeably in Apoc. xi. 17, xix. 6. And in this sense יְהוָה מָלַךְ is the watchword of the theocratic Psalms. Thus it is used even in Ps. xlvii. 9; but the first of the Psalms beginning with this watchword is Ps. xciii. They are all post-exilic. The prominent point from which this eschatological perspective opens out is the time of the new-born freedom and of the newly restored state.

Hitzig pertinently says: "This Psalm is already contained *in nuce* in ver. 9 of the preceding Psalm, which surely comes from the same author. This is at once manifest from the jerking start of the discourse in ver. 3 (cf. xcii. 10), which resolves the thought into two members, of which the first subsides into the vocative יהוה." The LXX. (*Codd. Vat.* and *Sin.*) inscribes it: Εἰς τὴν ἡμέρην τοῦ προσαββάτου, ὅτε κατῴκισται ἡ γῆ, αἶνος ᾠδῆς τῷ Δαυίδ. The third part of this inscription is worthless. The first part (for which *Cod. Alex.* erroneously has: τοῦ σαββάτου) is corroborated by the Talmudic tradition. Ps. xciii. was really the Friday Psalm, and that, as is said in *Rosh ha-shana* 31a, על שם שגמר מלאכתו (בששי) ומלך עליהן, because God then (on the sixth day) had completed His creative work and began to reign over them (His creatures); and that ὅτε κατῴκισται (al. κατῴκιστο) is to be explained in accordance therewith: when the earth had been peopled (with creatures, and more especially with men).

Vers. 1, 2. The sense of מָלָךְ (with *ā* beside *Zinnor* or *Sarka* as in xcvii. 1, xcix. 1 beside *Dechî**) is historical, and it stands in the middle between the present ה׳ מֹלֵךְ and the future ה׳ יִמְלֹךְ: Jahve has entered upon the kingship and now reigns. Jahve's rule heretofore, since He has given up the use of His omnipotence, has been self-abasement and self-renunciation: now, however, He shows Himself in all His majesty, which rises aloft above everything; He has put this on like a garment; He is King, and now too shows Himself to the world in the royal robe. The first לָבֵשׁ has *Olewejored;* then the accentuation

---

* It is well known that this pausal form of the 3d *masc. præt.* occurs in connection with *Zakeph;* but it is also found with *Rebia* in cxii. 10 (the reading וּכְעָס), Lev. v. 23 (נָזַל), Josh. x. 13 (עָמָד), Lam. ii. 17 (זָמָם; but not in Deut. xix. 19, Zech. i. 6, which passages Kimchi counts up with them in his grammar *Michlol*); with *Tarcha* in Isa. xiv. 27 (יָעַץ), Hos. vi. 1 (טָרָף), Amos iii. 8 (שָׁאָג); with *Tebîr* in Lev. v. 18 (שָׁגָג); and even with *Munach* in 1 Sam. vii. 17 (שָׁפַט), and according to Abulwalid with *Mercha* in 1 Kings xi. 2 (דָּבַק).

takes 'ה לָבֵשׁ together by means of *Dechî*, and עֹז הִתְאַזָּר together
by means of *Athnach*. עֹז, as in Ps. xxix., points to the enemies;
what is so named is God's invincibly triumphant omnipotence.
This He has put on (Isa. li. 9), with this He has girded Himself—a military word (Isa. viii. 9): Jahve makes war against
everything in antagonism to Himself, and casts it to the ground
with the weapons of His wrathful judgments. We find a
further and fuller description of this עֹז הִתְאַזֵּר in Isa. lix. 17,
lxiii. 1 sq., cf. Dan. vii. 9.* That which cannot fail to take
place in connection with the coming of this accession of Jahve
to the kingdom is introduced with אַף. The world, as being the
place of the kingdom of Jahve, shall stand without tottering in
opposition to all hostile powers (xcvi. 10). Hitherto hostility
towards God and its principal bulwark, the kingdom of the
world, have disturbed the equilibrium and threatened all God-
appointed relationships with dissolution; Jahve's interposition,
however, when He finally brings into effect all the abundant
might of His royal government, will secure immoveableness to
the shaken earth (cf. lxxv. 4). His throne stands, exalted
above all commotion, מֵאָז; it reaches back into the most distant
past. Jahve is מֵעוֹלָם; His being loses itself in the immemorial
and the immeasurable. The throne and nature of Jahve are
not incipient in time, and therefore too are not perishable; but
as without beginning, so also they are endless, infinite in duration.

Vers. 3–5. All the raging of the world, therefore, will not
be able to hinder the progress of the kingdom of God and its
final breaking through to the glory of victory. The sea with its
mighty mass of waters, with the constant unrest of its waves, with
its ceaseless pressing against the solid land and foaming against
the rocks, is an emblem of the Gentile world alienated from
and at enmity with God; and the rivers (floods) are emblems
of worldly kingdoms, as the Nile of the Egyptian (Jer. xlvi.
7 sq.), the Euphrates of the Assyrian (Isa. viii. 7 sq.), or more
exactly, the Tigris, swift as an arrow, of the Assyrian, and the

---

* These passages, together with Ps. xciii. 1, civ. 1, are cited in *Cant.
Rabba* 26*b* (cf. *Debarim Rabba* 291*d*), where it is said that the Holy One
calls Israel כלה (bride) ten times in the Scriptures, and that Israel on the
other hand ten times assigns kingly judicial robes to Him.

tortuous Euphrates of the Babylonian empire (Isa. xxvii. 1).
These rivers, as the poet says whilst he raises a plaintive but
comforted look upwards to Jahve, have lifted up, have lifted
up their murmur, the rivers lift up their roaring. The thought
is unfolded in a so-called "parallelism with reservation." The
perfects affirm what has taken place, the future that which
even now as yet is taking place. The ἅπαξ λεγ. דָּכְיָ signifies
a striking against (*collisio*), and a noise, a din. One now in
ver. 4 looks for the thought that Jahve is exalted above this
roaring of the waves. מִן will therefore be the *min* of comparison, not of the cause: "by reason of the roar of great waters
are the breakers of the sea glorious" (Starck, Geier),—which,
to say nothing more, is a tautological sentence. But if מִן is comparative, then it is impossible to get on with the accentuation
of אדירים, whether it be with *Mercha* (Ben-Asher) or *Dechî*
(Ben-Naphtali). For to render: More than the roar of great
waters are the breakers of the sea glorious (Mendelssohn), is
impracticable, since מים רבים are nothing less than ים (Isa. xvii.
12 sq.), and we are prohibited from taking אדירים משברי־ים as a
parenthesis (Köster) by the fact that it is just this clause that
is exceeded by אדיר במרום ה׳. Consequently אדירים has to be
looked upon as a second attributive to מים brought in afterwards, and מִשְׁבְּרֵי־יָם (the waves of the sea breaking upon the
rocks, or even only breaking upon one another) as a more
minute designation of these great and magnificent waters
(אדירים, according to Ex. xv. 10 *), and it should have been

accented: מִקֹּלוֹת ׀ מַיִם רַבִּים אַדִּירִים מִשְׁבְּרֵי יָם. Jahve's celestial
majesty towers far above all the noisy majesties here below,
whose waves, though lashed never so high, can still never reach
His throne. He is King of His people, Lord of His church,
which preserves His revelation and worships in His temple.
This revelation, by virtue of His unapproachable, all-overpower-
ing kingship, is inviolable; His testimonies, which minister to

---

* A Talmudic enigmatical utterance of R. Azaria runs: יבא אדיר ויפרע
לאדירים מאדירים באדירים, Let the glorious One (Jahve, Ps. xciii. 4, cf.
Isa. x. 34, xxxiii. 21) come and maintain the right of the glorious ones
(Israel, Ps. xvi. 3) against the glorious ones (the Egyptians, Ex. xv. 10
according to the construction of the Talmud) in the glorious ones (the
waves of the sea, Ps. xciii. 4).

the establishment of His kingdom and promise its future manifestation in glory, are λόγοι πιστοὶ καὶ ἀληθινοί, Apoc. xix. 9, xxii. 6. And holiness becometh His temple (נַאֲוָה־קֹּדֶשׁ, 3d *præt. Pilel*, or according to the better attested reading of Heidenheim and Baer, נָאֲוָה;* therefore the feminine of the adjective with a more loosened syllable next to the tone, like יְחַשְּׁב־לִי in xl. 18), that is to say, it is inviolable (sacrosanct), and when it is profaned, shall ever be vindicated again in its holiness. This clause, formulated after the manner of a prayer, is at the same time a petition that Jahve in all time to come would be pleased to thoroughly secure the place where His honour dwells here below against profanation.

PSALM XCIV.

THE CONSOLATION OF PRAYER UNDER THE OPPRESSION OF TYRANTS.

1 O GOD of vengeance, Jahve,
  O God of vengeance, shine forth!
2 Lift up Thyself, Judge of earth,
  Render recompense unto the haughty!
3 How long shall evil-doers, Jahve,
  How long shall evil-doers triumph?

4 They gush over, they speak arrogant things,
  They boast themselves, all the workers of evil.
5 Thy people, Jahve, they break in pieces,
  And they oppress Thine inheritance.
6 The widow and stranger they slay,
  And they murder the fatherless;
7 And say as they do it: "Jāh seeth not,
  And the God of Jacob hath no knowledge."

---

* The Masora on Ps. cxlvii. reckons four נָאֲוָה, one וְנָאֲוָה, and one נָאֲוָה, and therefore our נאוה is one of the י̇̇ז מלין דמפקין אלף וכל חד לית מפיק (cf. Frensdorf's *Ochla we-Ochla*, p. 123), *i.e.* one of the seventeen words whose *Aleph* is audible, whilst it is otherwise always quiescent; *e.g.* בְּמוֹצָאֵת, otherwise מוֹצָאת.

8 Be sensible, ye senseless among the people!
   And ye fools, when will ye become wise?
9 He who hath planted the ear, ought He not to hear?
   Or He who formed the eye, ought He not to see?
10 He who chastiseth the nations, ought He not to reprove,
   He who teacheth men knowledge?
11 Jahve knoweth the thoughts of men
   That they are vanity.

12 Blessed is the man whom Thou chastenest, Jāh,
   And teachest out of Thy Law;
13 To give him rest from the days of adversity,
   Until the pit be digged for the evil-doer.
14 For Jahve doth not thrust away His people,
   And He doth not forsake His inheritance.
15 But right must turn unto righteousness,
   And all the upright in heart shall follow it.

16 Who would rise up for me against the evil-doers?
   Who would stand up for me against the workers of
17 If Jahve had not been my help,   [iniquity?
   My soul would quickly have dwelt in the silence of death.
18 If I say: My foot tottereth,
   Then, Jahve, thy loving-kindness upholdeth me.
19 In the multitude of my cares within me
   Thy comforts delight my soul.

20 Hath the judgment-seat of corruption fellowship with Thee,
   Which frameth trouble by decree?
21 They press in upon the soul of the righteous,
   And condemn innocent blood.
22 But Jahve is a fortress for me,
   And my God is the high rock of my refuge.
23 He turneth back upon them their iniquity,
   And for their wickedness He will destroy them,
   Jahve our God will destroy them.

This Psalm, akin to Ps. xcii. and xciii. by the community of the anadiplosis, bears the inscription Ψαλμὸς ᾠδῆς τῷ Δαυίδ, τετράδι σαββάτου in the LXX. It is also a Talmudic tradi-

tion * that it was the Wednesday song in the Temple liturgy
(τετράδι σαββάτου = ברביעי בשבת). Athanasius explains it
by a reference to the fourth month (Jer. xxxix. 2). The τῷ
Δαυίδ, however, is worthless. It is a post-Davidic Psalm; for,
although it comes out of one mould, we still meet throughout
with reminiscences of older Davidic and Asaphic models. The
enemies against whom it supplicates the appearing of the God
of righteous retribution are, as follows from a comparison of
vers. 5, 8, 10, 12, non-Israelites, who despise the God of Israel
and fear not His vengeance, ver. 7; whose barbarous doings,
however, call forth, even among the oppressed people themselves, foolish doubts concerning Jahve's omniscient beholding
and judicial interposition. Accordingly the Psalm is one of
the latest, but not necessarily a Maccabæan Psalm. The later
Persian age, in which the Book of Ecclesiastes was written,
could also exhibit circumstances and moods such as these.

Vers. 1–3. The first strophe prays that God would at
length put a judicial restraint upon the arrogance of ungodliness. Instead of הוֹפִיעַ (a less frequent form of the imperative
for הוֹפַע, Ges. § 53, rem. 3) it was perhaps originally written
הופיעה (lxxx. 2), the *He* of which has been lost owing to the
He that follows. The plural נְקָמוֹת signifies not merely single
instances of taking vengeance (Ezek. xxv. 17, cf. *supra* xviii.
48), but also intensively complete revenge or recompense
(Judg. xi. 36, 2 Sam. iv. 8). The designation of God is
similar to אֵל גְּמֻלוֹת in Jer. li. 56, and the anadiplosis is like
vers. 3, 23, xciii. 1, 3. הִנָּשֵׂא, lift Thyself up, arise, viz. in
judicial majesty, calls to mind vii. 7. הָשִׁיב גְּמוּל is construed
with עַל (cf. לְ, xxviii. 4, Isa. lix. 18) as in Joel iv. 4. With
גֵּאִים accidentally accord ἀγανός and κύδεϊ γαίων in the epic poets.

---

* According to *B. Erachin* 11*a*, at the time of the Chaldæan destruction of Jerusalem the Levites on their pulpits were singing this 94th Psalm,
and as they came to the words " and He turneth back upon them their
iniquity" (ver. 23), the enemies pressed into the Temple, so that they were
not able to sing the closing words, " Jahve, our God, will destroy them."
To the scruple that Ps. xciv. is a Wednesday, not a Sunday, Psalm (that
fatal day, however, was a Sunday, מוצאי שבת), it is replied, it may have
been a lamentation song that had just been put into their mouths by the
circumstances of that time (אלייא בעלמא דנפל להו בפומייהו).

Vers. 4–7. The second strophe describes those over whom the first prays that the judgment of God may come. הִבִּיעַ (cf. הִטִּיף) is a tropical phrase used of that kind of speech that results from strong inward impulse and flows forth in rich abundance. The poet himself explains how it is here (cf. lix. 8) intended: they speak עָתָק, that which is unrestrained, unbridled, insolent (vid. xxxi. 19). The *Hithpa.* הִתְאַמֵּר Schultens interprets *ut Emiri* (أَمِير, a commander) *se gerunt;* but אָמִיר signifies in Hebrew the top of a tree (vid. on Isa. xvii. 9); and from the primary signification to tower aloft, whence too אָמַר, to speak, prop. *efferre = effari,* הִתְאַמֵּר, like הִתְיַמֵּר in Isa. lxi. 6, directly signifies to exalt one's self, to carry one's self high, to strut. On יְדַכְּאוּ cf. Prov. xxii. 22, Isa. iii. 15; and on their atheistical principle which וַיֹּאמְרוּ places in closest connection with their mode of action, cf. x. 11, lix. 8 *extrem.* The *Dagesh* in יָּהּ, distinct from the *Dag.* in the same word in ver. 12, cxviii. 5, 18, is the *Dag. forte conjunct.* according to the rule of the so-called דחיק (vol. ii. p. 354, note).

Vers. 8–11. The third strophe now turns from those bloodthirsty, blasphemous oppressors of the people of God whose conduct calls forth the vengeance of Jahve, to those among the people themselves, who have been puzzled about the omniscience and indirectly about the righteousness of God by the fact that this vengeance is delayed. They are called בֹּעֲרִים and כְּסִילִים in the sense of lxxiii. 21 sq. Those hitherto described against whom God's vengeance is supplicated are this also; but this appellation would be too one-sided for them, and בָּעָם refers the address expressly to a class of men among the people whom those oppress and slay. It is absurd that God, the planter of the ear (הַנֹּטַע, like שֹׁסַע in Lev. xi. 7, with an accented *ultima,* because the *præt. Kal* does not follow the rule for the drawing back of the accent called נסוג אחור) and the former of the eye (cf. xl. 7, Ex. iv. 11), should not be able to hear and to see; everything that is excellent in the creature, God must indeed possess in original, absolute perfection.* The

---

* The questions are not: ought He to have no ear, etc.; as Jerome pertinently observes in opposition to the anthropomorphites, *membra tulit, efficientias dedit.*

poet then points to the extra-Israelitish world and calls God יִסֵּר גּוֹיִם, which cannot be made to refer to a warning by means of the voice of conscience; יִסֵּר used thus without any closer definition does not signify "warning," but "chastening" (Prov. ix. 7). Taking his stand upon facts like those in Job xii. 23, the poet assumes the punitive judicial rule of God among the heathen to be an undeniable fact, and presents for consideration the question, whether He who chasteneth nations cannot and will not also punish the oppressors of His church (cf. Gen. xviii. 25), He who teacheth men knowledge, *i.e.* He who nevertheless must be the omnipotent One, since all knowledge comes originally from Him? Jahve,—thus does the course of argument close in ver. 11,—sees through (יֹדֵעַ of penetrative perceiving or knowing that goes to the very root of a matter) the thoughts of men that they are vanity. Thus it is to be interpreted, and not: for they (men) are vanity; for this ought to have been כִּי הֶבֶל הֵמָּה, whereas in the dependent clause, when the predicate is not intended to be rendered especially prominent, as in ix. 21, the pronominal subject may precede, Isa. lxi. 9, Jer. xlvi. 5 (Hitzig). The rendering of the LXX. (1 Cor. iii. 20), ὅτι εἰσὶ μάταιοι (Jerome, *quoniam vanœ sunt*), is therefore correct; הֵמָּה, with the customary want of exactness, stands for הֵנָּה. It is true men themselves are הבל; it is not, however, on this account that He who sees through all things sees through their thoughts, but He sees through them in their sinful vanity.

Vers. 12–15. The fourth strophe praises the pious sufferer, whose good cause God will at length aid in obtaining its right. The "blessed" reminds one of xxxiv. 9, xl. 5, and more especially of Job v. 17, cf. Prov. iii. 11 sq. Here what are meant are sufferings like those bewailed in vers. 5 sq., which are however, after all, the well-meant dispensations of God. Concerning the aim and fruit of purifying and testing afflictions God teaches the sufferer out of His Law (cf. *e.g.* Deut. viii. 5 sq.), in order to procure him rest, viz. inward rest (cf. Jer. xlix. 23 with Isa. xxx. 15), *i.e.* not to suffer him to be disheartened and tempted by days of wickedness, *i.e.* wicked, calamitous days (Ew. § 287, *b*), until (and it will inevitably come to pass) the pit is finished being dug into which the ungodly falls headlong (cf. cxii. 7 sq.). יִה has the emphatic *Dagesh*, which properly does not double, and still less unite, but requires an emphatic pronunciation of the letter, which might easily become inaudible. The initial *Jod* of the divine name might easily lose its consonantal value here in connection with the preceding toneless *û*,* and the *Dag.* guards against this: cf. cxviii. 5, 18. The certainty of the issue that is set in prospect by עַד is then confirmed with כִּי. It is impossible that God can desert His church—He cannot do this, because in general right must finally come to His right, or, as it is here expressed, מִשְׁפָּט must turn to צֶדֶק, *i.e.* the right that is now subdued must at length be again strictly maintained and justly administered, and "after it then all who are upright in heart," *i.e.* all such will side with it, joyously greeting that which has been long missed and yearned after. מִשְׁפָּט is fundamental right, which is at all times consistent with itself and raised above the casual circumstances of the time, and צֶדֶק, like אֱמֶת in Isa. xlii. 3, is righteousness (justice), which converts this right into a practical truth and reality.

Vers. 16–19. In the fifth strophe the poet celebrates the praise of the Lord as his sole, but also trusty and most consolatory help. The meaning of the question in ver. 16 is, that there is no man who would rise and succour him in the conflict with the evil-doers; לְ as in Ex. xiv. 25, Judg. vi. 31, and עִם (without נִלְחָם or the like) in the sense of *contra*, as in lv. 19, cf. 2 Chron. xx. 6. God alone is his help. He alone has rescued him from death. הָיָה is to be supplied to לוּלֵי: if He had not been, or: if He were not; and the apodosis is: then very little would have been wanting, then it would soon have come to this, that his soul would have taken up its abode, etc.; cf. on the construction cxix. 92, cxxiv. 1–5, Isa. i. 9, and

---

* If it is correct that, as Aben-Ezra and Parchon testify, the וּ, as being compounded of *o* (*u*) + *i*, was pronounced *ü* [like the *u* in the French word *pur*] by the inhabitants of Palestine, then this *Dagesh*, in accordance with its orthophonic function, is the more intelligible in cases like תִּיסְרֵנוּ יָהּ and קְרָאתִי יָהּ, cf. Pinsker, *Einleitung*, S. 153, and Geiger, *Urschrift*, S. 277. In קוּמוּ צֵאוּ, Gen. xix. 14, Ex. xii. 31, קוּמוּ סְעוּ, Deut. ii. 24, *Tsade* and *Samech* have this *Dagesh* for the same reason as the *Sin* in תִּשְׁבִּיתוּ שְּׂאוֹר, Ex. xii. 15 (*vid.* Heidenheim on that passage), viz. because there is a danger in all these cases of slurring over the sharp sibilant. Even Chajug' (*vid.* Ewald and Dukes' *Beiträge*, iii. 23) confuses this *Dag. orthophonicum* with the *Dag. forte conjunctivum*.

on כְּמְעַט with the *præt.* lxxiii. 2, cxix. 87, Gen. xxvi. 10 (on the other hand with the *fut.* lxxxi. 15). דּוּמָה is, as in cxv. 17, the silence of the grave and of Hades; here it is the object to שָׁכְנָה, as in xxxvii. 3, Prov. viii. 12, and frequently. When he appears to himself already as one that has fallen, God's mercy holds him up. And when thoughts, viz. sad and fearful thoughts, are multiplied within him, God's comforts delight him, viz. the encouragement of His word and the inward utterances of His Spirit. שַׂרְעַפִּים, as in cxxxix. 23, is equivalent to שְׂעִפִּים, from שָׂעַף, סָעַף, شعب, to split, branch off (*Psychology*, S. 181; tr. p. 214). The plural form יְשַׁעֲשְׁעוּ, like the plural of the imperative in Isa. xxix. 9, has two *Pathachs*, the second of which is the "independentification" of the *Chateph* of יְשַׁעֲשַׁע.

Vers. 20—23. In the sixth strophe the poet confidently expects the inevitable divine retribution for which he has earnestly prayed in the introduction. יְחָבְרְךָ is erroneously accounted by many (and by Gesenius too) as *fut. Pual* = יְחֻבָּרְךָ = יְחֻבַּר עִמָּךְ, a vocal contraction together with a giving up of the reduplication in favour of which no example can be advanced. It is *fut. Kal* = יֶחְבָּרְךָ, from יַחְבֹּר = יֶחְבַּר, with the same regression of the modification of the vowel* as in יְחָנְךָ = יְחָנֶּךָ in Gen. xliii. 29, Isa. xxx. 19 (Hupfeld), but as in verbs *primæ gutturalis*, so also in כְּתָבָם, כְּתָבֵם, inflected from כָּתֹב, Ew. § 251, *d.* It might be more readily regarded as *Poel* than as *Pual* (like תֹּאכְלֵהוּ, Job xx. 26), but the *Kal* too already signifies to enter into fellowship (Gen. xiv. 3, Hos. iv. 17), therefore (similarly to יְגָרְךָ, v. 5) it is: *num consociabitur tecum.* כִּסֵּא is here the judgment-seat, just as the Arabic *cursi* directly denotes the tribunal of God (in distinction from العَرْش, the throne of His majesty). With reference to הַוּוֹת *vid.* on v. 10. Assuming that חֹק is a divine statute, we obtain this meaning for עֲלֵי־חֹק: which frameth (*i.e.* plots and executes) trouble, by making

---

* By means of a similar transposition of the vowel as is to be assumed in תֶּאֱהֲבוּ, Prov. i. 22, it also appears that מוּסַבִּין = מְסוּבִּין (lying upon the table, ἀνακείμενοι) of the Pesach-Haggada has to be explained, which Joseph Kimchi finds so inexplicable that he regards it as a clerical error that has become traditional.

the written divine right into a rightful title for unrighteous
conduct, by means of which the innocent are plunged into
misfortune. Hitzig renders: contrary to order, after Prov.
xvii. 26, where, however, עַל־יֹשֶׁר is intended like ἕνεκεν δικαιοσύνης, Matt. v. 10. Olshausen proposes to read יָגוּרוּ (lvi.
7, lix. 4) instead of יָגוֹדוּ, just as conversely Aben-Ezra in lvi.
7 reads יָגוֹדוּ. But גָּדַד, גּוּד, has the secured signification of

scindere, incidere (cf. جَدّ, but also خَدّ, *supra*, i. 399), from
which the signification *invadere* can be easily derived (whence
גְּדוּד, a breaking in, invasion, an invading host). With reference to דָּם נָקִי *vid. Psychology*, S. 243 (tr. p. 286): because
the blood is the soul, that is said of the blood which applies
properly to the person. The subject to יגודו are the seat of corruption (by which a high council consisting of many may be
meant, just as much as a princely throne) and its accomplices.
Prophetic certainty is expressed in וַיְהִי and וַיָּשָׁב. The figure
of God as מִשְׂגָּב is Davidic and Korahitic. צוּר מַחְסִי is explained from xviii. 2. Since הֵשִׁיב designates the retribution as
a return of guilt incurred in the form of actual punishment,
it might be rendered " requite " just as well as " cause to
return ;" עֲלֵיהֶם, however, instead of לָהֶם (liv. 7) makes the
idea expressed in vii. 17 more natural. On בְּרָעָתָם Hitzig correctly compares 2 Sam. xiv. 7, iii. 27. The Psalm closes with
an anadiplosis, just as it began with one ; and אֱלֹהֵינוּ affirms
that the destruction of the persecutor will follow as surely as
the church is able to call Jahve its God.

PSALM XCV.

CALL TO THE WORSHIP OF GOD AND TO OBEDIENCE TO HIS WORD.

1 COME, let us exult unto Jahve,
  Let us make a joyful noise to the Rock of our salvation !
2 Let us come before His face with thanksgiving,
  Let us make a joyful noise unto Him in songs !

3 For a great God is Jahve,
  And a great King above all gods ;

4 He, in whose hand are the deep places of the earth,
   And to whom belong the tops of the mountains;
5 To whom belongeth the sea, and HE hath made it,
   And His hands have formed the dry land.
6 Come, let us worship and bow down,
   Let us kneel before Jahve our Maker!
7 For He is our God,
   And we are the people of His pasture and the flock of His
      hand.

   To-day if ye will but hearken to His voice!
8 Harden not your hearts as at Meríbah,
   As on the day of Massah in the wilderness,
9 When your fathers tempted Me,
   Proved me, although they saw My work.
10 Forty years was I vexed with a generation,
   And said: " They are a people that do err in their heart."
   But they knew not My ways,
11 So that I sware in My wrath:
   " Verily they shall not enter into My rest!"

This Psalm is related to the preceding by the celebration
of Jahve as a " Rock." If it has any definite occasion, it is
at any rate not manifest what that occasion is. It consists of
a four-line introduction and two groups of ten lines.

Vers. 1, 2. Jahve is called the Rock of our salvation (as
in lxxxix. 27, cf. xciv. 22) as being its firm and sure ground.
Visiting the house of God, one comes before God's face; קַדֵּם
פָּנָי, *præoccupare faciem*, is equivalent to *visere* (*visitare*). תּוֹדָה
is not *confessio peccati*, but *laudis*. The *Beth* before תודה is
the *Beth* of accompaniment, as in Mic. vi. 6; that before זְמִרוֹת
(according to 2 Sam. xxiii. 1 a name for psalms, whilst מִזְמוֹר
can only be used as a technical expression) is the *Beth* of the
medium.

Vers. 3–7b. The adorableness of God receives a threefold
confirmation: He is exalted above all gods as King, above all
things as Creator, and above His people as Shepherd and
Leader. אֱלֹהִים (gods) here, as in xcvi. 4 sq., xcvii. 7, 9, and
frequently, are the powers of the natural world and of the

world of men, which the Gentiles deify and call kings (as
Moloch (Molech), the deified fire), which, however, all stand
under the lordship of Jahve, who is infinitely exalted above
everything that is otherwise called god (xcvi. 4, xcvii. 9).   The
supposition that תּוֹעֲפוֹת הָרִים denotes the pit-works (μέταλλα) of
the mountains (Böttcher), is at once improbable, because to all
appearance it is intended to be the antithesis to מֶחְקְרֵי־אָרֶץ, the
shafts of the earth.   The derivation from וָעַף (יָעַף), κάμνειν,
κοπιᾶν, also does not suit תועפות in Num. xxiii. 22, xxiv. 8, for
"fatigues" and "indefatigableness" are notions that lie very
wide apart.   The כֶּסֶף תּוֹעָפוֹת of Job xxii. 25 might more readily
be explained according to this "silver of fatigues," *i.e.* silver
that the fatiguing labour of mining brings to light, and תועפות
הרים in the passage before us, with Gussetius, Geier, and
Hengstenberg : *cacumina montium quia defatigantur qui eo
ascendunt*, prop. ascendings = summits of the mountains, after
which כסף תועפות, Job xxii. 25, might also signify "silver of
the mountain-heights."   But the LXX., which renders δόξα
in the passages in Numbers and τὰ ὕψη τῶν ὀρέων in the passage before us, leads one to a more correct track.   The verb
יָעַף (וָעַף), transposed from יפע (ופע), goes back to the root וף, יף,
to stand forth, tower above, to be high, according to which
תועפות = תופעות signifies *eminentiæ*, *i.e.* towerings = summits, or
prominences = high (the highest) perfection (*vid.* on Job xxii.
25).   In the passage before us it is a synonym of the Arabic
ميفاة، مِيفًى, *pars terræ eminens* (from وفى = יפע, prop. instrumentally : a means of rising above, viz. by climbing), and of
the names of eminences derived from يفع (after which Hitzig
renders : the teeth of the mountains).   By reason of the fact
that Jahve is the Owner (cf. 1 Sam. ii. 8), because the Creator
of all things, the call to worship, which concerns no one so
nearly as it does Israel, the people, which before other peoples
is Jahve's creation, viz. the creation of His miraculously
mighty grace, is repeated.   In the call or invitation, הִשְׁתַּחֲוָה
signifies to stretch one's self out full length upon the ground,
the proper attitude of adoration ; כָּרַע, to curtsey, to totter ;
and בָּרַך, Arabic *baraka*, starting from the radical signification
flectere, to kneel down, *in genua* (πρόχνυ, *pronum* = *procnum*)
procumbere, 2 Chron. vi. 13 (cf. Hölemann, *Bibelstudien*, i.

135 f.). Beside עַם מַרְעִיתוֹ, people of His pasture, צֹאן יָדוֹ is not the flock formed by His creating hand (Augustine: *ipse gratiâ suâ nos oves fecit*), but, after Gen. xxx. 35, the flock under His protection, the flock led and defended by His skilful, powerful hand. Böttcher renders: flock of His charge; but יָד in this sense (Jer. vi. 3) signifies only a place, and "flock of His place" would be poetry and prose in one figure.

Vers. 7c–11. The second decastich begins in the midst of the Masoretic ver. 7. Up to this point the church stirs itself up to a worshipping appearing before its God; now the voice of God (Heb. iv. 7), earnestly admonishing, meets it, resounding from out of the sanctuary. Since שָׁמַע בְּ signifies not merely to hear, but to hear obediently, ver. 7c cannot be a conditioning protasis to what follows. Hengstenberg wishes to supply the apodosis: "then will He bless you, His people;" but אִם in other instances too (lxxxi. 9, cxxxix. 19, Prov. xxiv. 11), like לֹא, has an optative signification, which it certainly has gained by a suppression of a promissory apodosis, but yet without the genius of the language having any such in mind in every instance. The word הַיּוֹם placed first gives prominence to the present, in which this call to obedience goes forth, as a decisive turning-point. The divine voice warningly calls to mind the self-hardening of Israel, which came to light at Merîbah, on the day of Massah. What is referred to, as also in lxxxi. 8, is the tempting of God in the second year of the Exodus on account of the failing of water in the neighbourhood of Horeb, at the place which is for this reason called *Massah u-Merîbah* (Ex. xvii. 1–7); from which is to be distinguished the tempting of God in the fortieth year of the Exodus at *Merîbah*, viz. at the waters of contention near Kadesh (written fully *Mê-Merîbath Kadesh*, or more briefly *Mê-Merîbah*), Num. xx. 2–13 (cf. on lxxviii. 20). Strictly כמריבה signifies nothing but *instar Meribæ*, as in lxxxiii. 10 *instar Midianitarum*; but according to the sense, בְּ is equivalent to כְּעַל, cvi. 32, just as כְּיוֹם is equivalent to כְּבַיּוֹם. On אֲשֶׁר, *quum*, cf. Deut. xi. 6. The meaning of גַּם־רָאוּ פָעֳלִי is not they also (גם as in lii. 7) saw His work; for the reference to the giving of water out of the rock would give a thought that is devoid of purpose here, and the assertion is too indefinite for **it to** be understood of the judgment upon those who tempted

God (Hupfeld and Hitzig). It is therefore rather to be rendered: notwithstanding ($\ddot{o}\mu\omega\varsigma$, Ew. § 354, a) they had (= although they had, cf. גם in Isa. xlix. 15) seen His work (His wondrous guiding and governing), and might therefore be sure that He would not suffer them to be destroyed. The verb קוט coincides with $\kappa o\tau\acute{\epsilon}\omega$, $\kappa\acute{o}\tau o\varsigma$. בְּדוֹר, for which the LXX. has $\tau\hat{\eta}\ \gamma\epsilon\nu\epsilon\hat{q}\ \acute{\epsilon}\kappa\epsilon\acute{\iota}\nu\eta$, is anarthrous in order that the notion may be conceived of more qualitatively than relatively: with a (whole) generation. With וָאֹמַר Jahve calls to mind the repeated declarations of His vexation concerning their heart, which was always inclined towards error which leads to destruction—declarations, however, which bore no fruit. Just this ineffectiveness of His indignation had as its result that (אֲשֶׁר, not $\ddot{o}\tau\iota$ but $\ddot{\omega}\sigma\tau\epsilon$, as in Gen. xiii. 16, Deut. xxviii. 27, 51, 2 Kings ix. 37, and frequently) He sware, etc. (אִם = verily not, Ges. § 155, 2, f, with the emphatic future form in $\hat{u}n$ which follows). It is the oath in Num. xiv. 27 sqq. that is meant. The older generation died in the desert, and therefore lost the entering into the rest of God, by reason of their disobedience. If now, many centuries after Moses, they are invited in the Davidic Psalter to submissive adoration of Jahve, with the significant call: "To-day if ye will hearken to His voice!" and with a reference to the warning example of the fathers, the obedience of faith, now as formerly, has therefore to look forward to the gracious reward of entering into God's rest, which the disobedient at that time lost; and the taking possession of Canaan was, therefore, not as yet the final מְנוּחָה (Deut. xii. 9). This is the connection of the wider train of thought which to the writer of the Epistle to the Hebrews, ch. iii., iv., follows from this text of the Psalm.

PSALM XCVI.

A GREETING OF THE COMING KINGDOM OF GOD.

1 SING unto Jahve a new song,
  Sing unto Jahve, all lands.
2 Sing unto Jahve, bless His Name,
  Cheerfully proclaim His salvation from day to day.

3 Declare His glory among the heathen,
  His wonders among all peoples.

4 For great is Jahve and worthy to be praised exceedingly,
  Terrible is He above all gods.
5 For all the gods of the peoples are idols,
  But Jahve hath made the heavens.
6 Brightness and splendour are before Him,
  Might and beauty are in His sanctuary.

7 Give unto Jahve, O ye races of the peoples,
  Give unto Jahve glory and might.
8 Give unto Jahve the honour of His Name,
  Take offerings and come into His courts.
9 Worship Jahve in holy attire,
  Tremble before Him, all lands.

10 Say among the heathen: "Jahve is now King,
  Therefore the world will stand without tottering,
  He will govern the peoples in uprightness."
11 The heavens shall rejoice
  And the earth be glad,
  The sea shall roar and its fulness.

12 The field shall exult and all that is therein,
  Then shall all the trees of the wood shout for joy—
13 Before Jahve, for He cometh,
  For He cometh to judge the earth—
  He shall judge the world in righteousness
  And the peoples in His faithfulness.

What Ps. xcv. 3 says: "*A great God is Jahve, and a great King above all gods*," is repeated in Ps. xcvi. The LXX. inscribes it (1) ᾠδὴ τῷ Δαυίδ, and the chronicler has really taken it up almost entire in the song which was sung on the day when the Ark was brought in (1 Chron. xvi. 23–33); but, as the coarse seams between vers. 22 and 23, 33 and 34 show, he there strings together familiar reminiscences of the Psalms (*vid.* on Ps. cv.) as a sort of mosaic, in order approximately to express the festive mood and festive strains of that day. And

(2) ὅτε ὁ οἶκος ᾠκοδομεῖτο (*Cod. Vat.* ᾠκοδόμηται) μετὰ τὴν αἰχμαλωσίαν. By this the LXX. correctly interprets the Psalm as a post-exilic song: and the Psalm corresponds throughout to the advance which the mind of Israel has experienced in the Exile concerning its mission in the world. The fact that the religion of Jahve is destined for mankind at large, here receives the most triumphantly joyous, lyrical expression. And so far as this is concerned, the key-note of the Psalm is even deutero-Isaianic. For it is one chief aim of Isa. ch. xl.–lxvi. to declare the pinnacle of glory of the Messianic apostolic mission on to which Israel is being raised through the depth of affliction of the Exile. All these post-exilic songs come much nearer to the spirit of the New Testament than the pre-exilic; for the New Testament, which is the intrinsic character of the Old Testament freed from its barriers and limitations, is in process of coming into being (*im Werden begriffen*) throughout the Old Testament, and the Exile was one of the most important crises in this progressive process.

Ps. xcvi.–xcviii. are more Messianic than many in the strict sense of the word Messianic; for the central (gravitating) point of the Old Testament gospel (*Heilsverkündigung*) lies not in the Messiah, but in the appearing (parusia) of Jahve—a fact which is explained by the circumstance that the mystery of the incarnation still lies beyond the Old Testament knowledge or perception of salvation. All human intervention in the matter of salvation accordingly appears as purely human, and still more, it preserves a national and therefore outward and natural impress by virtue of the national limit within which the revelation of salvation has entered. If the ideal Davidic king who is expected even does anything superhuman, he is nevertheless only a man—a man of God, it is true, without his equal, but not the God-man. The mystery of the incarnation does, it is true, the nearer it comes to actual revelation, cast rays of its dawning upon prophecy, but the sun itself remains below the horizon: redemption is looked for as Jahve's own act, and "Jahve cometh" is also still the watchword of the last prophet (Mal. iii. 1).

The five six-line strophes of the Psalm before us are not to be mistaken. The chronicler has done away with five lines, and thereby disorganized the strophic structure; and one line (ver. 10*a*) he has removed from its position. The originality of the Psalm in the Psalter, too, is revealed thereby, and the non-independence of the chronicler, who treats the Psalm as an historian.

Vers. 1–3. Call to the nation of Jahve to sing praise to its God and to evangelize the heathen. שִׁירוּ is repeated three times. The new song assumes a new form of things, and the call thereto, a present which appeared to be a beginning that furnished a guarantee of this new state of things, a beginning viz. of the recognition of Jahve throughout the whole world of nations, and of His accession to the lordship over the whole earth. The new song is an echo of the approaching revelation of salvation and of glory, and this is also the inexhaustible material of the joyful tidings that go forth from day to day (מִיּוֹם לְיוֹם as in Esth. iii. 7, whereas in the Chronicles it is מִיּוֹם אֶל־יוֹם as in Num. xxx. 15). We read ver. 1*a* verbally the same in Isa. xlii. 10; ver. 2 calls to mind Isa. lii. 7, lx. 6; and ver. 3*a*, Isa. lxvi. 19.

Vers. 4–6. Confirmation of the call from the glory of Jahve that is now become manifest. The clause ver. 4*a*, as also cxlv. 3, is taken out of xlviii. 2. כָּל־אֱלֹהִים is the plural of כָּל־אֱלוֹהַּ, every god, 2 Chron. xxxii. 15; the article may stand here or be omitted (xcv. 3, cf. cxiii. 4). All the elohim, *i.e.* gods, of the peoples are אֱלִילִים (from the negative אַל), nothings and good-for-nothings, unreal and useless. The LXX. renders δαιμόνια, as though the expression were שֵׁדִים (cf. 1 Cor. x. 20), more correctly εἴδωλα in Apoc. ix. 20. What ver. 5 says is wrought out in Isa. ch. xl., xliv., and elsewhere; אֱלִילִים is a name of idols that occurs nowhere more frequently than in Isaiah. The sanctuary (ver. 6) is here the earthly sanctuary. From Jerusalem, over which the light arises first of all (Isa. ch. lx.), Jahve's superterrestrial doxa now reveals itself in the world. הוֹד־וְהָדָר is the usual pair of words for royal glory. The chronicler reads ver. 6*b* עֹז וְחֶדְוָה בִּמְקֹמוֹ, might and joy are in His place (חֶדְוָה a late word, like אַחֲוָה, brotherhood, brotherly affection, from an old root, Ex. xviii. 9). With the place of God one might associate the thought of the celestial place of God transcending space; the chronicler may, however, have altered בְּמִקְדָּשׁוֹ into בִּמְקוֹמוֹ because when the Ark was brought in, the Temple (בֵּית הַמִּקְדָּשׁ) was not yet built.

Vers. 7–9. Call to the families of the peoples to worship God, the One, living, and glorious God. הָבוּ is repeated three times here as Ps. xxix., of which the whole strophe is an echo. Isaiah (ch. lx.) sees them coming in with the gifts which they are admonished to bring with them into the courts of Jahve (in Chron. only: לְפָנָיו). Instead of בְּהַדְרַת קֹדֶשׁ here and in the chronicler, the LXX. brings the courts (חצרת) in once more; but the dependence of the strophe upon Ps. xxix. furnishes a guarantee for the "holy attire," similar to the wedding garment in the New Testament parable. Instead of מִפָּנָיו, ver. 9b, the chronicler has מִלְּפָנָיו, just as he also alternates with both forms, 2 Chron. xxxii. 7, cf. 1 Chron. xix. 18.

Vers. 10, 11. That which is to be said among the peoples is the joyous evangel of the kingdom of heaven which is now come and realized. The watchword is "Jahve is King," as in Isa. lii. 7. The LXX. correctly renders: ὁ κύριος ἐβασίλευσε,* for מָלַךְ is intended historically (Apoc. xi. 17). אַף, as in xciii. 1, introduces that which results from this fact, and therefore to a certain extent goes beyond it. The world below, hitherto shaken by war and anarchy, now stands upon foundations that cannot be shaken in time to come, under Jahve's righteous and gentle sway. This is the joyful tidings of the new era which the poet predicts from out of his own times, when he depicts the joy that will then pervade the whole creation; in connection with which it is hardly intentional that ver. 11a and 11b acrostically contain the divine names יהוה and יהו. This joining of all creatures in the joy at Jahve's appearing is a characteristic feature of Isa. ch. xl.–lxii. These cords are already struck in Isa. xxxv. 1 sq. "The sea and its fulness" as in Isa. xlii. 10. In the chronicler ver. 10a (ויאמרו instead of אמרו) stands between ver. 11b and 11c,—according to Hitzig, who uses all his ingenuity here in favour of that other recension of the text, by an oversight of the copyist.

---

* In the *Psalterium Veronense* with the addition *apo xylu*, Cod. 156, Latinizing ἀπὸ τῷ ξύλῳ; in the Latin Psalters (the Vulgate excepted) *a ligno*, undoubtedly an addition by an early Christian hand, upon which, however, great value is set by Justin and all the early Latin Fathers.

Vers. 12, 13. The chronicler changes שָׂדַי into the prosaic הַשָּׂדֶה, and כָּל־עֲצֵי־יַעַר with the omission of the כל into עֲצֵי הַיַּעַר. The psalmist on his part follows the model of Isaiah, who makes the trees of the wood exult and clap their hands, ch. lv. 12, xliv. 23. The אָז, which points into this festive time of all creatures which begins with Jahve's coming, is as in Isa. xxxv. 5 sq. Instead of לִפְנֵי, "before," the chronicler has the מִלִּפְנֵי so familiar to him, by which the joy is denoted as being occasioned by Jahve's appearing. The lines ver. 13*bc* sound very much like ix. 9. The chronicler has abridged ver. 13, by hurrying on to the mosaic-work portion taken from Ps. cv. The poet at the close glances from the ideal past into the future. The two-fold בָא is a participle, Ew. § 200. Being come to judgment, after He has judged and sifted, executing punishment, Jahve will govern in the righteousness of mercy and in faithfulness to the promises.

PSALM XCVII.

THE BREAKING THROUGH OF THE KINGDOM OF GOD, THE JUDGE AND SAVIOUR.

1 JAHVE is now King, the earth shouteth for joy,
  Many islands rejoice.
2 Clouds and darkness are round about Him,
  Righteousness and judgment are the pillars of His throne.
3 Fire goeth before Him
  And burneth up His enemies round about.

4 His lightnings lighten the world;
  The earth seeth it, and trembleth because of it.
5 Mountains melt like wax before Jahve,
  Before the Lord of the whole earth.
6 The heavens declare His righteousness,
  And all the peoples see His glory.

7 Confounded are all those who serve graven images,
  Who boast themselves of idols;
  All the gods cast themselves down to Him.
8 Zion heareth it and rejoiceth thereat,

And the daughters of Judah shout for joy—
Because of Thy judgments, Jahve!

9 For Thou, Jahve, art the Most High over all the earth,
Thou art highly exalted above all gods.

10 Ye who love Jahve, hate evil :
He who guardeth the souls of His saints,
Out of the hand of the evil-doer will He rescue them.
11 Light is sown for the righteous,
And for the upright-minded joy.
12 Rejoice, ye righteous, in Jahve,
And sing praise unto His holy Name.

This Psalm, too, has the coming of Jahve, who enters upon His kingdom through judgment, as its theme, and the watchword " Jahve is King" as its key-note. The LXX. inscribes it : τῷ Δαυίδ, ὅτε ἡ γῆ αὐτοῦ καθίσταται (καθίστατο) ; Jerome : *quando terra ejus restituta est.* The τῷ Δαυίδ is worthless ; the time of restoration, from which it takes its rise, is the post-exilic, for it is composed, as mosaic-work, out of the earlier original passages of Davidic and Asaphic Psalms and of the prophets, more especially of Isaiah, and is entirely an expression of the religious consciousness which resulted from the Exile.

Vers. 1-3. We have here nothing but echoes of the older literature : ver. 1, cf. Isa. xlii. 10-12, li. 5 ; ver. 2*a*, cf. xviii. 10, 12 ; ver. 2*b* = lxxxix. 15 ; ver. 3*a*, cf. l. 3, xviii. 9 ; ver. 3*b*, cf. Isa. xlii. 25. Beginning with the visible coming of the kingdom of God in the present, with ה׳ מָלָךְ the poet takes his stand upon the standpoint of the kingdom which is come. With it also comes rich material for universal joy. תָּגֵל is indicative, as in xcvi. 11 and frequently. רַבִּים are all, for all of them are in fact many (cf. Isa. lii. 15). The description of the theophany, for which the way is preparing in ver. 2, also reminds one of Hab. ch. iii. God's enshrouding Himself in darkness bears witness to His judicial earnestness. Because He comes as Judge, the basis of His royal throne and of His judgment-seat is also called to mind. His harbinger is

fire, which consumes His adversaries on every side, as that
which broke forth out of the pillar of cloud once consumed
the Egyptians.

Vers. 4–6. Again we have nothing but echoes of the older
literature: ver. 4*a* = lxxvii. 19; ver. 4*b*, cf. lxxvii. 17; ver. 5*a*,
cf. Mic. i. 4; ver. 5*b*, cf. Mic. iv. 13; ver. 6*a* = l. 6; ver. 6*b*,
cf. Isa. xxxv. 2, xl. 5, lii. 10, lxvi. 18. The poet goes on to
describe that which is future with historical certainty. That
which lxxvii. 19 says of the manifestation of God in the earlier
times he transfers to the revelation of God in the last time.
The earth sees it, and begins to tremble in consequence of it.
The reading וַתָּחֶל, according to Hitzig (cf. Ew. § 232, *b*) traditional, is, however, only an error of pointing that has been
propagated; the correct reading is the reading of Heidenheim
and Baer, restored according to MSS., וַתָּחֶל (cf. 1 Sam. xxxi. 3),
like וַתָּבֶן, וַתָּקָם, וַתָּרֶם, and וַתָּשֶׂם. The figure of the wax is found
even in lxviii. 3; and Jahve is also called "Lord of the whole
earth" in Zech. iv. 14, vi. 5. The proclamation of the heavens
is an expression of joy, xcvi. 11. They proclaim the judicial
strictness with which Jahve, in accordance with His promises,
carries out His plan of salvation, the realization of which has
reached its goal in the fact that all men see the glory of God.

Vers. 7, 8. When the glory of Jahve becomes manifest,
everything that is opposed to it will be punished and consumed by
its light. Those who serve idols will become conscious of their
delusion with shame and terror, Isa. xlii. 17, Jer. x. 14. The
superhuman powers (LXX. ἄγγελοι), deified by the heathen,
then bow down to Him who alone is *Elohim* in absolute personality. הִשְׁתַּחֲווּ is not imperative (LXX., Syriac), for as a
command this clause would be abrupt and inconsequential, but
the perfect of that which actually takes place. The quotation
in Heb. i. 6 is taken from Deut. xxxii. 43, LXX. In ver. 8
(after xlviii. 12) the survey of the poet again comes back to his
own nation. When Zion hears that Jahve has appeared, and all
the world and all the powers bow down to Him, she rejoices;
for it is in fact her God whose kingship has come to be acknowledged. And all the daughter-churches of the Jewish
land exult together with the mother-church over the salvation
which dawns through judgments.

Ver. 9. This distichic epiphonema (ver. 9*a* = lxxxiii. 19;

ver. 9*b*, cf. xlvii. 3, 10) might close the Psalm; there follows
still, however, a hortatory strophe (which was perhaps not
added till later on).

Vers. 10–12. It is true ver. 12*a* is = xxxii. 11, ver. 12*b*
= xxx. 5, and the promise in ver. 10 is the same as in xxxvii.
28, xxxiv. 21; but as to the rest, particularly ver. 11, this
strophe is original. It is an encouraging admonition to fidelity
in an age in which an effeminate spirit of looking longingly
towards [**lit.** ogling] heathenism was rife, and stedfast adherence to Jahve was threatened with loss of life. Those who
are faithful in their confession, as in the Maccabæan age (᾽Ασι-
δαῖοι), are called חֲסִידָיו. The beautiful figure in ver. 11 is misapprehended by the ancient versions, inasmuch as they read
זרח (cxii. 4) instead of זרע. זָרֻעַ does not here signify sown
= strewn into the earth, but strewn along his life's way, so
that he, the righteous one, advances step by step in the light.
Hitzig rightly compares κίδναται, σκίδναται, used of the dawn
and of the sun. Of the former Virgil also says, *Et jam prima
novo spargebat lumine terras.*

PSALM XCVIII.

GREETING TO HIM WHO IS BECOME KNOWN IN RIGHTEOUS-NESS AND SALVATION.

1 SING unto Jahve a new song,
  For He hath done marvellous things,
  His right hand and His holy arm helped Him.
2 Jahve hath made known His salvation,
  He hath revealed His righteousness before the eyes of the
      nations.
3 He remembered His loving-kindness and His faithfulness to
      the house of Israel,
  All the ends of the earth saw the salvation of our God.

4 Make a joyful noise unto Jahve, all ye lands,
  Break forth into rejoicing and play—
5 Play unto Jahve with the cithern,
  With the cithern and the voice of song.

6 With trumpets and the sound of the horn,
  Make a joyful noise before the King Jahve!

7 Let the sea roar, and that which filleth it,
  The world, and those who dwell therein.
8 Let the rivers clap their hands,
  Together let the mountains rejoice
9 Before Jahve, for He cometh to judge the earth—
  He shall judge the world with righteousness,
  And the peoples with uprightness.

This is the only Psalm which is inscribed מִזְמוֹר without further addition, whence it is called in *B. Aboda Zara*, 24*b*, מזמורא יתומא (the orphan Psalm). The Peshîto Syriac inscribes it *De redemtione populi ex Ægypto;* the " new song," however, is not the song of Moses, but the counterpart of this, cf. Apoc. xv. 3. There " the Lord reigneth " resounded for the first time, at the sea; here the completion of the beginning there commenced is sung, viz. the final glory of the divine kingdom, which through judgment breaks through to its full reality. The beginning and end are taken from Ps. xcvi. Almost all that lies between is taken from the second part of Isaiah. This book of consolation for the exiles is become as it were a Castalian spring for the religious lyric.

Vers. 1–3. Ver. 1*ab* we have already read in xcvi. 1. What follows in ver. 1*c*–3 is taken from Isa. lii. 10, lxiii. 5, cf. 7, lix. 16, cf. xl. 10. The primary passage, Isa. lii. 10, shows that the *Athnach* of ver. 2 is correctly placed. לְעֵינֵי is the opposite of hearsay (cf. للعيـن, from one's own observation, *opp.* للخـبـر, from the narrative of another person). The dative לְבֵית יִשְׂרָאֵל depends upon וַיִּזְכֹּר, according to cvi. 45, cf. Luke i. 54 sq.

Vers. 4–6. The call in ver. 4 demands some joyful manifestation of the mouth, which can be done in many ways; in ver. 5 the union of song and the music of stringed instruments, as of the Levites; and in ver. 6 the sound of wind instruments, as of the priests. On ver. 4 cf. Isa. xliv. 23, xlix.

13, lii. 9, together with xiv. 7 (inasmuch as פִּצְחוּ וְרַנְּנוּ is equivalent to פִּצְחוּ רִנָּה). קוֹל זִמְרָה is found also in Isa. li. 3.

Vers. 7–9. Here, too, it is all an echo of the earlier language of Psalms and prophets: ver. 7*a* = xcvi. 11; ver. 7*b*
like xxiv. 1; ver. 8 after Isa. lv. 12 (where we find מָחָא כַּף
instead of the otherwise customary תָּקַע כַּף, xlvii. 2; or הִכָּה כַּף,
2 Kings xi. 12, is said of the trees of the field); ver. 9 = xcvi.
13, cf. 10. In the bringing in of nature to participate in the
joy of mankind, the clapping rivers (נְהָרוֹת) are original to this
Psalm: the rivers cast up high waves, which flow into one
another like clapping hands;* cf. Hab. iii. 10, where the abyss
of the sea lifts up its hands on high, *i.e.* causes its waves to
run mountain-high.

PSALM XCIX.

SONG OF PRAISE IN HONOUR OF THE THRICE HOLY ONE.

1 JAHVE reigneth, the peoples tremble;
　　He sitteth upon the cherubim, the earth tottereth.
2 Jahve in Zion is great,
　　And HE is exalted above all the peoples.
3 They shall praise Thy great and fearful name—
　　Holy is HE.

4 And the might of a king who loveth the right
　　Hast THOU established in righteousness;
　　Right and righteousness hast THOU executed in Jacob.
5 Exalt ye Jahve our God,
　　And prostrate yourselves at His footstool—
　　Holy is HE.

6 Moses and Aaron among His priests,
　　And Samuel among those who call upon His name—
　　They called unto Jahve and HE answered them;

---

* Luther renders: "the water-floods exult" (*frohlocken*); and Eychman's
Vocabularius predicantium explains *plaudere* by " to exult (*frohlocken*)
for joy, to smite the hands together *præ gaudio*;" cf. Luther's version of
Ezek. xxi. 17.

7 In a pillar of cloud He spoke to them;
  They kept His testimonies,
  And the law which He gave them.
8 Jahve our God, Thou hast answered them;
  A forgiving God wast Thou unto them,
  And one taking vengeance of their deeds.
9 Exalt ye Jahve our God,
  And prostrate yourselves at His holy mountain,
  For holy is Jahve our God.

This is the third of the Psalms (xciii., xcvii., xcix.) which begin with the watchword ה' מָלָךְ. It falls into three parts, of which the first (vers. 1–3) closes with קָדוֹשׁ הוּא, the second (vers. 4, 5) with קָדוֹשׁ הוּא, and the third, more full-toned, with קָדוֹשׁ ה' אֱלֹהֵינוּ—an earthly echo of the trisagion of the seraphim. The first two Sanctuses are two hexastichs; and two hexastichs form the third, according to the very same law by which the third and the sixth days of creation each consists of two creative works. This artistic form bears witness against Olshausen in favour of the integrity of the text; but the clare-obscure of the language and expression makes no small demands upon the reader.

Bengel has seen deepest into the internal character of this Psalm. He says, " The 99th Psalm has three parts, in which the Lord is celebrated as He who is to come, as He who is, and as He who was, and each part is closed with the ascription of praise: He is holy." The Psalm is laid out accordingly by Oettinger, Burk, and C. H. Rieger.

Vers. 1–3. The three futures express facts of the time to come, which are the inevitable result of Jahve's kingly dominion bearing sway from heaven, and here below from Zion, over the world; they therefore declare what must and will happen. The participle *insidens cherubis* (lxxx. 2, cf. xviii. 11) is a definition of the manner (Olshausen): He reigns, sitting enthroned above the cherubim. נוּט, like نون, is a further formation of the root נא, *vv*, to bend, nod. What is meant is not a trembling that is the absolute opposite of joy, but a trembling that leads on to salvation. The *Breviarium in Psal-*

terium, which bears the name of Jerome, observes : *Terra quamdiu immota fuerit, sanari non potest ; quando vero mota fuerit et intremuerit, tunc recipiet sanitatem.* In ver. 3a declaration passes over into invocation. One can feel how the hope that the " great and fearful Name" (Deut. x. 17) will be universally acknowledged, and therefore that the religion of Israel will become the religion of the world, moves and elates the poet. The fact that the expression notwithstanding is not קָדוֹשׁ אַתָּה, but קָדוֹשׁ הוּא, is explained from the close connection with the seraphic trisagion in Isa. vi. 3. הוּא refers to Jahve ; He and His Name are notions that easily glide over into one another.

Vers. 4, 5. The second *Sanctus* celebrates Jahve with respect to His continuous righteous rule in Israel. The majority of expositors construe it : " And (they shall praise) the might of the king, who loves right ;" but this joining of the clause on to יוֹדוּ over the refrain that stands in the way is hazardous. Neither can וְעֹז מֶלֶךְ מִשְׁפָּט אָהֵב, however, be an independent clause, since אָהֵב cannot be said of עֹז, but only of its possessor. And the dividing of the verse at אהב, adopted by the LXX., will therefore not hold good. משׁפט אהב is an attributive clause to מלך in the same position as in xi. 7 ; and עֹז, with what appertains to it, is the object to כּוֹנַנְתָּ placed first, which has the king's throne as its object elsewhere (ix. 8, 2 Sam. vii. 13, 1 Chron. xvii. 12), just as it here has the might of the king, which, however, here at the same time in מֵישָׁרִים takes another and permutative object (cf. the permutative subject in lxxii. 17), as Hitzig observes ; or rather, since מישרים is most generally used as an adverbial notion, this מישרים (lviii. 2, lxxv. 3, ix. 9, and frequently), usually as a definition of the mode of the judging and reigning, is subordinated : and the might of a king who loves the right, *i.e.* of one who governs not according to dynastic caprice but moral precepts, hast Thou established in spirit and aim (directed to righteousness and equity). What is meant is the theocratic kingship, and ver. 4c says what Jahve has constantly accomplished by means of this kingship : He has thus maintained right and righteousness (cf. *e.g.* 2 Sam. viii. 15, 1 Chron. xviii. 14, 1 Kings x. 9, Isa. xvi. 5) among His people. Out of this manifestation of God's righteousness, which is more conspicuous, and can be better estimated, within the nation of the history of redemption than

elsewhere, grows the call to highly exalt Jahve the God of
Israel, and to bow one's self very low at His footstool.   לַהֲדֹם
רַגְלָיו, as in cxxxii. 7, is not a statement of the object (for Isa.
xlv. 14 is of another kind), but (like אֶל in other instances) of
the place in which, or of the direction (cf. vii. 14) in which
the προσκύνησις is to take place. The temple is called Jahve's
footstool (1 Chron. xxviii. 2, cf. Lam. ii. 1, Isa. lx. 13) with
reference to the ark, the *capporeth* of which corresponds to the
transparent sapphire (Ex. xxiv. 10) and to the crystal-like
firmament of the *mercaba* (Ezek. i. 22, cf. 1 Chron. xxviii. 18).

Vers. 6–9. The vision of the third *Sanctus* looks into the
history of the olden time prior to the kings. In support of the
statement that Jahve is a living God, and a God who proves
Himself in mercy and in judgment, the poet appeals to three
heroes of the olden time, and the events recorded of them.
The expression certainly sounds as though it had reference to
something belonging to the present time ; and Hitzig therefore
believes that it must be explained of the three as heavenly
intercessors, after the manner of Onias and Jeremiah in the
vision 2 Macc. xv. 12–14. But apart from this presupposing an
active manifestation of life on the part of those who have fallen
happily asleep, which is at variance with the ideas of the latest
as well as of the earliest Psalms concerning the other world,
this interpretation founders upon ver. 7*a*, according to which
a celestial discourse of God with the three " in the pillar of
cloud" ought also to be supposed. The substantival clauses
ver. 6*ab* bear sufficient evidence in themselves of being a
retrospect, by which the futures that follow are stamped as
being the expression of the cotemporaneous past. The distribution of the predicates to the three is well conceived.
Moses was also a mighty man in prayer, for with his hands
uplifted for prayer he obtained the victory for his people over
Amalek (Ex. xvii. 11 sq.), and on another occasion placed himself in the breach, and rescued them from the wrath of God
and from destruction (cvi. 23, Ex. xxxii. 30–32 ; cf. also Num.
xii. 13) ; and Samuel, it is true, is only a Levite by descent,
but by office in a time of urgent need a priest (*cohen*), for he
sacrifices independently in places where, by reason of the absence of the holy tabernacle with the ark of the covenant, it
was not lawful, according to the letter of the law, to offer

sacrifices, he builds an altar in Ramah, his residence as judge, and has, in connection with the divine services on the high place (*Bama*) there, a more than high-priestly position, inasmuch as the people do not begin the sacrificial repasts before he has blessed the sacrifice (1 Sam. ix. 13). But the character of a mighty man in prayer is outweighed in the case of Moses by the character of the priest; for he is, so to speak, the proto-priest of Israel, inasmuch as he twice performed priestly acts which laid as it were a foundation for all times to come, viz. the sprinkling of the blood at the ratification of the covenant under Sinai (Ex. ch. xxiv.), and the whole ritual which was a model for the consecrated priesthood, at the consecration of the priests (Lev. ch. viii.). It was he, too, who performed the service in the sanctuary prior to the consecration of the priests: he set the shew-bread in order, prepared the candlestick, and burnt incense upon the golden altar (Ex. xl. 22–27). In the case of Samuel, on the other hand, the character of the mediator in the religious services is outweighed by that of the man mighty in prayer: by prayer he obtained Israel the victory of Ebenezer over the Philistines (1 Sam. vii. 8 sq.), and confirmed his words of warning with the miraculous sign, that at his calling upon God it would thunder and rain in the midst of a cloudless season (1 Sam. xii. 16, cf. Sir. xlvi. 16 sq.).

The poet designedly says: Moses and Aaron were among His priests, and Samuel among His praying ones. This third twelve-line strophe holds good, not only of the three in particular, but of the twelve-tribe nation of priests and praying ones to which they belong. For ver. 7a cannot be meant of the three, since, with the exception of a single instance (Num. xii. 5), it is always Moses only, not Aaron, much less Samuel, with whom God negotiates in such a manner. אֲלֵיהֶם refers to the whole people, which is proved by their interest in the divine revelation given by the hand of Moses out of the cloudy pillar (Ex. xxxiii. 7 sq.). Nor can ver. 6c therefore be understood of the three exclusively, since there is nothing to indicate the transition from them to the people: crying (קֹרְאִים, syncopated like הֹטְמָאִים, 1 Sam. xiv. 33) to Jahve, *i.e.* as often as they (these priests and praying ones, to whom a Moses, Aaron, and Samuel belong) cried unto Jahve, He answered them—He revealed Himself to this people who had such leaders (*choragi*), in the cloudy pillar, to those who kept His testimonies and the law which He gave them. A glance at ver. 8 shows that in Israel itself the good and the bad, good and evil, are distinguished. God answered those who could pray to Him with a claim to be answered. Ver. 7bc is, virtually at least, a relative clause, declaring the prerequisite of a prayer that may be granted. In ver. 8 is added the thought that the history of Israel, in the time of its redemption out of Egypt, is not less a mirror of the righteousness of God than of the pardoning grace of God. If vers. 7, 8 are referred entirely to the three, then עֲלִילוֹת and נְקַם, referred to their sins of infirmity, appear to be too strong expressions. But to take the suffix of עֲלִילוֹתָם objectively (*ea quæ in eos sunt moliti Core et socii ejus*), with Symmachus (καὶ ἔκδικος ἐπὶ ταῖς ἐπηρείαις αὐτῶν) and Kimchi, as the *ulciscens in omnes adinventiones eorum* of the Vulgate is interpreted,* is to do violence to it. The reference to the people explains it all without any constraint, and even the flight of prayer that comes in here (cf. Mic. vii. 18). The calling to mind of the generation of the desert, which fell short of the promise, is an earnest admonition for the generation of the present time. The God of Israel is holy in love and in wrath, as He Himself unfolds His Name in Ex. xxxiv. 6, 7. Hence the poet calls upon his fellow-countrymen to exalt this God, whom they may with pride call their **own**, *i.e.* to acknowledge and confess His majesty, and to fall down and worship at (ל cf. אֶל, v. 8) the mountain of His holiness, the place of His choice and of His presence.

PSALM C.

CALL OF ALL THE WORLD TO THE SERVICE OF THE TRUE GOD.

1 MAKE a joyful noise unto Jahve, all ye lands!
2 Serve Jahve with gladness,
   Come before Him with rejoicing.

---

* *Vid.* Raemdonck in his *David propheta cet.* 1800 : *in omnes injurias ipsis illatas, uti patuit in Core cet*

3 Know ye that Jahve is God:
He hath made us, and His we are,
His people, and the flock of His pasture.

4 Come into His gates with thanksgiving,
Into His courts with praise.
Give thanks unto Him, bless His name.
5 For Jahve is good,
His mercy is everlasting,
And to generation and generation His faithfulness.

This Psalm closes the series of deutero-Isaianic Psalms, which began with Ps. xci. There is common to all of them that mild sublimity, sunny cheerfulness, unsorrowful spiritual character, and New Testament expandedness, which we wonder at in the second part of the Book of Isaiah; and besides all this, they are also linked together by the figure anadiplosis, and manifold consonances and accords.

The arrangement, too, at least from Ps. xciii. onwards, is Isaianic: it is parallel with the relation of Isa. ch. xxiv.–xxvii. to ch. xiii.–xxiii. Just as the former cycle of prophecies closes that concerning the nations, after the manner of a musical finale, so the Psalms celebrating the dominion of God, from Ps. xciii. onwards, which vividly portray the unfolded glory of the kingship of Jahve, have *Jubilate* and *Cantate* Psalms in succession.

From the fact that this last Jubilate is entirely the echo of the first, viz. of the first half of Ps. xcv., we see how ingenious the arrangement is. There we find all the thoughts which recur here. There it is said in ver. 7, *He is our God, and we are the people of His pasture and the flock of His hand.* And in ver. 2, *Let us come before His face with thanksgiving* (בְּתוֹדָה)*, let us make a joyful noise unto Him in songs!*

This תודה is found here in the title of the Psalm, מִזְמוֹר לְתוֹדָה. Taken in the sense of a " Psalm for thanksgiving," it would say but little. We may take לתודה in a liturgical sense (with the Targum, Mendelssohn, Ewald, and Hitzig), like ליום הֹשַׁבּת, xcii. 1, in this series, and like להזכיר in xxxviii. 1, lxx. 1. What is intended is not merely the *tôda* of the heart, but the *shela-mîm-tôda,* זֶבַח תּוֹדָה, cvii. 22, cxvi. 17, which is also called ab-

solutely תודה in lvi. 13, 2 Chron. xxix. 31. That kind of
shelamîm is thus called which is presented על־תודה, *i.e.* as
thankful praise for divine benefits received, more particularly
marvellous protection and deliverance (*vid.* Ps. cvii.).

Vers. 1–3. The call in ver. 1 sounds like xcviii. 4, lxvi. 1.
כָּל־הָאָרֶץ are all lands, or rather all men belonging to the earth's
population. The first verse, without any parallelism and in
so far monostichic, is like the signal for a blowing of the trumpets. Instead of "serve Jahve with gladness (בְּשִׂמְחָה)," it is
expressed in ii. 11, "serve Jahve with fear (בְּיִרְאָה)." Fear and
joy do not exclude one another. Fear becomes the exalted
Lord, and the holy gravity of His requirements; joy becomes
the gracious Lord, and His blessed service. The summons to
manifest this joy in a religious, festive manner springs up out of
an all-hopeful, world-embracing love, and this love is the spontaneous result of living faith in the promise that all tribes of
the earth shall be blessed in the seed of Abraham, and in the
prophecies in which this promise is unfolded. דְּעוּ (as in iv. 4)
Theodoret well interprets δι᾽ αὐτῶν μάθετε τῶν πραγμάτων.
They are to know from facts of outward and inward experience
that Jahve is God: *He hath made us, and not we ourselves.*
Thus runs the *Chethîb*, which the LXX. follows, αὐτὸς ἐποίησεν
ἡμᾶς καὶ οὐχ ἡμεῖς (as also the Syriac and Vulgate); but Symmachus (like Rashi), contrary to all possibilities of language,
renders αὐτὸς ἐποίησεν ἡμᾶς οὐκ ὄντας. Even the Midrash (*Bere-
shith Rabba,* ch. c. *init.*) finds in this confession the reverse of the
arrogant words in the mouth of Pharaoh: "I myself have made
myself" (Ezek. xxix. 3). The *Kerî,* on the other hand, reads לוֹ,*
which the Targum, Jerome, and Saadia follow and render: *et
ipsius nos sumus.* Hengstenberg calls this *Kerî* quite unsuitable
and bad; and Hupfeld, on the other hand, calls the *Chethîb* an
" unspeakable insipidity." But in reality both readings accord
with the context, and it is clear that they are both in harmony

------

* According to the reckoning of the Masora, there are fifteen passages
in the Old Testament in which לֹא is written and לוֹ is read, viz. Ex. xxi. 8,
Lev. xi. 21, xxv. 30, 1 Sam. ii. 3, 2 Sam. xvi. 18, 2 Kings viii. 10, Isa. ix.
2, lxiii. 9, Ps. c. 3, cxxxix. 16, Job xiii. 15 [cf. the note there], xli. 4, Prov.
xix. 7, xxvi. 2, Ezra iv. 2. Because doubtful, Isa. xlix. 5, 1 Chron. xi. 20
are not reckoned with these.

with Scripture. Many a one has drawn balsamic consolation from the words *ipse fecit nos et non ipsi nos; e.g.* Melancthon when disconsolately sorrowful over the body of his son in Dresden on the 12th July 1559. But in *ipse fecit nos et ipsius nos sumus* there is also a rich mine of comfort and of admonition, for the Creator is also the Owner, His heart clings to His creature, and the creature owes itself entirely to Him, without whom it would not have had a being, and would not continue in being. Since, however, the parallel passage, xcv. 7, favours וְלוֹ rather than וְלֹא; since, further, וְלֹא is the easier reading, inasmuch as הוּא leads one to expect that an antithesis will follow (Hitzig); and since the "His people and the sheep of His pasture" that follows is a more natural continuation of a preceding וְלוֹ אנחנו than that it should be attached as a predicative object to עָשָׂנוּ over a parenthetical וְלֹא אנחנו: the *Kerî* decidedly maintains the preference. In connection with both readings, עָשָׂה has a sense related to the history of redemption, as in 1 Sam. xii. 6. Israel is Jahve's work (מעשׂה), Isa. xxix. 23, lx. 21, cf. Deut. xxxii. 6, 15, not merely as a people, but as the people of God, who were kept in view even in the calling of Abram.

Vers. 4, 5. Therefore shall the men of all nations enter with thanksgiving into the gates of His Temple and into the courts of His Temple with praise (xcvi. 8), in order to join themselves in worship to His church, which—a creation of Jahve for the good of the whole earth—is congregated about this Temple and has it as the place of its worship. The pilgrimage of all peoples to the holy mountain is an Old Testament dress of the hope for the conversion of all peoples to the God of revelation, and the close union of all with the people of this God. His Temple is open to them all. They may enter, and when they enter they have to look for great things. For the God of revelation (lii. 11, liv. 8) is "good" (xxv. 8, xxxiv. 9), and His loving-kindness and faithfulness endure for ever —the thought that recurs frequently in the later Hallelujah and Hodu Psalms and is become a liturgical formula (Jer. xxxiii. 11). The mercy or loving-kindness of God is the generosity, and His faithfulness the constancy, of His love.

PSALM CI.

THE VOWS OF A KING.

1 OF mercy and right will I sing,
　　　　　To Thee, Jahve, will I harp,
2 I will give heed to the way of uprightness—
　　　　　When wilt Thou come unto me?!
　I will walk in the innocence of my heart
　　　　　within my house,
3 I will not set before mine eyes
　　　　　a worthless action;
　The commission of excesses I hate,
　　　　　nothing shall cleave to me.
4 A false heart shall keep far from me,
　　　　　I will not cherish an evil thing.
5 Whoso secretly slandereth his neighbour,
　　　　　him will I destroy;
　Whoso hath a high look and puffed-up heart,
　　　　　him will I not suffer.
6 Mine eyes are upon the faithful of the land,
　　　　　that they may be round about me;
　Whoso walketh in the way of uprightness,
　　　　　he shall serve me.
7 He shall not sit within my house
　　　　　who practiseth deceit;
　He who speaketh lies shall not continue
　　　　　before mine eyes.
8 Every morning will I destroy
　　　　　all the wicked of the earth,
　That I may root out of Jahve's city
　　　　　all workers of iniquity.

This is the "prince's Psalm,"* or as it is inscribed in

---

* Eyring, in his *Vita* of Ernest the Pious [Duke of Saxe-Gotha, b. 1601, d. 1675], relates that he sent an unfaithful minister a copy of the 101st Psalm, and that it became a proverb in the country, when an official had done anything wrong: He will certainly soon receive the prince's Psalm to read.

Luther's version, " David's mirror of a monarch."   Can there
be any more appropriate motto for it than what is said of
Jahve's government in xcix. 4 ?   In respect of this passage
of Ps. xcix., to which Ps. c. is the finale, Ps. ci. seems to be
appended as an echo out of the heart of David.   The appro-
priateness of the words לְדָוִד מִזְמוֹר (the position of the words is
as in Ps. xxiv., xl., cix., cx., cxxxix.) is corroborated by the
form and contents.   Probably the great historical work from
which the chronicler has taken excerpts furnished the post-
exilic collector with a further gleaning of Davidic songs, or at
least songs that were ascribed to David.   The Psalm before us
belongs to the time during which the Ark was in the house of
Obed-Edom, where David had left it behind through terror at
the misfortune of Uzzah.   David said at that time : " *How
shall the Ark of Jahve come to me* (the unholy one) ? " 2 Sam.
vi. 8.   He did not venture to bring the Ark of the Fearful and
Holy One within the range of his own house.   In our Psalm,
however, he gives utterance to his determination as king to give
earnest heed to the sanctity of his walk, of his rule, and of his
house ; and this resolve he brings before Jahve as a vow, to
whom, in regard to the rich blessing which the Ark of God
diffuses around it (2 Sam. vi. 11 sq.), he longingly sighs :
" *When wilt Thou come to me ?!* "   This cotemporaneous
reference has been recognised by Hammond and Venema.
From the fact that Jahve comes to David, Jerusalem becomes
" the city of Jahve," ver. 8 ; and to defend the holiness of this
the city of His habitation in all faithfulness, and with all his
might, is the thing to which David here pledges himself.

The contents of the first verse refer not merely to the
Psalm that follows as an announcement of its theme, but to
David's whole life : graciousness and right, the self-manifesta-
tions united ideally and, for the king who governs His people,
typically in Jahve, shall be the subject of his song.   Jahve,
the primal source of graciousness and of right, it shall be, to
whom he consecrates his poetic talent, as also his playing upon
the harp.   חֶסֶד is condescension which flows from the principle
of free love, and מִשְׁפָּט legality which binds itself impartially
and uncapriciously to the rule (norm) of that which is right
and good.   They are two modes of conduct, mutually temper-

ing each other, which God requires of every man (Mic. vi. 8, cf. Matt. xxiii. 23: τὴν κρίσιν καὶ τὸν ἔλεον), and more especially of a king. Further, he has resolved to give heed, thoughtfully and with an endeavour to pursue it (בְּ הִשְׂכִּיל as in Dan. ix. 13), unto the way of that which is perfect, *i.e.* blameless. What is further said might now be rendered as a relative clause: when Thou comest to me. But not until then ?! Hitzig renders it differently: I will take up the lot of the just when it comes to me, *i.e.* as often as it is brought to my knowledge. But if this had been the meaning, בִּדְבַר would have been said instead of בְּדֶרֶךְ (Ex. xviii. 16, 19, 2 Sam. xix. 12 [11]); for, according to both its parts, the expression דרך תמים is an ethical notion, and is therefore not used in a different sense from that in ver. 6. Moreover, the relative use of the interrogative מָתַי in Hebrew cannot be supported, with the exception, perhaps, of Prov. xxiii. 35. Athanasius correctly interprets: ποθῶ σου τὴν παρουσίαν, ὦ δέσποτα, ἱμείρομαί σου τῆς ἐπιφανείας, ἀλλὰ δὸς τὸ ποθούμενον. It is a question of strong yearning: when wilt Thou come to me? is the time near at hand when Thou wilt erect Thy throne near to me? If his longing should be fulfilled, David is resolved to, and will then, behave himself as he further sets forth in the vows he makes. He pledges himself to walk within his house, *i.e.* his palace, in the innocence or simplicity of his heart (lxxviii. 72, Prov. xx. 7), without allowing himself to be led away from this frame of mind which has become his through grace. He will not set before his eyes, viz. as a proposition or purpose (Deut. xv. 9, Ex. x. 10, 1 Sam. xxix. 10, LXX.), any morally worthless or vile matter whatsoever (xli. 9, cf. concerning בְּלִיַּעַל, xviii. 5). The commission of excesses he hates: עָשׂה is *infin. constr.* instead of עֲשׂוֹת as in Gen. xxxi. 28, l. 20, Prov. xxi. 3, cf. רְאֹה Gen. xlviii. 11, שְׁתוֹ Prov. xxxi. 4. סֵטִים (like שֵׂטִים in Hos. v. 2), as the object of עָשׂה, has not a personal (Kimchi, Ewald) signification (cf. on the other hand xl. 5), but material signification: (*facta*) *declinantia* (like זֵדִים, xix. 14, *insolentia*; חֹבְלִים, Zech. xi. 7, *vincientia*); all temptations and incitements of this sort he shakes off from himself, so that nothing of the kind cleaves to him. The confessions in ver. 4 refer to his own inward nature: לֵב עִקֵּשׁ (not עִקֶּשׁ־לֵב, Prov. xvii. 20), a false heart that is not faithful in its intentions

either to God or to men, shall remain far from him; wickedness (רָע as in xxxvi 5) he does not wish to know, *i.e.* does
not wish to foster and nurture within him. Whoso secretly
slanders his neighbour, him will he destroy; it will therefore
be so little possible for any to curry favour with him by un-
charitable perfidious tale-bearing, of the wiliness of which
David himself had had abundant experience in his relation to
Saul, that it will rather call forth his anger upon him (Prov.
xxx. 10). Instead of the regularly pointed מְלוֹשְׁנִי the *Kerî*
reads מְלָשְׁנִי, *m'lŏshnî*, a *Poel* (לָשֵׁן *linguâ petere*, like עֵין *oculo
petere*, elsewhere הִלְשִׁין, Prov. xxx. 10) with ŏ instead of ō (*vid.*
on cix. 10, lxii. 4) and with *Chirek compaginis* (*vid.* on Ps.
cxiii.). The "lofty of eyes," *i.e.* supercilious, haughty, and
the "broad of heart," *i.e.* boastful, puffed up, self-conceited
(Prov. xxviii. 25, cf. xxi. 4), him he cannot endure (אוּכָל, properly *fut. Hoph.*, I am incapable of, viz. לָשֵׂאת, which is to be
supplied as in Isa. i. 13, after Prov. xxx. 21, Jer. xliv. 22).*
On the other hand, his eyes rest upon the faithful of the land,
with the view, viz., of drawing them into his vicinity. Whoso
walks in the way of uprightness, he shall serve him (שָׁרֵת, θερα-
πεύειν, akin to עָבַד, δουλεύειν). He who practises deceit shall
not stay within his house; he who speaks lies shall have no
continuance (יִכּוֹן is more than equivalent to נָכוֹן) before (under)
his eyes. Every morning (לַבְּקָרִים as in lxxiii. 14, Isa. xxxiii. 2,
Lam. iii. 23, and לִבְקָרִים, Job vii. 18), when Jahve shall have
taken up His abode in Jerusalem, will he destroy all evil-doers
(רִשְׁעֵי as in cxix. 119), *i.e.* incorrigibly wicked ones, wherever
he may meet them upon the earth, in order that all workers of
evil may be rooted out of the royal city, which is now become
the city of Jahve.

---

* In both instances the Masora writes אוֹתוֹ (*plene*), but the Talmud,
B. Erachin 15*b*, had אתו before it when it says: "Of the slanderer God
says: I and he cannot dwell together in the world, I cannot bear it any
longer with him (אִתּוֹ)."

PSALM CII.

PRAYER OF A PATIENT SUFFERER FOR HIMSELF AND FOR
THE JERUSALEM THAT LIES IN RUINS.

2 O JAHVE, hear my prayer,
  And let my cry come unto Thee.
3 Hide not Thy face from me in the day that I am in trouble,
  Incline Thine ear unto me,
  In the day that I call answer me speedily.

4 For my days are vanished in smoke,
  And my bones are heated through as a hearth.
5 Smitten like a green herb and dried up is my heart,
  For I have forgotten to eat my bread,
6 Because of my loud crying my bones cleave to my flesh.

7 I am like a pelican of the wilderness,
  I am become as an owl of the ruins.
8 Keeping watch I am as a lonely bird on the house-top.
9 All the day mine enemies reproach me;
  Those who are mad against me swear by me.

10 For I have eaten ashes like bread,
   And mingled my drink with weeping,
11 Because of Thine indignation and Thy raging,
   That Thou hast lifted me up and cast me down.
12 My days are like a lengthened shadow,
   And I myself am dried up like the green herb.

13 But THOU, Jahve, sittest enthroned for ever,
   And Thy remembrance endureth into all generations.
14 THOU wilt arise, have mercy upon Zion,
   For it is time to favour her, yea the time is come—
15 For Thy servants cling lovingly to her stones,
   And they cry sore over her dust.

16 And the heathen shall fear the Name of Jahve,
   And all the kings of the earth Thy glory,

17 Because Jahve hath rebuilt Zion,
     He hath appeared in His glory,
18 He hath turned to the prayer of the destitute,
     And not despised their prayer.

19 It shall be written for the generation to come,
     And a people yet to be created shall praise Jāh,
20 That He hath looked down from His holy height,
     From heaven unto earth hath Jahve looked,
21 To hear the sighing of the prisoner,
     To set at liberty those who are appointed to death,
22 That they may declare in Zion the Name of Jahve,
     And His praise in Jerusalem,
23 When the peoples are gathered together,
     And the kingdoms, to serve Jahve.

24 He hath bowed down my strength in the way,
     He hath shortened my days.
25 I said, My God, take me not away in the midst of my
          days—
     Into all generations Thy years endure.
26 Of old hast Thou founded the earth,
     And the heavens are the work of Thy hands.
27 Those shall perish, but Thou remainest,
     They all shall wax old like a garment,
     As a vesture dost Thou change them and they change—
28 But Thou art the same and Thy years have no end!
29 The children of Thy servants shall dwell,
     And their seed shall continue before Thee.

Ps. ci. utters the sigh: *When wilt Thou come to me?* and
Ps. cii. with the inscription: *Prayer for an afflicted one when
he pineth away and poureth forth his complaint before Jahve,*
prays, *Let my prayer come unto Thee.* It is to be taken, too,
just as personally as it sounds, and the person is not to be construed into a nation. The song of the עָנִי is, however, certainly
a national song; the poet is a servant of Jahve, who shares
the calamity that has befallen Jerusalem and its homeless
people, both in outward circumstances and in the very depth
of his soul. עָטַף signifies to pine away, languish, as in lxi. 3,

Isa. lvii. 16; and שָׁפַךְ שִׂיחוֹ to pour out one's thoughts and complaints, one's anxious care, as in cxlii. 3, cf. 1 Sam. i. 15 sq.

As is the case already with many of the preceding Psalms, the deutero-Isaianic impression accompanies us in connection with this Psalm also, even to the end; and the further we get in it the more marked does the echo of its prophetical proto-type become. The poet also allies himself with earlier Psalms, such as xxii., lxix., and lxxix., although himself capable of lofty poetic flight, in return for which he makes us feel the absence of any safely progressive unfolding of the thoughts.

Vers. 2, 3. The Psalm opens with familiar expressions of prayer, such as rise in the heart and mouth of the praying one without his feeling that they are of foreign origin; cf. more especially xxxix. 13, xviii. 7, lxxxviii. 3; and on ver. 3: xxvii. 9 (*Hide not Thy face from me*); lix. 17 (ביום צר לי); xxxi. 3 and frequently (*Incline Thine ear unto me*); lvi. 10 (ביום אקרא); lxix. 18, cxliii. 7 (מַהֵר עֲנֵנִי).

Vers. 4—6. From this point onward the Psalm becomes original. Concerning the *Beth* in בְעָשָׁן, *vid.* on xxxvii. 20. The reading כְּמוֹ קָד (in the Karaite Ben-Jerucham) enriches the lexicon in the same sense with a word which has scarcely had any existence. מוֹקֵד (Arabic *maukid*) signifies here, as in other instances, a hearth. נִחָרוּ is, as in lxix. 4, *Niphal*: my bones are heated through with a fever-heat, as a hearth with the smouldering fire that is on it. הוּכָּה (cf. יְגוֹדוּ, xciv. 21) is used exactly as in Hos. ix. 16, cf. Ps. cxxi. 6. The heart is said to dry up when the life's blood, of which it is the reser-voir, fails. The verb שָׁכַח is followed by מִן of dislike. On the cleaving of the bones to the flesh from being baked, *i.e.* to the skin (Arabic بِشْر, in accordance with the radical signification, the surface of the body = the skin, from בשר, to brush along, rub, scrape, scratch on the surface), cf. Job xix. 20, Lam. iv. 8. לְ (אֶל) with דָּבַק is used just like בְּ. It is unnecessary, with Böttcher, to draw מִקּוֹל אֲנַחְתִי to ver. 5. Continuous straining of the voice, especially in connection with persevering prayer arising from inward conflict, does really make the body waste away.

Vers. 7—9. קָאַת (construct of קָאַת or קָאָת from קָאָה, *vid.*

Isaiah, ii. 73), according to the LXX., is the pelican, and כּוֹס is the night-raven or the little horned-owl.* דָּמָה obtains the signification to be like, equal (*æqualem esse*), from the radical signification to be flat, even, and to spread out flat (as the Dutch have already recognised). They are both unclean creatures, which are fond of the loneliness of the desert and ruined places. To such a wilderness, that of the exile, is the poet unwillingly transported. He passes the nights without sleep (שָׁקַד, to watch during the time for sleep), and is therefore like a bird sitting lonesome (בּוֹדֵד, Syriac erroneously נוֹדֵד) upon the roof whilst all in the house beneath are sleeping. The *Athnach* in ver. 8 separates that which is come to be from the ground of the "becoming" and the "becoming" itself. His grief is that his enemies reproach him as one forsaken of God. מְהוֹלָל, *part. Poal*, is one made or become mad, Eccles. ii. 2: my mad ones = those who are mad against me. These swear by him, inasmuch as they say when they want to curse: "God do unto thee as unto this man," which is to be explained according to Isa. lxv. 15, Jer. xxix. 22.

Vers. 10–12. Ashes are his bread (cf. Lam. iii. 16), inasmuch as he, a mourner, sits in ashes, and has thrown ashes all over himself, Job ii. 8, Ezek. xxvii. 30. The inflected שִׁקֻּוַי

---

* The LXX. renders it: I am like a pelican of the desert, I am become as a night-raven upon a ruined place (οἰκοπέδῳ). In harmony with the LXX., Saadia (as also the Arabic version edited by Erpenius, the Samaritan Arabic, and Abulwalîd) renders קָאַת by قوق (here and in Lev. xi. 18, Deut. xiv. 17, Isa. xxxiv. 17), and כּוֹס by بوم ; the latter (*bum*) is an onomatopoetic name of the owl, and the former (*kuk*) does not even signify the owl or horned-owl (although the small horned-owl is called *um kuéik* in Egypt, and in Africa *abu kuéik; vid.* the dictionaries of Bocthor and Marcel s. v. *chouette*), but the pelican, the " long-necked water-bird" (Damiri after the lexicon *el-ʿObâb* of Hasan ben-Mohammed el-Saghani). The Græco-Veneta also renders קָאַת with πελεκάν,—the Peshito, however, with ܩܩ. What Ephrem on Deut. xiv. 17 and the *Physiologus Syrus* (ed. *Tychsen*, p. 13, cf. pp. 110 sq.) say of ܩܩ, viz. that it is a marsh-bird, is very fond of its young ones, dwells in desolate places, and is incessantly noisy, likewise points to the pelican, although the Syrian lexicographers vary. Cf. also Oedmann, *Vermischte Sammlungen*, Heft 3, Cap. 6. (Fleischer after a communication from Rödiger.)

has שִׁקּוּ = שִׁקּוּי for its principal form, instead of which it is שִׁקּוּי
in Hos. ii. 7. "That Thou hast lifted me up and cast me down"
is to be understood according to Job xxx. 22. First of all God
has taken away the firm ground from under his feet, then from
aloft He has cast him to the ground—an emblem of the lot of
Israel, which is removed from its fatherland and cast into
exile, *i.e.* into a strange land. In that passage the days of
his life are כְּצֵל נָטוּי, like a lengthened shadow, which grows
longer and longer until it is entirely lost in darkness, cix. 23.
Another figure follows: he there becomes like an (uprooted)
plant which dries up.

Vers. 13–15. When the church in its individual members
dies off on a foreign soil, still its God, the unchangeable One,
remains, and therein the promise has the guarantee of its fulfilment. Faith lays hold upon this guarantee as in Ps. xc. It
becomes clear from ix. 8 and Lam. v. 19 how תֵּשֵׁב is to be
understood. The Name which Jahve makes Himself by self-
attestation never falls a prey to the dead past, it is His ever-
living memorial (זֵכֶר, Ex. iii. 15). Thus, too, will He restore
Jerusalem; the limit, or appointed time, to which the promise
points is, as his longing tells the poet, now come. מוֹעֵד, according to lxxv. 3, Hab. ii. 3, is the juncture, when the redemption
by means of the judgment on the enemies of Israel shall dawn.
לְחֶנְנָהּ, from the infinitive חֵנַן, has ĕ, flattened from ă, in an
entirely closed syllable. רָצָה *seq. acc.* signifies to have pleasure
in anything, to cling to it with delight; and חָנַן, according to
Prov. xiv. 21, affirms a compassionate, tender love of the object.
The servants of God do not feel at home in Babylon, but their
loving yearning lingers over the ruins, the stones and the heaps
of the rubbish (Neh. iii. 34 [iv. 2]), of Jerusalem.

Vers. 16–18. With וְיִירְאוּ we are told what will take place
when that which is expected in ver. 14 comes to pass, and at
the same time the fulfilment of that which is longed for is
thereby urged home upon God: Jahve's own honour depends
upon it, since the restoration of Jerusalem will become the
means of the conversion of the world—a fundamental thought
of Isa. ch. xl.–lxvi. (cf. more particularly ch. lix. 19, lx. 2),
which is also called to mind in the expression of this strophe.
This prophetic prospect (Isa. xl. 1–5) that the restoration of
Jerusalem will take place simultaneously with the glorious

parusia of Jahve re-echoes here in a lyric form. כִּי, ver. 17,
states the ground of the reverence, just as ver. 20 the ground
of the praise. The people of the Exile are called in ver. 18
הָעַרְעָר, from עָרַר, to be naked : homeless, powerless, honourless,
and in the eyes of men, prospectless. The LXX. renders this
word in Jer. xvii. 6 *ἀγριομυρίκη*, and its plural, formed by an
internal change of vowel, עֲרוֹעֵר, in Jer. xlviii. 6 *ὄνος ἄγριος*,
which are only particularizations of the primary notion of that
which is stark naked, neglected, wild. Ver. 18*b* is an echo of
Ps. xxii. 25. In the mirror of this and of other Psalms written
in times of affliction the Israel of the Exile saw itself reflected.

Vers. 19–23. The poet goes on advancing motives to
Jahve for the fulfilment of his desire, by holding up to Him
what will take place when He shall have restored Zion. The
evangel of God's redemptive deed will be written down for
succeeding generations, and a new, created people, *i.e.* a people
coming into existence, the church of the future, shall praise
God the Redeemer for it. דּוֹר אַחֲרוֹן as in xlviii. 14, lxxviii. 4.
עַם נִבְרָא like עַם נוֹלָד xxii. 32, perhaps with reference to deutero-
Isaianic passages like Isa. xliii. 7. On ver. 20, cf. Isa. lxiii.
15 ; in ver. 21 (cf. Isa. xlii. 7, lxi. 1) the deutero-Isaianic
colouring is very evident. And ver. 21 rests still more verbally upon lxxix. 11. The people of the Exile are as it were
in prison and chains (אָסִיר), and are advancing towards their
destruction (בְּנֵי תְמוּתָה), if God does not interpose. Those who
have returned home are the subject to לְסַפֵּר. בְּ in ver. 23 introduces that which takes place simultaneously : with the release
of Israel from servitude is united the conversion of the world.
נִקְבַּץ occurs in the same connection as in Isa. lx. 4. After
having thus revelled in the glory of the time of redemption the
poet comes back to himself and gives form to his prayer on his
own behalf.

Vers. 24–29. On the way (ב as in cx. 7)—not "by means
of the way" (ב as in cv. 18), in connection with which one
would expect to find some attributive minuter definition of the
way—God hath bowed down his strength (cf. Deut. viii. 2) ; it
was therefore a troublous, toilsome way which he has been led,
together with his people. He has shortened his days, so that
he only drags on wearily, and has only a short distance still
before him before he is entirely overcome. The *Chethîb* כחו

(LXX. ἰσχύος αὐτοῦ) may be understood of God's irresistible might, as in Job xxiii. 6, xxx. 18, but in connection with it the designation of the object is felt to be wanting. The introductory אֹמַר (cf. Job x. 2), which announces a definite moulding of the utterance, serves to give prominence to the petition that follows. In the expression אַל־תַּעֲלֵנִי life is conceived of as a line the length of which accords with nature; to die before one's time is a being taken up out of this course, so that the second half of the line is not lived through (lv. 24, Isa. xxxviii. 10). The prayer not to sweep him away before his time, the poet supports not by the eternity of God in itself, but by the work of the rejuvenation of the world and of the restoration of Israel that is to be looked for, which He can and will bring to an accomplishment, because He is the ever-living One. The longing to see this new time is the final ground of the poet's prayer for the prolonging of his life. The confession of God the Creator in ver. 26 reminds one in its form of Isa. xlviii. 13, cf. xliv. 24. הֵמָּה in ver. 27 refers to the two great divisions of the universe. The fact that God will create heaven and earth anew is a revelation that is indicated even in Isa. xxxiv. 4, but is first of all expressed more fully and in many ways in the second part of the Book of Isaiah, viz. li. 6, 16, lxv. 17, lxvi. 22. It is clear from the agreement in the figure of the garment (Isa. li. 6, cf. l. 9) and in the expression (עָמַד, *perstare*, as in Isa. lxvi. 22) that the poet has gained this knowledge from the prophet. The expressive אַתָּה הוּא, Thou art He, *i.e.* unalterably the same One, is also taken from the mouth of the prophet, Isa. xli. 4, xliii. 10, xlvi. 4, xlviii. 12 ; הוּא is a predicate, and denotes the identity (sameness) of Jahve (Hofmann, *Schriftbeweis*, i. 63). In ver. 29 also, in which the prayer for a lengthening of life tapers off to a point, we hear Isa. lxv. 9, lxvi. 22 re-echoed. And from the fact that in the mind of the poet as of the prophet the post-exilic Jerusalem and the final new Jerusalem upon the new earth under a new heaven blend together, it is evident that not merely in the time of Hezekiah or of Manasseh (assuming that Isa. ch. xl.–lxvi. are by the old Isaiah), but also even in the second half of the Exile, such a perspectively foreshortened view was possible. When, moreover, the writer of the Epistle to the Hebrews at once refers vers. 26-28 to Christ, this is justified by the fact that

the God whom the poet confesses as the unchangeable One is
Jahve who is to come.

PSALM CIII.

HYMN IN HONOUR OF GOD THE ALL-COMPASSIONATE ONE.

1 BLESS, O my soul, Jahve,
  And all that is within me, His holy Name.
2 Bless, O my soul, Jahve,
  And forget not all His benefits—
3 Who forgiveth all thine iniquity,
  Who healeth all thine infirmities,
4 Who redeemeth thy life from the pit,
  Who crowneth thee with loving-kindness and tender
5 Who satisfieth thy mouth with good,   [mercies,
  So that thy youth renews itself like the eagle.

6 Deeds of righteousness doth Jahve perform,
  And judgments on behalf of all that are oppressed.
7 He made known His ways unto Moses,
  To the children of Israel His mighty acts.
8 Merciful and gracious is Jahve,
  Slow to anger and plenteous in mercy.
9 Not always doth He contend,
  And not for ever doth He keep anger.
10 He doth not deal with us after our sins,
  Nor recompense us after our iniquities.

11 For as the heaven is high above the earth,
  So mighty is His mercy upon those who fear Him.
12 As far as the east is from the west,
  So far doth He remove our transgressions from us.
13 Like as a father pitieth his children,
  So Jahve pitieth those who fear Him.
14 For He knoweth our nature,
  He is mindful, that we are dust.

15 A mortal man—his days are as grass,
  As a flower of the field, so he flourisheth.

16 If the wind passeth over him, he is not,
   And his place knoweth him no more.
17 But the mercy of Jahve is from everlasting to everlasting
        upon those who fear Him,
   And His righteousness is manifested to children's children,
18 To those who keep His covenant
   And are mindful of His statutes to do them.

19 Jahve hath established His throne in the heavens,
   And His kingdom ruleth over all.
20 Bless Jahve, ye His angels,
   Ye strong heroes doing His word,
   Hearkening to the call of His word.
21 Bless Jahve, all ye His hosts,
   His servants doing His pleasure.
22 Bless Jahve, all ye His works,
   In all places of His dominion.
   Bless, O my soul, Jahve!

To the " *Thou wilt have compassion upon Zion*" of cii. 14
is appended Ps. ciii., which has this as its substance throughout; but in other respects the two Psalms stand in contrast to
one another. The inscription לדוד is also found thus by itself
without any further addition even before Psalms of the First
Book (xxvi.–xxviii., xxxv., xxxvii.). It undoubtedly does not
rest merely on conjecture, but upon tradition. For no internal
grounds which might have given rise to the annotation לדוד can
be traced. The form of the language does not favour it. This
pensive song, so powerful in its tone, has an Aramaic colouring
like Ps. cxvi., cxxiv., cxxix. In the heaping up of Aramaizing
suffix-forms it has its equal only in the story of Elisha, 2 Kings
iv. 1–7, where, moreover, the *Kerî* throughout substitutes the
usual forms, whilst here, where these suffix-forms are intentional ornaments of the expression, the *Chethîb* rightly remains
unaltered. The forms are *2d sing. fem. ēchi* for *ēch*, and *2d sing.
plur. ājchi* for *ajich*. The *i* without the tone which is added
here is just the one with which originally the pronunciation
was אַתְּי instead of אַתְּ and לְכִי for לָךְ. Out of the Psalter (here
and cxvi. 7, 19) these suffix-forms *echi* and *ajchi* occur only in

Jer. xi. 15, and in the North-Palestinian history of the prophet in the Book of Kings.

The groups or strophes into which the Psalm falls are vers. 1–5, 6–10, 11–14, 15–18, 19–22. If we count their lines we obtain the schema 10. 10. 8. 8. 10. The Coptic version accordingly reckons 46 *CTYXOC*, *i.e.* στίχοι.

Vers. 1–5. In the strophe vers. 1–5 the poet càlls upon his soul to arise to praiseful gratitude for God's justifying, redeeming, and renewing grace. In such soliloquies it is the Ego that speaks, gathering itself up with the spirit, the stronger, more manly part of man (*Psychology*, S. 104 sq.; tr. p. 126), or even, because the soul as the spiritual medium of the spirit and of the body represents the whole person of man (*Psychology*, S. 203; tr. p. 240), the Ego rendering objective in the soul the whole of its own personality. So here in vers. 3–5 the soul, which is addressed, represents the whole man. The קְרָבִים which occurs here is a more choice expression for (מֵעַיִם) מֵעִים: the heart, which is called קֶרֶב κατ' ἐξοχήν, the reins, the liver, etc.; for according to the scriptural conception (*Psychology*, S. 266; tr. p. 313) these organs of the cavities of the breast and abdomen serve not merely for the bodily life, but also the psycho-spiritual life. The summoning בָּרְכִי is repeated *per anaphoram*. There is nothing the soul of man is so prone to forget as to render thanks that are due, and more especially thanks that are due to God. It therefore needs to be expressly aroused in order that it may not leave the blessing with which God blesses it unacknowledged, and may not forget all His acts performed (גָּמַר = גְּמָר) on it (גְּמוּל, ῥῆμα μέσον, *e.g.* in cxxxvii. 8), which are purely deeds of loving-kindness (benefits). Now follow attributive participles, which attach themselves to אַתְּ־ה'. Most prominent stands mercy (loving-kindness), which is the primal condition and the foundation of all the others, viz. sin-pardoning mercy. The verbs סָלַח and רָפָא with a dative of the object denote the bestowment of that which is expressed by the verbal notion. תַּחֲלוּאִים (taken from Deut. xxix. 21, cf. 1 Chron. xxi. 19, from חָלָה = חָלָא, root חל, *solutum, laxum esse*) are not merely bodily diseases, but all kinds of inward and outward sufferings. מִשַּׁחַת the LXX. renders ἐκ φθορᾶς (from שַׁחַת, as in Job xvii. 14); but in this antithesis to life it is more natural to render the "pit" (from שׁוּחַ) as a name of Hades, as in xvi. 10. Just as the soul owes its deliverance from guilt and distress and death to God, so also does it owe to God that with which it is endowed out of the riches of divine love. The verb עִטֵּר, without any such addition as in v. 13, is "to crown," cf. viii. 6. As is usually the case, it is construed with a double accusative; the crown is as it were woven out of loving-kindness and compassion. The *Beth* of בַּטּוֹב in ver. 5 instead of the accusative (civ. 28) denotes the means of satisfaction, which is at the same time that which satisfies. עֶדְיֵךְ the Targum renders: *dies senectutis tuæ*, whereas in xxxii. 9 it has *ornatus ejus;* the Peshîto renders : *corpus tuum*, and in xxxii. 9 inversely, *juventus eorum.* These significations, "old age" or "youth," are pure inventions. And since the words are addressed to the soul, עֶדְי cannot also, like כָּבוֹד in other instances, be a name of the soul itself (Aben-Ezra, Mendelssohn, Philipp-sohn, Hengstenberg, and others). We, therefore, with Hitzig, fall back upon the sense of the word in xxxii. 9, where the LXX. renders τὰς σιαγόνας αὐτῶν, but here more freely, ap-parently starting from the primary notion of עדי = Arabic *chadd*, the cheek : τὸν ἐμπιπλῶντα ἐν ἀγαθοῖς τὴν ἐπιθυμίαν σου (whereas Saadia's *victum tuum* is based upon a comparison

of the Arabic غَذَا, to nourish). The poet tells the soul (*i.e.* his

own person, himself) that God satisfies it with good, so that it as it were gets its cheeks full of it (cf. lxxxi. 11). The com-parison כַּנֶּשֶׁר is, as in Mic. i. 16 (cf. Isa. xl. 31), to be referred to the annual moulting of the eagle. Its renewing of its plumage is an emblem of the renovation of his youth by grace. The predicate to נְעוּרָיְכִי (plural of extension in relation to time) stands first regularly in the *sing. fem.*

Vers. 6–10. His range of vision being widened from him-self, the poet now in vers. 6–18 describes God's gracious and fatherly conduct towards sinful and perishing men, and that as it shines forth from the history of Israel and is known and re-cognised in the light of revelation. What ver. 6 says is a common-place drawn from the history of Israel. מִשְׁפָּטִים is an accusative governed by the עֹשֵׂה that is to be borrowed out of עֹשֵׂה (so Baer after the Masora). And because ver. 6 is the result of an historical retrospect and survey, יוֹדִיעַ in ver. 7 can

affirm that which happened in the past (cf. xcix. 6 sq.) ; for
the supposition of Hengstenberg and Hitzig, that *Moses* here
represents Israel like *Jacob, Isaac,* and *Joseph* in other instances,
is without example in the whole Israelitish literature. It becomes clear from ver. 8 in what sense the making of His ways
known is meant. The poet has in his mind Moses' prayer :
"make known to me now Thy way" (Ex. xxxiii. 13), which
Jahve fulfilled by passing by him as he stood in the cleft of
the rock and making Himself visible to him as he looked after
Him, amidst the proclamation of His attributes. The ways of
Jahve are therefore in this passage not those in which men are
to walk in accordance with His precepts (xxv. 4), but those
which He Himself follows in the course of His redemptive
history (lxvii. 3). The confession drawn from Ex. xxxiv. 6 sq.
is become a formula of the Israelitish faith (lxxxvi. 15, cxlv. 8,
Joel ii. 13, Neh. ix. 17, and frequently). In vers. 9 sqq. the
fourth attribute (וְרַב־חֶסֶד) is made the object of further praise.
He is not only long (אֶרֶךְ from אָרֵךְ, like כָּבֵד from כָּבֵד) in anger,
i.e. waiting a long time before He lets His anger loose, but
when He contends, *i.e.* interposes judicially, this too is not
carried to the full extent (lxxviii. 38), He is not angry for
ever (נָטַר, to keep, viz. anger, Amos i. 11 ; cf. the parallels
both as to matter and words, Jer. iii. 5, Isa. lvii. 16). The
procedure of His righteousness is regulated not according to
our sins, but according to His purpose of mercy. The perfects in ver. 10 state that which God has constantly not done,
and the futures in ver. 9 what He continually will not do.

Vers. 11–14. The ingenious figures in vers. 11 sq. (cf.
xxxvi. 6, lvii. 11) illustrate the infinite power and complete
unreservedness of mercy (loving-kindness). הִרְחִיק has *Gaja*
(as have also הִשְׁחִיתוּ and הִתְעִיבוּ, xiv. 1, liii. 2, in exact texts),
in order to render possible the distinct pronunciation of the
guttural in the combination רח. Ver. 13 sounds just as much
like the spirit of the New Testament as vers. 11, 12. The relationship to Jahve in which those stand who fear Him is a
filial relationship based upon free reciprocity (Mal. iii. 11).
His Fatherly compassion is (ver. 14) based upon the frailty
and perishableness of man, which are known to God, much the
same as God's promise after the Flood not to decree a like
judgment again (Gen. viii. 21). According to this passage

and Deut. xxxi. 21, יִצְרֵנוּ appears to be intended of the moral nature ; but according to ver. 14*b*, one is obliged to think rather of the natural form which man possesses from God the Creator (וַיִּיצֶר, Gen. ii. 7) than of the form of heart which he has by his own choice and, so far as its groundwork is concerned, by inheritance (li. 7). In זָכוּר, mindful, the passive, according to Böttcher's correct apprehension of it, expresses a passive state after an action that is completed by the person himself, as in יָדוּעַ בָּטוּחַ, and the like. In its form ver. 14*a* reminds one of the Book of Job ch. xi. 11, xxviii. 23, and ver. 14*b* as to subject-matter recalls Job vii. 7, and other passages (cf. Ps. lxxviii. 39, lxxxix. 48) ; but the following figurative representation of human frailty, with which the poet contrasts the eternal nature of the divine mercy as the sure stay of all God-fearing ones in the midst of the rise and decay of things here below, still more strongly recalls that book.

Vers. 15–18. The figure of the grass recalls xc. 5 sq., cf. Isa. xl. 6–8, li. 12 ; that of the flower, Job xiv. 2. אֱנוֹשׁ is man as a mortal being ; his life's duration is likened to that of a blade of grass, and his beauty and glory to a flower of the field, whose fullest bloom is also the beginning of its fading. In ver. 16 בּוֹ (the same as in Isa. xl. 7 sq.) refers to man, who is compared to grass and flowers. כִּי is ἐάν with a hypothetical perfect ; and the wind that scorches up the plants, referred to man, is an emblem of every form of peril that threatens life : often enough it is really a breath of wind which snaps off a man's life. The bold designation of vanishing away without leaving any trace, " and his place knoweth him no more," is taken from Job vii. 10, cf. *ibid.* viii. 18, xx. 9. In the midst of this plant-like, frail destiny, there is, however, one strong ground of comfort. There is an everlasting power, which raises all those who link themselves with it above the transitoriness involved in nature's laws, and makes them eternal like itself. This power is the mercy of God, which spans itself above (עַל) all those who fear Him like an eternal heaven. This is God's righteousness, which rewards faithful adherence to His covenant and conscientious fulfilment of His precepts in accordance with the order of redemption, and shows itself even to (לְ) children's children, according to Ex. xx. 6, xxxiv. 7, Deut. vii. 9 : on into a thousand generations, *i.e.* into infinity.

Vers. 19–22.   He is able to show Himself thus gracious to His own, for He is the supra-mundane, all-ruling King.   With this thought the poet draws on to the close of his song of praise. The heavens in opposition to the earth, as in cxv.3, Eccles. v. 1 [2], is the unchangeable realm above the rise and fall of things here below.   On ver. 19*b* cf. 1 Chron. xxix. 12.   בַּכֹּל refers to everything created without exception, the universe of created things.   In connection with the heavens of glory the poet cannot but call to mind the angels.   His call to these to join in the praise of Jahve has its parallel only in Ps. xxix. and cxlviii.   It arises from the consciousness of the church on earth that it stands in living like-minded fellowship with the angels of God, and that it possesses a dignity which rises above all created things, even the angels which are appointed to serve it (xci. 11).   They are called גִּבֹּרִים as in Joel iv. [iii.] 11, and in fact גִּבֹּרֵי כֹחַ, as the strong to whom belongs strength un-equalled.   Their life endowed with heroic strength is spent entirely—an example for mortals—in an obedient execution of the word of God.   לִשְׁמֹעַ is a definition not of the purpose, but of the manner : *obediendo* (as in Gen. ii. 3 *perficiendo*).   Hear-ing the call of His word, they also forthwith put it into exe-cution.   The hosts (צְבָאָיו), as מְשָׁרְתָיו shows, are the celestial spirits gathered around the angels of a higher rank (cf. Luke ii. 13), the innumerable λειτουργικὰ πνεύματα (civ. 4, Dan. vii. 10, Heb. i. 14), for there is a *hierarchia cœlestis*.   From the archangels the poet comes to the myriads of the heavenly hosts, and from these to all creatures, that they, wheresoever they may be throughout Jahve's wide domain, may join in the song of praise that is to be struck up ; and from this point he comes back to his own soul, which he modestly includes among the creatures mentioned in the third passage.   A threefold בָּרְכִי נַפְשִׁי now corresponds to the threefold בָּרְכוּ ; and inasmuch as the poet thus comes back to his own soul, his Psalm also turns back into itself and assumes the form of a converging circle.

PSALM CIV.

HYMN IN HONOUR OF THE GOD OF THE SEVEN DAYS.

1 BLESS, O my soul, Jahve!
Jahve, my God, Thou art very great,
In splendour and glory hast Thou clothed Thyself;
2 Enwrapping Thyself in light as a garment,
Spreading out the heavens like a tent-cloth,
3 Who layeth the beams of His chambers in the waters,
Who maketh the clouds His chariot,
Who walketh upon the wings of the wind,
4 Making His messengers out of the winds,
His servants out of flaming fire.

5 He hath founded the earth upon its pillars,
That it may not totter for ever and ever.
6 The deep as a garment didst Thou cover over it,
Upon the mountains stood the waters.
7 At Thy rebuke they fled,
At the voice of Thy thunder they hasted away—
8 The mountains rose, the valleys sank—
To the place which Thou hast founded for them.
9 A bound hast Thou set, they may not pass over,
They may not turn back to cover the earth.

10 Who sendeth forth springs in the bottoms of the
         valleys,
Between the mountains they take their course.
11 They give drink to all the beasts of the field,
The wild asses quench their thirst.
12 Upon them the birds of the heaven have their habi-
         tation,
From among the branches they raise their voice.
13 He watereth the mountains out of His chambers—
With the fruit of Thy works is the earth satisfied.
14 He causeth grass to grow for the cattle,
And herb for the service of man—

To bring forth bread out of the earth,
15 And that wine may make glad the heart of mortal man,
To make his face shining from oil,
And that bread may support the heart of mortal man.
16 The trees of Jahve are satisfied,
The cedars of Lebanon, which He hath planted;
17 Where the birds make their nests,
The stork which hath its house upon the cypresses.
18 Mountains, the high ones, are for the wild goats,
The rocks are a refuge for the rock-badgers.

19 He hath made the moon for a measuring of the times,
The sun knoweth its going down.
20 Thou makest darkness, and it is night,
Wherein all the beasts of the forest do move.
21 The young lions roar after their prey,
And seek from God their food.
22 The sun ariseth, they retreat
And lay themselves down in their dens.
23 Man goeth forth to his work,
And to his labour, until the evening.

24 How manifold are Thy works, Jahve,
With wisdom hast Thou executed them altogether,
The earth is full of Thy creatures!
25 Yonder sea, great and far extended—
There it teems with life, innumerable,
Small beasts together with great.
26 There the ships move along,
The leviathan which Thou hast formed to sport
therein.
27 They all wait upon Thee,
That Thou mayest give them their food in its season.
28 Thou givest it to them, they gather it up;
Thou openest Thy hand, they are satisfied with good.
29 Thou hidest Thy face, they are troubled;
Thou takest back their breath, they expire,
And return to their dust.
30 Thou sendest forth Thy breath, they are created,
And Thou renewest the face of the ground.

31 Let the glory of Jahve endure for ever,
   Let Jahve rejoice in His works;
32 He, who looketh on the earth and it trembleth,
   He toucheth the mountains and they smoke.
33 I will sing unto Jahve as long as I live,
   I will harp unto my God as long as I have my being.
34 May my meditation be acceptable to Him,
   I, even I will rejoice in Jahve.
35 Let the sinful disappear from the earth,
   And evil-doers be no more—
   Bless, O my soul, Jahve,
       Hallelujah.

With *Bless, O my soul, Jahve*, as Ps. ciii., begins this anonymous Ps. civ. also, in which God's rule in the kingdom of nature, as there in the kingdom of grace, is the theme of praise, and as there the angels are associated with it. The poet sings the God-ordained present condition of the world with respect to the creative beginnings recorded in Gen. i. 1–ii. 3; and closes with the wish that evil may be expelled from this good creation, which so thoroughly and fully reveals God's power, and wisdom, and goodness. It is a Psalm of nature, but such as no poet among the Gentiles could have written. The Israelitish poet stands free and unfettered in the presence of nature as his object, and all things appear to him as brought forth and sustained by the creative might of the one God, brought into being and preserved in existence on purpose that He, the self-sufficient One, may impart Himself in free condescending love —as the creatures and orders of the Holy One, in themselves good and pure, but spotted and disorganized only by the self-corruption of man in sin and wickedness, which self-corruption must be turned out in order that the joy of God in His works and the joy of these works in their Creator may be perfected. The Psalm is altogether an echo of the heptahemeron (or history of the seven days of creation) in Gen. i. 1–ii. 3. Corresponding to the seven days it falls into seven groups, in which the הנה־טוב מאד of Gen. i. 31 is expanded. It is not, however, so worked out that each single group celebrates the work of a day of creation; the Psalm has the commingling whole of the finished creation as its standpoint, and is there-

fore not so conformed to any plan. Nevertheless it begins
with the light and closes with an allusion to the divine Sabbath. When it is considered that ver. 8*a* is only with violence
accommodated to the context, that ver. 18 is forced in without
any connection and contrary to any plan, and that ver. 32 can
only be made intelligible in that position by means of an artificial combination of the thoughts, then the supposition of
Hitzig, ingeniously wrought out by him in his own way, is
forced upon one, viz. that this glorious hymn has decoyed some
later poet-hand into enlarging upon it.

Vers. 1–4. The first decastich begins the celebration with
work of the first and second days. הוֹד וְהָדָר here is not the
doxa belonging to God πρὸ παντὸς τοῦ αἰῶνος (Jude, ver. 25),
but the doxa which He has put on (Job xl. 10) since He
created the world, over against which He stands in kingly
glory, or rather in which He is immanent, and which reflects
this kingly glory in various gradations, yea, to a certain extent
is this glory itself. For inasmuch as God began the work of
creation with the creation of light, He has covered Himself
with this created light itself as with a garment. That which
once happened in connection with the creation may, as in Amos
iv. 13, Isa. xliv. 24, xlv. 7, Jer. x. 12, and frequently, be expressed by participles of the present, because the original setting
is continued in the preservation of the world; and determinate
participles alternate with participles without the article, as in Isa.
xliv. 24–28, with no other difference than that the former are
more predicative and the latter more attributive. With ver. 2*b*
the poet comes upon the work of the second day: the creation
of the expanse (רקיע) which divides between the waters. God
has spread this out (cf. Isa. xl. 22) like a tent-cloth (Isa. liv. 2),
of such light and of such fine transparent work; נוֹטֶה here
rhymes with עֹטֶה. In those waters which the " expanse" holds
aloft over the earth God lays the beams of His upper chambers (עֲלִיּוֹתָיו, instead of which we find מֲעֲלוֹתָיו in Amos ix. 6,
from עֲלִיָּה, ascent, elevation, then an upper story, an upper
chamber, which would be more accurately עִלִּיָּה after the Aramaic and Arabic); but not as though the waters were the
material for them, they are only the place for them, that is
exalted above the earth, and are able to be this because to the

Immaterial One even that which is fluid is solid, and that which is dense is transparent. The reservoirs of the upper waters, the clouds, God makes, as the lightning, thunder, and rain indicate, into His chariot (רְכוּב), upon which He rides along in order to make His power felt below upon the earth judicially (Isa. xix. 1), or in rescuing and blessing men. רְכוּב (only here) accords in sound with כְּרוּב, xviii. 11. For ver. 3c also recalls this primary passage, where the wings of the wind take the place of the cloud-chariot. In ver. 4 the LXX. (Heb. i. 7) makes the first substantive into an accusative of the object, and the second into an accusative of the predicate: Ὁ ποιῶν τοὺς ἀγγέλους αὐτοῦ πνεύματα καὶ τοὺς λειτουργοὺς αὐτοῦ πυρὸς φλόγα. It is usually translated the reverse way: making the winds into His angels, etc. This rendering is possible so far as the language is concerned (cf. c. 3 *Chethîb*, and on the position of the words, Amos iv. 13 with v. 8), and the plural מְשָׁרְתָיו is explicable in connection with this rendering from the force of the parallelism, and the singular אֵשׁ from the fact that this word has no plural. Since, however, עָשָׂה with two accusatives usually signifies to produce something out of something, so that the second accusative (viz. the accusative of the predicate, which is logically the second, but according to the position of the words may just as well be the first, Ex. xxv. 39, xxx. 25, as the second, Ex. xxxvii. 23, xxxviii. 3, Gen. ii. 7, 2 Chron. iv. 18–22) denotes the *materia ex qua*, it may with equal right at least be interpreted: Who makes His messengers out of the winds, His servants out of flaming or consuming (*vid.* on lvii. 5) fire (אֵשׁ, as in Jer. xlviii. 45, *masc.*). And this may affirm either that God makes use of wind and fire for special missions (cf. cxlviii. 8), or (cf. Hofmann, *Schriftbeweis*, i. 325 f.) that He gives wind and fire to His angels for the purpose of His operations in the world which are effected through their agency, as the materials of their outward manifestation, and as it were of their self-embodiment,[*] as then in xviii. 11 wind and cherub are both to be associated

------

[*] It is a Talmudic view that God really makes the angels out of fire, *B. Chagiga*, 14a (cf. *Koran*, xxxviii. 77): Day by day are the angels of the service created out of the stream of fire (נהר דינור), and sing their song of praise and perish.

together in thought as the vehicle of the divine activity in the world, and in xxxv. 5 the angel of Jahve represents the energy of the wind.

Vers. 5–9. In a second decastich the poet speaks of the restraining of the lower waters and the establishing of the land standing out of the water. The suffix, referring back to אֶרֶץ, is intended to say that the earth hanging free in space (Job xxvi. 7) has its internal supports. Its eternal stability is preserved even amidst the judgment predicted in Isa. xxiv. 16 sq., since it comes forth out of it, unremoved from its former station, as a transformed, glorified earth. The deep (תְּהוֹם) with which God covers it is that primordial mass of water in which it lay first of all as it were in embryo, for it came into being ἐξ ὕδατος καὶ δι' ὕδατος (2 Pet. iii. 5). כִּסִּיתוֹ does not refer to תהום (*masc.* as in Job xxviii. 14), because then עָלֶיהָ would be required, but to אֶרֶץ, and the masculine is to be explained either by attraction (according to the model of 1 Sam. ii. 4*a*), or by a reversion to the masculine ground-form as the discourse proceeds (cf. the same thing with עִיר 2 Sam. xvii. 13, צְעָקָה Ex. xi. 6, יָד Ezek. ii. 9). According to ver. 6*b*, the earth thus overflowed with water was already mountainous; the primal formation of the mountains is therefore just as old as the תהום mentioned in direct succession to the תהו ובהו. After this, vers. 7–9 describe the subduing of the primordial waters by raising up the dry land and the confining of these waters in basins surrounded by banks. Terrified by the despotic command of God, they started asunder, and mountains rose aloft, the dry land with its heights and its low grounds appeared. The rendering that the waters, thrown into wild excitement, rose up the mountains and descended again (Hengstenberg), does not harmonize with the fact that they are represented in ver. 6 as standing above the mountains. Accordingly, too, it is not to be interpreted after cvii. 26: they (the waters) rose mountain-high, they sunk down like valleys. The reference of the description to the coming forth of the dry land on the third day of creation requires that הָרִים should be taken as subject to יַעֲלוּ. But then, too, the בְּקָעוֹת are the subject to יֵרְדוּ, as Hilary of Poictiers renders it in his *Genesis*, v. 97, etc. : *subsidunt valles*, and not the waters as subsiding into the valleys. Hupfeld is correct ; ver. 8*a* is a parenthesis which affirms that, inasmuch as the waters retreating laid the solid land bare, mountains and valleys as such came forth visibly; cf. Ovid, *Metam.* i. 344:

Flumina subsidunt, montes exire videntur.

Ver. 8 continues with the words אֶל־מָקוֹם (cf. Gen. i. 9, אֶחָד): the waters retreat to the place which (זֶ, cf. ver. 26, for אֲשֶׁר, Gen. xxxix. 20) God has assigned to them as that which should contain them. He hath set a bound (גְּבוּל, synon. חֹק, Prov. viii. 29, Jer. v. 22) for them beyond which they may not flow forth again to cover the earth, as the primordial waters of chaos have done.

Vers. 10–14*b*. The third decastich, passing on to the third day of creation, sings the benefit which the shore-surrounded waters are to the animal creation and the growth of the plants out of the earth, which is irrigated from below and moistened from above. God, the blessed One, being the principal subject of the Psalm, the poet (in ver. 10 and further on) is able to go on in attributive and predicative participles: Who sendeth springs בַּנְּחָלִים, into the wadîs (not: בִּנְחָלִים, as brooks). נַחַל, as ver. 10*b* shows, is here a synonym of בִּקְעָה, and there is no need for saying that, flowing on in the plains, they grow into rivers. The LXX. has ἐν φάραγξιν. חַיְתוֹ שָׂדָי is doubly poetic for חַיַּת הַשָּׂדֶה. God has also provided for all the beasts that roam far from men; and the wild ass, swift as an arrow, difficult to be hunted, and living in troops (פֶּרֶא, Arabic *ferâ*, root פר, فر, to move quickly, to whiz, to flee; the wild ass, the *onager*, Arabic *ḥimâr el-waḥs*, whose home is on the steppes), is made prominent by way of example. The phrase "to break the thirst" occurs only here. עֲלֵיהֶם, ver. 12*a*, refers to the מַעְיָנִים, which are also still the subject in ver. 11*a*. The pointing עֳפָאיִם needlessly creates a hybrid form in addition to עֳפָאים (like לְבָאים) and עֳפָיִים. From the tangled branches by the springs the poet insensibly reaches the second half of the third day. The vegetable kingdom at the same time reminds him of the rain which, descending out of the upper chambers of the heavens, waters the waterless mountain-tops. Like the Talmud (*B. Ta'anîth*, 10*a*), by the "fruit of Thy work" (מעשׂיך as singular) Hitzig understands the rain; but rain is rather that which fertilizes; and why might not the fruit be meant which God's works (מעשׂיך, plural) here below (ver. 24), viz. the vegetable creations, bear, and from which the earth, *i.e.* its population, is satisfied, inasmuch as vegetable food springs up as much for the beasts as for man? In connection with עֵשֶׂב the poet is thinking of cultivated plants, more especially wheat; לַעֲבֹדַת, however, does not signify: *for cultivation by man*, since, according to Hitzig's correct remonstrance, they do not say עבד העשב, and להוציא has not man, but rather God, as its subject, but as in 1 Chron. xxvi. 30, *for the service* (use) *of man.*

Vers. 14*c*–18. In the fourth decastich the poet goes further among the creatures of the field and of the forest. The subject to לְהוֹצִיא is מַצְמִיחַ. The clause expressing the purpose, which twice begins with an infinitive, is continued in both instances, as in Isa. xiii. 9, but with a change of subject (cf. *e.g.* Amos i. 11, ii. 4), in the finite verb. On what is said of wine we may compare Eccles. x. 19, Sir. xl. 20, and more especially Isaiah, who frequently mentions wine as a representative of all the natural sources of joy. The assertion that מִשֶּׁמֶן signifies "before oil = brighter than oil," is an error that is rightly combated by Böttcher in his *Proben* and two of his "Gleanings,"* which imputes to the poet a mention of oil that is contrary to his purpose in this connection and inappropriate. Corn, wine, and oil are mentioned as the three chief products of the vegetable kingdom (Luther, Calvin, Grotius, Dathe, and Hupfeld), and are assumed under עֵשֶׂב in ver. 14*b*, as is also the case in other instances where distinction would be superfluous, *e.g.* in Ex. ix. 22. With oil God makes the countenance shining, or bright and cheerful, not by means of anointing,— since it was not the face but the head that was anointed (Matt. vi. 17),—but by the fact of its increasing the savouriness and nutritiveness of the food. לְהַצְהִיל is chosen with reference to יִצְהָר. In ver. 15*c* לְבַב־אֱנוֹשׁ does not stand after, as in ver. 15*a* (where it is לְבַב־ with *Gaja* on account of the distinctive), but before the verb, because לבב as that which is inward stands in antithesis to פנים as that which is outside. Since the fertilization of the earth by the rain is the chief subject of the predi-

---

cation in vers. 13–15, ver. 16 is naturally attached to what precedes without arousing critical suspicion. That which satisfies is here the rain itself, and not, as in ver. 13*b*, that which the rain matures. The "trees of Jahve" are those which before all others proclaim the greatness of their Creator. אֲשֶׁר־שָׁם refers to these trees, of which the cedars and then the cypresses (בְּרוֹשִׁים, root בר, to cut) are mentioned. They are places where small and large birds build their nests and lodge, more particularly the stork, which is called the חֲסִידָה as being πτηνῶν εὐσεβέστατον ζῷων (Babrius, *Fab.* xiii.), as *avis pia* (*pietaticultrix* in Petronius, lv. 6), *i.e.* on account of its love of family life, on account of which it is also regarded as bringing good fortune to a house.* The care of God for the lodging of His creatures leads the poet from the trees to the heights of the mountains and the hiding-places of the rocks, in a manner that is certainly abrupt and that disturbs the sketch taken from the account of the creation. הַגְּבֹהִים is an apposition. יָעֵל (Arabic *waʻil*) is the steinboc, wild-goat, as being an inhabitant of יָעֵל (*waʻl, waʻla*), *i.e.* the high places of the rocks, as יָעֵן, Lam. iv. 3, according to Wetzstein, is the ostrich as being an inhabitant of the *waʻna*, *i.e.* the sterile desert; and שָׁפָן is the rock-badger, which dwells in the clefts of the rocks (Prov. xxx. 26), and resembles the marmot—South Arabic تُفَّن, *Hyrax Syriacus* (distinct from the African). By שָׁפָן the Jewish tradition understands the coney, after which the Peshito here renders it לְחַגְסָא (חֲגַם, *cuniculus*). Both animals, the coney and the rock-badger, may be meant in Lev. xi. 5, Deut. xiv. 7; for the sign of the cloven hoof (פַּרְסָה שְׁסוּעָה) is wanting in both. The coney has four toes, and the *hyrax* has a peculiar formation of hoof, not cloven, but divided into several parts.

Vers. 19–23. The fifth decastich, in which the poet passes over from the third to the fourth day, shows that he has the

---

* In the *Merg'* district, where the stork is not called *leklek* as it is elsewhere, but *charnuk* on account of its bill like a long horn (خرن) standing out in front, the women and children call it أبو سعد, "bringer of good luck." Like the חסידה, the long-legged carrion-vulture (*Vultur percnopterus*) or mountain-stork, ὀρειπελαργός, is called רָחָם (رخم) on account of its στοργή.

order of the days of creation before his mind. The moon is mentioned first of all, because the poet wishes to make the picture of the day follow that of the night. He describes it in ver. 19 as the calendarial principal star. מוֹעֲדִים are points and divisions of time (epochs), and the principal measurer of these for civil and ecclesiastical life is the moon (cf. Sir. xliii. 7, ἀπὸ σελήνης σημεῖον ἑορτῆς), just as the sun, knowing when he is to set, is the infallible measurer of the day. In ver. 20 the description, which throughout is drawn in the presence of God in His honour, passes over into direct address: jussives (וִיהִי, תָּשֶׁת) stand in the hypothetical protasis and in its apodosis (Ew. § 357, *b*). It depends upon God's willing only, and it is night, and the wakeful life of the wild beasts begins to be astir. The young lions then roar after their prey, and *flagitaturi sunt a Deo cibum suum*. The infinitive with *Lamed* is an elliptical expression of a *conjugatio periphrastica* (*vid.* on Hab. i. 17), and becomes a varying expression of the future in general in the later language in approximation to the Aramaic. The roar of the lions and their going forth in quest of prey is an asking of God which He Himself has implanted in their nature. With the rising of the sun the aspect of things becomes very different. שֶׁמֶשׁ is feminine here, where the poet drops the personification (cf. Ps. xix.). The day which dawns with sunrise is the time for man. Both as to matter and style, vers. 21–23 call to mind Job xxiv. 5, xxxvii. 8, xxxviii. 40.

Vers. 24–30. Fixing his eye upon the sea with its small and great creatures, and the care of God for all self-living beings, the poet passes over to the fifth and sixth days of creation. The rich contents of this sixth group flow over and exceed the decastich. With מָה־רַבּוּ (not מַה־גָּדְלוּ, xcii. 6) the poet expresses his wonder at the great number of God's works, each one at the same time having its adjustment in accordance with its design, and all, mutually serving one another, co-operating one with another. קָנָה, which signifies both bringing forth and acquiring, has the former meaning here according to the predicate: full of creatures, which bear in themselves the traces of the Name of their Creator (קָנָה). Beside קִנְיָנֶיךָ, however, we also find the reading קִנְיָנֶךָ, which is adopted by Norzi, Heidenheim, and Baer, represented by the versions (LXX., Vulgate, and Jerome), by expositors (Rashi: קִנְיָן שֶׁלָּךְ), by the majority of the mss. (according to Norzi) and old printed copies, which would signify τῆς κτίσεώς σου, or according to the Latin versions κτήσεώς σου (*possessione tua*, Luther "thy possessions"), but is inferior to the plural κτισμάτων σου, as an accusative of the object to מְלָאָה. The sea more particularly is a world of moving creatures innumerable (lxix. 35). זֶה הַיָּם does not properly signify this sea, but that sea, yonder sea (cf. lxviii. 9, Isa. xxiii. 13, Josh. ix. 13). The attributes follow in an appositional relation, the looseness of which admits of the non-determination (cf. lxviii. 28, Jer. ii. 21, Gen. xliii. 14, and the reverse case above in ver. 18*a*). אֳנִיָּה in relation to אֳנִי is a *nomen unitatis* (the single ship). It is an old word, which is also Egyptian in the form *hani* and *ana*.* *Leviathan*, in the Book of Job, the crocodile, is in this passage the name of the whale (*vid*. Lewysohn, *Zoologie des Talmuds*, §§ 178–180, 505). Ewald and Hitzig, with the Jewish tradition, understand בּוֹ in ver. 26 according to Job xl. 29 [xli. 5]: in order to play with him, which, however, gives no idea that is worthy of God. It may be taken as an alternative word for שָׁם (cf. בוֹ in ver. 20, Job xl. 20): to play therein, viz. in the sea (Saadia). In כֻּלָּם, ver. 27, the range of vision is widened from the creatures of the sea to all the living things of the earth; cf. the borrowed passages cxlv. 15 sq., cxlvii. 9. כֻּלָּם, by an obliteration of the suffix, signifies directly "altogether," and בְּעִתּוֹ (cf. Job xxxviii. 32): when it is time for it. With reference to the change of the subject in the principal and in the infinitival clause, *vid*. Ew. § 338, *a*. The existence, passing away, and origin of all beings is conditioned by God. His hand provides everything; the turning of His countenance towards them upholds everything; and His breath, the creative breath, animates and renews all things. The spirit of life of every creature is the disposing of the divine Spirit, which hovered over the primordial waters and transformed the chaos into the cosmos. תֹּסֵף in ver. 29 is equivalent to תֶּאֱסֹף, as in 1 Sam. xv. 6, and frequently. The full future forms accented

---

* *Vide* Chabas, *Le papyrus magique Harris*, p. 246, No. 826: HANI (אנֹי), *vaisseau, navire*, and the *Book of the Dead* i. 10, where *hani* occurs with the determinative picture of a ship. As to the form *ana, vid*. Chabas *loc. cit.* p. 33.

on the *ultima*, from ver. 27 onwards, give emphasis to the statements. Job xxxiv. 14 sq. may be compared with ver. 29.

Vers. 31–35. The poet has now come to an end with the review of the wonders of the creation, and closes in this seventh group, which is again substantially decastichic, with a sabbatic meditation, inasmuch as he wishes that the glory of God, which He has put upon His creatures, and which is reflected and echoed back by them to Him, may continue for ever, and that His works may ever be so constituted that He who was satisfied at the completion of His six days' work may be able to rejoice in them. For if they cease to give Him pleasure, He can indeed blot them out as He did at the time of the Flood, since He is always able by a look to put the earth in a tremble, and by a touch to set the mountains on fire (וַתִּרְעָד of the result of the looking, as in Amos v. 8, ix. 6, and וַיֶּעֱשָׁנוּ of that which takes place simultaneously with the touching, as in cxliv. 5, Zech. ix. 5, cf. on Hab. iii. 10). The poet, however, on his part, will not suffer there to be any lack of the glorifying of Jahve, inasmuch as he makes it his life's work to praise his God with music and song (בְּחַיָּי as in lxiii. 5, cf. Bar. iv. 20, ἐν ταῖς ἡμέραις μου). Oh that this his quiet and his audible meditation upon the honour of God may be pleasing to Him (עָרֵב עַל synonymous with טוֹב עַל, but also שָׁפַר עַל, xvi. 6)! Oh that Jahve may be able to rejoice in him, as he himself will rejoice in his God! Between "I will rejoice," ver. 34, and "He shall rejoice," ver. 31, there exists a reciprocal relation, as between the Sabbath of the creature in God and the Sabbath of God in the creature. When the Psalmist wishes that God may have joy in His works of creation, and seeks on his part to please God and to have his joy in God, he is also warranted in wishing that those who take pleasure in wickedness, and instead of giving God joy excite His wrath, may be removed from the earth (יִתַּמּוּ, cf. Num. xiv. 35); for they are contrary to the purpose of the good creation of God, they imperil its continuance, and mar the joy of His creatures. The expression is not: may sins (חֲטָאִים, as it is meant to be read in *B. Berachoth*, 10a, and as some editions, *e.g.* Bomberg's of 1521, actually have it), but: may sinners, be no more, for there is no other existence of sin than the personal one.

With the words *Bless, O my soul, Jahve*, the Psalm recurs

to its introduction, and to this call upon himself is appended the *Hallelujah* which summons all creatures to the praise of God—a call of devotion which occurs nowhere out of the Psalter, and within the Psalter is found here for the first time, and consequently was only coined in the later age. In modern printed copies it is sometimes written הַלְלוּ־יָהּ, sometimes הַלְלוּ יָהּ, but in the earlier copies (*e.g.* Venice 1521, Wittenberg 1566) mostly as one word הַלְלוּיָהּ.* In the majority of MSS. it is also found thus as one word,† and that always with ה, except the first הַלְלוּיָהּ which occurs here at the

end of Ps. civ., which has ה *raphe* in good MSS. and old printed copies. This mode of writing is that attested by the Masora (*vid.* Baer's *Psalterium*, p. 132). The Talmud and Midrash observe this first Hallelujah is connected in a significant manner with the prospect of the final overthrow of the wicked. Ben-Pazzi (*B. Berachoth* 10a) counts 103 פרשיות up to this Hallelujah, reckoning Ps. i. and ii. as one פרשתא.

---

* More accurately הַלְלוּיָהּ with *Chateph*, as Jekuthiël ha-Nakdan expressly demands. Moreover the mode of writing it as one word is the rule, since the Masora notes the הַלְלוּ־יָהּ, occurring only once, in cxxxv. 3, with לית בטעם as being the only instance of the kind.

† Yet even in the Talmud (*J. Megilla* i. 9, *Sofrim* v. 10) it is a matter of controversy concerning the mode of writing this word, whether it is to be separate or combined; and in *B. Pesachim* 117a Rab appeals to a Psalter of the school of Chabibi (תילי דבי חביבי) that he has seen, in which הללו stood in one line and יה in the other. In the same place Rab Chasda appeals to a תילי דבי רב חנין that he has seen, in which the *Hallelujah* standing between two Psalms, which might be regarded as the close of the Psalm preceding it or as the beginning of the Psalm following it, was written in the middle between the two (באמצע פירקא). In the הללויה written as one word, יה is not regarded as strictly the divine name, only as an addition strengthening the notion of the הללו, as in במרחביה cxviii. 5; with reference to this, *vide* Geiger, *Urschrift*, S. 275.

PSALM CV.

THANKSGIVING HYMN IN HONOUR OF GOD WHO IS ATTESTED IN THE EARLIEST HISTORY OF ISRAEL.

1 GIVE thanks unto Jahve, publish His Name,
Make known among the peoples His deeds.
2 Sing unto Him, harp unto Him,
Speak of all His wondrous works.
3 Glory ye in His holy Name,
Let the heart of those rejoice who seek Jahve.
4 Follow after Jahve and His strength,
Seek ye His face evermore.
5 Remember His wondrous works which He hath done,
His rare deeds and the decisions of His mouth,
6 O seed of Abraham His servant,
Ye sons of Jacob, His chosen ones.

7 He, Jahve, is our God,
His judgments go forth over all lands.
8 He remembereth for ever His covenant,
The word which He hath established to a thousand generations,
9 Which He made with Abraham,
And His oath unto Isaac.
10 And He hath established it for Jacob as a statute,
For Israel as an everlasting covenant,
11 Saying : " Unto thee do I give the land of Canaan
As the line of your inheritance."

12 When they were a countable people,
Very small, and sojourning therein,
13 And went to and fro from nation to nation,
From one kingdom to another people :
14 He suffered no man to oppress them,
And He reproved kings for their sakes :
15 " Touch not Mine anointed ones,
And to My prophets do no harm ! "

16 Then He called up a famine over the land,
   Every staff of bread He brake.
17 He sent before them a man,
   As a slave was Joseph sold.
18 They hurt his feet with fetters,
   Iron came upon his soul,
19 Until the time that his word came,
   The word of Jahve had proved him.
20 The king sent and loosed him,
   The ruler of the peoples, and let him go free;
21 He made him lord of his house,
   And ruler over all his possession,
22 To bind his princes at his will,
   And to make his elders wiser.
23 Thus Israel came to Egypt,
   And Jacob sojourned in the land of Ham.
24 And He made His people fruitful exceedingly,
   And made them more powerful than their enemies.

25 He turned their heart to hate His people,
   To practise cunning on His servants;
26 He sent Moses His servant,
   Aaron, whom He had chosen.
27 They performed upon them facts of His signs,
   And strange things in the land of Ham.
28 He sent darkness and made it dark,
   And they rebelled not against His words;
29 He turned their waters into blood,
   And thus killed their fish.
30 Their land swarmed forth frogs
   In the chambers of their kings.
31 He spake, and the gad-fly came,
   Gnats in all their border.
32 He gave them as rain hail,
   Flaming fire in their land,
33 And He smote down their vines and fig-trees,
   And brake the trees of their border.
34 He spake, and the locusts came,
   And the grasshopper without number,

35 And devoured all the green herb in their land,
And devoured the fruit of their ground.
36 Then He smote all the first-born in their land,
The firstlings of all their strength,
37 And led them forth with silver and gold,
And there was no stumbling one among His tribes.
38 Egypt rejoiced at their departure,
For dread of them had fallen upon them.

39 He spread a cloud for a covering,
And fire to lighten the night;
40 They desired, and He brought quails,
And satisfied them with the bread of heaven;
41 He opened a rock, and waters gushed out,
They flowed through the steppes as a river.
42 For He remembered His holy word,
Abraham His servant;
43 And He led forth His people with gladness,
And with exulting His chosen ones;
44 And He gave them the lands of the heathen,
And that gained by the labour of the nations they in-
herited;
45 That they might observe His laws
And keep His instructions.
Hallelujah !

We have here another Psalm closing with *Hallelujah*, which opens the series of the *Hodu*-Psalms. Such is the name we give only to Psalms which begin with הודו (cv., cvii., cxviii., cxxxvi.), just as we call those which begin with הללויה (cvi., cxi.–cxiii., cxvii., cxxxv., cxlvi.–cl.) *Hallelujah*-Psalms (*alleluia-tici.*) The expression לְהַלֵּל וּלְהוֹדוֹת, which frequently occurs in the books of Chronicles, Ezra, and Nehemiah, points to these two kinds of Psalms, or at least to their key-notes.

The festival song which David, according to 1 Chron. xvi. 7, handed over to Asaph and his brethren for musical execution at the setting down of the Ark and the opening of divine service on Zion, is, so far as its first part is concerned (1 Chron. xvi. 8–22), taken from our Psalm (vers. 1–15), which is then followed by Ps. xcvi. as a second part, and is closed with Ps.

cvi. 1, 47, 48. Hitzig regards the festival song in the chronicler as the original, and the respective parallels in the Psalms as " layers or shoots." " The chronicler," says he, " there produces with labour, and therefore himself seeking foreign aid, a song for a past that is dead." But the transition from ver. 22 to ver. 23 and from ver. 33 to ver. 34, so devoid of connection, the taking over of the verse out of Ps. cvi. referring to the Babylonian exile into ver. 35, and even of the doxology of the Fourth Book, regarded as an integral part of the Psalm, into ver. 36, refute that perversion of the right relation, which has been attempted in the interest of the Maccabæan Psalms. That festival song in the chronicler, as has been shown again very recently by Riehm and Köhler, is a compilation of parts of songs already at hand, arranged for a definite purpose. Starting on the assumption that the Psalms as a whole are Davidic (just as all the Proverbs are Salomonic), because David called the poetry of the Psalms used in religious worship into existence, the attempt is made in that festival song to represent the opening of the worship on Zion at that time in strains belonging to the Davidic Psalms.

So far as the subject-matter is concerned, Ps. cv. attaches itself to the Asaph Psalm lxxviii., which recapitulates the history of Israel. The recapitulation here, however, is made not with any didactic purpose, but with the purpose of forming a hymn, and does not come down beyond the time of Moses and Joshua. Its source is likewise the Tôra as it now lies before us. The poet epitomizes what the Tôra narrates, and clothes it in a poetic garb.

Vers. 1–6. Invitation to the praise—praise that resounds far and wide among the peoples—of the God who has become manifest wondrously in the deeds and words connected with the history of the founding of Israel. הוֹדָה לָה׳, as in xxxiii. 2, lxxv. 2, of a praising and thankful confession offered to God ; קְרָא בְּשֵׁם ה׳, to call with the name of Jahve, *i.e.* to call upon it, of an audible, solemn attestation of God in prayer and in discourse (Symmachus, κηρύσσετε). The joy of heart *

---

* The *Mugrash* of יִשְׂמַח with the following *Legarme* seems here to be of equal value with *Zakeph*, 1 Chron. xvi. 10.

that is desired is the condition of a joyous opening of the
mouth and Israel's own stedfast turning towards Jahve, the
condition of all salutary result; for it is only His " strength"
that breaks through all dangers, and His " face" that lightens
up all darkness. מִשְׁפְּטֵי־פִיו, as ver. 7 teaches, are God's judicial
utterances, which have been executed without any hindrance,
more particularly in the case of the Egyptians, their Pharaoh,
and their gods. The chronicler has פִּיהוּ and זֶרַע יִשְׂרָאֵל, which
is so far unsuitable as one does not know whether עבדו is to
be referred to " Israel" the patriarch, or to the " seed of
Israel," the nation; the latter reference would be deutero-
Isaianic. In both texts the LXX. reads עֲבָדָיו (ye His servants).

Vers. 7–11. The poet now begins himself to do that to
which he encourages Israel. Jahve is Israel's God: His righteous rule extends over the whole earth, whilst His people
experience His inviolable faithfulness to His covenant. יהוה
in ver. 7a is in apposition to הוּא, for the God who bears this
name is as a matter of course the object of the song of
praise. זָכַר is the perfect of practically pledged certainty (cf.
cxi. 5, where we find instead the future of confident prospect).
The chronicler has זִכְרוּ instead (LXX. again something different : μνημονεύωμεν); but the object is not the demanding
but the promissory side of the covenant, so that consequently
it is not Israel's remembering but God's that is spoken of. He
remembers His covenant in all time to come, so that exile and
want of independence as a state are only temporary, exceptional conditions. צִוָּה has its radical signification here, to
establish, institute, cxi. 9. לְאֶלֶף דּוֹר (in which expression דור is
a specifying accusative) is taken from Deut. vii. 9. And since
דָּבָר is the covenant word of promise, it can be continued אֲשֶׁר
כָּרַת ; and Hagg. ii. 5 (vid. Köhler thereon) shows that אשר is
not joined to בריתו over ver. 8b. וּשְׁבוּעָתוֹ, however, is a second
object to זָכַר (since דָּבָר with what belongs to it as an apposition is out of the question). It is the oath on Moriah (Gen.
xxii. 16) that is meant, which applied to Abraham and his
seed. לְיִשְׂחָק (chronicler לְיִצְחָק), as in Amos vii. 9, Jer. xxxiii.
26. To זָכַר is appended וַיַּעֲמִידֶהָ; the suffix, intended as neuter,
points to what follows, viz. this, that Canaan shall be Israel's
hereditary land. From Abraham and Isaac we come to Jacob-
Israel, who as being the father of the twelve is the twelve-tribe

nation itself that is coming into existence; hence the plural can alternate with the singular in ver. 11. אֶת־אֶרֶץ כְּנַעַן (chronicler, without the אֵת) is an accusative of the object, and חֶבֶל נַחֲלַתְכֶם accusative of the predicate: the land of Canaan as the province of your own hereditary possession measured out with a measuring line (lxxviii. 55).

Vers. 12–15. The poet now celebrates the divine preservation which had sway over the small beginnings of Israel, when it made the patriarchs proof against harm on their wanderings. "Men of number" are such as can be easily counted, *vid.* the confessions in Gen. xxxiv. 30, Deut. xxvi. 5; וַיִּתְהַלְּכוּ places the claim upon the hospitality at one time of this people and at another time of that people in the connection with it of cause and effect. כִּמְעַט, as a small number, only such a small number, signifies, as being virtually an adjective: inconsiderable, insignificant, worthless (Prov. x. 20). בָּהּ refers to Canaan. In ver. 13 the way in which the words גּוֹי and עַם alternate is instructive: the former signifies the nation, bound together by a common origin, language, country, and descent; the latter the people, bound together by unity of government.* The apodosis does not begin until ver. 14. It is different in connection with בִּהְיוֹתְכֶם in the text of the chronicler, and in this passage in the Psalter of the Syriac version, according to which ver. 12 ought to be joined to the preceding group. The variation וממלכה instead of ממלכה is of no consequence; but לְאִישׁ (to any one whomsoever) instead of אָדָם, in connection with הניח, restores the current mode of expression (Eccles. v. 11, 2 Sam. xvi. 11, Hos. iv. 17) instead of one which is without support elsewhere, but which follows the model of נָתַן, נָטַשׁ, Gen. xxxi. 28 (cf. *supra* i. 274); whilst on the other hand וּבִנְבִיאַי instead of וְלִנְבִיאַי substitutes an expression that cannot be supported for the current one (Gen. xix. 9, Ruth i. 21). In ver. 14 the poet has the three histories of the preservation of

---

* For this reason a king says עַמִּי, not גּוֹיִי; and גּוֹי only occurs twice with a suffix, which refers to Jahve (cvi. 5, Zeph. ii. 9); for this reason גּוֹי, frequently side by side with עַם, is the nobler word, *e.g.* in Deut. xxxii. 21, Jer. ii. 11; for this reason עַם is frequently added to גּוֹי as a dignitative predicate, Ex. xxxiii. 13, Deut. iv. 6; and for this reason גּוֹיִם and עַם ה׳ are used antithetically.

the wives of the patriarchs in his mind, viz. of Sarah in Egypt (Gen. ch. xii.), and of Sarah and of Rebekah both in Philistia (ch. xx., xxvi., cf. especially xxvi. 11). In the second instance God declares the patriarch to be a " prophet" (ch. xx. 7). The one mention has reference to this and the other to Gen. ch. xvii., where Abram is set apart to be the father of peoples and kings, and Sarai to be a princess. They are called מְשִׁיחִים (a passive form) as being God-chosen princes, and נְבִיאִים (an intensive active form, from נְבָא, root נב, to divulge), not as being inspired ones (Hupfeld), but as being God's spokesmen (cf. Ex. vii. 1 sq. with iv. 15 sq.), therefore as being the recipients and mediators of a divine revelation.

Vers. 16–24. " To call up a famine" is also a prose expression in 2 Kings viii. 1. *To break the staff of bread* (*i.e.* the staff which bread is to man) is a very old metaphor, Lev. xxvi. 26. That the selling of Joseph was, providentially regarded, a " sending before," he himself says in Gen. xlv. 5. Ps. cii. 24 throws light upon the meaning of עָנָּה בְ. The *Keri* רַגְלוֹ is just as much without any occasion to justify it as עֵינוֹ in Eccles. iv. 8 (for עֵינָיו). The statement that iron came upon his soul is intended to say that he had to endure in iron fetters sufferings that threatened his life. Most expositors take בַּרְזֶל as equivalent to בְּבַרְזֶל, but Hitzig rightly takes נפשׁו as an object, following the Targum; for ברזל as a name of an iron fetter* can change its gender, as do, *e.g.*, צפון as a name of the north wind, and כבוד as a name of the soul. The imprisonment (so harsh at the commencement) lasted over ten years, until at last Joseph's word came to pass, viz. the word concerning his exaltation which had been revealed to him in dreams (Gen. xlii. 9). According to cvii. 20, דְּבָרוֹ appears to be the word of Jahve, but then one would expect from ver. 19*b* a more parallel turn of expression. What is meant is Joseph's open-hearted word

---

* Also in ancient Arabic فِرْزِل (after the Aramaic פִּרְזְלָא) directly signifies an iron fetter (and the large smith's shears for cutting the iron), whence the *verb. denom.* فَرْزَل *c. acc. pers.*, to put any one into iron chains. Iron is called בַּרְזֶל from בָּרַן, to pierce, like the Arabic حَدِيد, as being the material of which pointed tools are made.

concerning his visions, and אִמְרַת ה׳ is the revelation of God conveying His promises, which came to him in the same form, which had to try, to prove, and to purify him (צָרַף as in xvii. 3, and frequently), inasmuch as he was not to be raised to honour without having in a state of deep abasement proved a faithfulness that wavered not, and a confidence that knew no despair. The divine "word" is conceived of as a living effectual power, as in cxix. 50. The representation of the exaltation begins, according to Gen. xli. 14, with שָׁלַח־מֶלֶךְ,* and follows Gen. xli. 39–41, 44, very closely as to the rest, according to which בְּנַפְשׁוֹ is a collateral definition to לֶאְסֹר (with an orthophonic *Dag.*) in the sense of בִּרְצוֹנוֹ : by his soul, *i.e.* by virtue of his will (*vid. Psychology*, S. 202 ; tr. p. 239). In consequence of this exaltation of Joseph, Jacob-Israel came then into Egypt, and sojourned there as in a protecting house of shelter (concerning גּוּר, *vid. supra*, ii. 203). Egypt is called (vers. 23, 27) the land of *Chām*, as in lxxviii. 51 ; according to Plutarch, in the vernacular the black land, from the dark ashy grey colouring which the deposited mud of the Nile gives to the ground. There Israel became a powerful, numerous people (Ex. i. 7, Deut. xxvi. 5), greater than their oppressors.

Vers. 25–38. Narration of the exodus out of Egypt after the plagues that went forth over that land. Ver. 25 tells how the Egyptians became their " oppressors." It was indirectly God's work, inasmuch as He gave increasing might to His people, which excited their jealousy. The craft reached its highest pitch in the weakening of the Israelites that was aimed at by killing all the male children that were born. דִּבְרֵי signifies facts, instances, as in lxv. 4, cxlv. 5. Here, too, as in Ps. lxxviii., the miraculous judgments of the ten plagues do not stand in exactly historical order. The poet begins with the ninth, which was the most distinct self-representation of divine wrath, viz. the darkness (Ex. x. 21–29): *shā'lach chō'-shech*. The former word (שָׁלַח) has an orthophonic *Gaja* by

---

* Here שׁלח is united by *Makkeph* with the following word, to which it hurries on, whereas in ver. 28 it has its own accent, a circumstance to which the Masora has directed attention in the apophthegm : שלוחי דמלכא זריזין שלוחי דחשוכא מתינין (the emissaries of the king are in haste, those of darkness are tardy) ; *vid.* Baer, *Thorath Emeth*, p. 22.

the final syllable, which warns the reader audibly to utter the
guttural of the toneless final syllable, which might here be
easily slurred over. The *Hiph.* הֶחְשִׁיךְ has its causative signification here, as also in Jer. xiii. 16; the contracted mode of
writing with *i* instead of *î* may be occasioned by the *Waw convers.* Ver. 28*b* cannot be referred to the Egyptians; for the
expression would be a mistaken one for the final compliance,
which was wrung from them, and the interrogative way of
taking it: *nonne rebellarunt,* is forced: the cancelling of the לא,
however (LXX. and Syriac), makes the thought halting.
Hitzig proposes ולא שמרו: they observed not His words; but
this, too, sounds flat and awkward when said of the Egyptians.
The subject will therefore be the same as the subject of שָׂמוּ;
and of Moses and Aaron, in contrast to the behaviour at *Mê-
Merîbah* (Num. xx. 24, xxvii. 14; cf. 1 Kings xiii. 21, 26), it
is said that this time they rebelled not against the words (*Kerî,*
without any ground: the word) of God, but executed the
terrible commands accurately and willingly. From the ninth
plague the poet in ver. 29 passes over to the first (Ex. vii.
14–25), viz. the red blood is appended to the black darkness.
The second plague follows, viz. the frogs (Ex. vii. 26 [viii. 1]
–viii. 11 [15]); ver. 30*b* looks as though it were stunted, but
neither has the LXX. read any ויבאו (ויעלו), Ex. vii. 28. In
ver. 31 he next briefly touches upon the fourth plague, viz.
the gad-fly, עָרֹב, LXX. κυνόμυια (Ex. viii. 16–28 [20–32], *vid.*
on lxxviii. 45), and the third (Ex. viii. 12–15 [16–19]), viz. the
gnats, which are passed over in Ps. lxxviii. From the third
plague the poet in vers. 32, 33 takes a leap over to the seventh,
viz. the hail (Ex. ix. 13–35). In ver. 32 he has Ex. ix. 24
before his mind, according to which masses of fire descended
with the hail; and in ver. 33 (as in lxxviii. 47) he fills in the
details of Ex. ix. 25. The seventh plague is followed by the
eighth in vers. 34, 35, viz. the locust (Ex. x. 1–20), to which יֶלֶק
(the grasshopper) is the parallel word here, just as חָסִיל (the
cricket) is in lxxviii. 46. The expression of innumerableness
is the same as in civ. 25. The fifth plague, viz. the pestilence,
murrain (Ex. ix. 1–7), and the sixth, viz. שְׁחִין, boils (Ex. ix.
8–12), are left unmentioned; and the tenth plague closes, viz.
the smiting of the first-born (Ex. xi. 1 sqq.), which ver. 36
expresses in the Asaphic language of lxxviii. 51. Without

any mention of the institution of the Passover, the tenth plague is followed by the departure with the vessels of silver and gold asked for from the Egyptians (Ex. xii. 35, xi. 2, iii. 22). The Egyptians were glad to get rid of the people whose detention threatened them with total destruction (Ex. xii. 33). The poet here draws from Isa. v. 27, xiv. 31, lxiii. 13, and Ex. xv. 16. The suffix of שְׁבָטָיו refers to the chief subject of the assertion, viz. to God, according to cxxii. 4, although manifestly enough the reference to Israel is also possible (Num. xxiv. 2).

Vers. 39–45. Now follows the miraculous guidance through the desert to the taking possession of Canaan. The fact that the cloud (עָנָן, root עַן, to meet, to present itself to view, whence the Arabic 'ănăn, the visible outward side of the vault of heaven) by day, and becoming like fire by night, was their guide (Ex. xiii. 21), is left out of consideration in ver. 39a. With לְמָסָךְ we are not to associate the idea of a covering against foes, Ex. xiv. 19 sq., but of a covering from the smiting sun, for פָּרַשׂ (Ex. xl. 19), as in Isa. iv. 5 sq., points to the idea of a canopy. In connection with the sending of the quails the tempting character of the desire is only momentarily dwelt upon, the greater emphasis is laid on the omnipotence of the divine goodness which responded to it. שָׁאֲלוּ is to be read instead of שָׁאַל, the וּ before וַ having been overlooked; and the *Keri* writes and points שְׂלָיו (like סְתָיו, עֲנָיו) in order to secure the correct pronunciation, after the analogy of the plural termination ־ָיו. The bread of heaven (lxxviii. 24 sq.) is the manna. In ver. 41 the giving of water out of the rock at Rephidim and at Kadesh are brought together; the expression corresponds better to the former instance (Ex. xvii. 6, cf. Num. xx. 11). הָלְכוּ refers to the waters, and נָהָר for כִּנְהָרוֹת, lxxviii. 16, is, as in xxii. 14, an equation instead of a comparison. In this miraculous escort the patriarchal promise moves on towards its fulfilment; the holy word of promise, and the stedfast, proved faith of Abraham—these were the two motives. The second את is, like the first, a sign of the object, not a preposition (LXX., Targum), in connection with which ver. 42b would be a continuation of ver. 42a, dragging on without any parallelism. Joy and exulting are mentioned as the mood of the redeemed ones with reference to the festive joy displayed at the Red Sea and at Sinai. By ver. 43 one is reminded of the same descriptions of the antitype in Isaiah, ch. xxxv. 10, li. 11, lv. 12, just as ver. 41 recalls Isa. xlviii. 21. " The lands of the heathen" are the territories of the tribes of Canaan. עָמָל is equivalent to יְגִיעַ in Isa. xlv. 14 : the cultivated ground, the habitable cities, and the accumulated treasures. Israel entered upon the inheritance of these peoples in every direction. As an independent people upon ground that is theirs by inheritance, keeping the revealed law of their God, was Israel to exhibit the pattern of a holy nation moulded after the divine will; and, as the beginning of the Psalm shows, to unite the peoples to themselves and their God, the God of redemption, by the proclamation of the redemption which has fallen to their own lot.

PSALM CVI.

ISRAEL'S UNFAITHFULNESS FROM EGYPT ONWARDS, AND GOD'S FAITHFULNESS DOWN TO THE PRESENT TIME.

HALLELUJAH !
1 GIVE thanks unto Jahve, for He is good,
For His graciousness endureth for ever.
2 Who can utter the mighty acts of Jahve,
[Who] make all His praise to be heard?
3 Blessed are they who keep the right,
He who doeth righteousness at all times.
4 Remember me, Jahve, at the favouring of Thy people,
Visit me with Thy help,
5 That I too may see the prosperity of Thy chosen ones,
That I too may be glad at the gladness of Thy people,
That I too may glory with Thine inheritance.

6 We have sinned like unto our fathers,
We have committed iniquity, we have done wickedly.
7 Our fathers in Egypt heeded not Thy wonders,
They remembered not the abundance of Thy loving-kindnesses,
And were rebellious at the sea, at the Red Sea.

8 Yet He saved them for His Name's sake,
To make His strength known.
9 He rebuked the Red Sea, and it dried up,
And led them through the floods as upon a plain;
10 And He saved them out of the hand of the hater,
And redeemed them out of the hand of the enemy.
11 The waters covered their oppressors,
Not one of them was left—
12 Then they believed His words,
They sang His praise.

13 They quickly forgat His works,
They waited not for His counsel.
14 They lusted greedily in the desert,
And tempted God in the wilderness.
15 Then He gave them their desire,
And sent consumption into their soul.
16 They manifested envy against Moses in the camp,
Against Aaron, the holy one of Jahve—
17 The earth opened and swallowed up Dathan,
And covered the band of Abiram;
18 And fire seized upon their band,
A flame consumed the evil-doers.
19 They made a calf in Horeb,
Then they worshipped the molten image,
20 And they bartered their glory
For the likeness of an ox that eateth grass.
21 They had forgotten God their Saviour,
Who did great deeds in Egypt,
22 Wondrous works in the land of Ham,
Terrible deeds at the Red Sea.
23 Then He thought to exterminate them,
Had not Moses His chosen one
Stepped into the breach before Him
To calm His wrath, that He should not destroy.

24 They despised the pleasant land,
They believed not His word.
25 They murmured in their tents,
They hearkened not to the voice of Jahve.

26 Then He lifted up His hand against them
 To cast them down in the desert,
27 And to disperse their seed among the heathen,
 And to scatter them in the lands.
28 They joined themselves unto Baal-Peôr,
 And ate the sacrifices for the dead,
29 And excited provocation by their doings;
 And the plague brake in among them.
30 Then stood up Phinehas and arranged,
 And the plague was stayed.
31 And it was counted unto him for righteousness
 Unto all generations for ever.
32 Then they excited displeasure at the waters of strife,
 And it went ill with Moses for their sakes.
33 For they rebelled against God's Spirit,
 And he erred with his lips.

34 They did not exterminate the peoples
 Which Jahve had said to them;
35 But mixed themselves among the heathen,
 And learned their works.
36 They served their idols,
 And they became to them a snare.
37 They sacrificed their sons and their daughters to demons,
38 And shed innocent blood,
 The blood of their sons and their daughters,
 Whom they sacrificed to the idols of Canaan,
 So that the land was polluted by blood-guiltiness.
39 They became impure by their works,
 And became fornicators by their doings.
40 Then was the wrath of Jahve kindled against His
 people,
 And He abhorred His own inheritance.
41 He gave them over into the hand of the heathen,
 And their haters became their oppressors.
42 Their enemies oppressed them,
 And they were obliged to bow down under their hand.
43 Many times did He rescue them,
 Yet they rebelled in their self-will—
 Then they perished in their iniquity.

44 But He saw how hard it went with them,
    When He heard their cry of grief.
45 He remembered for them His covenant,
    And had compassion according to the abundance of His
        mercies.
46 And He caused them to be compassionated
    In the presence of all who carried them into captivity.
47 Save us, Jahve our God,
    And bring us together out of the heathen,
    To give thanks unto Thy holy Name,
    And to glory in Thy praise.
48 Blessed be Jahve the God of Israel from ever-
       lasting to everlasting,
    And let all people say Amen!
      Hallelujah!!

With this anonymous Psalm begins the series of the strictly Hallelujah-Psalms, *i.e.* of those Psalms which have הללריה for their arsis-like beginning and for their inscription (cvi., cxi.–cxiii., cxvii., cxxxv., cxlvi.–cl.). The chronicler in his cento, 1 Chron. xvi. 8 sqq., and in fact in ch. xvi. 34–36, puts the first and last verses of this Psalm (vers. 1, 47), together with the *Beracha* (ver. 48) which closes the Fourth Book of the Psalms, into the mouth of David, from which it is to be inferred that this Psalm is no more Maccabæan than Ps. xcvi. and cv. (which see), and that the Psalter was divided into five books which were marked off by the doxologies even in the time of the chronicler. The Beracha, ver. 48, appears even at that period to have been read as an integral part of the Psalm, according to liturgical usage. The Hallelujah Ps. cvi., like the Hodu Ps. cv. and the Asaph Ps. lxxviii., recapitulates the history of the olden times of the Israelitish nation. But the purpose and mode of the recapitulation differ in each of these three Psalms. In Ps. lxxviii. it is didactic; in Ps. cv. hymnic; and here in Ps. cvi. penitential. It is a penitential Psalm, or Psalm of confession, a וִדּוּי (from הִתְוַדָּה to confess, Lev. xvi. 21). The oldest types of such liturgical prayers are the two formularies at the offering of the first-fruits, Deut. ch. xxvi., and Solomon's prayer at the dedication of the Temple, 1 Kings ch. viii. And to this kind of *tephilla*, the *Vidduj*,

belong, beyond the range of the Psalter, the prayer of Daniel,
ch. ix. (*vid.* the way in which it is introduced in ver. 4), and
the prayer (Neh. ix. 5–x. 1 [ix. 38]) which eight Levites uttered
in the name of the people at the celebration of the fast-day
on the twenty-fourth of Tishri. It is true Ps. cvi. is distinguished from these prayers of confession in the prose style as
being a Psalm; but it has three points in common with them
and with the liturgical tephilla in general, viz. (1) the fondness for inflexional rhyming, *i.e.* for rhyming terminations
of the same suffixes; (2) the heaping up of synonyms; and
(3) the unfolding of the thoughts in a continuous line. These
three peculiarities are found not only in the liturgical border,
vers. 1–6, 47, but also in the middle historical portion, which
forms the bulk of the Psalm. The law of parallelism is, it is
true, still observed; but apart from these distichic wave-like
ridges of the thoughts, it is all one direct, straight-line flow
without technical division.

Vers. 1–5. The Psalm begins with the liturgical call,
which was not coined for the first time in the Maccabæan age
(1 Macc. iv. 24), but was already in use in Jeremiah's time
(ch. xxxiii. 11). The LXX. appropriately renders טוֹב by
χρηστός, for God is called " good" not so much in respect of
His nature as of the revelation of His nature. The fulness of
this revelation, says ver. 2 (like xl. 6), is inexhaustible. גְּבוּרוֹת
are the manifestations of His all-conquering power which
makes everything subservient to His redemptive purposes (xx.
7); and תְּהִלָּה is the glory (praise or celebration) of His self-
attestation in history. The proclaiming of these on the part
of man can never be an exhaustive echo of them. In ver. 3
the poet tells what is the character of those who experience
such manifestations of God; and to the assertion of the blessedness of these men he appends the petition in ver. 4, that God
would grant him a share in the experiences of the whole nation
which is the object of these manifestations. עַמֶּךָ beside בִּרְצוֹן
is a genitive of the object: with the pleasure which Thou
turnest towards Thy people, *i.e.* when Thou again (cf. ver. 47)
showest Thyself gracious unto them. On פָּקַד cf. viii. 5, lxxx.
15, and on רָאָה בְּ, Jer. xxix. 32; a similar *Beth* is that beside
לְשִׂמֹחַ (at, on account of, not: in connection with), xxi. 2, cxxii.

1. God's " inheritance" is His people ; the name for them is
varied four times, and thereby גּוֹי is also exceptionally brought
into use, as in Zeph. ii. 9.

Vers. 6–12. The key-note of the *vidduj*, which is a
settled expression since 1 Kings viii. 47 (Dan. ix. 5, cf. Bar.
ii. 12), makes itself heard here in ver. 6 ; Israel is bearing at
this time the punishment of its sins, by which it has made itself
like its forefathers. In this needy and helpless condition the
poet, who all along speaks as a member of the assembly, takes
the way of the confession of sin, which leads to the forgiveness
of sin and to the removal of the punishment of sin. רָשַׁע,
1 Kings viii. 47, signifies to be, and the *Hiph.* to prove one's
self to be, a רָשָׁע. עִם in ver. 6 is equivalent to *æque ac*, as in
Eccles. ii. 16, Job ix. 26. With ver. 7 the retrospect begins.
The fathers contended with Moses and Aaron in Egypt (Ex.
v. 21), and gave no heed to the prospect of redemption (Ex.
vi. 9). The miraculous judgments which Moses executed (Ex.
iii. 20) had no more effect in bringing them to a right state of
mind, and the abundant tokens of loving-kindness (Isa. lxiii. 7)
amidst which God redeemed them made so little impression on
their memories that they began to despair and to murmur even
at the Red Sea (Ex. xiv. 11 sq.). With עַל, ver. 7*b*, alternates בְּ
(as in Ezek. x. 15, בִּנְהַר) ; cf. the alternation of prepositions in
Joel iv. 8*b*. When they behaved thus, Jahve might have left
their redemption unaccomplished, but out of unmerited mercy
He nevertheless redeemed them. Vers. 8–11 are closely dependent upon Ex. ch. xiv. Ver. 11*b* is a transposition (cf.
xxxiv. 21, Isa. xxxiv. 16) from Ex. xiv. 28. On the other
hand, ver. 9*b* is taken out of Isa. lxiii. 13 (cf. Wisd. xix. 9) ;
Isa. lxiii. 7–lxiv. is a prayer for redemption which has a similar
ground-colouring. The sea through which they passed is called,
as in the Tôra, יַם־סוּף, which seems, according to Ex. ii. 3, Isa.
xix. 3, to signify the sea of reed or sedge, although the sedge
does not grow in the Red Sea itself, but only on the marshy
places of the coast ; but it can also signify the sea of sea-weed,
mare algosum, after the Egyptian *sippe*, wool and sea-weed
(just as صوف also signifies both these). The word is certainly
Egyptian, whether it is to be referred back to the Egyptian
word *sippe* (sea-weed) or *sēbe* (sedge), and is therefore used

after the manner of a proper name; so that the inference drawn
by Knobel on Ex. xiii. 18 from the absence of the article, that
סוּף is the name of a town on the northern point of the gulf, is
groundless. The miracle at the sea of sedge or sea-weed—as
ver. 12 says—also was not without effect. Ex. xiv. 31 tells us
that they believed on Jahve and Moses His servant, and the
song which they sang follows in Ex. ch. xv. But they then
only too quickly added sins of ingratitude.

Vers. 13–23. The first of the principal sins on the other
side of the Red Sea was the unthankful, impatient, unbelieving
murmuring about their meat and drink, vers. 13–15. For what
ver. 13 places foremost was the root of the whole evil, that,
falling away from faith in God's promise, they forgot the works
of God which had been wrought in confirmation of it, and did
not wait for the carrying out of His counsel. The poet has
before his eye the murmuring for water on the third day after
the miraculous deliverance (Ex. xv. 22–24) and in Rephidim
(Ex. xvii. 2). Then the murmuring for flesh in the first and
second years of the exodus which was followed by the sending
of the quails (Ex. ch. xvi. and Num. ch. xi.), together with the
wrathful judgment by which the murmuring for the second
time was punished (*Kibrôth ha-Ta'avah*, Num. xi. 33–35).
This dispensation of wrath the poet calls רָזוֹן (LXX., Vulgate,
and Syriac erroneously πλησμονήν, perhaps מָזוֹן, nourishment),
inasmuch as he interprets Num. xi. 33–35 of a wasting disease,
which swept away the people in consequence of eating inordi-
nately of the flesh, and in the expression (cf. lxxviii. 31) he
closely follows Isa. x. 16. The "counsel" of God for which
they would not wait, is His plan with respect to the time and
manner of the help. חִכָּה, root حَكَ, a weaker power of حَقّ,
whence also حَكَل, i. 180, حَكَم, i. 84 note, signifies prop. to
make firm, *e.g.* a knot (cf. on xxxiii. 20), and starting from this
(without the intervention of the metaphor *moras nectere*, as
Schultens thinks) is transferred to a firm bent of mind, and
the tension of long expectation. The epigrammatic expression
וַיִּתְאַוּוּ תַאֲוָה (plural of וַיִּתְאָו, xlv. 12, for which codices, as also in
Prov. xxiii. 3, 6, xxiv. 1, the Complutensian, Venetian 1521,
Elias Levita, and Baer have וַיִתְאָו without the tonic lengthening)
is taken from Num. xi. 4.

The second principal sin was the insurrection against their superiors, vers. 16–18. The poet has Num. ch. xvi. xvii. in his eye. The rebellious ones were swallowed up by the earth, and their two hundred and fifty noble, non-Levite partisans consumed by fire. The fact that the poet does not mention Korah among those who were swallowed up is in perfect harmony with Num. xvi. 25 sqq., Deut. xi. 6; cf. however Num. xxvi. 10. The elliptical תְּפְתַּח in ver. 17 is explained from Num. xvi. 32, xxvi. 10.

The third principal sin was the worship of the calf, vers. 19–23. The poet here glances back at Ex. ch. xxxii., but not without at the same time having Deut. ix. 8–12 in his mind; for the expression " in Horeb" is Deuteronomic, *e.g.* Deut. iv. 15, v. 2, and frequently. Ver. 20 is also based upon the Book of Deuteronomy: they exchanged their glory, *i.e.* the God who was their distinction before all peoples according to Deut. iv. 6–8, x. 21 (cf. also Jer. ii. 11), for the likeness (תַּבְנִית) of a plough-ox (for this is pre-eminently called שׁוֹר, in the dialects תּוֹר), contrary to the prohibition in Deut. iv. 17. On ver. 21*a* cf. the warning in Deut. vi. 12. " Land of Cham" = Egypt, as in lxxviii. 51, cv. 23, 27. With וַיֹּאמֶר in ver. 23 the expression becomes again Deuteronomic: Deut. ix. 25, cf. Ex. xxxii. 10. God made and also expressed the resolve to destroy Israel. Then Moses stepped into the gap (before the gap), *i.e.* as it were covered the breach, inasmuch as he placed himself in it and exposed his own life; cf. on the fact, besides Ex. ch. xxxii., also Deut. ix. 18 sq., x. 10, and on the expression, Ezek. xxii. 30 and also Jer. xviii. 20.

Vers. 24–33. The fact to which the poet refers in ver. 24, viz. the rebellion in consequence of the report of the spies, which he brings forward as the fourth principal sin, is narrated in Num. ch. xiii., xiv. The appellation אֶרֶץ חֶמְדָּה is also found in Jer. iii. 19, Zech. vii. 14. As to the rest, the expression is altogether Pentateuchal. " They despised the land," after Num. xiv. 31; "they murmured in their tents," after Deut. i. 27; "to lift up the hand" = to swear, after Ex. vi. 8, Deut. xxxii. 40; the threat לְהַפִּיל, to make them fall down, fall away, after Num. xiv. 29, 32. The threat of exile is founded upon the two great threatening chapters, Lev. xxvi., Deut. xxviii.; cf. more particularly Lev. xxvi. 33 (together with the echoes in

Ezek. v. 12, xii. 14, etc.), Deut. xxviii. 64 (together with the echoes in Jer. ix. 15, Ezek. xxii. 15, etc.). Ezek. xx. 23 stands in a not accidental relationship to ver. 26 sq.; and according to that passage, וּלְהַפִּיל is an error of the copyist for וּלְהָפִיץ (Hitzig).

Now follows in ver. 28–31 the fifth of the principal sins, viz. the taking part in the Moabitish worship of Baal. The verb נִצְמַד (to be bound or chained), taken from Num. xxv. 3, 5, points to the prostitution with which Baal Peôr, this Moabitish Priapus, was worshipped. The sacrificial feastings in which, according to Num. xxv. 2, they took part, are called eating the sacrifices of the dead, because the idols are dead beings (νεκροί, Wisd. xiii. 10–18) as opposed to God, the living One. The catena on Apoc. ii. 14 correctly interprets: τὰ τοῖς εἰδώλοις τελεσθέντα κρέα.* The object of "they made angry" is omitted; the author is fond of this, cf. vers. 7 and 32. The expression in ver. 29b is like Ex. xix. 24. The verb עָמַד is chosen with reference to Num. xvii. 13 [xvi. 48]. The result is expressed in ver. 30b after Num. xxv. 8, 18 sq., xvii. 13 [xvi. 48]. With פִּלֵּל, to adjust, to judge adjustingly (LXX., Vulgate, correctly according to the sense, ἐξιλάσατο), the poet associates the thought of the satisfaction due to divine right, which Phinehas executed with the javelin. This act of zeal for Jahve, which compensated for Israel's unfaithfulness, was accounted unto him for righteousness, by his being rewarded for it with the priesthood unto everlasting ages, Num. xxv. 10–13. This accounting of a work for righteousness is only apparently contradictory to Gen. xv. 5 sq.: it was indeed an act which sprang from a constancy in faith, and one which obtained for him the acceptation of a righteous man for the sake of this upon which it was based, by proving him to be such.

---

* In the second section of *Aboda zara*, on the words of the Mishna: "The flesh which is intended to be offered first of all to idols is allowed, but that which comes out of the temple is forbidden, because it is like sacrifices of the dead," it is observed, fol. 32b: "Whence, said R. Jehuda ben Bethêra, do I know that that which is offered to idols (תקרובת לעבודה זרה) pollutes like a dead body? From Ps. cvi. 28. As the dead body pollutes everything that is under the same roof with it, so also does everything that is offered to idols." The Apostle Paul declares the objectivity of this pollution to be vain, cf. more particularly 1 Cor. x. 28 sq.

In vers. 32, 33 follows the sixth of the principal sins, viz. the insurrection against Moses and Aaron at the waters of strife in the fortieth year, in connection with which Moses forfeited the entrance with them into the Land of Promise (Num. xx. 11 sq., Deut. i. 37, xxxii. 51), since he suffered himself to be carried away by the persevering obstinacy of the people against the Spirit of God (הִמְרָה mostly providing the future for מָרָה, as in vers. 7, 43, lxxviii. 17, 40, 56, of obstinacy against God; on אֶת־רוּחוֹ cf. Isa. lxiii. 10) into uttering the words addressed to the people, Num. xx. 10, in which, as the smiting of the rock which was twice repeated shows, is expressed impatience together with a tinge of unbelief. The poet distinguishes, as does the narrative in Num. ch. xx., between the obstinacy of the people and the transgression of Moses, which is there designated, according to that which lay at the root of it, as unbelief. The retrospective reference to Num. xxvii. 14 needs adjustment accordingly.

Vers. 34–43. The sins in Canaan: the failing to exterminate the idolatrous peoples and sharing in their idolatry. In ver. 34 the poet appeals to the command, frequently enjoined upon them from Ex. xxiii. 32 sq. onwards, to extirpate the inhabitants of Canaan. Since they did not execute this command (vid. Judg. ch. i.–iii. 6), that which it was intended to prevent came to pass: the heathen became to them a snare (מוֹקֵשׁ), Ex. xxiii. 33, xxxiv. 12, Deut. vii. 16. They intermarried with them, and fell into the Canaanitish custom in which the abominations of heathenism culminate, viz. the human sacrifice, which Jahve abhorreth (Deut. xii. 31), and only the demons (שֵׁדִים, Deut. xxxii. 17) delight in. Thus then the land was defiled by blood-guiltiness (חָנַף, Num. xxv. 33, cf. Isa. xxiv. 5, xxvi. 21), and they themselves became unclean (Ezek. xx. 43) by the whoredom of idolatry. In vers. 40–43 the poet (as in Neh. ix. 26 sqq.) sketches the alternation of apostasy, captivity, redemption, and relapse which followed upon the possession of Canaan, and more especially that which characterized the period of the judges. God's "counsel" was to make Israel free and glorious, but they leaned upon themselves, following their own intentions (בַּעֲצָתָם); wherefore they perished in their sins. The poet uses מָכַךְ (to sink down, fall away) instead of the נָמַק (to moulder, rot) of the primary pas-

sage, Lev. xxvi. 39, retained in Ezek. xxiv. 23, xxxiii. 10, which
is no blunder (Hitzig), but a deliberate change.

Vers. 44–46. The poet's range of vision here widens from
the time of the judges to the history of the whole of the succeeding age down to the present; for the whole history of
Israel has essentially the same fundamental character, viz. that
Israel's unfaithfulness does not annul God's faithfulness. That
verifies itself even now. That which Solomon in 1 Kings viii.
50 prays for on behalf of his people when they may be betrayed
into the hands of the enemy, has been fulfilled in the case of
the dispersion of Israel in all countries (cvii. 3), Babylonia,
Egypt, etc.: God has turned the hearts of their oppressors
towards them. On רָאָה בְ, to regard compassionately, cf. Gen.
xxix. 32, 1 Sam. i. 11. בַּצַּר לָהֶם belong together, as in cvii. 6,
and frequently. רִנָּה is a cry of lamentation, as in 1 Kings viii.
28 in Solomon's prayer at the dedication of the Temple. From
this source comes ver. 6, and also from this source ver. 46, cf.
1 Kings viii. 50 together with Neh. i. 11. In וַיִּנָּחֵם the drawing back of the tone does not take place, as in Gen. xxiv. 67.
חסדו beside כְּרֹב is not pointed by the *Kerî* חֲסָדוֹ, as in v. 8, lxix.
14, but as in Lam. iii. 32, according to ver. 7, Isa. lxiii. 7, חֲסָדָו:
in accordance with the fulness (riches) of His manifold mercy
or loving-kindness. The expression in ver. 46 is like Gen.
xliii. 14. Although the condition of the poet's fellow-countrymen in the dispersion may have been tolerable in itself, yet this
involuntary scattering of the members of the nation is always
a state of punishment. The poet prays in ver. 47 that God
may be pleased to put an end to this.

Ver. 47. He has now reached the goal, to which his whole
Psalm struggles forth, by the way of self-accusation and the
praise of the faithfulness of God. הִשְׁתַּבֵּחַ (found only here) is
the reflexive of the *Piel*, to account happy, Eccles. iv. 2, therefore: in order that we may esteem ourselves happy to be able
to praise Thee. In this reflexive (and also passive) sense
השתבח is customary in Aramaic and post-biblical Hebrew.

Ver. 48. The closing doxology of the Fourth Book. The
chronicler has וְאָמְרוּ before ver. 47 (which with him differs only
very slightly), an indispensable rivet, so to speak, in the fitting
together of cvi. 1 (cvii. 1) and cvi. 47. The means this
historian, who joins passages together like mosaic-work, calls

to his aid are palpable enough.   He has also taken over ver. 48 by transforming *and let all the people say Amen, Hallelujah!* in accordance with his style (cf. 1 Chron. xxv. 3, 2 Chron. v. 13, and frequently, Ezra iii. 11), into an historical clause: וַיֹּאמְרוּ כָל־הָעָם אָמֵן וְהַלֵּל לַיהוָה.   Hitzig, by regarding the echoes of the Psalms in the chronicler as the originals of the corresponding Psalms in the Psalter, and consequently 1 Chron. xvi. 36 as the original of the *Beracha* placed after our Psalm, reverses the true relation; *vid.* with reference to this point, Riehm in the *Theolog. Literat. Blatt*, 1866, No. 30, and Köhler in the *Luther. Zeitschrift*, 1867, S. 297 ff.   The priority of Ps. cvi. is clear from the fact that ver. 1 gives a liturgical key-note that was in use even in Jeremiah's time (ch. xxxiii. 11), and that ver. 47 reverts to the tephilla-style of the introit, vers. 4 sq.   And the priority of ver. 48 as a concluding formula of the Fourth Book is clear from the fact that it has been fashioned, like that of the Second Book (lxxii. 18 sq.), under the influence of the foregoing Psalm.   The *Hallelujah* is an echo of the Hallelujah-Psalm, just as there the *Jahve Elohim* is an echo of the Elohim-Psalm.   And "let all the people say Amen" is the same closing thought as in ver. 6 of Ps. cl., which is made into the closing doxology of the whole Psalter.   Ἀμὴν ἀλληλούϊα together (Apoc. xix. 4) is a laudatory confirmation.

FIFTH BOOK OF THE PSALTER

Ps. CVII.–CL.

PSALM CVII.

1 " GIVE thanks unto Jahve, for He is good,
   For His loving-kindness endureth for ever,"
2 Let the redeemed of Jahve say,
   Whom He hath redeemed out of the hand of oppression
3 And gathered out of the lands,
   From the east and from the west, from the north and
      from the sea.

4 They wandered in the desert in a waste of a way,
   They found not a city of habitation.
5 Under hunger and thirst
   Their soul fainted in them.
6 *Then they cried unto Jahve in their trouble—*
   Out of their distresses He delivered them,
7 And led them by a right way
   To arrive at a city of habitation.—
8 *Let them praise to Jahve His loving-kindness,*
   And His wonders to the children of men,
9 That He hath satisfied the thirsty soul,
   And filled the hungry soul with good.

10 Those who dwelt in darkness and the shadow of death,
   Being bound in torture and iron,
11 Because they rebelled against the words of God
   And derided the counsel of the Most High,

12 And He humbled their heart by labour,
They fell down, and there was none to help.
13 *Then they cried unto Jahve in their trouble—*
Out of their distresses He saved them;
14 He led them forth out of darkness and the shadow of death,
And burst their bonds asunder.
15 *Let them praise to Jahve His goodness,*
And His wonders to the children of men,
16 That He hath broken in pieces the brazen doors
And smitten down the iron bars.

17 The foolish, on account of the way of their transgression,
And on account of their iniquity, had to suffer.
18 All food their soul abhorred,
And they drew near to the gates of death.
19 *Then they cried unto Jahve in their trouble—*
Out of their distresses He saved them.
20 He sent His word and healed them,
And caused them to escape out of their pit-falls.
21 *Let them praise to Jahve His goodness,*
And His wonders to the children of men,
22 And let them sacrifice sacrifices of thanksgiving
And declare His works with a shout of joy.

23 Those who go down to the sea in ships,
Who do business in great waters—
24 These have seen the works of Jahve,
And His wonders in the deep.
25 He spake and raised a stormy wind,
Which forced up its waves on high.
26 They went up towards heaven, they went down into the
Their soul was melted in trouble.   [depths,
27 They whirled and staggered like a drunken man,
And all their wisdom came of itself to nought.
28 *Then they cried unto Jahve in their trouble,*
And out of their distresses He brought them forth.
29 He changed the storm into a gentle breeze,
And their waves were still.
30 Then were they glad that they were abated,
And He led them to the haven of their desire.

31 *Let them praise to Jahve His goodness,*
   And His wonders to the children of men,
32 And let them exalt Him in the congregation of the people,
   And praise Him in the council of the elders.

33 He changed rivers into a desert
   And water-springs into drought,
34 A fruitful land into a salt-plain,
   Because of the wickedness of those who dwelt therein.
35 He changed the desert into a pool of water,
   And the dry land into water-springs;
36 And made the hungry to dwell there,
   And they built a city of habitation.
37 They sowed fields and planted vineyards,
   And obtained profitable fruit.
38 He blessed them and they multiplied greatly,
   And their cattle He made into not a few.

39 Then they became few and were reduced
   By the pressure of misfortune and sorrow—
40 He who poureth contempt on princes
   And causeth them to wander in the pathless waste:
41 He removed the needy out of the way of affliction,
   And made the families like a flock.
42 The upright see it and rejoice,
   And all knavery stoppeth its mouth.

       *   *   *

43 Whoso is wise let him observe these things,
   And let them consider the loving-kindnesses of Jahve!

With this Psalm begins the Fifth Book, the Book אלה הדברים of the Psalter. With Ps. cvi. closed the Fourth Book, or the Book במדבר, the first Psalm of which, Ps. xc., bewailed the manifestation of God's wrath in the case of the generation of the desert, and in the presence of the prevailing death took refuge in God the eternal and unchangeable One. Ps. cvi., which closes the book, has בַּמִּדְבָּר (vers. 14, 26) as its favourite word, and makes confession of the sins of Israel on the way to Canaan. Now, just as at the beginning of the Book of Deuteronomy Israel stands on the threshold of the Land of

Promise, after the two tribes and a half have already established themselves on the other side of the Jordan, so at the beginning of this Fifth Book of the Psalter we see Israel restored to the soil of its fatherland. There it is the Israel redeemed out of Egypt, here it is the Israel redeemed out of the lands of the Exile. There the lawgiver once more admonishes Israel to yield the obedience of love to the Law of Jahve, here the psalmist calls upon Israel to show gratitude towards Him, who has redeemed it from exile and distress and death.

We must not therefore be surprised if Ps. cvi. and cvii. are closely connected, in spite of the fact that the boundary of the two Books lies between them. "Ps. cvii. stands in close relationship to Ps. cvi. The similarity of the beginning at once points back to this Psalm. Thanks are here given in ver. 3 for what was there desired in ver. 47. The praise of the Lord which was promised in Ps. cvi. 47 in the case of redemption being vouchsafed, is here presented to Him after redemption vouchsafed." This observation of Hengstenberg is fully confirmed. The Psalms civ.–cvii. really to a certain extent form a tetralogy. Ps. civ. derives its material from the history of the creation, Ps. cv. from the preparatory and early history of Israel, Ps. cvi. from the history of Israel in Egypt, in the desert, and in the Land of Promise down to the Exile, and Ps. cvii. from the time of the restoration.

Nevertheless the connection of Ps. civ. with cv.–cvii. is by far not so close as that of these three Psalms among themselves. These three anonymous Psalms form a trilogy in the strictest sense; they are a tripartite whole from the hand of one author. The observation is an old one. The *Harpffe Davids mit Teutschen Saiten bespannet* (Harp of David strung with German Strings), a translation of the Psalms which appeared in Augsburg in the year 1659, begins Ps. cvi. with the words: "For the third time already am I now come, and I make bold to spread abroad, with grateful acknowledgment, Thy great kindnesses." God's wondrous deeds of loving-kindness and compassion towards Israel from the time of their forefathers down to the redemption out of Egypt according to the promise, and giving them possession of Canaan, are the theme of Ps. cv. The theme of Ps. cvi. is the sinful conduct of Israel from Egypt onwards during the journey through the desert, and then in the

Land of Promise, by which they brought about the fulfilment
of the threat of exile (ver. 27) ; but even there God's mercy
was not suffered to go unattested (ver. 46). The theme of Ps.
cvii., finally, is the sacrifice of praise that is due to Him who
redeemed them out of exile and all kinds of destruction. We
may compare cv. 44, *He gave them the lands* (אֲרָצוֹת) *of the
heathen;* cvi. 27, (*He threatened*) *to cast forth their seed among
the heathen and to scatter them in the lands* (בָּאֲרָצוֹת) ; *and* cvii. 3,
out of the lands (מֵאֲרָצוֹת) *hath He brought them together, out of
east and west, out of north and south.* The designed similarity
of the expression, the internal connection, and the progression
in accordance with a definite plan, are not to be mistaken here.
In other respects, too, these three Psalms are intimately interwoven. In them Egypt is called " the land of Ham " (cv. 23,
27, cvi. 22), and Israel " the chosen ones of Jahve " (cv. 6, 43,
cvi. 5, cf. 23). They are fond of the interrogative form of
exclamation (cvi. 2, cvii. 43). There is an approach in them
to the hypostatic conception of the Word (דָּבָר, cv. 19, cvi. 20).
Compare also יְשִׂימוֹן cvi. 14, cvii. 4 ; and the *Hithpa.* הִתְהַלֵּל cv.
3, cvi. 5, הִשְׁתַּבַּח cvi. 47, הִתְבַּלָּע cvii. 27. In all three the poet
shows himself to be especially familiar with Isa. ch. xl.–lxvi.,
and also with the Book of Job. Ps. cvii. is the fullest in reminiscences taken from both these Books, and in this Psalm
the movement of the poet is more free without recapitulating
history that has been committed to writing. Everything therefore favours the assertion that Ps. cv., cvi., and cvii. are a
" trefoil " (*trifolium*),—two Hodu-Psalms, and a Hallelujah-
Psalm in the middle.

Ps. cvii. consists of six groups with an introit, vers. 1–3,
and an epiphonem, ver. 43. The poet unrolls before the dispersion of Israel that has again attained to the possession of
its native land the pictures of divine deliverances in which
human history, and more especially the history of the exiles, is
so rich. The epiphonem at the same time stamps the hymn as
a consolatory Psalm ; for those who were gathered again out
of the lands of the heathen nevertheless still looked for the
final redemption under the now milder, now more despotic
sceptre of the secular power.

Vers. 1–3. The introit, with the call upon them to grateful

praise, is addressed to the returned exiles. The Psalm carries
the marks of its deutero-Isaianic character on the very front of
it, viz. : " the redeemed of Jahve," taken from Isa. lxii. 12, cf.
lxiii. 4, xxxv. 9 sq. ; קִבֵּץ as in Isa. lvi. 8, and frequently ; "from
the north and from the sea," as in Isa. xlix. 12 : " the sea" (יָם)
here (as perhaps there also), side by side with east, west, and
north, is the south, or rather (since יָם is an established *usus
loquendi* for the west) the south-west, viz. the southern portion
of the Mediterranean washing the shores of Egypt. With this
the poet associates the thought of the exiles of Egypt, as with
וּמִמַּעֲרָב the exiles of the islands, *i.e.* of Asia Minor and Europe ;
he is therefore writing at a period in which the Jewish state
newly founded by the release of the Babylonian exiles had
induced the scattered fellow-countrymen in all countries to
return home. Calling upon the redeemed ones to give thanks
to God the Redeemer in order that the work of the restoration
of Israel may be gloriously perfected amidst the thanksgiving
of the redeemed ones, he forthwith formulates the thanksgiving by putting the language of thanksgiving of the ancient
liturgy (Jer. xxxiii. 11) into their mouth. The nation, now
again established upon the soil of the fatherland, has, until it
had acquired this again, seen destruction in every form in a
strange land, and can tell of the most manifold divine deliverances. The call to sacrifice the sacrifices of thanksgiving
is expanded accordingly into several pictures portraying the
dangers of the strange land, which are not so much allegorical,
personifying the Exile, as rather exemplificative.

Vers. 4–9. It has actually come to pass, the first strophe
tells us, that they wandered in a strange land through deserts
and wastes, and seemed likely to have to succumb to death
from hunger. According to ver. 40 and Isa. xliii. 19, it appears
that ver. 4a ought to be read לֹא־דֶרֶךְ (Olshausen, Baur, and
Thenius) ; but the line is thereby lengthened inelegantly. The
two words, joined by *Munach*, stand in the construct state, like
פֶּרֶא אָדָם, Gen. xvi. 12 : a waste of a way = ἔρημος ὁδός, Acts
viii. 26 (Ewald, Hitzig), which is better suited to the poetical
style than that דֶּרֶךְ, as in מִשְׁנֶה־כֶּסֶף, and the like, should be an
accusative of nearer definition (Hengstenberg). In connection
with עִיר מוֹשָׁב the poet, who is fond of this combination (vers.
7, 36, cf. בֵּית־מוֹשָׁב, Lev. xxv. 29), means any city whatever

which might afford the homeless ones a habitable, hospitable reception. With the perfects, which describe what has been experienced, alternates in ver. 5*b* the imperfect, which shifts to the way in which anything comes about : their soul in them enveloped itself (*vid.* lxi. 3), *i.e.* was nigh upon extinction. With the *fut. consec.* then follows in ver. 6 the fact which gave the turn to the change in their misfortune. Their cry for help, as the imperfect יַצִּילֵם implies, was accompanied by their deliverance, the fact of which is expressed by the following *fut. consec.* וַיַּדְרִיכֵם. Those who have experienced such things are to confess to the Lord, with thanksgiving, His loving-kindness and His wonderful works to the children of men. It is not to be rendered : His wonders (supply אֲשֶׁר עָשָׂה) *towards* the children of men (Luther, Olshausen, and others). The two לְ coincide : their thankful confession of the divine loving-kindness and wondrous acts is not to be addressed alone to Jahve Himself, but also to men, in order that out of what they have experienced a wholesome fruit may spring forth for the multitude. נֶפֶשׁ שֹׁקֵקָה (*part. Polel*, the *ē* of which is retained as a pre-tonic vowel in pause, cf. lxviii. 26 and on Job xx. 27, Ew. § 188, *b*) is, as in Isa. xxix. 9, the thirsting soul (from שׁוּק, ساق, to urge forward, of the impulse and drawing of the emotions, in Hebrew to desire ardently). The preterites are here an expression of that which has been experienced, and therefore of that which has become a fact of experience. In superabundant measure does God uphold the languishing soul that is in imminent danger of languishing away.

Vers. 10–16. Others suffered imprisonment and bonds ; but through Him who had decreed this as punishment for them, they also again reached the light of freedom. Just as in the first strophe, here too, as far as יוֹדוּ in ver. 15, is all a compound subject ; and in view of this the poet begins with participles. " Darkness and the shadow of death" (*vid.* xxiii. 4) is an Isaianic expression, Isa. ix. 1 (where יֹשְׁבֵי is construed with בְּ), xlii. 7 (where יֹשְׁבֵי is construed as here, cf. Gen. iv. 20, Zech. ii. 11), just as " bound in torture and iron" takes its rise from Job xxxvi. 8. The old expositors call it a hendiadys for " torturing iron" (after cv. 18) ; but it is more correct to take the one as the general term and the other as the particular :

bound in all sorts of affliction from which they could not break away, and more particularly in iron bonds (בַּרְזֶל, like the Arabic *firzil*, an iron fetter, *vid.* on cv. 18). In ver. 11, which calls to mind Isa. v. 19, and with respect to ver. 12, Isa. iii. 8, the double play upon the sound of the words is unmistakeable. By עֵצָה is meant the plan in accordance with which God governs, more particularly His final purpose, which lies at the basis of His leadings of Israel. Not only had they nullified this purpose of mercy by defiant resistance (הִמְרָה) against God's commandments (אִמְרֵי, Arabic *awâmir, âmireh*) on their part, but they had even blasphemed it; נָאַץ, Deut. xxxii. 19, and frequently, or נָאַץ (prop. to pierce, then to treat roughly), is an old Mosaic designation of blasphemy, Deut. xxxi. 20, Num. xiv. 11, 23, xvi. 30. Therefore God thoroughly humbled them by afflictive labour, and caused them to stumble (כָּשַׁל). But when they were driven to it, and prayed importunately to Him, He helped them out of their straits. The refrain varies according to recognised custom. Twice the expression is ויצעקו, twice ויזעקו; once יצילם, then twice יושיעם, and last of all יוציאם, which follows here in ver. 14 as an alliteration. The summary condensation of the deliverance experienced (ver. 16) is moulded after Isa. xlv. 2. The Exile, too, may be regarded as such like a large jail (*vid. e.g.* Isa. xlii. 7, 22); but the descriptions of the poet are not pictures, but examples.

Vers. 17–22. Others were brought to the brink of the grave by severe sickness; but when they draw nigh in earnest prayer to Him who appointed that they should suffer thus on account of their sins, He became their Saviour. אֱוִיל (cf. *e.g.* Job v. 3), like נָבָל (*vid.* xiv. 1), is also an ethical notion, and not confined to the idea of defective intellect merely. It is one who insanely lives only for the passing hour, and ruins health, calling, family, and in short himself and everything belonging to him. Those who were thus minded, the poet begins by saying, were obliged to suffer by reason of (in consequence of) their wicked course of life. The cause of their days of pain and sorrow is placed first by way of emphasis; and because it has a meaning that is related to the past יִתְעַנּוּ thereby comes all the more easily to express that which took place simultaneously in the past. The *Hithpa.* in 1 Kings ii. 26 signifies to suffer willingly or intentionally; here: to be

obliged to submit to suffering against one's will. Hengstenberg, for example, construes it differently : " Fools because of
their walk in transgression (more than ' because of their transgression'), and those who because of their iniquities were
afflicted—all food," etc. But מִן beside יִתְעַנּוּ has the assumption in its favour of being an affirmation of the cause of the
affliction. In ver. 18 the poet has the Book of Job (ch. xxxiii.
20, 22) before his eye. And in connection with ver. 20, ἀπέστειλεν τὸν λόγον αὐτοῦ καὶ ἰάσατο αὐτούς (LXX.), no passage
of the Old Testament is more vividly recalled to one's mind
than cv. 19, even more than cxlvii. 18 ; because here, as in cv.
19, it treats of the intervention of divine acts within the sphere
of human history, and not of the intervention of divine operations within the sphere of the natural world. In the natural
world and in history the word (דְּבָר) is God's messenger (cv. 19,
cf. Isa. lv. 10 sq.), and appears here as a mediator of the divine
healing. Here, as in Job xxxiii. 23 sq., the fundamental fact
of the New Testament is announced, which Theodoret on this
passage expresses in the words : Ὁ Θεὸς Λόγος ἐνανθρωπήσας
καὶ ἀποσταλεὶς ὡς ἄνθρωπος τὰ παντοδαπὰ τῶν ψυχῶν ἰάσατο
τραύματα καὶ τοὺς διαφθαρέντας ἀνέρρωσε λογισμούς. The
LXX. goes on to render it : καὶ ἐρρύσατο αὐτοὺς ἐκ τῶν
διαφθορῶν αὐτῶν, inasmuch as the translators derive שְׁחִיתוֹתָם
from שְׁחִיתָה (Dan. vi. 5), and this, as שַׁחַת elsewhere (vid. xvi.
10), from שַׁחַת, διαφθείρειν, which is approved by Hitzig. But
Lam. iv. 20 is against this. From שָׁחָה is formed a noun שְׁחוּת
(שִׁחוּת) in the signification a hollow place (Prov. xxviii. 10), the
collateral form of which, שְׁחִית (שִׁחִית), is inflected like חֲנִית, plur.
חֲנִיתוֹת with a retention of the substantival termination. The
" pits " are the deep afflictions into which they were plunged,
and out of which God caused them to escape. The suffix of
וִירַפְּאֵם avails also for יְמַלֵּט, as in Gen. xxvii. 5, xxx. 31, Ps.
cxxxix. 1, Isa. xlvi. 5.

Vers. 23–32. Others have returned to tell of the perils of
the sea. Without any allegory (Hengstenberg) it speaks of
those who by reason of their calling traverse (which is expressed
by יָרַד because the surface of the sea lies below the dry land
which slopes off towards the coast) the sea in ships (read
boŏnijoth without the article), and that not as fishermen, but
(as Luther has correctly understood the choice of the word) in

commercial enterprises. These have seen the works and wonders of God in the eddying deep, *i.e.* they have seen with their own eyes what God can do when in His anger He calls up the powers of nature, and on the other hand when He compassionately orders them back into their bounds. God's mandate (וַיֹּאמֶר as in cv. 31, 34) brought it to pass that a stormy wind arose (cf. עָמַד, xxxiii. 9), and it drove its (the sea's) waves on high, so that the seafarers at one time were tossed up to the sky and then hurled down again into deep abysses, and their soul melted בְּרָעָה, in an evil, anxious mood, *i.e.* lost all its firmness. They turned about in a circle (יָחוֹגּוּ from חָגַג = חוג) and reeled after the manner of a drunken man; all their wisdom swallowed itself up, *i.e.* consumed itself within itself, came of itself to nought, just as Ovid, *Trist.* i. 2, says in connection with a similar description of a storm at sea: *ambiguis ars stupet ipsa malis.* The poet here writes under the influence of Isa. xix. 3, cf. 14. But at their importunate supplication God led them forth out of their distresses (xxv. 17). He turned the raging storm into a gentle blowing (= דְּמָמָה דַקָּה, 1 Kings xix. 12). הֵקִים construed with לְ here has the sense of transporting (carrying over) into another condition or state, as Apollinaris renders: αὐτίκα δ᾽ εἰς αὔρην προτέρην μετέθηκε θύελλαν. The suffix of גַּלֵּיהֶם cannot refer to the מַיִם רַבִּים in ver. 23, which is so far removed; "their waves" are those with which they had to battle. These to their joy became calm (חָשָׁה) and were still (שָׁתַק as in Jonah i. 11), and God guided them ἐπὶ λιμένα θελήματος αὐτῶν (LXX.). מָחוֹז, a hapax-legomenon, from حاز (حوز), to shut in on all sides and to draw to one's self (root حوز, *gyravit, in gyrum egit*), signifies a place enclosed round, therefore a haven, and first of all perhaps a creek, to use a northern word, a fiord. The verb שָׁתַק in relation to חָשָׁה is the stronger word, like יָבֵשׁ in relation to חָרַם in the history of the Flood. Those who have been thus marvellously rescued are then called upon thankfully to praise God their Deliverer in the place where the national church assembles, and where the chiefs of the nation sit in council; therefore, as it seems, in the Temple and in the Forum.*

------

* In exact editions like Norzi, Heidenheim, and Baer's, before vers. 23,

Now follow two more groups without the two beautiful and
impressive refrains with which the four preceding groups are
interspersed.   The structure is less artistic, and the transitions
here and there abrupt and awkward.   One might say that these
two groups are inferior to the rest, much as the speeches of
Elihu are inferior to the rest of the Book of Job.   That they
are, however, nevertheless from the hand of the very same poet
is at once seen from the continued dependence upon the Book
of Job and Isaiah.   Hengstenberg sees in vers. 33–42 "the
song with which they exalt the Lord in the assembly of the
people and upon the seat of the elders."   But the *materia laudis*
is altogether different from that which is to be expected according to the preceding calls to praise.   Nor is it any the more
clear to us that vers. 33 sq. refer to the overthrow of Babylon,
and vers. 35 sqq. to the happy turn of affairs that took place
simultaneously for Israel; ver. 35 does not suit Canaan, and
the expressions in vers. 36 sq. would be understood in too low a
sense.   No, the poet goes on further to illustrate the helpful
government of God the just and gracious One, inasmuch as he
has experiences in his mind in connection therewith, of which
the dispersion of Israel in all places can sing and speak.

Vers. 33–38.   Since in ver. 36 the historical narration is
still continued, a meaning relating to the cotemporaneous past
is also retrospectively given to the two correlative יָשֵׂם.   It now
goes on to tell what those who have now returned have observed
and experienced in their own case.   Ver. 33a sounds like Isa.
l. 2b; ver. 33b like Isa. xxxv. 7a; and ver. 35 takes its rise
from Isa. xli. 18b.   The juxtaposition of מוֹצָאֵי and צִמָּאוֹן, since
Deut. viii. 15, belongs to the favourite antithetical alliterations,
e.g. Isa. lxi. 3.   מְלֵחָה, that which is salty (LXX. cf. Sir. xxxix.
23 : ἅλμη), is, as in Job xxxix. 6, the name for the uncultivated,
barren steppe.   A land that has been laid waste for the punishment of its inhabitants has very often been changed into
flourishing fruitful fields under the hands of a poor and grateful generation; and very often a land that has hitherto lain
uncultivated and to all appearance absolutely unprofitable has

---

24, 25, 26, 27, 28, and 40 there stand reversed *Nuns* (נונין הפוכין, in the
language of the Masora נונין מנוזרות), as before Num. x. 35 and between
x. 36 and xi. 1 (nine in all).   Their signification is unknown.

developed an unexpected fertility. The exiles to whom Jeremiah writes, ch. xxix. 5 : *Build ye houses and settle down, and plant gardens and eat their fruit,* may frequently have experienced this divine blessing. Their industry and their knowledge also did their part, but looked at in a right light, it was not their own work but God's work that their settlement prospered, and that they continually spread themselves wider and possessed a not small, *i.e.* (cf. 2 Kings iv. 3) a very large, stock of cattle.

Vers. 39–43. But it also came to pass that it went ill with them, inasmuch as their flourishing prosperous condition drew down upon them the envy of the powerful and tyrannical; nevertheless God put an end to tyranny, and always brought His people again to honour and strength. Hitzig is of opinion that ver. 39 goes back into the time when things were different with those who, according to vers. 36–38, had thriven. The *modus consecutivus* is sometimes used thus retrospectively (*vid.* Isa. xxxvii. 5) ; here, however, the symmetry of the continuation from vers. 36–38, and the change which is expressed in ver. 39*a* in comparison with ver. 38*b*, require an actual consecution in that which is narrated. They became few and came down, were reduced (שָׁחַח, cf. Prov. xiv. 19 : to come to ruin, or to be overthrown), *a coarctatione malitiæ et mœroris.* עֹצֶר is the restraint of despotic rule, רָעָה the evil they had to suffer under such restraint, and יָגוֹן sorrow, which consumed their life. מעצר has *Tarcha* and רעה *Munach* (instead of *Mercha* and *Mugrash, vid. Accentuationssystem,* xviii. 2). There is no reason for departing from this interpunction and rendering : " through tyranny, evil, and sorrow." What is stiff and awkward in the progress of the description arises from the fact that ver. 40 is borrowed from Job xii. 21, 24, and that the poet is not willing to make any change in these sublime words. The version shows how we think the relation of the clauses is to be apprehended. Whilst He pours out His wrath upon tyrants in the contempt of men that comes upon them, and makes them fugitives who lose themselves in the terrible waste, He raises the needy and those hitherto despised and ill-treated on high out of the depth of their affliction, and makes families like a flock, *i.e.* makes their families so increase, that they come to have the appearance of a merrily gamboling and numerous flock. Just as this figure points back to Job xxi. 11, so ver. 42 is made up out of Job xxii. 19, v. 16. The sight of this act of recognition on the part of God of those who have been wrongfully oppressed gives joy to the upright, and all roguery (עַוְלָה, *vid.* xcii. 16) has its mouth closed, *i.e.* its boastful insolence is once for all put to silence. In ver. 43 the poet makes the strains of his Psalm die away after the example of Hosea, ch. xiv. 10 [9], in the *nota bene* expressed after the manner of a question : Who is wise—he will or let him keep this, *i.e.* bear it well in mind. The transition to the jussive together with a change of number is rendered natural by the fact that מִי חָכָם, as in Hos. *loc. cit.* (cf. Jer. ix. 11, Esth. v. 6, and without *Waw apod.* Judg. vii. 3, Prov. ix. 4, 16), is equivalent to *quisquis sapiens est.* חַסְדֵי ה׳ (חַסְדֵי) are the manifestations of mercy or loving-kindness in which God's ever-enduring mercy unfolds itself in history. He who is wise has a good memory for and a clear understanding of this.

PSALM CVIII.

TWO ELOHIMIC FRAGMENTS BROUGHT TOGETHER.

2 CONFIDENT is my heart, Elohim,
  I will sing and play upon the harp,
  Yea, this shall my glory do.
3 Awake up, O harp and cithern,
  I will awake the morning dawn !

4 I will praise Thee among the peoples, Jahve,
  And praise Thee upon the harp among the nations.
5 For great beyond the heavens is Thy mercy, Elohim,
  And unto the clouds Thy truth.
6 Oh show Thyself exalted above the heavens, Elohim,
  And above the whole earth Thy glory !

7 In order that Thy beloved may be delivered—
  Save now with Thy right hand and answer me !

8 Elohim hath promised in His holiness :

I shall rejoice, I shall portion out Shechem,
And measure out the valley of Succoth.
9 Mine is Gilead, mine Manasseh,
And Ephraim is the helm of my head,
Judah is my sceptre,
10 Moab is my wash-pot,
Upon Edom I cast my shoe,
Over Philistia I shout for joy.

11 Who will conduct me to the fortified city,
Who will bring me to Edom?!
12 Hast not Thou, Elohim, cast us off,
And goest not forth, Elohim, with our armies?—
13 Grant us deliverance from the oppressor,
Yea, vain is the help of man.
14 In Elohim shall we obtain the victory,
And HE will tread down our oppressors.

The אוֹדְךָ in ver. 4 and the whole contents of this Psalm
is the echo to the הוֹדוּ of the preceding Psalm. It is inscribed
a *Psalm-song by David*, but only because it is compiled out of
ancient Davidic materials. The fact of the absence of the
למנצח makes it natural to suppose that it is of later origin.
Two Davidic Psalm-pieces in the Elohimic style are here, with
trifling variations, just put together, not soldered together, and
taken out of their original historical connection. That a poet
like David would thus compile a third out of two of his own
songs (Hengstenberg) is not conceivable.

Vers. 2–6. This first half is taken from Ps. lvii. 8–12.
The repetition of *confident is my heart* in Ps. lvii. is here
omitted; and in place of it the " my glory" of the exclamation, *awake my glory*, is taken up to "I will sing and will harp"
as a more minute definition of the subject (*vid.* on iii. 5): He
will do it, yea, his soul with all its godlike powers shall do it.
Jahve in ver. 4 is transformed out of the *Adonaj*; and *Waw
copul.* is inserted both before ver. 4*b* and ver. 6*b*, contrary to
Ps. lvii. מֵעַל, ver. 5*a* (as in Esth. iii. 1), would be a pleasing
change for עַד if ver. 5*a* followed 5*b* and the definition of
magnitude did not retrograde instead of heightening. More-

over xxxvi. 6, Jer. li. 9 (cf. עַל in cxiii. 4, cxlviii. 13) favour עַד in opposition to מֵעַל.

Vers. 7–14. Ps. lx. 7–14 forms this second half. The clause expressing the purpose with לְמַעַן, as in its original, has the following הוֹשִׁיעָה for its principal clause upon which it depends. Instead of וַעֲנֵנוּ, which one might have expected, the expression used here is וַעֲנֵנִי without any interchange of the mode of writing and of reading it; many printed copies have וַעֲנֵנוּ here also; Baer, following Norzi, correctly has וַעֲנֵנִי. Instead of וְלִי ... לִי, lx. 9, we here read לִי ... לִי, which is less soaring. And instead of *Cry aloud concerning me, O Philistia* (the plaintive cry of the vanquished), it here is, *Over Philistia do I shout for joy* (the triumphant cry of the victor); in accordance with which Hupfeld wishes to take הִתְרוֹעָעִי in the former as infinitive: "over (עֲלֵי instead of עָלַי) Philistia is my shouting for joy" (הִתְרוֹעֲעִי instead of הִתְרוֹעָעִי, since the infinitive does not admit of this pausal form of the imperative). For עִיר מָצוֹר we have here the more usual form of expression עִיר מִבְצָר. Ver. 12a is weakened by the omission of the אַתָּה (הֲלֹא).

PSALM CIX.

IMPRECATION UPON THE CURSER WHO PREFERS THE CURSE TO THE BLESSING.

1 GOD of my praise, be not silent!
2 For a wicked mouth and a deceitful mouth have they
    opened against me,
They have spoken against me with a lying tongue,
3 And with animosities have they surrounded me
And fought against me without cause.
4 For my love they make themselves hostile to me,
Whilst I am all prayer;
5 And have requited me with evil for good,
And with hatred for my love.

6 Set Thou a wicked man over him,
And let Satan stand at his right hand;

7 If he is judged, let him come off as a wicked man,
  And let his prayer become sin.
8 Let his days be few,
  His office let another take.
9 Let his children become orphans,
  And his wife a widow,
10 And let his children wander to and fro begging,
  And let them entreat far from their ruins.

11 Let the creditor surround with snares all that he hath,
  And let strangers spoil what his labour hath gained.
12 Let there be no one to continue kindness to him,
  And let no one bestow [anything] upon his orphans.
13 Let his posterity be rooted out,
  In the next generation let their name be blotted out.
14 Let the guilt of his fathers be remembered with Jahve,
  And let the sin of his mother not be blotted out,
15 Let them be always before Jahve,
  And may He cut off their memory from the earth.

16 Because he hath not remembered to show kindness,
  And hath persecuted a man wretched and poor,
  And terrified of heart, to put him to death.
17 He hath loved the curse, and it hath come upon him ;
  And he delighted not in blessing, and it remained far
    from him.
18 He clothed himself in cursing as his garment,
  And it pressed like water into his bowels,
  And like oil into his bones.
19 So let it become unto him as a coat in which he covereth
    himself,
  And as a girdle which he continually putteth on.
20 This is the reward of mine adversaries from Jahve,
  And of those who speak evil concerning my soul.

21 But do THOU, Jahve Lord, act for me for Thy Name's
    sake ;
  Because Thy loving-kindness is good, deliver Thou me !
22 For I am wretched and poor,
  And my heart is pierced within me.

23 As a shadow, when it lengtheneth, am I gone,
　　I am scared away as a locust.
24 My knees knock together through fasting,
　　And my flesh is fallen away from fatness.
25 And I am become a reproach to them,
　　They see me, they shake their head.

26 Succour me, Jahve my God,
　　Help me according to Thy loving-kindness,
27 That they may know that this is Thy hand,
　　Thou, Jahve, hast done it.
28 *They* curse, but THOU blessest;
　　They arise and are ashamed, and Thy servant is glad.
29 Mine adversaries shall clothe themselves with reproach,
　　And envelope themselves as with a mantle with their own
　　　　shame.
30 I will give thanks greatly unto Jahve with my mouth,
　　And in the midst of many will I praise Him,
31 That He placeth Himself at the right hand of the poor,
　　To help him against the judges of his soul.

The אוֹדֶה, corresponding like an echo to the הודו of Ps. cvii.,
is also found here in ver. 30. But Ps. cix. is most closely
related to Ps. lxix. Anger concerning the ungodly who requite
love with ingratitude, who persecute innocence and desire the
curse instead of the blessing, has here reached its utmost bound.
The imprecations are not, however, directed against a multitude as in Ps. lxix., but their whole current is turned against
one person. Is this Doeg the Edomite, or Cush the Benjamite?
We do not know. The marks of Jeremiah's hand, which raised
a doubt about the לדוד of Ps. lxix., are wanting here; and if
the development of the thoughts appears too diffuse and overloaded to be suited to David, and also many expressions (as the
inflected מְעַט in ver. 8, the נִכְאֵה, which is explained by the
Syriac, in ver. 16, and the half-passive חָלַל in ver. 22) look as
though they belong to the later period of the language, yet we
feel on the other hand the absence of any certain echoes of
older models. For in the parallels ver. 6, cf. Zech. iii. 1, and
vers. 18, 29b, cf. Isa. lix. 17, it is surely not the mutual relationship but the priority that is doubtful; ver. 22, however, in

relation to lv. 5 (cf. ver. 4 with lv. 5) is a variation such as is also allowable in one and the same poet (*e.g.* in the refrains). The anathemas that are here poured forth more extensively than anywhere else speak in favour of David, or at least of his situation. They are explained by the depth of David's consciousness that he is the anointed of Jahve, and by his contemplation of himself in Christ. The persecution of David was a sin not only against David himself, but also against the Christ in him; and because Christ is in David, the outbursts of the Old Testament wrathful spirit take the prophetic form, so that this Psalm also, like Ps. xxii. and lxix., is a typically prophetic Psalm, inasmuch as the utterance of the type concerning himself is carried by the Spirit of prophecy beyond himself, and thus the ἀρά is raised to the προφητεία ἐν εἴδει ἀρᾶς (Chrysostom). These imprecations are not, however, appropriate in the mouth of the suffering Saviour. It is not the spirit of Zion but of Sinai which here speaks out of the mouth of David; the spirit of Elias, which, according to Luke ix. 55, is not the spirit of the New Testament. This wrathful spirit is overpowered in the New Testament by the spirit of love. But these anathemas are still not on this account so many beatings of the air. There is in them a divine energy, as in the blessing and cursing of every man who is united to God, and more especially of a man whose temper of mind is such as David's. They possess the same power as the prophetical threatenings, and in this sense they are regarded in the New Testament as fulfilled in the son of perdition (John xvii. 12). To the generation of the time of Jesus they were a deterrent warning not to offend against the Holy One of God, and this *Psalmus Ischarioticus* (Acts i. 20) will ever be such a mirror of warning to the enemies and persecutors of Christ and His Church.

Vers. 1–5. A sigh for help and complaints of ungrateful persecutors form the beginning of the Psalm. "God of my praise" is equivalent to God, who art my praise, Jer. xvii. 14, cf. Deut. x. 21. The God whom the Psalmist has hitherto had reason to praise will also now show Himself to him as worthy to be praised. Upon this faith he bases the prayer: be not silent (xxviii. 1, xxxv. 22)! A mouth such as belongs to the "wicked," a mouth out of which comes "deceit," have they

opened against him; they have spoken with him a tongue
(accusative, *vid.* on lxiv. 6), *i.e.* a language, of falsehood.   דִּבְרֵי
of things and utterances as in xxxv. 20.   It would be capricious to take the suffix of אַהֲבָתִי in ver. 4 as *genit. object.* (love
which they owe me), and in ver. 5 as *genit. subject.*; from
xxxviii. 21 it may be seen that the love which he has shown to
them is also meant in ver. 4.   The assertion that he is " prayer"
is intended to say that he, repudiating all revenge of himself,
takes refuge in God in prayer and commits his cause into His
hands.   They have loaded him with evil for good, and hatred
for the love he has shown to them.   Twice he lays emphasis
on the fact that it is love which they have requited to him with
its opposite.   Perfects alternate with aorists: it is no enmity
of yesterday; the imprecations that follow presuppose an inflexible obduracy on the side of the enemies.

Vers. 6–10.   The writer now turns to one among the many,
and in the angry zealous fervour of despised love calls down
God's judgment upon him.   To call down a higher power,
more particularly for punishment, upon any one is expressed
by עַל (הִפְקִיד) פָּקַד, Jer. xv. 3, Lev. xxvi. 16.   The tormentor of
innocence shall find a superior executor who will bring him
before the tribunal (which is expressed in Latin by *legis actio
per manus injectionem*).   The judgment scene in vers. 6*b*, 7*a*
shows that this is what is intended in ver. 6*a*: At the right
hand is the place of the accuser, who in this instance will not
rest before the *damnatus es* has been pronounced.   He is called
שָׂטָן, which is not to be understood here after 1 Sam. xxix. 4,
2 Sam. xix. 23 [22], but after Zech. iii. 1, 1 Chron. xxi. 1, if
not directly of Satan, still of a superhuman (cf. Num. xxii. 22)
being which opposes him, by appearing before God as his
κατήγωρ; for according to ver. 7*a* the שׂטן is to be thought of as
accuser, and according to 7*b* God as Judge.   רָשָׁע has the sense
of *reus*, and יֵצֵא refers to the publication of the sentence.   Ver.
7*b* wishes that his prayer, viz. that by which he would wish to
avert the divine sentence of condemnation, may become לַחֲטָאָה,
not: a missing of the mark, *i.e.* ineffectual (Thenius), but,
according to the usual signification of the word: a sin, viz.
because it proceeds from despair, not from true penitence.   In
ver. 8 the incorrigible one is wished an untimely death (מְעַטִּים
as in one other instance only, Eccles. v. 1) and the loss of his

office. The LXX. renders: τὴν ἐπισκοπὴν αὐτοῦ λάβοι ἕτερος. פְּקֻדָּה really signifies the office of overseer, oversight, office, and the one individual must have held a prominent position among the enemies of the psalmist. Having died off from this position before his time, he shall leave behind him a family deeply reduced in circumstances, whose former dwelling-place—he was therefore wealthy—becomes "ruins." His children wander up and down far from these ruins (מִן as *e.g.* in Judg. v. 11, Job xxviii. 4) and beg (דָּרַשׁ, like προσαιτεῖν, ἐπαιτεῖν, Sir. xl. 28 = בִּקֵּשׁ לֶחֶם, xxxvii. 25). Instead of וְדֹרְשׁוּ the reading וְדָרְשׁוּ is also found. A *Poel* is now and then formed from the strong verbs also,* in the inflexion of which the *Cholem* is sometimes shortened to *Kametz chatuph; vid.* the forms of לֹשֵׁן, to slander, in ci. 5, תֹּאַר, to sketch, mark out in outline, Isa. xliv. 13, cf. also Job xx. 26 (תְּאָכְלֵהוּ) and Isa. lxii. 9 (according to the reading מְאָסְפָיו). To read the *Kametz* in these instances as *ā*, and to regard these forms as resolved *Piels*, is, in connection with the absence of the *Metheg*, contrary to the meaning of the pointing; on purpose to guard against this way of reading it, correct codices have וְדָרְשׁוּ (cf. lxix. 19), which Baer has adopted.

Vers. 11–15. The *Piel* נִקֵּשׁ properly signifies to catch in snares; here, like the Arabic نَقَشَ, II., IV., corresponding to the Latin *obligare* (as referring to the creditor's right of claim); נֹשֶׁה is the name for the creditor as he who gives time for payment, gives credit (*vid.* Isa. xxiv. 2). In ver. 12 מָשַׁךְ חֶסֶד, to draw out mercy, is equivalent to causing it to continue and last, xxxvi. 11, cf. Jer. xxxi. 3. אַחֲרִיתוֹ, ver. 13*a*, does not signify his future, but as ver. 13*b* (cf. xxxvii. 38) shows: his posterity. יְהִי לְהַכְרִית is not merely *exscindatur*, but *exscindenda sit* (Ezek. xxx. 16, cf. Josh. ii. 6), just as in other instances הָיָה לְ corresponds to the active *fut. periphrasticum, e.g.* Gen. xv. 12, Isa. xxxvii. 26. With reference to יִמַּח instead of יִמַּח (contracted from יִמָּחֶה), *vid.* Ges. § 75, rem. 8. A Jewish acrostic

---

* In connection with the strong verb it frequently represents the *Piel* which does not occur, as with דָּרַשׁ, לֹשֵׁן, שָׁפַט, or even represents the *Piel* which, as in the case of שֵׁרֵשׁ, is already made use of in another signification (*Piel*, to root out; *Poel*, to take root).

interpretation of the name יֵשׁוּ runs: יִמַּח שְׁמוֹ וְזִכְרוֹ. This curse shall overtake the family of the υἱὸς τῆς ἀπωλείας. All the sins of his parents and ancestors shall remain indelible above before God the Judge, and here below the race, equally guilty, shall be rooted out even to its memory, *i.e.* to the last trace of it.

Vers. 16–20. He whom he persecuted with a thirst for blood, was, apart from this, a great sufferer, bowed down and poor and נִכְאֵה לֵבָב, of terrified, confounded heart. LXX. κατανενυγμένον (Jerome, *compunctum*); but the stem-word is not נכא (נכה), root נך (vol. i. 425), but כָּאָה, Syriac ܟܐܐ, cogn. כָּהָה, to cause to come near, to meet. The verb, and more especially in *Niph.*, is proved to be Hebrew by Dan. xi. 30. Such an one who without anything else is of a terrified heart, inasmuch as he has been made to feel the wrath of God most keenly, this man has persecuted with a deadly hatred. He had experienced kindness (חֶסֶד) in a high degree, but he blotted out of his memory that which he had experienced, not for an instant imagining that he too on his part had to exercise חֶסֶד. The *Poel* מוֹתֵת instead of הֵמִית points to the agonizing death (Isa. liii. 9, cf. Ezek. xxviii. 10 מוֹתֵי) to which he exposes God's anointed. The fate of the shedder of blood is not expressed after the manner of a wish in vers. 16–18, but in the historical form, as being the result that followed of inward necessity from the matter of fact of the course which he had himself determined upon. The verb בּוֹא *seq. acc.* signifies to surprise, suddenly attack any one, as in Isa. xli. 25. The three figures in ver. 18 are climactic: he has clothed himself in cursing, he has drunk it in like water (Job xv. 16, xxxiv. 7), it has penetrated even to the marrow of his bones, like the oily preparations which are rubbed in and penetrate to the bones. In ver. 19 the emphasis rests upon יַעְטֶה and upon תָּמִיד. The summarizing ver. 20 is the close of a strophe. פְּעֻלָּה, an earned reward, here punishment incurred, is especially frequent in Isa. ch. xl.–lxvi., *e.g.* xlix. 4, xl. 10; it also occurs once even in the Tôra, Lev. xix. 13. Those who answer the loving acts of the righteous with such malevolence in word and in deed commit a satanic sin for which there is no forgiveness. The curse is the fruit of their own choice and deed. Arnobius: *Nota ex arbitrio evenisse ut nollet, propter hæresim, quæ dicit Deum alios præ-destinasse ad benedictionem, alios ad maledictionem.*

Vers. 21–25. The thunder and lightning are now as it were followed by a shower of tears of deep sorrowful complaint. Ps. cix. here just as strikingly accords with Ps. lxix., as Ps. lxix. does with Ps. xxii. in the last strophe but one. The twofold name *Jahve Adonaj* (*vid. Symbolæ,* p. 16) corresponds to the deep-breathed complaint. עֲשֵׂה אִתִּי, deal with me, *i.e.* succouring me, does not greatly differ from לִי in 1 Sam. xiv. 6. The confirmation, ver. 21*b*, runs like lxix. 17: Thy loving-kindness is טוֹב, absolutely good, the ground of everything that is good and the end of all evil. Hitzig conjectures, as in lxix. 17, כְּטוֹב חסדך, "according to the goodness of Thy loving-kindness;" but this formula is without example: "for Thy loving-kindness is good" is a statement of the motive placed first and corresponding to the "for Thy Name's sake." In ver. 22 (a variation of lv. 5) חָלַל, not חָלָל, is traditional; this חָלַל, as being *verb. denom.* from חָלָל, signifies to be pierced, and is therefore equivalent to חוֹלַל (cf. Luke ii. 35). The metaphor of the shadow in ver. 23 is as in cii. 12. When the day declines, the shadow lengthens, it becomes longer and longer (Virgil, *majoresque cadunt altis de montibus umbræ*), till it vanishes in the universal darkness. Thus does the life of the sufferer pass away. The poet intentionally uses the *Niph.* נֶהֱלָכְתִּי (another reading is נֶהֱלַכְתִּי); it is a power rushing upon him from without that drives him away thus after the manner of a shadow into the night. The locust or grasshopper (apart from the plague of the locusts) is proverbial as being a defence-less, inoffensive little creature that is soon driven away, Job xxxix. 20. נִנְעַר, to be shaken out or off (cf. Arabic *na'ûra*, a water-wheel that fills its clay-vessels in the river and empties them out above, and הַנַּעַר, Zech. xi. 16, where Hitzig wishes to read הַנַּעֵר, *dispulsio = dispulsi*). The fasting in ver. 24 is the result of the loathing of all food which sets in with deep grief. כָּחַשׁ מִשָּׁמֶן signifies to waste away so that there is no more fat left.* In ver. 25 אֲנִי is designedly rendered prominent: in this

---

* The verbal group כחש, כחד, جَهَدَ, كَاذَبَ, etc. has the primary signi-fication of withdrawal and taking away or decrease; to deny is the same as to withdraw from agreement, and he becomes thin from whom the fat

the form of his affliction he is the butt of their reproaching, and they shake their heads doubtfully, looking upon him as one who is punished of God beyond all hope, and giving him up for lost. It is to be interpreted thus after lxix. 11 sq.

Vers. 26–31. The cry for help is renewed in the closing strophe, and the Psalm draws to a close very similarly to Ps. lxix. and xxii., with a joyful prospect of the end of the affliction. In ver. 27 the hand of God stands in contrast to accident, the work of men, and his own efforts. All and each one will undeniably perceive, when God at length interposes, that it is His hand which here does that which was impossible in the eyes of men, and that it is His work which has been accomplished in this affliction and in the issue of it. He blesses him whom men curse: they arise without attaining their object, whereas His servant can rejoice in the end of his affliction. The futures in ver. 29 are not now again imprecations, but an expression of believingly confident hope. In correct texts כְּמְעִיל has *Mem raphatum*. The "many" are the "congregation" (*vid.* xxii. 23). In the case of the marvellous deliverance of this sufferer the congregation or church has the pledge of its own deliverance, and a bright mirror of the loving-kindness of its God. The sum of the praise and thanksgiving follows in ver. 31, where כִּי signifies *quod*, and is therefore allied to the ὅτι *recitativum* (cf. xxii. 25). The three Good Friday Psalms all sum up the comfort that springs from David's affliction for all suffering ones in just such a pithy sentence (xxii. 25, lxix. 34). Jahve comes forward at the right hand of the poor, contending for him (cf. cx. 5), to save (him) from those who judge (xxxvii. 33), *i.e.* condemn, his soul. The contrast between this closing thought and vers. 6 sq. is unmistakeable. At the right hand of the tormentor stands Satan as an accuser, at the right hand of the tormented one stands God as his vindicator; he who delivered him over to human judges is condemned, and he who was delivered up is "taken away out of distress and from judgment" (Isa. liii. 8) by the Judge of the judges, in order that, as we now hear in the following

---

withdraws, goes away. Saadia compares on this passage (פרה) בהמה כחושה, a lean cow, *Berachoth* 32a. In like manner Targum II. renders Gen. xli. 27 תּוֹרָתָא בְחִישָׁתָא, the lean kine.

Psalm, he may sit at the right hand of the heavenly King.
Ἐδικαιώθη ἐν πνεύματι . . . ἀνελήμφθη ἐν δόξῃ! (1 Tim.
iii. 16.)

PSALM CX.

TO THE PRIEST-KING AT THE RIGHT HAND OF GOD.

1 THE oracle of Jahve unto my Lord :
" Sit thou at My right hand,
Until I make thine enemies
The stool of thy feet."

2 The sceptre of thy might
Will Jahve stretch forth out of Zion :
" Rule thou in the midst of thine enemies ! "
*

3 Thy people are most willing on thy field-day ;
In holy festive garments,
Out of the womb of the morning's dawn
Cometh the dew of thy young men.

4 Jahve hath sworn and will not repent :
" Thou shalt be a priest for ever
After the manner of Melchizedek."
*   *

5 The Lord at thy right hand
Dasheth kings in pieces in the day of His wrath,
6 He shall judge among the nations,
It becometh full of corpses.

He dasheth in pieces a head upon a broad country ;
7 Of the brook in the way shall he drink,
Therefore shall he lift up the head on high.

*   *   *

While the Pharisees were gathered together, Jesus asked
them : What think ye of Christ ? Whose Son is He ? They
say unto Him : David's. He saith unto them : How then doth
David in the spirit call Him Lord, saying : " The LORD hath

said unto my Lord : Sit Thou on My right hand until I make Thine enemies the stool of Thy feet ? " If David then calls Him Lord, how is He his Son ? And no man was able to answer Him a word, neither durst any one from that day forth question Him further.

So we read in Matt. xxii. 41–46, Mark xii. 35–37, Luke xx. 41–44. The inference which it is left for the Pharisees to draw rests upon the two premises, which are granted, that Ps. cx. is Davidic, and that it is prophetico-Messianic, *i.e.* that in it the future Messiah stands objectively before the mind of David. For if those who were interrogated had been able to reply that David does not there speak of the future Messiah, but puts into the mouth of the people words concerning himself, or, as Hofmann has now modified the view he formerly held (*Schriftbeweis*, ii. 1, 496–500), concerning the Davidic king in a general way,* then the question would lack the background of cogency as an argument. Since, however, the pro-

---

* *Vid.* the refutation of this modified view in Kurtz, *Zur Theologie der Psalmen*, in the *Dorpater Zeitschrift* for the year 1861, S. 516.

Supplementary Note.—Von Hofmann now interprets Ps. cx. as prophetico-Messianic. We are glad to be able to give it in his own words. " As the utterance of a prophet who speaks the word of God to the person addressed, the Psalm begins, and this it is then all through, even where it does not, as in ver. 4, expressly make known to the person addressed what God swears to him. God intends to finally subdue his foes to him. Until then, until his day of victory is come, he shall have a dominion in the midst of them, the sceptre of which shall be mighty through the succour of God. His final triumph is, however, pledged to him by the word of God, which appoints him, as another Melchizedek, to an eternal priesthood, that excludes the priesthood of Aaron, and by the victory which God has already given him in the day of His wrath.

" This is a picture of a king on Zion who still looks forward to that which in Ps. lxxii. 8 sqq. has already taken place,—of a victorious, mighty king, who however is still ruling in the midst of foes,—therefore of a king such as Jesus now is, to whom God has given the victory over heathen Rome, and to whom He will subdue all his enemies when he shall again reveal himself in the world ; meanwhile he is the kingly priest and the priestly king of the people of God. The prophet who utters this is David. He whom he addresses as Lord is the king who is appointed to become that which Ps. lxxii. describes him ; it is therefore he of whom God has spoken according to 2 Sam. xxiii. 3. David beholds him in a moment of his ruling to which the moment in his own ruling in which we find him in 2 Sam. xi. 1 is typically parallel."

phetico-Messianic character of the Psalm was acknowledged at that time (even as the later synagogue, in spite of the dilemma into which this Psalm brought it in opposition to the church, has never been able entirely to avoid this confession), the conclusion to be drawn from this Psalm must have been felt by the Pharisees themselves, that the Messiah, because the Son of David and Lord at the same time, was of human and at the same time of superhuman nature; that it was therefore in accordance with Scripture if this Jesus, who represented Himself to be the predicted Christ, should as such profess to be the Son of God and of divine nature.

The New Testament also assumes elsewhere that David in this Psalm speaks not of himself, but directly of Him, in whom the Davidic kingship should finally and for ever fulfil that of which the promise speaks. For ver. 1 is regarded elsewhere too as a prophecy of the exaltation of Christ at the right hand of the Father, and of His final victory over all His enemies: Acts ii. 34 sq., 1 Cor. xv. 25, Heb. i. 13, x. 13; and the Epistle to the Hebrews (ch. v. 6, vii. 17, 21) bases its demonstration of the abrogation of the Levitical priesthood by the Melchizedek priesthood of Jesus Christ upon ver. 4. But if even David, who raised the Levitical priesthood to the pinnacle of splendour that had never existed before, was a priest after the manner of Melchizedek, it is not intelligible how the priesthood of Jesus Christ after the manner of Melchizedek is meant to be a proof in favour of the termination of the Levitical priesthood, and to absolutely preclude its continuance.

We will not therefore deceive ourselves concerning the apprehension of the Psalm which is presented to us in the New Testament Scriptures. According to the New Testament Scriptures, David speaks in Ps. cx. not merely of Christ in so far as the Spirit of God has directed him to speak of the Anointed of Jahve in a typical form, but directly and objectively in a prophetical representation of the Future One. And would this be impossible? Certainly there is no other Psalm in which David distinguishes between himself and the Messiah, and has the latter before him: the other Messianic Psalms of David are reflections of his radical, ideal contemplation of himself, reflected images of his own typical history; they contain prophetic elements, because David there too speaks ἐν πνεύματι, but elements that are not solved by the person of David. Nevertheless the last words of David in 2 Sam. xxiii. 1–7 prove to us that we need not be surprised to find even a directly Messianic Psalm coming from his lips. After the splendour of all that pertained to David individually had almost entirely expired in his own eyes and in the eyes of those about him, he must have been still more strongly conscious of the distance between what had been realized in himself and the idea of the Anointed of God, as he lay on his death-bed, as his sun was going down. Since, however, all the glory with which God has favoured him comes up once more before his soul, he feels himself, to the glory of God, to be " the man raised up on high, the anointed of the God of Jacob, the sweet singer of Israel," and the instrument of the Spirit of Jahve. This he has been, and he, who as such contemplated himself as the immortal one, must now die : then in dying he seizes the pillars of the divine promise, he lets go the ground of his own present, and looks as a prophet into the future of his seed : *The God of Israel hath said, to me hath the Rock of Israel spoken : " A ruler of men, a just one, a ruler in the fear of God; and as the light of the morning, when the sun riseth, a cloudless morning, when after sunshine, after rain it becomes green out of the earth."* For not little (לֹא־כֵן to be explained according to Job ix. 35, cf. Num. xiii. 33, Isa. li. 6) *is my house with God, but an everlasting covenant hath He made with me, one ordered in all things and sure, for all my salvation and all my favour—ought He not to cause it to sprout?* The idea of the Messiah shall notwithstanding be realized, in accordance with the promise, within his own house. The vision of the future which passes before his soul is none other than the picture of the Messiah detached from its subjectivity. And if so there, why may it not also have been so even in Ps. cx. ?

The fact that Ps. cx. has points of connection with cotemporaneous history is notwithstanding the less to be denied, as its position in the Fifth Book leads one to suppose that it is taken out of its cotemporary annalistic connection. The first of these connecting links is the bringing of the Ark home to Zion. Girded with the linen ephod of the priest, David had accompanied the Ark up to Zion with signs of rejoicing. There upon Zion Jahve, whose earthly throne is the Ark, now took

His place at the side of David; but, spiritually considered, the matter stood properly thus, that Jahve, when He established Himself upon Zion, granted to David to sit henceforth enthroned at His side. The second connecting link is the victorious termination of the Syro-Ammonitish war, and also of the Edomitish war that came in between. The war with the Ammonites and their allies, the greatest, longest, and most glorious of David's wars, ended in the second year, when David himself joined the army, with the conquest of Rabbah. These two cotemporary connecting links are to be recognised, but they only furnish the Psalm with the typical ground-colour for its prophetical contents.

In this Psalm David looks forth from the height upon which Jahve has raised him by the victory over Ammon into the future of his seed, and there He who carries forward the work begun by him to the highest pitch is his Lord. Over against this King of the future, David is not king, but subject. He calls him, as one out of the people, " my Lord." This is the situation of the prophetico-kingly poet. He has received new revelations concerning the future of his seed. He has come down from his throne and the height of his power, and looks up to the Future One. He too sits enthroned on Zion. He too is victorious from thence. But His fellowship with God is the most intimate imaginable, and the last enemy is also laid at His feet. And He is not merely king, who as a priest provides for the salvation of His people, He is an eternal Priest by virtue of a sworn promise. The Psalm therefore relates to the history of the future upon a typical ground-work. It is also explicable why the triumph in the case of Ammon and the Messianic image have been thus to David's mind disconnected from himself. In the midst of that war comes the sin of David, which cast a shadow of sorrow over the whole of his future life and reduced its typical glory to ashes. Out of these ashes the phœnix of Messianic prophecy here arises. The type, come back to the conscious of himself, here lays down his crown at the feet of the Antitype.

Ps. cx. consists of three sevens, a tetrastich together with a tristich following three times upon one another. The *Rebia magnum* in ver. 2 is a security for this stichic division, and in like manner the *Olewejored* by חֵילֶךָ in ver. 3, and in general

the interpunction required by the sense. And vers. 1 and 2
show decisively that it is to be thus divided into 4 + 3 lines;
for ver. 1 with its rhyming inflexions makes itself known as
a tetrastich, and to take it together with ver. 2 as a heptastich
is opposed by the new turn which the Psalm takes in ver. 2.
It is also just the same with ver. 4 in relation to ver. 3: these
seven stichs stand in just the same organic relation to the
second divine utterance as the preceding seven to the first
utterance. And since vers. 1–4 give twice 4 + 3 lines, vers.
5–7 also will be organized accordingly. There are really seven
lines, of which the fifth, contrary to the Masoretic division of
the verse, forms with ver. 7 the final tristich.

The Psalm therefore bears the threefold impress of the
number seven, which is the number of an oath and of a covenant. Its impress, then, is thoroughly prophetic. Two divine
utterances are introduced, and that not such as are familiar to
us from the history of David and only reproduced here in a
poetic form, as with Ps. lxxxix. and cxxxii., but utterances of
which nothing is known from the history of David, and such
as we hear for the first time here. The divine name *Jahve*
occurs three times. God is designedly called *Adonaj* the
fourth time. The Psalm is consequently prophetic; and in
order to bring the inviolable and mysterious nature even of its
contents into comparison with the contemplation of its outward
character, it has been organized as a threefold septiad, which
is sealed with the thrice recurring tetragramma.

Vers. 1, 2. In Ps. xx. and xxi. we see at once in the
openings that what we have before us is the language of the
people concerning their king. Here לַאדֹנִי in ver. 1 does not
favour this, and נְאֻם is decidedly against it. The former does
not favour it, for it is indeed correct that the subject calls his
king " my lord," *e.g.* 1 Sam. xxii. 12, although the more exact
form of address is " my lord the king," *e.g.* 1 Sam. xxiv. 9 [8];
but if the people are speaking here, what is the object of the
title of honour being expressed as if coming from the mouth
of an individual, and why not rather, as in Ps. xx., xxi., לְמֶלֶךְ
or לִמְשִׁיחוֹ? נְאֻם is, however, decisive against the supposition
that it is an Israelite who here expresses himself concerning
the relation of his king to Jahve. For it is absurd to suppose

that an Israelite speaking in the name of the people would begin in the manner of the prophets with נְאֻם, more particularly since this נְאֻם ה׳ placed thus at the head of the discourse is without any perfectly analogous example (1 Sam. ii. 30, Isa. i. 24 are only similar) elsewhere, and is therefore extremely important. In general this opening position of נְאֻם, even in cases where other genitives than יהוה follow, is very rare; נְאֻם is found besides, so placed, only in the mouth of Balaam in Num. xxiv. 3 sq., 15 sq., of David in 2 Sam. xxiii. 1, of Agur in Prov. xxx. 1, and always (even in Ps. xxxvi. 2) in an oracular signification. Moreover, if one from among the people were speaking, the declaration ought to be a retrospective glance at a past utterance of God. But, first, the history knows nothing of any such divine utterance; and secondly, נְאֻם ה׳ always introduces God as actually speaking, to which even the passage cited by Hofmann to the contrary, Num. xiv. 28, forms no exception. Thus it will consequently not be a past utterance of God to which the poet glances back here, but one which David has just now heard ἐν πνεύματι (Matt. xxii. 43), and is therefore not a declaration of the people concerning David, but of David concerning Christ. The unique character of the declaration confirms this. Of the king of Israel it is said that he sits on the throne of Jahve (1 Chron. xxix. 23), viz. as visible representative of the invisible King (1 Chron. xxviii. 5); Jahve, however, commands the person here addressed to take his place at His right hand. The right hand of a king is the highest place of honour, 1 Kings ii. 19.* Here the sitting at the right hand signifies not merely an idle honour, but reception into the fellowship of God as regards dignity and dominion, exaltation to a participation in God's reigning (βασιλεύειν, 1 Cor. xv. 25). Just as Jahve sits enthroned in the heavens and laughs at the rebels here below, so shall he who is exalted henceforth share this blessed calm with Him, until He subdues all enemies to him, and therefore makes him the unlimited, universally acknowledged ruler. עַד as in Hos. x. 12, for עַד־כִּי or עַד־אֲשֶׁר, does not exclude the time that lies beyond,

---

* Cf. the custom of the old Arabian kings to have their viceroy (*ridf*) sitting at their right hand, *Monumenta antiquiss. hist. Arabum, ed. Eichhorn*, p. 220.

but as in cxii. 8, Gen. xlix. 10, includes it, and in fact so that
it at any rate marks the final subjugation of the enemies as a
turning-point with which something else comes about (*vid.* Acts
iii. 21, 1 Cor. xv. 28).   הֲדֹם is an accusative of the predicate.
The enemies shall come to lie under his feet (1 Kings v. 17 [3]),
his feet tread upon the necks of the vanquished (Josh. x. 24),
so that the resistance that is overcome becomes as it were the
dark ground upon which the glory of his victorious rule arises.
For the history of time ends with the triumph of good over
evil,—not, however, with the annihilation of evil, but with its
subjugation.   This is the issue, inasmuch as absolute omnipotence is effectual on behalf of and through the exalted Christ.
In ver. 2, springing from the utterance of Jahve, follow words
expressing a prophetic prospect.   Zion is the imperial abode of
the great future King (ii. 6).   מַטֵּה עֻזְּךָ (cf. Jer. xlviii. 17,
Ezek. xix. 11–14) signifies " the sceptre (as insignia and the
medium of exercise) of the authority delegated to thee" (1 Sam.
ii. 10, Mic. v. 3 [4]).   Jahve will stretch this sceptre far forth
from Zion : no goal is mentioned up to which it shall extend,
but passages like Zech. ix. 10 show how the prophets understand such Psalms.   In ver. 2b follow the words with which
Jahve accompanies this extension of the dominion of the exalted One.   Jahve will lay all his enemies at his feet, but not
in such a manner that he himself remains idle in the matter.
Thus, then, having come into the midst of the sphere (בְּקֶרֶב) of
his enemies, shall he reign, forcing them to submission and
holding them down.   We read this רְדֵה in a Messianic connection in lxxii. 8.   So even in the prophecy of Balaam (Num.
xxiv. 19), where the sceptre (ch. xxiv. 17) is an emblem of the
Messiah Himself.

Vers. 3, 4.   In order that he may rule thus victoriously, it
is necessary that there should be a people and an army.   In
accordance with this union of the thoughts which ver. 3a
anticipates, בְּיוֹם חֵילֶךָ signifies in the day of thy arriere ban, *i.e.*
when thou callest up thy "power of an army" (2 Chron. xxvi.
13) to muster and go forth to battle.   In this day are the
people of the king willingnesses (נְדָבֹת), *i.e.* entirely cheerful
readiness ; ready for any sacrifices, they bring themselves with
all that they are and have to meet him.   There is no need of
any compulsory, lengthy proclamation calling them out : it is

no army of mercenaries, but willingly and quickly they present themselves from inward impulse (מִתְנַדֵּב, Judg. v. 2, 9). The punctuation, which makes the principal cæsura at חֵילֶךָ with *Olewejored*, makes the parallelism of חיל and יַלְדוּתֶךָ distinctly prominent. Just as the former does not signify *roboris tui*, so now too the latter does not, according to Eccles. xi. 9, signify παιδιότητός σου (Aquila), and not, as Hofmann interprets, the dew-like freshness of youthful vigour, which the morning of the great day sheds over the king. Just as גָּלוּת signifies both exile and the exiled ones, so יַלְדוּת, like νεότης, *juventus, juventa*, signifies both the time and age of youth, youthfulness, and youthful, young men (the youth). Moreover one does not, after ver. 3*a*, look for any further declaration concerning the nature of the king, but of his people who place themselves at his service. The young men are likened to dew which gently descends upon the king out of the womb (*uterus*) of the morning-red.* מִשְׁחָר is related to שַׁחַר just as מַחֲשָׁךְ is to חֹשֶׁךְ; the notion of שׁחר and חֹשׁךְ appears to be more sharply defined, and as it were apprehended more massively, in משׁחר and מחשׁךְ. The host of young men is likened to the dew both on account of its vigorousness and its multitude, which are like the freshness of the mountain dew and the immense number of its drops, 2 Sam. xvii. 12 (cf. Num. xxiii. 10), and on account of the silent concealment out of which it wondrously and suddenly comes to light, Mic. v. 6 [7]. After not having understood "thy youth" of the youthfulness of the king, we shall now also not, with Hofmann, refer בְּהַדְרֵי־קֹדֶשׁ to the king, the holy attire of his armour. הַדְרַת קֹדֶשׁ is the vestment of the priest

---

* The LXX. renders it: ἐν ταῖς λαμπρότησι τῶν ἁγίων σου (belonging to the preceding clause), ἐκ γαστρὸς πρὸ ἑωσφόρου ἐγέννησά σε (Psalt. Veron. *exegennesa se*; Bamberg. *gegennica se*). The Vulgate, following the Italic closely: *in splendoribus sanctorum; ex utero ante luciferum genui te.* The Fathers in some cases interpret it of the birth of the Lord at Christmas, but most of them of His antemundane birth, and accordingly Apollinaris paraphrases: γαστρὸς καρπὸς ἐμῆς πρὸ ἑωσφόρου αὐτὸς ἐτύχθης. In his own independent translation Jerome reads בהררי (as in lxxxvii. 1), *in montibus sanctis quasi de vulva orietur tibi ros adolescentiæ tuæ*, as Symmachus ἐν ὄρεσιν ἁγίοις,—elsewhere, however, ἐν δόξῃ ἁγίων. The substitution is not unmeaning, since the ideas of dew and of mountains (cxxxiii. 3) are easily united; but it was more important to give prominence to the holiness of the equipment than to that of the place of meeting.

for performing divine service : the Levite singers went forth
before the army in " holy attire " in 2 Chron. xx. 21; here,
however, the people without distinction wear holy festive garments.   Thus they surround the divine king as dew that is
born out of the womb of the morning-red.   It is a priestly
people which he leads forth to holy battle, just as in Apoc. xix.
14 heavenly armies follow the Logos of God upon white horses,
ἐνδεδυμένοι βύσσινον λευκὸν καθαρόν—a new generation, wonderful as if born out of heavenly light, numerous, fresh, and
vigorous like the dew-drops, the offspring of the dawn.   The
thought that it is a priestly people leads over to ver. 4.   The
king who leads this priestly people is, as we hear in ver. 4, himself a priest (cohen).   As has been shown by Hupfeld and
Fleischer, the priest is so called as one who stands (from כָּהַן =
כּוּן in an intransitive signification), viz. before God (Deut. x.
8, cf. Ps. cxxxiv. 1, Heb. x. 11), like נָבִיא the spokesman, viz.
of God.*   To stand before God is the same as to serve Him,
viz. as priest.   The ruler whom the Psalm celebrates is a priest
who intervenes in the reciprocal dealings between God and
His people within the province of divine worship; the priestly
character of the people who suffer themselves to be led forth to
battle and victory by him, stands in causal connection with the
priestly character of this their king.   He is a priest by virtue
of the promise of God confirmed by an oath.   The oath is not
merely a pledge of the fulfilment of the promise, but also a seal
of the high significance of its purport.   God the absolutely truthful One (Num. xiii. 19) swears—this is the highest enhancement of the נְאֻם ה׳ of which prophecy is capable (Amos vi. 8).

He appoints the person addressed as a priest for ever " after
the manner of Melchizedek" in this most solemn manner.   The
i of דברתי is the same ancient connecting vowel as in the מלכי
of the name Melchizedek; and it has the tone, which it loses
when, as in Lam. i. 1, a tone-syllable follows.   The wide-

---

* The Arabic lexicographers explain كَاهِن by من يقوم بامر الرجل
ويسعى فى حاجته, " he who stands and does any one's business and
manages his affair."   That قام, קום, and مثل, מָשַׁל, side by side with
עָמַד are synonyms of כהן in this sense of standing ready for service and in
an official capacity.

meaning עַל־דִּבְרַת, "in respect to, on account of," Eccles. iii. 18, vii. 14, viii. 2, is here specialized to the signification "after the manner, measure of," LXX. κατὰ τὴν τάξιν. The priesthood is to be united with the kingship in him who rules out of Zion, just as it was in Melchizedek, king of Salem, and that for ever. According to De Wette, Ewald, and Hofmann, it is not any special priesthood that is meant here, but that which was bestowed directly with the kingship, consisting in the fact that the king of Israel, by reason of his office, commended his people in prayer to God and blessed them in the name of God, and also had the ordering of Jahve's sanctuary and service. Now it is true all Israel is a "kingdom of priests" (Ex. xix. 6, cf. Num. xvi. 3, Isa. lxi. 6), and the kingly vocation in Israel must therefore also be regarded as in its way a priestly vocation. But this spiritual priesthood, and, if one will, this princely oversight of sacred things, needed not to come to David first of all by solemn promise; and that of Melchizedek, after which the relationship is here defined, is incongruous to him; for the king of Salem was, according to Canaanitish custom, which admitted of the union of the kingship and priesthood, really a high priest, and therefore, regarded from an Israelitish point of view, united in his own person the offices of David and of Aaron. How could David be called a priest after the manner of Melchizedek, he who had no claim upon the tithes of the priests like Melchizedek, and to whom was denied the authority to offer sacrifice * inseparable from the idea of the priesthood in the Old Testament? (cf. 2 Chron. xxvi. 20.) If David were the person addressed, the declaration would stand in antagonism with the right of Melchizedek as priest recorded in Gen. ch. xiv., which, according to the indisputable representation of the Epistle to the Hebrews, was equal in compass to the Levitico-Aaronic right, and, since "after the manner of" requires a coincident reciprocal relation, in antagonism to itself also.†

One might get on more easily with ver. 4 by referring the

---

* G. Enjedin the Socinian (died 1597) accordingly, in referring this Psalm to David, started from the assumption that priestly functions have been granted exceptionally by God to this king as to no other; *vid.* the literature of the controversy to which this gave rise in Serpilius, *Personalia Davidis,* S. 268–274.

† Just so Kurtz, *Zur Theologie der Psalmen, loc. cit.* S. 523.

Psalm to one of the Maccabæan priest-princes (Hitzig, von
Lengerke, and Olshausen); and we should then prefer to the
reference to Jonathan who put on the holy *stola*, 1 Macc. x.
21 (so Hitzig formerly), or Alexander Jannæus who actually
bore the title of king (so Hitzig now), the reference to Simon,
whom the people appointed to "be their governor and high
priest for ever, until there should arise a faithful prophet"
(1 Macc. xiv. 41), after the death of Jonathan his brother—a
union of the two offices which, although an irregularity, was not
one, however, that was absolutely illegal. But the priesthood,
which the Maccabæans, however, possessed originally as being
priests born, is promised to the person addressed here in ver. 4;
and even supposing that in ver. 4 the emphasis lay not on a
union of the priesthood with the kingship, but of the kingship
with the priesthood, then the retrospective reference to it in
Zechariah forbids our removing the Psalm to a so much later
period. Why should we not rather be guided in our understanding of this divine utterance, which is unique in the Old
Testament, by this prophet, whose prophecy in ch. vi. 12 sq. is
the key to it? Zechariah removes the fulfilment of the Psalm
out of the Old Testament present, with its blunt separation
between the monarchical and hierarchical dignity, into the
domain of the future, and refers it to Jahve's Branch (צֶמַח)
that is to come. He, who will build the true temple of God,
satisfactorily unites in his one person the priestly with the
kingly office, which were at that time assigned to Joshua the
high priest and Zerubbabel the prince. Thus this Psalm was
understood by the later prophecy; and in what other sense
could the post-Davidic church have appropriated it as a prayer
and hymn, than in the eschatological Messianic sense? But
this sense is also verified as the original. David here hears
that the king of the future exalted at the right hand of God,
and whom he calls his Lord, is at the same time an eternal
priest. And because he is both these his battle itself is a
priestly royal work, and just on this account his people fighting
with him also wear priestly garments.

Vers. 5–7. Just as in ver. 2 after ver. 1, so now here too
after the divine utterance, the poet continues in a reflective
strain. The Lord, says ver. 5, dashes in pieces kings at the
right hand of this priest-king, in the day when His wrath is

kindled (ii. 12, cf. xxi. 10). אֲדֹנָי is rightly accented as subject.
The fact that the victorious work of the person addressed is
not his own work, but the work of Jahve on his behalf and
through him, harmonizes with ver. 1b. The sitting of the
exalted one at the right hand of Jahve denotes his uniform
participation in His high dignity and dominion. But in the fact
that the Lord, standing at his right hand (cf. the counterpart
in cix. 6), helps him to victory, that unchangeable relationship
is shown in its historical working. The right hand of the
exalted one is at the same time not inactive (see Num. xxiv.
17, cf. ver. 8), and the Lord does not fail him when he is obliged
to use his arm against his foes. The subject to יָדִין and to the
two מָחַץ is the Lord as acting through him. "He shall judge
among the peoples" is an eschatological hope, vii. 9, ix. 9, xcvi.
10, cf. 1 Sam. ii. 10. What the result of this judgment of the
peoples is, is stated by the neutrally used verb מָלֵא with its
accusative גְּוִיּוֹת (cf. on the construction lxv. 10, Deut. xxxiv.
9): it there becomes full of corpses, there is there a multitude
of corpses covering everything. This is the same thought as
in Isa. lxvi. 24, and wrought out in closely related connection
in Apoc. xix. 17, xviii. 21. Like the first מָחַץ, the second (ver.
6c) is also a perfect of the ideal past. Accordingly אֶרֶץ רַבָּה
seems to signify the earth or a country (cf. אֶרֶץ רְחָבָה, Ex. iii. 8,
Neh. ix. 35) broad and wide, like תְּהוֹם רַבָּה the great far-
stretching deep. But it might also be understood the "land
of Rabbah," as they say the "land of Jazer" (Num. xxxii. 1),
the "country of Goshen" (Josh. x. 41), and the like; therefore
the land of the Ammonites, whose chief city is Rabbah. It is
also questionable whether רֹאשׁ עַל־אֶרֶץ רַבָּה is to be taken like
κεφαλὴν ὑπὲρ πάντα, Eph. i. 22 (Hofmann), or whether עַל־ארץ
רבה belongs to מָחַץ as a designation of the battle-field. The
parallels as to the word and the thing itself, lxviii. 22, Hab.
iii. 13 sq., speak for רֹאשׁ signifying not the chief, but the head;
not, however, in a collective sense (LXX., Targum), but the
head of the רָשָׁע κατ᾽ ἐξοχήν (vid. Isa. xi. 4). If this is the case,
and the construction רֹאשׁ עַל is accordingly to be given up,
neither is it now to be rendered: He breaks in pieces a head
upon the land of Rabbah, but upon a great (broad) land; in
connection with which, however, this designation of the place
of battle takes its rise from the fact that the head of the ruler

over this great territory is intended, and the choice of the word
may have been determined by an allusion to David's Ammonitish war. The subject of ver. 7 is now not that arch-fiend, as
he who in the course of history renews his youth, that shall rise
up again (as we explained it formerly), but he whom the Psalm,
which is thus rounded off with unity of plan, celebrates. Ver.
7*a* expresses the toil of his battle, and ver. 7*b* the reward of
undertaking the toil. עַל־כֵּן is therefore equivalent to *ἀντὶ
τούτου.* בַּדֶּרֶךְ, however, although it might belong to מִנַּחַל (of
the brook by the wayside, lxxxiii. 10, cvi. 7), is correctly drawn
to יִשְׁתֶּה by the accentuation: he shall on his arduous way, the
way of his mission (cf. cii. 24), be satisfied with a drink from
the brook. He will stand still only for a short time to refresh
himself, and in order then to fight afresh; he will unceasingly
pursue his work of victory without giving himself any time for
rest and sojourn, and therefore (as the reward for it) it shall
come to pass that he may lift his head on high as victor; and
this, understood in a christological sense, harmonizes essentially
with Phil. ii. 8 sq., Heb. xii. 2, Apoc. v. 9 sq.

PSALM CXI.

ALPHABETICAL SONG IN PRAISE OF GOD.

HALLELUJAH.

1 א I WILL give thanks unto Jahve with the whole heart,
  ב In the council of the upright and the congregation.
2 ג Great are the deeds of Jahve,
  ד Worthy of being sought after in all their purposes.
3 ה Glory and splendour is His work,
  ו And His righteousness endureth for ever.
4 ז A memorial of His wonderful works hath He founded,
  ח Gracious and compassionate is Jahve.
5 ט Meat hath He given to those who fear Him,
  י He remembereth His covenant for ever.   [works,
6 כ He hath made known to His people the power of His
  ל Giving to them the heritage of the heathen.
7 מ The works of His hands are truth and right,
  נ Faithful are all His statutes,
8 ס Firm for ever and ever,
  ע Established according to truth, and upright.

9 פ He hath sent redemption unto His people,
  צ He hath pledged His covenant for ever—
  ק Holy and reverend is His Name.
10 ר The beginning of wisdom is the fear of Jahve,
  ש A good understanding have all dutiful ones;
  ת He shall have eternal praise.

With Ps. cxi. begins a trilogy of Hallelujah-Psalms. It may be appended to Ps. cx., because it places the "for ever" of cx. 4 in broader light in relation to the history of redemption, by stringing praise upon praise of the deeds of Jahve and of His appointments. It stands in the closest relationship to Ps. cxii. Whilst Ps. cxi., as Hitzig correctly says, celebrates the glory, might, and loving-kindness of Jahve in the circle of the "upright," Ps. cxii. celebrates the glory flowing therefrom and the happiness of the "upright" themselves, of those who fear Jahve. The two Psalms are twin in form as in contents. They are a mixture of materials taken from older Psalms and gnomical utterances; both are sententious, and both alphabetical. Each consists of twenty-two lines with the twenty-two letters of the alphabet at the beginning,* and every line for the most part consists of three words. Both songs are only chains of acrostic lines without any strophic grouping, and therefore cannot be divided out. The analogous accentuation shows how strong is the impression of the close relationship of this twin pair; and both Psalms also close, in vers. 9 and 10, with two verses of three members, being up to this point divided into verses of two members.

That which the poet purposes doing in ver. 1, he puts into execution from ver. 2 onwards. וְעֵדָה, according to lxiv. 7, cxviii. 14, is equivalent to וְעֵדְתָם. According to ver. 10*b*, חֶפְצֵיהֶם in ver. 2*b* apparently signifies those who find pleasure in them (the works of God); but חֶפְצֵי=חֶפְצִי (like שִׂמְחִי, Isa. xxiv. 7 = שִׂמְחִי) is less natural than that it should be the construct form of the plural of חֵפֶץ, that occurs in three instances,

---

* Böttcher transposes the verses in Ps. cxi., and in cxii. 5 corrects יכלכל into וכלכל; in the warmth of his critical zeal he runs against the boundary-posts of the letters marking the order, without observing it.

and there was no need for saying that those who make the works of God the object of their research are such as interest themselves in them. We are led to the right meaning by לְכָל־חֶפְצוֹ in 1 Kings ix. 11 in comparison with Isa. xliv. 28, xlvi. 10, cf. liii. 10, where חֵפֶץ signifies God's purpose in accordance with His counsel: constantly searched into, and therefore a worthy object of research (דרשׁ, root דר, to seek to know by rubbing, and in general experimentally, cf. درى of knowledge empirically acquired) according to all their aims, *i.e.* in all phases of that which they have in view. In ver. 4 זֵכֶר points to the festival which propagates the remembrance of the deeds of God in the Mosaic age; טֶרֶף, ver. 5, therefore points to the food provided for the Exodus, and to the Passover meal, together with the feast of unleavened bread, this memorial (זִכָּרוֹן, Ex. xii. 14) of the exemption in faithfulness to the covenant which was experienced in Egypt. This Psalm, says Luther, looks to me as though it had been composed for the festival of Easter. Even from the time of Theodoret and Augustine the thought of the Eucharist has been connected with ver. 5 in the New Testament mind; and it is not without good reason that Ps. cxi. has become the Psalm of the church at the celebration of the Lord's Supper. In connection with הִגִּיד one is reminded of the Pesach-Haggada. The deed of redemption which it relates has a power that continues in operation; for to the church of Jahve is assigned the victory not only over the peoples of Canaan, but over the whole world. The power of Jahve's deeds, which He has made known to His people, and which they tell over again among themselves, aims at giving them the inheritance of the peoples. The works of His hands are truth and right, for they are the realization of that which is true and which lasts and verifies itself, and of that which is right, that triumphantly maintains its ground. His ordinances are נְאֱמָנִים (occasionally pointed נֶאֱמָנִים), established, attested, in themselves and in their results authorizing a firm confidence in their salutariness (cf. xix. 8). סְמוּכִים, supported, stayed, viz. not outwardly, but in themselves, therefore imperturbable (cf. סָמוּךְ used of the state of mind, cxii. 8, Isa. xxvi. 3). עֲשׂוּיִם, moulded, arranged, viz. on the part of God, "in truth, and upright;" יָשָׁר is accusative of the predicate

(cf. cxix. 37), but without its being clear why it is not pointed
וַיֹּשֶׁר. If we have understood vers. 4–6 correctly, then פְּדוּת
glances back at the deliverance out of Egypt. Upon this
followed the ratification of the covenant on Sinai, which still
remains inviolable down to the present time of the poet, and
has the holiness and terribleness of the divine Name for a
guarantee of its inviolability. The fear of Jahve, this holy
and terrible God, is the beginning of wisdom—the motto of
the *Chokma* in Job (ch. xxviii. 28) and Proverbs (ch. i. 7,
ix. 10), the Books of the *Chokma*. Ver. 10*b* goes on in this
Proverbs-like strain: the fear of God, which manifests itself
in obedience, is to those who practise them (the divine precepts, פקודים) שֵׂכֶל טוֹב (Prov. xiii. 15, iii. 4, cf. 2 Chron. xxx.
22), a fine sagacity, praiseworthy discernment—such a (dutiful) one partakes of everlasting praise. It is true, in glancing
back to ver. 3*b*, תְּהִלָּתוֹ seems to refer to God, but a glance forward to cxii. 3*b* shows that the praise of him who fears God
is meant. The old observation therefore holds good: *ubi hæc
ode desinit, sequens incipit* (Bakius).

PSALM CXII.

ALPHABETICAL SONG IN PRAISE OF THOSE WHO FEAR GOD.

HALLELUJAH.

1 א BLESSED is the man who feareth Jahve,
  ב Who delighteth greatly in His commandments!
2 ג His seed shall become mighty upon earth,
  ד The generation of the upright is blessed.
3 ה Wealth and riches are in his house,
  ו And his righteousness standeth for ever.
4 ז There ariseth in darkness for the upright a light,
  ח Gracious and compassionate and righteous.
5 ט Blessed is he who giveth and lendeth,
  י In the judgment doth he maintain his cause.
6 כ He tottereth not for ever,
  ל The righteous is had in everlasting remembrance.
7 מ By evil tidings he is not affrighted,
  נ His heart is stedfast, confident in Jahve.

8 ס His heart is firm, it doth not fear;
   ע Until he see his desire upon his adversaries.
9 פ Freely doth he give to the needy,
   צ His righteousness standeth for ever.
   ק His horn groweth up into honour,
10 ר The wicked seeth it, and is vexed,
   ש Gnashing his teeth and melting away—
   ת The desire of the wicked shall perish.

The alphabetical Hallelujah Ps. cxi., which celebrated the government of God, is now followed by another coinciding with it in structure (*CTYXOC K̄B̄, i.e.* 22 στίχοι, as the Coptic version correctly counts), which celebrates the men whose conduct is ordered after the divine pattern.

As in the preceding Psalm, ver. 1 here also sets forth the theme of that which follows. What is there said in ver. 3 concerning the righteousness of God, ver. 3 here says of the righteousness of him who fears God: this also standeth fast for ever, it is indeed the copy of the divine, it is the work and gift of God (xxiv. 5), inasmuch as God's salutary action and behaviour, laid hold of in faith, works a like form of action and behaviour to it in man, which, as ver. 9 says, is, according to its nature, love. The promise in ver. 4 sounds like Isa. lx. 2. Hengstenberg renders: " There ariseth in the darkness light to the upright who is gracious and compassionate and just." But this is impossible as a matter of style. The three adjectives (as in cxi. 4, pointing back to Ex. xxxiv. 6, cf. cxlv. 8, cxvi. 5) are a mention of God according to His attributes. חַנּוּן and רַחוּם never take the article in Biblical Hebrew, and צַדִּיק follows their example here (cf. on the contrary, Ex. ix. 27). God Himself is the light which arises in darkness for those who are sincere in their dealings with Him; He is the Sun of right-eousness with wings of rays dispensing " grace" and " tender mercies," Mal. iii. 20 [iv. 2]. The fact that He arises for those who are compassionate as He is compassionate, is evident from ver. 5. טוֹב being, as in Isa. iii. 10, Jer. xliv. 17, in-tended of well-being, prosperity, טוֹב אִישׁ is here equivalent to אַשְׁרֵי אִישׁ, which is rendered טוּבֵיה דְּגַבְרָא in Targumic phrase. חוֹנֵן signifies, as in xxxvii. 26, 21, one who charitably dispenses his gifts around.   Ver. 5*b* is not an extension of the picture of virtue, but, as in cxxvii. 5*c*, a promissory prospect: he will uphold in integrity (בְּמִשְׁפָּט, lxxii. 2, Isa. ix. 6 [7], and frequently), or rather (=בַּמִּשְׁפָּט) in the cause (cxliii. 2, Prov. xxiv. 23, and frequently), the things which depend upon him, or with which he has to do; for כִּלְכֵּל, *sustinere*, signifies to sustain, *i.e.* to nourish, to sustain, *i.e.* endure, and also to support, maintain, *i.e.* carry through.   This is explanatorily confirmed in ver. 6: he stands, as a general thing, imperturbably fast.   And when he dies he becomes the object of everlasting remembrance, his name is still blessed (Prov. x. 7).   Because he has a cheerful conscience, his heart too is not disconcerted by any evil tidings (Jer. xlix. 23): it remains נָכוֹן, erect, straight and firm, without suffering itself to bend or warp; בָּטֻחַ בְּה׳, full of confidence (passive, "in the sense of a passive state after a completed action of the person himself," like זָכוּר, ciii. 14); סָמוּךְ, stayed in itself and established.   The last two designations are taken from Isa. xxvi. 3, where it is the church of the last times that is spoken of.   Ps. xci. 8 gives us information with reference to the meaning of רָאָה בְצָרָיו; עַד, as in xciv. 13, of the inevitable goal, on this side of which he remains undismayed.   2 Cor. ix. 9, where Paul makes use of ver. 9 of the Psalm before us as an encouragement to Christian beneficence, shows how little the assertion "his righteousness standeth for ever" is opposed to the New Testament consciousness.   פִּזַּר of giving away liberally and in manifold ways, as in Prov. xi. 24.   רוּם, ver. 9*c*, stands in opposition to the egoistical הָרִים in lxxv. 5 as a vegetative sprouting up (cxxxii. 17).   The evil-doer must see this and, confounded, vex himself over it; he gnashes his teeth with the rage of envy and chagrin, and melts away, *i.e.* loses consistency, becomes unhinged, dies off (נָמֵס, 3d *præt. Niph.* as in Ex. xvi. 21, pausal form of נָמֵס=נָמַס).   How often has he desired the ruin of him whom he must now see in honour! The tables are turned; this and his ungodly desire in general come to nought, inasmuch as the opposite is realized.   On יִרְאָה, with its self-evident object, cf. Mic. vii. 10.   Concerning the pausal form וְכָעַס, *vid.* xciii. 1.   Hupfeld wishes to read תִּקְוַת after ix. 19, Prov. x. 28.   In defence of the traditional reading, Hitzig rightly points to Prov. x. 24 together with ver. 28.

PSALM CXIII.

HALLELUJAH TO HIM WHO RAISETH OUT OF LOW ESTATE.

HALLELUJAH.

1 PRAISE, ye servants of Jahve,
　Praise the Name of Jahve!
2 Blessed be the Name of Jahve
　From this time forth and for evermore!
3 From the rising of the sun unto its going down
　Is the Name of Jahve to be praised.

4 Exalted above all peoples is Jahve,
　Above the heavens His glory.
5 Who is like Jahve our God,
　He who sitteth enthroned on high,
6 He who looketh far below
　In heaven and upon earth?

7 Who raiseth up the lowly out of the dust,
　Who lifteth the poor from the heap of ashes,
8 To set him with nobles,
　With the nobles of His people.
9 Who maketh the barren woman to keep house,
　As a joyful mother of the sons,
　　　　Hallelujah.

With this Psalm begins the *Hallel*, which is recited at the three great feasts, at the feast of the Dedication (*Chanucca*) and at the new moons, and not on New Year's day and the day of Atonement, because a cheerful song of praise does not harmonize with the mournful solemnity of these days. And they are recited only in fragments during the last days of the Passover, for " my creatures, saith the Holy One, blessed be He, were drowned in the sea, and ought ye to break out into songs of rejoicing?" In the family celebration of the Passover night it is divided into two parts, the one half, Ps. cxiii., cxiv., being sung before the repast, before the emptying of the second festal cup, and the other half, Ps. cxv.–cxviii., after

the repast, after the filling of the fourth cup, to which the
ὑμνήσαντες (Matt. xxvi. 30, Mark xiv. 26) after the institution
of the Lord's Supper, which was connected with the fourth
festal cup, may refer. Paulus Burgensis styles Ps. cxiii.–cxviii.
Alleluja Judæorum magnum. This designation is also frequently
found elsewhere. But according to the prevailing custom, Ps.
cxiii.–cxviii., and more particularly Ps. cxv.–cxviii., are called
only *Hallel*, and Ps. cxxxvi., with its " for His mercy endureth
for ever" repeated twenty-six times, bears the name of " *the
Great Hallel*" (הַלֵּל הַגָּדוֹל).*

A heaping up, without example elsewhere, of the so-called
Chirek compaginis is peculiar to Ps. cxiii. Gesenius and others
call the connecting vowels *i* and *o* (in proper names also *u*) the
remains of old case terminations ; with the former the Arabic
genitive termination is compared, and with the latter the
Arabic nominative termination. But in opposition to this it
has been rightly observed, that this *i* and *o* are not attached to
the dependent word (the genitive), but to the governing word.
According to the more probable view of Ewald, § 211, *i* and *o*
are equivalent connecting vowels which mark the relation of the
genitive case, and are to be explained from the original oneness
of the Semitic and Indo-Germanic languages.

The *i* is found most frequently appended to the first member
of the *stat. constr.*, and both to the *masc.*, viz. in Deut. xxxiii.
16, Zech. xi. 17 (perhaps twice, *vid.* Köhler *in loc.*), and to the
femin., viz. in Gen. xxxi. 39, Ps. cx. 4, Isa. i. 21. Lev. xxvi.
42, Ps. cxvi. 1 hardly belong here. Then this *i* is also fre-

---

* *Vid.* the tractate *Sofrim*, xviii. § 2. Apart from the new moons, a
which the recitation of the *Hallel* κατ᾽ ἐξοχήν, *i.e.* Ps. cxiii.–cxviii., is only
according to custom (מנהג), not according to the law, the *Hallel* was
recited eighteen times a year during the continuance of the Temple (and
in Palestine even in the present day), viz. once at the Passover, once at
Shabuoth, eight times at Succoth, eight times at Chanucca (the feast of
the Dedication) ; and now in the Exile twenty-one times, because the
Passover and Succoth have received two feast-days and Shabuoth one as
an addition, viz. twice at the Passover, twice at Shabuoth, nine times at
Succoth. Instead of *Hallel* absolutely we also find the appellation " the
Egyptian Hallel" (הַלֵּל הַמִּצְרִי) for Ps. cxiii.–cxviii. The ancient ritual only
makes a distinction between this (Egyptian) Hallel and the Great Hallel,
Ps. cxxxvi. (see there).

quently found when the second member of the *stat. constr.* has
a preposition, and this preposition is consequently in process of
being resolved: Gen. xlix. 11, Ex. xv. 6, Obad. ver. 3 (Jer.
xlix. 16), Hos. x. 11, Lam. i. 1, Ps. cxxiii. 1, and perhaps
Cant. i. 9. Also in the *Chethîb*, Jer. xxii. 23, li. 13, Ezek.
xxvii. 3. Thirdly, where a word stands between the two notions
that belong together according to the genitival relation, and
the *stat. construct.* is consequently really resolved: Ps. ci. 5,
Isa. xxii. 16, Mic. vii. 14. It is the same *i* which is found in a
great many proper names, both Israelitish, *e.g. Gamaliel* (benefit
of God), and Phœnician, *e.g. Melchizedek, Hanniba'al* (the
favour of Baal), and is also added to many Hebrew prepositions, like בִּלְתִּי (where the *i* however can, according to the
context, also be a pronominal suffix), זוּלָתִי (where *i* can likewise be a suffix), מִנִּי (poetical). In אַפְסִי, on the other hand,
the *i* is always a suffix. The tone of the *i* only retreats in
accordance with rhythmical rule (*vid.* cx. 4), otherwise *i* is
always accented. Ver. 8 shows how our Ps. cxiii. in particular delights in this ancient *i*, where it is even affixed to the
infinitive as an ornament, a thing which occurs nowhere else,
so that לְהוֹשִׁיבִי excites the suspicion of being written in error for
לְהוֹשִׁיבוֹ.

Among those things which make God worthy to be praised
the Psalm gives prominence to the condescension of the infinitely exalted One towards the lowly one. It is the lowliness of
God lowering itself for the exaltation of the lowly which performs its utmost in the work of redemption. Thus it becomes
explicable that Mary in her *Magnificat* breaks forth into the
same strain with the song of Hannah (1 Sam. ch. ii.) and this
Psalm.

Vers. 1–3. The call, not limited by any addition as in
cxxxiv. 1, or even, after the manner of ciii. 20 sq., extended
over the earth, is given to the whole of the true Israel that corresponds to its election by grace and is faithful to its mission;
and its designation by " servants of Jahve" (lxix. 37, cf.
xxxiv. 23), or even " servant of Jahve" (cxxxvi. 22), has
come into vogue more especially through the second part of
Isaiah. This Israel is called upon to praise Jahve; for the
praise and celebration of His Name, *i.e.* of His nature, which

is disclosed by means of its manifestation, is a principal element, yea, the proper ground and aim, of the service, and shall
finally become that which fills all time and all space. מְהֻלָּל,
laudatum (*est*), is equivalent to αἰνετόν, *laudabile* (LXX., Vulgate), and this does not differ greatly from *laudetur*. The predictive interpretation *laudabitur* is opposed to the context (cf.
moreover Köhler on Mal. i. 11).

Vers. 4–6. This praiseworthiness is now confirmed. The
opening reminds one of xcix. 2. *Pasek* stands between גוים
and יהוה in order to keep them apart. The totality of the
nations is great, but Jahve is raised above it; the heavens
are glorious, but Jahve's glory is exalted above them. It is
not to be explained according to cxlviii. 13; but according to
lvii. 6, 12, רם belongs to ver. 4*b* too as predicate. He is the
incomparable One who has set up His throne in the height,
but at the same time directs His gaze deep downwards (expression according to Ges. § 142, rem. 1) in the heavens and
upon earth, *i.e.* nothing in all the realm of the creatures that
are beneath Him escapes His sight, and nothing is so low that
it remains unnoticed by Him; on the contrary, it is just that
which is lowly, as the following strophe presents to us in a
series of portraits so to speak, that is the special object of His
regard. The structure of vers. 5, 6 militates against the construction of " in the heavens and upon the earth" with the
interrogatory " who is like unto Jahve our God?" after Deut.
iii. 24.

Vers. 7–9. The thoughts of vers. 7*a* and 8*a* are transplanted from the song of Hannah. עָפָר, according to 1 Kings
xvi. 2, cf. xiv. 7, is an emblem of lowly estate (Hitzig), and
אַשְׁפֹּת (from שָׁפַת) an emblem of the deepest poverty and desertion; for in Syria and Palestine the man who is shut out
from society lies upon the *mezbele* (the dunghill or heap of
ashes), by day calling upon the passers-by for alms, and by
night hiding himself in the ashes that have been warmed by
the sun (*Job*, ii. 152). The movement of the thoughts in ver. 8,
as in ver. 1, follows the model of the epizeuxis. Together with
the song of Hannah the poet has before his eye Hannah's
exaltation out of sorrow and reproach. He does not, however,
repeat the words of her song which have reference to this
(1 Sam. ii. 5), but clothes his generalization of her experience

in his own language. If he intended that עֲקֶרֶת should be understood out of the genitival relation after the form עֲטֶרֶת, why
did he not write מוֹשִׁיבִי הַבַּיִת עֲקָרָה? הַבַּיִת would then be equivalent to בֵּיתָה, lxviii. 7. עֲקֶרֶת הַבַּיִת is the expression for a woman
who is a wife, and therefore housewife, נְוַת (בְּעֲלַת) הַבַּיִת, but yet
not a mother. Such an one has no settled position in the house
of the husband, the firm bond is wanting in her relationship
to her husband. If God gives her children, He thereby makes
her then thoroughly at home and rooted-in in her position. In
the predicate notion אֵם הַבָּנִים שְׂמֵחָה the definiteness attaches to
the second member of the string of words, as in Gen. xlviii. 19,
2 Sam. xii. 30 (cf. the reverse instance in Jer. xxiii. 26, נִבְּאֵי
הַשֶּׁקֶר, those prophesying that which is false), therefore: a mother
of the children. The poet brings the matter so vividly before
him, that he points as it were with his finger to the children
with which God blesses her.

PSALM CXIV.

COMMOTION OF NATURE BEFORE GOD THE REDEEMER OUT OF EGYPT.

1 WHEN Israel went forth out of Egypt,
  The house of Jacob out of a people of strange language,
2 Then Judah became His sanctuary,
  Israel His dominion.

3 The sea saw it, and fled,
  Jordan turned backwards,
4 The mountains skipped like rams,
  The hills like young sheep.

5 What aileth thee, O sea, that thou fleest?
  O Jordan, that thou turnest backwards?
6 Ye mountains, that ye skip like rams?
  Ye hills, like young sheep?—

7 Before the face of the Lord tremble, O earth,
  Before the face of the God of Jacob,

8 Who changeth the rock into a pool of water,
　The flinty rock into water-springs!

To the side of the general Hallelujah Ps. cxiii. comes an historical one, which is likewise adorned in ver. 8 with the *Chirek compaginis*, and still further with *Cholem compaginis*, and is the festival Psalm of the eighth Passover day in the Jewish ritual. The deeds of God at the time of the Exodus are here brought together to form a picture in miniature which is as majestic as it is charming. There are four tetrastichs, which pass by with the swiftness of a bird as it were with four flappings of its wings. The church sings this Psalm in a *tonus peregrinus* distinct from the eight Psalm-tones.

Vers. 1–4. Egypt is called עַם לֹעֵז (from לָעַז, cogn. לָעֵג, לָעָה), because the people spoke a language unintelligible to Israel (lxxxi. 6), and as it were a stammering language. The LXX., and just so the Targum, renders ἐκ λαοῦ βαρβάρου (from the Sanscrit *barbaras*, just as onomatopoetic as *balbus*, cf. Fleischer in Levy's *Chaldäisches Wörterbuch*, i. 420). The redeemed nation is called *Judah*, inasmuch as God made it His sanctuary (קֹדֶשׁ) by setting up His sanctuary (מִקְדָּשׁ, Ex. xv. 17) in the midst of it, for Jerusalem (*el-kuds*) was Benjamitish Judæan, and from the time of David was accounted directly as Judæan. In so far, however, as He made this people His kingdom (מַמְשְׁלוֹתָיו, an amplificative plural with *Mem pathacha-tum*), by placing Himself in the relation of King (Deut. xxxiii. 5) to the people of possession which by a revealed law He established characteristically as His own, it is called *Israel*. The predicate takes the form וַתְּהִי, for peoples together with country and city are represented as feminine (cf. Jer. viii. 5). The foundation of that new beginning in connection with the history of redemption was laid amidst majestic wonders, inasmuch as nature was brought into service, co-operating and sympathizing in the work (cf. lxxvii. 15 sqq.). The dividing of the sea opens, and the dividing of the Jordan closes, the journey through the desert to Canaan. The sea stood aside, Jordan halted and was dammed up on the north in order that the redeemed people might pass through. And in the middle, between these great wonders of the exodus from Egypt and the entrance into Canaan, arises the not less mighty wonder of the giving of the Law: the skipping of the mountains like rams, of the hills like בְּנֵי־צֹאן, *i.e.* lambs (Wisd. xix. 9), depicts the quaking of Sinai and its environs (Ex. xix. 18, cf. *supra* lxviii. 9, and on the figure xxix. 6).

Vers. 5–8. The poet, when he asks, "What aileth thee, O sea, that thou fleest . . . ?" lives and moves in this olden time as a cotemporary, or the present and the olden time as it were flow together to his mind; hence the answer he himself gives to the question propounded takes the form of a triumphant mandate. The Lord, the God of Jacob, thus mighty in wondrous works, it is before whom the earth must tremble. אָדוֹן does not take the article because it finds its completion in the following יַעֲקֹב (אֱלוֹהַּ); it is the same *epizeuxis* as in cxiii. 8, xciv. 3, xcvi. 7, 13. הַהֹפְכִי has the constructive *i* out of the genitival relation; and in לְמַעְיְנוֹ in this relation we have the constructive *ô*, which as a rule occurs only in the genitival combination, with the exception of this passage and בְּנוֹ בְעֹר, Num. xxiv. 3, 15 (not, however, in Prov. xiii. 4, "his, the sluggard's, soul"), found only in the name for wild animals חַיְתוֹ־אֶרֶץ, which occurs frequently, and first of all in Gen. i. 24. The expression calls to mind cvii. 35. הַצּוּר is taken from Ex. xvii. 6; and חַלָּמִישׁ (LXX. τὴν ἀκρότομον, that which is rugged, abrupt) * stands, according to Deut. viii. 15, poetically for סֶלַע, Num. xx. 11, for it is these two histories of the giving of water

---

* One usually compares خلنبوس, *chalnabûs* [the Karaite lexicographer Abraham ben David writes חלמבום]; but this obsolete word, as a compound from خلس, to be black-grey, and خنبس, to be hard, may originally signify a hard black-grey stone, whereas חלמיש looks like a mingling of the verbal stems حمس, to be hard, and حلس, to be black-brown (as جلمود, a detached block of rock, is of the verbal stems جلد, to be hard, and جمد, to be massive). In Hauran the doors of the houses and the window-shutters are called خلمسة when they consist of a massive slab of dolerite, probably from their blackish hue. Perhaps חלמיש is the ancient name for basalt; and in connection with the hardness of this form of rock, which resembles a mass of cast metal, the breaking through of springs is a great miracle.—WETZSTEIN. For other views *vid.* on Isa. xlix. 21, l. 7.

to which the poet points back.   But why to these in particular?
The causing of water to gush forth out of the flinty rock is a
practical proof of unlimited omnipotence and of the grace
which converts death into life.   Let the earth then tremble
before the Lord, the God of Jacob.   It has already trembled
before Him, and before Him let it tremble.   For that which
He has been He still ever is; and as He came once, He will
come again.

PSALM CXV.

CALL TO THE GOD OF ISRAEL, THE LIVING GOD, TO RESCUE THE HONOUR OF HIS NAME.

1 NOT unto us, Jahve, not unto us,
  But unto Thy Name give glory,
  Because of Thy loving-kindness, because of Thy truth.
2 Wherefore shall the heathen say:
  " Where is now their God? "

3 And our God is in the heavens,
  Whatsoever He willeth He carrieth out.
4 Their gods, however, are silver and gold,
  The work of men's hands.
5 They have a mouth and speak not,
  They have eyes and see not,
6 They have ears and· hear not,
  They have a nose and smell not.
7 Their hands, with which they handle not,
  Their feet, with which they walk not,
  They speak not with their throat.
8 Like unto them do those who make them become,
  Every one who trusteth in them.

9 Israel, trust thou in Jahve,
  Their help and their shield is He.
10 O house of Aaron, trust ye in Jahve,
  Their help and their shield is He.
11 Ye who fear Jahve, trust in Jahve,
  Their help and their shield is He.

12 Jahve hath been mindful of us, He will bless—
   He will bless the house of Israel,
   He will bless the house of Aaron,
13 He will bless those who fear Jahve,
   The small together with the great.
14 Jahve will add to you,
   To you and your children.

15 Blessed be ye of Jahve,
   The Creator of heaven and earth.
16 The heavens are heavens for Jahve,
   And the earth hath He given to the children of men.
17 The dead praise not Jāh,
   Nor all those who go down into the silence of death;
18 We, however, we will bless Jāh
   From henceforth and for evermore,
                 Hallelujah.

This Psalm, which has scarcely anything in common with
the preceding Psalm except that the expression "house of
Jacob," cxiv. 1, is here broken up into its several members in
vers. 12 sq., is found joined with it, making one Psalm, in the
LXX., Syriac, Arabic, and Æthiopic versions, just as on the
other hand Ps. cxvi. is split up into two. This arbitrary
arrangement condemns itself. Nevertheless Kimchi favours
it, and it has found admission into not a few Hebrew manu-
scripts.

It is a prayer of Israel for God's aid, probably in the presence of an expedition against heathen enemies. The two
middle strophes of the four are of the same compass. Ewald's
conjecture, that whilst the Psalm was being sung the sacrifice
was proceeded with, and that in ver. 12 the voice of a priest
proclaims the gracious acceptance of the sacrifice, is pleasing.
But the change of voices begins even with ver. 9, as Olshausen
also supposes.

Vers. 1, 2. It has to do not so much with the honour of
Israel, which is not worthy of the honour (Ezek. xxxvi. 22 sq.)
and has to recognise in its reproach a well-merited chastisement, as with the honour of Him who cannot suffer the

reproaching of His holy name to continue long. He willeth
that His name should be sanctified. In the consciousness of
his oneness with this will, the poet bases his petition, in so far
as it is at the same time a petition on behalf of Israel, upon
God's χάρις and ἀλήθεια as upon two columns. The second
עַל, according to an express note of the Masora, has no *Waw*
before it, although the LXX. and Targum insert one. The
thought in ver. 2 is moulded after lxxix. 10, or after Joel ii.
17, cf. Ps. xlii. 4, Mic. vii. 10. אַיֵּה־נָא is the same style as
נֶגְדָה־נָּא in cxvi. 18, cf. in the older language אָם־נָא, אַל־נָא, and
the like.

Vers. 3–8. The poet, with "And our God," in the name
of Israel opposes the scornful question of the heathen by the
believingly joyous confession of the exaltation of Jahve above
the false gods. Israel's God is in the heavens, and is therefore
supramundane in nature and life, and the absolutely unlimited
One, who is able to do all things with a freedom that is conditioned only by Himself: *quod vult, valet* (ver. 3*b* = cxxxv. 6,
Wisd. xii. 18, and frequently). The carved gods (עָצָב, from
עָצַב, cogn. קָצַב, חָצַב) of the heathen, on the contrary, are dead
images, which are devoid of all life, even of the sensuous life
the outward organs of which are imaged upon them. It cannot
be proved with Eccles. v. 16 that יְדֵיהֶם and רַגְלֵיהֶם are equivalent
to רגלים ידים, להם. They are either subjects which the *Waw*
apodosis (cf. Gen. xxii. 24, Prov. xxiii. 24, Hab. ii. 5) renders
prominent, or *casus absoluti* (Ges. § 145, 2), since both verbs
have the idols themselves as their subjects less on account of
their gender (יד and רגל are feminine, but the Hebrew usage of
genders is very free and not carried out uniformly) as in respect
of ver. 7*c*: with reference to their hands, etc. יְמִישׁוּן is the
energetic future form, which goes over from מָשַׁשׁ into מוּשׁ, for
יְמֻשׁוּ. It is said once again in ver. 7*c* that speech is wanting to
them; for the other negations only deny life to them, this at the
same time denies all personality. The author might know from
his own experience how little was the distinction made by the
heathen worship between the symbol and the thing symbolized.
Accordingly the worship of idols seems to him, as to the later
prophets, to be the extreme of self-stupefaction and of the destruction of human consciousness; and the final destiny of the
worshippers of false gods, as he says in ver. 8, is, that they

become like to their idols, that is to say, being deprived of their consciousness, life, and existence, they come to nothing, like those their nothingnesses (Isa. xliv. 9). This whole section of the Psalm is repeated in Ps. cxxxv. (vers. 6, 15–18).

Vers. 9–14. After this confession of Israel there now arises a voice that addresses itself to Israel. The threefold division into Israel, the house of Aaron, and those who fear Jahve is the same as in cxviii. 2–4. In Ps. cxxxv. the " house of Levi" is further added to the house of Aaron. Those who fear Jahve, who also stand in the last passage, are probably the proselytes (in the Acts of the Apostles σεβόμενοι τὸν Θεόν, or merely σεβόμενοι*); at any rate these are included even if Israel in ver. 9 is meant to signify the laity, for the notion of " those who fear Jahve" extends beyond Israel. The fact that the threefold refrain of the summons does not run, as in xxxiii. 20, *our help and shield is He*, is to be explained from its being an antiphonal song. In so far, however, as the Psalm supplicates God's protection and help in a campaign the declaration of confident hope, *their help and shield is He*, may, with Hitzig, be referred to the army that is gone or is going forth. It is the same voice which bids Israel to be of good courage and announces to the people the well-pleased acceptance of the sacrifice with the words " Jahve hath been mindful of us" (זְכָרָנוּ 'ה, cf. עַתָּה יָדַעְתִּי, xx. 7), perhaps simultaneously with the presentation of the memorial portion (אזכרה) of the meat-offering (xxxviii. 1). The יְבָרֶךְ placed at the head is particularized threefold, corresponding to the threefold summons. The special promise of blessing which is added in ver. 14 is an echo of Deut. i. 11, as in 2 Sam. xxiv. 3. The contracted future יֹסֵף we take in a consolatory sense; for as an optative it would be too isolated here. In spite of all oppression on the part of the heathen, God will make His people ever more numerous, more capable of offering resistance, and more awe-inspiring.

Vers. 15–18. The voice of consolation is continued in ver. 15, but it becomes the voice of hope by being blended with

---

* The appellation φοβούμενοι does not however occur, if we do not bring Acts x. 2 in here; but in Latin inscriptions in Orelli-Hentzen No. 2523, and in Auer in the *Zeitschrift für katholische Theologie* 1852, S. 80, the proselyte (*religionis Judaicæ*) is called *metuens.*

the newly strengthened believing tone of the congregation.
Jahve is here called the Creator of heaven and earth because
the worth and magnitude of His blessing are measured thereby.
He has reserved the heavens to Himself, but given the earth to
men. This separation of heaven and earth is a fundamental characteristic of the post-diluvian history. The throne of God is
in the heavens, and the promise, which is given to the patriarchs
on behalf of all mankind, does not refer to heaven, but to the
possession of the earth (xxxvii. 22). The promise is as yet
limited to this present world, whereas in the New Testament
this limitation is removed and the κληρονομία embraces heaven
and earth. This Old Testament limitedness finds further expression in ver. 17, where דוּמָה, as in xciv. 17, signifies the
silent land of Hades. The Old Testament knows nothing of
a heavenly *ecclesia* that praises God without intermission, consisting not merely of angels, but also of the spirits of all men
who die in the faith. Nevertheless there are not wanting hints
that point upwards which were even better understood by the
post-exilic than by the pre-exilic church. The New Testament
morn began to dawn even upon the post-exilic church. We
must not therefore be astonished to find the tone of vi. 6, xxx.
10, lxxxviii. 11–13, struck up here, although the echo of those
earlier Psalms here is only the dark foil of the confession
which the church makes in ver. 18 concerning its immortality.
The church of Jahve as such does not die. That it also does
not remain among the dead, in whatever degree it may die off
in its existing members, the psalmist might know from Isa.
xxvi. 19, xxv. 8. But the close of the Psalm shows that such
predictions which light up the life beyond only gradually became
elements of the church's consciousness, and, so to speak, dogmas.

PSALM CXVI.

THANKSGIVING SONG OF ONE WHO HAS ESCAPED FROM
DEATH.

1 I LOVE, for Jahve heareth
  My cry, my heartfelt supplication.
2 For He hath inclined His ear unto me,
  Therefore will I call as long as I live.

3 The cords of death compassed me,
  And the straitnesses of Hades came upon me,
  Distress and sorrow did I experience.
4 Then upon the name of Jahve did I call:
  O Jahve, deliver my soul.

5 Gracious is Jahve and righteous,
  And our God a compassionate One.
6 A Guardian of the simple is Jahve;
  I was brought low, and He helped me.
7 Turn in, my soul, unto thy rest,
  For Jahve dealeth bountifully with thee.
8 Yea, Thou hast delivered my soul from death,
  Mine eyes from tears,
  My feet from falling.
9 I will walk before Jahve
  In the lands of the living.

10 I believe now, when I must speak:
  "I, I am afflicted very greatly."
11 I have said to myself in my despair:
  "All men are liars."
12 How can I repay Jahve
  All His benefits toward me?
13 The cup of salvation will I raise,
  And proclaim the Name of Jahve.
14 My vows will I pay unto Jahve,
  I will do it in the presence of all His people.

15 Precious in the eyes of Jahve
  Is the death of His saints.
16 Yea, O Jahve, for I am Thy servant,
  I am Thy servant, the son of Thy handmaid,
  Thou hast loosed my bonds.
17 Unto Thee will I sacrifice a sacrifice of thanksgiving
  And proclaim the Name of Jahve.
18 My vows will I pay unto Jahve,
  I will do it in the presence of all His people,
19 In the courts of Jahve's house,
  In the midst of thee, O Jerusalem!
        Hallelujah.

We have here another anonymous Psalm closing with *Hallelujah*. It is not a supplicatory song with a hopeful prospect before it like Ps. cxv., but a thanksgiving song with a fresh recollection of some deadly peril that has just been got the better of ; and is not, like Ps. cxv., from the mouth of the church, but from the lips of an individual who distinguishes himself from the church. It is an individual that has been delivered who here praises the loving-kindness he has experienced in the language of the tenderest affection. The LXX. has divided this deeply fervent song into two parts, cxvi. 1–9, 10–19, and made two Hallelujah-Psalms out of it ; whereas it unites Ps. cxiv. and cxv. into one. The four sections or strophes, the beginnings of which correspond to one another (vers. 1 and 10, 5 and 15), are distinctly separate. The words וּבְשֵׁם ה' אֶקְרָא are repeated three times. In the first instance they are retrospective, but then swell into an always more full-toned vow of thanksgiving. The late period of its composition makes itself known not only in the strong Aramaic colouring of the form of the language, which adopts all kinds of embellishments, but also in many passages borrowed from the pre-exilic Psalms. The very opening, and still more so the progress, of the first strophe reminds one of Ps. xviii., and becomes an important hint for the exposition of the Psalm.

Vers. 1–4. Not only is אָהַבְתִּי כִּי, " I love (like, am well pleased) that," like ἀγαπῶ ὅτι, Thucydides vi. 36, contrary to the usage of the language, but the thought, " I love that Jahve answereth me," is also tame and flat, and inappropriate to the continuation in ver. 2. Since vers. 3, 4 have come from xviii. 5–17, אָהַבְתִּי is to be understood according to אֶרְחָמְךָ in xviii. 2, so that it has the following יהוה as its object, not it is true grammatically, but logically. The poet is fond of this pregnant use of the verb without an expressed object, cf. אֶקְרָא in ver. 2, and הֶאֱמַנְתִּי in ver. 10. The *Pasek* after יִשְׁמַע is intended to guard against the blending of the final aʿ with the initial ʾa of אדני (cf. lxvi. 18, v. 2, in Baer). In ver. 1*b* the accentuation prevents the rendering *vocem orationis meæ* (Vulgate, LXX.) by means of *Mugrash*. The î of קוֹלִי will therefore no more be the archaic connecting vowel (Ew. § 211, *b*) than in Lev. xxvi. 42 ; the poet has varied the genitival construction of xxviii.

6 to the permutative. The second כִּי, following close upon the
first, makes the continuation of the confirmation retrospective.
" In my days" is, as in Isa. xxxix. 8, Bar. iv. 20, cf. בְּחַיָּי in
lxiii. 5, and frequently, equivalent to "so long as I live." We
even here hear the tone of Ps. xviii. (ver. 2), which is continued in vers. 3, 4 as a freely borrowed passage. Instead of
the " bands" (of Hades) there, the expression here is מְצָרֵי,
angustiæ, plural of מֵצַר, after the form מֵסַב in cxviii. 5, Lam. i.
3 (Böttcher, *De inferis*, § 423); the straitnesses of Hades are
deadly perils which can scarcely be escaped. The futures
אֶמְצָא and אֶקְרָא, by virtue of the connection, refer to the cotemporaneous past. אָנָּה (viz. בליש בקשה, *i.e.* in a suppliant sense)
is written with *He* instead of *Aleph* here and in five other
instances, as the Masora observes. It has its fixed *Metheg* in
the first syllable, in accordance with which it is to be pronounced *ānna* (like בָּתִּים, *bāttim*), and has an accented *ultima*
not merely on account of the following אֲדֹנָי = יהוה (*vid.* on iii.
8), but in every instance; for even where (the *Metheg* having
been changed into a conjunctive) it is supplied with two different accents, as in Gen. l. 17, Ex. xxxii. 31, the second
indicates the tone-syllable.* Instead now of repeating "and
Jahve answered me," the poet indulges in a laudatory confession
of general truths which have been brought vividly to his mind
by the answering of his prayer that he has experienced.

Vers. 5—9. With "gracious" and "compassionate" is
here associated, as in cxii. 4, the term "righteous," which
comprehends within itself everything that Jahve asserts concerning Himself in Ex. xxxiv. 6 sq. from the words " and
abundant in goodness and truth" onwards. His love is turned
especially toward the simple (LXX. τὰ νήπια, cf. Matt. xi. 25),

---

* Kimchi, mistaking the vocation of the *Metheg*, regards אָנָּה (אָנָּא) as
Milel. But the Palestinian and the Babylonian systems of pointing coincide in this, that the beseeching אנא (אנה) is *Milra*, and the interrogatory
אנה *Milel* (with only two exceptions in our text, which is fixed according
to the Palestinian Masora, viz. cxxxix. 7, Deut. i. 28, where the following
word begins with *Aleph*), and these modes of accenting accord with the
origin of the two particles. Pinsker (*Einleitung*, S. xiii.) insinuates against
the Palestinian system, that in the cases where אנא has two accents the
pointing was not certain of the correct accentuation, only from a deficient
knowledge of the bearings of the case.

who stand in need of His protection and give themselves over to it. פְּתָאיִם, as in Prov. ix. 6, is a mode of writing blended out of פְּתָאיִם and פְּתָיִים. The poet also has experienced this love in a time of impotent need. דַּלּוֹתִי is accented on the ultima here, and not as in cxlii. 7 on the penult. The accentuation is regulated by some phonetic or rhythmical law that has not yet been made clear (vid. on Job xix. 17).* יְהוֹשִׁיעַ is a resolved Hiphil form, the use of which became common in the later period of the language, but is not alien to the earlier period, especially in poetry (xlv. 18, cf. lxxxi. 6, 1 Sam. xvii. 47, Isa. lii. 5). In ver. 7 we hear the form of soliloquy which has become familiar to us from Ps. xlii., xliii., ciii. שׁוּבִי is Milra here, as also in two other instances. The plural מְנוּחִים signifies full, complete rest, as it is found only in God; and the suffix in the address to the soul is ajchi for ajich, as in ciii. 3–5. The perfect נָּמַל states that which is a matter of actual experience, and is corroborated in ver. 8 in retrospective perfects. In vers. 8, 9 we hear lvi. 14 again amplified; and if we add xxvii. 13, then we see as it were to the bottom of the origin of the poet's thoughts. מִן־דִּמְעָה belongs still more decidedly than יְהוֹשִׁיעַ to the resolved forms which multiply in the later period of the language. In ver. 9 the poet declares the result of the divine deliverance. The Hithpa. אֶתְהַלֵּךְ denotes a free and contented going to and fro; and instead of "the land of the living," xxvii. 13, the expression here is "the lands (אֲרָצוֹת), i.e. the broad land, of the living." There he walks forth, with nothing to hinder his feet or limit his view, in the presence of Jahve, i.e. having his Deliverer from death ever before his eyes.

Vers. 10–14. Since כִּי אֲדַבֵּר does not introduce anything that could become an object of belief, הֶאֱמִין is absolute here: to have faith, just as in Job xxiv. 22, xxix. 24, with לֹא it signifies "to be without faith, i.e. to despair." But how does it now proceed? The LXX. renders ἐπίστευσα, διὸ ἐλάλησα, which the apostle makes use of in 2 Cor. iv. 13, without our being

---

* The national grammarians, so far as we are acquainted with them, furnish no explanation. De Balmis believes that these Milra forms דַּלּוֹתִי, בַּלּוֹתִי, and the like, must be regarded as infinitives, but at the same time confirms the difference of views existing on this point.

therefore obliged with Luther to render: *I believe, therefore I speak;* כִּי does not signify διό. Nevertheless כִּי might according to the sense be used for לְכֵן, if it had to be rendered with Hengstenberg: "I believed, therefore I spake, but I was very much plagued." But this assertion does not suit this connection, and has, moreover, no support in the syntax. It might more readily be rendered: "I have believed that I should yet speak, *i.e.* that I should once more have a deliverance of God to celebrate;" but the connection of the parallel members, which is then only lax, is opposed to this. Hitzig's attempted interpretation, "I trust, when (כִּי as in Jer. xii. 1) I should speak: I am greatly afflicted," *i.e.* "I have henceforth confidence, so that I shall not suffer myself to be drawn away into the expression of despondency," does not commend itself, since ver. 10*b* is a complaining, but not therefore as yet a desponding assertion of the reality. Assuming that הֶאֱמַנְתִּי and אָמַרְתִּי in ver. 11*a* stand on the same line in point of time, it seems that it must be interpreted *I had faith, for I spake* (was obliged to speak); but אדבר, separated from האמנתי by כי, is opposed to the colouring relating to the cotemporaneous past. Thus ver. 10 will consequently contain the issue of that which has been hitherto experienced: *I have gathered up faith and believe* henceforth, *when I speak* (have to speak, must speak): *I am deeply afflicted* (עָנָה as in cxix. 67, cf. عنى, to be bowed down, more particularly in captivity, whence العُناة, those who are bowed down). On the other hand, ver. 11 is manifestly a retrospect. He believes now, for he is thoroughly weaned from putting trust in men: *I said in my despair* (taken from xxxi. 23), the result of my deeply bowed down condition: *All men are liars* (πᾶς ἄνθρωπος ψεύστης, Rom. iii. 4). Forsaken by all the men from whom he expected succour and help, he experienced the truth and faithfulness of God. Striding away over this thought, he asks in ver. 12 how he is to give thanks to God for all His benefits. מָה is an adverbial accusative for בַּמֶּה, as in Gen. xliv. 16, and the substantive תַּגְמוּל, in itself a later formation, has besides the Chaldaic plural suffix *ôhi*, which is without example elsewhere in Hebrew. The poet says in ver. 13 how alone he can and will give thanks to his Deliverer, by using a figure taken from the Passover (Matt. xxvi. 27),

the memorial repast in celebration of the redemption out of
Egypt. The cup of salvation is that which is raised aloft and
drunk amidst thanksgiving for the manifold and abundant
salvation (יְשׁוּעוֹת) experienced.   קָרָא בְשֵׁם ה׳ is the usual expression for a solemn and public calling upon and proclamation of
the Name of God. In ver. 14 this thanksgiving is more
minutely designated as שַׁלְמֵי נֶדֶר, which the poet now discharges.
A common and joyous eating and drinking in the presence of
God was associated with the *shelamim*. נָא (*vid.* cxv. 2) in the
freest application gives a more animated tone to the word with
which it stands. Because he is impelled frankly and freely to
give thanks before the whole congregation, נא stands beside נֶגֶד,
and נֶגֶד, moreover, has the intentional *ah.*

Vers. 15—19. From what he has experienced the poet
infers that the saints of Jahve are under His most especial
providence. Instead of הַמָּוֶת the poet, who is fond of such
embellishments, chooses the pathetic form הַמָּוְתָה, and consequently, instead of the genitival construct state (מוֹת), the construction with the *Lamed* of " belonging to." It ought properly
to be " soul " or " blood," as in the primary passage lxxii. 14.
But the observation of Grotius: *quæ pretiosa sunt, non facile
largimur,* applies also to the expression " death." The death of
His saints is no trifling matter with God; He does not lightly
suffer it to come about; He does not suffer His own to be
torn away from Him by death.* After this the poet goes on
beseechingly: *ānnáh Adonaj.* The prayer itself is not contained in פִּתַּחְתָּ לְמוֹסֵרָי,—for he is already rescued, and the
perfect as a precative is limited to such utterances spoken in
the tone of an exclamation as we find in Job xxi. 16,—but
remains unexpressed; it lies wrapped up as it were in this
heartfelt *ānnáh:* Oh remain still so gracious to me as Thou
hast already proved Thyself to me. The poet rejoices in and
is proud of the fact that he may call himself the servant of
God. With אֲמָתֶךָ he is mindful of his pious mother (cf. lxxxvi.

---

* The Apostolic Constitutions (vi. 30) commend the singing of these
and other words of the Psalms at the funerals of those who have departed
in the faith (cf. Augusti, *Denkwürdigkeiten,* ix. 563). In the reign of the
Emperor Decius, Babylas Bishop of Antioch, full of blessed hope, met
death singing these words.

16). The Hebrew does not form a feminine, עַבְדָּה ; أَمَة signifies a maid, who is not, as such, also عَبْدَة, a slave. The dative
of the object, לְמֹסְרִי (from מֹסְרִים for the more usual מֹסְרוֹת), is
used with פתחת instead of the accusative after the Aramaic
manner, but it does also occur in the older Hebrew (*e.g.* Job
xix. 3, Isa. liii. 11). The purpose of publicly giving thanks to
the Gracious One is now more full-toned here at the close.
Since such emphasis is laid on the Temple and the congregation, what is meant is literal thank-offerings in payment of
vows. In בְּתוֹכֵכִי (as in cxxxv. 9) we have in the suffix the
ancient and Aramaic *i* (cf. ver. 7) for the third time. With
אָנָּה the poet clings to Jahve, with נֶגְדָּה־נָּא to the congregation,
and with בְּתוֹכֵכִי to the holy city. The one thought that fills
his whole soul, and in which the song which breathes forth
his soul dies away, is *Hallelujah*.

PSALM CXVII.

INVITATION TO THE PEOPLES TO COME INTO THE KINGDOM OF GOD.

 1 PRAISE Jahve, all peoples,
   Praise Him, all ye nations !
 2 For mighty over us is His loving-kindness,
   And the truth of Jahve endureth for ever,
      Hallelujah !

The thanksgiving Psalm ending in *Hallelujah* is followed
by this shortest of all the Psalms, a Hallelujah addressed to
the heathen world. In its very brevity it is one of the grandest
witnesses of the might with which, in the midst of the Old
Testament, the world-wide mission of the religion of revelation
struck against or undermined the national limitation. It is
stamped by the apostle in Rom. xv. 11 as a *locus classicus* for
the fore-ordained (*gnadenrathschlussmässig*) participation of the
heathen in the promised salvation of Israel.

Even this shortest Psalm has its peculiarities in point of

language.   אֻמִּים (Aramaic אֻמַּיָּא, Arabic اُمَّة) is otherwise alien
to Old Testament Hebrew. The Old Testament Hebrew is
acquainted only with אֻמּוֹת as an appellation of Ismaelitish or
Midianitish tribes. כָּל־גּוֹיִם are, as in lxxii. 11, 17, all peoples
without distinction, and כָּל־הָאֻמִּים all nations without exception.
The call is confirmed from the might of the mercy or loving-
kindness of Jahve, which proves itself mighty over Israel, *i.e.*
by its intensity and fulness superabundantly covering (גָּבַר as
in ciii. 11; cf. ὑπερεπερίσσευσε, Rom. v. 20, ὑπερεπλεόνασε,
1 Tim. i. 14) human sin and infirmity; and from His truth,
by virtue of which history on into eternity ends in a verifying
of His promises. Mercy and truth are the two divine powers
which shall one day be perfectly developed and displayed in
Israel, and going forth from Israel, shall conquer the world.

PSALM CXVIII.

FESTIVAL PSALM AT THE DEDICATION OF THE NEW TEMPLE.

(*At the setting out.*)

1 GIVE thanks unto Jahve, for He is good,
  Yea, His mercy endureth for ever.
2 Let Israel say:
  " Yea, His mercy endureth for ever."
3 Let the house of Aaron say:
  " Yea, His mercy endureth for ever."
4 Let those who fear Jahve say:
  " Yea, His mercy endureth for ever."

(*On the way.*)

5 Out of straitness I cried unto Jah,
  Jah answered me upon a broad plain.
6 Jahve is for me—I do not fear,
  What can men do unto me?
7 Jahve is for me as my help,
  Therefore shall I see my desire upon those who hate me.

8 It is better to hide one's self in Jahve
   Than to put confidence in men.
9 It is better to take refuge in Jahve
   Than to put confidence in princes.
10 Let all the heathen compass me about—
   In the name of Jahve will I verily cut them in pieces.
11 Let them compass me about on all sides—
   In the name of Jahve will I verily cut them in pieces.
12 Let them compass me about like bees—
   They are extinguished like a fire of thorns,
   In the name of Jahve will I verily cut them in pieces.
13 Thou gavest me indeed a thrust that I might fall,
   But Jahve hath helped me.
14 My pride and my song is Jah,
   And He became my salvation.
15 The cry of exultation and of salvation resoundeth in the
      tents of the righteous :
   The right hand of Jahve getteth the victory.
16 The right hand of Jahve is highly exalted,
   The right hand of Jahve getteth the victory.
17 I shall not die, nay I shall live,
   And declare the deeds of Jah.
18 Jah hath chastened me sore,
   But hath not given me over unto death.

(At the going in.)

19 Open to me the gates of righteousness,
   That I may enter into them, that I may give thanks to Jah!

(Those who receive the festal procession.)

20 This is the gate of Jahve,
   The righteous may enter there.
21 I give thanks unto Thee, for Thou hast answered me,
   And art become my salvation.
22 The stone, which the builders despised,
   Is become the corner and head stone.
23 From Jahve is this come to pass,
   It is marvellous in our eyes.
24 This is the day which Jahve hath made,
   Let us exult and rejoice at it!

25 O Jahve, save I beseech Thee,
   O Jahve, grant I beseech Thee prosperity ! !
26 Blessed be he who cometh in the name of Jahve,
   We bless you from the house of Jahve.
27 God is Jahve and hath given us light—
   Bind the festive sacrifice with cords
   Even up to the horns of the altar !

(Answer of those who have arrived.)

28 My God art Thou, therefore will I give Thee thanks,
   My Deity, I will exalt Thee.

(All together.)

29 Give thanks unto Jahve, for He is good,
   Yea, His mercy endureth for ever.

What the close of Ps. cxvii. says of God's truth, viz. that it endureth for ever, the beginning of Ps. cxviii. says of its sister, His mercy or loving-kindness. It is the closing Psalm of the *Hallel*, which begins with Ps. cxiii., and the third *Hodu* (*vid.* on Ps. cv.). It was Luther's favourite Psalm : his beauteous *Confitemini*, which " had helped him out of troubles out of which neither emperor nor king, nor any other man on earth, could have helped him." With the exposition of this his noblest jewel, his defence and his treasure, he occupied himself in the solitude of his Patmos.

It is without any doubt a post-exilic song. Here too Hupfeld sweeps away everything into vague generality; but the history of the period after the Exile, without any necessity for our coming down to the Maccabæan period, as do De Wette and Hitzig, presents three occasions which might have given birth to it; viz. (1) The first celebration of the Feast of Tabernacles in the seventh month of the first year of the Return, when there was only a plain altar as yet erected on the holy place, Ezra iii. 1–4 (to be distinguished from a later celebration of the Feast of Tabernacles on a large scale and in exact accordance with the directions of the Law, Neh. ch. viii.). So Ewald. (2) The laying of the foundation-stone of the Temple in the second month of the second year, Ezra iii. 8 sqq. So Hengstenberg. (3) The dedication of the completed Temple

in the twelfth month of the sixth year of Darius, Ezra vi. 15
sqq. So Stier. These references to cotemporary history have
all three more or less in their favour. The first is favoured
more especially by the fact, that at the time of the second
Temple ver. 25 was the festal cry amidst which the altar of
burnt-offering was solemnly compassed on the first six days of
the Feast of Tabernacles once, and on the seventh day seven
times. This seventh day was called the great Hosanna (*Hosanna rabba*), and not only the prayers for the Feast of Tabernacles, but even the branches of willow trees (including the
myrtles) which are bound to the palm-branch (*lulab*), were
called *Hosannas* (הוֹשַׁעְנוֹת, Aramaic הוֹשַׁעְנֵי).* The second historical reference is favoured by the fact, that the narrative
appears to point directly to our Psalm when it says: *And the
builders laid the foundation of the Temple of Jahve, and the
priests were drawn up there in official robes with trumpets, and
the Levites the descendants of Asaph with cymbals, to praise
Jahve after the direction of David king of Israel, and they sang*
בְּהַלֵּל וּבְהוֹדֹת לַיהוָה כִּי טוֹב כִּי־לְעוֹלָם חַסְדּוֹ עַל־יִשְׂרָאֵל; *and all the
people raised a great shout* בְּהָלֵּל לַיהוָה, *because the house of Jahve
was founded.* But both of these derivations of the Psalm are
opposed by the fact that vers. 19 and 20 assume that the
Temple-building is already finished; whereas the unmistakeable allusions to the events that transpired during the building
of the Temple, viz. the intrigues of the Samaritans, the hostility of the neighbouring peoples, and the capriciousness of the
Persian kings, favour the third. In connection with this reference of the Psalm to the post-exilic dedication of the Temple,
vers. 19, 20, too, now present no difficulty. Ver. 22 is better
understood as spoken in the presence of the now upreared
Temple-building, than as spoken in the presence of the foundation-stone; and the words " unto the horns of the altar" in
ver. 27, interpreted in many different ways, come into the light
of Ezra vi. 17.

The Psalm falls into two divisions. The first division
(vers. 1–19) is sung by the festive procession brought up by
the priests and Levites, which is ascending to the Temple with

---

* *Vid.* my Talmudic Studies, **vi.** (*Der Hosianna-Ruf*), in the *Lutherische
Zeitschrift*, 1855, S. 653–656.

the animals for sacrifice. With ver. 19 the procession stands
at the entrance. The second part (vers. 20–27) is sung by
the body of Levites who receive the festive procession. Then
ver. 28 is the answer of those who have arrived, and ver. 29
the concluding song of all of them. This antiphonal arrangement is recognised even by the Talmud (*B. Pesachim* 119*a*)
and Midrash. The whole Psalm, too, has moreover a peculiar
formation. It resembles the *Mashal* Psalms, for each verse
has of itself its completed sense, its own scent and hue ; one
thought is joined to another as branch to branch and flower to
flower.

Vers. 1–18. The Hodu-cry is addressed first to all and
every one ; then the whole body of the laity of Israel and the
priests, and at last (as it appears) the proselytes (*vid.* on cxv.
9–11) who fear the God of revelation, are urgently admonished
to echo it back ; for " yea, His mercy endureth for ever," is
the required hypophon. In ver. 5, Israel too then begins as
one man to praise the ever-gracious goodness of God. יָהּ, the
Jod of which might easily become inaudible after קָרָאתִי, has an
emphatic *Dagesh* as in ver. 18*a*, and הַמֵּצַר has the orthophonic
stroke beside צַר (the so-called מַקֵּל), which points to the correct
tone-syllable of the word that has *Dechî.** Instead of עֲנָנִי it is
here pointed עֲנָנִי, which also occurs in other instances not only
with distinctive, but also (though not uniformly) with conjunctive accents.† The construction is a pregnant one (as in xxii.
22, xxviii. 1, lxxiv. 7, 2 Sam. xviii. 19, Ezra ii. 62, 2 Chron.
xxxii. 1) : He answered me by removing me to a free space

---

* *Vid.* Baer's *Thorath Emeth*, p. 7 note, and p. 21, end of note 1.

† Hitzig on Prov. viii. 22 considers the pointing קָנָנִי to be occasioned
by *Dechî*, and in fact עֲנָנִי in the passage before us has *Tarcha*, and in
1 Sam. xxviii. 15 *Munach;* but in the passage before us, if we read בַּמֶּרְחַבְיָה
as one word according to the Masora, עֲנָנִי is rather to be accented with
Mugrash; and in 1 Sam. xxviii. 15 the reading עֲנָנִי is found side by side
with עֲנָנִי (*e.g.* in *Bibl. Bomberg.* 1521). Nevertheless צְרַפְתַּנִי xvii. 3, and
הֹרֵנִי Job xxx. 19 (according to Kimchi's *Michlol*, 30*a*), beside *Mercha*,
show that the pointing beside conjunctive as beside disjunctive accents
wavers between *á* and *ā*, although *ā* is properly only justified beside disjunctive accents, and צֻנֵּנִי also really only occurs in pause.

(xviii. 20). Both lines end with יָהּ; nevertheless the reading בַּמֶּרְחַבְיָה is attested by the Masora (*vid.* Baer's *Psalterium*, pp. 132 sq.), instead of בַּמֶּרְחָב יָהּ. It has its advocates even in the Talmud (*B. Pesachim* 117a), and signifies a boundless extent, יה expressing the highest degree of comparison, like מַאְפֵּלְיָה in Jer. ii. 31, the deepest darkness. Even the LXX. appears to have read מרחביה thus as one word (εἰς πλατυσμόν, Symmachus εἰς εὐρυχωρίαν). The Targum and Jerome, however, render it as we do; it is highly improbable that in one and the same verse the divine name should not be intended to be used in the same force of meaning. Ps. lvi. (vers. 10; 5, 12) echoes in ver. 6; and in ver. 7 Ps. liv. (ver. 6) is in the mind of the later poet. In that passage it is still more clear than in the passage before us that by the *Beth* of בְּעֹזְרִי Jahve is not meant to be designated as *unus e multis*, but as a helper who outweighs the greatest multitude of helpers. The Jewish people had experienced this helpful succour of Jahve in opposition to the persecutions of the Samaritans and the satraps during the building of the Temple; and had at the same time learned what is expressed in vers. 7, 8 (cf. cxlvi. 3), that trust in Jahve (for which חָסָה בְּ is the proper word) proves true, and trust in men, on the contrary, and especially in princes, is deceptive; for under Pseudo-Smerdis the work, begun under Cyrus, and re-presented as open to suspicion even in the reign of Cambyses, was interdicted. But in the reign of Darius it again became free: Jahve showed that He disposes events and the hearts of men in favour of His people, so that out of this has grown up in the minds of His people the confident expectation of a world-subduing supremacy expressed in ver. 10.

The clauses vers. 10a, 11a, and 12a, expressed in the perfect form, are intended more hypothetically than as describing facts. The perfect is here set out in relief as a hypothetical tense by the following future. כָּל־גּוֹיִם signifies, as in cxvii. 1, the heathen of every kind. דְּבֹרִים (in the Aramaic and Arabic with ז) are both bees and wasps, which make themselves especially trouble-some in harvest time. The suffix of אֲמִילַם (from מוּל = מָלַל, to hew down, cut in pieces) is the same as in Ex. xxix. 30, ii. 17, and also beside a conjunctive accent in lxxiv. 8. Yet the reading אֲמִילֵם, like יְחִיתַן Hab. ii. 17, is here the better supported

(*vid.* Gesenius, *Lehrgebäude*, S. 177), and it has been adopted
by Norzi, Heidenheim, and Baer. The כִּי is that which states
the ground or reason, and then becomes directly confirmatory
and assuring (cxxviii. 2, 4), which here, after the "in the name
of Jahve" that precedes it, is applied and placed just as in
the oath in 1 Sam. xiv. 44.   And in general, as Redslob has
demonstrated, כִּי has not originally a relative, but a positive
(determining) signification, כ being just as much a demonstrative sound as ד, ז, שׁ, and ת (cf. ἐκεῖ, ἐκεῖνος, κεῖνος, ecce, hic,
illic, with the Doric τηνεί, τῆνος).   The notion of compassing
round about is heightened in ver. 11*a* by the juxtaposition of
two forms of the same verb (Ges. § 67, rem. 10), as in Hos.
iv. 18, Hab. i. 5, Zeph. ii. 1, and frequently.   The figure of
the bees is taken from Deut. i. 44.   The perfect דֹּעֲכוּ (cf. Isa.
xliii. 17) describes their destruction, which takes place instantly
and unexpectedly.   The *Pual* points to the punishing power
that comes upon them: they are extinguished (*exstinguuntur*)
like a fire of thorns, the crackling flame of which expires
as quickly as it has blazed up (lviii. 10).   In ver. 13 the
language of Israel is addressed to the hostile worldly power, as
the antithesis shows.   It thrust, yea thrust (*inf. intens.*) Israel,
that it might fall (לִנְפֹּל; with reference to the pointing, *vid.* on
xl. 15); but Jahve's help would not suffer it to come to that
pass.   Therefore the song at the Red Sea is revived in the
heart and mouth of Israel.   Ver. 14 (like Isa. xii. 2) is taken
from Ex. xv. 2.   עָזִּי (in MSS. also written עֻזִּי) is a collateral
form of עֹז (Ew. § 255, *a*), and here signifies the lofty self-
consciousness which is united with the possession of power:
pride and its expression an exclamation of joy.   Concerning
זִמְרָת *vid.* on xvi. 6.   As at that time, the cry of exultation and
of salvation (*i.e.* of deliverance and of victory) is in the tabernacles of the righteous: the right hand of Jahve—they sing
—עֹשָׂה חָיִל (Num. xxiv. 18), practises valour, proves itself
energetic, gains (maintains) the victory.   רוֹמֵמָה is *Milra*, and
therefore an adjective: *victoriosa* (Ew. § 120, *d*), from רָמֵם =
רוּם like שׁוֹמֵם from שָׁמֵם.   It is not the *part. Pil.* (cf. Hos. xi.
7), since the rejection of the participial *Mem* occurs in connection with *Poal* and *Pual*, but not elsewhere with *Pilel* (רוֹמֵם =
מְרוֹמֵם from רוּם).   The word yields a simpler sense, too, as *adject.
participiale Kal; romēmā'h* is only the fuller form for *ramā'h*,

Ex. xiv. 8 (cf. *rā'mah*, Isa. xxvi. 11). It is not its own strength
that avails for Israel's exultation of victory, but the energy of
the right hand of Jahve. Being come to the brink of the
abyss, Israel is become anew sure of its immortality through
Him. God has, it is true, most severely chastened it (יִסְּרַנִּי with
the suffix *anni* as in Gen. xxx. 6, and יָהּ with the emphatic
Dagesh, which neither reduplicates nor connects, cf. ver. 5,
xciv. 12), but still with moderation (Isa. xxvii. 7 sq.). He has
not suffered Israel to fall a prey to death, but reserved it for
its high vocation, that it may see the mighty deeds of God and
proclaim them to all the world. Amidst such celebration of
Jahve the festive procession of the dedication of the Temple
has arrived at the enclosure wall of the Temple.

Vers. 19–29. The gates of the Temple are called gates of
righteousness because they are the entrance to the place of the
mutual intercourse between God and His church in accordance
with the order of salvation. First the "gates" are spoken of,
and then the one "gate," the principal entrance. Those entering in must be "righteous ones;" only conformity with the
divine loving will gives the right to enter. With reference to
the formation of the conclusion ver. 19*b*, *vid*. Ew. § 347, *b*.
In the Temple-building Israel has before it a reflection of that
which, being freed from the punishment it had had to endure,
it is become through the mercy of its God. With the exultation of the multitude over the happy beginning of the rebuilding there was mingled, at the laying of the foundation-stone, the
loud weeping of many of the grey-headed priests, Levites, and
heads of the tribes who had also seen the first Temple (Ezra
iii. 12 sq.). It was the troublous character of the present
which made them thus sad in spirit; the consideration of the
depressing circumstances of the time, the incongruity of which
weighed so heavily upon their soul in connection with the
remembrance of the former Temple, that memorably glorious
monument of the royal power of David and Solomon.* And
even further on there towered aloft before Zerubbabel, the
leader of the building, a great mountain; gigantic difficulties
and hindrances arose between the powerlessness of the present

---

* Kurtz, in combating our interpretation, reduces the number of the
weeping ones to "some few," but the narrative says the very opposite.

position of Zerubbabel and the completion of the building of the Temple, which had it is true been begun, but was impeded. This mountain God has made into a plain, and qualified Zerubbabel to bring forth the top and key-stone (הָאֶבֶן הָרֹאשָׁה) out of its past concealment, and thus to complete the building, which is now consecrated amidst a loud outburst of incessant shouts of joy (Zech. iv. 7). Ver. 22 points back to that disheartened disdain of the small troublous beginning, which was at work among the builders (Ezra iii. 10) at the laying of the foundation-stone, and then further at the interruption of the building. That rejected (disdained) corner-stone is nevertheless become רֹאשׁ פִּנָּה, *i.e.* the head-stone of the corner (Job xxxviii. 6), which being laid upon the corner, supports and protects the stately edifice—an emblem of the power and dignity to which Israel has attained in the midst of the peoples out of deep humiliation.

In connection with this only indirect reference of the assertion to Israel we avoid the question,—perplexing in connection with the direct reference to the people despised by the heathen, —how can the heathen be called "the builders?" Kurtz answers: "For the building which the heathen world considers it to be its life's mission and its mission in history to rear, viz. the Babel-tower of worldly power and worldly glory, they have neither been able nor willing to make use of Israel . . ." But this conjunction of ideas is devoid of scriptural support and without historical reality; for the empire of the world has set just as much value, according to political relations, upon the incorporation of Israel as upon that of every other people. Further, if what is meant is Israel's own despising of the small beginning of a new era that is dawning, it is then better explained as in connection with the reference of the declaration to Jesus the Christ in Matt. xxi. 42–44, Mark xii. 10 sq., Acts iv. 11 (ὑφ' ὑμῶν τῶν οἰκοδομούντων), 1 Pet. ii. 7, the builders are the chiefs and members of Israel itself, and not the heathen. From 1 Pet. ii. 6, Rom. ix. 33, we see how this reference to Christ is brought about, viz. by means of Isa. xxviii. 16, where Jahve says: *Behold I am He who hath laid in Zion a stone, a stone of trial, a precious corner-stone of well-founded founding— whoever believeth shall not totter.* In the light of this Messianic prophecy of Isaiah ver. 22 of our Psalm also comes to have a Messianic meaning, which is warranted by the fact, that the

history of Israel is recapitulated and culminates in the history
of Christ; or, according to John ii. 19–21 (cf. Zech. vi. 12 sq.),
still more accurately by the fact, that He who in His state of
humiliation is the despised and rejected One is become in His
state of glorification the eternal glorious Temple in which
dwelleth all the fulness of the Godhead bodily, and is united
with humanity which has been once for all atoned for. In the
joy of the church at the Temple of the body of Christ which
arose after the three days of burial, the joy which is here
typically expressed in the words: "From with Jahve, *i.e.*
by the might which dwells with Him, is this come to pass,
wonderful is it become (has it been carried out) in our
eyes," therefore received its fulfilment. It is not נִפְלָאת but
נִפְלָאת, like הֻבָאת in Gen. xxxiii. 11, קָרָאת from קָרָא = קָרָה in
Deut. xxxi. 29, Jer. xliv. 23, קָרָאת from קָרָא, to call, Isa. vii.
14. We can hear Isa. xxv. 9 sounding through this passage,
as above in vers. 19 sq., Isa. xxvi. 1 sq. The God of Israel has
given this turn, so full of glory for His people, to the history.*
He is able now to plead for more distant salvation and prosperity with all the more fervent confidence. אָנָּא (six times
אָנָּה) is, as in every other instance (*vid.* on cxvi. 4), *Milra.*
הוֹשִׁיעָה is accented regularly on the *penult.*, and draws the following נָא towards itself by means of *Dag. forte conj.*; הַצְלִיחָה
on the other hand is *Milra* according to the Masora and other
ancient testimonies, and נָא is not dageshed, without Norzi
being able to state any reason for this different accentuation.
After this watchword of prayer of the thanksgiving feast, in
ver. 26 those who receive them bless those who are coming
(הַבָּא with *Dechî*) in the name of Jahve, *i.e.* bid them welcome
in His name. The expression " from the house of Jahve,"
like " from the fountain of Israel" in lxviii. 27, is equivalent
to, ye who belong to His house and to the church congregated
around it. In the mouth of the people welcoming Jesus as the
Messiah, Ὡσαννά was a " God save the king" (*vid.* on xx. 10);
they scattered palm branches at the same time, like the *lulabs*
at the joyous cry of the Feast of Tabernacles, and saluted Him

------

* The verse, " This is the day which the Lord hath made," etc., was,
according to Chrysostom, an ancient hypophon of the church. It has a
glorious history.

with the cry, " Blessed is He who cometh in the name of the Lord," as being the longed-for guest of the Feast (Matt. xxi. 9). According to the Midrash, in ver. 26 it is the people of Jerusalem who thus greet the pilgrims. In the original sense of the Psalm, however, it is the body of Levites and priests above on the Temple-hill who thus receive the congregation that has come up. The many animals for sacrifice which they brought with them are enumerated in Ezra vi. 17. On the ground of the fact that Jahve has proved Himself to be אֵל,·the absolutely mighty One, by having granted light to His people, viz. lovingkindness, liberty, and joy, there then issues forth the ejaculation, " Bind the sacrifice," etc. The LXX. renders συστήσασθε ἑορτὴν ἐν τοῖς πυκάζουσιν, which is reproduced by the *Psalterium Romanum : constituite diem solemnem in confrequentationibus*, as Eusebius, Theodoret, and Chrysostom (although the last waveringly) also interpret it ; on the other hand, it is rendered by the *Psalterium Gallicum : in condensis*, as Apollinaris and Jerome (*in frondosis*) also understand it. But much as Luther's version, which follows the latter interpretation, " Adorn the feast with green branches even to the horns of the altar," accords with our German taste, it is still untenable ; for אָסַר cannot signify to encircle with garlands and the like, nor would it be altogether suited to חַג in this signification.* Thus then in this instance A. Lobwasser renders it comparatively more correctly, although devoid of taste : " The Lord is great and mighty of strength who lighteneth us all ; *fasten your bullocks to the horns beside the altar*." To the horns ?! So even Hitzig and others render it. But such a " binding to" is unheard of. And can אָסַר עַד possibly signify to bind on to anything ? And what would be the object of binding them to the horns of the altar ? In order that they might not run away ?! Hengstenberg and von Lengerke at least disconnect the words " unto the horns of the altar " from any relation to this precautionary measure, by interpreting : until it (the animal for the festal

---

* Symmachus has felt this, for instead of συστήσασθε ἑορτὴν ἐν τοῖς πυκάζουσιν (*in condensis*) of the LXX., he renders it, transposing the notions, συνδήσατε ἐν πανηγύρει πυκάσματα. Chrysostom interprets this : στεφανώματα καὶ κλάδους ἀνάψατε τῷ ναῷ, for Montfaucon, who regards this as the version of the *Sexta*, is in error.

sacrifice) is raised upon the horns of the altar and sacrificed.
But how much is then imputed to these words! No indeed,
חַג denotes the animals for the feast-offering, and there was so
vast a number of these (according to Ezra *loc. cit.* seven hundred and twelve) that the whole space of the court of the priests
was full of them, and the binding of them consequently had
to go on as far as to the horns of the altar. Ainsworth (1627)
correctly renders: " unto the hornes, that is, all the Court
over, untill you come even to the hornes of the altar, intending
hereby many sacrifices or boughs." The meaning of the call
is therefore: Bring your hecatombs and make them ready for
sacrifice.* The words " unto (as far as) the horns of the
altar" have the principal accent. In ver. 28 (cf. Ex. xv. 2)
the festal procession replies in accordance with the character of
the feast, and then the Psalm closes, in correspondence with its
beginning, with a *Hodu* in which all voices join.

PSALM CXIX.

A TWENTY-TWO-FOLD STRING OF APHORISMS BY ONE WHO IS PERSECUTED FOR THE SAKE OF HIS FAITH.

Aleph.

1 BLESSED are those whose ways are blameless,
  Who walk in the law of Jahve!
2 Blessed are those who keep His testimonies,
  Who seek Him with the whole heart,
3 They also do no unrighteousness—
  They walk in His ways.
4 THOU hast enjoined Thy precepts
  To keep them diligently.
5 Oh that my ways were directed
  To keep Thy statutes!
6 Then shall I not be ashamed,
  When I have respect unto all Thy commandments.

---

* In the language of the Jewish ritual *Isru-chag* is become the name
of the after-feast day which follows the last day of the feast. Ps. cxviii.
is the customary Psalm for the *Isru-chag* of all מוֹעֲדִים.

7 I will give thanks to Thee with an upright heart,
When I learn the judgments of Thy righteousness.
8 I will keep Thy statutes:
Forsake me not utterly.

Beth.

9 Wherewithal shall a young man keep his way pure ?
If he taketh heed according to Thy word.
10 With the whole heart have I sought Thee :
Let me not wander from Thy commandments.
11 In my heart do I treasure up Thy word,
That I may not sin against Thee.
12 Blessed art Thou, Jahve,
Teach me Thy statutes.
13 With my lips do I recount
All the judgments of Thy mouth.
14 In the way of Thy testimonies do I rejoice,
As in all manner of possession.
15 I will meditate in Thy precepts,
And have respect unto Thy paths.
16 In Thy statutes do I delight myself,
I will not forget Thy word.

Gimel.

17 Deal bountifully with Thy servant, that I may live,
So will I keep Thy word.
18 Open Thou mine eyes, that I may behold
Wondrous things out of Thy law.
19 I am a stranger in the earth :
Hide not Thy commandments from me
20 My soul is crushed with longing
After Thy judgments at all times.
21 Thou hast rebuked the proud ;
Cursed are those who do err from Thy commandments.
22 Remove from me reproach and contempt;
For I keep Thy testimonies.
23 Though princes sit and deliberate against me,
Thy servant doth meditate in Thy statutes.
24 Nevertheless Thy testimonies are my delight,
The men of my counsel.

Daleth.

25 My soul cleaveth unto the dust:
Quicken Thou me according to Thy word.

26 I declared my ways, and Thou heardest me:
Teach me Thy statutes.

27 Make me to understand the way of Thy precepts:
So will I meditate on Thy wondrous works.

28 My soul melteth for heaviness:
Strengthen Thou me according to Thy word.

29 Remove from me the way of lying,
And with Thy law be gracious unto me.

30 The way of truth I have chosen:
Thy judgments have I set before me.

31 I have given myself up to Thy testimonies:
Jahve, put me not to shame.

32 I run the way of Thy commandments,
For Thou dost enlarge my heart.

He.

33 Teach me, Jahve, the way of Thy statutes,
That I may keep it unto the end.

34 Give me understanding, that I may keep Thy instruction,
And observe it with the whole heart.

35 Make me to walk in the path of Thy commandments;
For therein do I delight.

36 Incline my heart unto Thy testimonies,
And not to covetousness.

37 Turn away mine eyes from beholding vanity;
In Thy way quicken Thou me.

38 Stablish Thy word unto Thy servant,
As that which makes them fear Thee.

39 Take away my reproach which I fear;
For Thy judgments are good.

40 Behold, I long after Thy precepts:
Quicken me in Thy righteousness.

Vav.

41 And let Thy mercies come unto me, Jahve,
Thy salvation, according to Thy word,

42 And I will answer him who reproacheth me;
   For I trust in Thy word.
43 And take not the word of truth utterly out of my mouth;
   For I hope in Thy judgments.
44 And I will keep Thy law continually,
   For ever and ever,
45 And I will walk at liberty;
   For I seek Thy precepts.
46 And I will speak of Thy testimonies before kings,
   And will not be ashamed.
47 And I will delight myself in Thy commandments,
   Which I love.
48 And my hands will I lift up unto Thy commandments
     [which I love],
   And I will meditate in Thy statutes.

Zajin.

49 Remember the word unto Thy servant,
   Because Thou hast caused me to hope.
50 This is my comfort in my affliction,
   That Thy word hath quickened me.
51 The proud have had me greatly in derision—
   I have not declined from Thy law.
52 I remembered Thy judgments of old, Jahve,
   And comforted myself.
53 Indignation hath taken hold upon me because of the wicked,
   Who forsake Thy law.
54 Thy statutes are my songs
   In the house of my pilgrimage.
55 I have remembered Thy name, Jahve, in the night,
   And I have kept Thy law.
56 This is appointed to me,
   That I should keep Thy precepts.

Heth.

57 Thou art my portion, Jahve:
   I have said that I would keep Thy words.
58 I entreated Thee with the whole heart:
   Be merciful unto me according to Thy word.

59 I thought on my ways,
   And turned my feet unto Thy testimonies.
60 I make haste, and delay not
   To keep Thy commandments.
61 The cords of the wicked are round about me—
   I do not forget Thy law.
62 At midnight I will rise to give thanks unto Thee
   Because of the judgments of Thy righteousness.
63 I am a companion of all those who fear Thee,
   And of those who keep Thy precepts.
64 The earth, Jahve, is full of Thy mercy:
   Teach me Thy statutes.

Teth.

65 Thou hast dealt well with Thy servant,
   Jahve, according unto Thy word.
66 Teach me good judgment and knowledge,
   For I believe in Thy commandments.
67 Before I was afflicted I went astray,
   And now I keep Thy word.
68 Thou art good, and doest good ;
   Teach me Thy statutes.
69 The proud have forged a lie against me—
   I will keep Thy precepts with the whole heart.
70 Their heart is as fat as grease—
   I delight in Thy law.
71 It was good for me that I was afflicted,
   That I might learn Thy statutes.
72 The law of Thy mouth is better unto me
   Than thousands of gold and silver.

Jod.

73 Thy hands have made me and fashioned me :   [ments.
   Give me understanding, that I may learn Thy command-
74 Let those who fear Thee be glad when they see me ;
   For I hope in Thy word.
75 I know, Jahve, that righteousness are Thy judgments,
   And that Thou in faithfulness hast afflicted me.
76 Let Thy merciful kindness be for my comfort,
   According to Thy promise unto Thy servant.

77 Let Thy tender mercies come unto me, that I may live;
   For Thy law is my delight.
78 Let the proud be ashamed that they dealt falsely with me—
   But I meditate on Thy precepts.
79 Let those who fear Thee turn unto me,
   And those who know Thy testimonies.
80 Let my heart be sound in Thy statutes,
   That I be not ashamed.

Kaph.

81 My soul fainteth for Thy salvation:
   I hope in Thy word.
82 Mine eyes fail with longing for Thy word,
   Saying, When wilt Thou comfort me?—
83 Verily, though I am become like a bottle in the smoke,
   Do I not forget Thy statutes.
84 Short indeed are the days of Thy servant,
   When wilt Thou execute judgment on those who persecute
85 The proud have digged pits for me,   [me?
   They who are not after Thy law.
86 All Thy commandments are faithful:
   They persecute me wrongfully; help Thou me!
87 They had almost consumed me in the land;
   Yet do I not forsake Thy precepts.
88 Quicken me after Thy loving-kindness,
   So will I keep the testimony of Thy mouth.

Lamed.

89 For ever, Jahve,
   Thy word is settled in heaven.
90 Thy faithfulness is unto all generations:
   Thou hast established the earth, and it abideth.
91 They continue this day according to Thy judgments;
   For all beings are Thy servants.
92 Unless Thy law had been my delight,
   I should then have perished in mine affliction.
93 I will never forget Thy precepts;
   For with them Thou hast quickened me.
94 I am Thine, save me;
   For I seek Thy precepts.

95 If the wicked lie in wait for me to destroy me—
     I consider Thy testimonies.
96 To all perfection, as I have seen, there is an end,
     Yet Thy commandment is without any limits.

Mem.

97 O how love I Thy law!
     It is my meditation all the day.
98 Thy commandments make me wiser than mine enemies;
     For they are ever my portion.
99 I have more understanding than all my teachers;
     For Thy testimonies are my meditation.
100 I understand more than aged men;
     For I keep Thy precepts.
101 I refrain my feet from every evil way,
     That I may keep Thy word.
102 I have not departed from Thy judgments;
     For Thou hast taught me.
103 How sweet are Thy words unto my taste,
     Sweeter than honey to my mouth!
104 From Thy precepts I get understanding:
     Therefore I hate every false way.

Nun.

105 Thy word is a lamp unto my feet,
     And a light unto my path.
106 I have sworn, and I will perform it,
     That I will keep Thy righteous judgments.
107 I am afflicted very much—
     Quicken me, Jahve, according unto Thy word!
108 Accept the freewill offerings of my mouth, Jahve,
     And teach me Thy judgments.
109 My soul is continually in my hand:
     Yet do I not forget Thy law.
110 The wicked have laid a snare for me:
     Yet do I not err from Thy precepts.
111 Thy testimonies have I taken as a heritage for ever;
     For they are the rejoicing of my heart.
112 I have inclined mine heart to perform Thy statutes
     For ever, even unto the end.

Samech.

113 I hate the double-minded,
And Thy law do I love.
114 My hiding-place and my shield art Thou:
I hope in Thy word.
115 Depart from me, ye evil-doers—
I will keep the commandments of my God.
116 Uphold me according unto Thy word, and I shall live,
And let me not be ashamed of my hope.
117 Hold Thou me up, and I shall be safe,
And I will have respect unto Thy statutes continually.
118 Thou hast trodden down all them that err from Thy
For their intrigue is falsehood.   [statutes;
119 Thou puttest away all the wicked of the earth like dross:
Therefore I love Thy testimonies.
120 My flesh is rigid for terror of Thee,
And I am afraid of Thy judgments.

Ajin.

121 I have done judgment and righteousness:
Thou wilt not leave me to mine oppressors.
122 Be surety for Thy servant for good:
Let not the proud oppress me.
123 Mine eyes fail for Thy salvation,
And for the word of Thy righteousness.
124 Deal with Thy servant according unto Thy mercy,
And teach me Thy statutes.
125 Thy servant am I, give me understanding,
That I may know Thy testimonies.
126 It is time to interpose for Jahve:
They have made void Thy law.
127 Therefore I love Thy commandments
More than gold, and than fine gold.
128 Therefore I esteem all precepts concerning all things to
I hate every false way.   [be right;

Phe (Pe).

129 Wonderful are Thy testimonies:
Therefore doth my soul keep them.

130 The unfolding of Thy words giveth light;
Giving understanding unto the simple.
131 I opened my mouth, and panted;
For I long for Thy commandments.
132 Look Thou upon me, and be merciful unto me,
As is right towards those who love Thy name.
133 Establish my steps by Thy word,
And let not any iniquity have dominion over me.
134 Deliver me from the oppression of man,
And I will keep Thy precepts.
135 Make Thy face to shine upon Thy servant,
And teach me Thy statutes.
136 Mine eyes run down rivers of waters,
Because they keep not Thy law.

Tsade.

137 Righteous art Thou, Jahve,
And upright are Thy judgments.
138 Thou hast commanded Thy testimonies in righteousness,
And in very faithfulness.
139 My zeal consumeth me,
For mine adversaries have forgotten Thy words.
140 Thy word is very pure,
And Thy servant loveth it.
141 I am young and despised:
Yet do not I forget Thy precepts.
142 Thy righteousness is that which is right for ever,
And Thy law truth.
143 Trouble and anguish have taken hold on me:
Yet thy commandments are my delight.
144 Thy testimonies are that which is right for ever:
Give me understanding that I may live.

Koph.

145 I call with the whole heart—answer me;
Jahve, Thy statutes will I keep!
146 When I cry unto Thee, save me,
And I will keep Thy testimonies!
147 Early, even before the dawning of the morning, did I
I hoped in Thy word.   [make supplication:

148 Mine eyes anticipate the night-watches,
    To meditate on Thy word.
149 Hear my voice according unto Thy loving-kindness ;
    Jahve, quicken me according to Thy judgments.
150 They draw nigh who follow after mischief,
    Who are far from Thy law :
151 Thou comest all the nearer, O Jahve,
    And all Thy commandments are truth.
152 From Thy testimonies I have known for a long time
    That Thou hast founded them for ever.

Resh.

153 Look upon mine affliction, and deliver me ;
    For I do not forget Thy law.
154 Plead my cause and deliver me,
    Quicken me according to Thy word.
155 Salvation is far from the wicked,
    For they seek not Thy statutes.
156 Abundant are Thy tender mercies, Jahve ;
    Quicken me according to Thy judgments.
157 Many are my persecutors and mine oppressors ;
    I decline not from Thy testimonies.
158 I beheld the transgressors, and was grieved,
    Because they kept not Thy word.
159 Consider that I love Thy precepts :
    Quicken me, Jahve, according to Thy loving-kindness.
160 The sum of Thy word is truth,   [for ever.
    And every one of the judgments of Thy righteousness is

Sin, Shin.

161 Princes have persecuted me without a cause,
    But my heart standeth in awe of Thy words.
162 I rejoice over Thy word,
    As one that findeth great spoil.
163 Pretended faith I hate, and I abhor it :
    Thy law do I love.
164 Seven times a day do I praise Thee
    Because of the judgments of Thy righteousness.
165 Great peace have they who love Thy law,
    And nothing causeth them to stumble.

166 Jahve, I hope for Thy salvation,
   And do Thy commandments.
167 My soul keepeth Thy testimonies,
   And I love them exceedingly.
168 I keep Thy precepts and Thy testimonies,
   For all my ways are before Thee.

Thav (Tav).

169 Let my cry come up before Thee, Jahve;
   Give me understanding according to Thy word.
170 Let my supplication come up before Thee,
   Deliver me according to Thy promise.
171 My lips shall utter praise,
   That Thou dost teach me Thy statutes.
172 My tongue doth speak of Thy word,
   For all Thy commandments are righteousness.
173 Let Thy hand be a help unto me,
   For I have chosen Thy precepts.
174 I have longed for Thy salvation, Jahve,
   And Thy law is my delight.
175 Let my soul live and praise Thee,
   And let Thy judgments help me.
176 If I should go astray—as a lost sheep seek Thy servant,
   For I do not forget Thy commandments.

To the *Hodu* Ps. cxviii., written in gnome-like, wreathed style, is appended the throughout gnomico-didactic Ps. cxix., consisting of one hundred and seventy-six Masoretic verses, or regarded in relation to the strophe, distichs, which according to the twenty-two letters of the alphabet fall into twenty-two groups (called by the old expositors the ὀγδοάδες or *octonarii* of this *Psalmus literatus s. alphabetites*); for each group contains eight verses (distichs), each of which begins with the same consecutive letter ($8 \times 22 = 176$). The Latin Psalters (as the *Psalterium Veronense*, and originally perhaps all the old Greek Psalters) have the name of the letter before each group; the Syriac has the signs of the letters; and in the Complutensian Bible, as also elsewhere, a new line begins with each group. The Talmud, *B. Berachoth*, says of this Psalm: "it consists of eight *Alephs*," etc.; the Masora styles it אלפא ביתא רבא; the Midrash on it is called מדרש אלפא ביתא, and the Pesikta פסיקתא דתמניא אפי. In our German version it has the appropriate inscription, "The Christian's golden A B C of the praise, love, power, and use of the word of God;" for here we have set forth in inexhaustible fulness what the word of God is to a man, and how a man is to behave himself in relation to it. The Masora observes that the Psalm contains only the one verse 122, in which some reference or other to the word of revelation is not found as in all the 175 others *—a many-linked chain of synonyms which runs through the whole Psalm. In connection with this ingenious arrangement, so artfully devised and carried out, it may also not be merely accidental that the address *Jahve* occurs twenty-two times, as Bengel has observed : *bis et vicesies pro numero octonariorum.*

All kinds of erroneous views have, however, been put forth concerning this Psalm. Köster, von Gerlach, Hengstenberg, and Hupfeld renounce all attempts to show that there is any accordance whatever with a set plan, and find here a series of maxims without any internal progression and connection. Ewald begins at once with the error, that we have before us the long prayer of an old experienced teacher. But from vers. 9 sq. it is clear that the poet himself is a " young man," a fact that is also corroborated by vers. 99 and 100. The poet is a young man, who finds himself in a situation which is clearly described : he is derided, oppressed, persecuted, and that by those who despise the divine word (for apostasy encompasses him round about), and more particularly by a government hostile to the true religion, vers. 23, 46, 161. He is lying in bonds (ver. 61, cf. 83), expecting death (ver. 109), and recognises in his affliction, it is true, God's salutary humbling, and in the midst of it God's word is his comfort and his wisdom, but he also yearns for help, and earnestly prays for it.—The whole Psalm is a prayer for stedfastness in the midst of an ungodly, degenerate race, and in the midst of great trouble, which is heightened by the

---

* " In every verse," this is the observation of the Masora on ver. 122, " ver. 122 only excepted, we find one of the ten (pointing to the ten fundamental words or decalogue of the Sinaitic Law) expressions: *word, saying, testimonies, way, judgment, precept, commandment* (צוני), *law, statute, truth* " (according to another reading, *righteousness*).

pain he feels at the prevailing apostasy, and a prayer for ultimate deliverance which rises in group *Kaph* to an urgent *how
long!*   If this sharply-defined physiognomy of the Psalm is
recognised, then the internal progression will not fail to be discerned.

After the poet has praised fidelity to the word of God
(*Aleph*), and described it as the virtue of all virtues which is
of service to the young man and to which he devotes himself
(*Beth*), he prays, in the midst of the scoffing and persecuting
persons that surround him, for the grace of enlightenment
(*Gimel*), of strengthening (*Daleth*), of preservation (*He*), of
suitable and joyful confession (*Vav*); God's word is all his
thought and pursuit (*Zajin*), he cleaves to those who fear God
(*Heth*), and recognises the salutary element of His humbling
(*Teth*), but is in need of comfort (*Jod*) and sighs: how long!
(*Kaph.*)   Without the eternal, sure, mighty word of God he
would despair (*Lamed*); this is his wisdom in difficult circumstances (*Mem*); he has sworn fidelity to it, and maintains his
fidelity as being one who is persecuted (*Nun*), and abhors and
despises the apostates (*Samech*).   He is oppressed, but God
will not suffer him to be crushed (*Ajin*); He will not suffer the
doings of the ungodly, which wring from him floods of tears,
to prevail over him (*Phe*)—over him, the small (still youthful)
and despised one whom zeal concerning the prevailing godlessness is consuming away (*Tsade*).   Oh that God would hear
his crying by day and by night (*Koph*), would revive him
speedily with His helpful pity (*Resh*)—him, viz., who being persecuted by princes clings fast to Him (*Shin*), and would seek
him the isolated and so sorely imperilled sheep! (*Tav.*)   This outline does not exhaust the fundamental thoughts of the separate
ogdoades, and they might surely be still more aptly reproduced,
but this is sufficient to show that the Psalm is not wanting in
coherence and progressive movement, and that it is not an
ideal situation and mood, but a situation and mood based upon
public relationships, from which this manifold celebration of
the divine word, as a fruit of its teaching, has sprung.

It is natural to suppose that the composition of the Psalm
falls in those times of the Greek domination in which the
government was hostile, and a large party from among the
Jews themselves, that was friendly towards the government,

persecuted all decided confessors of the Tôra. Hitzig says, "It can be safely maintained that the Psalm was written in the Maccabæan age by a renowned Israelite who was in imprisonment under Gentile authorities." It is at least probable that the plaited work of so long a Psalm, which, in connection with all that is artificial about it, from beginning to end gives us a glimpse of the subdued afflicted mien of a confessor, is the work of one in prison, who whiled away his time with this plaiting together of his complaints and his consolatory thoughts.

Vers. 1–8. The eightfold *Aleph*. Blessed are those who act according to the word of God; the poet wishes to be one of these. The alphabetical Psalm on the largest scale begins appropriately, not merely with a simple (cxii. 1), but with a twofold *ashrê*. It refers principally to those *integri viæ* (*vitæ*). In ver. 3 the description of those who are accounted blessed is carried further. Perfects, as denoting that which is habitual, alternate with futures used as presents. In ver. 4 לִשְׁמֹר expresses the purpose of the enjoining, as in ver. 5 the goal of the directing. אַחֲלַי (whence אֲחַלֵי, 2 Kings v. 3) is compounded of אָח (*vid. supra*, i. 428) and לַ (לְוַי), and consequently signifies *o si*. On יִכֹּנוּ cf. Prov. iv. 26 (LXX. κατευθυνθείησαν). The retrospective אָז is expanded anew in ver. 6*b*: then, when I namely. "Judgments of Thy righteousness" are the decisions concerning right and wrong which give expression to and put in execution the righteousness of God.* בְּלָמְדִי refers to Scripture in comparison with history.

Vers. 9–16. The eightfold *Beth*. Acting in accordance with the word of God, a young man walks blamelessly; the poet desires this, and supplicates God's gracious assistance in order to it. To purify or cleanse one's way or walk (זִכָּה, cf. lxxiii. 13, Prov. xx. 9) signifies to maintain it pure (זַךְ, root זך,

---

* The word "judgments" of our English authorized version is retained in the text as being the most convenient word; it must, however, be borne in mind that in this Psalm it belongs to the "chain of synonyms," and does not mean God's acts of judgment, its more usual meaning in the Old Testament Scriptures, but is used as defined above, and is the equivalent here of the German *Rechte*, not *Gerichte*.—Tr.

زك, to prick, to strike the eye, *nitere;*[*] *vid.* Fleischer in Levy's *Chaldäisches Wörterbuch*, i. 424) from the spotting of sin, or to free it from it. Ver. 9*b* is the answer to the question in ver. 9*a*; לִשְׁמֹר signifies *custodiendo semetipsum*, for שָׁמַר can also signify " to be on one's guard" without נַפְשׁוֹ (Josh. vi. 18). The old classic (*e.g.* xviii. 31) אִמְרָתֶךָ alternates throughout with דְּבָרֶךָ; both are intended collectively. One is said to hide (צָפַן) the word in one's heart when one has it continually present with him, not merely as an outward precept, but as an inward motive power in opposition to selfish action (Job xxiii. 12). In ver. 12 the poet makes his way through adoration to petition. סִפַּרְתִּי in ver. 13 does not mean enumeration, but recounting, as in Deut. vi. 7. עֵדוֹת is the plural to עֵדוּת; עֵדֹת, on the contrary, in ver. 138 is the plural to עֵדָה: both are used of God's attestation of Himself and of His will in the word of revelation. כְּעַל signifies, according to ver. 162, " as over" (short for כַּאֲשֶׁר עַל), not: as it were more than (Olshausen); the כ would only be troublesome in connection with this interpretation. With reference to הוֹן, which has occurred already in xliv. 13, cxii. 3 (from הוֹן, هون, to be light, *levem*), *aisance*, ease, opulence, and concrete, goods, property, *vid.* Fleischer in Levy's *Chald. Wörterb.* i. 423 sq. אָרְחֹתֶיךָ, ver. 15, are the paths traced out in the word of God; these he will studiously keep in his eye.

Vers. 17–24. The eightfold *Gimel.* This is his life's aim : he will do it under fear of the curse of apostasy; he will do it also though he suffer persecution on account of it. In ver. 17 the expression is only אֶחְיֶה as cxviii. 19, not וְאֶחְיֶה as in vers. 77, 116, 144 : the *apodosis imper.* only begins with וְאֶשְׁמְרָה, whereas אחיה is the good itself for the bestowment of which the poet prays. גַּל in ver. 18*a* is *imper. apoc. Piel* for גַּלֵּה, like נַס in Dan. i. 12. נִפְלָאוֹת is the expression for everything supernatural and mysterious which is incomprehensible to the ordinary understanding and is left to the perception of faith. The Tôra beneath the surface of its letter contains an abundance of such " wondrous things," into which only eyes from which

---

[*] The word receives the meaning of νιχᾶν (*vid. supra*, ii. 136), like ظهر and بهر, from the signification of outshining = overpowering.

God has removed the covering of natural short-sightedness penetrate; hence the prayer in ver. 18. Upon earth we have no abiding resting-place, we sojourn here as in a strange land (ver. 19, xxxix. 13, 1 Chron. xxix. 15). Hence the poet prays in ver. 19 that God would keep His commandments, these rules of conduct for the journey of life, in living consciousness for him. Towards this, according to ver. 20, his longing tends. גֵּרַס (*Hiph.* in Lam. iii. 16) signifies to crush in pieces, جَرَشَ and here, like the Aramaic גְּרַס, גְּרֵס, to be crushed, broken in pieces. לְתַאֲבָה (from תָּאַב, vers. 40, 174, a secondary form of אָבָה) states the bias of mind in or at which the soul feels itself thus overpowered even to being crushed: it is crushing from longing after God's judgments, viz. after a more and more thorough knowledge of them. In ver. 21 the LXX. has probably caught the meaning of the poet better than the pointing has done, inasmuch as it draws ἐπικατάρατοι to ver. 21*b*, so that ver. 21*a* consists of two words, just like vers. 59*a*, 89*a*; and Kamphausen also follows this in his rendering. For אֲרוּרִים as an attribute is unpoetical, and as an accusative of the predicate far-fetched; whereas it comes in naturally as a predicate before הַשֹּׁגִים מִמִּצְוֹתֶיךָ: cursed (אָרַר = هَجَرَ, detestari), viz. by God. Instead of גֹּל, "roll" (from גָּלַל, Josh. v. 9), it is pointed in ver. 22 (מעל) גַּל, "uncover" = גִּלָּה, as in ver. 18, reproach being conceived of as a covering or veil (as *e.g.* in lxix. 8), cf. Isa. xxii. 8 (perhaps also Lam. ii. 14, iv. 22, if גִּלָּה עַל there signifies " to remove the covering upon anything"). גַּם in ver. 23*a*, as in Jer. xxxvi. 25, has the sense of גַּם־כִּי, etiamsi; and גַּם in ver. 24*a* the sense of nevertheless, ὅμως, Ew. § 354, *a*. On נִדְבַּר בְּ (reciprocal), cf. Ezek. xxxiii. 30. As in a criminal tribunal, princes sit and deliberate how they may be able to render him harmless.

Vers. 25–32. The eightfold *Daleth*. He is in deep trouble, and prays for consolation and strengthening by means of God's word, to which he resigns himself. His soul is fixed to the dust (xliv. 26) in connection with such non-recognition and proscription, and is incapable of raising itself. In ver. 25*b* he implores new strength and spirits (חִיָּה as in lxxi. 20, lxxxv. 7) from God, in conformity with and by reason of His word. He has rehearsed his walk in every detail to God,

and has not been left without an answer, which has assured
him of His good pleasure : may He then be pleased to advance
him ever further and further in the understanding of His word,
in order that, though men are against him, he may nevertheless
have God on his side, vers. 26, 27. The complaint and request
expressed in ver. 25 are renewed in ver. 28. דָּלַף refers to the
soul, which is as it were melting away in the trickling down of
tears ; קַיֵּם is a *Piel* of Aramaic formation belonging to the later
language. In vers. 29, 30 the way of lies or of treachery, and
the way of faithfulness or of perseverance in the truth, stand
in opposition to one another. חָנֵן is construed with a double
accusative, inasmuch as תּוֹרָה has not the rigid notion of a fixed
teaching, but of living empirical instruction. שִׁוָּה (short for
שִׁוָּה לְנֶגֶד, xvi. 8) signifies to put or set, viz. as a *norma normans*
that stands before one's eyes. He cleaves to the testimonies of
God ; may Jahve not disappoint the hope which to him springs
up out of them, according to the promise, ver. 31. He runs,
i.e. walks vigorously and cheerfully, in the way of God's commandments, for He has widened his heart, by granting and
preserving to the persecuted one the joyfulness of confession
and the confidence of hope.

Vers. 33–40. The eightfold *He.* He further prays for
instruction and guidance that he may escape the by-paths of
selfishness and of disavowal. The noun עֵקֶב, used also elsewhere as an *accus. adverb.*, in the signification *ad extremum*
(vers. 33 and 112) is peculiar to our poet. אֶצְּרֶנָּה (with a
Shebâ which takes a colouring in accordance with the principal
form) refers back to דֶּרֶךְ. In the petition " give me understanding " (which occurs six times in this Psalm) הֲבִין is causative, as in Job xxxii. 8, and frequently in the post-exilic
writings. בֶּצַע (from בָּצַע, *abscindere,* as κέρδος accords in sound
with κείρειν) signifies gain and acquisition by means of the
damage which one does to his neighbour by depreciating his
property, by robbery, deceit, and extortion (1 Sam. viii. 3), and
as a name of a vice, covetousness, and in general selfishness.
שָׁוְא is that which is without real, *i.e.* without divine, contents
or intrinsic worth,—God-opposed teaching and life. בִּדְרָכֶךָ *

---

* Heidenheim and Baer erroneously have בִּדְרָכֶיךָ with *Jod. plural.*, contrary to the Masora.

is a defective plural; cf. חַסְדֶּךָ, ver. 41, וּמִשְׁפָּטֶךָ, ver. 43, and frequently. Establishing, in ver. 38, is equivalent to a realizing
of the divine word or promise. The relative clause אֲשֶׁר לְיִרְאָתֶךָ
is not to be referred to לְעַבְדְּךָ according to ver. 85 (where the
expression is different), but to אִמְרָתֶךָ: fulfil to Thy servant
Thy word or promise, as that which (*quippe quœ*) aims at men
attaining the fear of Thee and increasing therein (cf. cxxx. 4,
xl. 4). The reproach which the poet fears in ver. 39 is not
the reproach of confessing, but of denying God. Accordingly
מִשְׁפָּטֶיךָ are not God's judgments [*i.e.* acts of judgment], but
revealed decisions or judgments: these are good, inasmuch as
it is well with him who keeps them. He can appeal before
God to the fact that he is set upon the knowledge and experience of these with longing of heart; and he bases his request
upon the fact that God by virtue of His righteousness, *i.e.* the
stringency with which He maintains His order of grace, both
as to its promises and its duties, would quicken him, who is at
present as it were dead with sorrow and weariness.

Vers. 41–48. The eightfold *Vav*. He prays for the grace
of true and fearlessly joyous confession. The LXX. renders
ver. 41*a*: καὶ ἔλθοι ἐπ' ἐμὲ τὸ ἔλεός σου; but the Targum
and Jerome rightly (cf. ver. 77, Isa. lxiii. 7) have the plural:
God's proofs of loving-kindness in accordance with His promises will put him in the position that he will not be obliged
to be dumb in the presence of him who reproaches him (חֹרְף,
prop. a plucker, cf. خَروف, a lamb = a plucker of leaves or
grass), but will be able to answer him on the ground of his
own experience. The verb עָנָה, which in itself has many
meanings, acquires the signification "to give an answer"
through the word, דָּבָר, that is added (synon. הֵשִׁיב דָּבָר). Ver.
43 also refers to the duty of confessing God. The meaning
of the prayer is, that God may not suffer him to come to such
a pass that he will be utterly unable to witness for the truth;
for language dies away in the mouth of him who is unworthy
of it before God. The writer has no fear of this for himself,
for his hope is set towards God's judgments (לְמִשְׁפָּטֶךָ, defective
plural, as also in ver. 149; in proof of which, compare vers.
156 and 175), his confidence takes its stand upon them. The
futures which follow from vers. 44 to 48 declare that what he

would willingly do by the grace of God, and strives to do, is
to walk בִּרְחָבָה, in a broad space (elsewhere בַּמֶּרְחָב), therefore
unstraitened, which in this instance is not equivalent to happily,
but courageously and unconstrainedly, without allowing myself
to be intimidated, and said of inward freedom which makes
itself known outwardly. In ver. 46 the Vulgate renders: *Et
loquebar de* (*in*) *testimoniis tuis in conspectu regum et non con-
fundebar*—the motto of the Augsburg Confession, to which it
was adapted especially in connection with this historical interpretation of the two verbs, which does not correspond to the
original text. The lifting up of the hands in ver. 48 is an
expression of fervent longing desire, as in connection with
prayer, xxviii. 2, lxiii. 5, cxxxiv. 2, cxli. 2, and frequently.
The second אֲשֶׁר אָהַבְתִּי is open to the suspicion of being an
inadvertent repetition. שִׂיחַ בְּ (synon. הָגָה בְּ) signifies a still
or audible meditating that is absorbed in the object.

Vers. 49–56. The eightfold *Zajin*. God's word is his
hope and his trust amidst all derision; and when he burns
with indignation at the apostates, God's word is his solace.
Since in ver. 49 the expression is not דְּבָרְךָ but דָּבָר, it is not to
be interpreted according to xcviii. 3, cvi. 45, but: remember
the word addressed to Thy servant, because Thou hast made
me hope (*Piel causat.* as *e.g.* נִשָּׁה, to cause to forget, Gen. xli.
51), *i.e.* hast comforted me by promising me a blessed issue,
and hast directed my expectation thereunto. This is his comfort in his dejected condition, that God's promissory declaration has quickened him and proved its reviving power in his
case. In הֱלִיצֻנִי (הַלִּיצוּנִי), *ludificantur*, it is implied that the
זֵדִים are just לֵצִים, frivolous persons, libertines, free-thinkers
(Prov. xxi. 24). מִשְׁפָּטֶיךָ, ver. 52, are the valid, verified decisions
(judgments) of God revealed from the veriest olden times. In
the remembrance of these, which determine the lot of a man
according to the relation he holds towards them, the poet found
comfort. It can be rendered: then I comforted myself; or
according to a later usage of the *Hithpa.*: I was comforted.
Concerning זַלְעָפָה, *æstus*, *vid.* xi. 6, and on the subject-matter,
vers. 21, 104. The poet calls his earthly life "the house of
his pilgrimage;" for it is true the earth is man's (cxv. 16), but
he has no abiding resting-place there (1 Chron. xxix. 15), his
בֵּית עוֹלָם (Eccles. xii. 5) is elsewhere (*vid. supra*, ver. 19, xxxix.

13). God's statutes are here his "songs," which give him spiritual refreshing, sweeten the hardships of the pilgrimage, and measure and hasten his steps. The Name of God has been in his mind hitherto, not merely by day, but also by night; and in consequence of this he has kept God's law (וָאֶשְׁמְרָה, as five times besides in this Psalm, cf. iii. 6, and to be distinguished from וְאֶשְׁמְרָה, ver. 44). Just this, that he keeps (*observat*) God's precepts, has fallen to his lot. To others something else is allotted (iv. 8), to him this one most needful thing.

Vers. 57–64. The eightfold *Heth*. To understand and to keep God's word is his portion, the object of his incessant praying and thanksgiving, the highest grace or favour that can come to him. According to xvi. 5, lxxiii. 26, the words חֶלְקִי ה׳ belong together. Ver. 57*b* is an inference drawn from it (אָמַר לְ as in Ex. ii. 14, and frequently), and the existing division of the verse is verified. חִלָּה פְנֵי, as in xlv. 13, is an expression of caressing, flattering entreaty; in Latin, *caput mulcere* (*demulcere*). His turning to the word of God the poet describes in ver. 59 as a result of a careful trying of his actions. After that he quickly and cheerfully, ver. 60, determined to keep it without any long deliberation with flesh and blood, although the snares of wicked men surround him. The meaning of חֶבְלֵי is determined according to ver. 110: the pointing does not distinguish so sharply as one might have expected between חֶבְלֵי, ὠδῖνας, and חַבְלֵי, snares, bonds (*vid.* xviii. 5 sq.); but the plural nowhere, according to the usage of the language as we now have it, signifies bands (companies), from the singular in 1 Sam. x. 5 (Böttcher, § 800). Thankfulness urges him to get up at midnight (*acc. temp.* as in Job xxxiv. 20) to prostrate himself before God and to pray. Accordingly he is on friendly terms with, he is closely connected with (Prov. xxviii. 24), all who fear God. Out of the fulness of the loving-kindness of God, which is nowhere unattested upon earth (ver. 64*a* = xxxiii. 5), he implores for himself the inward teaching concerning His word as the highest and most cherished of mercies.

Vers. 65–72. The eightfold *Teth*. The good word of the gracious God is the fountain of all good; and it is learned in the way of lowliness. He reviews his life, and sees in everything that has befallen him the good and well-meaning appointment of the God of salvation in accordance with the plan

and order of salvation of His word. The form עַבְדְּךָ, which is
the form out of pause, is retained in ver. 65a beside *Athnach*,
although not preceded by *Olewejored* (cf. xxxv. 19, xlviii. 11,
Prov. xxx. 21). Clinging believingly to the commandments of
God, he is able confidently to pray that He would teach him
"good discernment" and "knowledge." טַעַם is ethically the
capacity of distinguishing between good and evil, and of dis-
covering the latter as it were by touch ; טוּב טַעַם, good discernment, is a coupling of words like טוּב לֵב, a happy disposition,
cheerfulness. God has brought him into this relationship to
His word by humbling him, and thus setting him right out of
his having gone astray. אִמְרָה in ver. 67b, as in ver. 11, is not
God's utterance conveying a promise, but imposing a duty.
God is called טוֹב as He who is graciously disposed towards
man, and מֵטִיב as He who acts out this disposition ; this loving
and gracious God he implores to become his Teacher. In his
fidelity to God's word he does not allow himself to be led astray
by any of the lies which the proud try to impose upon him
(Böttcher), or better absolutely (cf. Job xiii. 4) : to patch together over him, making the true nature unrecognisable as it
were by means of false plaster or whitewash (טָפַל, to smear
over, bedaub, as the Targumic, Talmudic, and Syriac show).
If the heart of these men, who by slander make him into a
caricature of himself, is covered as it were with thick fat (a
figure of insensibility and obduracy, xvii. 10, lxxiii. 7, Isa. vi.
10, LXX. ἐτυρώθη, Aquila ἐλιπάνθη, Symmachus ἐμυαλώθη)
against all the impressions of the word of God, he, on the
other hand, has his delight in the law of God (שִׁעֲשַׁע with
an accusative of the object, not of that which is delighted,
xciv. 19, but of that which delights). How beneficial has the
school of affliction through which he has attained to this, been
to him ! The word proceeding from the mouth of God is now
more precious to him than the greatest earthly riches.

Vers. 73–80. The eightfold *Jod.* God humbles, but He
also exalts again according to His word ; for this the poet prays
in order that he may be a consolatory example to the God-
fearing, to the confusion of his enemies. It is impossible that
God should forsake man, who is His creature, and deny to him
that which makes him truly happy, viz. the understanding and
knowledge of His word. For this spiritual gift the poet prays

in ver. 73 (cf. on 73*a*, Deut. xxxii. 6, Job x. 8, xxxi. 15); and he wishes in ver. 74 that all who fear God may see in him with joy an example of the way in which trust in the word of God is rewarded (cf. xxxiv. 3, xxxv. 27, lxix. 33, cvii. 42, and other passages). He knows that God's acts of judgment are pure righteousness, *i.e.* are regulated by God's holiness, out of which they spring, and by the salvation of men, at which they aim; and he knows that God has humbled him אֱמוּנָה (*accus. adverb.* for בֶּאֱמוּנָה), being faithful in His intentions towards him; for it is just in the school of affliction that one first learns rightly to estimate the worth of His word, and comes to feel its power. But trouble, though sweetened by an insight into God's salutary design, is nevertheless always bitter; hence the well-justified prayer of ver. 76, that God's mercy may notwithstanding be bestowed upon him for his consolation, in accordance with the promise which is become his (לְ as in ver. 49*a*), His servant's. עִוַּת, ver. 78, instead of being construed with the accusative of the right, or of the cause, that is perverted, is construed with the accusative of the person upon whom such perversion of right, such oppression by means of misrepresentation, is inflicted, as in Job xix. 6, Lam. iii. 36. Chajug′ reads עִוְּדוּנִי as in ver. 61. The wish expressed in ver. 79 is to be understood according to lxxiii. 10, Jer. xv. 19, cf. Prov. ix. 4, 16. If instead of וְיֹדְעֵי (which is favoured by ver. 63), we read according to the *Chethîb* וְיֵדְעוּ (cf. ver. 125), then what is meant by יָשׁוּבוּ לִי is a turning towards him for the purpose of learning: may their knowledge be enriched from his experience. For himself, however, in ver. 80 he desires unreserved, faultless, unwavering adherence to God's word, for only thus is he secure against being ignominiously undeceived.

Vers. 81–88. The eightfold *Kaph*. This strengthening according to God's promise is his earnest desire (כָּלָה) now, when within a very little his enemies have compassed his ruin (כִּלָּה). His soul and eyes languish (כָּלָה as in lxix. 4, lxxxiv. 3, cf. Job xix. 27) for God's salvation, that it may be unto him according to God's word or promise, that this word may be fulfilled. In ver. 83 כִּי is hypothetical, as in xxi. 12 and frequently; here, as perhaps also in xxvii. 10, in the sense of "although" (Ew. § 362, *b*). He does not suffer anything to drive God's word out of his mind, although he is already become

like a leathern bottle blackened and shrivelled up in the smoke.
The custom of the ancients of placing jars with wine over the
smoke in order to make the wine prematurely old, *i.e.* to mellow
it (*vid.* Rosenmüller), does not yield anything towards the
understanding of this passage: the skin-bottle that is not intended for present use is hung up on high; and the fact that it
had to withstand the upward ascending smoke is intelligible,
notwithstanding the absence of any mention of the chimney.
The point of comparison, in which we agree for the most part
with Hitzig, is the removal of him who in his dungeon is continually exposed to the drudgery of his persecutors. כַּמָּה in
ver. 84 is equivalent to "how few." Our life here below is
short, so also is the period within which the divine righteousness can reveal itself. שִׁיחוֹת (instead of which the LXX.
erroneously reads שִׂיחוֹת), pits, is an old word, lvii. 7. The
relative clause, ver. 85*b*, describes the "proud" as being a
contradiction to the revealed law; for there was no necessity for
saying that to dig a pit for others is not in accordance with
this law. All God's commandments are an emanation of His
faithfulness, and therefore too demand faithfulness; but it is
just this faithfulness that makes the poet an object of deadly
hatred. They have already almost destroyed him "in the
land." It is generally rendered "on earth;" but "in heaven"
at the beginning of the following octonary is too far removed
to be an antithesis to it, nor does it sound like one (cf. on the
other hand ἐν τοῖς οὐρανοῖς, Matt. v. 12). It is therefore: in
the land (cf. lviii. 3, lxxiii. 9), where they think they are the
only ones who have any right there, they have almost destroyed
him, without shaking the constancy of his faith. But he stands
in need of fresh grace in order that he may not, however, at
last succumb.

Vers. 89–96. The eightfold *Lamed*. Eternal and imperishable in the constant verifying of itself is the vigorous
and consolatory word of God, to which the poet will ever
cling. It has heaven as its standing-place, and therefore it
also has the qualities of heaven, and before all others, heaven-
like stability. Ps. lxxxix. (ver. 3) uses similar language in
reference to God's faithfulness, of which here ver. 90 says that
it endureth into all generations. The earth hath He creatively
set up, and it standeth, viz. as a practical proof and as a scene

of His infinite, unchangeable faithfulness. Heaven and earth are not the subjects of ver. 91 (Hupfeld), for only the earth is previously mentioned; the reference to the heavens in ver. 89 is of a very different character. Hitzig and others see the subject in לְמִשְׁפָּטֶיךָ: with respect to Thy judgments, they stand fast unto this day; but the עֲבָדֶיךָ which follows requires another meaning to be assigned to עָמְדוּ: either of taking up one's place ready for service, or, since עמד למשפט is a current phrase in Num. xxxv. 12, Josh. xx. 6, Ezek. xliv. 24, of placing one's self ready to obey (Böttcher). The subject of עָמְדוּ, as the following הַכֹּל shows, is meant to be thought of in the most general sense (cf. Job xxxviii. 14): all beings are God's servants (subjects), and have accordingly to be obedient and humble before His judicial decisions—הַיּוֹם, " even to this day," the poet adds, for these judicial decisions are those which are formulated beforehand in the Tôra. Joy in this ever sure, all-conditioning word has upheld the poet in his affliction, ver. 92. He who has been persecuted and cast down as it were to death, owes his reviving to it, ver. 93. From Him whose possession or property he is in faith and love he also further looks for his salvation, ver. 94. Let evildoers lie in wait for him (קִוּוּ in a hostile sense, as in lvi. 7, קִוָּה, cf. חִכָּה, going back to קָוָה, قَوِيَ, with the broad primary signification, to be tight, firm, strong) to destroy him, he meditates on God's testimonies. He knows from experience that all (earthly) perfection (תִּכְלָה) has an end (inasmuch as, having reached its height, it changes into its opposite); God's commandment (singular as in Deut. xi. 22), on the contrary, is exceeding broad (cf. Job xi. 9), unlimited in its duration and verification.

Vers. 97–104. The eightfold *Mem*. The poet praises the practical wisdom which the word of God, on this very account so sweet to him, teaches. God's precious law, with which he unceasingly occupies himself, makes him superior in wisdom (Deut. iv. 6), intelligence, and judgment to his enemies, his teachers, and the aged (Job xii. 20). There were therefore at that time teachers and elders (πρεσβύτεροι), who (like the Hellenizing Sadducees) were not far from apostasy in their laxness, and hostilely persecuted the young and strenuous zealot for God's law. The construction of ver. 98*a* is like Joel i. 20,

Isa. lix. 12, and frequently. הִיא refers to the commandments
in their unity: he has taken possession of them for ever (cf.
ver. 111*a*).   The Mishna (*Aboth* iv. 1) erroneously interprets:
from all my teachers do I acquire understanding.   All three מִן
in vers. 98–100 signify *præ* (LXX. ὑπέρ).   In כָּלִאתִי, ver. 101*a*,
from the mode of writing we see the verb *Lamed Aleph* passing
over into the verb *Lamed He*.   הוֹרִתָנִי is, as in Prov. iv. 11 (cf.
Ex. iv. 15), a defective mode of writing for הוֹרִיתני.   נִמְלְצוּ, ver.
103*a*, is not equivalent to נִמְרְצוּ, Job vi. 25 (*vid. Job*, i. 118, 279),
but signifies, in consequence of the dative of the object לְחִכִּי,
that which easily enters, or that which tastes good (LXX. ὡς
γλυκέα); therefore surely from מָלַץ = מָלַט, to be smooth: how
smooth, entering easily (Prov. xxiii. 31), are Thy words (promises) to my palate or taste!   The collective singular אִמְרָתֶךָ is
construed with a plural of the predicate (cf. Ex. i. 10).   He
has no taste for the God-estranged present, but all the stronger
taste for God's promised future.   From God's laws he acquires
the capacity for proving the spirits, therefore he hates every
path of falsehood (= ver. 128*b*), *i.e.* all the heterodox tendencies
which agree with the spirit of the age.

   Vers. 105–112.   The eightfold *Nun*.   The word of God is
his constant guide, to which he has entrusted himself for ever.
The way here below is a way through darkness, and leads close
past abysses: in this danger of falling and of going astray the
word of God is a lamp to his feet, *i.e.* to his course, and a light
to his path (Prov. vi. 23); his lamp or torch and his sun
That which he has sworn, viz. to keep God's righteous requirements, he has also set up, *i.e.* brought to fulfilment, but not
without being bowed down under heavy afflictions in confessing
God; wherefore he prays (as in ver. 25) that God would revive
him in accordance with His word, which promises life to those
who keep it.   The confessions of prayer coming from the
inmost impulse of his whole heart, in which he owns his in-
debtedness and gives himself up entirely to God's mercy, he
calls the free-will offerings of his mouth in ver. 108 (cf. l. 14,
xix. 15).   He bases the prayer for a gracious acceptance of
these upon the fact of his being reduced to extremity.   "To
have one's soul in one's hand" is the same as to be in conscious
peril of one's life, just as " to take one's soul into one's hand"
(Judg. xii. 3, 1 Sam. xix. 5, xxviii. 21, Job xiii. 14) is the

same as to be ready to give one's life for it, to risk one's life.*
Although his life is threatened (ver. 87), yet he does not waver
and depart from God's word; he has taken and obtained possession of God's testimonies for ever (cf. ver. 98); they are his
"heritage," for which he willingly gives up everything else, for
they (הֵמָּה inexactly for הֵנָּה) it is which bless and entrance him
in his inmost soul. In ver. 112 it is not to be interpreted after
xix. 12: eternal is the reward (of the carrying out of Thy
precepts), but in ver. 33 עֵקֶב is equivalent to לָעַד, and ver. 44
proves that ver. 112b need not be a thought that is complete in
itself.

Vers. 113–120. The eightfold *Samech*. His hope rests
on God's word, without allowing itself to be led astray by
doubters and apostates. סֵעֲפִים (the form of nouns which indicate defects or failings) are those inwardly divided, halting
between two opinions (סְעִפִּים), 1 Kings xviii. 21, who do
homage partly to the worship of Jahve, partly to heathenism,
and therefore are trying to combine faith and naturalism. In
contrast to such, the poet's love, faith, and hope are devoted
entirely to the God of revelation; and to all those who are
desirous of drawing him away he addresses in ver. 115 (cf. vi.
9) an indignant " depart." He, however, stands in need of
grace in order to persevere and to conquer. For this he prays
in vers. 116, 117. The מִן in מִשְּׂבְרִי is the same as in בּוֹשׁ מִן.
The *ah* of וְאֶשְׁעָה is the intentional *ah* (Ew. § 228, c), as in Isa.
xli. 23. The statement of the ground of the סָלִיתָ, *vilipendis*,
does not mean: unsuccessful is their deceit (Hengstenberg,
Olshausen), but falsehood without the consistency of truth is
their self-deceptive and seductive tendency. The LXX. and
Syriac read תַּרְעִיתָם, " their sentiment;" but this is an Aramaic
word that is unintelligible in Hebrew, which the old translators
have conjured into the text only on account of an apparent
tautology. The reading חִשַּׁבְתָּ or חָשַׁבְתָּ (Aquila, Symmachus,
and Jerome; LXX. ἐλογισάμην, therefore חשבתי) instead of
הִשְׁבַּתָּ might more readily be justified in ver. 119a; but the
former gives too narrow a meaning, and the reading rests on a
mistaking of the construction of השבית with an accusative of

---

* Cf. *B. Taanith 8a*: " The prayer of a man is not answered אלא אם כן
משים נפשו בכפו, *i.e.* if he is not ready to sacrifice his life."

the object and of the effect : all the wicked, as many of them
as are on the earth, dost Thou put away as dross (סִגִים). Accordingly מִשְׁפָּטֶיךָ in ver. 120 are God's punitive judgments, or
rather (cf. ver. 91) God's laws (judgments) according to which
He judges. What is meant are sentences of punishment, as
in Lev. ch. xxvi., Deut. ch. xxviii. Of these the poet is afraid,
for omnipotence can change words into deeds forthwith. In
fear of the God who has attested Himself in Ex. xxxiv. 7 and
elsewhere, his skin shudders and his hair stands on end.

Vers. 121–128. The eightfold *Ajin*. In the present time
of apostasy and persecution he keeps all the more strictly to
the direction of the divine word, and commends himself to the
protection and teaching of God. In the consciousness of his
godly behaviour (elsewhere always צֶדֶק וּמִשְׁפָּט, here in one
instance מִשְׁפָּט וָצֶדֶק) the poet hopes that God will surely not
(בַּל) leave him to the arbitrary disposal of his oppressors. This
hope does not, however, raise him above the necessity and duty
of constant prayer that Jahve would place Himself between
him and his enemies. עָרַב *seq. acc.* signifies to stand in any
one's place as furnishing a guarantee, and in general as a
mediator, Job xvii. 3, Isa. xxxviii. 14 ; לְטוֹב similar to לְטוֹבָה,
lxxxvi. 17, Neh. v. 19 : in my behalf, for my real advantage. The expression of longing after redemption in ver. 123
sounds like vers. 81 sq. " The word of Thy righteousness" is
the promise which proceeds from God's " righteousness," and
as surely as He is " righteous" cannot remain unfulfilled.
The one chief petition of the poet, however, to which he comes
back in vers. 124 sq., has reference to the ever deeper knowledge of the word of God ; for this knowledge is in itself at
once life and blessedness, and the present calls most urgently
for it. For the great multitude (which is the subject to הֵפֵרוּ)
practically and fundamentally break God's law ; it is therefore
time to act for Jahve (עָשָׂה לְ as in Gen. xxx. 30, Isa. lxiv. 3
[4], Ezek. xxix. 20), and just in order to this there is need of
well-grounded, reliable knowledge. Therefore the poet attaches
himself with all his love to God's commandments ; to him they
are above gold and fine gold (xix. 11), which he might perhaps
gain by a disavowal of them. Therefore he is as strict as he
possibly can be with God's word, inasmuch as he acknowledges
and observes all precepts of all things (כָּל־פִּקּוּדֵי כֹל), *i.e.* all

divine precepts, let them have reference to whatsoever they will, as יְשָׁרִים, right (יָשַׁר, to declare both in avowal and deed to be right); and every false (lying) tendency, all pseudo-Judaism, he hates. It is true ver. 126*a* may be also explained: it is time that Jahve should act, *i.e.* interpose judicially; but this thought is foreign to the context, and affords no equally close union for עַל־כֵּן; moreover it ought then to have been accented עֵת לַעֲשׂוֹת לַיהוָה. On כָּל־פִּקּוּדֵי כֹל, "all commands of every purport," cf. Isa. xxix. 11, and more as to form, Num. viii. 16, Ezek. xliv. 30. The expression is purposely thus heightened; and the correction כָל־פִּקּוּדֶיךָ (Ewald, Olshausen, and Hupfeld) is also superfluous, because the reference of what is said to the God of revelation is self-evident in this connection.

Vers. 129–136. The eightfold *Phe*. The deeper his depression of spirit concerning those who despise the word of God, the more ardently does he yearn after the light and food of that word. The testimonies of God are פְּלָאוֹת, wonderful and strange (paradoxical) things, exalted above every-day life and the common understanding. In this connection of the thoughts נְצָרָתַם is not intended of careful observance, but of attentive contemplation that is prolonged until a clear penetrating understanding of the matter is attained. The opening, disclosure (פֵּתַח, *apertio*, with *Tsere* in distinction from פֶּתַח, *porta*) of God's word giveth light, inasmuch as it makes the simple (פְּתָיִים as in Prov. xxii. 3) wise or sagacious; in connection with which it is assumed that it is God Himself who unfolds the mysteries of His word to those who are anxious to learn. Such an one, anxious to learn, is the poet: he pants with open mouth, viz. for the heavenly fare of such disclosures (פָּעַר like פָּעַר פֶּה in Job xxix. 23, cf. Ps. lxxxi. 11). יָאַב is a hapaxlegomenon, just as תָּאַב is also exclusively peculiar to the Psalm before us; both are secondary forms of אָבָה. Love to God cannot indeed remain unresponded to. The experience of helping grace is a right belonging to those who love the God of revelation; love in return for love, salvation in return for the longing for salvation, is their prerogative. On the ground of this reciprocal relation the petitions in vers. 133–135 are then put up, coming back at last to the one chief prayer "teach me." אִמְרָה, ver. 133, is not merely a "promise" in this instance, but the declared will of God in general. כָּל־אָוֶן refers pre-

eminently to all sin of disavowal (denying God), into which
he might fall under outward and inward pressure (עָשֶׁק). For
he has round about him those who do not keep God's law. On
account of these apostates (עַל לֹא as in Isa. liii. 9, equivalent
to עַל־אֲשֶׁר לֹא) his eyes run down rivers of water (יָרַד as in Lam.
iii. 48, with an accusative of the object). His mood is not that
of unfeeling self-glorying, but of sorrow like that of Jeremiah,
because of the contempt of Jahve, and the self-destruction of
those who contemn Him.

Vers. 137–144. The eightfold *Tsade*. God rules righteously and faithfully according to His word, for which the
poet is accordingly zealous, although young and despised. The
predicate יָשָׁר in ver. 137*b* precedes its subject מִשְׁפָּטֶיךָ (God's
decisions in word and in deed) in the primary form (after the
model of the verbal clause cxxiv. 5), just as in German [and
English] the predicative adjective remains undeclined. The
accusatives צֶדֶק and אֱמוּנָה in ver. 138 are not predicative
(Hitzig), to which the former (" as righteousness")—not the
latter however—is not suited, but adverbial accusatives (in
righteousness, in faithfulness), and מְאֹד according to its position is subordinate to ואמונה as a virtual adjective (cf. Isa. xlvii.
9) : the requirements of the revealed law proceed from a disposition towards and mode of dealing with men which is strictly
determined by His holiness (צדק), and beyond measure faithfully and honestly designs the well-being of men (אמונה מאד).
To see this good law of God despised by his persecutors stirs
the poet up with a zeal, which brings him, from their side, to
the brink of extreme destruction (lxix. 10, cf. צִמְּתַת, lxxxviii. 17).
God's own utterance is indeed without spot, and therefore not
to be carped at ; it is pure, fire-proved, noblest metal (xviii. 31,
xii. 7), therefore he loves it, and does not, though young
(LXX. νεώτερος, Vulgate *adolescentulus*) and lightly esteemed,
care for the remonstrances of his proud opponents who are old
and more learned than himself (the organization of ver. 141 is
like ver. 95, and frequently). The righteousness (צְדָקָה) of the
God of revelation becomes eternal righteousness (צֶדֶק), and His
law remains eternal truth (אֱמֶת). צדקה is here the name of the
attribute and of the action that is conditioned in accordance
with it ; צדק the name of the state that thoroughly accords
with the idea of that which is right. So too in ver. 144 : צדק

are Jahve's testimonies for ever, so that all creatures must give glory to their harmony with that which is absolutely right. To look ever deeper and deeper into this their perfection is the growing life of the spirit. The poet prays for this vivifying insight.

Vers. 145–152. The eightfold *Koph*. Fidelity to God's word, and deliverance according to His promise, is the purport of his unceasing prayer. Even in the morning twilight (נֶשֶׁף) he was awake praying. It is not הַנֶּשֶׁף, I anticipated the twilight; nor is קִדַּמְתִּי, according to lxxxiv. 14, equivalent to קדמתיך, but קִדַּמְתִּי ... וָאֲשַׁוֵּעַ is the resolution of the otherwise customary construction קדמתי לְשַׁוֵּעַ, Jonah iv. 2, inasmuch as קָדַם may signify "to go before" (lxviii. 26), and also "to make haste (with anything):" even early before the morning's dawn I cried. Instead of לדבריך the *Kerî* (Targum, Syriac, Jerome) more appropriately reads לִדְבָרְךָ after vers. 74, 81, 114. But his eyes also anticipated the night-watches, inasmuch as they did not allow themselves to be caught not sleeping by any of them at their beginning (cf. לְרֹאשׁ, Lam. ii. 19). אִמְרָה is here, as in vers. 140, 158, and frequently, the whole word of God, whether in its requirements or its promises. In ver. 149 כְּמִשְׁפָּטֶךָ is a defective plural as in ver. 43 (*vid.* on ver. 37), according to ver. 156, although according to ver. 132 the singular (LXX., Targum, Jerome) would also be admissible: what is meant is God's order of salvation, or His appointments that relate thereto. The correlative relation of vers. 150 and 151 is rendered natural by the position of the words. With קָרְבוּ (cf. קָרֵב) is associated the idea of rushing upon him with hostile purpose, and with קָרוֹב, as in lxix. 19, Isa. lviii. 2, of hastening to his succour. זִמָּה is infamy that is branded by the law: they go forth purposing this, but God's law is altogether self-verifying truth. And the poet has long gained the knowledge from it that it does not aim at merely temporary recompense. The sophisms of the apostates cannot therefore lead him astray. יְסַדְתָּם for יְסַדְתָּן, like הֵמָּה in ver. 111.

Vers. 153–160. The eightfold *Resh*. Because God cannot suffer those who are faithful to His word to succumb, he supplicates His help against his persecutors. רִיבָה is *Milra* before the initial (half-guttural) *Resh*, as in xliii. 1, lxxiv. 22. The *Lamed* of לְאִמְרָתְךָ is the *Lamed* of reference (with respect

to Thine utterance), whether the reference be normative
(=כְּאִמְרָתֶךָ, ver. 58), as in Isa. xi. 3, or causal, xxv. 2, Isa. lv. 5,
Job xlii. 5. The predicate רָחוֹק, like יָשָׁר in ver. 137, stands
first in the primary, as yet indefinite form. Concerning ver.
156*b* *vid.* on ver. 149. At the sight of the faithless he felt a
profound disgust; וָאֶתְקוֹטָטָה, pausal aorist, supply בָּהֶם, cxxxix.
21. It is all the same in the end whether we render אֲשֶׁר *quippe
qui* or *siquidem*. רֹאשׁ in ver. 160 signifies the head-number or
sum. If he reckons up the word of God in its separate parts
and as a whole, truth is the denominator of the whole, truth is
the sum-total. This supplicatory חַיֵּנִי is repeated three times
in this group. The nearer it draws towards its end the more
importunate does the Psalm become.

Vers. 161–168. The eightfold שׁ (both *Shin* and *Sin* *).
In the midst of persecution God's word was still his fear, his
joy, and his love, the object of his thanksgiving, and the ground
of his hope. Princes persecute him without adequate cause,
but his heart does not fear before them, but before God's words
(the *Kerî* likes the singular, as in ver. 147), to deny which would
be to him the greatest possible evil. It is, however, a fear that
is associated with heartfelt joy (ver. 111). It is the joy of a
conflict that is rewarded by rich spoil (Judg. v. 30, Isa. ix. 2
[3]). Not merely morning and evening, not merely three times
a day (lv. 18), but seven times (שֶׁבַע as in Lev. xxvi. 18, Prov.
xxiv. 16), *i.e.* ever again and again, availing himself of every
prayerful impulse, he gives thanks to God for His word, which
so righteously decides and so correctly guides, is a source of
transcendent peace to all who love it, and beside which one is
not exposed to any danger of stumbling (מִכְשׁוֹל, LXX. σκάνδαλον, cf. 1 John ii. 10) without some effectual counter-working.
In ver. 166*a* he speaks like Jacob in Gen. xlix. 18, and can
speak thus, inasmuch as he has followed earnestly and untir-
ingly after sanctification. He endeavours to keep God's law
most conscientiously, in proof of which he is able to appeal to
God, the Omniscient One. שָׁמְרָה is here the 3*d praet.*, where-

---

* Whilst even in the oldest alphabetical *Pijutim* the *Sin* perhaps represents the *Samech* as well, but never the *Shin*, it is the reverse in the Biblical
alphabetical pieces. Here *Sin* and *Shin* coincide, and *Samech* is specially
represented.

as in lxxxvi. 2 it is *imperat.* The future of אָהֵב is both אֹהַב and אֱהַב, just as of אָחַז both אֹחֵז and אֶאֱחֹז.

Vers. 169–176. The eightfold *Tav.* May God answer this his supplication as He has heard his praise, and interest Himself on behalf of His servant, the sheep that is exposed to great danger. The petitions " give me understanding " and " deliver me " go hand-in-hand, because the poet is one who is persecuted for the sake of his faith, and is just as much in need of the fortifying of his faith as of deliverance from the outward restraint that is put upon him. רִנָּה is a shrill audible prayer; תְּחִנָּה, a fervent and urgent prayer. עָנָה, prop. to answer, signi-fies in ver. 172 to begin, strike up, attune (as does ἀποκρίνεσθαι also sometimes). According to the rule in l. 23 the poet bases his petition for help upon the purpose of thankful praise of God and of His word. Knowing how to value rightly what he possesses, he is warranted in further supplicating and hoping for the good that he does not as yet possess. The " salvation " for which he longs (תָּאַב as in vers. 40, 20) is redemption from the evil world, in which the life of his own soul is imperilled. May then God's judgments (defective plural, as in vers. 43, 149, which the Syriac only takes as singular) succour him (יַעַזְרֻנִי, not יְעַזְרֻנִי). God's hand, ver. 173, and God's word afford him succour; the two are involved in one another, the word is the medium of His hand. After this relationship of the poet to God's word, which is attested a hundredfold in the Psalm, it may seem strange that he can say of himself תָּעִיתִי כְּשֶׂה אֹבֵד; and perhaps the accentuation is correct when it does not allow itself to be determined by Isa. liii. 6, but interprets: If I have gone astray—seek Thou like a lost sheep Thy servant. שֶׂה אֹבֵד is a sheep that is lost (cf. אֹבְדִים as an appellation of the dispersion, Isa. xxvii. 13) and in imminent danger of total destruction (cf. xxxi. 13 with Lev. xxvi. 38). In connection with that inter-pretation which is followed by the interpunction, ver. 176*b* is also more easily connected with what precedes: his going astray is no apostasy; his home, to which he longs to return when he has been betrayed into by-ways, is beside the Lord.

THE FIFTEEN SONGS OF DEGREES,
OR GRADUAL PSALMS.

Ps. CXX.–CXXXIV.

These songs are all inscribed שִׁיר הַמַּעֲלוֹת. The LXX., according to the most natural signification of the word, renders: ᾠδὴ τῶν ἀναβαθμῶν; the Italic and Vulgate, *canticum graduum* (whence the liturgical term " gradual Psalms"). The meaning at the same time remains obscure. When, however, Theodotion renders ᾆσμα τῶν ἀναβάσεων, Aquila and Symmachus ᾠδὴ εἰς τὰς ἀναβάσεις (as though it were absolutely לַמַּעֲלוֹת, as in cxxi. 1), it looks even like an explanation. The fathers, more particularly Theodoret, and in general the Syrian church, associate with it the idea of ἡ ἀπὸ Βαβυλῶνος ἐπάνοδος. Ewald has long advocated this view. In his Introduction to *Die poetischen Bücher des Alten Bundes* (1839), and elsewhere, he translated it " Songs of the Pilgrim caravans" or " of the homeward marches," and explained these fifteen Psalms as old and new travelling songs of those returning from the Exile. The verb עָלָה certainly is the usual word for journeying to Palestine out of the Babylonian low country, as out of the country of the Egyptian Nile Valley. And the fact that the Return from the Exile is called הַמַּעֲלָה מִבָּבֶל in Ezra vii. 9 is enticing. Some of these Psalms, as cxxi., cxxiii.–cxxv., cxxix., cxxx., cxxxii., cxxxiii., are also suited to this situation, or can at least be adapted to it. But Ps. cxx., if it is to be referred to the Exile, is a song that comes out of the midst of it; Ps. cxxvi. might, so far as its first half is concerned, be a travelling song of those returning, but according to its second half it is a prayer of those who have returned for the restoration of the whole of Israel, based upon thanksgiving; and Ps. cxxii. assumes the existence and frequenting of the Temple and of the holy city, and Ps. cxxxiv. the full exercise of the Temple-service. It is also inconvenient that מַעֲלָה, which in itself only expresses a journey up, not a journey homewards, is without any closer definition ; and more particularly since, in connection with this form of the word, the signification of a something (a step, a sun-dial, rising thoughts, Ezek. xi. 5) is at least just as natural as that of an action. שִׁיר הָעֲלָיִם would have been at once palpable. And what is meant by the plural? The interpretation of the plural of the different caravans or companies in which the exiles returned, assumes a *usus loquendi* with which we are altogether unacquainted.

Relatively more probable is the reference to the pilgrimage-journeyings at the three great feasts,—according to a later Hebrew expression, the שָׁלֹשׁ רְגָלִים. This going up to Jerusalem required by the Law is also usually called עלה. So Agellius (1606), Herder, Eichhorn, Maurer, Hengstenberg, Keil, and others, and so now even Ewald in the second edition (1866) of the Introduction to *Die Dichter des Alten Bundes*, so Kamphausen, and Reuss in his treatise *Chants de Pèlerinage ou petit Psautier des Pèlerins du second temple* (in the *Nouvelle Revue de Théologie*, i. 273–311), and Liebusch in the Quedlinburg Easter Programm, 1866: " The pilgrim songs in the Fifth Book of the Psalter." But מַעֲלָה in this signification is without precedent; and when Hupfeld says in opposition to this, " the fact that a noun accidentally does not occur in the Old Testament does not matter, since here at any rate it is a question of the interpretation of a later usage of the language," we may reply that neither does the whole range of the post-biblical Hebrew exhibit any trace of this usage. Thenius accordingly tries another way of doing justice to the word. He understands מעלות of the different stations, *i.e.* stages of the journey up, that are to be found in connection with the festive journeys to high-lying Jerusalem. But the right name for " stations" would be מַסָּעוֹת or מַעֲמָדוֹת; and besides, the notion borrowed from the processions to Mount Calvary is without historical support in the religious observances of Israel. Thus, then, the needful ground in language and custom for referring this title of the Psalms to the journeyings up to the feasts is taken from under us; and the consideration that the first three and the last three songs are suited to the hymn-book of a festal pilgrimage, and that they all bear in them, as Liebusch has demonstrated, the characteristic features of the spiritual national song, is not able to decide the doubtful meaning of מעלות.

We will now put the later Jewish interpretation to the proof. According to *Middoth* ii. 5, *Succa* 15*b*, a semi-circular

staircase with fifteen steps led out of the court of the Israelitish
men (עזרת ישׂראל) down into the court of the women (עזרת נשׁים),
and upon these fifteen steps, which correspond to the fifteen
gradual Psalms, the Levites played musical instruments on the
evening of the first day of the Feast of Tabernacles in connection with the joyful celebration of the water-drawing,* and
above them in the portal (upon the threshold of the Nicanor-
gate or Agrippa-gate†) stood two priests with trumpets. It
has been said that this is a Talmudic fable invented on behalf
of the inscription שׁיר המעלות, and that the fifteen steps are got
out of Ezek. xl. 26, 31 by reading the two verses together.
This aspersion is founded on ignorance. For the Talmud does
not say in that passage that the fifteen Psalms have taken their
name from the fifteen steps; it does not once say that these
Psalms in particular were read aloud upon the fifteen steps, but
it only places the fifteen steps on a parallel with the fifteen
Psalms; and, moreover, interprets the name שׁיר המעלות quite
differently, viz. from a legend concerning David and Ahithophel, *Succa* 53*a*, *Maccoth* 11*a* (differently rendered in the section *Chelek* of the tractate *Sanhedrin* in the Jerusalem Talmud).
This legend to which the Targum inscription relates (*vid.* Buxtorf, *Lex. Talmud. s.v.* קפא) is absurd enough, but it has nothing
to do with the fifteen steps. It is not until a later period that
Jewish expositors say that the fifteen Psalms had their name
from the fifteen steps.‡ Even Hippolytus must have heard
something similar when he says (p. 190, *ed. Lagarde*): πάλιν
τε αὐτοῦ εἰσί τινες τῶν ἀναβαθμῶν ᾠδαί, τὸν ἀριθμὸν πεντεκαί-
δεκα, ὅσοι καὶ οἱ ἀναβαθμοὶ τοῦ ναοῦ, τάχα δελοῦσαι τὰς ἀναβάσεις περιέχεσθαι ἐν τῷ ἑβδόμῳ καὶ ὀγδόῳ ἀριθμῷ, upon which
Hilary relies: *esse autem in templo gradus quindecim historia*

---

* *Vid.* my *Geschichte der jüdischen Poesie*, S. 193 f.

† It was called the Nicanor-gate in the Temple of Zerubbabel, and the
Agrippa-gate in the Temple of Herod: in both of them they ascended to
its threshold by fifteen steps; *vid.* Unruh, *Das alte Jerusalem und seine
Bauwerke* (1861), S. 137, cf. 194.

‡ Lyra in his *Postillæ*, and Jacob Leonitius in his Hebrew *Libellus
effigiei templi Salomonis* (Amsterdam 1650, 4to), even say that the Levites
sang one of the fifteen songs of degrees on each step. Luther has again
generalized this view; for his rendering "a song in the higher choir" is
intended to say, *cantores harum odarum stetisse in loco eminentiori* (Bakius).

nobis locuta est; viz. 15 (7 + 8) steps leading out of the court of the priests into the Holy of holies. In this, then, the allegory in which the interpretation of the church delighted for a long time seemed naturally at hand, viz., as Otmar Nachtgal explains, " Song of the steps or ascents, which indicate the spirit of those who ascend from earthly things to God." The Furtmaier Codex in Maihingen accordingly inscribes them " Psalm of the first step" (*Psalm der ersten staffeln*), and so on. If we leave this *sensus anagogicus* to itself, then the title, referred to the fifteen steps, would indeed not be inappropriate in itself (cf. *Graduale* or *Gradale* in the service of the Romish Church), but is of an external character such as we find nowhere else.*

Gesenius has the merit of having first discerned the true meaning of the questioned inscription, inasmuch as first in 1812 (*Hallische Lit. Zeitschrift*, 1812, Nr. 205), and frequently since that time, he has taught that the fifteen songs have their name from their step-like progressive rhythm of the thoughts, and that consequently the name, like the triolet (roundelay) in Western poetry, does not refer to the liturgical usage, but to the technical structure. The correctness of this view has been duly appraised more particularly by De Wette, who adduces this rhythm of steps or degrees, too, among the more artificial rhythms. The songs are called Songs of degrees or Gradual Psalms as being songs that move onward towards a climax, and that by means of πλοκή (ἐπιπλοκή), *i.e.* a taking up again of the immediately preceding word by way of giving intensity to the expression ; and they are placed together on account of this common characteristic, just like the *Michtammim*, which bear that name from a similar characteristic. The fact, as Liebusch objects, that there is no trace of מעלות in this figurative signification elsewhere, is of no consequence, since in the inscriptions of the Psalms in general we become acquainted with a technical language which (apart from a few echoes in the Chronicles) is without example elsewhere, in relation to poetical and musical technology. Neither are we refuted by the fact that this as it were climbing movement of the thoughts which plants upon a

---

* Hitzig, in his Commentary (1865), has attempted a new combination of these Psalms, in regard to the number of verses of cxx. and cxxi. (7 + 8) and their total number, with the steps of the Temple.

preceding word, and thus carries itself forward, is not without example even outside the range of these fifteen songs in the Psalter itself (*e.g.* xciii., xcvi.), as also elsewhere (Isa. xvii. 12 sq., xxvi. 5 sq., and more particularly in the song of Deborah, Judg. v. 3, 5, 6, etc.), and that it is not always carried out in the same manner in the fifteen Psalms. It is quite sufficient that the parallelism retires into the background here as nowhere else in fifteen songs that are linked together (even in cxxv., cxxvii., cxxviii., cxxxii.); and the onward course is represented with decided preference as a gradation or advance step by step, that which follows being based upon what goes before, and from that point advancing and ascending still higher.

PSALM CXX.

CRY OF DISTRESS WHEN SURROUNDED BY CONTENTIOUS MEN.

1 TO Jahve in my distress
  Do I cry, and He answereth me.
2 O Jahve, deliver my soul from a lying lip,
  From a crafty tongue!

3 What shall He give to thee, and what shall He further give
  Thou crafty tongue? [to thee,
4 Arrows of a mighty one, sharpened,
  Together with coals of broom.

5 Woe is me that I sojourn in Meshech,
  That I *dwell* beside the tents of Kedar!
6 Long enough hath my soul *dwelt*
  With those who hate *peace.*
7 I am *peace;* yet when I speak,
  They are for war.

This first song of degrees attaches itself to Ps. cxix. 176. The writer of Ps. cxix., surrounded on all sides by apostasy and persecution, compares himself to a sheep that is easily lost, which the shepherd has to seek and bring home if it is not to perish; and the writer of Ps. cxx. is also "as a sheep in the midst of wolves." The period at which he lived is uncertain, and it is consequently also uncertain whether he had to endure such endless malignant attacks from foreign barbarians or from his own worldly-minded fellow-countrymen. E. Tilling has sought to establish a third possible occasion in his *Disquisitio de ratione inscript. XV Pss. grad.* (1765). He derives this and the following songs of degrees from the time immediately succeeding the Return from the Exile, when the secret and open hostility of the Samaritans and other neighbouring peoples (Neh. ii. 10, 19, iv. 1 [7], vi. 1) sought to keep down the rise of the young colony.

Vers. 1–4. According to the pointing וַיַּעֲנֵנִי, the poet appears to base his present petition, which from ver. 2 onwards is the substance of the whole Psalm, upon the fact of a previous answering of his prayers. For the petition in ver. 2 manifestly arises out of his deplorable situation, which is described in vers. 5 sqq. Nevertheless there are also other instances in which וְיַעֲנֵנִי might have been expected, where the pointing is וַיַּעֲנֵנִי (iii. 5, Jonah ii. 3), so that consequently וַיַּעֲנֵנִי may, without any prejudice to the pointing, be taken as a believing expression of the result (cf. the future of the consequence in Job ix. 16) of the present cry for help. צָרָתָה, according to the original signification, is a form of the definition of a state or condition, as in iii. 3, xliv. 27, lxiii. 8, Jonah ii. 10, Hos. viii. 7, and בַּצָּרָתָה לִּי = בַּצַּר־לִי, xviii. 7, is based upon the customary expression צַר לִי. In ver. 2 follows the petition which the poet sends up to Jahve in the certainty of being answered. רְמִיָּה beside לָשׁוֹן, although there is no *masc.* רָמִי (cf. however the Aramaic רַמַּי, רַמָּאי), is taken as an adjective after the form עֲנִיָּה, טְרִיָּה, which it is also perhaps in Mic. vi. 12. The parallelism would make לָשׁוֹן natural, like לְשׁוֹן מִרְמָה in lii. 6; the pointing, which nevertheless disregarded this, will therefore rest upon tradition. The apostrophe in ver. 3 is addressed to the crafty tongue. לָשׁוֹן is certainly feminine as a rule; but whilst the tongue as such is feminine, the לְשׁוֹן רְמִיָּה of the address, as in lii. 6, refers to him who has such a kind of tongue (cf. Hitzig on Prov. xii. 27), and thereby the לְךָ is justified; whereas the rendering, "what does it bring to thee, and what does it profit thee?" or, "of what use to thee and what advancement to thee is the crafty tongue?" is indeed possible so far as concerns the syntax (Ges. § 147, *e*), but is unlikely as being ambiguous and confusing in expression. It is also to be inferred from the correspondence between מַה־יִּתֵּן לְךָ וּמַה־יֹּסִיף לָךְ and the formula of an oath כֹּה יַעֲשֶׂה־לְּךָ אֱלֹהִים וְכֹה יוֹסִיף, 1 Sam. iii. 17, xx. 13, xxv. 22, 2 Sam. iii. 35, Ruth i. 17, that God is to be thought of as the subject of יתן and יסיף: "what will," or rather, in accordance with the otherwise precative use of the formula and with the petition that here precedes: "what shall He (is He to) give to thee (נָתַן as in Hos. ix. 14), and what shall He add to thee, thou crafty tongue?" The reciprocal relation of ver. 4*a* to מה־יתן, and of ver. 4*b* with the superadding עם to מה־יסיף, shows that ver. 4 is not now a characterizing of the tongue that continues the apostrophe to it, as Ewald supposes. Consequently ver. 4 gives the answer to ver. 3 with the twofold punishment which Jahve will cause the false tongue to feel. The question which the poet, sure of the answering of his cry for help, puts to the false tongue is designed to let the person addressed hear by a flight of sarcasm what he has to expect. The evil tongue is a sharp sword (lvii. 5), a pointed arrow (Jer. ix. 7 [8]), and it is like a fire kindled of hell (Jas. iii. 6). The punishment, too, corresponds to this its nature and conduct (lxiv. 4). The "mighty one" (LXX. δυνατός) is God Himself, as it is observed in *B. Erachin* 15*b* with a reference to Isa. xlii. 13: "There is none mighty but the Holy One, blessed is He." He requites the evil tongue like with like. Arrows and coals (cxl. 11) appear also in other instances among His means of punishment. It, which shot piercing arrows, is pierced by the sharpened arrows of an irresistibly mighty One; it, which set its neighbour in a fever of anguish, must endure the lasting, sure, and torturingly consuming heat of broom-coals. The LXX. renders it in a general sense, σὺν τοῖς ἄνθραξι τοῖς ἐρημικοῖς; Aquila, following Jewish tradition, ἀρκευθίναις; but רֶתֶם, Arabic رتم, *ratem*, is the broom-shrub (*e.g.* uncommonly frequent in the *Belkâ*).

Vers. 5–7. Since arrows and broom-fire, with which the evil tongue is requited, even now proceed from the tongue itself, the poet goes on with the deep heaving אוֹיָה (only found here). גּוּר with the accusative of that beside which one sojourns, as in v. 5, Isa. xxxiii. 14, Judg. v. 17. The Moschi (מֶשֶׁךְ, the name of which the LXX. takes as an appellative in the signification of long continuance; cf. the reverse instance in Isa. lxvi. 19 LXX.) dwelt between the Black and the Caspian Seas, and it is impossible to dwell among them and the inhabitants of Kedar (vid. lxxxiii. 7) at one and the same time. Accordingly both these names of peoples are to be understood emblematically, with Saadia, Calvin, Amyraldus, and others, of *homines similes ejusmodi barbaris et truculentis nationibus.** Meshech is reckoned to Magog in Ezek. xxxviii. 2, and the Kedarites are possessed by the lust of possession (Gen. xvi. 12) of the *bellum omnium contra omnes.* These rough and quarrelsome characters have surrounded the poet (and his fellow-countrymen, with whom he perhaps comprehends himself) too long already. רַבַּת, abundantly (vid. lxv. 10), appears, more particularly in 2 Chron. xxx. 17 sq., as a later prose word. The הּ, which throws the action back upon the subject, gives a pleasant, lively colouring to the declaration, as in cxxii. 3, cxxiii. 4. He on his part is peace (cf. Mic. v. 4 [5], Ps. cix. 4, cx. 3), inasmuch as the love of peace, willingness to be at peace, and a desire for peace fill his soul; but if he only opens his mouth, they are for war, they are abroad intent on war, their mood and their behaviour become forthwith hostile. Ewald (§ 362, b) construes it (following Saadia): and I—although I speak peace; but if כִּי (like עַד, cxli. 10) might even have this position in the clause, yet וְכִי cannot. שָׁלוֹם is not on any account to be supplied in thought to אֲדַבֵּר, as Hitzig suggests (after xxii. 8, xxviii. 3, xxxv. 20). With the shrill dissonance of שלום and מלחמה the Psalm closes; and the cry for help with which it opens hovers over it, earnestly desiring its removal.

---

* If the Psalm were a Maccabæan Psalm, one might think מֶשֶׁךְ, from מָשַׁךְ, σύρειν, alluded to the Syrians or even to the Jewish apostates with reference to מָשַׁךְ עָרְלָה, ἐπισπᾶσθαι τὴν ἀκροβυστίαν (1 Cor. vii. 18).

PSALM CXXI.

THE CONSOLATION OF DIVINE PROTECTION.

1 I LIFT up mine eyes unto the mountains:
　Whence shall come *my help?*
2 *My help* cometh from Jahve,
　The Creator of heaven and earth.

3 He will not indeed suffer thy foot to totter,
　Thy Keeper will not slumber.
4 Behold *slumbereth not* and sleepeth not
　The Keeper of Israel.

5 *Jahve* is *thy Keeper,*
　Jahve is thy shade upon thy right hand:
6 By day the sun shall not smite thee,
　And the moon in the night.

7 *Jahve* shall *keep thee* from all evil,
　He *shall keep* thy soul.
8 Jahve *shall keep* thy going out and thy coming in
　From this time forth and for evermore.

This song of degrees is the only one that is inscribed שִׁיר לַמַּעֲלוֹת and not שִׁיר הַמַּעֲלוֹת. The LXX., Targum, and Jerome render it as in the other instances; Aquila and Symmachus, on the contrary, ᾠδὴ (ᾆσμα) εἰς τὰς ἀναβάσεις, as the Midrash *Sifrî* also mystically interprets it: Song upon the steps, upon which God leads the righteous up into the other world. Those who explain המעלות of the homeward caravans or of the pilgrimages rightly regard this למעלות, occurring only once, as favouring their explanation. But the *Lamed* is that of the rule or standard. The most prominent distinguishing mark of Ps. cxxi. is the step-like movement of the thoughts: it is formed לְמַעֲלוֹת, after the manner of steps. The view that we have a pilgrim song before us is opposed by the beginning, which leads one to infer a firmly limited range of vision, and therefore a fixed place of abode and far removed from his native mountains. The tetrastichic arrangement of the Psalm is unmistakeable.

Vers. 1–4. Apollinaris renders as meaninglessly as possible: ὄμματα δενδροκόμων ὀρέων ὑπερεξετάνυσσα—with a reproduction of the misapprehended ἦρα of the LXX. The expression in fact is אֶשָּׂא, and not נָשָׂאתִי. And the mountains towards which the psalmist raises his eyes are not any mountains whatsoever. In Ezekiel the designation of his native land from the standpoint of the Mesopotamian plain is "the mountains of Israel." His longing gaze is directed towards the district of these mountains, they are his *kibla*, *i.e.* the sight-point of his prayer, as of Daniel's, ch. vi. 11 [10]. To render " from which my help cometh" (Luther) is inadmissible. מֵאַיִן is an interrogative even in Josh. ii. 4, where the question is an indirect one. The poet looks up to the mountains, the mountains of his native land, the holy mountains (cxxxiii. 3, lxxxvii. 1, cxxv. 2), when he longingly asks : whence will my help come? and to this question his longing desire itself returns the answer, that his help comes from no other quarter than from Jahve, the Maker of heaven and earth, from Him who sits enthroned behind and upon these mountains, whose helpful power reaches to the remotest ends and corners of His creation, and with (עִם) whom is help, *i.e.* both the willingness and the power to help, so that therefore help comes from nowhere but from (מִן) Him alone. In ver. 1*b* the poet has propounded a question, and in ver. 2 replies to this question himself. In ver. 3 and further the answering one goes on speaking to the questioner. The poet is himself become objective, and his Ego, calm in God, promises him comfort, by unfolding to him the joyful prospects contained in that hope in Jahve. The subjective אַל expresses a negative in both cases with an emotional rejection of that which is absolutely impossible. The poet says to himself : He will, indeed, surely not abandon thy foot to the tottering (לַמּוֹט, as in lxvi. 9, cf. lv. 23), thy Keeper will surely not slumber; and then confirms the assertion that this shall not come to pass by heightening the expression in accordance with the step-like character of the Psalm : Behold the Keeper of Israel slumbereth not and sleepeth not, *i.e.* He does not fall into slumber from weariness, and His life is not an alternate waking and sleeping. The eyes of His providence are ever open over Israel.

Vers. 5–8. That which holds good of " the Keeper of

Israel" the poet applies believingly to himself, the individual among God's people, in ver. 5 after Gen. xxviii. 15. Jahve is his Keeper, He is his shade upon his right hand (הַיָּמִין as in Judg. xx. 16, 2 Sam. xx. 9, and frequently; the construct state instead of an apposition, cf. *e.g.* جانب الغربيِ, the side of the western = the western side), which protecting him and keeping him fresh and cool, covers him from the sun's burning heat. עַל, as in cix. 6, cx. 5, with the idea of an overshadowing that screens and spreads itself out over anything (cf. Num. xiv. 9). To the figure of the shadow is appended the consolation in ver. 6. הִכָּה of the sun signifies to smite injuriously (Isa. xlix. 10), plants, so that they wither (cii. 5), and the head (Jonah iv. 8), so that symptoms of sun-stroke (2 Kings iv. 19, Judith viii. 2 sq.) appear. The transferring of the word to the moon is not zeugmatic. Even the moon's rays may become insupportable, may affect the eyes injuriously, and (more particularly in the equatorial regions) produce fatal inflammation of the brain.* From the hurtful influences of nature that are round about him the promise extends in vers. 7, 8 in every direction. Jahve, says the poet to himself, will keep (guard) thee against all evil, of whatever kind it may be and whencesoever it may threaten; He will keep thy soul, and therefore thy life both inwardly and outwardly; He will keep (יִשְׁמָר־, cf. on the other hand יִשְׁפֹּט־ in ix. 9) thy going out and coming in, *i.e.* all thy business and intercourse of life (Deut. xxviii. 6, and frequently); for, as Chrysostom observes, ἐν τούτοις ὁ βίος ἅπας, ἐν εἰσόδοις καὶ ἐξόδοις, therefore: everywhere and at all times; and that from this time forth even for ever. In connection with this the thought is natural, that the life of him who stands under the so universal and unbounded protection of eternal love can suffer no injury.

---

* Many expositors, nevertheless, understand the destructive influence of the moon meant here of the nightly cold, which is mentioned elsewhere in the same antithesis, Gen. xxxi. 40, Jer. xxxvi. 30. De Sacy observes also: *On dit quelquefois d'un grand froid, comme d'un grand chaud, qu'il est brûlant.* The Arabs also say of snow and of cold as of fire: *jaḥrik,* it burns.

PSALM CXXII.

A WELL-WISHING GLANCE BACK AT THE PILGRIMS' CITY.

1 I REJOICED in those who said to me:
   "Let us go into the house of Jahve!"
2 Our feet stood still
   Within thy gates, *O Jerusalem,*
3 *Jerusalem,* thou that art built up again
   As a city which is compact in itself!

4 Whither *the tribes* went up,
   The tribes of Jāh—
   A precept for Israel—
   To give thanks unto the Name of Jahve.
5 For there were set *thrones* for judgment,
   Thrones for the house of David.

6 Wish ye Jerusalem *peace:*
   May it be well with those who love thee!
7 *Peace* be within thy walls,
   Prosperity within thy palaces!
8 For my brethren and my friends' sakes
   Will I speak *peace* concerning thee.
9 For the sake of the house of Jahve, our God,
   Will I seek thy good.

If by "the mountains" in cxxi. 1 the mountains of the
Holy Land are to be understood, it is also clear for what reason
the collector placed this Song of degrees, which begins with
the expression of joy at the pilgrimage to the house of Jahve,
and therefore to the holy mountain, immediately after the preceding song. By its peace-breathing (שׁלוֹם) contents it also,
however, touches closely upon Ps. cxx. The poet utters aloud
his hearty benedictory salutation to the holy city in remembrance of the delightful time during which he sojourned there
as a visitor at the feast, and enjoyed its inspiring aspect. If
in respect of the לְדָוִד the Psalm were to be regarded as an old
Davidic Psalm, it would belong to the series of those Psalms of

the time of the persecution by Absalom, which cast a yearning
look back towards home, the house of God (xxiii., xxvi., lv. 15,
lxi., and more particularly lxiii.).   But the לְדָוִד is wanting in
the LXX., *Codd. Alex.* and *Vat.*; and the *Cod. Sinait.*, which
has *TΩ ΔΑΔ*, puts this before Ps. cxxiv., εἰ μὴ ὅτι κύριος,
κ.τ.λ., also, contrary to *Codd. Alex.* and *Vat.*   Here it is occasioned by ver. 5, but without any critical discernment.   The
measures adopted by Jeroboam I. show, moreover, that the
pilgrimages to the feasts were customary even in the time of
David and Solomon.   The images of calves in Dan and Bethel,
and the changing of the Feast of Tabernacles to another month,
were intended to strengthen the political rupture, by breaking
up the religious unity of the people and weaning them from
visiting Jerusalem.   The poet of the Psalm before us, however, lived much later.   He lived, as is to be inferred with
Hupfeld from ver. 3, in the time of the post-exilic Jerusalem
which rose again out of its ruins.   Thither he had been at one
of the great feasts, and here, still quite full of the inspiring
memory, he looks back towards the holy city; for, in spite of
Reuss, Hupfeld, and Hitzig, vers. 1 sq., so far as the style is
concerned, are manifestly a retrospect.

Vers. 1–3.   The preterite שָׂמַחְתִּי may signify: I rejoice
(1 Sam. ii. 1), just as much as: I rejoiced.   Here in comparison with ver. 2*a* it is a retrospect; for הָיָה with the participle
has for the most part a retrospective signification, Gen. xxxix.
22, Deut. ix. 22, 24, Judg. i. 7, Job i. 14.   True, עֹמְדוֹת הָיוּ
might also signify: they have been standing and still stand (as
in x. 14, Isa. lix. 2, xxx. 20); but then why was it not more
briefly expressed by עָמְדוּ (xxvi. 12)?   The LXX. correctly
renders: εὐφράνθην and ἑστῶτες ἦσαν.   The poet, now again
on the journey homewards, or having returned home, calls to
mind the joy with which the cry for setting out, " Let us go
up to the house of Jahve!" filled him.   When he and the
other visitors to the feast had reached the goal of their pilgrimage, their feet came to a stand-still, as if spell-bound by
the overpowering, glorious sight.*   Reviving this memory, he

---

* So also Veith in his, in many points, beautiful Lectures on twelve
gradual Psalms (Vienna 1863), S. 72, " They arrested their steps, in order

exclaims: Jerusalem, O thou who art built up again—true, בָּנָה in itself only signifies " to build," but here, where, if there is nothing to the contrary, a closed sense is to be assumed for the line of the verse, and in the midst of songs which reflect the joy and sorrow of the post-exilic restoration period, it obtains the same meaning as in cii. 17, cxlvii. 2, and frequently (Gesenius: *O Hierosolyma restituta*). The parallel member, ver. 3*b*, does not indeed require this sense, but is at least favourable to it. Luther's earlier rendering, " as a city which is compacted together," was happier than his later rendering, " a city where they shall come together," which requires a *Niph.* or *Hithpa.* instead of the passive. חֻבַּר signifies, as in Ex. xxviii. 7, to be joined together, to be united into a whole; and יַחְדָּו strengthens the idea of that which is harmoniously, perfectly, and snugly closed up (cf. cxxxiii. 1). The *Kaph* of כְּעִיר is the so-called *Kaph veritatis:* Jerusalem has risen again out of its ruined and razed condition, the breaches and gaps are done away with (Isa. lviii. 12), it stands there as a closely compacted city, in which house joins on to house. Thus has the poet seen it, and the recollection fills him with rapture.*

Vers. 4, 5. The imposing character of the impression was still greatly enhanced by the consideration, that this is the city where at all times the twelve tribes of God's nation (which were still distinguished as its elements even after the Exile, Rom. xi. 1, Luke ii. 36, Jas. i. 1) came together at the three great feasts. The use of the שֶׁ twice as equivalent to אֲשֶׁר is (as in Canticles) appropriate to the ornamental, happy, miniature-like manner of these Songs of degrees. In שָׁשָּׁם the שָׁם is, as in Eccles. i. 7, equivalent to שָׁמָּה, which on the other hand in ver. 5 is no more than an emphatic שָׁם (cf. lxxvi. 4, lxviii. 7). עָלוּ affirms a habit (cf. Job i. 4) of the past, which extends into the present. עֵדוּת לְיִשְׂרָאֵל is not an accusative of the definition or destination (Ew. § 300, *c*), but an apposition to the previous clause, as *e.g.* in Lev. xxiii. 14, 21, 31 (Hitzig), referring to the appointment in Ex. xxiii. 17, xxxiv. 23, Deut.

---

to give time to the amazement with which the sight of the Temple, the citadel of the king, and the magnificent city filled them."

　* In synagogue and church it is become customary to interpret ver. 3 of the parallelism of the heavenly and the earthly Jerusalem.

xvi. 16. The custom, which arose thus, is confirmed in ver. 5 from the fact, that Jerusalem, the city of the one national sanctuary, was at the same time the city of the Davidic kingship. The phrase יָשַׁב לְמִשְׁפָּט is here transferred from the judicial persons (cf. xxix. 10 with ix. 5, Isa. xxviii. 6), who sit in judgment, to the seats (thrones) which are set down and stand there for judgment (cf. cxxv. 1, and θρόνος ἔκειτο, Apoc. iv. 2). The Targum is thinking of seats in the Temple, viz. the raised (in the second Temple resting upon pillars) seat of the king in the court of the Israelitish men near the שַׁעַר הָעֶלְיוֹן, but לְמִשְׁפָּט points to the palace, 1 Kings vii. 7. In the flourishing age of the Davidic kingship this was also the highest court of judgment of the land; the king was the chief judge (2 Sam. xv. 2, 1 Kings iii. 16), and the sons, brothers, or kinsmen of the king were his assessors and advisers. In the time of the poet it is different; but the attractiveness of Jerusalem, not only as the city of Jahve, but also as the city of David, remains the same for all times.

Vers. 6–9. When the poet thus calls up the picture of his country's "city of peace" before his mind, the picture of the glory which it still ever possesses, and of the greater glory which it had formerly, he spreads out his hands over it in the distance, blessing it in the kindling of his love, and calls upon all his fellow-countrymen round about and in all places: *apprecamini salutem Hierosolymis.* So Gesenius correctly (*Thesaurus*, p. 1347); for just as שָׁאַל לוֹ לְשָׁלוֹם signifies to inquire after any one's well-being, and to greet him with the question: הֲשָׁלוֹם לָךְ (Jer. xv. 5), so שָׁאַל שָׁלוֹם signifies to find out any one's prosperity by asking, to gladly know and gladly see that it is well with him, and therefore to be animated by the wish that he may prosper; Syriac, שְׁאֵל שְׁלָמָא דְּ directly: to salute any one; for the interrogatory הֲשָׁלוֹם לָךְ and the well-wishing שָׁלוֹם לָךְ, εἰρήνη σοί (Luke x. 5, John xx. 19 sqq.), have both of them the same source and meaning. The reading אֹהָלָיִךְ, commended by Ewald, is a recollection of Job xii. 6 that is violently brought in here. The loving ones are comprehended with the beloved one, the children with the mother. שָׁלָה forms an alliteration with שָׁלוֹם; the emphatic form יִשְׁלָיוּ occurs even in other instances out of pause (*e.g.* lvii. 2). In ver. 7 the alliteration of שָׁלוֹם and שַׁלְוָה is again taken up, and both accord with the name of Jerusalem. *Ad elegantiam facit,* as Venema observes, *perpetua vocum ad se invicem et omnium ad nomen Hierosolymœ alliteratio.* Both together mark the Song of degrees as such. Happiness, cries out the poet to the holy city from afar, be within thy bulwarks, prosperity within thy palaces, *i.e.* without and within. חֵיל, ramparts, circumvallation (from חגל, to surround, Arabic حول, round about, equally correct whether written חֵיל or חֵל), and אַרְמְנוֹת as the parallel word, as in xlviii. 14. The twofold motive of such an earnest wish for peace is love for the brethren and love for the house of God. For the sake of the brethren is he cheerfully resolved to speak peace (τὰ πρὸς εἰρήνην αὐτῆς, Luke xix. 42) concerning (דִּבֶּר בְּ, as in lxxxvii. 3, Deut. vi. 7, LXX. περὶ σοῦ; cf. דִּבֶּר שָׁלוֹם with אֶל and לְ, to speak peace to, lxxxv. 9, Esth. x. 3) Jerusalem, for the sake of the house of Jahve will he strive after good (*i.e.* that which tends to her well-being) to her (like בִּקֵּשׁ טוֹבָה לְ in Neh. ii. 10, cf. דָּרַשׁ שָׁלוֹם, Deut. xxiii. 7 [6], Jer. xxix. 7). For although he is now again far from Jerusalem after the visit that is over, he still remains united in love to the holy city as being the goal of his longing, and to those who dwell there as being his brethren and friends. Jerusalem is and will remain the heart of all Israel as surely as Jahve, who has His house there, is the God of all Israel.

PSALM CXXIII.

UPWARD GLANCE TO THE LORD IN TIMES OF CONTEMPT.

1 TO Thee do I lift up mine *eyes,*
    Thou who art enthroned in the heavens!
2 Behold, *as the eyes* of servants
    unto the hand of their master,
 As the eyes of a maid unto the hand
    of her mistress:
So our *eyes* are unto Jahve our God,
    until He *be gracious* unto us.

3 *Be gracious* unto us, Jahve, *be gracious* unto us,
    for of *contempt* are we *full enough.*

> 4 *Full enough* is our soul
>   With the scorn of the haughty,
>   the *contempt* of despots.

This Psalm is joined to the preceding Psalm by the community of the divine name *Jahve our God*.   Alsted (died 1638) gives it the brief, ingenious inscription *oculus sperans*.   It is an upward glance of waiting faith to Jahve under tyrannical oppression.   The fact that this Psalm appears in a rhyming form, "as scarcely any other piece in the Old Testament" (Reuss), comes only from those inflexional rhymes which creep in of themselves in the tephilla style.

Vers. 1, 2.   The destinies of all men, and in particular of the church, are in the hand of the King who sits enthroned in the unapproachable glory of the heavens and rules over all things, and of the Judge who decides all things.   Up to Him the poet raises his eyes, and to Him the church, together with which he may call Him "Jahve our God," just as the eyes of servants are directed towards the hand of their lord, the eyes of a maid towards the hand of her mistress; for this hand regulates the whole house, and they wait upon their winks and signs with most eager attention.   Those of Israel are Jahve's servants, Israel the church is Jahve's maid.   In His hand lies its future.   At length He will take compassion on His own.   Therefore its longing gaze goes forth towards Him, without being wearied, until He shall graciously turn its distress.   With reference to the *i* of הַיֹּשְׁבִי, *vid.* on cxiii., cxiv.   אֲדוֹנֵיהֶם is their common lord; for since in the antitype the sovereign Lord is meant, it will be conceived of as *plur. excellentiæ*, just as in general it occurs only rarely (Gen. xix. 2, 18, Jer. xxvii. 4) as an actual plural.

Vers. 3, 4.   The second strophe takes up the "be gracious unto us" as it were in echo.   It begins with a *Kyrie eleison*, which is confirmed in a *crescendo* manner after the form of steps.   The church is already abundantly satiated with ignominy.   רַב is an abstract "much," and רַבַּת (cf. lxv. 10, cxx. 6) is concrete, "a great measure," like רַבָּה, lxii. 3, something great (*vid.* Böttcher, *Lehrbuch*, § 624).   The subjectivizing, intensive לָהּ accords with cxx. 6—probably an indication of

one and the same author.   בּוּ is strengthened by לָעֵג, like בַּ in
Ezek. xxxvi. 4.   The article of הַלַּעַג is retrospectively demonstrative: full of such scorn of the haughty (Ew. § 290, *d*).
הַבּוּז is also retrospectively demonstrative; but since a repetition of the article for the fourth time would have been inelegant, the poet here says לִגְאֵיוֹנִים with the *Lamed,* which serves
as a circumlocution of the genitive.   The Masora reckons this
word among the fifteen " words that are written as one and are
to be read as two."   The *Kerî* runs viz. לִגְאֵי יוֹנִים, *superbis
oppressorum* (יוֹנִים, *part. Kal,* like הַיּוֹנָה Zeph. iii. 1, and frequently).   But apart from the consideration that instead of
גְּאֵי, from the unknown גָּאָה, it might more readily be pointed
גְּאֵי, from גֵּאֶה (a form of nouns indicating defects, contracted
גֵּא), this genitival construction appears to be far-fetched, and,
inasmuch as it makes a distinction among the oppressors, inappropriate.   The poet surely meant לִגְאֵיוֹנִים or לַגֵּאֵיוֹנִים.   This
word גֵּאָיוֹן (after the form עֶלְיוֹן, אֶבְיוֹן, רַעֲיוֹן) is perhaps an intentional new formation of the poet.   Saadia interprets it after
the Talmudic לִגְיוֹן, *legio;* but how could one expect to find such
a Grecized Latin word (λεγεών) in the Psalter!   Dunash ben-
Labrat (about 960) regards גאיונים as a compound word in the
signification of הַגֵּאִים הַיּוֹנִים.   In fact the poet may have chosen
the otherwise unused adjectival form גֵּאָיוֹנִים because it reminds
one of יוֹנִים, although it is not a compound word like דְּבִיוֹנִים.   If
the Psalm is a Maccabæan Psalm, it is natural to find in לִגְאֵיוֹנִים
an allusion to the despotic domination of the יְוָנִים.

PSALM CXXIV.

THE DELIVERER FROM DEATH IN WATERS AND IN A SNARE.

> 1 *HAD not Jahve been for us,*
>   Let Israel say—
> 2 *Had not Jahve been for us,*
>   When men rose up against us:
>
> 3 *Then* had they swallowed us up alive,
>   When their anger was kindled against us—
> 4 *Then* had the *waters* overwhelmed us,
>   The stream *had gone over our soul*—

5 *Then had gone over our soul*
　The proudly swelling *waters.*

6 Blessed be Jahve, who hath not abandoned **us**
　A prey to their teeth !
7 Our soul, like a bird hath it *escaped*
　Out of *the snare* of the fowlers:
　The snare was broken
　And we—we *escaped.*

8 Our help is in the Name of Jahve,
　The Creator of heaven and earth.

The statement "the stream had gone over our soul" of this fifth Song of degrees, coincides with the statement "our soul is full enough" of the fourth; the two Psalms also meet in the synonymous new formations גֵּאֲיוֹנִים and זֵידוֹנִים, which also look very much as though they were formed in allusion to cotemporary history.   The לְדָוִד is wanting in the LXX., *Codd. Alex.* and *Vat.*, here as in Ps. cxxii., and with the exception of the Targum is wanting in general in the ancient versions, and therefore is not so much as established as a point of textual criticism.   It is a Psalm in the manner of the Davidic Psalms, to which it is closely allied in the metaphors of the overwhelming waters, xviii. 5, 17 (cf. cxliv. 7), lxix. 2 sq., and of the little bird; cf. also on לוּלֵי xxvii. 13, on אָדָם used of hostile men lvi. 12, on בָּלַע חַיִּים lv. 16, on בָּרוּךְ ה׳ xxviii. 6, xxxi. 22.   This beautiful song makes its modern origin known by its Aramaizing character, and by the delight, after the manner of the later poetry, in all kinds of embellishments of language.   The art of the form consists less in strophic symmetry than in this, that in order to take one step forward it always goes back half a step.   Luther's imitation (1524), "Were God not with us at this time" (*Wäre Gott nicht mit uns diese Zeit*), bears the inscription "The true believers' safeguard."

Vers. 1–5.   It is commonly rendered, "If it had not been Jahve who was for us."   But, notwithstanding the subject that is placed first (cf. Gen. xxiii. 13), the שֶׁ belongs to the לוּלֵי;

since in the Aramaizing Hebrew (cf. on the other hand Gen.
xxxi. 42) לוּלֵי שֶׁ (cf. لَوْلَا أَنْ) signifies *nisi* (prop. *nisi quod*), as
in the Aramaic (דְּ) שֶׁ (לְוָאִי) לְוָי, *o si* (prop. *o si quod*). The אֲזַי,
peculiar to this Psalm in the Old Testament, instead of אָז
follows the model of the dialectic (הָדֵין, הֵידֵין) אֲדַיִן, וَאֲنَا, וَسَمَّ.

In order to begin the apodosis of לוּלֵי (לוּלֵא) emphatically the
older language makes use of the confirmatory כִּי, Gen. xxxi.
42, xliii. 10; here we have אֲזַי (well rendered by the LXX.
ἄρα), as in cxix. 92. The *Lamed* of הָיָה לָנוּ is *raphe* in both
instances, according to the rule discussed above, vol. ii. 145.
When men (אָדָם) rose up against Israel and their anger was
kindled against them, they who were feeble in themselves over
against the hostile world would have been swallowed up alive
if they had not had Jahve for them, if they had not had Him
on their side. This "swallowing up alive" is said elsewhere
of Hades, which suddenly and forcibly snatches away its
victims, lv. 16, Prov. i. 12; here, however, as ver. 6 shows, it
is said of the enemies, who are represented as wild beasts. In
ver. 4 the hostile power which rolls over them is likened to an
overflowing stream, as in Isa. viii. 7 sq., the Assyrian. נַחְלָה, a
stream or river, is *Milel*; it is first of all accusative: towards
the stream (Num. xxxiv. 5); then, however, it is also used as a
nominative, like הַמְּוֹתָה, לַיְלָה, and the like (cf. common Greek
ἡ νύχθα, ἡ νεότητα); so that תָה‎ֶ is related to חַ‎ֶ (ה‎ָ) as נָה‎ָ,
מוֹ‎ָ to ן‎ָ and ם‎ָ (Böttcher, § 615). These latest Psalms are
fond of such embellishments by means of adorned forms and
Aramaic or Aramaizing words. זֵידוֹנִים is a word which is
indeed not unhebraic in its formation, but is more indigenous
to Chaldee; it is the Targum word for זֵדִים in lxxxvi. 14, cxix.
51, 78 (also in liv. 5 for זָרִים), although according to Levy the
MSS. do not present זֵידוֹנִין but זֵידָנִין. In the passage before us
the Targum renders: the king who is like to the proud waters
(לְמוֹי זֵידוֹנַיָּא) of the sea (Antiochus Epiphanes?—A scholium
explains οἱ ὑπερήφανοι). With reference to עָבַר before a plural
subject, *vid.* Ges. § 147.

Vers. 6–8. After the fact of the divine succour has been
expressed, in ver. 6 follows the thanksgiving for it, and in ver.
7 the joyful shout of the rescued one. In ver. 6 the enemies

are conceived of as beasts of prey on account of their blood-thirstiness, just as the worldly empires are in the Book of Daniel; in ver. 7 as "fowlers" on account of their cunning. According to the punctuation it is not to be rendered: Our soul is like a bird that is escaped, in which case it would have been accented נַפְשֵׁנוּ כְצִפּוֹר, but: our soul (subject with *Rebia magnum*) is as a bird (כְּצִפּוֹר as in Hos. xi. 11, Prov. xxiii. 32, Job xiv. 2, instead of the syntactically more usual כַּצִּפּוֹר) escaped out of the snare of him who lays snares (יוֹקֵשׁ, elsewhere יָקוֹשׁ, יָקוּשׁ, a fowler, xci. 3). נִשְׁבָּר (with *a* beside *Rebia*) is 3d *prœt.*: the snare was burst, and we—we became free. In ver. 8 (cf. cxxi. 2, cxxxiv. 3) the universal, and here pertinent thought, viz. the help of Israel is in the name of Jahve, the Creator of the world, *i.e.* in Him who is manifest as such and is continually verifying Himself, forms the epiphonematic close. Whether the power of the world seeks to make the church of Jahve like to itself or to annihilate it, it is not a disavowal of its God, but a faithful confession, stedfast even to death, that leads to its deliverance.

PSALM CXXV.

ISRAEL'S BULWARK AGAINST TEMPTATION TO APOSTASY.

1 THEY who trust in Jahve are as Mount Zion,
   Which doth not totter, it standeth fast *for ever.*
2 As for Jerusalem—mountains are *round about* her,
   And Jahve is *round about* His people
   From this time and *for evermore.*

3 For the sceptre of wickedness shall not rest
   Upon the lot of *the righteous,*
   Lest *the righteous* stretch out
   Their hands unto iniquity.

4 O show Thyself *good,* Jahve, unto the *good*
   And to those who are upright in their hearts.

5 But those who turn aside their crooked paths—
  Jahve cause them to pass away with the workers of iniquity.
  Peace be upon Israel!

The favourite word *Israel* furnished the outward occasion for annexing this Psalm to the preceding. The situation is like that in Ps. cxxiii. and cxxiv. The people are under foreign dominion. In this lies the seductive inducement to apostasy. The pious and the apostate ones are already separated. Those who have remained faithful shall not, however, always remain enslaved. Round about Jerusalem are mountains, but more important still: Jahve, of rocks the firmest, Jahve encompasses His people.

That this Psalm is one of the latest, appears from the circumstantial expression " the upright in their hearts," instead of the old one, " the upright of heart," from פֹּעֲלֵי הָאָוֶן instead of the former פֹּעֲלֵי אָוֶן, and also from לְמַעַן לֹא (beside this passage occurring only in cxix. 11, 80, Ezek. xix. 9, xxvi. 20, Zech. xii. 7) instead of לְמַעַן אֲשֶׁר לֹא or פֶּן.

Vers. 1, 2. The stedfastness which those who trust in Jahve prove in the midst of every kind of temptation and assault is likened to Mount Zion, because the God to whom they believingly cling is He who sits enthroned on Zion. The future יֵשֵׁב signifies: He sits and will sit, that is to say, He continues to sit, cf. ix. 8, cxxii. 5. Older expositors are of opinion that the heavenly Zion must be understood on account of the Chaldæan and the Roman catastrophes; but these, in fact, only came upon the buildings on the mountain, not upon the mountain itself, which in itself and according to its appointed destiny (*vid.* Mic. iii. 12, iv. 1) remained unshaken. In ver. 2 also it is none other than the earthly Jerusalem that is meant. The holy city has a natural circumvallation of mountains, and the holy nation that dwells and worships therein has a still infinitely higher defence in Jahve, who encompasses it round (*vid.* on xxxiv. 8), as perhaps a wall of fire (Zech. ii. 9 [5]), or an impassably broad and mighty river (Isa. xxxiii. 21); a statement which is also now confirmed, for, etc. Instead of inferring from the clause ver. 2 that which is to be expected with לכן, the poet confirms it with כי by that which is surely to be expected.

Ver. 3. The pressure of the worldly power, which now lies heavily upon the holy land, will not last for ever; the duration of the calamity is exactly proportioned to the power of resistance of the righteous, whom God proves and purifies by calamity, but not without at the same time graciously preserving them. "The rod of wickedness" is the heathen sceptre, and "the righteous" are the Israelites who hold fast to the religion of their fathers. The holy land, whose sole entitled inheritors are these righteous, is called their "lot" (גורל, κλῆρος = κληρονομία). נוּחַ signifies to alight or settle down anywhere, and having alighted, to lean upon or rest (cf. Isa. xi. 2 with John i. 32, ἔμεινεν). The LXX. renders οὐκ ἀφήσει, i.e. לֹא יַנִּיחַ (cf. on the other hand יָנִיחַ, He shall let down, cause to come down, in Isa. xxx. 32). Not for a continuance shall the sceptre of heathen tyranny rest upon the holy land, God will not suffer that: in order that the righteous may not at length, by virtue of the power which pressure and use exercises over men, also participate in the prevailing ungodly doings. שָׁלַח with *Beth*: to seize upon anything wrongfully, or even only (as in Job xxviii. 9) to lay one's hand upon anything (frequently with עַל). As here in the case of עֻלָּתָה, in lxxx. 3 too the form that is the same as the locative is combined with a preposition.

Vers. 4, 5. On the ground of the strong faith in vers. 1 sq. and of the confident hope in ver. 3, the petition now arises that Jahve would speedily bestow the earnestly desired blessing of freedom upon the faithful ones, and on the other hand remove the cowardly [lit. those afraid to confess God] and those who have fellowship with apostasy, together with the declared wicked ones, out of the way. For such is the meaning of vers. 4 sq. טובים (in Proverbs alternating with the "righteous," ch. ii. 20, the opposite being the "wicked," רשעים, ch. xiv. 19) are here those who truly believe and rightly act in accordance with the good will of God,* or, as the parallel

---

* The Midrash here calls to mind a Talmudic riddle: There came a good one (Moses, Ex. ii. 2) and received a good thing (the Tôra, Prov. iv. 2) from the good One (God, Ps. cxlv. 9) for the good ones (Israel, Ps. cxxv. 4).

member of the verse explains (where לִישָׁרִים did not require the
article on account of the addition), those who in the bottom of
their heart are uprightly disposed, as God desires to have it.
The poet supplicates good for them, viz. preservation against
denying God and deliverance out of slavery; for those, on the
contrary, who bend (הִטָּה) their crooked paths, *i.e.* turn aside
their paths in a crooked direction from the right way (עֲקַלְקַלּוֹתָם,
cf. Judg. v. 6, no less than in Amos ii. 7, Prov. xvii. 23, an accusative of the object, which is more natural than that it is the
accusative of the direction, after Num. xxii. 23 *extrem.*, cf. Job
xxiii. 11, Isa. xxx. 11)—for these he wishes that Jahve would

clear them away (הוֹלִיךְ like أهلك, *perire facere* = *perdere*)

together with the workers of evil, *i.e.* the open, manifest sinners,
to whom these lukewarm and sly, false and equivocal ones are
in no way inferior as a source of danger to the church. LXX.
correctly: τοὺς δὲ ἐκκλίνοντας εἰς τὰς στραγγαλιὰς (Aquila
διαπλοκάς, Symmachus σκολιότητας, Theodotion διεστραμμένα)
ἀπάξει κύριος μετὰ, κ.τ.λ.   Finally, the poet, stretching out his
hand over Israel as if pronouncing the benediction of the
priest, gathers up all his hopes, prayers, and wishes into the
one prayer: "Peace be upon Israel." He means "the Israel
of God," Gal. vi. 16. Upon this Israel he calls down peace
from above. Peace is the end of tyranny, hostility, dismem-
berment, unrest, and terror; peace is freedom and harmony
and unity and security and blessedness.

PSALM CXXVI.

THE HARVEST OF JOY AFTER THE SOWING OF TEARS.

1 WHEN Jahve brought back the returning ones of Zion,
  We were as those who dream.
2 *Then* laughter filled our mouth,
  And our tongue a shout of joy.
 Then said they among the heathen :
   " *Great things hath Jahve done for them*"—
3 *Great things hath Jahve done for us,*
  We became glad.

4 Oh lead back, Jahve, our captive ones,
        As streams in the south country !
5 Those who sow with tears,
        Shall reap with a shout of joy.
6 He goeth to and fro amidst weeping,
        Bearing the scattering of the seed—
He cometh along with a shout of joy,
        Bearing his sheaves.

It is with this Psalm, which the favourite word *Zion* connects with the preceding Psalm, exactly as with Ps. lxxxv., which also gives thanks for the restoration of the captive ones of Israel on the one hand, and on the other hand has to complain of the wrath that is still not entirely removed, and prays for a national restoration. There are expositors indeed who also transfer the grateful retrospect with which this Song of degrees (vers. 1–3), like that Korahitic Psalm (vers. 2–4), begins, into the future (among the translators Luther is at least more consistent than the earlier ones) ; but they do this for reasons which are refuted by Ps. lxxxv., and which are at once silenced when brought face to face with the requirements of the syntax.

Vers. 1–3. When passages like Isa. i. 9, Gen. xlvii. 25, or others where וְהָיִינוּ is *perf. consec.*, are appealed to in order to prove that הָיִינוּ כְּחֹלְמִים may signify *erimus quasi somniantes*, they are instances that are different in point of syntax. Any other rendering than that of the LXX. is here impossible, viz. : Ἐν τῷ ἐπιστρέψαι κύριον τὴν αἰχμαλωσίαν Σιὼν ἐγενήθημεν ὡς παρακεκλημένοι (כְּנֻחָמִים ?—Jerome correctly, *quasi somniantes*). It is, however, just as erroneous when Jerome goes on to render : *tunc implebitur risu os nostrum ;* for it is true the future after אָז has a future signification in passages where the context relates to matters of future history, as in xcvi. 12, Zeph. iii. 9, but it always has the signification of the imperfect after the key-note of the historical past has once been struck, Ex. xv. 1, Josh. viii. 30, x. 12, 1 Kings xi. 7, xvi. 21, 2 Kings xv. 16, Job xxxviii. 21 ; it is therefore, *tunc implebatur*. It is the exiles at home again upon the soil of their fatherland who here cast back a glance into the happy time when their destiny suddenly took another turn, by the God of Israel disposing the heart of the conqueror of Babylon to set them at liberty, and to send them to their native land in an honourable manner. שִׁיבַת is not equivalent to שְׁבִית, nor is there any necessity to read it thus (Olshausen, Böttcher, and Hupfeld). שִׁיבָה (from שׁוּב, like בִּיאָה, קִימָה) signifies the return, and then those returning; it is, certainly, an innovation of this very late poet. When Jahve brought home the homeward-bound ones of Zion —the poet means to say—we were as dreamers. Does he mean by this that the long seventy years' term of affliction lay behind us like a vanished dream (Joseph Kimchi), or that the redemption that broke upon us so suddenly seemed to us at first not to be a reality but a beautiful dream? The tenor of the language favours the latter: as those not really passing through such circumstances, but only dreaming. Then—the poet goes on to say—our mouth was filled with laughter (Job viii. 21) and our tongue with a shout of joy, inasmuch, namely, as the impression of the good fortune which contrasted so strongly with our trouble hitherto, compelled us to open our mouth wide in order that our joy might break forth in a full stream, and our jubilant mood impelled our tongue to utter shouts of joy, which knew no limit because of the inexhaustible matter of our rejoicing. And how awe-inspiring was Israel's position at that time among the peoples! and what astonishment the marvellous change of Israel's lot produced upon them! Even the heathen confessed that it was Jahve's work, and that He had done great things for them (Joel ii. 20 sq., 1 Sam. xii. 24)—the glorious predictions of Isaiah, as in ch. xlv. 14, lii. 10, and elsewhere, were being fulfilled. The church on its part seals that confession coming from the mouth of the heathen. This it is that made them so joyful, that God had acknowledged them by such a mighty deed.

Vers. 4–6. But still the work so mightily and graciously begun is not completed. Those who up to the present time have returned, out of whose heart this Psalm is, as it were, composed, are only like a small vanguard in relation to the whole nation. Instead of שבותנו the *Keri* here reads שְׁבִיתֵנוּ, from שְׁבִית, Num. xxi. 29, after the form בְּכִית in Gen. l. 4. As we read elsewhere that Jerusalem yearns after her children, and Jahve solemnly assures her, " thou shalt put them all on

as jewels and gird thyself like a bride" (Isa. xlix. 18), so here
the poet proceeds from the idea that the holy land yearns after
an abundant, reanimating influx of population, as the *Negeb*
(*i.e.* the Judæan south country, Gen. xx. 1, and in general the
south country lying towards the desert of Sinai) thirsts for the
rain-water streams, which disappear in the summer season and
regularly return in the winter season. Concerning אֲפִיק, " a
water-holding channel," *vid.* on xviii. 16. If we translate
converte captivitatem nostram (as Jerome does, following the
LXX.), we shall not know what to do with the figure, whereas
in connection with the rendering *reduc captivos nostros* it is just
as beautifully adapted to the object as to the governing verb. If
we have rightly referred *negeb* not to the land of the Exile but
to the Land of Promise, whose appearance at this time is still
so unlike the promise, we shall now also understand by those
who sow in tears not the exiles, but those who have already
returned home, who are again sowing the old soil of their native
land, and that with tears, because the ground is so parched
that there is little hope of the seed springing up. But this
tearful sowing will be followed by a joyful harvest. One is
reminded here of the drought and failure of the crops with
which the new colony was visited in the time of Haggai, and
of the coming blessing promised by the prophet with a view
to the work of the building of the Temple being vigorously
carried forward. Here, however, the tearful sowing is only
an emblem of the new foundation-laying, which really took
place not without many tears (Ezra iii. 12), amidst sorrowful
and depressed circumstances; but in its general sense the language of the Psalm coincides with the language of the Preacher
on the Mount, Matt. v. 4 : Blessed are those who mourn, for
they shall be comforted. The subject to ver. 6 is the husbandman, and without a figure, every member of the *ecclesia pressa*.
The gerundial construction in ver. 6*a* (as in 2 Sam. iii. 16,
Jer. l. 4, cf. the more Indo-Germanic style of expression in
2 Sam. xv. 30) depicts the continual passing along, here the
going to and fro of the sorrowfully pensive man ; and ver. 6*b*
the undoubted coming and sure appearing of him who is highly
blessed beyond expectation. The former bears מֶשֶׁךְ הַזָּרַע, the
seed-draught, *i.e.* the handful of seed taken from the rest for
casting out (for מֶשֶׁךְ הַזֶּרַע in Amos ix. 13 signifies to cast forth

the seed along the furrows); the latter his sheaves, the produce
(תְּבוּאָה), such as puts him to the blush, of his, as it appeared
to him, forlorn sowing. As by the sowing we are to understand everything that each individual contributes towards the
building up of the kingdom of God, so by the sheaves, the
wholesome fruit which, by God bestowing His blessing upon it
beyond our prayer and comprehension, springs up from it.

PSALM CXXVII.

EVERYTHING DEPENDS UPON THE BLESSING OF GOD.*

1 *IF Jahve build not* the house,
  They labour *in vain* thereon who *build* it.
  If Jahve watch not over the city,
  In vain doth he keep awake *who watcheth over it.*

2 *In vain* is it that ye rise up early
  And only sit down late,
  Eating the bread of sorrowful labour
  Even so He giveth to His beloved in sleep.

3 Behold a heritage of Jahve are *sons*,
  A reward is the fruit of the womb.
4 As arrows in the hand of a mighty man,
  So are *sons* of the youth.

5 Blessed is the man
  Who hath his quiver full of them :
  They shall not be ashamed,
  When they speak with enemies in the gate.

The inscribed לִשְׁלֹמֹה is only added to this Song of degrees
because there was found in ver. 2 not only an allusion to the
name *Jedidiah*, which Solomon received from Nathan (2 Sam.
xii. 25), but also to his being endowed with wisdom and riches
in the dream at Gibeon (1 Kings iii. 5 sqq.). And to these is

---

* *An Gottes Segen ist alles gelegen.*

still to be added the Proverbs-like form of the Psalm; for, like the proverb-song, the extended form of the *Mashal*, it consists of a double string of proverbs, the expression of which reminds one in many ways of the Book of Proverbs (עֲצָבִים in ver. 2, toilsome efforts, as in Prov. v. 10; מְאַחֲרֵי, as in Prov. xxiii. 30; בְּנֵי הַנְּעוּרִים in ver. 4, sons begotten in one's youth, as in Prov. v. 18 אֵשֶׁת נְעוּרִים, a wife married in one's youth; בַּשַּׁעַר in ver. 5, as in Prov. xxii. 22, xxiv. 7), and which together are like the unfolding of the proverb, ch. x. 22: *The blessing of Jahve, it maketh rich, and labour addeth nothing beside it.* Even Theodoret observes, on the natural assumption that ver. 1 points to the building of the Temple, how much better the Psalm suits the time of Zerubbabel and Joshua, when the building of the Temple was imperilled by the hostile neighbouring peoples; and in connection with the relatively small number of those who had returned home out of the Exile, a numerous family, and more especially many sons, must have seemed to be a doubly and threefoldly precious blessing from God.

Vers. 1, 2. The poet proves that everything depends upon the blessing of God from examples taken from the God-ordained life of the family and of the state. The rearing of the house which affords us protection, and the stability of the city in which we securely and peaceably dwell, the acquisition of possessions that maintain and adorn life, the begetting and rearing of sons that may contribute substantial support to the father as he grows old—all these are things which depend upon the blessing of God without natural preliminary conditions being able to guarantee them, well-devised arrangements to ensure them, unwearied labours to obtain them by force, or impatient care and murmuring to get them by defiance. Many a man builds himself a house, but he is not able to carry out the building of it, or he dies before he is able to take possession of it, or the building fails through unforeseen misfortunes, or, if it succeeds, becomes a prey to violent destruction: if God Himself do not build it, they labour thereon (עָמֵל בְּ, Jonah iv. 10, Eccles. ii. 21) in vain who build it. Many a city is well-ordered, and seems to be secured by wise precautions against every misfortune, against fire and sudden attack; but if God Himself do not guard it, it is in vain that those to whom its protection is entrusted give themselves no sleep and perform (שָׁקַד, a word that has only come into frequent use since the literature of the Salomonic age) the duties of their office with the utmost devotion. The perfect in the apodosis affirms what has been done on the part of man to be ineffectual if the former is not done on God's part; cf. Num. xxxii. 23. Many rise up early in order to get to their work, and delay the sitting down as long as possible; *i.e.* not: the lying down (Hupfeld), for that is שָׁכַב, not יָשַׁב; but to take a seat in order to rest a little, and, as what follows shows, to eat (Hitzig). קוּם and שֶׁבֶת stand opposed to one another: the latter cannot therefore mean to remain sitting at one's work, in favour of which Isa. v. 11 (where בַּבֹּקֶר and בַּנֶּשֶׁף form an antithesis) cannot be properly compared. 1 Sam. xx. 24 shows that prior to the incursion of the Grecian custom they did not take their meals lying or reclining (ἀνα- or κατακείμενος), but sitting. It is vain for you—the poet exclaims to them—it will not after all bring what you think to be able to acquire; in so doing you eat only the bread of sorrow, *i.e.* bread that is procured with toil and trouble (cf. Gen. iii. 17, בְּעִצָּבוֹן): כֵּן, in like manner, *i.e.* the same as you are able to procure only by toilsome and anxious efforts, God gives to His beloved (lx. 7, Deut. xxxiii. 12) שֵׁנָא (= שֵׁנָה), in sleep (an adverbial accusative like עֶרֶב, לַיְלָה, בֹּקֶר), *i.e.* without restless self-activity, in a state of self-forgetful renunciation, and modest, calm surrender to Him: " God bestows His gifts during the night," says a German proverb, and a Greek proverb even says: εὕδοντι κύρτος αἱρεῖ. Böttcher takes כֵּן in the sense of " so = without anything further;" and כן certainly has this meaning sometimes (*vid.* introduction to Ps. cx.), but not in this passage, where, as referring back, it stands at the head of the clause, and where what this mimic כן would import lies in the word שנא.

Vers. 3–5. With הִנֵּה it goes on to refer to a specially striking example in support of the maxim that everything depends upon God's blessing. פְּרִי הַבֶּטֶן (Gen. xxx. 2, Deut. vii. 13) beside בָּנִים also admits of the including of daughters. It is with שָׂכָר (recalling Gen. xxx. 18) just as with נַחֲלַת. Just as the latter in this passage denotes an inheritance not according to hereditary right, but in accordance with the free-will of the

giver, so the former denotes not a reward that is paid out as in
duty bound, but a recompense that is bestowed according to
one's free judgment, and in fact looked for in accordance with
a promise given, but cannot by any means be demanded.   Sons
are a blessed gift from above.   They are—especially when
they are the offspring of a youthful marriage (*opp.* בֶּן־זְקֻנִים,
Gen. xxxvii. 3, xliv. 20), and accordingly themselves strong
and hearty (Gen. xlix. 3), and at the time that the father is
growing old are in the bloom of their years—like arrows in
the hand of a warrior.   This is a comparison which the circumstances of his time made natural to the poet, in which the
sword was carried side by side with the trowel, and the work
of national restoration had to be defended step by step against
open enemies, envious neighbours, and false brethren.   It was
not sufficient then to have arrows in the quiver; one was
obliged to have them not merely at hand, but in the hand
(בְּיַד), in order to be able to discharge them and defend one's
self.   What a treasure, in such a time when it was needful to
be constantly ready for fighting, defensive or offensive, was
that which youthful sons afforded to the elderly father and
weaker members of the family!   Happy is the man—the poet
exclaims—who has his quiver, *i.e.* his house, full of such arrows,
in order to be able to deal out to the enemies as many arrows
as may be needed.   The father and such a host of sons surrounding him (this is the complex notion of the subject) form
a phalanx not to be broken through.   If they have to speak
with enemies in the gate—*i.e.* candidly to upbraid them with
their wrong, or to ward off their unjust accusation—they shall
not be ashamed, *i.e.* not be overawed, disheartened, or disarmed.
Gesenius in his *Thesaurus*, as Ibn-Jachja has already done,
takes דִּבֶּר here in the signification " to destroy;" but in Gen.
xxxiv. 13 this *Piel* signifies to deal behind one's back (deceitfully), and in 2 Chron. xxii. 10 to get rid of by assassination.

This shade of the notion, which proceeds from دبر, *pone esse*

(*vid.* xviii. 48, xxviii. 2), does not suit the passage before us,
and the expression לֹא־יֵבֹשׁוּ is favourable to the idea of the gate
as being the forum, which arises from taking ידברו in its ordinary signification.   Unjust judges, malicious accusers, and
false witnesses retire shy and faint-hearted before a family so

capable of defending itself. We read the opposite of this in
Job v. 4 of sons upon whom the curse of their fathers rests.

PSALM CXXVIII.

THE FAMILY PROSPERITY OF THE GOD-FEARING MAN.

1 *HAPPY* is every one who feareth Jahve,
  Who walketh in His ways.
2 The labour of thy hands shalt thou surely eat,
  Happy art thou, and it is well with thee.

3 Thy wife, like a fruitful vine is she,
  In the inner part of thy house ;
  Thy children are like shoots of olive-trees
  Round about thy table.

4 Behold, surely thus is the man *blessed*
  Who feareth Jahve.
5 Jahve *bless* thee out of Zion,
  And see thou the prosperity of Jerusalem
  All the days of thy life,
6 *And see thou* thy children's children—
  Peace be upon Israel !

Just as Ps. cxxvii. is appended to Ps. cxxvi. because the
fact that Israel was so surprised by the redemption out of
exile that they thought they were dreaming, finds its interpretation in the universal truth that God bestows upon him whom
He loves, in sleep, that which others are not able to acquire by
toiling and moiling day and night: so Ps. cxxviii. follows Ps.
cxxvii. for the same reason as Ps. ii. follows Ps. i. In both
instances they are Psalms placed together, of which one begins
with *ashrê* and one ends with *ashrê*. In other respects Ps.
cxxviii. and cxxvii. supplement one another. They are related to one another much as the New Testament parables of
the treasure in the field and the one pearl are related. That
which makes man happy is represented in Ps. cxxvii. as a gift
coming as a blessing, and in Ps. cxxviii. as a reward coming as
a blessing, that which is briefly indicated in the word שָׂכָר in

cxxvii. 3 being here expanded and unfolded. There it appears as a gift of grace in contrast to the God-estranged self-activity of man, here as a fruit of the *ora et labora*. Ewald considers this and the preceding Psalm to be songs to be sung at table. But they are ill-suited for this purpose; for they contain personal mirrorings instead of petitions, and instead of benedictions of those who are about to partake of the food provided.

Vers. 1–3. The כִּי in ver. 2 signifies neither "for" (Aquila, κόπον τῶν ταρσῶν σου ὅτι φάγεσαι), nor "when" (Symmachus, κόπον χειρῶν σου ἐσθίων); it is the directly affirmative כִּי, which is sometimes thus placed after other words in a clause (cxviii. 10–12, Gen. xviii. 20, xli. 32). The proof in favour of this asseverating כִּי is the very usual כִּי עַתָּה in the apodoses of hypothetical protases, or even כִּי־אָז in Job xi. 15, or also only כִּי in Isa. vii. 9, 1 Sam. xiv. 39 : "surely then ;" the transition from the confirmative to the affirmative signification is evident from ver. 4 of the Psalm before us. To support one's self by one's own labour is a duty which even a Paul did not wish to avoid (Acts xx. 34), and so it is a great good fortune (טוֹב לְךָ as in cxix. 71) to eat the produce of the labour of one's own hands (LXX. τοὺς καρποὺς τῶν πόνων, or according to an original reading, τοὺς πόνους τῶν καρπῶν *) ; for he who can make himself useful to others and still is also independent of them, he eats the bread of blessing which God gives, which is sweeter than the bread of charity which men give. In close connection with this is the prosperity of a house that is at peace and contented within itself, of an amiable and tranquil and hopeful (rich in hope) family life. " Thy wife (אֶשְׁתְּךָ, found only here, for אִשְׁתְּךָ) is as a fruit-producing vine." פֹּרִיָּה for פָּרָה, from פָּרָה = פָּרִי, with the *Jod* of the root retained, like בּוֹכִיָּה, Lam. i. 16. The figure of the vine is admirably suited to the wife, who is a shoot or sprig of the husband, and stands in need of the man's support as the vine needs a stick or the wall of a house (*pergula*). בְּיַרְכְּתֵי בֵיתֶךָ does not belong to the figure,

____

* The fact that the τῶν καρπῶν of the LXX. here, as in Prov. xxxi. 20, is intended to refer to the hands is noted by Theodoret and also by Didymus (in Rosenmüller): καρπούς φησι νῦν ὡς ἀπὸ μέρους τὰς χεῖρας (i.e. *per synecdochen partis pro toto*), τουτέστι τῶν πρακτικῶν σου δυνάμεων φάγεσαι τοὺς πόνους.

as Kimchi is of opinion, who thinks of a vine starting out of the room and climbing up in the open air outside. What is meant is the angle, corner, or nook (יַרְכְּתֵי, in relation to things and artificial, equivalent to the natural יְרֵכֵי), *i.e.* the background, the privacy of the house, where the housewife, who is not to be seen much out of doors, leads a quiet life, entirely devoted to the happiness of her husband and her family. The children springing from such a noble vine, planted around the family table, are like olive shoots or cuttings; cf. in Euripides, *Medea*, 1098: τέκνων ἐν οἴκοις γλυκερὸν βλάστημα, and *Herc. Fur.* 839: καλλίπαις στέφανος. Thus fresh as young layered small olive-trees and thus promising are they.

Vers. 4–6. Pointing back to this charming picture of family life, the poet goes on to say: behold, for thus = behold, thus is the man actually blessed who fears Jahve. כִּי confirms the reality of the matter of fact to which the הִנֵּה points. The promissory future in ver. 5*a* is followed by imperatives which call upon the God-fearing man at once to do that which, in accordance with the promises, stands before him as certain. מִצִּיּוֹן as in cxxxiv. 3, xx. 3. בָּנִים לְבָנֶיךָ instead of בְּנֵי בָנֶיךָ gives a designed indefiniteness to the first member of the combination. Every blessing the individual enjoys comes from the God of salvation, who has taken up His abode in Zion, and is perfected in participation in the prosperity of the holy city and of the whole church, of which it is the centre. A New Testament song would here open up the prospect of the heavenly Jerusalem. But the character of limitation to this present world that is stamped upon the Old Testament does not admit of this. The promise refers only to a present participation in the well-being of Jerusalem (Zech. viii. 15) and to long life prolonged in one's children's children; and in this sense calls down intercessorily peace upon Israel in all its members, and in all places and all ages.

PSALM CXXIX.

THE END OF THE OPPRESSORS OF ZION.

1 *ENOUGH have they oppressed me from my youth up,*
Let Israel say—

   2 *Enough have they oppressed me from my youth up,*
     Nevertheless they have not prevailed against me.

   3 Upon my back the ploughers ploughed,
     They made long their furrow-strip.
   4 Jahve is righteous :
     He hath cut asunder the cords of the wicked.
   5 They must be ashamed and turn back,
     All who hate Zion.

   6 They must become as grass of the house-tops,
     Which, ere it shooteth up, withereth—
   7 Wherewith the reaper filleth not his hand,
     Nor he who bindeth sheaves his bosom,
   8 Neither do they who pass by say :
     The blessing of Jahve be upon you!
     " We bless you in the name of Jahve ! !"

Just as Ps. cxxiv. with the words " *let Israel say*" was followed by Ps. cxxv. with " *peace be upon Israel,*" so Ps. cxxviii. with " *peace be upon Israel*" is followed by Ps. cxxix. with " *let Israel say.*" This Ps. cxxix. has not only the call " *let Israel say,*" but also the situation of a deliverance that has been experienced (cf. ver. 4 with cxxiv. 6 sq.), from which point it looks gratefully back and confidently forward into the future, and an Aramaic tinge that is noticeable here and there by the side of all other classical character of form, in common with Ps. cxxiv.

Vers. 1, 2.   Israel is gratefully to confess that, however much and sorely it was oppressed, it still has not succumbed. רַבַּת, together with רַבָּה, has occurred already in lxv. 10, lxii. 3, and it becomes usual in the post-exilic language, cxx. 6, cxxiii. 4, 2 Chron. xxx. 18 ; Syriac *rebath.*   The expression " from my youth " glances back to the time of the Egyptian bondage ; for the time of the sojourn in Egypt was the time of Israel's youth (Hos. ii. 17 [15], xi. 1, Jer. ii. 2, Ezek. xxiii. 3).   The protasis ver. 1*a* is repeated in an interlinked, chain-like conjunction in order to complete the thought ; for ver. 2*b* is the turning-point, where גַּם, having reference to the whole negative clause, signifies " also" in the sense of " nevertheless," ὅμως (synon. בְּכָל־זֹאת), as in Ezek. xvi. 28, Eccles. vi. 7, cf. above, cxix. 24 : although they oppressed me much and sore, yet have they not overpowered me (the construction is like Num. xiii. 30, and frequently).

Vers. 3–5. Elsewhere it is said that the enemies have driven over Israel (lxvi. 12), or have gone over its back (Isa. li. 23) ; here the customary figurative language חָרַשׁ אָוֶן in Job iv. 8 (cf. Hos. x. 13) is extended to another figure of hostile dealing : without compassion and without consideration they ill-treated the stretched-forth back of the people who were held in subjection, as though it were arable land, and, without restraining their ferocity and setting a limit to their spoiling of the enslaved people and country, they drew their furrow-strip (מַעֲנִיתָם, according to the *Keri* מַעֲנוֹתָם) long. But מַעֲנָה does not signify (as Keil on 1 Sam. xiv. 14 is of opinion, although explaining the passage more correctly than Thenius) the furrow

(= תֶּלֶם, גְּדוּד), but, like مَعْنَاةٌ, a strip of arable land which the ploughman takes in hand at one time, at both ends of which consequently the ploughing team (צֶמֶד) always comes to a stand, turns round, and ploughs a new furrow ; from עָנָה, to bend, turn (*vid.* Wetzstein's Excursus II. at the end of this volume). It is therefore : they drew their furrow-turning long (dative of the object instead of the accusative with *Hiph.*, as *e.g.* in Isa. xxix. 2, cf. with *Piel* in xxxiv. 4, cxvi. 16, and *Kal* lxix. 6, after the Aramaic style, although it is not unhebraic). Righteous is Jahve—this is an universal truth, which has been verified in the present circumstances ;—He hath cut asunder the cords of the wicked (עֲבוֹת as in ii. 3 ; here, however, it is suggested by the metaphor in ver. 3, cf. Job xxxix. 10 ; LXX. αὐχένας, *i.e.* עֲנוּק), with which they held Israel bound. From that which has just been experienced Israel derives the hope that *all* Zion's haters (a newly coined name for the enemies of the religion of Israel) will be obliged to retreat with shame and confusion.

Vers. 6–8. The poet illustrates the fate that overtakes them by means of a picture borrowed from Isaiah and worked up (ch. xxxvii. 27) : they become like " grass of the house-tops," etc. שֶׁ is a relative to יָבֵשׁ (*quod exarescit*), and קַדְמַת,

priusquam, is Hebraized after מִן־קַדְמַת דְּנָה in Dan. vi. 11, or מִקַּדְמַת דְּנָה in Ezra v. 11. שָׁלַף elsewhere has the signification " to draw forth" of a sword, shoe, or arrow, which is followed by the LXX., Theodotion, and the Quinta: πρὸ τοῦ ἐκσπασθῆναι, before it is plucked. But side by side with the ἐκσπασθῆναι of the LXX. we also find the reading ἐξανθῆσαι; and in this sense Jerome renders (*statim ut*) *viruerit*, Symmachus ἐκκαυλῆσαι (to shoot into a stalk), Aquila ἀνέθαλεν, the Sexta ἐκστερεῶσαι (to attain to full solidity). The Targum paraphrases שלף in both senses: to shoot up and to pluck off. The former signification, after which Venema interprets: *antequam se evaginet vel evaginetur, i.e. antequam e vaginulis suis se evolvat et succrescat*, is also advocated by Parchon, Kimchi, and Aben-Ezra. In the same sense von Ortenberg conjectures שְׁחָלַף. Since the grass of the house-tops or roofs, if one wishes to pull it up, can be pulled up just as well when it is withered as when it is green, and since it is the most natural thing to take חָצִיר as the subject to שלף, we decide in favour of the intransitive signification, " to put itself forth, to develope, shoot forth into ear." The roof-grass withers before it has put forth ears or blossoms, just because it has no deep root, and therefore cannot stand against the heat of the sun.* The poet pursues the figure of the grass of the house-tops still further. The encompassing lap or bosom (κόλπος) is called elsewhere חֹצֶן (Isa. xlix. 22, Neh. v. 13); here it is חֶצֶן, like the Arabic *hidn* (diminutive *hodein*), of the same root with מָחוֹז, a creek, in cvii. 30. The enemies of Israel are as grass upon the house-tops, which is not garnered in; their life closes with sure destruction, the germ of which they (without any need for any rooting out) carry within themselves. The observation of Knapp, that any Western poet would have left off with ver. 6, is based upon the error that vers. 7, 8 are an idle embellishment. The greeting addressed to the reapers in ver. 8 is taken from life; it is not denied even to heathen reapers. Similarly Boaz (Ruth

---

* So, too, Geiger in the *Deutsche Morgenländische Zeitschrift*, xiv. 278 f., according to whom سلف (شلف) occurs in Saadia and Abu-Said in the signification " to be in the first maturity, to blossom,"—a sense שלף may also have here; cf. the Talmudic שלופפי used of unripe dates that are still in blossom.

ii. 4) greets them with " Jahve be with you," and receives
the counter-salutation, " Jahve bless thee."   Here it is the
passers-by who call out to those who are harvesting: *The
blessing* (בִּרְכַּת) *of Jahve happen to you* (אֲלֵיכֶם,* as in the Aaronitish blessing), and (since " we bless you in the name of
Jahve" would be a purposeless excess of politeness in the
mouth of the same speakers) receive in their turn the counter-
salutation: *We bless you in the name of Jahve.*   As a contrast it
follows that there is before the righteous a garnering in of
that which they have sown amidst the exchange of joyful benedictory greetings.

PSALM CXXX.

DE PROFUNDIS.

1 OUT of the depths do I call unto Thee, Jahve.
2 Lord, O hearken to my voice,
  Let Thine ears be attentive
  To the voice of my supplication !

3 If Thou keepest iniquities, Jāh—
  Lord, who can stand ? !
4 Yet with Thee is the forgiveness,
  That Thou mayest be feared.

5 *I hope* in Jahve, *my soul hopeth,*
  And upon His word do I wait.
6 *My soul waiteth for the Lord,*
  More than the night-watchers for the morning,
  The night-watchers for the morning.

7 Wait, *Israel,* for Jahve,
  For with Jahve is the mercy,
  And abundantly is there with Him *redemption.*
8 And HE will *redeem Israel*
  From all its iniquities.

---

* Here and there עֲלֵיכֶם is found as an error of the copyist.   The
Hebrew Psalter, Basel 1547, 12mo, notes it as a various reading.

Luther, being once asked which were the best Psalms, replied, *Psalmi Paulini;* and when his companions at table pressed him to say which these were, he answered: Ps. xxxii., li., cxxx., and cxliii. In fact in Ps. cxxx. the condemnability of the natural man, the freeness of mercy, and the spiritual nature of redemption are expressed in a manner thoroughly Pauline. It is the sixth among the seven *Psalmi pœnitentiales* (vi., xxxii., xxxviii., li., cii., cxxx., cxliii.).

Even the chronicler had this Psalm before him in the present classification, which puts it near to Ps. cxxxii.; for the independent addition with which he enriches Solomon's prayer at the dedication of the Temple, 2 Chron. vi. 40–42, is compiled out of passages of Ps. cxxx. (ver. 2, cf. the divine response, 2 Chron. vii. 15) and Ps. cxxxii. (vers. 8, 16, 10).

The mutual relation of Ps. cxxx. to Ps. lxxxvi. has been already noticed there. The two Psalms are first attempts at adding a third, Adonajic style to the Jehovic and Elohimic Psalm-style. There *Adonaj* is repeated seven times, and three times in this Psalm. There are also other indications that the writer of Ps. cxxx. was acquainted with that Ps. lxxxvi. (compare ver. 2*a*, שִׁמְעָה בְקוֹלִי, with lxxxvi. 6, וְהַקְשִׁיבָה בְּקוֹל; ver. 2*b*, לְקוֹל תַּחֲנוּנָי, with lxxxvi. 6, בְּקוֹל תַּחֲנוּנוֹתָי; ver. 4, עִמְּךָ הַסְּלִיחָה, with lxxxvi. 5, וְסַלָּח; ver. 8, עִם ה' הַחֶסֶד, with lxxxvi. 5, 15, רַב־חֶסֶד). The fact that קָשׁוּב (after the form שַׁכּוּל) occurs besides only in those dependent passages of the chronicler, and קַשֵּׁב only in Neh. i. 6, 11, as סְלִיחָה besides only in Dan. ix. 9, Neh. ix. 17, brings our Psalm down into a later period of the language; and moreover Ps. lxxxvi. is not Davidic.

Vers. 1–4. The depths (מַעֲמַקִּים) are not the depths of the soul, but the deep outward and inward distress in which the poet is sunk as in deep waters (lxix. 3, 15). Out of these depths he cries to the God of salvation, and importunately prays Him who rules all things and can do all things to grant him a compliant hearing (שָׁמַע בְּ, Gen. xxi. 12, xxvii. 13, xxx. 6, and other passages). God hears indeed even in Himself, as being the omniscient One, the softest and most secret as well as the loudest utterance; but, as Hilary observes, *fides officium suum exsequitur, ut Dei auditionem roget, ut qui per naturam suam audit per orantis precem dignetur audire.* In this sense the poet prays that His ears may be turned קַשֻּׁבוֹת (duller collateral form of קַשָּׁב, to be in the condition of *arrectæ aures*), with strained attention, to his loud and urgent petition (xxviii. 2). His life hangs upon the thread of the divine compassion. If God preserves iniquities, who can stand before Him?! He preserves them (שָׁמַר) when He puts them down to one (xxxii. 2) and keeps them in remembrance (Gen. xxxvii. 11), or, as it is figuratively expressed in Job xiv. 17, sealed up as it were in custody in order to punish them when the measure is full. The inevitable consequence of this is the destruction of the sinner, for nothing can stand against the punitive justice of God (Nah. i. 6, Mal. iii. 2, Ezra ix. 15). If God should show Himself as Jāh,* no creature would be able to stand before Him, who is *Adonaj*, and can therefore carry out His judicial will or purpose (Isa. li. 16). He does not, however, act thus. He does not proceed according to the legal stringency of recompensative justice. This thought, which fills up the pause after the question, but is not directly expressed, is confirmed by the following כִּי, which therefore, as in Job xxii. 2, xxxi. 18, xxxix. 14, Isa. xxviii. 28 (cf. Eccles. v. 6), introduces the opposite. With the Lord is the willingness to forgive (הַסְּלִיחָה), in order that He may be feared; *i.e.* He forgives, as it is expressed elsewhere (*e.g.* lxxix. 9), for His Name's sake: He seeks therein the glorifying of His Name. He will, as the sole Author of our salvation, who, putting all vain-glorying to shame, causes mercy instead of justice to take its course with us (cf. li. 6), be reverenced; and gives the sinner occasion, ground, and material for reverential thanksgiving and praise by bestowing " forgiveness" upon him in the plenitude of absolutely free grace.

Vers. 5–8. Therefore the sinner need not, therefore too the poet will not, despair. He hopes in Jahve (*acc. obj.* as in xxv. 5, 21, xl. 2), his soul hopes; hoping in and waiting upon God is the mood of his inmost and of his whole being. He waits upon God's word, the word of His salvation (cxix. 81), which, if it penetrates into the soul and cleaves there, calms

---

* Eusebius on Ps. lxviii. (lxvii.) 5 observes that the Logos is called ῎Ια as μορφὴν δούλου λαβὼν καὶ τὰς ἀκτῖνας τῆς ἑαυτοῦ θεότητος συστείλας καὶ ὥσπερ καταδὺς ἐν τῷ σώματι. There is a similar passage in Vincentius Ciconia (1567), which we introduced into our larger Commentary on the Psalms (1859–60).

all unrest, and by the appropriated consolation of forgiveness
transforms and enlightens for it everything in it and outside
of it.   His soul is לַאדֹנָי, *i.e.* stedfastly and continually directed
towards Him; as Chr. A. Crusius when on his death-bed, with
hands and eyes uplifted to heaven, joyfully exclaimed : " My
soul is full of the mercy of Jesus Christ. *My whole soul is
towards God.*"   The meaning of לאדני becomes at once clear
in itself from cxliii. 6, and is defined moreover, without supplying שֹׁמֶרֶת (Hitzig), according to the following לַבֹּקֶר.   Towards the Lord he is expectantly turned, like those who in the
night-time wait for the morning.   The repetition of the expression " those who watch for the morning" (cf. Isa. xxi. 11)
gives the impression of protracted, painful waiting.   The
wrath, in the sphere of which the poet now finds himself, is a
nightly darkness, out of which he wishes to be removed into
the sunny realm of love (Mal. iii. 20 [iv. 2]); not he alone,
however, but at the same time all Israel, whose need is the
same, and for whom therefore believing waiting is likewise the
way to salvation.   With Jahve, and with Him exclusively,
with Him, however, also in all its fulness, is הַחֶסֶד (contrary to
lxii. 13, without any pausal change in accordance with the
varying of the segolates), the mercy, which removes the guilt
of sin and its consequences, and puts freedom, peace, and joy
into the heart.   And plenteous (הַרְבֵּה, an adverbial *infin. absol.*,
used here, as in Ezek. xxi. 20, as an adjective) is with Him redemption; *i.e.* He possesses in the richest measure the willingness, the power, and the wisdom, which are needed to procure
redemption, which rises up as a wall of partition (Ex. viii. 19)
between destruction and those imperilled.   To Him, therefore,
must the individual, if he will obtain mercy, to Him must His
people, look up hopingly; and this hope directed to Him shall
not be put to shame: He, in the fulness of the might of His
free grace (Isa. xliii. 25), will redeem Israel from all its iniquities, by forgiving them and removing their unhappy inward
and outward consequences.   With this promise (cf. xxv. 22)
the poet comforts himself.   He means complete and final redemption, above all, in the genuinely New Testament manner,
spiritual redemption.

PSALM CXXXI.

CHILD-LIKE RESIGNATION TO GOD.

1 JAHVE, my heart is not haughty, and mine eyes are not
  Neither have I to do with great things   [lofty,
  And extraordinary which are beyond me.

2 Verily I have smoothed down and calmed my soul;
  Like a child that is weaned beside its mother,
  Like the child that is weaned is my soul beside me.

3 Wait, Israel, upon Jahve
  From henceforth and for ever.

This little song is inscribed לְדָוִד because it is like an echo
of the answer (2 Sam. vi. 21 sq.) with which David repelled
the mocking observation of Michal when he danced before the
Ark in a linen ephod, and therefore not in kingly attire, but in
the common raiment of the priests: *I esteem myself still less
than I now show it, and I appear base in mine own eyes.* In
general David is the model of the state of mind which the poet
expresses here. He did not push himself forward, but suffered
himself to be drawn forth out of seclusion. He did not take
possession of the throne violently, but after Samuel has anointed
him he willingly and patiently traverses the long, thorny, cir-
cuitous way of deep abasement, until he receives from God's
hand that which God's promise had assured to him. The persecution by Saul lasted about ten years, and his kingship in
Hebron, at first only incipient, seven years and a half. He
left it entirely to God to remove Saul and Ishbosheth. He
let Shimei curse. He left Jerusalem before Absalom. Submission to God's guidance, resignation to His dispensations,
contentment with that which was allotted to him, are the
distinguishing traits of his noble character, which the poet of
this Psalm indirectly holds up to himself and to his cotemporaries as a mirror, viz. to the Israel of the period after the Exile,
which, in connection with small beginnings under difficult
circumstances, had been taught humbly contented and calm
waiting.

With לֹא־גָבַהּ לִבִּי the poet repudiates pride as being the state of his soul; with לֹא־רָמוּ עֵינָי (*lo-ramū'* as in Prov. xxx. 13, and before *Ajin, e.g.*, also in Gen. xxvi. 10, Isa. xi. 2, in accordance with which the erroneous placing of the accent in Baer's text is to be corrected), pride of countenance and bearing; and with וְלֹא־הִלַּכְתִּי, pride of endeavour and mode of action. Pride has its seat in the heart, in the eyes especially it finds its expression, and great things are its sphere in which it diligently exercises itself. The opposite of "great things" (Jer. xxiii. 3, xlv. 5) is not that which is little, mean, but that which is small; and the opposite of "things too wonderful for me" (Gen. xviii. 14) is not that which is trivial, but that which is attainable.

אִם־לֹא does not open a conditional protasis, for where is the indication of the apodosis to be found? Nor does it signify "but," a meaning it also has not in Gen. xxiv. 38, Ezek. iii. 6. In these passages too, as in the passage before us, it is asseverating, being derived from the usual formula of an oath: verily I have, etc. שִׁוָּה signifies (Isa. xxviii. 25) to level the surface of a field by ploughing it up, and has an ethical sense here, like יָשָׁר with its opposites עָקֹב and עָפָל. The *Poel* דּוֹמֵם is to be understood according to דּוּמִיָּה in lxii. 2, and דּוּמָם in Lam. iii. 26. He has levelled or made smooth his soul, so that humility is its entire and uniform state; he has calmed it so that it is silent and at rest, and lets God speak and work in it and for it: it is like an even surface, and like the calm surface of a lake. Ewald and Hupfeld's rendering: "as a weaned child on its mother, so my soul, being weaned, lies on me," is refuted by the consideration that it ought at least to be כִּגְמוּלָה, but more correctly כֵּן גמולה; but it is also besides opposed by the article which is swallowed up in כַּגָּמֻל, according to which it is to be rendered: like one weaned beside its mother (here כִּגְמוּל on account of the determinative collateral definition), like the weaned one (here כַּגָּמוּל because without any collateral definition: cf., with Hitzig, Deut. xxxii. 2, and the like; moreover, also, because referring back to the first גמול, cf. Hab. iii. 8), is my soul beside me (Hitzig, Hengstenberg, and most expositors). As a weaned child—viz. not one that is only just begun to be weaned, but an actually weaned child (גָּמַל, cognate גָּמַר, to bring to an end, more particularly to bring suckling to an end, to wean)—lies upon its mother without crying impatiently and

craving for its mother's breast, but contented with the fact
that it has its mother—like such a weaned child is his soul
upon him, *i.e.* in relation to his Ego (which is conceived of
in עָלַי as having the soul upon itself, cf. xlii. 7, Jer. viii. 18;
Psychology, S. 151 f., tr. p. 180): his soul, which is by nature
restless and craving, is stilled; it does not long after earthly
enjoyment and earthly good that God should give these to it,
but it is satisfied in the fellowship of God, it finds full satisfaction in Him, it is satisfied (satiated) in Him.

By the closing strain, ver. 3, the individual language of the
Psalm comes to have a reference to the congregation at large.
Israel is to renounce all self-boasting and all self-activity, and
to wait in lowliness and quietness upon its God from now and
for evermore. For He resisteth the proud, but giveth grace
unto the humble.

PSALM CXXXII.

PRAYER FOR THE HOUSE OF GOD AND THE HOUSE OF DAVID.

1 REMEMBER, Jahve, to DAVID
  All the trouble endured by him,
2 Him who hath sworn unto Jahve,
  Hath vowed unto *the Mighty One of Jacob:*
3 "I will not enter into the tent of my house,
  I will not go up to the bed of my couch;
4 I will not give sleep to mine eyes,
  Slumber to mine eyelids,
5 Until I find a place for Jahve,
  A dwelling-tent for *the Mighty One of Jacob!*"

6 Behold it was, we heard it, in Ephrâthah,
  We found it in the fields of Ja'ar.
7 So let us go into His dwelling-tent,
  Let us prostrate ourselves before His footstool.
8 Arise, Jahve, to Thy rest,
  Thou and the Ark of Thy majesty!

9 *Let Thy priests clothe themselves with righteousness,*
  And Thy saints shout for joy.
10 For the sake of DAVID Thy servant
  Turn not back the face of Thine anointed!

11 Jahve hath sworn to DAVID
  In truth that which He will not recall:
  " Of the fruit of thy body
  Do I appoint a possessor of thy throne.
12. If thy children keep My covenant
  And My testimony, which I teach them:
  Their children also shall for ever
  Sit upon thy throne."
13 For Jahve hath chosen Zion,
  He hath desired it as an abode for Himself.

14 " This is my rest for ever,
  Here will I dwell, *for I have desired it.*"
15 Her provision will I bless abundantly,
  Her poor will I satisfy with bread,
16 *And her priests will I clothe with salvation,*
  And her saints shall shout aloud for joy.
17 There will I make a horn to shoot forth for DAVID,
  I will prepare a lamp for mine anointed.
18 His enemies will I clothe with shame,
  And upon himself shall his crown blossom.

Ps. cxxxi. designedly precedes Ps. cxxxii. The former has grown out of the memory of an utterance of David when he brought home the Ark, and the latter begins with the remembrance of David's humbly zealous endeavour to obtain a settled and worthy abode for the God who sits enthroned above the Ark among His people. It is the only Psalm in which the sacred Ark is mentioned. The chronicler put vers. 8–10 into the mouth of Solomon at the dedication of the Temple (2 Chron. vi. 41 sq.). After a passage borrowed from Ps. cxxx. 2 which is attached by עַתָּה to Solomon's Temple-dedication prayer, he appends further borrowed passages out of Ps. cxxxii. with וְעַתָּה. The variations in these verses of the Psalms, which are annexed by him with a free hand and from memory (*Jahve Elohim* for

Jahve, יַרְנֵנוּ) for יִשְׂמְחוּ בַטּוֹב for צֶדֶק, לְמְנוּחָתֶךָ תְּשׁוּעָה for לְנוּחֶךָ,
just as much prove that he has altered the Psalm, and not
reversely (as Hitzig persistently maintains), that the psalmist
has borrowed from the Chronicles. It is even still distinctly
to be seen how the memory of Isa. lv. 3 has influenced the close
of ver. 42 in the chronicler, just as the memory of Isa. lv. 2
has perhaps also influenced the close of ver. 41.

The psalmist supplicates the divine favour for the anointed
of Jahve for David's sake. In this connection this anointed
one is neither the high priest, nor Israel, which is never so
named (*vid.* Hab. iii. 13), nor David himself, who "in all the
necessities of his race and people stands before God," as Hengstenberg asserts, in order to be able to assign this Song of
degrees, as others, likewise to the post-exilic time of the new
colony. Zerubbabel might more readily be understood (Baur),
with whom, according to the closing prophecy of the Book of
Haggai, a new period of the Davidic dominion is said to begin.
But even Zerubbabel, the פַּחַת יְהוּדָה, could not be called מָשִׁיחַ,
for this he was not. The chronicler applies the Psalm in
accordance with its contents. It is suited to the mouth of
Solomon. The view that it was composed by Solomon himself
when the Ark of the covenant was removed out of the tent-
temple on Zion into the Temple-building (Amyraldus, De
Wette, Tholuck, and others), is favoured by the relation of the
circumstances, as they are narrated in 2 Chron. v. 5 sqq., to the
desires of the Psalm, and a close kinship of the Psalm with Ps.
lxxii. in breadth, repetitions of words, and a laboured forward
movement which is here and there a somewhat uncertain
advance. At all events it belongs to a time in which the
Davidic throne was still standing and the sacred Ark was not
as yet irrecoverably lost. That which, according to 2 Sam.
ch. vi., vii., David did for the glory of Jahve, and on the other
hand is promised to him by Jahve, is here made by a post-
Davidic poet into the foundation of a hopeful intercessory
prayer for the kingship and priesthood of Zion and the church
presided over by both.

The Psalm consists of four ten-line strophes. Only in connection with the first could any objection be raised, and the
strophe be looked upon as only consisting of nine lines. But
the other strophes decide the question of its measure; and the

breaking up of the weighty ver. 1 into two lines follows the
accentuation, which divides it into two parts and places אֵת by
itself as being אֵת (according to *Accentssystem*, xviii. 2, with
Mugrash).   Each strophe is adorned once with the name of
David; and moreover the step-like progress which comes back
to what has been said, and takes up the thread and carries it
forward, cannot fail to be recognised.

Vers. 1–5. One is said to remember anything to another
when he requites him something that he has done for him, or
when he does for him what he has promised him.   It is the post-
Davidic church which here reminds Jahve of the hereinafter
mentioned promises (of the " mercies of David," 2 Chron. vi.
42, cf. Isa. lv. 3) with which He has responded to David's עֻנּוֹת.
By this verbal substantive of the *Pual* is meant all the care and
trouble which David had in order to procure a worthy abode
for the sanctuary of Jahve.   עֻנָּה בְ signifies to trouble or harass
one's self about anything, *afflictari* (as frequently in the Book
of Ecclesiastes) ; the *Pual* here denotes the self-imposed trouble,
or even that imposed by outward circumstances, such as the
tedious wars, of long, unsuccessful, and yet never relaxed
endeavours (1 Kings v. 17 [3]).   For he had vowed unto God
that he would give himself absolutely no rest until he had
obtained a fixed abode for Jahve.   What he said to Nathan
(2 Sam. vii. 2) is an indication of this vowed resolve, which
was now in a time of triumphant peace, as it seemed, ready for
being ·carried out, after the first step towards it had already
been taken in the removal of the Ark of the covenant to Zion
(2 Sam. ch. vi.) ; for 2 Sam. ch. vii. is appended to 2 Sam. ch.
vi. out of its chronological order and only on account of the
internal connection.   After the bringing home of the Ark,
which had been long yearned for (cf. ci. 2), and did not take
place without difficulties and terrors, was accomplished, a series
of years again passed over, during which David always carried
about with him the thought of erecting God a Temple-building.
And when he had received the tidings through Nathan that he
should not build God a house, but that it should be done by his
son and successor, he nevertheless did as much towards the
carrying out of the desire of his heart as was possible in connection with this declaration of the will of Jahve.   He conse-

crated the site of the future Temple, he procured the necessary
means and materials for the building of it, he made all the
necessary arrangements for the future Temple-service, he in-
spirited the people for the gigantic work of building that was
before them, and handed over to his son the model for it, as it
is all related to us in detail by the chronicler. The divine name
" the mighty One of Jacob " is taken from Gen. xlix. 24, as in
Isa. i. 24, xlix. 26, lx. 16. The Philistines with their Dagon
had been made to feel this mighty Rock of Jacob when they
took the sacred Ark along with them (1 Sam. ch. v.). With
אִם David solemnly declares what he is resolved not to do. The
meaning of the hyperbolically expressed vow in the form of an
oath is that for so long he will not rejoice at his own dwelling-
house, nor give himself up to sleep that is free from anxiety;
in fine, for so long he will not rest. The genitives after אֹהֶל
and עֶרֶשׂ are appositional genitives; Ps. xliv. delights in similar
combinations of synonyms. יְצוּעָי (Latin *strata mea*) is a poetical plural, as also is מִשְׁכְּנוֹת. With תְּנוּמָה (which is always said
of the eyelids, Gen. xxxi. 40, Prov. vi. 4, Eccles. viii. 16, not
of the eyes) alternates שְׁנַת (according to another reading שֵׁנַת)
for שֵׁנָה. The *âth* is the same as in נַחֲלַת in xvi. 6, cf. lx. 13,
Ex. xv. 2, and frequently. This Aramaizing rejection of the
syllable before the tone is, however, without example elsewhere. The LXX. adds to ver. 4, καὶ ἀνάπαυσιν τοῖς κροτά-
φοις μου (וּמְנוּחָה לְרַקּוֹתָי), but this is a disagreeable overloading
of the verse.

Vers. 6–10. In ver. 6 begins the language of the church,
which in this Psalm reminds Jahve of His promises and comforts itself with them. Olshausen regards this ver. 6 as altogether inexplicable. The interpretation nevertheless has some
safe starting-points. (1) Since the subject spoken of is the
founding of a fixed sanctuary, and one worthy of Jahve, the
suffix of שְׁמַעֲנוּהָ (with *Chateph* as in Hos. viii. 2, Ew. § 60, *a*) and
מְצָאנוּהָ refers to the Ark of the covenant, which is *fem.* also in
other instances (1 Sam. iv. 17, 2 Chron. viii. 11). (2) The
Ark of the covenant, fetched up out of Shiloh by the Israelites
to the battle at Ebenezer, fell into the hands of the victors, and
remained, having been again given up by them, for twenty
years in Kirjath-Jearim (1 Sam. vii. 1 sq.), until David removed
it out of this Judæan district to Zion (2 Sam. vi. 2–4; cf.

2 Chron. i. 4). What is then more natural than that שְׂדֵי־יָעַר is a poetical appellation of Kirjath-Jearim (cf. "the field of Zoan" in lxxviii. 12)? Kirjath-Jearim has, as a general thing, very varying names. It is also called *Kirjath-ha-jearim* in Jer. xxvi. 20 (*Kirjath-ʿarim* in Ezra ii. 25, cf. Josh. xviii. 28), *Kirjath-baʿal* in Josh. xv. 60, *Baʿalah* in Josh. xv. 9, 1 Chron. xiii. 6 (cf. *Har-ha-baʿalah*, Josh. xv. 11, with *Har-Jearim* in Josh. xv. 10), and, as it seems, even *Baʿalê Jehudah* in 2 Sam. vi. 2. Why should it not also have been called *Jaʿar* side by side with *Kirjath-Jearim*, and more especially if the mountainous district, to which the mention of a hill and mountain of *Jearim* points, was, as the name "city of the wood" implies, at the same time a wooded district? We therefore fall in with Kühnöl's (1799) rendering: we found it in the meadows of Jaar, and with his remark: "Jaar is a shortened name of the city of Kirjath-Jearim."

The question now further arises as to what *Ephrathah* is intended to mean. This is an ancient name of Bethlehem; but the Ark of the covenant never was in Bethlehem. Accordingly Hengstenberg interprets, "We knew of it in Bethlehem (where David had spent his youth) only by hearsay, no one had seen it; we found it in Kirjath-Jearim, yonder in the wooded environs of the city, where it was as it were buried in darkness and solitude." So even Anton Hulsius (1650): *Ipse David loquitur, qui dicit illam ipsam arcam, de qua quum adhuc Bethlehemi versaretur inaudivisset, postea a se (vel majoribus suis ipso adhuc minorenni) inventam fuisse in campis Jaar.* But (1) the supposition that David's words are continued here does not harmonize with the way in which they are introduced in ver. 2, according to which they cannot possibly extend beyond the vow that follows. (2) If the church is speaking, one does not see why Bethlehem is mentioned in particular as the place of the hearsay. (3) *We heard it in Ephrathah* cannot well mean anything else than, *per antiptosin* (as in Gen. i. 4, but without כִּי), we heard that it was in Ephrathah. But the Ark was before Kirjath-Jearim in Shiloh. The former lay in the tribe of Judah close to the western borders of Benjamin, the latter in the midst of the tribe of Ephraim. Now since אֶפְרָתִי quite as often means an Ephraimite as it does a Bethlehemite, it may be asked whether *Ephrathah* is not intended of the

Ephraimitish territory (Kühnöl, Gesenius, Maurer, Tholuck,
and others). The meaning would then be: we had heard that
the sacred Ark was in Shiloh, but we found it not there, but
in Kirjath-Jearim. And we can easily understand why the
poet has mentioned the two places just in this way. *Ephrâth*,
according to its etymon, is fruitful fields, with which are contrasted the fields of the wood—the sacred Ark had fallen from
its original, more worthy abode, as it were, into the wilderness.
But is it probable, more especially in view of Mic. v. 1, that in
a connection in which the memory of David is the ruling idea,
Ephrathah signifies the land of Ephraim? No, *Ephrathah*
is the name of the district in which Kirjath-Jearim lay.
Caleb had, for instance, by Ephrath, his third wife, a son
named Hûr (Chûr), 1 Chron. ii. 19. This Hûr, the first-born
of Ephrathah, is the father of the population of Bethlehem
(1 Chron. iv. 4), and Shobal, a son of this Hûr, is father of
the population of Kirjath-Jearim (1 Chron. ii. 50). Kirjath-
Jearim is therefore, so to speak, the daughter of Bethlehem.
This was called Ephrathah in ancient times, and this name
of Bethlehem became the name of its district (Mic. v. 1).
Kirjath-Jearim belonged to *Caleb-Ephrathah* (1 Chron. ii. 24),
as the northern part of this district seems to have been called
in distinction from *Negeb-Caleb* (1 Sam. xxx. 14).

But מִשְׁכְּנוֹתָיו in ver. 7 is now neither a designation of the
house of Abinadab in Kirjath-Jearim, for the expression would
be too grand, and in relation to ver. 5 even confusing, nor a
designation of the Salomonic Temple-building, for the expression standing thus by itself is not enough alone to designate it.
What is meant will therefore be the tent-temple erected by
David for the Ark when removed to Zion (2 Sam. vii. 2, יְרִיעָה).
The church arouses itself to enter this, and to prostrate itself
in adoration towards (*vid.* xcix. 5) the footstool of Jahve, *i.e.*
the Ark; and to what purpose? The Ark of the covenant is
now to have a place more worthy of it; the מְנוּחָה, *i.e.* the
בֵּית מְנוּחָה, 1 Chron. xxviii. 2, in which David's endeavours
have through Solomon reached their goal, is erected: let Jahve
and the Ark of His sovereign power, that may not be touched
(see the examples of its inviolable character in 1 Sam. ch. v.,
vi., 2 Sam. vi. 6 sq.), now enter this fixed abode! Let His
priests who are to serve Him there clothe themselves in "right-

eousness," *i.e.* in conduct that is according to His will and pleasure; let His saints, who shall there seek and find mercy, shout for joy! More especially, however, let Jahve for David's sake, His servant, to whose restless longing this place of rest owes its origin, not turn back the face of His anointed one, *i.e.* not reject his face which there turns towards Him in the attitude of prayer (cf. lxxxiv. 10). The chronicler has understood ver. 10 as an intercession on behalf of Solomon, and the situation into which we are introduced by vers. 6–8 seems to require this. It is, however, possible that a more recent poet here, in vers. 7, 8, reproduces words taken from the heart of the church in Solomon's time, and blends petitions of the church of the present with them. The subject all through is the church, which is ever identical although changing in the persons of its members. The Israel that brought the sacred Ark out of Kirjath-Jearim to Zion and accompanied it thence to the Temple-hill, and now worships in the sanctuary raised by David's zeal for the glory of Jahve, is one and the same. The prayer for the priests, for all the saints, and more especially for the reigning king, that then resounded at the dedication of the Temple, is continued so long as the history of Israel lasts, even in a time when Israel has no king, but has all the stronger longing for the fulfilment of the Messianic promise.

Vers. 11–13. The "for the sake of David" is here set forth in detail. אֱמֶת in ver. 11*a* is not the accusative of the object, but an adverbial accusative. The first member of the verse closes with לְדָוִד, which has the distinctive *Pazer*, which is preceded by *Legarmeh* as a sub-distinctive; then follows at the head of the second member אֱמֶת with *Zinnor*, then לֹא־יָשׁוּב מִמֶּנָּה with *Olewejored* and its conjunctive *Galgal*, which regularly precedes after the sub-distinctive *Zinnor*. The suffix of מִמֶּנָּה refers to that which was affirmed by oath, as in Jer. iv. 28. Lineal descendants of David will Jahve place on the throne (לְכִסֵּא like לְרֹאשׁ in xxi. 4) to him, *i.e.* so that they shall follow him as possessors of the throne. David's children shall for ever (which has been finally fulfilled in Christ) sit לְכִסֵּא to him (cf. ix. 5, Job xxxvi. 7). Thus has Jahve promised, and expects in return from the sons of David the observance of His Law. Instead of עֵדֹתִי זוֹ it is pointed עֵדֹתִי זוֹ. In Hahn's edition עֵדֹתִי has *Mercha* in the *penult.* (cf. the retreat of the tone in אֲדֹנִי זֶה, Dan. x. 17), and in Baer's edition the still better attested reading *Mahpach* instead of the counter-tone *Metheg*, and *Mercha* on the *ultima*. It is not plural with a singular suffix (cf. Deut. xxviii. 59, Ges. § 91, 3), but, as זו = זאת indicates, the singular for עֵדוּתִי, like תְּחָנֹתִי for תְּחֻנֹתִי in 2 Kings vi. 8; and signifies the revelation of God as an attestation of His will. אֲלַמְּדֵם has *Mercha mahpach.*, זו *Rebia parvum*, and עֵדֹתִי *Mercha;* and according to the interpunction it would have to be rendered: "and My self-attestation there" (*vid.* on ix. 16), but זו is relative: My self-attestation (revelation), which I teach them. The divine words extend to the end of ver. 12. The hypotheses with אִם, as the fulfilment in history shows, were conditions of the continuity of the Davidic succession; not, however,—because human unfaithfulness does not annul the faithfulness of God,—of the endlessness of the Davidic throne. In ver. 13 the poet states the ground of such promissory mercy. It is based on the universal mercy of the election of Jerusalem. אִוָּהּ has *He mappic.* like עִנָּה in Deut. xxii. 29, or the stroke of *Raphe* (Ew. § 247, *d*), although the suffix is not absolutely necessary. In the following strophe the purport of the election of Jerusalem is also unfolded in Jahve's own words.

Vers. 14–18. Shiloh has been rejected (lxxviii. 60), for a time only was the sacred Ark in Bethel (Judg. xx. 27) and Mizpah (Judg. xxi. 5), only somewhat over twenty years was it sheltered by the house of Abinadab in Kirjath-Jearim (1 Sam. vii. 2), only three months by the house of Obed-Edom in Perez-Uzzah (2 Sam. vi. 11)—but Zion is Jahve's abiding dwelling-place, His own proper settlement, מְנוּחָה (as in Isa. xi. 10, lxvi. 1, and besides 1 Chron. xxviii. 2). In Zion, His chosen and beloved dwelling-place, Jahve blesses everything that belongs to her temporal need (צֵידָהּ for צֵידָתָהּ, *vid.* on xxvii. 5, note); so that her poor do not suffer want, for divine love loves the poor most especially. His second blessing refers to the priests, for by means of these He will keep up His intercourse with His people. He makes the priesthood of Zion a real institution of salvation: He clothes her priests with salvation, so that they do not merely bring it about instrumentally, but personally possess it, and their whole outward appearance is one which proclaims salvation. And to all her saints He

gives cause and matter for high and lasting joy, by making
Himself known also to the church, in which He has taken
up His abode, in deeds of mercy (loving-kindness or grace).
There (שָׁם, cxxxiii. 3) in Zion is indeed the kingship of promise, which cannot fail of fulfilment. He will cause a horn
to shoot forth, He will prepare a lamp, for the house of David,
which David here represents as being its ancestor and the
anointed one of God reigning at that time ; and all who hostilely
rise up against David in his seed, He will cover with shame as
with a garment (Job viii. 22), and the crown consecrated by
promise, which the seed of David wears, shall blossom like an
unfading wreath. The horn is an emblem of defensive might
and victorious dominion, and the lamp (נֵר, 2 Sam. xxi. 17, cf.
נִיר, 2 Chron. xxi. 7, LXX. λύχνον) an emblem of brilliant
dignity and joyfulness. In view of Ezek. xxix. 21, of the
predictions concerning the Branch (*zemach*) in Isa. iv. 2, Jer.
xxiii. 5, xxxiii. 15, Zech. iii. 8, vi. 12 (cf. Heb. vii. 14), and of
the fifteenth Beracha of the *Shemone-Esre* (the daily Jewish
prayer consisting of eighteen benedictions) : " make the branch
(*zemach*) of David Thy servant to shoot forth speedily, and let
his horn rise high by virtue of Thy salvation,"—it is hardly to
be doubted that the poet attached a Messianic meaning to this
promise. With reference to our Psalm, Zacharias, the father
of John the Baptist, changes that supplicatory beracha of his
nation (Luke i. 68–70) into a praiseful one, joyfully anticipating the fulfilment that is at hand in Jesus.

PSALM CXXXIII.

PRAISE OF BROTHERLY FELLOWSHIP.

1 BEHOLD how good it is, and how delightful,
   That brethren also dwell together !
2 Like the fine oil upon the head,
   Flowing gently down upon the beard, the beard of Aaron,
   Which flows gently down upon the hem of his garments—
3 Like the dew of Hermon, *which flows gently down* upon the
     mountains of Zion,
   For there hath Jahve commanded the blessing,
   Life, for evermore.

In this Psalm, says Hengstenberg, " David brings to the consciousness of the church the glory of the fellowship of the saints, that had so long been wanting, the restoration of which had begun with the setting up of the Ark in Zion." The Psalm, in fact, does not speak of the termination of the dispersion, but of the uniting of the people of all parts of the land for the purpose of divine worship in the one place of the sanctuary; and, as in the case of Ps. cxxii., its counterpart, occasions can be found in the history of David adapted to the לדוד of the inscription. But the language witnesses against David; for the construction of שׁ with the participle, as שֶׁיֹּרֵד, *qui descendit* (cf. cxxxv. 2, שֶׁעֹמְדִים, *qui stant*), is unknown in the usage of the language prior to the Exile. Moreover the inscription לדוד is wanting in the LXX. *Cod. Vat.* and the Targum; and the Psalm may only have been so inscribed because it entirely breathes David's spirit, and is as though it had sprung out of his love for Jonathan.

With גַּם the assertion passes on from the community of nature and sentiment which the word " brethren" expresses to the outward active manifestation and realization that correspond to it: good and delightful (cxxxv. 3) it is when brethren united by blood and heart also (corresponding to this their brotherly nature) dwell together—a blessed joy which Israel has enjoyed during the three great Feasts, although only for a brief period (*vid.* Ps. cxxii.). Because the high priest, in whom the priestly mediatorial office culminates, is the chief personage in the celebration of the feast, the nature and value of that local reunion is first of all expressed by a metaphor taken from him. שֶׁמֶן הַטּוֹב is the oil for anointing described in Ex. xxx. 22–33, which consisted of a mixture of oil and aromatic spices strictly forbidden to be used in common life. The sons of Aaron were only sprinkled with this anointing oil; but Aaron was expressly anointed with it, inasmuch as Moses poured it upon his head; hence he is called *par excellence* " the anointed priest " (הַכֹּהֵן הַמָּשִׁיחַ), whilst the other priests are only " anointed" (מְשֻׁחִים, Num. iii. 3) in so far as their garments, like Aaron's, were also sprinkled with the oil (together with the blood of the ram of consecration), Lev. viii. 12, 30. In the time of the second Temple, to which the holy oil of

anointing was wanting, the installation into the office of high
priest took place by his being invested in the pontifical robes.
The poet, however, when he calls the high priest as such
Aaron, has the high-priesthood in all the fulness of its divine
consecration (Lev. xxi. 10) before his eyes. Two drops of the
holy oil of anointing, says a Haggada, remained for ever hanging
on the beard of Aaron like two pearls, as an emblem of atonement and of peace. In the act of the anointing itself the
precious oil freely poured out ran gently down upon his beard,
which in accordance with Lev. xxi. 5 was unshortened.

In that part of the Tôra which describes the robe of the
high priest, שׁוּלֵי is its hems, פִּי רֹאשׁוֹ, or even absolutely פֶּה, the
opening for the head, or the collar, by means of which the
sleeveless garment was put on, and שָׂפָה the binding, the em-
broidery, the border of this collar (*vid.* Ex. xxviii. 32, xxxix.
23; cf. Job xxx. 18, פִּי כֻתָּנְתִּי, the collar of my shirt). פִּי must
apparently be understood according to these passages of the
Tôra, as also the appellation מִדּוֹת (only here for מַדִּים, מְדִים),
beginning with Lev. vi. 3, denotes the whole vestment of the
high priest, yet without more exact distinction. But the
Targum translates פִּי with אִמְרָא (*ora* = *fimbria*) — a word
which is related to אִמְרָא, *agnus*, like ᾦα to ὄϊς. This ᾦα is used
both of the upper and lower edge of a garment. Accordingly
Apollinaris and the Latin versions understand the ἐπὶ τὴν ᾦαν
of the LXX. of the hem (*in oram vestimenti*); Theodoret,
on the other hand, understands it to mean the upper edging:
ᾦαν ἐκάλεσεν ὃ καλοῦμεν περιτραχήλιον, τοῦτο δὲ καὶ ὁ Ἀκύλας
στόμα ἐνδυμάτων εἴρηκε. So also De Sacy: *sur le bord de son
vêtement, c'est-à-dire, sur le haut de ses habits pontificaux.* The
decision of the question depends upon the aim of this and the
following figure in ver. 3. If we compare the two figures, we
find that the point of the comparison is the uniting power of
brotherly feeling, as that which unites in heart and soul those
who are most distant from one another locally, and also brings
them together in outward circumstance. If this is the point
of the comparison, then Aaron's beard and the hem of his
garments stand just as diametrically opposed to one another as
the dew of Hermon and the mountains of Zion. פִּי is not the
collar above, which gives no advance, much less the antithesis
of two extremes, but the hem at the bottom (cf. שָׂפָה, Ex. xxvi.

4, of the edge of a curtain). It is also clear that שִׁירָיו cannot
now refer to the beard of Aaron, either as flowing down over
the upper border of his robe, or as flowing down upon its hem ;
it must refer to the oil, for peaceable love that brings the most
widely separated together is likened to the oil. This reference
is also more appropriate to the style of the onward movement
of the gradual Psalms, and is confirmed by ver. 3, where it
refers to the dew, which takes the place of the oil in the other
metaphor. When brethren united in harmonious love also
meet together in one place, as is the case in Israel at the great
Feasts, it is as when the holy, precious chrism, breathing forth
the blended odour of many spices, upon the head of Aaron
trickles down upon his beard, and from thence to the extreme
end of his vestment. It becomes thoroughly perceptible, and
also outwardly visible, that Israel, far and near, is pervaded by
one spirit and bound together in unity of spirit.

This uniting spirit of brotherly love is now symbolized also
by the dew of Hermon, which descends in drops upon the
mountains of Zion. " What we read in the 133d Psalm of
the dew of Hermon descending upon the mountains of Zion,"
says Van de Velde in his *Travels* (Bd. i. S. 97), " is now
become quite clear to me. Here, as I sat at the foot of Hermon, I understood how the water-drops which rose from its
forest-mantled heights, and out of the highest ravines, which
are filled the whole year round with snow, after the sun's rays
have attenuated them and moistened the atmosphere with them,
descend at evening-time as a heavy dew upon the lower mountains which lie round about as its spurs. One ought to have
seen Hermon with its white-golden crown glistening aloft in
the blue sky, in order to be able rightly to understand the
figure. Nowhere in the whole country is so heavy a dew perceptible as in the districts near to Hermon." To this dew the
poet likens brotherly love. This is as the dew of Hermon : of
such pristine freshness and thus refreshing, possessing such
pristine power and thus quickening, thus born from above
(cx. 3), and in fact like the dew of Hermon which comes
down upon the mountains of Zion—a feature in the picture
which is taken from the natural reality ; for an abundant dew,
when warm days have preceded, might very well be diverted
to Jerusalem by the operation of the cold current of air

sweeping down from the north over Hermon. We know,
indeed, from our own experience how far off a cold air coming
from the Alps is perceptible and produces its effects. The
figure of the poet is therefore as true to nature as it is beautiful. When brethren bound together in love also meet
together in one place, and in fact when brethren out of the
north unite with brethren in the south in Jerusalem, the city
which is the mother of all, at the great Feasts, it is as when
the dew of Mount Hermon, which is covered with deep, almost
eternal snow,* descends upon the bare, unfruitful—and therefore longing for such quickening—mountains round about
Zion. In Jerusalem must love and all that is good meet.
For there (שָׁם as in cxxxii. 17) hath Jahve commanded (צִוָּה as
in Lev. xxv. 21, cf. Ps. xlii. 9, lxviii. 29) the blessing, *i.e.* there
allotted to the blessing its rendezvous and its place of issue.
אֶת־הַבְּרָכָה is appositionally explained by חַיִּים : life is the substance and goal of the blessing, the possession of all possessions, the blessing of all blessings. The closing words
עַד־הָעוֹלָם (cf. xxviii. 9) belong to צִוָּה : such is God's inviolable,
ever-enduring order.

PSALM CXXXIV.

NIGHT-WATCH GREETING AND COUNTER-GREETING.

The Call.

1 BEHOLD, *bless ye Jahve*, all ye servants of Jahve,
  Who serve in the house of Jahve by night !
2 Lift up your hands to the sanctuary
  And bless ye Jahve !

---

* A Hauranitish poem in Wetzstein's *Lieder-Sammlungen* begins :

‫البارحة هبّت علينا شرارة | من عالى الثلج‬ — — ‫‬, " Yesterday
there blew across to me a spark | from the lofty snow-mountain (the
Hermon)," on which the commentator dictated to him the remark, that
‫شرارة‬, the glowing spark, is either the snow-capped summit of the mountain glowing in the morning sun or a burning cold breath of air, for one
says in everyday life ‫الصقّع يحرق‬, the frost burns [*vid.* note to cxxi. 6].

The Answer.

3 *Jahve bless thee* out of Zion,
The Creator of heaven and earth !

This Psalm consists of a greeting, vers. 1, 2, and the reply thereto. The greeting is addressed to those priests and Levites who have the night-watch in the Temple; and this antiphon is purposely placed at the end of the collection of Songs of degrees in order to take the place of a final beracha. In this sense Luther styles this Psalm *epiphonema superiorum.* It is also in other respects (*vid. Symbolæ,* p. 66) an appropriate finale.

Vers. 1, 2. The Psalm begins, like its predecessor, with הִנֵּה; there it directs attention to an attractive phenomenon, here to a duty which springs from the office. For that it is not the persons frequenting the Temple who are addressed is at once clear from the fact that the tarrying of these in the Temple through the night, when such a thing did actually occur (Luke ii. 37), was only an exception. And then, however, from the fact that עָמַד is the customary word for the service of the priests and Levites, Deut. x. 8, xviii. 7, 1 Chron. xxiii. 30, 2 Chron. xxix. 11 (cf. on Isa. lxi. 10, and Ps. cx. 4), which is also continued in the night, 1 Chron. ix. 33. Even the Targum refers ver. 1*b* to the Temple-watch. In the second Temple the matter was arranged thus. After midnight the chief over the gate-keepers took the keys of the inner Temple and went with some of the priests through the little wicket of the Fire Gate (שַׁעַר בֵּית הַמּוֹקֵד). In the inner court this patrol divided into two companies, each with a burning torch; one company turned west, the other east, and so they compassed the court to see whether everything was in readiness for the service of the dawning day. At the bakers' chamber, in which the *Mincha* of the high priest was baked (לִשְׁכַּת עוֹשֵׂי הֲבִיתִּין), they met with the cry: All is well. In the meanwhile the rest of the priests also arose, bathed, and put on their garments. Then they went into the stone chamber (one half of which was the place of session of the Sanhedrim), where, under the superintendence of the chief over the drawing of the lots and of a judge, around whom stood all the priests in their robes of office, the functions of the priests in the service of the coming day were assigned to them by lot (Luke i. 9). Accordingly Tholuck, with Köster, regards vers. 1 sq. and 3 as the antiphon of the Temple-watch going off duty and those coming on. It might also be the call and counter-call with which the watchmen greeted one another when they met. But according to the general keeping of the Psalm, vers. 1 sq. have rather to be regarded as a call to devotion and intercession, which the congregation addresses to the priests and Levites entrusted with the night-service in the Temple. It is an error to suppose that "in the nights" can be equivalent to "early and late." If the Psalter contains Morning Psalms (iii., lxiii.) and Evening Psalms (iv., cxli.), why should it then not contain a vigil Psalm? On this very ground Venema's idea too, that בַּלֵּילוֹת is syncopated from בְּהַלֵּילוֹת, "with *Hallels, i.e.* praises," is useless. Nor is there any reason for drawing ἐν ταῖς νυξίν, as the LXX. does, to ver. 2,* or, what would be more natural, to the בָּרֲכוּ that opens the Psalm, since it is surely not strange that, so long as the sanctuary was standing, a portion of the servants of God who ministered in it had to remain up at night to guard it, and to see to it that nothing was wanting in the preparations for the early service. That this ministering watching should be combined with devotional praying is the purport of the admonition in ver. 2. Raising suppliant hands (יְדֵכֶם, negligently written for יְדֵיכֶם) towards the Most Holy Place (τὰ ἅγια), they are to bless Jahve. קֹדֶשׁ (according to *B. Sota* 39a, the accusative of definition: in holiness, *i.e.* after washing of hands), in view of xxviii. 2, v. 8, cxxxviii. 2 (cf. רוֹם in Hab. iii. 10), has to be regarded as the accusative of the direction.

Ver. 3. Calling thus up to the Temple-hill, the church receives from above the benedictory counter-greeting: Jahve bless thee out of Zion (as in cxxviii. 5), the Creator of heaven and earth (as in cxv. 15, cxxi. 2, cxxiv. 8). From the time of Num. vi. 24 *jebaréchja* is the ground-form of the priestly benediction. It is addressed to the church as one person, and to each individual in this united, unit-like church.

---

* The LXX. adjusts the shortening of ver. 1*b* arising from this, by reading העמדים בבית ה׳ בחצרות בית אלהינו after cxxxv. 2.

PSALM CXXXV.

FOUR-VOICED HALLELUJAH TO THE GOD OF ISRAEL, THE GOD OF GODS.

HALLELUJAH.

1 PRAISE ye the Name of Jahve,
  Praise ye, O ye servants of Jahve,
2 Who stand in the house of Jahve,
  In the courts of the house of our God!
3 Praise ye Jāh, for Jahve is good;
  Harp unto His Name, for it is lovely;
4 For Jacob hath Jāh chosen for Himself,
  Israel as His possession.

5 For I know that Jahve is great
  And our Lord above all gods.
6 All that Jahve willeth He carrieth out
  In heaven and upon earth,
  In the seas and in all the depths;
7 Who bringeth the vapours up from the end of the earth,
  He maketh lightnings for the rain,
  Who bringeth forth wind out of His treasuries.

8 Who smote the first-born of Egypt
  From man down to the cattle,
9 Sent signs and wonders
  Into the midst of thee, O Egypt,
  Against Pharaoh and all his servants!

10 Who smote great nations
   And slew mighty kings,
11 Sihon, king of the Amorites,
   And Og, king of Bashan,
   And all the kingdoms of Canaan;
12 And gave over their land as a heritage,
   As a heritage to Israel His people.

13 Jahve, Thy Name endureth for ever,
   Thy memorial, Jahve, unto all generations.

14 For Jahve will render justice to His people,
    And repent Himself concerning His servants.

15 The idols of the heathen are silver and gold,
    The work of men's hands.
16 A mouth have they and cannot speak,
    Eyes have they and cannot see,
17 Ears have they and cannot hear,
    Nor is there any breath at all in their mouth.
18 Like unto them must they who made them become,
    Every one who trusted in them.

19 O house of Israel, bless ye Jahve!
    O house of Aaron, bless ye Jahve!
20 O house of Levi, bless ye Jahve!
    Ye who fear Jahve, bless Jahve!—
21 Blessed be Jahve out of Zion,
    Who dwelleth in Jerusalem,
            Hallelujah!

Ps. cxxxv. is here and there (*vid. Tôsefôth Pesachim* 117*a*)
taken together with Ps. cxxxiv. as one Psalm. The combining
of Ps. cxv. with cxiv. is a misapprehension caused by the in-
scriptionless character of Ps. cxv., whereas Ps. cxxxv. and
cxxxiv. certainly stand in connection with one another. For
the Hallelujah Ps. cxxxv. is, as the mutual relation between
the beginning and close of Ps. cxxxiv. shows, a Psalm-song
expanded out of this shorter hymn, that is in part drawn from
Ps. cxv.

It is a Psalm in the mosaic style. Even the Latin poet
Lucilius transfers the figure of mosaic-work to style, when he
says: *quam lepide lexeis compostæ ut tesserulæ omnes* . . . In
the case of Ps. cxxxv. it is not the first time that we have met
with this kind of style. We have already had a glimpse of it
in Ps. xcvii. and xcviii. These Psalms were composed more
especially of deutero-Isaianic passages, whereas Ps. cxxxv.
takes its *tesserulæ* out of the Law, Prophets, and Psalms.

Vers. 1–4. The beginning is taken from cxxxiv. 1; ver. 2*b*

recalls cxvi. 19 (cf. xcii. 14); and ver. 4 is an echo of Deut.
vii. 6. The servants of Jahve to whom the summons is addressed, are not, as in cxxxiv. 1 sq., His official servants in
particular, but according to ver. 2b, where the courts, in the
plural, are allotted to them as their standing-place, and according to vers. 19, 20, those who fear Him as a body. The threefold *Jahve* at the beginning is then repeated in *Jāh* (הַלְלוּ־יָהּ, cf.
note * to civ. 35), *Jahve*, and *Jāh*. The subject of כִּי נָעִים is
by no means Jahve (Hupfeld), whom they did not dare to call
נעים in the Old Testament, but either the Name, according to
liv. 8 (Luther, Hitzig), or, which is favoured by cxlvii. 1 (cf.
Prov. xxii. 18), the praising of His Name (Apollinaris: ἐπεὶ
τόδε καλὸν ἀείδειν): His Name to praise is a delightful employ,
which is incumbent on Israel as the people of His choice and
of His possession.

Vers. 5–7. The praise itself now begins. כִּי in ver. 4a set
forth the ground of the pleasant duty, and the כי that begins
this strophe confirms that which warrants the summons out of
the riches of the material existing for such a hymn of praise.
Worthy is He to be praised, for Israel knows full well that
He who hath chosen it is the God of gods. The beginning
is taken from cxv. 3, and ver. 7 from Jer. x. 13 (li. 16).
Heaven, earth, and water are the three kingdoms of created
things, as in Ex. xx. 4. נְשִׂיא signifies that which is lifted up,
ascended; here, as in Jeremiah, a cloud. The meaning of
בְּרָקִים לַמָּטָר עָשָׂה is not: He makes lightnings into rain, *i.e.*
resolves them as it were into rain, which is unnatural; but
either according to Zech. x. 1: He produces lightnings in behalf of rain, in order that the rain may pour down in consequence of the thunder and lightning, or poetically: He makes
lightnings for the rain, so that the rain is announced (Apollinaris) and accompanied by them. Instead of מוֹצִא (cf. lxxviii.
16, cv. 43), which does not admit of the retreating of the tone,
the expression is מוֹצֵא, the ground-form of the *part. Hiph.* for
plurals like מַעֲזְרִים, מַחֲלְמִים, מַחֲצְרִים, perhaps not without being
influenced by the וַיּוֹצֵא in Jeremiah, for it is not מוֹצֵא from
מָצָא that signifies "producing," but מֵפִיק = מוֹצִיא. The metaphor of the treasuries is like Job xxxviii. 22. What is intended
is the fulness of divine power, in which lie the grounds of the
origin and the impulses of all things in nature.

Vers. 8, 9. Worthy is He to be praised, for He is the Redeemer out of Egypt. בְּתוֹכֵכִי as in cxvi. 19, cf. cv. 27.

Vers. 10–12. Worthy is He to be praised, for He is the Conqueror of the Land of Promise. In connection with ver. 10 one is reminded of Deut. iv. 38, vii. 1, ix. 1, xi. 23, Josh. xxiii. 9. גּוֹיִם רַבִּים are here not many, but great peoples (cf. גְּדֹלִים in cxxxvi. 17), since the parallel word עֲצוּמִים is by no means intended of a powerful number, but of powerful might (cf. Isa. liii. 12). As to the rest also, the poet follows the Book of Deuteronomy: viz. לְכֹל מַמְלְכוֹת as in Deut. iii. 21, and נָתַן נַחֲלָה as in Deut. iv. 38 and other passages. It is all Deuteronomic with the exception of the שׁ, and the לְ in ver. 11 as the *nota accus.* (as in cxxxvi. 19 sq., cf. lxix. 6, cxvi. 16, cxxix. 3); the construction of הָרַג is just as Aramaizing in Job v. 2, 2 Sam. iii. 30 (where vers. 30, 31, like vers. 36, 37, are a later explanatory addition). The הָרַג alternating with הִכָּה is, next to the two kings, also referred to the kingdoms of Canaan, viz. their inhabitants. Og was also an Amoritish king, Deut. iii. 8.

Vers. 13, 14. This God who rules so praiseworthily in the universe and in the history of Israel is the same yesterday, and to-day, and for ever. Just as ver. 13 (cf. cii. 13) is taken from Ex. iii. 15, so ver. 14 is taken from Deut. xxxii. 36, cf. xc. 13, and *vid.* on Heb. x. 30, 31 (vol. ii. 191).

Vers. 15–18. For the good of His proved church He ever proves Himself to be the Living God, whereas idols and idol-worshippers are vain—throughout following cxv. 4–8, but with some abridgments. Here only the אַף used as a particle recalls what is said there of the organ of smell (אַף) of the idols that smells not, just as the רוּחַ which is here (as in Jer. x. 14) denied to the idols recalls the הָרִיחַ denied to them there. It is to be rendered: also there is not a being of breath, *i.e.* there is no breath at all, not a trace thereof, in their mouth. It is different in 1 Sam. xxi. 9, where יֶשׁ אִין (not אַיִן) is meant to be equivalent to the Aramaic אִית אִין, *num (an) est;* אִין is North-Palestinian, and equivalent to the interrogatory אִם (after which the Targum renders אֲלּוּ אִית).

Vers. 19–21. A call to the praise of Jahve, who is exalted above the gods of the nations, addressed to Israel as a whole, rounds off the Psalm by recurring to its beginning. The three-fold call in cxv. 9–11, cxviii. 2–4, is rendered fourfold here by

the introduction of the house of the Levites, and the wishing of
a blessing in cxxxiv. 3 is turned into an ascription of praise.
Zion, whence Jahve's self-attestation, so rich in power and
loving-kindness, is spread abroad, is also to be the place whence
His glorious attestation by the mouth of men is spread abroad.
History has realized this.

PSALM CXXXVI.

O GIVE THANKS UNTO THE LORD, FOR HE IS GOOD.

1 GIVE thanks unto Jahve, for He is good,
   For His goodness endureth for ever.
2 Give thanks unto the God of gods,
   For His goodness endureth for ever.
3 Give thanks unto the Lord of lords—
   For His goodness endureth for ever.

4 To Him who alone doeth great wonders,
   For His goodness endureth for ever.
5 To Him who by wisdom made the heavens,
   For His goodness endureth for ever.
6 To Him who stretched out the earth above the waters—
   For His goodness endureth for ever.

7 To Him who made great lights,
   For His goodness endureth for ever.
8 The sun for dominion by day,
   For His goodness endureth for ever.
9 The moon and stars for dominions by night—
   For His goodness endureth for ever.

10 To Him who smote the Egyptians in their first-born,
   For His goodness endureth for ever.
11 And brought forth Israel out of their midst,
   For His goodness endureth for ever.
12 With a strong hand and a stretched-out arm—
   For His goodness endureth for ever.

13 To Him who divided the Red Sea into parts,
   For His goodness endureth for ever.

14 And made Israel to pass through in the midst of it,
    For His goodness endureth for ever.
15 And overthrew Pharaoh and his host in the Red Sea—
    For His goodness endureth for ever.

16 To Him who led His people in the desert,
    For His goodness endureth for ever.
17 To Him who smote great kings,
    For His goodness endureth for ever.
18 And slew glorious kings—
    For His goodness endureth for ever.

19 Sihon, king of the Amorites,
    For His goodness endureth for ever.
20 And Og, king of Bashan,
    For His goodness endureth for ever.
21 And gave their land as a heritage,
    For His goodness endureth for ever.
22 As a heritage to Israel His servant—
    For His goodness endureth for ever.

23 Who in our low estate remembered us,
    For His goodness endureth for ever.
24 And redeemed us from our adversaries,
    For His goodness endureth for ever.
25 Giving bread to all flesh—
    For His goodness endureth for ever.
26 Give thanks unto the God of heaven,
    For His goodness endureth for ever.

The cry cxxxv. 3, *Praise ye Jāh, for good is Jahve*, is here followed by a *Hodu*, the last of the collection, with " for His goodness endureth for ever" repeated twenty-six times as a *versus intercalaris*. In the liturgical language this Psalm is called *par excellence* the great Hallel, for according to its broadest compass the great Hallel comprehends Ps. cxx. to cxxxvi.,*

---

* There are three opinious in the Talmud and Midrash concerning the compass of the " Great Hallel," viz. (1) Ps. cxxxvi., (2) Ps. cxxxv. 4–cxxxvi., (3) Ps. cxx.–cxxxvi.

whilst the Hallel which is absolutely so called extends from Ps. cxiii. to cxviii. Down to ver. 18 the song and counter-song organize themselves into hexastichic groups or strophes, which, however, from ver. 19 (and therefore from the point where the dependence on Ps. cxxxv., already begun with ver. 17, becomes a borrowing, onwards) pass over into octastichs. In Heidenheim's Psalter the Psalm appears (after Norzi) in two columns (like Deut. ch. xxxii.), which it is true has neither tradition (*vid.* on Ps. xviii.) nor MSS. precedent in its favour, but really corresponds to its structure.

Vers. 1–9. Like the preceding Psalm, this Psalm allies itself to the Book of Deuteronomy. Vers. 2a and 3a (*God of gods and Lord of lords*) are taken from Deut. x. 17; ver. 12a (*with a strong hand and stretched-out arm*) from Deut. iv. 34, v. 15, and frequently (cf. Jer. xxxii. 21); ver. 16a like Deut. viii. 15 (cf. Jer. ii. 6). With reference to the Deuteronomic colouring of vers. 19–22, *vid.* on cxxxv. 10–12; also the expression "Israel His servant" recalls Deut. xxxii. 36 (cf. cxxxv. 14, xc. 13), and still more Isa. xl.–lxvi., where the comprehension of Israel under the unity of this notion has its own proper place. In other respects, too, the Psalm is an echo of earlier model passages. *Who alone doeth great wonders* sounds like lxxii. 18 (lxxxvi. 10); and the adjective "great" that is added to "wonders" shows that the poet found the formula already in existence. In connection with ver. 5a he has Prov. iii. 19 or Jer. x. 12 in his mind; תְּבוּנָה, like חָכְמָה, is the demiurgic wisdom. Ver. 6a calls to mind Isa. xlii. 5, xliv. 24; the expression is "above the waters," as in xxiv. 2 "upon the seas," because the water is partly visible and partly invisible מִתַּחַת לָאָרֶץ (Ex. xx. 4). The plural אוֹרִים, *luces*, instead of מְאֹרוֹת, *lumina* (cf. Ezek. xxxii. 8, מְאוֹרֵי אוֹר), is without precedent. It is a controverted point whether אֹרֹת in Isa. xxvi. 19 signifies lights (cf. אוֹרָה, cxxxix. 12) or herbs (2 Kings iv. 39). The plural מֶמְשָׁלוֹת is also rare (occurring only besides in cxiv. 2): it here denotes the dominion of the moon on the one hand, and (going beyond Gen. i. 16) of the stars on the other. בַּלַּיְלָה, like בַּיּוֹם, is the second member of the *stat. construct.*

Vers. 10–26. Up to this point it is God the absolute in general, the Creator of all things, to the celebration of whose praise they are summoned; and from this point onwards the God of the history of salvation. In ver. 13*a* וְגָזֵר (instead of בָּקַע, lxxviii. 13, Ex. xiv. 21, Neh. ix. 11) of the dividing of the Red Sea is peculiar; גְּזָרִים (Gen. xv. 17, side by side with בְּתָרִים) are the pieces or parts of a thing that is cut up into pieces. נִעֵר is a favourite word taken from Ex. xiv. 27. With reference to the name of the Egyptian ruler *Pharaoh* (Herodotus also, ii. 111, calls the Pharaoh of the Exodus the son of Sesostris-Rameses Miumun, not Μενόφθας, as he is properly called, but absolutely Φερῶν), *vid.* on lxxiii. 22. After the God to whom the praise is to be ascribed has been introduced with לְ by always fresh attributes, the לְ before the names of Sihon and of Og is perplexing. The words are taken over, as are the six lines of vers. 17*a*–22*a* in the main, from cxxxv. 10–12, with only a slight alteration in the expression. In ver. 23 the continued influence of the construction הוֹדוּ לְ is at an end. The connection by means of שֶׁ (cf. cxxxv. 8, 10) therefore has reference to the preceding " for His goodness endureth for ever." The language here has the stamp of the latest period. It is true זָכַר with *Lamed* of the object is used even in the earliest Hebrew, but שָׁפֵל is only authenticated by Eccles. x. 6, and פָּרַק, to break loose = to rescue (the customary Aramaic word for redemption), by Lam. v. 8, just as in the closing verse, which recurs to the beginning, " God of heaven " is a name for God belonging to the latest literature, Neh. i. 4, ii. 4. In ver. 23 the praise changes suddenly to that which has been experienced very recently. The attribute in ver. 25*a* (cf. cxlvii. 9, cxlv. 15) leads one to look back to a time in which famine befell them together with slavery.

PSALM CXXXVII.

BY THE RIVERS OF BABYLON.

1 BY the rivers of Babylon, there we sat and wept,
  When we remembered Zion.
2 Upon the willows in the midst thereof
  We hung our citherns.

3 For there our oppressors asked of us
    The words of songs,
    And our tormentors joy:
    Sing us a song of Zion!

4 How are we to sing Jahve's songs
    Upon strange soil?!
5 If I forget thee, O Jerusalem,
    Let my right hand become lame!

6 Let my tongue cleave to the roof of my mouth,
    If I do not remember thee,
    If I do not set Jerusalem
    Above all my joys!

7 Remember, Jahve, the children of Edom
    In the day of Jerusalem,
    Who said: Raze, raze it
    Even to the foundation!

8 O daughter of Babylon, thou wasted one, blessed is he who
            giveth thee thy reward,
    Which thou hast merited for us!
9 Blessed is he who taketh and dasheth thy little ones
    Against the rock!

The Hallelujah Ps. cxxxv. and the Hodu Ps. cxxxvi. are
followed by a Psalm which glances back into the time of the
Exile, when such cheerful songs as they once sang to the
accompaniment of the music of the Levites at the worship of
God on Mount Zion were obliged to be silent. It is anony-
mous. The inscription $T\hat{\wp}$ $\varDelta\alpha\upsilon\grave{\imath}\delta$ ($\delta\iota\grave{\alpha}$) ʻ$I\epsilon\rho\epsilon\mu\acute{\iota}o\upsilon$ found in
codices of the LXX., which is meant to say that it is a Davidic
song coming from the heart of Jeremiah,* is all the more
erroneous as Jeremiah never was one of the Babylonian exiles.
The ש, which is repeated three times in vers. 8 sq., corre-

---

* Reversely Ellies du Pin (in the preface of his *Bibliothèque des Auteurs
Ecclésiastiques*) says: *Le Pseaume 136 porte le nom de David et de Jeremie,
ce qu'il faut apparement entendre ainsi: Pseaume de Jeremie fait à l'imitation
de David.*

sponds to the time of the composition of the Psalm which is required by its contents. It is just the same with the paragogic *i* in the future in ver. 6. But in other respects the language is classic; and the rhythm, at the beginning softly elegiac, then more and more excited, and abounding in guttural and sibilant sounds, is so expressive that scarcely any Psalm is so easily impressed on the memory as this, which is so pictorial even in sound.

The metre resembles the elegiac as it appears in the so-called cæsura schema of the Lamentations and in the cadence of Isa. xvi. 9, 10, which is like the Sapphic strophe. Every second line corresponds to the pentameter of the elegiac metre.

Vers. 1–6. Beginning with perfects, the Psalm has the appearance of being a Psalm not belonging to the Exile, but written in memory of the Exile. The bank of a river, like the seashore, is a favourite place of sojourn of those whom deep grief drives forth from the bustle of men into solitude. The boundary line of the river gives to solitude a safe back; the monotonous splashing of the waves keeps up the dull, melancholy alternation of thoughts and feelings; and at the same time the sight of the cool, fresh water exercises a soothing influence upon the consuming fever within the heart. The rivers of Babylon are here those of the Babylonian empire: not merely the Euphrates with its canals, and the Tigris, but also the Chaboras (*Chebar*) and Eulæos (’*Ulai*), on whose lonesome banks Ezekiel (ch. i. 3) and Daniel (ch. viii. 2) beheld divine visions. The שָׁם is important: there, in a strange land, as captives under the dominion of the power of the world. And גַּם is purposely chosen instead of וְ: with the sitting down in the solitude of the river's banks weeping immediately came on; when the natural scenery around contrasted so strongly with that of their native land, the remembrance of Zion only forced itself upon them all the more powerfully, and the pain at the isolation from their home would have all the freer course where no hostilely observant eyes were present to suppress it. The willow (צַפְצָפָה) and viburnum, those trees which are associated with flowing water in hot low-lying districts, are indigenous in the richly watered lowlands of Babylonia. עֲרָב (עֲרָבָה), if one and the same with غرب, is not the willow, least of all the weeping-willow, which is

called *ṣafsâf mustaḥî* in Arabic, "the bending-down willow,"
but the viburnum with dentate leaves, described by Wetzstein
on Isa. xliv. 4. The Talmud even distinguishes between *tsaph-
tsapha* and *'araba,* but without our being able to obtain any sure
botanic picture from it. The עֲרָבָה, whose branches belong to the
constituents of the *lulab* of the Feast of Tabernacles (Lev. xxiii.
40), is understood of the crack-willow [*Salix fragilis*], and even
in the passage before us is surely not distinguished with such
botanical precision but that the *gharab* and willow together with
the weeping-willow (*Salix Babylonica*) might be comprehended
under the word עֲרָבָה. On these trees of the country abounding
in streams the exiles hung their citherns. The time to take
delight in music was past, for μουσικὰ ἐν πένθει ἄκαιρος διή-
γησις, Sir. xxii. 6. Joyous songs, as the word שִׁיר designates
them, were ill suited to their situation.

In order to understand the כִּי in ver. 3, vers. 3 and 4 must
be taken together. They hung up their citherns; for though
their lords called upon them to sing in order that they might
divert themselves with their national songs, they did not feel
themselves in the mind for singing songs as they once resounded
at the divine services of their native land. The LXX., Targum, and Syriac take תּוֹלָלֵינוּ as a synonym of שׁוֹבֵינוּ, synonymous
with שׁוֹלָלֵינוּ, and so, in fact, that it signifies not, like שׁוֹלָל, the
spoiled and captive one, but the spoiler and he who takes others
prisoners. But there is no Aramaic שָׁלַל = תְּלַל. It might more
readily be referred back to a *Poel* תּוֹלֵל (= הֵתֵל), to disappoint,
deride (Hitzig); but the usage of the language does not favour
this, and a stronger meaning for the word would be welcome.
Either תּוֹלָל = תְּהוֹלָל, like מְהוֹלָל, cii. 9, signifies the raving one,
i.e. a bloodthirsty man or a tyrant, or from יָלַל, *ejulare,* one who
causes the cry of woe or a tormentor,—a signification which
commends itself in view of the words תּוֹשָׁב and תַּלְמִיד, which are
likewise formed with the preformative ת. According to the
sense the word ranks itself with an *Hiph.* הוֹלִיל, like תּוֹכֵחָה, תּוֹעֶלֶת,
with הוֹעִיל and הוֹכִיחַ, in a mainly abstract signification (Dietrich,
Abhandlungen, S. 160 f.). The דִּבְרֵי beside שִׁיר is used as in
xxxv. 20, lxv. 4, cv. 27, cxlv. 5, viz. partitively, dividing up the
genitival notion of the species: words of songs as being parts
or fragments of the national treasury of song, similar to מִשִּׁיר a
little further on, on which Rosenmüller correctly says: *sacrum*

aliquod carmen ex veteribus illis suis Sionicis. With the expression "song of Zion" alternates in ver. 4 "song of Jahve,"
which, as in 2 Chron. xxix. 27, cf. 1 Chron. xxv. 7, denotes
sacred or liturgical songs, that is to say, songs belonging to
Psalm poesy (including the *Cantica*).

Before ver. 4 we have to imagine that they answered the
request of the Babylonians at that time in the language that
follows, or thought thus within themselves when they withdrew
themselves from them. The meaning of the interrogatory exclamation is not that the singing of sacred songs in a foreign
land (חוּצה לארץ) is contrary to the law, for the Psalms continued to be sung even during the Exile, and were also enriched
by new ones. But the *shir* had an end during the Exile, in so
far as that it was obliged to retire from publicity into the quiet
of the family worship and of the houses of prayer, in order that
that which is holy might not be profaned; and since it was not,
as at home, accompanied by the trumpets of the priests and the
music of the Levites, it became more recitative than singing
properly so called, and therefore could not afford any idea of
the singing of their native land in connection with the worship
of God on Zion. From the striking contrast between the
present and the former times the people of the Exile had in
fact to come to the knowledge of their sins, in order that they
might get back by the way of penitence and earnest longing to
that which they had lost. Penitence and home-sickness were
at that time inseparable; for all those in whom the remembrance of Zion was lost gave themselves over to heathenism
and were excluded from the redemption. The poet, translated
into the situation of the exiles, and arming himself against the
temptation to apostasy and the danger of denying God, there-
fore says: If I forget thee, O Jerusalem, תִּשְׁכַּח יְמִינִי.   תִּשְׁכַּח has
been taken as an address to Jahve: *obliviscaris dexteræ meæ*
(*e.g.* Wolfgang Dachstein in his song "*An Wasserflüssen Babylon*"), but it is far from natural that Jerusalem and Jahve
should be addressed in one clause. Others take יְמִינִי as the subject and תִּשְׁכַּח transitively: *obliviscatur dextera mea, scil. artem
psallendi* (Aben-Ezra, Kimchi, Pagninus, Grotius, Hengstenberg, and others); but this ellipsis is arbitrary, and the interpolation of מִנִּי after יְמִינִי (von Ortenberg, following Olshausen)
produces an inelegant cadence. Others again assign a passive

sense to תִּשְׁכַּח: *oblivioni detur* (LXX., Italic, Vulgate, and Luther), or a half-passive sense, *in oblivione sit* (Jerome) ; but the thought : let my right hand be forgotten, is awkward and tame. *Obliviscatur me* (Syriac, Saadia, and the Psalterium Romanum) comes nearer to the true meaning. תִּשְׁכַּח is to be taken reflexively : *obliviscatur sui ipsius*, let it forget itself, or its service (Amyraldus, Schultens, Ewald, and Hitzig), which is equivalent to let it refuse or fail, become lame, become benumbed, much the same as we say of the arms or legs that they " go to sleep," and just as the Arabic نسى signifies both to forget and to become lame (cf. Gesenius, *Thesaurus*, p. 921*b*). La Harpe correctly renders : *O Jerusalem ! si je t'oublie jamais, que ma main oublie aussi le mouvement !* Thus there is a correspondence between vers. 5 and 6 : My tongue shall cleave to my palate if I do not remember thee, if I do not raise Jerusalem above the sum of my joy. אַזְכְּרֵכִי has the affixed *Chirek*, with which these later Psalms are so fond of adorning themselves. רֹאשׁ is apparently used as in cxix. 160 : *supra summam* (the totality) *lætitiæ meæ*, as Coccejus explains, *h.e. supra omnem lætitiam meam*. But why not then more simply עַל כֹּל, above the totality ? רֹאשׁ here signifies not κεφάλαιον, but κεφαλή : if I do not place Jerusalem upon the summit of my joy, *i.e.* my highest joy ; therefore, if I do not cause Jerusalem to be my very highest joy. His spiritual joy over the city of God is to soar above all earthly joys.

Vers. 7–9. The second part of the Psalm supplicates vengeance upon Edom and Babylon. We see from Obadiah's prophecy, which is taken up again by Jeremiah, how shamefully the Edomites, that brother-people related by descent to Israel and yet pre-eminently hostile to it, behaved in connection with the destruction of Jerusalem by the Chaldæans as their malignant, rapacious, and inhuman helpers. The repeated *imper. Piel* עָרוּ, from עָרָה (not *imper. Kal* from עָרַר, which would be עֹרוּ), ought to have been accented on the *ult.* ; it is, however, in both cases accented on the first syllable, the pausal עָרוּ (cf. כְּלוּ in xxxvii. 20, and also הַסּוּ, Neh. viii. 11) giving rise to the same accentuation of the other (in order that two tone-syllables might not come together). The *Pasek* also stands between the two repeated words in order that they may be duly separated, and secures, moreover, to the guttural initial of the second עָרוּ its distinct pronunciation (cf. Gen. xxvi. 28, Num. xxxv. 16). It is to be construed: lay bare, lay bare (as in Hab. iii. 13, cf. גִּלָּה in Mic. i. 6) in it (*Beth* of the place), or in respect of it (*Beth* of the object), even to the foundation, *i.e* raze it even to the ground, leave not one stone upon another. From the false brethren the imprecation turns to Babylon, the city of the imperial power of the world. The daughter, *i.e.* the population, of Babylon is addressed as הַשְּׁדוּדָה. It certainly seems the most natural to take this epithet as a designation of its doings which cry for vengeance. But it cannot in any case be translated: thou plunderer (Syriac like the Targum: *bozuzto;* Symmachus ἡ λῃστρίς), for שָׁדַד does not mean to rob and plunder, but to offer violence and to devastate. Therefore: thou devastator; but the word so pointed as we have it before us cannot have this signification: it ought to be הַשֹּׁדֵרָה, like בֹּגֵדָה in Jer. iii. 7, 10, or הַשַּׁדּוּדָה (with an unchangeable *ā*), corresponding to the Syriac active intensive form *âlûso*, oppressor, *gôdûfo*, slanderer, and the Arabic likewise active intensive form فَاعُول, *e.g.* *fâshûs*, a boaster, and also as an adjective: *gôz fâshûs*, empty nuts, cf. יָקוּשׁ = יָקֹשׁ, a fowler, like *nâtûr* (נאטור), a field-watcher. The form as it stands is *partic. pass.*, and signifies προνενομευμένη (Aquila), *vastata* (Jerome). It is possible that this may be said in the sense of *vastanda*, although in this sense of a *part. fut. pass.* the participles of the *Niphal* (*e.g.* xxii. 32, cii. 19) and of the *Pual* (xviii. 4) are more commonly used. It cannot at any rate signify *vastata* in an historical sense, with reference to the destruction of Babylon by Darius Hystaspes (Hengstenberg); for ver. 7 only prays that the retribution may come: it cannot therefore as yet have been executed; but if השדודה signified the already devastated one, it must (at least in the main) have been executed already. It might be more readily understood as a prophetical representation of the executed judgment of devastation; but this prophetic rendering coincides with the imprecative: the imagination of the Semite when he utters a curse sees the future as a realized fact. "Didst thou see the smitten one (*madrûb*)," *i.e.* he whom God must smite? Thus the Arab inquires for a person who is detested. "Pursue him who is

seized (*ilhak el-ma'chûdh*)," *i.e.* him whom God must allow thee
to seize! They speak thus inasmuch as the imagination at
once anticipates the seizure at the same time with the pursuit.
Just as here both *madrûb* and *ma'chûdh* are participles of *Kal*,
so therefore הַשְּׁדוּדָה may also have the sense of *vastanda* (which
must be laid waste!). That which is then further desired for
Babylon is the requital of that which it has done to Israel, Isa.
xlvii. 6. It is the same penal destiny, comprehending the children also, which is predicted against it in Isa. xiii. 16–18, as
that which was to be executed by the Medes. The young children (with reference to עוֹלָל, עוֹלֵל, *vid.* on viii. 3) are to be dashed
to pieces in order that a new generation may not raise up again
the world-wide dominion that has been overthrown, Isa. xiv.
21 sq. It is zeal for God that puts such harsh words into the
mouth of the poet. "That which is Israel's excellency and
special good fortune the believing Israelite desires to have bestowed upon the whole world, but for this very reason he desires
to see the hostility of the present world of nations against the
church of God broken" (Hofmann). On the other hand, it
cannot be denied that the "blessed" of this Psalm is not suited
to the mouth of the New Testament church. In the Old
Testament the church as yet had the form of a nation, and the
longing for the revelation of divine righteousness clothed itself
accordingly in a warlike garb.

PSALM CXXXVIII.

THE MEDIATOR AND PERFECTER.

1 I WILL give thanks unto Thee with my whole heart,
    Before the gods will I harp unto Thee.
2 I will worship towards Thy holy Temple,
    And give thanks unto Thy Name because of Thy mercy and
        Thy truth,
    That Thou hast magnified Thy promise above all Thy Name.

3 In the day that I called Thou didst answer me,
    Thou didst inspire me with courage—a lofty feeling per-
        vaded my soul.

4 All the kings of the earth shall give thanks unto Thee, Jahve,
   When they have heard the utterances of Thy mouth;
5 And they shall sing of the ways of Jahve,
   That great is the glory of Jahve:
6 For exalted is Jahve and He seeth the lowly,
   And the proud He knoweth well afar off.

7 If I walk in the midst of trouble, Thou dost revive me,
   Over the wrath of mine enemies dost Thou stretch forth
         Thy hand,
   And Thy right hand saveth me.
8 Jahve will perfect for me;
   Jahve, Thy mercy endureth for ever,
   The work of Thy hands—Thou wilt not forsake it.

There will come a time when the praise of Jahve, which
according to cxxxvii. 3 was obliged to be dumb in the presence
of the heathen, will, according to cxxxviii. 5, be sung by the
kings of the heathen themselves. In the LXX. Ps. cxxxvii.
side by side with $\tau\hat{\omega}$ $\Delta av\acute{\iota}\delta$ also has the inscription $'I\epsilon\rho\epsilon\mu\acute{\iota}ov$,
and Ps. cxxxviii. has $'A\gamma\gamma a\acute{\iota}ov$ $\kappa a\grave{\iota}$ $Z a\chi a\rho\acute{\iota}ov$. Perhaps these
statements are meant to refer back the existing recension of
the text of the respective Psalms to the prophets named (*vid.*
Köhler, *Haggai*, S. 33). From the fact that these names of
psalmodists added by the LXX. do not come down beyond
Malachi, it follows that the Psalm-collection in the mind of
the LXX. was made not later than in the time of Nehemiah.

The speaker in Ps. cxxxviii., to follow the lofty expectation
expressed in ver. 4, is himself a king, and according to the inscription, David. There is, however, nothing to favour his
being the author; the Psalm is, in respect of the Davidic
Psalms, composed as it were out of the soul of David—an echo
of 2 Sam. ch. vii. (1 Chron. ch. xvii.). The superabundant
promise which made the throne of David and of his seed an
eternal throne is here gratefully glorified. The Psalm can
at any rate be understood, if with Hengstenberg we suppose
that it expresses the lofty self-consciousness to which David
was raised after victorious battles, when he humbly ascribed the
glory to God and resolved to build Him a Temple in place of
the tent upon Zion.

Vers. 1, 2   The poet will give thanks to Him, whom he means without mentioning Him by name, for His mercy, *i.e.* His anticipating, condescending love, and for His truth, *i.e.* truthfulness and faithfulness, and more definitely for having magnified His promise (אִמְרָה) above all His Name, *i.e.* that He has given a promise which infinitely surpasses everything by which He has hitherto established a name and memorial for Himself (עַל־כָּל־שִׁמְךָ, with ō instead of ŭ, an anomaly that is noted by the Masora, *vid.* Baer's *Psalterium*, p. 133). If the promise by the mouth of Nathan (2 Sam. ch. vii.) is meant, then we may compare 2 Sam. vii. 21.   גְּדֻלָּה, גָּדוֹל, גָּדַל are repeated in that promise and its echo coming from the heart of David so frequently, that this הִגְדַּלְתָּ seems like a hint pointing to that history, which is one of the most important crises in the history of salvation. The expression נגד אלהים also becomes intelligible from this history. Ewald renders it: "in the presence of God!" which is surely meant to say: in the holy place (De Wette, Olshausen). But "before God will I sing praise to Thee (O God!)"—what a jumble! The LXX. renders ἐναντίον ἀγγέλων, which is in itself admissible and full of meaning,* but without coherence in the context of the Psalm, and also is to be rejected because it is on the whole very questionable whether the Old Testament language uses אלהים thus, without anything further to define it, in the sense of "angels." It might be more readily rendered "in the presence of the gods," viz. of the gods of the peoples (Hengstenberg, Hupfeld, and Hitzig); but in order to be understood of gods which are only seemingly such, it would require some addition. Whereas אלהים can without any addition denote the magisterial possessors of the dignity that is the type of the divine, as follows from lxxxii. 1 (cf. xlv. 7) in spite of Knobel, Graf, and Hupfeld; and thus, too (cf. נֶגֶד מְלָכִים in cxix. 46), we understand it here, with Rashi, Aben-Ezra, Kimchi, Flaminius, Bucer, Clericus, and others. What is meant are "the great who are in the earth," 2 Sam. vii. 9, with whom David, inasmuch as he became king from being a shepherd, is ranked, and

---

* Bellarmine: *Scio me psallentem tibi ab angelis, qui tibi assistunt, videri et attendi et ideo ita considerate me geram in psallendo, ut qui intelligam, in quo theatro consistam.*

above whom he has been lifted up by the promise of an eternal
kingship. Before these earthly "gods" will David praise the
God of the promise; they shall hear for their salutary confusion, for their willing rendering of homage, that God hath
made him "the highest with respect to the kings of the earth"
(lxxxix. 28).

Vers. 3-6. There are two things for which the poet gives
thanks to God: He has answered him in the days of trouble
connected with his persecution by Saul and in all distresses;
and by raising him to the throne, and granting him victory
upon victory, and promising him the everlasting possession of
the throne, He has filled him with a proud courage, so that
lofty feeling has taken up its abode in his soul, which was
formerly fearful about help. Just as רהב signifies impetuosity,
vehemence, and then also a monster, so הִרְהִיב signifies both to
break in upon one violently and overpoweringly (Cant. vi. 5;
cf. Syriac *arheb*, Arabic *arhaba*, to terrify), and to make any
one courageous, bold, and confident of victory. בְּנַפְשִׁי עֹז forms
a corollary to the verb that is marked by *Mugrash* or *Dechî*:
so that in my soul there was עֹז, *i.e.* power, viz. a consciousness
of power (cf. Judg. v. 21). The thanksgiving, which he, the
king of the promise, offers to God on account of this, will be
transmitted to all the kings of the earth when they shall hear
(שָׁמְעוּ in the sense of a *fut. exactum*) the words of His mouth,
i.e. the divine אִמְרָה, and they shall sing of (שִׁיר with בְּ, like
דִּבֶּר בְּ in lxxxvii. 3, שִׂיחַ בְּ in cv. 2 and frequently, הַלֵּל בְּ in xliv.
9, הִזְכִּיר בְּ in xx. 8, and the like) the ways of the God of the
history of salvation, they shall sing that great is the glory of
Jahve. Ver. 6 tells us by what means He has so super-glori-
ously manifested Himself in His leadings of David. He has
shown Himself to be the Exalted One who in His all-embracing
rule does not leave the lowly (cf. David's confessions in cxxxi.
1, 2 Sam. vi. 22) unnoticed (cxiii. 6), but on the contrary
makes him the especial object of His regard; and on the other
hand even from afar (cf. cxxxix. 2) He sees through (יֵדָע as in
xciv. 11, Jer. xxix. 23) the lofty one who thinks himself unobserved and conducts himself as if he were answerable to no
higher being (x. 4). In correct texts וגבה has *Mugrash*, and
ממרחק *Mercha*. The form of the *fut. Kal* יֵירַע is formed after
the analogy of the *Hiphil* forms יֵילִיל in Isa. xvi. 7, and fre-

quently, and יֵטִיב in Job xxiv. 21; probably the word is intended to be all the more emphatic, inasmuch as the first radical, which disappears in יֵדַע, is thus in a certain measure restored.*

Vers. 7, 8. Out of these experiences—so important for all mankind—of David, who has been exalted by passing through humiliation, there arise for him confident hopes concerning the future. The beginning of this strophe calls xxiii. 4 to mind. Though his way may lead through the midst of heart-oppressing trouble, Jahve will loose these bands of death and quicken him afresh (חִיָּה as in xxx. 4, lxxi. 20, and frequently). Though his enemies may rage, Jahve will stretch forth His hand threateningly and tranquillizingly over their wrath, and His right hand will save him. יְמִינְךָ is the subject according to cxxxix. 10 and other passages, and not (for why should it be supposed to be this?) *accus. instrumenti* (*vid.* lx. 7). In ver. 8 יִגְמֹר is intended just as in lvii. 3: the work begun He will carry out, ἐπιτελεῖν (Phil. i. 6); and בַּעֲדִי (according to its meaning, properly: covering me) is the same as עָלַי in that passage (cf. xiii. 6, cxlii. 8). The pledge of this completion is Jahve's everlasting mercy, which will not rest until the promise is become perfect truth and reality. Thus, therefore, He will not leave, forsake the works of His hands (*vid.* xc. 16 sq.), *i.e.*, as Hengstenberg correctly explains, everything that He has hitherto accomplished for David, from his deliverance out of the hands of Saul down to the bestowment of the promise— He will not let one of His works stand still, and least of all one that has been so gloriously begun. הִרְפָּה (whence תֶּרֶף) signifies to slacken, to leave slack, *i.e.* leave uncarried out, to leave to

---

* The Greek imperfects with the double (syllabic and temporal) augment, as ἑώρων, ἀνέῳγον, are similar. Chajug' also regards the first *Jod* in these forms as the preformative and the second as the radical, whereas Abulwalîd, *Gramm.* ch. xxvi. p. 170, explains the first as a prosthesis and the second as the preformative. According to the view of others, *e.g.* of Kimchi, יֵידַע might be *fut. Hiph.* weakened from יְהֵדַע (יְהֵידִיעַ), which, apart from the unsuitable meaning, assumes a change of consonants that is all the more inadmissible as ידע itself springs from וְדַע. Nor is it to be supposed that יֵידַע is modified from יֵידַע (Luzzatto, § 197), because it is nowhere written יֵידַע.

itself, as in Neh. vi. 3. אַל expresses a negation with a measure of inward excitement.

PSALM CXXXIX.

ADORATION OF THE OMNISCIENT AND OMNIPRESENT ONE.

1 JAHVE, Thou searchest and knowest me!
2 THOU knowest my sitting down and my rising up,
Thou understandest my thought afar off.
3 My path and my lying down Thou searchest,
And with all my ways art Thou familiar.
4 For there is not a word on my tongue—
Lo, Thou, O Jahve, knowest it altogether.
5 Behind and before dost Thou surround me,
And hast laid Thy hand upon me.
6 Incomprehensible to me is such knowledge,
It is too high, I have not grown up to it.
7 Whither could I go from Thy Spirit,
And whither could I flee from Thy presence?!
8 If I should ascend to heaven, there art THOU ;
And if I should make Hades my resting-place, here art
Thou also.
9 If I should raise the wings of the morning,
If I should settle down at the extremity of the sea—
10 There also Thy hand would guide me,
And Thy right hand lay hold of me.
11 And if I should say: Let nothing but darkness enwrap me,
And let the light round about me become night—
12 Even the darkness would not be too dark for Thee,
And the night would be to Thee bright as the day;
Darkness and light are alike to Thee.

13 For THOU hast brought forth my reins,
Thou didst interweave me in my mother's womb.
14 I give Thee thanks that I am fearfully, wonderfully made;
Wonderful are Thy works,
And my soul knoweth it right well.

15 My bones were not hidden from Thee,
   I who was wrought in secret,
   Curiously wrought in the depths of the earth.
16 When an embryo Thine eyes saw me,
   And in Thy book were they all written:
   Days which were already sketched out,
   And for it one among them.
17 And how precious are Thy thoughts unto me, O God,
   How mighty is their sum!
18 If I would count them, they are more than the sand;
   I awake and I am still with Thee.

19 Oh that Thou wouldest slay the wicked, Eloah;
   And ye men of blood-guiltiness, depart from me!
20 They who mention Thee craftily,
   Speak out deceitfully—Thine adversaries.
21 Should I not hate those who hate Thee, Jahve,
   And be indignant at those who rise up against Thee?!
22 With the utmost hatred do I hate them,
   They are to me as mine own enemies.
23 Search me, O God, and know my heart,
   Prove me and know my thoughts,
24 And see whether there is in me any way of pain,
   And lead me in the everlasting way!

In this Aramaizing Psalm what the preceding Psalm says in ver. 6 comes to be carried into effect, viz.: *for Jahve is exalted and He seeth the lowly, and the proud He knoweth from afar.* This Psalm has manifold points of contact with its predecessor. From a theological point of view it is one of the most instructive of the Psalms, and both as regards its contents and poetic character in every way worthy of David. But it is only inscribed לדוד because it is composed after the Davidic model, and is a counterpart to such Psalms as Ps. xix. and to other Davidic didactic Psalms. For the addition למנצח neither proves its ancient Davidic origin, nor in a general way its origin in the period prior to the Exile, as Ps. lxxiv. for example shows, which was at any rate not composed prior to the time of the Chaldæan catastrophe.

The Psalm falls into three parts: vers. 1b–12, 13–18,

19–24; the strophic arrangement is not clear. The first part celebrates the Omniscient and Omnipresent One. The poet knows that he is surrounded on all sides by God's knowledge and His presence; His Spirit is everywhere and cannot be avoided; and His countenance is turned in every direction and inevitably, in wrath or in love. In the second part the poet continues this celebration with reference to the origin of man; and in the third part he turns in profound vexation of spirit towards the enemies of such a God, and supplicates for himself His proving and guidance. In vers. 1 and 4 God is called *Jahve*, in ver. 17 *El*, in ver. 19 *Eloah*, in ver. 21 again *Jahve*, and in ver. 23 again *El*. Strongly as this Psalm is marked by the depth and pristine freshness of its ideas and feeling, the form of its language is still such as is without precedent in the Davidic age. To all appearance it is the Aramæo-Hebrew idiom of the post-exilic period pressed into the service of poetry. The Psalm apparently belongs to those Psalms which, in connection with a thoroughly classical cha- racter of form, bear marks of the influence which the Aramaic language of the Babylonian kingdom exerted over the exiles. This influence affected the popular dialect in the first instance, but the written language also did not escape it, as the Books of Daniel and Ezra show; and even the poetry of the Psalms is not without traces of this retrograde movement of the lan- guage of Israel towards the language of the patriarchal an- cestral house. In the *Cod. Alex.* Ζαχαρίου is added to the τῷ Δαυὶδ ψαλμός, and by a second hand ἐν τῇ διασπορᾷ, which Origen also met with " in some copies."

Vers. 1–7. The Aramaic forms in this strophe are the ἅπαξ λεγομ. רֵעַ (ground-form רֶעְיִ) in vers. 2 and 17, endea- vour, desire, thinking, like רְעוּת and רַעְיוֹן in the post-exilic books, from רָעָה (רְעָא), *cupere, cogitare;* and the ἅπ. λεγ. רֶבַע in ver. 3, equivalent to רֵבֶץ, a lying down, if רִבְעִי be not rather an infinitive like בִּלְעִי in Job vii. 19, since אָרְחִי is undoubtedly not inflected from אֹרַח, but, as being infinitive, like עָבְרִי in Deut. iv. 21, from אָרַח; and the verb אָרַח also, with the ex- ception of this passage, only occurs in the speeches of Elihu (Job xxxiv. 8), which are almost more strongly Aramaizing than the Book of Job itself. Further, as an Aramaizing feature we have the objective relation marked by *Lamed* in the expression בַּנְתָּה לְרֵעִי, Thou understandest my thinking, as in cxvi. 16, cxxix. 3, cxxxv. 11, cxxxvi. 19 sq. The monostichic opening is after the Davidic style, *e.g.* xxiii. 1*b*. Among the prophets, Isaiah in particular is fond of such thematic introductions as we have here in ver. 1*b*. On וַתֵּדַע instead of וַתֵּדָעֵנִי *vid.* on cvii. 20; the pronominal object stands once beside the first verb, or even beside the second (2 Kings ix. 25), instead of twice (Hitzig). The " me" is then expanded: sitting down, rising up, walking and lying, are the sum of human conditions or states. רֵעִי is the totality or sum of the life of the spirit and soul of man, and דְּרָכַי the sum of human action. The divine knowledge, as וַתֵּדַע says, is the result of the scrutiny of man. The poet, however, in vers. 2 and 3 uses the perfect throughout as a mood of that which is practically existing, because that scrutiny is a scrutiny that is never unexecuted, and the knowledge is consequently an ever-present knowledge. מֵרָחוֹק is meant to say that He sees into not merely the thought that is fully fashioned and matured, but even that which is being evolved. זֵרִיתָ from זֵרָה is combined by Luther (with Azulai and others) with זֵר, *a wreath* (from זֵרַר, *constringere, cingere*), inasmuch as he renders: whether I walk or lie down, Thou art round about me (*Ich gehe oder lige, so bistu vmb mich*). זֵרָה ought to have the same meaning here, if with Wetzstein one were to compare the Arabic, and more particularly Beduin, نرى, *dherâ*, to protect; the notion of affording protection does not accord with this train of thought, which has reference to God's omniscience: what ought therefore to be meant is a hedging round which secures its object to the knowledge, or even a protecting that places it in security against any exchanging, which will not suffer the object to escape it.*

---

* This *Verb. tert.* و *et* ى is old, and the derivative *dherâ*, protection, is an elegant word; with reference to another derivative, *dherwe*, a wall of rock protecting one from the winds, *vid. Job*, ii. 23, note. The II. form (*Piel*) signifies to protect in the widest possible sense, *e.g.* (in *Neshwân*, ii. 343*b*), " نرى الشاء, he protected the sheep (against being exchanged) by leaving a lock of wool upon their backs when they were shorn, by which they might be recognised among other sheep."

The Arabic دری, to know, which is far removed in sound, is
by no means to be compared; it is related to دأ, to push, urge
forward, and denotes knowledge that is gained by testing and
experimenting. But we also have no need of that ذری, to
protect, since we can remain within the range of the guaranteed Hebrew usage, inasmuch as זָרָה, to winnow, *i.e.* to spread
out that which has been threshed and expose it to the current
of the wind, in Arabic likewise ذری (whence מִזְרֶה, *midhrâ*, a
winnowing-fork, like רַחַת, *racht*, a winnowing-shovel), gives an
appropriate metaphor. Here it is equivalent to: to investigate
and search out to the very bottom; LXX., Symmachus, and
Theodotion, ἐξιχνίασας, after which the Italic renders *investi-
gasti*, and Jerome *eventilasti*. הִסְכִּין with the accusative, as in
Job xxii. 21 with עִם: to enter into neighbourly, close, familiar
relationship, or to stand in such relationship, with any one;
cogn. שָׁכֵן, سكن. God is acquainted with all our ways not only
superficially, but closely and thoroughly, as that to which He
is accustomed.

In ver. 4 this omniscience of God is illustratively corroborated with כִּי; ver. 4*b* has the value of a relative clause, which,
however, takes the form of an independent clause. מִלָּה (pronounced by Jerome in his letter to Sunnia and Fretela, § 82,
MALA) is an Aramaic word that has been already incorporated in the poetry of the Davidico-Salomonic age. כֻּלָּהּ signifies both all of it and every one. In ver. 5 Luther has been
misled by the LXX. and Vulgate, which take צוּר in the signification *formare* (whence צוּרָה, *forma*); it signifies, as the
definition " behind and before" shows, to surround, encompass.
God is acquainted with man, for He holds him surrounded on
all sides, and man can do nothing, if God, whose confining
hand he has lying upon him (Job ix. 23), does not allow him
the requisite freedom of motion. Instead of דַּעְתְּךָ (LXX. ἡ
γνῶσίς σου) the poet purposely says in ver. 6*a* merely דַּעַת: a
knowledge, so all-penetrating, all-comprehensive as God's knowledge. The *Kerî* reads פְּלִיאָה, but the *Chethîb* פְּלִאיָה is supported by the *Chethîb* פִּלְאִי in Judg. xiii. 18, the *Kerî* of which
there is not פֶּלִיא, but פֶּלִי (the pausal form of an adjective פְּלִי,

the feminine of which would be פְּלִיָּה). With מִמֶּנִּי the transcendence, with נִשְׂגְּבָה the unattainableness, and with לֹא־אוּכַל
לָהּ the incomprehensibleness of the fact of the omniscience of
God is expressed, and with this, to the mind of the poet, coincides God's omnipresence; for true, not merely phenomenal,
knowledge is not possible without the immanence of the knowing one in the thing known. God, however, is omnipresent,
sustaining the life of all things by His Spirit, and revealing
Himself either in love or in wrath,—what the poet styles His
countenance. To flee from this omnipresence (מִן, away from),
as the sinner and he who is conscious of his guilt would gladly
do, is impossible. Concerning the first אָנָה, which is here
accented on the *ultima*, *vid.* on cxvi. 4.

Vers. 8–12. The future form אֶפַּק, customary in the Aramaic,
may be derived just as well from סָלַק (סְלִק), by means of the
same mode of assimilation as in יִסֹּב=יְסַבֵּב, as from נָסַק (נְסֵק),
which latter is certainly only insecurely established by Dan.
vi. 24, לְהַנְסָקָה (cf. לְהַנְזָקַת, Ezra iv. 22; הַנְפֵּק, Dan. v. 2), since
the *Nun*, as in לְהַנְעָלָה, Dan. iv. 3, can also be a compensation
for the resolved doubling (*vid.* Bernstein in the *Lexicon Chrestom. Kirschianæ*, and Levy *s.v.* נְסַק). אִם with the simple future
is followed by cohortatives (*vid.* on lxxiii. 16) with the equivalent אַצִּיעָה among them: *et si stratum facerem (mihi) infernum*
(accusative of the object as in Isa. lviii. 5), etc. In other
passages the wings of the sun (Mal. iii. 20 [iv. 2]) and of the
wind (xviii. 11) are mentioned, here we have the wings of the
morning's dawn. *Pennæ auroræ*, Eugubinus observes (1548),
est velocissimus auroræ per omnem mundum decursus. It is
therefore to be rendered: If I should lift wings (נָשָׂא כְנָפַיִם as
in Ezek. x. 16, and frequently) such as the dawn of the morning
has, *i.e.* could I fly with the swiftness with which the dawn of
the morning spreads itself over the eastern sky, towards the
extreme west and alight there. Heaven and Hades, as being
that which is superterrestrial and subterrestrial, and the east and
west are set over against one another. אַחֲרִית יָם is the extreme
end of the sea (of the Mediterranean with the " isles of the Gentiles "). In ver. 10 follows the apodosis: nowhere is the hand
of God, which governs everything, to be escaped, for *dextera
Dei ubique est.* וָאֹמַר (not וָאֹמֵר, Ezek. xiii. 15), "therefore I
spake," also has the value of a hypothetical protasis: *quodsi*

dixerim. אַךְ and חֹשֶׁךְ belong together: *meræ tenebræ* (*vid:* xxxix. 6 sq.); but יְשׁוּפֵנִי is obscure. The signification secured to it of *conterere, contundere*, in Gen. iii. 15, Job ix. 17, which is followed by the LXX. (Vulgate) καταπατήσει, is inappropriate to darkness. The signification *inhiare*, which may be deduced as possible from שָׁאַף, suits relatively better, yet not thoroughly well (why should it not have been יְבַלְעֵנִי?). The signification *obvelare*, however, which one expects to find, and after which the Targum, Symmachus, Jerome, Saadia, and others render it, seems only to be guessed at from the connection, since שׁוּף has not this signification in any other instance, and in favour of it we cannot appeal either to נָשַׁף—whence נֶשֶׁף, which belongs together with נָשַׁב, נָשַׁם, and נָפַשׁ—or to עָטַף, the root of which is עט (עָטָה), or to צָעַף, whence צָעִיף, which does not signify to cover, veil, but according to ضعف, to fold, fold together, to double. We must therefore either assign to יְשׁוּפֵנִי the signification *operiat me* without being able to prove it, or we must put a verb of this signification in its place, viz. יְשׁוּכֵנִי (Ewald) or יְעוּפֵנִי (Böttcher), which latter is the more commendable here, where darkness (חֹשֶׁךְ, synon. מָעוּף, עֵיפָה) is the subject: And if I should say, let nothing but darkness cover me, and as night (the predicate placed first, as in Amos iv. 13) let the light become about me, *i.e.* let the light become night that shall surround and cover me (בַּעֲדֵנִי, poetic for בַּעֲדִי, like תַּחְתֵּנִי in 2 Sam. ch. xxii.)—the darkness would spread abroad no obscurity (cv. 28) that should extend beyond (מִן) Thy piercing eye and remove me from Thee. In the word יָאִיר, too, the *Hiphil* signification is not lost: the night would give out light from itself, as if it were the day; for the distinction of day and night has no conditioning influence upon God, who is above and superior to all created things (*der Uebercreatürliche*), who is light in Himself. The two כ are correlative, as *e.g.* in 1 Kings xxii. 4. חֲשֵׁיכָה (with a superfluous *Jod*) is an old word, but אוֹרָה (cf. Aramaic אוֹרְתָּא) is a later one.

Vers. 13–18. The fact that man is manifest to God even to the very bottom of his nature, and in every place, is now confirmed from the origin of man. The development of the child in the womb was looked upon by the Israelitish Chokma as one of the greatest mysteries, Eccles. xi. 5; and here the poet praises this coming into being as a marvellous work of the omniscient and omnipresent omnipotence of God. קָנָה here signifies *condere*; and סָכַךְ not: to cover, protect, as in cxl. 8, Job. xl. 22, prop. to cover with network, to hedge in, but: to plait, interweave, viz. with bones, sinews, and veins, like יְשֹׁכֵךְ in Job x. 11. The reins are made specially prominent in order to mark them, the seat of the tenderest, most secret emotions, as the work of Him who trieth the heart and the reins. The προσευχή becomes in ver. 14 the εὐχαριστία: I give thanks unto Thee that I have wonderfully come into being under fearful circumstances, *i.e.* circumstances exciting a shudder, viz. of astonishment (נוֹרָאוֹת as in lxv. 6). נִפְלָה (= נִפְלָא) is the passive to הִפְלָה, iv. 4, xvii. 7. Hitzig regards נִפְלֵיתָ (Thou hast shown Thyself wonderful), after the LXX., Syriac, Vulgate, and Jerome, as the only correct reading; but the thought which is thereby gained comes indeed to be expressed in the following line, ver. 14*b*, which sinks down into tautology in connection with this reading. עֹצֶם (collectively equivalent to עֲצָמִים, Eccles. xi. 5) is the bones, the skeleton, and, starting from that idea, more generally the state of being as a sum-total of elements of being. אֲשֶׁר, without being necessarily a conjunction (Ew. § 333, *a*), attaches itself to the suffix of עָצְמִי. רֻקַּם, " to be worked in different colours, or also embroidered," of the system of veins ramifying the body, and of the variegated colouring of its individual members, more particularly of the inward parts; perhaps, however, more generally with a retrospective conception of the colours of the outline following the undeveloped beginning, and of the forming of the members and of the organism in general.* The mother's womb is here called not merely סֵתֶר (cf. Æschylus' *Eumenides*, 665: ἐν σκότοισι νηδύος τεθραμμένη, and the designation of the place where the fœtus is formed as " a threefold darkness" in the Koran, *Sur.* xxxix. 8), the *ē* of which is retained here in pause (*vid.* Böttcher, *Lehrbuch*, § 298), but by a bolder appellation תַּחְתִּיּוֹת אָרֶץ, the lowest parts of the earth, *i.e.* the interior of the earth (*vid.* on lxiii. 10) as being the secret laboratory of the earthly origin, with the same retro-

---

* In the Talmud the egg of a bird or of a reptile is called מְרֻקֶּמֶת, when the outlines of the developed embryo are visible in it; and likewise the mole (*mola*), when traces of human organization can be discerned in it.

spective reference to the first formation of the human body out
of the dust of the earth, as when Job says, ch. i. 21: "naked
came I out of my mother's womb, and naked shall I return
thither"—שָׁמָּה, viz. εἰς τὴν γῆν τὴν μητέρα πάντων, Sir. xl. 1.
The interior of Hades is also called בֶּטֶן שְׁאוֹל in Jonah ii. 3 [2],
Sir. li. 5. According to the view of Scripture the mode of
Adam's creation is repeated in the formation of every man, Job
xxxiii. 6, cf. 4. The earth was the mother's womb of Adam,
and the mother's womb out of which the child of Adam comes
forth is the earth out of which it is taken.

(Ver. 16.) The embryo folded up in the shape of an egg is
here called גֹּלֶם, from גָּלַם, to roll or wrap together (cf. *glomus*, a
ball), in the Talmud said of any kind of unshapen mass (LXX.
ἀκατέργαστον, Symmachus ἀμόρφωτον) and raw material, *e.g.*
of the wood or metal that is to be formed into a vessel (*Chullin*
25*a*, to which Saadia has already referred).* As to the rest, compare similar retrospective glances into the embryonic state in Job
x. 8–12, 2 Macc. vii. 22 sq. (*Psychology*, S. 209 ff., tr. pp. 247
sq.). On the words *in libro tuo* Bellarmine makes the following correct observation: *quia habes apud te exemplaria sive
ideas omnium, quomodo pictor vel sculptor scit ex informi materia
quid futurum sit, quia videt exemplar.* The signification of the
future יִכָּתֵבוּ is regulated by רָאוּ, and becomes, as relating to the
synchronous past, *scribebantur.* The days יֻצָּרוּ, which were already formed, are the subject. It is usually rendered: "the
days which had first to be formed." If יֻצָּרוּ could be equivalent to יִיָּצְרוּ, it would be to be preferred; but this rejection of
the *præform. fut.* is only allowed in the *fut. Piel* of the verbs
Pe Jod, and that after a *Waw convertens, e.g.* וַיִּבֶּשׁ = וַיְיַבֵּשׁ,
Nah. i. 4 (cf. Caspari on Obad. ver. 11).† Accordingly,
assuming the original character of the לֹא in a negative signification, it is to be rendered: The days which were (already)
formed, and there was not one among them, *i.e.* when none
among them had as yet become a reality. The suffix of כֻּלָּם

---

* Epiphanius, *Hær.* xxx. § 31, says the Hebrew γολμη signifies the
peeled grains of spelt or wheat before they are mixed up and backed, the
still raw (only bruised) flour-grains—a signification that can now no longer
be supported by examples.

† But outside the Old Testament it also occurs in the *Pual*, though as a
wrong use of the word; *vide* my *Anekdota* (1841), S. 372 f.

points to the succeeding יָמִים, to which יֻצָּרוּ is appended as an attributive clause; וְלֹא אֶחָד בָּהֶם is subordinated to this יֻצָּרוּ: *cum non* or *nondum* (Job xxii. 16) *unus inter eos = unus eorum* (Ex. xiv. 28) *esset*. But the expression (instead of וְעוֹד לֹא הָיָה or טֶרֶם יִהְיֶה) remains doubtful, and it becomes a question whether the *Kerî* ולו (*vid.* on c. 3), which stands side by side with the *Chethîb* ולא (which the LXX., Aquila, Symmachus, Theodotion, the Targum, Syriac, Jerome, and Saadia follow), is not to be preferred. This ולו, referred to גלמי, gives the acceptable meaning: and for it (viz. its birth) one among them (these days), without our needing to make any change in the proposed exposition down to יצרו. We decide in favour of this, because this ולו אחד בהם does not, as ולא אחד בהם, make one feel to miss any הָיָה, and because the וְלִי which begins ver. 17 connects itself to it by way of continuation. The accentuation has failed to discern the reference of כלם to the following ימים, inasmuch as it places *Olewejored* against יכתבו. Hupfeld follows this accentuation, referring כלם back to גלמי as a coil of days of one's life; and Hitzig does the same, referring it to the embryos. But the precedence of the relative pronoun occurs in other instances also,* and is devoid of all harshness, especially in connection with כֻּלָּם, which directly signifies altogether (*e.g.* Isa. xliii. 14). It is the confession of the omniscience that is united with the omnipotence of God, which the poet here gives utterance to with reference to himself, just as Jahve says with reference to Jeremiah, Jer. i. 5. Among the days which were preformed in the idea of God (cf. on יצרו, Isa. xxii. 11, xxxvii. 26) there was also one, says the poet, for the embryonic beginning of my life. The divine knowledge embraces the beginning, development, and completion of all things (*Psychology*, S. 37 ff., tr. pp. 46 sqq.). The knowledge of the thoughts of God which are written in the book of creation and revelation is the poet's cherished possession, and to ponder over them is his favourite pursuit: they are precious to him, יָקְרוּ (after xxxvi. 8), not: difficult of comprehension (*schwerbegreiflich*, Maurer, Olshausen), after Dan. ii. 11, which

---

* The Hebrew poet, says Gesenius (*Lehrgebäude*, S. 739 f.), sometimes uses the pronoun before the thing to which it referred has even been spoken of. This phenomenon belongs to the Hebrew style generally, *vid.* my *Anekdota* (1841), S. 382.

would surely have been expressed by עֲמְקוּ (xcii. 6), more readily:
very weighty (*schwergewichtig*, Hitzig), but better according to
the prevailing Hebrew usage: highly valued (*schwergewerthet*),
cara.*   "Their sums" are powerful, prodigious (xl. 6), and
cannot be brought to a *summa summarum*. If he desires to
count them (*fut. hypothet.* as in xci. 7, Job xx. 24), they prove
themselves to be more than the sand with its grains, that is to
say, innumerable. He falls asleep over the pondering upon
them, wearied out; and when he wakes up, he is still with God,
i.e. still ever absorbed in the contemplation of the Unsearchable
One, which even the sleep of fatigue could not entirely inter-
rupt. Ewald explains it somewhat differently: if I am lost in
the stream of thoughts and images, and recover myself from
this state of reverie, yet I am still ever with Thee, without
coming to an end. But it could only perhaps be interpreted
thus if it were הַעִירוֹתִי or הִתְעוֹרַרְתִּי. Hofmann's interpretation
is altogether different: I will count them, the more numerous
than the sand, when I awake and am continually with Thee,
viz. in the other world, after the awaking from the sleep of
death. This is at once impossible, because הקיצתי cannot here,
according to its position, be a *perf. hypotheticum*. Also in connection with this interpretation עוֹד would be an inappropriate
expression for "continually," since the word only has the sense
of the continual duration of an action or a state already existing; here of one that has not even been closed and broken off
by sleep. He has not done; waking and dreaming and waking
up, he is carried away by that endless, and yet also endlessly
attractive, pursuit, the most fitting occupation of one who is
awake, and the sweetest (cf. Jer. xxxi. 26) of one who is asleep
and dreaming.

Vers. 19–21. And this God is by many not only not believed in and loved, but even hated and blasphemed! The
poet now turns towards these enemies of God in profound vexation of spirit. The אִם, which is conditional in ver. 8, here is
an optative *o si*, as in lxxxi. 9, xcv. 7. The expression תִּקְטֹל
אֱלוֹהַּ reminds one of the Book of Job, for, with the exception of
our Psalm, this is the only book that uses the verb קָטַל, which

---

* It should be noted that the radical idea of the verb, viz. being heavy
(German *schwer*), is retained in all these renderings.—TR.

is more Aramaic than Hebrew, and the divine name *Eloah*
occurs more frequently in it than anywhere else. The transition from the optative to the imperative סוּרוּ is difficult ; it
would have been less so if the *Waw copul.* had been left out :
cf. the easier expression in vi. 9, cxix. 115. But we may not
on this account seek to read יָסֻרוּ, as Olshausen does. Everything here is remarkable ; the whole Psalm has a characteristic
form in respect to the language. מֶנִּי is the ground-form of the
overloaded מִמֶּנִּי, and is also like the Book of Job, ch. xxi. 16,
cf. מֶנְהוּ ch. iv. 12, Ps. lxviii. 24. The mode of writing יֹמְרֻוךָ
(instead of which, however, the Babylonian texts had יֹאמְרֻוךָ) is
the same as in 2 Sam. xix. 15, cf. in 2 Sam. xx. 9 the same
melting away of the *Aleph* into the preceding vowel in connection with אָחַז, in 2 Sam. xxii. 40 in connection with אַוּר, and
in Isa. xiii. 20 with אָהַל. Construed with the accusative of the
person, אָמַר here signifies to declare any one, *profiteri*, a meaning which, we confess, does not occur elsewhere. But לִמְזִמָּה
(cf. לְמִרְמָה, xxiv. 4 ; the Targum : who swear by Thy name for
wantonness) and the parallel member of the verse, which as it
runs is moulded after Ex. xx. 7, show that it has not to be
read יַמְרֻוךָ (Quinta : παρεπίκρανάν σε). The form נָשׂוּא, with
Aleph otians, is also remarkable ; it ought at least to have been
written נָשֻׂאוּ (cf. נִרְפּוּא, Ezek. xlvii. 8) instead of the customary
נָשְׂאוּ ; yet the same mode of writing is found in the *Niphal* in
Jer. x. 5, יִנָּשׂוּא, it assumes a ground-form נשׂה (xxxii. 1) = נָשָׂא,
and is to be judged of according to אָבוּא in Isa. xxviii. 12 [Ges.
§ 23, 3, rem. 3]. Also one feels the absence of the object to
נָשׂוּא לַשָּׁוְא. It is meant to be supplied according to the decalogue,
Ex. xx. 7, which certainly makes the alteration שְׁמֶךָ (Böttcher,
Olsh.) or זִכְרְךָ (Hitzig on Isa. xxvi. 13), instead of עָרֶיךָ, natural.
But the text as we now have it is also intelligible : the object to נשׂוא is derived from יִמְרֻוךָ, and the following עָרֶיךָ is
an explanation of the subject intended in נשׂוּא that is introduced subsequently. Ps. lxxxix. 52 proves the possibility of this
structure of a clause. It is correctly rendered by Aquila ἀντί-
ζηλοί σου, and Symmachus οἱ ἐναντίοι σου. עָר, an enemy, prop.
one who is zealous, a zealot (from עוּר, or rather עִיר, = غَار *med.*
Je, ζηλοῦν, whence עִיר, غَيَرٌ = קִנְאָה), is a word that is guaranteed by 1 Sam. xxviii. 16, Dan. iv. 16, and as being an Ara-

maism is appropriate to this Psalm. The form תְּקוֹמֵם for
מִתְקוֹמֵם has cast away the preformative *Mem* (cf. שְׂפָתִים and
מִקְרֵה, מִשְׁפָּתִים in Deut. xxiii. 11 for מִמְקְרֵה); the suffix is to be
understood according to xvii. 7. *Pasek* stands between יהוה
and אֶשְׂנָא in order that the two words may not be read together
(cf. Job xxvii. 13, and above x. 3). הִתְקוֹטֵט as in the recent
Ps. cxix. 158. The emphasis in ver. 22*b* lies on לִי; the poet
regards the adversaries of God as enemies of his own. תַּכְלִית
takes the place of the adjective: *extremo (odio) odi eos*. Such
is the relation of the poet to the enemies of God, but without
indulging any self-glorying.

Vers. 23, 24. He sees in them the danger which threatens
himself, and prays God not to give him over to the judgment of
self-delusion, but to lay bare the true state of his soul. The fact
"Thou hast searched me," which the beginning of the Psalm
confesses, is here turned into a petitioning "search me." Instead of רֵעַים in ver. 17, the poet here says שַׂרְעַפִּים, which signifies branches (Ezek. xxxi. 5) and branchings of the act of
thinking (thoughts and cares, xciv. 19). The *Resh* is epen-
thetic, for the first form is שְׂעִפִּים, Job iv. 13, xx. 2. The poet
thus sets the very ground and life of his heart, with all its outward manifestations, in the light of the divine omniscience.
And in ver. 24 he prays that God would see whether any
דֶּרֶךְ־עֹצֶב cleaves to him (בִּי as in 1 Sam. xxv. 24), by which is
not meant "a way of idols" (Rosenmüller, Gesenius, and
Maurer), after Isa. xlviii. 5, since an inclination towards, or
even apostasy to, heathenism cannot be an unknown sin; nor
to a man like the writer of this Psalm is heathenism any
power of temptation. דרך בֶּצַע (Grätz) might more readily be
admissible, but דרך עֹצֶב is a more comprehensive notion, and
one more in accordance with this closing petition. The poet
gives this name to the way that leads to the pain, torture, viz.
of the inward and outward punishments of sin; and, on the
other hand, the way along which he wishes to be guided he
calls דֶּרֶךְ עוֹלָם, the way of endless continuance (LXX., Vulgate, Luther), not the way of the former times, after Jer. vi.
16 (Maurer, Olshausen), which thus by itself is ambiguous (as
becomes evident from Job xxii. 15, Jer. xviii. 15), and also
does not furnish any direct antithesis. The "everlasting
way" is the way of God (xxvii. 11), the way of the righteous,
which stands fast for ever and shall not "perish" (i. 6).

PSALM CXL.

PRAYER FOR PROTECTION AGAINST WICKED, CRAFTY MEN

2 DELIVER me, Jahve, from wicked men,
  From the violent man preserve me,
3 Who plot wickedness in the heart,
  Daily do they stir up wars.
4 They sharpen their tongue like a serpent,
  Adder's poison is under their lips.   (*Sela.*)

5 Keep me, Jahve, from the hands of the wicked,
  From the violent man preserve me,
  Who purpose to thrust aside my footsteps.
6 The proud hide snares for me and cords,
  They spread nets close by the path,
  They set traps for me.   (*Sela.*)

7 I say to Jahve : My God art Thou,
  Oh give ear, Jahve, to the cry of my supplication.
8 Jahve the Lord is the stronghold of my salvation,
  Thou coverest my head in the day of equipment.
9 Grant not, Jahve, the desires of the wicked ;
  Let not his device prosper, that they may not be lifted up.
      (*Sela.*)

10 The head of those who compass me about—let the trouble
        of their lips cover them !
11 Let burning coals be cast down upon them, let them be
        cast into the fire,
   Into abysses out of which they may never rise up !
12 Let not the man of the tongue be established on the earth,
   The man of violence—let wickedness hunt him in violent
        haste !

13 I know that Jahve will carry through the cause of the
        afflicted,
   The right of the poor.
14 Yea, the righteous shall give thanks unto Thy Name,
   The upright shall dwell beside Thy countenance.

The close of the preceding Psalm is the key to David's position and mood in the presence of his enemies which find expression in this Psalm. He complains here of serpent-like, crafty, slanderous adversaries, who are preparing themselves for war against him, and with whom he will at length have to fight in open battle. The Psalm, in its form more bold than beautiful, justifies its לדוד in so far as it is Davidic in thoughts and figures, and may be explained from the circumstances of the rebellion of Absalom, to which as an outbreak of Ephraim-itish jealousy the rebellion of Sheba ben Bichri the Benjamite attached itself. Ps. lviii. and lxiv. are very similar. The close of all three Psalms sounds much alike, they agree in the use of rare forms of expression, and their language becomes fearfully obscure in style and sound where they are directed against the enemies.

Vers. 2–4. The assimilation of the *Nun* of the verb נָצַר is given up, as in lxi. 8, lxxviii. 7, and frequently, in order to make the form more full-toned. The relative clause shows that אִישׁ חֲמָסִים (*vid.* vol. i. 277) is not intended to be understood exclusively of one person. בְּלֵב strengthens the notion of that which is deeply concealed and premeditated. It is doubtful whether יָגוּרוּ signifies to form into troops or to stir up. But from the fact that גוּר in lvi. 7, lix. 4, Isa. liv. 15, signifies not *congregare* but *se congregare*, it is to be inferred that גוּר in the passage before us, like גֵּרָה (or הִתְגָּרָה in Deut. ii. 9, 24), in Syriac and Targumic גְּרַג, signifies *concitare*, to excite (cf. שׁוּר together with שָׂרָה, Hos. xii. 4 sq.). In ver. 4 the Psalm coincides with lxiv. 4, lviii. 5. They sharpen their tongue, so that it inflicts a fatal sting like the tongue of a serpent, and under their lips, shooting out from thence, is the poison of the adder (cf. Cant. iv. 11). עַכְשׁוּב is a ἅπαξ λεγομ. not from כָּשַׁב (*Jesurun*, p. 207), but from עָכַשׁ, عكس and عكش, root علك (*vid.* Fleischer on Isa. lix. 5, עַכָּבִישׁ), both of which have the significations of bending, turning, and coiling after the manner of a serpent; the *Beth* is an organic addition modifying the meaning of the root.*

---

* According to the original Lexicons عكس signifies to bend one's self, to wriggle, to creep sideways like the roots of the vine, in the V. form to

Vers. 5, 6. The course of this second strophe is exactly parallel with the first. The perfects describe their conduct hitherto, as a comparison of ver. 3*b* with 3*a* shows. פְּעָמִים is poetically equivalent to רַגְלַיִם, and signifies both the foot that steps (lvii. 7, lviii. 11) and the step that is made by the foot (lxxxv. 14, cxix. 133), and here the two senses are undistinguishable. They are called גֵּאִים on account of the inordinate ambition that infatuates them. The metaphors taken from the life of the hunter (cxli. 9, cxlii. 4) are here brought together as it were into a body of synonyms. The meaning of לְיַד־מַעְגָּל becomes explicable from cxlii. 4; לְיַד, at hand, is equivalent to "immediately beside" (1 Chron. xviii. 17, Neh. xi. 24). Close by the path along which he has to pass, lie gins ready to spring together and ensnare him when he appears.

Vers. 7–9. Such is the conduct of his enemies; he, however, prays to his God and gets his weapons from beside Him. The day of equipment is the day of the crisis when the battle is fought in full array. The perfect סַכּוֹתָה states what will then take place on the part of God: He protects the head of His anointed against the deadly blow. Both ver. 8*a* and 8*b* point to the helmet as being מָעוֹז רֹאשׁ, lx. 9; cf. the expression "the helmet of salvation" in Isa. lix. 17. Beside מַאֲוַיֵּי, from the ἅπ. λεγ. מַאֲוָה, there is also the reading מַאֲוַיֵּי, which Abulwalîd found in his Jerusalem codex (in Saragossa). The

---

move one's self like an adder (according to the *Kamûs*) and to walk like a drunken man (according to *Neshwân*); but عكش signifies to be intertwined, knit or closely united together, said of hairs and of the branches of trees, in the V. form to fight hand to hand and to get in among the crowd. The root is apparently expanded into עֲכְשׁוּב by an added *Beth* which serves as a notional speciality, as in عرقوب the convex bend of the steep side of a rock, or in the case of the knee of the hind-legs of animals, and in خرنوب (in the dialect of the country along the coast of Palestine, where the tree is plentiful, in Neshwân *churnûb*), the horn-like curved pod of the carob-tree (*Ceratonia Siliqua*), syncopated خروب, *charrûb* (not *charûb*), from خرن, cogn. قرن a horn, cf. خرناية the beak of a bird of prey, خرنوق the stork [*vid.* on civ. 17], خرنين the rhinoceros [*vid.* on xxix. 6], خرنيت the unicorn [*vid. ibid.*].—WETZSTEIN.

regular form would be מְאַוַּי, and the doubly irregular *ma'awajjê*
follows the example of מְחַשַּׁבַּי, מַחֲמַדַּי, and the like, in a manner
that is without example elsewhere. זְמָמוֹ for מְזִמָּתוֹ is also a
hapaxlegomenon; according to Gesenius the principal form is
זֵמָם, but surely more correctly זְמָם (like קְרָב), which in Aramaic
signifies a bridle, and here a plan, device. The *Hiph.* הֵפִיק
(root פק, whence נֶפֶק, نفق) signifies *educere* in the sense of
reportare, Prov. iii. 13, viii. 35, xii. 2, xviii. 22, and of *por-
rigere*, cxliv. 13, Isa. lviii. 10. A reaching forth of the plan
is equivalent to the reaching forth of that which is projected.
The choice of the words used in this Psalm coincides here, as
already in מַעְגָּל, with Proverbs and Isaiah. The future יָרוּמוּ
expresses the consequence (cf. lxi. 8) against which the poet
wishes to guard.

Vers. 10–12. The strophic symmetry is now at an end.
The longer the poet lingers over the contemplation of the
rebels the more lofty and dignified does his language become,
the more particular the choice of the expressions, and the more
difficult and unmanageable the construction. The *Hiph.* הֵסֵב
signifies, causatively, to cause to go round about (Ex. xiii. 18),
and to raise round about (2 Chron. xiv. 6); here, after Josh.
vi. 11, where with an accusative following it signifies to go
round about: to make the circuit of anything, as enemies who
surround a city on all sides and seek the most favourable point
for assault; מְסִבַּי from the participle מֵסֵב. Even when derived
from the substantive מֵסַב (Hupfeld), "my surroundings" is
equivalent to אֹיְבַי סְבִיבוֹתַי in xxvii. 6. Hitzig, on the other hand,
renders it: the head of my slanderers, from סָבַב, to go round
about, Arabic to tell tales of any one, defame; but the Arabic

سبّ, *fut. u*, to abuse, the IV. form (*Hiphil*) of which moreover is not used either in the ancient or in the modern language,
has nothing to do with the Hebrew סבב, but signifies originally
to cut off round about, then to clip (injure) any one's honour
and good name.* The fact that the enemies who surround

---

* The lexicographer *Neshwân* says, i. 279b: السبّ الشتم وقيل ان
اصل السبّ القطع ثم صار الشتم, "*sebb* is to abuse; still, the more
original signification of cutting off is said to lie at the foundation of this

the psalmist on every side are just such calumniators, is intimated here in the word שְׂפָתֵימוֹ. He wishes that the trouble which the enemies' slanderous lips occasion him may fall back upon their own head. רֹאשׁ is head in the first and literal sense according to vii. 17; and יְכַסֵּימוֹ (with the *Jod* of the groundform כסי, as in Deut. xxxii. 26, 1 Kings xx. 35; *Chethîb* יְכַסּוּמוֹ,* after the attractional schema, 2 Sam. ii. 4, Isa. ii. 11, and frequently; cf. on the masculine form, Prov. v. 2, x. 21) refers back to רֹאשׁ, which is meant of the heads of all persons individually. In ver. 11 יָמִיטוּ (with an indefinite subject of the higher punitive powers, Ges. § 137, note), in the signification to cause to descend, has a support in lv. 4, whereas the *Niph.* נָמוֹט, fut. יִפּוֹט, which is preferred by the *Kerî*, in the signification to be made to descend, is contrary to the usage of the language. The ἅπ. λεγ. מַהֲמֹרוֹת has been combined by Parchon and others with the Arabic همر, which, together with other significations (to strike, stamp, cast down, and the like), also has the signification to flow (whence *e.g.* in the Koran, *mâ' munhamir*, flowing water). "Fire" and "water" are emblems of perils that cannot be escaped, lxvi. 12, and the mention of fire is therefore appropriately succeeded by places of flowing water, pits of water. The signification "pits" is attested by the Targum, Symmachus, Jerome, and the quotation in Kimchi: "first of all they buried them in מהמורות; when the flesh was consumed they collected the bones and buried them in coffins." On בַּל־יְקוּמוּ cf. Isa. xxvi. 14. Like vers. 10, 11, ver. 12 is also not to be taken as a general maxim, but as expressing a wish in accordance with the excited tone of this strophe. אִישׁ לָשׁוֹן is not a great talker, *i.e.* boaster, but an idle talker, *i.e.* slanderer (LXX. ἀνὴρ γλωσσώδης, cf. Sir. viii. 4). According to the accents, אִישׁ חָמָס רָע is the parallel; but what would be the object of this designation of violence as worse or more malignant? With Sommer, Olshausen, and others, we take רָע as the subject

---

signification." That قطع is synonymous with it, *e.g.* ليش تقطع فينا, why dost thou cut into us? *i.e.* why dost thou insult our honour?— WETZSTEIN.

* Which is favoured by Ex. xv. 5, *j'chasjûmû* with *mû* instead of *mô*, which is otherwise without example.

to יְצוּדֶנּוּ : let evil, *i.e.* the punishment-which arises out of evil, hunt him; cf. Prov. xiii. 21, חַטָּאִים תְּרַדֵּף רָעָה, and the opposite in xxiii. 6. It would have to be accented, according to this our construction of the words, אִישׁ חָמָס רָע יְצוֹדֶנִי לְמַדְחֵפֹת. The ἅπ. λεγ. לְמַדְחֵפֹת we do not render, with Hengstenberg, Olshausen, and others: push upon push, with repeated pushes, which, to say nothing more, is not suited to the figure of hunting, but, since דָּחַף always has the signification of precipitate hastening: by hastenings, that is to say, forced marches.

Vers. 13, 14. With ver. 13 the mood and language now again become cheerful, the rage has spent itself; therefore the style and tone are now changed, and the Psalm trips along merrily as it were to the close. With reference to ידעת for ידעתי (as in Job xlii. 2), *vid.* xvi. 2. That which David in ix. 5. confidently expects on his own behalf is here generalized into the certain prospect of the triumph of the good cause in the person of all its representatives at that time oppressed. אַךְ, like יָדַעְתִּי, is an expression of certainty. After seeming abandonment God again makes Himself known to His own, and those whom they wanted to sweep away out of the land of the living have an ever sure dwelling-place with His joyful countenance (xvi. 11).

PSALM CXLI.

EVENING PSALM IN THE TIMES OF ABSALOM.

1 JAHVE, I call upon Thee, Oh haste Thee unto me;
  Oh hearken to my voice, when I call upon Thee!
2 Let my prayer be accounted as incense before Thee,
  The lifting up of my hands as the evening meat-offering.

3 Oh set a watch, Jahve, upon my mouth,
  A protection upon the door of my lips.
4 Incline not my heart to an evil matter,
  To practise knavish things in iniquity
  With the lords who rule wickedly,
  And let me not taste their dainties.

5 Let a righteous man smite me lovingly and rebuke me,

Such oil upon the head let not my head refuse,
For still do I meet their wickedness only with prayer.
6 Hurled down upon the sides of the rock are their judges,
And they hear my words as welcome.
7 As when one furroweth and breaketh up the earth,
Are our bones sowed at the gate of Hades.

8 For unto Thee, Jahve Lord! do mine eyes look,
In Thee do I hide, pour not my soul out!
9 Keep me from the hands of the snare of those who lay
snares for me,
And from the traps of those who rule wickedly.
10 Let the wicked fall into their own net,
Whilst *I* altogether escape.

The four Psalms, cxl., cxli., cxlii., and cxliii., are interwoven
with one another in many ways (*Symbolæ*, pp. 67 sq.).   The
following passages are very similar, viz. cxl. 7, cxli. 1, cxlii. 2,
and cxliii. 1.   Just as the poet complains in cxlii. 4, " when
my spirit veils itself within me," so too in cxliii. 4; as he prays
in cxlii. 8, " Oh bring my soul out of prison," so in cxliii. 11,
" bring my soul out of distress," where צרה takes the place of
the metaphorical מסגר.   Besides these, compare cxl. 5, 6 with
cxli. 9; cxlii. 7 with cxliii. 9; cxl. 3 with cxli. 5, רעות; cxl. 14
with cxlii. 8; cxlii. 4 with cxliii. 8.
The right understanding of the Psalm depends upon the
right understanding of the situation.   Since it is inscribed
לדוד, it is presumably a situation corresponding to the history
of David, out of the midst of which the Psalm is composed,
either by David himself or by some one else who desired to
give expression in Davidic strains to David's mood when in
this situation.   For the gleaning of Davidic Psalms which we
find in the last two Books of the Psalter is for the most part
derived from historical works in which these Psalms, in some
instances only free reproductions of the feelings of David with
respect to old Davidic models, adorned the historic narrative.
The Psalm before us adorned the history of the time of the
persecution by Absalom.   At that time David was driven out
of Jerusalem, and consequently cut off from the sacrificial
worship of God upon Zion; and our Psalm is an evening

hymn of one of those troublous days. The ancient church, even prior to the time of Gregory (*Constitutiones Apostolicæ*, ii. 59), had chosen it for its evening hymn, just as it had chosen Ps. lxiii. for its morning hymn. Just as Ps. lxiii. was called ὁ ὀρθρινός (*ibid.* viii. 37), so this Psalm, as being the Vesper Psalm, was called ὁ ἐπιλύχνιος (*ibid.* viii. 35).

Vers. 1, 2. The very beginning of Ps. cxli. is more after the manner of David than really Davidic; for instead of *haste thee to me*, David always says, *haste thee for my help*, xxii. 20, xxxviii. 23, xl. 14. The לְךָ that is added to בְּקָרְאִי (as in iv. 2) is to be explained, as in lvii. 3: when I call to Thee, *i.e.* when I call Thee, who art now far from me, to me. The general cry for help is followed in ver. 2 by a petition for the answering of his prayer. Luther has given an excellent rendering: Let my prayer avail to Thee as an offering of incense; the lifting up of my hands, as an evening sacrifice (*Mein Gebet müsse fur dir tügen wie ein Reuchopffer, Meine Hende auffheben, wie ein Abendopffer*). תִּכּוֹן is the *fut. Niph.* of כּן, and signifies properly to be set up, and to be established, or reflexive: to place and arrange or prepare one's self, Amos iv. 12; then to continue, *e.g.* ci. 7; therefore, either let it place itself, let it appear, *sistat se*, or better: let it stand, continue, *i.e.* let my prayer find acceptance, recognition with Thee קְטֹרֶת, and the lifting up of my hands מִנְחַת־עָרֶב. Expositors say that this in both instances is the *comparatio decurtata*, as in xi. 1 and elsewhere: as an incense-offering, as an evening *mincha*. But the poet purposely omits the כְּ of the comparison. He wishes that God may be pleased to regard his prayer as sweet-smelling smoke or as incense, just as this was added to the *azcara* of the meal-offering, and gave it, in its ascending perfume, the direction upward to God,* and that He may be pleased to regard the

---

* It is not the priestly קְטֹרֶת תָּמִיד, *i.e.* the daily morning and evening incense-offering upon the golden altar of the holy place, Ex. xxx. 8, that is meant (since it is a non-priest who is speaking, according to Hitzig, of course John Hyrcanus), but rather, as also in Isa. i. 13, the incense of the *azcara* of the meal-offering which the priest burnt (הִקְטִיר) upon the altar; the incense (Isa. lxvi. 3) was entirely consumed, and not merely a handful taken from it.

lifting up of his hands (מַשְׂאַת, the construct with the reduplication given up, from מַשְׂאֵת, or even, after the form מַתְּנַת, from מַשְׂאָה, here not *oblatio*, but according to the phrase נְשָׂא כַפַּיִם [יָדַיִם], *elevatio*, Judg. xx. 38, 40, cf. Ps. xxviii. 2, and frequently) as an evening *mincha*, just as it was added to the evening *tamîd* according to Ex. xxix. 38–42, and concluded the work of the service of the day.*

Vers. 3, 4. The prayer now begins to be particularized, and that in the first instance as a petition for the grace of silence, calling to mind old Davidic passages like xxxix. 2, xxxiv. 14. The situation of David, the betrayed one, requires caution in speaking; and the consciousness of having sinned, not indeed against the rebels, but against God, who would not visit him thus without his deserving it, stood in the way of any outspoken self-vindication. In *pone custodiam ori meo* שָׁמְרָה is ἅπ. λεγ., after the infinitive form עָצְמָה, עָזְבָה, דָּבְקָה. In ver. 3*b* דַּל is ἅπ. λεγ. for דֶּלֶת; cf. "doors of the mouth" in Mic. vii. 5, and πύλαι στόματος in Euripides. נִצְּרָה might be *imper. Kal*: keep I pray, with *Dag. dirimens* as in Prov. iv. 13. But נְצָר עַל is not in use; and also as the parallel word to שָׁמְרָה, which likewise has the appearance of being imperative, נִצְּרָה is explicable as regards its pointing by a comparison of יִקְּהָה in Gen. xlix. 10, דִּבְּרָה in Deut. xxxiii. 3, and קָרְבָה in lxxiii. 28. The prayer for the grace of silence is followed in ver. 4 by a prayer for the breaking off of all fellowship with the existing rulers. By a flight of irony they are called אִישִׁים, lords, in the sense of בְּנֵי אִישׁ, iv. 3 (cf. the Spanish *hidalgos* = *hìjos d'algo*, sons of somebody). The evil thing (דָּבָר ׀ רָע, with *Pasek* between the two ר, as in Num. vii. 13, Deut. vii. 1 between the two מ, and in 1 Chron. xxii. 3 between the two ל), to which Jahve may be pleased never to incline his heart (תֵּט, *fut. apoc. Hiph.* as in xxvii. 9), is forthwith more particularly designated: *perpetrare faci-*

---

* The reason of it is this, that the evening *mincha* is oftener mentioned than the morning *mincha* (see, however, 2 Kings iii. 20). The whole burnt-offering of the morning and the meat-offering of the evening (2 Kings xvi. 15, 1 Kings xviii. 29, 36) are the beginning and close of the daily principal service; whence, according to the example of the *usus loquendi* in Dan. ix. 21, Ezra ix. 4 sq., later on *mincha* directly signifies the afternoon or evening.

nora maligne cum dominis, etc. עֲלִלוֹת of great achievements in the sense of infamous deeds, also occurs in xiv. 1, xcix. 8. Here, however, we have the *Hithpo.* הִתְעַלֵּל, which, with the accusative of the object עֲלִלוֹת, signifies: wilfully to make such actions the object of one's acting (cf. تَعَلَّلَ بِالشَّيْ, to meddle with any matter, to amuse, entertain one's self with a thing). The expression is made to express disgust as strongly as possible; this poet is fond of glaring colouring in his language. In the dependent passage *neve eorum vescar cupediis*, לָחַם is used poetically for אָכַל, and בְּ is the partitive *Beth*, as in Job xxi. 25. מַנְעַמִּים is another hapaxlegomenon, but as being a designation of dainties (from נָעֵם, to be mild, tender, pleasant), it may not have been an unusual word. It is a well-known thing that usurpers revel in the *cuisine* and cellars of those whom they have driven away.

Vers. 5–7. Thus far the Psalm is comparatively easy of exposition; but now it becomes difficult, yet not hopelessly so. David, thoroughly conscious of his sins against God and of his imperfection as a monarch, says, in opposition to the abuse which he is now suffering, that he would gladly accept any friendly reproof: " let a righteous man smite in kindness and reprove me—head-oil (*i.e.* oil upon the head, to which such reproof is likened) shall my head not refuse." So we render it, following the accents, and not as Hupfeld, Kurtz, and Hitzig do: " if a righteous man smites me, it is love; if he reproves me, an anointing of the head is it unto me;" in connection with which the designation of the subject with הִיא would be twice wanting, which is more than is admissible. צַדִּיק stands here as an abstract substantive: the righteous man, whoever he may be, in antithesis, namely, to the rebels and to the people who have joined them. Amyraldus, Maurer, and Hengstenberg understand it of God; but it only occurs of God as an attribute, and never as a direct appellation. חֶסֶד, as in Jer. xxxi. 3, is equivalent to בְּחֶסֶד, *cum benignitate* = *benigne.* What is meant is, as in Job vi. 14, what Paul (Gal. vi. 1) styles πνεῦμα πραΰτητος. And הָלַם, *tundere*, is used of the strokes of earnest but well-meant reproof, which is called " the blows of a friend" in Prov. xxvii. 6. Such reproof shall be to him as head-oil (xxiii. 5, cxxxiii. 2), which his head does not despise. יָנִי, written defectively for יָנִיא, like יֵשִׁי in lv. 16, אָבִי, 1 Kings xxi. 29 and frequently; הֵנִיא (root נא, نٰا, with the nasal *n*, which also expresses the negation in the Indo-Germanic languages) here signifies to deny, as in xxxiii. 10 to bring to nought, to destroy. On the other hand, the LXX. renders μὴ λιπανάτω τὴν κεφαλήν μου, which is also followed by the Syriac and Jerome, perhaps after the Arabic نَوَى, to become or to be fat, which is, however, altogether foreign to the Aramaic, and is, moreover, only used of fatness of the body, and in fact of camels. The meaning of the figure is this: well-meant reproof shall be acceptable and spiritually useful to him. The confirmation כִּי־עוֹד וגו׳ follows, which is enigmatical both in meaning and expression. This עוֹד is the cipher of a whole clause, and the following ו is related to this עוֹד as the *Waw* that introduces the apodosis, not to כִּי, as in 2 Chron. xxiv. 20, since no progression and connection is discernible if כי is taken as a subordinating *quia*. We interpret thus: *for it is still so* (the matter still stands thus), *that my prayer is against their wickednesses; i.e.* that I use no weapon but that of prayer against these, therefore let me always be in that spiritual state of mind which is alive to well-meant reproof. Mendelssohn's rendering is similar: I still pray, whilst they practise infamy. On עוֹד ו cf. Zech. viii. 20 עוֹד אֲשֶׁר (*vid.* Köhler), and Prov. xxiv. 27 אַחַר ו. He who has prayed God in ver. 3 to set a watch upon his mouth is dumb in the presence of those who now have dominion, and seeks to keep himself clear of their sinful doings, whereas he willingly allows himself to be chastened by the righteous; and the more silent he is towards the world (see Amos v. 13), the more constant is he in his intercourse with God. But there will come a time when those who now behave as lords shall fall a prey to the revenge of the people who have been misled by them; and on the other hand, the confession of the salvation, and of the order of the salvation, of God, that has hitherto been put to silence, will again be able to make itself freely heard, and find a ready hearing.

As ver. 6 says, the new rulers fall a prey to the indignation of the people and are thrown down the precipices, whilst the people, having again come to their right mind, obey the words

of David and find them pleasant and beneficial (*vid.* Prov. xv.
26, xvi. 24). נִשְׁמְטוּ is to be explained according to 2 Kings
ix. 33. The casting of persons down from the rock was not an
unusual mode of execution (2 Chron. xxv. 12). יְדֵי־סָלַע are the
sides (cxl. 6, Judg. xi. 26) of the rock, after which the expression ἐχόμενα πέτρας of the LXX., which has been misunderstood by Jerome, is intended to be understood;* they are therefore
the sides of the rock conceived of as it were as the hands of the
body of rock, if we are not rather with Böttcher to compare the
expressions בְּיָדֵי and עַל־יְדֵי construed with verbs of abandoning
and casting down, Lam. i. 14, Job xvi. 11, and frequently. In
ver. 7 there follows a further statement of the issue on the side
of David and his followers: *instar findentis et secantis terram*
(בָּקַע with *Beth*, elsewhere in the hostile signification of *irrumpere*)
dispersa sunt ossa nostra ad ostium (לְפִי as in Prov. viii. 3) *orci*;
Symmachus: ὥσπερ γεωργὸς ὅταν ῥήσσῃ τὴν γῆν, οὕτως ἐσκορ-
πίσθη τὰ ὀστᾶ ἡμῶν εἰς στόμα ᾅδου; Quinta: ὡς καλλιεργῶν
καὶ σκάπτων ἐν τῇ γῇ, κ.τ.λ. Assuming the very extreme, it is
a look of hope into the future: should his bones and the bones
of his followers be even scattered about the mouth of Sheôl (cf.
the Syrian picture of Sheôl: "the dust upon its threshold ʿal-
escûfteh," *Deutsche Morgenländ. Zeitschrift*, xx. 513), their soul
below, their bones above—it would nevertheless be only as
when one in ploughing cleaves the earth; *i.e.* they do not lie
there in order that they may continue lying, but that they may
rise up anew, as the seed that is sown sprouts up out of the up-
turned earth. LXX. *Codd. Vat. et Sinait.* τὰ ὀστᾶ ἡμῶν, beside
which, however, is found the reading αὐτῶν (*Cod. Alex.* by a
second hand, and the Syriac, Arabic, and Æthiopic versions),
as Böttcher also, *pro ineptissimo utcunque*, thinks עצמינו must be
read, understanding this, according to 2 Chron. xxv. 12 *extrem.*,
of the mangled bodies of those cast down from the rock. We
here discern the hope of a resurrection, if not directly, at least
(cf. Oehler in Herzog's *Real-Encyklopädie*, concluding volume,
S. 422) as an emblem of victory in spite of having succumbed.
That which authorizes this interpretation lies in the figure of

---

* Beda Pieringer in his *Psalterium Romana Lyra Redditum* (Ratisbonæ
1859) interprets κατεπόθησαν ἐχόμενα πέτρας οἱ κραταιοὶ αὐτῶν, absorpti, i.e.
operti sunt loco ad petram pertinente signiferi turpis consilii eorum.

the husbandman, and in the conditional clause (ver. 8), which
leads to the true point of the comparison; for as a complaint
concerning a defeat that had been suffered: " so are our bones
scattered for the mouth of the grave (in order to be swallowed
up by it)," ver. 7, would be alien and isolated with respect to
what precedes and what follows.

Vers. 8–10. If ver. 7 is not merely an expression of the
complaint, but at the same time of hope, we now have no need
to give the כִּי the adversative sense of *imo*, but we may leave it
its most natural confirmatory signification *namque*. From this
point the Psalm gradually dies away in strains comparatively
easy to be understood and in perfect keeping with the situation.
In connection with ver. 8 one is reminded of xxv. 15, xxxi. 2;
with vers. 9 sq., of vii. 16, lxix. 23, and other passages. In
" pour not out (תְּעַר with sharpened vowel instead of תְּעָר, Ges.
§ 75, rem. 8) my soul," עָרָה, *Piel*, is equivalent to the *Hiph.* הֶעֱרָה
in Isa. liii. 12. יְדֵי פַּח are as it were the hands of the seizing
and capturing snare; and יָקְשׁוּ לִי is virtually a genitive: *qui in-
sidias tendunt mihi*, since one cannot say יָקֹשׁ פַּח, *ponere laqueum.*
מַכְמֹרִים, nets, in ver. 10 is another hapaxlegomenon; the *enallage numeri* is as in lxii. 5, Isa. ii. 8, v. 23,—the singular that
slips in refers what is said of the many to each individual in
particular. The plural מִקְשׁוֹת for מִקְשִׁים, xviii. 6, lxiv. 6, also
occurs only here. יַחַד is to be explained as in iv. 9: it is intended
to express the coincidence of the overthrow of the enemies and
the going forth free of the persecuted one. With יַחַד אָנֹכִי the
poet gives prominence to his simultaneous, distinct destiny:
simul ego dum (עַד as in Job viii. 21, cf. i. 18) *prætereo h. e.
evado.* The inverted position of the כִּי in cxviii. 10–12 may be
compared; with cxx. 7 and 2 Kings ii. 14, however (where
instead of אַף־הוּא it is with Thenius to be read אֵפוֹא), the case is
different.

PSALM CXLII.

CRY SENT FORTH FROM THE PRISON TO THE
BEST OF FRIENDS.

2 WITH my voice to Jahve do I cry,
   With my voice to Jahve do I make supplication,

3 I pour forth before Him my complaint,
My trouble do I make known before Him.
4 When my spirit veils itself within me,
Thou indeed art acquainted with my way.

     On the path along which I must go,
         they hide a trap for me.
5 Look to the right and see,
         no friend appeareth for me;
All refuge hath failed me,
         no one careth for my soul.
6 I cry unto Thee, Jahve,
I say: THOU art my refuge,
My portion in the land of the living.

7 Oh hearken to my cry of woe,
         for I am very weak;
Deliver me from my persecutors,
         for they are too strong for me.
8 Oh lead my soul out of imprisonment,
         to praise Thy Name—
In me shall the righteous glory:
         that Thou dealest bountifully with me.

This the last of the eight Davidic Psalms, which are derived by their inscriptions from the time of the persecution by Saul (*vid.* on Ps. xxxiv.), is inscribed: *A Meditation by David, when he was in the cave, a Prayer.* Of these eight Psalms, Ps. lii. and liv. also bear the name of *Maskîl* (*vid.* on Ps. xxxii.); and in this instance תְּפִלָּה (which occurs besides as an inscription only in xc. 1, cii. 1, Hab. iii. 1) is further added, which looks like an explanation of the word *maskîl* (not in use out of the range of Psalm-poetry). The article of בַּמְּעָרה, as in lvii. 1, points to the cave of Adullam (1 Sam. ch. xxii.) or the cave of Engedi (1 Sam. ch. xxiv.), which latter, starting from a narrow concealed entrance, forms such a labyrinthine maze of passages and vaults that the torches and lines of explorers have not to the present time been able to reach the extremities of it.

The Psalm does not contain any sure signs of a post-Davidic age; still it appears throughout to be an imitation of

older models, and pre-eminently by means of vers. 2 sq. (cf.
lxxvii. 2 sq.) and ver. 4 (cf. lxxvii. 4) it comes into a relation
of dependence to Ps. lxxvii., which is also noticeable in Ps.
cxliii. (cf. ver. 5 with lxxvii. 12 sq.). The referring back of the
two Psalms to David comes under one and the same judgment.

Vers. 2–4a. The emphasis of the first two lines rests upon
אֶל־ה׳. Forsaken by all created beings, he confides in Jahve.
He turns to Him in pathetic and importunate prayer (אֶזְעָק, the
parallel word being אֶתְחַנָּן, as in xxx. 9), and that not merely
inwardly (Ex. xiv. 15), but with his voice (*vid.* on iii. 5)—for
audible prayer reacts soothingly, strengtheningly, and sancti-
fyingly upon the praying one—he pours out before Him his
trouble which distracts his thoughts (שָׁפַךְ שִׂיחַ as in cii. 1, cf.
lxii. 9, lxiv. 2, 1 Sam. i. 16), he lays open before Him everything
that burdens and distresses him. Not as though He did not also
know it without all this; on the contrary, when his spirit (רוּחִי
as in cxliii. 4, lxxvii. 4, cf. נַפְשִׁי Jonah ii. 8 [7], Ps. cvii. 5, לִבִּי
lxi. 3) within him (עָלַי, see xlii. 5) is enshrouded and languishes,
just this is his consolation, that Jahve is intimately acquainted
with his way together with the dangers that threaten him at
every step, and therefore also understands how to estimate the
title (right) and meaning of his complaints. The *Waw* of וְאַתָּה
is the same as in 1 Kings viii. 36, cf. 35. Instead of saying:
then I comfort myself with the fact that, etc., he at once declares
the fact with which he comforts himself. Supposing this to be
the case, there is no need for any alteration of the text in order
to get over that which is apparently incongruous in the relation
of ver. 4b to 4a.

Vers. 4b–6. The prayer of the poet now becomes deep-
breathed and excited, inasmuch as he goes more minutely into
the details of his straitened situation. Everywhere, whithersoever he has to go (cf. on cxliii. 8), the snares of craftily calcu-
lating foes threaten him. Even God's all-seeing eye will not
discover any one who would right faithfully and carefully interest himself in him. הַבִּיט, look! is a graphic hybrid form of
הַבֵּט and הַבִּיט, the usual and the rare imperative form; cf. הָבִיא
1 Sam. xx. 40 (cf. Jer. xvii. 18), and the same modes of writing
the *inf. absol.* in Judg. i. 28, Amos ix. 8, and the *fut. conv.* in
Ezek. xl. 3. מַכִּיר is, as in Ruth ii. 19, cf. 10, one who looks

kindly upon any one, a considerate (cf. the phrase הִכִּיר פָּנִים)
well-wisher and friend.   Such an one, if he had one, would be
עָמַד עַל־יְמִינוֹ or מִימִינוֹ (xvi. 8), for an open attack is directed to
the arms-bearing right side (cix. 6), and there too the helper in
battle (cx. 5) and the defender or advocate (cix. 31) takes his
place in order to cover him who is imperilled (cxxi. 5).   But
then if God looks in that direction, He will find him, who is
praying to Him, unprotected.   Instead of וְאֵין one would certainly
have sooner expected אֲשֶׁר or כִּי as the form of introducing the
condition in which he is found; but Hitzig's conjecture, הַבֵּט יָמִין
וּרְאֵה, "looking for days and seeing," gives us in the place of this
difficulty a confusing half-Aramaism in יֹמִין = יָמִין in the sense
of יָמִים in Dan. viii. 27, Neh. i. 4.   Ewald's rendering is better:
" though I look to the right hand and see (וְרָאֵה), yet no friend
appears for me ; " but this use of the *inf. absol.* with an adversative apodosis is without example.   Thus therefore the pointing
appears to have lighted upon the correct idea, inasmuch as it
recognises here the current formula הַבֵּט וּרְאֵה, *e.g.* Job xxxv. 5,
Lam. v. 1.   The fact that David, although surrounded by a
band of loyal subjects, confesses to having no true friend, is to
be understood similarly to the language of Paul when he says
in Phil. ii. 20: " I have no man like-minded."   All human
love, since sin has taken possession of humanity, is more or less
selfish, and all fellowship of faith and of love imperfect; and
there are circumstances in life in which these dark sides make
themselves felt overpoweringly, so that a man seems to himself
to be perfectly isolated and turns all the more urgently to God,
who alone is able to supply the soul's want of some object to
love, whose love is absolutely unselfish, and unchangeable, and
unbeclouded, to whom the soul can confide without reserve
whatever burdens it, and who not only honestly desires its good,
but is able also to compass it in spite of every obstacle.   Surrounded by bloodthirsty enemies, and misunderstood, or at least
not thoroughly understood, by his friends, David feels himself
broken off from all created beings.   On this earth every kind
of refuge is for him lost (the expression is like Job xi. 20).
There is no one there who should ask after or care for his soul,
and should right earnestly exert himself for its deliverance.
Thus, then, despairing of all visible things, he cries to the Invisible One.   He is his " refuge " (xci. 9) and his " portion " (xvi. 5,

lxxiii. 26), *i.e.* the share in a possession that satisfies him. To be allowed to call Him his God—this it is which suffices him and outweighs everything. For Jahve is the Living One, and he who possesses Him as his own finds himself thereby " in the land of the living " (xxvii. 13, lii. 7). He cannot die, he cannot perish.

Vers. 7, 8. His request now ascends all the more confident of being answered, and becomes calm, being well-grounded in his feebleness and the superiority of his enemies, and aiming at the glorifying of the divine Name. In ver. 7 רִנָּתִי calls to mind xvii. 1; the first confirmation, lxxix. 8, and the second, xviii. 18. But this is the only passage in the whole Psalter where the poet designates the " distress" in which he finds himself as a prison (מַסְגֵּר). Ver. 8*b* brings the whole congregation of the righteous in in the praising of the divine Name. The poet therefore does not after all find himself so absolutely alone, as it might seem according to ver. 5. He is far from regarding himself as the only righteous person. He is only a member of a community or church whose destiny is interwoven with his own, and which will glory in his deliverance as its own; for "if one member is honoured, all the members rejoice with it " (1 Cor. xii. 26). We understand the differently interpreted יַכְתִּירוּ after this "rejoicing with " (συγχαίρει). The LXX., Syriac, and Aquila render : the righteous wait for me; but to wait is כִּתֵּר and not הִכְתִּיר. The modern versions, on the other hand, almost universally, like Luther after Felix Pratensis, render : the righteous shall surround me (flock about me), in connection with which, as Hengstenberg observes, בִּי denotes the tender sympathy they feel with him : crowding closely upon me. But there is no instance of a verb of surrounding (הִקִּיף, עָטַר, עוּד, סֹבֵב, סָבַב, אָפַף) taking בְּ; the accusative stands with הִכְתִּיר in Hab. i. 4, and כִּתֵּר in xxii. 13, in the signification *cingere*. Symmachus (although erroneously rendering : τὸ ὄνομά σου στεφανώσονται δίκαιοι), Jerome (*in me coronabuntur justi*), Parchon, Aben-Ezra, Coccejus, and others, rightly take יַכְתִּירוּ as a denominative from כֶּתֶר, to put on a crown or to crown (cf. Prov. xiv. 18): on account of me the righteous shall adorn themselves as with crowns, *i.e.* shall triumph, that Thou dealest bountifully with me (an echo of xiii. 6). According to passages like lxiv. 11, xl. 17, one might have expected בּוֹ instead of בִּי. But the close of Ps. xxii. (vers. 23

sqq.), cf. cxl. 12 sq., shows that בִּי is also admissible. The very fact that David contemplates his own destiny and the destiny of his foes in a not merely ideal but foreordainedly causal connection with the general end of the two powers that stand opposed to one another in the world, belongs to the characteristic impress of the Psalms of David that come from the time of Saul's persecution.

PSALM CXLIII.

LONGING AFTER MERCY IN THE MIDST OF DARK IMPRISONMENT.

1 JAHVE, hear my prayer, oh give ear to my supplication;
  In Thy faithfulness answer me, in Thy righteousness.
2 And enter not into judgment with Thy servant,
  For before Thee no man living is righteous.
3 For the enemy hath persecuted my soul,
  He hath crushed my life to the ground,
  He hath made me to lie down in terrible darkness, like
     those for ever dead.

4 And my spirit languisheth within me,
  In my inward part my heart is benumbed.
5 I remember the days of old,
  I meditate upon all Thy doing,
  I muse upon the work of Thy hands.
6 I stretch forth my hands unto Thee,
  My soul is as a thirsty land unto Thee!   (*Sela.*)

7 Answer me speedily, Jahve, my spirit yearneth:
  Hide not Thy face from me,
  I should become like those who go down to the pit.
8 Let me hear Thy loving-kindness with the dawn of the
  For I trust in Thee.   [morning,
  Make known to me the way in which I am to go,
  For unto Thee do I lift up my soul.

9 Deliver me from mine enemies, Jahve!
  I have hidden myself with Thee.

10 Teach me to do Thy will,
   For Thou art my God;
   Let Thy good Spirit lead me in an even land.
11 For Thy Name's sake, Jahve, quicken me again,
   In Thy righteousness be pleased to bring my soul out of
      trouble,
12 And in Thy loving-kindness cut off mine enemies,
   And destroy all the oppressors of my soul,
   For I am Thy servant.

In some codices of the LXX. this Psalm (as Euthymius also bears witness) has no inscription at all; in others, however, it has the inscription: Ψαλμὸς τῷ Δαυεὶδ ὅτε αὐτὸν ἐδίωκεν Ἀβεσσαλὼμ ὁ υἱὸς αὐτοῦ (*Cod. Sinait.* οτε αυτον ο υσ κατα-διωκει). Perhaps by the same poet as Ps. cxlii., with which it accords in vers. 4, 8, 11 (cf. cxlii. 4, 8), it is like this a modern offshoot of the Davidic Psalm-poetry, and is certainly composed as coming out of the situation of him who was persecuted by Absalom. The Psalms of this time of persecution are distinguished from those of the time of the persecution by Saul by the deep melancholy into which the mourning of the dethroned king was turned by blending with the penitential sorrowfulness of one conscious of his own guilt. On account of this fundamental feature the church has chosen Ps. cxliii. for the last of its seven *Psalmi pœnitentiales.* The *Sela* at the close of ver. 6 divides the Psalm into two halves.

Vers. 1–6. The poet pleads two motives for the answering of his prayer which are to be found in God Himself, viz. God's אֱמוּנָה, truthfulness, with which He verifies the truth of His promises, that is to say, His faithfulness to His promises; and His צְדָקָה, righteousness, not in a recompensative legal sense, but in an evangelical sense, in accordance with His counsel, *i.e.* the strictness and earnestness with which He maintains the order of salvation established by His holy love, both against the ungratefully disobedient and against those who insolently despise Him. Having entered into this order of salvation, and within the sphere of it serving Jahve as his God and Lord, the poet is the servant of Jahve. And because the conduct of the God of salvation, ruled by this order of

salvation, or His "righteousness" according to its fundamental
manifestation, consists in His justifying the sinful man who
has no righteousness that he can show corresponding to the
divine holiness, but penitently confesses this disorganized relationship, and, eager for salvation, longs for it to be set right
again,—because of all this, the poet prays that He would not
also enter into judgment (בּוֹא בְמִשְׁפָּט as in Job ix. 32, xxii. 4,
xiv. 3) with him, that He therefore would let mercy instead
of justice have its course with him.　For, apart from the fact
that even the holiness of the good spirits does not coincide with
God's absolute holiness, and that this defect must still be very
far greater in the case of spirit-corporeal man, who has earthi-
ness as the basis of his origin,—yea, according to li. 7, man is
conceived in sin, so that he is sinful from the point at which he
begins to live onward,—his life is indissolubly interwoven with
sin, no living man possesses a righteousness that avails before
God (Job iv. 17, ix. 2, xiv. 3 sq., xv. 14, and frequently).*

With כִּי (ver. 3) the poet introduces the ground of his
petition for an answer, and more particularly for the forgiveness
of his guilt.　He is persecuted by deadly foes and is already
nigh unto death, and that not without transgression of his own,
so that consequently his deliverance depends upon the forgiveness of his sins, and will coincide with this.　"The enemy per-
secuteth my soul" is a variation of language taken from vii. 6
(חַיָּה for חַיִּים, as in lxxviii. 50, and frequently in the Book of
Job, more particularly in the speeches of Elihu).　Ver. 3c also
recalls vii. 6, but as to the words it sounds like Lam. iii. 6 (cf.
lxxxviii. 7).　מֵתֵי עוֹלָם (LXX. νεκροὺς αἰῶνος) are either those
for ever dead (the Syriac), after שְׁנַת עוֹלָם in Jer. li. 39, cf.
בֵּית עוֹלָמוֹ in Eccles. xii. 5, or those dead time out of mind
(Jerome), after עַם עוֹלָם in Ezek. xxvi. 20.　The genitive construction admits both senses; the former, however, is rendered
more natural by the consideration that הוֹשִׁיבַנִי glances back to
the beginning that seems to have no end: the poet seems to
himself like one who is buried alive for ever.　In consequence

---

* Gerson observes on this point (vid. Thomasius, Dogmatik, iv. 251): I
desire the righteousness of pity, which Thou bestowest in the present life,
not the judgment of that righteousness which Thou wilt put into operation
in the future life—the righteousness which justifies the repentant one.

of this hostility which aims at his destruction, the poet feels his spirit within him, and consequently his inmost life, veil itself (the expression is the same as cxlii. 4, lxxvii. 4); and in his inward part his heart falls into a state of disturbance (יִשְׁתּוֹמֵם, a *Hithpo.* peculiar to the later language), so that it almost ceases to beat. He calls to mind the former days, in which Jahve was manifestly with him; he reflects upon the great redemptive work of God, with all the deeds of might and mercy in which it has hitherto been unfolded; he meditates upon the doing (בְּמַעֲשֵׂה, Ben-Naphtali בְּמַעֲשֵׂה) of His hands, *i.e.* the hitherto so wondrously moulded history of himself and of his people. They are echoes out of lxxvii. 4–7, 12 sq. The contrast which presents itself to the Psalmist in connection with this comparison of his present circumstances with the past opens his wounds still deeper, and makes his prayer for help all the more urgent. He stretches forth his hands to God that He may protect and assist him (*vid.* Hölemann, *Bibelstudien*, i. 150 f.). Like a parched land is his soul turned towards Him,—language in which we recognise a bending round of the primary passage lxiii. 2. Instead of לְךָ it would be לָךְ, if סֶלָה (Targum לְעָלְמִין) were not, as it always is, taken up and included in the sequence of the accents.

Vers. 7–12. In this second half the Psalm seems still more like a reproduction of the thoughts of earlier Psalms. The prayer, " answer me speedily, hide not Thy face from me," sounds like lxix. 18, xxvii. 9, cf. cii. 3. The expression of languishing longing, כָּלְתָה רוּחִי, is like lxxxiv. 3. And the apodosis, " else I should become like those who go down into the pit," agrees word for word with xxviii. 1, cf. lxxxviii. 5. In connection with the words, " cause me to hear Thy lovingkindness in the early morning," one is reminded of the similar prayer of Moses in xc. 14, and with the confirmatory " for in Thee do I trust" of xxv. 2, and frequently. With the prayer that the night of affliction may have an end with the next morning's dawn, and that God's helping loving-kindness may make itself felt by him, is joined the prayer that God would be pleased to grant him to know the way that he has to go in order to escape the destruction into which they are anxious to ensnare him. This last prayer has its type in Ex. xxxiii. 13, and in the Psalter in xxv. 4 (cf. cxlii. 4); and its confirmation :

for to Thee have I lifted up my soul, viz. in a craving after salvation and in the confidence of faith, has its type in xxv. 1, lxxxvi. 4.   But the words אֵלֶיךָ כִפִּיתִי, which are added to the petition " deliver me from mine enemies" (lix. 2, xxxi. 16), are peculiar, and in their expression without example. The Syriac version leaves them untranslated. The LXX. renders: ὅτι πρὸς σὲ κατέφυγον, by which the defective mode of writing כסתי is indirectly attested, instead of which the translators read נסתי (cf. נוס עַל in Isa. x. 3) ; for elsewhere not חָסָה but נוס is reproduced with καταφυγεῖν. The Targum renders it מֵימְרָךְ מַנֵּיתִי לְפָרִיק, Thy Logos do I account as (my) Redeemer (i.e. regard it as such), as if the Hebrew words were to be rendered : upon Thee do I reckon or count, כַּסְתִּי = כִּפִּיתִי, Ex. xii. 4.   Luther closely follows the LXX. : " to Thee have I fled for refuge." Jerome, however, inasmuch as he renders : ad te protectus sum, has pointed כִּסֵּיתִי (כָּסֵיתִי). Hitzig (on the passage before us and Prov. vii. 20) reads כָּסְתִי from כָּסָא = סְכָא, to look (" towards Thee do I look"). But the Hebrew contains no trace of that verb ; the full moon is called כסא (כסה), not as being " a sight or vision, species," but from its covered orb (vol. ii. 394).

The כִפִּתי before us only admits of two interpretations : (1) Ad (apud) te texi = to Thee have I secretly confided it (Rashi, Aben-Ezra, Kimchi, Coccejus, J. H. Michaelis, J. D. Michaelis, Rosenmüller, Gesenius, and De Wette). But such a constructio prægnans, in connection with which כִּפָּה would veer round from the signification to veil (cf. כסה מן, Gen. xviii. 17) into its opposite, and the clause have the meaning of כִּי אֵלֶיךָ גִּלִּיתִי, Jer. xi. 20, xx. 12, is hardly conceivable. (2) Ad (apud) te abscondidi, scil. me (Saadia, Calvin, Maurer, Ewald, and Hengstenberg), in favour of which we decide ; for it is evident from Gen. xxxviii. 14, Deut. xxii. 12, cf. Jonah iii. 6, that כִּפָּה can express the act of covering as an act that is referred to the person himself who covers, and so can obtain a reflexive meaning. Therefore: towards Thee, with Thee have I made a hiding = hidden myself, which according to the sense is equivalent to חָסִיתִי (vid. vol. i. 99), as Hupfeld (with a few MSS.) wishes to read ; but Abulwalîd has already remarked that the same goal is reached with כִּפִּתי. Jahve, with whom he hides himself, is alone able to make known to him

what is right and beneficial in the position in which he finds
himself, in which he is exposed to temporal and spiritual
dangers, and is able to teach him to carry out the recognised
will of God ("the will of God, good and well-pleasing and
perfect," Rom. xii. 2); and this it is for which he prays to Him
in ver. 10 (רְצוֹנֶךָ; another reading, רְצוֹנֶךָ). For Jahve is indeed
his God, who cannot leave him, who is assailed and tempted
without and within, in error; may His good Spirit then (רוּחֲךָ
טוֹבָה for הַטּוֹבָה, Neh. ix. 20*) lead him in a level country, for,
as it is said in Isaiah, ch. xxvi. 7, in looking up to Jahve, "the
path which the righteous man takes is smoothness; Thou
makest the course of the righteous smooth." The geographical
term אֶרֶץ מִישׁוֹר, Deut. iv. 43, Jer. xlviii. 21, is here applied
spiritually. Here, too, reminiscences of Psalms already read
meet us everywhere: cf. on "to do Thy will," xl. 9; on "for
Thou art my God," xl. 6, and frequently; on "Thy good
Spirit," li. 14; on "a level country," and the whole petition,
xxvii. 11 (where the expresssion is "a level path"), together
with v. 9, xxv. 4 sq., xxxi. 4. And the Psalm also further
unrolls itself in such now well-known thoughts of the Psalms:
For Thy Name's sake, Jahve (xxv. 11), quicken me again (lxxi.
20, and frequently); by virtue of Thy righteousness be pleased
to bring my soul out of distress (cxlii. 8, xxv. 17, and frequently); and by virtue of Thy loving-kindness cut off mine
enemies (liv. 7). As in ver. 1 faithfulness and righteousness,
here loving-kindness (mercy) and righteousness, are coupled
together; and that so that mercy is not named beside תּוֹצִיא, nor
righteousness beside תַּצְמִית, but the reverse (*vid.* on ver. 1). It
is impossible that God should suffer him who has hidden himself in Him to die and perish, and should suffer his enemies
on the other hand to triumph. Therefore the poet confirms

---

* Properly, "Thy Spirit, a good one," so that טוֹבָה is an adjectival
apposition; as we can also say רוּחַ הַטּוֹבָה, a spirit, the good one, although
such irregularities may also be a negligent usage of the language, like the
Arabic مَسْجِدُ الجَامِعِ, the chief mosque, which many grammarians
regard as a construct relationship, others as an ellipsis (inasmuch as they
supply المكان between the words); the former is confirmed from the
Hebrew, *vid.* Ewald, § 287, *a.*

the prayer for the cutting off (הִצְמִית as in xciv. 23) of his
enemies and the destruction (הַאֲבִיד, elsewhere אִבֵּד) of the
oppressors of his soul (elsewhere צֹרְרִי) with the words: *for I
am Thy servant.*

PSALM CXLIV.

TAKING COURAGE IN GOD BEFORE A DECISIVE COMBAT.

The blessed condition of God's people.

1 BLESSED be Jahve my Rock,
  Who traineth my hands for the fight,
  My fingers for the war—
2 My loving-kindness and my fortress,
  My high tower and my deliverer for me,
  My shield and He in whom I hide,
  Who subdueth my people under me !

3 Jahve, what is man that Thou takest knowledge of him,
  The child of mortal man that Thou heedest him !
4 As for man, he is like a breath,
  His days are as a shadow that vanisheth away.

5 Jahve, bow Thy heavens and come down,
  Touch the mountains that they smoke.
6 Cast forth lightnings to scatter them ;
  Send forth Thine arrows to destroy them.
7 Send Thy hands from above,
  Rescue me and deliver me out of great waters :
  Out of the hand of the sons of the strange land,
8 Whose mouth speaketh vanity,
  And whose right hand is a right hand of falsehood.

9 Elohim, a new song will I sing unto Thee,
  Upon a ten-stringed nabla will I play unto Thee,
10 Who giveth salvation unto kings,
  Who rescueth David His servant from the evil sword,
11 Rescue and deliver me out of the hand of the sons of the
     strange land,

Whose mouth speaketh vanity,
Whose right hand is a right hand of falsehood.

12 *Because our sons are as high-reared plants in their youthful
   vigour,
   Our daughters as adorned corners after the mode of structure
   of a palace;*
13 *Our garners full, affording every kind of store;
   Our sheep bringing forth by thousands, multiplying by tens
   of thousands in our pastures;*
14 *Our kine bearing without mishap and without loss,
   And no lamentation in our streets.*
15 *Blessed is the people that is in such a case,
   Blessed is the people whose God is Jahve!*

Praised be Jahve who teacheth me to fight and conquer
(vers. 1, 2), me the feeble mortal, who am strong only in Him,
vers. 3, 4. May Jahve then be pleased to grant a victory this
time also over the boastful, lying enemies, vers. 5–8; so will I
sing new songs of thanksgiving unto Him, the bestower of
victory, vers. 9, 10. May He be pleased to deliver me out of
the hand of the barbarians who envy us our prosperity, which
is the result of our having Jahve as our God, vers. 11–15. A
glance at this course of the thought commends the additional
inscription of the LXX. (according to Origen only "in a few
copies"), πρὸς τὸν Γολιάδ, and the Targumist's reference of the
" evil sword" in ver. 10 to the sword of Goliath (after the
example of the Midrash). Read 1 Sam. xvii. 47. The Psalm
has grown out of this utterance of David. In one of the old
histories, just as several of these lie at the foundation of our
Books of Samuel as sources of information that are still recognisable, it was intended to express the feelings with which
David entered upon the single-handed combat with Goliath
and decided the victory of Israel over the Philistines. At that
time he had already been anointed by Samuel, as both the
narratives which have been worked up together in the First
Book of Samuel assume: see 1 Sam. xvi. 13, x. 1. And this
victory was for him a gigantic stride to the throne.

If אֲשֶׁר in ver. 12a is taken as *eo quod*, so that envy is
brought under consideration as a motive for the causeless (שָׁוְא),

lyingly treacherous rising (יְמִין שָׁקֶר) of the neighbouring peoples,
then the passage vers. 12–15 can at any rate be comprehended
as a part of the form of the whole. But only thus, and not
otherwise; for אֲשֶׁר cannot be intended as a statement of the
aim or purpose: in order that they may be . . . (Jerome, De
Wette, Hengstenberg, and others), since nothing but illustra-
tive substantival clauses follow; nor do these clauses admit of
an optative sense: We, whose sons, may they be . . . (Maurer);
and אֲשֶׁר never has an assuring sense (Vaihinger). It is also
evident that we cannot, with Saadia, go back to ver. 9 for the
interpretation of the אֲשֶׁר (اسمم على ما). But that junction
by means of *eo quod* is hazardous, since envy or ill-will (קנאה)
is not previously mentioned, and וִימִינָם יְמִין שָׁקֶר expresses a fact,
and not an action. If it is further considered that nothing is
wanting in the way of finish to the Psalm if it closes with ver.
11, it becomes all the more doubtful whether vers. 12–15 belonged originally to the Psalm. And yet we cannot discover
any Psalm in its immediate neighbourhood to which this piece
might be attached. It might the most readily, as Hitzig correctly judges, be inserted between vers. 13 and 14 of Ps. cxlvii.
But the rhythm and style differ from this Psalm, and we must
therefore rest satisfied with the fact that a fragment of another
Psalm is here added to Ps. cxliv., which of necessity may be
accounted as an integral part of it; but in spite of the fact
that the whole Psalm is built up on a gigantic scale, this was
not its original corner-stone, just as one does not indeed look
for anything further after the refrain, together with the mention of David in vers. 10 sq., cf. xviii. 51.

Vers. 1, 2. The whole of this first strophe is an imitation
of David's great song of thanksgiving, Ps. xviii. Hence the
calling of Jahve "my rock," xviii. 3, 47; hence the heaping
up of other appellations in ver. 2*a*, in which xviii. 3 is echoed;
but וּמְפַלְטִי־לִי (with Lamed deprived of the *Dagesh*) follows the
model of 2 Sam. xxii. 2. The naming of Jahve with חַסְדִּי is a
bold abbreviation of אֱלֹהֵי חַסְדִּי in lix. 11, 18, as also in Jonah
ii. 9 [8] the God whom the idolatrous ones forsake is called
חַסְדָּם. Instead of מִלְחָמָה the Davidic Psalms also poetically
say קְרָב, lv. 22, cf. lxxviii. 9. The expression "who traineth

my hands for the fight" we have already read in xviii. 35. The last words of the strophe, too, are after xviii. 48 ; but instead of וַיְדַבֵּר this poet says הָרוֹדֵד, from רָדָה = רָדַד (cf. Isa. xlv. 1, xli. 2), perhaps under the influence of וּמֹרִיד in 2 Sam. xxii. 48. In Ps. xviii. 48 we however read עַמִּים, and the Masora has enumerated Ps. cxliv. 2, together with 2 Sam. xxii. 44, Lam. iii. 14, as the three passages in which it is written עמי, whilst one expects עמים (ג' דסבירין עמים), as the Targum, Syriac, and Jerome (yet not the LXX.) in fact render it. But neither from the language of the books nor from the popular dialect can it be reasonably expected that they would say עַמִּי for עַמִּים in such an ambiguous connection. Either, therefore, we have to read עמים,* or we must fall in with the strong expression, and this is possible: there is, indeed, no necessity for the subduing to be intended of the use of despotic power, it can also be intended of God-given power, and of subjugating authority. David, the anointed one, but not having as yet ascended the throne, here gives expression to the hope that Jahve will grant him deeds of victory which will compel Israel to submit to him, whether willingly or reluctantly.

Vers. 3, 4. It is evident that ver. 3 is a variation of viii. 5 with the use of other verbs. יָדַע in the sense of loving intimacy; חָשַׁב, properly to count, compute, here *rationem habere*. Instead of כִּי followed by the future there are consecutive futures here, and בֶּן־אָדָם is aramaizingly (בַּר אֱנָשׁ) metamorphosed into בֶּן־אֱנוֹשׁ. Ver. 4 is just such another imitation, like a miniature of xxxix. 6 sq., 11, cf. lxii. 10. The figure of the shadow is the same as in cii. 12, cf. cix. 23. The connection of the third stanza with the second is still more disrupt than that of the second with the first.

Vers. 5–8. The deeds of God which Ps. xviii. celebrates are here made an object of prayer. We see from xviii. 10 that וַתֵּרַד, ver. 5a, has Jahve and not the heavens as its subject; and from xviii. 15 that the suffix *em* in ver. 6 is meant in both instances to be referred to the enemies. The enemies are called sons of a foreign country, *i.e.* barbarians, as in xviii. 45 sq. The fact that Jahve stretches forth His hand out of

---

* Rashi is acquainted with an otherwise unknown note of the Masora: תחתיו קרי ; but this *Kerî* is imaginary.

the heavens and rescues David out of great waters, is taken verbatim from xviii. 17; and the poet has added the interpretation to the figure here. On ver. 8a cf. xii. 3, xli. 7. The combination of words "right hand of falsehood" is the same as in cix. 2. But our poet, although so great an imitator, has, however, much also that is peculiar to himself. The verb בָּרַק, "to send forth lightning;" the verb פָּצָה in the Aramæo-Arabic signification "to tear out of, rescue," which in David always only signifies "to tear open, open wide" (one's mouth), xxii. 14, lxvi. 14; and the combination "the right hand of falsehood" (like "the tongue of falsehood" in cix. 2), i.e. the hand raised for a false oath, are only found here. The figure of Omnipotence, "He toucheth the mountains and they smoke," is, as in civ. 32, taken from the mountains that smoked at the giving of the Law, Ex. xix. 18, xx. 15. The mountains, as in lxviii. 17 (cf. lxxvi. 5), point to the worldly powers. God only needs to touch these as with the tip of His finger, and the inward fire, which will consume them, at once makes itself known by the smoke, which ascends from them. The prayer for victory is followed by a vow of thanksgiving for that which is to be bestowed.

Vers. 9–11. With the exception of Ps. cviii., which is composed of two Davidic Elohim-Psalms, the *Elohim* in ver. 9 of this strophe is the only one in the last two Books of the Psalter, and is therefore a feeble attempt also to reproduce the Davidic Elohimic style. The "new song" calls to mind xxxiii. 3, xl. 4; and נֵבֶל עָשׂוֹר also recalls xxxiii. 2 (which see). The fact that David mentions himself by name in his own song comes about in imitation of xviii. 51. From the eminence of thanksgiving the song finally descends again to petition, vers. 7c, 8 being repeated as a refrain. The petition developes itself afresh out of the attributes of the Being invoked (ver. 10), and these are a pledge of its fulfilment. For how could the God to whom all victorious kings owe their victory (xxxiii. 16, cf. 2 Kings v. 1, 1 Sam. xvii. 47) possibly suffer His servant David to succumb to the sword of the enemy! חֶרֶב רָעָה is the sword that is engaged in the service of evil.

Vers. 12–15. With reference to the relation of this passage to the preceding, *vid.* the introduction. אֲשֶׁר (it is uncertain whether this is a word belonging originally to this piece or one added by the person who appended it as a sort of clasp or rivet) signifies here *quoniam*, as in Judg. ix. 17, Jer. xvi. 13, and frequently. LXX. ὧν οἱ υἱοί (אשר בניהם); so that the temporal prosperity of the enemies is pictured here, and in ver. 15 the spiritual possession of Israel is contrasted with it. The union becomes satisfactorily close in connection with this reading, but the reference of the description, so designedly set forth, to the enemies is improbable. In vers. 12–14 we hear a language that is altogether peculiar, without any assignable earlier model. Instead of נְטִעִים we read נְטָעִים elsewhere; "in their youth" belongs to "our sons." מְזָוֵינוּ, our garners or treasuries, from a singular מֶזֶו or מָזוּ (apparently from a verb מָזָה, but contracted out of מְזֶוֶה), is a hapaxlegomenon; the older language has the words מִמְּגוּרָה, אוֹצָר, אָסָם instead of it. In like manner זַן, *genus* (*vid.* Ewald, *Lehrbuch*, S. 380), is a later word (found besides only in 2 Chron. xvi. 14, where וּזְנִים signifies *et varia quidem*, Syriac *zᵉnonoje*, or directly spices from *species*); the older language has מִין for this word. Instead of אַלּוּפִים, kine, which signifies "princes" in the older language, the older language says אֲלָפִים in viii. 8. The *plena scriptio* צֹאונֵנוּ, in which the *Waw* is even inaccurate, corresponds to the later period; and to this corresponds שׁ‎=אֲשֶׁר in ver. 15, cf. on the other hand xxxiii. 12. Also מְסֻבָּלִים, laden = bearing, like the Latin *forda* from *ferre* (cf. מְעֻבָּר in Job xxi. 10), is not found elsewhere. צֹאן is (contrary to Gen. xxx. 39) treated as a feminine collective, and אַלּוּף (cf. שׁוֹר in Job xxi. 10) as a *nomen epicœnum*. Contrary to the usage of the word, Maurer, Köster, Von Lengerke, and Fürst render it: our princes are set up (after Ezra vi. 3); also, after the mention of animals of the fold upon the meadows out-of-doors, one does not expect the mention of princes, but of horned cattle that are to be found in the stalls. זָוִית elsewhere signifies a corner, and here, according to the prevailing view, the corner-pillars; so that the elegant slender daughters are likened to tastefully sculptured Caryatides—not to sculptured projections (Luther). For (1) זָוִית does not signify a projection, but a corner, an angle, Arabic زَاوِيَة, *zâwîa* (in the terminology of the stone-mason the square-stone = אֶבֶן פִּנָּה, in the terminology of the carpenter the square), from زوى, *abdere* (cf. *e.g.* the proverb: *fî 'l zawâjâ* *chabâjâ*, in the corners are treasures). (2) The upstanding pillar is better adapted to the comparison than the overhanging projection. But that other prevailing interpretation is also doubtful. The architecture of Syria and Palestine—the ancient, so far as it can be known to us from its remains, and the new—exhibits nothing in connection with which one would be led to think of "corner-pillars." Nor is there any trace of that signification to be found in the Semitic זָוִית. On the other hand, the corners of large rooms in the houses of persons of position are ornamented with carved work even in the present day, and since this ornamentation is variegated, it may be asked whether מְחֻטָּבוֹת does here signify "sculptured," and not rather "striped in colours, variegated," which we prefer, since חָטַב (cogn. חָצֵב) signifies nothing more than to hew firewood;* and on the other side, the signification of the Arabic خطب, to be striped, many-coloured (IV. to become green-striped, of the coloquintida), is also secured to the verb חָטַב side by side with that signification by Prov. vii. 16. It is therefore to be rendered : our daughters are as corners adorned in varied colours after the architecture of palaces.† The words הָאֲלִיף,

---

* In every instance where חטב (cogn. חצב) occurs, frequently side by side with שָׁאַב מִים (to draw water), it signifies to hew wood for kindling; wherefore in Arabic, in which the verb has been lost, حطب signifies firewood (in distinction from خشب, wood for building, timber), and not merely this, but fuel in the widest sense, *e.g.* in villages where wood is scarce, cow-dung (*vid. Job*, i. 377, note), and the hemp-stalk, or stalk of the maize, in the desert the بعّر, *i.e.* camel-dung (which blazes up with a blue flame), and the perennial steppe-plant or its root. In relation to حطب, أحطب signifies lopped, pruned, robbed of its branches (of a tree), and حرب حاطب a pruning war, which devastates a country, just as the wood-gathering women of a settlement (styled الحاطبات or الحواطت) with their small hatchet (محطب) lay a district covered with tall plants bare in a few days. In the villages of the *Merg'* the little girls who collect the dry cow-dung upon the pastures are called بنات حاطبات, בְּנוֹת חֹטְבוֹת.—WETZSTEIN.

† Corners with variegated carved work are found even in the present

to bring forth by thousands, and מִרְבָּב (denominative from רְבָבָה), which surpasses it, multiplied by tens of thousands, are freely formed. Concerning חוּצוֹת, meadows, *vid.* on Job xviii. 17. פֶּרֶץ, in a martial sense a defeat, *clades*, *e.g.* in Judg. xxi. 15, is here any violent misfortune whatever, as murrain, which causes a breach, and יוֹצֵאת any head of cattle which goes off by a single misfortune. The lamentation in the streets is intended as in Jer. xiv. 2. שֶׁכָּכָה is also found in Cant. v. 9; nor does the poet, however, hesitate to blend this שׁ with the tetragrammaton into one word. The *Jod* is not dageshed (cf. cxxiii. 2), because it is to be read שֶׁאֲדֹנָי, cf. מֶיְהֹוָה = מֵאֲדֹנָי in Gen. xviii. 14. Luther takes ver. 15*a* and 15*b* as contrasts: Blessed is the people that is in such a case, But blessed is the people whose God is the Lord. There is, however, no antithesis intended, but only an exceeding of the first declaration by the second. For to be allowed to call the God from whom every blessing comes his God, is still infinitely more than the richest abundance of material blessing. The pinnacle of Israel's good fortune consists in being, by the election of grace, the people of the Lord (xxxii. 12).

---

day in Damascus in every reception-room (the so-called قَاعَة) of respectable houses [cf. Lane, *Manners and Customs of the Modern Egyptians*, Introduction]. An architectural ornament composed with much good taste and laborious art out of wood carvings, and glittering with gold and brilliant colours, covers the upper part of the corners, of which a *ḳâʿa* may have as many as sixteen, since three wings frequently abut upon the *bêt el-baḥăra*, *i.e.* the square with its marble basin. This decoration, which has a most pleasing effect to the eye, is a great advantage to saloons from two to three storeys high, and is evidently designed to get rid of the darker corners above on the ceiling, comes down from the ceiling in the corners of the room for the length of six to nine feet, gradually becoming narrower as it descends. It is the broadest above, so that it there also covers the ends of the horizontal corners formed by the walls and the ceiling. If this crowning of the corners, the technical designation of which, if I remember rightly, is القَرْنِيَة, *ḳornia*, might be said to go back into Biblical antiquity, the Psalmist would have used it as a simile to mark the beauty, gorgeous dress, and rich adornment of women. Perhaps, too, because they are not only modest and chaste (cf. Arabic *mesturât*, a veiled woman, in opposition to *memshushât*, one shone on by the sun), but also, like the children of respectable families, hidden from the eyes of strangers; for the Arabic proverb quoted above says, "treasures are hidden in the corners," and the superscription of a letter addressed to a lady of position runs: "May it kiss the hand of the protected lady and of the hidden jewel."—WETZSTEIN.

PSALM CXLV.

HYMN IN PRAISE OF THE ALL-BOUNTIFUL KING.

1 א I will extol Thee, my God O King,
And I will bless Thy Name for ever and ever.

2 ב Every day will I bless Thee,
And I will glorify Thy Name for ever and ever.

3 ג Great is Jahve, and greatly worthy to be praised,
And His greatness is unsearchable.

4 ד One generation to another praiseth Thy works,
And they declare Thy mighty deeds.

5 ה On the glorious honour of Thy majesty
And on Thy wondrous works will I meditate.

6 ו And they shall speak forth thy mightily terrible deeds,
And Thy mighty acts will I declare.

7 ז The praise of Thy great goodness shall they abundantly
utter,
And sing aloud of Thy righteousness.

8 ח Gracious and full of compassion is Jahve,
Long-suffering and great in goodness.

9 ט Good is Jahve unto all,
And His tender mercies are over all His works.

10 י All Thy works praise Thee, Jahve,
And Thy saints do bless Thee.

11 כ They talk of the glory of Thy kingship,
And confess Thy might—

12 ל To make known to the sons of men His mighty acts,
And the stately glory of His kingship.

13 מ Thy kingship is a kingship for all ages,
And Thy dominion endureth into all generations.

14 ס Jahve upholdeth all those who fall,
And raiseth up all those who are bowed down.

15 ע The eyes of all wait upon Thee,
And Thou givest them their food in due season;

16 פ Thou openest out Thine abundance,
And satisfiest every living thing with delight.

17 צ Jahve is righteous in all His ways,
   And gracious in all His works.
18 ק Jahve is nigh unto all those who call upon Him,
   To all who call upon Him in truth;
19 ר He fulfilleth the desire of those who fear Him,
   And He heareth their cry and delivereth them.
20 שׁ Jahve preserveth all those who love Him,
   And all the wicked doth He destroy.
21 ת Let my mouth then speak the praise of Jahve,
   And let all flesh bless His holy Name for ever and ever!

With Ps. cxliv. the collection draws doxologically towards its close. This Psalm, which begins in the form of the *beracha* (ברוך ה׳), is followed by another in which *benedicam* (vers. 1, 2) and *benedicat* (ver. 21) is the favourite word. It is the only Psalm that bears the title תְּהִלָּה, whose plural תְּהִלִּים is become the collective name of the Psalms. In *B. Berachoth* 4b it is distinguished by the apophthegm: "Every one who repeats the תהלה לדוד three times a day may be sure that he is a child of the world to come (בן העולם הבא)." And why? Not merely because this Psalm, as the Gemara says, אתיא באלף בית, *i.e.* follows the course of the alphabet (for Ps. cxix. is in fact also alphabetical, and that in an eightfold degree), and not merely because it celebrates God's care for all creatures (for this the Great Hallel also does, Ps. cxxxvi. 25), but because it unites both these prominent qualities in itself (משום דאית ביה תרתי). In fact, Ps. cxlv. 16 is a celebration of the goodness of God which embraces every living thing, with which only cxxxvi. 25, and not cxi. 5, can be compared. *Valde sententiosus hic Psalmus est*, says Bakius; and do we not find in this Psalm our favourite *Benedicite* and *Oculi omnium* which our children repeat before a meal? It is the ancient church's Psalm for the noon-day repast (*vid.* Armknecht, *Die heilige Psalmodie*, 1855, S. 54); ver. 15 was also used at the holy communion, hence Chrysostom says it contains τὰ ῥήματα ταῦτα, ἅπερ οἱ μεμυη-μένοι συνεχῶς ὑποψάλλουσι λέγοντες· Οἱ ὀφθαλμοὶ πάντων εἰς σὲ ἐλπίζουσιν καὶ σὺ δίδως τὴν τροφὴν αὐτῶν ἐν εὐκαιρίᾳ.

Κατὰ στοιχεῖον, observes Theodoret, καὶ οὗτος ὁ ὕμνος σύγ-κειται. The Psalm is distichic, and every first line of the distich has the ordinal letter; but the distich *Nun* is wanting.

The Talmud (*loc. cit.*) is of opinion that it is because the fatal נָפְלָה (Amos v. 2), which David, going on at once with ה' סוֹמֵךְ לְכָל־הַנֹּפְלִים, skips over, begins with *Nun.* On the other hand, Ewald, Vaihinger, and Sommer, like Grotius, think that the *Nun*-strophe has been lost. The LXX. (but not Aquila, Symmachus, Theodotion, nor Jerome in his translation after the original text) gives such a strophe, perhaps out of a MS. (like the Dublin *Cod. Kennicot,* 142) in which it was supplied: Πιστὸς (נאמן as in cxi. 7) κύριος ἐν (πᾶσι) τοῖς λόγοις αὐτοῦ καὶ ὅσιος ἐν πᾶσι τοῖς ἔργοις αὐτοῦ (according with ver. 17, with the change only of two words of this distich). Hitzig is of opinion that the original *Nun*-strophe has been welded into Ps. cxli.; but only his clairvoyant-like historical discernment is able to amalgamate ver. 6 of this Psalm with our Ps. cxlv. We are contented to see in the omission of the *Nun*-strophe an example of that freedom with which the Old Testament poets are wont to handle this kind of forms. Likewise there is no reason apparent for the fact that Jeremiah has chosen in ch. ii., iii., and iv. of the Lamentations to make the *Ajin*-strophe follow the *Pe*-strophe three times, whilst in ch. i. it precedes it.

Vers. 1–7. The strains with which this hymn opens are familiar Psalm-strains. We are reminded of xxx. 2, and the likewise alphabetical song of praise and thanksgiving xxxiv. 2. The *plena scriptio* אֱלוֹהַי in cxliii. 10 is repeated here. God is called "the King" as in xx. 10, xcviii. 6. The language of address "my God the King," which sounds harsh in comparison with the otherwise usual "my King and my God" (v. 3, lxxxiv. 4), purposely calls God with unrelated generality, that is to say in the most absolute manner, the King. If the poet is himself a king, the occasion for this appellation of God is all the more natural and the signification all the more pertinent. But even in the mouth of any other person it is significant. Whosoever calls God by such a name acknowledges His royal prerogative, and at the same time does homage to Him and binds himself to allegiance; and it is just this confessory act of exalting Him who in Himself is the absolutely lofty One that is here called רוֹמֵם. But how can the poet express the purpose of praising God's Name *for ever?* Because the praise of God is a need of his inmost nature, he has a perfect right to forget his own

drops the form of address. God's kingdom is a kingdom of all æons, and His dominion is manifested without exception and continually in all periods or generations (בְּכָל־דּוֹר וָדֹר as in xlv. 18, Esth. ix. 28, a pleonastic strengthening of the expression בְּדֹר וָדֹר, xc. 1). It is the eternal circumference of the history of time, but at the same time its eternal substance, which more and more unfolds and achieves itself in the succession of the periods that mark its course. For that all things in heaven and on earth shall be gathered up together (ἀνακεφαλαιώ-σασθαι, Eph. i. 10) in the all-embracing kingdom of God in His Christ, is the goal of all history, and therefore the substance of history which is working itself out. With ver. 13 (cf. Dan. iii. 33 [iv. 3], iv. 31 [34], according to Hitzig the primary passages) another paragraph is brought to a close.

Vers. 14–21. The poet now celebrates in detail the deeds of the gracious King. The words with לְ are pure datives, cf. the accusative expression in cxlvi. 8. He in person is the support which holds fast the falling ones (נֹפְלִים, here not the fallen ones, see xxviii. 1) in the midst of falling (Nicephorus: τοὺς καταπεσεῖν μέλλοντας ἑδραιοῖ, ὥστε μὴ καταπεσεῖν), and the stay by which those who are bowed together raise themselves. He is the Provider for all beings, the Father of the house, to whom in the great house of the world the eyes (עֵינֵי with the second ê toneless, Ew. § 100, b) of all beings, endowed with reason and irrational, are directed with calm confidence (Matt. vi. 26), and who gives them their food in its, i.e. in due season. The language of civ. 27 is very similar, and it proceeds here, too, as there in ver. 28 (cf. Sir. xl. 14). He opens His hand, which is ever full, much as a man who feeds the doves in his court does, and gives רָצוֹן, pleasure, i.e. that which is good, which is the fulfilling of their desire, in sufficient fulness to all living things (and therefore those in need of support for the body and the life). Thus it is to be interpreted, according to Deut. xxxiii. 23 (after which here in the LXX. the reading varies between εὐδοκίας and εὐλογίας), cf. Acts xiv. 17, ἐμπιπλῶν τροφῆς καὶ εὐφροσύνης τὰς καρδίας ἡμῶν. הִשְׂבִּיעַ is construed with a dative and accusative of the object instead of with two accusatives of the object (Ges. § 139. 1, 2). The usage of the language is unacquainted with רצון as an adverb in the sense of "willingly" (Hitzig), which would rather be

בִּרְצוֹנְךָ‎. In all the ways that Jahve takes in His historical rule
He is "righteous," *i.e.* He keeps strictly to the rule (norm) of
His holy love; and in all His works which He accomplishes in
the course of history He is merciful (חָסִיד‎), *i.e.* He practises
mercy (חֶסֶד‎, see xii. 2); for during the present time of mercy
the primary essence of His active manifestation is free pre-
venting mercy, condescending love. True, He remains at a
distance from the hypocrites, just as their heart remains far
from Him (Isa. xxix. 13); but as for the rest, with impartial
equality He is nigh (קָרוֹב‎ as in xxxiv. 19) to all who call upon
Him בֶּאֱמֶת‎, in firmness, certainty, truth, *i.e.* so that the prayer
comes from their heart and is holy fervour (cf. Isa. x. 20,
xlviii. 1). What is meant is true and real prayer in opposition
to the νεκρὸν ἔργον, as is also meant in the main in John iv.
23 sq. To such true praying ones Jahve is present, viz. in
mercy (for in respect of His power He is everywhere); He
makes the desire of those who fear Him a reality, their will
being also His; and He grants them the salvation (σωτηρία)
prayed for. Those who are called in ver. 19 those who fear
Him, are called in ver. 20 those who love Him. Fear and
love of God belong inseparably together; for fear without love
is an unfree, servile disposition, and love without fear, bold-
faced familiarity: the one dishonours the all-gracious One, and
the other the all-exalted One. But all who love and fear Him
He preserves, and on the other hand exterminates all wanton
sinners. Having reached the *Tav*, the hymn of praise, which
has traversed all the elements of the language, is at an end.
The poet does not, however, close without saying that praising
God shall be his everlasting employment (יְדַבֶּר‏ ֿ פִּי‎ with *Olewejored*, the *Mahpach* or rather *Jethib* sign of which above represents the *Makkeph*), and without wishing that all flesh, *i.e.* all
men, who are σὰρξ καὶ αἷμα, בָּשָׂר וָדָם‎, may bless God's holy
Name to all eternity. The realization of this wish is the final
goal of history. It will then have reached ver. 43 of the great
song in Deut. ch. xxxii.—Jahve one and His Name one (Zech.
xiv. 9), Israel praising God ὑπὲρ ἀληθείας, and the Gentiles
ὑπὲρ ἐλέους (Rom. xv. 8 sq.).

PSALM CXLVI.

HALLELUJAH TO GOD THE ONE TRUE HELPER.

HALLELUJAH.

1 PRAISE, O my soul, Jahve!
2 I will praise Jahve as long as I live,
  I will harp unto my God as long as I have any being.
3 Trust not in princes,
  In the son of man, who is not capable of help!
4 If his breath goeth forth, he returneth to his clod—
  In that day his devices perish.

5 Happy is he whose help is the God of Jacob,
  Whose confidence is in Jahve his God,
6 The Creator of heaven and earth,
  Of the sea and all that is therein—
  Who keepeth truth for ever,
7 Obtaining judgment for the oppressed,
  Giving bread to the hungry.

  Jahve looseth those who are bound,
8 Jahve maketh the blind to see,
  Jahve raiseth up those who are bowed down,
  Jahve loveth the righteous,
9 Jahve preserveth the strangers,
  He helpeth up the orphan and widow,
  And the way of the wicked He turneth down.
10 Jahve reigneth as King for ever,
  Thy God, O Zion, unto all generations—
    Hallelujah.

The Psalter now draws to a close with five Hallelujah Psalms. This first closing Hallelujah has many points of coincidence with the foregoing alphabetical hymn (compare אֲהַלְלָה in ver. 2 with cxlv. 2; שִׂבְרוֹ in ver. 5 with cxlv. 15; "who giveth bread to the hungry" in ver. 7 with cxlv. 15 sq.; "who maketh the blind to see" in ver. 8 with cxlv. 14; "Jahve reigneth, etc.," in ver. 10 with cxlv. 13)—the same range of thought betrays one author.   In the LXX. Ps. cxlvi.–cxlviii. (according to its enumeration four Psalms, viz. cxlv.–cxlviii., Ps. cxlvii. being split up into two) have the inscription Ἀλληλούια. Ἀγγαίου καὶ Ζαχαρίου, which is repeated four times.   These Psalms appear to have formed a separate Hallel, which is referred back to these prophets, in the old liturgy of the second Temple.   Later on they became, together with Ps. cxlix., cl., an integral part of the daily morning prayer, and in fact of the פסוקי דזמרה, i.e. of the mosaic-work of Psalms and other poetical pieces that was incorporated in the morning prayer, and are called even in *Shabbath* 118b *Hallel*,* but expressly distinguished from the Hallel to be recited at the Passover and other feasts, which is called "the Egyptian Hallel." In distinction from this, Krochmal calls these five Psalms the Greek Hallel.   But there is nothing to oblige us to come down beyond the time of Ezra and Nehemiah.   The agreement between 1 Macc. ii. 63 (ἔστρεψεν εἰς τὸν χοῦν αὐτοῦ, καὶ ὁ διαλογισμὸς αὐτοῦ ἀπώλετο) and ver. 4 of our Psalm, which Hitzig has turned to good account, does not decide anything concerning the age of the Psalm, but only shows that it was in existence at the time of the author of the First Book of Maccabees,—a point in favour of which we were not in need of any proof.   But there was just as much ground for dissuading against putting confidence in princes in the time of the Persians as in that of the Grecian domination.

Vers. 1–4.   Instead of "bless," as in ciii. 1, civ. 1, the poet of this Psalm says "praise."   When he attunes his soul to the praise of God, he puts himself personally into this mood of mind, and therefore goes on to say "I will praise."   He will, however, not only praise God in the song which he is beginning, but בְּחַיָּי (*vid.* on lxiii. 5), filling up his life with it, or בְּעוֹדִי (prop. "in my yet-being," with the suffix of the noun, whereas עוֹדֶנִּי with the verbal suffix is "I still am"), so that his continued life is also a constant continued praising, viz. (and this is in the mind of the poet here, even at the commencement of the Psalm) of the God and King who, as being the Almighty, Eternal, and

---

* Rashi, however, understands only Ps. cxlviii. and cl. by פסוקי דזמרה in that passage.

unchangeably Faithful One, is the true ground of confidence.
The warning against putting trust in princes calls to mind
cxviii. 8 sq. The clause: the son of man, who has no help
that he could afford, is to be understood according to lx. 13.
The following לְאַדְמָתוֹ shows that the poet by the expression
בֶּן־אָדָם combines the thoughts of Gen. ii. 7 and iii. 19. If his
breath goes forth, he says, basing the untrustworthiness and
feebleness of the son of Adam upon the inevitable final destiny
of the son of Adam taken out of the ground, then he returns
to his earth, *i.e.* the earth of his first beginning; cf. the more
exact expression אֶל־עֲפָרָם, after which the εἰς τὴν γῆν αὐτοῦ of
the LXX. is exchanged for εἰς τὸν χοῦν αὐτοῦ in 1 Macc. ii.
63: On the hypothetical relation of the first future clause to
the second, cf. cxxxix. 8–10, 18; Ew. § 357, *b*. In that day,
the inevitable day of death, the projects or plans of man are
at once and for ever at an end. The ἅπ. λεγ. עֶשְׁתֹּנֹת describes
these with the collateral notion of subtleness and magnitude.

Vers. 5–7*a*. Man's help is of no avail; blessed is he
(this is the last of the twenty-five אַשְׁרֵי of the Psalter), on the
contrary, who has the God of Jacob (שֶׁאֵל like שֶׁיְהֹוָה in cxliv.
15) as Him in whom is his succour (בְּעֶזְרוֹ with *Beth essentiæ*,
vid. on xxxv. 2),—he, whose confidence (שֵׂבֶר as in cxix. 116)
rests on Jahve, whom he can by faith call his God. Men often
are not able to give help although they might be willing to do
so: He, however, is the Almighty, the Creator of the heavens,
the earth, and the sea, and of all living things that fill these
three (cf. Neh. ix. 6). Men easily change their mind and do
not keep their word: He, however, is He who keepeth truth or
faithfulness, inasmuch as He unchangeably adheres to the fulfilling of His promises. שֹׁמֵר אֱמֶת is in form equivalent substantially to שֹׁמֵר חֶסֶד and שֹׁמֵר הַבְּרִית. And that which He is
able to do as being the Almighty, and cannot as being the
Truthful One leave undone, is also really His mode of active
manifestation made evident in practical proofs: He obtains
right for the oppressed, gives bread to the hungry, and consequently proves Himself to be the succour of those who suffer
wrong without doing wrong, and as the provider for those who
look for their daily bread from His gracious hand. With
הַשֹּׁמֵר, the only determinate participle, the faithfulness of God
to His promises is made especially prominent.

Vers. 7*b*–10. The five lines beginning with *Jahve* belong together. Each consists of three words, which in the main is also the favourite measure of the lines in the Book of Job. The expression is as brief as possible. הַתִּיר is transferred from the yoke and chains to the person himself who is bound, and פָּקַח is transferred from the eyes of the blind to the person himself. The five lines celebrate the God of the five-divisioned Tôra, which furnishes abundant examples for these celebrations, and is directed with most considerate tenderness towards the strangers, orphans, and widows in particular. The orphan and the widow, says the sixth line, doth He recover, strengthen (with reference to עוֹדֵד see xx. 9, xxxi. 12). *Valde gratus mihi est hic Psalmus*, Bakius observes, *ob Trifolium illud Dei: Advenas, Pupillos, et Viduas, versu uno luculentissime depictum, id quod in toto Psalterio nullibi fit.* Whilst Jahve, however, makes the manifold sorrows of His saints to have a blessed issue, He bends (יְעַוֵּת) the way of the wicked, so that it leads into error and ends in the abyss (i. 6). This judicial manifestation of Jahve has only one line devoted to it. For He rules in love and in wrath, but delights most of all to rule in love. Jahve is, however, the God of Zion. The eternal duration of His kingdom is also the guarantee for its future glorious completion, for the victory of love. Hallelujah!

PSALM CXLVII.

HALLELUJAH TO THE SUSTAINER OF ALL THINGS, THE RESTORER OF JERUSALEM.

1   HALLELUJAH,
　　For it is good to celebrate our God in song,
　　For it is lovely, comely is a hymn of praise.
2　The builder up of Jerusalem is Jahve,
　　The outcasts of Israel He gathereth together;
3　He healeth the broken in heart,
　　And bindeth up their wounds;
4　Telling the number of the stars,
　　He calleth them all by names.
5　Great is our Lord and rich in strength,
　　To His understanding there is no number.

6 Jahve helpeth up the afflicted,
   He casteth the wicked down to the ground.

7 Sing unto Jahve a thanksgiving song,
   Play unto our God upon the cithern !
8 Who covereth the heaven with clouds,
   Who prepareth rain for the earth,
   Who maketh the mountains shoot forth grass ;
9 Giving to the beast its food,
   To the young ravens which call.
10 Not in the strength of the horse doth He delight,
   Not in the legs of a man doth He take pleasure—
11 Jahve hath pleasure in those who fear Him,
   In those who hope in His mercy.

12 Celebrate, O Jerusalem, Jahve,
   Praise Thy God, O Zion !
13 For He hath made the bolts of thy gates fast,
   He hath blessed thy children in the midst of thee--
14 He it is who giveth thy border peace,
   He satisfieth thee with the fat of wheat;
15 Who sendeth forth His commandment to the earth,
   His word runneth very swiftly ;
16 Who giveth snow like wool,
   He scattereth hoar-frost like ashes,
17 He casteth down His ice like morsels—
   Before His cold, who can stand ? !
18 He sendeth forth His word and causeth everything to melt ,
   He causeth His wind to blow, forthwith the waters flow.
19 He made known His word unto Jacob,
   His statutes and His judgments unto Israel.
20 He hath not dealt so with any nation ;
   And as for His judgments—they do not know them,
        Hallelujah.

It is the tone of the restoration-period of Ezra and Nehemiah that meets us sounding forth out of this and the two following Psalms, even more distinctly and recognisably than out of the nearly related preceding Psalm (cf. ver. 6 with cxlvi. 9).   In Ps. cxlvii. thanksgiving is rendered to God for the restoration of Jerusalem, which is now once more a city with walls and gates; in Ps. cxlviii. for the restoration of the national independence; and in Ps. cxlix. for the restoration of the capacity of joyously and triumphantly defending themselves to the people so long rendered defenceless and so ignominiously enslaved.

In the seventh year of Artachshasta (Artaxerxes i. Longimanus) Ezra the priest entered Jerusalem, after a journey of five months, with about two thousand exiles, mostly out of the families of the Levites (458 B.C.). In the twentieth year of this same clement king, that is to say, thirteen years later (445 B.C.), came Nehemiah, his cup-bearer, in the capacity of a *Tirshâtha* (*vid. Isaiah*, vol. i. 2). Whilst Ezra did everything for introducing the Mosaic Law again into the mind and commonwealth of the nation, Nehemiah furthered the building of the city, and more particularly of the walls and gates. We hear from his own mouth, in ch. ii.–vii. of the Book that is extracted from his memoirs, how indefatigably and cautiously he laboured to accomplish this work. Ch. xii. 27–45 is closely connected with these notes of Nehemiah's own hand. After having been again in the meanwhile in Susa, and there neutralized the slanderous reports that had reached the court of Persia, he appointed, at his second stay in Jerusalem, a feast in dedication of the walls. The Levite musicians, who had settled down for the most part round about Jerusalem, were summoned to appear in Jerusalem. Then the priests and Levites were purified; and they purified the people, the gates, and the walls, the bones of the dead (as we must with Herzfeld picture this to ourselves) being taken out of all the tombs within the city and buried before the city; and then came that sprinkling, according to the Law, with the sacred lye of the red heifer, which is said (*Para* iii. 5) to have been introduced again by Ezra for the first time after the Exile. Next the princes of Judah, the priests, and Levite musicians were placed in the west of the city in two great choirs (תּוֹדֹת*) and processions

---

* The word has been so understood by Menahem, Juda ben Koreish, and Abulwalîd; whereas Herzfeld is thinking of hecatombs for a thank-offering, which might have formed the beginning of both festive processions.

(תְּהִלָּכֹת). The one festal choir, which was led by the one half
of the princes, and among the priests of which Ezra went on
in front, marched round the right half of the city, and the
other round the left, whilst the people looked down from the
walls and towers. The two processions met on the east side of
the city and drew up in the Temple, where the festive sacrifices
were offered amidst music and shouts of joy.

The supposition that Ps. cxlvii.–cl. were all sung at this
dedication of the walls under Nehemiah (Hengstenberg) cannot
be supported; but as regards Ps. cxlvii., the composition of
which in the time of Nehemiah is acknowledged by the
most diverse parties (Keil, Ewald, Dillmann, Zunz), the
reference to the Feast of the Dedication of the walls is very
probable. The Psalm falls into two parts, vers. 1–11, 12–20,
which exhibit a progression both in respect of the building
of the walls (vers. 2, 13), and in respect of the circumstances of the weather, from which the poet takes occasion
to sing the praise of God (vers. 8 sq., 16–18). It is a
double Psalm, the first part of which seems to have been composed, as Hitzig suggests, on the appearing of the November
rain, and the second in the midst of the rainy part of the
winter, when the mild spring breezes and a thaw were already
in prospect.

Vers. 1–6. The Hallelujah, as in cxxxv. 3, is based upon
the fact, that to sing of our God, or to celebrate our God in
song (זַמֵּר with an accusative of the object, as in xxx. 13, and
frequently), is a discharge of duty that reacts healthfully and
beneficially upon ourselves: " comely is a hymn of praise "
(taken from xxxiii. 1), both in respect of the worthiness of
God to be praised, and of the gratitude that is due to Him.
Instead of זַמֵּר or לְזַמֵּר, xcii. 2, the expression is זִמְרָה, a form
of the *infin. Piel*, which at least can still be proved to be
possible by לְיִסְרָה in Lev. xxvi. 18. The two כִּי are co-ordinate, and כִּי־נָעִים no more refers to God here than in cxxxv. 3,
as Hitzig supposes when he alters ver. 1 so that it reads:
" Praise ye Jah because He is good, play unto our God
because He is lovely." Ps. xcii. 2 shows that כִּי־טוֹב can refer
to God; but נָעִים said of God is contrary to the custom and
spirit of the Old Testament, whereas טוֹב and נעים are also in

cxxxiii. 1 neuter predicates of a subject that is set forth in the infinitive form. In ver. 2 the praise begins, and at the same time the confirmation of the delightful duty. Jahve is the builder up of Jerusalem, He brings together (כָּנַס as in Ezekiel, the later word for אָסַף and קִבֵּץ) the outcasts of Israel (as in Isa. xi. 12, lvi. 8); the building of Jerusalem is therefore intended of the rebuilding up, and to the dispersion of Israel corresponds the holy city laid in ruins. Jahve healeth the heart-broken, as He has shown in the case of the exiles, and bindeth up their pains (xvi. 4), *i.e.* smarting wounds; רָפָא, which is here followed by חִבֵּשׁ, also takes to itself a dative object in other instances, both in an active and (Isa. vi. 10) an impersonal application; but for שְׁבוּרֵי לֵב the older language says נִשְׁבְּרֵי לֵב, xxxiv. 19, Isa. lxi. 1. The connection of the thoughts, which the poet now brings to the stars, becomes clear from the primary passage, Isa. xl. 26, cf. 27. To be acquainted with human woe and to relieve it is an easy and small matter to Him who allots a number to the stars, that are to man innumerable (Gen. xv. 5), *i.e.* who has called them into being by His creative power in whatever number He has pleased, and yet a number known to Him (מֹנֶה, the *part. præs.*, which occurs frequently in descriptions of the Creator), and calls to them all names, *i.e.* names them all by names which are the expression of their true nature, which is well known to Him, the Creator. What Isaiah says (ch. xl. 26) with the words, " because of the greatness of might, and as being strong in power," and (ver. 28) " His understanding is unsearchable," is here asserted in ver. 5 (cf. cxlv. 3): great is our Lord, and capable of much (as in Job xxxvii. 23, שַׂגִּיא כֹחַ), and to His understanding there is no number, *i.e.* in its depth and fulness it cannot be defined by any number. What a comfort for the church as it traverses its ways, that are often so labyrinthine and entangled! Its Lord is the Omniscient as well as the Almighty One. Its history, like the universe, is a work of God's infinitely profound and rich understanding. It is a mirror of gracious love and righteous anger. The patient sufferers (עֲנָוִים) He strengthens (מְעוֹדֵד as in cxlvi. 9); malevolent sinners (רְשָׁעִים), on the other hand, He casts down to the earth (עֲדֵי־אָרֶץ, cf. Isa. xxvi. 5), casting deep down to the ground those who exalt themselves to the skies.

Vers. 7–11. With ver. 7 the song takes a new flight. עָנָה לְ signifies to strike up or sing in honour of any one, Num. xxi. 27, Isa. xxvii. 2. The object of the action is conceived of in בְּתוֹדָה as the medium of it (cf. *e.g.* Job xvi. 4). The participles in vers. 8 sq. are attributive clauses that are attached in a free manner to לֵאלֹהֵינוּ. הֵכִין signifies to prepare, procure, as *e.g.* in Job xxxviii. 41—a passage which the psalmist has had in his mind in connection with ver. 9. מַצְמִיחַ, as being the causative of a *verb. crescendi*, is construed with a double accusative: " making mountains (whither human agriculture does not reach) to bring forth grass;" and the advance to the thought that God gives to the cattle the bread that they need is occasioned by the " He causeth grass to grow for the cattle " of the model passage civ. 14, just as the only hinting אֲשֶׁר יִקְרָאוּ, which is said of the young of the raven (which are forsaken and cast off by their mothers very early), is explained from יְלָדָיו אֶל־אֵל יְשַׁוֵּעוּ in Job *loc. cit.* The verb קָרָא, κράζειν (cf. κρώζειν), is still more expressive for the cry of the raven, κόραξ, Sanscrit *kârava*, than that שִׁוַּע; κοράττειν and κορακεύεσθαι signify directly to implore incessantly, without taking any refusal. Towards Him, the gracious Sustainer of all beings, are the ravens croaking for their food pointed (cf. Luke xii. 24, " Consider the ravens "), just like the earth that thirsts for rain. He is the all-conditioning One. Man, who is able to know that which the irrational creature unconsciously acknowledges, is in the feeling of his dependence to trust in Him and not in himself. In all those things to which the God-estranged self-confidence of man so readily clings, God has no delight (יֶחְפָּץ, pausal form like יֶחְבָּשׁ) and no pleasure, neither in the strength of the horse, whose rider imagines himself invincible, and, if he is obliged to flee, that he cannot be overtaken, nor in the legs of a man, upon which he imagines himself so firm that he cannot be thrown down, and which, when he is pursued, will presumptively carry him far enough away into safety. שׁוֹק, ساق, is the leg from the knee to the foot, from ساق, root سوق, to drive, urge forward, more particularly to urge on to a gallop (like *crus*, according to Pott, from the root *car*, to go). What is meant here is, not that the strength of the horse and muscular power are of no avail when God wills to destroy a man (xxxiii. 16 sq., Amos ii. 14

sq.), but only that God has no pleasure in the warrior's horse and in athletic strength. Those who fear Him, *i.e.* with a knowledge of the impotency of all power possessed by the creature in itself, and in humble trust feel themselves dependent upon His omnipotence—these are they in whom He takes pleasure (רָצָה with the accusative), those who, renouncing all carnal defiance and self-confident self-working, hope in His mercy.

Vers. 12–20. In the LXX. this strophe is a Psalm (*Lauda Jerusalem*) of itself. The call goes forth to the church again on the soil of the land of promise assembled round about Jerusalem. The holy city has again risen out of its ruins; it now once more has gates which can stand open in the broad daylight, and can be closed and bolted when the darkness comes on for the security of the municipality that is only just growing into power (Neh. vii. 1–4). The blessing of God again rests upon the children of the sacred metropolis. Its territory, which has experienced all the sufferings of war, and formerly resounded with the tumult of arms and cries of woe and destruction, God has now, from being an arena of conflict, made into peace (the accusative of the effect, and therefore different from Isa. lx. 17); and since the land can now again be cultivated in peace, the ancient promise (lxxxi. 17) is fulfilled, that God would feed His people, if they would only obey Him, with the fat of wheat. The God of Israel is the almighty Governor of nature. It is He who sends His fiat (אִמְרָתוֹ after the manner of the וַיֹּאמֶר of the history of creation, cf. xxxiii. 9) earthwards (אֶרֶץ, the accusative of the direction). The word is His messenger (*vid.* on cvii. 20), עַד־מְהֵרָה, *i.e.* it runs as swiftly as possible, viz. in order to execute the errand on which it is sent. He it is who sends down snow-flakes like flocks of wool, so that the fields are covered with snow as with a white-woollen warming covering.* He scatters hoar-frost (כְּפוֹר from כָּפַר, to cover over) about like ashes, so that trees, roofs, etc., are crusted over with the fine frozen dew or mist as though they were powdered with ashes that the wind had blown about. Another time He casts His

---

* Bochart in his *Hierozoicon* on this passage compares an observation of Eustathius on Dionysius Periegetes: τὴν χιόνα ἐριώδες ὕδωρ ἀστείως οἱ παλαιοὶ ἐκάλουν.

ice * (קַרְחוֹ from קֶרַח; or according to another reading, קָרְחוֹ from
קֹרַח) down like morsels, fragments, כְפִתִּים, viz. as hail-stones, or
as sleet. The question : before His cold—who can stand? is
formed as in Nah. i. 6, cf. cxxx. 3. It further comes to pass
that God sends forth His word and causes them (snow, hoar-
frost, and ice) to melt away : He makes His thawing wind
blow, waters flow ; *i.e.* as soon as the one comes about, the other
also takes place forthwith. This God now, who rules all things
by His word and moulds all things according to His will, is the
God of the revelation pertaining to the history of salvation,
which is come to Israel, and as the bearer of which Israel takes
the place of honour among the nations, Deut. iv. 7 sq., 32–34.
Since the poet says מַגִּיד and not הִגִּיד, he is thinking not only of
the Tôra, but also of prophecy as the continuous self-attestation of God, the Lawgiver. The *Kerî* דְּבָרָיו, occasioned by the
plurals of the parallel member of the verse, gives an unlimited
indistinct idea. We must keep to דְּבָרוֹ, with the LXX., Aquila,
Theodotion, the Quinta, Sexta, and Jerome. The word, which
is the medium of God's cosmical rule, is gone forth as a word
of salvation to Israel, and, unfolding itself in statutes and judgments, has raised Israel to a legal state founded upon a positive
divine law or judgment such as no Gentile nation possesses.
The Hallelujah does not exult over the fact that these other
nations are not acquainted with any such positive divine law,
but (cf. Deut. iv. 7 sq., Baruch iv. 4) over the fact that Israel
is put into possession of such a law. It is frequently attested
elsewhere that this possession of Israel is only meant to be a
means of making salvation a common property of the world at
large.

PSALM CXLVIII.

HALLELUJAH OF ALL HEAVENLY AND EARTHLY BEINGS.

HALLELUJAH.

1 PRAISE ye Jahve from the heavens,
  Praise ye Him in the heights.

---

* LXX. (Italic, Vulgate) κρύσταλλον, *i.e.* ice, from the root κρυ, to
freeze, to congeal (Jerome *glaciem*). *Quid est crystallum?* asks Augustine,
and replies : *Nix est glacie durata per multos annos ita ut a sole vel igne acile
dissolvi non possit.*

2 Praise ye Him, all His angels,
  Praise ye Him, all His host.
3 Praise ye Him, sun and moon,
  Praise Him all ye stars of light.
4 Praise Him ye heavens of heavens,
  And ye waters that are above the heavens.
5 Let them praise the Name of Jahve,
  For HE commanded and they were created,
6 And He set them there for ever and ever;
  He gave a law, and not one transgresseth it.

7 Praise ye Jahve from the earth,
  Sea-monsters and all deeps;
8 Fire and hail, snow and vapour,
  Stormy wind fulfilling His word;
9 Ye mountains and all hills,
  Fruit-trees and all cedars;
10 Ye wild beasts and all cattle,
  Creeping things and winged birds;
11 Kings of the earth and all tribes,
  Princes and all judges of the earth;
12 Young men and also maidens,
  Old men together with youths—
13 Let them praise the Name of Jahve,
  For His Name is highly exalted, He alone,
  His glory is above earth and heaven.
14 And He hath raised a horn for His people,
  For a praise for all His saints,
  For the children of Israel, for the people near unto Him
      Hallelujah.

After the Psalmist in the foregoing Hallelujah has made the gracious self-attestation of Jahve in the case of the people of revelation, in connection with the general government of the almighty and all-benevolent One in the world, the theme of his praise, he calls upon all creatures in heaven and on earth, and more especially mankind of all peoples and classes and races and ages, to join in concert in praise of the Name of Jahve, and that on the ground of the might and honour which He has bestowed upon His people, *i.e.* has bestowed upon them once more now when they are gathered together again out of exile and Jerusalem has risen again out of the ruins of its overthrow. The hymn of the three in the fiery furnace, which has been interpolated in ch. iii. of the Book of Daniel in the LXX., is for the most part an imitation of this Psalm. In the language of the liturgy this Psalm has the special name of *Laudes* among the twenty *Psalmi alleluiatici*, and all the three Psalms cxlviii.–cl. which close the Psalter are called αἶνοι, Syriac *shabchûh* (praise ye Him).

In this Psalm the loftiest consciousness of faith is united with the grandest contemplation of the world. The church appears here as the choir-leader of the universe. It knows that its experiences have a central and universal significance for the whole life of creation; that the loving-kindness which has fallen to its lot is worthy to excite joy among all beings in heaven and on earth. And it calls not only upon everything in heaven and on earth that stands in fellowship of thought, of word, and of freedom with it to praise God, but also the sun, moon, and stars, water, earth, fire, and air, mountains, trees, and beasts, yea even such natural phenomena as hail, snow, and mist. How is this to be explained? The easiest way of explaining is to say that it is a figure of speech (Hupfeld); but this explanation explains nothing. Does the invitation in the exuberance of feeling, without any clearness of conception, here overstep the boundary of that which is possible? Or does the poet, when he calls upon these lifeless and unconscious things to praise God, mean that we are to praise God on their behalf—ἀφορᾶν εἰς ταῦτα, as Theodoret says, καὶ τοῦ Θεοῦ τὴν σοφίαν καταμανθάνειν καὶ διὰ πάντων αὐτῷ πλέκειν τὴν ὑμνῳδίαν? Or does the " praise ye " in its reference to these things of nature proceed on the assumption that they praise God when they redound to the praise of God, and find its justification in the fact that the human will enters into this matter of fact which relates to things, and is devoid of any will, and seizes it and drags it into the concert of angels and men? All these explanations are unsatisfactory. The call to praise proceeds rather from the wish that all creatures, by becoming after their own manner an echo and reflection of the divine glory, may participate in the joy at the glory which God has bestowed upon His people after their deep humiliation. This wish, however, after all rests upon the great truth, that the way through suffering to glory which the church is traversing, has not only the glorifying of God in itself, but by means of this glorifying, the glorifying of God in all creatures and by all creatures, too, as its final aim, and that these, finally transformed (glorified) in the likeness of transformed (glorified) humanity, will become the bright mirror of the divine doxa and an embodied hymn of a thousand voices. The calls also in Isa. xliv. 23, xlix. 13, cf. lii. 9, and the descriptions in Isa. xxxv. 1 sq., xli. 19, lv. 12 sq., proceed from the view to which Paul gives clear expression from the stand-point of the New Testament in Rom. viii. 18 sqq.

Vers. 1–6. The call does not rise step by step from below upwards, but begins forthwith from above in the highest and outermost spheres of creation. The place whence, before all others, the praise is to resound is the heavens; it is to resound in the heights, viz. the heights of heaven (Job xvi. 19, xxv. 2, xxxi. 2). The מִן might, it is true, also denote the birth or origin: ye of the heavens, *i.e.* ye celestial beings (cf. lxviii. 27), but the parallel בַּמְּרוֹמִים renders the immediate construction with הַלְלוּ more natural. Vers. 2–4 tell who are to praise Jahve there: first of all, all His angels, the messengers of the Ruler of the world—all His host, *i.e.* angels and stars, for צְבָאוֹ (*Chethîb*) or צְבָאָיו (*Kerî* as in ciii. 21) is the name of the heavenly host armed with light which God Tsebaoth commands (*vid.* on Gen. ii. 1),—a name including both stars (*e.g.* in Deut. iv. 19) and angels (*e.g.* in Josh. v. 14 sq., 1 Kings xxii. 19); angels and stars are also united in the Scriptures in other instances (*e.g.* Job xxxviii. 7). When the psalmist calls upon these beings of light to praise Jahve, he does not merely express his delight in that which they do under any circumstances (Hengstenberg), but comprehends the heavenly world with the earthly, the church above with the church here below (*vid.* on Ps. xxix., ciii.), and gives a special turn to the praise of the former, making it into an echo of the praise of the latter, and blending both harmoniously together. The heavens of heavens are, as in Deut. x. 14, 1 Kings viii. 27, Sir. xvi. 18, and frequently, those which lie beyond the heavens of the earth which were created on the fourth day, therefore they are the outermost and highest spheres. The waters which are above the heavens are, according to Hupfeld, "a product of the fancy, like the upper heavens and the whole of the inhabitants of heaven." But if in general the other world is not a notion to which there is no corresponding entity, this notion may also have things for its substance which lie beyond our knowledge of nature. The Scriptures, from the first page to the last, acknowledge the existence of celestial waters, to which the rain-waters stand in the relation as it were of a finger-post pointing upwards (see Gen. i. 7). All these beings belonging to the superterrestrial world are to praise the Name of Jahve, for HE, the God of Israel, it is by whose fiat (צִוָּה, like אָמַר in xxxiii. 9*) the heavens and all their host are created (xxxiii. 6). He has set them, which did not previously exist, up (הֶעֱמִיד as *e.g.* in Neh. vi. 7, the causative to עָמַד in xxxiii. 9, cf. cxix. 91), and that for ever and ever (cxi. 8), *i.e.* in order for ever to maintain the position in the whole of creation which He has assigned to them. He hath given a law (חֹק) by which its distinctive characteristic is stamped upon each of these heavenly beings, and a fixed bound is set to the nature and activity of each in its mutual relation to all, and not one transgresses (the individualizing singular) this law given to it. Thus וְלֹא יַעֲבֹר is to be understood, according to Job xiv. 5, cf. Jer. v. 22, Job xxxviii. 10, Ps. civ. 9. Hitzig makes the Creator Himself the subject; but then the poet would have at least been obliged to say חֹק־נתן לָמוֹ, and moreover it may be clearly seen from Jer. xxxi. 36, xxxiii. 20, how the thought that God inviolably keeps the orders of nature in check is expressed θεοπρεπῶς. Jer. v. 22, by way of example, shows that the law itself is not, with Ewald, Maurer, and others, following the LXX., Syriac, Italic, Jerome, and Kimchi, to be made the subject: a law hath He given, and it passes not away (an imperishable one). In combination with חֹק, עָבַר always signifies " to pass over, transgress."

Vers. 7–14. The call to the praise of Jahve is now turned, in the second group of verses, to the earth and everything belonging to it in the widest extent. Here too מִן־הָאָרֶץ, like מִן־הַשָּׁמַיִם, ver. 1, is intended of the place whence the praise is to resound, and not according to x. 18 of earthly beings. The call

---

is addressed in the first instance to the sea-monsters or dragons
(lxxiv. 13), *i.e.*, as Pindar (*Nem.* iii. 23 sq.) expresses it, θῆρας
ἐν πελάγεϊ ὑπερόχους, and to the surging mass of waters (תְּהֹמוֹת)
above and within the earth. Then to four phenomena of
nature, coming down from heaven and ascending heavenwards,
which are so arranged in ver. 8*a*, after the model of the chiasmus (crosswise position), that fire and smoke (קִיטוֹר), more
especially of the mountains (Ex. xix. 18), hail and snow stand
in reciprocal relation; and to the storm-wind (רוּחַ סְעָרָה, an appositional construction, as in cvii. 25), which, beside a seeming
freeness and untractableness, performs God's word. What is
said of this last applies also to the fire, etc.; all these phenomena of nature are messengers and servants of God, civ. 4, cf.
ciii. 20. When the poet wishes that they all may join in concert with the rest of the creatures to the praise of God, he ex-
cepts the fact that they frequently become destructive powers
executing judicial punishment, and only has before his mind
their (more especially to the inhabitant of Palestine, to whom
the opportunity of seeing hail, snow, and ice was more rare
than with us, imposing) grandeur and their relatedness to the
whole of creation, which is destined to glorify God and to be
itself glorified. He next passes over to the mountains towering
towards the skies and to all the heights of earth; to the fruit-
trees, and to the cedars, the kings among the trees of the forest;
to the wild beasts, which are called הַחַיָּה because they represent the most active and powerful life in the animal world, and
to all quadrupeds, which, more particularly the four-footed
domestic animals, are called בְּהֵמָה; to the creeping things (רֶמֶשׂ)
which cleave to the ground as they move along; and to the
birds, which are named with the descriptive epithet winged
(צִפּוֹר כָּנָף as in Deut. iv. 17, cf. Gen. vii. 14, Ezek. xxxix. 17,
instead of עוֹף כָּנָף, Gen. i. 21). And just as the call in Ps. ciii.
finds its centre of gravity, so to speak, at last in the soul of man,
so here it is addressed finally to humanity, and that, because
mankind lives in nations and is comprehended under the law
of a state commonwealth, in the first instance to its heads:
the kings of the earth, *i.e.* those who rule over the earth by
countries, to the princes and all who have the administration
of justice and are possessed of supreme power on the earth,
then to men of both sexes and of every age.

All the beings mentioned from ver. 1 onwards are to praise the Name of Jahve; for His Name, He (the God of this Name) alone (Isa. ii. 11, Ps. lxxii. 18) is נִשְׂגָּב, so high that no name reaches up to Him, not even from afar; His glory (His glorious self-attestation) extends over earth and heaven (*vid.* viii. 2). כִּי, without our being able and obliged to decide which, introduces the matter and the ground of the praise; and the fact that the desire of the poet comprehends in יְהַלְלוּ all the beings mentioned is seen from his saying "earth and heaven," as he glances back from the nearer things mentioned to those mentioned farther off (cf. Gen. ii. 4). In ver. 14 the statement of the object and of the ground of the praise is continued. The motive from which the call to all creatures to Hallelujah proceeds, viz. the new mercy which God has shown towards His people, is also the final ground of the Hallelujah which is to sound forth; for the church of God on earth is the central-point of the universe, the aim of the history of the world, and the glorifying of this church is the turning-point for the transformation of the world. It is not to be rendered: He hath exalted the horn of His people, any more than in cxxxii. 17: I will make the horn of David to shoot forth. The horn in both instances is one such as the person named does not already possess, but which is given him (different from lxxxix. 18, 25, xcii. 11, and frequently). The Israel of the Exile had lost its horn, *i.e.* its comeliness and its defensive and offensive power. God has now given it a horn again, and that a high one, *i.e.* has helped Israel to attain again an independence among the nations that commands respect. In Ps. cxxxii., where the horn is an object of the promise, we might directly understand by it the Branch (*Zemach*). Here, where the poet speaks out of his own present age, this is at least not the meaning which he associates with the words. What now follows is an apposition to וַיָּרֶם קֶרֶן לְעַמּוֹ: He has raised up a horn for His people —praise (we say: to the praise of; cf. the New Testament εἰς ἔπαινον) to all His saints, the children of Israel, the people who stand near Him. Others, as Hengstenberg, take תְּהִלָּה as a second object, but we cannot say הֵרִים תְּהִלָּה. Israel is called עַם קְרֹבוֹ, the people of His near = of His nearness or vicinity (Köster), as Jerusalem is called in Eccles. viii. 10 מְקוֹם קָדוֹשׁ

instead of מְקוֹם קֹדֶשׁ (Ew. § 287, *a, b*). It might also be said, according to Lev. x. 3, עַם קְרֹבָיו, the nation of those who are near to Him (as the Targum renders it). In both instances עַם is the governing noun, as, too, surely גֶּבֶר is in גֶּבֶר עֲמִיתִי, Zech. xiii. 7, which need not signify, by going back to the abstract primary signification of עָמִית, a man of my near fellowship, but can also signify a man of my neighbour, *i.e.* my nearest man, according to Ew. *loc. cit.* (cf. above on cxliii. 10, lxxviii. 49). As a rule, the principal form of עַם is pointed עָם; and it is all the more unnecessary, with Olshausen and Hupfeld, to take the construction as adjectival for עַם קָרוֹב לוֹ. It might, with Hitzig after Aben-Ezra, be more readily regarded as appositional (to a people, His near, *i.e.* standing near to Him). We have here an example of the genitival subordination, which is very extensive in Hebrew, instead of an appositional co-ordination : *populo propinqui sui,* in connection with which *propinqui* may be referred back to *propinquum = propinquitas,* but also to *propinquus* (literally : a people of the kind of one that is near to Him). Thus is Israel styled in Deut. iv. 7. In the consciousness of the dignity which lies in this name, the nation of the God of the history of salvation comes forward in this Psalm as the leader (*choragus*) of all creatures, and strikes up a Hallelujah that is to be followed by heaven and earth.

PSALM CXLIX.

HALLELUJAH TO THE GOD OF VICTORY OF HIS PEOPLE.

HALLELUJAH.

1 SING unto Jahve a new song,
His praise in the congregation of the saints.
2 Let Israel rejoice in its Maker,
Let the children of Zion be joyful in their King
3 Let them praise His Name with dance,
With timbrel and cithern let them play unto Him
4 For Jahve taketh pleasure in His people,
He adorneth the humble with salvation.

> 5 Let the saints exult in glory,
>   Let them shout aloud upon their beds.
>
> 6 Hymns of God fill their throats,
>   And a two-edged sword is in their hand,
> 7 To execute vengeance among the nations,
>   Punishments among the peoples;
> 8 To bind their kings with chains
>   And their nobles with iron fetters,
> 9 To execute upon them the written judgment—
>   It is glory for all His saints,
>   Hallelujah.

This Psalm is also explained, as we have already seen on Ps. cxlvii., from the time of the restoration under Ezra and Nehemiah. The new song to which it summons has the supreme power which Israel has attained over the world of nations for its substance. As in cxlviii. 14 the fact that Jahve has raised up a horn for His people is called תְּהִלָּה לְכָל־חֲסִידָיו, so here in cxlix. 9 the fact that Israel takes vengeance upon the nations and their rulers is called הָדָר לְכָל־חֲסִידָיו. The writer of the two Psalms is one and the same. The fathers are of opinion that it is the wars and victories of the Maccabees that are here prophetically spoken of. But the Psalm is sufficiently explicable from the newly strengthened national self-consciousness of the period after Cyrus. The stand-point is somewhere about the stand-point of the Book of Esther. The New Testament spiritual church cannot pray as the Old Testament national church here prays. Under the illusion that it might be used as a prayer without any spiritual transmutation, Ps. cxlix. has become the watchword of the most horrible errors. It was by means of this Psalm that Caspar Scloppius in his *Classicum Belli Sacri*, which, as Bakius says, is written not with ink, but with blood, inflamed the Roman Catholic princes to the Thirty Years' religious War. And in the Protestant Church Thomas Münzer stirred up the War of the Peasants by means of this Psalm. We see that the Christian cannot make such a Psalm directly his own without disavowing the apostolic warning, " the weapons of our warfare are not carnal " (2 Cor. x. 4). The praying Christian must therefore trans-

pose the letter of this Psalm into the spirit of the New Covenant; the Christian expositor, however, has to ascertain the
literal meaning of this portion of the Scriptures of the Old
Testament in its relation to cotemporary history.

Vers. 1–5. A period, in which the church is renewing its
youth and drawing nearer to the form it is finally to assume,
also of inward necessity puts forth new songs. Such a new
era has now dawned for the church of the saints, the Israel
that has remained faithful to its God and the faith of its
fathers. The Creator of Israel (עֹשָׂיו, plural, with the plural
suffix, like עֹשָׂי in Job xxxv. 10, עֹשֵׂיִךְ in Isa. liv. 5, cf. עֹשֵׂהוּ in
Job xl. 19; according to Hupfeld and Hitzig, cf. Ew. §
256, b, Ges. § 93, 9, singular; but *aj, ajich, aw*, are always
really plural suffixes) has shown that He is also Israel's Pre-
server and the King of Zion, that He cannot leave the children
of Zion for any length of time under foreign dominion, and
has heard the sighing of the exiles (Isa. lxiii. 19, xxvi. 13).
Therefore the church newly appropriated by its God and King
is to celebrate Him, whose Name shines forth anew out of its
history, with festive dance, timbrel, and cithern. For (as the
occasion, hitherto only hinted at, is now expressly stated) Jahve
takes a pleasure in His people; His wrath in comparison with
His mercy is only like a swiftly passing moment (Isa. liv. 7 sq.).
The futures that follow state that which is going on at the
present time. עֲנָוִים is, as frequently, a designation of the
ecclesia pressa, which has hitherto, amidst patient endurance of
suffering, waited for God's own act of redemption. He now
adorns them with יְשׁוּעָה, help against and victory over the hostile world; now the saints, hitherto enslaved and contemned,
exult בְּכָבוֹד, in honour, or on account of the honour which
vindicates them before the world and is anew bestowed upon
them (בְּ of the reason, or, which is more probable in connection
with the boldness of the expression, of the state and mood*);
they shout for joy upon their beds, upon which they have
hitherto poured forth their complaints over the present (cf.
Hos. vii. 14), and ardently longed for a better future (Isa

---

* Such, too (with pomp, not " with an army "), is the meaning of μετὰ
δόξης in 1 Macc. x. 60, xiv. 4, 5, *vid.* Grimm *in loc.*

xxvi. 8); for the bed is the place of soliloquy (iv. 5), and the tears shed there (vi. 7) are turned into shouts of joy in the case of Israel.

Vers. 6–9. The glance is here directed to the future. The people of the present have again, in their God, attained to a lofty self-consciousness, the consciousness of their destiny, viz. to subjugate the whole world of nations to the God of Israel. In the presence of the re-exaltation which they have experienced their throat is full of words and songs exalting Jahve (רוֹמֲמוֹת, plural of רוֹמָם, or, according to another reading, רוֹמַם, lvi. 17), and as servants of this God, the rightful Lord of all the heathen (lxxxii. 8), they hold in their hand a many-mouthed, *i.e.* many-edged sword (*vid. supra,* p. 28), in order to take the field on behalf of the true religion, as the Maccabees actually did, not long after: ταῖς μὲν χερσὶν ἀγωνιζόμενοι, ταῖς δὲ καρδίαις πρὸς τὸν Θεὸν εὐχόμενοι (2 Macc. xv. 27). The meaning of ver. 9a becomes a different one, according as we take this line as co-ordinate or subordinate to what goes before. Subordinated, it would imply the execution of a penal jurisdiction over those whom they carried away, and כָּתוּב would refer to prescriptive facts such as are recorded in Num. xxxi. 8, 1 Sam. xv. 32 sq. (Hïtzig). But it would become the religious lyric poet least of all to entertain such an unconditional prospect of the execution of the conquered worldly rulers. There is just as little ground for thinking of the judgment of extermination pronounced upon the nations of Canaan, which was pronounced upon them for an especial reason. If ver. 9a is taken as co-ordinate, the "written judgment" (*Recht*) consists in the complete carrying out of the subjugation; and this is commended by the perfectly valid parallel, Isa. xlv. 14. The poet, however, in connection with the expression "written," has neither this nor that passage of Scripture in his mind, but the testimony of the Law and of prophecy in general, that all kingdoms shall become God's and His Christ's. Subjugation (and certainly not without bloodshed) is the scriptural מִשְׁפָּט for the execution of which Jahve makes use of His own nation. Because the God who thus vindicates Himself is Israel's God, this subjugation of the world is הָדָר, splendour and glory, to all who are in love devoted to Him. The glorifying of Jahve is also the glorifying of Israel.

PSALM CL.

THE FINAL HALLELUJAH.

1   HALLELUJAH,
  PRAISE YE GOD IN HIS SANCTUARY,
  PRAISE HIM IN HIS STRONG FIRMAMENT!
2 PRAISE HIM IN HIS MIGHTY ACTS,
  PRAISE HIM ACCORDING TO THE ABUNDANCE OF HIS
      GREATNESS!
3 PRAISE HIM WITH THE SOUND OF HORNS,
  PRAISE HIM WITH HARP AND CITHERN!
4 PRAISE HIM WITH TIMBREL AND DANCE,
  PRAISE HIM WITH STRINGS AND SHALM!
5 PRAISE HIM WITH CLEAR CYMBALS,
  PRAISE HIM WITH CLASHING CYMBALS!

6 LET EVERYTHING THAT HATH BREATH PRAISE JAH,
      HALLELUJAH.

The call to praise Jahve "with dance and with timbrel" in cxlix. 3 is put forth here anew in ver. 4, but with the introduction of all the instruments ; and is addressed not merely to Israel, but to every individual soul.

Vers. 1–5. The Synagogue reckons up thirteen divine attributes according to Ex. xxxiv. 6 sq. (שְׁלשׁ עֶשְׂרֵה מִדּוֹת), to which, according to an observation of Kimchi, correspond the thirteen הַלֵּל of this Psalm. It is, however, more probable that in the mind of the poet the tenfold הַלְלוּ encompassed by Hallelujahs is significative ; for ten is the number of rounding off, completeness, exclusiveness, and of the extreme of exhaustibleness. The local definitions in ver. 1 are related attributively to God, and designate that which is heavenly, belonging to the other world, as an object of praise. קָדְשׁוֹ (the possible local meaning of which is proved by the קֹדֶשׁ and קֹדֶשׁ קָדָשִׁים of the Tabernacle and of the Temple) is in this passage the heavenly הֵיכָל ; and רְקִיעַ עֻזּוֹ is the firmament spread out by God's omnipotence and testifying of God's omnipotence (lxviii. 35), not according to its front side, which is turned towards the earth, but according to the reverse or inner side, which is turned towards the celestial world, and which marks it off from the earthly world. The third and fourth *hălᵃlu* give as the object of the praise that which is at the same time the ground of the praise: the tokens of His גְּבוּרָה, *i.e.* of His all-subduing strength, and the plenitude of His greatness (גֻּדְלוֹ = גָּדְלוֹ), *i.e.* His absolute, infinite greatness. The fifth and sixth *hălᵃlu* bring into the concert in praise of God the ram's horn, שׁוֹפָר, the name of which came to be improperly used as the name also of the metallic חֲצֹצְרָה (*vid.* on lxxxi. 4), and the two kinds of stringed instruments (*vid.* xxxiii. 2), viz. the nabla (*i.e.* the harp and lyre) and the kinnor (the cithern), the ψαλτήριον and the κιθάρα (κινύρα). The seventh *hălᵃlu* invites to the festive dance, of which the chief instrumental accompaniment is the תֹּף (Arabic *duff*, Spanish *adufe*, derived from the Moorish) or tambourine. The eighth *hălᵃlu* brings on the stringed instruments in their widest compass, מִנִּים (cf. xlv. 9) from מֵן, Syriac *menîn*, and the shepherd's pipe, עֻגָב (with the *Gimel raphe* = עוּנָב); and the ninth and tenth, the two kinds of castanets (צִלְצְלֵי, construct form of צֶלְצְלִים, singular צֶלְצַל), viz. the smaller clear-sounding, and the larger deeper-toned, more noisy kinds (cf. κύμβαλον ἀλαλάζον, 1 Cor. xiii. 1), as צִלְצְלֵי שָׁמַע (pausal form of שֶׁמַע = שֵׁמַע, like סָתֵר in Deut. xxvii. 15, and frequently, from סֵתֶר = סָתֵר) and צִלְצְלֵי תְרוּעָה are, with Schultens, Pfeifer, Burk, Köster, and others, to be distinguished.

Ver. 6. The call to praise has thus far been addressed to persons not mentioned by name, but, as the names of instruments thus heaped up show, to Israel especially. It is now generalized to "the totality of breath," *i.e.* all the beings who are endowed by God with the breath of life (נִשְׁמַת חַיִּים), *i.e.* to all mankind.

With this full-toned Finale the Psalter closes. Having risen as it were by five steps, in this closing Psalm it hovers over the blissful summit of the end, where, as Gregory of Nyssa says, all creatures, after the disunion and disorder caused by sin have been removed, are harmoniously united for one choral dance (εἰς μίαν χοροστασίαν), and the chorus of mankind concerting with the angel chorus are become one cymbal of divine praise, and the final song of victory shall salute God, the triumphant Conqueror ($\tau\hat{\omega}$ $\tau\rho o\pi a\iota o\acute{\upsilon}\chi\omega$), with shouts of joy. There is now no need for any special closing *beracha*. This whole closing Psalm is such. Nor is there any need even of an *Amen* (cvi. 48, cf. 1 Chron. xvi. 36). The *Hallelujah* includes it within itself and exceeds it.

EXCURSUS BY J. G. WETZSTEIN.

I.—CONCERNING דרור, THE NAME OF A BIRD.

On Ps. lxxxiv. 4 (p. 4).

SAADIA GAON explains דְּרוֹר by the Arabic دُورِيّة, a word the correctness of which has been doubted. It is, however, perfectly correct; for in Syria and Palestine the common sparrow is called دُورِيّ, *dûrî*, whence the *nomen unitatis* دُورِيّة. The word is to be traced back to دُور, the plural of دَار, the "farm-yard one," and signifies properly "that which is found or dwells in the farm-yards;" thus the *Ḳamûs* (*s.v.* دار) cites the phrase ما بِه دُورِيّ (used of a desolated locality), "there is no being that dwells in farm-yards therein," where we should say: "no living soul." In this phrase it is exchanged at pleasure for the synonyms دَيَّار, دَارِي, and دَيُّور, which are likewise denominatives of دَار.

The word *dûrî* is a thoroughly characteristic appellation for the sparrow, which inhabits the villages in immense flocks, where the standing corn and the corn lying on the threshing-floors in the open fields feed it for one half of the year, whilst it finds its food during the other half in the courts of the houses. It builds its nest in the walls by digging out the mortar between the air-dried bricks. These holes are stopped up once a year, because they injure the walls; and the birds that are then taken out always furnish an abundant repast, the only one of the kind, moreover, in the year, for no one takes the trouble to make a sport of shooting sparrows.

It is another question, whether the *derôr*, also, really corresponds to the *dûrî?* This would be impossible if the

ṣippôr, which is connected with *derôr* in Ps. lxxxiv. 4 and Prov.
xxvi. 2, as is supposed, signifies the sparrow. Saadia is consequently obliged to interpret צִפּוֹר differently. But is צפור then
the sparrow? Is it possible for a word which the Bible uses
to designate almost all kinds of birds to be the name of a
particular species? Its comparison with the Arabic عصفور,
from which it certainly differs only dialectically, does not support that supposition; for this word is a collective name for
the whole bulk of the small chirping and singing birds, side by
side with which the separate species must also have its special
name. The fact that in Syria one rarely sees and hears anything of any other *'oṣfûr* than the sparrow, arises from the fact
that the sparrow has multiplied so excessively there, whilst the
land, that has been deprived of its woods and is overrun with
birds of prey, is very poor in singing birds of all kinds. But
if the *ṣippôr* corresponds to the *'oṣfûr* in this sense, then the
derôr might well be the *dûrî*. The *swallow*, which one usually
thinks of, has its own name; and the *wood-pigeon*, which others
suppose to be the *derôr*, does not suit Prov. xxvi. 2.

The etymology of the word *derôr* is obscure. If it signifies
the sparrow, it will be a so-called primitive; at least it is then
more natural to regard the Syro-Arabic *dûrî* as a *derôr* that
has been corrupted by a later supposition of a more transparent
etymology, than to regard *derôr* as a defectively written and
hence erroneously pointed פְּעלול form (perhaps like פָּרוּר) from
the root דור.

II.—CONCERNING THE SIGNIFICATION OF THE WORD מענה
IN ITS APPLICATION TO AGRICULTURE.

On Ps. cxxix. 3 (p. 299), cf. on Ps. lxv. 11 (vol. ii. p. 230).

THE word מַעֲנָה, Arabic معانة, signifies a strip of arable land
which the ploughman takes in hand at one time, at both ends
of which consequently the ploughing-team always comes to a
stand, turns round, and begins a new furrow. The length of
the *ma'nâh* is of course the same as the length of the furrows.
Since the ordinary ox of Palestine is smaller and weaker than

ours, and easily becomes tired under the yoke, which presses
heavily on the nape of its neck and confines its neck, they are
obliged to give it time to recover its strength by frequent resting.   This always takes place at the termination of a furrow,
when the peasant raises the unwieldy plough out of the earth,
and turns it over, when he is obliged to clear off the moist
earth with the *jábút* (יָאבוּת, a small iron shovel at the lower end
of the oxen-stick or goad) and to hammer the loosened wedges
and rings tight again, during which time the team is able to
recover itself by resting.   Hence, too, they do not make the
furrows a great length.   If the field is under two hundred feet
long, it forms only one *ma'náh;* but when in level districts the
long parcels of ground (*sihám* from the singular שֶׁהֶם) of the
separate peasant farmers of a village frequently extend to the
distance of a mile and a half, the ploughman is compelled to
divide his parcel of ground into several معانى (מֶעֱנוֹת), each of
which is ploughed by itself.   The furrows, that is to say,
cannot be made breadthwise, because the small plots are mostly
far too narrow, and because the fields of his neighbours on
either side that might be already tilled would be injured by it;
for the boundaries of the fields (*hudûd* from the singular חַד)
are not formed, as with us, by rows, *i.e.* by broad strips of green
sward, but only by isolated heaps of stones, of which two larger
ones lie between every two fields, and are called *amâmí* (from
the singular אַמֶּיה, "mother ridge, *i.e.* main ridge"), and a
number of smaller ones called *ka'âkîr* (from the singular קְעָקוּר).
Moreover cross-ploughing would be rendered difficult by these
boundary stones, and the plough would often be seriously
injured.   In my collection of Hauranitish peasants' proverbs
and maxims the following is to be found: " One ox is as much
use to thee as two, and the shortness of the *ma'náh* as much
as its length " (يغنيك عن ثورين ثور ويغنيك عن طول المعانى
قصرها), on which I have recorded the following original interpretation: If it does not make any difference to the produce of
the field whether the *ma'náh* be greater or less, but in connection with the former the ploughing oxen are exhausted even
after half a day's work, whereas in connection with the latter
they remain fit for work the whole day, it is more profitable to
the peasant to make his *ma'náh* as short as practicable.

The word מענה only occurs besides in 1 Sam. xiv. 14, where it is said that Jonathan with his armour-bearer, in connection with an attack upon one of the posts of the enemy, slew twenty men, and that within the short space of about half a מענה, *i.e.* not during a long pursuit and by degrees, but in a brief hot battle on an arena of about a hundred paces. In the passage in the Psalm the back is conceived of as a field which is divided into several long מענות. To our taste the plural is certainly disturbing; the comparison of the back to one long-extended מענה, which may indeed have a hundred furrows, is simpler, and the impression produced by it more forcible; hence the *Kerî* supposes the singular מַעֲנִית, which must be regarded as an Aramaizing collateral form of the singular מענה, for the difference in forms like مصفاة, مصفاية, مصفية, مصفيّة, and مصفيت in connection with *Lamed He* stems is for the most part only idiomatic.

According to its derivation, מענה (with local *Mem*) is perhaps the portion of a field taken in hand by the ploughman, from עָנָה, to work; or with reference to the two ends, within the limit of which the ploughing is done, the furrow-turning, στροφή, from עָנָה, to turn; or a tract or space of a certain length, from ענה, to strive after, to seek to attain, whence the well-known Arabic word معنى (masculine of מְעֲנָה), that which is striven after, the desired object, then specially that which is aimed at by the language, the drift (the meaning and sense).

The Arabic معناة, together with the greater part of the agrarian terminology, is not found in the original lexicons, because it was not regarded as purely Arabic, but as belonging to the Nabatæan and Syrian dialects. The terms must therefore still be collected among the peasants. I found a good many in the *Merg'*-country, where I had my country estate; but the most interesting were in the *Haurân*, where, too, معناة still belongs to the living language.